THE FACTS ON FILE
COMPANION TO THE

WORLD NOVEL

1900 TO THE PRESENT
VOLUME I

MICHAEL D. SOLLARS
Editor

ARBOLINA LLAMAS JENNINGS
Assistant Editor

Facts On File
An imprint of Infobase Publishing

Facts On File, Inc.
An imprint of Infobase Publishing
132 West 31st Street
New York NY 10001

Library of Congress Cataloging-in-Publication Data

The Facts on File companion to the world novel, 1900 to the present /
[edited by] Michael Sollars.
      p. cm.
  Includes bibliographical references and index.
  ISBN 978-0-8160-6233-1 (set : alk. paper) 1. Fiction—20th century—
Bio-bibliography—Dictionaries. I. Sollars, Michael. II. Facts on
File, Inc. III. Title: Companion to the 20th-century World novel.
  PN3503.F33 2007
  808.83'04—dc22   2006033416

Facts On File books are available at special discounts when purchased in bulk quantities for businesses, associations, institutions, or sales promotions. Please call our Special Sales Department in New York at (212) 967-8800 or (800) 322-8755.

You can find Facts On File on the World Wide Web at http://www.factsonfile.com

Text design adapted by James Scotto-Lavino
Cover design by Salvatore Luongo

Printed in the United States of America

VB Hermitage 10 9 8 7 6 5 4 3 2 1

This book is printed on acid-free paper and contains 30% post-consumer recycled content.

CONTENTS

INTRODUCTION

A SURVEY OF THE WORLD NOVEL SINCE 1900
The 20th century was perhaps the most significant period in the development of the novel since the genre's introduction. We can track the origin of the novel back to such works as Lady Murasaki Shikubu's *The Tale of Genji* (*Genji Monogatari*), Miguel de Cervantes's *La Galatea* (1585) and *Don Quixote de la Mancha* (1605), and John Bunyan's *The Pilgrim's Progress* (1678). These forerunners possess many of the narrative devices associated with what we know today as the novel. The Mexican writer Carlos Fuentes is only one of many novelists who credit Cervantes as a significant influence on modern literature. In fact, a poll of writers conducted by the Norwegian Nobel Institute in 2002 found *Don Quixote* to be the best work of fiction ever published. This point also underscores the importance of what we can today consider the world novel, or geonovel. From the beginning, the novel has never been exclusively an American or British literary export.

Compiling this volume has afforded this editor a unique opportunity to discern the significant trends and changes in the form and purpose of the novel. These literary and aesthetic upheavals have been seismic, coming unannounced and sometimes unexpectedly, as when Franz Kafka's Gregor Samsa in *The Metamorphosis* awakens one morning to find that he has suddenly and inexplicably been transformed into a bug. Six major movements have been identified below to illustrate the scope and degree of significant shifts in the novel in the last century.

First, just as Cervantes gave the novel its beginning, Marcel Proust gave the novel a new lease. According to the French writer Colette, *Swann's Way* was "everything one would have wished to write, everything one neither dared nor knew how to write." And Graham Greene commented, "Proust was the greatest novelist of the twentieth century, just as Tolstoy was in the nineteenth." Proust's *In Search of Lost Time* (or *Remembrance of Things Past*) marked the end of the 19th-century novel influenced by social realism, as practiced by such giants as Gustave Flaubert, Victor Hugo, Thomas Hardy, Leo Tolstoy, Ivan Turgenev, and Fyodor Dostoevsky. *In Search of Lost Time* awakened the literary scene to fresh approaches and ideas, disregarding what had long been viewed as standard conventions of the well-written novel. Proust's fluid style and disregard for formal time and linear action allowed him to dispense with the causal plotline, dramatic action, and standard character development. Writing before James Joyce's *Ulysses* appeared in 1922, Proust inaugurated such literary devices as stream of consciousness and began a new focus on perception, fragmentation in plot and expression, metanarrative, and subjectivity.

Second, the century witnessed a change in the purpose of the novel as a form of artistic expression. Early modernists such as Thomas Mann and Tanizaki Jun'ichirō maintained what they considered an important distinction between art and history or life: Art deals in the universal, history in the particular. Art is not a fictionalized rendering of historical or personal experience. According to Tanizaki, fiction's role or domain is artifice. The artist, although his or her work may reflect social and political concerns, creates imaginary characters and worlds. These constructs may or may not mirror reality. The ability of an author like Mann to create the universal rather than actual incidence allows a work like his *The Magic Mountain,* for example, to endure in its universal expression, like Cervantes's *Don Quixote.*

The Magic Mountain has been heralded as a world masterpiece since its publication in 1924. Lacking Proust's stylistic innovations, Mann's work succeeds by virtue of its sensitive treatment of prewar Europe. The plight of the characters, who are seriously ill patients in a therapeutic spa, is representative of the illness of all of Europe after World War I and during the buildup to World War II. Illness becomes the controlling metaphor that functions within the novel and continues to reach far beyond the book's temporal story. Albert Camus's later work *The Plague,* written during World War II, is also representative of how a writer presents the universal rather than an actual historical event.

This aesthetic focus on art for art's sake remained evident throughout the first half of the 20th century until new attitudes prevailed. Writers began to more directly embrace art as a social tool, a tool for power and change. Pablo Picasso's 1937 painting *Guernica,* depicting the German bombing of the Basque city of the same name during the Spanish civil war, illustrated how an artist can become engaged in world events and in history. Writers began to do the same.

Gabriel García Márquez's *One Hundred Years of Solitude* further introduced changes to the 20th-century novel. The most important was the concept of magic realism (pioneered by Jorge Luis Borges), a blend of magical elements in a realistic setting. In one sense, magic realism is a way to respond to the social problems of a country or region. García Márquez's fictional biographies describe dictators, echoing the aphorism that the pen is mightier than the sword. In crafting his small fictional world, García Márquez also writes about all of Colombia and all of Latin America and, by extension, any country ravaged by brutal dictators or colonial rule. He reminds readers that violence cannot be swept away, even by the art of the novelist. Violence persists, as the world cannot seem to get beyond it.

Some authors have become directly involved in politics. The Peruvian writer Mario Vargas Llosa made an unsuccessful run for the presidency of his country during 1988–1990. He was actually surprised and dismayed by his resounding defeat at the polls. His work reflects this inability to know and to control reality. Vargas Llosa came to realize that artists can impose form on art but not on life, which is too elusive and unpredictable. An earlier Peruvian writer, Ciro Alegría, after years of forced exile from his homeland, returned in 1957 to become a high-ranking member of the party headed by a friend. The 20th century's most famous example of the writer-politician is perhaps the noted playwright Válcav Havel (not included in this collection), the popularity of whose dramatic work catapulted him to the presidency of the Czech Republic.

The third important movement was the novel as re-creation, or even source or authenticator, of history. Works by such writers as Ramón del Valle-Incán and Patrick Chamoiseau are often viewed by readers as portraying actual events. In many respects, the novelist has emerged as society's new historian. For example, Valle-Inclán's most important novel, *Tirano Banderas* (1926), is a fictional account of a Latin American country that is ruled by a cruel and corrupt dictator. It has been called the first dictator novel and thus created a new genre that remains popular today. Valle-Inclán wrote *Tirano Banderas* to denounce Miguel Primo de Rivera, the dictator of Spain from 1923 to 1930, and the forced exile of fellow novelist, playwright, and philosopher Miguel de Unamuno.

In this historical guise, the novel was perhaps returning to an older tradition, since this admixture of artifice and fact in artistic expression is centuries, even millennia, old. In ancient Greece, Aristophanes' comedy *The Clouds,* which cast Socrates in the central role, was so seriously regarded by the Athenian populace that, according to Plato's *Apology,* this fictional portrayal became a factor in the people's decision to condemn the philosopher to death.

A fourth remarkable change in the novel in the last 100 years has been its increasing imperviousness to definition. Through the years, various attempts have been made to capture, if not constrain, the novel through formal delineation. One attempt at clarification or signification that persisted for many decades came from E. M. Forster's *Aspects of the Novel,* which stated that the novel is "a fiction in prose of a certain extent," and that its length is "over 50,000 words." Another part of the traditional definition is that the writer should seek to depict and interpret the human character swept up in a struggle.

But in the last century, unexpected and unforeseen dimensions to the novel have emerged. In the 20th century, the length of the novel became even more debatable, with works far shorter than Forester's prescribed length of 50,000 words. Additionally, collections of what may have traditionally been judged as short stories are in fact often seen as related tales that together constitute a unified narrative. This is certainly the case with Tadeusz Borowski's *This Way for the Gas, Ladies and Gentlemen.* In postmodern considerations, a work's unity does not depend exclusively on characteristics within the work so much as on considerations outside the work—social, cultural, and political. Another way of looking at this aesthetic attitude is that the reader rather than the author brings unity to the work.

Fifth, the novel has expanded its geographical range dramatically. The extensive collection of novelists and novels in this companion affords a reader with a unique opportunity to study this range. In the early years of the century the novel was widely viewed as a Western, Eurocentric product, but as the century progressed, writers from other parts of the globe, such as Patrick Chamoiseau of Martinique, Paulo Coelho of Brazil, Dai Sijie of China, and Simin Daneshvar of Iran, came to the attention of the Western and world readers. Such a development cannot be underestimated.

For the sixth development of the novel form in the 20th century, we turn to the role of the reader. How does the reader—an outsider to the writing of a work—become an active force with regard to it? The reader has historically been a passive element (though certainly furnishing an active imagination), trusting the author, the narrator, and defined narrative forms.

However, the role of the reader has been redefined and expanded, especially in the last two decades of the 20th century. These transformations are part of what today is seen as the postmodern movement. As artists have challenged the traditional and formal modes of writing—including the trusted narrator, single point of view, logical plot, and other tenets—this opposition to, even defiance of, the old guard of narrative techniques has tested the complacency of readers. Novelists such as Alain Robbe-Grillet in *Jealousy* have challenged readers to keep up—to be more vigilant and observant. In essence, the postmodern artist, unlike his or her 19th-century counterpart, seeks not to communicate directly with the reader but deliberately to evade the reader's grasp.

ABOUT THIS BOOK

The Facts On File Companion to the World Novel, 1900 to the Present offers the reader a collection of writings on almost 600 novelists and novels that emerged during arguably the most dramatic and transformative period in world literature.

Each of the articles was written by a scholar with research background in his or her topic. Each entry is substantive, detailed, and accompanied by a bibliographical listing. The companion's purpose is not only to answer students' immediate questions but also to engage them and encourage them to dig deeper into their research subjects. Another goal of this companion is to outline the emergence of what can be termed the geonovel, the novel as an artistic expression that exists outside defined political, cultural, or social borders and definitions. The emergence of voluminous translations of novels from around the globe into English has propelled this accomplishment.

Selecting the authors and works to be included in this volume was difficult and painstaking. The decision process, weaving objective and subjective considerations, evolved over time. For the most part, authors had to write in a language other than English, though some exceptions were made for English-language authors from developing nations, such as Chinua Achebe and Amos Tutola. Such authors are often considered to write outside the dominant English-language tradition. Author selection was further based on the influence that a writer's work has had with readers and their cultural and social significance. Since this companion was written for the young scholar in college and high school, classroom reading lists were consulted, as well as various published lists on what constitutes the canon, or the leading or "best" novels. Significantly, our selection did not include only what is currently being taught but also what—according to faculty members—students could look forward to studying in future decades. The editor's expectation has been to contribute a serious research source that will continue to be valuable for many decades ahead.

The collection is organized alphabetically, with novelists and novels together. Names of novelists or authors are given in SMALL CAPITAL LETTERS in the text of an entry to indicate a cross-reference. Readers may also benefit from looking through the appendices, such as the geographical listing of authors and the general bibliography of secondary sources, which supplements the further reading lists given at the end of entries.

Michael D. Sollars

A

ABE KŌBŌ (1924–1993) *Japanese novelist, playwright, short story writer* Abe Kōbō is a well-known writer in both Japan and the wider world. Abe's works, particularly The WOMAN IN THE DUNES (*Suna na Onna,* 1962), are famous for their absurd and fantastic elements. This absurdity often causes critics to equate Abe with authors such as FRANZ KAFKA, ALBERT CAMUS, Samuel Beckett, and Eugene Ionesco, although an equally appropriate comparison might also be made to Kurt Vonnegut, inasmuch as a number of Abe's works contain an idiosyncratic mix of straight narrative, science fiction, and absurdity.

To characterize Abe's works as "absurd" implies a certain level of cultural collusion in Abe's writing that is not entirely accurate. Recognizing that the absurdists were writing mainly in the 1950s, the reader would be forgiven in assuming that Abe merely wrote Japanese versions of Western novels (which enjoyed much popularity in postwar Japan). However, this omits Abe's own feelings on contemporary life. It is important to realize the Japanese national context of postwar economic depression and decline of central authority in which his novels were written. That is, although Abe partially shares the "existentialist" position of writers such as Camus and JEAN-PAUL SARTRE (in which modern man is without roots and without recourse to absolute truths and morals), Abe's form of absurdity is grounded in Japanese cultural experience and his own early life.

Abe was born Abe Kimifusa ("Kōbō" is a bastardized form of the name) in Tokyo on March 7, 1924. His father, a doctor with the Imperial Medical College of Manchuria, raised Abe in Manchuria, then a Japanese occupied state known as Manchukuo. However, he was educated primarily in Japan, first at an elite high school (from 1941) and then at Tokyo Imperial University (from 1943), where he studied medicine. Abe's dual "nationality" led him to feel like an outsider with regard both to Japan and Manchukuo, and his experiences differed quite significantly from those of many of his contemporaries. His upbringing was firmly rooted not only in Japan and Japanese culture but also in a particular region of Japan, compelling Abe to assimilate a number of disparate experiences. This sense of dislocation had a major effect on his works and perhaps explains the sense of isolation—and often desolation—within them, as well as the openness Abe exhibited toward new genres and methods of writing.

Despite studying medicine, Abe never practiced as a doctor (stories exist that he was awarded the degree solely on the condition that he would not practice medicine), and soon after the war he began writing novels and short stories. In fact, Abe's writing seems to stem directly from the impact that World War II had on Japanese life. After the war, Manchuria reverted to Chinese rule, and the United States occupied Japan. Such radical upheavals exacerbated his already present sense of homelessness even further—especially when coupled with the death of his father in 1946. Abe's first novel was published only two years later. *The Signpost at the End of the Road* (*Owarishi Michi no Shirube Ni,*

1

1948) explicitly explores the theme of rootedness in terms of both domestic and personal life. As a result of his own experiences of trying to find a place to call "home," works such as *The Signpost at the End of the Road* explore ideas of community and belonging, also seen in the collection of poems he self-published in 1947.

Despite a relatively productive decade in the immediate postwar era, there is a large gap in translated works by Abe for this period. In many ways, however, these years were formative for the writer, as he joined a literary and philosophical group, the Night Association, which debated ideas of Marxism and surrealism in literature. He also began to explore different styles and genres of writing. Because of the group's founder, Hanada Kiyoteru (who had recommended *The Signpost at the End of the Road* for publication), Abe also became affiliated with the Japanese Communist Party at this time, although he was expelled in February 1962 as he became increasingly frustrated with their approach, perhaps because of the influence of Isikawa Jun, a vehement anti-Marxist.

It was with his works of the late 1950s and 1960s that Abe was to gain worldwide acclaim, beginning with the publication of *Inter Ice Age Four* (*Dai-Yon Kampyoki,* 1959). This novel differs remarkably from the traditional Japanese novel by blurring the primarily Western genres of science fiction and mystery (hence the comparisons to authors like Kurt Vonnegut). The surreal content of *Inter Ice Age Four* and its questioning of genre led Abe toward an increasingly experimental approach to writing and a period of substantial productivity. In the following decade, he wrote a number of novels and plays, including *The Face of Another* (*Tanin no Kao,* 1964); *The Ruined Map* (*Moetsukita Chizu,* 1967); and a play *Friends* (*Tomodachi,* 1959), which is clearly a criticism of Marxist ideals of "brotherly love." However, his most famous work of this period is undoubtedly *The Woman in the Dunes,* which won the Yomiuri Prize and which, along with *The Face of Another* and a screenplay, *Pitfall* (*Otoshi Ana*), was filmed by Teshigahara Hiroshi.

Although Abe is most famous for his works of this period, he continued writing until his death in 1993. Toward the end of his career, Abe focused more emphatically on drama, writing plays and directing his own experimental drama group, the Abe Kōbō Studio. He still produced novels, however, including *The Box Man* (*Hako Otako,* 1973), *Secret Rendezvous* (*Mikkai,* 1977), *The Ark Sakura* (*Hakobune Sakura Maru,* 1984), and *The Kangaroo Notebook* (*Kangaru Noto,* 1991).

BIBLIOGRAPHY

Abe Kōbō. *Three Plays.* Translated by Donald Keene. New York: Columbia University Press, 1993.

Iles, Timothy. *Abe Kōbō. An Exploration of His Prose, Drama and Theatre.* Fucecchio, Italy: European Press Academic, 2000.

William Slocombe

ABOUZEID, LEILA (1950–   ) *Moroccan novelist, short story writer*

The distinguished Moroccan writer Leila Abouzeid is among the first Arab women writers to gain critical acclaim for her literary oeuvre. Her work reflects a keen and informed critical outlook on the social and cultural changes within Morocco during a crucial transition from pre- to postindependent Morocco. Although she received a bilingual education, in both French and Arabic, Abouzeid chose deliberately to write in Arabic as a political choice and as an anticolonialist gesture. Most of her novels describe the plights and anxieties of her generation, especially those of women who are victimized by a patriarchal social system. She explores the nationalist movement that led to independence as well as relations between parents and children and those between husbands and wives. She also writes about contemporary Moroccan society and how it manages the colonial legacy in terms of its social relations and cultural identity. Her work is highly autobiographical.

Abouzeid was born in El Ksiba in central Morocco but raised and educated in Rabat, the capital. After high school, she joined Mohammed V University, where she received an undergraduate degree. Since then she has worked as a scriptwriter, journalist, and author. She first worked in a television anchor post (1972–73), then as press secretary for numerous ministers and other officials in government. Because of the French colonial enterprise in Morocco, she resisted writing in French and instead read voraciously a great variety of books in Arabic. As an undergraduate student, she wrote many articles that were published in Moroccan newspapers and also contributed short stories to the Arabic Service of the London-based British Broadcasting Corporation (BBC).

Leila Abouzeid's first novel, *Year of the Elephant* (*Am Al-fil*), was published in 1983. It was greatly acclaimed by critics and was the first Arabic-language novel by a Moroccan woman to be translated into English. It is an autobiographical novel that deals with the coming of age of a woman named Zahra, who is both the narrator and central character. Zahra, divorced by her husband after many years of marriage, returns to her hometown and becomes involved in a fierce struggle for self-actualization in postindependence Morocco. While describing her endeavors to rebuild her independent self and gain social and financial independence, the protagonist reveals, through a series of recollections, her childhood, marriage, and involvement in the nationalist struggle for independence. Zahra had been able to actively help the resistance movement by helping in the dissemination of nationalist literature, smuggling arms, organizing strikes, and collecting money. With the help of her friends Safia and Roukia, Zahra also realized that the value of independence requires education. In the novel, these women organize special schooling sessions for women and literacy classes to prepare women for the real struggle of development.

In *Return to Childhood: The Memoir of a Modern Moroccan Woman* (*Ruju'lla Tufula,* 1993), Abouzeid explores some of the same themes and issues that she developed in *Year of the Elephant.* This story takes place in the 1950s, against a background of Morocco's struggle for independence from French colonial rule. When it first appeared in Arabic, it was a best seller in Morocco and became a reference point for contemporary North African literature in Arabic.

In this work, Abouzeid reinvents the genre of autobiography through her dexterous ability to use personal recollections as a template to expose the social, cultural, and political vicissitudes of her generation from multiple female perspectives, namely the writer's mother, her grandmother, and herself. Thus the choice of autobiography assumes political and ideological implications in a society in which women have been silenced in public as well as private. Abouzeid's preface

and Elizabeth Fernea's foreword discuss the development of this genre in Arabic literature, and for the writer it is an empowering gesture intended for a non-Moroccan audience that enables her to correct some misconceptions about Muslim women. Through women's eyes and with rich and poetic oral descriptions, Abouzeid's work charts the strange world of her childhood and family dramas, but she also conveys vividly the ways they are intertwined with social issues and political conflict. The memoir opens some years before independence, exactly on the day her father, a resistance fighter, was imprisoned by the French colonial authority.

Abouzeid's father is a central figure in the narrative. Because of his strong opposition to the French and advocacy of Moroccan independence, he was repeatedly imprisoned by the French. As a result, his family found themselves forced to flee the capital and to frequently relocate to other parts of Morocco to the safety of relatives. Abouzeid recalls the dramatic times that ensued after her father's imprisonment and reports these events through the eyes of a young child trying to make sense of life through the stories of her mother and grandmother. Thus we learn about family disputes, domestic dramas and intrigues, herbal remedies, magic, and political changes. The writer also details her relationship with her father, who insisted she go to school and helped her to pave the way for other females as the prototypical figure of the "modern Moroccan woman" of the title.

Through an experimental narrative method of nonlinearity, the reader becomes alerted to the maturing voice of the protagonist, whose observations provide a critical stance on the complex issues involved in building a modern Morocco as well as a critique of the political system with both its establishment and its opposition parties. What emerges through the memoir is the development of personal relationships between generations as well as between husbands and wives.

The Last Chapter (*al-Fasl al-akhir,* 2000) was written in Arabic and published in an English translation (by the author and John Liechety) in the same year. In this semiautobiographical novel, Aisha, the narrator, recounts her life story from schooldays till the time she becomes a single accomplished woman. The narrative voice remains consistent throughout all the chapters except the final one.

Aisha is a well-educated, intellectual, and independent woman who traces her life from early childhood, as one of two girls in a school full of boys, to her early adult life as a successful but lonely woman. Through a series of vignettes, the narrator exposes the sexist attitudes of her society, which are the reasons why Aisha has decided to remain unmarried. This male chauvinistic mindset is illustrated through the husband of one of her schoolmates who later in life sees Aisha on television, consulted for public opinion, and reportedly says: "I'll bet you anything she's dying to exchange that nonsense for a husband."

Building on this example and others from her entourage, Aisha casts an ironic look on the miserable lot of the majority of Moroccan women who find themselves stuck in these types of marital situations. As an intellectual and independent woman, Aisha is comparatively privileged, despite the series of failed love relationships. In spite of her cynical and regretful moments, Aisha is represented by the writer as faring better than her married sisters. However, Abouzeid surprisingly suggests that women could also be the cause of women's unhappiness through ruthless exploitation and plotting, as the story of Aisha with her school friend and other stories about magic and sorcery show.

In terms of its portrayal and critique of society, the novel draws a parallel between domestic exploitation and political corruption. Aisha, who is unable to succumb to the sexual advances of her boss in the Ministry of Education, decides to resign her position. This line of criticism of male dishonesty and betrayal is shown in her failed love affairs. Even the most promising love relationship with Karim, which is based on an intense passionate attraction, is doomed to failure when she visits him in Spain and finds that he has a wife and a baby.

BIBLIOGRAPHY

Hassan, Ihab. "Queries for Postcolonial Studies." *Philosophy and Literature* 22, no. 2 (1998): 328–342.

Majid, Anouar. "The Politics of Feminism in Islam." *Signs* 23, no. 2 (Winter 1998): 321–361.

Malti-Douglas, Fadwa. *Men, Women and God(s): Nawal El Saadawi and Arab Feminist Poetics.* Berkeley: University of California Press, 1995.

Moukhlis, Salah. "A History of Hopes Postponed": Women's Identity and the Postcolonial State in *Year of the Elephant: A Moroccan Woman's Journey Toward Independence. Research in African Literatures* 34, no. 3 (Fall 2003): 66–83.

Rausch, Margaret. *Bodies, Boundaries and Spirit Possession: Moroccan Women and the Revision of Tradition.* Berlin: Transcript Verlag, 2000.

Ahmed Idrissi Alami

ABSENT WITHOUT LEAVE (ENTFERNUNG VON DER TRUPPE) Heinrich Böll (1964)

The post–World War II novel *Absent without Leave* represents something of a change of literary pace for Heinrich Böll (1917–85), at least in terms of its formal and stylistic strategies. Although some thematic concerns persist from his earlier work of the 1940s and 1950s—years that established his reputation as one of Germany's most important writers—*Absent without Leave* was written in a self-consciously playful avant-garde style until then unseen in Böll's prose fiction, which tended to offer a demanding, retooled form of modernism. This change of stylistic direction, however, is well suited to the overarching thrust of the work: The formal changes match the content's focus on aggressive nonconformity. The German title of the text, *Entfernung von der Truppe,* emphasizes, instead of mere absence, an act of deliberate distanciation, or distancing (the *Entfernung*), from some kind of group (the *Truppe*). This deliberate self-isolation from the masses or pack references a literal desertion as well as the moral lesson of more general nonconformity.

The text is a first-person narration by Wilhelm Schmölder, who declares that his humanity began when his state service ended, a declaration likewise applicable to Böll's own nonconformist attitudes toward the maturing 1960s West-German society as well as toward the literary establishment in the wake of a controversy about his novel *The Clown* (1963). *Absent without Leave* was not well received by critics at the time of publication, but it remains unique in Böll's canon of work, admirable for its rigorous critique of society, intriguing for its unprecedented experimentation in form, and important for its "almost autobiographical" (as he put it) insights into Böll's evolving attitudes.

In an ironic and colloquial tone, Wilhelm Schmölder (whose full name has to be cobbled together by readers) playfully relates a series of flashbacks to the late 1930s and 1940s from the narrative present of 1963, by which time West German society had consolidated the breathtaking material gains of its 1950s "Economic Miracle." These flashbacks focus, in particular, on September 22, 1938, the day on which Schmölder entered the house of his wife's family, the Bechtolds, and also the day he recognized that humanity starts when one decides to reject unreflective conformity. To understand this particular moment, Schmölder has to explain his previous work in the Reich Labor Service, how "service" (literally for the state, but also more generally) always filled him with anxiety. After his marriage to Hildegard Bechtold, Schmölder does not return to his service, eponymously distancing himself from others, but after a week he is arrested, sent to prison, and then mustered into the army. Among other episodes, he reports how his wife and two brothers-in-law died in the Allies' bombing of Germany, leaving only his wife's younger brother, Johannes, a staff sergeant turned successful businessman and a poster child for the economic miracle of the 1950s, whose selective memories allow him to disown his brothers who died for family and country.

This surviving Bechthold brother is despised by his own mother, Anna Bechtold, Schmölder's mother-in-law and an inspiration in the text. An "instinct Catholic" who does not allow the pope to dictate her faith to her, Anna was the leader of a communist cell during the war and had been imprisoned for attacking an officer who had come to search for her deserter son. The heroic figure of Anna also represents a bit of a change of tactics for Böll, one that anticipates his direction in his celebrated GROUP PORTRAIT WITH LADY (1971), for she offers a positive and female model for opposition at a time of high social, political, and cultural conformity (late 1950s, early 1960s). Schmölder writes that she and he are like "Neanderthals," out of time, rather like the unearthed statue he feels himself to be before his estranged daughter and son-in-law.

Out-of-time, nonconformist, distanced—all also describe the stylistic and formal approach of *Absent without Leave,* which deliberately departs the modified modernism that Böll had been cultivating since the 1940s and that had culminated in his much-lauded BILLIARDS AT HALF PAST NINE. In *Absent without Leave,* the ironic tone of the first-person narration of memory creates an unusual hybrid of memoirs and fiction: The narrative is constantly interrupted, digressing, and adamantly nonlinear. The drop-out attitudes of the narrator are thus reflected in the form of the work itself. Many critics have highlighted the unorthodox (ungrammatical) sentence structure, the subversive manipulation of narrative verb tenses, and especially the contradictory intertextual references to both Nazi propaganda and literary forebears that are like fairy tales. The text also applies documentary sources (like newspaper articles pasted into a journal) as well as, for Böll's work, rare direct address to the reader (at one point the text suggests the reader take a break to make a wish list). But even these kinds of postmodern games fit the thematic agenda of the text in encouraging active participation and energetic engagement on the part of the reader. Schmölder—like Anna Bechtold and, one presumes, Böll himself—cannot forget the repressed past or reconcile the compromised present, so he demands, aggressively and mischievously, that readers do not either.

BIBLIOGRAPHY

Böll, Victor and Jochen Schubert. *Heinrich Böll.* Munich: Deutscher Taschenbuch Verlag, 2002.

Butler, Michael, ed. *The Narrative Fiction of Heinrich Böll: Social Conscience and Literary Achievement.* Cambridge and New York: Cambridge University Press, 1994.

Conrad, Robert C. *Understanding Heinrich Böll.* Columbia, S.C.: Camden House 1992.

Crampton, Patricia, trans. *Heinrich Böll, on His Death: Selected Obituaries and the Last Interview.* Bonn: Inter Nationes, 1985.

Prodanuik, Ihor. *The Imagery in Heinrich Böll's Novels.* Bonn: Bouvier, 1979.

Reed, Donna K. *The Novels of the Nazi Past.* New York: Peter Lang, 1985.

Zachau, Reinhard K. *Heinrich Böll: Forty Years of Criticism.* Columbia, S.C.: Camden House, 1994.

Jaimey Fisher

ACHEBE, CHINUA (1930–) *Nigerian novelist*   When asked about his writing, Chinua Achebe said that "it was important to teach my readers that

their past—with all its imperfections—was not one long night of savagery from which the first Europeans acting on God's behalf delivered them." It is this idea, the vindication of voices long silenced, that epitomizes Achebe's image as the father of African literature. His first novel, THINGS FALL APART (1958), which communicates the complexities and crisis of the Igbo society, is considered to be one of the most important works in postcolonial literature and introduced readers to Achebe's elegant prose and mixture of English and Igbo. The Igbo society, located in southeastern Nigeria, is an agrarian community whose people have long been subject to internal and external political strife. Achebe's desire to rewrite, or "write back to," the traditional colonial narrative inspired his career as a novelist, a political activist, and an editor who has shaped the world's perspective of African literature.

Achebe was born in Ogidi, Nigeria, on November 16, 1930. The fifth of six children, he was christened Albert Chinualumogu Achebe by his parents, Isaiah Okafor Achebe and Janet Achebe. He attended English schools in Ogidi and was encouraged to read English primers by his father, one of Ogidi's first converts to Christianity and the founder of the first Anglican church there. However, his mother countered his father's influence by telling the young boy African stories and thus exposing him to indigenous Igbo culture as well. Achebe often points out that he was discouraged from participating in Igbo rituals as a child, but "took it all in" nevertheless. Therefore, through his parents he developed a sense of dualism and balance early in life and became increasingly curious about the boundaries between East and West, which he later explored in novels such as *Things Fall Apart, No Longer at Ease* (1960), and *Arrow of God* (1964).

As a young adult, Achebe excelled at the government college in Umuahia and at University College, Ibadan, where he began his studies in medicine in 1948. After his first year, however, he became interested in Nigerian history and religious studies and subsequently changed from medicine to a major in the liberal arts. Like his literary contemporaries, Achebe began to notice discrepancies between his knowledge of Nigeria and the perceptions of Africa depicted in popular British colonial novels such as Joseph Conrad's

Heart of Darkness (1902) and Joyce Cary's *Mister Johnson* (1939).

As a student, Achebe was a prolific writer, contributing articles, sketches, and short fiction to the university newspaper, the *University Herald.* In 1953 he completed his bachelor's degree and joined the Nigerian Broadcasting Service, where he was promoted in 1961 to director of external services in charge of the Voice of Nigeria. He trained briefly at the BBC in London and quickly became influential in the formation of a new Nigerian national identity through broadcasting. During the same year, he married Christie Chinwe Okoli, and they began a family that would eventually include four children.

As an emerging successful author and radio personality, Achebe felt compelled to speak out against the civil war that erupted in Nigeria during the late 1960s and early 1970s. Three major ethnic linguistic groups existed in Nigeria at this time: the Yoruba, Hausa, Fulani, and Igbo. These groups, locked in civil war as they struggled to escape the remaining vestiges of colonialism, became the topic for Achebe's third novel, *A Man of the People* (1966), an indictment of Nigeria's domestic military. Committed to using his art and language as a way to teach people about society, Achebe traveled to Europe, endorsing support for the newly seceded Igbo nation of Biafra. As a result of his activism, he and his family were driven out of their home in Lagos in 1966 during an anti-Igbo rebellion. They quickly relocated to Nsukka, where Achebe took a post as a professor of literature at the University of Nigeria.

Achebe has said that these initial years of his career were dedicated to cultural revitalization through language. He chose to write in both English and Igbo and thus recast the image of colonialism in Africa from a bicultural viewpoint. As the founding editor of the journal *Okike* and the African Writers Series, Achebe opened the door to other African authors seeking to broaden the scope of postcolonial and postmodern literature. Achebe supports reciprocity between personal and political truths and the influence of the human imagination and the written word.

When asked about his intentions as he composed *Things Fall Apart,* Achebe responded that "there is no such thing as absolute power over narrative. Those who secure this privilege for themselves can arrange stories about others pretty much where, and as, they like. Just as in corrupt, totalitarian regimes, those who exercise power over others can do anything." In this same vein, Achebe published *Girls at War and Other Stories* in 1972, the first of several publications about Nigeria's problematic and unstable postindependence years.

In the late 1970s, Achebe published little. He moved to the United States for a three-year teaching position at the University of Massachusetts at Amherst (a post he returned to from 1987 to 1988). However, after returning to Nsukka in 1976, he continued his activism and subsequently published "The Trouble with Nigeria" (1983) and ANTHILLS OF THE SAVANNAH (1987). The former, a political essay, and the latter, a novel, examine ruthless politicians and the culture surrounding political coups. In 1988 his first three novels—*Things Fall Apart, No Longer at Ease,* and *Arrow of God*—were published together as *The African Trilogy.*

Achebe began his career as a bold but lone voice focusing on the way historic events impact the ordinary individual. He views postcolonial Africa with irony and compassion and portrays his characters honestly as complicated and fallible. As the first authentic interpreter of Africa to the world, Achebe sees writing as a social responsibility and art as a communal experience. A main proponent of the African literary diaspora, Achebe encourages other authors to explore the power of the human soul through experimental works. His many honors include the Margaret Wong Memorial Prize, the Nigerian National Trophy for Literature, the Commonwealth Poetry Prize, and the Nigerian National Merit Award.

In 1990 Achebe was in a near-fatal car accident while visiting Lagos with his son. Despite a quick rescue after the accident, he suffered injuries that paralyzed him from the waist down. He later relocated to the United States, where he accepted a teaching position at Bard College in Annandale-on-Hudson, New York. There he continues to lecture and to write about the African experience.

BIBLIOGRAPHY

Achebe, Chinua. *Home and Exile.* Oxford: Oxford University Press, 2000.

Muoneke, Romanus Okey. *Art, Rebellion and Redemption: A Reading of the Novels of Chinua Achebe.* New York: Peter Lang, 1994.

Njoku, Benedict Chiaka. *The Four Novels of Chinua Achebe: A Critical Study.* New York: Peter Lang, 1984.

Ohaeto, Ezenwa. *Chinua Achebe: A Biography.* Bloomington: Indiana University Press, 1997.

Olakunle, George. *Relocating Agency: Modernity and African Letters.* Albany: State University of New York Press, 2003.

Palmer, Eustace. *An Introduction to the African Novel: A Critical Study of Twelve Books by Chinua Achebe, James Ngugi, Camara Laye, Elechi Amadi, Ayi Kwei Armach, Mongo Beti, and Gabriel Okara.* New York: Africana Publications, 1972.

Parker, Michael, and Roger Starkey, eds. *Postcolonialism Literatures: Achebe, Ngugi, Desai, Walcott.* Basingstoke, U.K.: Macmillan, 1995.

Soonsik, Kim. *Colonialism and Postcolonialism Discourse in the Novels of Yom Sang-sop, Chinua Achebe and Salman Rushdie.* New York: Peter Lang, 2004.

Yousaf, Nahem. *Chinua Achebe.* Tavistock, U.K.: Northcote House in Association with the British Council, 2003.

Emily Clark

ADNAN, ETEL (1925–   ) *Lebanese novelist, playwright, poet, short story writer*

Born in Beirut, Lebanon, Etel Adnan is one of the foremost Arab-American writers and thinkers, with her work including fiction, poetry, drama, essays, and visual art. Born to a Syrian Muslim father and a Greek Christian mother, Adnan grew up in a multilingual environment that encompassed Greek, Turkish, Arabic, French, and English. She writes in English and French, and her works have been translated into numerous languages, including Arabic, Italian, Dutch, German, and Urdu.

Even though Adnan does not write in Arabic and has lived in the United States and Europe most of her life, the themes and issues she examines in her work firmly situate her in the Arab as well as the Arab-American and European literary and cultural traditions. The split between her Western education and her Arab heritage has greatly influenced her perspective, surfacing as a recurring thematic concern in her work. Her essay "To Write in a Foreign Language" (1996), for instance, focuses on her ongoing negotiation of varying cultural and linguistic traditions, delineating the ways in which her poems and prose are entrenched in a rich background and a complex personal history. This autobiographical essay highlights such a complexity by describing Adnan's rejection of the French language during the Algerian war of independence (1954–62). She states that expressing herself in French made her feel an accomplice in the brutality of imperial power, a dilemma that she could resolve only through the process of painting.

Living in the United States during the Vietnam War in the 1960s triggered Adnan's need to express her reactions to the war through poetry. She published several antiwar poems in English, including "The Ballad of the Lonely Knight in Present-Day America" and "The Enemy's Testament." Other poems written in English followed, resulting in the publication of Adnan's first book of poetry, *Moonshots* (1966). *Five Senses for One Death* (1971), a love poem written for a female friend who had committed suicide, followed. Although she had never mastered Arabic as a child, Adnan deeply felt the tug of this language and heritage on her creative thought. She found a way to achieve a solid link to this language that until then had remained beyond her grasp by joining together Arabic script and watercolor painting, thus uniting word and image. The act of joining these two media was done by copying the works of major Arab poets in unconventional calligraphic form on scrolls of Japanese folded paper, transforming them into visual pieces of art. Such works have been displayed in galleries across the United States as well as in the Arab world.

Adnan's education and career has spanned several countries and continents. In 1955, after studying philosophy at the Sorbonne in Paris, she pursued her postgraduate work at the University of California, Berkeley; she also spent a year at Harvard. The shift between the French and American educational and linguistic systems had a profound influence on Adnan, greatly shaping her intellectual and literary outlooks. Between 1958 and 1972, she taught philosophy at the Dominican College of San Rafael, California, after which she returned to Beirut to work as the cultural editor of the French-language newspaper *Al-Safa*. In Beirut she switched back to writing in French, and in 1973 she published two long political poems, "Jebu" and "L'express Beyrouth→Enfer" ("The Beirut-Hell Express"), in one book. Her other works written dur-

ing this period include the poem "Pablo Neruda is a Banana Tree" (later published as a book in 1982), and the book-length poem *The Arab Apocalypse* (*L'Apocalypse arabe,* 1989), which also intermingles visual and verbal expressions.

In 1977, during the Lebanese civil war (1975–90), Adnan left for France. In Paris her novel SITT MARIE ROSE took shape after she learned about an acquaintance being kidnapped, tortured, and killed at the hands of Christian Lebanese militiamen. Written in French and published in Paris in 1977, the novel is a fictionalized account of Marie Rose Boulos's ordeal and a portrayal of Adnan's feminist and political attitudes toward the Lebanese civil war. Translated into six languages, including Arabic (1979) and English (1982), *Sitt Marie Rose* is Adnan's most widely read and best-known work.

As the war in Lebanon intensified in 1979, Adnan returned to California, where she continued writing and painting. She published a long poem, *From A to Z* (1982), and a collection entitled *The Indian Never Had a Horse and Other Poems* (1985), which probes the dispossession of Native Americans. *Journey to Mount Tamalpais* followed in 1986, a work in which Adnan further explores elaborate connections among visual art, prose, and poetry. *The Spring Flowers Own & Manifestations of the Voyage,* a collection of poems, was published in 1990.

The 1990s witnessed the publication of several more volumes of Adnan's work, including *Paris When It's Naked* (1993), a rumination in prose on the city of Paris, and *Of Cities and Women: Letters to Fawwaz* (1993), a collection of letters revolving around gender and feminism, written by Adnan to fellow Arab writer and exile Fawwaz Traboulsi. Adnan currently spends her time in Beirut, Paris, and California and continues to write and publish new works as well as translations of her earlier works. She has been instrumental in shaping intellectual explorations of such themes as Arab exile, language, displacement, and equality, and continues to influence Arab and Arab-American writers and thinkers.

BIBLIOGRAPHY
Kilpatrick, Hilary: "Interview with Etel Adnan (Lebanon)."
    In *Unheard Words: Women and Literature in Africa, the*

Arab World, Asia, the Caribbean and Latin America, edited by Mineke Schipper, 114–120. London: Allison & Busby, 1985.

Majaj, Lisa Suheir, and Amal Amireh, eds. *Etel Adnan: Critical Essays on the Arab-American Writer and Artist.* Jefferson, N.C.: McFarland and Company, 2002.

Carol Fadda-Conrey

AĞAOĞLU, ADALET (1929–) *Turkish essayist, novelist, playwright, poet*

Adalet Ağaoğlu, a leading contemporary Turkish writer, was born in 1929 in Nallihan, a small town near Ankara. Her father was a small tradesman whose conservative stand in life shaped many ideas in Ağaoğlu's life. She lived in this small town until 1949, when she went to Ankara to study at the high school for girls. She later studied French language and literature at Ankara University, and thus French became the language through which she was exposed to many important writers of world literature. In 1951 she started to work for Ankara Radio, from which she resigned in 1970, but she devoted all her energy to writing, composing critical essays on drama as early as 1946. She also wrote plays for the stage and for radio, bringing her considerable success as a playwright. In the years 1948–50, her poems appeared in various journals. She released her first novel, *Lying Down to Die* (*Ölmeye Yatmak,* 1973), to wide popularity and acclaim. She added to her reputation as a novelist with a number of finely honed short stories. Since the publication of her first novel, she has attracted a wide reading public and is acknowledged as one of the premier modern Turkish novelists.

Ağaoğlu's early childhood, coinciding with the early years when the Turkish Republic was characterized by the nation-building project of Kemalist ideology, had a profound impact on her writing. She created most of her characters against the background of the sociopolitical context of the new Turkish Republic; this backdrop is often considered as important as the characters themselves in the author's novels. Other issues she persistently puts at the center of her works include women's rights in an Islamic context, the correlation between the community and the individual, the social and financial handicaps that trap or demonize the individual, the cultural metamorphoses of Turkish society after Kemalist ideology, hypocrisy and double standards in both right- and left-wing groups, political oppression, and class and national identity.

A close look at her novels offers insight into Ağaoğlu's career in fiction. *Lying Down to Die,* the first novel in her trilogy *Hard Times* (*Dar Zamanlar*), tells the story of Aysel, an academician who locks herself in a hotel room in Ankara to prepare for her death. She looks back on her past in order to come to terms with her recent crisis—a sexual liaison with one of her students. In this process, her mind moves back and forth through her personal history, and this personal perspective merges into the national history. Ağaoğlu gives a panoramic picture of the early and later years of the modern Turkish Republic through Aysel, concentrating on the people in her immediate surroundings who were born and raised in the previous Islamic traditions. These same individuals are caught up in national change and suddenly expected to live within a totally different framework of the modern, secular, and democratic system. The changes and expectations produce conflicts and tension between this generation and their children, who are regarded as the future of the new republic.

The novel traces the 1938 graduates (eight students) of a provincial primary school through World War II and into the political turmoil of the late 1960s. The reader witnesses the metamorphoses that these characters live through in the process. There is a strong emphasis on anxiety, displacement, and alienation experienced by the members of both generations.

Aysel looks back on her past as a form of purgation. In this process, she discovers her own physical body, which she has suppressed in her efforts to build up her "imagined" identity. In the end, she does not commit suicide, as earlier suspected, but leaves the hotel room feeling revitalized both physically and intellectually. However, whether she goes back to her life with her husband or starts a new life on her own terms remains ambiguous.

Lying Down to Die looks at the main character's attempts to make sense of her past, with her ultimate decision about her future hanging in the balance. In *A Wedding Night* (*Bir Düğün Gecesi,* 1972), the second novel of the trilogy, the author Ağaoğlu presents the mature years of the young people whom the reader sees traced from their early schooling onward in the previous work. Despite the illusion of social promotion, these characters cannot escape the previous social network. *A Wedding Night* tells the story of these characters on a matrimonial evening, which brings together two small shop-owning families from Nallihan. In the first generation, their fathers could exist only on the margin of the dominant discourse, but now their children climb up the social ladder, moving into the upper-middle class.

Social mobility again rests at the center of the novel, in which these characters seem to undergo changes in appearance without absorbing the spirit of the age. The wedding takes place in the Anatolian Club, where the segmented nature of Anatolia is reflected through its guests, who are heterogeneous in terms of their social, political, and religious standing. The attempt to look Westernized in *Lying Down to Die* is also visible here. There is an absurd combination of foods, drinks, and music: Raki is served with whiskey, characters dance a tango before the performance of the belly dancer, and Western-style food is served with Turkish food.

Despite the illusion of stability, these people of small-town origin have not been able to secure their positions. Everybody judges one another by appearance and cannot go beyond it. Issues of shallow relationships, mistrust, solipsism of the intellectual, suffocating family ties, lack of a sense of belonging, and a widely shared framework of thought and favoritism dominate the work. Another point that the novel emphasizes is the discrepancy between fact and illusion. Some of the characters like Aysel, her husband, Omer, and her sister Tezel are aware of this discrepancy; however, they are marginalized within their social circle.

In *No* (*Hayir,* 1987), the last novel of the trilogy, Ağaoğlu puts Aysel's consciousness at the center of her fictional universe. There are occasional references to the familiar characters from the previous novels of the trilogy, but now the idealism of the early years of the Republic is totally gone. In this book the reader can see certain groups of individuals who only move about in life with a self-serving interest. Except for a very few people, most of the characters, including the members of the academic world, are conformists, and compared to them the pathetic bureaucrats of the first generation

in *Lying Down to Die* are much more dignified. In the 1980s, Aysel feels even more marginalized and lonely. To make matters worse, she is dismissed from her position at the university without valid reason. At the same time, her husband breaks off the marriage for Aysen, Aysel's nephew, the bride in *Lying Down to Die*. Friends or students in her life replace family ties.

The novel gives an account of a day at the end of which Aysel is supposed to go to a ceremony where she will be given the New Echoes Award by the Institute of Social Anthropology. She spends the day making preparations, but she is also half aware that going to that ceremony implies being integrated into the conventional network once again and saying "yes" to the official recognition that is granted to her after long years of neglect. She cannot bring herself to comply and chooses a mysterious disappearance, leaving the members of the awards committee in amazement. Hers is a very unrealistic way of suicide, which is more metaphorical than literal. Here the title of the novel becomes significant, as it is also the culmination of Aysel's quest since her primary school years.

In *Summer's End* (*Yaz Sonu,* 1980), Ağaoğlu tells the story of an intellectual woman who finds loss all around her. She loses her son in a terrorist attack and then also loses her social network, including her husband. The story is told by a frame narrator, who, encouraged by her doctor, leaves all her work in the city for a relaxing holiday in a Mediterranean seaside motel. Despite her decision not to get involved in any kind of process of writing, her imagination is mesmerized by the associations evoked by an abandoned cottage near her motel, and she fictionalizes whatever she hears about the cottage and the woman who once lived in it and had been killed by one of the construction workers. The nameless narrator makes her the protagonist of her story and creates her own shadow in the image of this woman, who also writes her journal. The narrator casts her own features over her protagonist: Both have the same attitude to life, and even their taste in food and drink is the same. The frame narrator names her Nevin and integrates her, somehow, to her own spatial and temporal reality.

Nevin arranges an end-of-summer meeting with some people from her past: Her ex-husband, her brother, a friend and his girlfriend, and a friend of her dead son come together in her small sea cottage, which is situated in a deserted coastal area. This meeting turns into a pitiful attempt to get in touch with their past and to renew their foregone intimacy. However, despite the absorbing warmth of the present moment, all are aware that they cannot extend this warmth into the future. The meeting therefore turns into an abortive attempt to relive the sense of intersubjective continuity left in the past. After her guests depart, a crippled construction worker who seeks intimacy with a woman murders her.

As in her other novels, Ağaoğlu focuses on different segments in Turkish society; however, in this one, there is an unbridgeable gap between the social classes: between the rich and the poor, between the intellectual and the simple-minded, between the traditional and the modern-minded. Traditions appear as obstacles for all the classes, who live in their own pit, unable to reach beyond its imitations. The novel also refers to the political turmoil and the resulting sense of uncertainty and anxiety in the country. Nevin's son was killed in a terrorist attack, for example. Her husband is now impotent, which, according to Nevin, is caused by the anxiety of the times. Thus, there are three women writers in the novel: Ağaoğlu herself, the frame narrator, and Nevin. One can also say that the novel fictionalizes the process of novel writing. Despite her will, the frame narrator is absorbed in the fiction-making process. In her life, the line between fact and fiction is blurred, and she integrates the things she sees around into Nevin's fictional universe.

Ağaoğlu wrote The SLENDER ROSE OF MY DESIRE as her second novel, following Lying Down to Die. The book describes one day in the life of Bayram, a migrant Turkish worker in Germany. In Curfew (Üç Beş Kişi, 1984), Ağaoğlu deals with social mobility in Eskisehir, a big city in Anatolia. Instead of one consciousness, the narration focuses on six different consciousnesses, making each character the protagonist of each section. Thus, the same events are reflected from six different perspectives as the consciousness of each character travels back and forth in time. In this novel Ağaoğlu tells the metamorphoses of a rural upper-middle-class family with references to the characters from different segments of society. Again, they are defined according to

their positions and traditions, which seem to be the biggest obstacle on their way to self-realization. Women are trapped by the traditional expectations while men are given utmost freedom in their lives on the same issues. Still, all the male characters, except for the liberal-minded businessman Ferit Sakarya, cannot escape being feminized by the traditions. They are not actors, despite the illusion, but acted upon within their social networks.

Interestingly, the most lovable character is Ferit, the businessman. Ağaoğlu faced intense criticism from the leftist media because of the character's portrayal. He is a liberal humanist and immune from the political and social ills of the time. Another sympathetic character is Kardelen, the underprivileged girl who struggles to survive but who can "be" even in the conservative context of Eskisehir, while her friend Kismet, though rich, is devastated by her mother's conventional expectations. Murat, Kismet's brother, suffers from the same predicament as his sister's: He is victimized by his role as the only son of the family. He is sandwiched between his own aspirations to become a musician and those of his mother to make him the future head of the family. He moves to Istanbul, and as he falls in love with a touring singer, Selmin, he vanishes from sight.

Through the love affair between Murat and Selmin, this conservative Eskisehir family is juxtaposed with another family that is also old but fell from grace and sacrificed all its virtues for lavish living. Selmin's family (her mother and sister) are an old aristocratic Istanbul family who have enjoyed relative prosperity. They are loose in morals and feel that they must stoop to the level of these rural "rough" people for financial reasons; ironically, they are taken as predators by these same rough people.

The novel takes place on a June evening in 1980 and revolves around Kismet's decision to escape from her husband to Istanbul, where her brother, Murat, lives. In the end she dares to make her decision and takes the train, but the novel ends in ambiguity as Murat has been attacked by some ambiguous characters just before the curfew. He will not be able to come to meet Kismet, who has never been away from home on her own and who is ignorant of the possible dangers of starting a new life in a big metropolis like Istanbul.

Ağaoğlu has also released "a chamber novel," *Ruh Üşümesi* (*Desolation of the Soul,* 1991), which reflects the emotional misery of the inhabitants of a big city in modern times. It is an experimental novel based on a chance encounter of two people at a restaurant. The woman and man, who have an ordinary look of professional people having their lunch, are placed at the same table by the waiter. As the novel proceeds, we learn that they suffer from an incurable loneliness of their souls in their solipsistic but fragmented worlds. Nothing happens in the novel except that these two people share the same table for a brief time. However, despite the exchange of a few insignificant remarks, each makes the other the focus of his or her fantasies of marriage and a possible sexual intimacy. The narration is based on stream of consciousness and generates many fragmented scenes of fantasy, which make the novel difficult to follow. The lack of a discernible and traditional plotline can leave readers frustrated. This frustration reaches a peak at the end of the novel, when the nameless woman leaves the restaurant as if nothing has happened after sharing the most intimate experiences, though imaginary, with a nameless man.

BIBLIOGRAPHY

Ağaoğlu, Adalet. *Curfew*. Translated by John Goulden. Austin: University of Texas Press, 1997.

Nurten Birlik

AGNON, SAMUEL JOSEPH (SHMUEL YOSEF AGNON, SHMUEL YOSEF HALEVI CZACZKES) (1888–1970) *Hebrew novelist, short story writer*

Shmuel Yosef Agnon (pseudonym of Shmuel Yosef Halevi Czaczkes) was one of the leading Hebrew novelists and short story writers of the 20th century. He was the first Hebrew writer to be awarded the Nobel Prize in literature. In 1966 he shared the Nobel Prize with corecipient Nelly Sachs (1891–1970), a German poet and dramatist. Agnon's works often deal with fading traditions and the conflict between traditional Jewish ways and the evolving modern world. In 1932 he became recognized as one of the central figures of modern Hebrew literature when he published the first edition of his collected works, including the folk epic *The Bridal Canopy* (*Hakhnasat kalah,* 1919).

Agnon was born in Buczacz, eastern Galicia, Austria-Hungary (now Buchach, Ukraine). Growing up in a family of Polish Jewish merchants, scholars, and rabbis, he studied Yiddish, the language spoken at home, and Hebrew, the language of the Bible. He also acquired knowledge of the German language from his mother. His education came in the family home under the direction of his father. As a young writer of short stories and poetry, Agnon wrote in Yiddish and Hebrew at first under his own name and several pseudonyms. It was after immigrating to Palestine in 1907 that the author adopted the surname Agnon and began to write predominately in the Hebrew language. He made his home in Palestine, where he lived the rest of his life.

Agnon's debut as a writer came with his first story about Palestine: "Forsaken Wives" ("Agunot," 1908). His first major work was the novel *The Bridal Canopy* in 1919. Reb Yudel Hasid, the work's central figure, represents the wandering Jew. Readers will readily appreciate Agnon's second novel—one of his most significant works—*A Guest for the Night* (*Ore'ah Nata' Lalun,* 1938). This story describes the bleak circumstances of Jews in eastern Europe after World War I. An anonymous narrator returns from Israel to his home in Galicia (Europe) to find a tragic world: people devastated by war, pogrom and disease. (Agnon once described his hometown of Buczacz as a "city of the dead.") The narrator is also disillusioned by witnessing the loss of traditional values, along with evident material, moral, and spiritual decay. The autobiographical core of this story was Agnon's own return to Buczacz in 1930.

The early pioneer immigrants living in the new state in Palestine are portrayed in his epic *Only Yesterday* (*Temol Shilshom,* 1945), which is critically regarded as Agnon's greatest novel. This work is a powerful description of Palestine in the days of the Second Aliyah, the period of intense emigration into Palestine after World War II, and explores the author's familiar theme of a Westernized Jew who leaves his homeland behind to emigrate to Israel. *Only Yesterday* reflects Agnon's own actual and spiritual experiences; its tone also reveals the somber remembrance of the Holocaust, a time during which the novel was written. Robert Alter in the *Los Angeles Times Book Review* describes the work as "[A] scathing vision of God and man, Zionism and Jewish history, desire and guilt, language, and meaning . . . a novel that deserves comparison with Franz Kafka's *The Trial*. . . . Its appearance in English now, delayed for half a century by the formidable difficulties of translating its Hebrew, makes available to American readers a work of powerful, and eccentric, originality."

Students of Agnon's fiction should know that there exist two different versions of his collected works. This has resulted from the many revisions that the author incorporated into his manuscripts as he reworked his fiction. One collection appears in 11 volumes as *Kol Sipurav Shel Shmuel Yosef Agnon* (vols. 1–6, Berlin, 1931–35; vols. 7–11, Jerusalem and Tel Aviv, 1939–52). The second collection comprises eight volumes, published in Tel Aviv (1953–62).

Critical studies of Agnon's writing include Nitza Ben-Dov's *Agnon's Art of Indirection: Uncovering Latent Content in the Form of S. Y. Agnon* (1993); Anne Golomb Hoffman's *Between Exile and Return: S. Y. Agnon and the Drama of Writing* (1991); David Aberbach's *At the Handles of the Lock: Themes in the Fiction of S. Y. Agnon* (1984); and Baruch Hochman's *The Fiction of S. Y. Agnon* (1970). Hoffman writes in *Between Exile and Return*: "S. Y. Agnon . . . ranks with the major modernists of [the 20th] century, but differs from his European peers in his intense engagement in a universe of sacred language."

Agnon received many prestigious awards, including the Israel Prize in 1954 and 1958. His crowning honor was the Nobel Prize in literature in 1966, the first granted to a Hebrew writer. He died in Rehovot, Israel, on February 17, 1970.

BIBLIOGRAPHY

Aberbach, David. *At the Handles of the Lock: Themes in the Fiction of S. Y. Agnon.* Oxford and New York: Oxford University Press, 1984.

Band, Arnold J. *Studies in Modern Jewish Literature.* Philadelphia: Jewish Publication Society, 2003.

Ben-Dov, Nitza. *Agnon's Art of Indirection: Uncovering Latent Content in the Fiction of S. Y. Agnon.* Leiden and New York: E. J. Brill, 1993.

Frisch, Harold. *S. Y. Agnon.* New York: F. Ungar Publications, 1975.

Hoffman, Anne Golomb. *Between Exile and Return: S. Y. Agnon and the Drama of Writing.* Albany: State University of New York Press, 1991.

Katz, Stephen. *The Centrifugal Novel: S. Y. Agnon's Poetics of Composition.* Madison, N.J.: Fairleigh Dickinson University Press, 1999.

Michael D. Sollars

ALCHEMIST, THE (*O ALQUIMISTA*) PAULO COELHO (1988)

The most popular novel of the Brazilian writer PAULO COELHO (1947–   ), *The Alchemist* combines philosophical ideas and words of wisdom about ambition, perseverance, and success. Since its publication in 1988, the novel has sold over 27 million copies worldwide and has been translated into more than 40 languages. It has topped the best-seller lists in more than 35 countries, bringing international acclaim and honors to Coelho.

The Alchemist narrates the story of a shepherd boy called Santiago who travels with his flock, looking for the best pastures for his sheep in the Andalusian countryside. The conflict arises early in the novel's plot when Santiago chooses to seek an interpretation of a recent dream and is advised to travel to the pyramids in Egypt and look for a hidden treasure. The novel narrates the mystical experiences of Santiago as he travels from Spain, through the Egyptian desert and on to the great pyramids, seeking the fulfillment of his dream.

Coelho's novel is almost mythical in structure, with a linear plot and single story line recounted in simple language. The tightly written narrative is not embellished by elaborate characterization, explanations, or historical details, and any detail irrelevant to the main plot is conspicuously absent. The entire emphasis of the novel remains on eternally valid truths, which Coelho attempts to convey through the story. The symbolic elements in the narrative, the universal quality of the protagonist's experiences, and the message the novel suggests to the reader account for much of *The Alchemist*'s popularity.

The Alchemist underlines an idea or wish that human beings strongly want to believe: If one sincerely desires something, the whole universe conspires to fulfill that dream. Coelho conveys, through the novel, that this sentiment is a lie and that at some point in life people lose the ability to control their lives and become the playthings of fate. He suggests that by listening to one's heart and by heeding omens and signs, one can control destiny.

The strong undercurrent of optimism, which runs through the narrative, is the novel's greatest charm.

It is notable that in the tale Santiago's chance encounters with people bring him closer to his aim and motivate him to continue his quest despite his complacence at times. His meeting with the Gypsy fortune-teller in the beginning is followed immediately by a meeting with the old king of Salem, Melchizedek, who is aware of Santiago's past and future and urges the boy to pursue his vision. An unfortunate experience with a thief in Tangier disheartens the searcher for a time, but his memories of the words of the king guide him to the right course of action. The crystal merchant for whom Santiago works for almost a year prefers to dream of going on a pilgrimage instead of embarking on a journey to Mecca in real life. The crystal merchant's fear of failure shakes Santiago into resolving to follow his dream.

Santiago later meets an Englishman who harbors the hope of meeting the mysterious alchemist, an Arab who lives at the Al-Fayoum oasis and possesses exceptional powers. Santiago joins the caravan with the Englishman to travel to Egypt, and it is during this journey that the shepherd boy comes to know about the soul of the world, the language of the heart, and the intricacies of the science of alchemy. The shepherd boy's budding love for an Arabian girl, Fatima, whom he meets during his voyage through the desert, tempts him into giving up his quest for the treasure, but aptly enough Fatima plays the role of a soul mate and coaxes Santiago to continue his difficult expedition. Toward the end of the novel, Santiago's meeting with the alchemist in the desert helps the young seeker to discover his inner strengths and brings him closer to realizing his destiny.

Omens, signs, dreams, and visions pervade the narrative and act like refrains in this song of the desert. It is only by taking note of these subtle revelations of his subconscious mind that Santiago rises to the alchemist's expectations and bravely faces all the trials that await him. In *The Alchemist,* Coelho suggests through Santiago's tale that it is only by finding and following one's "personal myth" that one can hope to achieve success, contentment, and happiness. Those who do not have the courage to pursue their deepest desires end up living an empty and doomed life plagued by dissatisfaction and frustration.

BIBLIOGRAPHY

Arias, Juan. *Paulo Coelho: The Confessions of a Pilgrim.* London: HarperCollins, 1999.

Coelho, Paulo. *Like the Flowing River: Thoughts and Reflections.* London: HarperCollins, 2006.

Preeti Bhatt

ALEGRÍA, CIRO (1909–67) *Peruvian essayist, novelist*

Ciro Alegría remains one of the most respected Spanish-American writers of the 1940s and 1950s. His work typically focuses on the colonial and postcolonial oppression of the Peruvian Indians. He is often linked with other literary pathbreakers such as Brazil's Joaquim Maria Machado de Assis (1839–1908) and GRACILIANO RAMOS (1892–1953) and Venezuela's RÓMULO GALLEGOS (1884–1969), each of whom wrote, in their own native voices, themes that diverged from the dominant European notion of what the traditional novel and subject should entail. His work is also associated with later fellow Peruvians like Julio Ramón Ribeyro (1929–   ), Alfredo Bryce Echenique (1939–   ), and MARIO VARGAS LLOSA (1936–   ). Alegría became a catalytic revolutionary in Peruvian literature and politics. One of his best-known novels is *Broad and Alien Is the World* (*El mundo es ancho y ajeno,* 1941), a work that lays bare despotic landowners, corrupt governmental officials, and the ubiquitous poverty that haunted the Andean Indians.

Alegría was born in 1909 to Spanish-Irish parents, José Alegría and Herminia Bazán Lynch. He grew up in Sartimbanba, Peru's Marañón River region, where the young Alegría witnessed the oppression of the native people by European colonialist ideology. These experiences became embedded in his mind and later became the content and emphasis of his literary oeuvre. The young Alegría's elementary and secondary education came in Trujillo. Alegría's biographers often highlight the fact that one of the young boy's elementary teachers was the renowned poet and militant Marxist César Vallejo (1892–1938). After finishing his secondary education at the National College of San Juan in Trujillo, he worked briefly as a reporter and in manual labor jobs. He later attended the University of Trujillo and worked for newspaper *El Norte.*

Alegría lived through one of the world's most violent political periods. He was continuously caught up in the violent political intrigue sweeping through his country. During the first part of the 1930s, Alegría took part in political reforms in Peru. In 1930 he joined a radical group of dissidents who overtly pushed for economic and social change to improve the lives of the impoverished Indian people. He was incarcerated in the infamous prison El Sixto in Lima. His political actions forced the activist to flee Peru to Chile. Exiled in South America, Alegría wrote numerous articles and short stories for newspapers in Buenos Aires and other cities. It was while in exile that Alegría penned his first novel, *The Golden Serpent* (*La serpiente de oro,* 1935). This novel brought the author his first serious literary recognition. His second novel, *Los perros hambrientos,* 1938), followed three years later.

Broad and Alien Is the World, one of Alegría's most acclaimed novels, again returns in its subject matter to life in his homeland. The work depicts in vivid detail an Indian tribe struggling to survive against the exploitation from European colonialists. The novel won the author the Latin American Novel Prize in 1941.

Alegría remained in exile from Peru during and after World War II. Between 1941 and 1948 he lived in New York City, where he continued writing. After the war he taught at the University of Puerto Rico, and later, living in Cuba, he wrote articles on the revolution stirring in that island country. It was not until 1957—a decade and a half after he had left Peru—that the author finally returned to his home country. Ironically, it was politics that called him home. Back in Peru, Alegría became a member of the party headed by his friend, President Fernando Belaúnde Terry (1912–2002). Terry held two terms as Peru's president (1963–68; 1980–85). Alegría was elected to the Chamber of Deputies in 1963 when Terry first took control of the country.

Ciro Alegría's unexpected death at the age of 57 was a shock to the literary world. He died in Trujillo on February 17, 1967.

BIBLIOGRAPHY

Barbas-Rhoden, Laura. *Writing Women in Central America: Gender and the Fictionalization of History.* Athens: Ohio University Press, 2003.

Craft, Linda J. *Novels of Testimony and Resistance from Central America.* Gainesville: University of Florida Press, 1997.

Varona, Dora. *Ciro Alegría: trayectoria y mensaje.* Lima: Ediciones Varona, 1972.

Vazquez Amaral, Jose. *The Contemporary Latin American Narrative.* New York: Las Americas Publishing, 1970.

Michael D. Sollars

ALLENDE, ISABEL (1942–   ) *Peruvian essayist, novelist*   Publication of the Peruvian-born Isabel Allende's The HOUSE OF THE SPIRITS (*La casa de los espíritus,* 1982) presaged a new generation of Latin American literature. Allende's novel reveals significant similarities to the work of the authors of the "Boom" period, the literary explosion of Latin American narrative in the 1960s and 1970s—most notably GABRIEL GARCÍA MÁRQUEZ's ONE HUNDRED YEARS OF SOLITUDE. While these comparisons are evident, Allende's first novel has often been designated as marking the beginnings of the post-Boom period in Latin American literature. In any case, *The House of the Spirits* brought a new dimension to Latin American writing. Allende applies a distinctly female point of view to her frequently political subjects and alters or completely discards the magical realism of her male predecessors in literature.

The House of the Spirits also brought Allende international acclaim and attention. Although her subsequent works have also sold well, these later novels owe a great deal of their success to the foundation laid by this early work. Indeed, *The House of the Spirits* reveals themes and motifs that reappear in Allende's following works. Although she eventually progresses away from the overt political concerns of *The House of the Spirits* and her second novel, OF LOVE AND SHADOWS (*De amor y de sombra,* 1984), Allende never completely discards her feminist interests and preoccupation with emotional relationships, even in more recent novels with male protagonists, The INFINITE PLAN and *Zorro.*

Her works are often intensely personal and subjective, exploring the internal motivations and conflicts of the characters even as the novels reveal more universal problems, such as the difficulties of life under a dictatorship or the flaws in a materialistic lifestyle. Allende's novels are also inextricably linked to her own life and background, and her characters and subjects frequently evolve from people or forces in her own experience. There is often little separation between life and art in her novels, whose subjects and emotions often spring from Allende's own experiences and beliefs.

Allende's works feature a panorama of characters from a wide variety of cultures and lifestyles, and they perhaps owe that diversity to the migratory nature of her childhood. Isabel Allende was born in Lima, Peru, in 1942, but she is generally considered a Chilean author. Her mother, named Francisca Llona Barros but called Panchita, left Isabel's father, Tomás Allende, several times, and the two finally annulled their marriage in 1945. Allende's absent father returns in various forms in her novels, and the author's real-life Chilean grandfather, who took in Panchita and her three children, forms the basis for Esteban Trueba in *The House of the Spirits*. Panchita soon fell in love with Ramón Huidobro, and the young Isabel Allende accompanied her stepfather, Tío Ramón, to diplomatic assignments in Bolivia and Beirut. Travel marks intermittent periods of Allende's life, from her exile from Chile under its dictatorship to more recent times, when she lives in the United States in California but regularly visits Spain and Latin America.

Allende's early career as a journalist gives little indication for her later vocation as a novelist, beyond providing evidence of the young woman's remarkable imagination. Her work in journalism does, however, bring to the surface many of the themes central to her books—including feminism. From 1959 to 1965, Allende worked for the Food and Agriculture Organization of the United Nations, and in 1962 she married Miguel Frías. In 1967 she wrote for magazines where she polished her writing skills and developed her feminist ideals. A collection of articles later published as *Civilize Your Troglodyte* (*Civilice a su troglodita,* 1974) is a compilation of witty attacks on male machismo. Despite the critical tone of such essays, Allende's humor tempered her censure, and her writings—as well as the television programs she became involved in—were popular.

In 1973, however, Allende's popularity and success came to an abrupt halt. On September 11, 1973, General Augusto Pinochet Ugarte led a military coup that ended with the death (a speculated assassination) of elected President Salvador Allende, Isabel Allende's uncle. The revolt also dissolved Chile's democracy, and in 1975 Allende left Chile for voluntary exile in Venezuela. Her early years there reflect a sharp contrast to the prosperity she and her family had enjoyed in Chile in the years before the Pinochet dictatorship changed her world. Both she and her husband struggled to find employment, and Allende was unable to find steady work with either magazines or newspapers. In 1981, while writing the volume that eventually became *The House of the Spirits,* Allende was also working 12-hour days at a local school.

Allende did not begin *The House of the Spirits* with the intention of producing a great book—or even any kind of book at all. Instead, *The House of the Spirits* began as an extended letter to her 90-year-old grandfather, the man whose constant presence in her childhood and early adulthood made him one of the most powerful emotional and intellectual influences in her life. The "letter" was intended to preserve her grandfather's memory and the stories of his family. Allende followed this same form of writing years later after another monumental loss: The book *Paula* began as a letter to her daughter who had fallen into a coma.

Many of the characters in *The House of the Spirits* resemble members of Allende's family. Her grandmother underlies the characterization of Clara, although Allende admits that Clara's magical or supernatural attributes are exaggerated. Likewise, Esteban Trueba is not a true portrayal of Allende's grandfather, who, Allende observes, was more benevolent. Other characters in the novel are also drawn from real life; the Candidate represents Salvador Allende, and the Poet is Pablo Neruda. Allende's uncles also provided inspiration for characters in the book. Despite the novel's foundation in real-life characters and political situations, however, the work cannot be considered autobiographical. The elements of magic realism present in *The House of the Spirits* even further disconnect the novel from autobiography or history.

Allende's first work bears some similarity to García Márquez's *One Hundred Years of Solitude*. She has recognized her debt to her predecessors, noting the influence of previous Latin American writers. Allende's feminist viewpoint directs the novel's movement through the lives of Rosa, Clara, Blanca, and Alba. *The House of the Spirits* is, finally, a book concerned with exploring women's lives during a period of entrenched social patriarchy and political turmoil.

Despite the eventual phenomenal success of *The House of the Spirits,* however, Allende did not at first find a publisher for a work written by an unknown female author. Rejected in Latin America, the novel was published in Spain by Plaza y Janés, and it was quickly translated around the world, with the first English translation in 1985. Despite its popularity abroad, the book was banned in Chile, although copies were smuggled into the country. Ironically, after a 15-year exile, Allende returned to Chile in 1990 to receive the Gabriela Mistral prize after the restoration of the country's democracy.

Allende's second novel, *Of Love and Shadows,* continues the political themes of *The House of the Spirits.* Based on a real political crime uncovered in 1978, the book examines the abuses of power under Pinochet's dictatorship. Like *The House of the Spirits,* the book does not directly name the country in which it takes place, but in both books the setting is recognizably Chile.

The English edition of *Eva Luna* (1987) and *The Stories of Eva Luna* (*Cuentos de Eva Luna,* 1990) followed *Of Love and Shadows* in 1988 and 1991, respectively. The novel *Eva Luna* deals with two themes, feminism and narration, which Allende says she was only able to identify after reading criticism on the book itself. Both *Eva Luna* and *Of Love and Shadows* are set in Venezuela, but the novel *Eva Luna* also reflects the end of Allende's first marriage and her growing awareness of her own identity as a woman and a writer. Though the collection of short fiction pieces continues to echo Allende's appreciation of Venezuela, *The Stories of Eva Luna,* represents her experimentation with a different narrative form: short stories.

Allende adopted the short story formula out of necessity in order to adjust to changes in her life. In 1987 she met William (Willie) Gordon, and the following year they married. While writing the collection of tales in *The Stories of Eva Luna,* Allende was living in Gordon's chaotic, noisy household, and she found that the shorter time required to create short stories—as opposed to the much more prolonged period of concentration for a

novel—better fitted her lifestyle at that time. The stories—primarily love stories—also suggest her new married life.

Willie Gordon also influenced Allende's next novel, *The Infinite Plan* (*El plan infinito,* 1991), first published in English in 1993. As in Allende's first book, she took the inspiration for *The Infinite Plan* from real people in her life. Gordon is the model for the novel's central protagonist, Gregory Reeves. *The Infinite Plan* is also Allende's first novel set in the United States as well as her first with a male protagonist. While the book sold well, critical reactions were mixed, probably because of its distinct differences from Allende's earlier books.

In 1991 Allende experienced a great personal tragedy: Her daughter, Paula, fell into a coma from complications of porphyria, a genetic illness. On December 6, 1992, Paula died at the house Allende shared with her husband in California. For Allende, the period of Paula's long illness and dying was devastating, and it eventually resulted in a book-length antidote to her pain, *Paula* (1994), published in English in 1995. Her long letter to her daughter is distinctly autobiographical, an expulsion of pain and acceptance of loss.

After *Paula,* Allende did not immediately return to the style and themes of previous books. Instead, as part of a continuing reaction to the loss of her daughter, Allende turned again to nonfiction with *Aphrodite* (*Afrodita,* 1997), published in English in 1998. Like previous works, the book deals with love and passion; unlike earlier books, it does so in the more lighthearted context of what might be called an erotic cookbook.

In subsequent years, Allende returned to the feminist context and Latin American setting of her early novels. *DAUGHTER OF FORTUNE* (*Hija de la fortuna,* 1998) and *Portrait in Sepia* (*Retrato en sepia,* 2000), published in English respectively in 1999 and 2001, form a trilogy with her first book, *The House of the Spirits. Daughter of Fortune,* set in the middle 1800s, and *Portrait in Sepia,* dealing with the years between 1860 and 1910, provide background to *The House of the Spirits,* which looks at the 20th century. Both *Daughter of Fortune* and *Portrait in Sepia* deal less with criticism of grand social injustice—the tyrannies of a dictatorship, for example—than with the oppression and marginalization of women. The two later books also demonstrate Allende's progressive movement away from the earlier style of magic realism toward a more realistic historical perspective.

Allende's latest books suggest her truest motivation for writing. Famously, she denies interest in the reviews or criticism of her novels; her primary motivation for writing, she says, has always been simply to tell a story. Her recent movement toward children's or young adult literature emphasizes her desire to reach her readers in this narrative, rather than critical, way. *City of the Beasts* (*La ciudad de las bestias,* 2002), *Kingdom of the Golden Dragon* (*El reino del dragon de oro,* 2003), and *Forest of the Pygmies* (*El bosque de los pigmeos,* 2004), published respectively in English in 2002, 2004, and 2005, address a younger audience than that attracted by her earlier books.

But Allende has not lost her political edge. A memoir published in 2003, *My Invented Country* (*Mi país inventado*), closely examines the dark realities of her homeland, Chile, as well as her own sometimes fantastic responses to it. The military coup of September 11, 1973, in which Salvador Allende lost his life and Chile lost its democracy, and the violent attack upon the United States by terrorists of September 11, 2001, precipitated the writing of a new novel and influenced its subject. In her book *Zorro: A Novel* (2005), Allende returns to the California setting of *The Infinite Plan* but examines an earlier time and setting in which political strife and social injustice recall frequent themes found in her earlier books.

Allende's narrative strengths have greatly changed and matured since the 1982 publication of her first novel, *The House of the Spirits.* While her interests in female characters and social structures have remained constant, she can no longer be accused of a simple mimicry of the magic realism of other writers like García Márquez. Isabel Allende has mastered a wide range of narrative forms, from the novel to the short story to the memoir, and she has developed her own unique and valuable voice—a distinctly female voice—among Latin American writers.

BIBLIOGRAPHY

Antoni, Robert. "Parody or Piracy: The Relationship of *The House of the Spirits* to *One Hundred Years of Solitude.*" *Latin American Literary Review* 16, no. 32 (1988): 16–28.

Correas Zapata, Celia. *Isabel Allende: Life and Spirits.* Translated by Margaret Sayers Peden. Houston: Arte Público Press, 2002.

Crystall, Elyse, et al. "An Interview with Isabel Allende." *Contemporary Literature* 33, no. 4 (1992): 585–600.

Graham, Philip. "A Less Magical Realism." *New Leader* 84, no. 6 (2001): 38–39.

Hart, Patricia. *Narrative Magic in the Fiction of Isabel Allende.* Rutherford, N.J.: Fairleigh Dickinson University Press, 1989.

Jenkins, Ruth Y. "Authorizing Female Voice and Experience: Ghosts and Spirits in Kingston's *The Woman Warrior* and Allende's *The House of the Spirits.*" *Melus* 19, no. 3 (1994): 61–73.

Rodden, John, ed. *Conversations with Isabel Allende.* Austin: University of Texas Press, 1999.

Rojas, Sonia Riguelme, and Edna Aguirre Rehbeim, eds. *Critical Approaches to Isabel Allende's Novels.* New York: Peter Lang, 1991.

Shea, Maureen E. "Love, Eroticism, and Pornography in the Works of Isabel Allende." *Women's Studies* 18 (1990): 223–231.

Tasker, Fred. "Writings Mirror Isabel Allende's Personal Odyssey," *The Miami Herald,* 1 April 1998.

Toms, Michael. "Interview with Isabel Allende." *Common Boundary* (May/June 1994): 16–23.

Elliott Winter

ALL MEN ARE MORTAL (*TOUS LES HOMMES SONT MORTELS*) SIMONE DE BEAUVOIR (1946)

Published just following World War II, *All Men Are Mortal* by SIMONE DE BEAUVOIR (1908–86) speaks vehemently and passionately against vanity, the desire to control, and the desire for dictatorial power. Curious and existential, it is a type of philosophical ghost story. Like many of Beauvoir's other novels, *All Men Are Mortal* begins from within the emotional life and social situations of an upper-middle-class artist. Unlike Beauvoir's other novels, however, it does not stay in that realm—instead, it departs for a supernatural sphere while at the same time navigating through centuries of European political history. Throughout one artist's odd relationship with a supernatural being, the story depicts self-serving mortality and immortality in such a way that each makes the other seem both meaningless and horrifying. Above all, *All Men Are Mortal* emphasizes the futility of living with the desire to control, to enslave, or to rise above others.

The novel begins with the presentation of an excessively vain and jealous actress, Regina, who secretly rages against the happiness of others, including that of her friends. She suffers in the knowledge that her life, beauty, and joy are not individual to her. Even romantic love, or the "great human drama," is unsatisfying for her because she knows, as Beauvoir seems to indicate, that the experience is not unique. She finds life unbearable because she must share attention with others and must acknowledge that she is not the center of all things and people. Alongside Regina's somewhat tormented path, Beauvoir places "middle-class houses" with "heart-shaped vents," perhaps representative of bourgeois mediocrity and love within a mediocre existence. Most painful to Regina, it seems, is the idea that time is passing and one day she will grow old and cease to exist.

Regina's dissatisfaction and jealousy culminate when, in the courtyard of the hotel where she stays with her male companion, Roger, she sees a man who hardly moves and does not seem to desire to eat or sleep. She is sure the man "doesn't know what boredom is." He seems so self-assured that in his presence she thinks that she may not even exist. Regina's insecurity draws her closer to the strange man, as though she thinks she might be capable of appropriating his peculiar form of enlightenment. After some investigating, she learns that his name is Raymond Fosca and that he has recently been released from an insane asylum. Regina makes his acquaintance and announces that she plans to cure him, which seems neither to startle nor interest him. There is nevertheless an attraction between them, as they both continually return to the subject of the passing of time. Fosca's problem, he says, is not that he is insane but that he is immortal.

After only a brief time, Regina begins to believe in Fosca's condition of immortality and falls in love with him. She seems convinced that she might, by being close to Fosca, also become immortal. Time, as an idea, becomes repugnant to Regina, and she makes that aversion known by occasionally lashing out at her friends if they even mention the time. It is unclear if Regina behaves as her true self when she spends time with her friends, who accept temporality, or when she

spends time with Fosca, who persistently avers that he is immortal and timeless. Naturally, Regina's love affair with a man her friends declare to be a lunatic isolates her from them and from her previous life. To everyone else it seems that Regina is falling into a type of insanity with this man Fosca, while she seems to believe that she is falling into a type of timeless immortality, or at least an enlightened state.

It is Regina's ambition that Fosca become a playwright and write parts for her, but he does not share her enthusiasm for artistic creation and seems uninspired. Regina begs to be allowed to understand his lethargy or depression, and finally Fosca tells her the story of how he became immortal. Fosca's tale, which constitutes the major part of the book, begins in medieval Italy, when he drinks a magic potion that, after causing several days of unconsciousness, makes him immortal. Already an important official and warrior of the city of Carmona, the newly supernatural Fosca becomes a master strategist, dictator, and murderer, first only in Italy and then in all of Europe. With the ability to live beyond all loved ones and enemies, there seems to be nothing for him to do except win battles and accumulate political power, century after century.

Fosca describes making his way through the time of the Hapsburg Empire, the exploration and colonization of the New World, the English Reformation, and the French Revolution, among other events. In the course of Fosca's life, or his living condition, he loves and loses several women partners, his son, and many friends. His relationships are deep and meaningful and at the same time empty and meaningless, since he knows that he will retain his life and his power long after his companions have expired and faded away. The men he befriends envy his condition but make use of it in their political endeavors. The women who become aware of Fosca's immortality feel disgust and fear for his condition and, quite reasonably, do not believe in his love for them. Fosca himself discovers that a life without end does not have much meaning; the future, he realizes, stretches out before him as an endless, gloomy plain. He becomes a scientist, coldly examining the world without truly caring for anything. His curiosities, desires, and hopes all vanish, and his life becomes an even path of destruction and loss.

Fosca's story reveals that he has lived with what the fame-seeking Regina initially desires—immortality, eternal youth, and ultimate power over others—but finally it horrifies her, as it does many other women in Fosca's history. His condition indicates that mortality and helplessness, or the weight of events within a normal life span, define humanness or give meaning to one's life. According to *All Men Are Mortal*, Fosca is not a man but something else, even something monstrous. His immortality and dictatorial successes have brought him nothing but torturous over-satiation, the endless desire for desire, and the yearning for death or for freedom from existence.

Fosca's observations also reveal that what many men and women strive toward, to rise above their stations, is also a futile endeavor, since all men and women will eventually cease to exist and will be forgotten. Fosca's exposure of the insignificance of all things and people leaves Regina "defeated," as Beauvoir says in one of the novel's final lines. After Fosca has coldly taken his leave of her, she releases "the first scream," with which she expresses the ultimate realization of her insignificance. It is a scream in fear of death, but also of living a futile life; it is certainly a scream akin to the existential terror felt by the World War–period intellectuals. Through Fosca's dismal immortality and Regina's neuroses, Beauvoir seems to ponder the essence of cruel, selfish, and psychotic dictatorships. With the "first" of Regina's screams, Beauvoir gives voice to the horror, contempt, and revulsion she and her contemporaries must have felt for Hitler's domination of Europe during World War II.

BIBLIOGRAPHY

Bair, Deirdre. *Simone de Beauvoir*. New York: Summit Books, 1990.

Beauvoir, Simone de. *Adieux: A Farewell to Sartre*. Translated by Patrick O'Brian. New York: Pantheon Books, 1984.

Crosland, Margaret. *Simone de Beauvoir: The Woman and Her Work*. London: Heinemann, 1992.

Evans, Mary. *Simone de Beauvoir*. London and Thousand Oaks, Calif.: Sage, 1996.

Fullbrook, Kate, and Edward Fullbrook. *Simone de Beauvoir and Jean-Paul Sartre*. New York: Harvester Wheatsheaf, 1993.

Grosholz, Emily R. *The Legacy of Simone de Beauvoir*. Oxford: Clarendon Press, 2004.

Johnson, Christopher. *Thinking in Dialogue*. Nottingham, U.K.: University of Nottingham, 2003.

Okley, Judith. *Simone de Beauvoir: A Re-Reading*. London: Virago Press, 1986.

Simons, Margaret A. *Beauvoir and the Second Sex: Feminism, Race, and the Origin of Existentialism*. Lanham, Md.: Rowman & Littlefield, 1999.

Tidd, Ursula. *Simone de Beauvoir, Gender and Testimony*. Cambridge and New York: Cambridge University Press, 1999.

Susan Kirby-Smith

ALL QUIET ON THE WESTERN FRONT (IM WESTEN NICHTS NEUES) ERICH MARIA REMARQUE (1929)

All Quiet on the Western Front depicts the disillusionment of Paul Baumer, a young foot soldier fighting in World War I. Written by ERICH MARIA REMARQUE (1898–1970), this depiction of the horrors of war is one of the most renowned German works of the 20th century. Drawing on his own experience as a young man conscripted into military service for Germany, Remarque not only uses the character of Paul as his own mouthpiece but also makes his protagonist symbolic of the situation of all the soldiers who fought on either side of the western front. Stretching 440 miles from the Swiss border to the North Sea, the line of trenches and barbed wire fences moved little between 1914 and 1918, despite incessant attempts on both sides to break through. This infamous front became a symbol of the most futile and meaningless aspects of World War I.

Of particular importance in *All Quiet on the Western Front* is the novel's style. The down-to-earth and unassuming narrative voice of Paul Baumer avoids anything in the way of high or polished rhetoric. The style is clean and reportorial, working deliberately against an idiom of heroic adventure or romantic patriotism. Although the young Paul is shown to possess a lyrical and sensitive side, nothing in his narrative is inflated or elevated; indeed, even his death is deliberately made to seem anticlimactic.

The setting of this novel is also of utmost importance. The *Western Front* of the title is the name for the most important sequence of battlefields in the war. It was here that such modern weapons as poison gas, powerful explosives, and machine guns were first deployed, making the scale of injury and death catastrophic. In addition, individual soldiers were considered disposable in a military strategy of attrition; battles continued for months while corpses and casualties mounted. To Paul, who is thrown into this world with little preparation, the battles on the front are mad, meaningless, and frightening; when ordinary days with his comrades are interrupted by chaotic periods of battle, it is as if he has been plunged into a waking nightmare.

While most of the vivid narrative episodes take place on the front lines, a section of the book depicts Paul's return to his home, which serves as a contrast to his horrific experience on the front lines. Paul's books, his butterfly collection, and all personal mementoes of his previous life now seem part of a world he has left behind forever. While suffering deprivation, the people back home have no idea of the dimension and depth of the suffering on the battlefields of the western front. In fact, Paul feels that he must lie to his family and the others in the town because they would not be able to handle or understand the truth. This trip home consolidates Paul's sense that he is part of a generational shift involving a dramatic break with the past.

A prominent demonstration of this alienation occurs when Corporal Himmelstoss, who had sadistically hazed the boys when they were undergoing basic training, is posted to the front. Instead of viewing him as a member of their unit, the comrades attack him at an opportune moment, beating him severely. The reader comes to understand that for the young soldiers, the war is against not only the enemy, but also against the elders of the former generation who are responsible for its carnage and for stealing the youth of the men who had to fight in it. These father figures, once assumed to be guides to the adult world, are now perceived as having no insight or wisdom—indeed as having betrayed the younger generation. Paul and his skeptical, mocking comrades see the authorities to whom they had previously deferred as impervious to the realities of loss and suffering they have caused. In addition, contrary to the official patriotic optimism of the higher-ranked soldiers, the younger comrades suspect that, in reality, their country will not emerge victorious at the end of the day.

With the exception of the resourceful Stanislaus Katczinsky, a fortyish man known as Kat, Paul and the other soldiers are all very young men who have gone straight from the schoolroom to the battlefield. As a result, a generation of young men comes of age in a crisis environment. For Paul and his generation, initiation into adulthood is unusually brutal and traumatic—even those who survive will be psychologically scarred for life. One incident that fills Paul with rage and remorse, for instance, is the way in which his former classmate Kemmerich receives a wound which, because it is poorly cared for by medical officials, turns fatal. By the time Kemmerich dies, however, both Paul and his fellow soldier Muller are more concerned about the fate of Kemmerich's boots. This is a result of the failure on the part of the authorities to supply the troops with necessary clothing and equipment; it is also a sign of a general dehumanizing set of values in which the dying man's boots become more important than the dying man himself.

Another traumatic episode concerns Paul's killing of a French soldier, Gerard Duval. Horrified and conscience-stricken, Paul looks through the soldier's personal belongings and realizes that this Duval, although not German, was not his enemy but a fellow victim of a war machine that destroyed their generation and its aspirations. Episodes such as this remind the reader that this is a universal story depicting not simply the German point of view but the experience of all of the young men on the battlefields of Europe at the time. Not long after this event, Paul falls in battle. The last survivor of the group of comrades we have been following throughout the novel, Paul is shot by random enemy fire on a quiet, ordinary day not long before the war officially ends. The cold impersonality and absurdity of Paul's death is described in a very short paragraph which abruptly and shockingly concludes the novel, reinforcing the novel's basic purpose: to foreground the individual victim of a conflict fought with advanced, lethal weapons for inexplicable reasons. At the same time, Paul's death represents the experience of a generation of young men sacrificed to a senseless, devastating war that emphasized how an entire civilization teetered on the verge of self-destruction.

A literary sensation when first published, *All Quiet on the Western Front* has remained among the most read and most memorable of all antiwar novels. Banned in the 1930s by the Nazis, who subjected all Remarque's work to public burnings, the novel has survived as one of the most indispensable literary documents of the 20th century.

BIBLIOGRAPHY

Barker, Christine R., and R. W. Last. *Erich Maria Remarque.* New York: Barnes & Noble, 1979.

Firda, Richard Arthur. *All Quiet on the Western Front: Literary Analysis and Cultural Context.* New York: Twayne Publishing, 1993.

Tims, Hilton. *Erich Maria Remarque: The Last Romantic.* New York: Carroll & Graf, 2003.

Wagener, Hans. *Understanding Erich Maria Remarque.* Columbia: University of South Carolina Press, 1991.

Margaret Boe Birns

AMADO, JORGE (1912–2001) *Brazilian novelist, screenwriter*

The works of modernist Jorge Amado, one of the most famous Brazilian writers of the 20th century, have been read around the globe. He is particularly remembered for the book and screen adaptation of *Dona Flor and Her Two Husbands* (*Dona Flor e seus dois maridos*) in 1978.

Amado was born the son of cocoa planters on a farm called Auricidia, in the outskirts of the town of Itabuna, in the state of Bahia, Brazil. He attended elementary and high school in the capital of Salvador and studied law in the Faculdade de Direito da Universidade do Brasil, in Rio de Janeiro. Married twice, first to Matilde Garcia Rosa and later to Zelia Gattai, he died in Salvador in 2001.

Amado wrote more than 20 romances. Even a sampling of his oeuvre makes an impressive list: *Land of Carnival* (*O país do carnaval*); CACAO (*Cacau*); *Sweat* (*Suor*); *Sea of Death* (*Mar morto*); *Captains of the Sand* (*Capitães da areia*); *The War of the Saints* (*Jubiabá*); *The* VIOLENT LAND (*Terras do sem fim*); *The Golden Harvest* (*São Jorge dos Ilheus*); *Gabriela Clove and Cinnamon* (*Gabriela cravo e clanela*); *Shepherds in the Night* (*Os pastores da noite*); *Dona Flor and Her Two Husbands*; *Tent of Miracles* (*Tenda dos milagres*); *Tereza Batista—The Home of Wars* (*Tereza Batista cansada de guerra*); *Pen, Sword, Camisole: A Fable to Kindle Hope* (*Farda, fardão e camisola de dormir*); *Showdown* (*Tocaia Grande*); and *Tieta: A Novel* (*Tieta do Agreste*). A highly versatile author, he also wrote historical essays, short stories, plays, newspaper articles, and screenplays, and he experimented in writing poetry and songs. Many of his novels were adapted for the silver screen, stage, and television.

Amado's presence in the literary world began in 1930 and ended only with his death, as he remained active in writing throughout his life. His works have been translated for readers in more than 50 countries. His literary success began with his first book, *Land of Carnival,* written when he was 18 years old. He would go on to influence generations of writers in terms of subject matter and style. It is interesting that for years many of the Brazilian Livias, Marianas, and Gabrielas born in Brazil were named after the characters of Amado's romances, such as *Sea of Death* and *Gabriela Clove and Cinnamon.*

Amado's works reflect the movement conventionally called the Rediscovery of Brazil in the decade of the 1930s, as well as during the reevaluation of the country that took place in the 1960s and the 1970s. This was a period when the sociopolitical-economic bases of Brazilian society saw much change, including a new bourgeois morality regarding sexual behavior and increasing lack of understanding between the social classes and races in Brazil.

Amado's extraordinary sense of the necessity of communication compelled him to relate to the writers of his time. He contributed to the translation into Portuguese of works by such Latin-American artists as RÓMULO GALLEGOS, Enrique Amorim, Jorge Icaza, and CIRO ALEGRÍA. The extraordinary reception to his work was certainly a result of the author's devotion to social causes, including his fight against oppression and the exploitation of the workers. To that he added, later in time, an involvement with the fight for a complete, or existential, liberty. His modernist tendencies would echo those of the French leader of existentialism, JEAN-PAUL SARTRE.

In 1932 Amado joined the Brazilian Communist Party, at the time an illegal organization with which he had become familiar through the noted writer Rachel de Queiroz. He was arrested on several occasions, and in 1936 he was detained in the city of Natal for taking part in the frustrated communist revolution of 1935. Later he traveled through Latin America, visited the

United States, and resided in São Paulo and Rio de Janeiro. He took part in the movements to end Getulio Vargas's dictatorship and for the amnesty of the political prisoners of that regime.

In 1945 Amado was elected federal deputy for the Brazilian Constituent Assembly as a representative of the Brazilian Communist Party, which had gained its legal status by then. He assumed office the following year, but in 1948 his mandate was extinguished, as the party was once again declared illegal. On behalf of the Communist Party, he traveled to Paris on a mission to share his countrymen's ideas; his departure, as a coincidence, saved him from an arrest order that had just been issued for him. While in Paris, he communicated with various personalities in the arts and literature, including Sartre, Pablo Picasso, Pablo Neruda, and Louis Aragon. Later he traveled through Europe and the Soviet Union and participated in the World Congress of Writers for Peace, held in Poland. During that time, he also visited China, Mongolia, and, later, several countries of South America. In 1951 he was granted the Lenin Peace Prize.

In 1956 Amado left the Communist Party, alleging that he wanted to concentrate on his writing. Five years later he was unanimously elected a member of the Brazilian Academy of Letters (Academia Brasileira de Letras) in the first voting. To some extent he was boycotted by governmental leaders and repudiated by some Brazilian literary critics. In 1994 he established permanent residence in Salvador, where he was granted the Camões Ward (Prêmio Camões), the most prestigious literary award to a writer in Portuguese.

Amado's works often focus on the life of the poor social classes of Bahia. His novels portray the exploitation of workers and the greed and insensitivity of business production owners. In contrast, his romances steer clear of gloom and hopelessness. Rather, they emphasize the force and ability of the poor classes to fight their unfavorable situation for better living conditions and happiness.

Many Brazilian literary critics have considered Amado's fiction works, mainly the part published in and after 1956, too steeped in prejudice against the owners of commerce and in favor of the poor classes. According to these detractors, Amado's characters disguise Brazilian problems and conflicts in a mixture of sensuality and mysticism, methods that avoid real discussions of the country's dire problems. A new generation of critics—among them Eduardo de Assis Duarte, who wrote *Jorge Amado: Romance em tempo de utopia* (*Jorge Amado: Romance in Utopia Times*)—has offered a fresh view of Amado's oeuvre. De Assis Duarte, in valorizing Amado's work, gives the novels deserved merit based on his analysis of their romantic tradition and adventurous characteristics rather than a social or Marxist reading.

Cacau and *Dona Flor and Her Two Husbands* are two of Amado's most celebrated works. These two books also reflect the tone, subject, and characters found in many of his other fictional pieces. *Cacau* was published in 1933 and inaugurated the so-called Cocoa Cycle, a series of books focused on cocoa plantations. Its first edition was sold out in little more than one month. This romance and Amado's subsequent work, *Sweat*, clandestinely reached Portugal, where they were banned, influencing the formation of the Portuguese Neorealism movement. In fact, in a provocative introductory note to *Cacau*, the author declares: "I tried to describe in this book, in a minimum of literature and a maximum of honest realism, the sub-human conditions of the life of the workers of cocoa farms in Southern Bahia State. Will it be considered a proletarian romance?"

The story is entirely narrated by the character Jose Cordeiro, a middle-class young man from the Brazilian state of Sergipe, who, having lost everything, looks for work in southern Bahia in the hope of getting back on his feet. He discovers that love and politics make for strange bedfellows. He finds work on the farm owned by "Colonel" Manoel Misael de Souza Telles, a man who is called Mané Flagel by his employees for his questionable moral qualities. On the farm, Jose Cordeiro makes friends with some coworkers, who nickname him "The Sergipe Man." He then experiences the subhuman working conditions experienced by all the poor workers on the cocoa plantation. Meanwhile, he is attracted to Maria, the colonel's daughter. She falls in love with Cordero, proposes marriage, and offers him an administrator's position on her father's farm. Cordeiro resists her, seeing her as an enemy of the working class. He leaves the farm abruptly, journeys to São Paulo, and joins the Communist Party.

Dona Flor and Her Two Husbands, written in 1967, is set in the city of Salvador. It narrates in third person the story of Floripedes, nicknamed Dona Flor, a young and attractive teacher of the culinary arts. Her first husband, Vadinho, an easygoing gambler and bohemian, dies on a Mardi Gras Sunday, leaving her terribly heartbroken. Shortly after, though, she marries the local pharmacist, the meticulous Teodoro Madureira, with whom she begins to live a tranquil and undemanding life, very much the way she always dreamed.

One day the phantom of Vadinho appears to her, proposing that she and he resume their former sexual and emotional interplay. Dona Flor tries to resist his proposal and goes to the point ordering of a powerful hex to be made to make this apparition disappear. Complications mount. The hex takes too long to start working, leaving Vadinho sufficient time to convince Dona Flor that he is still her husband and that he can produce the best of all worlds for her. She can have both husbands to complete her life. With the pharmacist Madureira she will have a stable life, and with Vadinho she will enjoy her old conjugal passion. She finally gives in to him. At that moment, however, the hex starts working, and Vadinho's phantom begins to weaken, nearly disappearing. Faced with the possibility of losing Vadinho forever, and the promise of passion, Dona Flor gathers all her will to oppose the hex that she herself had ordered. From this chaos comes a new order. The three characters begin to compose a triangle that only Dona Flor can perceive, and she willingly accepts both husbands, receiving from each what she desires. This is one of Jorge Amado's most intriguing romances, painting the constructive force of desire.

Dona Flor and her Two Husbands was adapted for a movie directed by Bruno Barreto in 1976, becoming the greatest box-office success of the Brazilian cinema. The romance was also adapted for television by Dias Gomes of Globo TV NetWork and in 1997 for a musical play, then named *Sarava,* by Richard Nash, with musical scores by Mitch Leigh, directed and choreographed by Rick Atwell and Santo Loquasto.

BIBLIOGRAPHY

Amado, Jorge. *Cacao.* Translated by Estela Dos Santos. Caracas: Biblioteca Ayacucho, 1991.

———. *Dona Flor and Her Two Husbands.* Translated by Harriet de Onis. New York: Knopf, 1969.

———. *Pen, Sword, Camisole: A Fable to Kindle Hope.* Translated by Helen R. Lane. New York: Avon Books, 1985.

Brower, Keith, et al., eds. *Jorge Amado: New Critical Essays.* New York; London: Routledge, 2001.

Denning, Michael. *Culture in the Age of Three Worlds.* London and New York: Verso, 2004.

Eliana Bueno-Ribeiro

AMERIKA FRANZ KAFKA **(1927)** The Czech writer FRANZ KAFKA (1883–1924) wrote *Amerika* between 1911 and 1914, but the novel was not published until 1927, several years after the author's death. Kafka never crossed the Atlantic to America, and much of his knowledge of the New World was drawn from family lore and writings by Charles Dickens (who wrote of his travels in the United States) and the fantasist Karl May. Kafka's narrative depicts the inconclusive struggle of a young man named Karl Rossman who ventures to the United States in order to escape a pregnancy scandal in his homeland. Karl's attempts to gain a foothold in an alien, incomprehensible country are perpetually stymied by various restrictive scenarios and domineering personalities.

America is represented as alternately emancipatory and confining. Upon his arrival and serendipitous encounter with his Uncle Jacob, Karl feels relatively positive about his new environment. But despite his preconceived idealization of America and the luxurious accommodation at his uncle's home, Karl becomes increasingly claustrophobic. Effectively imprisoned in his room, he is governed by his uncle, who "frowned with annoyance if he ever found Karl out on the balcony." When the pair visit Mr. Pollunder's country house, Karl feels oppressed by its "endless corridors, the chapel, the empty rooms, the darkness everywhere" and by Pollunder's daughter Clara, who attempts to seduce him.

Eventually expelled by his uncle for breaking curfew, Karl travels deeper into the country and hooks up with two scoundrels, Robinson and Delamarche. In the town of Ramses, Karl becomes "the lowest and most dispensable employee in the enormous hierarchy of the hotel's domestics." The work is grueling, and the exhaustion it produces in Karl compounds his sense of alienation: "After a twelve-hour shift, coming off duty at six o'clock in the morning, he was so weary that he went straight to bed without heeding anyone." Karl does, however, befriend a young secretary named Therese, but after being falsely accused of thievery, Karl is once again dismissed. One regime is swiftly exchanged for another, as Karl moves on to work for a despotic, obese woman named Brunelda, who is Delamarche's mistress. Robinson warns Karl that "this isn't service here, it's slavery."

Karl's sense of conscription is expressed by the physical "embraces" he receives from people he encounters. An interrogating Mr. Pollunder "put his arm round Karl and drew him between his knees" and "involuntarily [Karl] struggled to free himself from Pollunder's arm." Later, when Karl finds himself literally suffocated by Brunelda's fleshiness, "he flinched in an involuntary but unsuccessful attempt to escape from the pressure of her body." These episodes of forced engagement are micro-illustrations of the larger restrictive systems within which the immigrant Karl must function. In each case, Karl's attempts to extricate himself from the embrace are described as "involuntary"—as if his aversion to this form of contact is a reflexive matter of self-preservation and not merely discomfort. The incidents with Brunelda, where "his head, which was pressed against her breast . . . could move neither backwards nor sideways," as well as Clara Pollunder's erotic advances, recall Karl's earlier experience with a maidservant. It was she who forcibly seduced him and became pregnant—the instance of physical coercion that had led to Karl's exile in the first place.

Instead of a land of freedom, America, both materially and symbolically, becomes Karl's land of bondage. The Nature Theater of Oklahoma—whose advertisement banners declare "Everyone is welcome!"—becomes the next and (in the context of this unfinished novel) "final" means of escape. The theater's recruitment event abounds in the metaphors and rhetoric of salvation: A group of trumpet players dressed up as angels greet the prospective employees, and Karl notes that even "destitute, disreputable characters" are hired. Furthermore, the train journey to Oklahoma is an optimistic one, if only because it impresses upon Karl the sheer enormity of his adoptive country: "Everything that went on in the little compartment, which was

thick with cigarette-smoke in spite of the open window, faded into comparative insignificance before the grandeur of the scene outside." Images of wide-open landscapes abound in the novel's final scene: "Masses of blue-black rock rose in sheer wedges to the railway line; even craning one's neck out the window, one could not see their summits."

The religious resonances in *Amerika* are profound. Parallels can be drawn between Karl and the biblical Joseph, who is blamed for an older woman's sexual advances and is forced to leave his home. Like the Israelites' exodus, which is guided by a pillar of fire, Karl's arrival in America is marked by a bright light: "A sudden burst of sunshine seemed to illumine the Statue of Liberty." Rather than a torch, however, the Statue of Liberty holds a sword, foreshadowing, perhaps, impending conflict and struggle. Karl is entering territory which may prove to be the antithesis of the promised land he expects, in the same way that that Joseph discovered in Egypt the land of his people's eventual enslavement. As the Jews fled Egypt, so too does Karl leave the land of slave labor for an unknown but promising territory; as he departs, "hundreds of women dressed as angels in white robes with great wings on their shoulders were blowing on long trumpets that glittered like gold." Moreover, the Nature Theater's claim that it "can find employment for everyone, a place for everyone" echoes Moses' insistence on everyone's inclusion in the new land.

Since Kafka never finished writing *Amerika* (the manuscript, along with his other work, was edited and published by Max Brod after Kafka's death from tuberculosis), it remains unclear whether Oklahoma will offer the freedom that Karl seeks. Kafka had told Brod that the Nature Theater of Oklahoma chapter was going to be the novel's last, and that the story would end with Karl finding a job, a home, freedom, and even his parents in this "almost limitless" environment. However, on another occasion, Kafka said that Karl would eventually be executed. The original (working) title of the novel, *The Man Who Disappeared,* would affirm this moribund prediction; Karl's decision to join the theater and, in particular, the name he provides to the recruiters—"Negro"—may signal a final acquiescence to marginality and oppression, an opting out of the social and economic systems in which he had formerly been eager to participate. The theater may thus be less a salvation and more, as the German Marxist literary critic and philosopher Walter Benjamin has asserted, "a place where the self is disconfirmed."

BIBLIOGRAPHY

Bridgwater, Patrick. *Kafka's Novels: An Interpretation.* Amsterdam: Rodopi, 2003.

Brod, Max. *Franz Kafka, a Biography.* New York: Schocken Books, 1960.

Cooper, Gabriele von Natzmer. *Kafka and Language: In the Stream of Thoughts and Life.* Riverside, Calif.: Ariadne Press, 1991.

Kafka, Franz. *Kafka—The Complete Stories.* Edited by Nahum N. Glatzer. New York: Schocken Books, 1976.

Karl, Frederick Robert. *Franz Kafka: Representative Man.* New York: Ticknor & Fields, 1991.

Loose, Gerhard. *Franz Kafka and Amerika.* Frankfurt am Main: V. Klostermann, 1968.

Mailloux, Peter Alden. *A Hesitation before Birth: The Life of Franz Kafka.* Newark: University of Delaware Press, 1989.

Pawel Ernst. *The Nightmare of Reason: The Life of Franz Kafka.* New York: Farrar, Straus and Giroux, 1983.

Kiki Benson

ANDRADE, MARIO DE (MÁRIO SOBRAL)
(1893–1945) *Brazilian novelist, poet* In his preface to *Hallucinated City* (1922), Mario de Andrade elegantly states that "there are certain figures of speech in which we can see the embryo of oral harmony, just as we can find the germ of musical harmony in the reading of the symphonies of Pythagoras." This marriage of music, literature, and aesthetics typifies Andrade's life and work. Born to middle-class parents in São Paulo, Brazil, Mario de Andrade demonstrated exceptional musical skill at a very young age. He pursued musical studies at the Music and Drama Conservatory in São Paulo and upon graduation in 1917 published his first book of poems, entitled *There Is A Drop of Blood in Each Poem* (*Há uma gota de sangue em cada poema*) under the pseudonym Mário Sobral.

Andrade's first publication was not well received, and he moved to the rural countryside, where he began documenting both the history and culture of the Brazilian interior. By 1922 he had not only broadened the scope of his writing but also formed a group of artists interested in experimenting with both form and content. Andrade and Grupo dos Cinco, or the Group of Five, shared an intense commitment to the incorporation of nationalism in all forms of artistic expression. All modernists, the Group of Five helped Andrade formulate what would become a distinctly Brazilian form of the flourishing European movement. As a result of the group's new artistic manifesto, Andrade collaborated with artist Anita Malfetti and poet Oswald de Andrade in 1922 to host the Week of Modern Art, an event that would introduce their work as well as modernism to a wider audience. While planning the exhibition, Andrade also composed what became Brazil's first piece of avant-garde literature, a book of poems dedicated to São Paulo and aptly named *Hallucinated City*.

Andrade's poetic musings on São Paulo represented his developing artistic philosophy and, unlike his first poetic endeavor, integrated fragmented descriptions and Brazilian folklore with local dialect. His readings from *Hallucinated City* served as the focal point for the week-long exhibition and drew a considerable audience. However, despite the success of the Week of Modern Art, the Group of Five disbanded in 1929, and Andrade resumed his travels throughout the country. His growing fascination with the languages, music, and cultures of Brazil is deeply reflected in all of his work but especially in the pieces following the early 1920s. During this time Andrade's exploration of relationships between artistic compositions and the music of the street and country began to translate into poetry and prose that resulted in his most successful project: his novel *Macunaíma* (1928).

Translated into numerous languages and made into several film adaptations, *Macunaíma* is a novel that combines magical realism with a blend of Brazilian dialects and a poetic prose style. The novel chronicles the adventures of Macunaíma, a man who is both adult and child, powerful and fearful, central and isolated. His journey from his indigenous tribe in the jungle to the streets of São Paulo and back home documents the complications that occur when two cultures meet. Andrade, a mulatto himself, creates Macunaíma as a man of complex heritage who must find a new identity in metropolitan São Paulo before returning home. *Macunaíma* was heralded by critics as the cornerstone of the Brazilian modernist movement and continues to influence authors today. Andrade also wrote *Amar, Verbo Intransitivo* (1927) which has not been translated into English.

After his unparalleled success of the 1920s, Mario de Andrade continued to study and document the culture and music of Brazil. However, when Getúlio Vargas came to power in 1930, Andrade's success as an author declined, although he did retain his position as Chair of History of Music and Aesthetics at the São Paulo Conservatory. Despite the political upheaval of the revolution and Vargas's control of the country, Andrade and archeologist Paulo Duarte created the São Paulo Department of Culture, which fostered cultural and demographic research. Andrade and Duarte's programs remained functional until 1937, when Vargas exiled Duarte and Andrade became the director of the Congress of National Musical Language in Rio de Janeiro. Andrade returned to his post as chair at the conservatory in 1941 and continued his work on music and folklore until he unexpectedly died of a heart attack at home in São Paulo in 1945.

BIBLIOGRAPHY

Lopez, Kimberele S. "Modernismo and the Ambivalence of the Postcolonial Experience: Cannabalism, Primitivism, and Exoticism in Mario de Andrade's *Macunaíma.*" *Luso-Brazilian Review* 35, no. 1 (1998): 25–39.

Nunes, Zita. "Race and Ruins." In *Exploration in Anthropology and Literary Studies,* edited by Daniel E. Valentine and Jeffrey M. Peck, 235–248. Berkeley: University of California Press, 1996.

Emily Clark

ANDRIĆ, IVO (1892–1975) *Croatian novelist, poet, short-story writer*

Ivo Andrić was one of the most distinguished writers of former Yugoslavia. A prolific novelist, poet, and short story writer, he made an international reputation with his historical trilogy on Bosnia, written during the final years of World War II (1944–45): *The Bosnian Chronicle* (*Travnička Hronika*), *The BRIDGE ON THE DRINA* (*Na Drini Ćuprija*), and *The Woman from Sarajevo* (*Gospodica*). In 1961 Andrić was awarded the Nobel Prize in literature for "the epic force with which he traced themes and depicted human destinies drawn from the history of his country."

The material for his narratives mainly stemmed from Andrić's careful exploration and wide knowledge of the cultural heritage and historical circumstances of the peoples and religions inhabiting the area of the former Yugoslavia. Andrić's apprehension of the Balkans as a bridge between the East and the West and his early attentiveness to the multicultural intertwine in the Bosnian region may easily position him in the much later postcolonial literary context. On the other hand, the emphatically intimate nature of his writing as "epic force," his refined psychological analysis, and a prevailing sense of Kierkegaardian pessimism situate his fiction in the semimodernist reframing of the realist novel. Andrić's vibrant prose, characterized by long sentence structure and mellifluous style, has been most frequently compared to the narrative techniques of such contemporaries as ANDRÉ GIDE or MARCEL PROUST.

Born in Travnik, Bosnia (then in the Austro-Hungarian Empire), Andrić spent his childhood in the picturesque Oriental town of Višegrad, the city that would capture his literary imagination. In 1903 he moved to Sarajevo, where he completed grammar school. At about this time, he began to write poetry. He also joined the youth revolutionary movement Mlada Bosna (Young Bosnia), which fought for the liberation and independence of the South Slavs under the Austro-Hungarian Empire. In 1912 Andrić moved to Zagreb (now in Croatia), where he finished his education at the Royal University.

The Mlada Bosna organization was to make history on June 28, 1914, when one of its members, Gavrilo Princip, assassinated the Austrian archduke Francis Ferdinand, thereby inciting World War I. Soon after the assassination, Andrić himself was arrested; he spent nearly eight months in prison. While incarcerated and during his subsequent house confinement, Andrić wrote his prose poems, later published in the book *Ex Ponto* (1918).

With the collapse of the Austro-Hungarian monarchy in 1918, the South Slavs unified and created the Kingdom of the Serbs, Croats, and Slovenes (later Yugoslavia). Andrić moved to its capital, Belgrade, and the end of the war saw the beginning of his successful diplomatic career. (His consular posts were to include Bucharest, Trieste, Marseilles, Madrid, Berlin, and other cities). This period was also highlighted by his move toward prose writing.

In the next two literary decades, Andrić wrote some of his most powerful short fiction, including "The Journey of Ali Djerzelez" ("Putovanje Alije Derzeleza"), "Love in a Small Town" ("Ljubav u Kasabi"), "Anika's Times" ("Anikina Vremena"), and "The Pasha's Concubine" ("Mara Milosnica"). These and other stories were published in the collection *The Pasha's Concubine and Other Tales* (1968). These short stories deal with life in the multiethnic and proto-urban Bosnian crucible. Alongside his diplomatic career and creative work, Andrić devoted much time to an intensive study of documents of the Turkish and the Austro-Hungarian rule in Bosnia. In 1924 he earned his Ph.D. in history at the University of Graz in Austria, defending his doctorate thesis on "The Development of Spiritual Life in Bosnia under the Influence of Turkish Rule."

The beginning of World War II found Andrić in an unenviable post as an envoy to Germany. Upon the German bombardment of Belgrade (April 1941), he left Berlin and returned to Belgrade, where he retired from the diplomatic service, spending the war years in solitude.

The end of the war witnessed the almost simultaneous publication of Andrić's most famous work, a trilogy of novels published in 1945: *The Bosnian Chronicle, The Bridge on the Drina,* and *The Woman from Sarajevo. The Bosnian Chronicle* is exemplary of the writer's prominent usage of a narrative intertwining fact and fiction. Grounded in Andrić's meticulous study of the correspondence of the French consul in Travnik in the years 1807–14, the novel is a comprehensive account of an intriguing mixture of diplomatic influences in Bosnia at the time: While the different international forces (the French, the Austro-Hungarians, and the Turks) engage in lengthy and complex political machinations, the people of the area bear the consequences of what appears to them as a ludicrous political game.

The second part of the trilogy, *The Bridge on the Drina,* is a pseudohistorical chronicle of a small Bosnian town. It is also the most expressive embodiment of Andrić's interest in the issues of cultural interaction and of his belief in the specific function of the Balkans as the bridge between the East and the West. This chronicle spans four centuries in which the multiethnic fictional characters and historical figures mingle and vanish in a series of narrative sketches, whereas the role of the main character is assigned to the sole transhistorical and preserving constituent of the story—the bridge itself.

The third novel of the trilogy, *The Woman from Sarajevo,* takes place in a more proximate historical setting: Sarajevo and Belgrade in the first decades of the 20th century. The novel focuses on a single female character, a spinster whose personal life is shaped by her unconquerable stinginess, as much a matter of personal makeup as a product of concrete sociohistorical circumstances.

During the initial postwar years, Andrić became one of the most distinctive voices in Yugoslav arts and science as well as in the country's political life: He became the president of the Yugoslav Writers Association and a member of the Serbian Academy of Science and Arts. In the following decades, he wrote a number of short and long works, the most important among which are *The Vizier's Elephant* (*Vezirov Slon,* 1947) and the narrative triptych *Jelena, the Woman of My Dream* (*Jelena, Žena Koje Nema,* 1965).

During his lifetime, Andrić published only one more novel, a complex existentialist narrative entitled *The Doomed Yard* (*Prokleta Avlija,* 1954; also translated as *The Devil's Yard,* 1962). The novel, structured as a series of frame narratives, weaves together the life story of a wealthy young man from Smyrna in the last years of the Ottoman Empire and that of the ill-fated brother of a Turkish sultan in the 15th century. As the stories intertwine, the main characters and their respective political-historical times also fuse. Read variously as the parable of the tyranny of the state and the fatalistic symbolist picture of human intrinsic "doom" and ignorance, this novel remains one of the most complex narratives in Yugoslav literature.

Receipt of the 1961 Nobel Prize in literature put Andrić in the center of international acclaim. In the following years, he wrote little. He died in Belgrade in March 1975. Posthumously, his literary executors published one more of Andrić's novels, *Omer Paša Latas,* a chronicle of Sarajevo in the 19th century. The depiction of the town in the novel is rendered through the historical personality of Omer Paša Latas, a Christian who converted to Islam, fled the Austro-Hungarian army, and became a famous Ottoman soldier and statesman. The end of the novel is a narrative of the grim viewpoint expressed by the Austrian consul to Bosnia in an actual piece of correspondence of 1851; its central comparison of Bosnia to a prison remains evocative and politically pertinent today.

Ivo Andrić possessed strong imagination and verbal mastery, with a pronounced taste for localisms. Poetic in its impetus, Andrić's narrative style is that of high precision and well-wrought syntax. His extraordinary knowledge of the historical circumstances of Bosnia and Herzegovina furnished him with topics that spoke well to multicultural and postcolonial concerns and are particularly engaging for those interested in Balkan history today.

The expressive combination of facts from historical archives and ethnic oral fiction (legends, word of mouths, and oral storytelling) made Andrić's novels formal explorations of the relationship between fact and fiction. Thus conceived in fragile epistemological space, the stories became for Andrić the superhistorical keepers of the secrets of human nature and absurdity of the human condition. In this description it is correct to recognize his intimate literary affiliation with ALBERT CAMUS, an alliance Andrić himself acknowledged in his Nobel Prize acceptance address in 1961. Andrić is also an astute observer of human nature; psychological veracity and a disenchanted view of humankind are distinctive features of his novels. Yet it is precisely through the act of storytelling that the human race may preserve its importance, the writer believed. According to Andrić, narration and renarration comprise the utmost achievement in the humankind's endeavor to understand itself and to move on through history.

BIBLIOGRAPHY

Cooper, Henry R., Jr. "The Structure of *The Bridge on the Drina*." *The Slavic and East European Journal* 27, no. 3 (1983): 365–373.

Hawkesworth, Celia. *Ivo Andric: Bridge Between East and West*. London and Dover, N.H.: Athlone Press, 1984.

Juričić, Želimir B. *The Man and the Artist: Essays on Ivo Andrić*. Lanham, Md.: University Press of America, 1986.

Singh Mukerji, Vanita. *Ivo Andric: A Critical Biography*. Jefferson, N.C.: McFarland, 1990.

Vucinich, Wayne, ed. *Ivo Andrić Revisited: The Bridge Still Stands*. Berkeley: University of California Regents, 1996.

Sanja Bahun-Radunovic

ANTHILLS OF THE SAVANNAH CHINUA ACHEBE (1987)

This later novel by Nigerian author CHINUA ACHEBE (1930–) is markedly different from his most well-known work, *Things Fall Apart* (1958), in both form and content. The novel, set in a fictional 20th-century African country representative of Nigeria, examines the political and cultural problems plaguing a modern postcolonial society. Achebe describes "Kangan" as a nation struggling to regain political stability and to cope with increasingly complex issues of race, class, and gender after emancipation from Britain.

The events of the novel are relayed by several narrators, or "witnesses," whose voices are often difficult to distinguish from each other. Chris Oriko, Ikem Osodi, Beatrice Okoh, and an unnamed person guide the reader through the events leading up to the latest political coup and the exiles or deaths of members of the administration. The narration begins by introducing the reader to the inner workings of the current administration, which include both Chris, the commissioner for information, and Ikem, the editor of the government-controlled newspaper, *The National Gazette*. The president, known as His Excellency or simply as Sam to his childhood friends, is quickly distancing himself from his cabinet and becoming increasingly dictatorial.

However, the novel focuses less on the political upheaval of this regime and more on the relationships between Chris, Ikem, and Sam, who attended Lord Lugard College together, and Beatrice, Chris's lover. Although the central event of the story is the President's refusal to address a lack of water in the rural area of Abazon, it is the narrators' responses to his negligence that drive the plot. Ikem's open criticism of the President's handling of the situation causes Sam to demand that Chris fire Ikem. Although he has mediated between his two friends for many years, Chris refuses to participate in their present feud occurring on the national stage. Nevertheless, Ikem is indeed terminated from his position and, in his anger, delivers a lecture at the University of Bassa on propaganda and freedom. Ikem's speech and his ties to Abazonian protestors quickly result in his murder by the regime. Chris suspects that Ikem's death also signals a threat to his own life, and he goes into hiding, aided by Beatrice and Emmanuel, the leader of the University of Bassa Students Union.

At this point in the novel, Beatrice takes over not only as the main narrator but also as a metaphor for the past, present, and future of Kangan. Although Achebe alludes to class and gender throughout the text, he now refocuses the narration on Beatrice and her relationships with the few other women in the novel. Described by the novelist as part modern woman and part ancient priestess, Beatrice brings the book and its message of integrating old customs with new traditions to its conclusion. She coordinates Chris's hiding places and cares for Elewa, Ikem's pregnant widow, situations that force her to confront the class differences in Kangan society. Beatrice realizes that ordinarily she would not develop relationships with Elewa, a working-class girl, and the taxi drivers who arrange Chris's transfer from one locale to another. Her dependence upon these people for strength and information challenges the hierarchical system of class so strongly present in Kangan society. Additionally, Beatrice grows closer to her maid, Agatha, a practicing Christian who consistently reacts to guests according to their economic class.

Amid Beatrice's adjustments to her new support system, Chris arrives safely in Abazon and the current regime crumbles, marking Chris's release from exile. However, within minutes of learning the news, he is fatally wounded while attempting to stop the rape of a young girl by a police sergeant. Although disheartened by Chris's ironic death, Beatrice quickly finds solace in the birth of Ikem's daughter and her naming ceremony. Breaking with tradition, Beatrice and the group present all name the girl instead of the father or uncle performing the rite. Ikem's and Elewa's daughter is named Amaechina, or "May-the-path-never-close," a masculine name, therefore ending the narrative with an affirmation of feminine power and hope for the future of a new Kangan/Nigeria.

BIBLIOGRAPHY

Erritouni, Ali. "Contradictions and Alternatives in Chinua Achebe's *Anthills of the Savannah*." *Journal of Modern Literature* 29, no. 2 (2006): 50–74.

Ikegami, Robin. "Knowledge and Power, the Story and the Storyteller: Achebe's *Anthills of the Savannah*." *Modern Fiction Studies* 37, no. 3 (1991): 493–507.

Emily Clark

APPELFELD, AHARON (1932–) *Israeli novelist*

The duality of memory and imagination have captivated Aharon Appelfeld since childhood and remain a theme in the more than 20 books that he has published. He was born in Czernowitz, Romania, to Bonia and Michael Appelfeld. His official country of birth was Bukovina, which was annexed to Romania. Appelfeld was seven years old and had only finished his first year of school when World War II broke out, transforming his pastoral years of a childhood enveloped in love and warmth into terror and a growing awareness of anti-Semitism and its violent consequences. Appelfeld's novel BADENHEIM 1939 (1975) particularly reflects the months during the summer of 1939, which the author remembers as a life now beyond recognition, as the world around him deteriorated from month to month.

Prior to the war, despite Michael Appelfeld's telegrams to relatives and friends in such countries as Uruguay and Chile, and even attempts to obtain a visa to America, the Appelfeld family became cognizant of how trapped they were as Jews under the increasing might of Adolf Hitler and Germany. Aharon Appelfeld has characterized his home as a place without religious belief, resembling a modern urban rather than kosher Jewish lifestyle. However, the later presence of his Orthodox grandfather enforced kosher practices, Torah laws, and the eating of only foods allowed by their religion. Although Appelfeld's father endeavored to find passages out of Romania for the family, he was unable to prevent their being sent to the ghetto after the end of summer 1938.

The ghetto in Czernowitz compressed all elements of the Jewish social sphere, collapsing previous social frameworks. As an eight-year-old, Appelfeld soon learned how to distinguish between the friendly and violent mentally ill patients who had been released into the ghetto. He enjoyed observing their gestures, such as the way they held a plate or tore off chunks of bread to eat. He was eventually deported with his father and

35,000 others to Trans-Dniestria in a freight train. Altogether, 40,000 residents of the ghetto were deported; Appelfeld's mother had been shot and killed.

From Trans-Dniestria, Appelfeld was forced to march with his father and other prisoners to a concentration camp in Ukraine. The march took two months, during which they passed dead bodies along the road and were surrounded by Romanian soldiers and Ukrainian militia who beat them with their whips and randomly shot at them. Walking through the melting snow, many children and adults sank and drowned in the mud. Appelfeld's father was a constant source of strength to him during this time, but their closeness disappeared as soon as they arrived at the camp, first when Appelfeld was separated from his father and then when he alone escaped. He was 10 years old.

After spending many days in the forest following his escape from the concentration camp, Appelfeld found refuge in a peasant home. He was fortunate in having blond looks and knowledge of the Ukrainian language. Encountering a woman on the village outskirts, he told her he had been born in Lutschintz and that his parents had been killed in an air raid, leaving him to fend for himself. He was able to safely board with this woman, named Maria, in exchange for domestic chores and shopping expeditions to the nearest village. His fright of being recognized as Jewish was realized one day when he heard the shout of "Jew-boy" from a Ukrainian child. From that moment, he dressed in peasant's clothes and, upon further interrogation, even told Maria that his parents had been Ukrainian. Although his parents were already dead, Appelfeld clung to the belief that they were waiting for him and that he would be reunited with them if only he could find them. After he left Maria's house, he worked for a blind old peasant who was also kind to him.

Appelfeld was 12 years old when the Russians recaptured Ukraine in 1944. He then served in a mobile Russian army as a kitchen aide for a year before escaping with eight other boys and making his way to Yugoslavia and then to Italy. He spent time in a refugee camp in Italy, where he learned the Hebrew alphabet and how to pray, before traveling to Palestine. He finally took a ship with hundreds of people to the Haifa coast in 1946. Appelfeld was then interned at the camp at Alit, a British settlement, where he learned Hebrew words.

During his first year in Israel, Appelfeld worked in the fields and also increased his knowledge of the Hebrew language, the Bible, and the poems of Hayyim Nachman Bialik. Although he was an orphan, he did have a few distant relatives who lived in Jaffa. While he recognized the inevitable connection between German, the language of his mother, and the slaughter of the Jews during the war, he felt that his mother and her language were one. The pain of losing his mother at the beginning of the war was felt all over again as he begin to replace her language with Hebrew.

Appelfeld took part in the Aliyat Hano'ar Youth Movement during 1946 and 1948, and then was an apprentice at an agricultural school on the outskirts of Jerusalem during the following two years, working in the orchards. He continued to quench his thirst for the Hebrew language and its literature, and also wrote extensively in his diary. After these four years, Appelfeld prepared for the military exam, wanting to be accepted into a fighting unit to become a regular soldier or even officer. He was accepted into the army, but on the restricted basis of Fit for Service (FFS), a soldier who administers those in active combat.

Appelfeld was emotionally and geographically displaced and alienated while in the army, continuously transferred to various locations for guard duty. While his diary reflects his sense of emptiness, he did have time in which to continue reading whatever he was able to get his hands on. Appelfeld's time in the army reinforced his own questions of personal identity. He would also later serve in the Yom Kippur War as a lecturer in the army's Educational Corps, stationed at the Suez Canal.

Following his two-year service in the Israeli army in the early 1950s, Appelfeld studied at the Hebrew University of Jerusalem for four years. He also joined the New Life Club, established in 1950 by Holocaust survivors from Galicia and Bukovina, and enjoyed the poetry evenings, conversations, and, most of all, the company of those he considered his own extended family. (After decades of political and internal turmoil, the New Life Club closed permanently at the end of the 1980s, but it would continue to influence and permeate Appelfeld's writing.)

Before Appelfeld could attend the Hebrew University, he had to pass a preliminary examination, a daunting prospect considering that he had only been to the first grade before the war began. He therefore studied volumes of material for a year and a half before receiving his matriculation certificate. At the university, where courses were taught by a mixture of teachers and students who were fellow émigrés, Appelfeld learned Yiddish as well as Hebrew, and also found interests in Kabbalah and Hasidism. At the same time he worked on his own literary voice. He spent his years at the Hebrew University cultivating both his literary interests, which now ranged from FRANZ KAFKA and ALBERT CAMUS to Russian authors, and religious preoccupations, searching for an authentic form of Judaism.

Appelfeld did not begin to write until the 1950s, and only a little then. It was a time when pages and pages of notebooks, booklets, and memories about the war were being written. Appelfeld has described a barrier of repression about his experiences during the war that initially prevented his own "witnessing." He was suspicious of literature produced about World War II, and he believed that testimonies were more authentic than fiction. Nonetheless, Appelfeld also believed it was possible to create what he referred to as an "interior narrative" that would allow for expressions of truth in emotion and essence of feeling rather than the simple naming of people and places. He began publishing narratives in the form of poetry in the periodical *B-Ma'ale* in the early 1950s.

Although he had given up his ambition to become an Israeli writer in the late 1950s, Appelfeld's quest to reconcile his multiple identities of orphan, child of war, refugee, and émigré resulted in his first book *Smoke* (1962), a collection of stories in which he wrote imaginatively about the Holocaust. In reviews of *Smoke*, critics labeled the author as a "Holocaust writer" despite his decision not to witness or testify to his own wartime experiences; he was also labelled as restrained and unsentimental. His own childhood memories revived during the 1970s, influencing such novels as *The Age of Wonders* (1978) and *The Searing Light* (1980). *The Immortal Bartfuss* (1989) won him the National Jewish Book Award. Appelfeld did not write about his wartime experiences until the novel *Mesilat Barzel*

(1991), which testifies to his forced march amid exhaustion, hunger, and death to a concentration camp in Ukraine.

Appelfeld currently resides in Jerusalem and is a professor of Hebrew literature at Ben Gurion University of the Negev. Despite his early struggles with the language, Appelfeld writes in Hebrew, and his works have been translated into numerous other languages. His writing has won him international recognition and critical and popular acclaim, including the prestigious Israel Prize.

BIBLIOGRAPHY

Appelfeld, Aharon. *Beyond Despair: Three Lectures and a Conversation with Philip Roth.* Translated by Jeffrey M. Green. New York: Fromm International, 1994.

———. *The Story of a Life.* Translated by Aloma Halter. New York: Schocken Books, 2004.

Cohen, Joseph. *Voices of Israel: Essays on and Interviews with Yehuda Amichai, A. B. Yehoshua, T. Carmi, Aharon Appelfeld, and Amos Oz.* Albany: State University of New York Press, 1990.

Ramras-Rauch, Gila. *Aharon Appelfeld: The Holocaust and Beyond.* Bloomington: Indiana University Press, 1994.

Tara J. Johnson

ARCH OF TRIUMPH (ARC DE TRIOMPHE) ERICH MARIA REMARQUE (1945)

The fifth published novel by Germany's ERICH MARIA REMARQUE (1898–1970), *Arch of Triumph* was first published in the United States in 1945; the German edition followed in 1946. The story takes place in Paris between November 11, 1938, and the first days of September 1939. The significance of the narration's framing dates—the 20th anniversary of the World War I armistice and the outbreak of World War II—contribute to the dark climate of the novel, which is dominated by the feeling of general instability and desperation during the interwar period. Two main plots set the dynamics and the fateful conflicts of the narration. The first is the story of the revenge of the main character, Ravic, on his sadistic Nazi persecutor, Haake, who has ruined Ravic's life. The other is the love relationship between Ravic and Joan Madou, an actress and singer.

Ravic, whose real name is Ludwig Fresenburg, is a German doctor living illegally in Paris. He supports himself by conducting "ghost" surgical operations for his French medical colleagues, Veber and Durant. Both doctors seek Ravic's assistance for his extraordinary skills, which had made him chief surgeon in one of the best hospitals in Germany. His promising career had been suddenly interrupted in 1933, when he helped two friends avoid Nazi persecution and was arrested by the Gestapo. Tortured by Haake, Ravic managed to escape from the concentration camp hospital. On his way abroad, the fugitive received news about the suicide of his girlfriend, who had collapsed after Haake's interrogation.

Five years later, Ravic accidentally spots Haake in a street cafe in Paris. With help from a friend, the Russian refugee Boris Morosow, Ravic lures Haake into a trap and kills him. The protagonist does not feel remorse for the cold-blooded murder; rather, he sees the act of vengeance as necessary to regaining his dignity and obtaining relief from the traumatic memories of the past.

The story of hate and revenge interlaces in the narration with the story of love between Ravic and Joan. In the beginning of the novel, Ravic meets Joan wandering aimlessly through Paris. Sympathizing with her confusion and suicidal moods after the death of her partner, Ravic takes care of the woman and eventually falls in love with her. The relationship is troubled by Joan's possessiveness, emotional instability, and desire to live life to the full, all manifested in her reckless behavior and love affairs with other men. In addition, Ravic's distrust of his own feelings and his attempts to rationalize his and Joan's actions prevent him from fulfilling Joan's expectations and from finding his place in their complicated emotional situation.

Ravic breaks away from Joan after a brief passionate relationship that culminates during a getaway to southern France, yet he is not able to fully separate from her, even when he refuses to react to her reconciliation attempts. Joan calls him for the last time when she is shot by her jealous new lover. Ravic goes to her aid, but the wound is fatal. Joan's death coincides with the outbreak of the war. Ravic, who has lost the woman he loves and has taken his revenge on Haake, does not see any reason to hide anymore and surrenders to the police.

The figure of Ravic is one of Remarque's most memorable protagonists: He is self-sufficient, cynical, and distant. He carries no illusions about the ruthlessness of human nature, but still tries to protect what he understands as elementary human dignity, even when his actions put him in danger. His opinions about interpersonal relations are marked by Social Darwinism and are strongly influenced by what he, as a doctor and outsider, observes of everyday life in the metropolis. Through portraits of prostitutes and their clients, back-street abortionists, and hypocritical doctors, Remarque draws a rich image of prewar Paris, where the romantic notion of love interweaves with the booming sex market. Dark forebodings of the coming world catastrophe set free decadent tendencies: The figure constellation of the novel includes émigrés from countries struck by emerging totalitarianisms, living from day to day, seeking forgetfulness in alcohol and sex, and awaiting the unavoidable war.

The depiction of the passion between Ravic and Joan is often interpreted as Remarque's artistic rendering of his real-life relationship with the famed actress Marlene Dietrich. Although the representation of love in *Arch of Triumph* does not lack moving moments and elements that have become pop culture icons (such as the lovers' favorite drink, Calvados), it is not as convincing as similar motifs in Remarque's other works, such as the more subtle portrayal of love in his novel *Three Comrades* (1937). The reader's compassion leans not toward the ambivalent figure of Joan Madou but instead toward Kate Hegström, Ravic's cancer-sick patient, whose friendship with the male protagonist and grace and dignity while facing her terminal disease remind one of other sympathetic female characters in Remarque's works.

Arch of Triumph, received rather coldly in Remarque's native Germany, became an instant market hit in the United States and was filmed for the first time in 1948. Unfortunately, the star cast and the director of the Oscar-winning adaptation of ALL QUIET ON THE WESTERN FRONT, Lewis Milestone, were not enough to ensure the movie's success. The novel, however, confirmed Remarque's reputation as an author of works that skillfully catch the spirit of their time.

BIBLIOGRAPHY
Gordon, Hayim. *Heroism and Friendship in the Novels of Erich Maria Remarque.* New York: Peter Lang, 2003.

Owen, C. R. *Erich Maria Remarque: A Critical Bio-Bibliography*. Amsterdam: Rodopi, 1984.

Tims, Hilton. *Erich Maria Remarque: The Last Romantic*. New York: Carroll & Graf, 2003.

Wagner, Hans. *Understanding Erich Maria Remarque*. Columbia: University of South Carolina Press, 1991.

Jakub Kazecki

ARGUEDAS, JOSÉ MARÍA (1911–1969)

Peruvian novelist, short story writer Many decades after the death of José María Arguedas, his work continues to be recognized as one of the best instances of transcultural literature in Latin American fiction. During his lifetime, the Peruvian author received diverse prizes that acknowledged his literary and cultural impact on society: the Javier Prado Prize (1958), Ricardo Palma Prize (1959, 1962), William Faulkner Certificate of Merit (1963), and Inca Garcilaso de la Vega Prize (1968). To date, some of his works have been translated into English, Italian, German, French, Russian, Hungarian, Dutch, and Romanian, which reveals his worldwide readership.

José María Arguedas Altamirano was born in the southern Andean town of Andahuaylas, Peru, to Víctor Manuel Arguedas, an itinerant lawyer from Cuzco, and Victoria Altamirano, a member of a distinguished upper-class family. Born in the early part of the 20th century, Arguedas was introduced into a world shaped at the crossroads of modernization in Peru. He lived painfully within the basic cultural dichotomy of the country: indigenous versus colonial or European languages and cultures. In that context, both his life and work act as a human and cultural bridge.

As a young boy, Arguedas accompanied his father on many travels through diverse towns in the southern Peruvian Andes; he later portrayed its landscape and people in a powerful language, displaying their lyrical and magical-mythical visions of the world. Arguedas was only three years old when his mother died in 1914, a tragedy that shaped his life forever. The young boy soon found that he was the target of his stepmother's disdain, and he was relegated to living with the indigenous servants at his stepmother's hacienda. It was from these farm workers that Arguedas learned to appreciate the spiritual dimensions of the land and its working people. He also acquired an appreciation for the Quechuan people and their language that he adopted as his native language.

Not only as a child but also as an adult, Arguedas saw the world from the Quechuan magical and mythical viewpoint. The indelible scars of hate from the side of his stepmother and love from the Quechua people who raised him motivated his coming to terms with reality and creativity in a never-ending struggle with language—a struggle that, indeed, embodied his life and magnificent work.

Although Arguedas was born into a privileged social position in Peru, he was emotionally Quechua. The fact that he was not born into that Quechuan world to which he felt he belonged was a source of constant suffering. This frustration later became an aching acknowledgment that the project of rescuing his beloved Andean world and culture through the creation of a national mestizo project was doomed. He knew and loved the Quechuan world—its language, culture, myths, and rituals—with *warma kuyay* (a Quechuan expression referring to child's love). Thus, he dedicated his life to creating a possible bridge between those opposed worlds that coexisted within him.

Arguedas studied literature and anthropology at San Marcos University in Lima, where he later became a professor of Quechua and ethnic studies. As novelist, storyteller, poet, folklorist, ethnographer, and educator, Arguedas wrote extensively. And yet he never considered himself a professional writer. He saw his writing as the very embodiment of his life, and as a means of portraying the reality he knew and lived. In that sense, he felt close to the poet César Vallejo and the novelist JUAN RULFO, two authors he knew and deeply admired.

Arguedas wrote as a spokesman of the Quechua Andean world, setting out to correct the distorted stereotyped image of the indigenous people presented by earlier fiction. His works, written in Spanish for a nonindigenous public, offer deep insight into the Quechuan mentality, more probing than any works published before. The reader is shown that the basis of Andean culture is a magical-religious view of the world that regards the world not merely as something to be conquered and exploited but as a unified cosmic order animated by supernatural forces and linked in a universal harmony.

In his early fiction, Arguedas's success in communicating his worldview was somehow restricted by his continued reliance on a conventional realist manner. Moreover, in his first writings he portrayed a closed rural sphere. But from DEEP RIVERS (*Los ríos profundos,* 1958) onward, he evolved a more effective lyrical-magical style. Artistically, he faced the problem of translating the sensibility of people who express themselves in Quechua into what appeared to him to be the alien medium of Spanish. His initial solution was to modify Spanish in such a way as to incorporate the basic features of Quechuan syntax and thus reproduce something of the special character of indigenous speech. But these experiments were only partially successful, so subsequently he opted for a correct Spanish skillfully reshaped to convey Andean thoughts and sensibilities.

Quechua was the author's mother tongue. His writings convey his profound awareness of being bilingual in language and culture. For Arguedas, Spanish was a learned language that he did not feel was his own; produced in him a profound estrangement between the word and the perception of reality. His writing thus became a battleground over language and expression. As Arguedas finally opted to translate the Quechuan sensibility into correct Spanish, he believed in the authenticity of the Quechua language, a mythical living entity for which he could not find any adequate Spanish equivalent. He strove for a literary medium that would suggest the cultural reality he wanted to communicate; he wanted both form and culture to become one.

In terms of scope and narrative complexity, Arguedas's work evolves from the small indigenous communities, villages, and towns of the Andes, to more complex geocultural spheres. This is shown by the spatial and narrative distance that goes from *Water* (*Agua,* 1935) to the posthumous *The Fox of Above and the Fox of Below* (*El zorro de arriba y el zorro de abajo,* 1971). In the stories of *Water* and the short novel *Diamonds and Flint* (*Diamantes y pedernales,* 1954), the universe is perceived as an unavoidable dichotomy. In *Yawar Feast* (*Yawar fiesta,* 1941) and *Deep Rivers* (1958), the Andean rural world is seen as opposed to the coastal white cities, but they are dialogically related. In *All Bloods* (*Todas las sangres,* 1964) and *The Fox of Above,* Arguedas echoes the painful, contradictory, and necessary approach between these two worlds. Arguedas wrote other books of short stories dealing with these same themes as well as an impressive novel on his experience in prison, *The Sixth* (*El sexto,* 1961).

The context of Arguedas's fiction is the semifeudal socioeconomic order that prevailed in the Andean highlands from the Spanish conquest until recent times. However, while some earlier writers had simplistically depicted a black-and-white confrontation between oppressive white landowners and a downtrodden indigenous peasantry, Arguedas presented a more complex picture of Andean society. Furthermore, he demonstrated that centuries of coexistence have brought about a process of transcultural exchange between the two existing civilizations. While the Western presence dominates socially and economically, the indigenous culture predominates and informs Arguedas's worldview.

Most of Arguedas's novels are socially conscious. Nonetheless, the main strand in his work draws on his personal experience to depict the clash of Peru's two main cultures while focusing on a young boy torn between two cultural influences. This boy, who is evidently a narrative echo of Arguedas, appears in such texts as the stories in *Water* and the novel *Deep Rivers.* This autobiographical element emerged again, and even more straightforwardly, in Arguedas's last novel, *The Fox of Above,* where the narrative is interspersed with sections of diary, recording the crisis that led him to suicide in 1969.

Arguedas's work also explores the impact of change on Andean society. Thus, in *Yawar Fiesta* the region emerges from its isolation, progress being symbolized by a government decree banning nonprofessional bullfights. However, the novel highlights the paradox that the very modernity that promises to liberate the indigenous people from their isolation also threatens to destroy their culture. *All Bloods* reflects the political and economic changes that had been taking place in Peru since the mid-1950s. This extraordinary social novel portrays the breakup of the traditional semifeudal order and the emergence of the newly mobilized indigenous community as a political force. The novels also express confidence in the ability of the Quechua culture to adapt to a modern industrial society without losing its distinctive identity.

Later Arguedas became disillusioned as the country embarked on an uncontrolled process of capitalist development that threatened a depopulation of the countryside and the erosion of traditional ways of life. *The Fox of Above,* which seems to exist somewhere between the fiction of a novel and the fact of an ethnographic account, offers a crude picture of this new reality, epitomized by the coastal boomtown of Chimbote. Nonetheless, the presence of the Quechuan culture of the Andean migrants who live in the city points out the possibility of cultural survival, adaptation, and even progress.

Displaying a pioneering transcultural perspective in his narrative, Arguedas was able to create a space for himself between the two different worlds, interweaving knowledge, dialects, systems, worldviews, and inheritances. Avoiding rigid polarization and binary extremism, his fiction accounts for the importance of interstices and liminal spaces where one perception blends or crosses over into another, showing how it is possible to stand by more than one culture and yet belong irrevocably to both.

Arguedas attached himself, both emotionally and creatively, to both past and present popular culture. His commitment to Quechuan sources and knowledge is both intellectual and emotional. Arguedas hoped that the cultural traumas of invasion and usurpation could be reassessed in new ways, opening up positive perspectives for the future of his beloved Peru. His works show the importance for modern industrial technology and culture to intersect or to incorporate magic, nature, and preindustrialized culture. Arguedas's work shows a belief that a new Andeanized national culture would emerge out of the melting pot of diversity in Peru. A persistent theme is that the Quechuan people and culture could not only survive but could also become the foundation of an original national culture.

Arguedas's writings represent the unavoidable, often tragic, bicultural blending of Andean and Spanish worlds in Peru's past, present, and future. A new criti-

cal appreciation of this author's work and legacy continues. Arguedas is considered one of the most important authors to speak out on issues such as the survival of native cultures and the dynamics between tradition and modernity. The significance and influence of his work, sometimes misunderstood during his lifetime and during the years immediately following his death, have acquired a full meaning in this multicultural and globalized world. Thus, José María Arguedas remains very much alive in the hearts of readers.

BIBLIOGRAPHY

Cornejo Polar, Antonio. *Los Universos narrativos de José María Arguedas.* Buenos Aires: Losada, 1973.

Díaz Ruiz, Ignacio. *Literatura y biografía en José María Arguedas.* Cuadernos del Instituto de Investigaciones Filológicas, no. 18, México City: Universidad Nacional Autónoma de México, 1991.

Escobar, Alberto. *Arguedas o la utopía de la lengua.* Serie Lengua y Sociedad, no. 6. Lima: Instituto de Estudios Peruanos, 1984.

Forgues, Roland. *José María Arguedas: Del pensamiento dialéctico al pensamiento trágico.* Lima: Horizonte, 1989.

Kemper Columbus, Claudette. *Mythological Consciousness and the Future. José María Arguedas.* New York, Bern, and Frankfurt: Peter Lang, 1986.

Pinilla, Carmen María. *Arguedas: Conocimiento y vida.* Lima: Pontificia Universidad Católica del Perú, 1994.

Sandoval, Ciro A., and Sandra M. Boschetto-Sandoval, eds. *José María Arguedas. Reconsiderations for Latin American Cultural Studies.* Latin American Series Number 29. Athens: Ohio University Center for International Studies, 1998.

Dora Sales-Salvador

ARIYOSHI SAWAKO (1931–1984) *Japanese essayist, novelist, playwright, short story writer*

Ariyoshi Sawako, one of Japan's most popular 20th-century writers, wrote more than 100 short stories, novels, plays, musicals, and movie scripts in her 53 years of life. By combining skillful writing, poignant social criticism, and a deep love of humanity, she created sensitive, insightful works and established a respected place for herself in the literary world.

Ariyoshi was born in Wakayama City, Japan, on January 20, 1931. With the exception of four years when she lived in Java, she grew up in Wakayama Prefecture. She attended Tokyo Women's Christian College from 1949 to 1952, then worked for Okura Publishing Company in 1952 and 1953. In 1954 she began her writing career. Ariyoshi won a fellowship from the Rockefeller Foundation in 1959 to study for one year at Sarah Lawrence College in New York State. There she continued her earlier study of the performing arts. She married in 1962 but divorced in 1964; she had one daughter.

The author started her literary profession by writing short stories. Many of them—such as "Ballad" ("Jiuta," 1956) and "The Ink Stick" ("Sumi," 1961)—picture traditional artists struggling in the modern world. In "The Tomoshibi" ("Tomoshibi," 1961), Ariyoshi shows the transformation of an insecure barmaid into a confident woman through the acceptance and love of the proprietress of the bar.

At the end of the 1950s Ariyoshi turned to novels as a literary form for expressing her social concerns. She based a number of her works on historical characters and situations. She reveals problems faced by women in traditional Japanese households in *The RIVER KI* (*Kinokawa*, 1959) and *The DOCTOR'S WIFE* (*Hanaoka Seishū no tsuma*, 1966). *Hishoku* (1964) deals with racial segregation in the United States. Ariyoshi's most popular novel, *The TWILIGHT YEARS* (*Kōkōtsu no hito*, 1972), shows the difficulties faced by senior citizens and the family members who care for them. In *Kabuki Dancer* (*Izumo no Okuni*, 1972), Ariyoshi tells the story of Okuni, the temple dancer who founded kabuki, and presents some of the social issues in imperial Kyoto in the late 16th and early 17th centuries. *Fukugō osen* (1975) examines the problem of environmental pollution. *Her Highness Princess Kazu* (*Kazunokiya iama otome*, 1978), a historical novel set in 1860–61 and based on the personage of Princess Kazu, who lived from 1846 to 1877, received the Mainichi Cultural Prize in 1979. It relates the Tokugawa shogunate's attempts to unite the imperial court and the shogunate and exposes some of the social problems of the time.

Ariyoshi had a great love for the theater—both modern drama and traditional Kabuki—which began when she was a student. As a result, her fiction relies a great deal on dialogue to reveal the thoughts and motivations of her characters and to show the relationships of characters with one another. She wrote a number of plays, some still performed in Japan today, and adapted some of her fiction for the stage and screen. She also wrote radio and television scripts.

On August 30, 1984, Ariyoshi died in her sleep. Besides being one of the most popular 20th-century writers in Japan, she earned international acclaim with the translation of a number of her works into other languages. A French translation of *The Doctor's Wife* became a best seller in France in 1981, and English translations of *The River Ki, The Doctor's Wife,* and *The Twilight Years* have a large audience in the United States and around the world.

BIBLIOGRAPHY

"Ariyoshi, Sawako." *Contemporary Authors*. Vol. 105. Detroit: Gale Research, 1982.

Ueda, Makoto. "Ariyoshi Sawako." *The Mother of Dreams and Other Short Stories*. Edited by Ueda. Tokyo: Kodansha International, 1989, 240.

Charlotte S. Pfeiffer

ASSAULT, THE (DE AANSLAG) HARRY MULISCH (1982)

A gripping novel that challenges the notions of innocence and guilt, *The Assault* is considered among the greatest works of contemporary European fiction. Broken into five episodes, spanning 1945 to 1981, the novel by Dutch author HARRY MULISCH (1927–   ) is termed within the prologue "the story of an incident." This "incident" and its ensuing tale follow Anton Steenwijk, the protagonist, through his personal journey in postwar Holland.

The novel begins in Haarlem in the home of Anton Steenwijk, a 12-year-old boy, as he and his family are engaged in playing a board game. Six shots ring out in the darkness of the night. Peter, Anton's older brother, discovers that Fake Ploeg, the chief inspector of police and a Nazi collaborator, has been assassinated. Further, the Kortewegs, the Steenwijks' neighbors, are carrying Fake's lifeless body from their own house to deposit it at the Steenwijks' house. Recognizing that the Nazis will retaliate for Fake's murder, Peter runs out to move the carcass. As Peter approaches the body, the Nazis arrive. Chaos ensues. Peter runs into the darkness. Gunshots are fired. The Steenwijks' home is set ablaze, and Anton is separated from his family.

Driven by the German convoy, Anton is taken to prison by the Germans and then to Amsterdam, where he is finally retrieved by his uncle.

The second episode of the novel jumps to 1952, revealing that Anton has entered medical school. An invitation to a birthday party from a fellow classmate living in Haarlem brings Anton back to his hometown. Anton leaves the party and begins to walk. He makes his way to the quay and discovers that the Beumers, his family's other neighbors, still inhabit the same home as they had before the war. Mrs. Beumer invites Anton in, and he reluctantly accepts. Mrs. Beumer's recollection of the incident jars Anton's thoughts. He ventures out from the Beumers' house and toward a monument that stands at the place of the incident. Anton reads the names of his parents, and the episode concludes as Anton returns back to his aunt and uncle's home in Amsterdam.

Four years later, in 1956, the third episode begins. Anton, having recently finished medical school, has begun to specialize in anesthesiology. Now living in an apartment in Amsterdam, he encounters Fake Ploeg, Jr., at an anticommunist rally. Uncertain as to why, Anton invites Fake upstairs to his apartment. After exchanging comments regarding their present occupations, their conversation develops into a charged debate over the past incident, innocence, and accountability. Each contests the veracity of the other's arguments. Their meeting climaxes, and Fake exits the apartment. Anton reflects upon the meeting's instructiveness, and the episode ends.

Episode four, dated 1966, describes Anton, now married and with a daughter, and his relationship with Mr. Takes. Initially unknown to one another, each character possesses knowledge of the other's secrets. Mr. Takes reveals to Anton his knowledge of and participation in the incident, while Anton divulges his memories of Mr. Takes's confidant. Though both Anton and Mr. Takes gain insight from the other's information, neither character finds solace through their discoveries. Instead, the complexities of innocence, guilt, and accountability are furthered as the fourth episode concludes.

Fifteen years pass, and the last episode begins. Anton, now remarried and with a son, suffers an anxiety attack while away on vacation. He recovers and, upon his daughter's 16th birthday, following her request, travels to Haarlem to revisit the place of the incident. Despite its changed appearance, Anton describes the site to his daughter. They gaze upon the monument and the names of Anton's parents. At lunch, Anton tells his daughter about Truus Coster, Mr. Takes's confidant. Memories of her, and the incident, seep back into Anton's mind. His emotional response prompts him and his daughter to visit her grave.

Later in the episode, Anton joins his son in a march against atomic weaponry. Amidst the crowds of people, Anton discovers Karin Korteweg, his childhood neighbor from Haarlem. Deciding that fate has brought them together at this peace rally, Karin reveals to Anton her recollection of the incident and, with it, the final wrinkle in *The Assault*. She details the events of that night, her memories of Anton's brother, and the war's aftereffects upon her family. Finally, Karin exposes why she and her father deposited Fake Ploeg before the Steenwijks' home, as opposed to another home. Karin's tale gives Anton complete understanding of the incident. He leaves Karin and walks amid the stream of protestors. Anton finds his son and again probes the idea of innocence and guilt, asking, "Was guilt innocent, and innocence guilty?" Finally overcome by a feeling of acceptance, Anton marches alongside his son, among the crowd, as the novel closes.

Noted for its brilliance, *The Assault* is both a psychological thriller and a discourse on humanity. Through the novel, Mulisch penetrates the innermost regions of Anton's soul while carrying the reader along a thematic journey of accountability, betrayal, catharsis, and deliverance. Popularized by its many translations, *The Assault* is among Mulisch's better-known works. Following its conversion from text into film, *The Assault* received both the 1987 Oscar and Golden Globe awards for Best Foreign Language Film. The richness of the text and the complexity of its concerns render *The Assault,* for much of its audience, something more than just "the story of an incident."

BIBLIOGRAPHY
Mulisch, Harry. *Criminal Case 40/61, the Trial of Adolph Eichmann.* Translated by Robert Naborn. Philadelphia: University of Pennsylvania Press, 2005.

————. *The Discovery of Heaven: A Novel.* Translated by Paul Vincent. New York: Viking, 1996.

————. *Siegfried.* Translated by Paul Vincent. New York: Viking, 2003.

————. *The Stone Bridal Bed.* Translated by Adrienne Dixon. London; New York: Abelard-Schuman, 1962.

Adam Reinherz

ASTURIAS, MIGUEL ANGEL (1899–1974)

Guatemalan novelist, poet   Poet, novelist, and diplomat Miguel Angel Asturias is one of the most celebrated figures in the history of Latin American letters. Asturias drew upon his experiences with the indigenous cultures of Guatemala and the political reality of life in Latin America in crafting his fiction. The uniqueness and force of his work comes from his break with the common forms of realist fiction as a form of social protest prevalent at the time. His fiction is at once imaginative, poetic, and structurally complex in its presentation of themes of violence and social injustice. In 1967 Asturias was awarded the Nobel Prize in literature.

Miguel Angel Asturias was born in Guatemala City in October 1899. At the time of his birth, Guatemala was in the grip of an oppressive dictatorship under Manuel Estrada Cabrera. Because of Miguel's father's political differences with the new regime, the Asturias family was forced to flee the capital to a rural area outside the city. It was here that Asturias first came into contact with the indigenous people of Guatemala who would play such an intimate role in his work later.

After receiving his law degree from the Universidad de San Carlos in 1922, Asturias published his thesis "The Social Problem of the Indian" ("El problema social del indio," 1923). A year later he embarked on a 10-year stay in Europe, a time during which he produced some of his greatest work. Once in Paris, Asturias began studying under the acclaimed anthropologist and expert on Central American indigenous culture, Georges Raynaud, and successfully translated the Mayan holy book *Popol Vuh* into Spanish from Raynaud's French version.

Asturias's first major published work, *Legends of Guatemala* (*Leyendas de Guatemala,* 1930), was praised by French critic Paul Valéry and became an instant success, winning the Silla Monsegur prize for best book written by a Latin American published in France.

In *Leyendas* Asturias combined his extensive knowledge of Mayan mythology with a writing style influenced by the surrealist movement in Europe. The result is a poetic and lyrical presentation of Mayan myths set against the trauma of Spanish colonization.

In 1933 Asturias returned to Guatemala, only to find his country gripped by another dictatorship under Jorge Ubico. The political climate made it impossible for Asturias to publish what would become his most famous work, *The PRESIDENT* (*El señor presidente,* 1946), a novel that is fiercely critical of all dictatorships. The inspiration for the novel came from Asturias's early experiences as a child and young man under the dictatorship of Estrada Cabrera. In this brilliant piece of fiction, he explores the way a totalitarian regime can affect the individual and community psychologically. He achieves this by creating a world in which light and dark are separate yet mutually involved in creating a chaotic landscape where natural human relationships are warped into grotesque caricatures. The silent center of the novel is the dictator. Although he rarely speaks and appears only occasionally throughout the unfolding of the plot, the dictator nevertheless exists ubiquitously in the minds of every character, governing their actions and robbing them of personal autonomy. The negative psychological effects of dictatorship are further enhanced by Asturias's prose style. His use of dream sequences, wordplay, and surreal scenarios blur the lines between appearance and reality, making the nightmare of life under totalitarianism all the more jarring.

After the success of *The President,* Asturias returned to the myths and plight of the indigenous people of Latin America in his next novel, *Men of Corn* (*Hombres de maíz,* 1949). The novel chronicles the devastation experienced by native people at the hands of agricultural companies looking to profit from the commercialization of land. Asturias uses magical realism to foreground the mythic qualities of the indigenous experience being challenged by the sheer political and economic might of foreign capital interests.

The period from 1950 to 1960 marked a significant shift in Asturias's work. His novels began to take a more direct approach in their criticism of political corruption and imperialist impositions on Guatemala. The books in his *Banana Trilogy* (*Trilogia bananera*) best exemplify this transition. The trilogy, which is composed of *The Cyclone* (*Viento fuerte,* 1950), *The Green Pope* (*El papa verde,* 1954), and *The Eyes of the Interred* (*Los ojos de los enterrados,* 1960), attacks the United Fruit Company of the United States for its exploitation of the Guatemalan people and the strong-arm tactics it utilized in seizing land.

In 1966 Asturias received the Lenin Peace Prize and was named ambassador to France. A year later he won the Nobel Prize in literature. Toward the end of his life, he continued to write works like the ardently anti-imperialist *Weekend in Guatemala* (*Weekend en Guatemala,* 1954) and *Mulatta* (*Mulatta de tal,* 1963), an ambitious novel that exhibits his exceptional ability to channel his vast knowledge of myth into a work of masterful fiction. Asturias died in Madrid in 1974.

Miguel Angel Asturias will be best remembered for his ability to combine magical realism and the literary stylistics of surrealism with the myths of the indigenous people of Latin America to create a new kind of social protest literature that addressed the most pressing political and humanitarian issues of his time. It is this remarkable synthesis that has made Asturias's work a landmark in the history of Latin American literature.

BIBLIOGRAPHY

Callan, Richard J. *Miguel Angel Asturias*. New York: Twayne Publishers, 1970.

Franco, Jean. *An Introduction to Spanish American Literature*. 3rd ed. New York: Cambridge University Press, 1994.

Martin, Gerald. "Miguel Angel Asturias: El Señor presidente." In *Landmarks in Modern Latin American Fiction*, edited by Philip Swanson. London: Routledge, 1990.

Prieto, René. *Miguel Angel Asturias's Archeology of Return*. New York: Cambridge University Press, 1993.

Vazquez Amaral, Jose. *The Contemporary Latin American Narrative*. New York: Las Americas Publishing, 1970.

Albert Sergio Laguna

AUSTERLITZ W. G. Sebald (2001)   *Austerlitz* is the name of a famous battle in the Napoleonic wars and of a train station in Paris. It is also the name of a novel and a beautifully drawn character by German author W. G. Sebald (1944–2001). Who is Jacques Austerlitz? This question drives the protagonist of the novel *Austerlitz,* an architectural historian whom the nameless narrator meets in the waiting room of the Antwerp train station in 1967. Austerlitz investigates grandiose architecture, such as train stations, forts, or hospitals, in order to write a definitive architectural history, but his vast research and encyclopaedic knowledge compromise his ability to go through with his project, and he gives it up when he realizes that his frantic work serves the single purpose of blocking his access to his own past.

Adopted by a Welsh minister and his sickly wife and growing up as Dafydd Elias, Austerlitz learned his real name at the age of 12, knowing—without, however, understanding—that he came from a family and a country he had been forced to leave irreversibly behind as a five-year-old during one of the 1939 Kindertransportes (Children's Transports) from Prague. Early childhood memory fragments begin to emerge slowly, then accelerate to overcome the adult Austerlitz with violent urgency, growing and condensing to knowledge of a Jewish family that was exterminated during the Holocaust, of which Austerlitz is the only survivor.

Thirty years pass between the initial meeting of the narrator and Austerlitz and the continuation of their "Antwerp conversation" in London and Paris—30 years during which Austerlitz travels to Prague to meet his childhood nanny Véra and to learn about his Francophile parents, Agáta Austerlitz and Maximilian Aychenwald. Unable to remember their faces, Austerlitz becomes obsessed with tracing his parents' fate. Their paths lead him to Theresienstadt and, at the end of the book, the Austerlitz train station, from which Maximilian was sent to Drancy, to be deported to the East and the death camps.

The quest to uncover his forgotten childhood had begun at another train station, the Liverpool Street Station in London, which Austerlitz had visited in the 1980s before its complete remodelling. Inside the old station, he discovers the Ladies' Waiting Room, and suddenly he sees his Welsh foster parents and the boy they have come to meet: the small boy from Prague, the young Jacques. Here, in the train station, the adult self and the child self connect for the first time and begin the journey to Prague. After his meetings with his childhood nanny Véra, the adult Austerlitz sets out to travel to Great Britain for a second time; but, haunted by his childhood memories of the first train ride through Germany, he suffers from a complete mental and physical breakdown. As part of his recovery, he reads extensively about the Theresienstadt ghetto; the narrator reproduces Austerlitz's impression of the ghetto in the longest sentence in the book, which covers more than 10 pages in the German edition. In the fabricated documentary film of the ghetto shot by the Nazis, which Austerlitz subsequently watches, he believes he sees an image of his mother, and during his second visit to Prague, he digs up a photograph of an anonymous actress whom he feverishly wants to be Agáta. Austerlitz urgently needs to embrace an image of the loved one who has left no trace in his memory— if only to know himself.

Austerlitz's obsession with his mother's image is an example of Sebald's deep concern for the visual and its relationship to memory. One prominent aspect of Sebald's work that always elicits comment is his use of photographs: In all his prose works, the author includes images that run parallel to the text, without, however, submitting to it. Bare of inscriptions, the "stray photographs" (Sebald) tell their own version of the story, or a different story altogether. One of the results of Sebald's particular technique is to alert the reader to the imbalance between so-called historical truths (the photographs) and individual memory (the texts), and it is up to the sensitive reader to reconcile this imbalance by honoring memory as much as "history," if not more.

BIBLIOGRAPHY

Görner, Rüdiger. *The Anatomist of Melancholy: Essays in Memory of W. G. Sebald.* Munich: IUDICIUM, 2003.

Long, J. J., and Anne Whitehead, eds. *W. G. Sebald: A Critical Companion.* Edinburgh: Edinburgh University Press, 2004.

McCulloh, Mark Richard. *Understanding W. G. Sebald.* Columbia: University of South Carolina Press, 2003.

Santner, Eric L. *On Creaturely Life: Rilke, Benjamin, Sebald.* Chicago: University of Chicago Press, 2006.

Melanie Steiner

AUTUMN OF THE PATRIARCH, THE (EL OTOÑO DEL PATRIARCA) GABRIEL GARCÍA MÁRQUEZ (1975)   This novel appeared seven years

after ONE HUNDRED YEARS OF SOLITUDE (*Cien años de soledad,* 1967), but the author has said that he began it much earlier, as early as January 1958, when as a journalist he witnessed the ouster of President Pérez Jiménez in Venezuela. In August 1967, at a conference in Caracas, a group of writers of the Boom movement, including CARLOS FUENTES, announced that several of them would collaborate on a novel about the archetypal Latin American dictator. The project was never carried out, but the idea produced outstanding works by, among others, Augusto Roa Bastos, ALEJO CARPENTIER, MARIO VARGAS, LLOSA, Carlos Fuentes, and, of course, by GABRIEL GARCÍA MÁRQUEZ. *The Autumn of the Patriarch* is not the only book about the dictator, the *cacique* of Latin American history, or about corruption and power, but it is one of the finest by any writer.

Many of the details of the *cacique* portrayed in *The Autumn of the Patriarch* are based of the life of Juan Vicente Gómez, a military general and president of Venezuela from 1908 until his death in 1935, but the protagonist in the novel is a composite of leaders including, but not limited to, Gustavo Rojas Pinilla of Colombia, the Duvaliers of Haiti, Maximiliano Hernández Martínez of El Salvador, Marcos Pérez Jiménez and Juan Vicente Gómez of Venezuela, Juan Perón and Eva Duarte de Perón of Argentina, Joseph Stalin, and Francisco Franco, who was still in power in Spain where García Márquez worked on this novel. Historical anecdotes are incorporated into the narrative, such as the one about the mother saying that if she had known that her son would become dictator, she would have insisted he learn to read.

This book is a meditative treatise and analysis of dictators and power on both mythical and historical levels but based in an unnamed Caribbean country that includes parts of many different shores. There, a dictator rules for 100 years from inside a multilocked room with a window overlooking the Caribbean Sea. The author plays with both time and geography. New inventions are introduced to mark the passage of time, but the rule of the tyrant seems eternal. The chronology is not linear but spiral, and there are anachronisms, such as the arrival of Christopher Columbus and the landing of the U.S. Marines in the same scene.

One of the most remarkable aspects of this novel is its intricate narrative style. It is divided into six chapters—

relentless blocks of prose, without paragraph divisions, in long unpunctuated sentences, laid out as poetry in unmarked words, cadences of colloquial phrases, popular expressions, and snatches of familiar songs and verse by well-known writers, such as Rubén Darío (1867–1916), the Nicaraguan poet who invigorated the Spanish lyric. The pace is swift; the words flow in a torrent from various sources: the tyrant, an onlooker, or the all-knowing narrator. Reality and illusion are both themes and devices. The episodes employ hyperbole, allusion, paradox, shifts in narrative voice, and intermittent insights into minds and characters.

The novel moves in a series of anecdotes that relate to the life of the dictator, identified as the General, from the autumn of his reign to its end. In the first chapter the General's rotting corpse is discovered in the presidential palace, but there is suspicion because this is the second death discovered there. The first was that of his officially appointed double. The General had, therefore, been able to observe the spectacle of popular celebration over his demise and later assassinate the celebrants, and reward the mourners.

The second chapter begins with the discovery of the first corpse of the General, which is really that of Patricio Aragones. As the discoverers wait for verification and identification, they recall the General's brutal appetites, including his obsessive love for Manuela Sánchez, a working-class woman of stunning beauty, before whom the General was impotent. The third chapter is about limitless power and utter ruthlessness. It portrays the arrival of the General's best friend at a banquet, a friend whom the General suspected of involvement in a plot. The friend arrives stretched out full length on a silver platter, garnished with cauliflower and laurel, almonds, gold medals, and pine nuts, ready for carving and serving to the petrified guests. In the fourth chapter the General tries to have his aging mother canonized and instead names her patroness of the nation. He initiates intimacy with his intended wife and instead defecates in his shorts.

As the narration continues through the stages of trussing the General's body, managing the public announcement, and preparing the official funeral, there are flashbacks to the beginning of the end. In the last two chapters the bodies of the General's wife and child are thrown into the plaza and ripped apart by dogs. The General puts into motion a sadistic cleansing and celebrates his 100th anniversary in power. He dies in solitude and utter desolation, in power but powerless, never knowing what he was like, or even if he was a figment of the imagination, an uncertain vision of pitiful eyes, through a life arduous and ephemeral, "through the dark sound of the frozen leaves of his autumn toward the homeland of the shadows of the truth of oblivion."

Despite the irony, the satire, and the moments of humorous delight, the novel reads like a Greek tragedy of a tyrant blinded by power to everything including his own nature. The General rains pestilence and corruption through his land, and evokes pity and fear in his subjects, who celebrate in choral hymns of joy at his demise.

BIBLIOGRAPHY

Bloom, Harold, ed. *Gabriel García Márquez.* New York: Chelsea House, 1989.

Fernández-Braso, Miguel. *Gabriel García Márquez.* Madrid: Editorial Azur, 1969.

Fuentes, Carlos. *La nueva novela hispanoamericana.* Mexico City: Cuadernos de Joaquin Mortiz, 1969.

Janes, Regina. *Gabriel García Márquez: Revolutions in Wonderland.* Columbia: University of Missouri Press, 1981.

McGuirk, Bernard and Richard Cardwell, eds. *Gabriel Garcia Marquez: New Readings.* Cambridge: Cambridge University Press, 1987.

Menton, Seymour. *Latin America's New Historical Novel.* Austin: The University of Texas Press, 1993.

Williams, Raymond L. *Gabriel Garcia Marquez.* Boston: G. K. Hall & Co., 1984.

Arbolina Llamas Jennings

AXE OF WANDSBEK, THE (DAS BEIL VON WANDSBEK) ARNOLD ZWEIG (1948)

The German author ARNOLD ZWEIG (1887–1968) started work in 1938 on one of his major novels, *The Axe of Wandsbek,* a psychological analysis of individual behavior in everyday life under the Third Reich. It depicts the evil in the structures of German society and tries to explain its receptivity to malevolent impulses and wrongdoing, as well as the psychological mechanisms that prohibited the people from protesting against crimes committed by the supporters of the Nazi regime.

The novel continued Zweig's considerations about the relationship between justice and morality to which the writer had dedicated his earlier prose work.

The creative impulse for the novel was an article found by Zweig in a German exile newspaper in 1937. The news event from Hamburg, telling the story of the suicide of a Hamburg butcher and his wife, served as the culmination point of the narration. The novel begins in August 1937, when Albert Tetjeen, a butcher from Wandsbek, a city district of Hamburg, encounters business problems. He loses customers in favor of modern department stores and asks his comrade from World War I, Hans Peter Footh, for help. Footh finds a solution that he thinks would satisfy several needs: For generous financial remuneration, Tetjeen is to execute by decapitation political prisoners held in the Hamburg city jail. The four prisoners are communists who have been sentenced to death after being falsely accused of the shooting death of an officer of the Nazi Stormtroopers. Footh obtains this position for Tetjeen in order to help not only his friend but also the father of his girlfriend, Anette Koldeway. The young woman's father is the director of Hamburg's central prison, and in the novel the director is having trouble finding a replacement for the prison's executioner, who is out sick. Last but not least, finding an executioner is a gesture of Footh's support of the Nazi government, for Hitler has refused to visit Hamburg while the communists remain alive. In return, Footh, a dynamic shipping dealer, hopes for lucrative business opportunities.

Tetjeen agrees to the deal with Footh and executes the prisoners with his butcher's axe. Although he is disguised to keep his anonymity, a prison doctor present during the procedure, Käte Neumeier, recognizes him and spreads the word among the butcher's customers. The worker population of Wandsbek, sympathizing with the falsely indicted victims and disgusted by the use of Tetjeen's professional skills to kill innocent people, boycotts his store. Tetjeen's wife, Stine, discovers the truth about her husband's source of income and the real reason for the boycott. The story ends in September 1938, when remorse, financial ruin, and the community's moral condemnation lead Stine to suicide. After finding her body, Tetjeen also takes his own life.

Like Zweig's first success, *The Case of Sergeant Grischa,* the novel *The Axe of Wandsbek* is a story about individuals, both guilty and innocent, who are involved in legal murder. This time, though, Zweig left the reality of World War I and used the conditions of the Nazi dictatorship as the background for the narrative events. The thematic similarities between the two novels form a dialectic relationship that allowed Zweig to create an effective image of a corrupted social system—the continuation of the same machinery powered by political and economic interests that swallowed the young man Grischa in *The Case of Sergeant Grischa* 20 years before. The difference is that the legal murder in *The Axe of Wandsbek* cannot be explained by the special circumstances of war, state of emergency, or possible external thread. The majority of the society passively observes the imprisonment and execution of the communists. Placing the victims against the indifference or active support of "good burghers" permits Zweig to question the origins and omnipresence of evil in German society. The explanation offered by Zweig resembles his thoughts from *Insulted and Exiled:* National Socialism, as much as the war, was a manifestation of the unconscious effects that contradict reason and civilization. However, he also goes beyond this interpretational framework to show the striking contradiction in the worldview of cultured and independently thinking people, such as Dr. Koldewey or Käte Neumeier, who could convince themselves by some means to support a regime based on brutality and crime.

The brutal and criminal actions of the regime find reflection in other figures of the story. The question of how Albert Tetjeen, a sensitive and decent man and war veteran, could become the instrument of power and not have second thoughts about the moral responsibility for his actions constitutes the main tension of the work. This lack of reflection becomes his undoing. An interesting figure is also Albert's counterpoint, his wife, Stina, who finds herself caught in a tragic conflict between her love for her husband and the voice of her conscience. Stina is one of the most complex female characters in Zweig's literary oeuvre.

On the political level, the story's message leaves room for optimism: The fate of the murderer Tetjeen, who is broken by the workers' boycott and cruel business competition, demonstrates that the fall of the Nazi regime was contained at its conception and growth. Zweig attributed to fascism the characteristics of a last state of capitalism and foresaw the next development phase in communism, looking to the Soviet Union as an example. His transition to communist ideology, supported by extended readings of Karl Marx's works, was becoming evident.

The time of the publication of *The Axe of Wandsbek* (finished in 1943) coincided with the writer's return to Germany from exile. In 1948, after the end of the war, Zweig settled down in ruined Berlin. He became involved in the democratization of the country's political and cultural institutions, happy to free himself from the isolation of the immigrant and eager to see his dream of a just society become reality. In 1949, when the German Democratic Republic was created from the eastern part of Germany that remained under Russian control, Zweig decided to support the socialist system that meant, for him, the promise of a peaceful future.

BIBLIOGRAPHY
Isenberg, Noah W. *Between Redemption and Doom: The Strains of German-Jewish Modernism.* Lincoln: University of Nebraska Press, 1999.

Rost, Maritta. *Bibliographie Arnold Zweig.* Berlin and Weimar: Aufbau-Verlag, 1987.

Salamon, George. *Arnold Zweig.* New York: Twayne Publishers, 1975.

Steffin, Margarete. *Briefe an Berühmte Männer: Walter Benjamin, Bertolt Brecht, Arnold Zweig.* Hamburg: Verlagsanst, 1999.

Jakub Kazecki

AZUELA, MARIANO (1873–1952) *Mexican novelist*

Mariano Azuela, best known for writing the first major novel of the Mexican Revolution, *The* UNDERDOGS (*Los de abajo,* 1915), was born in Lagos de Moreno, Jalisco, Mexico, the son of a modest middle-class family. In his lifetime he successfully practiced his two great passions: writing and medicine. A prolific author of 16 novels, literary criticism, and other works, Azuela launched his writing career with the publication of "Impressions of a Student" in a Mexico City weekly in 1896. In 1903, in a contest sponsored by the Juegos Florales de Lagos, he obtained an award for his narrative piece "Of My Land" ("De mi tierra"). These forays into writing were followed by a series of published novels, including *María Luisa* (1907), *Los fracasados* (1908), *Mala yerba* (1909), *Andrés Pérez, maderista* (1911), *Sin amor* (1912), *Los de abajo* (1916), *The Bosses* (*Los caciques,* 1917), *The Flies* (*Las moscas,* 1932), *El camarada Pantoja* (1937), *An English Translation of San Gabriel De Valdivias* (*San Gabriel de Valdivias,* 1936), *Regina Landa* (1939), *Avanzada* (1940), *La nueva burguesía* (1941), *La marchanta* (1944), *La mujer domada* (1944), *Sendas perdidas* (1949), and *Esa sangre* and *La maldición.* (published posthumously in 1955). His *Complete Works* (*Obras completas*) appeared in three volumes between 1958 and 1960.

After finishing his studies in Guadalajara, Jalisco, Azuela began to practice medicine in 1909 in his native Lagos. The start of his professional career coincided with what was to become one of Mexico's most turbulent and influential periods of the 20th century, the Mexican Revolution (1910–20s). The overall corruption under the dictator Porfirio Díaz's 34-year regime was the catalyst that initiated a decade of violent struggles for land redistribution and social reforms in Mexico. As a liberal and a moralist, Azuela subscribed to egalitarian ideals which prompted him to become politically active and to support Francisco I. Madero's 1910 uprising overthrowing the Díaz government. He was appointed chief of political affairs in Lagos de Moreno, and in 1911 he was made director of education of the state of Jalisco. Madero's time in office was short-lived, however, and he was soon betrayed, overthrown, and assassinated by Díaz supporter General Victoriano Huerta, his minister of war. Several rebellions broke out in opposition to the reactionary general. Rebel leaders included Venustiano Carranza, Alvaro Obregón, Plutarco Elías Calles, Francisco (Pancho) Villa, and Emiliano Zapata, each of whom would play fundamental roles in the revolution. Mariano Azuela joined one of Villa's armies led by Julián Medina and served as a physician. It was in this capacity that he gained firsthand knowledge of the revolution, its complexities, and its contradictions, experiences he would later describe and analyze in his now-famous novel *The Underdogs.*

In 1915, when counterrevolutionary forces temporarily gained control of Mexico, Azuela moved to El

Paso, Texas. There he wrote *The Underdogs*. This novel gave voice to his mounting disappointment with the new forms of corruption that the revolution had unleashed. For Azuela, there was no apparent organized platform to unite the revolutionaries; only the unbridled quest for power seemed to be their motivating force. Though the novel went largely unnoticed initially, it was later was heralded as the first serious attempt to understand and give form and meaning to the revolution. Mexico slowly began to take notice of Azuela's novel when *The Underdogs* was published in weekly installments in the periodical *El Universal ilustrado* in 1915. A year later it was rereleased in complete book form, which gained it acclaim. The novel's success prompted the translations and subsequent publications in English, French, German, Japanese, Serbian, Russian, Yiddish, and Italian. The English version, *The Underdogs,* was translated by Enrique Munguía and published in New York in 1929. The author adapted the novel for the stage, and his adaptation was later used to produce a film version directed by Chano Urueta and released in 1939.

The Underdogs is momentous because it was the first of what was to become a robust subgenre of Mexican letters: "the novel of the Mexican Revolution." Many Mexican novelists, including Agustín Yáñez, JUAN RULFO, CARLOS FUENTES, and Rosario Castellanos, followed Azuela's example, each contributing works that attempted to make sense of a brutal yet defining moment of Mexican history.

In 1917 Azuela returned to Mexico and lived in the capital, where he wrote and worked among the poor. The subsequent novels written after his return continued to show the disappointment with the revolution's failures—in particular *Los Caciques* (1917) and *Las Moscas* (1918), both of which also deal with the revolution of 1910. Azuela's narratives showcase characters who are often vehicles for the author's preoccupations and insights. His works all evince a strong allegiance to the poor and working-class mestizo and Indian populations whom the author served in his capacity as doctor.

Mariano Azuela received the National Prize in literature in 1949. He died in 1952 and is buried beneath the Rotonda de Hombres Illustres, Mexico's most prestigious monument devoted to its greatest heroes.

BIBLIOGRAPHY

Azuela, Mariano. *Correspondence: Selections.* Mexico City: Fondo de Cultura Económica, 2000.

Martinez, Eliud. *The Art of Mariano Azuela: Modernism in La malhora, El desquite, La lucérnaga.* Pittsburgh, Pa.: Latin American Literary Review Press, 1980.

Robe, Stanley Linn. *Azuela and the Mexican Underdogs.* Berkeley: University of California Press, 1979.

Vazquez Amaral, Jose. *The Contemporary Latin American Narrative.* New York: Las Americas Publishing, 1970.

Laura Pirott-Quintero

B

BÂ, MARIAMA (1929–1981) *Sengalese essayist, novelist* Mariama Bâ considered herself "a modern Muslim woman," a politically loaded term that indicates Bâ's strong commitment to both Islamic values and women's rights. The Senegal author believed that the two concepts complemented rather than opposed each other. Her writings, which include several essays, newspaper articles, and two novels, explore the position of women and the choices available to them in postindependence Senegal. She was particularly concerned with the place of women in the changing African politics at the dawn of independence. African traditional society, while patriarchal in nature, did acknowledge the contributions of women to community survival and provided avenues through which to maintain balance, however delicate, in gender relationships. Colonization introduced new values and initiated new modes of thinking that compromised the already fragile status of women in society. Bâ's work called attention to the further marginal status of women in the new society and their disenfranchisement from the decision-making process on both personal and public levels. Her writing advocates for a society that encourages and promotes the well-being of all its peoples, where race, gender, and class prejudices are not the basis of personal and public decisions and policies.

Bâ was born in Dakar, Senegal, in 1929 into a politically prominent and affluent family. Her father was actively involved in political activities in Senegal before and after the country's independence from France. He served as the country's first minister of health in 1956. After her mother's death, Bâ was raised by her maternal grandparents, who provided her with a strong background in traditional and Islamic values. Her father insisted that she also receive formal education by attending the public schools taught in French. Consequently, while growing up, Bâ attended the public primary school during the day and the Koranic (Qu'ranic) school at evenings and school holidays. At the end of her primary education, Bâ, unlike many women of her generation, continued her education at the École Nomale de Rufisque, a teacher's training college near Dakar where she was trained as a primary school teacher. She excelled in her studies and graduated in 1948. She then served as a primary school teacher for 12 years, during which time she married Obeye Diop, a member of the Senegalese Parliament. They had nine children. When her marriage to Diop failed, she raised the children alone.

Due to poor health, Bâ resigned from teaching in 1950 to take up a position as the Senegalese Regional Inspectorate of Teaching. For the next 30 years, she used her position to advocate for the importance of education as well as the rights of women in the Senegalese society. Her combination of formal and traditional education gave her insights on many issues facing the women of her generation. She was actively involved in many Senegalese women's organizations that kept the "woman question" at the forefront of the national debate on the future of the country. Bâ was troubled by the tendency of postindependence African society to redefine and pervert traditional practices for the social and political disenfranchisement of women. Her first novel, *So Long a Letter* (*Une si longue lettre,* 1979), explores these issues. Bâ uses the life story of her protagonist, Ramatoulaye, to reflect on the lives of women and the many issues they have to confront daily as they tried to negotiate their place within the new society. Many of the events in Ramatoulaye's life parallel the facts of Bâ's own life. Ramatoulaye's husband abandons her after 25 years of marriage for a younger woman, her daughter's age. Ramatoulaye has 10 children she has to raise alone because of her husband's abandonment, not unlike Bâ, who had to raise her nine children alone after her divorce from her husband. But *So Long a Letter* is far from sentimental. Its narrative powerfully questions the place of old rituals, customs, and beliefs in the new society. The author also calls attention to the fact that the choices women make affect not only their individual lives but those of their daughters as well. Empathy and self-reflective choices are necessary to promote the welfare and self-growth of all peoples, both male and female, in any given community.

So Long a Letter received the Noma Prize in 1980, a high honor that helped establish Bâ as an influential African writer of the 20th century. The novel has been translated into several languages, including English. Her second novel, *Scarlet Letter* (*Un chant écarlate*), also received international acclaim. This work moves the discussion of women's issue to the international scale by exploring the interracial relationship between a young Senegalese man and a young French woman. The ultimate failure of the relationship highlights the difficulties of trying to negotiate racial and gender issues in an unforgiving personal and political environment.

Bâ died in 1981 of cancer at the age of 51, just before the publication of *Scarlet Letter.* Her unfortunate and untimely death at the onset of a rather promising literary career left many readers wondering what further contributions she would have made to African literature had she not died so young.

BIBLIOGRAPHY

Azodo, Ada Uzoamaka, ed. *Emerging Perspectives on Mariama Bâ: Postcolonialism, Feminism, and Postmodernism.* Trenton, N.J.: Africa World, 2003.

Kamara, Gibreel M. "The Feminist Struggle in the Senegalese Novel: Mariama Bâ and Sembene Ousmane." *Journal of Black Studies* 32, no. 2 (2001): 212–228.

Klaw, Barbara. "Mariama Ba's *Une si longue letter* and Subverting a Mythology of Sex-Based Oppression." *Research in African Literatures* 31, no. 2 (2000): 132–150.

McElaney-Johnson, Ann. "Epistolary Friendship: *La prise de parole* in Mariama Bâ's *Une si longue letter.*" *Research in African Literatures* 30, no. 2 (1999): 110–121.

Pritchett, James A. "Mariama Bâ's *So Long a Letter.*" In *African Novels in the Classroom,* edited by Margaret Jean Hay, 49–62. Boulder, Colo.: Rienner, 2000.

Salome C. Nnoromele

BACHMANN, INGEBORG (1926–1973)

Austrian novelist, poet   Ingeborg Bachmann, born in Austria, was a highly noted novelist and poet. Having grown up in war-ravaged central Europe during World War II, Bachmann wrote on the central topic of violence. In addition to the general effects of violence, Bachmann's work looks particularly at violence against women. Fascism's brutality, which Bachmann witnessed as a young woman in her occupied native Austria, became a metaphor for human relationships in her writing. Her work also shows her interest in philosophy, especially the limits of language. Influenced by the philosophy of Ludwig Wittgenstein, her work plumbs the inadequacy and limits of linguistic expression. As a novelist, poet, and dramatist, Bachmann became a leading voice in postwar German-language literature and is today regarded as one of the most important Austrian writers of the 20th century.

Bachmann was born in 1926 in Klagenfurt, Austria, the daughter of a high school teacher who joined the Austrian Nazi Party in 1932. At the age of 12, she witnessed Nazi troops marching into her small town in the southern region of Austria. This early impression of foreign dominance and violence became a central motif in her work and the model for her autobiographical novella *Youth in an Austrian Town* (*Jugend in einer Österreichischen Stadt,* 1961). After World War II, Bachmann left Klagenfurt to study philosophy, German literature, and psychology in Innsbruck and Graz in Austria. In 1950 she received her doctorate from the University of Vienna with a dissertation on the philosopher Martin Heidegger.

During the following years, Bachmann worked as a scriptwriter for the radio station Rot-Weiss-Rot, an institution of the American occupying forces. Her first radio play, *A Deal in Dreams* (*Ein Geschäft mit Träumen*), was broadcast in 1952. One year later Bachmann's first collection of poems was published and awarded a literary prize of the most influential German literary movement of this period, the Gruppe 47. (An informal association of German-speaking writers founded in 1947, Group 47 [hence its name] sought to reestablish German literature after its corruption by Nazi propaganda during World War II.)

Other volumes of poetry quickly followed, including *Invocation of the Great Bear* (1956), in which Bachmann shows a society where the former Nazi authorities are again in charge and where only poetic language offers a possibility for personal and social redemption. During the following years, Bachmann received many literary prizes, and at the age of 33 she became the first holder of the chair of poetics at the University of Frankfurt.

It was in the 1960s that Bachmann's skill in writing novels and short prose gained critical attention. Her prose, filled with isolation, betrayal, and violence, focuses on the life stories of women. In the mid–1960s she completed *Ways of Death Project* (*Todesarten-Projekt*), an ambitious work dealing with fascism and with men's subtle violation of others, especially women. The conception of *Todesarten* envisaged a trilogy, but only one part of the work was published during Bachmann's lifetime: *Malina,* the "overture." In this novel, which anticipated later feminist discussions about female subjectivity, the female character is defeated by a patriarchal society, and her voice dies away unheard. In earlier works such as the radio play *The Good God of Manhattan* (*Der Gute Gott von Manhattan,* 1958), this same theme of male versus female striving for existence is evident. In *Malina* the female first-person narrator appears to live with a man named Malina, but through the course of the novel, in which Bachmann weaves together quotations from other authors' writings (for example, Goethe and Shakespeare) as well as echoes from pieces of music, such as Richard Wagner's *Tristan und Isolde* and Arnold Schönberg's *O alter Duft aus Märchenzeit,* the reader uncovers a surprising discovery about Malina's identity. It becomes more and more evident that Malina is the male alter ego of the female "I," the imagined extension of the narrator's personality. At the end of the novel, after all efforts have failed to find a common language with the beloved second man named Ivan and after a nightmare encounter with the third man, the father—a Nazi—the female character disappears into a crack in the wall. Surprisingly, there never was a woman, says the remaining Malina, and the novel ends with the expression: "It was murder."

Though contemporary critics remained more enthusiastic about Bachmann's poetry than her prose, in 1961 she received the Berlin Critics Prize for her story collection *The Thirtieth Year* (*Das Dreißigste Jahr*), and in 1964 she was awarded the prestigious Georg Büchner Prize.

Bachmann died tragically in a mysterious fire at the age of 47 in 1973. Her death came in Rome two years after *Malina* was published. The other two novels of the trilogy *Todesarten*—*The Book of Franza* (*Der Fall Franza*) and *Requiem for Fanny Goldmann* (*Requiem für Fanny Goldmann*)—remained unfinished at her death.

BIBLIOGRAPHY

Bird, Stephanie. *Women Writers and National Identity: Bachmann, Duden, Özdamar.* Cambridge and New York: Cambridge University Press, 2003.

Brinker-Gabler, Gisela, and Markus Zisselsberger. *"If we had the word": Ingelborg Bachmann, View and Review.* Riverside, Calif.: Ariadne Press, 2004.

Brokoph-Mauch, Gudrum, ed. *Thunder Rumbling at My Heels: Tracing Ingelborg Bachmann.* Riverside, Calif.: Ariadne Press, 2004.

Gölz, Sabine I. *The Split Scene of Reading: Nietzsche/Derrida/Kafka/Bachmann.* Atlantic Heights, N.J.: Humanities Press, 1998.

Redwitz, Eckenbert. *The Image of the Woman in the Works of Ingeborg Bachmann.* New York: Peter Lang, 1993.

Nikola Herweg

BADENHEIM 1939 AHARON APPELFELD (1980)

Badenheim 1939 is a skillful fictional answer to the question that many have asked about the Holocaust: Why was there not more resistance? Perhaps the answer to the question is something much more simple than has been considered, as Holocaust survivor and acclaimed author AHARON APPELFELD (1932–) suggests in one of his best-known novels.

Although Badenheim is the name of a fictional town, the year 1939 has complications outside of Appelfeld's fictional treatise. The author raises hysteria through an acute portrayal of characters caught in a world that without doubt resembles the real world of 1939. The months before Adolf Hitler began his campaign to conquer lands throughout Europe and systematically massacre millions of human beings. Appelfeld situates his narrative—and admittedly lackluster characters—in a time that both rejects and anticipates the violence and monstrosity of World War II. The realism of Appelfeld's fictional creation, thoroughly echoing a very real and unforgettable historical time period, allows for the despair to rise like a crescendo throughout the actions and minds of the characters. Readers are made to feel as though they are as complicit as the characters that both witness and assist their own destruction.

On the surface, *Badenheim 1939* is the simple tale of a group of characters who gather in 1939 at a resort town, presumably near Vienna, for relaxation and entertainment. The primary concern of both the town's residents and vacationers at the beginning of the novel is whether the impresario, Dr. Pappenheim, will deliver on his promises of committing prominent musical artists to the town's festivities. The characters assume that the gradually more visible Sanitation Department is working with Dr. Pappenheim to provide them with an unforgettable Music Festival and celebration. The status of Dr. Pappenheim as an able impresario and the town of Badenheim as an enviable resort become connected, almost inevitably, with the progressive work of the Sanitation Department. Dr. Pappenheim's Jewishness is spotlighted by the Sanitation Department's "modest announcement" requiring all Jews to register with them. The townspeople, the vacationers, and the visiting musicians assume that Dr. Pappenheim is connected with the Sanitation Department because he is Jewish. After registration begins for emigration to Poland, Dr. Pappenheim becomes representative of life in an alien country; people swear allegiance to his Jewish Order to go even if they are not Jewish. Dr. Pappenheim, with his knowledge of such details as the impending train journey to Poland, is increasingly recognized as having an authority that has been delegated to him by the Sanitation Department.

Underlying the novel's events is a rising despair, a feeling that what has been will never be again and, even more so, cannot be regained by the characters and by the town of Badenheim. The Sanitation Department's requirement that all Jews register, according to its regulations, transforms both visitors and inhabitants of Badenheim: "[I]t was as if some alien spirit had descended on the town." While Appelfeld's dreary, naïve characters do not verbalize their questions about the Sanitation Department's actions, there is a growing feeling of forced capitulation to an authorized system that has overtaken them. The festiveness of the advertisements for life in Poland that soon adorn the Sanitation Department's office mocks the characters' belief in their annual artists' festival. The increasing confinement of Badenheim is ironically coupled with the growth of the Sanitation Department into a reference center and Poland souvenir shop for all of the townspeople, vacationers, and musicians. As the food supply in the hotel decreases, there is a collective frightening awareness: "[T]hey understood: there was no more going back."

One of the guiding questions of the events of *Badenheim 1939* is the trouble with reconciling the characters' attitudes and actions with what is going on around them in the resort town. Specifically, the characters do not seem to be aware of the consequences of what appear to be standard yet peculiar events in Badenheim. They replace their questions about the work of the Sanitation Department with the cheeriness of springtime and future events to look forward to. Certainly one of the more crushing early moments in the novel occurs when the characters allow their concerns about the Sanitation Department to be pacified by an increasing and unfulfilled appetite for sweets from the pastry shop. Appelfeld plays with the characters' trusted assumptions about the Sanitation Department's work and authority in order to slowly reveal its sinister nature. The Department's order and efficiency echo the frightening systematization of murder that would come to be the hallmark of Hitler's Nazi regime. As will occur in an overwhelming number of European cities, the Sanitation Department becomes a cog in the wheel of a bureaucracy designed to register, confine, transfer, and eradicate entire populations of human beings.

Perhaps what causes *Badenheim 1939* to stand out among Appelfeld's works is the intensity and hopelessness felt by readers of this novel. *Badenheim 1939* is yet another one of Appelfeld's distinctly profound, emotionally and psychologically challenging explorations of the Holocaust. One of the most poignant moments in the novel occurs after the Jews have registered, the town of Badenheim has been barred and gated with sentries, the post office has been closed, and the water supply to the hotel's swimming pool has been shut off. Letters to the various vacationers begin to arrive, causing the people to become aware of their deprivation of personal freedom. However, the rising despair and confusion of the townspeople and vacationers give way to relief when the Sanitation Department posts emigration procedures; at that point hope returns to a group of people who live in their expectations of an illusive life in Poland. The majesty of Appelfeld's prose captures the twin emotions of anxiety and festiveness as the people, released from their isolation, walk to the train station. Only the dirtiness of the train cars that arrive to transport them hint at the conclusion of their lives that they have been inevitably living for during the spring of 1939 in Badenheim.

BIBLIOGRAPHY

Budick, Emily Miller. "Literature, Ideology, and the Measure of Moral Freedom: The Case of Aharon Appelfeld's Badenhaim 'ir nofesh." *Modern Language Quarterly: A Journal of Literary History* 60, no. 2 (1999): 223–249.

Shacham, Chaya. "Language on the Verge of Death: On Language and Language Criticism in *Badenheim 1939* by Aharon Appelfeld." Orbis Litterarum: *International Review of Literary Studies* 59, no. 3 (2004): 188–203.

Walden, Daniel. "Psychoanalysis of Dreams: Dream Theory and its Relationship to Literature and Popular Culture: Freud, Billy Joel, Appelfeld, and Abe." *Journal of Popular Culture* 32, no. 1 (1998): 113–120.

Tara J. Johnson

BA JIN (LI FEIGAN) (1904–2005) *Chinese essayist, novelist*

The real name of the author who wrote under the pen name Ba Jin is Li Feigan. He was born into a large, wealthy family in Chengdu, Sichuan Province, China. After receiving an initial education under private tutorship in his childhood, Ba Jin entered Chengdu Foreign Language School in 1923. He had accepted the out-of-date and domestic ideas after the May Fourth Movement in 1919 and later moved to Shanghai and Nanjing to continue his studies. In 1927 he traveled to France, where he stayed for two years while finishing his first novel, *Destruction,* in Paris. In 1931 he finished his representative work, FAMILY, which is regarded as a semiautobiographical novel, in addition to being the first volume of the *Trilogy of Torrent* (*Jiliu*). The novel, which is often used in history courses, describes the decline of a big family in the early 20th century; it is a work that has influenced many thousands of young people in China. With the publication of *Family,* Ba Jin became a noted writer.

Later Ba Jin published numerous books such as the *Spring, Autumn* trilogy, consisting of *Love,* COLD NIGHT, and *A Garden of Repose.* While writing novels and essays, Ba Jin also edited many magazines. He was the editor in chief of *Culture Life* and Pingming Publishing House before 1949 and worked for Harvest and Shanghai Literature after that. The total of his works amounted to 13 million Chinese characters, and he was one of the few writers in China who lived not on government pay but on royalties from his writing.

Ba Jin gained high respect from readers. He was not only a great writer but also a true humanist. He once said: "Loving truth and living honestly is my attitude to life." Ba Jin expressed true feeling in all of his works, including descriptions of his inside thoughts during the period of the Cultural Revolution. The name of his collection of essays was *Random Thoughts* (*Sui Xiang Lu*), published in 1984. He also finished *Ward Four: A Novel of Wartime China* in 2001.

BIBLIOGRAPHY

Kubler, Cornelius C. *Vocabulary and Notes to Ba Jin's Jia.* Ithaca, N.Y.: Cornell University, 1976,

Lang, Olga. *Pa Chin and His Writings: Chinese Youth between the Two Revolutions.* Cambridge: Harvard University Press, 1967.

Mao, Nathan K. *Pa Chin.* Boston: Twayne Publishers, 1978.

Ru, Yi-ling. *The Family Novel: Toward a Generic Definition.* New York: Peter Lang, 1992.

Mei Han

BALTASAR AND BLIMUNDA (MEMORIAL DO CONVENTO) JOSÉ SARAMAGO (1922)

The novel *Memorial do convento,* written in 1984, advanced JOSÉ SARAMAGO (1922–) from national popularity to international recognition. The historical novel was translated from the Portuguese into English by Giovanni Pontiero in 1986. José Saramago was awarded the Nobel Prize in literature in 1998. History, fantasy, romance, and Saramago's distinctive critique of social inequities converge in this multifaceted literary work. His unique narrative style established the groundwork for his later novels. Saramago experimented with his distinctive blend of dialogue, description, and commentary in densely packed yet flowing text.

Historicity blends with fantasy and romance in the novel, called a "romance" in the Portuguese. The actual construction of the convent and palace of Mafra near Lisbon was ordered by King João V during the early 18th century. He promised a Franciscan monk that he would build the Memorial of the Convent to God if he and his wife were blessed with a child. When his wish was granted—Queen Maria Ana Josefa conceived an heir to the throne after years of a barren reign—the king proposed· an extravagant copy of the Vatican. While constructed on a smaller scale, his memorial pays homage to the nameless peasants who joined Baltasar and Blimunda in its construction. The immense undertaking required an inexhaustible supply of peasant labor. Peasants were dispensable to royalty, a footnote at most in recorded history. In his novel, Saramago parallels their personal history with the official story, that of church and state. The lovers of his book portray the sorrows and joys of the masses of humanity left unwritten in the annals of history.

Saramago unites an unlikely cast of characters who reveal humanity's saving grace amid the fires of international wars and the Inquisition. The wise female protagonist, Blimunda, possesses a second sight that perceives the interior life sources of others. She sees their wills rather than their souls, which belong to the church. She also chooses her circle of intimates through her acute perception. While witnessing her mother's execution in an auto-da-fé with more than 100 other Portuguese peasants in the Plaza Rocio, she approaches Baltasar to tell him that he is already known to her. Blimunda's mother, although a converted Christian, was burned for being one-fourth Jewish. Her last earthly sight was of her daughter united with her soul mate. The indivisible couple bond with an inventor-priest, Fray Bartolomeu Lourenço de Gusmão, who warns them that he may also be condemned for heretical ideas. His insatiable and unorthodox quest for knowledge and truth frees them all. Together they form an earthly trinity. Their union preserves their tenuous humanity as their joint efforts enable them to rise above their lowly condition.

The unlikely friends come together while witnessing an auto-da-fé, or mass execution, in the public square. While she does not reveal that she is witnessing her own mother's execution, Blimunda communicates silently with the woman at the stake who searches for her daughter in the crowd of onlookers as she burns. Blimunda's mother manages to convey to her that Baltasar Sete-Sóis (Seven Suns), the man whom she has just chosen, will accompany her throughout her life. The condemned mother then dies knowing that Blimunda is not left alone in the world.

The founding of the Convent of Mafra results from the convergence of various levels of Portuguese society. King João V, who has fathered many illegitimate children, is unable to produce an heir to the throne with Queen Maria. He makes a deal with God through a Franciscan mediator, Fray Bartolomeu, to fund the memorial if God grants them an heir. His prayers, and those of the Franciscan priest deal broker, are answered. His memorial is built upon countless invisible peasant lives.

Blimunda's pure vision counterbalances the hubris and greed of the ruling classes. She sees clearly through every person and every "body." When she does not see the body of Christ in the Eucharistic host, she surmises that Christ does not dwell there, nor does He reside in humans. Saramago portrays Blimunda as a pure but not celestial being. Her transparency enables her to perceive the interior of every human being. Blimunda does not find souls there, which belong to a distant, and in Saramago's novel, absent god. Rather, she collects wills. As she gathers human wills into her mystical yet commonplace basket, Blimunda empowers her friend to create a flying machine and motivates her beloved to travel the world in search of her when they are separated. The "passarola," a great mechanical bird, releases this earthly trinity from the constraints of their positions.

Domenico Scarlatti, the Italian composer, is also befriended by Fray Bartolomeu. His official post as musical director of the convent's choirs and music teacher to the royal Portuguese heirs is affected by Blimunda's purity. Moved by her clarity of vision while grounded firmly in the natural world, Scarlatti is inspired to create sounds as ethereal as her way of perceiving that world. Scarlatti seeks to compose music that will break away from the instruments and ascend like the lovers who take to the sky in the "passarola," or great bird.

Baltasar's blind loyalty is guided by his lover's acute vision. Despite the loss of one hand in battle, he works on the construction site as well as on the flying machine, the invention of the visionary monk whom they have befriended.

One allegorical quest is the success of the passarola, Father Bartolomeu's flying machine. His lifelong obsession allows the lovers to rise above the squalor, suffering, and injustice of their condition. The earthly trinity is temporarily able to leave earthly misery behind and share a private paradise. Autocratic and dogmatic powers of Church and State cannot reach them in their private space on the passarola.

When Blimunda discovers Baltasar years after his final voyage, their freedom is preserved. Upon landing from a solo flight to a distant region of Portugal, he was captured as a heretic. After searching nine years throughout Portugal, she finds Baltasar last in line to be burned at the stake in Lisbon. This auto-da-fé closes the circle opened by her mother's execution. Upon his death, Baltasar's own will reunites with Blimunda to rest with her, the constant and all-seeing keeper of wills. Their indomitable love is of earth, not of heaven. Blimunda, the keeper of wills, preserves their earthly paradise in her personal *Memorial*. Readers may experience this personal paradise and parallel history of Portugal for themselves by entering the earthly kingdom of *Baltasar and Blimunda*.

BIBLIOGRAPHY

Barroso, Conzelina. "José Saramago: The Art of Fiction." *The Paris Review*, Vol. 40, No. 149 (Winter 1998): 54–74.

Bloom, Harold, ed. *José Saramago* (Bloom's Modern Critical Views). New York: Chelsea House, 2005.

Cole, Kevin L. "José Saramago's Blindness." *The Explicator* vol. 64, no. 2, (Winter 2006): 109–112.

Engdahl, Horace, ed. "José Saramago," *Literature, 1996–2000* (Nobel Lectures: Including presentation Speeches and Laureates' Biographies). Singapore: World Scientific, 2003. 87–107.

MacLehose, Christopher. *Turning the Page: Essays, Memoirs, Fiction, Poetry.* London: Harvill, 1993.

Saramago, José. *Blindness.* Translated by Giovanni Pontiero. San Diego, Calif.: Harcourt, 1997.

———. *Baltasar and Blimunda.* Translated by Giovanni Pontiero. San Diego, Calif.: Harcourt, 1987.

———. *The Double.* Translated by Margaret Jull Costa. London: Harvill, 2004.

Carole Champagne

BALZAC AND THE LITTLE CHINESE SEAMSTRESS (*BALZAC ET LA PETITE TAILLEUSE CHINOISE*) Dai Sijie (2000)

Balzac and the Little Chinese Seamstress was an instant sensation upon its publication in French. The novel by Chinese author Dai Sijie (1954–) fictionalizes the lives of two urban youths sent to the Chinese countryside for reeducation during the Cultural Revolution of the 1960s and 1970s. Dai describes the first flush of adolescent love felt by his two protagonists—love for a local young woman and love for a hidden cache of Western literary classics—against the backdrop of political and social upheaval. The result is a slender, poetic novel about both the universal trials of adolescence and the more specific turmoil experienced by the so-called Lost Generation, the young men and women forcibly taken by the Mao government from their schools and families and sent to work as laborers in small rural villages across China.

The parabolic novel begins in 1971, as 18-year-old Luo, the son of a famous dentist who once treated Communist Party chairman Mao Zedong, and the 17-year-old nameless narrator, the son of two doctors, are sent to the remote mountain region known as Phoenix of the Sky to be reeducated among former opium growers. Forced to work in coal mines, the two best friends entertain themselves by showing off Western novelties to their peasant hosts, including an alarm clock and a violin, and by dramatically retelling the plots of movies to crowds of villagers. The pair also befriend the young woman whom the author refers to as the Little Seamstress, daughter of the local tailor, gradually falling in love with her charming beauty. One day Luo and the narrator visit an old friend nick-named Four Eyes, the son of a famous poet, and become convinced that Four Eyes has several volumes of forbidden literature hidden in a fancy suitcase. Steal-ing their friend's luggage, Luo and the narrator undergo a "Balzacian reeducation" by devouring novel after novel by Honoré Balzac, Alexandre Dumas, Gustave Flaubert, Herman Melville, and other canonical Euro-pean and American authors.

Much as the friendship with the young woman awakens new feelings of passion within the young admirers, so too does their avid reading awaken a new sense of political oppression. The novels teach Luo and the narrator about emotion, love, idealism, individual-ism, and spontaneous action—values discouraged by the repressive communist system that has given rise to the Cultural Revolution. The clandestine readings inspire in the boys and in the beautiful seamstress a longing for a fuller, richer life.

In 1966 Chairman Mao Zedong and his wife, Jiang Qin, convinced that bourgeois capitalism and Western culture were eroding China, decided to revamp the Communist Party and Chinese culture by destroying traditional lifestyles, the so-called Four Olds—old hab-its, old customs, old behaviors, and old ideas. A sig-nificant aspect of this destruction involved sending "young intellectuals," or men and women between the ages of 15 and 25 who had attended secondary school, to the countryside, where hard labor would rid them of any progressive memories and attitudes of Western influence. Denied access to education, books, music, and art, the so-called Lost Generation, the approxi-mately 12 million young people thus reeducated were plied with communist propaganda, encouraged to spy on fellow citizens, asked to report subversive activities to the authorities, and sometimes forced to join the Red Guard, the revolutionary youth army created to maintain order as well as to compulsorily institute the large-scale collective changes deemed necessary by the dictatorial Mao. The horrifying atmosphere ended with Mao's death in 1976.

Dai, an expatriate Chinese novelist and filmmaker and who has lived and worked in France since 1984, based some of the novel's key plot points on his own three-year reeducation in rural Sichuan Province in China. In inter-views he has acknowledged the real-life existence of both the Little Seamstress and a hidden hoard of Western clas-sics. As a work of fiction, however, *Balzac and the Little Chinese Seamstress* blends magical realism (a literary device that juxtaposes elements of fantasy with straight-forward narrative) with bitter lamentation for the lives destroyed by Mao's sweeping cultural reforms.

Balzac and the Little Chinese Seamstress suggests the possibilities of literature to spur mental growth while harshly criticizing any political system that seeks to limit the capacity for independent thinking. It longs for a more open cultural exchange, one that would enable the East and the West to mingle their myriad artistic outputs—from *The Count of Monte Cristo* to folk songs sung by Chinese peasants—as well as to mourn those who suffered under a tyrannical regime that favored ignorance over intelligent, individualist inquiry. After reading Balzac's *Ursule Mirouët* to the Little Seamstress, Luo says to the narrator: "This fellow Balzac is a wiz-ard. . . . He touched the head of this mountain girl with an invisible finger, and she was transformed." Dai's melancholic novel has a similarly powerful effect: It ensures that a painful past remains present in the mem-ories of his readers, and it engenders a compelling sense of the privilege of possessing a free imagination.

Among other awards, the novel won the 2003 Inter-national IMPAC Dublin Literary Award. In 2002 Dai directed a movie version of his novel in Mandarin; it went on to receive a 2003 Golden Globe nomination for Best Foreign Language Film.

BIBLIOGRAPHY

Dai Sijie. *Balzac and the Little Chinese Seamstress.* Translated by Ina Rilke. London: Chatto & Windus, 2001.
———. *Le complex de Di: roman.* Paris: Gallimard, 2003.
———. *Mr. Muo's Travelling Couch.* Translated by Ina Rilke. London: Chatto & Windus, 2005.

Jessica Allen

BARBUSSE, HENRI (1873–1935) *French novelist*

The French novelist Henri Barbusse was one of the exemplar writers during and following World War I. His work is recognized for its visceral critique of war and the lives changed by the carnage of trench warfare. He is regarded as one of the first novelists to offer an honest and realistic portrayal of soldiers in combat during World War I. His novels revived respect for the power of art to transform society and politics. Even so, Barbusse's life remains paradoxical: the pacifist in military uniform, the artist as social reformer.

Barbusse was born on May 17, 1873, in Asnieres, outside of Paris. His first writings—poetry—appeared in *Mourners* (*Pleureuses,* 1895), and were written in the author's youth and well before the opening of the First World War. These early works are today sometimes identified as neosymbolist. In 1908 he published his first important novel, *The Inferno* (*L'Enfer*), a work closely identified with neonaturalism. This work broke many taboos, sparking controversy for its voyeuristic glimpse into bedroom life. The story is highly realistic and exact in its portrayal, relating the voyeurism of a young Parisian who lives in a boardinghouse. Barbusse describes how the young Peeping Tom spies on the other boarders through a hole in his bedroom wall. Graphically, the author describes scenes of birth, death, adultery, and lesbianism. The novel proved not only shocking but daring at the time, crossing conventional moral boundaries.

In 1914 Barbusse volunteered for wartime service despite his antiwar stance. Forty-one years old at the beginning of World War I, he served in the front trenches, was wounded in action on several occasions, fought at the battle of Verdun, and was cited for gallantry. He was mustered out of the service in 1917 due to his wounds. Those long years steeled Barbusse in his pacifism, and this philosophical stance was given much weight in his next novels.

Barbusse's novel *Under Fire* (*Le feu,* 1916) was finished during World War I, gaining him fame. This work represents one of the first and most firm criticisms of not only the French but other nations involved in the global conflict. The novel, told from the first-person point of view, bravely depicts in accurate and close-up detail the bloodshed, mangled bodies, and death resulting from trench warfare. The book's dedication is "To the memory of the comrades who fell by my side at Crouÿ and on Hill 119, January, May, and September, 1915." Internationally acclaimed, the novel won the Prix Goncourt based on the book's threaded language of realism and poetics. The author describes moments in the trenches in the chapter entitled "Under Fire": "There is a swift illumination up above—a rocket. The scene in which I am stranded is picked out in sketchy incipience around me. The crest of our trench stands forth, jagged and disheveled, and I see, stuck to the wall every five paces like upright caterpillars, the shadows of the watchers."

Barbusse was openly a pacifist and stood against the horrific consequences of the long years of warfare. Following the war, he became a member of the Communist Party in France. He continued writing, producing such political novels as *Light* (*Clarte,* 1919), *Chains* (*Les enchainements,* 1924), and *The Judas of Jesus* (*Le Judas de Jesus,* 1927). The novel *Chains,* in particular, brought criticism from American readers, and Barbusse found himself on the defensive. The embattled author published a response to the criticism in *The Nation* (June 23, 1926), addressing his message to the "Free Spirits of America." *The Nation's* abstract summarizes Barbusse's lengthy essay: "American opinion accepts too uncritically the myths and distortions with which constituted authority and its official apologists. Barbusse describes that, to be a revolutionist does not mean that one is consumed by a sick need of disturbing the existing order; that one must wave the flag, threaten, and make excited demonstrations after the manner of the demagogue."

For Barbusse there existed no division between art and politics. Art, in part, functioned as a tool to help reshape human attitudes and social action. Barbusse's progressive social role for art fell into direct conflict with other newly emerging aesthetic attitudes toward art and politics. These include dadaism and surrealism, two social and artistic movements in the first decades of the 20th century that denounced traditional forms and purposes of art. While Barbusse attempted to write the past in order to change the future, surrealists such as ANDRÉ BRETON sought to destroy the past in order to shape a new beginning.

Barbusse's communist leanings later led him to take up residence in the Soviet Union. He died in Moscow on August 30, 1935, at the age of 62, while writing the work *Stalin* (*Staline,* 1935). He is buried in Paris.

BIBLIOGRAPHY
Baudorre, Philipe. *Barbusse.* Paris: Flammarion, 1995.
Relinger, Jean. *Henri Barbusse: Ecrivain combattant.* Paris: PUF, 1994.
Vidal, Annette. *Henri Barbusse, soldat de la paix.* Paris: Editeurs Français R'eunis, 1953.

Michael D. Sollars

BARICCO, ALESSANDRO (1958–   ) *Italian novelist*

The Italian novelist Alessandro Baricco gained rapid popularity late in the 20th century with the publication of a series of short but poetic and passionate works. The author's popular fiction, such as *Ocean Sea* and *Silk,* reveals his ability to paint character and setting from a diverse pallete. He draws from ballad, fable, poetry, history, and modern sensibility to produce some of Italy's most intriguing and captivating prose. His imaginative, minimalist prose has been compared to that of his fellow Italian writer, ITALO CALVINO.

Baricco was born in Turin, Italy, and still resides there. He began his artistic career as a music critic for the Italian daily *La Repubblica.* He later became a cultural correspondent for *La Stampa.* He has spent many years studying music, particularly opera. His operatic musical work *Love Is a Dart* (*L'amore è un dardo*) first appeared as a successful program on Italian public television in 1993. The following year he produced *Pickwick: Of Reading and Writing* (*Pickwick, del leggere e dello scrivere*), a literary program, with the journalist Giovanna Zucconi. It is the author's passion for music that has inspired his writing as a storyteller. Baricco founded the Holden School in Turin, a writing workshop dedicated to narrative expression.

The eclectic Baricco has written a handful of novels to date, including *Ocean Sea,* (*Oceano mare,* 1993), *Silk* (*Seta,* 1996), *Without Blood* (*Senza sangre,* 2002), *City* (2003), and *Castles of Anger* (*Castelli di rabbia,* 2004). *Castles of Anger* won the Prix Médicis in France and the Selezione Campiello prize in Italy. Baricco's *Ocean Sea* won the Viareggio and Palazzo del Bosco prizes in Italy.

Ocean Sea is Baricco's postmodern fable of human desire and longing. The novel is set in the Almayer Inn, a remote shoreline hotel. An unusual group of strangers have gathered at the inn. A painter, a scientist, an adulteress, a young woman, and others are thrown into an unexpected web of relationships. Their meeting seems predestined, with their fates intertwined in a classical form. A strange mariner, easily recalling Samuel Taylor Coleridge's *Rime of the Ancient Mariner,* suddenly enters the inn, bringing with him a desire for vengeance.

Baricco's *Silk,* a passionate fable, is a timeless story of adventure, exotic lands, the impossible quest, and love gained and lost. Set in 1861, *Silk* relates the story of Frenchman Hervé Joncour, who as a young man decides to become a silk merchant instead of pursuing a promising military career. He resides in the town of Lavilledieu, a small French community that has thrived economically on its silk industry until a disaster strikes. An epidemic has devastated the silk worms in France and other parts of the West, bringing economic collapse to the little town's silk manufacturing. In an attempt to save the local economy, Hervé Joncour, leaving his wife, Hélène, behind, travels to the faraway islands of Japan, where it is believed that silkworms remain uninfected by the plague due to the country's isolation as an island nation and because of its rigid policies against outside traffic to the nation. Baricco sets his story several years after the time when the American commodore Matthew C. Perry first opened Japan to outside trade in 1854, ending 200 years of the country's isolation. Regardless of the country's remaining trade restrictions, especially on silk worms, Hervé Joncour proceeds on his quest to carry this tiny and delicate cargo outside of the Japanese border.

After a long and arduous journey to the Far East, Hervé Joncour finds himself in the court of a powerful and yet mysterious warlord. His eyes instantly become riveted on a beautiful woman in the warlord's tent. The traveler is uncertain if she is the man's wife, concubine, or daughter. He notices that the young beauty has round eyes, not those of oriental women. Her mystery and beauty entrap Hervé Joncour, who falls in love with her. They never exchange words or long glances. The balance of the novel describes his desire for the woman and his repeated journeys from France to Japan, ostensibly to secure the precious silk cargo but in reality to see the young woman again.

Silk became an overnight best seller in the author's home country and has been translated into 27 languages. The book is slated to be made into an opera by André Previn and a film produced by Miramax.

BIBLIOGRAPHY

Baricco, Alessandro. *Lands of Glass.* Translated by Alastair McEwen. London: Hamish Hamilton, 2002.

————. *Ocean Sea.* Translated by Alastair McEwen. New York: Knopf, 1999.

————. *Silk.* Translated by Guido Waldman. London: Harvill Press, 1997.

————. *Without Blood.* Translated by Ann Goldstein. Edinburgh: Canongate, 2004.

Michael D. Sollars

BAROJA, PÍO (PÍO BAROJA Y NESSI) (1872–1956) *Spanish novelist*

The Spanish author Pío Baroja authored nearly 100 novels, making him not only one of the most celebrated Spanish writers of the 20th century but also one of the most prolific. Though he resisted being too closely associated with any particular political or ideological faction, Baroja in his early work embodied the spirit of the Generation of 1898, a diverse intellectual movement that grew out of Spain's defeat in the Spanish-American War. Seeking the regeneration and modernization of Spanish society, Baroja's novels frequently indict the Catholic Church, the Spanish education system, the military, and the concepts of democracy and marriage. Having flirted with anarchism in his youth, Baroja resisted institutions of power that controlled individuals and all mass political or religious movements. As such, his novels tend to celebrate the individual and indict those who conform to social and institutional norms. What many critics regard as Baroja's best fiction—such as *The Quest* (*La busca*, 1904)—chronicles the toil-filled lives of lower classes. His commitment to social realism and sympathy for the disenfranchised led José Ortega y Gosset to call Baroja "el Homero de la canalla" (the Homer of the rabble).

Baroja also insisted upon the absurdity and randomness of human existence, which his writing style reflects. Informal, conversational prose and loosely structured plots—sometimes criticized for being excessively chaotic—are the hallmarks of Baroja's fiction. His penchant for the "open novel" makes him a forerunner of later 20th-century modern novels, as Baroja eschewed 19th-century literary conventions that favored tightly woven plots and linear narrative development. Baroja's chief influences include Charles Darwin, Friedrich Nietzsche, and Immanuel Kant, as well as Charles Dickens and Fyodor Dostoyevsky. Like others of the Generation of 1898, Baroja desired that contemporary European ideas would gain acceptance in relatively traditional Spain.

Of Basque heritage, Baroja was born in San Sebastían and spent most of his life in Madrid, though he also lived in Pamplona, Cestona, and Valencia. He earned a medical degree, writing a thesis on pain, but his short career as a doctor left him dissatisfied. He and his brother Ricardo, also a writer of Basque-themed adventures who later became a renowned impressionist painter, helped an aunt run her Madrid bakery.

In 1900 Baroja published his first novel, *The House of Aizgorri* (*La casa de Aizgorri*), which became part of a trilogy entitled *The Basque Country* (*La tierra vasca*, 1900–09). In 1901 the author formed an alliance called Los Tres with two other writers, Ramiro de Maeztu and José Martínez Ruiz, the famous Spanish literary critic who coined the phrase *Generation of 1898*. Los Tres rather broadly sought to improve Spain's troubled economy and educational system, though the group met little success and dissolved soon after its inception. Baroja twice attempted to secure a position with the Spanish parliament, called the Cortes. Though social activism clearly appealed to him, his disdain for rigid political dogma of all kinds seems to have ultimately rendered him more fit for the quiet, independent writing life, a man of words rather than deeds. It is no surprise, then, that Baroja's fiction tackles the very issues that Los Tres sought to improve, as his novels attend to the economic and social hardships faced by his characters.

The main characters of his early novels, such as those of *The Way to Perfection* (*Camino de perfection*, 1902), *The Lord of Labraz* (*El mayorazgo de Labraz*, 1903) and another trilogy, *The Struggle for Life* (*La lucha por la vida*), more successfully retain their individuality and resist social conformity than those characters of his later novels, who tend to be defeated by social forces. The novels *The Quest* (*La busca,* 1904), *Weeds* (*Mala hierba,* 1904), and *Red Dawn* (*Aurora roja,* 1905) comprise *The Struggle for Life.* *The Quest* in particular brought Baroja international acclaim, as the novel exposes the difficulties of urban lower-class life in Madrid. While the theme of social and economic stratification dominates much of Baroja's work, he was also concerned with Spain's future and its relationship with other countries. Attention to Spain's position is paid in *The Way to Perfection, Caesar or Nothing* (*César o nada,* 1910), and *The World Is Like That* (*El mundo es ansí,* 1912).

Baroja's later novels, which hardly received the critical acclaim and popularity his earlier works engendered, are suspense-driven adventure tales that more palpably reflect the Spanish picaresque tradition. Between 1913 and 1935 Baroja published a cycle of 22 novels, collectively entitled *Memoirs of a Man of Action* (*Memorias de un hombre de acción*). The books track the episodic adventures of 19th-century liberal spy and conspirator Eugenio de Aviraneta, a relative of Baroja's mother.

American novelists John Dos Passos and Ernest Hemingway, who visited the Spanish author just before his death in 1956, have each recognized Baroja's influence on their own fiction. Spanish novelist CAMILO JOSÉ CELA, who felt that Baroja ought to have been awarded a Nobel Prize in literature, also considered himself indebted to the author's work.

BIBLIOGRAPHY

Barrow, Leo L. *Negation in Baroja: A Key to his Novelistic Creativity.* Tucson: University of Arizona Press, 1971.

Close, Glen S. *La imprenta enterrada: Baroja.* Rosario, Argentina: Beatriz Viterbo, 2000.

Fernández Urtasun, Rosa. *Poéticas del modernismo español.* Pamplona, Spain: Ediciones Universidad de Navarra, 2002.

Jessica Gravely

BARON IN THE TREES, THE (*IL BARONE RAMPANTE*) ITALO CALVINO (1957)

Published first in Italian in 1957 and translated into English in 1959, *The Baron in the Trees* is an enchanting novel by ITALO CALVINO (1923–85). Because of the book's mixture of fantasy and allegory, *The Baron in the Trees* is viewed by many readers to be among Calvino's best work. The author is often regarded as one of the best fiction writers in Italian in the latter half of the 20th century. *The Baron in the Trees* is, in fact, part of a trilogy of books that also includes *The Cloven Viscount* (*Il visconte dimezzato,* 1952) and *The Nonexistent Knight* (*Il cavaliere inesistente,* 1959). These three tales were published collectively under the title *Our Ancestors* (*I nostri antenati,* 1960), for which Calvino was awarded the Salento Prize. The books were inspired by Ludovico Ariosto's mock epic *Orlando Furioso* (1516), which satirizes the chivalric conventions of the Middle Ages.

The Baron in the Trees, however, does not take the Middle Ages as its time period, but rather the Enlightenment of the 18th century. The book bears witness to the passing of this Age of Reason and Enlightenment and the time of Voltaire, a figure with whom the narrator of the book converses during a visit to Paris. The novel is not so much about this narrator, who admits the limits of his narrative ability, as it is about his brother, Cosimo Piovasco di Rondo—the baron of the book's title. It opens with the definitive event in Cosimo's life: On June 15, 1767, Cosimo declares that he will not eat the snails his parents put in front of him and out of protest he decides to climb into the trees near his home. The book subsequently follows Cosimo's life as the young man spends his entire existence above ground in the branches and leaves of tall trees. The community tenderly cares for him even though he appears to have gone mad. Cosimo never touches the ground again, but grows old living above the world. As he nears death, the protagonist grabs onto a balloon that passes by his tree and floats away, never to be seen again.

Not long after initially climbing into the trees, Cosimo meets the love of his life: a young girl known as Viola. Soon Viola moves away with her family, leaving Cosimo brokenhearted. Viola reappears late in the novel, and Cosimo admits to her that he has longed all these years for her return. After a brief period of shared happiness, the two are finally parted by jealousy, as Viola uses two expatriate officers, one English and the other Neapolitan, to push Cosimo into an envious fury that ruins their relationship. Unable to reconcile, Viola moves away again, never to return, and Cosimo is haunted for the rest of his life by his lack of understanding of her.

Aside from his love for Viola, Cosimo spends his years in the trees engaged in a number of adventures, all the while accompanied by a dachshund he names Ottimo Massimo, who turns out to be Viola's pet from her youth. Cosimo sabotages the clandestine work of pirates, he cleverly eliminates a wolf pack that invades his home of Ombrosa, and he even finds time to impress luminaries such as Napoleon. Despite his rugged life in the trees, Cosimo becomes a well-read and educated man who corresponds with prominent thinkers of his time, such as the 18th-century French encyclopedist Denis Diderot, and catches the attention of even the famed satirist Voltaire himself. Nevertheless, Cosimo remains a mystery to the townsfolk and to his family, particularly his father, who is both embarrassed and dumbfounded by Cosimo's resistance to quit his arboreal life.

Through the historical time period covered in the book, Calvino is able to represent an important transformation in ideas and art, particularly in Europe where the Age of Reason gave way to romanticism and new ideas about liberty, revolution, and nation. In the midst of Cosimo's strange stubbornness to live apart from others, he lends a helping hand when he can, such as when he begins to design elaborate hanging aqueducts. The book thus comments on what it means to be part of a community, as Cosimo, despite his seeming aloofness, remains quite engaged with those around him. The reader also finds in the book a simple love story that ultimately teaches the importance of communication and mutual respect.

BIBLIOGRAPHY

Bloom, Harold, ed. *Italo Calvino. Bloom's Modern Critical Views.* New York: Chelsea House, 2000.

Bondanella, Peter and Andrea Ciccarelli, eds. *The Cambridge Companion to the Italian Novel.* New York: Cambridge University Press, 2003.

Weiss, Beno. *Understanding Italo Calvino.* Columbia: University of South Carolina Press, 1993.

Joe W. Moffett

BARRÈS, MAURICE (1862–1923) *French essayist, novelist* Maurice Barrès left his mark on fin-de-siècle France as a famous political figure and respected novelist. Two images are associated with him: the portrait made by the fashionable painter Jacques-Émile Blanche, depicting a pale young dandy with a white flower on his lapel, and the picture of the revered patriotic writer/politician draped in a French flag. These illustrate his dual life, as "Prince of Youth" for fin-de-siècle France and as the prince or founder of modern French nationalism. Barrès's novels and articles stress individual thought and action, which must be transposed into concrete political involvement; the man himself strove to make his life into a continuation of his literary ideas and work.

In his lifetime Barrès had a huge impact on a whole generation of French writers, such as young ANDRÉ GIDE, MARCEL PROUST, Drieu La Rochelle, Henri de Montherlant, ANDRÉ MALRAUX, FRANÇOIS MAURIAC, Jacques Nimier, and Luis Aragon; his articles in *L'Echo de Paris* galvanized the Generation of 1914, members of an artistic group who fought in the trenches of World War I. Barrès's novels are now outdated, out of print, and mostly read by researchers for their influence on other writers. On the other hand, Barrès's pioneer use of two commonly used terms—*intellectual* and *nationalism*—caught the attention of linguists, and he is noted for that. He is also a crucial part of 20th-century French political theory, and discussions abound on Barrès as a proto-Fascist; historians raise questions on whether his brand of exclusive nationalism led to controversial doctrines such as Mussolini's Fascism or Hitler's National Socialism. Historians of contemporary French political thought also compare Barrès's view of the French nation to the Front National party of Jean-Marie Le Pen with its conservative platform. Barring the literary revival of his novels, Barrès's legacy is that of a political theorist.

Auguste-Maurice Barrès was born on August 19, 1862, at Charmes-sur-Moselle, Vosges, an eastern region of France close to the German border. The occupation of Lorraine by Prussia during the Franco-Prussian War (1870–71) undoubtedly affected his life, and Barrès traced his subsequent fierce nationalist feelings back to this childhood trauma. The publication of his anticonformist trilogy *The Cult of the Self* (*Le culte du moi,* 1888–91) gave him immediate literary fame at an early age.

Barrès started questioning corrupt Republican institutions and wanted to change them. In 1889, at the age of 27, he was elected a representative (*député*) for his native Lorraine at the French National Assembly. He then represented a Boulangiste faction (from the name of General Boulanger, a short-lived anti-Republican leader). For Maurice Barrès, direct political activity would systematically coexist with writing; through his life he was altogether a novelist, a journalist, and a politician. With novelist Émile Zola, he proved to be one of the first French politically involved (*engagé*) intellectuals by his stance and his articles at the time of the Dreyfus affair (1894–1906).

The Dreyfus affair, which dominated French political life for over a decade, sprang from the 1894 conviction for high treason of Captain Alfred Dreyfus, an officer in the French army. Dreyfus was a Jewish man from Alsace, a part of France bordering Germany; for nationalists, he was in essence a potential foreigner who had opted for French citizenship after the German annexation of his native province. Dreyfus was convicted of spying for Germany upon flimsy evidence, but he was the ideal culprit for a society that viewed Jews as outsiders to mainstream Catholic France. The publication in the newspaper *L'Aurore* of the famous "I Accuse . . . ! Letter to the President of the Republic by Émile Zola" ("*J'Accuse . . . ! Lettre au Président de la République par Émile Zola*") on January 13, 1898, transformed the forgotten court sentence of an obscure Jewish officer into a national matter. All of France took sides for or against Dreyfus's conviction; Maurice Barrès, as one of the main anti-Dreyfus writers, published his response to Zola, "The Protest of the Intellectuals" ("*La protestation des intellectuels*"), on February 1, 1898, in *Le Journal* and denounced supporters of Dreyfus as foreigners who had no right to meddle with French affairs.

The time of the Dreyfus affair was when Barrès laid the foundations for the nationalist doctrine that he further developed in later texts and articles. Anti-Dreyfusards stood for law and order, exclusionary nationalism, and patriotism and felt that the good of the French

nation was more important than the rights of a single foreign individual. Extreme anti-Dreyfusards like Barrès viewed the affair as a way to cripple the Republic, which they saw as weak and corrupt, and bring about its collapse. Despite his 1889 election to the National Assembly on a secular platform, Barrès did not hesitate to take a traditional anti-Semitic position at the time of the Dreyfus affair. His nationalism dictated that only individuals whose family history was rooted in France's past could be considered as truly French; French ancestry could not possibly be adopted, "naturalization" was de facto impossible. Catholicism, as the religion of most French people, became part of the cultural heritage of being French; Protestants, Jews, or FreeMasons were construed as foreign undesirable elements for a united nation. Barrès's nationalism was not based on racial characteristics, though, and in that sense he cannot be considered as a precursor to Hitler's National Socialism; only visceral ties to the soil of the homeland (*la terre et les morts,* the earth and the dead) allow people to belong to the French nation; Jews, the wandering nation par excellence, could not possibly be construed as French. In his racism, Barrès joined a famous theorist of anti-Semitic France, Edouard Drumont, the author of *Jewish France* (*La France juive,* 1886).

In 1898 Barrès, as leader of the anti-Dreyfus camp, was again a man of action as he assembled a group of literary men into the League of the French Homeland (Ligue de la Patrie Française); he even subsequently published anti-Semitic texts collected into *Scenes and Doctrines of Nationalism* (*Scènes et doctrines du nationalisme,* 1902). While the year 1906 saw Captain Dreyfus's pardon and the ultimate failure of anti-Dreyfus efforts, it was also the year Maurice Barrès attained literary and political recognition. He was elected both to the French Academy and as a representative (*député*) for a district of Paris at the National Assembly.

During World War I (1914–18), Barrès published daily articles in the newspaper *L'Echo de Paris*; these were later collected in the 14 volumes of *The Great War Chronicles* (*Chroniques de la Grande Guerre*). His patriotic ardor galvanized the French troops, and victory in 1918 also represented the ultimate recognition of his efforts. By this time Barrès was mellowing out with age, and his *Journals* (*Cahiers*) show that he was slipping from nationalism into Catholicism. His post-war publications, such as *The Genius of the Rhine* (*Le génie du Rhin,* 1921), even advocated reconciliation between French and German people toward a common task. During his later years, Barrès traveled to the Orient and published an Orientalist romance, *A Garden on the Orontes* (*Un jardin sur l'Oronte,* 1922), which many critics of the time found out of character and distastefully erotic. Before he died on December 4, 1923, Barrès was working on the manuscript of a text with Catholic overtones, *The Mystery in Full Daylight* (*Le mystère en pleine lumière*).

The two trilogies published by Maurice Barrès express his commitment to ideas he deeply believed in: fierce individualism and the importance of maintaining one's provincial roots. *Cult of the Self* (*Culte du moi,* 1888–91) and *The Novel of National Vigor* (*Le roman de l'énergie nationale,* 1897–1902) both show the scope of Barrès's didactic ambition as a writer of philosophical and political texts.

The fictional trilogy *Cult of the Self* was Maurice Barrès's first major contribution to French literature. He was then under the age of 30, and literary recognition as the Prince of Youth came following this publication, as a whole generation of young men identified with the protagonist's solitude and his rejection of the common people. The collective title of *Cult of the Self* comprises three volumes: *Under the Gaze of the Barbarians* (*Sous l' œil des barbares,* 1888), *A Free Man* (*Un homme libre,* 1889), and finally *Berenice's Garden* (*Le jardin de Bérénice,* 1891). These novels have a very loose narrative plot, and the allegorical characters' lyrical tone gives the writing a stilted quality that does not carry well over time. *Cult of the Self* is in essence an egotistical manifesto in which the author lays out principles of conscious individualism; precepts are needed since the ego, for Barrès, constantly fights in order to establish or preserve its identity and recreate itself. This is an earlier version of JEAN-PAUL SARTRE's famous "Hell is other people" statement, and the existence of others (the Barbarians of the first title) makes life a permanent fight for self-assertion.

For human egos in that constant strife, emotions are important, since in Barrès's own words, "It is not reason that gives us our moral orientation, it is our sensi-tivity." The protagonist of *A Free Man* establishes for his life three governing principles. A cursory reading of these precepts shows how emotions precede reason; as a first principle, Barrès considers that exaltation is what brings men most happiness; second, that the best thing about exaltation is to analyze it; and third, that men must feel as much as possible while analyzing as much as possible. True to his later dispositions, Barrès also uses the trilogy to advocate discipleship to Great Men as well as devotion to one's native land. These rules of life served as a model to a whole generation; the impact of his defense of individualism was enormous.

Barrès published his second trilogy, *The Novel of National Vigor* (*Le roman de l'énergie nationale,* 1897–1902) 10 years later, at the time of the Dreyfus affair. At this point he showed himself at his dogmatic best and defended the values of the native environment and region; authors such as Gide, who had adored his first trilogy, were very critical of the second one. *The Novel of National Vigor* consists of *The Uprooted* (*Les déracinés,* 1897), *The Call to the Soldier* (*L'appel au soldat,* 1900), and *Their Figures* (*Leurs figures,* 1902). This second trilogy is partly autobiographical in that it tells the story of seven young men who leave their native Lorraine for Paris. As they seek fortune in Paris, these youths meet with the problems and disillusions of adulthood. This is the main theme of the first volume, *The Uprooted.* The second novel of the trilogy, *The Call to the Soldier,* looks at the history of the Boulangiste Party, which Barrès joined and represented in 1889; and finally the third volume, *The Call to the Soldier,* deals with the corruption of the Republican system and the Panama scandal. The series has been viewed by critics as "a plea for local patriotism, and for the preservation of the distinctive qualities of the old French provinces," and it was in line with Barrès's nationalism at the time.

A Garden on the Orontes (*Un jardin sur l'Oronte,* 1922), the novel Maurice Barrès wrote two years before he died, is radically different from anything he published earlier. Critics of the time were surprised and looked unsuccessfully for a political or religious meaning to this conventional orientalist tale; others later spoke of Barrès's artistic liberation from the constraints of ideological writing, calling this light romance his

1001 Nights. The plot is fairly simple: Western travelers in 1914 Syria buy from locals an old Arab manuscript recounting the love story of Guillaume, a crusader, and Orante, the widow of the emir of Qalaat. This story of passion, lust, and female ambition takes place in 12th-century Syria and finds its inspiration in the medieval vision of love; Barrès uses the 12th-century romance of *Tristan and Iseult* as a constant reference in his text. It is a conventional romance novel with the usual ingredients of love and betrayal; The author sprinkles the plot with a few erotic scenes which were risqué for the time and for his usual readership. Characters are flat and conventional; they betray Barrès's inexperience at this form of fiction. The somber end to the novel shows juvenile disillusion on the part of the author, as the protagonist concludes that "Now . . . I know that men cannot count on any other love than their mother's."

BIBLIOGRAPHY

Barrès, Maurice. *Une enquête aux pays du Levant.* Paris: Manucius, 2005.

Carroll, David. *French Literary Fascism: Nationalism, Anti-Semitism, and the Ideology of Culture.* Princeton, N.J.: Princeton University Press, 1995.

Drake, David. *French Intellectuals and Politics from the Dreyfus Affair to the Occupation.* New York: Palgrave Macmillan, 2005.

Mauriac, François. *La Rencontre avec Barrès.* Paris: La Table Ronde, 1993.

Sternell, Zeev. *Maurice Barrès et le Nationalisme Français.* Paris: Armand Colin, 1972.

Annick Durand

BATAILLE, GEORGES (LORD AUCH, PIERRE ANGELIQUE) (1897–1962) *French essayist, novelist*

Georges Bataille was one of the most influential French writers of the 20th century. A novelist, essayist, and frequent journal editor, Bataille was a leading voice in literary and artist movements. His work has long been linked to philosophical and religious explorations of eroticism, surrealism, and death. His novels often explore the paradoxes of man's relationship with his own nature and with God. Bataille is often compared to fellow French novelists JEAN-PAUL SARTRE, and ALBERT CAMUS, as well as other postwar writers who created philosophical novels to explain the prevalence of evil evidenced by the two world wars, the Holocaust, and the bombing of Hiroshima and other cities during these conflicts. While Bataille was a philosophical and psychological writer like Sartre and Camus, he was also greatly influenced by what he considered the evil nature of humankind, the church, the community, and the individual self. Bataille's relationship with other French writers and artists during his lifetime was compounded by rifts brought on by sharp intellectual differences.

The son of a syphilitic and paralytic father, Joseph Aristide-Bataille, Georges Bataille often lived life with wild abandon. He craved to be seen in public, engaged in unashamed acts of debauchery, and frolicked in infidelity. He also forsook his devout relationship with God as a young man. Bataille had numerous love affairs and wives, and he visited brothels and engaged in sexual exhibition until he became infirm in his old age. He regretted that he had to work as a librarian for most of his life because his novels produced little in literary accolades or monetary recompense. While his work avoids easy classification, the nature of his erotic literature is more philosophical and psychological than merely pornographic.

Bataille's father became paralytic only three years after the writer was born, and over the ensuing 12 years the young child witnessed his father's continuing physical decline, including blindness. Images of his father with his eyes rolled backward into his head, relieving himself in his chair and in his bedpan, influenced Bataille's erotic literature, including STORY OF THE EYE (*Histoire de l'oeil,* 1928) written in the late 1920s and early 1930s.

Perhaps even worse than his father's declining physical health and inability to serve as a patriarchal mentor to his son was his mother's decision for her and young Georges to leave Rheims without his father when the French city was evacuated in August 1914 during World War I. Bataille believed that his father had been abandoned because he was too crippled and insane to flee with the family. When his father died in November 1915, Bataille, who had converted to Catholicism in the same month that he had left his father in Rheims, fell into despair that his father had died without acknowledging God.

Bataille had already received two baccalaureate degrees in 1914 and 1915 when he was called up to fight in World War I; however, he was released from the military in 1916 because he suffered from tuberculosis. Bataille's early devotion to Christianity and his newfound relationship with God led to the writing of the pious, six-page article "Notre Dame de Rheims" while he was a student in the seminary of Saint-Flour from 1917 to 1918. Although the essay is about the Notre Dame cathedral in the recently bombed Paris, it can also be read as an homage to the father left behind. Bataille's article, which appeared in 1919, is the only religious work that he published.

After the submission of his thesis, "The Order of Chivalry in the Thirteenth Century," Bataille graduated second in his class from the École Nationale des Chartes in 1922 and received a fellowship to the School of Advanced Hispanic Studies in Madrid. During his stay in Madrid, he witnessed the death of 20-year-old bullfighter Manuel Granero. Bataille incorporated aspects of this story in *Story of the Eye,* published in 1928 under the pseudonym of Lord Auch. (Many years after the author's death, the canon of his works began to take a more complete shape through the discovery of his multiple pseudonyms, including Lord Auch and Pierre Angelique.)

While in Madrid, Bataille embraced the Nietzschean statement that God is dead, and when he returned to Paris in 1923, he became involved with the surrealist movement, frequented bordellos, and engaged in debauchery. He became even more fascinated with the paradoxes of eroticism and death when the psychoanalyst Adrien Borel gave him the photographs of Chinese torture as 100 forms of punishment. Bataille wrote a short book, *W. C.,* and later destroyed it in 1926. In 1927 he began psychoanalysis with Adrien Borel and wrote *Story of the Eye* and *The Solar Anus* (*L'anus solaire,* 1931). In 1928 he married his first wife, Sylvia Makles; they divorced six years later, and she later married the French psychoanalyst Jacques Lacan. Bataille's first daughter, Laurence, was born in 1930.

The 1930s was a stormy decade for Bataille. Heated arguments with other writers and artists broke out, particularly with ANDRÉ BRETON, the impassioned leader of the surrealists. Bataille also became associated with numerous publications. He was the editor of the journal *Documents,* published the pamphlet *Un Cadavre,* and joined Boris Souvarine's anti-Stalinist Cercle Communiste Democratique. After *Documents* folded due to financial losses, Bataille established the journal *Minotaure,* which was later adopted by the surrealists (1931–33). With Rene Lefebvre, Bataille also founded Masses, a seminar to discuss socialist issues between intellectuals and workers. He wrote essays for *La Critique Sociale* in 1933. During the years 1934–38 Bataille separated from his wife and had an affair with Colette Peignot (known as Laure). Near the end of the 1930s, he founded the journal *Acephale,* dedicated to the work of Nietzsche, which printed four issues from 1936 to 1939. Colette Peignot died of tuberculosis at the age of 35 in November 1938, and Bataille submerged himself in beginning to write *Guilty* (*Le coupable,* 1944) within the next year. He also wrote *The Blue of the Moon* (*Le bleu du ciel,* 1945).

During the 1940s and 1950s, Bataille penned several novels under various pseudonyms. *Madame Edwarda* (1937) was published under the name Pierre Angelique. *Inner Experience* (*L'expérience intérieure,* 1943) was published the same year that the author met Diane Kotchoubey de Beauharnais (Mme. Snopko), whom he married in 1946; they had one daughter.

Bataille wrote seven more works, including *My Mother* (*Ma mère,* 1966), which was published posthumously. He also founded the journal *Critique* and wrote essays on surrealism and on other artists and artistic movements. One of his most important publications, *The Tears of Eros* (*Les larmes d'Éros,* 1961), was placed on the index of forbidden books by the Roman Catholic Church in 1961. He also experienced recurrent bouts with tuberculosis.

Bataille's writings were influenced by Friedrich Nietzsche, by the Marquis de Sade, and Gilles de Rais, as well as by the anthropologist Marcel Mauss. His works reject traditional values and focus on eroticism and violence and on the similarity between horror and voluptuousness, between pain and joy. Georges Bataille died on July 8, 1962.

BIBLIOGRAPHY

Gemerchak, Christopher M. *The Sunday of the Negative: Reading Bataille, Reading Hegel.* Albany: State University of New York Press, 2003.

Goldhammer, Jesse. *The Headless Republic: Sacrificial Violence in Modern French Thought.* Ithaca, N.Y.: Cornell University Press, 2005.

Irwin, Alexander. *Saints of the Impossible: Bataille, Weil, and the Politics of the Sacred.* Minneapolis: University of Minnesota Press, 2002.

Surya, Michel. *Georges Bataille: An Intellectual Biography.* London; New York: Verso, 2002.

Tara J. Johnson

BAUDOLINO UMBERTO ECO (2000)

The fourth novel by the prolific Italian novelist UMBERTO ECO (1932–) charts the adventurous life of the eponymous hero, a medieval adventurer and consummate liar with a gift for making the most of chance. The book opens with Baudolino rescuing the hapless historian and Byzantine court official Niketas from the marauding knights of the Fourth Crusade during the sack of Constantinople in April 1204. As he and Niketas wait for the chaos in the burning city to subside, Baudolino narrates the story of his extraordinary life and his continuing quest for the mythical kingdom of Prester John.

Baudolino has certainly had an interesting life. Born in 1137, in what later becomes the city of Alessandria, a chance childhood encounter with Holy Roman Emperor Frederick the Great rescues Baudolino from his impoverished environment. As Frederick's adopted son, he is given an excellent education, but Baudolino is soon stealing historical parchments written by Frederick's uncle, Bishop Otto, in order to write the first draft of his life story. The young Baudolino's desire to construct his own version of reality is to become a recurring theme in the novel, for when his theft of Otto's manuscripts appears to be on the brink of discovery, Baudolino simply forges new ones from his own imagination. Even when he is sent to Paris to be schooled (and to avoid his growing attraction to Frederick's new wife, the young Empress Beatrice), his habit of generating false realities continues. In the company of Abdul, a musician with a taste for intoxicating "green honey," and the Poet, whose poems are actually written by Baudolino, our hero writes a fake letter to Frederick from Prester John, the legendary priest-king of the Orient. This act marks the beginning of the quest that dominates Baudolino's life; he dedicates all his energies to locating the magical kingdom of Prester John, but he and his friends only set off on their journey after the death of Frederick in 1190.

Up until this point, *Baudolino* follows Eco's previous novels in its mixing of detective fiction with philosophical speculation, producing a complex discussion about the nature of history. It is clear to Niketas, and the reader, that Baudolino is not to be trusted. He constructs elaborate lies about his life and his involvement in historical events, but we are carried away by the sheer innovation of Baudolino's implausible narration. Eco uses this focus on lies and lying to interrogate our understanding of history, presenting it as a collective illusion that is constructed to fit the demands of the present rather than the events of the past. For Eco, language constantly struggles under its dual nature, for it is both a source of imaginative creativity and a vehicle for conveying truth. Baudolino's colorful accounts manipulate these functions of language, blurring the border between real and possible worlds.

However, *Baudolino* differs from Eco's previous fictions in that after the death of Frederick, the novel's attention shifts from historical events to the medieval obsession with the fantastic journey. In their search for Prester John, Baudolino and his friends travel through lands inhabited by every imaginable sort of monster, all of which originate in classical and medieval texts. Conflicts between the monster tribes are grounded in religious differences, and here the novel draws attention to the often spurious ideological distinctions that provoke mutual animosity. Amid all the basilisks, manticores, and harpies, Eco is making a comment about the human desire to classify and differentiate in order to create systems of order and give structure to our lives and our histories. And yet, as Baudolino's lies indicate, these orders and systems often eclipse the very histories they were intended to preserve, until it is impossible to identify the true nature of the past. So beneath the entertaining exotica of Baudolino's narrative lies Eco's real interest: How do we narrate the past when language itself becomes untrustworthy?

Eco's trademark games with language and narrative structure are just as apparent in *Baudolino* as they are in his previous novels, as is the humor with which he broaches these difficult ideas about history and language.

Even so, Baudolino is one of the most mysterious of Eco's characters, a man whose past and sense of self are constantly being remade by his own imagination, and who no longer knows where his own lies end and reality begin. In Baudolino we see the individual lost in language and isolated by the compulsion to create new versions of reality. The relationship between the sign and its object is destabilized in the hectic extravagance of Baudolino's world, and Eco's novel asks us to question the extent to which our own worlds are similarly disordered by the deceptively slippery nature of language.

BIBLIOGRAPHY

Farronato, Cristina. "Umberto Eco's *Baudolino* and the Language of Monsters." In *Umberto Eco,* 3 vols., edited by Mike Gane and Nicholas Gane, 3:147–167. London: SAGE Publications, 2005.

Rochelle Sibley

BEAUVOIR, SIMONE DE (1908–86) *French novelist*

Unconventional in her life and in her writing, Simone de Beauvoir is best known for her seminal feminist text *The Second Sex* (1949) and for her long relationship with French writer and philosopher JEAN-PAUL SARTRE. Interesting as these two facts are, they provide an incomplete representation of the writer and person. In fact, to be remembered as Sartre's mistress relegates Beauvoir to the "relative identity" she fought against for herself and for other women. Educator, social activist, existential philosopher, biographer, essayist, dramatist, and novelist, Beauvoir created a remarkable body of work that not only influenced literary circles but also changed 20th-century perspectives.

Her life spanned 78 years of the 20th century, making her a witness to Europe's tumultuous modern history. Beauvoir's writing was both a celebration of her own writing life and a quest for her place as a female intellectual amid the perplexity of the modern world. Beauvoir gave prominence to the existential ideas of the "gaze" and the "other" in the establishment of female identity, ideas that later writers such as Jacques Lacan expanded. She also experimented with multiple points of view and narrative sequence in her fiction and dealt openly with the topics of aging and death.

Although Beauvoir traveled extensively, she lived most of her life within a small area of Paris near where she was born. The older of two daughters, Simone was the child of a wealthy and very conventional Parisian couple. Georges, who aspired to the aristocratic life, became an attorney. Also a theatre devotee, he was often involved in amateur community theatre. Georges Beauvoir's prosperous father owned a 500-acre estate where Simone spent her childhood summers. An agnostic, Georges took little interest in his daughters' spiritual training. On the other hand, Simone's mother Françoise, a member of a well-to-do banking family, was a devout Catholic whose conservatism and extreme piety manifested itself in her domineering treatment of her daughters. She sent them to a private Catholic school, Le Cours Desir, where Simone was made to feel her intelligence was more an oddity than an asset. Madame Beauvoir also strictly censored the books her daughters were allowed to read by cutting, marking, or pinning pages together. One of Simone's first acts of rebellion was to sneak into her father's study and lose herself in the forbidden books. The books she devoured encouraged her entrance into what she called, in *Memoirs of a Dutiful Daughter* (1958), "the enemy territory of the intellectuals."

Georges Beauvoir's law practice and personal wealth suffered severe setbacks during World War I, making it impossible for the family to continue to live in the luxury they had become accustomed to. Although he could not afford a dowry for his daughters, Beauvoir expected them to settle into lives as wives and mothers, befitting their former class. When Simone was a child, her father was proud of her intelligence, but as she became older, he was embarrassed by what he considered her unfeminine interest in learning. Now Simone rebelled against the idea of being a commodity in the financial and social transaction of marriage, shocking her family by announcing that she planned to continue her education and become a teacher, a position considered totally unsuitable for a woman of her class.

Beauvoir received her baccalaureate in 1925 and then attended the Institut Saint-Marie, where she devoted herself to the study of philosophy and literature. Enrolling in the Sorbonne in 1927, she received a philosophy degree in 1929. Her continued affiliation with intellectuals further estranged her from her father. In her autobiography, Beauvoir reports a recurring dream during these years. She sees herself on trial in a crowded courtroom, prosecuted for some heinous crime for which she alone bears responsibility. Eventually she realizes that her transgression is her independence, her autonomy apart from male approval of her existence.

Writing enabled Beauvoir to maintain her autonomy and to explore what it meant to be both female and a writer. Throughout her life, she was to associate books and writing with rebellion against the constraints society imposed on her sex.

At the time she was studying at the Sorbonne, Beauvoir met Jean-Paul Sartre, another philosophy student, and they began a relationship that was to last until his death. When final exam results for philosophy degrees were announced, Sartre had placed first and Beauvoir second, although professors admitted they had difficulty making the decision. Beauvoir was only the ninth woman and, at the age of 21, the youngest person to ever be awarded such a degree.

By the time Sartre met Beauvoir, he had already established a sort of philosophical triumvirate with fellow students Paul Nizan and Andre Herbaud. The three were fascinated with the depth and breadth of Beauvoir's intellect and began to include her in their circle. Beyond her relationship with Sartre, Beauvoir achieved what she had been seeking all her life: acceptance as an intellectual. Sartre and Beauvoir felt their relationship was an "essential" love, but eschewing the bourgeois ideas of marriage, monogamy, and family, they decided that each should be free to find "contingent loves" to enhance their experience. The two each had a number of lovers during their 50-year relationship and only lived together for a short period before World War II. During this brief period, one of Beauvoir's lycée students became a third partner with them. This arrangement provided material for Beauvoir's first novel, SHE CAME TO STAY (1943), but also made her lifestyle the target of criticism and scandal.

Shortly after their graduation, both Sartre and Beauvoir received appointments as instructors at lycées; Beauvoir in Marseilles and later Rouen and Paris, and Sartre in Le Harve and Lyons. During her early years as a teacher, Beauvoir began to write intently but discarded some of her early attempts. By 1937 her only literary output was a small collection of short stories. When Beauvoir began to write *She Came to Stay,* she was not only delving into her personal relationships but was also considering the psychological confrontation between self and other. The novel chronicles the lives of a couple after a young girl moves into their home and disrupts their complacency. In the fictional triangle, the older woman murders the younger "intruder" and simultaneously frees herself from her attachment to the man. In the real Sartre-Beauvoir-Olga triangle, Olga met and married a student of Sartre's. The two couples remained good friends for many years.

In 1945 Sartre and Beauvoir founded *Les Temps modernes,* an independent socialist magazine that became influential among French intellectuals. Beauvoir's second novel was *The Blood of Others* (1946), a tale of Paris before World War II and during the Resistance. The book raises moral and ethical questions Beauvoir was to return to in later works: the nature of responsibility and choice, the importance of the individual in the march of history, and the fundamental nature of freedom. During these years, Beauvoir was also producing philosophical treatises on the principles of existentialism, including *Pyrrhus et Cineas* (1943) and *The Ethics of Ambiguity* (1947).

Normally writing in a realistic vein, Beauvoir departed from this in ALL MEN ARE MORTAL (1946), a novel centering on death and immortality. The protagonist is a 13th-century immortal Italian, Fosca, who falls in love with Regine, a modern actress terrified of death. As Fosca recounts the political atrocities he has witnessed through the centuries and the disappointments he has experienced, readers realize that immortality is a curse and that life's meaning is derived from one's relationships with contemporaries and the dangers and possibilities inherent in those relationships.

For the first half of her life, Beauvoir had tried to deny that her identity as a woman had made any difference in her life. She was an intellectual individual practicing the radical individualism of existentialism, and that was all. However, now Beauvoir was beginning to understand that she must begin to answer what it had meant to her to be a woman in the 20th century. In taking up this question for herself, Beauvoir also helped many other women confront it. *The Second Sex*

(1949) was published in two parts, to both acclaim and disparagement. Beauvoir was attacking some of the most hallowed tenets of patriarchal society and facing forthright the issues of power and privilege. She realized that being a female had indeed made a difference in her life: It was a man's world, one that relegated women to a class of nonpaid domesticity and motherhood in which they had little individual freedom. In addition, culture had fashioned conditions that were perpetuating the deplorable situations in which women found themselves, and women were often complicit in their own fate. A major redistribution of economic resources and the possibility of true choices for women were necessary before women's lives could improve.

The complexity of Beauvoir's two-volume study cannot be adequately conveyed here, and many later feminists have found key points of disagreement with her, especially her views of motherhood. However, two facts are important in considering *The Second Sex*. First of all, Beauvoir was writing as much to answer her own questions as she was for others. If her argument sometimes seems contradictory or too colored by existentialism, it should be remembered that Beauvoir was herself struggling to comprehend reasons for the female condition, something that was also a means to continue a long-standing debate with Sartre about the nature of freedom. Second, Beauvoir wrote in a specific time about the circumstances of her own life and the lives of other women she knew. Her arguments may seem lacking or conciliatory to third-wave feminists, but Beauvoir was most definitely revolutionary and visionary in her time.

For her novel The *Mandarins* (1954), Beauvoir won France's highest literary prize, the Prix Goncourt. This novel provides a realistic picture of the conflict faced among French intellectuals after World War II. During the French Resistance, diverse groups had united for the cause of freedom from Nazi Germany. No longer united in a common cause, the essential differences among the groups led to confrontation and conflict that eventually destroyed the hope held by intellectuals for a new world order. Characters must come to terms with their disillusionment and try to reconcile their hopes for the future with the reality of the present.

Although *The Mandarins* was immensely successful, Beauvoir primarily devoted the remainder of her career to nonfiction, especially to her three-volume autobiography: *Memoirs of a Dutiful Daughter* (1958), *The Prime of Life* (1960), and *The Force of Circumstance* (1963). Other works include a collection of essays, *Privileges* (1955); an accurate depiction of her mother's death in *A Very Easy Death* (1964); travel works about China and America; a sociological treatise on the treatment of the aged entitled, in English, *The Coming of Age* (1970); and an account of the last years of Sartre's life called *Adieux: A Farewell to Sartre* (1981). Beauvoir was also an outspoken social critic, protesting the French treatment of Algeria in the 1960s, advocating the legalization of abortion, and promoting the political and economic rights of women.

Simone de Beauvoir died in Paris on April 18, 1986. She was buried in Montparnasse Cemetery next to John-Paul Sartre, with more than 5,000 people in attendance, a testimony to the extent of her influence and admiration.

The significance of *The Second Sex* on the feminist movement cannot be overestimated, and much of the attention given to Beauvoir has been related to this important work. However, in recent years critics have turned to the remainder of the remarkable body of writing Beauvoir produced and are reevaluating her impact as a novelist, autobiographer, and social critic, understanding her as an individual who charted the unconventional, intellectual course of her own life.

BIBLIOGRAPHY

Bair, Deirdre. *Simone de Beauvoir.* New York: Summit Books, 1990.

Beauvoir, Simone de. *Adieux: A Farewell to Sartre.* Translated by Patrick O'Brian. New York: Pantheon Books, 1984.

———. *The Prime of Life.* Translated by Peter Green. Cleveland and New York: World Publishing, 1962.

Crosland, Margaret. *Simone de Beauvoir: The Woman and Her Work.* London: Heinemann, 1992.

Evans, Mary. *Simone de Beauvoir.* London and Thousand Oaks, Calif.: Sage, 1996.

Fullbrook, Kate, and Edward Fullbrook. *Simone de Beauvoir and Jean-Paul Sartre.* New York: Harvester Wheatsheaf, 1993.

Grosholz, Emily R. *The Legacy of Simone de Beauvoir.* Oxford: Clarendon Press, 2004.

Johnson, Christopher. *Thinking in Dialogue.* Nottingham,
    U.K.: University of Nottingham, 2003.
Okley, Judith. *Simone de Beauvoir: A Re-Reading.* London:
    Virago Press, 1986.
Simons, Margaret A. *Beauvoir and the Second Sex: Feminism,
    Race, and the Origin of Existentialism.* Lanham, Md.: Row-
    man & Littlefield, 1999.
Tidd, Ursula. *Simone de Beauvoir, Gender and Testimony.*
    Cambridge and New York: Cambridge University Press,
    1999.

Jean Hamm

BEIRUT BLUES (BARID BAYRUT) Hanan
al-Shaykh (1992) Written in Arabic by Lebanese
writer Hanan al-Shaykh (1945–) and translated into
English as *Beirut Blues* by Catherine Cobham in 1995,
Barid Bayrut is one of most haunting and compelling
novels about enduring the day-to-day challenges of the
Lebanese civil war (1975–90). Often referred to as an
epistolary novel, *Beirut Blues* comprises a collection of
letters written by the protagonist, Asmahan, an independent Lebanese Muslim woman who opts to remain in
Lebanon despite the ravages of the civil war. The letters,
which remain unsent, offer insightful glimpses into
Asmahan's emotional and intellectual state.

Each letter is addressed to a particular character or
location that has had a marked influence on Asmahan,
including the narrator's emigrant friend Hanan, her ex-
lover Naser, her family's land in a Lebanese village, her
grandmother, Billie Holiday, the war, and Beirut itself.
As she does in some of her other novels, al-Shaykh
delves once again into the personal and communal
effects of civil war, with the collection of letters in *Beirut Blues* amounting to Asmahan's account of living
through a war. In this way al-Shaykh offers a layered
and multidimensional version of this intensely complex milestone in recent Lebanese history.

One of the important roles carried out by *Beirut
Blues* is that it emphasizes a strong and deep-seated
connection between the Lebanese in the diaspora and
those who have stayed behind, delineating the emotional and national ties that unite these two groups, as
well as their deep attachment, whether it be direct or
indirect, to the city of Beirut. When all other vital
modes of communication have been cut as a result of
the raging war, Asmahan's letters (and by extension the
novel itself) act as a lifeline linking the Lebanese in
exile to their friends and families back home and
redraw, from Asmahan's personal point of view, the
overall trajectory of the war for Lebanese and foreign
readers alike.

Originally written in Arabic and published in 1992,
Beirut Blues is al-Shaykh's retrospective look at the personal and communal effects of Lebanon's civil war,
which has instilled lingering psychological traumas in
its citizens. By recreating the 1985 tensions between
two Muslim militias in Beirut—Amal on the one hand
and Hezbollah on the other—al-Shaykh reinstates in
Beirut Blues the necessity to assess the war's impact
from a retrospective point of view. She does this revi-
sionary act by segmenting the war into isolated incidents and events, highlighting in the process its
senseless and purely destructive causes. Avoiding nostalgic sentimentality, this novel brings under intense
scrutiny the readiness of a nation to delve into a bloody
war, at the same time alluding to the harmful effects
that might result from the Lebanese community's ready
and unquestioning postwar erasure of its traumatic
memories.

Furthermore, *Beirut Blues* not only brings into dialogue such complex notions as home and exile, but
also complicates the notion of home itself by incorporating within the novel's framework diverse elements
that are at odds with each other on the Lebanese home
front, such as the village on the one hand and the city
on the other, as well as the geographical and ideological border separating East from West Beirut during the
civil war. The physical and psychological effects of this
war are so overpoweringly present in this novel (primarily through Asmahan's letters) that the war itself
becomes a primary, if not the primary, character in the
narrative.

Asmahan's characterization is also important to
reach a fuller understanding of the war's conditions.
One of the most poignant portrayals in *Beirut Blues* is
Asmahan wavering between her longing to be with her
lover Jawad in Paris and yet her inability to renounce
her attachment to Beirut. Even though she often
expresses a sense of being imprisoned within the city,
she still regards the option of leaving the country and
the war behind as an act of deception. Yet *Beirut Blues*

cannot be accused in any way of offering a romanticized portrayal of Beirut. In fact, it is precisely sentimentality and nostalgia that al-Shaykh fights against in this novel. For this reason, underscoring the political dimensions of the war becomes a focal point in the novel, so much so that a more accurate, albeit fragmented, portrayal of Lebanon emerges.

Beirut Blues remains one of the most poignant literary representations of the civil war in Lebanon, mixing the personal with the communal to offer an intensely emotional yet critical look at such devastating circumstances. al-Shaykh has been celebrated for her incisive portrayals in Beirut Blues, which not only attest to the resilience of a people's will but also bear witness to the importance of coming to terms with a country's traumatic history.

BIBLIOGRAPHY

Adams, Ann Marie. "Writing Self, Writing Nation: Imagined Geographies in the Fiction of Hanan al-Shaykh." Tulsa Studies in Women's Literature 20, no. 2 (2001): 201–216.

Fadda-Conrey, Carol. "Exilic Memories of War: Lebanese Women Writers Looking Back." In Arabesque: Arabic Literature in Translation and Arab Diasporic Writing, edited by Maysa Abou-Youssef Hayward. Special issue of Studies in the Humanities 30, nos. 1–2 (2003): 7–20.

Manganaro, Elise Salem. "Lebanon Mythologized or Lebanon Deconstructed: Two Narratives of National Consciousness." In Women and War in Lebanon, edited by Lamia Rustum Shehadeh, 112–128. Gainesville: University Press of Florida, 1999.

Carol Fadda-Conrey

BENEATH THE RED BANNER (ZHENG HONG QI XIA) LAO SHE (1980)

Beneath the Red Banner is an unfinished autobiographical novel by LAO SHE (1899–1966), one of the most famous modern Chinese authors. It is also his last work, left unfinished when Lao She committed suicide before he came to develop the main body of this opus. The work describes the Manchu folk customs and Chinese social crisis at the end of 19th century vividly and truthfully.

The novel is narrated from the perspective of a Manchu boy who is born on December 23, 1898, by the lunar calendar. His birth date is regarded a lucky day because that is the opportune day that the God of the Stove left for heaven to report the business of the household he had supervised during the whole year. The book's narrator is the youngest child of a poor family, and his father is a soldier of the Pure Red Banner.

In the Qing Dynasty, the emperor has instituted an eight-banner system to guard the country. All the banner men are divided into eight groups (Pure Yellow Banner, Band Yellow Banner, Pure White Banner, Band White Banner, Pure Blue Banner, Band Blue Banner, Pure Red Banner, Band Red Banner) and can receive a monthly allowance from the government. The banner men are well regarded for their skill of riding and shooting at the same time. As time goes by, many of these soldiers begin paying more attention to pleasurable activities such as feeding birds, training pigeons, and collecting antiques than they do their military training. The boy's elder sister marries a low-level military officer, but this man prefers talking about his pigeons to discussing military issues, as does the boy's father. These military men have no idea how to make a living by themselves and have never thought about the future. All they are interested in is how to idle away their afternoons, though their monthly pay from the government is a paltry amount and does not go far in their households. The boy's aunt, a widow, also gets money from the government in the name of her dead husband. She lives with the boy's family but never offers a hand to help her sister-in-law. On the contrary, she asks to be served well.

The boy's father is a city gate guard. He had two daughters and two sons before the birth of the youngest boy, but since both of the older boys had died due to illness, he cherishes his only remaining son very much. The boy's mother is a diligent woman and arranges the housework well on very limited budget. Despite their economic predicament, the family manages to hold a decent birth ceremony for their new son, under the help of Fu Hai, the boy's cousin. The ceremony, called the Third Day washing ceremony, is a very important event in the boy's life. All the relatives gather in a yard to celebrate the birth of a new baby. They bring gifts and the host treats them to a rich banquet. After that the boy is put in a big copper basin full of warm water boiled with leaves of wormwood. A venerable old lady is invited to bless the boy, and she washes him from head to toe, as a cleansing portion of the ritual, then finally beats him with a scallion. This causes the boy's cry to reach a high pitch. His father then throws the scallion to the roof of the house. The ceremony is successful, as the boy's cry implies his fortune.

As the boy grows up, the country's economic situation becomes worse and worse. The family dwells in the downtown of the capital, which is packed with ordinary citizens of different nationalities. For example, Uncle Jin-si is a Muslim, and Lao Wang is of Han nationality. These two shopkeepers feel it is harder than ever to support their businesses, while the boy's mother finds it more difficult to pay all the bills on her husband's meager salary. Lao Wang ascribes it to the foreign goods and foreign religion, and he has a problem related to the foreign churches and their Chinese hangers-on. One day Duo Lao-da, a rascally Banner man, demands a free chicken; Lao Wang refuses him firmly. Although the banner men are used to buying anything on credit, they usually give Lao Wang money the next month. Duo Lao-da stops paying his bill at Lao Wang's store. Lao Wang is threatened by Duo Lao-da and asks Fu Hai and some other Banner men for help.

Beneath the Red Banner ends before solving this predicament among the characters. As the novel remained incomplete at the author's death, the book is only a fraction of the novel that Lao She planned to write. He had planned to develop a tragedy of a nation through the history of his own family. We can sense his profound self-examination and consciousness through his reminiscent narration. His vivid descriptions of the Manchu system, etiquette, religion, ceremony, appellation, finery, dietary dialect, and other images create a poignant and visceral sense of folklore.

BIBLIOGRAPHY

Guan Ji-xin. *The Treasure of Contemporary ManZu Literature, Study on Beneath the Red Banner. Papers Collected on Laoshe Study.* Shandong: People's Press, 1983.
Zhao Yuan. *Beijing: The City and the People.* Beijing: Beijing University Press, 2002.

Mei Han

BENNI, STEFANO (1947–) *Italian novelist, poet, short story writer*

Stefano Benni is one of the most prominent and prolific Italian authors of the late 20th and early 21st centuries. While Benni's significance to contemporary Italy is certainly rooted in his literary fame, his contributions to several media will no doubt mark his tenure in the age of technology. In addition to his novels, Benni has published volumes of poetry and collections of short stories and plays, made voice recordings of live performances of some of his works accompanied by music, contributed to comic books, and directed a live-action film.

Born on August 12, 1947, in Bologna, a northern Italian city known for its leftist tendencies, Benni lived in the surrounding countryside until he was 16. Removed from the distractions of an urban setting in his youth, he exhibited early signs of narrative creativity by rewriting the endings of famous novels and stories. The rapid social and cultural changes brought about by the economic boom that Italy experienced in the late 1950s and early 1960s was not yet reflected in the restricted atmosphere of the 1960s school system, whose curricula had not changed since before the Fascist era. High school furnished Benni with a traditional understanding of the great classical and Italian poets (including Catullus, Pascoli, and Montale), whom he would come to imitate and parody in his collected volumes of poetry (*Prima o poi l'amore arriva,* 1981, and *Ballads* [*Ballate*], 1991). He began to study philosophy at university, although his formal education was interrupted by obligatory military service. Coming of age in the turbulent political era of the late 1960s and early 1970s left its mark on Benni, who often satirizes contemporary politics and culture in his narratives. He began his career as a journalist, contributing regularly to the left-wing newspaper *Il Manifesto* in the 1970s, as well as to *l'Espresso* and *la Repubblica* after gaining literary acclaim as a novelist-poet.

The single trait that unifies Benni's oeuvre is humor, although it would be difficult to pin him down as a writer of one specific genre, since he employs a mixture of fantasy, science fiction, children's literature, fairy tales, romance, adventure, and the hard-boiled detective story, often in one novel. A postapocalyptic, underground Paris of the not-too-distant future provides the opening setting for his first novel, *Terra!* (1983), whose main protagonists include a Japanese samurai general, the Russian-American tyrant Great

Scorpion, the nine-year-old computer prodigy Frank Einstein, and the old Chinese guru Fang, who vie to unravel ancient Incan riddles in order to find a new Earth. Globalization and tyrannical governments again take center stage in 2000's *Spiriti,* a thinly veiled satire of big business, commercialization, and puppet politicians, that also serves as a prescient warning of actual events of the Second Gulf War following the terrorist attacks of 9/11. One cannot help but mention thematic similarities between the apocalyptic conclusions of *Spiriti* (as well as that of 1992's *La compagnia dei Celestini*) and ITALO SVEVO's *Confessions of Zeno,* although the latter posited the general malaise of modernity while the former seems to lay blame on the superpowers of politics, culture, and business as the cause of humanity's inevitable demise.

The backdrop of many of Benni's novels envisions a futuristic or fantastic metropolis encumbered by corrupted adult values and a polluted environment, populated by children and adolescents either wise beyond their years or possessing magical, salvational characteristics. The fugitive orphans of *La compagnia dei Celestini* overcome personal fears and maleficent truant officers to compete and win the first World Cup of Street Soccer, only to meet a tragic end. The eponymous hero of 1996's *Elianto* lies ill with a mysterious malady while a small group of children search out the elixir that will cure him. The main protagonist of *Saltatempo* (2001) receives a biological clock from a pagan divinity that allows him to jump ahead in time. Benni's latest novel, *Margherita Dolcevita* (2005), relates the story of one young girl who is the only person in her village able to resist the competitive consumerist impulses that pervade her hometown when the Del Bene family moves in next door.

The allegorical and fantastic qualities found in much of Benni's narrative can be attributed to ITALO CALVINO's influence, and the presence of political satire owes not little to the legacy of playwright and actor Dario Fo (1926–   ). The novelty of Benni's unique narrative voice is an innovation entirely his own, which includes dialects and colloquial Italian (although the author is from Bologna, his grandparents hail from Naples and the Molise region of southern Italy), French, German, Latin, Greek, English, and a host of neologisms formed by mixtures of the above. Benni's linguistic originality, however, creates problems for would-be translators of his novels; although some of his publications have been translated into many European and some Asian languages, very few are available in English, which lessens his fame in the English-speaking world of letters.

Benni's other novels include forays into the hard-boiled genre with *Baol* (1990) and *Achille più veloce* (2003), which reimagines Odyssean characters in a contemporary setting. His first publication of short stories, *Bar Sport,* appeared in 1976; other collections of short stories include *Il bar sotto il mare* (*The Café Under the Sea,* 1987), which was well received critically and commercially; *L'ultima lacrima* (*The Last Tear,* 1994) and *Bar sport duemila* (1997). *Blues in sedici* (1998) is his most recent collection of poetry.

BIBLIOGRAPHY

Boria, Monica. "Echoes of Counterculture in Stefano Benni's Humour." *Romance Studies* 23, no. 1 (2005): 29–42.

Degli Esposti, Cristina. "Interview with Stefano Benni: A Postmodern Moraliste." *Italian Quarterly* 32, no. 123–124 (1995): 99–105.

Jansen, Monica. "Verso il nuovo millenio: Rappresentazione dell'apocalisse nella narrativa italiana contemporanea (Benni, Busi, Vassalli)." *Narrativa* 20, no. 21 (2001): 131–150.

Perissinotto, Cristina. "Di vincitori, di vinti, e d'idee: Fanciulli e filosofia nei romanzi di Stefano Benni." *RLA: Romance Languages Annual* 9 (1997): 300–304.

———. "The Pen and the Prophet." *RLA: Romance Languages Annual* 8 (1996): 287–291.

Sandra A. Waters

BERLIN ALEXANDERPLATZ ALFRED DÖBLIN (1929)

Berlin Alexanderplatz is considered by some to be the most significant urban novel in German literature. Franz Biberkopf, the protagonist of this novel by ALFRED DÖBLIN (1878–1957), is an ex-convict who gains his freedom after serving a four-year sentence in a prison in Berlin Tegel. He seeks to become a decent citizen but is drawn into the underworld soon after his release. Attempting to make a living by selling bow ties, the unwary Franz falls under the influence of the criminal Reinhold and ends up losing an arm. Reinhold murders Franz's girlfriend Mieze, the only stabilizing force in Franz's life, the woman who had given him hope in his struggle for human decency. Franz is wrongly accused of her murder and put into a mental clinic. A surprising as well as ambiguous ending allows Biberkopf finally to find his way in the metropolitan environment. The novel's action is confined to a small area in Alexanderplatz, the dynamic urban center of Berlin, where police, prostitutes, small tradesmen, and crooks determine the metropolitan picture.

It is not merely the fable that makes *Berlin Alexanderplatz* so outstanding but its avant-garde narrative style, which achieves a new intensity of expression. Döblin attempted to grasp the modern metropolis's totality by employing a montage technique that was already common in film. Walter Benjamin, in his *Selected Writings*, remarked the year after the novel's appearance: "The stylistic principle governing this book is that of montage. . . . The montage explodes the framework of the novel, bursts its limits both stylistically and structurally, and clears the way for new, epic possibilities. Formally, above all. The material of the montage is anything but arbitrary. Authentic montage is based on the document." In a variety of narrative registers, Döblin incorporates printed matter (ads and market reports), public dialogue (political speech, weather reports) and bits of common and familiar songs. Language is not merely a referential medium in *Berlin Alexanderplatz*; it is deliberately employed as the reality that Döblin hopes to depict. The novel achieves a density and complexity that require a high degree of concentration from the reader.

The immediate response to Döblin's novel was diverse: Communist authors of "Group 25," of which Döblin himself was a member, criticized the depicted primitiveness of the proletariat. They claimed that Franz Biberkopf was a tragic, petty bourgeois, a difficult figure and as such not at all representative of the German proletariat. In addition, many critics accused Döblin of plagiarism. There are indeed clear similarities between Döblin's novel on the one hand and James Joyce's *Ulysses* (1922) and John Dos Passos's *Manhattan Transfer* (1925) on the other. Yet while *Berlin Alexanderplatz* was certainly inspired in its montage and associative techniques, Döblin rightly rejected the accusations, pointing out his experimentations with expressionist and dadaist techniques that had to be considered a stylistic breakthrough. In 1932 he concluded his indebtedness to Joyce, stating that the book *Ulysses* "meant for him a helpful breeze in his sails." Döblin's creative appropriation of the styles of foreign writers as well as his highly original adaptation of psychoanalysis and cinematic techniques must be considered major contributions to the avant-garde movement.

The novel became an overwhelming literary and monetary success. For the first time it allowed Döblin a life without financial worries, and he gained a reputation in Germany and around the world. In November 1929 the well-respected critic Herbert Ihering wrote: "Döblin is probably the only German candidate for the Nobel Prize. . . . It would repair the damaged reputation of the prize and regain it some acceptance."

In 1930 Döblin, with broadcast director Max Brings, worked on a version of *Berlin Alexanderplatz* for the radio. The radio show was first broadcast on September 30, 1930, starring Heinrich George as Biberkopf. The novel's popularity was further ensured by Phil Jutzi's 1931 cinematic adaptation, again starring Heinrich George. Döblin and Hans Wilhelm had collaboratively written the screenplay. Rainer Werner Fassbinder's 1980 version for TV added to the novel's ongoing resonance. By no means should these adaptations be downplayed or understood as the merely monetary exploitation of Döblin's novel. They were, rather, a central sociopolitical interest of his: In a lecture of September 30, 1929, entitled "Literature and Radio," Döblin explicitly called it the task of the radio to reduce the gap between literature and the people and to disseminate literary language by exploiting radio's specific acoustic possibilities.

BIBLIOGRAPHY
Barta, Peter I. *Bely, Joyce, and Döblin: Peripatetics in the City Novel*. Gainesville: University Press of Florida, 1996.

Bekes, Peter. *Alfred Döblin Berlin Alexanderplatz: Interpretation*. Munich: Oldenbourg, 1995.

Jelavich, Peter. *Berlin Alexanderplatz: Radio, Film, and the Death of Weimar Culture*. Berkeley: University of California Press, 2006.

Sander, Gabriele. *Alfred Döblin, Berlin Alexanderplatz*. Stuttgart: P. Reclam, 1998.

Schoonover, Henrietta S. *The Humorous and Grotesque Elements in Döblin's Berlin Alexanderplatz.* Berne and Las Vegas: Peter Lang, 1977.

Martin Blumenthal-Barby

BERNANOS, GEORGES (1888–1948) *French essayist, novelist*

Georges Bernanos was one of France's premier journalists, novelists, and essayists writing during the second quarter of the 20th century. Bernanos belonged to that succession of French Catholic writers who, from Léon Bloy (1846–1917) to Paul Claudel (1868–1955) and FRANÇOIS MAURIAC (1885–1970), explored the darkest depths of human nature and searched above all for the means to find salvation for the immortal soul. His masterpiece, *The Diary of a Country Priest (Journal d'un curé de campagne,* 1936), a novel about an idealistic village priest in spiritual and psychological turmoil, shows the author to be one of the most original writers of his time. A passionate nationalist, Georges Bernanos supported the French monarchy, denounced the evils of both communism and totalitarianism, and called for a world order inspired not by materialism but by Christian mysticism and a return to the ideals of historic France.

Bernanos was born in Paris on February 20, 1888, to a family of craftsmen, and from early childhood he was steeped in a traditionalist, conservative, and antirepublican atmosphere. As a child he spent his vacations in his father's country house in Fressin, in Pas-de-Calais, northern France, the setting he would use for most of his fictional narratives. He attended religious schools including the Collège des Jésuits, Collège Notre-Dame-des-Champs (1901–03), Collège Saint-Célestin, Bourges (1903–04), Collège Sainte-Marie, and Aire-sur-la-Lys. Charles de Gaulle, the future president of France, was a classmate. Bernanos's correspondence with Father Lagrange, his literature teacher from the school at Bourges, reveals a spiritually tormented adolescence. He considered the priesthood but concluded this was not his calling.

At the Sorbonne (1906–09), Bernanos earned degrees in both law and literature. In 1908, at the age of 20, he joined the Camelots du Roi, a militant royalist organization that paraded through the Latin quarter of Paris provoking the partisans of the bourgeois and materialistic republic, which had driven God from the schools and from public life. Bernanos also rallied several protests organized by Action Française, the official organization to restore the monarchy to France, formed by Charles Maurras in 1908. After a protest in March 1909, Bernanos was incarcerated for a brief time in La Santé prison. In 1913 he took charge of *L'Avant-Garde de Normandie,* a weekly monarchist newspaper located in Rouen. It was there that he met his future wife, Jeanne Talbert d'Arc, a descendant of the family of Joan of Arc.

During World War I Bernanos enlisted as part of the Sixth Dragons Regiment in the French army, witnessed the battles of Somme and Verdun, and was wounded several times. In 1918, after the war, he withdrew from active involvement with Action Française because the monarchist movement was being sacrificed to parliamentary democracy and the electoral process. He broke with Maurras but still defended the ideals of Action Française, even when the organization was condemned by Pope Pius XI in 1926.

In 1917 Bernanos married Jeanne Talbert d'Arc, and they subsequently had three sons and three daughters. Following the war, he worked as an inspector for an insurance company until 1927, when he attempted to provide for his family primarily through his writing, which he considered a divine vocation. He wrote for a variety of journals, including a column for *Le Figaro* from 1930 to 1932.

The novels of Bernanos are powerful accounts of intense spiritual struggle that reflect his passionate Catholicism and reveal a visionary writer gifted with a rare evocative power. In his first novel, *The Star of Satan/Under the Sun of Satan (Sous le soleil de Satan,* 1926), a priest fights the devil for the soul of his village. *The Impostor (L'imposture,* 1927) and its sequel *Joy (La joie,* 1928) dramatize the spiritual crisis of a prominent member of the Parisian clergy. The struggle against the devil is reenacted with even greater personal anguish in *The Diary of a Country Priest,* in which a young, inexperienced priest battles physical pain, spiritual despair, and the moral indifference of his small-town flock. *Mouchette (Nouvelle histoire de Mouchette,* 1937) is the story of a teenager so abused by everyone in her village that death becomes a solace if not a salvation. In the fictional universe of Georges Bernanos, evil is a constant, and innocence and heroism do not save individuals; they make saints and martyrs.

Literary success did not translate into financial security for the author. In 1933 Bernanos became disabled in a traffic accident, and because of debts, he was evicted from his family home. In 1934 Bernanos relocated with his wife and six children to Palma de Mallorca in the Balearic Islands. From this vantage point off the coast of Spain, he was a witness to the conflagration in Spain that would forever change his predilection for the politics of the extreme Right. His experiences of the Spanish civil war (1936–39) impelled him to write *Diary of My Times* (*Les Grandes cimetères sous la lune,* 1938). This fiery book attacked Catholics for favoring Franco in the civil war. "The Spanish experience," he wrote, "is probably the principal event of my life."

After living in Mallorca, Bernanos moved to Brazil, where he tried farming unsuccessfully. He continued to write polemical essays and articles and called for a spiritual and moral return to the mystical vision of ancient France, which he saw personified in the figure of Joan of Arc, the lowly maiden who, through faith, revitalized the French aristocracy. He gave lectures in Switzerland, Belgium, and North Africa and contributed to various journals, including *Carrefour, La Bataille, L'Intransigeant,* and *Combat,* which was edited for some time by ALBERT CAMUS.

After returning to France in 1945 at the request of General Charles de Gaulle, Bernanos quickly became disgusted by the corruption in his country and left for Tunisia. It was there that he wrote *The Fearless Heart* (*Dialogues des Carmélites,* 1949), in which nuns are martyred during the French Revolution. His last meditation on faith, agony, and death, *Dialogues des Carmélites,* was adapted for the stage in 1952.

Bernano's first prize came in December 1929, when he received the Prix Femina-La Vie Heureuse for *Joy,* the sequel to *The Impostor.* The novel *The Diary of a Country Priest* received the Grand Prix du Roman of the French Academy in 1936.

Robert Bresson's film adaptation of *The Diary of a Country Priest* won the Golden Lion at the 12th annual Venice International Film Festival. Bresson's adaptation of *Mouchette* for the screen premiered to great acclaim in 1966.

Georges Bernanos died of cancer in Paris on July 5, 1948.

BIBLIOGRAPHY

Balthasar, Hans Urs von. *Bernanos: An Eccesiastical Existence.* Translated by Erasmo Leiva-Merikakis. San Francisco: Ignatius Press, 1996.

Bush, William. *George Bernanos.* New York: Twayne Publishers, 1969.

Cooke, John E. *Georges Bernanos: A Study of Christian Commitment.* Amersham, U.K.: Avebury, 1981.

Fitch, Brian T. *Dimensions et structures chez Bernanos; essai de méthode critique.* Paris: Lettres Modernes, 1969.

Molnar, Thomas Steven. *Bernanos: His Political Thought & Prophecy.* New Brunswick, N.J.: Transaction Publishers, 1997.

Arbolina L. Jennings

BETI, MONGO (ALEXANDRE BIYIDI AWALA) (1932–2001) *African novelist*   Mongo Beti of Cameroon is considered one of the preeminent Francophone African writers of the period preceding and following the country's African independence in 1960. Mongo Beti is a pseudonym of Alexandre Biyidi Awala. The author's trenchant satires of French colonialism made him an icon of the struggle against neocolonialism—the continued exploitation of African countries by European powers after they had achieved independence.

Born in Cameroon and educated in Catholic missions and public schools in the Cameroon capital of Yaoundé, Beti later studied literature in France and lived most of his life in Rouen, where he taught high school at the Lycée Corneille and where he met and married a French colleague, Odile Tobner. In 1954 he published his first novel, *The Cruel City* (*Ville cruelle,* 1954), which describes the exploitation of the African peasant class. The novel was published under the pseudonym Eza Boto—a name that the author used only once in his career. It was in 1956 that he adopted the pen name Mongo Beti (which signifies "son of the Béti people" in Ewondo, the language of the Bétis in West-Central Africa). Under this name, which announced his fidelity to his African roots, he published what many consider to be his masterpiece, the novel *The Poor Christ of Bomba* (*Le pauvre Christ de*

Bomba, 1956). The novel is a biting satire of the brutality and folly of the colonial administration and the Catholic Church in Africa. Its wide acclaim and critical success made Beti one of the leading writers of Présence Africaine, a publishing house based in Paris and started by the Senegalese writer Alioune Diop.

Beti continued to teach and write in France, but he could not ignore the turmoil of his native Cameroon, from which he would remain a political exile for over 30 years. His novel MISSION TO KALA (*Mission terminée,* 1957) was awarded the prestigious French Prix Sainte-Beuve. In 1958 he published *King Lazarus* (*Le roi miraculé,* 1958), which was eventually translated into English, Russian, and other languages, garnering him international renown.

The respect won by Beti from the literary establishment was not shared by the French government, however. Cameroon became officially independent from France in 1960, but there continued a bitter war of repression against the independence movement, l'Union des Populations du Cameroun (UPC). Its secretary general, Ruben Um Nyobé, was assassinated in 1958 by French troops, and its president, Félix-Roland Moumié, already in exile, was assassinated in Geneva by a former agent of the French intelligence organization Service de Documentation Extérieure et de Contre-espionnage (SDECE). Ernest Ouandé, a vice president of the organization, returned from exile and was arrested and executed after a hasty court trial. Osende Afana, another high official in the UPC, was killed in an ambush in Ghana.

For 15 years Beti ceased to publish. Then, in 1972, his pamphlet *The Rape of Cameroon* (*Main basse sur le Cameroun*) appeared, denouncing the neocolonial influence of France in Cameroon and the brutal dictatorship of Cameroon's president, Amadou Ahidjo. The French government banned the pamphlet's publication and seized copies of it, counter to the laws of the Third Republic guaranteeing freedom of thought and expression. However, the French justified their actions by relying on a 1936 amendment that permits the seizure of writings of "foreign provenance."

The French minister of the interior attempted to revoke Beti's French nationality and to force him to seek refuge in Canada or Switzerland, both countries having offered him asylum and teaching posts. Beti refused to concede, and in 1973 the newly created African civil rights organization AFASPA (Association Française d'Amitié et de Solidarité avec les Peuples d'Afrique) interceded on his behalf, sponsoring a campaign of petitions to French president Valéry Giscard d'Estaing and the minister of the interior.

As Beti's French nationality remained uncertain, he continued his polemics, publishing the novel *Remember Ruben* (1974), his homage to the slain secretary general of the UPC, Ruben Um Nyobé; and the allegorical novel *Perpetua and the Habit of Unhappiness* (*Perpetue et l'habitude du malheur,* 1974). In 1978, with his wife Odile Tobner, Beti founded the literary journal *Black People, African People* (*Peuples noirs, peuples africains*)—a forum of protest against neocolonialism in Africa. He would write for and oversee publication of the review until the mid-1980s.

Beti retired from teaching in 1996 and returned to Cameroon after more than 30 years of political exile in France. There he opened a bookstore, Librairie des Peuples Noirs. He found Cameroon to be much the same after independence as it had been during colonialism—a country replete with vice and arbitrarily administered. He never ceased to air his grievances, alienating several renowned francophone African writers of his generation—FERDINAND OYONO (Cameroon), CAMARA LAYE (Guinea), Sony Labou Tansi (Congo), and Léopold Senghor (Senegal)—when he accused them of appeasing the former colonial power and writing for an European audience. His last book, *Too Much Sun Kills Love* (*Trop de soleil tue l'amour,* 1999), is a comical and yet scathing attack on dictatorships.

Upon the author's death from complications due to renal failure in 2001, Beti's family, observing his wishes, held a private funeral service and refused any posthumous honors from Cameroon on his behalf. As Beti himself stated before his death, "Even dead, I do not wish to lower myself."

BIBLIOGRAPHY

Arnold, Stephen H., ed. *Critical Perspectives on Mongo Beti.* Boulder, Colo.: Lynne Rienner Publishers, 1998.

Bjornson, Richard. "The Concept of Neocolonialism in the Later Works of Mongo Beti." In *Mapping Intersections: African Literature and Africa's Development,* edited by Anne

V. Adams and Janis A. Mayes, 137–149. Trenton, N.J.: Africa World Press, 1998.

Ihom, Cletus. "The Significance of the Cyclical Technique in the Novels of Mongo Beti." In *Themes in African Literature in French: A Collection of Essays,* edited by Sam Ade Ojo and Olusola Oke, 107–116. Ibadan, Nigeria: Spectrum Books, 2000.

Palmer, Eustace. *An Introduction to the African Novel: A Critical Study of Twelve Books by Chinua Achebe, James Ngugi, Camara Laye, Elechi Amadi, Ayi Kwei Armach, Mongo Beti, and Gabriel Okara.* New York: Africana Publications, 1972.

Patrick L. Day

BIENEK, HORST (1930–1990) *German editor, essayist, novelist, poet, scriptwriter* Horst

Bienek was a writer and filmmaker whose works include poems, novels, and essays. Although he was German, his linguistic and cultural background reflected strong elements of Polish as well as German influence. Bienek was born in Silesia, the mining region in eastern Germany which, as a border land, contained a population that was equally at home with or distanced from Germany and Poland. Like GÜNTER GRASS, whose Danzig novels reveal a strong sense of place and cultural orientation, Bienek's most famous work, *Gleiwitz Quartet,* paints in concrete detail the nature of a unique environment.

Gleiwitz, where Bienek was born and lived until 1946, was a small town that, in September 1939, became the center of the world's attention when a German radio station was allegedly attacked by Polish soldiers. In actuality, the attack was staged to provide a pretext for the German invasion of Poland. Following the war, Bienek left Gleiwitz when he moved to Berlin in 1946. He worked at various small-scale literary jobs until 1951, when he was accepted into Bertolt Brecht's drama school. His time there was very short as he was arrested in that year for anti-Soviet agitation. Sentenced to 25 years of hard labor, Bienek was sent to Vorkuta, one of the major sites in the infamous Soviet gulag. It was here, in this complex of 13 mining centers, that Bienek spent the next four years until pardoned in 1955. Returning to Germany, he moved to West Germany in 1956 and for a while worked as a writer and editor for Hesse State Radio. In the late 1950s and early 1960s, Bienek was a magazine editor. In 1966 he

moved to Munich, where he remained for the rest of his life, working as a writer and editor.

Although his theatrical career was cut short by his imprisonment in the 1950s, Bienek returned to this venue as a scriptwriter and filmmaker. One of his projects was the filming of his 1968 novel *The CELL* (*Die Zelle*) in the 1970s. He won several awards for his film work. As a writer, he began composing poetry, much of which is available in *Selected Poems, 1957–1987* (*Ausgewählte Geilichte,* 1989). These poems are very concrete in their approach and their subject, a reflection of what happens to individuals caught in the great and destructive movements of the 20th century in Central Europe. One poem, "Boyhood in Gleiwitz," ("Knabenalterin Gleiwitz"), describes, in a patois of combined German and Polish slang, his experiences, before the war, playing near a river where later he saw concentration camp prisoners being executed. While not shrinking from the horrors, Bienek also depicts the experience of childhood. It is similar to *The UNBEARABLE LIGHTNESS OF BEING,* in which MILAN KUNDERA describes a strong feeling of fairly pleasant nostalgia whenever he sees a photograph of Hitler, because it reminds him of not always unpleasant times as a boy in occupied Czechoslovakia. In reading Bienek's poem, one sees the logic of his later decision to convert the experience in those years to the four novels that became the *Gleiwitz Quartet.*

Bienek's poems also bear a very strong lineage to his first novel, *The Cell.* The experience of Vorkuta is described in short poems describing the landscape and the specific experiences of working. He also manages to describe the alienation between those forced to become political prisoners and those who were not. In one poem he refers to those remaining as "unworthy of death" while so many "die with dignity." Like the poetry of Zbigniew Herbert and others of central Europe in the mid-20th century, nothing is abstract. Everything is concrete, in part a reaction against prewar formalism but also because the political and cultural situation called for concrete expression. And, as is often the case with the poetry of this region and this time, it is written within a wider context of power, politics, and victims with or without dignity. *The Cell* is heavily influenced by Bienek's own experience in what he referred to as "silos of torment." It does not clearly show how the narrator came to be incarcerated but conveys with great clarity the physical, emotional, and mental disintegration of an individual in prison. In the same year that *The Cell* was published (1968), Bienek's collection of essays, *Bakunin, an Invention,* was published.

Bienek's greatest work, however, is the set of four novels that depict happenings in his hometown at the time of World War II. Each novel is very definite not only about the locale but the particular day on which occur specific incidents that are removed from the larger arena of the world. *The First Polka* (*Die erste Polka,* 1975) takes place on the day before World War II begins. *September Light* (*Septemberlicht,* 1977) describes events that happen four days later, and *Time Without Bells* (*Zeit ohne Glocken,* 1979) is set on Good Friday in 1943. *Earth and Fire's* (*Erde und Feuer,* 1982) temporal scope is wider and concludes with its major characters either fleeing west to Dresden or remaining in Gleiwitz to face inevitable outcomes. These books, by their wealth of incident and characters that appear throughout the narrative, bring alive the experience of life in Hitler's Germany, making it less abstract for those who have lived in different times and in different political climates. Bienek was influenced by William Faulkner (1897–1962), particularly in the way the American author cultivated a particular patch of ground and developed it as a universe, not unaware of the outside world and certainly not insulated from it, but definitely affected by it.

Horst Bienek died in Munich in 1990.

BIBLIOGRAPHY

Bienek, Horst. *Aufsätze, Materialen, Bibliographie.* Munich: C. Hanser, 1990.

———. *The Cell.* Translated by Ursula Mahlendorf. Santa Barbara, Calif.: Unicorn, 1972.

———. *Earth and Fire.* Translated by Ralph Manheim. New York: Atheneum, 1988.

———. *Selected Poems, 1957–1987.* Translated by Ruth and Matthew Meade. Greensboro, N.C.: Unicorn, 1989.

———. *Time Without Bells.* Translated by Ralph R. Read. New York: Atheneum, 1988.

Robert Stacy

BILLIARDS AT HALF PAST NINE (BILLIARD UM HALBZEHN) HEINRICH BÖLL (1959)

One of the most celebrated novels by HEINRICH BÖLL (1917–85), *Billiards at Half Past Nine* appeared in 1959, the same year as *The TIN DRUM* by GÜNTER GRASS and *Speculations about Jacob* by Uwe Johnson, two other seminal works of German literature that attempt to come to terms with Germany's unmastered past and what this war past means for the present. Although the novel focuses on one day—September 6, 1958, the 80th birthday of the patriarch of the Fähmel family, Heinrich Fähmel—it narrates how history produces, illuminates, and transforms this single day through flashbacks, memories, and reflections.

With a wide array of stylistic devices, the story narrates the history of three generations of the Fähmel family, three generations that came of age in entirely different eras: Heinrich in the imperial (pre-Weimar Republic) era, his son Robert in the Nazi years, and Robert's son Joseph in the postwar period. All of these Fähmels are architects, and the novel focuses on a building as a central symbol—namely, the Abbey of St. Anton, which Heinrich built, Robert demolished during the war, and Joseph is rebuilding in the 1950s. The abbey underscores the complicity of institutions, such as the church, and individuals, such as Heinrich, with the Nazis; consequently, the Fähmels' relations to the building become the means to come to terms with the past. The novel has been criticized, including by Böll, for its reductive and overly schematic understanding of perpetrators versus victims (which it breaks down metaphorically into categories like "buffaloes" and "lambs"), but its ambitious formal approach and rigorous critique of sociopolitical institutions as well as individual behavior render it a major breakthrough in Böll's illustrious career.

Billiards at Half Past Nine starts with monologues by Dr. Robert Fähmel, who plays billiards at the Prince Heinrich Hotel every morning at 9:30, during which time he thinks about and narrates the past to an elevator boy, Hugo. Robert's inner monologue and solipsistic conversations with Hugo are just two of the ways that the novel delivers, in wide-ranging and fragmentary manner, the broad strokes of its narrative: There are at least 10 other narrative perspectives, including other inner and outer monologues, free indirect speech, and streams of consciousness. In this complex manner, the reader learns that Robert's father, Heinrich, received a commission in 1907 to build the Abbey of St. Anton, a prize contract that initiated his meteoric rise both professionally and socially. Heinrich's ambition and subsequent success, especially his obsessive focus on the future, blind him to the historical realities of the present. He understood World War I, which killed his wife Johanna's two brothers, as a "higher" violence; only with Nazism and World War II, which claims his son Otto, first ideologically and then fatally, does he begin to understand how individuals make war and history.

Heinrich's son Robert has more insight into the violent character of the Nazis, but after initially more public dissent, he settles into a silent mode of resistance—namely, putting his expertise to work as a demolitions expert for the army. His work includes the demolition of the very same abbey, officially to create a free fire zone but also to punish the monks of the abbey for supporting the Nazis. Heinrich's wife actually has the most insight into the danger the Nazis have brought, but she has been committed to a mental institution since 1942 for her "insane" resistance to Hitler, including an attempt to board a deportation train full of Jews. Böll's work implies that she, who possesses the most insight, has to be treated as insane by an insane society.

The novel divides its large ensemble of characters into metaphorical categories of varying complicity: the buffalo who believe in, oversee, and practice violence in the name of power; the lambs who remain the pacifistic, passive victims; and the all-too-often absent shepherds of those lambs. By the end of the novel, on the 80th birthday of her husband, Johanna decides to strike out against one such "buffalo" by attempting to assassinate a postwar minister who has managed to overcome an ugly Nazi past. She wants to kill him before he can kill her grandchildren, as those who have partaken of the "buffalo sacrament" have also killed her brothers and her children.

Most criticism of the novel has focused on this typology, which confirms and augments Böll's tendency to the "mythological-theological problematic" (as he once put it). In the 1970s, Böll himself said this approach was too simplistic, that relations of power were far more complicated and that he would do it differently if he were to do it again. His main interest was in drawing a line from the nationalist elites (such as Paul von Hindenburg) who drove Germany into World War I to the Nazis and then into the postwar period, which rehabilitated many of the same political, social, and economic elites. Whatever the weaknesses of this schema, the complex and arresting style, which has drawn comparisons with William Faulkner as well as the French *nouveau roman,* and the message it carries about making memory a moral act continues to be positively received. Johanna's attempted assassination does not succeed, and she seems headed back to the mental institution, but her shot rings out as an meaningful *acte de la résistance,* a shot not only sealing the past but starting the race anew.

BIBLIOGRAPHY

Böll, Victor, and Jochen Schubert. *Heinrich Böll.* Munich: Deutscher Taschenbuch Verlag, 2002.

Butler, Michael, ed. *The Narrative Fiction of Heinrich Böll: Social Conscience and Literary Achievement.* Cambridge and New York: Cambridge University Press, 1994.

Conrad, Robert C. *Understanding Heinrich Böll.* Columbia, S.C.: Camden House, 1992.

Crampton, Patricia, trans. *Heinrich Böll, on his Death: Selected Obituaries and the Last Interview.* Bonn: Inter Nationes, 1985.

Prodanuik, Ihor. *The Imagery in Heinrich Böll's Novels.* Bonn: Bouvier, 1979.

Reed, Donna K. *The Novels of the Nazi Past.* New York: Peter Lang, 1985.

Zachau, Reinhard K. *Heinrich Böll: Forty Years of Criticism.* Columbia, S.C.: Camden House, 1994.

Jaimey Fisher

BIOY CASARES, ADOLFO (1914–1999)
Argentinean essayist, novelist, poet, short story writer   The prolific Argentinean writer Adolfo Bioy Casares is one of the most important names in 20th-century fantastic literature. His numerous novels and collections of short stories, articles, essays, letters, and works in collaboration with Jorge Luis Borges, published under the pseudonyms H. Bustos Domecq and B. Suárez Lynch, are all praised for their impeccable style and elegant use of the Spanish language. Together with Borges, 15 years his senior, and Silvina Ocampo, his wife, Bioy Casares also edited influential anthologies

of fantastic short stories and crime novels. His work is characterized by a deep sympathy for the individual, someone who fails again and again due to the complexity of the world and to the uncertainties of love, which itself is as strange as the fantastic in literature.

Bioy Casares was born into an upper-class Argentinean family and raised on a large estate, Rincón Viejo in Pardo, and in Buenos Aires. In the 1920s he traveled to Europe and Africa with his parents. At the early age of 11 he fell in love with his cousin, a passion that compelled him to write his first novel. His first publication, when he was only 15 years old, was a collection of short stories called *Prólogo,* published with the help of his father. Bioy's motto was, "For writing there is no better recipe than to write," which he truly lived by. And by the age of 25, he had published five more collections of short stories and a novel.

Decisive for Bioy's career as an author was his meeting with fellow Argentinean author Jorge Luis Borges in 1932 in the house of Victoria Ocampo, the editor of the literary magazine *Sur* and one of the most influential figures in cultural Argentina. In 1940 Bioy married Victoria's sister, Silvina Ocampo, and in the same year he published his first masterpiece, *The INVENTION OF MOREL* (*La invención de Morel,* 1940). Borges wrote in a now famous prologue to this novel that "to classify it as perfect is neither an imprecision nor a hyperbole." Bioy thought that Borges praised only the plot and not the way he executed the story, although the elder author insisted that Bioy was his "secret master" for helping to lead him toward a leaner, more classical style. In 1942 this fertile friendship between the two South American writers brought to light their first work in collaboration, *Six Problems for Don Isidro Parodi,* a series of splendidly written parodies of crime stories.

After his novel *A Plan for Escape* (*Plan de evasion,* 1945), a claustrophobic story of a penal colony, where he applied Arthur Schopenhauer's philosophy of "The World as Will and Representation," and after writing many stories with classical topics of fantastic literature, Bioy turned, under pressure from Argentina's dictator, Juan Perón, toward subjects in contemporary Argentinean life. Although Bioy Casares never liked political interpretations of his works, *Dream of Heroes* (*El sueño de los heroes,* 1954) can easily be read as a critical account of the Perón regime. Buenos Aires was, and remains, a world capital of psychoanalysis, which is reflected in this novel: Beneath the dream of the heroes there is a layer of shifts and senseless cruelty against the innocent. It is equally possible to read his texts *Diary of the War of the Pig* (*Diario de la guerra del cerdo,* 1969) and *Asleep in the Sun* (*Dormir al sol,* 1973) as political allegories. In the first work the whole population of Buenos Aires suddenly turns violent against a segment of their society (here the old), and in the latter work the protagonist finds out that his wife's soul has been changed into that of a shepherd dog in a mental hospital. This work can be read as a fable of modern politics, of brainwashing through media, or it can be enjoyed as an elegantly written and witty novel.

Throughout Bioy Casares's work the fantastic plot is handled like in a crime novel. The text reveals barely noticeable hints that suddenly fit together and explain the story's surprising solution. Although there is always something fantastic in the air, the author relates his stories with great sympathy for the sorrows of the common life of ordinary people. Very detailed descriptions of suburban Buenos Aires and the struggle of common people go hand in hand with fantastic phenomena in Bioy Casares's writing until his last long novel, *A Fragile Champion* (*Un campeón desparejo,* 1993).

In December 1994 Bioy's wife Silvina Ocampo died at the age of 90. Just three weeks later his daughter Marta was killed in a car accident. These incidents led Bioy to reflect upon his own life, and his remaining work is more autobiographical in nature. He published his memories (*Memorias,* 1994), a book of quotations (*De jardines ajenos,* 1994), letters (*En viaje,* 1996), and an allegorical short novel, *From One World to Another* (*De un mundo a otro,* 1997). On March 8, 1999, he died without having fulfilled two of his last wishes. He had always wanted to write a book on Jorge Luis Borges and then, of course, he didn't want to die at all: "No one had asked me if I want to be born, but now that I am here, I don't want to go. The idea of death to me doesn't seem attractive at all."

BIBLIOGRAPHY

Bioy Casares, Adolfo. *Diary of the War of the Pig.* Translated by Gregory Woodruff and Donald A. Yates. New York: McGraw-Hill, 1972.

————. *The Dream of Heroes*. Translated by Diana Thorold. New York: Dutton, 1987.

————. *The Invention of Morel*. Translated by Ruth L. C. Simms. New York: New York Review Books, 2003.

————. *Selected Stories*. Translated by Suzanne Jill Levine. New York: New Directions, 1994.

Camurati, Mireya. *Bioy Casares y el alegre trabajo de la inteligencia*. Buenos Aires: Ediciones Corregidor, 1990.

Curia, Beatriz. *La concepción del cuento en Adolfo Bioy Casares*. Mendoza: Universidad Nacional de Cuyo, Facultad de Filosofía y Letras, Instituto de Literaturas Modernas, 1986.

Levine, Suzanne Jill. *Guía de Adolfo Bioy Casares*. Madrid: Fundamentos, 1982.

Martino, Daniel. *ABC de Adolfo Bioy Casares*. Madrid: Ediciones de la Universidad, 1991.

Snook, Margaret L. *In Search of Self: Gender and Identity in Bioy Casares's Fantastic Fiction*. New York: Peter Lang, 1998.

Suárez Coalla, Francisca. *Lo Fantástico en la obra de Adolfo Bioy Casares*. Toluca: Universidad Autónoma del Estado de México, 1994.

Toro, Alfonso de and Susanna Regazzoni, eds. *Coloquio Internacional en Homenaje a Adolfo Bioy Casares (2000: Universitat Leipzig): Homenaje a Adolfo Bioy Casares: una retrospectiva de su obra (literatura, ensayo, filosofía, teoría de la cultura, crítica literaria)*. Frankfurt, Vervuert and Madrid: Iberoamericana, 2002.

Stefan Kutzenberger

BLACK BOOK, THE (KARA KITAP) ORHAN PAMUK (1990)

In Turkey, where writer ORHAN PAMUK (1952–) is a foremost intellectual figure, the novel *The Black Book* has been praised and attacked by both left-wing and conservative critics and columnists. The work has also generated extensive debates about Turkish modernization and secularism as well as Islamic traditions. *The Black Book,* which was awarded the Prix France Culture in 1991, received accolades from Western critics who acknowledged Pamuk as the "eastern" counterpart to Jorge Luis Borges, ITALO CALVINO, and GABRIEL GARCÍA MÁRQUEZ—a label the Turkish author finds "as unsatisfactory as describing a new fruit as somewhere between a peach and an orange." Pamuk was the recipient of the Nobel Prize in literature in 2006.

Set in contemporary Istanbul, *The Black Book* is a nostalgic, intimate travelogue through the laced intricacies of modern Turkish identity, closely mirrored by the city's labyrinthine topography. The novel is framed as a fragmented detective story: On a winter night, Galip, an Istanbul lawyer, returns home to find that his wife, Rüya, has disappeared. So has Rüya's half brother Jelal, a famous Istanbul columnist whose life and journalistic fame Galip secretly covets. While trying to retrace Rüya and Jelal's steps, Galip enters the maze of the city with its subterranean passageways, central wealthy neighborhoods, and neglected marginal shantytowns, all rich with riddles, centuries-old secrets, and misleading clues. Galip's subsequent encounters—with a mannequin maker, an erstwhile Marxist militant, a retired army colonel interested in Sufism, a film celebrity–look-alike prostitute with a religious penchant, and a BBC team set to make a documentary on Jelal—engender intertwined and contradictory accounts of the fraught relationships between East and West, history, religion, and metaphysical inquiries into memory, identity, and contemporary Turkish realities.

According to Pamuk, Istanbul is in "a mesmerizing state of ruin." Bathed in neglect, among the wrecks and ghosts of past inhabitants or travelers and the "waste" of modern Western pop culture ("We Lost Our Memories at the Movies"), the city is in danger of "drying up." It is consumed by its own impossible ambition to keep up with a reality in which East and West, past and present, are continuously tearing each other apart. In one of his columns ("The Day the Bosphorus Dries Up"), Jelal writes about the city on the Golden Horn: "On the last day, when the waters suddenly recede, among the American transatlantics gone to ground and Ionic columns covered with seaweed, there will be Celtic and Ligurian skeletons. . . . Amidst mussel-encrusted Byzantine treasures . . . and soda-pop bottles, I can imagine a civilization whose energy needs . . . will be derived from a dilapidated Romanian tanker propelled into a mire-pit."

This parallels the case of Turkish identity, torn between ancestral, Muslim customs and beliefs and Atatürk's efforts to Westernize and secularize the Turkish state. The chapter titled "Do you remember me?" recounts the story of an Istanbul mannequin maker who informs the Western visitors to his underground, muddy, and dusty shop that his establishment is "an indicator of the Turkish achievement concerning modernization and industrialization." "All parts are made in

Turkey," he adds. The shop houses a micro-universe of unwanted mannequins, remnants of a civilization that has seemingly gone to waste. The wax and wooden life-like figures were banned from the above-ground realm, first by a "narrow-minded Sheik of Islam" and then by modern-day consumer culture, for they resemble Turkish people "too much." The mannequin maker sadly remarks that there are "historical forces which are against letting our nation be itself, in an effort to deprive us of our daily gestures which are our most precious treasure." However, as the underground multileveled structure of the city reveals, Turkish identity also has its subterranean passageways that "had always managed to wreak vengeance" on the surface level for having pushed it below. The identity conflict, Pamuk suggests, resides inside as much as outside.

The main narrative points of view in the novel alternate between Jelal's columns and Galip's stories and metaphysical inquiries rendered by an omnipresent narrator; in the end, the narrative voices collapse into a Jelal-Galip synchretic identity. The central female character is given no plausible existence. Rüya ("dream" in Turkish) exists only in Galip's version of the story. Described as obsessed with modern detective novels, Rüya is the silent heroine-victim of an unresolved, postmodern story of that genre.

Pamuk is a compelling writer who is not afraid to play with and display his influences, from Scheherazade (the Persian fictional storyteller of *The Book of One Thousand and One Nights*) and Sufi poets to Gustave Flaubert and MARCEL PROUST. Pamuk is a profuse master storyteller—an enabler of other people's stories—and an observer of intimate spaces—"museums" of Turkish daily life. In the final analysis, Pamuk is *à la recherche* of things past. It is precisely *a lack* that is at the origins of this story: the disappearance of Rüya-dream (an Albertine-like character from Proust), and also a nostalgia for the empire—the faded glory of the Ottomans, with their rich and inimitable customs.

BIBLIOGRAPHY

Freeman, John. "*In Snow*, an Apolitical Poet Mirrors Apolitical Pamuk." *Village Voice,* 17 August 2004.

Pamuk, Orhan. "The Anger of the Damned." *New York Review of Books,* 15 November 2001.

———. *The Black Book.* Translated by Güneli Gün. San Diego: Harcourt Brace, 1996.

———. "Freedom to Write." *New York Review of Books.* 25 May 2006.

———. *Istanbul: Memories of a City.* Translated by Maureen Freely. London: Faber and Faber, 2005.

Laura Ceia-Minjares

BLACK BOX (KUFSAH SHEHORAH) AMOS OZ (1987)

Written by Israeli writer AMOS OZ (1939–), *Black Box* appeared in Hebrew under the title *Kufsah Shehorah* in 1987. The novel immediately climbed to the top of the best-seller lists in Israel, breaking previously recorded book sales. It was translated by Nicholas de Lange and published in English a year later. In 1988 *Black Box* won Amos Oz the Prix Femina Etranger, France's top literary award for the best foreign novel of that year. The novel was made into a film by Ye'ud Levanon in 1994.

In *Black Box,* Oz focuses on the subject of family life as a means of examining the nation. Taking its name from the cockpit recorder found among the wreckage after a plane crash, the epistolary novel gives an account of the failed marriage of its central protagonists, Alexander Gideon and Ilana Sommo, seven years after a bitter divorce. The novel is set in 1976 and moves between London, Chicago, and Jerusalem. The story begins with a letter from Ilano Sommo to her estranged ex-husband Alexander Gideon, a former Israeli tank commander turned intellectual now living in Chicago. He has recently written a book on fanaticism that has confirmed his status as a scholar. Ostensibly at his mercy, Ilana asks Alex for financial assistance to help their wayward son Boaz, who at 16 years of age is drifting aimlessly through life, getting into trouble with the police. Before ending the letter, Ilana offers to do anything for Alex if he will share his substantial inheritance with her. Alex replies to her, his attorney Manfred Zakheim, and Ilana's current husband Michel Sommo, a Moroccan Jew who uses the money that Alex sends through Zakheim not only to help Boaz but also to invest in dubious right-wing Zionist enterprises.

Reflecting Oz's belief in a two-state solution to the Israeli-Palestinian conflict, *Black Box* thematically suggests that truth and reconciliation do not necessarily result in happiness or forgiveness, but perhaps a truce. Ilana and Alex's initial letters initiate a web of correspondence among Alex, Ilana, Michel, Zakheim, Boaz, and Ilana's sister Rahel, who warns Ilana not to resume relations with Alex Gideon. The correspondents hurl anger, abuse, complaint, reproach, love, and longing at each other in the letters, and in the process Ilana and Alex reconcile. She convinces the dying man to return to Jerusalem, to the childhood home that Boaz has inhabited and transformed into a commune, and she leaves Michel Sommo to take care of Alex in his final days. Boaz carries his father in his arms throughout the run-down castle, and Ilana takes care of Alex as if he were an infant. Meanwhile, Michel Sommo and his family ritualistically mourn the end of his marriage to Ilana, as if she had died.

In an interesting twist on the love triangle, Alex offers to bequeath Michel Sommo half his inheritance if the offended husband would permit his wife and young daughter to remain with the dying man until he expires. Michel Sommo refuses, claims his daughter from Ilana, and begins divorce proceedings. Ilana writes back after eight months have passed, requesting forgiveness and asking Michel to join her at the commune so that she, Alex, and Michel might live together as a family. She signs the letter "Mother." Michel Sommo pens the final letter, a self-righteous translation of Psalm 103 in which he offers forgiveness, based on a belief that his wronged innocence has been vindicated through Alexander Gideon's richly deserved suffering.

Perhaps due to its setting shortly after the Yom Kippur War and Alexander Gideon's characterization as a former tank commander, *Black Box* has been read as an allegory for the Zionist enterprise. In a review of the novel, Elizabeth Pochoda quotes Oz as having said that Zionism exacted a toll on women, and she goes on to state that Ilana's obsessions with both Alexander Gideon and Michel Sommo represent the "malaise" at the heart of Zionism—idealism and cruelty. Ilana's marriage to the arrogant and mercenary religious fanatic Michel represents blind trust in a vision of perfection, and her absolute devotion to the violent and abusive Alexander reflects a desire to be dominated. Torn between the world-weary despair of the old Ashkenazi elite represented in Alexander Gideon and the shrewd aspirations of recent immigrants such as Michel Sommo who have more in common with the Arabs of North Africa than the eastern European Ashkenazim, Ilana spends much of her time running between the two, searching for happiness. This servitude in women under Zionism far exceeds gender inequality, according to Pochoda. But, more important, she finds that as allegories of the state of Israel, *Black Box* and other works by Oz chronicle the suffocation and boredom of people forced to live in proximity with each other, everyone relinquishing something and no one owning the truth—"exactly what the Jews had for almost two millennia." And this irony, she concludes, accounts for the tragicomic nature of the novel.

Black Box does not end happily, yet it is perhaps the most lighthearted of Oz's novels, namely because the characters are so desperately flawed. Ilana's obsessions, Michel's fanaticism, Boaz's illiteracy and stupidity, Zakheim's exploitation of Alex as well as his devotion, and Alex's dark humor make their intertwining story utterly convincing—in the tradition of great literary realism, such as works by Russian writer and playwright Anton Chekhov.

BIBLIOGRAPHY

Balaban, Abraham. *Between God and Beast: An Examination of Amos Oz's Prose.* University Park: Pennsylvania State University Press, 1993.

Mazor, Yair. *Somber Lust: The Art of Amos Oz.* Translated by Marganit Weinberger-Rotman. Albany: State University of New York Press, 2002.

Wirth-Nesher, Hana. *City Codes: Reading the Modern Urban Novel.* Cambridge and New York: Cambridge University Press, 1996.

Deyonne Bryant

BLACK RAIN (KUROI AME) IBUSE MASUJI (1965–66)

Black Rain is one of the most powerful works of literature in any language dealing with the aftermath of a nuclear catastrophe. Comparable, at least on the surface, with American author John Hersey's *Hiroshima* (1946), *Black Rain* by Japanese author IBUSE MASUJI (1898–1993) deals with the events of August 6, 1945, when the atomic bomb was dropped on Hiroshima. Whereas Hersey's work is based upon the experiences of six survivors of the atomic blast, *Black Rain* is primarily the story of Shizuma Shigematsu and his family. Although based on diaries and testimonies of the bombing victims, the prevailing tone used throughout is novelistic and, were it not for the documentary material Ibuse includes, could easily be assumed a work of fiction. The work began life in serial form, published in *Showa* from January 1965 to September 1966 and then in translated form in *Japan Quarterly* in 1967–68, before being compiled into a book under the auspices of publisher Kodansha.

What sets *Black Rain* apart from other recollections of the tragedy at Hiroshima is the humanity central to the story. Written some two decades after the war, the novel's overarching story is concerned with the attempts to get Shigematsu's niece, Yasuko, married. She is having problems because of the stigma attached to those who suffer radiation sickness (in postwar Japan, there was a social underclass of those affected by the radiation called *hibakusha*). Although Yasuko shows no symptoms, Shigematsu and his wife, Shigeko, must produce evidence that she is unlikely to suffer any lasting effects from her exposure to radiation. So begins the rationale for the story, as Shigematsu, Shigeko, and Yasuko rewrite their diaries for the days immediately following the event. This technique (called an "embedded" or "framed" narrative) allows the reader to vicariously witness the bombing and its results while also distancing them from the actual event. It also allows Ibuse to insert secondary materials from other survivors, providing a more complete picture of those days, as well as a more "objective" view based on historical and scientific research conducted after the war.

One of the most remarkable points about *Black Rain* is the way in which Ibuse describes the bombing. Rather than call it an "atomic bomb," and thereby assume a later perspective, Ibuse builds up a picture of the bomb's effects slowly, using the characters' descriptions of tragedy. The account begins with characters talking about the flash and eventual appearance of the large, now famous image of a mushroom cloud. Confusion abounds as to what this is: Yasuko believes it is the result of a powerful "oil bomb," while others believe it is merely the result of a quantity of concentrated high explosives. The macabre descriptions of burnt bodies and symptoms of radiation sickness are met with confusion by characters and official reports alike. When people who survived the blast and the subse-quent fires that decimated the city begin dying, it is assumed that the bomb had poison mixed with explosives.

One of the most poignant accounts of this ignorance is the description of the "black rain" that began falling a few days after the initial blast, giving the book its title. Shigematsu and his family, traipsing through the ruins of Hiroshima, tripping over rubble and dead bodies, feel it raining and discover that the rain is black. They are later told that the rain is not harmful, but the reader is aware that with each drop that strikes them, the Shizumas are being exposed to potentially lethal radiation. When Yasuko later becomes ill with radiation sickness (in the novel's "present"), the full tragedy comes home to the reader: Although she had never before exhibited symptoms, she suffers years later—like the rain, the destruction caused by the bomb continued past the initial devastating blast. Shigematsu says: "When she first told me about it, in the living room, there was a moment when the living room vanished and I saw a great, mushroom-shaped cloud rising into a blue sky."

What the reader might see as naïveté is in actuality a very human response to an incomprehensible and unprecedented event. Rather than tell the reader that an atomic bomb exploded and then deal with its aftermath, Ibuse narrates the characters' growing concern as the full extent of the horror becomes known. In fact, Shigematsu only discovers the proper name of "atomic bomb" a week after the blast and very late in the text. This clearly reveals that the "bomb" is not the main focus of the text, although it is obviously an important part of it. Rather, Ibuse's primary concern is to paint a picture of wartime Japanese society alongside the bomb's effect on the Shizumas, the city of Hiroshima, and Japanese society.

Black Rain, therefore, does not shy away from confronting issues only tangentially related to the bomb. Aside from Shigematsu's carp farm, which he and his friends start because of their intermittent bouts of radiation sickness, the text also provides a picture of daily life in wartime Japan, talking about issues such as rationing and the relationship of civilians to military personnel. The book is also not partisan, as it does not demonize the Allies and celebrate Japanese involvement in World War II. Rather, the novel portrays Japanese society in an evenhanded manner, mentioning the war profiteering that occurred in Hiroshima after the devastation, the waste of human life in the formation of the kamikaze suicide pilots, and the incapacity of the military to give appropriate civilian aid.

Among depictions of mass crematoria and decaying corpses, *Black Rain* manages to convey something fundamentally human. The prevailing message of the text is that war, and especially atomic war, is never positive. At the conclusion of the tragic story, Ibuse writes, quoting from the emperor's declaration of surrender: "[T]he final result would be to bring about not only the annihilation of the Japanese race, but the destruction of human civilization as a whole." When coupled with the fact that the reader leaves the text assuming that Yasuko will not survive her radiation sickness, it is clear that *Black Rain* is a sobering yet not sombre account of the inhumanity of war.

BIBLIOGRAPHY

Cohn, Joel R. *Studies in the Comic Spirit in Modern Japanese Fiction.* Cambridge, Mass.: Harvard University Press, 1998.

Liman, Anthony V. *A Critical Study of the Literary Style of Ibuse Masuji.* Lewiston, N.Y.: E. Mellen Press, 1992.

Treat, John Whittier. *Poets of Water, Pillars of Fire: The Literature of Ibuse Masuji.* Seattle: University of Washington Press, 1988.

William George Slocombe

BLACK SHACK ALLEY (LA RUE CASES-NÈGRES, SUGAR CANE ALLEY) JOSEPH ZOBEL (1950)

Black Shack Alley is Keith Q. Warner's English translation of the classic French novel *La rue cases-nègres* by JOSEPH ZOBEL (1915–2006). The title of Zobel's work means "Breaking Negroes [Slaves] Street." *Black Shack Alley* is an autobiographical text that evolves around Zobel's coming of age in postslavery Martinique. José represents Zobel in the novel, and M'man Tine is José's grandmother and guardian.

Black Shack Alley discloses what life is like for José and M'man Tine, as well as for other impoverished blacks who live in shanty towns and work in the sugar cane fields of the French Indies. The novel delves into the hardships, culture, and spirituality of an otherwise invisible people. They are a people once enslaved by French aristocracy, and while they are "emancipated," they are still oppressed, poor, and inextricably bound to the cane fields. While *Black Shack Alley* sheds light on the perils of colonialism for those who are colonized, Zobel achieves this in a rather innovative way, one that distinguishes him among other writers in the Black Arts Movement and their predecessors, Harlem Renaissance writers.

Zobel intimately tells the story of an oppressed people instead of a story about how the oppressed interacts with their oppressors. Ironically, Zobel's book was influenced by Harlem Renaissance writer Richard Wright's autobiography *Black Boy*. Although Zobel's and Wright's works share common themes—poverty, oppression, and intellectual pursuits—they have distinctly different approaches. Wright's *Black Boy* is a blatant condemnation of racism and European domination; the work sustains itself on hostile encounters between whites and blacks. To the contrary, Zobel's *Black Shack Alley* focuses on a community of poor black Martinicans; thus, white people are rendered invisible.

Zobel's approach manifests indelible realities: Despite being colonized by the French, Africanisms thrive in black West Indian culture, and oppression and poverty go hand in hand. Zobel's vividly detailed descriptions also evoke an unforgettable sense of time, place, and circumstance. His approach to storytelling allows readers to glean the truth for themselves; *Black Shack Alley* condemns imperialism without overstatement. Throughout the novel there are rich examples of mores, taboos, and rituals that are rooted in African ideology. Nowhere is this more evident than in the belief that spirits are actively involved in daily life. Young José knows many of the superstitions by heart: "Never say good evening to a person you meet on the road when it is beginning to get dark. Because if it's a zombi, he'll carry your voice to the devil who could then take you away at any time. Always close the door when you're inside the shack at night. Because evil spirits could pelt stones after you, leaving you in pain the rest of your life."

Another enduring pastime of African culture is the African storytelling tradition. In *Black Shack Alley,* Mr.

Médouze embodies this tradition. He is an elder, a former slave and someone whom José greatly admires and enjoys listening to. Mr. Médouze's tales begin with the customary West Indian incantation "Eh cric!" and José responds "Eh crac!" This incantation exemplifies the call and response aspect of the African storytelling method, whereby the speaker ensures that he has the attention of his audience. Next, Mr. Médouze begins a fantastic tale that intrigues José: "Well, once upon a time . . . when Rabbit used to walk around dressed in white calico suit and Panama hat; when all the traces on Petit-Morne were paved with diamonds, rubies, topaz (all the streams ran gold and Grand Etang was a pool of honey). . . ." Mr. Médouze's stories provide José with an escape from an oftentimes bleak reality— the reality of abject poverty.

Zobel skillfully portrays the vast degree of poverty among the poor of Petit-Morne. He illustrates deprivation in every area of their lives, whether it be monetary, shelter, food, or clothing: "Indeed, the dingy jacket clothing Tortilla's body had shrunk, and if I couldn't see that the number of knots that made up the texture or if had increased, I was nonetheless aware that my good friend was all the more naked for it." Sadly, though M'man Tine labors from sunup to sundown, money is something that she never has enough of: ". . . M'man Tine came home, her rags and her skin weather-beaten, soaked like a sponge wanting to send me to the store, she looked in vain for the missing cent in every corner of the room."

The sugar cane fields undoubtedly serve as a catalyst of sorts for *Black Shack Alley* since so much of the novel is intertwined with the fields. José's attitude toward the fields is one of paradox and pain: "Despite all the pleasure I had nibbling on and sucking pieces of sugar cane, a field still represented in my eyes a damnable place where executioners, whom you couldn't even see, condemned black people from as young as eight years old, to weed, to dig, in storms that caused them to shrivel up and in the broiling sun that devoured them like mad dogs. . . ." The characters in *Black Shack Alley* spend a great deal of time in the fields; essentially their lives depend on sugar cane, but it is a difficult way of life. The cane fields symbolize oppression. Yet in spite of all the sorrow and

blighted conditions surrounding José, beauty, joy, and vitality are also present.

There are numerous scenes in the text redolent with aesthetic beauty, eroticism, and pleasure. Zobel creates this memorable imagery with well-crafted descriptive prose. The following passage depicts the exuberance and cadence of villagers dancing to the tom-tom: "Everything—the purulent feet, the quivering breasts, those male shoulders and frenzied hips, all those glassy eyes and rainbow smiles, all these people, satiated, drunk and forgetting all cares, blended into one burning, invading babel, like a fire, flaring into dancing, dancing, dancing."

Black Shack Alley offers a window into a specific time and place as it chronicles the evolution of an artist. Zobel's novel is successful on manifold levels. It demonstrates that while Africans can be taken out of Africa, it is harder still to take Africa out of the African, that subliminal prose can aptly reveal truth, and that one people's paradise is another people's hell.

BIBLIOGRAPHY

Gallagher, Mary. *Soundings in French Caribbean Writing 1950–2000. The Shock of Space and Time.* Oxford and New York: Oxford University Press.
Zobel, Joseph. *Black Shack Alley.* Translated by Keith Q. Warner. Boulder, Colo.: Lynne Reinner Publishers, 1980.

Cathy Clay

BLANCHOT, MAURICE (1907–2003) *French novelist, journalist*

The philosopher, literary theorist, and novelist Maurice Blanchot wrote more than 30 important works during his lifetime. He was born in the first decade of the 20th century into a Catholic family in eastern France in the village of Quain. Among his friends who influenced him were Emmanuel Levinas, with whom Blanchot studied at the University of Strasbourg. Levinas, of Jewish origin, would later play an important role in Blanchot's critical thoughts about the world. Levinas became a noted philosopher in France and was himself influenced by Edmund Husserl and Martin Heidegger, two German philosophers he had met at the University of Freiburg. He also translated works by these thinkers into French for the first time.

Blanchot lived at a time when the Nazi genocide, the inhuman nightmare of World War II, became an incessant leitmotif for the world's conscience. In the 1930s he wrote political editorials for *Journal des débats* about different issues, especially against humankind's ever-increasing focus on materialism. Blanchot was both anticommunist and anticapitalist. When France fell to the German army in 1940, he left the newspaper because of its affiliation with the Nazis, but he continued to contribute weekly literary articles to the publication. Following the war, he rejected Catholicism, turned to atheism, and became a recluse.

During the war, Blanchot participated in the French resistance against the German invaders. In 1943, still two years before the war's end, he published his first collection of criticism, entitled *Faux-Pas*. During the resistance, he hid Levinas's wife and son from persecution, and he also helped smuggle people over the French border to Switzerland.

One is surprised to see that Blanchot, a 20th-century philosopher, neither belonged to nor was defined by any literary trend. He is considered neither a surrealist nor dadaist nor an existentialist. It can be said that he was first and foremost a journalist, the profession he most admired, and then he was, secondly, a writer of fiction.

Blanchot's first novels were published in 1941 and 1942: *Thomas the Obscure* (*Thomas l'obscure*) and *Aminadab,* respectively. The influence of FRANZ KAFKA and that author's search to understand individual identity and the ego remain apparent in Blanchot's early fictional works. *Thomas the Obscure* poses the central enigma to the reader: Who *is* Thomas the Obscure? A reader is reminded of the French writer ALAIN ROBBE-GRILLET's intentionally obscure and elusive novels, such as *JEALOUSY*. The modernist, postmodernist work explores fundamental questions but never resolves them as the author and literature cannot reach any level of certainty. Others to influence Blanchot's writing include JEAN-PAUL SARTRE, Stéphane Mallarmé, and GEORGES BATAILLE. Blanchot's other novels include *Death Sentence* (*L'arrêt de mort,* 1948), *The Most High* (*Le très-haut,* 1949), and *The Step Not Beyond* (*Le pas au-delà,* 1973).

Blanchot's central theoretical works include "Literature and the Right to Death" in *The Work of Fire* (1995) and *The Gaze of Orpheus, The Space of Literature, The Infinite Conversation,* and *The Writing of Disaster.* Blan-

chot's influence on such later poststructural theorists as Jacques Derrida is clear.

It is important to mention that Kafka's writing helped to shape Blanchot's use of fragments in his work, a technique in which he excelled. An understanding of the use of these fragments is important to understanding Blanchot and his modernism. Through the feeling of anguish, to which the reader is exposed, Blanchot opens the door to another world. What is extraordinary is that in his works there is no more "I." The ego of the author and narrator is challenged. There is no more intrigue, there is no more ideology. Gone are the Freudian-founded psychological analyses and motivations found in other, earlier literature. What remains is the realization of the existence of a conscience without subject, of desire without object, and events without past or future.

Maurice Blanchot died on February 20, 2003, in Yvelines, France.

BIBLIOGRAPHY

Blanchot, Maurice. *Death Sentence.* Translated by Lydia Davis. Barrytown, N.Y.: Station Hill, 1978.
———. *The Gaze of Orpheus.* Translated by Lydia Davis. Barrytown, N.Y.: Station Hill, 1981.
———. *Madness of the Day.* Translated by Lydia Davis. Barrytown, N.Y.: Station Hill, 1988.
———. *Thomas the Obscure.* Translated by Robert Lamberton. New York: D. Lewis, 1973.
Clark, Timothy. *Derrida, Heidegger, Blanchot: Sources of Derrida's Notion and Practice of Literature.* Cambridge and New York: Cambridge University Press, 1992.
Gill, Carolyn Bailey, ed. *Maurice Blanchot: The Demand of Writing.* New York: Routledge, 1996.
Large, William. *Emmanuel Levinas and Maurice Blanchot: Ethics and Ambiguity of Writing.* Manchester: Clinamen Press, 2005.

Marcel Crespil

BLASCO IBÁÑEZ, VICENTE (1867–1928)

Spanish novelist   The Spanish novelist and politician Vicente Blasco Ibáñez wrote *Reeds and Mud* (*Cañas y barro,* 1902) and *The Cabin* (*La barraca,* 1898), realistic novels that dramatically depict the social problems affecting the Valencia region in Spain at the beginning of the 20th century. He achieved international popularity with his enormously popular novel about World

War I, *The Four Horsemen of the Apocalypse* (*Los cuatro jinetes del Apocalipsis,* 1916).

Blasco Ibáñez was born in Valencia, Spain, in 1867. He became a member of the Republican Party, was imprisoned many times for political activism, and exiled himself to Paris several times to escape prosecution. In France he read the works of Émile Zola and studied naturalism, the literary school that greatly influenced his regional Valencian novels. In 1894 he funded *El Pueblo,* an influential republican newspaper that voiced his political ideas (known as *blasquismo*), his support of federal republicanism, and his criticism of the governments of the Restoration. After serving as member of the Spanish parliament for six terms, he quit politics in 1908 and traveled to Argentina, where he tried to establish several utopian agricultural communities. He returned to Paris at the beginning of World War I when the president of France, Raymond Poincaré, asked him to write a novel about warfare to help the Allied cause. As a result, Blasco Ibáñez wrote *The Four Horsemen of the Apocalypse,* a novel so successful that it was published in over 200 editions, translated into almost every language, and adapted for film several times. *The Four Horsemen* made Blasco Ibáñez world famous. He died a very wealthy man on his large estate at Menton on the French Riviera in 1928; five years later he was ceremoniously reinterred in a cemetery in his native Valencia.

Blasco Ibáñez's voluminous novels can be classified into five main groups: the regional novels of his native Valencia, the international novels dealing with war and its consequences, novels of social revolt, psychological novels, and Spanish historical fiction.

His earliest works offer an intensely vivid depiction of the social problems affecting Valencia and realistically portray the lives of its population—peasants, farmers, fishermen, tradesmen, politicians. Most Hispanists consider these works superior to his later writings for their pictorial realism (very close to the naturalist style), their forceful and coloristic descriptions of rural and fishing life, and their imaginative elaboration. Blasco Ibáñez's masterpiece *Reeds and Mud* (1902) depicts the conflict between three generations of fishermen in the Albufera marshes in Valencia and shows the author's characteristic predilection for tragic love stories, unfortunate endings, and authentic colloquial language. The consequence of the force of heredity and of environmental determinism prevents significant psychological evolution; the characters of these works, such as *The Cabin* (1898) and *Rice and a Carriage* (*Arroz y tartana,* 1894), are usually regionalistic types driven by food, money, or sex.

Blasco Ibáñez achieved his greatest success from his more cosmopolitan European novels. These works move from the bonds of realist literature and, in keeping with the modernist movement, show anticonformism, a sense of disillusionment and despair, appreciation for different cultures, and the need to renovate and escape. His much-celebrated novel of World War I, *The Four Horsemen of the Apocalypse,* tells the tragic story of Julio Desnoyers, an Argentinean of French descent who returns to France once the conflict explodes. Published while the war was still being fought, this sincere and passionate best seller reflects the author's open support of the Allies. *The Four Horsemen* accurately describes the atmosphere, the sense of loss, and the overwhelming effects of World War I. Other novels in this genre include *Our Sea* (*Mare Nostrum,* 1918) and *The Enemies of Women* (*Los enemigos de la mujer,* 1919).

In the early years of the 20th century, Blasco Ibáñez wrote a series of novels in which the element of social protest is even more to the forefront and the characters are more developed. The settings are in different regions of Spain: *The Cathedral* (*La catedral,* 1903) in Toledo; *The Intruder* (*El intruso,* 1904) in Bilbao; *The Wine Cellar* (*La bodega,* 1904) in Jerez; and *The Horde* (*La horda,* 1905) in Madrid.

The popular *Blood and Sand* (*Sangre y arena,* 1908), about a bullfighter in a love triangle, was made into the movie *Blood and Sand* (1941) starring Tyrone Power and Linda Darnell. *Blood and Sand,* as well as *The Naked Maja* (*La maja desnuda,* 1906) and *The Will to Live* (*La voluntad de vivir,* 1907), marked a higher level of psychological and analytical development than earlier works.

With masterful prose, works such as *The Pope of the Sea* (*El papa del mar,* 1926), *In Search of the Great Khan* (*En busca del Gran Kan,* 1928), and *The Knight of the Virgin* (*El caballero de la Virgen,* 1929) glorify Spain's imperial past and counteract the anti-Spanish colonial legend.

BIBLIOGRAPHY
Alós Ferrando, Vicente R. *Vicente Blasco Ibáñez: biografía política.* Valencia: Institució Alfons el Magnanim, 1999.
Day, A. Grove. *V. Blasco Ibáñez.* New York: Twayne Publishers, 1972.
Oxford, Jeffrey Thomas. *Vicente Blasco Ibáñez: Color Symbolism in Selected Novels.* New York: Peter Lang, 1997.

Rosario Torres

BLINDNESS (ENSAIO SOBRE A CEGUEIRA) José Saramago (1995)

José Saramago (1922–   ), one of Portugal's most famous writers, was awarded the Nobel Prize in literature in 1988. His novel *Blindness* is considered one of his most outstanding literary achievements. A speculative parable reminiscent of Albert Camus's *The Plague, Blindness* examines the reasons for a mysterious social and moral breakdown in a typical modern city. Saramago's narrative uses the literal blindness of almost all the inhabitants of his city as a political, psychological, and spiritual metaphor.

Blindness is written in a distinctive style that Saramago developed when he returned to literature after a 20-year hiatus. This novel eschews conventional punctuation and paragraphs, moves between the first and third person, and shifts tense and perspective; it blends narrative, description, and dialogue to create a dreamlike flow of voices and episodes that reflect on the idea of blindness in all its permutations. The author effectively establishes the realistic consequences of a loss of vision and at the same time suggests the symbolic reverberations of a moral and spiritual condition.

Structured around a series of crises involving a mysterious epidemic of blindness, the novel presents as a major theme the demoralizing impact of the affliction and the way in which it leaves chaos and criminality in its wake. In an effort to cope with the epidemic, the authorities imprison the blind in a former mental institution where they must to fend for themselves. The scarce and putrid food and the crowding and squalid conditions are exacerbated by the increasingly unruly behavior of the institution's inmates. The breakdown of morality reaches its nadir with the rise of a band of blind men who victimize and humiliate other prisoners through such criminal transgressions as theft, rape, and terror. Humanity's worst instincts surface and social order disintegrates as individuals are overwhelmed by fear, confusion, and utter helplessness.

Saramago's narrative makes clear that the literal blindness of the inhabitants of the asylum is also a hysterical blindness, a pathology of consciousness that locks an individual within himself and deprives him of an ability to perceive his own humanity and the humanity of others. This isolating self-involvement, with its loss of genuine connection to other people, leads to a frightened, dehumanized society, a degraded world of predators and prey, criminals and victims—irreparable and hopeless.

Within this collapsing society, however, a little group of seven people begin to work together to regain a modicum of humanity. The leader of this group is the Doctor's Wife, the only sighted person in the novel, who has accompanied her ophthalmologist husband to the asylum, even though she is not blind. Her eyesight gives her practical and moral advantages. This sighted woman allows Saramago to explore not only the meaning of blindness but also the meaning of vision. She is instrumental in organizing the group, to keep it safe and fed, in addition to providing spiritual lucidity; she never loses her sympathetic feeling or her moral intelligence. Blindness in this regard is associated with the death of the heart and with the loss of concern for other human beings; the sight of the Doctor's Wife, on the other hand, is associated with compassion and the retention of an innate moral compass.

Another woman in the group, a prostitute known as the Girl with Dark Glasses, begins to display some of the virtues of the Doctor's Wife. She voluntarily assumes the care of a small boy and an old man, with whom she eventually falls in love. After the Doctor's Wife has led the group out of the asylum and into the city, which has also been universally afflicted with the same epidemic of sightlessness, another major character emerges, the Dog of Tears. When the Doctor's Wife breaks down in despair due to the seemingly impossible burdens she has assumed, the Dog of Tears comforts her and gives her the strength to continue. Looking into the woman's sighted eyes, he connects with her on a deeply spiritual level, once again allowing Saramago to remind the reader that, in this novel, seeing represents the sacred core of each living being.

The Doctor's Wife manages to secure safety for her little group by leading them to her apartment, a site of both literal and spiritual cleansing as they all bathe on her terrace in the rain. The social conditions elsewhere, however, deteriorate, with increasing scarcity, disorder, and confusion. It is at this point that the Doctor's Wife wanders into a church filled with those praying for rescue and consolation. She realizes that all the eyes of the statues of religious figures in the church are covered. A priest, radically, has blinded the icons upon whose intercession the people have come to depend. The blinding of the religious images has deprived the icons of the spiritual solace that they represent, rendering them equivalent to the unfeeling, unthinking, and blinded people who worship them. When the Doctor's Wife tells the assembled congregation that the holy images lack sight, the people abandon the church and soon regain their sight, as if the demystification of the religious symbols is somehow linked to the subsequent miraculous recovery. Vision allows the people in the city to begin to restore order. Symbolically, the powers associated with the images in the church have been transferred to humanity, who are empowered to use their own moral and spiritual resources—their own eyes—which are their birthright.

Throughout his novel, Saramago has skillfully woven the concepts of blindness and sight in such a way as to suggest that these two conditions metaphorically constitute the general situation of humanity, which is always vulnerable to a deadening moral blindness as well as capable of tremendous moral lucidity. The final words of the Doctor's Wife indicate just this when she tells her husband that the people of the city were blind and not sightless—blind people who can see but choose not to do so. Her glance at an empty, white sky at the end of the novel, which gives her the momentary impression that she, too, may be afflicted by blindness, encourages her to return her eyes to the happy sight of the revitalized city that has survived its dark journey.

The connection Saramago makes between blindness and humanity's deference to holy images specifically speaks to conditions in his home country of Portugal under the long dictatorship (1932–68) of António de Oliveira Salazar (1889–1970). Salazar, a fervently religious ruler, was committed to putting into action the social principles expressed by the Catholic Church under Pope Leo XIII. But on a more universal level, Saramago's narrative is a parable of good and evil. While he subjects his characters to a series of dispiriting ordeals stemming from an essentially pessimistic premise, the author also suggests that humanity's capacity for intelligence, hope, compassion, and moral strength can defeat the forces of blindness in any given society.

BIBLIOGRAPHY

Bloom, Harold, ed. *Jose Saramago.* New York: Chelsea House, 2005.

Cole, Kevin L. "Jose Saramago's *Blindness.*" *The Explicator* 64, no. 2, (Winter 2006): 109–112.

Carole A. Champagne

BLIND OWL, THE (BUF-E KUR) SADEQ HEDAYAT (1937)

SADEQ HEDAYAT (1903–51) was for many decades the best-known modern prose writer in Persian, the language of a country whose purified literary lexicon and restrictive linguistic formalism he sought to violate by introducing crude idioms and colloquial phrases. He has generally owed his reputation to his extraordinary and enigmatic novella *The Blind Owl,* which on the surface is reminiscent of Thomas DeQuincey's opiated phantasmagoria and Edgar Allan Poe's hysterical first-person narratives of obsessive morbidity, murder, and deathless corpses. These elements, together with the writer's personal habits, have given the work its unwarranted reputation as a drug-induced, formless, and singularly incomprehensible reverie suffused with intimations of mortality and populated by its harbingers. But while it may seem to sacrifice character development in favor of mood, in the manner of a prose poem, and while it does convey the trance-like states and hallucinations produced by the narrator's opium smoking, *The Blind Owl* is actually an intricate narrative exercise whose formal elements perfectly express the density of its metaphysical and metapsychological preoccupations.

The novella has a two-part structure. The first part is a dense, dreamlike narrative told by an unnamed narrator, who describes himself as having escaped beyond the city limits into the gravelike solitude of his coffin-like room. In order "to kill the time," he paints the covers of pen cases, obsessively reproducing the same scene each time: "a cypress tree under which a stooped, old man squatted on the ground shrouding himself in a cloak in the manner of Indian *yogis*. He wore a *shalma* around his head and had his index finger on his lips as if perplexed. Opposite him a girl in a long, black dress was bending to offer him a lily—because between them a brook intervened." One day he sees through an air vent in the wall a wondrous yet strangely familiar tableaux: the very scene he has been painting over and over again, except now the lilies are black. The narrator's visionary glimpse of this woman exalts and inspires him by instantaneously resolving "theological riddles"; but when he leaves his room to locate her, he finds only the remnants of a dead animal and a pile of trash where the old man had sat. Soon after, in a "coma-like limbo between sleep and wakefulness," he receives a mysterious visitation, an "ethereal," somnambulistic woman dressed in black. Without explanation, she enters his life like a transient angel of light, radiating an "intoxicating supernatural beam" from her mesmerizing, unnaturally large and "glistening" eyes—eyes that he alternately experiences, such is his ambivalence, as "wonder-stricken . . . condemning . . . "dreadful, enchanting, reproachful, . . . worried, threatening, and inviting." Although her whole being is unnervingly placid and her face expressionless, the narrator can see, behind her unfocused, unacknowledging eyes, "all my miserable life . . . the eternal night and the dense darkness that I had been looking for."

The woman seems to possess an exquisite, altogether unearthly, symmetry, "like a female mandrake separated from her mate." He senses that *he* is that mate, whose soul "had bordered on her soul" outside of time and that "we were doomed for a union." He feels himself "annihilate[d]" by her uncanny familiarity; only when she closes her eyes does he feel "sudden tranquility." When he finally touches her, he realizes by her coldness that she has been dead for days. "Her transient, brittle soul, which had no relation to the world of earthly beings . . . left the carcass that tortured it, and joined the world of wandering shadows. I think

it took my shadow with it as well." Yet he feels that she too has been an "angel of torture," that she had "poisoned my life or else my life had been susceptible to being poisoned and I could not have had any other type of life." Despite this, he also feels that "I had to be with her corpse. It seemed to me that from the dawn of creation, since the beginning of my existence, a cold feelingless corpse had shared my dark room with me." At this moment he experiences cosmic consciousness, the recognition that "My life was bound to . . . the eternal foolishness of all forms and species . . . far and near had all become united with my sentient life." He undertakes to paint, and thereby to preserve forever, the eyes of the woman and the impact they had had on him. As he is trying unsuccessfully to remember her gaze, her eyes open straight at him with a reproachful look, before returning to death and manifest decomposition. Bizarrely, as if under a compulsion, he then proceeds to dismember her body, place its fragments in a suitcase, and cart them away for burial, with the help of a corpse-carriage driver who is vaguely reminiscent of the old man in his paintings.

The narrator explains that in recording these events, he has been "writing only for my shadow on the wall" in the hope that "we can know each other better." And he refers to the woman as "the reflection of the Shadow of the soul." This emphasis on uncanny shadowings and doublings also pervades the second part of Hedayat's novella, which is slightly less eerie while altogether more perplexing in its refusal to provide any rationale for its obscure, disquieting incidents and scenes. The second part of the book constitutes a murky first-person description of the stages of a man's feverish illness and his unhappy marriage to a woman, always designated "the whore," who casts "a lustful shadow, very hopeful of itself." The exact relationship between the two parts remains a matter of speculation. It is not clear, for example, whether the narrators are the same man (and what *sameness* might mean) or whether the events of the second part occur before or after the first part. It is also unclear whether the mysterious female visitant who is dismembered and buried, and who may personify the promise of death, should be associated with or identified as the whorish wife, whom the narrator eventually stabs to death. Equally tortuous presences, both might be said to function as his anima, a feminine manifestation of the impulses of his soul.

What establishes the two parts as an integral whole is the recursive nature of the imagery—the uncanny repetitions, recurrences, and mirrorings that produce the novella's hypnotic quality. The same images appear again and again, while symbolic gestures and actions migrate from archetypal figure to archetypal figure (a motherly nanny, an erotic temple dancer, a butcher, and various avatars of old age, all of whom may or may not be aspects of the same composite archetype of the enlightened, liberated soul). Perhaps the most notable symbolic action is the "repulsive . . . ominous" laughter that issues from these old men. This laughter seems to break out at those moments when the narrator is deeply immersed in the network of desire-born illusions and misrecognitions that constitute this life. For example, immediately after hearing this laugh, the air vent that had allowed the narrator to gaze at the woman and the old man disappears: "I saw a dark, black wall in front of me . . . The same darkness that had obscured my vision all my life." Another example, of migrating gestures and acts, is a left-hand finger placed at the lips, between chewing teeth, or in the mouth. This possibly lewd or degraded action is first seen as a gesture of the old man under the cypress, but later the mysterious female visitant, the narrator's wife in childhood, and her younger brother are all identified by similar actions.

Hedayat's use of persistent motifs produces the impression of extraordinarily insistent, almost incantatory, obsessions. A few of the many other motifs that appear insistently throughout the text include: a flask of wine dating from the narrator's birth, which has been intermixed with a serpent's poison; the butcher's caressing dismemberment of dead sheep; golden "beeflies" that swarm corpses; an ancient jar (or funerary urn) covered in a glaze reminiscent of "broken-up golden bees" and painted with a woman's eyes and black lilies; a city of shadowy, seemingly uninhabitable houses of strange geometrical shapes (suggesting honeycombs) and darkened windows (suggesting death); and the act of lying prostrate with a great weight on the chest (the suitcase carrying the dismembered corpse,

the antique jar, and, finally, the narrator's own being). The same things seen and experienced, again and again, by the narrator of each part of the novella progressively combine to suggest the principle of karma that governs the cycles of birth, death, and rebirth. The narrator's (and the reader's) déjà vu also evokes Friedrich Nietzsche's conception of eternal recurrence inasmuch as the antique jar purchased by the narrator is likely to have been painted by "the same unfortunate painter of pencases" with whom the narrator is also identified. This uncanny doubling and self-distancing serves to suggest that the past and the present are coinherent. ("Weren't their experiences inherent in me? Did not the past exist in me?")

Hedayat's recursive narrative accretes associations between the images and establishes a feeling or tone that insinuates the dialectic of dissolution and regeneration. This serves to identify the essence of being alive as a repetition-compulsion—the most fundamental of repetition-compulsions that keeps beings subjected to the karmic wheel. Metaphysical coincidences seem to exist in reciprocal relation to metapsychological compulsions. Thus, the narrator comes to occupy (while lying in a fetal condition), "[t]he place where life and death meet and distorted images are created; past, dead desires, obliterated, choked desires come to life again and cry aloud for vengeance." This principle may also help to explain the uncanny relationship between the narrator and the other archetypal characters. Hallucinating a face that he recalls also having seen in childhood and which seems to resemble that of the butcher, the narrator speculates: "Perhaps it was the shadow of the spirit produced at my birth and was thus within the restricted circuit of my life." Similarly, he wonders, "Perhaps the old odds-and-ends seller, the butcher, nanny, and my whore of a wife had all been my shadows. Shadows among whom I had been a prisoner."

Recalling how in childhood he used to experience the characters in stories as if they were himself, the narrator considers, "Am I not writing my own story and myth? Stories are only a way of escape from unfulfilled desires; unfulfilled desires imagined by various story makers according to their inherited, narrow mentality." This last remark may help to explain Hedayat's convergence of philosophical perspectives (ranging from Zoroastrianism to Omar Khayyam to Schopen-hauer) and his experimental literary strategies. Hedayat was for many years an expatriate in Paris, and this may account in part for his syncretic imagination. Though nominally a Muslim, Hedayat apparently jettisoned his religious tradition for an eclectic mix of Western and Eastern ideas better suited to this philosophical pessimism and to a psychological nihilism that culminated in his suicide in Paris at the age of 48. Hedayat's familiarity with European modernism may account for *The Blind Owl*'s remarkable, perhaps unprecedented, originality: its audacious appropriation of incidents and images of another writer's book within a complex synthesis of Western and Eastern intimations about being and nonbeing. Hedayat sometimes goes beyond pastiche to the borders of plagiarism by dismembering and burying within his text extended passages from RAINER MARIA RILKE's *The NOTEBOOKS OF MALTE LAURIDS BRIGGE*, seemingly replicating at the formal level the book's persistent references to physical burial and decomposition. Among the passages he incorporates from Rilke's angst-ridden reverie is a catalogue of feverish sickbed intimations and a recognition before a mirror of multiple constituent selves "in me" but "not in my possession."

In the structural analysis that accompanies his translation of *The Blind Owl,* Iraj Bashiri attempts to demonstrate the paradigmatic presence of Buddhism, which was popular among Parisian intellectuals during the late 1920s, the period of Hedayat's residence. Bashiri argues, not entirely convincingly, that the incidents that comprise the second part of the novella are modeled on the *Buddha-carita,* which recounts legends of the Buddha's encounter with old age, sickness, and death, his repudiation of the desirability of women (after heavenly beings distort their bodies), his beggarly sojourn in a hovel, and his subsequent renunciation of asceticism prior to the achievement of enlightenment and the cessation of the cycles of "becoming" from incarnation to incarnation. There is no denying the book's substantial references to the desire to renounce the world of illusion ("this self-created night"), to the desire to resist being (re)born, and to the longing for death ("death that saves us from the deceits of life").

Hedayat, however, subjects Buddhist renunciation to an almost Gnostic emphasis on disgust that approximates contempt: "Perhaps [the odds-and-ends seller] himself was not aware of it, but these sufferings, these layers of misfortune encrusted on his head and face, the general misery that emanated from him, all these had created of him a demi-god. That dirty display in front of him was a personification of the creation." Yearning for his death and decomposition, the narrator is fearful "that the atoms of my body might blend with those of the bums. I could not bear this thought. Sometimes I wished myself to have long hands with big fingers by which I could gather the atoms of my body and keep them to myself so that they would not mix with those of the bums." That said, the long ordeal that constitutes the purgation of lust and the repudiation of material existence as intrinsically worthless is a fitful process. It is a process punctuated by the repeated flaring (and inevitable dwindling) of desires for his wife, who has long kept him from consummating their marriage, though she seems to have performed multiple infidelities with the most abject men.

Desire and annihilation are conflated in the ambiguous climax of part two. His wife makes immersion in desire painful by biting and splitting the narrator's upper lip as they unite sexually. In an impulsive response, he knifes and kills her. Does this act constitute, in symbolic terms, the necessarily violent severing by which the soul is finally able to divorce itself from fruitless desire and the insipid seductions of the dust-like flesh? Or is it an act that ensures further incarceration in the cycles of incarnation (symbolized by the book's final image of dead weight)? The ambiguities do not end there. The narrator finds that he has somehow come away with his wife's eyeball in the palm of his hand: Is this merely a grisly and macabre moment of horror, or does it constitute an esoteric image of mystical enlightenment? Going to the mirror, he discovers that he has suddenly become the odds-and-ends seller, an old man, a dealer in "meaningful forms" that have been "refused by life . . . rejected by life." Possessed by this otherness, he bursts into loud, raucous laughter that shakes his whole being: "The anguish of this woke me as if from a long deep sleep." He sees the odds-and-ends seller laughing and spiriting away the antique jar, leaving him surrounded by golden bee-flies and "the weight of a dead body," no doubt his own, "pressing on my chest."

BIBLIOGRAPHY

Bashiri, Iraj. *Hedayat's Ivory Tower: Structural Analysis of "The Blind Owl."* Minneapolis: Manor House, 1974.

Beard, Michael. *Hedayat's "Blind Owl" as a Western Novel.* Princeton, N.J.: Princeton University Press, 1990.

Fischer, Michael M. J. *Mute Dreams, Blind Owls, and Dispersed Knowledges: Persian Poesis in the Transnational Circuitry.* Durham, N.C.: Duke University Press, 2004.

Ghanoonparvar, M. R. *In a Persian Mirror: Images of the West and Westerners in Iranian Fiction.* Austin: University of Texas Press, 1993.

Hedayat, Sadeq. *The Blind Owl.* Translated by Iraj Bashiri. *Hedayat's Ivory Tower: Structural Analysis of "The Blind Owl."* Minneapolis: Manor House, 1974.

Hillmann, Michael C., ed. *Hedayat's "The Blind Owl" Forty Years After.* Austin: Center for Middle Eastern Studies, University of Texas, 1978.

Manoutchehr Mohandessi. "Hedayat and Rilke." *Comparative Literature* 23, no. 3 (Summer 1971): 209–216.

Milani, Abbas. "Hedayat and the Tragic Vision." In *Lost Wisdom: Rethinking Modernity in Iran.* Washington, D.C.: Mage Publishers, 2004. 93–100.

David Brottman

BODY SNATCHERS, THE (JUNTACADÁVERES) JUAN CARLOS ONETTI (1964)

The Body Snatchers is arguably the masterwork of Uruguay-born JUAN CARLOS ONETTI (1909–94), a distinction that ranks it above many other great novels. It was written at the margins of the so-called Latin American Boom— a period of intense literary creativity that spread throughout the continent for over a decade—and marks a break with tradition in terms of rejection of social and literary values. The fragmented and elusive narrative implies a split with conventional realism and its underlying assumptions.

Onetti's narrative is the story of the character Larsen, who is called to set up a brothel. He has been associated on and off with the world of prostitution, and his nickname Juntacadáveres (body snatcher) derives from this association. Barthé, the town councillor in Santa María, wishes to start the brothel as a legal institution. He has called on Larsen several times in the past to set up the brothel, but each time his plans have been frustrated by opposition within the town. When he finally has the permission, Barthé asks Díaz Grey to trace Larsen and to invite him to try again. When Díaz Grey finds him, he discovers that Larsen has long since given up his interest in the brothel and has taken a regular job with the local newspaper. Díaz Grey puts the offer to Larsen, who is at first sceptical. However, he finally accepts the job and finds three girls to work in the brothel. The entry of Larsen and the prostitutes in Santa María is not accepted by the populace, who finally expel Larsen and the girls from the town.

Jorge Malabia is an adolescent who is at the train station when Larsen and the prostitutes arrive. He accepts the brothel, although he is not one of the first to go there because he is involved in a relationship with his sister-in-law, Julita. At first Julita treats him as a substitute for her dead husband, Federico, but little by little Jorge manages to establish his own identity. Curiously enough, when Jorge and Julita initiate a sexual relationship, he seems able to go to the brothel.

Since Federico's death, Julita has been living in a hermetic world of her own as she tries to maintain the sense of fulfillment she had experienced with him. This rejection of the outer world is associated with madness. Her only contact is Jorge, and as she gradually accepts him as an individual person, his contact with Federico vanishes, and a closer relation with the reality of the world is established.

Jorge, meanwhile, is preoccupied with his relationship with the others since he is an outcast, despite their attempts to make him fit into their own moulds. His parents, who want him to take over the family newspaper when he grows up, try to prevent his going to the brothel. Jorge's independence is signalled by his visit there, which coincides with the official order for its closure. He associates with Larsen and the three prostitutes and goes to the station with them. He is about to get on the train when Padre Bergner prevents him from doing so by telling him that Julita has committed suicide. Though he returns to her wake, he still feels apart from everyone there.

The Body Snatchers is a novel in which heterogeneity is overly present. It derives from the number of central characters, whose links are mostly circumstantial.

There are certain metonymic links between them, however. They all live in Santa María at the same time, and they all react to the arrival of the brothel. But there is no unifying theme that binds them together. Larsen, whose nickname gives title to the novel, is not the central character, since Jorge and Díaz Grey are as important or even more so than he is. There is hardly a sense of characters changing in response to a situation; rather, they respond by reflecting inwardly and not by acting outwardly.

The heterogeneity is further emphasized by the lack of a global, linear narrative. There are very few consecutive chapters, and Onetti frequently switches between events and interjects flashbacks that relate past events. However, despite the heterogeneity, there is a certain consistency in the novel that derives from the individual narratives. The five main characters appear and reappear and constitute a focus of attention.

Some critics have argued that the sense of the break with tradition is a core concern of the novel, as seen in the multiplicity of main characters. This break is also brought out by sexuality and desire. In *The Body Snatchers,* the social nucleus is not the family but the brothel, which is presented as an outside threat to the order of the local community. Moreover, both Larsen and Jorge are essentially inverted representations of the hero of the 19th-century novel. Larsen, for instance, who had always dreamed of having a brothel, is doomed to failure from the very beginning, which makes the temporal accomplishment of his dream ironic. In all cases, the inversion of the ideal indicates a break with the assumptions of order and established values that underlie the realist tradition.

BIBLIOGRAPHY

Adams, Michael Ian. *Three Authors of Alienation: Bombal, Onetti, Carpentier.* Austin: University of Texas Press, 1975.

Craig, Linda. *Juan Carlos Onetti, Manuel Puig and Luisa Valenzuela: Marginality and Gender.* Rochester, N.Y.: Tamesis, 2005.

Fischer, Markus. *Was uns fehlt: Utopische Momente in Juntacadáveres von Juan Carlos Onetti.* Bern, Switzerland: Peter Lang, 1995.

Jones, Yvonne P. *The Formal Expression of Meaning in Juan Carlos Onetti's Narrative Art.* Cuernavaca, Mexico: Centro Intercultural de Documentacion, 1971.

Millington, Mark. *Reading Onetti: Language, Narrative and the Subject.* Liverpool, U.K.: F. Cairns, 1985.

Murray, Jack. *The Landscapes of Alienation: Ideological Subversion in Kafka, Céline and Onetti.* Palo Alto, Calif.: Stanford University Press, 1991.

San Roman, Gustavo, ed. *Onetti and Others: Comparative Essays.* Albany, N.Y.: State University of New York Press, 1999.

Santiago Rodriguez

BÖLL, HEINRICH (1917–1985) *German novelist*

The first citizen of the Federal Republic of Germany to win the Nobel Prize in literature, Heinrich Böll is considered one of postwar Germany's most important writers for both his incisive literary interventions and the keen moral sense that infused them. Böll's work was occupied primarily with Nazism, the war, and the Holocaust, as well as West Germany's uneven recovery from these nefarious events. Although his writings are often associated with Germany's "coming to terms with the past," he also insisted that Nazism was woven into German history of the entire 20th century, thus well before and after the allegedly aberrant years of 1933–45. His unflagging moral sense is driven, however, in part by the insight that Hitler was not inevitable, that events could have been different had Germans been more politically critical and civically active. His morally critical literature—often composed in a complex, modified modernist style—is built on a galvanizing solidarity with suffering, which is, in turn, the product of memory that Böll rendered an ethical act.

Böll's life spanned many of the astonishing historical transformations of 20th-century Germany: He was born toward the end of the Wilhelmine empire, came of age under the unstable Weimar democracy, entered his early adulthood under the Nazi dictatorship, was deployed to both fronts in World War II, lived under Allied occupation, and witnessed—with considerable skepticism—the rapid establishment of the Federal Republic of Germany (FRG). Born on December 21, 1917, in the western German city of Cologne, Böll was the third of five children of devout Catholics, Viktor and Maria (née Hermanns) Böll. This background— from a Catholic region and a devoutly Catholic family—influenced Böll's life and literature immensely: He often wrote of the shortcomings of the church as an institution, particularly of its complicity with Nazism. He maintained, however, the importance of Christian values and faith in leading a moral life.

During the increasing political chaos of Germany's Weimar Republic, his parents remained devoted to their Catholic religious and political beliefs, which provided Böll with something of a bulwark against the Nazi convictions that were engulfing Germany. In high school, Böll was the only one in his class to refuse to join the Hitler Youth, an act initiating a life and anticipating a key literary theme of nonconformity. Shortly after Böll's 1939 matriculation at the University of Cologne, an eight-week military training course overlapped with the beginning of World War II and stretched into six years of service in the army. His service carried him from the beginning of the war in September 1939 through September 1945, when he was released from an American POW camp. During a leave in 1942, he married Annemarie Cech, his childhood sweetheart, who later became an English teacher and translator and with whom he had three sons. His wartime experience, on both fronts as well as in the private refuge of love, instilled in him a deep skepticism toward militarism and hierarchies in general, a theme that continued to animate his work long after the war.

Böll wrote throughout the war, allegedly finishing six novels before its conclusion, all of which were lost in the bombing of Cologne. His first published book, *The Train Was on Time* (*Der Zug war pünktlich,* 1949), like many of Böll's early writings, was preoccupied with World War II, although not so much with its military details as with its psychological impact and moral implications. In this novella, he explores the behavior of a soldier who knows that he, an antiheroic everyman, will soon die. The text concentrates on this soldier's relationship to Olina, a Polish resistance fighter, a narrative thread later picked up in Böll's novel, *And Where Were You, Adam?* (*Wo warst du Adam?,* 1951), in which a German soldier on the eastern front falls in love with a Hungarian-Catholic-Jewish teacher. In *Adam,* Böll offers a rare depiction (for postwar German-gentile literature) of the concentration-camp murder of a Jewish person, a crime that is, for Böll, intertwined with the utter perversion of humanist and Christian values.

Böll was highly skeptical about the Federal Republic (FRG) that rose out of the ruins of Hitler's Germany and the Allied occupation. His fiction of the early 1950s turned increasingly to this new republic and engaged critically with its continuities from the Nazi time as well as with the vacuity of postwar materialism. These works also continued to highlight the perils of self-serving conformity as well as the abuses of power that mark his earlier work. His 1953 novel *And Never Said a Word* (*Und sagte kein einziges Wort*) and his *Tomorrow and Yesterday* (*Haus ohne Hüter,* 1954) are both concerned with the decline of the middle-class family and the withering of humanistic values in the wide wake of the war and the unreflective growth of West Germany.

The mid-1950s exacerbated Böll's concerns about the political and moral direction of West Germany: Its rearmament, its decision to join NATO, and its lax attitude toward former Nazis led Böll to question even more aggressively the moral foundations of the FRG. Amid his growing skepticism about the maturing republic, Böll published two of his most important novels, BILLIARDS AT HALF PAST NINE (*Billard um halbzehn,* 1959) and *The Clown* (*Ansichten eines Clowns,* 1963). *Billiards* traces the history of Germany from the pre–World War I imperial to the postwar period through three generations of the fictional Fähmel family. The central male figures of this family are all architects, and all have a tortured relationship to the novel's central symbol, the Abbey of St. Anton. Böll divides his characters into "buffaloes," "lambs," and "shepherds" depending on their relationship to violence and power; though he later criticized this schema as too reductive, it did demonstrate important historical continuities, especially among Germany's compromised ruling elite. *The Clown* was similarly critical of the restorationist postwar era, especially of the Catholic Church and its accommodations of prevailing military and economic interests. In the first-person narrator and eponymous clown, Hans Schnier, Böll offered the first in a string of radically nonconformist protagonists, but the narcissistic and self-involved clown hardly offers much hope, despite his social and political acuity.

The clown, Hans Schnier, was the first of a series of deliberately nonconformist protagonists, including those in Böll's next three major books. The short text ABSENT WITHOUT LEAVE (*Entfernung von der Truppe*, 1964) features an active resister to obligatory service who finds that his humanity started when his service ended. The text is written in a more emphatically avant-garde style than Böll's earlier work, including the use of documentary-literary techniques and direct reader address. In *End of a Mission* (*Ende einer Dienstfahrt*, 1966), a father and son burn an army jeep and have to defend themselves in court, which also allows for the introduction of different textual materials (testimony, court documents, and so on) into the narrative.

Both texts serve as formal and thematic rehearsal for Böll's next major novel, GROUP PORTRAIT WITH LADY (*Gruppenbild mit Dame*, 1971), which was decisive in his winning the Nobel Prize in literature a year later. In *Group Portrait*, a narrator is researching the life of the renegade Leni Pfeiffer in order to recast and reread Germany history from the 1920s through the narrative present of 1970/71. Leni's early biography corresponds to that of many middle-class women during the Nazi years, but there are also hints of her later nonconformity, including her coming under the guidance of a Jewish nun in school. During the war, she makes a small gesture of strictly forbidden charity by offering a Russian slave worker, Boris, a cup of coffee. By the end of the text, the narrator/researcher has become emotionally involved with Leni and rallies to her, as does a "Help-Leni-Committee," to save her house from predatory real-estate-speculator relatives, more critical symbols of the materialist Federal Republic.

Group Portrait with Lady was celebrated in part because of its summation and completion of Böll's engagement with Nazism and its consequences. The texts grouped together in Böll's last phase turn to the contemporary context of the 1970s and early 1980s. In *The Lost Honor of Katharina Blum, or: How Violence Develops and Where it Can Lead* (*Die verlorene Ehe der Katharina Blum oder: Wie Gewalt entstehen kann und wohin sie führt*, 1974), Böll attacks the way in which the national panic about, and sensationalist press preying upon, the threat of domestic terrorism can victimize the innocent—here a young, apolitical woman who unwittingly shelters a wanted man for one night. In *The Safety Net* (*Fürsorgliche Belagerung*, 1979), Böll

continued his investigation of terrorism and its impact on German society, although the novel also elaborates the interest in the elites of West German society that he had demonstrated as early as *Billiards*. Böll's last novel, published two months after his death on 16 July 1985, extends his development of female characters as mirrors for their times and as repositories for history. *Women in a River Landscape* (*Frauen vor Flußlandschaft*, 1985) tracks the lives of women (wives, girlfriends) of prominent families in and around Germany's new capital, Bonn, thereby creating a counternarrative, one weighed down by the past and dulled by the present, of the postwar "Bonner" Republic.

Böll's late works further and deepen his indefatigable skepticism about postwar German society, his deep-seated concern about the loss of humanism, and his unfaltering sense of the burden of German history. In an interview, Böll once said that "as an author," only two themes interested him, love and religion, but his comment obscures how his work insists that love and religion always unfold in a political and moral context. This political and moral concern did intermittently manifest itself in overt political activity for Böll: He was sporadically involved in politics in the 1970s and 1980s, coediting pamphlets on democracy and pacifism and giving speeches at protests against U.S. nuclear arms in Germany. He eventually supported the emergent Green Party, whose main foundation still bears Böll's name. But despite his public engagement, Böll maintained that his work concerned not so much contingent historical events or politics as the "mythological-theological" and the longer-term decay of bourgeois society. Böll's relentlessness in this examination extended to the rigors of his style. His point of literary departure is European realism, but he subjects this tradition to the mechanisms of memory, moral questioning, and ethical quandaries. Widely celebrated and deeply appreciated for both its literary and moral acumen, Böll's life and work spanned and addressed the vicissitudes of 20th-century German history and never shied from the country's responsibilities for its actions.

BIBLIOGRAPHY

Böll, Heinrich. *Short Stories*. Translated by Leila Vennewitz. Evanston, Ill.: Northwestern University Press, 1995.

———. *Stories, Political Writings, and Autobiographical Works*. Edited by Martin Black. New York: Continuum, 2006.

Butler, Michael. *The Narrative Fiction of Heinrich Böll: Social Conscience and Literary Achievement*. Cambridge and New York: Cambridge University Press, 1994.

Conrad, Robert C. *Understanding Heinrich Böll*. Columbia: University of South Carolina Press, 1992.

Reed, Donna K. *The Novel and the Nazi Past*. New York: Peter Lang, 1985.

Zachau, Reinhard K. *Heinrich Böll: Forty Years of Criticism*. Columbia, S.C.: Camden House, 1994.

Jaimey Fisher

BOOK OF LAUGHTER AND FORGET-TING, THE (KNIHA SMICHU A ZAPO-MNĚNI) MILAN KUNDERA (1978)

Set in postwar Czechoslovakia in the aftermath of the Stalinist purges of World War II, *The Book of Laughter and Forgetting* is "a novel in the form of variations" that explores how totalitarianism affects individual and collective, national and personal, memories. MILAN KUNDERA (1929–   ) traces the interrelated lives of a handful of characters who are each trying to recover or banish poignant memories. Much of the novel is based on Kundera's own knowledge of totalitarianism; following the Russian invasion of Czechoslovakia in 1968, Kundera lost his teaching post at the Academy of Music and Dramatic Arts, saw his books removed from the shelves of public libraries, and was banned from publishing in his homeland.

Divided into seven parts, the first section of the novel follows Mirek, a once-celebrated researcher who has been forced to leave his job and is surrounded by undercover agents. The character observes that "the struggle of man against power is the struggle of memory against forgetting." Yet throughout the novel, Kundera demonstrates that historical revision occurs not only at a national level but in private, everyday life as well. Kundera alternates between presenting characters' interior monologues and the narrator's reflections on philosophical and theoretical questions that arise, including: What constitutes history? Where do memories adhere and how are they recovered? What are the origins and characteristics of laughter? As usual, he presents these brief narratives using flashbacks, autho-

rial asides, and other frameworks. The novel is comprised of revealing episodes, often of a sexual nature, that function as studies of larger, pervasive themes.

The first and fourth sections of the novel—both entitled "Lost Letters"—introduce characters who are trying to track down documents from their past but are motivated by opposed impulses. Mirek tries to recover incriminating letters from his former mistress, Zdena, in order to put them out of reach of the state. Although she refuses to return the letters, he is compelled to reexamine their relationship, discovering that he had unwittingly falsified it. In contrast, Tamina, a waitress in a provincial town and the main heroine of the novel, yearns to preserve an accurate memory of her beloved late husband. Still mourning her loss, she tries to retrieve their love letters from her mother-in-law's house in Prague, hoping that they will restore her memory of her husband and their shared past. When Hugo, one of her regular customers, promises to retrieve the package, she halfheartedly enters into a relationship with him. When she discovers that Hugo has no intention of going to Prague, she becomes revolted by their relationship and her own dispassionate sexual submission.

Tamina reappears in part six in a surreal fantasy-adventure in which she is mysteriously led to an island inhabited entirely by children. Tamina, whose sexual maturity marks her as an outsider, faces a future of interminable, childish routines. At first the children fetishize her as a sexual object, then they begin to resent and torment her, and finally they regard her as an aberration and watch gloatingly as she drowns in an attempted escape from the island. In the course of her journey, Tamina discovers that sexuality, freed from the ties of love, becomes "a joy of *angelic* simplicity," but that the absence of weight or significance can also result in "a terrifying *burden of buoyancy*."

Laughter and Forgetting, like Kundera's later novels, investigates dichotomies such as weight and lightness; public and private; mind and body; and boundless love and *litost* (a Czech word meaning "a state of torment caused by a sudden insight into one's own miserable self") to uncover the origins of these oppositions. For example, the narrator posits that there are two kinds of laughter—angelic and demonic—and that, taken to their extreme, the former produces fanaticism, while the latter results in skepticism. He argues that individuals must maintain "equilibrium of power" between the two forms of laughter, since one would collapse under either the burden of uncontested meaning or the burden of meaningless buoyancy.

Throughout the novel, Kundera explores how history is constructed and how modernity has altered our perception of time. The narrator argues that whereas in the past, history served as a more or less static backdrop against which our personal lives unfolded, in the 20th century, history progresses rapidly, so that our private lives appear banal and plodding in contrast to the novelty of historical events. Kundera challenges the reader's assumptions about history, memory, love, and sex at every turn, placing distinctive characters in extraordinary situations in order to test and elucidate his theories. Above all else, *Laughter and Forgetting* examines the political and philosophical consequences of pushing human impulses to their furthest extremes; or, to put it another way, it explores the basic emotional origins of radical politics.

BIBLIOGRAPHY

Aji, Aron, ed. *Milan Kundera and the Art of Fiction: Critical Essays.* New York: Garland, 1992.

Pifer, Ellen. "*The Book of Laughter and Forgetting*: Kundera's Narration Against Narration." *Journal of Narrative Technique* 22, no. 2 (1992): 84–96.

Straus, Nina Pelikan. "Erasing History and Deconstructing the Text: Milan Kundera's *The Book of Laughter and Forgetting*." *Critique* 28, no. 2 (1987): 69–85.

Weeks, Mark. "Milan Kundera: A Modern History of Humor amid the Comedy of History." *Journal of Modern Literature* 28, no. 3 (2005): 130–148.

Shayna D. Skarf

BOROWSKI, TADEUSZ (1922–1951) *Polish novelist, poet, short story writer*

Tadeusz Borowski was part of a generation of Polish writers and poets (including Zbiegniew Herbert and Nobel laureate Wysława Szymborska) who came of age during the Nazi invasion of Poland and, after the war, the occupation by the Soviet Union. Although Polish, Borowski was born in what was part of the Soviet Union (Ukraine) in 1922. In 1926 his father was sent to a Soviet labor camp; four years later his mother was also arrested and deported. He was brought up by relatives until 1932, when his father was released and they both moved to Warsaw. Two years later, Borowski's mother joined them.

Borowski was a student until 1940, but by then Poland was occupied. As there was no formal education beyond the basic level in Poland, Borowski, like many, attended the underground universities that sprung up in Poland. To earn his living, he was actively engaged in the black market economy. His activities were typical in a country where the Germans not only ruled but sought to destroy national institutions.

In 1942 Borowski published his first book of poems through the underground Polish press. The following year he and his fiancée (the Maria of his poems and short stories) were arrested and sent to Auschwitz. Removed to Dachau in the summer of 1944, Borowski was liberated in May 1945. Until May 1946, when he returned to Poland, he remained mostly at an Allied-administered camp for displaced persons near Munich. His experience in this camp as a ward of the victorious Allies is also described in some of his short stories. In the meantime, Maria had gone to Sweden after the war. Although she did not want to return to communist Poland, she eventually relented and joined Borowski in November 1946.

Borowski's life took a significant turn when he became a journalist, eventually working for the Polish Bureau of Information. He was a political writer for the remaining years of his life, publishing no fiction, and committed suicide in 1951 at the age of 29. He did not leave a suicide note, and there has always been a cloud of speculation about the reasons that led to his death. At the time he was having marital problems, and a friend had been arrested by the state police. Additionally, according to some he may have had doubts about what he had done in becoming a polemicist for the new regime.

Borowski wrote two collections of short stories published after the war: *Farewell to Maria* (*Pożegnanie z Marią*, 1948) and *World of Stone* (*Kamienny Swiat*). Stories from these collections were published as a collective and unified narrative in English under the title *This Way for the Gas, Ladies and Gentlemen* (*Pożegnanie z Marią*, 1992). The stories are so unified that the complete work challenges traditional notions of the novel form.

In these linked narratives, the author describes the daily life of prisoners, those who struggle to live (and do so through their integration into the machinery that allows the camps to go on) and those who are doomed. With a high degree of precision, he categorizes the various places in the camp hierarchy, the different jobs with their privileges, and the accommodations that one must make to keep a job and thus hang on to life. In one story the narrator says that he and his fellows are not evoking evil irresponsibly or in vain because they have all become a party to it. In another story ("The People Who Walked On") the question raised—"Will evil ever be punished?"—finds no satisfactory answer, as of course there could be none after the experience of the concentration camps.

Borowski published two collections of poems during and immediately after the war: *When Ever the Earth* (*Gdziekolwiek*) and *The Names of Currents* (*Iniona Nurtu*). Poems from both collections were published in English as *Selected Poems*. His poetry is very bleak. In one verse he asks: "Who dares after this terrible war / to chant slogans in town squares?"—an ironic question given his role as a political propagandist in the years before his death.

Borowski's poems and stories remain highly disturbing. While he raised questions of complicity with evil years before Primo Levi's *The Grey Zone,* he did so in a way that makes very clear its self-loathing, disgust, and anger for all others who also struck a bargain with evil in order to survive.

The poet Czeslaw Milosz, in his analysis of the effects of the communist seizure of power over writers in *The Captive Mind* (*Zniewdony Umgel*) devoted a chapter to Borowski ("Beta, The Disappointed Lover"). According to Milosz, Borowski "had not faith, religious or other, and he had the courage to admit it in his poems." Also, Milosz notes that one of the lessons learned and articulated in the short stories was that hurting others in concentration camp society was permissible, provided they harmed you first. It needs to be remembered in assessing Borowski that he was the product of a time that included more than just the horror of German occupation and time spent in a concentration camp. In his youth, he saw not only the loss of his parents to the camps but also lived in Ukraine during the time of its collectivization and ensuing famines. Borowski was a poet of despair not from an internal perspective but as one who had observed and lived through the nightmare of European history in the first half of the 20th century.

BIBLIOGRAPHY

Borowski, Tadeusz. *This Way to the Gas, Ladies and Gentlemen.* Translated by Barbara Vedder. New York: Penguin Books, 1976.

Hatley, James. *Suffering Witness: The Quandary of Responsibility after the Irreparable.* Albany, N.Y.: State University of New York Press, 2000.

Robert N. Stacy

BOTCHAN Natsume Sōseki (1906)   *Botchan* is one of the best-loved novels in Japan and a true comic masterpiece. Written at the beginning of the 20th century by Natsume Sōseki (1867–1916), the novel tells the story of a gauche middle school teacher. Botchan, or "little master," is a 23-year-old Tokyoite who takes a teaching job in Shikoku, the smallest of the four main Japanese islands. Botchan quickly gets into a series of difficulties with students and fellow teachers, to whom he unabashedly gives his own private nicknames. In part these difficulties arise from his lack of social skills, which is to say his unwillingness to play social games. He is overly straightforward and honest in his encounters with students and fellow teachers.

The protagonist's bluntness, as well as an ardent passion for justice, is refreshing, especially when it affects his personal well-being. For instance, Botchan likes to frequent bathhouses and to indulge in his favorite dishes at dumpling restaurants. Although these activities are officially frowned upon, he believes that they are small compensations for his immurement in a remote provincial town. He also gets into a running battle with a group of students who play practical jokes on him in an effort to get rid of the "new teacher." However, the centerpiece of the novel is a quarrel between Botchan and the politically powerful, hypocritical Redshirt. So named because he wears a red flannel shirt all year, Redshirt has been plotting to steal the fiancée of Koga, the self-effacing, good-natured teacher of English. To achieve this, he bullies Koga into accepting a transfer to a school in a distant province.

This leads to a battle of wills between him and the head of mathematics, Porcupine, who in a meeting with Redshirt tells him that he must repeal the transfer. To further this intrigue, Redshirt invites Botchan out on a fishing trip with him and his ally, the sycophantic art teacher named Clown. On the boat, while Botchan is napping, the two men hold a conversation meant to be overheard and insinuate that Porcupine had instigated the students to put grasshoppers in Botchan's bed while he was off taking a bath during a recent night-duty stint at the school dormitory. Botchan and Porcupine fall out as a result, for in the interim Clown has also been scheming behind the scenes. Porcupine, who is Botchan's immediate superior, had helped him find lodgings when he first arrived in town. Hoping to take over these lodgings, however, Clown has pressured the landlord to tell tales to Porcupine and lie to him about Botchan's supposed rowdiness and insolence. Botchan and Porcupine are similar in temperament. Both are forthright and fiery, and for a moment there is a real danger that their altercation will be explosive. Fortunately, however, they discover Redshirt and Clown's machinations in the nick of time and quickly agree to patch up their differences.

Nevertheless, matters come to a head when Redshirt, through his brother, gets Botchan and Porcupine embroiled in a fight between rival school contingents at a ceremony commemorating a military victory. Not only are they hurt, they are wrongly implicated as instigators of the fight, and thus they will have to leave their positions at the school. In response, Botchan and Porcupine decide to teach Redshirt a lesson. Redshirt had rebuked Botchan at a staff meeting for indulging in essentially innocuous recreational activities. However the two men know about Redshirt's hypocrisy in these matters. They rent a room overlooking a brothel that they know he frequents. After a wait of several nights, they catch Redshirt and Clown leaving the premises. In a comic scene, they give the two groveling cowards a sound thrashing and a scolding. Fearful that his reputation will be ruined, Redshirt does not dare to tell the police; and with that the novel closes. Botchan and Porcupine leave Shikoku. Although they have lost their jobs, they are happy that they have won a great victory over the Redshirts and Clowns of the world. Botchan

returns to Tokyo, where he takes up a job at a transport company.

In a sense, *Botchan* is an idyll. It allows one to remember with affection the idealism that perhaps came easier at an earlier stage in life, before the compromises of adulthood set in. The novel produces a feeling of spiritual renewal through the picture of Botchan speaking his mind without fear or favor. His passion for the truth, his disregard for convention, and his disdain for self-advancement are hugely admirable qualities. Not surprisingly, they help the book transcend its historical and cultural setting, allowing it to win new readers with each subsequent generation.

BIBLIOGRAPHY

Gessel, Van C. *Three Modern Novelists: Soseki, Tanizaki, Kawabata.* Tokyo and New York: Kodansha, 1993.

Natsume, Soseki. *My Individualism and the Philosophical Foundations of Literature.* Translated by Sammy I. Tsunematsu. Boston: Tuttle, 2004.

———. *Rediscovering Natsume Soseki.* Translated by Sammy I. Tsunematsu. Folkestone, Kent, U.K.: Global Oriental, 2000.

Yiu, Angela. *Chaos and Order in the Works of Natsume Soseki.* Honolulu: University of Hawaii Press, 1998.

Wai-chew Sim

BOUDJEDRA, RACHID (1941–) *Algerian essayist, novelist, poet*

Rachid Boudjedra is one of the best-known Algerian authors. Writing in French, he began his career with a collection of poems, *Pour ne plus rêver,* published in 1965 by Editions Nouvelles D'Alger. Since then he has published more than 20 books, which have been translated into several languages, including the novel *The* REPUDIATION (*La répudiation,* 1969).

Born in 1941 in Ain Beida, east of Algeria, Boudjedra was brought up in a nationalist bourgeois family, with a polygamous father and 36 brothers and sisters. He started school in Constantine and went to high school in Tunis. During the Algerian War of Independence (1954–62), he dropped his studies to join the armed struggle against French colonialism in Algiers (1830–1962). Injured, he left the battlefield and later traveled to eastern Europe and Spain as a representative of the National Liberation Front.

After Algeria finally gained independence from France in 1962, Boudjedra returned to his home country. He took up studies in philosophy at Algiers University and then went to Paris, where he completed an undergraduate degree in philosophy at the Sorbonne in 1965. He later taught at the Lycée Abdelkader, a high school in Algiers. He was soon forced to give up his teaching post because of his critique of the government's policies. Considered politically dangerous, he was jailed for two years. After his release in 1967, Boudjedra was exiled to Blida, an area southwest of Algiers, where he taught philosophy, French, English, and arts at the Lycée El Feth. He spent a good deal of his time during this period urging schoolgirls to emancipate themselves from masculine domination. A defender of women's rights, Boudjedra remains an active member of the Algerian League for the Defense of Human Rights.

From 1969 to 1972, Boudjedra was compelled again to go into exile after his controversial novel *The Repudiation* was published in 1969 and was awarded the French Prix des Enfants Terribles. He subsequently moved to Morocco and taught in Rabat until 1975. The period following his six-year exile paradoxically saw the author settled in what resembles social conformity. He collaborated in 1977 with an authoritarian government which he formerly fulminated against, working as an adviser for the Ministry of Culture and Information. He fully endorsed the government's Arabization policies, begun in 1975, which replaced French with Arabic languages in administration and education, thus implicitly backing the dominant ideology that negates Algeria's cultural and linguistic diversity.

In 1981 Boudjedra was appointed as a reader for La Societé Nationale d'Edition et de Diffusion (SNED), known for its censorship and loyalty to the political establishment. At this time he was offered a teaching position at the prestigious Institute of Political Studies in Algiers. The apparent conformity did not, however, prevent him from pursuing social and political critiques in both his essays and fiction. Owing to his repeated virulent attack on Islam, which he dismissed as "absolutely incompatible with modernity," a death sentence was pronounced against him in 1983.

The year 1981 is a significant date in Boudjedra's writing career. It corresponds to the period during which he abandoned the French language to write exclusively in Arabic. Some of his detractors saw this shift as a sign of allegiance to the dominant ideology. Others viewed it as a symbolic return to the metaphor of the father, a person whom the author hated and severely criticized in the earlier fiction—all the more so as classical Arabic, the medium of his writing, is the language of the literate father, his illiterate mother's idiom being dialectical Arabic. Boudjedra argued in response to these critics that his choice was mainly motivated by the twin desire to "reconnect with the Algerian authentic identity" and to modernize Arabic and the Arab novel. He wanted, above all, to transgress Arabic culture by forcing it to address sexual and religious taboos that it would have traditionally shunned.

Boudjedra is an "organic intellectual," one who is engaged in the society he criticizes and tries to reform. Through a lyrical, incisive style mingling irony and derision, realism and fantasy, and gravity and mockery, he attacks the established order and strives for gender equality and social justice. He similarly tries to unsettle the very notion of literary genre by mixing rhetorical modes and literary registers that give his fiction a composite, polyphonic character.

Polygeneric, Boudjedra's novels are also meta-referential, filled with intertextual references that reveal his literary influences. These include CLAUDE SIMON, Boudjedra's "master" and stylistic model, Saint John Perse, ALBERT CAMUS, William Faulkner, GABRIEL GARCÍA MARQUEZ, LOUIS-FERDINAND CÉLINE, and GÜNTER GRASS. Structural and thematic repetition is another key feature of Boudjedra's writing. The same themes recur with slight variations, merging the different novels into an organic whole as well as connecting the author's two artistic phases. The Arabic phase continues the French one, and within the author's canon, *The Repudiation* stands for a thematic matrix of description and word purpose. It forms a supranarrative, determining the subsequent French and Arabic texts. While *Le démentelement* (1982) is the reference point of the Arabic novels, *Le désordre des choses* (1999) links up both creative periods. This book functions as a resonance chamber echoing novels in both French and Arabic version: *La répudiation; Topographie idéale pour un crime caractérisé* (1975); *Les 1001 années de nostalgie* (1979);

Le vainqueur de coupe (1981); *La macération* (1985); and *La prise de Gibraltar* (1987). It reiterates themes and sometimes copies whole pages from these works.

BIBLIOGRAPHY

Bensmain, Abdallah. *Crise du sujet, crise de l'identité: Une lecture psychanalytique de Rachid Boudjedra.* Casablanca: Afrique Orient, 1984.

Boudjedra, Rachid. *Lettres algériennes.* Paris: B. Grasset, 1995.

Gafaïti, Hafid. *Boudjedra ou la Passion de la modernité: Entretiens avec Rachid Boudjedra.* Paris: Denoël, 1987.

———. *Rachid Boudjedra: Autobiographie et Histoire, une poétique de la subversion.* Paris: L'Harmattan, 1999.

Ibnlfassi, Laïla, and Nicki Hitchcott, eds. *African Francophone Writing: A Critical Introduction.* Oxford: Berg, 1996.

Ibrahim-Ouali, Lila. *Rachid Boudjedra: Écriture poétique et structures romanesques.* Clermont-Ferrand: Association des publications de la Faculté des Lettres et Sciences humaines de Clermont-Ferrand, 1998.

Lyons, Tom. "Ambiguous narratives." *Cultural Anthropology* 16 (2001): 832–856.

———. "The ethnographic novel and ethnography in colonial Algeria." *Modern Philology* 100, no. 4 (2003): 576–596.

Zeliche, Mohamed-Salah. *Poét(h)ique des deux rives.* Paris: Karthala, 2005.

Amar Acheraiou

BOURGET, PAUL (CHARLES-JOSEPH-PAUL BOURGET) (1852–1935) *French essayist, novelist, poet* Though often overshadowed today by his contemporaries, Paul Bourget was a popular author and considered an important contributor to the French literary scene at the turn of the 20th century. Perhaps best known for the seeming split in his literary output—his early works characterized by a focus heavily inflected by Stendhal and his later works displaying a fervent, primarily Catholic moral drive—his oeuvre nevertheless stands as a testament to its author's psychological insight (influenced by William James) and technical acumen. In addition to his fiction, Bourget was an accomplished writer of literary criticism, travel narratives, and verse.

Paul Bourget was born in Amiens, in the Picardy region of northern France, to Justin Bourget and Anne-Adèle Valentin. His father was a professor of mathematics who boasted an admirable library, and young Bourget received throughout his youth a solid grounding in classical education, excelling at the prestigious Lycée Louis-le-Grand and proving to be exceptionally intellectually precocious. Despite the promise of his achievements while in school, instead of pursuing an academic career, as his father had, Bourget chose to become a writer.

His earliest works were not fiction but poetry (*La vie inquiète,* 1875; *Edel,* 1878; *Les aveux,* 1882) and criticism (*Les essais de psychologie contemporaine,* 1883; and *Les nouveaux essais de psychologie contemporaine,* 1886). Claude Debussy, a friend of Bourget, set a number of his poems to music. Bourget's *Essais,* a collection on current writers including Charles Baudelaire and Stendhal that came to define the pessimism of the age as a product of decadence, was particularly well received and established the author as a proponent of the developing study of the psyche, an interest that would later inform his fiction.

Bourget traveled extensively, leading to a number of important literary friendships as well as travel narratives, including *Etudes et portraits* (1888), in which he describes his travels in England and Ireland; *Sensations d'Italie* (1891), based on his experiences during his honeymoon with wife, Minnie David, whom he had married in 1890; and *Outre-Mer* (1895), detailing his impressions of America during his year-long tour of 1893. His reflections on his visit to America led Mark Twain to publish a scathing rebuttal: "What Paul Bourget Thinks of Us." Nevertheless, Bourget's travels to America, combined with sympathetic interests regarding the process of writing, led to friendships with Henry James, to whom *Cruelle énigme* (1885) is dedicated, and with Edith Wharton, who described their friendship in her 1934 work *A Backward Glance.*

While Bourget's reputation today rests on his critical writing, he was a prolific writer of fiction, producing dozens of novels and multiple collections of short stories. Regrettably, few of these works remain in print, demonstrating how far out of favor Bourget has become with the critical audience and the reading public. That said, his early fiction proved remarkably popular. His first novels focused on the psychology of love and include *Cruelle énigme* (1885), *André Cornélis* (1886), and *Mensonges* (1887). These works capitalized on the growing public (and critical) disdain for the naturalism of, for example, Émile Zola's works, and secured for Bourget a prominent place among popular writers. Beginning with The DISCIPLE (*Le disciple,* 1889), Bourget began moving away from the Taine-inflected spiritualism of his early novels to a more outwardly moralistic and monarchist tone (perhaps furthered by his conversion to Catholicism) that struck some critics and much of his public as heavy-handed. Later highlights of his vast oeuvre include COSMOPOLIS (1893), *The Emigrant* (*L'émigré,* 1907), and The NIGHT COMETH (*Le sens de la mort,* 1915). Often overlooked is Bourget's prolific output of *nouvelles*—he published some 21 volumes of short stories, many of which are thought to equal his best novels in quality. In the shorter frame, the didacticism of the longer works give way to discrete insight and character motivations.

Though he continued to write and publish into the last years of his life, after World War I Bourget's works failed to keep up with the quickly changing political, social, and literary attitudes of his world. He died on Christmas morning, 1935.

Paul Bourget's literary reputation, much like his fiction, is marked by a schism. His early standing in France can be witnessed by his admission to the Académie française in 1895 (an honor denied to Victor Hugo, Honoré de Balzac, and Émile Zola, among other writers), to that date the youngest man elected to the honor. With the passage of time, however, Bourget's contributions, while significant, have come under increasing scrutiny. The imprint of his moralistic overtones have become ever more important to the consideration of his works, which have often been labeled pedantic, even by critics who admit his powerful command of plot and psychological study of character. The escalation of conservatism in his political and personal beliefs cost him readership and popularity in his day, and the trend has continued, with little scholarly attention paid to Bourget's fiction in the decades since his death.

BIBLIOGRAPHY

Austin, Lloyd James. *Paul Bourget, sa vie et son oeuvre jusqu'en 1889.* Paris: E. Droz, 1940.

Autin, Albert. *Le disciple de Paul Bourget.* Paris: Société Française, 1930.

Mansuy, Michel. *Un moderne: Paul Bourget de l'enfance au Discipline.* Paris: Les Belles letters, 1960.

Singer, Armand E. *Paul Bourget.* Boston: Twayne Publishers, 1976.

Rebecca N. Mitchell

BRETON, ANDRÉ (1896–1966) *French essayist, novelist, poet*

The French poet, novelist, essayist, critic, and editor André Breton is best remembered as the chief theorist of the surrealist movement and one of its founders in 1924. Breton is also known as "le Pape du Surréalisme" (the pope of surrealism) since over the years he came to consider surrealism as an extension of his own vision of art and single-handedly expelled from the group anyone he did not agree with. His novel NADJA remains popular today for its illustration of surrealist art.

André Breton was born in the small town of Tinchebray, Normandy, on February 18, 1896. As was the case for most men of his generation and most surrealist artists, Breton's life was tremendously influenced by World War I. After briefly studying medicine and neuropsychiatry, he worked as a hospital orderly in various army psychiatric hospitals (Nantes, Pitié, Val-de-Grâce, Saint-Mammès) during the Great War. In this work he came across soldiers whose mental balance had been severely affected by the atrocities of war; he was also first exposed to the theories of Freud on the unconscious and the dream state, which had an enormous impact on surrealism. Breton vaguely tried Freudian psychoanalysis on his patients at the army wards and found their war-induced nightmares fascinating. At that time he made one of the crucial encounters of this life in a convalescing soldier called Jacques Vaché, whose rebellious stance toward war and social order Breton admired and emulated. In 1919 Vaché killed himself with an opium overdose, but his war letters collection (*War Letters* [*Lettres de guerre,* 1919]) published posthumously featured introductory essays by Breton. At the time, Vaché's letters had a significant impact on the newly founded dada movement.

With World War I came into existence an artistic revolution, an aesthetic upheaval called dadaism. Dada was chiefly a reaction to the absurdity of war and to prewar aesthetic values. In 1916 Breton briefly joined the dada movement, but quarrels prompted him to move on and leave dadaism behind. He had been writing poetry since early adolescence, when he discovered the works of the fellow French poets Charles Baudelaire and Stéphane Mallarmé. In 1919 in collaboration with Philippe Soupault, Breton wrote the first surrealist work, *The Magnetic Fields* (*Les champs magnétiques*). *The Magnetic Fields,* according to Philippe Soupault's 1968 interview for the French literary journal *Le magazine littéraire,* was "the invention of automatic writing, the rejection of literature," and that was for Breton "a discovery, a total liberation" since he then wrote about topics he rarely discussed, such as his childhood.

Surrealism was a word coined by French poet Guillaume Apollinaire, who called his 1918 play *The Breasts of Tiresias* (*Les mamelles de Tirésias*) "a surrealist drama"—namely, a nonnaturalistic representation of reality. As the theorist of surrealism par excellence, Breton gave ample definitions and discussions of the term in his first *Manifesto of Surrealism* (*Manifeste du Surréalisme,* 1924):

> SURREALISM, *n.* Psychic automatism in its pure state, by which one proposes to express—verbally, by means of the written word, or in any other manner—the actual functioning of thought. Dictated by the thought, in the absence of any control exercised by reason, exempt from any aesthetic or moral concern.

> ENCYCLOPEDIA. *Philosophy.* Surrealism is based on the belief in the superior reality of certain forms of previously neglected associations, in the omnipotence of dream, in the disinterested play of thought.

Whereas psychoanalytical theory widened the gap between dream and action, surrealism represented the resolution of these contradictory states and freed imagination from social and mental repression. In that sense, surrealism did not solely pertain to artistic expression but to life in general; it implied the rejection of all inherited bourgeois social values, as Breton wrote in this famous sentence from *Second Manifesto of Surrealism* (*Deuxième manifeste du Surréalisme,* 1929): "The simplest Surrealist act consists of dashing down the street, pistol in hand, and firing blindly, as fast as you can pull the trigger, into the crowd." Because of its ideological message, Breton envisioned surrealism as a group, like Marxist and Fourierist cells, with members sharing the belief that all passions are good. In *Interviews* (*Entretiens,* 1952) he stressed "the superiority of impassioned people to people with common sense."

Breton's *Manifestos,* his stance for a free expression of the unconscious through art, struck a cord with various artists in postwar Europe. French poets such as Paul Eluard, Philippe Soupault, Antonin Artaud, and Louis Aragon were at one point surrealists, as were Spanish director Luis Buñuel and Belgian artist René Magritte. Due to many inner ideological and personal conflicts, most members were, at some point, thrown out of the group by Breton. From its inception, surrealism was in a constant state of flux, but its first magazine, *The Surrealist Revolution* (*La Révolution surréaliste,* 1924–30), and its second one, *Surrealism at the Service of Revolution* (*Le Surréalisme au service de la révolution,* 1930–33), managed to spread its ideas beyond French borders.

Breton never lost touch with the politics of his time, and there was an effective link between surrealism and communism from 1927 to 1935. In 1927 Breton joined the French Communist Party, creating enormous tensions within the surrealist group. Through sheer disgust with the Stalinist purges of 1935, however, he broke off from communism but never ceased to believe in Marxism. In 1938 Breton met Leon Trotsky in Mexico and founded with him the Federation for the Independent Revolutionary Art (La Fédération de l'Art Révolutionnaire Indépendant).

André Breton's most important work of the 1920s is his novel *Nadja* (1928). Its starting point is an autobiographical event in Breton's life when he met, in October 1926, a woman called Leona, who had chosen the name Nadja "because in Russian it is the beginning of the word 'hope' and because it is only its beginning." Breton kept on seeing Nadja until February 1927, and the novel was written shortly after their split, between August and December that year. The end of the relationship with Nadja corresponded to a time of severe personal and ideological crisis in the writer's life: Breton had a tinge of guilt when Nadja, shortly after their relationship ended, had to be placed in a psychiatric ward, while at the same time he had to face the internal surrealist crisis generated by his public support for the French Communist Party.

André Breton systematically rejected writing conventions and, through *Nadja,* rejected the novel as a genre produced by 19th-century French bourgeois values. As Breton's personal papers prove, the many drawings, letters, and inventive phrases in the novel were generated by the real Leona; in that sense, *Nadja* could be viewed as traditional semiautobiographical narration. However, the numerous photographs and works of art that are an integral part of the text give a totally new topography to the novel and place it outside novelistic conventions. Breton used 44 photographs in the book, including portraits by Man Ray and various shots of Paris by Jacques-André Boiffard and Henri Manuel. *Nadja*'s "report" look was not coincidental at a time when surrealists had opened a Bureau for Surrealist Research at 15 rue de Grenelle, where people were invited to present testimonies in order to "gather all the information possible related to forms that might express the unconscious activity of the mind."

Breton presented *Nadja* as the product of automatic writing, a manifestation of unconscious activity and a series of ramblings set within Paris, a city that surrealists celebrated. It is a very loose narrative that begins with the narrator's question "Who am I?" and is then strung around a series of chance meetings, first with Nadja, then with various members of the surrealist group and unconventional characters. As a character, Nadja is beyond the bounds of reason, and the writer's fascination for the manifestations of the unconscious is very apparent. That attraction for madness precisely illustrates one of the most important chasms between surrealism and psychoanalysis: Unlike Freud, Breton failed to see madness as an illness.

Nadja has often been defined as a novel of "mad love" depicting the intense attraction for a mysterious woman-sorceress who endlessly enchants and surprises the narrator. It is hardly surprising that one of the numerous collections of poems that André Breton published in the 1930s was entitled *Mad Love* (*L'amour fou,* 1937),

which defended the irrational quality of love. At the end of that decade, Breton also started his rehabilitation work of various forgotten genres and unrecognized authors with the publication in 1940 of his *Anthology of Black Humor* (*Anthologie de l'humour noir*). He pursued it further with his homages to Marquis de Sade, Comte de Lautréamont, and Arthur Rimbaud.

During the Nazi occupation of France in 1941, Breton fled to Martinique and from there to the East Coast of the United States. In New York City he worked in broadcasting, organized a surrealist exhibit in 1942, and created the review *VVV*. When he returned to France in 1946, Breton, unlike many author intellectuals, refused to follow the official French Communist Party line. Through the 1950s and until his death in Paris on September 28, 1966, he gave his support to a second surrealist group through various exhibits and magazines.

BIBLIOGRAPHY

Breton, André. *Manifestes du Surréalisme.* Paris: Folio, 1985.
———. *Nadja.* Paris: Gallimard, 1928.
———. *Poems of André Breton: A Bilingual Anthology.* Translated by Jean-Pierre Cauvin and Mary Ann Caws. Boston: Commonwealth Books/Black Widow Press, 2006.
Durozoi, Gerard. *History of the Surrealist Movement.* Translated by Alison Anderson. Chicago: Chicago University Press, 2002.
Polizzotti, Mark. *Revolution of the Mind: The Life of André Breton.* New York: Farrar, Straus, 1995.
Le Surréalisme: Anthologie. Paris: Flammarion, 2002.

Annick Durand

BRIDGE ON THE DRINA, THE (*DA DRINI ĆUPRIJA*) Ivo Andrić (1945)

The Bridge on the Drina is the novel that brought international acclaim—as well as the 1961 Nobel Prize—to the Yugoslav writer Ivo Andrić (1892–1975). Written during World War II, this short novel is the best expression of Andrić's singular vision of the Balkan region as the bridge between the Orient and the Occident, the East and the West. *The Bridge on the Drina* is part of a trilogy, all published in 1945, that includes *Bosnia Story* (*Travnicka Hronika*) and *The Woman from Sarajevo* (*Gospodjica*).

The Balkans is the historic and geographic name used to describe a region of southeastern Europe. The area takes its name from the Balkan mountains running through the center of Bulgaria into eastern Serbia. Under the formal guise of emphatic localisms, the novel bespeaks the universal condition of struggle and suffering. This human toil, however, generates empathy and solidarity that cross ethnicities, religions, and races. Andrić's storytelling functions as the very point of human unification.

The Bridge on the Drina takes the form of a historical chronicle of Višegrad, a small town in eastern Bosnia where Andrić spent his childhood. The novel centers on a particular focal point in that community—a bridge across the Drina river, built upon the edict of the Turkish vizier Mehmed Pasha Sokolli in 1516. Through the image of the bridge, the novel traces Bosnian history from 1516 to 1914, interweaving several narratives in the transgenerational depiction of a borderline town in which different ethnicities—Orthodox Serbs, Catholic Croats, Muslims, Roma people, and Sephardic Jews—mingled and lived together, most of the time in peace. These diverse peoples reveal their struggles to conquer nature and survive in the turmoil of history. Throughout the centuries they forge a cohesive alternative history marked by a common cultural heritage, a shared mixed language, legends, anecdotes, and tales. The bridge and the river below it become the symbolic and dynamic representations of this human endeavor. More so, the bridge becomes the major character in this cross-generational tale. Its own history is emphatically that of an ethnic mélange.

In all his novels, Andrić is particularly interested in the characters whose ethnicity is marginalized or problematic or has undergone multiple historical vicissitudes. In *The Bridge on the Drina* such a character is Mehmed Pasha Sokolli, the Christian peasant snatched as a little boy by the Turks. Mehmed Pasha, one of many boys acquired in this forceful way, eventually becomes a Turkish vizier. Pained by the memory of his lost childhood and nationality, the vizier imagines the construction of a stone bridge in his hometown. This initiating story encapsulates the symbolic framing of the bridge. Spatially, the bridge is a meeting point metaphor, the location at which the diverse peoples get together and unite in its creation and protection. Temporally, the stone bridge is also a symbol of endurance

of human creation as contrasted with the transient lives of those who have lived by it.

The novel is structured as a series of narrative-historical vignettes around the unifying character of the bridge. Each chapter relates a historical and personal event or an anecdote from the bridge's construction. These narratives continue to the partial destruction of the bridge at the beginning of World War I. The stories span centuries and gain their meaning in interrelation: The legend about the stone builder who tried to prevent the bridge construction and finished his life impaled on its highest point gets refracted in the tale about a woman's tragic escape from a loveless marriage or in the mysterious anecdote about gambling with the devil. The bridge functions as the organizational device that strings this whole series of stories or chapters into a novel and is therefore the very epitome of the activity of storytelling.

The cultural events expressed as narrative movements across periods of time are given different weights by the author. Whereas much attention is dedicated to the construction of the bridge (three chapters) as well as to the history of the 19th century (10 chapters) and the early 20th century (nine chapters), the 17th and 18th centuries—the historically monolithic period of Ottoman rule in the area—are covered in only one chapter. This imbalance points to the real provenance of these stories: They are preserved and continuously reshaped by people's memory.

It is for this reason that some events in the novel acquire greater value and some—less picturesque ones—vanish in oblivion. In this way general history meets an altered history in Andrić's novel: The historical records are refracted through and even censored by the unrecorded history of personal or local events, of legends, anecdotes, and stories. The perseverance of the story—bridge-as-a story—brings to the fore the very act of narration. It is through this activity, according to Andrić, that the human suffering and toil may still acquire an intrinsic value.

Widely recognized as belonging to the heights of South Slavic literature, Andrić's *The Bridge on the Drina* elicits additional interest among readers in the light of the Kosovo and Sarajevo crises in the 1990s, including broader issues of geography, nationalism, and modern nation building in the region. Rich in evocative power, the novel is one of the best and most complex representations of the tumultuous, yet fascinating history of the Balkans.

BIBLIOGRAPHY

Cooper, Henry R., Jr. "The Structure of *The Bridge on the Drina*." *The Slavic and East European Journal* 27, no. 3 (1983).

Hawkesworth, Celia. *Ivo Andric: Bridge Between East and West.* London and Dover, N.H.: Athlone Press, 1984.

Juričić, Želimir B. *The Man and the Artist: Essays on Ivo Andrić.* Lanham, Md.: University Press of America, 1986.

Vucinich, Wayne, ed. *Ivo Andric Revisited: The Bridge Still Stands.* Berkeley: University of California Regents, 1996.

Sanja Bahun-Radunovic

BRIEF LIFE, A (*LA VIDA BREVE*) Juan Carlos Onetti (1950)   *A Brief Life* is the first major novel by Juan Carlos Onetti (1909–94), although the work is fourth in chronological order when placed with his related novels. It marks a watershed in the Uruguay-born Onetti's career as well as in Latin American novels. Onetti seemed well aware that the previous path of nativism was no longer acceptable and that the Latin American novel had to follow the path of modernization. *A Brief Life,* among other things, must be regarded as a central contribution to the coming of birth of a new novelistic pattern.

A Brief Life's main character is Juan María Brausen. The setting is Buenos Aires, where Brausen witnesses the arrival of the prostitute La Queca in the flat next to his, as well as the removal of his wife Gertrudis's left breast. This prompts a series of reflections about his life and his marriage. Gertrudis's operation and subsequent problems emphasize the split between the couple, and she eventually returns permanently to her mother in Temperley. As a consequence, Brausen begins a new relationship with La Queca and evolves a new identity, that of Arce. He then begins to imagine and write the story of Doctor Díaz Grey in Santa María. These two narratives interweave and run parallel throughout the rest of the novel.

When he loses his job, Brausen devotes himself to both projects. He visits Montevideo with La Queca and sees Gertrudis's sister, with whom he becomes involved, though he abandons her in the end. In this trip his identity as Arce develops and grows stronger. When they return to Buenos Aires, Brausen plans to murder La Queca in order to avoid the routine of their relationship. Meanwhile, the story of Díaz Grey has been developing from an initial scene to an adulterous relationship with the fictional Elena Sala. During Díaz Grey's search for Elena, he meets the young Annie Glaeson. Meanwhile Brausen has met Ernesto, one of La Queca's former lovers, and kills La Queca. Brausen and Ernesto flee to Santa María and are discovered by the police. In the final chapter, narrated by Díaz Grey himself, there is a confrontation with the police, but Díaz Grey and Annie seem to walk away unhindered.

As in most of his novels and short stories, Onetti shows that failure is an overwhelming pattern in *A Brief Life.* As some critics have argued, the novel deals with the issues of the uncertainty of the real and the process of degradation of the universe, which eventually means a lack of hope and of trust in humankind. Onetti is not concerned with the condition of Latin Americans. That is the reason why he does not involve himself in the dialectics of nativism versus civilization. His objective is the disillusioned analysis of universal humankind rooted in concrete characters and settings.

Central to Onetti's literary aim is the writing of a novel that goes beyond concrete realism. His are not fantastic novels, nor are his works realistic in a strict sense of the term. Onetti shared with the esteemed short story writer Jorge Luis Borges a concern for discrediting concrete reality and creating a vision that may oppose it. This is what may be clearly seen in *A Brief Life.* Naturally, to achieve his purpose the author had to reject traditional ways of storytelling and had to learn new narrative devices from authors other than Uruguayan (or Spanish-speaking) writers. The main narrative device present in the novel, as well as in the majority of the novels of his mature period, is the story filtered through various subjective narrators, which accounts for the ultimate subjectivity and unreality of the story. Onetti's other devices are the lack of a strict chronological sequence in the telling; an ultimate uncertainty about human personality, motive, or even events themselves; and the use of irony, ambivalence, paradox, and oxymoron. He acquired his narrative devices from the British and American modernists, namely Joseph Conrad and William Faulkner.

There is a more complex pattern of the narrative voice in *A Brief Life* than in the previous long narratives. Brausen is the main narrator of his own story, though when recalling past moments, the older Brausen acts as the primary storyteller. Díaz Grey's narrative is subordinated to Brausen's and is narrated mostly by Brausen, although at the end of the novel (part II, chapter XVII), Díaz Grey loses his subordinate status as a narrator and narrates the story himself while serving as a character as well.

Brausen's role as a narrator helps create the novel's fictional world. It introduces conjecture and speculative assertion in the world, while Brausen reacts against the world around him. Brausen's analysis of his own behavior and that of others does not lead to a psychological novel. In fact, Onetti's attempt is to move away from the psychological novel as practiced in the 19th century and establish a new sort of literary realism that may confront traditional realism and contemporary society. That is the final reason for the catalogue of misdemeanors that compound *A Brief Life*.

A Brief Life seems to be the resolution of the first novels in the chronology of Onetti's novels. If each protagonist in the previous novels struggles against dilemmas and problems, eventually Brausen has produced a resolution, and this may make the novel the culmination of Onetti's early writing.

BIBLIOGRAPHY

Adams, Michael Ian. *Three Authors of Alienation: Bombal, Onetti, Carpentier*. Austin: University of Texas Press, 1975.

Craig, Linda. *Juan Carlos Onetti, Manuel Puig and Luisa Valenzuela*. Rochester N.Y.: Tamesis, 2005.

Flores, Reyes E. "La vida breve: Brausen se lanza hacia un porvenir." *Revista de Crítica Literaria Latinoamericana* 29, no. 57 (2003): 151–157.

Gaspar, Catalina: "Ficción y realidad en la productividad metaficcional: A propósito de El obsceno pájaro de la noche y La vida breve." *Iberoamericana* 22, no. 2 (1998): 63–80.

Maier, Linda S. "A Mirror Game: Diffraction of Identity in La vida breve." *Romance Quarterly* 34, no. 2 (May 1987): 223–232.

Merrim, Stephanie. "La vida breve o la nostalgia de los orígenes." *Revista Iberoamericana* 52, nos. 135–136 (April, September 1986): 565–571.

Millington, Mark. *Reading Onetti: Language, Narrative and the Subject*. Liverpool: F. Cairns, 1985.

Murray, Jack. *The Landscapes of Alienation: Ideological Subversion in Kafka, Céline and Onetti*. Palo Alto, Calif.: Stanford University Press, 1991.

San Roman, Gustavo, ed. *Onetti and Others: Comparative Essays*. Albany, N.Y.: State University of New York Press, 1999.

Santiago Rodriguez

BROCH, HERMANN (1886–1951) *German essayist, novelist*

Austrian by birth, Hermann Broch is considered one of the major modernists in 20th-century German literature. His reputation rests on formally inventive and intellectually ambitious novels; critics place him next to James Joyce, ROBERT MUSIL, FRANZ KAFKA, and MARCEL PROUST. Broch's literary and philosophical ambition was not only to analyze history but also to foresee its future course. With his contributions to the fields of literature, philosophy, and the theory of human rights, he belonged to the avant-garde of his time, being a man of extraordinary insight into the human psyche as well as political constellations. Vision and exile are the two characteristics of his life and work. A first-rate theoretician in the fields of aesthetics, mass psychology, and politics, Broch saw his main topics as the loss of central values; dissolution of the traditional conception of the world; and the widening gap between art, science, and religion.

Broch was born into a prosperous Jewish family on November 1, 1886, in Vienna. The dutiful son of a textile manufacturer, he took his engineering degree and worked for some time in his family's factory. When his father retired in 1915, Broch took over the business. At the same time, he nurtured ambitions for an intellectual career. For years he wrote for various liberal journals and sporadically attended courses in mathematics, philosophy, and psychology at Vienna University, where the highly influential Vienna Circle was organized in 1929. The club's members campaigned against metaphysics as an outdated precursor of science. Broch himself believed that the task of literature was to deal with problems whose solutions elude the sciences. In

1927 he dismayed his family by selling the plant and declaring his intention to pursue a doctorate. But within a year, disappointed with his professors' reluctance to consider metaphysical questions, Broch abandoned his studies and turned to fiction writing.

At the age of 45, Broch published his first novel, the trilogy *The Sleepwalkers* (*Die Schlafwandler,* 1931), which reflects the author's conviction that history progresses in cycles of disintegrating and reintegrating value systems. After the failure of his second novel, *The Unknown Quantity* (*Die unbekannte Grösse,* 1933), Broch's literary output fell nearly silent. He occupied himself during 1936–37 with writing for the stage and working on political treatises such as *League of Nations Resolution* (*Völkerbund-Resolution,* published posthumously in 1973). The spread of fascism soon made Broch abandon his literary projects altogether. He was arrested by the Nazis in 1938. Inspired by a vision of impending death, he wrote a few elegies, which became the core of his later masterpiece *The Death of Virgil* (*Der Tod des Vergil,* 1945). With the help of Joyce, THOMAS MANN, Albert Einstein, and others, Broch was allowed to emigrate. He moved to London, then to Scotland, and finally to the United States.

Because Broch did not have academic degrees, he was unable to obtain regular faculty appointments, but he did receive a series of grants from various fellowships, including Guggenheim and Rockefeller. He was awarded by the American Academy of Arts and Sciences and was later even nominated for the Nobel Prize. From 1940 Broch was involved in refugee work. That same year he collaborated on a project called *The City of Man: A Declaration on World Democracy,* which directed his attention to social justice, the protection of human rights, and the peaceful solution of conflicts. Not only did he write essays on literary theory, but he also provided numerous comprehensive explanations of his texts.

The dilemma of the artist in a period of crisis is the subject of Broch's *The Death of Virgil.* Here Broch attempts to reconcile the rational scientific worldview with metaphysical and intuitive ideas. In *The Guiltless* (*Die Schuldlosen,* 1950), he traces the rise of Nazism to political apathy and spiritual disorientation. *The Spell* (*Die Verzauberung,* published posthumously in 1953) is set in a small Alpine village in the 1930s where farmers fall for the promises of a fanatic fundamentalist and even participate in ritual murder.

The Sleepwalkers is Broch's first novel and one of the towering achievements of 20th-century literature. This trilogy follows the transformation of central Europe from its fin-de-siècle glory to its post–World War I decline, depicted from different angles and perspectives in order to reach what Broch called *polyhistoricism.* His notion of history subscribes to the idea that the past is best revealed by following the development of the common man, who embodies ineluctable problems of a certain era. Broch's main characters represent different stages of moral disintegration within a bourgeois society; they experience the social, political, and economic troubles as phases of personal difficulties.

The first book of the trilogy, *The Romantic,* takes place in Berlin in 1888 and portrays 19th-century realism. Joachim von Pasenow is a Prussian aristocrat who clings to a code of ethical values that some consider outdated. The second book, *The Anarchist,* moves west to Cologne and Mannheim in 1903, with a shift in focus on the urban working class. The accountant August Esch is described as a transitional figure in search of a balance of values in unstable prewar Germany. Toward the end of World War I, the men from the two books meet one another in a small village on the Moselle, Pasenow as military commander and Esch as publisher of the local newspaper. They find hope in a fanatical religious sect waiting for a redeemer. However, both characters are defeated by Huguenau, the central character in Broch's third novel in the trilogy, *The Realist* (*Die Sachlichkeit*). The Realist is an army deserter who represents the new ethical standards of a society free of values. He swindles Esch out of his newspaper and bullies Pasenow into submitting to his authority. The romanticism and anarchy of the past have given way to the forces of objectivism. Huguenau is "the only adequate child of his age" and the inevitable harbinger of fascism.

According to Broch, sleepwalkers are people living between vanishing and emerging ethical systems, just as the somnambulist exists in a state between sleeping and waking. The kaleidoscopic narrative technique of the novel, which combines lyric, epic, and dramatic methods with a theoretical discourse, can therefore be understood as a formal transposition of the splintered modern world.

The philosophical focus of the trilogy should be searched for in Broch's essay "Disintegration of Values." Values are no longer shaped by a unifying philosophy or religion; history becomes a residue of an unconscious will to power and domination. Anyone ruthless or clever enough to manipulate the rest of the population is in charge.

The Sleepwalkers trilogy ends not with total destruction but rather with words of consolation and hope. Broch sees this situation as a turning point for a possible rebirth. It is this tension between the lament and the pragmatic understanding of how the world works that keeps his oeuvre as compelling today as it was in the 1930s.

Broch's novel *The Death of Virgil*, which he began to write while being interned as a political subversive, was first published in the United States in 1945. It is an extensive lyrical and philosophical meditation on the duties and limitations of writing, in which reality and hallucination, poetry and prose are inextricably mingled. The relationship between past, present, and future plays an important role; most of the novel takes place in that space between Here and There, or as is stated several times in the text, in that situation of "Not quite here, but yet at hand."

Broch reenacts the final 18 hours of the Roman poet Virgil's life. More radically than in any other of his texts, the plot is reduced to a minimum, creating a remarkable poetic-novelistic vision that consists of Virgil's long philosophical conversations and meditations about the moral responsibility of art in times of totalitarianism and murder. The four parts of the book are ruled by the elements water, fire, earth, and air. The first section consists of the poet's return to Italy through the slums of Brundisium. Virgil clings to his consciousness "with the strength of a man who feels the most significant thing of his life approaching." The second part is predominantly a fevered dream in the imperial palace. The third section consists of Virgil's conviction that his *Aeneid* must be burned because of poetry's uselessness. The emperor Augustus, however, wants the work preserved from destruction. Here,

Broch takes up again the subject of the disintegration of values already discussed in *The Sleepwalkers*, this time in the form of a dialogue between the dying poet and the emperor. In the last part, Virgil's pains and doubts dissolve into a euphoric vision of a newly found unity where death and creation coincide.

Broch's innovative narrative technique, which involves rhythmic cadences, almost creates a musical effect. Ceaseless sentence cycles with constant repetitions and word variations convey the complexity of a single thought. Over long passages, language is nothing but the expression of consciousness and emotion. Shaped by Broch's own demanding poetics, *The Death of Virgil* ultimately questions all literature and is one of the preeminent literary works of the 20th century.

On the eve of a planned return to Europe, Hermann Broch died at the age of 64 of a heart attack on May 30, 1951, in New Haven, Connecticut, where he had spent the last years of his life in close contact with Yale University and as an honorary lecturer there.

BIBLIOGRAPHY
Hardin, James, and Donald G. Daviau, eds. *Austrian Fiction Writers After 1914*. Detroit: Gale, 1989.
Lützeler, Paul Michael, ed. *Hermann Broch, Visionary in Exile*. Rochester, N.Y.: Camden House, 2003.
Schlant, Ernestine. *Hermann Broch*. Boston: Twayne Publishers, 1978.

Andrea Heiglmaier

BUDDENBROOKS (BUDDENBROOKS, VERFALL EINER FAMILIE) THOMAS MANN (1901)

Of the many works by the renowned German author THOMAS MANN (1875–1955), including DEATH IN VENICE and *The Magic Mountain*, none match the epic proportion or literary legacy of the novel *Buddenbrooks*. Written early in his career, this story of the decline of the family symbolized by the Buddenbrooks chronicles not simply an increase in generational disregard for familial responsibility, but also acts as a redefinition of the limitations imposed on the individual members of the family. The novel traces the transfer of importance from familial duty to self-fulfillment despite the hopes and expectations coveted by passing generations. Mann constructs a history covering four generations, beginning at the apex of business success for the Buddenbrook family and ending with their extinction as the sole surviving progeny succumbs to typhus. The basic plot of this first novel corresponds to Mann's own ambivalent feelings about the bourgeois life while reflecting the personal tension he experienced as a young artist to pursue his father's business interests.

Mann opens the novel in celebration. Three generations of the Buddenbrook family have moved into a house on Mengstraße and mark the festive occasion with friends. Through Mann's words a portrait emerges, one which gathers and reveals the underlying themes the novel will continue to explore in the pages to follow while subtly emphasizing the clear generational differences that provide the novel's tension. The reader receives a deep sense of the Napoleonic ideals reflected and opposed within the family.

Johann Buddenbrook, a genial patriarch who is a practical and serious businessman, leaves his grain business to his family-oriented son Jean. All fares well for the family until the time arrives for the Buddenbrooks' bourgeois legacy to pass down to Jean's children. The decay of the family fortune is narrated through Thomas, a cunning businessman who finds life progressively tiresome. His marriage produces a son, Hanno, and an increase in fortunes through his wife's dowry, but Thomas lacks the ability to manage and prosper his business affairs. The Buddenbrook fortune dwindles under his leadership and is liquidated upon his death at age 49. His other siblings, likewise, live short or unproductive lives. His sister Antonie (Tony) marries twice with the support and prompting of her family, yet both marriages end in divorce. A second sister dies at an early age from tuberculosis, and Thomas's only brother, Christian, crippled by hypochondria and psychopathic tendencies, fails to contribute to the success of the family business. The Buddenbrook legacy now falls into the hands of Thomas's son Hanno. Still a child himself, Hanno never has the opportunity to take up the family business, as he dies of typhus at the age of 15. As the last living family member, Hanno's death marks the completion of the family decline.

While the Buddenbrooks do succumb as a family unit, inner dynamics work diligently to bring about the family's demise, making the final collapse inevitable. Through Johann Buddenbrook a tradition is established in the family firm that requires different generations to work together to secure the business's success. Symbolized through the almost liturgical recordings of business achievements in the family's Gutenberg Bible, the house on Mengstraße becomes a symbol of tradition. The succeeding generations have an increasingly difficult time abiding by the traditional laws of the firm, which is demonstrated by the leitmotif of bad teeth. Thomas Buddenbrook is successful. He breaks every record in the firm's history despite numerous obstacles and becomes a senator in government activities. The decline of the Buddenbrooks therefore is not as a result of financial trouble but stems from physical and mental weakness. Readers know early on that Thomas has bad teeth, but it is not until a trip to the dentist at the age of 49 that his weakness, symbolized by a decayed, hollowed tooth, takes his life. Since all other heirs likewise demonstrate such weakness, the family business follows the natural progression into obscurity.

The house on Mengstraße also serves as a leitmotif. The original owners, the wealthy Ratenkamp family, experience their own decline within its walls. This fate seems inherited by the Buddenbrook family when they take over the residence. The reader is left to ponder if the Hagenström family (a rival family) will die out in a fashion similar to the Buddenbrooks and the Ratenkamps.

The depth of realism found within *Buddenbrooks* testifies to Mann's literary expertise. Through the character of Tony, Mann demonstrates the ever-increasing degree by which the interests of the family firm force family members to sacrifice their personal happiness. Tony falls in love with Morten Schwarzkopf, a man from a modest background. With him she finds happiness, the type of happiness that opens the doors of wonder and discovery such as the beauty of the sea and the political changes brewing within the country. With Morten, Tony experiences what her family cannot give her, yet when her family interferes and tears her away from Morten, Tony dutifully submits. Far more compelling, however, is the irony with which Mann completes Tony's role. The young woman will endure the failure of two family-approved marriages, yet Tony alone will not deter from feeling the need to protect the family tradition. She will uphold the principles of the firm even though they have become void of meaning, and it will be Tony who serves to symbolically represent the tenacity by which familial ideals cement individuals to old ideas. As a further ironic twist, she is the only character left alive at the conclusion of the novel.

Documenting the fictional history of four generations created a substantial compilation, even by 19th-century standards. The daunting manuscript generated a two-volume novel despite the publisher's fears of meager sales and unsuccessful attempts to persuade Mann to condense the book. By the second edition, *Buddenbrooks* catapulted him into celebrity status. Mann's vivid characterizations and meticulous detail brought life to the Buddenbrook family, but he would not attempt again the realism so well received by his reading audience. The novel would stand alone as Mann's testament to the individual within the family.

BIBLIOGRAPHY

Brennan, Joseph Gerard. *Thomas Mann's World.* New York: Russell & Russell, 1962.

Bruford, Walter Horace. *The German Tradition of Self-Cultivation: Bildung from Humboldt to Thomas Mann.* New York: Cambridge University Press, 1975.

Bürgin, Hans. *Thomas Mann, a Chronicle of His Life.* Mobile: University of Alabama Press, 1969.

Hatfield, Henry Caraway. *Thomas Mann: A Collection of Critical Essays.* Englewood Cliffs, N.J.: Prentice Hall, 1964.

Heilbut, Anthony. *Thomas Mann: Eros and Literature.* Riverside: University of California Press, 1997.

Heller, Erich. *The Ironic German, a Study of Thomas Mann.* London: Secker & Warburg, 1958.

———. *Thomas Mann, the Ironic German: A Study.* Mamaroneck, N.Y.: P. P. Appel, 1973.

Kahn, Robert L. *Studies in German Literature.* Houston: Rice University, 1964.

Masereel, Frans. *Mein Stundenbuch, 165 Holzschnitte Von Frans Masereel. Einleitung von Thomas Mann.* Munich: K. Wolff, 1926.

Mueller, William Randolph. *Celebration of Life: Studies in Modern Fiction.* New York: Sheed & Ward, 1972.

Reed, Terence. *Thomas Mann: The Uses of Tradition.* Oxford: Clarendon Press, 1974.

Robertson, Ritchie. *The Cambridge Companion to Thomas Mann.* Cambridge: Cambridge University Press, 2002.

Stock, Irvin. *Ironic Out of Love: The Novels of Thomas Mann.* Jefferson, N.C.: McFarland, 1994.

Christine Marie Hilger

BULGAKOV, MIKHAIL (MIKHAIL AFANASEVICH BULGAKOV) (1891–1940)

Russian novelist, playwright   As he left no autobiographical references, no diary, and no memoirs, a cloak of silence has surrounded the Russian-born Mikhail Afanasevich Bulgakov's life. Nevertheless, rediscovered in bits and pieces, his life proves as interesting as his work. He was born in Kiev on May 15, 1891, to Afanasi Ivanovich Bulgakov, a professor at the Kiev Theological Academy, and Varvara Mikhailova, née Pokrovskaya. Afanasi Bulgakov's theological erudition, as well as the religious ambiance of his workplace, contributed to his son's interest in the history of religions and Christianity, which were conveyed in his most acclaimed novel, The MASTER AND MARGARITA (*Master i Margarita,* 1966–67, published posthumously). Mikhail grew up with six brothers, of whom he was the eldest. In 1907 his father died from hypertonic nephrosclerosis, the disease that would eventually kill Mikhail as well. In 1916 Bulgakov became a physician certified with distinction from the University of Kiev. For several years he practiced his profession in various military hospitals and even as a field physician while enrolled in the Third Kazak Regiment. At the end of 1919, he resigned from the military service and turned to the vocation that would bring him international acclaim—writing.

In 1920 Bulgakov began his writing career at *Caucasus (Kavkaz),* a newspaper that was soon shut down by the Soviet rule. He then became engaged in organizing literary evenings for soldiers and citizens and tried his hand at playwriting, entertaining the passion for theater he had developed during his university years. He wrote a comic sketch, *Self-Defense (Samooborona),* and a four-act drama, *The Brothers Turbin (Brat'ia Turbiny).* Between 1920 and 1921 he wrote the prose work *Cuffnotes (Zapiski na Manzhetakh),* depicting the experiences of a novice writer in the tormented years following the October Revolution in Russia. In 1921 Bulgakov moved to Moscow, where he accepted any work available at various magazines and newspapers.

He published several sketches and stories in 1924, among which the most notable are "Diaboliad" (D'Yavoliada) and "Khan's Fire" (Khanskii Ogon). The same year, Bulgakov finished his first novel, *The White Guard* (*Belaya Gvardiya*) and the satires *The Fatal Eggs* (*Rokovye Yaytsa*) and *The Heart of a Dog* (*Sobach'ye Serdtse*). While the *The Fatal Eggs* found publication relatively easily, *The White Guard*'s first chapters were published in a journal that was shut down before the publication was completed. The novel was then submitted to another journal, which suffered the same ill fate as the earlier one.

The years 1926 to 1928 marked Bulgakov's peak as a playwright. He rewrote *The Brothers Turbin* and renamed it *The Days of the Turbins* (*Dni Turbinykh*). The play's approach to the October Revolution sparked virulent attacks from the regime's officials, who accused the author of being a supporter of the White Guardists, at the time a very dangerous political label. Bulgakov's bow tie, monocle, white starched collar, and cuffs also stood out as a provocation of the proletarian regime of his time. Soon after the successful premiere of *The Days of the Turbins,* a new play premiered, *Zoyka's Apartment* (*Zoikina Kvartira*). Bulgakov also wrote *The Crimson Island* (*Bagrovyi Ostrov*) and *Flight* (*Beg*), for whose productions he signed contracts with reputable theaters in Moscow. At this point Stalin himself saw *The Days of the Turbins*; as a consequence, the play was prohibited, the other productions were put on hold, and the advance money was requested back. By 1929 Bulgakov was altogether ousted from the theatrical world he loved so much. Disheartened, he began working on *A Cabal of Hypocrites* (*Kabala Sviatosh*), a play that depicts the last years of the French playwright Molière.

In 1930 it was again Stalin who, in response to Bulgakov's request, surprisingly allowed him to affiliate with the Moscow Art Theatre as a literary consultant and assistant producer. In this position he adapted for the stage Gogol's *Dead Souls* (*Mertvye Dushi*) and Tolstoy's *War and Peace* (*Voina i Mir*). In 1933 he submitted a biographical novel on Molière for publication, but the Soviet censorship, sensitive to the slightest allusions to the Bolshevik regime, required Bulgakov to rework the book, which he refused to do. The same year, he started writing *Bliss* (*Blazhenstvo*), a three-act

play that would be rewritten and performed as *Ivan Vasilevich* by the Theatre of Satire. Although Bulgakov's plays enjoyed great success, the Soviet critics launched new vitriolic attacks on the playwright's refusal to view art and history through the lens of the Bolshevik ideology. Soon it was only *The Days of the Turbins* and *Dead Souls* that were still performed; all the others were withdrawn from theaters.

In November 1936 Bulgakov started working on *Notes of a Dead Man*—later renamed *Theatrical Novel* (*Teatral'ny roman*)—based on his theatrical experiences. A year later he dedicated most of his time writing a novel on the devil, *The Master and Margarita.* He also adapted *Don Quixote* for the stage and worked as a librettist for the opera, writing *Peter the Great* (1988), *The Black Sea* (*Chernoe more,* 1937), and *Rachel* (1939), based on a story by Guy de Maupassant. The last theatrical project he worked on was *A Pastor,* a play known later as *Batum.*

On May 14, 1939, Bulgakov finished the epilogue of *The Master and Margarita.* In September that same year, he was diagnosed with the same disease his father had died of at the age of 48, hypertonic nephrosclerosis. He refused however to go to the hospital as he wanted to polish his novel. Very quickly his health declined dramatically and by the end of the year, Bulgakov knew his illness was terminal. He still dictated the last corrections to *The Master and Margarita,* to his wife until February 1940, when he was finally satisfied with the work.

Mikhail Bulgakov died on March 10, 1940. At the time of his death, he was known mainly as the author of one play, *The Days of the Turbins.* His national and international reputation as a major 20th-century author is entirely posthumous. Bulgakov's literary rehabilitation (or resurrection, according to some critics) began in 1955 with the publication of *The Days of the Turbins* and *Pushkin,* plays which had been performed but never published before. In 1966 and 1967 a highly censored edition of *The Master and Margarita* was published by the author's widow in the journal *Moscow* (*Moskva*). It was not until 1973 that the full edition of the novel was published. From then on, Bulgakov's appreciation and fame grew slowly but irreversibly. Especially after 1985, with the beginning of glasnost and perestroika, the Soviet Union's general public was exposed to Bulgakov's most daring pieces, such as *Adam and Eve* (*Adam i Eva,* 1931) and *Heart of a Dog* (1968), which had until then only been known to literary connoisseurs and the Western world. He soon became a cult figure for the Russian reader and internationally, one of the most important authors of the 20th century.

BIBLIOGRAPHY

Curtis, Julie A. E. *Bulgakov's Last Decade: The Writer as Hero.* Cambridge and New York: Cambridge University Press, 1987.

————. *Manuscripts Don't Burn: Mikhail Bulgakov, A Life in Letters and Diaries.* London: Bloomsbury, 1991.

Hunns, Derek, J. *Bulgakov's Apocalyptic Critique of Literature.* Lewiston, N.J.: Edwin Mellen Press, 1996.

Krugovoy, George. *The Gnostic Novel of Mikhail Bulgakov: Sources and Exegesis.* Lanham, Md.: University Press of America, 1991.

Milne, Lesley. *Mikhail Bulgakov: A Critical Biography.* New York: Cambridge University Press, 1990.

Sahni, Kalpana. *A Mind in Ferment: Mikhail Bulgakov's Prose.* Atlantic Highlands, N.J.: Humanities Press, 1986.

Terry, Garth M. *Mikhail Bulgakov in English: A Bibliography, 1891–1991.* Nottingham, Eng.: Astra Press, 1991.

Wright, A. Colin. *Mikhail Bulgakov: Life and Interpretations.* Toronto: University of Toronto Press, 1978.

Luminita M. Dragulescu

BUNIN, IVAN ALEKSEYEVICH (1870–1953) *Russian novelist, poet, short story writer*

Ivan Bunin was born October 22, 1870, on his family's estate in Voronezh, Russia. He was descended from nobility on both sides of his family, but his father, Aleksey Nikolayevich, squandered what remained of the family fortune on gambling and drink; this misfortune occurred after the tumultuous times of emancipation of the peasants in 1861 and industrialization during the late 19th century in Russia. Bunin began his education under a family tutor and continued it for four years at the gymnasium, or secondary school, where he did not distinguish himself. In 1885 he announced that he was leaving the school. His older brother, Yuly, who was under police supervision for political reasons, undertook to continue Ivan's education, assigning him readings in history, literature, and political philosophy.

Bunin published his first poem in 1887, and he continued to publish poems and short stories while he worked a variety of jobs—as an assistant to the editor of a journal; as a secretary in the local government of Poltava; as a cooper (one who makes or repairs barrels and casks); and as an unlicensed bookseller, which nearly landed him in trouble with the authorities. Bunin became acquainted with Leo Tolstoy and for a short time counted himself one of the elder author's disciples. After he left the provinces for Moscow and St. Petersburg in 1895, he became intimate with another esteemed Russian author, Anton Chekhov. Bunin married Anna Nikolaevna Tsakni in 1898, but this ill-advised union ended two years later. He published collections of short stories, poetry, and translations, and in 1903 he won the Pushkin Prize of the Russian Academy for his translation of Henry Wadsworth Longfellow's *The Song of Hiawatha.*

During the early years of the 20th century, Bunin traveled widely in Europe and the Near East. In preparation for a visit to Constantinople, he studied the Bible, the Koran, and Persian poetry, and the influence of these studies and this journey can be traced throughout the remainder of his career. Upon his return, he began translating these experiences into short stories and poems. The 1905 revolution in Russia caused Bunin to despair and helped foster his antipathy and contempt for modernity and revolt. In 1906 he met and married Vera Muromtseva, who remained his wife and close companion for the remainder of his life. He continued to publish original verse; translated Lord Byron, Alfred, Lord Tennyson, and Henry Wadsworth Longfellow; and was awarded a second Pushkin Prize in 1909. That same year Bunin was elected an honorary member of the Russian Academy.

Bunin published his first novel, *The VILLAGE* (*Derevnya*), in installments during 1909–10, when he was 40 years old. This tale of two brothers, Tikhon and Kuzma Ilitch Krasoff, was meant to capture the mundane facts of peasant life in a typical Russian village. The work received critical acclaim and immediately became the subject of controversy, but Bunin was disappointed by what he considered the lukewarm nature of both the praise and the criticism.

Beginning in 1911, Bunin traveled again in Europe, the Near East, and Asia. He felt stimulated, artistically and spiritually, by these travels, and details and reflections on this period of his life can be discovered in the stories he published afterward. The outbreak of World War I confirmed the essential pessimism of his judgment, and his attack on what he considered the moral and intellectual bankruptcy of modern Europe became more pronounced. During the war Bunin wrote several collections of short stories addressing the egocentrism and lack of tradition that he felt characterized modernity, which culminated in the short story for which he is best known in the West, "The Gentleman from San Francisco" ("Gospodin iz San-Frantzisko") .

After the February Revolution of 1917 and the Bolshevik Revolution in October of the same year, Bunin left Moscow for Kiev and then Odessa, where he lived for two uneasy years before immigrating to France. During this time, he kept a journal which he later published under the title *Cursed Days* (*Okainnye Dni*) in 1936. In it he recorded his impressions of the immediate effects of revolution: the random, constant violence and the way this violence coarsened everyone involved and destroyed centuries of Russian tradition. The work was banned during the Soviet period, but after 1989 it became immensely popular; according to Thomas Gaiton Marullo, who translated it into English, it had gone through at least 15 separate editions by 1991.

The Bunins fled from Odessa in late January and early February of 1920, eventually settling in France near the Alpine village of Grasse. During the 1920s, Bunin turned almost entirely to writing prose, and he wrote several collections of short stories in addition to the *The Life of Arsenieva* (*Zhizn Arsenieva*), which he began to publish serially in 1928. He intermittently revised and added to this work throughout the remainder of his life. Soon after Bunin arrived in France, various parties began promoting him as a possible Nobel candidate. In 1934 their efforts were rewarded when Bunin won the Nobel Prize in literature. He was the first writer in exile to win the award, and in his concise acceptance speech he called attention to the fact and also demonstrated his allegiance to old world traditions and courtesy, thanking the Swedish monarch for being "the chivalrous kind of a chivalrous people."

After winning the Nobel Prize, Bunin continued to write. He published an edition of his collected works in 1934–36; wrote more short stories, including, in 1939, "Lika," which was a continuation of *The Life of Arseniev;* and penned literary criticism on Tolstoy and Chekhov. During World War II, he remained in Grasse after France fell under German occupation. He suffered from poverty and wartime privations, and after the war his health worsened steadily and his financial problems became dire. Worse still, many suspected him of softening his position toward the Soviets and trading his sympathies for wealth and privilege, but in a letter to a friend he wrote that he had rejected their lucrative offers and had voluntarily chosen poverty rather than betray his principles. Bunin continued to write despite these hardships, but he was forced to stop when he was confined to bed in 1951. He died on November 8, 1953, and was mourned by many.

BIBLIOGRAPHY
Connolly, Julian W. *Ivan Bunin*. Boston: Twayne, 1982.
Kryzytski, Serge. *The Works of Ivan Bunin*. The Hague: Mouton, 1971.
Marullo, Thomas G., ed. *Ivan Bunin: Russian Requiem, 1885–1920*. Chicago: Ivan R. Dee, 1993.
Woodward, James B. *Ivan Bunin: A Study of his Fiction*. Chapel Hill: University of South Carolina Press, 1980.

Christopher Vilmar

BUZZATI, DINO (1906–1972) *Italian essayist, novelist, playwright, short story writer*   Dino Buzzati's unique blend of surrealism and existentialism gave rise to a new style of fiction and thought among Italian literati. Buzzati's works, a testament to his training as a journalist, involve prosaic individuals and experiences; however, his meticulous attention to detail magnifies the mundane. One is able to discern larger philosophical meaning in seemingly random, monotonous experiences. His simple, unadorned narrative style allows the reader to become more deeply absorbed in the experiences of the characters. His short stories, plays, novels, articles, and paintings attracted the attention of ALBERT CAMUS, who wrote an adaptation of one of Buzzati's plays.

Dino Buzzati was born on October 16, 1906, in San Pellegrino, Italy. He enjoyed a privileged youth at his family's ancestral home outside Belluno. In 1917, a year after he began studying at the Parini School in

Milan, Austrian soldiers seized and occupied his home; though they eventually left once the war ended, the villa was partially destroyed. Three years later his father, Giulio Cesare Buzzati, died. In 1924 Dino Buzzati enrolled at the University of Milan, where his father had been a professor of international law. He briefly served in the military from 1926 to 1927; a year later he began working for the *Corriere dell sera*, the Milan daily newspaper. While on assignment in Ethiopia in 1939, he was once again commissioned by the army; a year later he wrote his most famous novel, *The Tartar Steppe* (*Il deserto dei Tartari*, 1940). Despite the success of his novel, Buzzati continued as a war correspondent for the next three years. He gained international fame when *The Tartar Steppe* was translated into French in 1949.

The Tartar Steppe is set during World War II and takes place at Fort Bastiani. The novel concerns Giovanni Drogo, a newly commissioned military officer who eagerly awaits the thrill of combat from an imminent Tartar invasion. Months pass without incident; Drogo's greatest enemy is tedium. Though other officers accept opportunities to escape, Drogo clings to the hope of combat action. His life seamlessly melds into the monotony of regimentation and time drifts. One day the Tartar forces appear along the horizon; however, Drogo dies before the confrontation actually occurs. Thus, he never fulfills his desire for combat.

Buzzati also produced paintings, often depicting elements of pop culture, and in 1958 he held his first exhibition in Milan. In 1961 Alba Montovani, Buzzati's mother, died. Five years later he married Almeria Antoniazzi, in December 1966. Buzzati continued to write short stories and experiment with science fiction, in addition to creating a comic strip based on the myth of Orpheus. Around this time his writings began to reflect his awareness of mortality. On January 28, 1972, Dino Buzatti died of cancer.

BIBLIOGRAPHY

Quilliot, Roland. *Les Métaphores de l'inquiétude: Giraudoux, Hesse, Buzzatti.* Paris: Presses Universitaires de France, 1997.

Siddell, Felix. *Death or Deception: Sense of Place in Buzzatti and Morante.* Leicester, U.K.: Troubador, 2006.

Neshon Jackson

BYKAŬ, VASIL (1924–2003) *Belarusian novelist, short story writer*   For half a century, Vasil Bykaŭ played a major role in the political and literary life of his native Belarus. Through translations into Russian and other languages, Bykaŭ's work brought Belarusian literature to an international audience, despite the efforts of Soviet literary officialdom to present him as a Russian writer.

Vasil Bykaŭ was born on June 19, 1924, in the village of Bychki, Vitebsk Oblast, in the then Soviet Republic of Belarus. Belarus is situated above the Ukraine, bordering on Poland, Lithuania, Latvia, Ukraine, and Russia. Belarusian is a Slavonic language that uses the Cyrillic alphabet. Bykaŭ grew up during a period of intense political turmoil in his country. Invaded by the Soviet Red Army in 1918 and divided between Poland and Soviet Russia in 1921, the small nation of Belarus was locked behind the Iron Curtain until late in the 20th century.

Bykaŭ's studies at the Vitebsk Academy of Fine Arts were interrupted by the outbreak of World War II, and Bykaŭ joined the Soviet Red Army in 1942. Upon his demobilization in 1947, he started working for the newspaper *Grodnenskaia Pravda* in Grodno. His first stories were published in 1956. In 1959 Bykaŭ became a member of the Soviet Union of Writers. From 1978 on, he lived in Minsk; in the same year he was made a peoples' deputy of the Belarusian Soviet Socialist Republic, a post he held until 1990, although he was never a member of the Communist Party. Bykaŭ received many prestigious literary awards—State Prize and Order of the Red Labour Banner (1974), National Writer of Belarus (1980), Hero of Soviet Labour (1984), the "Triumph" Prize (a prestigious Russian award, 2000)—but he was also the target of sharp criticism for his refusal to toe the official party line. For most of his professional life he suffered low-level persecution at the hands of Soviet and Belarusian authorities. In 1997 he left Belarus following the repression of his work, moving first to Finland, then Germany and finally the Czech Republic. In 2003 he returned to Minsk, where he died of cancer at the age of 79.

The central theme of Bykaŭ's prose is World War II. His heroes are young soldiers and officers, fully credible characters who display the entire range of human vice and virtue, rather than the facile heroes so common in Soviet war writing. In the stories and novels, which are for the most part centered on insignificant missions at the home front, the action merely serves as the background against which the author examines the impact of events on the psyche of his characters. The extreme situations bring out the best and the worst in the protagonists—cowardice and treachery as well as loyalty unto death. Bykaŭ's grimly realistic prose never embellishes the confusion, fear, and suffering of simple soldiers, and his unromantic descriptions of chaos and death provide a striking contrast to the pompous solemnity of the traditional Soviet war novel. Bykaŭ was fortunate enough to start his literary career at a point of historical transition in the Soviet Union, as the relatively liberal climate of the "thaw" following Stalin's death in 1953 allowed him to break free from the prescribed treatment of the war as the heroic feat of the Soviet people that had prevailed during high Stalinism.

The tone for Bykaŭ's subsequent work was set by his first important work, the novella *The Cry of the Cranes* (*Zhuraŭliny kryk*, 1959). It tells the story of six young soldiers, only one of whom survives a mission. The action alternates with reminiscences, flashbacks, and dreams, a device Bykaŭ routinely employed in his later prose. The idealism of the 17-year-old recruit Glechik, who shoots one of his companions when he tries to desert his post, provides a moral point of reference against which the behavior of the other characters is judged. A Glechik-like figure who follows a strong moral imperative and serves as the conscience of the story would become a recurrent feature in Bykaŭ's work.

The writer's fame spread beyond the borders of Belarus with the novella *The Third Flare* (*Tretsiaia raketa*, 1961), again a portrait of a group of soldiers in action. It parallels *The Cry of the Cranes* in the end, when the hero and first-person narrator fires his last flare at a traitor. *Alpine Ballad* (*Alpiiskaia balada*, 1963) is one of Bykaŭ's weaker works, a somewhat contrived romance between two escaped prisoners of war.

Bykaŭ first aroused serious controversy with his short novel *The Dead Feel No Pain* (*Miortvym ne balits*, 1965); the Russian translation appeared in 1966 in the popular liberal journal *Novyi Mir*. The story inter-weaves past and present on two planes of narration, one of which hinges on the reminiscences of a veteran 21 years after the victory. Through the character of the veteran's superior captain, Sakhno, whose obsession with form and discipline caused the death of many Soviet soldiers while his own life was spared, Bykaŭ links the Stalinist cult of discipline to other wartime problems such as gross military inefficiency and desertion. More controversially, the present-day success of a reckless war tribunal chairman alleges that Stalinists continue to flourish in Soviet society despite the efforts at destalinization in the wake of the 20th Party Congress in 1956. Bykaŭ was hounded in the press and in the Writer's Union, and although *The Dead Feel No Pain* is one of his most popular works, it was not reprinted in book form until 1989 and is today curiously absent from Belarusian Web sites offering downloads of Bykaŭ's writings.

With the story *The Krugliany Bridge* (*Kruglianski most*, 1969), Bykaŭ broadened the war theme to include partisans. *Sotnikaŭ* (1970) appeared in English as *The Ordeal*, his first work to be published in the West. The novel allows the reader deep insight into the reasons that can turn an essentially virtuous man like the partisan Rybak into a traitor, as Rybak provides one of the two points of view in the narrative. But the quasi-objective device of double narrative only reinforces the unwavering moral absolute: by pointing out that Rybak ends up assisting at the hanging of his comrade because he wants to stay alive himself, the author attacks the widespread conviction that the end can justify all means.

In the 1970s Bykaŭ took to writing works that were less controversial and less psychologically complex. Lieutenant Ivanoŭski, the hero of *Live Until Dawn* (*Dashits da svitannia*, 1973), is an exemplary commander who is led to a rather pointless death by his feeling of obligation and the desire to avenge for a friend during an ill-conceived mission. Ivanoŭski's last night is depicted in excruciating detail over 70 pages. Other works of the 1970s include *Voŭtsaia zhaia* (*Pack of Wolves*) and *Paiti i ne viarnutstsa* (*To go and not return*).

Some of Bykaŭ's most important works were written during the 1980s. Included among them is *Sign of Misfortune* (*Znak biady*, 1982), a work charting the plight of simple village folk in German-occupied Belarus, linking it to their suffering during collectivization in the 1930s. *The Quarry* (*Karier,* 1986) forges a link between the war and present-day Belarus, emphasizing the importance of memory to avoid distortion of history. *In the Fog* (*U tumane,* 1987) examines the moral confusion Soviet society was plunged in by Stalinism on the example of a group of partisans.

Bykaŭ continued to write throughout the 1990s while becoming an active supporter of the Belarusian democratic and national movements in the aftermath of the Soviet Union's collapse. Among works from that time are a 1994 trilogy: *On Black Ice* (*Na chornych liadach*), *Before the End* (*Pierad kontsom*), and *Poor Folk* (*Biednyia liudtsi*). Bykaŭ became increasingly opposed to the Lukashenko regime when the latter moved toward autocracy in the mid-1990s, leading to his voluntary exile in 1997. In addition to his novels, Vasil

Bykaŭ left a large oeuvre of other works. Many of his novels and stories have been made into films.

BIBLIOGRAPHY

Dedkov, Igor A. *Povest o Cheloveke, Kotoryi Vystoial.* Moscow: Sovetskii Pisatel, 1990.

Kursunov, Dmitri. "Man in the War." *Soviet Literature* 4 (1985): 121–126.

McMillin, Arnold B. "Vasil Bykau and the Soviet Byelorussian Novel." In *The Languages and Literatures of the Non-Russian Peoples of the Soviet Union,* edited by George Thomas, 268–294. Hamilton, Ontario: McMaster University, 1977. 268–294.

Svirskii, Grigorii. *A History of Post-War Soviet Writing: The Literature of Moral Opposition.* Translated and edited by Robert Dessaix and Michael Ulman, 368–376. Ann Arbor, Mich.: Ardis, 1981.

Josephine von Zitzewitz

C

CABRERA INFANTE, GUILLERMO
(1929–2005) *Cuban essayist, novelist* Touted as one of the most original voices in Spanish-language literature, Guillermo Cabrera Infante skillfully blended his natural affinity for languages and dialects, his extensive readings of American and European writers, and his love of popular culture manifestations—primarily movies, music, and comic books—to produce his own unique, postmodern works that defy simple genre classification but have nonetheless intrigued a global audience. A novelist, essayist, translator, and critic, Cabrera Infante is most widely recognized as the writer of the hugely popular THREE TRAPPED TIGERS (*Tres tristes tigres,* 1967), a work that blurs fiction and reality and utilizes Cuban colloquialisms and sophisticated wordplay to depict cabaret nightlife and hustlers in pre-Castro Havana.

Born April 22, 1929, in Gibara on the northeast coast of Cuba, Guillermo Cabrera Infante was the oldest son of Zoila Infante Castro, a beautiful and congenial woman given to entertaining, and Guillermo Cabrera López, a staunch supporter of the Communist Party. This was a dangerous political stance to take in 1936 Cuba, and in one of the most traumatic events of Cabrera Infante's life, at only seven years of age, he witnessed two military policemen, with revolvers drawn, pursue his mother through his childhood home and arrest her for receiving propaganda materials from the Communist Party. Out of a strong sense of responsibility to his wife and to his political principles, Cabrera

Infante's father turned himself in to authorities later that same night, and for several months, Cabrera López and his wife remained incarcerated in a prison in Santiago de Cuba. During this time, Cabrera Infante lived with his maternal grandparents and suffered repeated nightmares and separation anxiety, a condition that would revisit him in 1962 when he left Cuba for Brussels to serve as a cultural attaché in the embassy there.

Soon after his parents were released from prison, the Cuban Communist Party was legalized, and the family moved to Havana, where Cabrera Infante enrolled in night school to learn English. He soon discovered that he harbored an exceptional talent for language learning and was awarded a certificate in the teaching of English in 1946. Although Cabrera Infante proved an unsuccessful instructor, his profound interest in words and language play led him to serve occasionally as a translator for *Hoy,* the Communist Party newspaper, and as a proofreader for *Luz,* another Cuban newspaper. During this time, he also avidly read works by such accomplished figures as William Faulkner, Ernest Hemingway, John Steinbeck, and James Joyce, writers who would prove highly influential in the development of his own writing style.

Cabrera Infante's first published story, written after a friend dared him to try his hand at writing, was a parody titled "Waters of Memory" ("Aguas de recuerdo"), which was published in 1947 by *Bohemia,* arguably the most famous Cuban magazine of that time. For this story, Cabrera Infante received a hefty sum of about $50, and he was hooked. From that point on, he devoted himself to writing, anything from literary notices for *Bohemia* to photographic essays and articles in another widely read magazine named *Carteles* to insightful film critiques. Even though his frank writing style and use of English obscenities landed him in jail for five days in October 1952, Cabrera Infante did not stop writing or alter his style or language. He merely began writing under pseudonyms, most commonly G. Caín and Jonás Castro, until the scandal had passed.

Success smiled upon Cabrera Infante in the early years of Fidel Castro's revolution. By 1968 he had been appointed editor of the cultural journal *Lunes de revolución* and had released a collection of short stories titled *Así en la paz como en la guerra* (1960), released in English under the title *Writes of Passage* (1994). He had also published a collection of film reviews interspersed with cultural debates called *Un oficio del siglo veinte* (1963), released in English as *A Twentieth Century Job* (1991), and he had penned his masterpiece *Tres tristes tigres* (1967; released in English as *Three Trapped Tigers,* 1971). But Cabrera Infante's fame did not bring great fortune, and the increasingly powerful Castro machine began to censor more harshly the materials that were allowed to reach the Cuban public. When the Cuban Film Institute, under the leadership of Alfredo Guevara, seized and banned a 23-minute documentary on Cuban nightlife filmed by Cabrera Infante's younger brother, Cabrera Infante and hundreds of others protested, provoking the Cuban government to denounce *Lunes de Revolución.*

Thus unemployed, Cabrera Infante had little choice but to take the Brussels embassy appointment when it was offered, but he grew increasingly frustrated with his native country's government, and he decided to cut ties with Cuba after he returned to Havana in 1965 to attend his mother's funeral and was detained without reason, unable to return to his job in Europe. Eventually he was permitted to go to Madrid, Spain, for the purpose of editing a manuscript. By this time, Cabrera Infante, his wife, and his two daughters had decided to go into exile, vowing never to return as long as Castro remained at the helm. He made good on his promise: He died in London on February 22, 2005, never having set foot on Cuban soil again.

After taking up residence in England, Cabrera Infante released several other books, including his memoir *Infante's Inferno* (*La Habana para un infante difunto,* 1979), an homage to the cigar written in English and entitled *Holy Smoke* (1985), and a collection of political essays titled *Mea Cuba* (1991). Though his name has been all but eradicated from Cuban letters as a traitor to the revolution (it does not appear in the 1980 *Dictionary of Cuban Literature,* published by the institute of Literature and Linguistics of the Cuban Academy of Sciences), Cabrera Infante remains an influential presence in the libraries of Cuban writers, and he maintains an impressive following in Europe, with a steadily increasing readership in the United States.

BIBLIOGRAPHY

Nelson, Ardis L., ed. *Guillermo Cabrera Infante: Assays, Essays, and Other Arts.* New York: Twayne Publishers, 1999.

Peavler, Terry J. "Guillermo Cabrera Infante's Debt to Ernest Hemingway." *Hispania* 62, no. 3 (1979): 289–296.

Souza, Raymond D. *Guillermo Cabrera Infante: Two Islands, Many Worlds.* Austin: University of Texas Press, 1996.

Dana Nichols

CACAO (CACAU) JORGE AMADO (1933)

The works of the 20th-century modernist JORGE AMADO (1912–2001), one of the most famous Brazilian writers of the 20th century, have been read around the globe. He is particularly remembered for his books *Cacao* and *Dona Flor and Her Two Husbands* (*Dona Flor e seus dois maridos*), as well as the screen adaptation of the latter.

Cacao and *Dona Flor and Her Two Husbands* are also two of Amado's most informative works, and they reflect the tone, subject, and characters found in many of the author's other fictional pieces. *Cacao* was published in 1933 and inaugurated the so-called Cocoa Cycle, a series of books based on the economic and social problems found on cocoa plantations. Its first edition was sold out in little more than one month. Some critics labeled it a novel and report in one, and it was deemed "socialist literature," causing the police to confiscate the first edition. But that did not stop the book's momentum, and Foreign Minister Osvaldo Aranha ensured that it would be available to the public.

Cacao sold out despite its shocking language and themes of the day.

This romance and the subsequent work, *Sweat,* clandestinely reached Portugal, where the books were banned, influencing the formation of the Portuguese neorealism movement. In fact, in a provocative introductory note to *Cacao,* the author declares: "I tried to describe in this book, in a minimum of literature and a maximum of honest realism, the sub-human conditions of the life of the workers of cocoa farms in Southern Bahia State. Will it be considered a proletarian romance?"

The story is entirely narrated by the character Jose Cordeiro, a middle-class young man from the Brazilian state of Sergipe who, having lost everything, looks for work in southern Bahia in the hope of getting back on his feet. He discovers that love and politics make for strange bedfellows. He finds work on the cocoa plantation owned by "Colonel" Manoel Misael de Souza Telles, a man called Mané Flagel by his employees for his questionable moral qualities. On the farm, Jose Cordeiro makes friends with some coworkers, who nickname him "The Sergipe Man," and along with other poor workers, he experiences the plantation's subhuman working conditions. Meanwhile, he is attracted to Maria, the colonel's daughter. She falls in love with Jose Cordeiro, proposes marriage, and offers him an administrator's position on her father's farm. Cordeiro resists her, seeing her as an enemy of the working class, and leaves the farm abruptly, journeying to São Paulo, where he joins the Communist Party.

Like Ayn Rand's *The Fountainhead, Cacao* is a sociopolitical tome that is very much of the time and of the minds of the people living in politically fractured countries. It is an accurate social commentary of the lives of those in Brazil at that time, and for that reason alone *Cacao* remains an important work of literature. It was also the first of Amado's books to be translated into another language, with Spanish being the first of many.

BIBLIOGRAPHY

Amado, Jorge. *Cacao.* Translated by Estela Dos Santos. Caracas: Biblioteca Ayacucho, 1991.

———. *Dona Flor and Her Two Husbands.* Translated by Harriet de Onis. New York: Knopf, 1969.

Brower, Keith, et al., eds. *Jorge Amado: New Critical Essays.* New York and London: Routledge, 2001.

Denning, Michael. *Culture in the Age of Three Worlds.* London and New York: Verso, 2004.

Stephanie Dickison

CAIRO TRILOGY, THE: PALACE WALK, PALACE OF DESIRE, SUGAR STREET (BAYN AL-QUASRAYN, QASR AL-CHAWQ, AL-SUKKARIYYA) NAGUIB MAHFOUZ (1956–1957)

The first great family saga of modern Arabic literature, *The Cairo Trilogy* tells the story of patriarch al-Sayyid Ahmad Abd al-Jawad and his family over the course of more than 30 years, from World War I to eight years before the overthrow of King Farouk in 1952. The titles of the trilogy's three novels—*Palace Walk* (*Bayn al-Quasrayn,* 1956), *Palace of Desire* (*Qasr al-Chawq,* 1957), and *Sugar Street* (*Al-Sukkariyya,* 1957)—are taken from actual street names in the Al-Jamaliyya district of Cairo. The trilogy is considered by many to be NAGUIB MAHFOUZ's magnum opus, written at the peak of his realist phase. The work has been hailed for its depiction of the changing conditions of Egypt's urban society as it underwent political, social, and religious struggles during the turbulent interwar period following the end of World War I, producing a conflict between Egypt's nationalist aspirations and Great Britain's imperialist and colonial power.

Having already spent over a decade examining contemporary national issues, particularly the conflict of the aspiring individual against a convulsively changing society, Mahfouz wrote *The Cairo Trilogy* with the intent of tracing this tension on a broader scale. In 1952, upon completing what he considered to be his best work, Mahfouz tried to publish it as a single novel. The colossal work, however, was refused by his publisher, Said al-Sahhar, who claimed the "calamity" would cost too much to publish on its own. It was upon the launch of Yusuf al-Siba'i's monthly review, *al-Risalah al-Jadidah,* that Mahfouz's work finally began to appear in print a few years later, albeit in serialized form. When *Palace Walk* was finally published and received success in 1956, Mahfouz divided the work into three parts, publishing the latter two portions in 1957.

Palace Walk introduces a middle-class Muslim family that functions as the heart of the entire narrative.

Around two-thirds of this first part is spent describing the everyday life of the family members—Amina, Yasin, Khadija, Fahmy, Aisha, and Kamal—as each negotiates issues of family, duty, and marriage under the strict authority of their father, al-Sayyad. Social rituals, especially surrounding food, are described in detail in Mahfouz's cross section of modern Egyptian family life. Covering the two years leading up to the 1919 revolution, the novel also mediates the nation's turbulent political events through the family members. The title of the novel, *Bayn al-Qasrayn,* meaning "between two places," refers to Egypt's liminal position both as part of the Ottoman Caliphate and as a newly emerging independent nation. In the second half of the book, the nation's political struggle is encapsulated in Fahmy, whose death as a revolutionary martyr marks the end of *Palace Walk.*

Palace of Desire depicts a changed family in the wake of Fahmy's death. The hypocritical al-Sayyad, partly characterized in *Palace Walk* by his nocturnal escapades with women and alcohol, is now declining in both health and patriarchal status due to the loss of his son five years ago. Change has also crept into his wife: The traditional coffee hour, previously held in the mother's space on the ground floor, has now been moved to the top floor of the house (al-Sayyad's domain) to reflect Amina's rising authority in the family. This part of the trilogy, however, centers primarily on her son Kamal's struggles with issues of national identity, class, friendship, and first love—the fundamental themes of the novel. Kamal embarks on an intellectual quest reminiscent of James Joyce's Stephen Dedalus. Despite his various conversations with friends and family, however, he remains a thwarted character at the novel's end, stunned by the death of Wafdist leader Sa'd Zaghlul (1857–1927). By this point in 1927, al-Sayyad has recovered from an illness that has caused him to become more pious, while Aisha has lost nearly her entire family to typhoid.

By 1935, the year marking the opening of *Sugar Street,* al-Sayyad's authority has come to a near total decline. Not only has the former patriarch's secret double life gradually been exposed to his sons, but both he and the coffee hour have also been forced to move to the ground floor on account of his weak heart, thus completing the household's shift from patriarchy to democracy. Aisha, already an old woman at 34 years of age, has taken to smoking, while Khadija is known for her regular rows with her mother-in-law. Yasin has finally discovered a measure of stability in his third marriage, and Kamal is now a professor and a member of the Wafdist Party fighting for Egypt's independence.

Politically, in *Sugar Street* Mahfouz continues to describe the state of revolution in Egypt as perpetual, with waves of oppression continually preventing the nation's rebirth. Despite brief moments of revolutionary progress, with the outbreak of World War II at the novel's end, Mahfouz remains pessimistic about the Egyptian people's ability to liberate their nation. In the novel's concluding chapters, Khadija's sons Abd al-Muni'm and Ahmad Shawkat, the next generation of freedom fighters, are arrested for distributing subversive tracts across Cairo. Thus, the central conflict of the trilogy—the tension between the individual and his or her society—remains a conflict at its end, despite the upheavals undergone by both the family and the nation. Following the pattern of the previous two novels, the final part of the trilogy comes to a powerful conclusion with a death and a birth: Amina's health fails her only a year after al-Sayyad's funeral, while the birth of Yasin's granddaughter marks yet another generational turn.

In the *Cairo Trilogy* as a whole, Mahfouz privileges a sense of the collective over the individual, represented by both al-Sayyad's family as well as the formation of the Wafdist Party. It is this feature that makes Mahfouz's novel uniquely Arab, for it deviates from the European novel's conventional centering on a single protagonist. Along with a skilled use of narrative perspective, Mahfouz's use of time is also unique in its dilation and contraction. While the events in *Palace Walk* (the longest of the three novels) occur gradually over the course of just two years, *Palace of Desire* quickens the pace of the story over four years, and in *Sugar Street* (the shortest) events are stretched across a span of 10 years. This distinctive use of time creates a sense of urgency that escalates over the course of the trilogy, mirroring the increasing urgency of a nation fighting to free itself of foreign rule.

The Cairo Trilogy is not just a literary masterpiece but also a valuable historical and anthropological document. Mahfouz's observations concerning the contemporary sociopolitical state of Egypt are astutely woven throughout an intensely personal family saga, creating a fictionalized record of a significant turbulent period in the nation's recent history. It is this combination of political and personal that has made the trilogy such an enormous success. Since it has been serialized for Arab television, al-Sayyad has become a household name in Egypt, as his larger-than-life character is seen to represent the archetypal Egyptian patriarch. *The Cairo Trilogy,* finally published in 2001 as the single volume Mahfouz intended, has been largely responsible for earning him Egypt's State Literary Prize for the Novel (1957) and the Nobel Prize in literature (1988).

BIBLIOGRAPHY

Beard, Michael, and Adnan Haydar, eds. *Naguib Mahfouz: From Regional Fame to Global Recognition.* Syracuse, N.Y.: Syracuse University Press, 1993.

El-Enany, Rashad. *Naguib Mahfouz: The Pursuit of Meaning.* London and New York: Routledge, 1993.

Gordon, Hayim. *Naguib Mahfouz's Egypt: Existential Themes in his Writings.* New York: Greenwood, 1990.

Hafez, Sabry. "Introduction." In *The Cairo Trilogy: Palace Walk, Palace of Desire, Sugar Street* (1956–57), translated by William Maynard Hutchins et al., vii–xxiii. New York: Alfred A. Knopf (Random House), 2001.

Milson, Menahem. *Naguib Mahfuz: The Novelist—Philosopher of Cairo.* New York: St. Martin's, 1998.

Moosa, Matti. *The Early Novels of Naguib Mahfouz: Images of Modern Egypt.* Gainesville: University Press of Florida, 1994.

Peled, Mattityahu. *Religion, My Own: The Literary Works of Najib Mahfuz.* New Brunswick, N.J., and London: Transaction Books, 1983.

Summer Pervez

CALVINO, ITALO (1923–1985) *Italian essayist, novelist, short story writer*

Because of his versatility, fertile imagination, and prolific nature, Italo Calvino is considered by many to be among the premier Italian fiction writers of the latter half of the 20th century. With an impressive list of novels, nonfiction, and short stories to his credit, Calvino produced a canon of literature of great variety and depth. The writer had a particular interest in revivifying native Italian folktales. He is remembered for the seeming ease with which he could spin tales, some realistic in detail, others quite otherworldly.

Calvino was born in Santiago de Las Vegas, Cuba, on October 15, 1923. His parents, Mario Calvino and Eva Mameli, both worked in the field of botany. They named their son Italo so that he would never forget his Italian heritage. In 1925 the family moved to San Remo on the Italian Riviera, where Calvino spent the next 20 years of his life. Here Calvino's father acted as curator of the botanical gardens and served as professor of tropical agriculture at the University of Turin. Intending to pursue studies in science like his parents, Calvino enrolled in the university where his father taught. He could not avoid his love for literature, however, and eventually graduated from the University of Turin in 1947 with a degree in letters after writing a thesis on the novelist Joseph Conrad.

Early in his life, Calvino was engaged in political action, first in 1940 as a member of the Young Fascists. He later joined the Italian resistance and fought the Germans from 1943 to 1945 in the Ligurian mountains. In 1945 he joined the Communist Party, but he eventually left it in 1957. Calvino's first book, *The Path to the Nest of Spiders* (1947), is based on his experiences as a partisan fighter and influenced in style by the neorealist mode popular at the time.

In 1947 Calvino began work at the Turin-based publisher Giulio Einaudi Editore in the publicity department. He worked off and on at Einaudi until 1984, eventually becoming an editor, and the firm published Calvino's work throughout his career. Over the years, Calvino worked in a number of areas of publishing and writing, including stints as a writer for various periodicals, from the leftist *Il Politecnico* in the 1940s to the newspaper *La Repubblica* in 1979. During the 1950s he traveled abroad. In 1952 he visited the former Soviet Union, and from 1959 to 1960 he was in the United States. He was particularly fond of New York City.

Calvino's stories from the 1950s are some of his most celebrated, particularly the trilogy of books he eventually published under the title *Our Ancestors* in 1960 and for which he won the Salento Prize. These books include *The Nonexistent Knight, The Cloven Vis-*

count, and *The* BARON IN THE TREES. In *The Nonexistent Knight,* the title figure represents Calvino's satiric take on the chivalric era, as the knight is literally nothing but a suit of armor. *The Cloven Viscount* is about the character Medardo of Terralba, who is halved in an Austro-Turkish battle but is eventually made whole again. *The Baron in the Trees* tells the tale of a young man who takes to living an arboreal existence out of distaste for the rules his parents force on him. Many critics point out the influence of Ludovico Ariosto and his *Orlando Furioso* on these stories, which use elements of satire, fantasy, and allegory.

Calvino met Judith Esther "Chichita" Singer in 1962, and the two married in 1964. An Argentine by birth, Singer worked as a translator for UNESCO in Paris. A daughter, Abigail, was born in 1965. At this same time Calvino published COSMICOMICS, a collection of stories narrated by the mysterious figure Qfwfq, who witnesses the creation and evolution of the universe. In 1967 he moved to Paris, where he lived intermittently for the next 15 years. While he was in Paris, Calvino met a number of members of French philosophical and literary circles such as the theorists Claude Levi-Straus and Roland Barthes, as well members of the experimental groups Tel Quel and Oulipo. The influence of the literary theories of the time, particularly the work on narrative by Barthes and the ideas of Swiss linguist Ferdinand de Saussure on the "sign" (the word and that to which it refers), would inform Calvino's thinking and writing.

The author was awarded the Premio Feltrinelli per la Narrativa for *Invisible Cities* in 1972. *Invisible Cites* consists of a series of reflections on reality hatched from imaginary dialogues between Kubla Kahn and the adventurer Marco Polo. *The Castle of Crossed Destinies* (1973) is a collection of stories linked together through Calvino's use of the Tarot deck as a story-generating device. The year 1979 witnessed the publication of perhaps Calvino's most-studied novel in colleges and universities: IF ON A WINTER'S NIGHT A TRAVELER (1979). This book ingeniously includes the "Reader" as its main character as Calvino begins 10 separate novels that each end as soon as they become intriguing. The novel is about reader expectations and the function of the narrator in the fictional text. The self-reflexive nature of this metafictional book has been influential on other writers, particularly American Lynn Emanuel, whose book *Then, Suddenly* (1999) self-consciously extends Calvino's approach into poetry.

Calvino and his family moved from Paris to Rome in 1980. That same year the writer published his first book of essays, entitled *The Uses of Literature.* His last novel, *Mr. Palomar,* appeared in 1983. Calvino died on September 19, 1985, of a cerebral hemorrhage. The last year of his life had been spent preparing lectures he had been scheduled to deliver for prestigious Charles Eliot Norton lecture series at Harvard University. Calvino was able to complete only five of the six projected talks, which expressed his thoughts on themes such as lightness, exactitude, and multiplicity in literature. They were later published under the title *Six Memos for the Next Millennium.*

BIBLIOGRAPHY

Bloom, Harold, ed. *Italo Calvino. Bloom's Modern Critical Views.* New York: Chelsea House, 2000.

Bondanella, Peter, and Andrea Ciccarelli, eds. *The Cambridge Companion to the Italian Novel.* New York: Cambridge University Press, 2003.

Weiss, Beno. *Understanding Italo Calvino.* Columbia: University of South Carolina Press, 1993.

Joe Moffett

CAMEL XIANG ZI (LUO TUO XIANG ZI)
LAO SHE (1939)   *Camel Xiang Zi* is one of the most touching and successful novels by the Chinese writer LAO SHE (1899–1966). Lao She, a patriotic people's writer, is a pseudonym of Shu Qingchun. The novel is based on the author's firsthand knowledge of rickshaw boys and typically shows the narrative style of this famous author: the vivid and sensitive portrayal of characters, biting and lively use of language, and, more important, the enlightened view toward his protagonists trapped in modern China's social turmoil.

The main character, Xiang Zi, is a healthy boy raised in the countryside. He moves to Beiping (today's Beijing) at the age of 18 and now makes a living as a rickshaw boy. He is tall and energetic, with a rubicund face and shaved head. He believes that he can transform his life by working hard, and sure enough he manages to buy his own new rickshaw three years later. This period proved to be a happy beginning for the young man, but the euphoria is short-lived as tragedy soon strikes. One day, while Xiang Zi is carrying a customer out of the city, he is robbed by a group of soldiers. They imprison him, forcing him to work for them. The young man quickly resolves to escape, and the opportunity soon comes. In the middle of the night, Xiang Zi flees the barracks, taking three camels with him that the soldiers had earlier stolen. He sells the camels to a villager for 35 yuan. The money makes up partially for Xiang Zi's loss, and for this experience he gains the nickname Camel.

Without enough money to buy a new rickshaw, Xiang Zi must borrow one from a rickshaw station named Harmony Yard. The boss of this station is Father Master Liu, an old man with only one daughter named Hu Niu. Xiang Zi is permitted to live in the yard, which is convenient for him as he has no home. His ambitions swell again. He has saved some of the money from the earlier sale of the camels, so he plans to work hard and save more money in order to buy his own rickshaw again.

His ambitions fall prey, though, to Hu Niu, an aging spinster and shrew who has helped her father run his business for many years. She notices Xiang Zi and tries to lure him into marriage. One night she persuades him to drink heavily, and they fall into bed together. The next morning Xiang Zi regrets his involvement with Hu Niu and decides that he must leave the station immediately. Feeling he has escaped another bleak and imprisoning situation, Xiang Zi finds a steady job working in Mr. Cao's house. Mr. Cao, a professor, treats the rickshaw boy well, but Xiang Zi enjoys his new job and improving spirits for only a few months. Hu Niu appears unexpectedly and tells Xiang Zi that she is pregnant with his baby and now wishes to marry soon. Xiang Zi is shocked by the news.

Having no choice, Xiang Zi returns to Harmony Yard, where he marries Hu Niu. He regrets his decision, however, and sees the marriage as ridiculous. Hu Niu is not only much older than he, but she is ugly, selfish, and lazy. He also learns of her deceit: She had faked her pregnancy by hiding a pillow under her coat. In their new home, Hu Niu employs a neighbor named Xiao Fu-zi as a maid, but she soon drives the young servant away because she fears that her husband is attracted to the younger woman. Xiang Zi is indeed attracted to the pretty young maid because she possesses all of the warm emotions and caring spirit that his wife lacks. Hu Niu soon dies of an infection, forcing Xiang Zi to sell the rickshaw to pay for his wife's burial. He decides that he cannot marry Xiao Fu-zi because he has no money to support her and her two younger brothers.

Despairing, Xiang Zi once again begins working as a rickshaw boy, but he also begins to smoke and drink heavily, and his temper turns volatile. He finds himself at the end of his rope, until one day he visits his former employer, Mr. Cao, who allows him to continue his old job. Mr. Cao also agrees to hire Xiao Fu-zi as a maidservant. Xiang Zi excitedly hurries to the tenement to tell his beloved the promising news, only to discover that Xiao Fu-zi has hanged herself in a grove outside the white cottage (the bawdyhouse).

This novel unfolds the collapse of a rickshaw boy, both in body and spirit. Xiang Zi comes from the countryside to live in the city. Although he prefers the urban life, he thinks and behaves as a farmer. He wishes to have his own rickshaw, just like a farmer wants to have his own land. He believes he can turn his dream into reality, but his efforts are in vain. His dreams—simple ones, he thought—die in front of him. He cannot have his own rickshaw and a caring, beautiful wife in Xiao Fu-zi.

The author Lao She describes the miserable career of rickshaw boys like Xiang Zi with mixed feelings. He shows his great sympathy to and understanding of the group of rickshaw workers, but he also reveals that one's own humanity is often too frail and powerless to withstand the onslaught of evil and destructive forces in the universe. Lao She's works are renowned for their compassion and profound understanding of human plight in the 20th century. In this sense, *Camel Xiang Zi* can be read as a mirror of modern Chinese sociocultural life during the early 20th century, and Lao She's works—others include the *Four Generations Under One Roof* (*Si Shi Tong Tang*) and the play *The Tea House* (*Chaguan*)—are regarded as the peak of civic literature in the history of Chinese modern literature.

BIBLIOGRAPHY

Fan Jun. "Recognizing Laoshe." *Literature Criticism* 5 and 6 (1996).

Zhan Kai-di. *Two Characteristics of Language in Camel Xiangzi. Papers Collected on Laoshe Study.* Shandong: People's Press, 1983.

Mei Han

CAMPAIGN, THE (*LA CAMPAÑA*) CARLOS FUENTES (1990)

Beginning in 1958 with *WHERE THE AIR IS CLEAR*, CARLOS FUENTES (1928–   ) has written several major novels, short stories, plays, screenplays, and numerous critical essays. With *The Campaign,* Fuentes recounts the history of the Americas and, more important, the origins of Hispanic culture. *The Campaign* is the first novel in a series of three planned works. *The Campaign* begins where *TERRA NOSTRA* (1975) leaves off: at the height of Spanish America's struggle for independence. The story in *The Campaign* unfolds via letters written by the protagonist, Baltasar Bustos, to a friend, Manuel Varela, who lives in Buenos Aires and whose manuscript becomes the text of this novel.

The setting encompasses a large geographical swath of what is modern-day Bolivia, Chile, Peru, Colombia, and Veracruz, and the novel spans the years from 1810 through 1920. Baltasar is young man deeply influenced (some would argue that he is seduced) by several facets of the Enlightenment and the Romantic periods. Baltasar is motivated by the writings of Voltaire, Rousseau, and Diderot; however, he is most intrigued by Rousseau's works. Baltasar believes that in order to rectify imbalances in all things, human desire and passion are integral factors in order to return to a state of perfect harmony.

As the son of a wealthy Argentinean landowner, Baltasar is a highly likeable character; he is romantic, passionate, insightful, and highly idealistic. Some critics argue that Baltasar's caring and idealistic nature make him vulnerable and thus fickle in the ideals he chooses (or chooses not) to believe. However, as philosophical as Baltasar is, he is also equally grounded in reality. His desire to correlate the philosophical ideals he gains from his readings and apply them to what is actually going on in his life makes him a complex thinker. Some critics, however, think of Baltasar as too much of an idealistic dreamer, akin to something like Cervantes's title character in *Don Quixote*. Some readers might also inquire whether or not Baltasar is actually certain what his ideals are and whether or not he is actually fighting for what he truly believes in. Other critics argue that the objectives Baltasar forms are never truly realized, despite his constant ruminating over them.

As philosophically inclined as Baltasar is, he is greatly moved by the teachings of the Catholic Church. However, this religious background directly challenges many of the ideals he has adopted from the Enlightenment school of thought. This collision of philosophies challenges Baltasar's existence, but it also functions as a method of explaining Fuentes's notion that everything in this novel—the characters, the incidents, even actual historical times, places, and events—represents a collective metaphor of ideas. These ideas do not exist separately; they exist simultaneously and function as a complementary text to the foundational makeup of Latin America's historical and cultural existence.

The Campaign can be regarded as a text detailing Latin America's development from a series of separate provinces to that of a complete yet still fledging republic. The contradiction of ideals and beliefs is central to very early Spanish-American formative thought principles. As Baltasar attempts to redeem both himself and the cause for which he is fighting, a newly developed consciousness is formed. Fuentes's account of Baltasar's campaign to remedy the contradictions and pacify the struggles regarding Spanish America's fight for independence is one that mirrors actual historical Spanish American historical struggles.

Fuentes has often regarded the large body of his fiction as one continual and total entity, and with *The Campaign* he embarks on what critics call his *el tiempo romántico,* or third cycle. This is the only novel by Fuentes focusing on Latin American countries other than Mexico; yet *The Campaign* still regards the search for truth and meaning in all Latin American countries. Existentially, truth is found within the school of Enlightenment thought, yet Baltasar still grapples to ascend to a greater plane of awareness because he is also torn by religious thought. This conflict functions as a way to not only help the readers define the central character but also to reinforce the idea that Fuentes's characters do not merely represent composites of reality, they represent ideas central to the earliest beginnings of Latin American independence and their subsequent newly formed republics.

A major theme of *The Campaign* is that of an ideal society, a utopic existence; yet this objective is in direct contrast with reality. This is similar to Baltasar's attempts to correlate the idealism he discovers in the writings of Rousseau and Voltaire to the reality of his present. Although an ideal and romantic endeavor, this is a highly unlikely outcome when one recalls the chaos and near-anarchy during the fall of the Spanish empire. However, since Baltasar represents the idealism and fervor that determinism affords, even in the face of impossibility, readers cannot blame him for remaining faithful to the hope that the destruction of war will raise the possibility of a better future.

The Campaign is a novel that lauds the philosophical and spiritual essence of the Enlightenment period; it supports the idea that reason can advocate the (re)evaluation of generally accepted ideas and institutions, and it begs to question the blind acceptance of that which is perceived as truth. When one regards Baltasar in this light, it is easy to see him as a positive figure and forgive his tendency to hope that a utopian reality transcends impossibility. *The Campaign* heralds the independent spirit of a new republic and posits the idea that a newly formed government can withstand the dystopic realities that inevitably challenge the best of man's intentions.

BIBLIOGRAPHY

Helmuth, Chalene. *The Postmodern Fuentes*. Lewisburg, Pa.: Bucknell University Press, 1997.

Langford, Walter M. *The Mexican Novel Comes of Age*. South Bend, Ind.: University of Notre Dame Press, 1971.

Van Delden, Maarten. *Carlos Fuentes, Mexico and Modernity*. Nashville, Tenn. Vanderbilt University Press, 1999.

Rosemary Briseño

CAMUS, ALBERT (1913–1960) *French essayist, novelist, playwright*

Albert Camus was one of the most influential French writers of the 20th century. A novelist, essayist, playwright, and journalist, Camus was a leading voice in literature as well as politics concerning human rights, freedom, and national independence. His work has long been linked to the philosophical ideas of existentialism and the absurd, two intellectual concepts prominent in the first half of the 20th century. His novels often explore the meaning of humankind's search for values, ethics, and purpose in a world devoid of God. Camus is often compared to ANDRÉ MALRAUX, JEAN-PAUL SARTRE, and other postwar writers in breaking with the traditional bourgeois novel. Camus's interest turned from then-popular psychological analysis toward philosophical problems such as humankind's existence in the state of the absurd.

Camus is perhaps best known for his novels *The STRANGER* (*L'étranger*, 1942), *The PLAGUE* (*La peste*, 1947), and *The FALL* (*La chute*, 1956), and for his short essay "The Myth of Sisyphus" ("Le mythe de Sisyphe," 1942). These philosophically enriched works sustain an intricate balance between the complexities of modern ideas and the simplicity of storytelling. Camus's writing plumbs such human conditions and frailties as war, suicide, revolt, absurdism, and atheism. Throughout his life, he was an ardent advocate of human rights and a steadfast denunciator of war and violence. He became a symbol for the conscience of humankind that abhorred inflexible political ideas. He saw no distinction between art and humanity, but rather viewed art as a means to bringing solutions to the problems facing the human race. In 1957 he was awarded the Nobel Prize in literature for his literary and political writing.

Albert Camus was born in Mondovia, Algeria, a French colony at the time, on November 7, 1913. His parents were Lucien Camus and Helen Sintes, French immigrants who sought a better economic life in the French colony. The family's hopes were soon dashed. Camus's father, a member of the First Zouave Regiment, died in 1914 during World War I's bloody battle of the Marne in France. The news of her husband's death caused Camus's mother to suffer a stroke that produced hearing loss and a speech impediment. The effects of war remained a continuous theme throughout the author's literary career.

Fatherless, Camus and his older brother grew up in extreme poverty. School life at the local Belcourt schools became an oasis from his squalid home circumstances. As a young student, Camus showed a keen ability in academics, the theater, and athletics. He was befriended by Louis Germain, a teacher, who tutored him to pass the entrance exams in 1923 for the lycée, an exclusive secondary school for students destined for the university. Camus was later accepted to the University of Algiers's school of philosophy. During his university studies, he contracted tuberculosis, a disease that undermined his health for the rest of his life. These health problems forced him to continue his studies intermittently at the university, and he received his *diplome d'études supérieures* (similar to an M.A.) from the University of Algiers in philosophy late in 1936. His goal of becoming a teacher was never realized because he could not pass the health examination due to his history of tuberculosis.

The decade between 1930 and 1940 produced turbulence and change on many fronts for the young Camus. He was searching for his place in the world as he entered his 20s. In 1934, while still a student, he joined the Communist Party. This began a period of fervent political activism that lasted throughout his life, although he soon broke with the communists. He became disillusioned with the strident political propaganda that called for change at the cost of human lives. While no longer a communist, Camus remained a socialist until his death in 1960.

In 1934 Camus married Simone Hie, but this union proved to be ill-fated. The daughter of a wealthy and upper-class ophthalmologist, Simone suffered from drug addiction. The marriage was short-lived. In 1940 Camus married again, this time to Francine Faure, a mathematics teacher from Oran; they had two children.

At the university between 1935 and 1939, Camus helped to found the Workers' Theater, a theatrical project designed to produce socialist plays for the benefit of Algerian workers. His foray into playwriting came as a collaboration with other young radical intellectuals on a political play, *Revolte dans les Asturies.* The theater company also produced plays by Malraux, John Millington Synge, ANDRÉ GIDE, and Fyodor Dostoyevsky.

Writing became Camus's direction in life. His professional writing career began as a reporter for the leftwing *Alger-Republicain,* an anticolonialist and socialist newspaper, and other journals. His work typically addressed ethnic discrimination faced by the Arabs, the poor, and other marginalized groups in Algeria, France, and the rest of Europe. He was particularly troubled by the barbarity of the Spanish civil war (1936–39). These writings were later published in *Actuelles III* (1958). In 1937 Camus published his first volume of writings, a collection of essays entitled *The Wrong Side and the Right Side* (*L'envers et l'endroit*). That same year he completed his first novel, *A Happy Death* (*La mort heureuse*), though it remained unpublished during his lifetime.

The first half of the 1940s brought Camus face-to-face with war once again. In 1940 he left his home in Algeria for Paris with the hope of becoming a reporter for the leftist press in the French center. The invasion of France by the German army put an end to these aspirations, and he fled Paris to North Africa. Upon his return to Algeria, Camus began teaching in Oran, where he met Francine Faure, who became his second wife. A pacifist, he wrote articles against the war in Europe, writings that placed him under the suspicion of the government in France and Algeria. He was soon declared a threat to national security and forced to leave the country.

Forced into exile, Camus returned to occupied France to work as a member of the French resistance. He was not well received and again fell under suspicion, becoming a man without a country, though he did secure a reporting post for the newspaper *Paris-Soir.* The newspaper staff was forced to relocate to the western port city of Bordeaux to escape capture by the Nazis. During this year—still 1940—Camus was constantly on the run, but he also wrote the manuscripts of a series of works for what he termed *The Absurds,* one of his most prolific achievements. *The Absurds* is a trilogy consisting of *The Stranger,* "The Myth of Sisyphus," and *The Plague,* works that brought Camus international literary recognition.

The two parts of *The Absurds* that best exemplify Camus's literary canon are the companion pieces *The Stranger* and "The Myth of Sisyphus," both published in 1942 and both addressing the philosophical subject of the absurd. In each text the central figures exist in an irrational and puzzling world.

Camus envisioned the absurd as a great divide between humankind's desire for happiness and a world that is unsuited for such an end. On the one hand, an individual seeks a world governed by the forces of justice and order, an existence he can comprehend rationally. In this world, good and justice are rewarded. On the other hand, the individual encounters the actual world, which is chaotic, irrational, and meaningless, and one which brings suffering before a meaningless death to mortals. Within this modern interpretation of the French philosopher René Descartes's fundamental premise—from "I think therefore I am" to "I exist therefore I am"—Camus concluded that man should not accept the absurdity of the universe but should revolt against this irrationality, this indifference. Revolt, for Camus and other existentialists, comes in the form of a new humanism: Old values are discarded in lieu of new values centered on the individual living in a social context.

Perhaps Camus's most widely read novel is *The Stranger,* which was published in 1942. *The Stranger* describes the tragic story of Meursault, a young man who is a stranger to those around him and an enigma to readers. The famous opening line of the short novel offers a glimpse into the action that occupies the entire work. Upon reading a telegram announcing his mother's death, Mersault is left uncertain whether she died on that day or the previous day. His reactions to his mother's passing also remain opaque. Throughout the novel, the reader is not availed of Mersault's thoughts and feelings toward his mother, his girlfriend, his murder of a stranger, and his acceptance of his conviction and execution for his senseless crime. Camus relates the story in the first person, a limited point of view that elides most of Mersault's feelings and reactions to the happenings in the novel.

The story of *The Stranger* is structured around three deaths and how Mersault faces the question of mortality. The death of his mother is announced at the opening of the novel. In the middle of the story, Mersault senselessly kills a stranger, and at the book's end, he faces execution for his crime. What has continuously appealed to readers is Mersault's indifference to all emotion and passion. He appears apathetic toward the three deaths, even the approach of his own execution. In one way, readers can see Mersault as the absurd character because he mirrors the indifference of the universe. While readers traditionally may seek to understand and comprehend Mersault as a fictional character, he remains outside of the boundary of definitive exegesis.

Mersault is the quintessential antihero. He is tough although ultimately vulnerable. Camus admired the tough persona of the characters found in such Ernest Hemingway novels as *The Sun Also Rises* and *A Farewell to Arms.* He also attempted to imitate the restraint and conciseness in the writing style that had gained great popularity in the middle of the 20th century.

Camus's powerful essay "The Myth of Sisyphus," written in the same year as *The Stranger,* explains his notion of the absurd and the apparent indifference of the universe to humankind's innate desire for happiness and justice in the world. It also addresses the difference between individual despair and loss of hope. "The Myth of Sisyphus" is a retelling of the Greek story of the unfortunate Sisyphus, who had angered the gods and was sentenced to an inhuman fate: to ceaselessly roll a tremendous stone to the top of a mountain, whereupon the rock would roll back to the bottom of the mountain of its own weight. Sisyphus would again and again take up his toil.

The deities deemed that no more dreadful punishment than futile and hopeless labor existed; they thought they could relish watching Sisyphus's torment. Camus recognized the inherent parallel between Sisyphus's mindless and habitual toil and modern humankind's everyday, mechanical, clock-driven existence. Ironically, however, Camus considered that one must ultimately view Sisyphus as happy. This position sparked remarkable debate the world over, as the essay received widespread popularity. Given that hope is lost for Sisyphus's release from his eternal fate, how can the tragic figure be viewed as happy? Camus considered that happiness and victory or triumph of self can prevail only if—as in Sisyphus's dire and unalterable circumstances—the unfortunate figure accepts his absurd condition.

Camus imagines Sisyphus as becoming one with his fate; through his acceptance of it, he becomes defiant and rebellious. He finds freedom in his ability to rise above his fate, at least in his mind, and through this conscious position he defeats the gods and his fate. Thus the individual rises above his circumstances and makes the best of them, working his task without bemoaning his fate. Sisyphus would become a pathetic and unfortunate figure if, according to Camus, he wasted his strength and effort through wailing against the inevitability decreed by the gods. It is through this conscious position that Sisyphus raises himself up: By his defiance and rebellion against the gods, but not against his daily task, Sisyphus redeems himself. This can only occur if one thinks of Sisyphus as happy—defiant and rebellious.

Like "The Myth of Sisyphus," *The Plague,* published in 1947, works on a mythic level. The popular novel captures a sense of myth in modern language. Based on Daniel Defoe's account in *A Journal of the Plague Year* (1665), Camus's *The Plague* is an allegorical story of the German invasion of Europe during World War II. The metaphor of the plague becomes the faceless evil for the German occupation of France. In this novel, the city of Oran is overrun with rats carrying a devastating plague that infects its citizens. There seems to be no way out of this senseless devastation. Once the plague is finally diagnosed, the city undergoes strict quarantine, and no one is allowed in or out, cutting them off from the outside world. The dead count starts to mount in astronomical numbers. The question arises: Why has this disease come to Oran and what, if anything, can be done about it? Yet no human action, regardless of its degree or merit, proves helpful in stopping the carnage; human action pales in light of the plague's indomitable nature, an army indiscriminately destroying human life in Oran.

Criticism regarding *The Plague* at the time of publication in 1947 centered on Camus's description of the German occupation of France and other countries in Western Europe through the faceless image of a plague rather than a more direct graphic representation of evil human forces.

Despite the hardships of World War II, the war years had proven to be a turning point for Camus in terms of philosophy, social activism, and writing. During the mid-1940s, he became friends with Jean-Paul Sartre and SIMONE DE BEAUVOIR. The three French intellectuals met often at Café de Flore on the Boulevard St-Germain, in an area known as the Left Bank, to discuss literature and politics.

Camus and Sartre first met in 1943 in Paris at the opening of Sartre's allegorical play *The Flies,* which denounced German collaboration. They initially shared a close friendship despite their contrasting economic backgrounds. Sartre grew up in a well-to-do middle-class environment, as opposed to Camus's dire poverty. Philosophically, the two writers were both social radicals, denouncing conservative measures that were seen as imposing injustices on the impoverished. Sartre was the key proponent of existentialism, a philosophy espousing the doctrine that man is utterly free from all shaping or controlling forces like religion, economics, culture, and politics to make his life what he wants to. Sartre's tenet that "existence precedes essence" reverses the traditional precept that humankind is endowed with certain innate fundamental spiritual and moral characteristics.

Although often misunderstood as an existentialist, Camus rejected this extreme label. His belief, in contrast to Sartre, focused on social responsibility and value. Camus is more rightly considered an absurdist, viewing humankind as possessing longings, hopes, and aspirations to which the universe does not respond. This is the essence of his essay "The Myth of Sisyphus."

Both Camus's *The Stranger* (1942) and Sartre's novel NAUSEA (1938) expounded on the meaninglessness of human existence in a world fraught with war and a loss of God. World War II and the Nazi occupation of France offered graphic representation to their ideas exploring absurdism and existentialism. Prior to their first meeting in 1943, the two writers had written positive reviews of the other's writing. Camus had discovered Sartre's writing in 1938 when he reviewed *Nausea* for an Algerian left-wing daily paper. He was then in his early 20s, having published two small books of essays: *The Wrong Side and the Right Side* (*L'envers et l'endroit,* 1937) and *Nuptials.* (*Noces,* 1938). Camus showed remarkable talent and insight in his reviews of many new fictional works published in Paris: Gide's *The COUNTERFEITERS,* Paul Nizan's *The Conspiracy,* Ignazio Silone's *Bread and Wind,* Aldous Huxley's *Those Barren Leaves,* JORGE AMADO's *Bahia,* and Sartre's *Nausea* and *The Wall.* Sartre, meanwhile, in comparing Camus to Hemingway and FRANZ KAFKA, admired *The Stranger* for the novel's simplicity of language, plot, and character development.

The friendship between Camus and Sartre came to a halt in 1952. For nearly a decade the two men had gained a reputation as the two leading intellectuals in the French language. Though both had helped to shape the history and future of France, their aesthetic and political attitudes changed after World War II. Two reasons can be attributed to their break. First, both writers published harsh articles and reviews about the other's work, attacks that were primarily based on political terms. These articles produced wounds that would not heal. Second, Camus and Sartre had proceeded down divergent political paths. Camus had long previously condemned the Communist Party for its acceptance of radical violence. His anticommunism called into question leftist ideas that advocated revolutionary violence, particularly against innocent immigrants in Algeria. These themes were developed in essays published in the nonfiction work *The Rebel* (*L'homme revolte,* 1951). This work directly examines the dangers of absolute political and religious ideas, particularly the transformation of revolutions into tyrannies. *The Rebel* warns against the excesses of revolution that have often manifested themselves in brutality, poverty, and purges through death hunts. Sartre's reaction emerged as vitriolic and visceral. He felt that Camus's denunciation of revolution had bolstered the forces opposing communism. Sartre remained an extreme Marxist and communist who backed violent reprisals against colonialists in Algeria. Algeria, Camus's homeland, remained a wedge separating the two men. Sartre called for violent rebellion against the French occupation in North Africa. Camus, on the other hand, sought a peaceful solution. The two men remained estranged until Sartre read a eulogy at his rival's funeral in 1960.

For several years Camus remained silent as a novelist, until, in 1956, he published *The Fall.* The work investigates Camus's frequent theme of judgment that the author initiated in *The Stranger.* The central figure, Jean-Baptiste Clamence, travels from Paris, the city of light, to the decadent, fog-bound world of Amsterdam. The novel is a monologue by Clamence in which he judges his life, seeing himself as having fallen from grace. The tone of *The Fall* remains extremely ironic throughout as the narrator, a Parisian lawyer who has enjoyed his virtuous nature and hedonistic lifestyle, describes his descent from a privileged existence to an awareness of his impoverished regard for others. As a lawyer defending the accused in front of judges, Clamence has remained free from human and divine judgment. However, fallen from the heights of a penthouse in Paris to a bar in the depths of Amsterdam's low country, he finds himself assessing his own life.

In addition to his fame as a novelist, Camus was highly regarded as a playwright. His two most noteworthy dramatic writings include *Caligula* (1938) and *Cross Purpose* (1944). In *Caligula,* Camus addresses how power is used as a malignant force in response to a meaningless universe. A young and tyrannical Roman emperor, Caligula punishes the populace after the senseless death of his beloved sister Drusilla, terrorizing them by going on a killing spree, murdering his subjects at random. He eventually welcomes his own assassination. *Cross Purpose* is another play that addresses the absurdity of existence. The main figure returns home to the inn his mother and sister run after traveling the world for two decades. Uncertain how to explain his surprise return after a long absence, the prodigal son elects to spend the night at the inn, posing as a stranger. What he does not know is that his mother and sister murder and rob rich travelers. The prodigal son becomes the next victim. After the family members discover his true identity, they commit suicide, a popular outcome for Camus.

Among the many awards Camus received, the 1957 Nobel Prize in literature recognized the author's international and timeless qualities. He was only 43 years old, distinguishing him as one of the youngest recipients of the coveted prize. Regrettably, his promising life was cut short. Less than three years after his recognition in Stockholm, Camus was killed in an automobile accident near Sens, France, on January 4, 1960. He was returning to Paris in an automobile driven by his publisher and friend, Michel Gallimard. Found in his papers at the accident site was the manuscript of the novel *The First Man* (*Le premier homme*) a fictionalized account of his family history that was finally published in 1995.

BIBLIOGRAPHY
Akeroyd, Richard H. *The Spiritual Quest of Albert Camus.* Tuscaloosa, Ala.: Portals Press, 1976.

Aronson, Ronald. *Camus & Sartre.* Chicago: University of Chicago Press, 2004.

Beauclair, Michelle. *Albert Camus, Marguerite Duras, and the Legacy of Mourning.* New York: Peter Lang, 1998.

Bloom, Harold, ed. *Albert Camus.* New York: Chelsea House, 1989.

Braun, Lev. *Witness of Decline: Albert Camus.* Madison, N.J.: Fairleigh Dickinson University Press, 1974.

Ellison, David R. *Understanding Albert Camus.* Columbia: University of South Carolina Press, 1990.

Falk, Eugene H. *Types of Thematic Structure: The Nature and Function of Motifs in Gide, Camus, and Sartre.* Chicago: University of Chicago Press, 1967.

Freeman, E. *The Theatre of Albert Camus: A Critical Study.* London: Methuen, 1971.

Grenier, Jean. *Albert Camus: Souvenirs.* Paris: Gallimard, 1968.

Lazere, Donald. *The Unique Creation of Albert Camus.* New Haven, Conn.: Yale University Press, 1973.

Michael D. Sollars

CANAIMA RÓMULO GALLEGOS (1935)

Canaima takes place along the Orinoco River, deep in the Venezuelan jungle of the early 20th century. It poetically illustrates the region's exotic natural beauty while telling a story that is at once as romantic as it is political. The novel's author, RÓMULO GALLEGOS (1884–1969), was an essayist, novelist, and statesman who led a distinguished career in public service. Among other positions, he served as president of Venezuela and is considered one of its most important political and literary figures.

Along with Gallegos's *DOÑA BÁRBARA* (1929) and *Cantaclaro* (1931), *Canaima* is one of the most significant works in Venezuela's literary canon. The three books, which may be read as a trilogy, all take place in the nation's rural backlands, forming a complete picture of the undeveloped plains and lush tropical jungle. Each novel depicts the classic struggle between civilization and barbarism, a clash frequently represented in works written in the early stages of nation building in Latin America's postindependence period. Gallegos clearly articulates his preference in this conflict: His novels' heroes invariably symbolize civilization, consistently triumphing over the untamed wilds—in both their human and environmental forms. Like many intellectual elites of his time, Gallegos looked to Europe as a model for Venezuela, advocating a "civilizing mission" for his relatively undeveloped young nation.

Canaima narrates the journey of its main character, Marcos Vargas, who leaves the city for an adventure in the backlands. He arrives in the Orinoco river basin, where he eventually disappears to live among the Indians. As in Gallegos's other works, the protagonist represents the Europeanized city dweller who battles with the forces of unchecked rural power, in this case the uncivilized and ruthless Ardavines family. Vargas is a fascinating character, and it is interesting to compare him with the better-known hero of Gallegos's *Doña Bárbara,* Santos Luzardo. While both embody the educated, citified voice of "reason," the former clearly represents a more nuanced, conflicted, and passionate version of the latter. The relatively two-dimensional Luzardo travels to the plains simply to conquer and domesticate the backlands, while Vargas journeys not only to dominate but also to learn from the Indians and to fall in love. As Jorge Ruffinelli, a scholar and literary critic who teaches at the University of Uruguay, observes in *Latin American Writers,* the author's writings evolved over time, gradually reflecting a greater appreciation for the "natural" elements of his native land: "In the course of his career, Gallegos turned away from the stereotypical racist European point of view in favor of a more complex understanding of the autochthonous elements of the American experience." In this sense, *Canaima* emerges as a more complex portrayal of Venezuelan life in the early 20th century than its more famous counterpart, *Doña Bárbara,* and many consider it Gallegos's finest novel.

The book illustrates several of the region's social and political conflicts of the time, including the corrupt legal justice system and abuses of workers by local bosses. Vargas challenges the lawlessness of the backlands, always fighting for righteous justice. He also has relationships with three women: Aracelis, Maigualida, and Aymara. He eventually fathers a son by the latter, an Indian woman who represents his decision to go into the forest and live among the natives. In the end, however, civilization again conquers the "barbaric" countryside, as the novel ends with Vargas sending his son to the city to be educated by his "civilized" friend Gabriel Ureña.

Although the author was raised in the city of Caracas, and he wrote *Canaima* while in exile in Spain, his novel effectively captures the linguistic, cultural, and societal relationships of the Venezuelan countryside. Gallegos's works are considered among the greatest expressions of the regional novel, a subgenre that played an important role in Latin American literature in the first half of the 20th century, according to scholar Melvin S. Arrington, Jr. Rich with colloquialisms and indigenous idioms, *Canaima* is one of the most vivid expressions of Venezuelan rural life of its day. At the same time, the novel has a timeless, universal appeal and has been translated into numerous languages. Many of the socioeconomic realities depicted remain as unchanged today as the natural setting that surrounds the book's characters, and *Canaima* continues to be an important and highly relevant literary work.

BIBLIOGRAPHY

Carrera, Gustavo Luis, ed. *Canaima ante la crítica.* Caracas: Monte Avila Editores Latinoamericana, 1995.

Gallegos, Rómulo. *Canaima.* Caracas: Monte Avila Editores, 1977.

———. *Canaima.* Translated by Will Kirkland. Pittsburgh, Pa.: University of Pittsburgh Press, 1996.

———. *Canaima.* Translated by Jaime Tello. Norman and London: University of Oklahoma Press, 1988.

Jane Marcus-Delgado

CANCER WARD (RAKOVYI KORPUS)

ALEKSANDR SOLZHENITSYN (1968)   This intriguing novel by Russia's esteemed author ALEKSANDR SOLZHENITSYN (1918–) begins with a family's fretful abandonment of the pompous, self-serving apparatchik judge Pavel Nikolayevich Rusanov at a Soviet oncology ward, where he is cut off from his customary power and comforts. Even so, *Cancer Ward* revolves around and ends with the tale of another patient who arrives at the institution at the same time as the judge. Oleg Kostoglotov, a worker, war veteran, and permanent exile from rural Ush-Terek, has endured an ordeal just to be admitted to the ward. Kostoglotov flirts with a young doctor and begins an affair with her. The other patients include a young engineer, Vadim Zatsyrko, studying a problem to give his life meaning according to his custom, though his life will end soon; a former

prison camp guard, Yefrem Podduyev; and Shulubin, a former academic who exemplifies the best of Leninist values but has now been purged and is dying. They provide counterparts, but the novel revolves around Kostoglotov's relentless will to live and to love, and around his search to know "what men live by."

The first part of the novel clarifies the helplessness of the patients; most have large tumors that make ordinary actions difficult, so their mobility is largely restricted. The patients spend the vast majority of their time in bed inside the ward, though Kostoglotov occasionally takes walks. The patients become excited about possible cures; at one time they think that radioactive gold will cure them, though no one can get any; at another point they believe tea made from a tree fungus may be a cure. Kostoglotov remains curious, and as he studies the treatment of cancer, he begins to understand more of what is going on around him. He knows most of the patients will die. The hospital releases terminal cases in the final stages.

When Rusanov arrives in the ward, he tries to bully others because he has the higher Communist Party status. However, the newspaper reports events that make him now vulnerable, and he becomes frightened when he realizes that the cadre of Stalinist loyalists like himself has gone out of power. The other patients mock him for taking a bureaucratic track to power, and his daughter brings him the news that retaliation has begun against those who delivered false evidence against the victims of Stalinism, something Rusanov has done himself. The conversation in the ward includes several loud arguments about the corruption inherent in privileging those like Rusanov. Rusanov is left behind, in a way: His daughter chooses to study literature rather than law, though she appears mostly to affirm "socialist realism." Rusanov's son has become a petty judge, but he horrifies Rusanov with his leniency and lack of cunning. The ongoing changes, Rusanov must realize, have changed his own life radically for the worse. Everybody, however, is disoriented by the changing climate. Several of the patients must consider that their lives outside are at a dead end.

Kostoglotov has a different problem: His virility is at stake. He had served as a soldier in World War II and then was exiled to the steppes of Asia. When he realizes a brief improvement in his condition, he begins to enjoy the relative freedom he finds. While other patients lie about gloomily dying, he finds great satisfaction absorbing nature or listening to the music at a nearby dance. The world's beauty continues to invigorate him. Having been deprived for so long, he has two romances while in the ward. Then he flirts with two women, doctors who are treating him. He develops great admiration and respect for Vera Gangart, who is nearly his age; he also adores the younger doctor, Lyudmila Dontsova, for her beauty and her liveliness. A crucial part of the problem derives from the hormone treatment he has been taking, which will make him impotent. He avoids the treatment, with Dontsova's complicity. Both women eventually believe that he has betrayed them, for not submitting to the recommended treatment properly and for pursuing the other woman. He seems to gain a measure of forgiveness from them, but the relationships are never the same.

As a counterpoint, there is also a romance between Dyomka, a young trade-school student, and his girlfriend Asya. The doctors want to amputate Dyomka's leg, but Asya wants him to refuse because the amputation would rob him of physical and masculine prowess. Later, however, Asya comes in devastated because she has breast cancer and must have the afflicted breast removed. To these two, youth shapes the significance of the problem at hand, but the overall construction of the novel implies that vanity afflicts those at all ages, and that all overlook the depth and beauty of ordinary life.

A theory of art comes into play in the arguments between the patients and in the conversation with Rusanov's daughter. Beauty itself adds to the value of life, the novel implies, and since literature seeks both to create beauty and to seek what men live by, the novel indirectly affirms the importance of literature in Russian life via its many allusions.

Most important, though, in one of the novel's central scenes, Kostoglotov opens a discussion on "what do men live by," after reading Leo Tolstoy's story on that theme. The debate has resonance in Kostoglotov's wondering what it would mean to be "saved at any price." He believes that some sacrifices ought not to be made even to protect one's life. The story he has read proposes that the answer must be love, but none of the patients has been prepared to accept such an answer. They offer mechanistic and materialist philosophical or political propositions. But as the characters' conflicts in the novel develop, neither the power of the state nor science appears to offer anything substantively redemptive to them or to humanity.

The conflicts in the novel call political, philosophical, and metaphysical issues into question. Numerous plot threads offer potential political allegories. If the hospital is a metaphor for the nation, then it matters that the doctors in this tale also seem lost: Vera, too, apparently has cancer, so she goes home to see an old general practitioner. An inept doctor at the cancer ward, who is a party stooge, abets a "show trial" for a decent medical staffer, and Vera and Lev Leonidovich go to derail what they deem an obscene proceeding; they succeed, but the party stooge is still delighted to have come up with the idea of having show trials for doctors. Obviously, one of the main themes is that the "little people" are almost helpless against a blind totalitarian state, but they must resist.

Solzhenitsyn depicts the failures evenhandedly: He makes clear that human beings are complex, neither logical nor predictable, and that any state plan would struggle. For this reason, most of the subplots do not fit into neat allegories. Even Rusanov, though he eventually finds out that he does not like mere people at all, first loved the rhetoric and mythology of Lenin for its love of "the People." This goes to another question: What is natural and what is artificial, with the implication that new, artificially imposed, man-made solutions must be flawed.

Probably the most important question is whether a worthwhile life can be too oriented to material and physical acquisition or whether a spiritual dimension must be attained. This problem bears upon Kostoglotov's choice between the sexy younger doctor (whose name means "life") and the platonic attraction to Vera, or Vega as she is called (which suggests a heavenly body, "Star"). It also bears upon the life of contemplation, burdened with a rotten body that Shulubin and Kostoglotov both perhaps anticipate after a "cure." Shulubin's last words claim that not all of him will die—yet another reference to a spiritual eternity. But even though Kostoglotov feels that he has grown through his struggle, on his first day after being released from the hospital, he spends his money foolishly on quick pleasures—a piece of grilled meat on a stick, a drink. When he realizes with shame that he has simply accommodated the physical dimension greedily, he goes to the zoo as if to purge himself. He encounters with rage another incident of cruelty to animals. Perhaps he recognizes that solutions in this world will bear within them the flaw of senseless human brutality. Still, Kostoglotov's struggle to embrace life on each meaningful level gives the book its sympathy and its power. The novel ends suddenly, as he drifts off to sleep, but not without provoking contemplation of many of the world's most important questions. *Cancer Ward* is the most emotionally moving of Sozhenitsyn's novels, at least as profound as the other great ones and certainly one of the 20th century's greatest works.

BIBLIOGRAPHY

Dunlop, John B., ed. *Solzhenitsyn in Exile.* Palo Alto, Calif.: Hoover Institution, 1985.

Ericson, Edward E. *Solzhenitsyn and the Modern World.* Washington, D.C.: Regnery Gateway, 1993.

Krasnov, Valdislav. *Solzhenitsyn and Dostoevsky: A Study in the Polyphonic Novel.* Athens: University of Georgia Press, 1980.

Rothberg, Abraham. *Alexandr Solzhenitsyn: The Major Novels.* Ithaca, N.Y.: Cornell University Press, 1971.

Thomas, D. M. *Alexander Solzhenitsyn: A Century in His Life.* New York: St. Martin's Press, 1998.

James Potts

CAN XUE (DENG XIAOHUA) (1953–   )

Chinese novelist, short story writer   To term Can Xue "unique" in Chinese literature is to state her position mildly. Critic Charlotte Innes describes the author as an anomaly among Chinese writers because of her deliberate resistance to socialist-realist literature, the official literary mode in Maoist China. It is therefore unsurprising that Can Xue's writing is more celebrated in and acceptable to the West. Surrealistic atmosphere, horrifying representations, and the denial of closure make her narratives not only difficult to read but politically troubling as well because they indirectly question the fantasy of a harmonious and glorious nation that Communist China wants to present to the world.

Born Deng Xiaohua in 1953, Can Xue (which means "dirty snow that refuses to melt") is arguably the first woman writer in the literary avant-garde movement, initiated around 1985, that includes internationally renowned writers such as Mo Yan and Su Tong. Like many Chinese during Mao's rule, Can Xue's parents were condemned as ultraleftist, which led to their "reeducation" and the writer's bitter and difficult childhood. Raised by her grandmother, Can Xue was forced to leave school at the age of 13, and for the next 10 years she found employment as an iron worker. It was during this time that she taught herself to sew and subsequently became a self-employed tailor. She only began writing fiction seriously in 1983, and her published works immediately gained notoriety among Chinese critics, who are predominantly male. In an interview with Laura McCandlish, Can Xue has contended that "I differ from their points of view. Lots of them [male writers] hate me, or at least they just keep silent, hoping I'll disappear. No one discusses my works, either because they disagree or don't understand. . . . For a distinguished woman writer in China, the writing profession is very strange because the mainstream criticism is from traditional culture, man's culture, so they can't understand an individual woman's style."

Can Xue's narratives are peopled with grotesque individuals living in abject poverty and constant fear. Her stories are more or less plotless, detailing the everyday existence of the Chinese people under an oppressive communist regime. Here, suspicion, murderous intent, confusion, and superstition constitute the dominant way of life and thought, all of which are mirrored by her meandering prose. The following passage from "Skylight" in *Dialogues in Paradise* (1989) is typical of Can Xue's stories:

A man was crawling up from the bushes at the end of the graveyard. . . . That was my younger brother. Within one night, he had grown a mole's tail and fur. In his degenerated memory his image of me was vulgar. Slobbering, he tried to catch some yellow fantasy. Finally, driven by certain elusive ideas, he crawled here from the cellar. Mother was sitting on a barrel in the cellar, mumbling an odd, unfamiliar name. She was in the process of melting, a fine stream of black water ran out under her feet toward the door.

Clearly, any attempt at reading such stories "realistically" is impossible. Can Xue attributes her inspiration to Samuel Beckett and FRANZ KAFKA, and in her works she celebrates the absurd and often nightmarish images that break down narrative coherence and rational interpretation. In Can Xue's world, characters (who are often already "inhuman" to begin with) transform into beasts and even "things," metaphorically reflecting the harsh reality that subjugates and ultimately anthropomorphises and objectifies the Chinese people. References to scatological and perverse fantasies dominate, and death becomes an everyday occurrence that is at best annoying and at worst, troublesome. Indeed, a reverence for the human person is completely devoid.

To date, English translations of Can Xue's writing are confined to two collections of short stories, *Dialogues in Paradise* (*Tiantangli de duihua,* 1989) and *The Embroidered Shoes: Stories* (*Xiuhua xie,* 1997); two novellas collected in *Old Floating Cloud: Two Novellas* (*Canglao de fuyun,* 1991); and a few short stories. From her forward to *Dialogues in Paradise* entitled "A Summer Day in the Beautiful South" (the title itself is a parody of popular Chinese literature that whitewashes the vexing reality of life under Mao), it can be surmised that her grandmother continues to exert a strong influence in Can Xue's life and writing. A resilient, stubborn, and resourceful woman, the writer's grandmother represents an enduring spirit who would not be cowed by life's circumstances. Can Xue transforms daily suffering and incomprehensibility into fiction as a means to grapple with (not in the sense of controlling or understanding) the troubled times following the Cultural Revolution. Thus, although her writing plunges into the depths of human decadence, there is always a suggestion of hope and renewal even in the bleakest and harshest of situations.

In one of the two novellas, *Yellow Mud Street,* the shape-shifting, unidentifiable "thing" called Wang Ziguang functions as a "presence" that haunts the story. Like the Cultural Revolution, which purports an aim that is impossible to define, Wang is simultaneously a ghost, an official, a dead person, and a pseudonym for a fellow comrade. This suggests the anomalousness of Maoist ideology that persistently burdens the Chinese people with confusion and uncertainty. In fact, as the narrator tells us, although she is searching for "the yellow mud street," it cannot be found; and yet, detailed descriptions of its inhabitants and their activities (especially obscene ones) are carefully provided. This suggests the schizophrenic insinuation of Chinese history during Mao's regime, which denies the reality of the people's suffering despite its obviousness.

Old Floating Cloud continues in the vein of private entrapment due to political manipulation. In this tale, two families living opposite each other are constantly suspicious of the other's "imagined" attempts at scandalizing. But even more insidious is the fact that members of a family are also suspicious of one another. Indeed, the Cultural Revolution's effects of policing the self and others are taken to their absurd extreme in this story. Not only are neighbors wary of one another, but husbands are distrustful of their wives and parents chary of their children.

The title story of Can Xue's second English-translated collection of short stories is a frightening study of overwhelming suspicion that results in insanity. The narrator-protagonist accuses a neighbor of stealing her "beauty" and, directly, her lover because the latter refuses to return the narrator's pair of embroidered shoes. But as the story progresses, it becomes unclear if there really is such a neighbor, or if all these accusations and insinuations are really the perverse imagination of a woman whose vain and suspicious nature has finally taken a toll on her. A similar theme is repeated in "A Strange Kind of Brain Damage."

It is impossible to separate a political edge from Can Xue's stories, despite her downplaying of their sociopolitical element. Her narratives are sharp satires of the Communist regime and its literary expressions, both of which obfuscate the painful actuality of every day life in China. In *Yellow Mud Street,* for example, the narrative is occasionally peppered with popular Maoist axioms that merely reveal the absurdity of such principles in the face of reality. But to read Can Xue as largely political is to miss the power of her prose. As Ronald Janssen aptly notes in his forward to *Old Floating Cloud,* the best way to approach a writer like Can Xue is to free one's imagination from familiar, regimented methods of reading: "Readers need only to set their imaginations free. Even if they do not always understand Can Xue, they will invariably be challenged, fascinated, and provoked."

BIBLIOGRAPHY

Can Xue. *Dialogues in Paradise.* Translated by Ronald R. Janssen and Zhang Jian. Evanston, Ill.: Northwestern University Press, 1989.

———. *The Embroidered Shoes: Stories.* Translated by Ronald R. Janssen and Zhang Jian. New York: Henry Holt, 1997.

———. *Old Floating Cloud: Two Novellas.* Translated by Ronald R. Janssen and Zhang Jian. Evanston, Ill.: Northwestern University Press, 1991.

———. "The Summons." Translated by Ronald R. Janssen and Zhang Jian. In *Chairman Mao Would Not be Pleased: Fiction from Today's China,* edited by Howard Goldblatt, 206–214. New York: Grove Press, 1995.

Lu, Tonglin, "Can Xue: What Is so Paranoid in her Writing." In *Gender and Sexuality in Twentieth-Century Chinese Literature and Society,* edited by Lu Tonglin, 175–204. New York: State University of New York Press, 1993.

Solomon, Jon. "Taking Tiger Mountain: Can Xue's Resistance and Cultural Critique." In *Gender Politics in Modern Chinese Writing and Feminism,* edited by Tani E. Barlow, 238–265. Durham, N.C.: Duke University Press, 1993.

Wedell-Wedellsborg, Anne. "Ambiguous Subjectivity: Reading Can Xue." *Modern Chinese Literature* 8 (1994): 7–20.

Yue, Meng. "Female Images and National Myth." In *Gender Politics in Modern Chinese Writing and Feminism,* edited by Tani E. Barlow, 118–136. Durham, N.C.: Duke University Press, 1993.

Andrew Hock-Soon Ng

ČAPEK, KAREL (1890–1938) *Czech novelist, dramatist, poet*

Karel Čapek was born in Malé Svatonovice, Bohemia, Austria-Hungary (now in the Czech Republic) in 1890. Although critically regarded for his novels, Čapek was also held in great esteem as a dramatist and poet, in addition to making a foray into biography. As a companion, friend, and colleague of the first president of the Czechoslovak Republic, Tomáš Masaryk, Čapek compiled an extensive recording of his political ideologies, philosophies, and ruminations in *Masaryk on Thought and Life* (*Hovory s T. G. Masarykem*), published in three volumes between 1928 and 1935.

Karel Čapek came from an intellectually centered family: his father, Antonín Čapek, was a country doctor, and Čapek's elder brother, Josef (1887–1945), achieved acclaim as a painter, novelist, and dramatist who also collaborated with his younger brother. The word *robot* was coined by Josef Čapek; in Czech, *robot* means "forced labor" or "servitude." Čapek's sister Helena (1886–1969) was also an occasional novelist.

Karl Čapek attended Charles University in Prague, where he studied philosophy, continuing this line of research at institutions in Berlin and Paris. In 1915 he was awarded a doctorate for a thesis entitled "Objective Methods in Aesthetics, with Reference to Creative Art," a work highly regarded by his academic peers and superiors. His first novel, *Zárivé Hlubiny* (1916), resulted from a collaboration with Josef, and in 1917 *Wayside Crosses* (*Boži Muka*), a collection of characteristically moody vignettes, also made it into print.

During World War I, Čapek held positions as a librarian and a tutor, most notably for the son of Count Vladimir Lažanský, a prominent Czech nationalist figure. Later, Čapek took up residence in Prague and began his career as a man of letters, writing columns and commentaries for the daily newspaper *Lidové Noviny*. His subjects were panoramic in their scope and elegant in their execution, yet even at this point his identification with the speculative qualities of the literature he later wrote became apparent. Aside from his more lighthearted and parodic writings, Čapek also wrote eloquently about racism, democratic breakdowns in Europe, and Nazism, writings which remain as relevant in the contemporary climate as they did at the time of publication.

Čapek's main intellectual influences are regarded as being the philosophers William James, Ortega y Gasset, and Henri Bergson. Čapek himself may well have influenced novelists from George Orwell to Kurt Vonnegut and beyond with his propensity for speculative fiction and satire. His novel WAR WITH THE NEWTS (*Válka s Mloky*, 1936) attracted praise from THOMAS MANN, and his work in translating the French symbolist poets had a profound and lasting effect on Czech poetry.

As a dramatist, Čapek worked with his brother on a number of collaborations. His first play, *The Fateful*

Game of Love (*Lásky hra Osudná,* 1910), was eventually staged 20 years after its publication. In 1920 Čapek met the actress Olga Scvheinpflugová, who starred in his play *The Outlaw* (*Loupežník,* 1920) and whom he married in 1935. Like his novels, Čapek's drama addressed philosophical themes, drawing heavily on elements from science fiction and fantasy, steering clear of the realism of daily events. In his symbolic fantasy drama *Rossum's Universal Robots* (*R.U.R.* 1920), the character Dr. Goll creates robots that can experience feelings of pain, but the robots eventually come to subsume and replace the men as workers. When war looms, the robot formula is destroyed and all but one human is killed. In the conclusion, the robots discover love, making the creation of a new formula redundant. Similarly, the satiric comedy *The Insect Play* (*Ze Zivota Hmyzy,* 1922), written in collaboration with Josef Čapek, was produced in 1922. Karel Čapek used this play to represent human vices through dreams in which female butterflies flirt with males and kill one, a beetle steals a store of dung, and ants struggle for power, with the animal representing a recurrent trope in Čapek's oeuvre.

In September 1938 a settlement signed in Munich allowed Czechoslovakia to be invaded by Germany, and it is believed that this point in history contributed significantly to the swift deterioration in Čapek's health, given his unshakeable belief not only in democracy but also in peace. Furthermore, his obsessiveness with his writing and the onset of a spinal disease from which he suffered throughout his life all significantly affected his health. Consequently, he died of pneumonia in Prague on December 25, 1938. Following the German invasion of Czechoslovakia in 1939, his works were suppressed by the Nazis, and Čapek's brother was interned in a concentration camp. Similarly, the communist reign viewed Čapek with cautious disdain, regarding his work as counter to the party's political agenda.

BIBLIOGRAPHY

Čapek, Karl. *Cross Roads.* Translated by Norma Comrada. North Haven, Conn.: Catbird Press, 2002.

———. *Four Plays.* Translated by Peter Mayer and Cathy Porter. London: Methuen Drama, 1999.

———. *War with Newts.* Translated by Ewald Osers. North Haven, Conn.: Catbird Press, 1999.

Feinberg, Leonard. *The Satirist.* New Brunswick, N.J., and London: Transaction Publishing, 2006.

Russell, Bertrand. *In Praise of Idleness: And Other Essays.* London and New York: Routledge, 2004.

Martyn J. Colebrook

CARAGIALE, MATEIU ION (1885–1936)

Romanian novelist, poet   Born in Bucharest on March 25, 1885, Mateiu Caragiale wrote some of the most important poetic and fictional works in the Romanian language. Criticized at first by the mainstream critical establishment for what was believed to be morally decadent and mannerist aesthetics, Caragiale gained almost a cult following from a younger generation of critics and writers in the 1920s and 1930s. This unfailing, somewhat illicit admiration went underground but continued during several repressive communist regimes (1945–89), even during periods when his writings were suppressed or, if published, harshly criticized officially. Today his collected and complete works have been republished and are part of high school and university curricula. Even so, his artistically intricate, elusive style and an immensely rich vocabulary of expression have helped this author escape the danger of becoming blandly mainstream. Like their author, Caragiale's works elude generic definition and maintain a proud distance even from their most devout admirers.

Mateiu Caragiale was the natural son of the eminent playwright and prose writer Ion Luca Caragiale and Maria Constantinescu. Maria's lower-middle-class background was an obstacle in the path of Ion Luca's meteoric rise, and he therefore never married her. In 1889 Ion Luca married the daughter of a distinguished Bucharest architect; Mateiu grew up in their household. In this rich cultural and artistic environment, he received the same outstanding education as his half brother and half sister. Nonetheless, his talents were never acknowledged as being equal to theirs, and he published early poems under a pseudonym. Caragiale was a stellar young student, but when he was prompted by his father to study law in Berlin in 1904, he showed little enthusiasm and never completed his studies. A dandy and a snob, in the literal meaning of the word—*sine nobilitate* (without noble rank)—Caragiale was convinced that he was of noble birth and researched his aristocratic roots and connections throughout his entire life. He returned to Bucharest in 1905 and continued his law studies but gave them up after a year.

Even though severely estranged from his father, Caragiale sent him a cycle of sonnets, *Pajere* (translatable as either hawks, mythical birds, or coat of arms). Profoundly impressed, the elder Caragiale facilitated his son's debut by having these poems published in the journal *Viața românească* (*Romanian Life*) in April 1912, but critics received the poems coldly. The rupture between father and son was never mended before the former's death in June 1912. Mateiu Caragiale's life continued in Romania, always under great financial strain. He held appointments as the cabinet chief of the Minister of Public Works (1912–14) and as director of the press bureau in the Ministry of Internal Affair's foreign section (1919–21). In 1921 he published his novella *Remember* in *Viața românească*.

In 1923 Caragiale married Marica Sion, the distinguished daughter of the writer George Sion. Through her the writer gained a much-needed financial stability and intellectual companionship. Partly as a result of this, Caragiale was able to complete the novel begun sometime in 1910, *Craii de Curtea-Veche* (1928), while keeping a journal in French and preparing a monograph about Count von Hoditz, an 18th century Prussian count and a friend of Frederick the Great. He also continued his heraldic studies: *Regarding an Aberration* (*În chestia unei aberații*) in 1930 and *A Heraldic Contribution to the History of the Brancoveni Family* (*O contribuție heraldică la istoria Brâncovenilor*) in 1935. He died on January 17, 1936, from cerebral congestion.

The Romanian critic Barbu Cioculescu argues in the introductory study of Mateiu Caragiale's *Works* (*Opere,* 2001) that the sonnet "The Old Courts" ("Curțile Vechi," 1904) of the cycle *Pajere* is significant for being emblematic of the novelist's literary activity. The sonnet describes centuries-old, deserted royal courts, referring to his 1928 novel *Craii de Curtea-Veche.* Yet the poem is more than an invocation recalling the 19th-century cult of the ruin. Its final sestet explores the art of looking: The focus moves from ruins to a scene in which bearded boyars dart cunning looks at young ladies. The poet's voice is completely absent. This is a subtle example of *mise-en-abîme,* an image presented to the reader/viewer who watches the noblemen smiling at young ladies conscious of being watched oneself. A miniature painter as well, Caragiale was keenly interested in exploring perspective in fiction and in creating either vast canvases or miniature scenes with words. He developed this art to the fullest in his later works.

Caragiale's prose works, which resemble prose poems, were received both with some high praise, as art aspiring to music, and also with harsh criticism. Loosely connected plots, the breakup of narrative continuity, the lack of a temporal and spatial linearity and of teleology—all marks of high modernist experimentation—were considered defects. The novella *Remember* presents the author's *ars poetica:* The goal of writing is not discovering truth but enriching the ambiguity that defines it. *Remember* is the story of a Berlin encounter between the Narrator and Aubrey de Vere, a dandy modeled on George Brummel and Oscar Wilde. Aubrey, who is also a transvestite, dies in mysterious and violent circumstances, which the Narrator refuses to investigate further.

Caragiale's only completed novel, *Craii de Curtea-Veche,* was the first volume of a projected but unfinished trilogy. The title, like the entire work, is difficult to translate. It has contradictory connotations, implying a mixture of sacred and profane: *Crai* is a word of Slavic origin meaning emperor, king, or ruler; the expression *trei crai de la rasarit* means the three kings who bring gifts at the birth of Christ. The word *crai* is also part of *craidon* (crai and Don Juan), a man who leads an easy life of feasting and amorous adventure. The locution *crai de Curtea-Veche* denotes a tramp, thief, hooligan, and loiterer. It helps to think of Curtea-Veche—the royal palace ruins—as a kind of court of miracles, as in Victor Hugo's *Notre Dame de Paris.* Caragiale may have obtained the term from two 19th-century histories by Dionisie-Fotino and Ionescu-Gion, according to which, in 1801, Bucharest's governing nobility left en masse for fear of a Turkish invasion, and the city was taken over by outlaws and thieves—*crai.* This mixture of sacred and profane characterizes the entire work.

The *crai* are three friends (including the narrator) who lead strange and double lives of dignified nobility during the day, which unravels at night when they are guided by Gore Pirgu, the fourth person and an "abject buffoon," through the orgiastic, carnivalesque nightlife of 1910 Bucharest. Their aesthetically superior world is challenged and ultimately destroyed by that of Pirgu. Yet if Pirgu's world is inferior, it is also more dynamic, and it prevails as a symbol of the newly emerged, post-World War I brave new world for which the writer himself felt contempt and repulsion. *Craii de Curtea-Veche* is a narrative about journeys of the imagination, the spirit, and the flesh. It lacks a traditional, realist plot, and it is not clear whether the Narrator tells the story as he lives it or as he remembers it. He plays metafictional games with both narrative and chronological perspective, challenging the usual rules of the novelistic genre.

After the end of the last communist dictatorship in 1989, Mateiu Caragiale began to receive a well-deserved recognition as one of the most original and innovative authors in Romanian literature. In January 2001 an important Bucharest literary magazine, *The Cultural Observer* (*Observatorul Cultural*), published the results of an inquiry in which more than 100 Romanian literary historians and critics participated. *Craii de Curtea Veche* was selected the best Romanian novel of the 20th century.

BIBLIOGRAPHY

Caragiale, Mateiu I. *Pajere*. Bucharest: Cartea Románeasca, 1983.
Orlich, Lleana Alexandra. *Articulating Gender, Narrating the Nation*. Boulder, Colo.: Columbia University Press, 2004.
Parvu, Sorin. *The Romanian Novel*. New York: Columbia University Press, 1992.

Adriana Varga

CARPENTIER, ALEJO (1904–1980) *Cuban essayist, novelist, poet*

A true man of letters, the Cuban-born Alejo Carpentier is widely regarded as one of the most important Latin American intellectuals of the 20th century. Along with Argentina's Jorge Luis Borges and Mexico's JUAN RULFO, Carpentier was integral to the Latin American literary renaissance of the 1920s. Employing a remarkable diversity of forms, Carpentier published thousands of articles and arts reviews, along with many essays, lectures, and radio plays. Several of his poems have been put to music by Cuban and non-Cuban musicians such as Amadeo Roldán, Alejandro García Caturla, and Marius François Gaillard. Carpentier's most profound and enduring works are, arguably, his novels, which render the historical, cultural, and ethnic complexities of Latin America in his signature baroque prose style.

The son of a French architect father and a Cuban mother, Alejo Carpentier was born in Havana in 1904. He spent his early school years in France but returned to Cuba to study architecture at Havana University. His academic career was short-lived, however, and he left the university to pursue work in journalism. Deeply committed to revolutionary politics, Carpentier partook in a number of radical movements; in 1923 he joined Grupo Minorista, and he was active in the Protesta de los Trece, a rebellious faction headed by Rubén Martínez Villena. Around this time, Carpentier became active on the Cuban literary scene, cofounding *Avance* magazine, in which he published his famous poem "Liturgia." The young author began to cultivate friendships with a number of important cultural figures, including Diego Rivera, whom Carpentier met at a writer's congress in Mexico. While serving a brief prison sentence (he was found guilty of communist sympathies), Carpentier drafted his first novel, *Ecue-Yamba-O* (1933). Upon his release from prison, he wrote and edited several cultural magazines and worked with Roldán to organize concerts featuring Igor Stravinsky, Francis Poulenc, and Erik Satie.

Living in Paris between 1928 and 1939, Carpentier came into contact with an array of writers, artists, and intellectuals, including ANDRÉ BRETON, Louis Aragon, Tristan Tzara, Raymond Quenau, Edgard Varèse, Arthur Honegger, and Pablo Picasso. He drew particular inspiration from the work of Antonin Artaud and Jacques Prévert. From 1933 to 1939, Carpentier arranged musical recordings and radio programs at the Fonoric Studios and established close friendships with Federico García Lorca, Rafael Alberti, José Bergamín, and Pedro Salinas. In 1937 Carpentier was honored as the Cuban representative at the Second Congress in Defense of Culture in Madrid.

The early 1940s found Carpentier delving into musicological research, which focused on Cuban musicians such as Esteban Salas and Manuel Saumell. Upon moving to Venezuela, he produced work for radio and advertisements. With the 1949 publication of his second novel, The KINGDOM OF THIS WORLD (El reino de este mundo, 1957), Carpentier became recognized as an important Latin American voice, while his next three works, The Lost Steps (Los pasos perdidos, 1953), The Chase (El acoso, 1956) and Explosion in a Cathedral (El siglo de las luces, 1962), placed him in an international league of literary innovators.

In the triumphant wake of the Cuban revolution, Carpentier returned to his home country, and in 1959 he became vice president of the National Council of Culture. He taught history at Havana University, served as vice president of National Union of Writers and Artists, and, together with Nicolás Guillén and Roberto Fernández Retamar, ran Unión magazine. Carpentier directed the Editora Nacional de Cuba from 1963 to 1968, when he was designated consultant minister for cultural themes at the Cuban Embassy in Paris. Among the many honors awarded to Carpentier throughout his prolific career are the Cervantes Prize of Literature (1978) and an honorary doctorate in Hispanic Language and Literature at Havana University. He died of cancer in Paris on April 24, 1980.

Carpentier's novels are characterized by poetics of excess—an intricacy that is customary in baroque art, which Carpentier claimed to be "the legitimate style of the modern Latin American writer." As with the baroque tradition of Europe, which reacted against the rectangular symmetries of neoclassical art with distorted and complicated forms, the baroque to which Carpentier refers is one of formal complexity and artifice. Implied in this aesthetic of abundance is a critique of religious and political structures whose self-aggrandizing optimism too often results in violent atrocity, existential emptiness, and social disenchantment. As José Lezama Lima explains, the baroque reflects the "desperate overflow of the dispossessed," which characterized "the culture of the Counter Conquest: the response of the new cultures, the mestizo and syncretic cultures of the New World, to the European Conquest." Carpentier's narratives, probing issues of cultural identity and the colonial legacy in Latin America, are thus befittingly expressed in the ornate language and structures of the baroque.

Largely historiographic, Carpentier's fiction mixes "official" accounts of the past with regional legend and mythology. Throughout his professional life, Carpentier considered himself to be, above all other things, a journalist, and his novels reflect this journalistic impulse. Material concerning his travels along Venezuela's Orinoco River, for example, which first appeared as an article in Carteles magazine, was later used in his novel The Lost Steps. But for Carpentier, the drive to represent things realistically necessitated (with seeming paradox) the representation of the magical. He achieved this not by inserting magical elements into a realistic scenario, but by revealing the mysterious and marvelous which reside within—are already part of—the real. In his essay "Lo barroco y lo real maravilloso" ("The Baroque and the Marvelous Real"), Carpentier explains: "The marvelous real that I defend and that is our own marvelous real is encountered in its raw state, latent and omnipresent, in all that is Latin American. Here the strange is commonplace and always was commonplace."

Carpentier's work offers possibly the best example of magical realism, a term coined by German critic Franz Roh. An intrinsically subversive literary mode, magical realism, in Roh's conception, "employs various techniques that endow all things with a deeper meaning and reveal mysteries that always threaten the secure tranquility of simple and ingenuous things." No less "real" than traditional realism, magical realism is thus a stylistic means of transgressing boundaries and destabilizing normative positions. As a practitioner, Carpentier not only redefined conventional historical and cultural interpretations of Latin America but also advanced a literary appreciation of the unfathomable and the irrational. CARLOS FUENTES said of Carpentier: "He is, I think, one of the first novelists who, on purpose, goes beyond Realism, goes beyond Naturalism, goes beyond Romanticism, in order to find in the remote past of Latin America the fundamental myths which can nourish our contemporary novels."

BIBLIOGRAPHY

Gonzalez Echevarria, Roberto. *Alejo Carpentier: The Pilgrim at Home*. Ithaca, N.Y.: Cornell University Press, 1977.

Harvey, Sally. *Carpentier's Proustian Fiction: The Influence of Marcel Proust on Alejo Carpentier*. London: Tamesis, 1994.

Pancrazio, James J. *The Logic of Fetishism: Alejo Carpentier and the Cuban Tradition*. Lewisburg, Pa.: Bucknell University Press, 2004.

Shaw, Donald Leslie. *Alejo Carpentier*. Boston: Twayne Publishers, 1985.

Tulsay, Bobs M. *Alejo Carpentier: A Comprehensive Study*. Valencia and Chapel Hill, N.C.: Albatros Hispanófila, 1982.

Vazquez Amaral, Jose. *The Contemporary Latin American Narrative*. New York: Las Americas Publishing, 1970.

Kiki Benzon

CĂRTĂRESCU, MIRCEA (1956–) *Romanian novelist, poet*

Mircea Cărtărescu is one of the most outstanding representatives of Romanian postmodernism, the subject of his elaborate Ph.D. thesis published in 1999. He was born in Bucharest, the capital of Romania and a city with a paradoxical mixture of early modernist, French-oriented fading style and exuberance. That he remains infatuated with this city can be seen in the first two volumes of his work-in-progress autobiographical trilogy *Dazzling* (*Orbitor*): *The Left Wing* (*Aripa stinga*, 1996) and *The Body* (*Corpul*, 2002). *Dazzling* is Cărtărescu's most sophisticated novel, although his growing international reputation was established by *The Dream* (*Visul*, 1989). This latter novel was rewritten and published as *Nostalgia* in 1993. The French edition, published in 1992, was nominated for the Médicis Prize and was awarded a distinguished French literary prize for the best non-French book published in translation in 1992.

Mircea Cărtărescu belongs to the most influential group of contemporary Romanian writers who reached their intellectual maturity during the 1980s within a climate of cautious counterculture and incipient postmodernism. His models as poets were members of the Beat generation and their successors, with works including Allen Ginsberg's *Howl*, the lyrics of the psychedelic 1960s, and the songs of the Beatles, the Rolling Stones, or REM. His fictional narrative took up the style of Jack Kerouac's cult-status work *On the Road*.

The Romanian counterculture and early postmodernism movements evident in the country were viewed as neither insurgent nor radical, principally because of political censorship. Looking back in time, however, one can find well-defined counterculture aspects in Cărtărescu's first poems, such as the psychedelic rhythm of his lines, their inner, dream-like musicality, or the author's antiestablishment references. Even at the present time, when he is enjoying considerable literary fame both in Romania and abroad, Cărtărescu continues to be an antiestablishment figure with no political or social affiliation, except for his academic post at the University of Bucharest, where he teaches as an associate professor of Romanian literature.

Cărtărescu's penchant for solitude has tremendously increased in the decades since his debut in 1980 when a series of poems was selected for a volume entitled *Headlights, Shop Windows, Photographs* (*Faruri, Vitrine, Fotografii*). At that time the poet was taking active part with other writers in groups, resulting in group actions and collective volumes of poetry or prose (*Air and Diamonds* [*Aer cu diamante*, 1982]; *Commando '83* [*Desant '83*, 1983]). Cărtărescu was also a promising member of the innovative literary circle Cenaclul de Luni (Monday Literary Club), whose meetings were chaired at the Faculty of Letters of Bucharest University by the influential Romanian literary critic and professor, Nicolae Manolescu (currently president of the Romanian Writers' Union). Later on, and especially after the revolution of December 1989, Cărtărescu isolated himself from the public, publishing one masterpiece after another: the ironic epic *The Levant* (*Levantul*) in 1990; the poems *Love* (*Dragostea*) and *Double CD* in 1994 and 1998, respectively; the novels *Nostalgia* (1993), *Travesti* (1994), and *Dazzling* (two volumes so far in 1996 and 2002); and his personal *Diary* in two separate volumes (2001, 2005). The English-speaking reader can find the author's work in Adam J. Sorkin's poetry selection *Bebop Baby* (1999); in *Poetry at Annaghmakerring*, published together with Romulus Bucur in Dublin in 1994 (Dedalus Press); and in the English version of *Nostalgia* (2005), translated by Julian Semilian.

After graduating from Bucharest University (1980), Cărtărescu worked as a secondary school teacher (1980–89), then as clerk for the Romanian Writers'

Union and as editor of the literary journal *Caiete critice* (*Critical Scripts*) until autumn 1991, when he joined the faculty of Bucharest University. He took part in 1990 in the International Writers Program at the University of Iowa in the United States and delivered lectures at the University of Amsterdam and in Germany. He also wrote the huge epic poem *The Levant* (1990), which is a completely untranslatable ironical masterpiece, since it uses many strata—even archaic or medieval—of the Romanian language and terminology. Written in brave, heroic hexameters, like Homer's epic *The Iliad,* the poem deploys a secret political plot, set up by a young revolutionary to punish the greedy prince of 18th-century Bucharest. Inflated like a true romantic hero, the protagonist meets a monstrous buccaneer who fearlessly plunders the waters of the Levant (eastern Mediterranean) in order to keep his son at Cambridge to learn philosophy. The buccaneer is persuaded to join the revolutionary's expedition. The team members then descend into the underworld and travel to a remote island to ask for help from a skillful, rather fantastic zeppelin maker. All of them eventually land in Bucharest, hoping to bring prosperity to it and to enthrone the former bloody pirate, who becomes a generous watchdog of the new order, although his gory adventures have left him with a single-eye.

The Levant is obviously a postmodern parody of classical epic structures, which it deconstructs with highly enjoyable irony. The political subversion runs very deep, which explains why the author only ventured to propose the poem to a publisher after the death of Nicolae Ceauşescu, the Romanian dictator. Cărtărescu's genius lies in his programmatic rewriting of the entire stylistic history of Romanian poetry, molding it into a soft texture of intermingling rhetorical threads. The barrier between fiction and reality is also softened: After deposing the greedy prince, the merry group of revolutionaries pay their respects to the author's home, express their gratitude, and drink a bottle of wine together. Nothing like *The Levant* has been written in the Romanian literature for decades. One would have to learn Romanian in order to fully enjoy it, although a brilliant Transylvanian poet, Kovacs Andras Ferenc, has partially translated it into Hungarian by using archaic styles taken from various older strata of classical Hungarian literature.

Nostalgia (1993) can be considered a novel only because of the imaginative unity of its three sections, written at different moments in Cărtărescu's life, chiefly in the last years of the communist dictatorship (1987–89), which also marked the genesis of *The Levant. Nostalgia* appeared at first as *The Dream* in 1989, slightly tailored by censorship. Among the excised fragments, for instance, was the "Prologue," subtitled "The Roulette Player," which was based on a literary extension of the Russian roulette motif—a suggestion of spectacular and lucid self-suicide, which had failed to please the communist censors.

Nostalgia is a brilliant postmodern projection of subjective ideas, dreamlike images, and fluid personal recollections. Their outstanding core is the autobiographical story "REM," which starts as a fake bildungsroman, openly influenced by THOMAS MANN, only to continue as a dreamy succession of spiritual and corporeal metamorphoses, allegedly inspired by FRANZ KAFKA. By continuously changing the styles of his recollections, Cărtărescu fills the gap between modernity and postmodernity, writing the imaginative story of his own literary evolution. The text evolves as a series of fluid dreams and personal fantasies, going back in time to the author's childhood. The concrete setting is Bucharest in the early 1960s, but no relevant political or social details can be found in the story, except for those explaining the internal screen of the author's conscience. The projections are heterogeneous, volatile, and fantastic, resembling the magical realism promoted by Jorges Luis Borges (who is cited with his *Aleph*) and other South American novelists.

REM as an acronym stands for "rapid eye movement," defined by dictionaries as the "mentally active period when sleep occurs." In the medical literature concerning sleeping and imagination, *rem* is a process of extreme subconscious fluidity, when one bridges the gap between identity and nonidentity, projecting oneself into totalizing images. REM also stands for "Roentgen equivalent (of) man," which measures a person's permeability to X-rays. It is interesting to note that each person has a different, unique REM quota— that is, REM acts like an inner-body "fingerprint." It is also well known that the letters REM designate a famous rock band, founded in Athens, Georgia, in the early 1980s by Bill Berry, Peter Buck, Mike Mills, and Michael Stipe. Cărtărescu perhaps had in mind all these levels of imaginative syncretism when writing his text as a musical flow of corporeal intensities, full of dazzling, erotogenic fantasies.

Cărtărescu has said in an interview that "REM" started as a dreamy self-projection, inspired by Carl Gustav Jung's suggestion that our subconscious maintains the imprints of a reversed body image, i.e., inside a man there can be a woman. Two texts from the *Nostalgia*, "Twins" ("Gemenii") and "REM," evoke such an inverted psychic embodiment, conceived by the author as fantastic reenactments of his mirror-image memories as a child. The whole book is—in the terms of the psychiatrist and linguist Jacques Lacan—an "imaginary anatomy," incorporating volatile images, corporeal flows, dreamy heterogeneities, and extremely elaborate cultural references and symbols. The author's spiritual program, expressed in the very meaning of his body projections, lies in the desire to reenter the "totality" from which he has been separated by individuation. His key word is *totul* (everything)—also the title of some of his poems. The psychedelic urge to compose a text that reunites Cărtărescu with the cosmic totality of all beings, regardless of the species, is resumed in his trilogy *Dazzling,* with only two parts published so far: *The Left Wing* and *The Body.*

BIBLIOGRAPHY

Bodiu, Andrei. *Mircea Cărtărescu.* Brasov, Romania: Aula, 2000.

Cărtărescu, Mircea. *Postmodernismul Romanesc.* Bucuresti, Romania: Humanitas, 1999.

Cistelecan, Alexandru. "Zaciu, Mircea—Papahagi, Marian—Sasu, Aurel." In *Dictionar Esential al Scriitorilor Romani.* Bucuresti, Romania: Albatros, 2000.

Cornis-Pope, Marcel. *The Unfinished Battles. Romanian Postmodernism Before and After 1989.* Iasi, Romania: Polirom, 1996.

Lefter, Ion Bogdan. *A Guide to Romanian Literature: Novels, Experiment, and the Postcommunist Book Industry.* Pitesti, Romania: Paralela 45, 1999.

Musat, Carmen. *Perspective Asupra Romanului Romanesc Postmodern si alte Fictiuni Teoretice.* Pitesti, Romania: Paralela 45, 1998.

Orlich, Ileana Alexandra. *Articulating Gender, Narrating the Nation.* East European Monographs, 2005.

Parvu, Sorin. *The Romanian Novel.* New York: Columbia University Press, 1992.

Pop, Ion, ed. *Dictionar Analitic de Opere Literare Romaneşti.* Vol. 3. Entry by Stefan. Cluj-Napoca, Romania: Casa Cartii de Stiinta, 2001.

Stefan Borbély

CASE OF SERGEANT GRISCHA, THE (DER STREIT UM DEN SERGEANTEN GRISCHA) ARNOLD ZWEIG (1927)

German author ARNOLD ZWEIG (1887–1968) wrote his most famous novel, *The Case of Sergeant Grischa,* as an account of World War I. Upon its publication in Germany in 1927, the novel's readers acclaimed the story as the most moving account of the First World War to date. Critics credited the author with awaking anew the interest of the readers for war literature, which prepared the ground for the success of other war novels, such as the universal best seller ALL QUIET ON THE WESTERN FRONT (*Im Westen nichts Neues,* 1929) by ERICH MARIA REMARQUE, to which Zweig's novel has been often favorably compared.

Zweig had worked on the novel since 1917, intending to express his changing attitude against the war and to reflect the time he had worked in the headquarters of the German army on the eastern front. He had already used the authentic episode around which the novel is built and which took place on the eastern front in 1917 in his 1921 drama *The Play of Sergeant Grischa* (*Das Spiel vom Sergeanten Grischa*). However, the lack of interest from theater producers and the artistic weaknesses of the play prevented it from being performed until 1930, when the same material had already been transformed into a novel and was quite successful on the book market.

The plot of *The Case of Sergeant Grischa* starts with the escape of a Russian soldier, Grischa Paprotkin, from a German prison camp in the spring of 1917. On the way to freedom and his family back in Russia, he encounters a peasant girl and berry picker named Babka, who falls in love with Grischa and advises him to assume the identity of another Russian soldier, Bjuschew. Grischa does not know that the Germans believe that Bjuschew is a spy. After the German troops capture the soldier, he charged as a spy and goes on trial for his life. At this point, Grischa reveals his real identity, and his honesty and affability convince the military judge advocate Posnanski, in cooperation with the young officer Paul Winfried and his friend Werner Bertin, to defend Grischa's case. The center of the novel becomes the struggle for Grischa's life, waged between two groups of German soldiers representing two different attitudes against the code of military honor. Although witnesses from the prison camp are able to confirm Grischa's version of his true identity, the quartermaster of the German army in the East, General Schieffenzahn, insists that Grischa must be put to death for the sake of the army's morale and to prevent the spread of Bolshevist ideas. When the intervention of old General von Lychow fails, the last chance of legal rescue for the innocent victim is lost. Grischa's execution is carried out by firing squad in autumn 1917.

In *The Case of Sergeant Grischa,* Zweig exposes the faulty interdependencies of justice and politics that originated in the sociopolitical conditions of Kaiser Wilhelm's Germany, grew during World War I, and dominated public life in the Weimar Republic. Grischa's case demonstrates how the administration of justice is abused as it becomes a political weapon used to suppress political opponents. The legal murder of the innocent Russian soldier was for Zweig a symptom of the disease that tormented the postwar German state, in which court trials against the antagonists of the industrial and conservative establishment exhibited only the illusion of justice all too often.

Through the figure of Grischa, a common soldier who loses control over his own fate and is condemned to watch the fight for his life without means of intervention, Zweig also shows the effects of war on the individual. The military, political, and economic machinery of the state and the army entraps and destructs the helpless human being, treating an individual life as insignificant. The nonpolitical, deeply human motives of the innocent Grischa, who just wants to reunite with his wife and a daughter he has never seen, has no consequence in the trial. The trial has the character of a political power struggle.

General Schieffenzahn's political agenda and victory over Grischa (a disguised version of the actual historical figure of Erich Ludendorff, the German army chief of staff from 1916 on) contrasts sharply with the moral standards of the group concentrated around the more benevolent General von Lychow. For the author this was—as if under a magnifying glass—an exemplification of the gradual shift of power toward the state and the army. The defeat of soldiers educated in German idealism in the confrontation with the aggressive imperialist and annexationist ambitions of Schieffenzahn and his supporters is symbolic: Zweig strived to show the triumph of bourgeois mentality over the old aristocratic values that proclaim wars are to be fought for noble causes rather than for materialist interests. For Zweig, World War I announced the end of a world in which the categories of right and wrong were superior to the legal appearances of human and institutional actions.

The popularity of the novel after publication underscored the timeliness of Grischa's story. The author precisely caught the reasons behind the political developments in the Weimar Republic in the 1920s, without sacrificing the wide scope of the novel and the complexity of the figures. Characterized by a lengthy, naturalistic style, numerous plots, and historical and psychological details, the narrative follows the causal connections between events and moves from one situation to another without losing the consistency and tension built by the main plot. The omniscient and often ironic narrator provides a good balance between affection and distance, allowing for intellectual play with the reader. The writer's deft use of language and careful depiction of multidimensional figures were factors that made *The Case of Sergeant Grischa* such a successful and still appealing novel.

After writing Grischa's story, Zweig felt a need to write a prequel or pre-story as well as to continue the war adventures of selected characters from the novel. Through these treatments he could better explain their motivations, the psychological changes they underwent, and the historical background of the events. Zweig's initial intention to limit his World War I works to a trilogy and later to a tetralogy proved insufficient, and the cycle, which he entitled *The Great War of the White Man,* grew to encompass six finished novels, published between 1928 and 1957. From the point of view of the narrated time, the cycle opens in 1913 in the last published novel *The Time Is Ripe* (*Die Zeit is reif,* 1957). The next two parts, *Young Woman of 1914* (*Junge Frau von 1914,* 1931) and *Education before Verdun* (*Erziehung vor Verdun,* 1935) precede the events told in *The Case of Sergeanten Grischa. Ceasefire* (*Die Feuerpause,* 1954) tells the events on the eastern front after the time of Grischa's death, in the winter months of 1917–18.

BIBLIOGRAPHY

Isenberg, Noah W. *Between Redemption and Doom: The Strains of German-Jewish Modernism.* Lincoln: University of Nebraska Press, 1999.

Rost, Maritta. *Bibliographie Arnold Zweig.* Berlin and Weimar: Aufbau-Verlag, 1987.

Salamon, George. *Arnold Zweig.* New York: Twayne Publishers, 1975.

Steffin, Margarete. *Briefe an Berühmete Männer: Walter Benjamin, Bertolt Brecht, Arnold Zweig.* Hamburg: Verlagsanst, 1999.

Jakub Kazecki

CASSANDRA (KASSANDRA) CHRISTA WOLF

(1983) *Cassandra* was the fifth and final lecture of a series CHRISTA WOLF (1929–) presented in 1982. Shortly thereafter, the draft was reworked and published in 1983 with Jan Van Heurck's English translation appearing in 1984. *Cassandra* is a retelling of Homer's prophetess and the last moments before her execution by the Greeks. Narrated by Cassandra, the novel is a reflection on her life, on Troy, and on the long war that leads to Troy's destruction. The novel appealed to readers in East Germany, where reprints quickly sold out, and in West Germany, where the novel remained on the best-seller list for a year. German Democratic Republic (GDR) critics, however, gave the novel mixed reviews when it was first published in German.

Except for the opening and closing passages, *Cassandra* is a first-person interior monologue. The opening and closing passages take place in present-day Greece, and the third-person narrator muses that this is the spot upon which the mythical Cassandra stood. When the novel switches perspective, Cassandra is a prisoner of war and is awaiting her execution. She is in front of the Mycenaean palace with her servant and her sons. As she awaits her death, she reflects on her city and civilization and the sequence of events that led up to the war and happenings during the war. Since she tried to shape what happened to her city in foretelling its destruction, she was not only ignored but also left out of the decision-making process. As a result, Cassandra narrates from both inside and outside of her culture.

In 1982 Wolf served as guest lecturer at the University of Frankfurt and gave series of talks entitled "Lectures on Poetics." These lectures were based on a trip to Greece that she had undertaken in 1980 with her husband. Since Wolf was a celebrated writer and a "loyal dissident" of the GDR, she was allowed to travel abroad, a luxury not afforded the general public of East Germany. The first two lectures were travelogues, the third a work diary, and the fourth an open letter. The fifth lecture was a draft of the novel *Cassandra,* which was published a year later. Only the GDR publisher Aufbau-Verlag kept Wolf's original sequence of lectures, which is then followed by the novel. The West German publisher Luchterhand published the essays and novel separately, and the English translation (published by Farrar, Straus) contains the lectures and novel in one volume but places the novel first. However, the latter two publishers' choices are confounding since the lectures give the reader an insight into the creation and themes of the novel.

In 1980 Wolf won the Büchner Prize, and during the address accepting the award, she claimed that the survival of mankind depended on women since men have an inclination toward self-destruction. This theme is expressed in *Cassandra,* in which the main character warns her fellow citizens about Troy's doomed future, but no one listens to her predictions.

Although *Cassandra* is set in mythical Greece, the novel reflects present-day concerns through allegory. It explores the threat of nuclear war, self-destruction, war mongering rather than peace negotiations, and women's lack of importance in society. Critic Dieter Sevin has observed that the male power structures in the novel, which exclude not only women but also any dissenters, reflect Christa Wolf's need to speak out on world events and GDR politics, but he notes that her warnings, too, were not heeded. Feminist critics continue to value the novel as an important contribution to German-language literature and as an examination of the failure of male power structures.

BIBLIOGRAPHY

Baumer, Franz. *Christa Wolf.* Berlin: Colloquium, 1988.

Böthig, Peter. *Christa Wolf: Eine Biographie in Bildern und Texten.* Munich: Luchterhand, 2004.

Finney, Gail. *Christa Wolf.* New York: Twayne Publishers, 1999.

Resch, Margit. *Understanding Christia Wolf: Returning Home to a Foreign Land.* Columbia: University of South Carolina Press, 1977.

Karen Bell

CASTLE, THE (DAS SCHLOSS) FRANZ KAFKA (1922)

The Castle is the last novel written by Czech author FRANZ KAFKA (1883–1924). Kafka began to write the book in 1922 in a village and not, as it is tempting to imagine, in the shadow of Prague's legendary castle. A customarily Kafkaesque yoking of the absurd and the sinister, *The Castle* depicts an individual's fruitless efforts to achieve his objective within an incomprehensible authoritative structure.

The story of *The Castle* is roughly as follows: Joseph K. arrives at a village and claims to be the officially appointed land surveyor to the Castle, a mysterious domain that rules over the village: "The Castle hill was hidden, veiled in mist and darkness, nor was there even a glimmer of light to show that the castle was there." The novel proceeds in a manner that falls somewhere between bewilderment and burlesque. K. wants to meet Klamm, the castle superior. His assistants, Arthur and Jeremiah, are not helpful. K. makes love to the barmaid Frieda, a former mistress of Klamm. Frieda leaves K. when she discovers that he is merely using her.

As is the case with all of Kafka's major works, *The Castle* was never finished, but in this instance it would seem that death itself forced the truncation. An ailing Kafka wrote to Max Brod (1884–1968), editor of his major works published after Kafka's death: "I have not spent this week very cheerfully because I have had to give up the Castle story, evidently for good." The novel ends in mid-sentence.

The first two chapters of *The Castle* were originally written in the first person; Kafka's decision to change the "I" to a "K" (for "Kafka") invites speculation. In a letter to Oskar Pollak, Kafka opines, "Many a book is like a key to unknown chambers within the castle of one's own self." As with much of the author's other fiction, several elements of *The Castle* correspond to events and conditions of Kafka's own life. Living as a Jew during the waning years of the Hapsburgs, Kafka grew conscious and critical of the systematic exclusion effected by hierarchical governing regimes; his employment at the Workers Accident Insurance Institute in Prague immersed him in a wearisome and inefficient bureaucratic world. These experiences may be read into the novel's omnipotent yet ever-remote castle and the prohibitive protocols of its faceless tenants. Kafka's residence in the countryside at the time of writing *The Castle* probably informed the rural environment in which the novel is set. The deterioration of the author's health and the reality of his worsening tuberculosis likely catalyzed the issues of mortality that are prominent in *The Castle*. Kafka died in 1924 at the age of 41.

The castle's focal image is resonant on several levels. In terms of its place in the literary tradition, the castle—as both domicile and forbidding domain—evokes late 19th-century Gothicism and its propensity for menacing architecture. As a polysemous figure with multiple meanings in the narrative, the castle reflects the aesthetic practice of ascribing arbitrary and iconic representation to an object corresponding to the symbolist movement, which exerted a huge influence on the German-language writers in Prague around Kafka's time.

The imperious and unapproachable castle also alludes to the impenetrable and self-perpetuating nature of political power, a theme Kafka also explores in *The TRIAL*—the story of a man who is condemned to death without knowing the nature of his crime. Following a more abstract interpretation, the castle described in the novel may be seen as a representation for that which is sought or required but remains ever-elusive—a goal (social, religious, or personal) that looms visible but is ultimately unattainable.

The theme of futile enterprise runs throughout Kafka's work, as Walter Benjamin noted: "To do justice to the figure of Kafka in its purity and its peculiar beauty, one must never lose sight of one thing: it is the purity and beauty of a failure." Thus is there a beautiful universality in Kafka's short but enigmatic parable "Before the Law," where a man spends fruitless decades waiting for permission to pass through the gates of justice, and in the writer's novel AMERIKA, where a young immigrant searching for "the promised land" endures a string of oppressive situations. Given Kafka's study of Hebrew, his increasing interest in the Zionist movement, and his (unrealized) plans to move to Tel Aviv, the scenario depicted in *The Castle* may reflect his own stymied and unfulfilled search for a homeland.

There has been, as with most of Kafka's work, a tendency to overinterpret *The Castle*—whether through the lens of religion, politics, psychoanalysis, history, or some version of literary theory. The oblique character of Kafka's writing renders it particularly conducive to interpretation but, ultimately, resistant to resolution. Most analysis of Kafka's work is as easily refuted as it is supported by his writing. If Kafka is a modernist, he is, arguably, an accidental one: Although he is one of the most revolutionary authors of the 20th century, there is nothing of the literary manifesto in his work. If K. of *The Castle* is a pilgrim, he is certainly an awkward one, more Chaplin than chaplain; if he is a revolutionary, he is a sadly ineffectual one; and if the journey K. makes is an allegorical one, then there would appear to be no end in sight.

BIBLIOGRAPHY

Bridgwater, Patrick. *Kafka's Novels: An Interpretation.* Amsterdam: Rodopi, 2003.

Brod, Max. *Franz Kafka, a Biography.* New York: Schocken Books, 1960.

Cooper, Gabriele von Natzmer. *Kafka and Language: In the Stream of Thoughts and Life.* Riverside, Calif.: Ariadne Press, 1991.

Kafka, Franz. *Kafka—The Complete Stories.* Edited by Nahum N. Glatzer. New York: Schocken Books, 1976.

Karl, Frederick Robert. *Franz Kafka: Representative Man.* New York: Ticknor & Fields, 1991.

Mailloux, Peter Alden. *A Hesitation before Birth: The Life of Franz Kafka.* Newark: University of Delaware Press, 1989.

Pawel Ernst. *The Nightmare of Reason: The Life of Franz Kafka.* New York: Farrar, Straus, Giroux, 1983.

Kiki Benson

CAT, THE (*LA CHATTE*) COLETTE (1933)

The popular author COLETTE (1873–1954) was born on January 28, 1873, in Saint-Sauveur-en-Puisaye, Burgundy, France. Author of more than 50 novels and numerous short stories, and articles for periodicals, she wrote from her early 20s through her mid-70s. This acclaimed 20th-century French writer was known for blurring the lines of fiction and autobiography, describing the modern teenager, and being one of the first modern women to live in accordance with her sensual and artistic inclinations. As in Colette's other novels, animals play a crucial role; in this case, the principal character is a cat. Of her more slender novels, *The Cat* focuses on purity and impurity as the tragic struggle.

The Cat tells the story of 19-year-old Camille, who is to marry 24-year-old Alain. Alain is blond and beautiful and the heir to a family business which is slowly declining. Camille, a brunette with stubby and unattractive fingers, is the daughter of a family who has recently acquired a great deal of wealth. On one level, *The Cat* is a murder mystery ignited by jealousy. However, this novel also touches on themes from Colette's other novels: the incompatibility of women and men and the desire for the past rather than the present.

Alain fears what will happen to his cat if he marries. Alain and Camille decide to marry, but they must first to move into the Parisian apartment of a friend who will be away for three summer months while their home is built. One motif in *The Cat* is the number three. Camille and Alain live on the ninth floor. They can see the top of three poplar trees that grow in the garden below from their three terrace windows. Their bedroom has three walls and is referred to as the triangular bedroom.

These two lovers are exact opposites, which greatly complicates their life. Camille prefers modern inventions such as fast sports cars, Parisian apartments, and jazz. She is materialistic and uninhibited about her sexuality. Alain is attached to his parent's home and a shady garden where his cat, Saha, resides. Camille is contemptuous of the servant Alain has had since he was a child. Alain is appalled when Camille walks around their apartment nude. Camille has a voracious appetite for sex, and she begins to put on weight from their lovemaking. Alain, on the other hand, loses weight. The only dimension of their relationship that is satisfying is their sexual activities together.

For Alain, the cat is his way back to the past. Saha is graceful, beautiful, and mysterious, moving through the world in purity. Alain reveals that he is going to visit his parent's house to see his cat. Camille insists on joining him to meet her feline rival. During his absence, Saha has lost weight and appears listless. Alain decides to bring the cat to the apartment, unknowingly creating a ménage à trois. Alain dines at home to be with his cat. The couple argue, and Camille calls Alain a monster, for she has become increasingly jealous of Saha. Camille decides to push Saha off their balcony when Alain is out one evening. She paces back and forth across the narrow balcony, forcing the cat to jump from the railing to the floor. The cat lets out an anguished cry, but then grows silent. When Saha relaxes her guard, Camille thrusts her arm forward and pushes the cat off the railing. The cat survives after its fall is broken by an awning. Alain brings Saha back up to the apartment, and the cat stares accusingly at Camille. When Alain realizes what has occurred, he leaves Camille to return to the old family house.

BIBLIOGRAPHY

Bidder, Jane and Phil Powrie. "Lesbian Speculations on/in Colette's *Claudine Married.*" *Women's Studies* 23, no. 1 (1994): 57–68.

Ladimer, Bethany, and Mary Evans. "Colette, Beauvoir and Duras: Age and Women Writers." *Women's Studies International Forum* 23, no. 4, (July–August 2000): 517.

Laura Madeline Wiseman

CATACOMBS OF THE VATICAN   See LAF-CADIO'S ADVENTURES.

CELA, CAMILO JOSÉ (1916–2002) *Spanish novelist, poet*   Camilo José Cela is regarded as one of the most influential Spanish writers of the 20th century. The Spanish civil war (1936–39) and the conditions of isolation and scarcity under which Spain lived during the dictatorship of Francisco Franco (1939–75) left a strong impression on Cela, and these images are visibly reflected in his writing. Cela's work often moves from a philosophical scepticism toward experimenta-

tion with varieties of realism. His narrative style has been called "fragmented realism," reflecting a simplistic and straightforward style used to express the uncertainty, poverty, and malaise of a generation.

Although Cela was a prolific writer, his two early novels *The FAMILY OF PASCUAL DUARTE* (*La familia de Pascual Duarte,* 1942) and *The HIVE* (*La colmena,* 1951) are his most popular, and they remain two of the most translated works in modern Spanish literature. Both novels address metaphysical questions concerning the meaning of existence and the search for individual identity. He is often associated with French existentialism and authors like ALBERT CAMUS and JEAN-PAUL SARTRE.

Camilo José Cela was born in Iria Flavia, La Coruña, Spain, on May 11, 1916. His mother was of British and Italian origin, and his father was a customs officer. His family lived in several cities before settling in Madrid in 1925. At 15 years of age, Cela contracted tuberculosis. His long-term recovery in the Guadarrama Hospital became the material of his novel *Convalescence Wing* (*Pabellón de reposo,* 1943).

Cela studied medicine at the University of Madrid, but he was more interested in literature and soon became acquainted with some of the most popular writers of his time, such as Miguel Hernández, María Zambrano, and PÍO BAROJA. At the start of the Spanish civil war in 1936, Cela, being 20 years of age, was obligated to join the military. He served as a corporal with the Nationalist army under Francisco Franco until he was injured in battle and sent to a hospital in Logroño. His service in Franco's army is noteworthy since most literary personalities, particularly those from abroad, such as Ernest Hemingway or George Orwell, backed the Republican leftist side. Perhaps because of this military service, Cela, the passionate liberal with Republican roots, was suspiciously regarded by both left- and right-wing parties during his life.

In 1944 Cela married María Rosario Conde, who served as his collaborator and secretary for more than 40 years. The marriage produced a son, Camilo José Cela Conde.

Although Cela's literary production began with lyrical, disquieting, even surreal poetry, literary recognition came with the publication of his first novel, *The Family of Pascual Duarte* (1942). The manuscript was rejected by several editors before it was eventually published, but it became an immediate success in the eyes of the public and critics. The novel's brutal realism and gratuitous violence did not go unchallenged, however. Despite its popularity, *The Family of Pascual Duarte* met resistance from the Catholic Church, which banned it as immoral and offensive. Problems with governmental censors were to plague Cela during most of his literary career, despite the fact that he himself had been a government censor during the Franco years in the 1940s.

The main character and narrator of *The Family of Pascual Duarte,* Pascual Duarte, is a brutal and ignorant peasant. He writes from prison what can be regarded as his public confession for all the horrible sins he has committed. Undoubtedly the most disturbing fact of the novel is the protagonist's apparent lack of morality or remorse. He becomes a ruthless killer, and his mounting depravity goes from killing his dog to matricide. His public confession shows only a modicum of guilt, although Duarte's intention seems to be to justify his ruthless killings by narrating the savage details of his story.

With *The Hive,* Cela abandoned traditional writing techniques for narrative experimentation based on a highly fragmented depiction of reality. The novel, devoid of the traditional plot, is a series of brief sketches of ordinary people and sordid episodes of the post–Spanish civil war years. This extraordinary narrative work includes nearly 300 characters, although many of these people are merely mentioned in the story. Cela's technique is to constitute the reproduction of short, vivid interactions among people without apparent connection. Despite the use of seemingly disjointed dialogue, these narrative exchanges are revealing and interesting. The dialogue provides snapshots and compelling testimony of the economic, social, and moral problems facing Spain.

Franco's government censors immediately banned *The Hive,* which was published for the first time in Buenos Aires, Argentina, in 1951. While Cela was still looking for an editor for *The Hive,* the author published *Journey to the Alcarria* (*Viaje a la Alcarria,* 1948), a colorful travel book that brings aesthetic dimensions to reporting. *Journey* presents travel writing at its best,

and it is perhaps the most popular nonfiction work by Cela.

In 1954 the writer moved to Palma de Mallorca, where he met Ernest Hemingway. In 1956 Cela founded and became director of the monthly literary magazine *Papeles de Son Armadans,* a publication that would eventually enjoy cult status. His later novels, including *Mazurka for Two Dead Men* (*Mazurca para dos muertos,* 1983), *San Camilo* (1936), *Mrs. Caldwell Speaks to Her Son* (*Mrs. Caldwell habla con su hijo,* 1953), and *Christo Versus Arizona* (1988), display a virtuosity of narrative experimentation. The technique includes lack of paragraph divisions or punctuation and dialogue without identification of speakers. These experimental later works never reached the quality or brought the acclaim of his early great novels.

Cela was elected a member of the Spanish Academy in 1957. After Francisco Franco died in 1975, and Spain became a constitutional monarchy, Cela was appointed a senator by royal designation. His first marriage having ended, in 1991 he married the journalist Marina Castaño.

The last 15 years of his life brought worldwide recognition of Cela's work, and in 1989 he was awarded the Nobel Prize in literature. In his Nobel lecture "Eulogy to the Fable," Cela said that the award pays tribute to the Spanish language. "It is not difficult to write in Spanish; the Spanish language is a gift from the gods which we Spaniards take for granted. I take comfort therefore in the belief that you wished to pay tribute to a glorious language and not to the humble writer who uses it for everything it can express."

Camilo José Cela died of heart failure in Madrid on January 17, 2002.

BIBLIOGRAPHY

Gibson, Ian. *Cela, el hombre que quiso ganar.* Madrid: Aguilar, 2003.

Perez, Janet. *Camilo Jose Cela Revisited: The Later Novels.* New York: Twayne Publishers, 2000.

Sánchez Salas, Gaspar. *Cela: el hombre a quien vi llorar.* Barcelona: Carena Editorial, 2002.

Tudela, Mariano. *Cela.* Madrid: ESESA, 1970.

Umbra, Francisco. *Cela: un cadáver esquisito.* Barcelona: Planeta, 2002.

Rafael Ruiz Pleguezuelos

CÉLINE, LOUIS-FERDINAND (LOUIS-FERDINAND DESTOUCHES) (1894–1961)

French novelist   Celebrated as a war hero in World War I yet denounced as a Nazi collaborator at the end of World War II, the French novelist and physician Louis-Ferdinand Céline remains today a figure of controversy. While his first novel JOURNEY TO THE END OF THE NIGHT (*Voyage au bout de la nuit*) remains a defining work of 20th-century French fiction, his anti-Semitic rhetoric during World War II led to his being denounced and imprisoned as a traitor and collaborator.

Céline was the pseudonym of Louis-Ferdinand Destouches, who was born on May 27, 1894, at Courbevoie (Seine), a Paris suburb, the son of an insurance company employee and a Parisian lace maker. He grew up in Paris, where his mother owned a small shop, and attended local schools. Planning a commercial career for their son, his parents arranged for the boy to study in Germany and England to improve his language skills.

In 1912, at the age of 18, Céline enlisted for a three-year tour of duty in the French cavalry. At the commencement of hostilities in summer 1914, the 20-year-old sergeant volunteered for a dangerous military mission, winning the highest military honors but also receiving severe head and arm wounds, which led to his service discharge and a state disability allowance. In 1916 he traveled to Cameroon with the Occupational Services, and in 1918 he began his medical studies, receiving his degree from the University of Paris in 1924. Between 1925 and 1928, Céline was employed by the League of Nations, traveling extensively: to Cameroon to research tropical diseases, to the United States to study the health effects of industrial production at the Ford factory in Detroit, to Canada, and to Cuba. These experiences, together with his subsequent return to Paris and the establishment in 1928 of a medical practice in Clichy, are the autobiographical raw materials out of which Céline shaped his first novel, *Journey to the End of the Night,* written at night after his shifts at the clinic, between 1928 and 1932. Although its publication in 1932 gave the young doctor instant (and unwanted) fame and notoriety, Céline nevertheless maintained that his literary output was secondary to his medical vocation, "a sort of do-gooding idealism which I have very strongly: a total commitment to the relief of illness."

Although critical reception was mixed, *Journey to the End of the Night* was an enormous popular success. While critics generally admired his groundbreaking experimentation with the French vernacular and his ruthless attack on French bourgeois culture, there were reservations about its bleak, misanthropic tone. Stylistically, its use of colloquial, raw, uncensored, spoken Parisian street argot opened new territories of the French language to written prose expression. Semiautobiographical, it chronicles in picaresque style the life experiences of its first-person narrator from the outbreak of World War I through the mid-1930s, commenting in the process, with bitter, often misanthropic sarcasm, on the horrors and absurdities of war, colonialism, industrialism, and the social conditions of modern life.

Céline's second novel, *Death on the Installment Plan* (*Mort à crédit*), was published in 1936 to equal success and equal controversy. It, too, is narrated in the first person—hereby a character named Ferdinand—and, drawing on the author's childhood memories, relates the events immediately preceding those detailed in *Journey to the End of the Night*. It contains, if anything, even more innovative linguistic and stylistic explorations than its predecessor.

That same year, Céline traveled to the Soviet Union. His trip was financed largely by members of the French Left (and by Soviet royalties on his first novel), who mistakenly saw in the young writer an authentic and sympathetic proletarian voice. Instead, the journey resulted in *Mea Culpa,* the first of his political pamphlets, expressing his complete disenchantment with the "worker's paradise." The work also marked the beginning of Céline's political drift to the Right. Acutely aware of the growing push toward a second catastrophic European conflict, Céline's writings became increasingly pro-German and anti-Semitic, placing blame for the building European unrest on supposed international Jewish interests.

During World War II, Céline continued to practice medicine, working at municipal clinics and dispensaries in Satrouville and Bezons. In 1943 he published his third novel, *Guignol's Band,* a vivid portrait of the under-side of London society during the early days of the First World War. Again characteristically semiautobiograph-ical, the novel covers what, in *Journey to the End of the Night,* would be the period between Bardamu's dis-charge from military service and his subsequent African adventures. In the midst of the war, however, *Guignol's Band* received little public or critical notice.

Fearing for his life, with the Allied liberation of France now imminent, Céline fled Paris, first going to Berlin in 1944. Then, in March 1945, the author, his wife, and their cat crossed Germany to Denmark on foot, hiding from the bombs and battling armies as best they could. The story of their escape through war-torn Germany in the last months of the war furnished the material for his last novels, *From Castle to Castle* (*D'un château l'autre,* 1957), *North* (*Nord,* 1960), and *Rigodon* (1969). Following the Allied victory, Céline was arrested and briefly imprisoned in Denmark. In June 1951 the French courts granted him full amnesty, and he was allowed to return to France, where he died in 1961.

Despite his politics and his anti-Semitism, Céline remains an important figure in the history of the 20th-century novel, both for his innovative use of colloquial spoken French and for his first-person "outsider" recon-structions of humanity's survival instinct in the face of total war, industrial mechanization, mass consumer culture, and colonialism. He was a major influence on not only JEAN-PAUL SARTRE and the French existential-ists but on the post–World War II generation of Ameri-can writers that included Henry Miller, Kurt Vonnegut, Jack Kerouac, and William Burroughs.

BIBLIOGRAPHY

Ostrovsky, Erica. *Céline and His Vision.* New York: New York University Press, 1967.

Thomas, Merlin. *Louis Ferdinand Céline.* New York: New Directions, 1980.

Vitoux, Frederic. *Céline: A Biography.* New York: Paragon House, 1992.

Michael Zeitler

CELL, THE (DIE ZELLE) HORST BIENEK (1968)

Long before the 20th century, prison literature was an old and varied genre ranging from the *Consolations of Philosophy* by the late Roman Empire writer Boethius to Fyodor Dostoyevsky's *The Idiot.* Thus, while it is not new or unique to the 20th century, prison literature has been important in defining eras of political upheaval and the movement of millions of individuals into prisons, concentration camps, or the Soviet com-plex known as the gulag. *The Cell* by the German-Pol-ish writer HORST BIENEK (1930–90) was a significant addition to that body of literature. In some ways, how-ever, it was a departure in large part because of its ambiguity and its concentration on the present experi-ence rather than the circumstances that led to impris-onment. The larger political and cultural context that informs *Darkness at Noon* by Arthur Koestler or the novels and stories of Varlam Shalamov or ALEKSANDR SOLZHENITSYN is absent.

Bienek, who spent four years in the Vorkuta camps of the gulag as a political prisoner, has created in *The Cell* a nonstop monologue, a personal narrative that focuses inward. It seldom reaches beyond the cell, which is essentially his universe with only occasional references to the outside. The narrator's existence takes place in an eternal present, with only occasional forays into the past and none into a future. His poor health and isolation are his main reference points.

The narrator is 58 years old and German, from Sile-sia, the eastern section that borders on Poland and is known for its mixture of Polish and German language and culture. (In this respect the narrator reflects his creator; Bienek lived in and wrote extensively about Silesia.) As the book was published in 1968, the reader assumes a fairly specific set of historical events that would have shaped this individual as he grew, matured, and lived out his life. Before coming to his 12-foot by 5-foot cell, the narrator spent 35 years as an art teacher in a girls' school. As far as we know, he has no family and is not married. He has not been tried for his offense, and his time in the cell is revealed during odd circumstances. Despite the fact that he has a serious infection on his left leg and one that is developing on his right, he is never taken to the infirmary. Rather, a medical attendant comes to him to replace his dress-ings and medicate him.

The narrator tells us about his daily life and the details of finding a lock of hair on his cell floor and enshrining it (a detail that has a particularly disturbing resonance later in the book). He describes his system of marking the walls, keeping his diary in this fashion. Those marks, combined with the signs and graffiti of earlier prisoners, constitute his means of marking time and organizing his world.

He was not always alone. At some time, before we become observers of his world, he had had a friend named Alban who was in an adjoining cell. He talks about their discussions, which ended when Alban was taken out of his cell, never to return. Initially, we accept the fact of Alban's existence just as we accept nearly everything the narrator tells us, at least at first. He tells us how he passes the time, including reliving special days, such as one he refers to as his "path-to-the-river" day. In another portion of the monologue, the narrator talks about his mother and father, who died when he was 10 years old. They had been standing on the frozen river when the ice they were standing on broke off, and they were carried off with the current—or, as he tells us, perhaps they were "pushed off by someone."

Why is he there in a cell? We receive clues, but these are quite contradictory, and our temptation to read the reason from Bienek's own history may be misleading. The narrator tells of trouble at the school when a banned book somehow got into the library and was discovered. As the library's substitute supervisor, he may now be in prison for that incident. He describes his interrogation, and the subject of making contact with some sort of resistance organization is raised. He claims that this is the prime cause of his interrogation (and hence his imprisonment). Slowly, however, the reader begins to piece together another possibility. He may not be there at all for political or subversive activity but may actually have committed a criminal act.

Near the end of the narrative, Alban returns, this time physically in the narrator's cell and not as an inmate tapping messages from another cell. Alban is now an interrogator and asks the narrator not about politics but a murder. A child, age 12–15 years, was raped, killed, and dumped in a rubbish heap near a river. The corpse was found with locks of hair cut off. We are reminded of the lock of hair he enshrined earlier in the narrative. We wonder what his "river" day really was, and whether it had anything to do with the child or his parents 48 years

earlier. Alban's identity and actual existence become unclear. We further question if the narrator is guilty of a criminal action against a human being and not a political crime. Alternatively, is this something he wishes were true (criminals in the gulag were treated much better than political prisoners)?

The narrator finishes as he began, saying he cannot bear repetition and he will tell no stories—although he has told us, albeit in very indirect terms, a story that is chilling regardless of his guilt or innocence or guilt.

The question for us is whether the narrator is delusional or a rational, sane man trying to survive and come to terms with a world mostly deprived of human contact. We never know if he is guilty or innocent or, if guilty, whether he is guilty of political offenses or of performing heinous acts against the innocent. The ambiguity of *The Cell* is striking. We may assume that the narrator is a political prisoner at first, although we may question it, but what becomes less ambiguous is that we are dealing with and confronting a tortured mind that may or may not have been so before the imprisonment but most certainly is now.

BIBLIOGRAPHY

Bienek, Horst. *Reise en die Kindheit: Wiedersehen mit Schlesien*. Munich: C. Hanser, 1988.

———. *Selected Poems, 1957–1987*. Translated by Ruth and Matthew Mead. Greensboro, N.C.: Unicorn Press, 1989.

Urback, Telman, ed. *Horst Bienek: Aufsätze, Materialen, Bibliographie*. Munich: C. Hanser, 1990.

Robert N. Stacy

CH'AE MANSHIK (CH'AE MAN-SIK) (1902–1950) *Korean novelist*

One of the leading writers of modern Korean literature, Ch'ae Manshik is noted for his unique fictional style that describes in realistic honesty and vivid detail life in his homeland during and after the oppressive Japanese occupation of Korea from 1910 to 1945. Ch'ae lived and wrote during a unique time in Korean modern history. Most of his life was lived under occupying forces—Japanese and Russian. He grew up under Japanese colonial rule and then lived to witness Russian forces at the end of World War II replacing Japan's long imperial dominance. Ch'ae's writing often reflects life under these harsh political and military conditions. His range of writing includes the genres of the novel, short story, drama, and essay.

Ch'ae was born in Umnae, a coastal village in the North Cholla province of Korea. He studied in Japan, following the tradition of other intellectuals of his homeland to journey to mainland Japan for education and the indoctrination of colonial ideas. Returning home to Korea after his education, he honed his writing skills by working at various jobs in journalism.

Ch'ae's life in Korea during the Japanese occupation of his homeland became the source of much of the material in his writing. This was an age of lost cultural identity. The 19th century was a time of advancing colonialism by imperial powers, pitted Korea against China, Russia, and Japan, all seeking to dominate and exploit the free, unmodernized country. Japan triumphed and invaded the country. Under Japanese rule, Koreans like Ch'ae struggled to maintain their historical identity. The Japanese occupying forces banned any teaching of the Korean language and history. Koreans were compelled to assume Japanese names and speak the imperial language.

The end of Japan's rule in Korea in 1945 did not bring harmony to the peninsular country. Ch'ae witnessed his own country divided up, with Russia controlling what is today known as North Korea and the United States controlling South Korea.

Ch'ae's fiction, highly realistic, was strongly influenced by Western forms, particularly the modernism represented by Russian and French literature. His themes often reflect the problems associated with advancing modernization and industry, education, class difference, and the individual pitted against the powers of the state.

One of Ch'ae's early fiction works is the novella *Age of Transition* (*Kwadogi*, 1923), an autobiographical work. In this short prose piece, Ch'ae tells the story of Korean students, characters fashioned on his own experiences, who are forced to reject their country's culture by studying in Japanese universities.

Ch'ae's novel *Peace under Heaven* (*Taepyeong chunhe,* 1938) is a finely woven satire, set in Seoul during the Japanese occupation of Korea, that offers a distinctive look at a troubled protagonist who chooses material rewards over spiritual salvation. The main character, Yun Tusop, is sadly comic and yet darkly horrid. Ch'ae

portrays Yun as a greedy and selfish manipulator whose treacherous actions are overlooked and even sanctioned by the Japanese officials. Yun is a loathsome, absentee landlord preoccupied by wealth, pleasure, power, and social status. He often berates his tenants and family members. *Peace under Heaven,* the first full-length work about life in the Japanese colony, is considered a classic. The author's modernist treatment of the character Yun, suggesting a 20th-century interpretation of Goethe's story of Faust, reveals the timeless theme of the tragedy of the triumph of materialism over the individual's spirit.

Ch'ae Manshik died of tuberculosis in 1950 at the age of 48.

BIBLIOGRAPHY

Fulton, Bruce, et al., eds. *Land of Exile: Contemporary Korean Fiction, Expanded Edition.* Armonk, N.Y.: M. E. Sharpe, 2007.

Lee, Peter H., ed. *Modern Korean Literature.* Honolulu: University of Hawaii Press, 1990.

Yoon-shik, Kim. *Understanding Modern Korean Literature.* Edison, N.J.: Jimoondang International, 1998.

Michael D. Sollars

CHAMOISEAU, PATRICK (1953–) *Martinican essayist, novelist, short story writer*   Patrick Chamoiseau is a major voice in contemporary literature. He was born in Fort-de-France, on the Caribbean island of Martinique, where he still resides. He received his education in law, first at the University of Martinique and then in France.

Chamoiseau is the author of several nonfiction works, including a history of the Antilles under the reign of Napoleon Bonaparte. Other nonfiction works include the manifesto *In Praise of Creoleness* (*Eloge de la creolité,* 1989), authored with Jean Bernabe and Raphael Confiant; the autobiographies *School Days* (*Une enfance créole 1: Anton d'enfance*) and *Childhood* (*Une enfance créole 2: Chemin d'école*); and *To Write in a Dominated Country* (*Ecrire en pays dominé,* 1997). Chamoiseau's stories and novels, among them *Creole Folktales, Strange Words, Solibo the Magnificent, The Old Slave and the Watchdog, The End of Childhood, Epic of the Final Legends,* and *Chronique des sept misères* have received considerable praise; but his best-known book, and masterpiece,

Derek Walcott proclaimed in *The New York Review of Books* in 1997, is the novel TEXACO, awarded the Prix Goncourt in 1992.

Texaco is a magnificent and tantalizing blend of French and Creole, a celebration of voices and once-lost narratives. It is also a reclaiming of history and identity and a tremendous example of Caribbean literature as set forth in Chamoiseau's manifesto, entitled "In Praise of Creoleness" ("Eloge de la créolité"), which states: "We shall create a literature, which will obey all the demands of modern writing while taking roots in the traditional configurations of our orality." The story is set in Texaco—a ghetto in Martinique located on the oil company's land holdings—and narrated by Marie-Sophie Laborieux, an elderly repository of the settlement's history and also the founder of the poverty-stricken shantytown. Her life is interrupted one day when she meets an urban planner who has been authorized to raze the settlement. Laborieux hopes to ingratiate herself in the mind of the city official and thus thwart his commission to destroy her community by relating her life story, including that of her father. Her story eventually weaves its way back into history, to the time of slavery, when her father, Esternome, saved the life of his owner from an attack by a maroon (fugitive slave). The novel, encompassing most of the colonial history of the island and the varied culture of its inhabitants, is a monumental testament to the humanistic force of literature.

Chamoiseau believes the French language to be the embodiment of colonialism. In *School Days,* a wonderfully entertaining and provoking account of his childhood, he examines the power of language to corrupt Martinique schoolchildren into seeing their landscape and history as inferior and thus perpetuate French colonial superiority. The memoir considers and dramatizes the resistance inherent in Creole as well as the situations and landscape from which it arose and how it is used to undermine established order to accomplish historical and cultural reclamation and therefore new ways of seeing and questioning the world. The character Big Bellybutton, in particular, is responsible for assailing the teacher's classroom formality with tales of island heroes and animals, magic and history.

Chamoiseau has complained that "Martinique is cut off from the rest of the Caribbean," a result of the fragmentary and violent history of the region. Perhaps it is for this reason that he has also said: "Caribbean literature does not yet exist. We are still in a state of pre-literature." To this statement Derek Walcott, in his now-famous review in *The New York Review of Books,* "A Letter to Chamoiseau," replied: "Oh yeah? My exuberance about *Texaco* should be tempered by this typical Francophony, France's ambiguous bequest, but it is not."

Chamoiseau is a full-time probation officer in Fort-de-France who has worked with young offenders for 15 years. He has said, "It sounds terrible, but understanding these people's experiences has helped me hugely as a writer, as it has allowed me to look into aspects of life that you wouldn't normally encounter." He works evenings, weekends, holidays, and rejects being a full-time writer because "I'd miss my work, my involvement" with the community.

Chamoiseau is a much-respected literary figure in his native Martinique. His manifesto suggests new ways of looking at Martinique's relationship with France. The manifesto was written in formal French, a matter Walcott wonders about in his review of *Texaco*: "Why was it not written in Creole if it is that passionate about authenticity?" Despite this, Chamoiseau continues to use the example of his novels, stories, memoirs, and essays to argue for Creolese being the only way of getting at a deeper Caribbean reality. "If a writer can use Creolese, then he is much more in touch with the thoughts and expressions of ordinary people."

BIBLIOGRAPHY

Chamoiseau, Patrick. *Childhood.* London: Granta Books, 1999.

———. *Chronicle of the Seven Sorrows.* Lincoln: University of Nebraska Press, 1999.

———. *Texaco.* Translated by Rose-Myriam Rejouis and Val Vinokurov. New York: Pantheon Books, 1997.

Détrie, Catherine, ed. *Poétiques du divers.* Praxiling, France: Université Paul Valéry, 1998.

Keith Jardim

CHANGE OF SKIN, A (CAMBIO DE PIEL)

CARLOS FUENTES (1967) The sixth novel by CARLOS FUENTES (1928–), *A Change of Skin* demonstrates his use of nonlinear and irregular time regarding narrative structure. Published in Spanish and in English in 1967, it is considered a complementary text to Fuentes's *TERRA NOSTRA* (1975), a fictionalized account of the construction of the Escorial, Spain's 16th century monastery and mausoleum near Madrid beginning in contemporary times and harkening back to the 16th century. *A Change of Skin* is dedicated to JULIO CORTÁZAR, Fuentes's literary peer and a writer whose work Fuentes openly admired. Essentially, this experimental novel is about a journey of four characters giving up their identities in exchange for different ones as they relive old memories and learn new things about themselves and each other. On another level, the novel is a satirical look at Mexico's societal, political, and cultural existence. Each character assumes the identity of another, in a sense borrowing each other's skin, as the title of the novel suggests, allowing readers to discover what is both fundamentally fortifying and essentially prohibiting about the main characters.

A Change of Skin won the prestigious Biblioteca Breve prize for fiction, the Seix Barral; however, the novel was originally not published in Spain because of censorship threats. A leading Spanish publishing house was set to publish *A Change of Skin,* but its content was deemed too objectionable. The novel delves into existentialist modes dealing with issues of protest and racism. Critics also argue that this novel was denied publication in Spain due to Fuentes's use of a clearly omniscient narrator, one whose actual existence is not defined by one point of view but by many.

Fuentes's use of a unique literary device, *la mirada* (a stare, or gaze; a visual perspective to and from one character to another) functions as a literary discourse in which readers come to understand and familiarize themselves with the four main characters, regardless of any distances that might be separating the characters from what they might be flashbacking to in their minds.

The novel takes place in the city of Cholula, Mexico. Javier, Elizabeth, Franz, and Isabel are all driving to the beaches of Veracruz, but the car breaks down, and rather than attempt to fix the car and continue on to Veracruz, they decide to spend the night in a hotel. Two of the four, Javier and Isabel, are characters that readers might recognize from Fuentes's first novel, *WHERE THE AIR IS CLEAR.* These characters are reincarnations of Rodrigo Pola and Betina Régules.

As the night progresses, the partners switch, one sleeping with another, and back again. The night is a collage of dreams, hallucinations, and flashbacks that symbolize many of the characters' inner fears and desires. What might be difficult for some readers to understand is that many of the visions and dreams the characters experience do not necessarily contribute directly to any kind of plot or character development specific to the story itself; rather, these visions contribute to themes integral to the novel as a whole and do not complement a common thread of plot weaving throughout. In this way, Fuentes defines characters juggling with questions of internal confusion and feelings of isolation, and this contributes to the existing body of postmodernist texts.

A key scene in *A Change of Skin* occurs at the ancient Aztec pyramids at Cholula, where Franz, Javier, Elizabeth, and Isabel's pasts meet their present. Fuentes creates a communion of temporalities in which the merging of what has happened in the past has directly influenced the present of the characters. Each character is joined in spiritual communion to the other by their life experiences. Mythical temporality, symbolized by the setting of the Aztec pyramid, suggests that the past is not merely history; it is a continual influence on the present and future.

Explicating the events in the story is an omniscient narrator, a mysterious changeling of sorts in that he changes skins, or identities, just as often as the characters do. In some cases, he refers to himself in the first person, as if he were a character in the novel; oftentimes, he engages directly in conversations with the four main characters. This is especially so with Elizabeth, Javier's wife; yet the narrator also addresses Isabel, though he does so in the second person. Some critics argue that the narrator has no sexual orientation, no defining characteristic other than that of an omniscient narrator, but the pet names that he bestows on Isabel and Elizabeth strongly suggest that the narrator is male. Furthermore, at the end of novel, the narrator identifies himself as Freddy Lambert. Fuentes has said that this name is a combination of many things. For one, the last name, Lambert, comes from the title character in French author Honoré Balzac's semiautobiographical novel *Louis Lambert.* Fuentes has also said that the narrator's first name, Freddy, comes from the German philosopher Friedrich Nietzsche, one of Fuentes's many major early influences.

A Change of Skin not only regards many modes of temporality and raises questions of existentialism; it also questions Mexican modernity, including societal, cultural, and political effects. The novel focuses on how Mexico's advances are all based on the country's ancient indigenous roots. By bridging the past with the present and the future, and by not adhering to linear temporality, Fuentes revolutionizes the genre of (re)telling the history of an ancient country.

But Fuentes does not always recount Mexico's past and present and future in a positive light; he does so with criticism, yet tempers it with genuine affection for *patria* (his country). *A Change of Skin* challenges all conventional modes of fiction, but the novel also manages to challenge widely accepted views of Mexico's past and present in such a way that it raises compelling questions of consciousness about where Mexico's future is headed. For Fuentes, it seems that the country's past should not be allowed to dictate its future, but this ideal projection and its fulfillment seem uncertain.

BIBLIOGRAPHY

Giacoman, Hely F., ed. *Homenaje de Carlos Fuentes*. New York: Las Américas, 1971.

González, Alfonso. *Carlos Fuentes: Life, Work, and Criticism.* Fredericton, N.B.: York Press, 1987.

Ibsen, Kristine. *Author, Text, and Reader in the Novels of Carlos Fuentes*. New York: Lang, 1993.

Rosemary Briseño

CHAREF, MEHDI (1952–   ) *Algerian novelist, screenwriter, film director*

Mehdi Charef is considered the first Beur writer in France. *Beur*, originally slang for "Arab," is the canonical (albeit contested) term used in literary and cultural studies to refer to second-generation Algerian immigrants in France or, more appropriately, to Franco-Algerians and French people of Algerian descent. The publication of Charef's first novel, TEA IN THE HAREM (*Le thé au harem d'Archi Ahmed*), in 1983 signaled the emergence of a generation of Beur writers, including Azouz Begag, Akli Tadjer, Farida Belghoul, Nacer Kettane, Tassadit Imache, Nina Bouraoui, and others whose (auto)biographical fiction explores cultural tensions in postcolonial France. Although Charef's work shares some themes with other Beur writers, such as the Algerian war for independence (1954–62), identity and gender formation, social exclusion, and racism, his humanistic portrayal of multicultural France emphasizes solidarity and friendship.

Mehdi Charef was born in Maghnia, Algeria, on October 24, 1952, when Algeria was still a French colony. At the beginning of the 1950s, his father migrated to France, where he worked in public construction, returning to Algeria to visit his family every two years. Following Algeria's independence from France in 1962, Charef and his family joined his father in France. He grew up in slums in Nanterre, at the periphery of Paris, and later in the housing projects that came to replace them. After earning a professional degree in mechanics, he worked in a factory producing tools for gardening from 1970 to 1983. When he was 20 years old, he spent time in prison for a minor infraction; upon his release, he swore never to return to prison and went back to factory work.

Charef considers himself to have been "saved by French literature" and the process of writing. Encouraged by his professors of French, he started to write a script that would become his first novel. After beginning it in 1975, he took up the script again in 1978 as a reaction to negative portrayals of the Algerian minority by the French media. Published in 1983 as *Tea in the Harem* by Mercure de France when Charef was 31, this autobiographical fiction gives a complex and rich picture of life in the housing projects at the margins of mainstream French society.

Written in very direct language, *Tea in the Harem* centers on the friendship between two young men, one French and the other Franco-Algerian: Pat and Madjid. After quitting school, they wander the streets and enter a life of delinquency; they are arrested after stealing a car. Although this groundbreaking novel has come to be understood as portraying the despair of a young Beur generation excluded from French society and lost between two cultures, it is also a poignant statement about the general effect of social exclusion in the 1980s on both the immigrant and broader French community. The 1985 cinematographic adaptation of the novel, written and directed by Charef himself and produced by Constantin Costas-Gavras, was critically acclaimed and received the French César for the best first film, the Jean Vigo Prize, and the award for best film in Madrid.

Charef's second novel, *The Harki of Mériem* (*Le Harki de Mériem,* 1989), evokes the difficult situation of the Harkis, Algerian men who fought on the side of France during the war for independence and fled the country after the conflict ended. After his son Sélim is the victim of a racist crime in France, Azzedine recalls his choice to be a Harki, a choice dictated by economic necessity. Charef grew up in Algeria during the war and was traumatized by the violence to the degree that he only returned once to Algeria many years later. He has refused to turn this novel into a film, arguing that some issues are better dealt with during the solitary act of reading. However, he has also said in interviews that he feels compelled to talk about this period and is planning to do other films about the Algerian war of independence.

In his third novel, *The House of Alexina* (*La maison d'Alexina,* 1999), also published by Mercure de France, Charef turns to his childhood memories to tell the story of five teenagers from broken homes who attend a school program for at-risk children. After their elderly alcoholic teacher, Mr. Raffin, dies of a heart attack, Alexina, a young psychiatrist and speech therapist, transfers the program to a house in Normandy in order to bring these children out of their isolating silence.

A prolific screenwriter and film director, Charef took 10 years to publish his third novel and adapted it for television in 1999. After *Tea in the Harem,* he continued to explore marginal characters and unusual friendships in films such as *Miss Mona* (1987), *Camomille* (1988), and *Pigeon Flies* (*Pigeon vole,* 1996). In *Miss Mona,* an undocumented immigrant named Samir meets a transvestite, Miss Mona, played by the famous French actor Jean Carmet. They commit various crimes together to secure money for papers and a sex-change operation. In *Camomille,* a young man kidnaps a radio star who is misunderstood by her rich family and is addicted to drugs. He decides to impregnate her to save her from committing suicide. *Pigeon Flies,* a made-for-television movie, explores the friendship between a homeless man and a child.

Strongly affected by his father's absence during his own childhood, Charef develops his male characters as mostly antiheroes with absent fathers. Women, on the other hand, take center stage in his most recent films. *In the Country of Juliets* (1992), an official selection in the Cannes film festival, concerns the journey of three women who emerge from jail. *Marie-Line* (2000) explores the internal contradictions of the eponymous main character, a right-wing extremist who fiercely leads a team of cleaners, mostly composed of undocumented female immigrants, in a large suburban supermarket. Her initial authority is undermined by her evolving friendship with the workers. Sexually harassed by her boss, forced to join an extremist political party to get her job, she finds consolation in leading the fan club of Joe Dassin, a charismatic popular French singer of the 1970s. Marie-Line is played by Muriel Robin, a famous French stand-up comedian who was nominated for the French César for Best Actress.

After a trip to Algeria in the 1990s, Charef wanted to do a light film on his childhood, but after seeing his aunt repudiated by her husband, he changed his focus to women's issues and made *The Daughter of Keltoum* (2001). Rallia, the main protagonist, is a 19-year-old model who had been adopted as a child by a Swiss family and who returns to Algeria to find her mother, Keltoum. This road movie highlights the evolution of the character from resentment toward her mother to understanding after she meets her aunt Nedjma and discovers the difficulty of life in the desert, the weight of traditions, and the oppression of women.

Many Beur writers only published one or two autobiographical novels before disappearing from the public scene. Although Charef has written only three novels and is now widely known for his films, he continues to be an inspiration for many contemporary Beur writers. Azouz Begag, another prominent figure in Beur writing, has acknowledged that his writing was born out of his reading of Charef's *Tea in the Harem.* Charef has paved the way for other Beur writers to go beyond the specific challenges faced by the Algerian community, which makes his work fully postcolonial.

BIBLIOGRAPHY

Bhabha, Homi K., ed. *Nation and Narration.* London, New York: Routledge, 1990.

Ibnlfassi, Laila, and Nicki Hitchcott. *African Francophone Writing*. Oxford, Washington, D.C.: Berb, 1996.

King, Russell, et al., eds. *Writing Across Worlds: Literature and Migration*. London, New York: Routledge, 1995.

Majumdar, Margaret, ed. *Francophone Studies: The Essential Glossary*. New York: Oxford University Press, 2002.

Martine Fernandes

CHÉRI COLETTE (1920) Sidonie-Gabrielle COLETTE was born on January 28, 1873, in Saint-Sauveur-en-Puisaye, Burgundy, France. Author of more than 50 novels, numerous short stories, and articles for periodicals of her era, she wrote from her early 20s through her mid-70s. This popular 20th-century French writer was known for blurring the lines of fiction and autobiography, inventing the modern teenager in fiction, and being the first modern woman to live in accordance with her sensual and artistic inclinations.

Colette began *Chéri* in September 1919. Monthly installments of the novel began appearing in *La Vie Parisienne* in January 1920 and went from magazine to book publication with few changes. This slim text focuses on the character transformation of the central protagonist, someone who is vulgar and shallow but rises above her own limitations when touched by love. Other motifs include the struggle between the pure and the impure, love and suffering, and separation and indivisibility.

Chéri is the story of a love between the beautiful but spoiled 25-year-old Fred Peloux, called Chéri, and a 49-year-old woman of sensuality, Léa de Lonval. The book opens with Chéri demanding that Léa give him her pearls. Léa is a well-kept courtesan made wealthy by a benefactor. Their love affair began in 1906 on trip to Normandy. The young male Chéri was 19, and Léa was the much older woman at 43 years, though she has known Chéri since he was an infant. A solitary kiss turned their relationship into a sexual one. Chéri proved a terrible lover, but with Léa's help he learned the art of love and romance. Chéri is fatherless and assumes he will be nurtured indefinitely by the middle-aged women around him, a role Léa has performed during the past six years of their relationship. Léa is practical, maternal, protective, and immovable. She is the ideal and successful demimondaine, or promiscu-

ous woman. Chéri is the opposite. He is nervous, agitated, irresponsible, childlike, and handsome, casting a spell on the women he meets.

Chéri decides to marry the 18-year-old heiress Edmée in autumn 1912, and immediately they leave on their six-month honeymoon. However, the breakup of Chéri and Léa troubles both of them. Léa runs into old friends, also aging courtesans, and sees their aging bodies as repulsive and grotesque. Léa fears her own aging and takes to bed ill, but she soon leaves her convalescence and decides to travel. She tells no one where she's going or when she will return. Chéri and Edmée arrive in Paris, both suffering and arguing. Chéri walks out, moves into a hotel, and frequents opium dens where he stares at fake pearls. He waits for Léa to return and when she does, he arrives in her rose-colored bedroom unannounced, exclaiming that he has come home. Léa is startled and pleased. They fall into each other's arms for a few brief hours. However, the next morning Chéri critically observes Léa's aging body without her knowing. Léa is making plans for them to escape together, but when she realizes that Chéri now sees her differently, she lashes out and then sends him back home. Léa finally accepts who she is, a mature woman and learns to live without Chéri. Colette continues this tale in *The Last of Chéri,* where Chéri is still in love with Léa but stuck in his loveless marriage.

BIBLIOGRAPHY

Colette, Sidonie Gabrielle. *Earthly Paradise: An Autobiography, Drawn from Her Lifetime Writings.* New York: Farrar, Straus and Giroux, 1966.

Fell, Alison S. "Life after Léa: War and Trauma in Colette's *La Fin de Chérie.*" Translated by Herma Briffault et al. *French Studies,* 59, no. 4 (October 2005): 495–450.

Laura Madeline Wiseman

CHOI INHUN (1936–   ) *Korean novelist, short story writer, dramatist* Choi Inhun brought a new trend to the landscape of Korean literature in the 1960s by establishing a new tradition of intellectual novels. He is also known for his innovation in literary techniques and experimentation with various narrative forms. His novels heralded a break with the Korean literature of preceding decades, which was preoccupied, if not obsessed, with the chaos and moral collapse of the country after its independence from Japanese colonial rule in 1945, national division, and the Korean War (1950–53). However, Choi, a novelist of ideas, has never remained in the realm of metaphysics. Instead, he seeks to mediate tensions between individual freedom and the burden of history by exploring both inward realities of human psychology and concrete, social contexts.

Choi was born on April 13, 1936, to a well-to-do merchant family in a northern region of Korea that was then under Japanese rule. When the country's new communist government, supported by the force of the Soviet Union's military, began to wield its power after Korea's independence in 1945, his "bourgeois" family, branded "an enemy of the people," was forced to flee, ending up in a refugee camp in South Korea. This experience of displacement from his native soil and Choi's keen awareness of his country's tragic place in the political maneuvers of world powers after World War II profoundly affected his literary imagination.

At age 24, Choi gained instant recognition with the publication of *The Square* (1960). "Square" in the title signifies an "open space" where solidarity and collectivity prevail as a historical momentum. In contrast to the "square," Choi presents another space, a "private room," where individuals, drawing back a few steps from a tumultuous crowd in the square, pursue freedom and happiness. Pitting these two disparate spaces against each other, Choi subtly casts doubts on the conflicting ideologies of the two Koreas.

The protagonist, Myungjun Yi, is a Hamlet-like, sensitive college student caught between the square and the private room. Amid the political upheaval and ideological clash after the partitioning of the Korean Peninsula, Yi is disappointed with the social milieu of the South and decides to go to the North. To his dismay, what he finds in the North is squares overflowing with meaningless political slogans and propagandas. While serving in the North Korean army during the Korean War, he is captured and held at a prison camp. During the prisoner-of-war negotiations after the war, he chooses to go to a neutral country, India. It is not clear whether Yi finally finds a third place to transcend the binary of the square and the private room since Choi ends the novel with his protagonist jumping into the

sea on his voyage to India. But *The Square* provides avenues to reinterpret the national division and ideological conflicts from a new perspective, thereby prophetically prefiguring a brief utopian moment envisioned in the South Korean civil uprising of April 19, 1960, and the shattering of the dream by the military coup d'état of May 16, 1961.

A unifying characteristic that underlies Choi's earlier novels is his examination of individuals' interior world. The author opens up a space to investigate his characters' innermost consciousness by reducing the narrative time frame. The actual events in *The Square* take place in a day when Yi is on a voyage to India, and the story of his life around the Korean War is narrated in the form of the Yi's memory. *Dream of Nine Clouds* (1962) treats an hour's nightmare and death of a character. *A Journey to the Western Countries* (1966) transforms a brief moment of going down from the second floor to the first into a fantastic journey to the city of W and the Sokwang Temple in North Korea. *The Daily Life of Ku-poh the Novelist* (1972), as noted by the title itself, also reflects Choi's interest in the compression of time. Evoking modernist novelists in the early 20th century, particularly James Joyce, this exploration into the interior worlds of an individual added a new dimension to the modernity of Korean literature.

The turn to inner realities demands new narrative forms and techniques. The short stories "Life of Nolbu" (1966) and "Life of Ongojip" (1969) illustrate the ways in which Choi creatively engages and revises folklore tradition. In "The Voice of the Governor-General" (1967), Choi develops nuanced commentaries on Korea's political situation by employing an imaginary historical period in the form of allegory. *The Daily Life of Ku-poh the Novelist* is a rewriting and reinventing of Taewon Park's novel already published several decades earlier. Finally, the author's unflagging efforts to search out new narrative forms led him to abandon fiction writing for a period and dedicate his talents to plays.

After publishing critically acclaimed dramas such as *Moon Moon Bright Moon* and *Away, Away, Long Long Time Ago* in the 1970s, Choi returned to novel writing with *The Topic* (1993). The exact meaning of the title is a subject for meditation in Buddhism. The "topic" Choi poses to himself in this novel is how to locate an individual's destiny not only in a national context but also from a larger, global perspective. Choi even attempts to transcend the genre of fiction itself by combining fiction, poetry, drama, essay, and criticism in *The Topic*. Based on his childhood memories in North Korea, a stay in the United States in the 1970s, and a trip to Russia in the early 1990s, the work follows Choi as he goes on an Odyssean voyage through 20th-century world history. Both in the United States, the very heart of capitalism, and in Russia, once the center of communism, the narrator "I" (a persona of the author) feels himself a refugee, just as Choi (and his character Yi in *The Square*) did in his partitioned country. Delineating how the destiny of Choi himself, his family, and his country bears the imprint of the world history, Choi broadens the parameters of national literature. In this sense, *The Topic* is praised by critics as "a monumental novel written in Korean serving as a doorway to world history."

BIBLIOGRAPHY

Kim Hunggyu. *Understanding Korean Literature*. Translated by Robert J. Fouser. Armonk, N.Y.: M. E. Sharpe, 1997.
Kim Yoon-shik. *Understanding Modern Korean Literature*. Translated by Jang Gyung-ryul. Seoul: Jipmoondang, 1998.

Seongho Yoon

CHO SE-HEE (1942–   ) *Korean novelist, short story writer*

Cho Se-hee is a leading representative of contemporary Korean writers. He is best known for his novel *A LITTLE BALL LAUNCHED BY A DWARF*, a collection of 12 short stories about the lives of lower-class people facing industrialization and urbanization. Cho's edgy portrayal of land developers' demolition of poor families' shanties, factory owners' suppression of labor unions, and intellectuals' moral corruption as they pander to the rich and powerful truly captures the zeitgeist of Korean society under the military dictatorship of the 1970s and 1980s. The author has said, "I write not to become a great novelist but to fulfill my civic duty as one of the masses of ordinary Korean people." As an intellectual with deep humanistic compassion toward marginalized people, Cho has assumed an ethical responsibility to raise his literary voice up for social justice, especially where it concerns the tragic breakdown of communal relationships and the organic environment.

Cho was born to working-class parents on August 20, 1942, in Gapyeong, a rural county near the capital city, Seoul. At the age of 14, he moved to a relative's home in Seoul in order to continue his studies. He later recalled that as a young boy, he felt very lonely in the strange place and spent after-school hours playing various sports. One day he discovered a Red Cross–sponsored library in his school. He started borrowing books by Leo Tolstoy and Fyodor Dostoyevsky, as the popular novels had already been checked out by other boys. He read translated editions of *Crime and Punishment, The Brothers Karamazov, War and Peace,* works that made an indelible impact on his adolescent mind. Though he was not a model student in high school, he nurtured a wish to write a novel. With a few practice pieces submitted for publication, he was fortunate enough to attract the attention of Kim Dong-ni and Hwang Soon-won, two leading novelists of the time. He went on to graduate from the Sorabol College of Arts and Kyonghee University and finally achieved his dream of becoming a novelist in 1965 when his novel *The Funeral Boat* won the first prize at a prestigious literary contest. However, Cho stopped writing for a 10-year period beginning in 1965 because he doubted whether he could produce literary works as great as those of Western writers. Disillusioned, he chose not to waste his time and energy writing what he regarded as rubbish; instead, he decided to work at a publishing firm to support his family.

Cho's fiery literary spirit returned, however, when he witnessed the sociopolitical tyranny of Park Jung-hee's military dictatorial regime in the 1970s. Many students, political activists, artists, writers, and conscientious intellectuals who condemned Park's government and who called for democracy and freedom were imprisoned or sentenced to death as instigators. Masses of rural farmers and urban factory workers were driven out of their hometowns and suffered from excessive labor and poor wages under the catchphrases of *urbanization* and *industrialization*. Their suffering, pain, sorrow, and even untimely deaths were neither compensated by the law nor known to the public. As an intellectual and a Korean citizen, Cho could not just sit in his office and witness such tyranny without acting: He grabbed a pen and started writing the first story of his now-famous 12-story novel, *A Little Ball Launched by a Dwarf*. Publication of this book brought Cho the Dong-in Literary Award in 1979.

Cho's oeuvre is not expansive, as he was forced to stop writing again under Chun Doo-hwan's military dictatorial regime of the 1980s. After publishing *A Little Ball Launched by a Dwarf* (1979), *Nemo Shot Down Today* (1979), *A Large Panji-Hat* (1979), and *The Hope Factory of A Man at # 503, Time Travel* (1983), he rested his pen for a decade, until he published *In the Grass Lawn* in 1994. After that, however, he concentrated his energy on participating in political meetings and demonstrations of marginalized farmers, as well as photographing factory laborers condemning the tyranny of the military government. His political concern was crystallized into a collection of photo-essays entitled *The Root of Silence* (2000). In 1997 he launched a literary magazine, *Dangdae Bipyoeong,* and currently he works as a chief editor and professor at Kyonghee University.

Despite the limited number of his works, Cho is revered as a premier writer in the history of Korean literature, and his *A Little Ball Launched by a Dwarf* (*Nangaengyeega SSoaollin Jageun Gong*) is considered the most beloved novel in Korean literature. Abbreviated as *NanSsoGong,* it has sold more than 800,000 copies annually since 1979 and reached the status of a cultural icon, a story handed down from generation to generation. The longevity of *NanSsoGong* can perhaps be understood when it is seen that a dwarf family's hardships and their anxious hope for the way out from their daily struggle pull at readers' heartstrings, reminding them of their own present condition, which differs little from those of a dwarf father of the 1970s. Another possible reason for the book's status as a classic is because the novel was written based on Cho's real-life experiences of being poor, powerless, and uneducated in Korean society.

In *NanSsoGong,* Cho has recounted a real-life story about the struggle between wealthy landowners and the poor. One day Cho was dining with a poor family who had received a demolition notice that their house was to be destroyed for redevelopment. The family refused to move out of their home since they had nowhere else to go. The land developer nonetheless ordered the shanty to be torn down, and as Cho and the family sat at dinner in the house, the iron wrecking ball tore through the wall in front of them. Infuriated, Cho went out and tried to get evictees to fight against the demolishers. However, he realized that there was nothing they could do to stem the tide of the rich and powerful who used their legal property rights in courts to do as they wished. That night, Cho decided to report the selfishness and greed of the wealthy by writing stories about poor, unprivileged people. At that time, the author says, he felt Korean society was in an urgent state of falling apart, and he wanted to send a warning to the dictatorial government with his stories.

To accomplish this, however, he had to cloak his dissident voice and disguise his radical messages with various literary techniques, including short fragmentary sentences, allegories, lyrical passages, and imaginary scenes. He also covered dark, painful reality with a simple, fairy-tale atmosphere and style to highlight the spiritual deterioration and social injustice separating the haves from the have-nots. Drawing on the contemporary news of rocketry and satellites being launched and using an image of a dwarf, he created a title easily associated with a fairy tale: *A Little Ball Launched by a Dwarf*. The publisher also put much effort into making the book's design appear innocent. These subterfuges were necessary because of the dictatorial regime's tough censorship, and they proved effective in confusing the ordinarily scrupulous censors, who did not really understand what they read. *NanSsoGong* proceeded to be published in multiple editions and became widely known to the public. In the end, Cho's strategy paid off as he successfully foiled the military government's attempt to blacklist his novel.

Nearly three decades after the novel's appearance, Cho maintains his compassion toward farmers and laborers who struggled and died due to unbearable living conditions. On November 15, 2005, he was injured by water guns as policemen were subduing a demonstration of farmers who were protesting against the government's new policy to open the rice market to global agribusiness corporations. Two days later, Cho heard that a female farmer named Oh Chu-ok had committed suicide by drinking liquid insecticide. With deep feeling for the suffering and pain of these poor, powerless people, he read a passage of *A Little Ball Launched by a Dwarf* at the celebratory occasion of the novel's 200th edition: "Those who live in the paradise do not think of the hell. Yet our family, living in the hell, have always dreamed of the paradise. Never a day passed without our dreaming of the paradise because we were being worn out day after day. For us living was like fighting in the war." The oppressive reality of "ten million dwarfs of today's Korean society" has not been changed a bit, and those poor dwarves are still "grabbing his ankles" to speak for them. With a strong sense of ethical obligation and humanistic compassion, Cho continues to participate in their meetings, demonstrations, and strikes in order to better hear the cries of dwarves and to record their stories with his camera and pen.

BIBLIOGRAPHY

Choi Gap-jin. "A Study of Hwang Suhk-young and Cho Se-hee." *Woorimalgeul* 24 (Winter 2002): 149–164.
"Cho Se-hee." *Jakgasehgye* (special edition) 7 (1990).
Kim Woo-chang. "History and Human Reason: Twenty-five Years Since Cho Se-hee's *A Little Ball Launched by a Dwarf*." *Dongnam Uhmunnonjip* 7 (1997): 51–76.
Shin Myung-jik. *The Dream of Impossible Subversion*. Seoul: Shiinsa, 2002.
Yee Kyong-ho. "Interview with Cho Se-hee." *Jakgasehgye*, 54 (Autumn 2002): 18–35.

Jihee Han

CHRIST STOPPED AT EBOLI (*CRISTO SI È FERMATO A EBOLI*) CARLO LEVI (1947)

The Italian author and painter CARLO LEVI (1902–75) wrote *Christ Stopped at Eboli* while hiding in a room looking onto Florence's Palazzo Pitti during the final years of World War II. An Italian Jew, a painter with a degree in medicine, and a committed antifascist who had been arrested and sent to southern Italy (in Lucania, now called Basilicata), Levi wrote this famous book about his forced internal exile in 1935 and 1936.

Though called a novel, *Christ Stopped at Eboli* is really nonfiction. Levi changed the name of his town, Aliano, to Gagliano, but other than such minimal changes, most of the accounts in the "novel" are true. What is surprising, first of all, is Levi's clear literary vocation. Previously he had written essays about the

relationship between man, the state, and the sacred; however, *Christ Stopped at Eboli* is filled with gorgeously detailed descriptions of nature, faces of people, and movements of animals.

Levi titled his book *Cristo si è fermato a Eboli* because, as he explains, "Christ never arrived here, nor time, nor the individual soul, nor hope, nor the tie between cause and effect, reason and history." In other words, Christ never proceeded more south than Eboli (a city in the region of Campania, which is northwest of the region of Basilicata). In Gagliano/Aliano, the populace is pagan, according to Levi. There is no sense of time or redemption or heaven. There is only earthly sorrow, the whispers of spirits, the workings of witches with their magic, popular festivals, and fear and loathing of the church.

As an anthropologist and sociologist, Levi describes the rituals of the people and their customs and battles, almost always lost, with the local government. From the beginning of his arrival, the protagonist is asked by the townspeople to heal their families, but the young doctor runs into trouble, because there are two other local doctors, both incompetent, and Levi is a political prisoner under restraint. Generally he is allowed to go only a certain distance, and he is followed continually. He likes to walk to the cemetery on the heights of the town when it is extremely hot and lie down inside the cool graves. (Carlo Levi actually did lie down inside the graves, and he describes the narrow rectangular view of the sky from six feet under.)

Levi inimitably recounts the castrating of pigs and the skinning of goats, in which, at the end, the goat becomes "naked and peeled like a saint." Levi's gaze is never condescending or patronizing; he always maintains a sober yet fascinated tone. He becomes part of the story, more and more, as peasants gather around him and trust his medical skills (rusty since he had not practiced for many years). He speaks of the sorcery (believed to exist) among women, the potions they slip their men when they eat, the magic spells to kill enemies. Levi narrates as well his emigration to America and inevitable return to the inevitable misery in Gagliano.

There is no hope here, among the peasants: They are squeezed by both their local lords and the state. Levi introduces the reader to particular characters such as the town priest. Drunk and broken in his old age, once a promising theological student, continually berating the unbelieving peasants, he lives with his deaf mother in a ramshackle hovel with chickens that deface his collection of books. At the end of the novel, after he gives a stirring sermon against the colonial war in Libya, he is thrown out of Gagliano by the *podestà* (magistrate).

At one point Carlo Levi's sister, a practicing doctor, comes to visit Levi; she wants to introduce projects to change the peasants' lives and combat the raging malaria. Her optimism is not shared by Levi, and the book closes with his departure from the town.

In 1936 an amnesty was declared after a victorious Italian advance in Ethiopia, and Levi was one of many political prisoners released. Nevertheless, he did not abandon his passion for the "southern question" (*la questione meridionale*) in later life. In 1963 he was elected as a senator representing Basilicata in the Italian parliament (as an independent running on the Communist ticket); he served until 1972. He died on January 4, 1975, and was buried in Aliano.

BIBLIOGRAPHY

Brand, Peter, and Lino Pertile, eds. *Cambridge History of Italian Literature.* Rev. ed. Cambridge: Cambridge University Press, 1999.

Ward, David. *Antifascisms: Cultural Politics in Italy, 1943–1946: Benedetto Croce and the Liberals, Carlo Levi and the "Actionists."* Madison, N.J.: Fairleigh Dickinson University Press, 1996.

Jacob Blakesley

CHRONICLE OF A BLOOD MERCHANT (*XU SANGUAN MAIXUE JI*) YU HUA (1996)

A tragicomedy, *Chronicle of a Blood Merchant* relates the story of how Xu Sanguan, a silk factory worker, faces physical pain and sacrifice for the survival of his family. The novel by the Chinese author YU HUA (1960–   ) is also about the protagonist's frictions and reconciliation with his wife and sons, and his endurance against the hardship of life during Mao's era in China, from communist saturation during the Great Leap Forward Campaign (1958–60) to the social engineering of the Cultural Revolution (1969–76).

The story of Xu Sanguan unfolds as a series of incidents in which the main character becomes involved in selling his blood for money over a period of 30 years of living through hard economic times. Every blood transaction is strikingly different in terms of the reason, motivation, situation, function, experience, and effect.

The start of Xu Sanguan's immersion into the habit of selling his own blood for money is accidental. An encounter with two blood merchants from his grandfather's village inspires Xu Sanguan to have his first try, though his motivation is vague. The money from his first blood sale helps him defeat his rival in courting a girl named Xu Yulan. Xu Sanguan and Xu Yulan soon marry. However, Yile, the son born to the pair, is not Xu Sanguan's offspring. The next blood transaction, which takes place many years later, is for Yile, who cuts the skull of the blacksmith's son with a rock in a fight protecting his younger brothers Erle and Sanle, Xu Sanguan's real sons. Failing to persuade He Xiaoyong, presumably Yile's real father, to pay for the serious injury Yile inflicted on the blacksmith's son, Xu Sanguan has to sell his blood for the second time in his life. However, uneasy about his wife's "nonresistance" to her former boyfriend's "rape" many years ago and ashamed of having raised another man's son, he is reluctant to pay for Yile's troublemaking behavior. Then, partly for revenge and partly for comically libidinous reasons, Xu has sex with another woman who works in the same factory where he works. His third blood sale furnishes him with the money needed to carry on this affair.

These serial reactions create continuous discords between Xu and his wife, but not so seriously as to bring an end to their marriage. Indeed, these incidents seem to be what keeps the marriage going. When living conditions turn worse during the Great Famine and the Cultural Revolution, the story gradually takes on a tragic tone, even though more tender feelings and affections can be found in Xu's family. In the harder circumstances, Xu Sanguan sells his blood for the fourth time to get his hungry family a relatively nutritious meal. The several blood deals that follow are all for his sons. One is to support Yile and Erle, who are sent to the poor countryside to be reeducated by the peasant farmers according to Mao's policy. Another is for a dinner treating Erle's farm leader, who has the power to decide whether and when Erle is permitted to return home and live with his parents.

The final blood transactions are the climax of this novel. Yile's life is in danger due to contracting hepatitis, and the medical treatment in Shanghai is unaffordable. In a desperate effort to save Yile, Xu Sanguan journeys to Shanghai, selling blood to the hospitals one by one on his route, once in a couple of days, regardless of the effects on his health. His blood transactions even include "buying back" his own blood twice in order to resell it at higher prices. At one point the doctors who want to save Xu's life find that he has fallen unconscious because too much of his blood has been extracted. Another situation is created when Xu buys "one bowl of" dense blood from a healthy young man who would like to help him and then sells to the hospital "two bowls of" blood diluted by drinking water. This all-out, life-risking struggle against the death of his stepson, and against the limitedness of his body, is one of the most impressive and moving scenes in this novel.

The epilogue of this story is set in the post-Mao era, when Xu Sanguan is old, his three sons grown up and married. No real tragedy has happened to this family during the past years, nor has he had to sell a drop of blood for economic reasons again. One day, however, Xu Sanguan feels a strong inner drive and physical desire to sell his blood once more. Because of his age, a young blood chief refuses him, with humiliating jeers at his old, useless blood. None of his three sons understands Xu's fury and sadness. Only the fried pig livers ordered by his wife in a restaurant—plate after plate, three in all, when Xu used to have one plate after every blood drawing—gives him some comfort.

For Xu Sanguan, selling his blood has many functions: to serve his family, to satisfy his own needs, to prove his strength and value, and to survive a disastrous age. *Chronicle of a Blood Merchant* can therefore be understood basically as a story about a common person's efforts and struggle for better living conditions for his family in hard times. While this conclusion approximates the value Xu places in selling his blood, the novel implies greater and richer motives.

To illustrate this, attention should be focused on the start and end of Xu Sanguan's career as a blood mer-

chant. Even his family life is the result of his first blood deal. These series of events all begin with a purposeless and accidental act. It is not until after he has been paid for his blood for the first time that Xu discovers what he should do with his life. Then he becomes a husband and a father, and enters the stage of striving for his family. The starting point of the career as a blood merchant brings his life into a dynamic process.

For Xu Sanguan, selling his blood provides a way to cope with the world and to satisfy his needs. But the awareness of his own self is, in fact, his discovery of how to use his body. During his career as a blood merchant, he fosters his own body as an instrument, a money-making machine or an alienated self. The first time Xu attempts to sell blood is for himself, for the sheer experience of his body, but after a lifetime of exploitation, his body is at the point of uselessness. Here we find the tragic fact that the blood transaction, once seen as a way of making a living, has been internalized by the character as a way of living, an inner need of his life. The novel ends in his failed effort to reexperience the existence of his own self, which lies only in the physical sensibility of an exploited body.

This means-becomes-end transition also implies a nihilistic view of life, in which time plays a role. In the river of time, where significant things seem to become meaningless, strength and health belong to the blood merchants no more. Xu Sanguan's blood associates die or become disabled. The blood chief Li, a person of power in their blood transactions, cannot avoid death either. Only the blood business remains, and a new generation of blood merchants carry the profession on, as life itself goes on. The future of these newcomers can be foretold from Xu's present. Xu Sanguan once struggled at the edge of life and death, but in the end, the children, for whom Xu has been desperately striving, care only for their own interests. It seems that for every blood merchant, tragedy and the void follow.

Nevertheless, the novel does not suggest a pessimistic attitude toward life. On the contrary, what is of importance here is a quality of endurance, of carrying on while confronting not only the hardship but also the meaninglessness of life.

In this sense, Xu Sanguan is praiseworthy. However, he is just a common person, a nonhero. There are obvious defects and weaknesses in his character. Some of them might compromise our fondness of him, while other behaviors draw us close to him. On the one hand, he is so cruel as to deprive Yile of a bowl of noodles during a famine merely because he does not consider Yile to be his own son; on the other hand, he is kind enough to risk his own life to save Yile. This novel is a success in balancing and combining these two sides of Xu Sanguan's character in the development of the plot.

The story of the blood merchants takes place in a real historical milieu, but it is far from clear if it is a realistic novel. Some of the characters' behaviors are so ridiculous as to tint the story with unreal and cartoon-like color. The characters' dialogue and acts are incredibly frank, thus giving the writing style an impressive tone of absurdity. An example is the funny, sensational description of how Xu Yulan had sex with her former boyfriend and the controversial issue of whether it was a rape or a seduction. This is retold without reservation by Xu Sanguan to his three sons in the "family trial" of Xu Yulan, who is absurdly accused of "prostitution" by the revolutionary activists. The children are described as amazed by these erotic details of their mother's past, regarding it with curiosity and interest. On the other hand, as a parody of the "public criticism meetings," which were very popular during the Cultural Revolution, the "family trial" scene in this novel is not so absurd and unreal in the mind of those who bear the historical memory of that real and nightmarish era.

The traumatic historical memories of China are an important background to understanding the story. However, this novel treats people's sufferings and catastrophes in an easy way, much more mildly than Yu Hua's former works, which are full of violence and death. Here tragic happenings are represented mostly as comic and funny. This trait is epitomized in an analogy that consistently cheers up every male blood merchant in the novel: The physical weakness after a blood drawing is described as "the same as the experience after one just dismounts from a woman's body," although the blood drawing itself is by no means comparable to a sexual orgasm. There is an intentional mixture of suffering and pleasure in a blackly humorous way here, which can be found almost everywhere in the book. This is both the style of the narrative and the atti-

tude of the characters: It is a way of dealing with the hardship of life, to make it a little bit more bearable.

BIBLIOGRAPHY

Hong Zhigang. *Yuhua Pingzhuan* (*A Critical Biography of Yu Hua*). Zhengzhou: Zhengzhou University Press, 1998.
Knight, Deirdre Sabina. "Capitalist and Enlightenment Values in 1990s Chinese Fiction: The Case of Yu Hua's Blood Seller." *Textual Practice* 16, no. 3 (December 2002). 547–568.
Wu Yiqin. "Farewell to 'Illusory Forms'—The Significance of *Xu Sanguan Selling His Blood* to Yu Hua." *Forum in literature and the Arts* 1 (2000): 10–19.
Yu Hua. *Xu Sanguan Maixue Ji.* Shanghai: Shanghai Literary Press, 1996.

Tu Xianfeng

CITIES OF SALT (MUDUN AL-MILH)

ABDELRAHMAN MUNIF (1984–1989) The most celebrated, controversial, and critically acclaimed series of novels by ABDELRAHMAN MUNIF (1933–2004) merits the title of epic by way of the work's time span covering many years, the endless chain of memorable characters, and the many plot threads. A quintet that started as a trilogy, *Cities of Salt* has been translated into several languages and is recommended reading for many university courses around the world; it is also banned in some Arab countries.

The novel is a graphic and detailed account of the transformation of a fictional Gulf country (resembling Saudi Arabia) from a simple Bedouin life into an oil-producing state governed, albeit indirectly, and exploited by American oil companies. It records the shattering of people's lives and the violation of their own traditions. Driven out of their simple homes and tents, the people watch their villages being leveled to the ground while American ports and cities are erected in their place. They are left feeling not only bewildered by modern technological novelties but also totally betrayed by their own greedy rulers, who give the foreign corporations the green light to do whatever they want regardless of the country's people and traditions.

Munif started working on the novel while staying in France; the first two volumes were published between 1981 and 1986. He completed the other three volumes after settling in Syria. The first volume—in Arabic,

Al-Teeh (the labyrinth/the wilderness, 1984)—was translated in 1987 as *Cities of Salt* by Peter Theroux, who also translated the second volume, *al-Ukhdud* (1986) (*The Trench* [1993]) and the third, *Taqasim al-layl wa al-Nahar* (1989) (*Variations on Night and Day* [1993]). The fourth book, *Al-Munbatt* (the uprooted, or the exiled), and the fifth, *Badiyat Azzolumat* (desert of darkness), both published in 1989, have yet to be translated into English.

Cities of Salt is said to have appeared at an opportune time politically. In the second half of the 20th century, Arab people had suffered many setbacks, having been let down by their governments and foreign interventions. The continued battles between the Israelis and the Palestinians, the Lebanese civil war (1975–90), and the Saudi-Egyptian-American political accord (1990) all took their toll. There was a need for an epic work that reevaluated the Arab history and future. Characters in Munif's works are ordinary, broken, and trapped. They speak everyday language, are disillusioned by modern industries, and struggle within an intricate social, economic, and political matrix in an effort to assert their identities. Eventually they take the law into their own hands. These are the characters that many Arab readers wanted to read about.

Having lived in many Arab cities, Munif knew the Arab people and political conditions better, perhaps, than any other writer at the time *Cities of Salt* was written. By traveling constantly, he developed firsthand knowledge and a unique relationship with many Arab cities and their history, which his uncontrolled imagination transformed into a great panorama delineating the social, economic, and political contours of an epoch. Such documentation is rendered in a captivating literary style, evoking at times the *Arabian Nights* and creating a wonderful portrait of the tragic accommodation to modernity by an oasis community. The collective title of the quintet is symbolic. The oil-based cities are as fragile and soluble as salt (extracting salt from the sea was the people's traditional industry before the exploration of oil), indicating their ephemeral existence.

Munif's style, described as unhurried, varies in the five volumes. The first volume is more descriptive, whereas the other volumes are more realistic. The conventional first-person narration is sometimes interrupted by other points of view, while memories, letters, and diaries are used without complicating the flow of the plot. In this sense, *Cities of Salt* reads like popular literature, especially in the way Munif makes use of poetry, religious quotes, fables, and historical anecdotes (markedly by Ibn Bakhit in the third volume, *Variations on Night and Day*). What characterizes this novel is the dialogue, which uses everyday (spoken and informal language) rather than formal literary language, creating vibrant, plausible characters. In *The Clash of Fundamentalisms* (2002), Tariq Ali, the renowned British historian and novelist, referred to *Cities of Salt* for description of some historical figures such as the Arabist and British agent H. A. R. Philby.

Cities of Salt depicts a society as it falls apart. Although the rulers are main characters in the quintet, Munif presents numerous unforgettable, typical characters whose characterization and complex relationships with the ruling elite bring history alive. The opening novel of the quintet tells the story of a desert village located on a brook, Wadi al-Uyoun, in the early 1930s. The village witnesses the first strike of sudden transformation represented by the main character, Miteb al-Hathal, a simple Bedouin. His stubborn resistance during the death of Wadi al-Uyoun as the tractors cut down all the trees leads to his mysterious death and makes a legend out of him. He becomes a phantom, appearing whenever the villagers are stressed or rebel. Al-Hathal does not witness the building of the modern, steel-like Western town of Harran, but his son Fawaz, with whom the story continues, does.

In contrast to Miteb al-Hathal, Ibn Rashed, another Bedouin who hosts the Americans quite hospitably and cooperates with them, thinks that the Americans will come no matter what, so he finds no point in resisting them. The character of Mufaddai al-Jeddan, a traditional doctor who helps the sick without pay, is also contrasted and, indeed, left to die of his injuries at the end by Subhi al-Mahmilji, a modern doctor who establishes good relations with the emir and allows new technologies to take control. Dr. al-Mahmilji and Ibn Rashed, the opportunist, continue to be main characters in the second volume, *The Trench*—the story of Mooran, the modern capital of the desert. The killing of al-Jeddan rouses and disturbs the inhabitants, who had accepted the sudden transformation of their town and who have become enslaved to modern professional life.

Variations on Night and Day is set in an earlier period, when the British ruled the region. Sultan Khureybit, with the help of the conniving British Hamilton, restores his ancestral claim to power and rules over Mooran, the city that the British mushroomed in the middle of the desert, under the name of the Hudaibiya State, expanding his dominion mercilessly over surrounding towns. In this volume, we meet one of the most admirable characters, Shemran al-Oteibi, a man who single-handedly rebels against the government for unjustly jailing his son. The novel also portrays the sultan's domestic life at the palace, his polygamous household—wives, eunuchs, children, servants, mistress—and the conflicts, intrigues, and murders within the palace.

The Uprooted (or *The Exiled*) is about the life of Sultan Khzael, who is exiled to Geneva. Dr. al-Mahmilji's daughter, Salma, is the main tragic character in this fourth volume. Her marriage to the sultan does not last long, and she is puzzled why her marriage fails so quickly. Like Shakespeare's Ophelia, Salma's mysterious death symbolizes the loss of innocence. Female characters are as passive in the quintet as they are in real-life Saudi Arabia. Munif often criticized the treatment of women as third-class citizens in Saudi Arabia.

The last volume of the quintet, *Desert of Darkness,* follows the life of Prince Finner, son of Sultan Khureybit (of the third volume) and Khazael's brother (of the fourth volume). Now that the political center has clearly shifted from Britain to the United States, Dr. al-Mahmilji's son, Ghazwan, who has learned to use his father's relations with the political elite, establishes a trading company in the United States to be exploited by local government personnel. The quintet ends with Finner's death.

Cities of Salt arguably surpasses Noble laureate NAGUIB MAHFOUZ's *Cairo Trilogy* in its richness of characters, creation and analysis of typical characters, recreation of historical figures, and precise descriptions, tying the stories together in a heroic setting: the desert itself. It remains an unparalleled literary Arab epic.

BIBLIOGRAPHY

Allen, Roger. "Review of Munif, *Cities of Salt.*" *World Literature Today* 63 (1989): 358–359.

Boulata, Issa J. "Social Change in Munif's *Cities of Salt. Edebiyat* 8, no. 2 (1998): 191–215.

Munif, Abdelrahman. *Cities of Salt.* Translated by Peter Theroux. New York: Random House, 1987.

———. *Story of a City: A Childhood in Amman.* Translated by Samira Kawar. London: Quartet Books, 1996.

———. *The Trench.* Translated by Peter Theroux. New York: Pantheon Books, 1991.

———. *Variations on Night and Day.* Translated by Peter Theroux. New York: Pantheon Books, 1993.

Ahmad Al-Issa
Nawar Al-Hassan Golley

CLAUDINE AT SCHOOL (*CLAUDINE À L'ÉCOLE*) COLETTE (1900)

Sidonie-Gabrielle COLETTE was born on January 28, 1873, in Saint-Sauveur-en-Puisaye, Burgundy, France. Author of more than 50 novels and numerous short stories and articles for periodicals of her era, she wrote from her early 20s through her mid-70s. This popular 20th-century French writer was known for blurring the lines of fiction and autobiography and being one of the first modern women to live in accordance with her desires. *Claudine at School,* initially attributed to Colette's first husband, Willy, is one of the more autobiographical accounts of her life. As recalled by both Willy and Colette, Colette was forced to write the original version of *Claudine at School* in exercise books, and Willy originally dismissed it as unsellable. However, he rediscovered the books in a drawer two years later and suggested several revisions, such as developing a love affair between Claudine and one of the schoolmistresses. It took four years until a publisher would accept the manuscript for publication, in 1900. The Claudine sequence became immensely successful, and Colette, then using her husband's name, followed *Claudine at School* with three other novels: *Claudine in Paris* (1901), *Claudine Married* (1902), and *Claudine and Annie* (1903).

Claudine at School opens when Claudine is living in a small village on the northern edge of Burgundy, France, and she has just turned 15. Claudine spends time in the woods, wears her chestnut hair in long braids, and dons long skirts because, though still a child, she admits she resembles a woman. She is raised by her father, a science professor, since her mother died early in Claudine's childhood. At school, Claudine is witty, intelligent, and strong. Her classmates are the daughters of shopkeepers and farmers, which makes Claudine exceptional, though she is not sent off to a boarding school like other well-to-do offspring in the village. At the parochial school, desire runs rampant and does not follow heteronormative lines. The school's headmistress, Miss Sergent, has her way with her assistant, Aimée Lanthenay. Claudine is infatuated with Aimée herself and takes private English lessons with her, which rouses the headmistress's jealousy. The school's official medical inspector is intrigued with Claudine, though he is suspected to be Miss Sergent's lover. Aimée's younger sister, Luce, arrives and falls for Claudine, the same way Claudine fell for Aimée. The book concludes by following Claudine to the district capital for her final exam.

BIBLIOGRAPHY

Southworth, Helen. "Rooms of their Own: How Colette Uses Physical and Textual Space to Question a Gendered Literary Tradition." *Tulsa Studies in Women's Literature* 20, no. 2 (Fall 2001): 253–278.

Stewart, Joan Hinde. "The School and the Home." *Women's Studies* 8, no. 3 (1981): 259–259.

Laura Madeline Wiseman

CLENCHED FISTS (DE KNUTNA HÄNDERNA) Vilhelm Moberg (1930)

The second book in a two-novel set about life on the remote and isolated Ulvaskog farm in the early 1920s, *Clenched Fists* describes a time period and a geographical setting very familiar to novelist Carl Arthur Vilhelm Moberg (1898–1973). *Clenched Fists* has been called a Småland version of *King Lear*. The stubborn farmer Adolf of Ulvaskog plows and cultivates his land with his own hands and refuses to acknowledge the changes around him. When his children wish to leave the farm for the city, he clenches his fists and resists so fiercely that he ends up with nothing.

New opportunities and Adolf's need for total control result in open rebellion among the grown-up children. The oldest daughter, Signe, leaves to make a living by waiting tables in Växjö. Erik applies for and is accepted to business school. Emil, the oldest son, is so disgusted with Adolf's stubborn refusal to modernize the farming methods that he takes on work as a road builder. The

empire of Ulvaskog that Adolf has envisioned crumbles. Left behind is only Mari, the youngest daughter and Adolf's favorite.

Life in the city, however, is not as carefree as the children imagined. Having spent their inheritance from their mother's death, they soon find themselves in financial trouble. Moral erosion also threatens. A friend reveals to Adolf that the latter's niece Gärda, who has lived in Stockholm for many years, is not working in an office as she claims but makes her living as a prostitute. Meanwhile, Mari has fallen in love with Martin, a glassblower working at the mill. Adolf opposes the match with the objection that a glassblower will never marry and settle down on a farm but will always travel to where there is work. When he reveals to Mari his wishes for a new generation on Ulvaskog, one that will secure him in his old age, she promises to stay with him until he dies.

In an attempt to persuade Adolf to sell the farm and hand over the proceeds to them, the children return to Ulvaskog to confront their father one last time. Erik is facing personal bankruptcy, while Signe has married the snobbish Gustav Nord and is also in need of extra money. But Adolf clenches his fists and stubbornly refuses to sell his farm. The siblings turn their attentions to Mari, without whom, they reason correctly, Adolf cannot possibly remain on the farm. Mari is persuaded to break her promise in an attempt to secure the happiness of her sister and brothers. She has corresponded with her cousin Gärda and decides to join her in Stockholm, unaware of Gärda's real profession. When Adolf finds out about Mari's plans, rather than allowing her to go, he kills her the night before her departure.

The novel is an attempt to describe the personal tragedies that followed in the wake of the depopulation of the Swedish countryside in the early 20th century. The land has taken Adolf prisoner, and his stubborn refusal to invest in agricultural machines alienates the children on whose working hands he depends. But Moberg's descriptions of Adolf's selfish and thoughtless children also suggest that the author's allegiance does not lie with them either. Their failures exemplify how ill equipped people straight from the farms are to handle city life and the capitalist system that governs it. Like the first book in the Ulvaskog-series, *Far From* the Highway, the pessimism of the 19th-century German philosopher Arthur Schopenhauer and a strong element of determinism can be discerned in the plot of Clenched Fists. Moberg later adapted his novel into a five-act play with the same name, which was first performed in 1939.

BIBLIOGRAPHY

Holmes, Philip. Vilhelm Moberg. Boston: Twayne Publishers, 1980.

———. Vilhelm Moberg: En Introduktion Till Hans Författarskap. Stockholm: Carlsson, 2001.

Platen, Magnus von. Den Unge Vilhem Moberg: En Levnadsteckning. Stockholm: Bonniers, 1978.

Malin Lidström Brock

COELHO, PAULO (1947–   ) *Brazilian essayist, novelist, short story writer*   A Brazilian novelist and lyricist, Paulo Coelho has achieved national and international appreciation for works that focus on the discovery of the self as a means of spiritual fulfillment. Coelho's novel The ALCHEMIST (O Alquimista, 1988), his most popular novel, is highly symbolic and uses a linear sequential plot structure to emphasize the eternal struggle between deeply driven human ambitions and the tragic tendency to abandon one's dreams to complacency. Coelho's works, originally written in Portuguese, have been translated into more than 50 languages, and more than 35 million of his books have been sold in 140 countries across the world.

Coelho was born into a middle-class family in Rio de Janeiro, Brazil. His nature as a young man seemed to run to wild extremes. His excessive teenage rebelliousness, as well as his inordinate passion for writing, upset his parents' expectations. Coelho abandoned his studies early in life to join the theater and was deeply influenced by the free nature of the hippie movement of the 1960s. In the early 1970s, the Brazilian rock star Raul Seixas invited Coelho to write the lyrics to his songs. Their records were very successful and brought Coelho fame and money. His life, however, was still caught up in extreme ups and downs, and he returned to a somewhat normal life as he started working for the music companies CBS and Polygram. He also married. By 1978, though, he had given up his job and had left his wife.

In 1979 Coelho and Christina Oticica, an old friend whom he later married, visited several countries in Europe, including Germany, where they toured the concentration camp at Dachau. In 1986 Coelho walked the medieval pilgrim's route stretching between France and Spain to Santiago de Compostela, an exhausting journey that took 56 days. He experienced a spiritual awakening during this pilgrimage, which he describes in his first novel, The Diary of a Magus (O diário de um mago), written in 1987, a year after completing his journey, and rereleased as The Pilgrimage in 1995. This was followed in 1988 by The Alchemist, a mystical novel that stresses the importance of signs, omens, and the need to believe in one's aspirations. Coelho's immensely popular novel underlines the concept of the personal legend or myth—the possibility of experiencing self-discovery by following one's dreams. His next novel, Brida (1990), the true story of an Irish enchantress, received much critical attention and improved the sales of his earlier works. This was followed by The Gift (O dom supremo) in 1991 and The Valkyries (As Valkírias) in 1992, a nonfiction work that describes Coelho's journey with his wife through the Mojave Desert, a torturous quest that took them 40 days.

Coelho's success continued with fictional works By the River Piedra I Sat Down and Wept (Na margem do rio Piedra eu sentei e chorei, 1994), a love story in which he explores his feminine side and divine love; and Maktub (1994), a collection of short stories based on folk tales. The Fifth Mountain (O monte cinco), published in 1996, narrates the story of the trials and tribulations experienced by the biblical prophet Elijah and his inspiring response to them. In 1997 Coelho published two books: The Manual of the Warrior of Light (Manual do guerreiro da luz), a collection of philosophical essays; and Love Letters From a Prophet (Cartas de amor do profeta), which compiles selected love letters of the distinguished Lebanese writer KHALIL GIBRAN to his beloved Mary Haskell. Veronika Decides to Die (Veronika decide morrer), published in 1998, is a critique against arbitrary hospitalization and recalls Coelho's experiences during his treatment in a mental institution in his adolescence. This was followed by The Devil and Miss Prym (O Demônio e a Srta Prym) in 2000, a novel that explores the contemporary conflict between human values and vices through a complex plot based in a small imaginary town.

In 2001 Coelho wrote a collection of short stories, *Fathers, Sons and Grandsons* (*Histórias para pais, filhos e netos*) for children. He explored the sacred view of sex in ELEVEN MINUTES (*Onze minutos*, 2003), the story of a prostitute. In 2004 he published *The Genie and the Roses*, (*O genio e as rosas*), a collection of legendary tales for children. His book *The Zahir* (*O Zahir*, 2005) is the fictional story of a renowned writer's search for his missing wife, a war correspondent. The novel has been released in several countries across the world.

Coelho has received several prestigious literary awards from different countries, including the Crystal Award (Switzerland), the Rio Branco Order (Brazil), the Légion d'Honneur (France), and a nomination for the International IMPAC Dublin Literary Award for *Veronika Decides to Die*. In 2002 he was elected to the Brazilian Academy of Letters (ABL). Coelho lives with his wife, Christina, in Rio de Janerio and in Tarbes, France.

BIBLIOGRAPHY

Arias, Juan. *Paulo Coelho: The Confessions of a Pilgrim*. London: HarperCollins, 1999.

Coelho, Paulo. *Like the Flowing River: Thoughts and Reflections*. London: HarperCollins: 2006.

Preeti Bhatt

COLD NIGHT (HAN YE) BA JIN (1947)

Cold Night is one of the representative works by BA JIN (1904–2005), a highly respected Chinese novelist. It was finished in the middle of 1940s, when the author changed his literary style from fervid emotionalism to a more dispassionate analysis of human nature. Focusing on the destiny of ordinary people, *Cold Night* describes the happiness and misery of the China of that age. It also belongs to Ba Jin's trilogy *The World*, a work widely regarded as the quintessential achievement of his fiction.

The story, which is set in Chongqing, the temporary capital of China during World War II, is about one man and two women. The complexity of the novel comes in part because the two women both love the same man but look down on each other. Their love and their discord lead him ultimately to confusion, poverty, and death.

One cold night, Wang Wen-xuan returns home after an emergency air-raid siren ends. He feels depressed by the absence of his wife, Zeng Shu-sheng. They had quarreled the night before, prompting her to move to her friend's home. Wang Wen-xuan wants to apologize to his wife, but his mother opposes this. His father had died years earlier, and his mother had brought Wang Wen-xuan up alone. To complicate matters, the aging widow lives with her son's family. She loves her son and grandson but hates her daughter-in-law intensely.

Zeng Shu-sheng feels an equal resentment toward her mother-in-law. She and her husband had been classmates studying education at a university in Shanghai and decided to carry on an educational experiment called rural and family-style school. But the war shattered their dream. She had to work as a clerk in a bank, while her husband joined a publishing company as a press corrector. Life was hard financially during the war years. To make matters worse, Zeng Shu-sheng insisted on sending her son to an expensive boarding school, which the family can ill afford.

The day after they quarrel, Wang Wen-xuan goes to DaChuan Bank to meet his wife, in spite of his mother's objection. Over coffee, Zeng Shu-sheng informs her husband that she will not return to him unless his mother leaves the home. Wang Wen-xuan keeps silent. As both women are important in his heart, he faces an unsolvable problem.

The young man returns home disappointed. His mother is waiting and has prepared dinner. Wang Wen-xuan eats little. When his mother discovers that he has just met with Zeng Shu-sheng, she becomes angry. His mother persuades him to abandon Zeng Shu-sheng since she was not at all satisfied with her daughter-in-law. She considers Zeng a live-in girlfriend, not a formally wedded wife to her only son, although the couple have been together for many years and have a 13-year-old son. Wang Wen-xuan can calm neither his mother nor his wife. He flees the house and goes drinking with his former middle school classmate.

Zeng Shu-sheng happens to find Wang Wen-xuan in the street; otherwise, the drunken man might have spent the whole night vomiting and sleeping out in the open. Zeng Shu-sheng rebukes her husband gently and, supporting him, takes him back to their home. Wang Wen-xuan enjoys the feeling of being taken care by his wife, and he holds her hand like a pitiful kid and begs her not to leave again. Zeng Shu-sheng agrees.

The whole family is now together again, which Wang Wen-xuan owes to having been drunk. It was not good to his health, but he would rather be ill if only his mother and his wife could get along peacefully. In fact, he is a weak man. He coughs, has fevers, even vomits blood now and then, but he dares not take a day off from work for fear of being fired. He can hardly support his family on his paltry wages.

In contrast, Zeng Shu-sheng is a beautiful and energetic woman. She cannot suffer a boring life in a conflict-ridden family. She prefers to cheer herself up by dressing up, dancing, and dating. Her mother-in-law prefers to regard her as a waitress instead of a professional in the bank. Nevertheless, she earns more money than her husband, pays the exorbitant fee for her son's private school, and bears most of the family's expense. Wang Wen-xuan's mother does the housework as a servant and at one point sells her gold ring to buy medicine for her poor son.

The Japanese army soon invades the northwest of China and quickly closes in on Chongqing. The city finds itself thrown into chaos. The citizens, including Wang's family, consider fleeing. Problems mount for the family. Wang Wen-xuan's job is in jeopardy, and he is struck down with tuberculosis. Zeng Shu-sheng finds an opportunity for a job promotion and leaves for Lanzhou with her manager, a man who has loved her for a long time. Her decision comes with difficulty and not quickly. Even though she cannot bear the estrangement and discord in the family, she cannot discard her husband either, especially when he is ill and needs her support. But finally she makes up her mind to leave after a terrible quarrel with her mother-in-law. Wang Wen-xuan supports his wife's choice. As he realizes that his illness is incurable, he will not discourage her from finding another kind of life. The decision for Zeng Shu-sheng to leave will also make his mother happy.

Wang Wen-xuan returns to his office with the help of a friend, but his colleagues refuse to have lunch with him for fear of being infected by his illness. He endures their unkindly treatment and comforts himself with the letters received from his wife. Zeng Shu-sheng is now working in Lanzhou, from where she sends money monthly. He relishes her short notes. One day Wang Wen-xuan receives a long letter from his wife, which at first greatly raises his spirits. But his happiness plummets as he reads further that Zeng Shu-sheng is asking for a divorce. He cries sadly, although he has known for some time that the end of their marriage would come sooner or later.

Wang Wen-xuan's health worsens. Soon he is unable to speak and feels a steady ache in his lungs and throat. He communicates with his mother by writing on paper as his life becomes empty and hopeless. When the Japanese finally surrender, the citizens of Chongqing celebrate the victory, but the good news cannot stop Wan Wen-xuan's slow and painful death from tuberculosis. He dies in a heartfelt moment, holding the hands of his mother and his son, with the clatter of a victory parade sounding outside the window.

Two months later, Zeng Shu-sheng flies back to Chongqing. She hurries home, where she finds that her husband has died and her mother-in-law has moved elsewhere with her son. She is shocked by the changes and wanders in the street aimlessly. Should she search for her son, or just fly back to Lanzhou?

The novel illustrates three typical figures. The reader finds Wang Wen-xuan as a timid man oppressed by the hardships of life. Growing up in a family lacking a father, the young man reveals overt oedipal tendencies. Married or not, he desires to be tended by his mother. His mother lives with him and acts the dual role of kind mother and severe father. Wang Wen-xuan is used to relying on his mother emotionally although he loves his wife, too. As for the relationship of the couple, expressions such as "like a child," "childish," and "childly" imply that Wang Wen-xuan prefers a mother-like woman for a mate. But Zeng Shu-sheng would rather have a lover than another (adult) son. She feels sorry for her husband but has no courage to continue her strife-filled life. The quarrels between the two women are the main reason for her leaving, in addition to which her emotional tie to her husband has changed from love to mercy. But in the eyes of Wang Wen-xuan's mother, it was this woman who robbed the love of her son and did not show her the proper respect. Theirs is a turbulent family in a turbulent nation. The feeling of the family is cold, leaving a sense of tragedy without hope.

BIBLIOGRAPHY

Chen Si-he. *Study on Bajin.* Beijing: People's Literature Press, 1986.

Wang Ying-guo. *Focus on Bajin.* Shanghai: Artistic Press, 1985.

Mei Han

COLETTE (SIDONIE-GABRIELLE CO-LETTE) (1873–1954) *French essayist, novelist, short story writer*

Sidonie-Gabrielle Collette was the author of more than 50 novels and numerous short stories and magazine articles. The widely celebrated 20th-century French writer, who published only under her last name, was known for blurring the lines between fiction and autobiography, creating characters that defy conventional sexual attitudes and cultivating a star persona on stage and in the press. Writing from her early 20s to her mid-70s, Colette penned many famous novels, including *The* VAGABOND (1910), CLAUDINE AT SCHOOL (1910), CHÉRI (1920), *The* CAT (1933), and the highly celebrated GIGI (1945). In her lifetime, Colette was one of the world's most celebrated female authors.

Colette was born on January 28, 1873, in Saint-Sauveur-en-Puisaye, Yonne, in the Burgundy region of France. She was the daughter of Jules-Joseph Colette and Adèle Eugénie Sidonie Landoy ("Sido"). Her childhood home overflowed with dogs, cats, and several siblings. Colette's parents experienced financial difficulty and eventually had to leave their village in 1890. Educated at the local village school, Colette spent much of her adolescence reading French writers of her time, but her real entrance into the literary world came with her marriage in 1893 to Henry Gauthiers-Villars (known as Willy), upon which she moved to Paris. Willy was a well-known writer and critic who employed several ghostwriters to pen his many publications. Soon into their marriage, Colette discovered Willy's extramarital affairs.

Colette's first novel, *Claudine at School,* was published in March 1900 under Willy's name. Willy encouraged Colette to jot down her ruminations about her childhood in exercise books. However, when the writing was first completed, her husband dismissed the work as lacking talent. Two years later, Willy rediscovered the texts in a drawer and suggested revisions to Colette. What was originally Colette's work and what were Willy's suggestions remains unclear. *Claudine at School* is a story of Claudine, a 15-year-old attending a parochial school in northern Burgundy, France. She is witty, intelligent, and strong. The book follows her adventures as well as several love affairs between individuals at the school. *Claudine at School* was followed by three other books featuring Claudine, which became immensely successful.

As Colette and Willy's marriage deteriorated, Colette also began having affairs. In 1904 she published *Dialogues de bêtes,* her first book published under her own name. This work is a collection of brief stories about household pets keenly aware of their human owners' obsessions. Colette's father died in 1905, and Willy and Colette separated in 1906. She then took up work in the music halls of Paris, under the watchful eye of the marquise de Belboeuf, known popularly as Missy, with whom Colette was openly and romantically involved. It was reported that Colette wore a black velvet collar inscribed: "I Belong to Missy." They spent time together in their beachside villa while they searched for their ideal house. Among Colette's other friends and lovers were the famous American lesbian Natalie Barney and the Italian writer Gabriele D'Annunzio. On stage the free-spirited Colette caused many sensations in Paris, miming copulation on one occasion (causing a riot at the Moulin Rouge) and exposing her breasts in a pantomime called *La Chair* (*The Flesh*).

Colette frequently wrote for magazines for income. Her novels did not bring in sufficient revenue on their own, in part because Willy had earlier sold the royalty rights of the Claudine novels. In 1910 Colette's novel *The Vagabond* appeared in segments in the magazine *La Vie Parisienne.* This work was written while the author was on tour with her musical troupe and composed in hotel rooms, backstage, and in train stations. In many ways it resembles Colette's life. The central character, Renée, is recently divorced, works in the theater, and writes novels. A man becomes infatuated with her, though she is only mildly interested in his advances. The novel was later adapted for film and stage. Meanwhile, Colette and Willy were officially divorced in 1910. As chapters of *The Vagabond* began appearing in monthly issues of *La Vie Parisienne,* Willy became angry at what Colette was writing and wrote a rebuttal novel.

Colette and Missy broke up as Colette became attracted to Henry de Jouvenel, editor of the magazine *Le Matin,* which Colette had begun writing for in December 1910. This publication had a wide readership across Europe, and Colette wrote a variety of articles, even covering court cases. Colette and Henry married at the end of 1912. The following year she gave birth to her only child, Colette de Jouvenel des Ursins. Though Colette had hoped to finish the sequel to *The Vagabond,* called *The Shackle* (1913), before the baby arrived, she was unable to do so and only completed the novel later that year.

In 1917 Colette wrote the novel *Mitsou,* but she lost her only manuscript on the subway and was forced to rewrite it. The book began appearing in installments in *La Vie Parisienne* in November and December of that year. During 1920, Colette's novel *Chéri* appeared in segments in periodicals. This novel tells the story of Léa, an experienced woman, and Chéri, a young man. After the two have been lovers for several years, Chéri decides to marry another woman. Léa and Chéri's breakup bears down hard on them both. When Chéri later quarrels with his new wife, he returns to Léa. Though Léa is thrilled to see him, she eventually sends him back to his young bride. *Chéri* was also adapted for the stage. During this time, the relationship between Colette and her second husband was failing, and they separated in 1923, divorcing in 1925.

Colette's next novel, *The Ripening Seed,* began appearing in serialized form in *Le Matin* in 1922. She met the man who would be her third husband, Maurice Goudeket, in 1925. She began working on *The Last of Chéri* (1926) but had to put the novel aside to write short articles for *Vogue* to earn an income. She also wrote *A Lesson in Love* (1928), *Sido* (1929), and *The Pure and the Impure* (1932). The novel *The Other One* (1929) tells the story of an egocentric playwright and his wife, both of whom have affairs. In 1927 the first academic work on Colette appeared, detailing her childhood history and her psychological approach to writing. Four years later, Claude Chauvière, who had once been her assistant, published a critical book on Colette and her work.

In 1933 Colette published *The Cat,* a story of a man in love with his cat rather than his wife. Jealousy permeates this book until the wife attempts to murder the cat. Later in 1935 Colette married Maurice, who remained her partner until her death. Her health soon began to deteriorate. The first signs of her long battle with arthritis began appearing in 1938. Another battle—World War II—was also breaking out. Her husband was captured by the Nazis and sent to a concentration camp. During the war, Colette wrote for *Le Petit Parisien* to earn money. She also wrote several other books during this time, including *Julie de Carneilhan* (1941), the story of a countess whose ex-husband lies and cheats to get money from her.

Between 1942 and 1943, Colette's arthritis advanced, compelling her to seek X-ray treatments, acupuncture, and intravenous injections of sulfur and iodine as medication. The treatments caused pain and weight loss. Meanwhile, Colette began a shorter work called *Gigi* (1944), which later became a popular Broadway play and an Oscar-winning film. In 1945 the author was elected to the Goncourt Academy, and in May 1953 the National Institute of Arts and Letters in New York elected her to membership. Colette died on August 3, 1954, and was given a state funeral in the cour d'honneur of the Palais-Royal. She is buried in the Père-Lachaise Cemetery in Paris.

BIBLIOGRAPHY

Henke, Suzette A. "Colette's Autofictions: Genre and Engenderment." In *Shattered Subjects: Trauma and Testimony in Women's Life-Writing.* New York: St. Martin's Press, 1998.

Mitchell, Yvonne. *Colette: A Taste for Life.* London: Weidenfeld and Nicolson, 1975.

Norell, Donna M. *Colette: An Annotated Primary and Secondary Bibliography.* New York: Garland Publishing, 1993.

Peebles, Catherine M. "What Does a Woman Enjoy? Colette's *Le pur et l'impur.*" In *The Psyche of Feminism: Sand, Colette, Sarraute.* West Lafayette, Ind.: Purdue University Press, 2004.

Southworth, Helen. *The Intersecting Realities and Fictions of Virginia Woolf and Colette.* Columbus: Ohio State University Press, 2004.

Stewart, Joan Hinde. *Colette*. Boston: Twayne Publishers, 1983.

Laura Madeline Wiseman

CONDÉ, MARYSE (1937–　) *Guadeloupean essayist, novelist, playwright*　Maryse Condé is a prolific Guadeloupean writer, dramatist, novelist, and critic. She was born February 11, 1937, in Guadeloupe, the West Indies, into a middle-class family, the daughter of Auguste Boucolon and Jeanne Quidal. Condé had a French education and obtained her doctoral degree from the Sorbonne in Paris in 1976; she has held many teaching posts in colleges and universities in France and America. In 1958 she married Mamadou Condé and had one son, but the marriage ended in divorce in 1981. She married her second husband, Richard Philcox, a translator, in 1982 and had three children with him. Richard Philcox has been responsible for the translation of many of her works into English.

Condé's works specialize in exploring the clash of cultures and races, particularly in Caribbean settings. Her main character, usually female, often finds herself trapped in a setting where her race, culture, gender, and sexuality conflict with what people in the surrounding society demand of her. In order to come to a recognition of her true self, this female protagonist will have to struggle between what she can discover inside herself and what her community expects of her. Very often this struggle is reflected in the conflict between the existing social order of the West African society and the effect of western European influence. The female protagonist has to come to terms with the land in which she lives as well. The character's frustrating experience sometimes reflects what Condé herself has gone through during her travels in West Africa, Paris, and her native Guadeloupe.

Condé has often been compared to other Caribbean postcolonial writers and evaluated in the context of the negritude movement promoted by Amie Cesaire and Edouard Glissant. She herself confesses that her mastery of the Creole language is inadequate for writing fiction, and therefore her readership remains fundamentally white and French. Her position on national identity is that this identity does not depend solely on speaking the Creole language, and that one can be a true Guadeloupean without speaking or writing perfect Creole. She calls her own language francophone-hybrid, meaning that she uses a hybrid language which shows the truly mixed nature of her identity, as someone who has received different kinds of cultural upbringing in one of the few remaining colonies in the world.

In many of Condé's novels, the search for a motherland and a mother culture ends in frustration because race is presented as only one factor that determines one's identity. Veronica, an Antillean student in Condé's first novel *Heremakhonon* (1976), has just such an experience. Eager to search for her roots in a newly liberated West African country, Veronica takes a flight and enters the new country, only to find that things are not as simple as she, an outsider, had expected. Under the mask of warm hospitality, the people still treat her as a foreigner, although she has tried to get involved in their daily lives. Unfortunately, her relationship with a local rebel leader and a powerful government official at the same time does not help her understand the forces at play in the revolution. Finally, realizing her powerlessness and incomprehension, she flies back to the West, which in a way is her homeland, none the wiser concerning the search for her cultural identity.

Condé's second novel, *A Season in Rihata* (*Une saison à Rihata,* 1981) tells a similar story, using a different perspective. The setting is also a West African country where the failure of a revolution throws light on the inner truth of the personalities involved. The main narrator this time is a young man, but the narrative flows in and out of this character's mind and very often allows other characters to speak their thoughts through him. The story gives equivalent value to the public and the private: While in the public sphere the planning and the failure of the revolution goes on, in the private sphere the characters involved reveal their real relationship with the land of the country.

It is probably *Segu* (1984), her third novel, that gave Condé a name as an important female writer on postcolonial issues. *Segu* traces the history of three generations of a West African family between 1797 and 1860, in the kingdom of Segou. The family of Dousika Traoré, a Bambara nobleman, is destroyed by direct and indirect results of external events such as colonialism, the slave trade, and the entrance of Islam and Christianity into Segou's culture. Traoré's three sons are all attracted away from the normal progression of family history because of the changing political and cultural influence of the times: His eldest son is converted to Islam; his second son is enslaved; and his third son enjoys great success in commerce. Condé includes a wealth of detail concerning personality, historical background, and even trivial daily happenings in African society over the decades in the story. Very often readers are not just given the details of the Traorés' experiences, but also the experiences of all those who come into contact with them, making the narrative a family saga on an epic scale set against the background of a tremendously rich and vigorous period in African history.

The cross-generational historical epic continues in *Segu*'s sequel, *The Children of Segu* (*Segu* II, 1985). This time the narrative moves to Central and Western North Africa, Brazil, and England, although the mechanism of colonialism, the slave trade, and Western religion continues into the following generations. Just as in the first volume, *Segu*, Condé has managed to incorporate complicated individual stories and characters' personal development into the larger picture of African history.

Land of Many Colours and Nanna-ya (*Pays-mêlé suivi de Nanna-ya*, 1985) is a double novella. In *Land of Many Colours* the narrative unfolds like a detective story, with the main narrator, the doctor, trying to find out about the life of a deceased young rebel. The doctor's search is like that of a historian, although he must finally claim that an objective, factual history is impossible to write because the human perspectives do not allow such logic and privileged, single perspective. "Colours" in the title denotes not only the color of skin but also the color of political belief.

I, TITUBA, BLACK WITCH OF SALEM (*Moi, Tituba, sorcière noire de Salem*, 1986) is a controversial fictional-autobiographical narrative recreating the life story of Tituba, a black female slave accused of witchcraft in the Salem witch trials at the end of the 17th century in Massachusetts. While the actual historical record is sparse, Condé "rescues" the protagonist by claiming a private confession from Tituba herself, who appears as a first-person narrator. The result is a highly personal, transgressive, and magical self-narrative revealing the hitherto unknown and unrepresented story of an unusual woman who survives difficult political and historical situations by means of personal strength and faith. Tituba comes across as not only a black woman with her own subjectivity, but also as one who sees through the patriarchal and imperialist hegemony, and who actively seeks ways to subvert it.

While *Segu* unfolds a family story from the 18th to the 19th centuries, *Tree of Life* (*La vie scélérate*, 1987) deals with the fortunes and misfortunes of a Guadeloupe family in the midst of 20th-century chaos. Told in the voice of a female descendant, Coco, the family story begins with Albert, who leaves his position on an island plantation to work on the Panama Canal but, horrified by the exploitation of the workers, leaves again and later makes a fortune for himself. His sons Jacob and Jean reject their inheritance from his fortune and choose other routes for their lives. The family history takes the readers through to the ambitious granddaughter Thecla and the unfortunate death of Albert II far away from home. Finally, at the end of the narration, Coco reconciles herself to the history of her own family and regains a sense of identity.

A similar narrative on an epic scale that crosses generations is also found in *The Last of the African Kings* (*Les derniers rois mages*, 1992), in which the fortunes of a noble African family are documented. Béhanzin is exiled to Martinique because of his opposition to French colonialism. His children are scattered through the Caribbean and the United States, where they experience the pain and horror of exile, isolation, and loss of origin, and they seek hope in the reconstruction of memory.

One of Condé's most celebrated works, CROSSING THE MANGROVE (*Traversée de la mangrove*, 1989), displays an interesting narrative structure reflective of a detective story. It opens with the discovery of Francis Sancher lying facedown in a mangrove swamp, which he had apparently been trying to cross. Although Sancher has lived in the village of Rivière au Sel for some time, he is a stranger to the villagers. What is known about him is that he had come to the village to end a strange curse that causes the death of all the male members of his family before their 50th birthday. The main focus of the story is the ceremony of the wake, organized by the villagers of Rivière au Sel, to show their respect to this stranger in their midst. Nineteen "mourners" reflect on their encounter with Sancher, who has touched their lives in different ways, although he has never been close to any of them. Remembering the past and trying to understand the significance of their past experiences, the 19 people who gather at the wake end up understanding their lives in new ways, and some even make resolutions for the future. Although the mystery of Sancher remains unsolved, at the end of the wake the mourners welcome the light of a new day which in many ways signifies a new beginning.

Windward Heights (*La migration des coeurs,* 1995) takes Emily Brontë's *Wuthering Heights* and reshapes it into a horrifying romance in which skin color is a determining factor. The story takes place at beginning of the 19th century in Cuba and Guadeloupe, detailing the obsessive and almost destructive love between a dark-skinned orphan Rayze and the mulatto Cathy Gagneur, who gives Rayze up to marry a lighter-skinned Creole husband. Just as in *Wuthering Heights,* the anger in Rayze has a strong influence on the life of his children.

Condé's *Desirada* (1997) engages once again the problem of West Indian identity from an outsider's position. Guadeloupe-born Marie-Noelle hates the life she is born into, a life confused by the secretive circumstances of her birth. She begins a journey of self-discovery that takes her to France and then to the United States. This investigation into her own history becomes a self-healing process. As she comes to understand her mother's circumstances, the sense of rejection in her own life evaporates. Although in the end she still cannot discover the truth about her identity, by tracing the narratives told by different people she gains an invaluable insight into the diasporic experience.

Condé claims that her work *Who Slashed Celanire's Throat?* (2000) "was inspired by an event that took place in Guadeloupe in 1995 when a baby was found with her throat slashed on a heap of garbage." In Condé's novel, Celanire, a girl born in the late 19th century, has been mutilated and left to die soon after birth. She survives, however, and grows to be a beautiful and strong woman determined to find out the mystery of her past. She travels from Guadeloupe to West Africa to Peru, stopping at nothing in an effort to uncover who was responsible for the crime done to her younger self. Although she works tirelessly for the weak and deprived of her community, her presence also seems to bring death and misfortune. The novel, subtitled "A Fantastical Tale," contains a blend of magic and realism very much in the style of GABRIEL GARCÍA MÁRQUEZ.

Maryse Condé has now been recognized as one of the leading female writers of postcolonial Caribbean literature. She has received many prizes and awards, including the Fulbright Scholarship, Prix Littéraire de la Femme, Prix Alain Boucheron, Guggenheim Fellowship, Puterbaugh Fellowship, Prix Carbet de la Caraibe, Marguerite Tourcenar Prize, a lifetime achievement award from New York University, and others. She was also named Commandeur de l'Order des Arts des Lettres by the French government in 2001. She now teaches at Princeton University and lives in New York and Montebello, Guadeloupe, with her husband and translator, Richard Philcox.

BIBLIOGRAPHY

Alexander, Simone A. James. *Mother Imagery in the Novels of Afro-Caribbean Women.* Columbia: University of Missouri Press, 2001.

Barbour, Sarah, and Gerise Herndon, eds. *Emerging Perspectives in Maryse Condé.* Trenton, N.J.: Africa World Press, 2006.

Condé, Maryse. *Tales from the Heart: True Tales from my Childhood.* Translated by Richard Philcox. New York: Soho Press, 2001.

Ouédraogo, Jean. *Maryse Condé et Ahmadou Kourouma.* New York: Peter Lang, 2004.

Pfaff, Francoise. *Conversations with Maryse Condé.* Lincoln: University of Nebraska Press, 1996.

Amy Wai-sum Lee

CONFESSIONS OF A MASK (KAMEN NO KOKUHAKU) MISHIMA YUKIO (1949)

Confessions of a Mask, a post war autobiographical novel, subverts the conventions of the traditional and dominant Japanese "I" novel of the 20th century. This book, MISHIMA YUKIO's (1925–70) first commercial success, received praise from the Japanese literary elite and paved the way for the author's prolific literary career spanning more than 20 years.

The novel's narrator, Kochan, begins by claiming that he witnessed his own birth and proceeds to detail his anomalous existence in a household tainted by illness, familial power struggles, and financial distress. Sequestered in his ill grandmother's stench-filled room, Kochan submits to the feminine domination his paternal grandmother imposes upon him and his entire family. His homosexual fantasies begin at the age of four when he sees a common laborer carrying buckets of excrement on his shoulders through the streets. The laborer's thigh-hugging pants and the occupation itself of transporting excrement, a symbol of the Earth Mother and a world fraught with pain and tragedy, function as a catalyst for the young boy's sexual awareness. Kochan desires to become this tragic figure.

Also at the age of four, Kochan recalls his discovery of a picture of a knight on a white horse, whose inevitably tragic end provokes his anticipation. He wishes for the knight's death and hopes to find it in the following pages in the book he is looking through. When the young boy's sick nurse informs him that the knight is in fact a woman named Joan of Arc, his world becomes destabilized. He explains this realization as a form of revenge thrust upon him by reality. Kochan puts the book aside forever.

Vivid memories—of the sweat of soldiers; his transvestism to express adoration of two melancholy women, Cleopatra and the female magician Tenkatsu; and fairy-tale stories of the death of princes—affect Kochan's early life. He concludes that his thirst for the tragic and for the bodies of young men is predetermined. This deterministic worldview threads together the chapters of the autobiography and ultimately lays the novel's philosophical groundwork. The youth's desire for death, night, and blood follows a trajectory traced by some malevolent force with no hope of being derailed.

The novel also probes the distinction between reality and illusion, making "mask" a fitting component of the book's title. Even as a boy, the narrator understands his social obligation to exert a certain masculinity, even with his female playmates. During a game of war, Kochan relishes the thought of his own death. His sadomasochistic fantasies increase in intricacy. He masturbates not only to magazine pictures he has altered, which show the bloody deaths of young men, but also to Guido Reni's depiction of Saint Sebastian. The focus of these fantasies eventually shifts from print media to a real-life acquaintance, a classmate named Omi.

The narrator falls in love with Omi, an older boy with primitive intellect and reputedly more sexual experience than Kochan's other classmates. Jealousy follows Kochan's first glimpse of Omi's body, an event for which he had longed for some time. The jealousy is of such potency that Kochan renounces his love and pursues his sickly, pensive adolescence. He philosophically considers the implications of attraction to the opposite sex and makes an effort to think, in amorous terms, of women such as bus conductresses, his second cousin Sumiko, and an anemic young woman he sees on a bus. His feelings, instead, remain amorphous. Any attraction he feels toward women is ill-defined and nonsexual.

The adolescent takes an interest in drinking, smoking, and kissing. He also begins to appreciate younger boys and continues to fantasize about his own death, this time as a soldier against the Allies during World War II. This glorious death never comes to fruition, as the war soon ends. He finally meets the sister of a friend whose piano playing has haunted him for years. The beauty of the girl Sonoko moves him, and he immediately acknowledges that he is not worthy of her. In any case, Kochan and Sonoko grow closer, with the young man fully aware that he is wearing a mask of normality, and that he is pretending to have the same desires as those he perceives in other young men of his age. The two stumble toward their predetermined fate.

The novel culminates in a congested, sweaty dance hall after a year of only occasional meetings between the two would-be lovers. Kochan notices a shirtless youth in his early 20s with a peony tattooed on his oiled, muscular chest. The narrator forgets Sonoko as sexual desire inundates him, and he imagines a dagger in the hand of a rival gang member slicing through the young man's torso. Sonoko's voice recenters him, and his world is subsequently split in two as he realizes that his neatly structured mask has crumbled into nothingness.

Mishima's *Confessions of a Mask* emphasizes the deterministic nature of the human condition. The text leaves the reader with a young man whose shadowy, ambiguous future is nothing if not chained to destiny. Mishima weaves darkness, violence, and sexual perversion throughout his autobiographical novel, the first rung on the ladder of his literary success.

BIBLIOGRAPHY

Abelsen, Peter. "Irony and Purity: Mishima." *Modern Asian Studies* 30, no. 3 (July 1996): 651–679.

Rhine, Marjorie. "Glossing Scripts and Scripting Pleasure in Mishima's *Confessions of a Mask.*" *Studies in the Novel* 31, no. 2 (Summer 1999): 222–234.

Wagenaar, Dick, and Yoshio Iwamoto. "Yukio Mishima: Dialectics of Mind and Body." *Contemporary Literature* 16, no. 1 (Winter 1975): 41–60.

Christy Nicole Wampole

CONFESSIONS OF FELIX KRULL, CONFIDENCE MAN (BEKENNTNISSE DES HOCHSTAPLERS FELIX KRULL) THOMAS MANN (1954)

The works of THOMAS MANN (1875–1955), a distinguished literary figure of the 20th century, epitomize the modern writer. The German author towered above the times in which he lived and has continued to be universally acclaimed, with readers today no less fascinated by his world and work, which characterize the best of creative thought. Mann's last composition, the magnum opus novel *Confessions of Felix Krull, Confidence Man,* and his earlier BUDDENBROOKS (1901) represent his best-known accomplishments. In 1929 the 54-year old Thomas Mann—who became one of the quintessential novelists of the modern period—was awarded the Nobel Prize in literature.

The writing of *Confessions of Felix Krull, Confidence Man: Memories, Part One*—a masterpiece novel about an elegant and intriguing con artist—took Mann a lifetime to complete. He had begun the work in 1910, publishing fragments in 1911 and 1919. In 1922 these pages appeared in hardbound book entitled *Bekenntnisse des Hochstaplers Felix Krull: Buch der Kindheit (Confessions of Felix Krull Confidence Man: The Early Years).* Not until 1936, under the succinct title *Felix Krull,* would an English translation of the 1922 version appear in *Stories of Three Decades,* an edition of Mann's selected short fiction written from 1897 to 1929.

Mann had intended to continue the *Krull* adventures, but various events interrupted him from further developing the still-fragmentary short work. Only some 40 years later—from 1951 to 1954—did Mann resume work on *Krull,* and he did so without any sign of stylistic interruption. After reading the final, still typewritten manuscript of the 1954 *Felix Krull* translation, his publisher, Alfred Knopf, sent his lifelong author-friend the following previously unknown radiogram (dated March 25, 1955): "The old master still puts the young ones to shame. *Krull* absolutely magnificent ditto [Denver] Lindley translation. Congratulations[.] Love Alfred."

Mann once remarked: "The conception [of *Krull*] has in it the germ of truly great humor; and I wrote the exciting fragment *Felix Krull* with such zest that I was not surprised to have many excellent judges pronounce it the best and happiest thing I had done. In a sense it may be the most personal; at least it expresses my personal attitude towards the traditional, which is both sympathetic and detached and which conditions my mission as an artist. Indeed, the inward laws which are the basis of that 'Bildungsroman' *The Magic Mountain* are the same in kind."

Felix Krull represents a work of social realism; yet on the whole its model was the genre of the picaresque novel, and many parallels relating to, for example, style, structure, and the main character's values are evident. Even Felix Krull's outlook on life demonstrates similarities with the picaresque novel. Furthermore, Felix follows the principle of self-regard and personal benefit, not integrity or compunction, and, in turn, lacks any concern or hesitation about cheating anyone if, by taking advantage of lucrative situations, he can accrue material gains. Though ruthless, Felix seems incapable of violent measures. In this regard, at the end of the novel Mann articulates what appears to represent the basis of Felix's value system. A particular incident necessitates that the protagonist authenticate the originality of a certain object, to which he responds: "Whether this procedure was artistic or fraudulent, I was not called upon to say, but I decided at once that, cheating or no, it was something I could do."

Mann's novel is related in the form of reminiscences in the first person by its main protagonist, Felix Krull. The entire work, with its action taking place in Germany, Paris, and Lisbon in the pre–World War I days, expresses a sense of playfulness and lightness of tone.

In doing this, the author allows his main character's confessions to surpass any vile criminality that normally would be associated with deceptive exploits. Such characteristics link Felix with many other picaresque characters of European fiction, such as Grimmelshausen's Simplicissimus, Defoe's Moll Flanders or Fielding's Tom Jones. Nevertheless, unlike the nobleman in Cervantes' *Don Quixote,* for example, the main character in *Felix Krull* is a lonely, poorly educated, irresistibly charismatic, romantic, and imaginative individual who also epitomizes the characteristics of a grand larcenist, embezzler, and con man.

Of course, Felix savors his outstandingly successful career as a high-class swindler (*Hochstapler*) for whom appearances are supreme and essence nothing. As the novel advances, Mann recounts Felix's development from near-impoverishment to a position of aristocratic privilege through his innate ability as a passionate confidence trickster. Of note, Felix's first name signifies "the happy one," whereas his surname, Krull, suggests *krumm* (crook, or dishonest), resulting in "a happy villain."

That Krull fully understands his spiritually oriented marriage with society and life, which is made possible only by his constant trickery and deceptive actions, becomes evident on almost every page of the work. But possibly his role-playing is best articulated in his comment: ". . . I could have found, had I desired it, abundant opportunity for conversation and companionship with a variety of individuals. . . . This . . . was by no means by intention; I either avoided such contacts entirely or took care that they never became intimate, for in early youth an inner voice had warned me that close association, friendship, and companionship were not to be my lot, but that I should be inescapably compelled to follow my strange path alone, dependent entirely upon myself, rigorously self-sufficient." Because Felix Krull has developed his own unique means of acquiring freedom from life's demands, he is undisturbed by the fact that his life actually is in conflict with society.

Felix's fascination with the impressions that an actor could create began early in his life, and as a young lad he had already begun to act out various deceptions, rapidly becoming an expert in impersonation. For a period, Felix was satisfied with his life, but when the family champagne business failed, his contentment altered, especially because the failure caused his father to commit suicide. Since Felix required a means to financially sustain himself, family members suggested that he obtain an apprenticeship in a Paris hotel. However, Felix's obligation of military conscription forbade his departure. Under these conditions, Mann paints a brilliantly colored word picture of Felix's thoughts, which momentarily depicts him as feeling limited in what he may do.

Initially, he responds to the present situation by assuming the role of an outside observer of life, but, like his picaresque predecessors, Krull rapidly garners self-control, believing himself capable of resolving any dilemma encountered positively. As he exclaims in the novel, "What an advantage it is to possess an easy and polished style of address, the gift of good form which that kind fairy thoughtfully laid in my cradle and which is so very necessary for the whole way of life I have adopted!" Realizing that travel to Paris requires that he either complete the military obligations or become excused, soon he acts out a fantastically convincing scene as an epileptic at the army inspection center that results in his exemption from military service. Then, after first stealing a woman's jewel case, the importance of which he only later discovers, he proceeds on his way to Paris.

In Paris a hotel director hires him as an elevator operator, but first changes his name to Armand. In this lighthearted Parisian environment of merriment and immoderation, Mann details Felix's countless exploits, which reveal, above all, the swindler's personal charm and beauty. The setting also illustrates the degree to which ladies find him attractive, and his uniquely astounding escapades and romantic conquests are possibly the most humorous of the entire novel. One such affair occurs with a rich hotel guest who happens to be the same woman whose jewels Felix had pocketed earlier. As that amorous encounter continues, Felix (or Armand, as he is known at the hotel) obtains numerous additional valuables from this same infatuated woman. Indeed, she insists that Felix accept her gifts, becoming robustly excited and animated when she learns that it was he who had stolen her other set of jewels. In such ways, the novel reveals that Felix does more than take advantage of others; he gratifies them as well, although these positive outcomes probably occur accidentally.

After selling his newly obtained riches, Felix acquires independence and begins to lead a double life: During the day he is Armand the hotel employee, while in the evening he is Felix Krull, man about town, a highly gifted and self-promoting confidence trickster. At one point a certain Marquis de Venosta uncovers Felix's double life, but the protagonist is quick to contrive how best to respond, immediately establishing a close friendship with the marquis and even becomes his trusted confidante. This friendship proves most advantageous for Felix, since the marquis's parents had intended for their son to travel around the world. However, with the approval of his aristocratic partner in deception, who loathes the idea of a world journey and delights in the idea of hoodwinking his parents, Felix agrees to impersonate the marquis, soon embarking on the world adventure.

Interestingly, Felix's explanation that material gain does not represent his primary motivation to undertake the adventure offers the reader much to ponder: "It was the change and renewal of my worn-out self, the fact that I had been able to put off the old Adam and slip on a new, that gave me such a sense of fulfillment and happiness."

Lisbon is the first stop on his journey, and here he meets interesting, wealthy intellectuals who hail from the highest circles of Europe's late aristocracy. Fascinated with them as well as with the variety of cultures and customs he confronts, Felix soon carries off his finest deception to date, executing remarkable acts of trickery that easily con his new acquaintances. His fabulously imaginative tales gain him much reward and considerably renewed confidence, aside from additional opportunities to engage in what he deems superlative amorous affairs.

However, Felix's final escapades—and the many intense, at times convoluted, deliberations that now occur—often focus on astonishingly complex matters, such as the "different forms and representations of life" or the Moorish, Gothic, and Italian elements, including the Hindu influence, of "architectural styles of castles and monasteries." Furthermore, extremely abstruse issues related to philosophy, mythology, romanticism, and religion, among other areas, also fill these discussions.

These debates almost seem like a competition at which one individual eventually triumphs over the other; in actuality, such a viewpoint represents the very reason that Felix participates in these verbal challenges, which he treats like a vigorous game. Yet these unduly but still spirited deliberations at times also seem to be intentionally challenging. Regardless of what constitutes the truth, one factor is certain: Their semantic dispute clearly initiates consideration about astoundingly complex issues that, at times, seem incomprehensible.

However, the very nature of this unusual situation seems to profoundly animate and entice Felix, who looks upon these supposedly problematical issues with a fervent and immediate desire to enact the best role he has ever played. In fact, his unexpected responses suggest he has achieved the epitome of his role as a comic criminal and arch deceiver. The confidence man Felix Krull understands only too well that to win the consensus and benevolence of others, one must express what the opponent wants to hear—or, as the situation may be, to enact the role his challenger desires of him. Nevertheless, it is here where the novel concludes, leaving the reader to contemplate the meaning of these puzzling and seemingly ambiguous matters.

Mann crafts his brilliantly funny and master comedy *Felix Krull* in a manner that allows it to continually provoke hilarity and arouse uproarious amusement. Indeed, amusement is found on nearly every page of *Felix Krull.* While the originality of Mann's humor, serenity, and buoyancy heighten the reader's positive experience, its author's best literary strength is found in a gift for parody and irony. Upon publication in America, *Confessions of Felix Krull Confidence Man: The Early Years* was passionately received by American readers.

BIBLIOGRAPHY

Berlin, Jeffrey B. "Additional Reflections on Thomas Mann as a Letter Writer: With the Unpublished Correspondences of Thomas Mann, Alfred A. Knopf, and H. T. Lowe-Porter about the Genesis of *Doctor Faustus, The Black Swan,* and *Confessions of Felix Krull—Confidence Man: The Early Years.*" *Oxford German Studies,* 34, no. ii (2005), 123–157.

————. ed.: *Approaches to Teaching Mann's* Death in Venice *and Other Short Fiction.* New York: Modern Language Association, 1992.

Hatfield, Henry. *From* The Magic Mountain: *Mann's Later Masterpieces.* Ithaca, N.Y., and London: Cornell University Press, 1979.

Heller, Erich. *The Ironic German: A Study of Thomas Mann.* London: Secker & Warburg, 1957.

Kurzhe, Hermann. *Thomas Mann. Life as a Work of Art. A Biography.* Translated by Leslie Willson. Princeton, N.J., Oxford: Princeton University Press, 2002.

Lesér, Esther H. *Thomas Mann's Short Fiction. An Intellectual Biography.* Rutherford, N.J.: Fairleigh Dickinson University Press, 1989.

Prater, Donald A. *Thomas Mann: A Life.* New York and Oxford: Oxford University Press, 1995.

Reed, Terence. *Thomas Mann: The Uses of Tradition.* 2nd ed. Oxford: Clarendon Press, 1996.

Robertson, Ritchie, ed. *The Cambridge Companion to Thomas Mann.* Cambridge: Cambridge University Press, 2002.

Steiner, George. "Thomas Mann's *Felix Krull.*" G. S., *Language and Silence.* Atheneum: New York, 1970, 269–279.

Jeffrey B. Berlin

CONVERSATION IN THE CATHEDRAL (CONVERSACIÓN EN LA CATEDRAL)

MARIO VARGAS LLOSA (1969)   Historically and politically important, this novel by MARIO VARGAS LLOSA (1936–   ) is based on the social conditions in Peru during the eight-year dictatorship of Manuel A. Odría. Lima, the capital of Peru, is the central stage of the narrative, where characters from different social classes—government officials, capitalists, left-wing students, servants, prostitutes, workers—present scenes of corruption, conspiracy, political struggles between left and right wings, poverty, and failure. The narrative reveals both the scandalous facts of Peruvian society and the absurdity of life in which many Peruvians find themselves.

The major narrative mode is the conversation between Santiago Zavala, a journalist and son of Don Fermín, Lima's famous capitalist, and Ambrosio, Don Fermín's former driver. They meet at a time after Odría's dictatorship and sit in a bar called The Cathedral to recall life during the past years and the fate of other characters in their lives. Their conversation forms a stream of dialogue to carry on various narrative threads involving the stories of different characters from various social backgrounds, all related to actual political events in Peruvian history. The stream of dialogue is a vehicle for many of Vargas Llosa's novels, but this one carries the technique to its extreme, including the stories of more than 30 characters over a large time span and multiple places, all within one single conversation. To grasp the story in a concise way, the reader needs to follow the fate of the four central figures: Santiago, Ambrosio, Don Fermín, and Bermúdez.

Santiago Zavala, while a young left-wing student, abandons his inheritance and leaves his wealthy upper-class family to pursue an independent life seeking truth through revolution. He is actively involved in the political movement against Odría's dictatorship, during which he and his partners are persecuted by Odría's secret service, led by Bermúdez. Santiago's father, Don Fermín, originally the financial supporter of the Odría government, maintains a friendship with Bermúdez until the Odría government encounters a fatal crisis on the political stage. Don Fermín's driver, Ambrosio, has also worked as a secret agent for Bermúdez. Disillusioned after many failures in his political activities, Santiago leaves school, marries a nurse named Ana, and starts working as a reporter for the detective and criminal section of a local newspaper. He then meets Ambrosio during a search for Ana's dog in a poor district of Lima.

Ambrosio is from a lower-class family whose father is a criminal. He seeks help from a friend from his youth, Bermúdez, after the latter becomes an official in the Odría government's ministry of internal affairs. He serves as Bermúdez's driver and hatchet man, directly handling his master's dirty business, such as collecting "protection fees" from the brothels and dispersing political protests. Bermúdez later sends him to work as chauffeur for Don Fermín, who actually takes him as a homosexual partner. Ambrosio falls in love with Amalia, the maid of Bermúdez's mistress, Musa. But when Musa threatens to reveal the sexual scandal between him and Don Fermín, Ambrosio kills her and runs away with Amalia to a remote town. Years later, after Amalia's death, Ambrosio returns to Lima to a hard-scrabble life, when he meets Santiago, the son of his former master.

Don Fermín Zavala is a representative of Peru's upper class in the novel. His success in business and the capital he possesses provide significant influence in Peru's political life. He uses his influence to help Odría come into power, but he also has a secret struggle with Odría's hit man, Bermúdez. When he observes the change in Peru's political situation, he turns to support the opposite parties and pushes Bermúdez out of office; then comes the end of Odría's reign. While a respectful public figure, with an apparently happy family, Don Fermín maintains a homosexual relationship with his chauffeur, Ambrosio, whom he instructs to murder Musa, who has blackmailed him. Don Fermín likes the intelligent and hardworking Santiago best among all of his children, but because of their political differences, the father and the son never reconcile.

Cayo Bermúdez, the official of the ministry of internal affairs, starts off as a playboy during his youth. With the help of Ambrosio, he secretly marries a milk merchant's daughter, Rosa. One of his high school friends helps Odría in the coup and later becomes minister of internal affairs in the Odría government. Bermúdez is then named an official in the ministry, and he later becomes the head of internal affairs. This figure is based on a real-life prototype, the Odría government's actual minister of internal affairs, whom the young Vargas Llosa once visited as a student representative in order to help some students arrested by the police. This meeting impressed Vargas Llosa so deeply that he wanted to write the actual figure into a fictional work, which he was able to do in this novel.

The dictator Odría is not represented directly in this novel, just indirectly through Bermúdez. Under the Odría government, Peru is turned into a prison. Bermúdez has his own hatchet men in the form of his secret service, and he arrests and expels the progressive people, declaring them to be illegal and suppressing the officers who attempt to overthrow him. On the other hand, Bermúdez also lives a scandalous life. He abandons his wife Rosa; has a mistress, Musa, in Lima; and tries to seduce other men's wives. He also uses his executive power to collect protection fees from local merchants. Following a sizable protest organized by the opposition parties, Odría is forced to dismiss Bermúdez from office, and Bermúdez flees abroad, taking chests filled with money with him.

This novel provides a panorama of Peru's political situations involving the various social classes and multiple aspects of political scandal. It manifests both the author's insight into the Peruvian society and the maturity of his insight and narrative skill.

BIBLIOGRAPHY

Kristal, Efraín. *Temptation of the Word: The Novels of Mario Vargas Llosa.* Nashville, Tenn.: Vanderbilt University Press, 1998.

Oviedo, José Miguel. *Mario Vargas Llosa: A Writer's Reality.* Barcelona: Seix Barral, 1985.

Vargas Llosa, Mario. *A Fish in the Water: A Memoir.* New York: Farrar, Straus, 1994.

Haiqing Sun

CORTÁZAR, JULIO (1914–1984) *Argentinean essayist, short story writer, novelist, poet*

Julio Cortázar is perhaps, after Jorge Luis Borges, the most influential Argentinean writer of the 20th century. His literary legacy includes poems, plays, and political writings, but it is prose fiction—both in collections of hallucinatory, startling short stories and in labyrinthine, intellectually charged novels—on which Cortázar's reputation rests. His many champions have included the Latin American litterateurs of the last century, among them Jorge Luis Borges, GABRIEL GARCÍA MÁRQUEZ, CARLOS FUENTES, and the poet Pablo Neruda, who famously remarked that "anyone who hasn't read Cortázar is doomed." Cortázar's readership, however, has not retained the numbers of his more famous contemporaries, and at present his work has been relegated predominantly—and perhaps unfairly—to the classroom.

Julio Cortázar was born in 1914, the son of Argentine parents who were living abroad in Brussels, Belgium, at the outbreak of World War I. His family would remain abroad for the duration of the war, seeking refuge in Switzerland and in Spain before returning to live in Banfield, Argentina, on the outskirts of Buenos Aires, in 1918. At the time of their relocation, the young Cortázar spoke only French.

Cortázar's difficult transition to Argentinean life—coupled with his father's desertion of the family in

1920—resulted in an introverted, sensitive childhood. Aware of the differences between himself and his Argentinean peers (including his unusual height of over six feet), Cortázar found respite both in his imagination and through the inventive fiction of such writers as Jules Verne and, in particular, Edgar Allan Poe, whose complete prose he would translate, years later, into Spanish. Young Cortázar's reading habits and interiority were so marked that his mother once took him to a physician to inquire about them.

Cortázar's formal education culminated in his certification to teach primary and secondary school from the Mariano Acosta teacher's college of Buenos Aires in 1932. After a single year of study at the University of Buenos Aires—his higher education abbreviated by his family's financial situation, with his mother and aunt taking care of both him and his younger sister, Ofelia—Cortázar began teaching high school in the nearby provinces of Bolivar and Chivilcoy. Though he had been writing since childhood, Cortázar was intensely critical of his own work and reluctant to publish. In 1938, while still a high school teacher, he released a thin volume of poetry under the pseudonym Julio Denis, entitled *Presence* (*Presencia*), a work he would later discount. Cortázar continued writing avidly throughout his tenure as a high school teacher, though he would not begin to publish fiction until his 30s.

In 1945 Cortázar was offered a position through a former college classmate to teach literature at the University of Cuyo in Mendoza, despite the fact he had no advanced degree. Though he would spend just a single academic year at the university, his stay would prove formative. The rise of the Perón regime in 1946 sparked protests throughout the university; Cortázar participated in these protests and was arrested. Feeling pressure from the pro-Perón university officials and aware of their disapproval of his political activism, Cortázar refused an offered chair and resigned his position to return to Buenos Aires. He would remain intensely and outspokenly political throughout the rest of his life, notably as a supporter of the Cuban and Nicaraguan revolutions, though he would consistently differentiate his political aims and beliefs from his aesthetic ones.

Of crucial importance to Cortázar was meeting Jorge Luis Borges in 1946. Editor of the literary magazine

Anales de Buenos Aires at the time, Borges would later recall the tall, somewhat disheveled young man entering his offices carrying the manuscript of his story "House Taken Over" ("Casa tomada"), the disquieting tale of a young couple, brother and sister, living in a large home that is being overrun, floor by floor, by otherworldly, never-named invaders. Cortázar left the manuscript, saying that he would return in 10 days to inquire about its status; when he returned in just seven, Borges informed him that the story had already been sent to the publisher. Thus began Cortázar's professional career as a writer.

In the years that followed, Cortázar continued to publish stories and essays, as well as a critically ignored play, *The Monarchs* (*Los reyes*), while supporting himself as a freelance translator. In 1951 he left Buenos Aires for Paris, traveling on a scholarship, and found expatriate life to his liking. In 1953 he established Parisian residency and married Aurora Bernandez. He would call Paris home for the rest of his life and was awarded French citizenship from President François Mitterand in July 1981, a distinction he accepted on the condition that he also retain his Argentinean citizenship.

In the same month as his relocation to Paris, Cortázar celebrated the publication of his first collection of short stories, *Bestiary* (*Bestiario*). Though he was 37 years old at the time, a relatively late age for a literary debut, his first years in expatriation proved prolific, producing material for two successive collections: *The END OF THE GAME* (*Final del juego,* 1956) and *Secret Weapons* (*Las armas secretas,* 1959). Though initial public and critical reaction was slow, Cortázar's work earned him a select, devoted audience that considered him an emerging master of the short story, a reputation he would continue to affirm with the publication of collections such as *All Fires the Fire* (*Todos los fuegos el fuego,* 1966), *A Change of Light* (published as *Octaedro,* 1974, and *Alguien que anda por ahí,* 1977), and *We Love Glenda So Much* (*Queremos tanto a Glenda,* 1981).

In 1960, however, Cortázar surprised his devotees and greatly increase his readership with the release of his novel *The WINNERS* (*Los premios*). The story of a social cross section of Argentineans selected by public lottery to sail on a ship manned by a mysterious, foreboding crew, *The Winners* proved not only that he could move successfully from the short form to the novel but that, in so doing, he could create a form of fiction as intricate and masterful.

Cortázar followed the success of *The Winners* with the work that most consider his masterpiece, the novel HOPSCOTCH (*Rayuela,* 1963), which brought him instant international acclaim and inaugurated a heyday of Cortázar scholarship and interest that flourished in the late 1960s and throughout the 1970s. In 1968 he published his third novel, *62: A Model Kit* (*62: Modelo para armar*), and in 1973 his fourth, *A MANUAL FOR MANUEL* (*Libro de Manuel*), for which he was awarded the Prix Médicis. Cortázar offered his prize money to the legal defense of South American political prisoners.

Cortázar continued to publish and push for political causes for the rest of his life. On February 12, 1984, Julio Cortázar died in his adopted Paris of complications from leukemia, the disease that had claimed his second wife, Carol Dunlop, in 1982. His death prompted numerous appreciations, including that of García Márquez, who claimed him to be "the most impressive man I've known."

BIBLIOGRAPHY

Moran, Dominic. *Questions of the Liminal in the Fiction of Julio Cortázar.* Oxford: European Humanities Research Centre, 2001.

Standish, Peter. *Understanding Julio Cortázar.* Columbia: University of South Carolina Press, 2001.

Stavans, Ilan. *Julio Cortázar: A Study of the Short Fiction.* New York: Twayne Publishers, 1996.

Vazquez Amaral, Jose. *The Contemporary Latin American Narrative.* New York: Las Americas Publishing, 1970.

Joseph Bates

COSMICOMICS (*LE COSMICOMICHE*)

ITALO CALVINO (1965)   *Cosmicomics* is a collection of linked short narratives written by the celebrated Italian writer ITALO CALVINO (1923–85). The stories prove to be a unified meditation on scientific theories of the inception and evolution of the universe as seen through the eyes of a narrator known simply as Qfwfq. Despite their scientific basis, the stories deal with such human issues as the nature of desire, love, and loneliness.

Calvino's parents were both researchers in botany, and when Calvino enrolled in college in 1941 (at the University of Turin, where his father taught) he too intended to pursue a career in science. Eventually, however, he turned to literature and graduated with a degree in letters, but his early scientific background clearly influenced *Cosmicomics*. The stories show Calvino confidently mixing scientific principles with fantasy and imagination, a technique that marks all of his work.

The book does not start at the beginning of creation and move toward the present, but it does move through time, marking the passage of ages. Each of its 12 stories begins with a short scientific quote—seemingly lifted from a textbook—and Qfwfq's response to that quote. In the first tale, Qfwfq relates a time in which the moon was closer to the earth than it is now and how those living on the earth would climb up on the moon to enjoy its different environment. In the story, Qfwfq reveals a desire for the wife of Captain Vhd Vhd, a passion that is unrequited. In the next story, which moves back in time to when the universe was in an earlier state, Qfwfq describes what it was like to live on a nebula. Another story, "All at One Point," similarly describes the very early claustrophobic moment in the history of the universe in which all of space was contracted to one point.

The story "A Sign in Space" tells of Qfwfq's desire to make a sign, despite the fact that at that time in the universe no one knew what a sign was. The theme of signs returns in the book's penultimate story, "The Light-Years," in which someone else in the universe makes a sign, which causes Qfwfq to question if he is being watched. These stories comment on the human need to communicate, and they illustrate the difficulty we often have when we set out to do so. They also reveal Calvino engaging the literary theory that was popular during his time. Calvino was deeply influenced by thinkers such as the linguist Ferdinand de Saussure and theorist Roland Barthes. Saussure was the father of structuralism, a theory that focused on the nature of language and the arbitrariness of what Saussure called the "sign," or word. The stories' focus on signs clearly evokes Saussure's work, and indeed the shortcomings of language haunt the book throughout.

Other stories deal with evolutionary issues such as the movement of organisms on the earth out of water and onto land (in "The Aquatic Uncle") and the dying out of the dinosaurs ("The Dinosaurs"). In the former story, the narrator's uncle refuses to leave water and eventually persuades Qfwfq's girlfriend, Lll, to come and live with him. In "The Dinosaurs," Qfwfq takes the form of the last dinosaur who is forced to live among a new species, simply called the "New Ones." These New Ones have heard tales of the once-ferocious race of dinosaurs, but they never suspect they have one in their midst. Eventually Qfwfq accepts his lonely fate as the last of his kind and journeys out on his own, but not before siring a son who will carry on his traits.

Other stories in the book manifest variations on these themes. "Without Colors," for instance, is another tale of unrequited love for Qfwfq; Calvino uses the coming of colors into the world as the basis for his story. "Games without End" shows Qfwfq as a boy who uses the complexities of the universe, such as the curvature of space, to his advantage in games with his friend Pfwfp. For their rich combination of science and human emotions, these stories are virtually unsurpassed in post–World War II literature. Calvino continued the stories of Qfwfq in his book *t zero* (1967).

BIBLIOGRAPHY

Bloom, Harold, ed. *Italo Calvino. Bloom's Modern Critical Views.* New York: Chelsea House, 2000.

Bondanella, Peter, and Andrea Ciccarelli, eds. *The Cambridge Companion to the Italian Novel.* New York: Cambridge University Press, 2003.

Weiss, Beno. *Understanding Italo Calvino.* Columbia: University of South Carolina Press, 1993.

Joe Moffett

COSMOPOLIS PAUL BOURGET (1893)

The French novel *Cosmopolis,* written in 1893 and translated into English the same year, is indicative of the earlier fiction of PAUL BOURGET (1852–1935), telling the story of a complicated love triangle set against the backdrop of Rome as the quintessential international city. Competing factions of lovers and their faithful or not-so-faithful friends are delineated not only by their allegiances but by their national origin, and often by their race. While *Cosmopolis* lacks the moralistic overtones of Bourget's later works, its ending does reinforce the necessity of a morally grounded life, offering a glimpse into the future of Bourget's oeuvre.

The central plot focuses on Catherine Steno, who leaves her lover, Boleslas Gorka, for the American painter Lincoln Maitland. Gorka is informed of Steno's actions through anonymous letters, and after returning to Rome to denounce Steno's new lover, he instead meets and insults Lincoln's longtime friend, Florent Chapron (brother to Lincoln's wife Lydia). To address their traded insults, the men agree to a duel.

The duel sequence forms a central component of the novel, demonstrating the futile violence that can ensue from bruised egos. When arrangements to avoid the duel cannot be made, Lydia, who wrote the anonymous letters to Gorka to retaliate against her husband's infidelity, realizes that she is to blame for the fate her brother faces, a fate she intended for her husband. Despite the attempts of Lydia and others to prevent the duel, it takes place.

Gorka escapes without injury, but Chapron takes a bullet to the leg. Following his exit, Gorka insults Julien Dorsenne—one of Chapron's seconds—and another duel is demanded on the spot. Ignoring the strict codes of dueling, the men face off, and while Dorsenne emerges unscathed, Gorka's arm is injured. His wife, insulted and demoralized but interested in protecting her young son from a fate like his father's, agrees to remain with her husband. Gorka accepts her two conditions: that he cease all communication with Mme. Steno and that they leave Rome.

Novelist Julien Dorsenne serves as a critical element to the novel's intrigue by serving as a confidante to many of the main characters. He demonstrates interest—perhaps romantic—in Alba Steno, daughter of Catherine Steno and best friend of Gorka's wife Maud. The injuries experienced by the men in the two duels are reflected in the emotional battles that the women fight. Ever determined to undermine her husband's affair, Lydia Maitland arranges for Alba to witness her mother and Lincoln Maitland embracing. The sight shatters Alba's little remaining faith in her mother, sending her into a suicidal depression, a seemingly natural course given that her father took his own life. After her declaration of love to novelist Julien Dorsenne is rebuffed, her determination deepens. Though she is recalled from the brink of a suicide by drowning, her excursion onto a lake exposes her to a fever that eventually kills her.

In addition to the convoluted social sparring in the author's novel, Bourget carves out space in *Cosmopolis* for an indictment of false religiosity in one of the text's subplots. Prince Pippino Ardea finds himself in financial straits and must sell his estate. He plans, with Mme. Steno's help, to marry the daughter of Justus Hafner, a match that would unite Hafner's money with Ardea's lineage. Hafner seeks Catholic legitimacy for his line through his daughter's marriage to the prince, who is descended from the pope. Young Fannie Hafner, genuinely devoted to her new Catholic faith, is upset by her betrothed's joking about his religion. Her interest in the marriage is further undermined through the discovery that her father's wealth was ill-gained. After breaking off the marriage, she too leaves Rome. The epilogue sees the freedom-loving novelist Dorsenne reconsidering his ways and finding solace in the pope's example.

Cosmopolis is thus a depiction of treacheries, lacking any significant, sustained, and untainted love and happiness. Rome functions as a cosmopolis, taken from the title, an internationally inflected locus of the impulses that undermine healthy and productive relationships; those who wish a life free from such psychical limitations and temptations must escape from the city. Character is determined in a positivist, or scientific, manner, by race and hereditary lines. By today's standards, Bourget's novel exhibits racism, especially toward Florent Chapron and his sister Lydia, who share one black grandparent. Bourget suggests that Chapron's dedication to Maitland is a vestige of the innate slave-master relationship, and his sister's "hypocrisy and perfidy" are due to her genetic heritage. Seen from today's perspective, this appears as an unseemly and ridiculous element of the story, one that undermines the otherwise nuanced character depictions throughout.

BIBLIOGRAPHY

Austin, Lloyd James. *Paul Bourget, sa vie et son oeuvre jusqu'en 1889*. Paris: E. Droz, 1940.

Autin, Albert. *Le Disciple de Paul Bourget*. Paris: Société Française, 1930.

Mansuy, Michel. *Un Moderne: Paul Bourget de l'enfance au Discipline*. Paris: Les Belles Letters, 1960.

Singer, Armand E. *Paul Bourget*. Boston: Twayne Publishers, 1976.

Rebecca N. Mitchell

COUNTERFEITERS, THE (LES FAUX-MONNAYEURS) ANDRÉ GIDE (1926)

The Counterfeiters was first published in Paris in 1926, although its French author, ANDRÉ GIDE (1869–1951), began the three-part novel in 1922. A winner of the 1947 Nobel Prize in literature, Gide considered *The Counterfeiters* his only true novel. Its style was influenced by the 19th-century Russian novelist Fyodor Dostoyevsky, about whom Gide wrote the important work, *Dostoyevsky through His Correspondence* (1908). Gide's Russian characters, such as the mysterious Strouvilhou, point to the strong influence of Dostoyevsky's *The Brothers Karamazov* in Gide's work.

The Counterfeiters is an experimental novel that reflects on Gide's engagement with the modern novel, the avant-garde literary milieu in the 1920s in Paris, and a wide range of sexual preferences. The main protagonist, Edouard, a novelist, sometimes acts as a second-person narrator. Edouard's lack of control over the narration is evidenced by the theft, early on in the story, of his novel, also titled *The Counterfeiters*. Arriving in Paris, ostensibly to visit his half sister (but actually owing to his attraction to his nephew, Olivier Molinier), Edouard loses his belongings to his nephew's schoolmate, Bernard Profitendieus. Bernard assumes narrative authority at times, as does Gide, who "reviews his characters" between the second and third parts of the book and provides insight into his writing process in the accompanying *Journal of the Counterfeiters*. As Gide writes in the First Notebook: "I am like a musician striving . . . to juxtapose and overlap an andante theme and an allegro theme."

This symphony of voices and stories represents the abstract qualities of the modernist movement in art and literature (ca. 1910–30), such as surrealist dreamscapes and experimental subjectivity. In contrast to French realism and 19th-century novelists such as Honoré de Balzac and Émile Zola, Gide illustrates the ways in which the modern character defies categorization or stereotyping.

Five Parisian families dominate Gide's story: the Profitendieus, Molinier, Passavant, Vedel-Azaïs, and La Pérouse families. Part one of the novel lays the foundation for several bourgeois hypocrisies, including adultery, prostitution, and illegitimate children. Bernard Profitendieus finds a love letter to his mother that indicates his father, the lawyer Albéric Profitendieus, is not his biological parent, inspiring him to leave home. Bernard spends one night with his friend and fellow graduating senior, Olivier, incidentally the son of his father's colleague, the judge Oscar Molinier. Though their parents are leaders in the community, they discover and cover up their middle-class children's use of a garret to have sexual orgies and later a counterfeiting ring at their sons' boarding school. As mentioned in news clippings included in the *Journal,* Gide based this subplot on a real crime ring in 1906 that used children to circulate counterfeit coins. The theme of counterfeiting is also an extended metaphor for understanding the hypocrisies of the bourgeois family.

The second part of the novel is set in Saas-Feé, Switzerland, where Bernard delays his final exam to accompany Edouard and his platonic friend, Laura Vedel-Azaïs Douviers, on a retreat. Laura is the daughter of Prosper Vedel, who runs the boarding school that is attended by males in *The Counterfeiters* at one time or another. Wife of a French professor in England, Laura is in Switzerland because she is pregnant by Olivier's brother Vincent, whom she meets while recovering from ostensibly fatal tuberculosis in a sanitarium. In Saas-Feé, Bernard, Edouard, and Laura meet Boris, the illegitimate grandson of their former music teacher, La Pérouse. La Pérouse's son died estranged from his father, and Boris's mother moved to Russia. Boris is accompanied by his Russian psychiatrist, who intimates that Boris suffers from mental illness related to precocious sexual activity. Edouard arranges for Boris to move to Paris and board at the academy where his grandfather teaches.

Meanwhile, Olivier becomes the editor of a literary review owned by Edouard's literary rival, Count Robert Passavant. The novel by Passavant, *The Horizontal Bar,* is popular, yet Gide mocks the literary pretensions of the symbolist school that surrounds Passavant. The turning point of the novel, for example, occurs during the Argonauts' dinner. A literary avant-garde society, the Argonauts slavishly follow fads. In a related subplot, Olivier's brother Vincent (the father of Laura's child) becomes romantically involved with Passavant's friend Lady Lilian Griffith, who finds her doctor friend's scientific observations on life "better than any novel." They disappear mysteriously in Africa, where Lilian dies in a boating accident and Vincent goes mad. Such tangents and attention to minor characters are meant to convey realism and underscore the artificiality of the novel. "In real life," Edouard remarks, "nothing is solved; everything continues." Gide posits that the art of fiction is forgery, whereas reality, with its messiness and untidiness, cannot be copied in a lucid manner.

The final chapters focus on suicide. Olivier is insulted at the Argonauts' dinner and goes home with his uncle Edouard. After they make love, Olivier attempts to kill himself but is saved at the last minute. La Pérouse muses about killing himself, but Boris commits suicide with the gun his grandfather keeps in his desk. Boris dies because of a dare by his schoolmates, proving the motto of the students' clique: *"The strong man cares nothing for life."* That such nihilism is introduced by the Russian Strouvilhou and his cousin Ghéridanisol is no coincidence.

Though Bernard reconciles with his father, and Laura returns to her husband Felix, several mysteries remain unsolved by the conclusion: the identity of Bernard's biological father, the future of Laura's illegitimate child, the fate of the counterfeit gang, and the direction of Edouard's novel. In fact, the final chapters of Gide's *The Counterfeiters* point to a continuance of adultery and pederasty. Edouard's sister (and Olivier's mother) Pauline discovers that her husband is unfaithful (an act for which her son, George, attempts to blackmail his father). Edouard is invited to dinner by M. Profitendieus, who ominously hints, in the final line of the novel, at a new liaison with Bernard's younger brother: "I feel very curious to know Caloub."

BIBLIOGRAPHY

Brée, Germaine. "Form and Content in Gide." *The French Review* 30, no. 6 (May 1957): 423–428.

Brosman, Catherine Savage. *An Annotated Bibliography of Criticism on André Gide.* New York: Garland, 1990.

O'Brien, Justin. "Gide's Fictional Technique." *Yale French Studies* 7 (1951): 81–90.

Rossi, Vinio. *André Gide: The Evolution of an Aesthetic.* New Brunswick, N.J.: Rutgers University Press, 1967.

Wendy C. Nielsen

COURAGE TO LOVE, THE (DEL-E DEL-DADEGI) SHAHRIAR MANDANIPOR (1989)

This important work by the Iranian author SHAHRIAR MANDANIPOR (1956–) is a two-volume novel about love, war, earthquake, and pre- and postrevolution Iran. It opens with a prologue entitled "The Four Mothers of Separation." Four angels—Gabriel, Michael, Seraphim (the trumpet blowing angel), and Death Angel—come to pick a little soil to create man; the first three fail to persuade the earth to hand over a little soil. The Death Angel succeeds in creating man, but then he blows everything to nonexistence.

Volume one consists of four parts; these sections represent the four elements of wind, earth, water, and fire. Part one starts with a description of the devastating earthquake in Rudbar, the northern part of Iran, 1990. Roja saves her youngest daughter, Zeitun, but her husband, Davud, manages to save himself while forgetting the older girl. He goes back to the ruins of their house and brings the injured girl, Golnar, but she has lost her legs and dies due to loss of blood. He gives the body to his wife and disappears. Roja buries her daughter and, carrying Zeitun, looks for her husband. The following parts go back and forth between earthquake, war, and the pre- and postrevolution events.

The novel revolves around the love of three men for Roja, who is the major character. She is a pretty wise village girl who has some high school education and chooses Davud, a university graduate and a semi-intellectual. Because of this marriage, Roja's father disinherits her and does not let her come to his house. Kakai, the second admirer of Roja, is an ugly, illiterate and simpleminded man who is in the battlefield most of the time. In part four he brings a grenade from the front with the intention of throwing it in Roja's house, but he never does it. The third admirer is Yahya, an albino who pretends to be Davud's friend in order to worm his way into Roja's heart. Women in this story are presented with more sympathy than men. In moments of misery and disaster, it is the memory of the women that gives the men the strength to go on, though the physical presence of a woman is sometimes disturbing and these men leave one woman to run after another.

Roja loses her daughter, husband, and mother in the earthquake. Parts two to five cover a 10-year conflict within the characters; the last two parts are flashbacks to the first year of the events. The novel ends with Roja adopting a girl who has lost her family in the earthquake, being exonerated from the death of her husband Davud, and reuniting with her father.

The language of this novel is not colloquial and informal; it is poetical in many parts and also embellished. As the story moves from the earthquake in the northern part of Iran to the war in the southern part, some words and expressions are presented through the narrator or the characters that imply a change in geography. Basically, though, even the uneducated characters' speech is reported in a rather formal and stylized manner. Mandanipor uses stream of consciousness quite often, especially when a disaster happens. Though the prologue hints at some Oriental fatalism, Roja's adoption of an orphan girl presents a picture of rebuilding a new life and some hope for the future, elements that are missing from most of Mandanipor's other works.

BIBLIOGRAPHY

Mozaffari, Nahid, and Ahmad Karimi Hakkak, eds. *Strange Times, My Dear. The PEN Anthology of Contemporary Iranian Literature.* New York: Arcade, 2005.

Farideh Pourgiv

CROSSING THE MANGROVE (TRAVERSÉE DE LA MANGROVE) MARYSE CONDÉ (1989)

Crossing the Mangrove has been regarded as one of the most self-reflective works of the Guadeloupean-born MARYSE CONDÉ (1937–), particularly in the way the author explores the cultural identity of the Caribbean people. The author's conscious inclusion of Creole, spoken by many of the characters in the novella, invites the reader to ponder the role of language in determining one's identity, especially in the case of the Caribbean people who are regarded by some as descendants of the African motherland.

Crossing the Mangrove is innovative in the sense of the narrative structure. The "main character" is found dead at the very beginning of the narrative, thus leaving Condé no traditional central narrator to tell a coherent and unified story. This absence of a dominant point of view and the presence of shifting viewpoints proved problematic for Condé's translator. In translating *Crossing the Mangrove* into English, Richard Philcox noted that to recapture the kind of fluid and floating discourse in and out of characters in the novel, he had to look for particular models in English literature; he was finally inspired by Virginia Woolf's stream of consciousness in dealing with characters and their thoughts.

Crossing the Mangrove marks a new phase of Condé's writing, particularly regarding the understanding and negotiation of the author's own cultural identity. Separated from her home in Guadeloupe in the West Indies, to which she later returned, Condé uses her fiction to offer a fresh recognition of her true position in relation to a mythical motherland. *Crossing the Mangrove* provides not only the context but also the symbol of how she, a Guadeloupean author writing in French, relates to her culture and the land of her birth. Some critics, especially those supporting the negritude movement, do not agree with her position concerning Creole, for they see the native dialect as the essence of the local identity. Condé, however, does not put the same emphasis on language as solely defining one's identity. Even in *Crossing the Mangrove,* in which she creates a cast of characters who sometimes express themselves through Creole, their identity is still not determined by their mastery of the language but through their own reflection of how the outsider or stranger affects the way these native people think of themselves.

The structure of the short novel follows a simple temporal development. The narrative begins with a sort of introduction to the story's action through the personal narrative of a retired elementary school teacher, Leocadie Tiomothée. At the opening of the narrative, she goes for a walk in the cool air of dusk. Reflecting on her own past, on the emptiness of her sister's life, and on the dreams she has had concerning her family's unfulfilled lives, she discovers the dead body of Francis Sancher lying facedown in the mud of a mangrove swamp. Having made sure of the dead man's identity, she proceeds to his house outside the village of Riviere au Sel to inform anyone who might be home.

Vilma Ramsaran, Sancher's pregnant mistress, emerges from the house to receive the news. Very soon the tragedy of Sancher's untimely death spreads throughout the village. His body is removed from the mangrove swamp and taken to the house of the Ramsarans, a local family, for the traditional wake, an all-night ceremony respecting the dead. A crowd of people, mostly villagers of Rivière au Sel, come to attend the wake, either to show their respect for the dead man publicly or for personal reasons of their own. The main content of the narrative is composed of the internal reflections of these people.

During his life, Francis Sancher was an enigma to the villagers, although he was even more puzzling in his death, for no obvious wounds or cause of death were discovered. Every villager living in Rivière au Sel had heard of Sancher, although no one had really been intimate with him, not even the two women who bore his children. He had simply arrived at the village one day, took a rather isolated house outside the village, obtained two huge Dobermans, and began living there. He claimed that he had come back to the village to end the curse that seemed to have fallen on the male members of his family: All of these men had died before they had reached the age of 50. Thus, he chose to keep to himself as much as possible, though ironically the air of mystery about him attracted attention of all sorts, resulting in his relations with the two women, Vilma and Mira.

Sancher's self-imposed isolation from the villagers was not only the result of his outsider status, but also because of the very different values he embraced. No one knew about his background. He spoke with a Cuban accent, yet no one could be sure about his origin; he seemed to have sufficient financial resources, and yet he did nothing the villagers considered work. The villagers watched with dismay the sight of Sancher sitting before his house, a typewriter in front of him all day. He said that that he would like to write a novel, which in itself did not amount to proper work in the eyes of the villagers. Moreover, the title he had chosen for his as yet unfinished novel, *Crossing the Mangrove,* did not find favor with the inhabitants who had long been living in the mangrove area.

In this way, the main part of the narrative has the appearance of an incidental collage comprising the individual reflections of the inhabitants of Rivière au Sel. Men and women think about their encounter with Sancher, what they knew of him, and what he made them think about their own lives. Although on the surface the wake is intended to pay respect to the dead, each person present is thinking about himself or herself, the past and the future. Instead of piecing together information about the enigmatic Sancher, these various reflections serve to reveal the lives and the concerns of the living.

It is already dawn by the time the narrative closes, yet the reader has no clearer idea concerning the mystery of Sancher's life and death. On the other hand, with the new day and after a whole night's pondering and recollection, some of the characters have undertaken new resolutions in their lives.

Vilma, Sancher's mistress at the time of his death, offers an intriguing comment which may also be seen as a direct reference to the novel's title. She says, "You don't cross a mangrove. You'd spike yourself on the roots of the mangrove tress. You'd be sucked down and suffocated by the brackish mud." Sancher's body was found in exactly such circumstances, making his own claim in the novel prophetic: "I'll never finish this book because before I've even written the first line and known what I'm going to put in the way of blood, laugher, tears, fears and hope, well, everything that makes a book a book and not a boring dissertation by a half-cracked individual, I've already found the title," which is the impossibility of crossing the mangrove swamp. The issue about the title of the book is self-referential. If crossing the swamp is an impossible task, what about the narrative bearing the same name that the readers are reading?

Many take the image of the mangrove as indicative of a pessimistic attitude toward discovering the truth of one's cultural identity. Vilma says that a mangrove swamp cannot be crossed. Sancher, the stranger, died trying and failing to cross the mangrove swamp. However, some critics construe the mangrove as a positive symbol of the infinite capacity of life to extend and establish roots away from the motherland. The durability of the mangrove comes from its extensive roots, indistinguishable from its trunk and eliminating the boundary between center and margins. Seen positively, the mangrove in the title of the novel may indicate a uniquely vigorous cultural identity that can flourish anywhere, no matter how far from home one is.

BIBLIOGRAPHY

Alexander, Simone A. James. *Mother Imagery in the Novels of Afro-Caribbean Women.* Columbia: University of Missouri Press, 2001.

Barbour, Sarah, and Gerise Herndon, eds. *Emerging Perspectives in Maryse Condé.* Trenton, N.J.: Africa World Press, 2006.

Condé, Maryse. *Tales from the Heart: True Tales from my Childhood.* Translated by Richard Philcox. New York: Soho Press, 2001.

Ouédraogo, Jean. *Maryse Condé et Ahmadou Kourouma.* New York: Peter Lang, 2004.

Pfaff, Francoise. *Conversations with Maryse Condé.* Lincoln: University of Nebraska Press, 1996.

Amy Wai-sum Lee

CROSSROADS (CAMINHOS CRUZADOS)

ERICO VERISSIMO (1935)   *Crossroads* is the second of 12 novels written by the Brazilian writer ERICO VERISSIMO (1905–75). In contrast to the writer's debut novel, *Clarissa* (1933), in which a teenager's life is told in a romantic, rather rosy tone, *Crossroads* is the work of a satirist and the expression of the novelist's protest against and nonconformity with the inequalities and injustices of bourgeois society. *Crossroads* is thus connected to the larger panorama of the Brazilian prose of the 1930s, which remained faithful to the romantic and naturalistic tradition that had used the novelistic genre as an instrument of social analysis and observation since the 19th century.

Following the transformations occasioned by industrialization, the Brazilian novel of the 1930s documented the passage of power from the traditional rural patriarchy to urban bourgeoisie. This literature of social denunciation found its expression in the novel of social color, especially in the northeast of Brazil, as in the novels of José Lins do Rego, JORGE AMADO, and GRACILIANO RAMOS. Regionalism, which had been masterfully explored by writers such as Simoes Lopes Neto and Alcides Maya in Rio Grande do Sul, did not seem a viable alternative to Verissimo. Preceding novelists such as Octavio de Faria, Marques Rebello, and Cyro dos Anjos, Verissimo became the first Brazilian writer of the 1930s to produce an urban novel of social analysis, an option that was first clearly manifested in *Crossroads*.

At a time in which Brazilian intellectuals sought inspiration in the French culture, Verissimo leaned toward Anglo-Saxon prose. Having developed a preference for realistic novels of social denunciation and for investigations of man in his dynamic relationships with the social fabric, Verissimo was naturally attracted to the American novel, which from the late 19th century had explored an undercurrent of social protest, as expressed in the naturalism of Stephen Crane and Theodore Dreiser; in the muckraking novelists; and in later socially engaged authors who showed a concern for the welfare of others, such as Sinclair Lewis, John Steinbeck, and John dos Passos.

In spite of the recurrent comparison between *Crossroads* and Aldous Huxley's *Point Counter Point* (1928), Verissimo acknowledged a much deeper influence from dos Passos's *Manhattan Transfer* (1925), whose representation of New York inspired him to attempt a similar collective representation of Pôrto Alegre. Huxley's *Point Counter Point* offered Verissimo an insight into the narrative possibilities offered by the use of the counterpoint technique—the crisscrossing of lives and intrigues, the absence of central characters, and the possibility of avoiding long descriptions and deep characterization. Both dos Passos and Huxley registered the crisis of individuality, the loss of meaningful interpersonal relationships, and the fragmentation of modern life, modern traits also found in Verissimo's *Crossroad*. However, similarities between these novels and *Crossroads* could be summarized by a remark made by Verissimo on the influence of Huxley's *Point Counter Point* on his novel: "The recipes are similar, but differ in nature and in the quality of the ingredients."

Crossroads lacks dos Passos's deterministic tone, which suggests unacknowledged forces shaping individual destinies. Unlike *Manhattan Transfer,* which, in spite of its multiple characters, centers around the romance of Jimmy Herf and Ellen Thatcher, Verissimo's novel, like Huxley's *Point Counter Point,* does not present a central character. Intending to trace a cross-sectional view of society, Verissimo opts for adopting a wide panorama of social life in Pôrto Alegre, much more encompassing than the one presented in *Point Counter Point*. Brief sentences lend a staccato quality to Verissimo's prose, and psychological characterization falls to a minimum.

Verissimo's novels show the author working with much-reduced time, place, and characterization. All action is compressed into five days, Saturday through Wednesday, and takes place either in Travessa das Acácias, where the have-nots live, or in the fancy neighborhoods inhabited by the haves, such as the Moinhos de Ventos, as well as in the clubs where the wealthy spend their leisure time. Narrative takes the form of short sketches in a succession of scenes that examine the lives of people from seven main households, whose stories run parallel. Story lines only occasionally crisscross to accentuate the contrast between the two worlds depicted in the novel; an exception is the intersection of the worlds of the rich and the poor through the romance of Noel and Fernanda. Action does not lead to conflict and resolution but serves, rather, to help build each of the recurrent characters, consisting of actions that typically reflect their behavior. Verissimo opts for plain, caricatured characters. The writer is well aware of the limitations and possibilities of caricature and acknowledges an oversimplification in his characters' psychology. He emphasizes, however, caricature as a widely accepted technique in the visual arts, used by painters like João Candido Portinari, Emiliano Di Cavalcanti, and Lasar Segall who, like him, engaged in social protest.

Characters belonging to the world of the wealthy are expertly drawn and represented. They include the Leitão Leirias, representing the well-established bourgeoisie who circulate among the upper class and the political circles; the Honorato Madeiras, a comfortably set middle-class family whose money comes from small business; and the Pedrosas, representative of the old rural patriarchy who, suddenly enriched by a lottery prize, come to town to dispute political and social power with the Leirias, the Madeiras, and their ilk.

The have-nots find expression in the household of the widow Eudoxia and her children, Fernanda and Pedro, who make just enough money to survive; and in the family of the unemployed Joao Benévolo and of Maximiliano, who, afflicted with tuberculosis, await death. Between these worlds circulates Professor Clarimundo, who earns his living in the regular school system and who also teaches private classes to well-to-do youngsters. The author also includes whores like Cacilda, who attends both the Leitão Leirias and the Pedrosas. The Leitão Leirias attract people like Salustiano (Salu), a handsome young man who uses his attractive athletic body to gain access to the upper circles and conquer the naïve Chinita; and the lawyer Armênio Albuquerque, who typifies pedantic shallow intellectuality. João Benévolo receives frequent visits from the down-to-earth Ponciano, who disputes his wife's love.

Besides representing different social segments, each family is composed of representative types. Dodó Leitão Leiria, businessman Honorato Leiria's wife, is an overly pious woman who is always engaged in promoting charity events but delights in having her efforts publicly acknowledged. In contrast with her mother's piousness, Vera is a worldly girl with lesbian tendencies. Virginia Madeira, uncomfortable in her role of mother and wife, forever dreaming of parties and attractive men, contrasts with her complacent husband and dreamy son Noel, who is unable to face the hardships of life. Nouveau riche Coronel Zé Maria Pedrosa curiously preserves his rural tastes, transplanting them into the urban scenery, and is a risible but respected character. His daughter Chinita is the provincial girl who, aspiring to a better and more glamorous life, imitates Hollywood artists. The family also includes Manuel, Chinita's brother, and Maria Luisa, Pedrosa's wife, the one who most deeply feels the dissolution of family ties in the new urban scenario. The poor at times try to escape their hardships through fantasy. They are typified by João Benévolo, who finds solace in the world of D'Artagnan, and his wife, the hard worker Laurentina, who, unhappily, does not make enough money to survive.

Crossroads offers, for the first time in Verissimo's prose, characters that embody the function of writers and readers, providing reflection on the role and social responsibility of the writer. Professor Clarimundo and Noel Madeira pursue writing projects; however, their projects never really prosper once they dissociate art from life, as they ignore the life that unfolds around them. It is Fernanda who suggests that Noel consider the drama of the dispossessed João Benévolo as a worthy theme. By doing so, she voices a concern with the kind of social realism that readers have come to identify with Verissimo as a writer of social investigation and denunciation.

BIBLIOGRAPHY

Chaves, Flavio L. *Erico Verissimo, realismo e sociedade.* Pôrto Alegre: Editora Globo, 1976.

Verissimom, Erico. *Brazilian Literature: An Outline.* New York: Macmillan, 1945.

———. *Solo de clarineta, memorias.* Pôrto Alegre: Editora Globo, 1974.

Denise Almeida Silva

CROWNING OF A KING, THE (EINSETZUNG EINES KÖNIGS) ARNOLD ZWEIG (1937)

The Crowning of a King is the concluding novel in a six-work magnum opus, *The Great War of the White Man,* by German author ARNOLD ZWEIG (1887–1968). Zweig called the series of novels about World War I "a literary document of the transition from imperialism to the socialist era." The author's heroes are confronted with the turbulent German postwar reality.

The subject of this part of the cycle is the power struggles and intrigues of a group of German high officers in occupied Lithuania in the last months of World War I (1914–18). The story starts in February 1918, when Captain Paul Winfried (a character who appears in Zweig's earlier novel *The CASE OF SERGEANT GRISCHA,* where he was engaged in the efforts to save the life of the Russian prisoner named Grischa) travels to Kovno to take a position in the political section of the Ober-Ost, the headquarters on the eastern front. Winfried's uncle, General von Lychow, sends the talented officer to serve under the chief of staff, General Clauss. Winfried, the central figure of *The Crowning of a King,* finds himself in a difficult situation: He has to find his own place in the conservative and elitist clique of the Officer Corps, and he must confront predatory political forces.

During the story, Winfried witnesses secret annexation plans that would ensure German economic and political control over the Baltic States. The plans foresee the connection of a kingdom of Lithuania (yet to be created) with Germany through the accession of a German candidate to the Lithuanian throne. The conflict in the decision-maker circles revolves around the question of which German dynasty should provide the new king. Winfried's involvement on the wrong side of the argument—his support for the liberal candidate who expresses the wishes of the Lithuanian people—turns out to have severe consequences for him. General Clauss allows the officers who oppose Winfried to teach him a lesson. As the result of a raid, when the military police catch Winfried without his proper documents, he is sent to a prison camp as a spy. He is soon released, but the scenes from the camp, where Jews and proletarians endure inhumane conditions, make him doubt the nobility of the German military command's intentions. After he learns that his colleagues and his superior from the headquarters are behind his imprisonment, he expresses his disdain for the military elite and breaks all relations with General Clauss, his former role model.

As with another novel in the author's series of six books, *Education before Verdun,* which shows Werner Bertin's enlightenment toward social consciousness, the story of Winfried in *The Crowing of a King* is also the story of the main character's change from innocence to experience. Zweig illustrates the transformation of the high-middle-class young man, who did not have much contact with society's masses and underdogs before his time in the Maljaty labor camp, into a disillusioned soldier sympathizing with the world's underprivileged. Winfried eventually sees through the German official lies and comes to understand that the main goal of the war is to secure the power and economic interests of the upper classes of the Wilhelm reich. Zweig stresses here once more his own ideological and moral position in the valuation of World War I.

Placing the action in the headquarters where the army command designed plans for the region's political future and where the interests of many powerful groups collided allowed Zweig to guide his readers through the morass of politics under Kaiser Wilhelm and to show them the hidden mechanisms of German decision making. The author's personal experiences

working in the information office on the eastern front provided invaluable background for the story. Switches in the narrative perspective, including third- to first-person narration and frequent use of internal monologue, made it possible to gain insights into the different characters' reasoning and psychological motivations. These stylistic devices are typically found in Zweig's conventional narrative approach.

The German readers' reaction to *The Crowning of a King* was not overwhelmingly fervent. Criticism focused on the point that the author loaded the narration with extraneous details that overshadowed Winfried's personal journey and sacrificed the individual story to that of historical considerations. The description of political forces and issues thus produced a sense of a historical novel. It broadened the understanding of the complex political and economical relationships that influenced the German "Drang nach Osten," the striving toward the east in the final year of the war. The novel aptly revealed how the Brest-Litovsk Treaty of March 3, 1918, created an opportunity to control practically the whole region. However, the wide range of problems depicted weakened the impact of the central plot.

Zweig finished *The Crowning of a King* in 1933 in the city of Haifa, in what was then Palestine and later became northern Israel. He considered the first printed copy of the novel to be a late present for his 50th birthday. The circumstances that led him to Palestine in December 1933 were a logical consequence of the writer's association with the relatively small but active and influential Zionist movement. His interest in Zionism was aroused prior to World War I. The idea of turning away from the anti-Semitic German society and the hope of establishing the ideal Israeli state in Palestine, in which the Jewish people could fully recover their ethnic and religious identity, was a utopian concept popularized by Zweig and other writers. After the war, the writer considered moving to Palestine, and many of his works were devoted to Jewish themes. These included *The Eastern Jewish Countenance* (*Das ostjüdische Antlitz,* 1920) and *New Canaan* (*Das neue Kanaan,* 1925). For a short time he was also editor of the Zionist newspaper *Jüdische Rundschau.* Zweig imagined Palestine as a new "left-wing Switzerland," where many ethnic groups could live together peacefully in a class-free society.

Zweig's visit to Palestine in 1932 became fictionalized in *De Vriendt Goes Home* (*De Vriendt kehrt Heim,* 1932), in which he expresses his relative disappointment with the actuality of life in that region of the world. Yet he returned there sooner than expected: Adolf Hitler's seizure of power the next year and the violent anti-Semitic actions by the Nazi party, including the burning of Zweig's books in May 1933, forced the writer to seek refuge in Palestine, the country he had long idealized.

BIBLIOGRAPHY

Isenberg, Noah W. *Between Redemption and Doom: The Strains of German-Jewish Modernism.* Lincoln: University of Nebraska Press, 1999.

Rost, Maritta. *Bibliographie Arnold Zweig.* Berlin; Weimar: Aufbau-Verlag, 1987.

Salamon, George. *Arnold Zweig.* New York: Twayne Publishers, 1975.

Steffin, Margarete. *Briefe an Berühmete Männer: Walter Benjamin, Bertolt Brecht, Arnold Zweig.* Hamburg: Verlagsanst, 1999.

White, Ray Lewis. *Arnold Zweig in the USA.* New York: Peter Lang, 1986.

Jakub Kazecki

CUNHA, EUCLIDES DA (1866–1909) *Brazilian novelist*   The reputation of the Brazilian engineer and journalist Euclides da Cunha rests on one book, REBELLION IN THE BACKLANDS (*Os Sertoes*), an account of the rise and destruction of a religious community in Brazil's northeast in 1897.

Born in 1866 outside of Rio de Janeiro, da Cunha was of mestizo (mixed race) ancestry, a fact that he apparently faced with a great deal of ambivalence. In writing of the mestizos of northeastern Brazil, he frequently described them as being degenerate, though in other passages he described them as the core and strength of Brazil. Although his mother died when he was very young, and his father detached himself from the family, Euclides was fortunate in being able to acquire an excellent education. At the age of 18 he was admitted to college to become a civil engineer. Two years later he went to Brazil's military college, from which he was commissioned in the army.

Da Cunha's technical education from both a military and engineering viewpoint informed his later writing as a journalist. His style is always clear, and his organization is logical. In *Rebellion in the Backlands* he not only manages scientific descriptions of the land and people of northeastern Brazil, he also breaks down in logical sequence the elements of the military campaign. In addition to describing the battles and skirmishes with clarity, he provides a clear sense of cause and effect in the military moves and countermoves of the Canudos campaign. The War de Canudos was a rebellion of peasants in northwestern Brazil against the newly formed Brazilian Republic in the 1890s. The revolt was led by a messianic priest and religious fanatic known as Antonio Conselheiro. The peoples of the Canudos, some 30,000 settlers, withstood the government's brutal campaign against them in a war that eventually destroyed them.

Da Cunha's own military career was not a success. Despite the fact that his wife was the daughter of a general, his pro-republican views (this before the declaration of the Brazilian Republic in 1889) and personal antagonism toward military life created serious problems. He had to leave the army the first time because of a lapse of conduct. Until 1896, when he left for good, he spent time in and out of the service. In 1897, only a year out of the army, he was sent as a war correspondent and covered the latter stages of the Canudos campaign against the community of Antonio the Counselor. Although his book describes the entire campaign, da Cunha was physically present only at the very end, when he witnessed the ending of the siege and the final assaults and house-to-house fighting.

At the conclusion of the war, da Cunha returned to engineering and surveying as his formal occupation. He supervised the building of bridges and conducted extensive survey work. In addition, he was a member of governmental border commissions. In his spare time, for five years after the battles around and in Canudos, he wrote *Rebellion in the Backlands.* Shortly before his death in 1909, he was appointed professor of philosophy at the Pedro II Institute.

Although his professional life flourished, da Cunha's personal life was unhappy. He and his wife were estranged, and he was shot by an army officer who was supposed to be his wife's lover and allegedly the father of one of da Cunha's children. At the time of his death, da Cunha was working on another book about northeast Brazil, titled *Paradise Lost.*

Although many Brazilians considered themselves not as advanced as Europeans, the country's intellectual circles were aware of and influenced by intellectual developments on the Continent. One such development was the philosophical school of positivism, which influenced many besides da Cunha throughout Latin America. Positivism's progressive and secular stance made it very popular within the Brazilian army as well as the rest of Brazil's early republican government. It did not support religion, especially established religion, and did not favor monarchies.

The republic, infused with this philosophy that da Cunha shared, was in opposition to the philosophy of Antonio and the belief system, however inchoate, of the peasants of Brazil's northeast. In his book, da Cunha expresses his modern disdain for their religion, superstition, and backwardness (as well as for their racial characteristics). Yet he cannot help but consider that the approaches taken by the republic were wrong in some ways. Like other positivists, he states quite explicitly that education and respect for these people should have been employed instead of their large-scale destruction.

As a soldier, engineer, and intellectual, da Cunha was well versed in current scientific thought. This knowledge of science informed his writing of the rebellion in terms of organization and in the extensive survey he provides of the land, climate, and population of the northeast. It is important to remember, however, that his judgments are based on the science of his time, which included theories and ideas long since discredited. In any event, his judgments cannot always be accepted at face value. As a mestizo himself and an accurate, dispassionate observer, he could not help but note the exceptions even when they contradicted widely accepted scientific theory.

Da Cunha's ambivalence about his own background and his ability to see both virtue and flaws in his countrymen, be they the mestizos of the northeast or from other parts, placed him in the position where he could see both sides. His views were not only expressed in his account of the strengths and weaknesses, the virtues and follies of the natives of the northeast but also in the weaknesses and errors of his fellow Brazilians elsewhere. In so doing, he was influential in articulating the meaning of Brazil and its people, a remarkable feat in a book that, while mythic, was only meant to be an account of a single expedition to quell an antirepublican community's opposition.

BIBLIOGRAPHY

Cunha, Euclides da. *Rebellion in the Backlands.* Translated by Euclides du Cunha. Chicago: University of Chicago Press, 1944.

Rabello, Sylvia. *Euclides da Cunha.* Rio de Janeiro: Editôra Civilização Brasileira, 1966.

Robert N. Stacy

D

DAI SIJIE (1954–) *Chinese novelist, screen-writer* Dai Sijie is an expatriate Chinese novelist and filmmaker who has lived in France since 1984. His books and movies examine contemporary China and its recent history, including the Cultural Revolution of the 1960s and 1970s, as well as the effects of an increasingly open cultural exchange between the East and the West.

Dai was born in the Fujian Province in southeastern China, where his parents worked as doctors. Between 1971 and 1974, Dai, still in his teens, was sent to the Sichuan Province to be "reeducated" as part of the larger Cultural Revolution sweeping China from 1966 to 1976. Approximately 12 million "young intellectu-als"—the pejorative label given to men and women between the ages of 15 and 25 who had attended secondary school—were forcibly removed from their homes and sent to work in rural farming villages across the country as part of this political crusade. After a period of two or three years, community leaders assessed whether there remained any traces of bour-geois influence within the young workers; those judged sufficiently cleansed were allowed to return home, and those judged insufficiently transformed were forced to remain in the countryside.

Later dubbed the "Lost Generation," the reeducated adolescents, like most members of Chinese society, were denied access to books, music, art, and other cul-tural pursuits deemed as corrupting by the restrictive government. Instead they were plied with communist propaganda and encouraged to spy on fellow citizens. They were also required to report subversive activities to the authorities and forced to join the Red Guard, the revolutionary youth army created to maintain order and institute the large-scale collective changes ordered by the dictatorial chairman of the Communist Party, Mao Zedong, and his wife, Jiang Qing. These changes were initiated to rid the party and the country of West-ern, middle-class influence. Mao's policies were fueled by the belief that the so-called traditional forms of life, named the Four Olds—old customs, old habits, old ideas, and old culture—must be destroyed to allow a more effective bureaucracy, complete with an idyllic philosophy based on rural values. The revolution suc-ceeded only in creating terrifying chaos.

After Mao died in 1976, and the ideological fervor relaxed somewhat, Dai entered Sichuan University to study art history and eventually received a fellowship for further study at the Sorbonne in Paris. He moved there permanently in 1984, specializing in film at the Institut Des Hautes Etudes Cinematographiques (Institute of Cinematographic Studies). Dai's screenwriting and direc-torial credits include *China, My Pain* (*Chine, ma douleur,* 1989), winner of the Jean Vigo Prize in 1989; *The Moon Eater* (*Le mangeur de lune,* 1993), winner of the Special Jury Prize at the 1994 Prague Film Festival; *Tang Onzieme* (*Tang le onzième,* 1998); and *Girls of the Chinese Botanist* (*Les filles du botaniste chinois,* 2004).

Dai also wrote and directed a film version of his best-selling novel *Balzac and the Little Chinese Seam-*

STRESS (2002), which was nominated for a Golden Globe for best foreign language film in 2003. Generally, he films on location in Southeast Asia in French, Mandarin, or Cantonese.

Balzac and the Little Chinese Seamstress (*Balzac et la petite tailleuse chinoise*), a slim, lyrical work that portrays the experiences of two adolescent boys during their reeducation in the Chinese countryside, catapulted Dai into international fame upon its publication in 2000. Loosely based on Dai's own reeducation experiences, the novel immediately sold more than 500,000 copies in France and has since been translated into many languages.

Dai blends magical realism (a literary style that combines a traditional and straightforward narration with fantastic characters and situations) with astringent memoir to recount the exploits of 18-year-old Luo and the 17-year-old unnamed narrator. Best friends since childhood, these "city youths" are sent to a mountain area known as "Phoenix of the Sky" to live with a group of farmers in early 1971. While there, they delight their peasant hosts with such modern inventions as an alarm clock, earn fame as storytellers by dramatically recounting the plots of movies, and discover—as well as devour—a friend's hoard of banned books translated into Chinese, including novels by Balzac and Alexandre Dumas. Each also falls in love with the beautiful Little Seamstress, daughter of a local tailor.

Mr. Muo's Travelling Couch (*Le complexe de Di,* 2003), Dai's second novel, received great acclaim when it appeared in France, winning the prestigious Prix Femina. The novel tells the story of Muo, a Chinese psychoanalyst who returns from a long exile in France to help his photographer-girlfriend, who has recently been jailed for political reasons. To save her from a long, harsh prison sentence, Muo travels around the countryside on a bicycle in search of the perfect present with which to bribe the judge. He also uses Freudian dream analysis to uncover the mysteries of the judge's subconscious motivations. These plot twists allow Dai to juxtapose the philosophies that undergird Western and Eastern cultural values—and ultimately to explore how and where and to what ends the West and East might meet.

BIBLIOGRAPHY
Dai Sijie. *Balzac and the Little Chinese Seamstress.* Translated by Ina Rilke. London: Chatto & Windus, 2001.
———. *Le complex de Di: Roman.* Paris: Gallimard, 2003.
———. *Mr. Muo's Travelling Couch.* Translated by Ina Rilke. London: Chatto & Windus, 2005.

Jessica Allen

DANESHVAR, SIMIN (1921–) *Iranian essayist, novelist, short story writer*   The publication in 1948 of Simin Daneshvar's *The Quenched Fire* (*Atash-e Khamoush*) ushered in a new age in Iranian literature, as it was the first collection of short stories by a woman writer to be published in Iran. Out of the 16 stories in the collection, seven of them had been inspired by the American short story writer O. Henry, whom Daneshvar had admired. Like O. Henry's work, these stories deal with issues of life, death, love, and sacrifice. Despite these comparisons, Daneshvar's mature style was already becoming evident. In any case, *The Quenched Fire,* with its focus on Iranian society, would lay the foundation for her second collection, *A City as Paradise* (*Shahri chon behesht*), which would focus on the lives of Persian women. In her second collection of short stories and in her subsequent works, Daneshvar would take a distinctly female perspective in her presentation of the life and culture of Iranian society.

Daneshvar's first novel, SAVUSHUN, published in 1969, brought her recognition as the foremost writer of Persian literature. As with her first collection of short stories, *Savushun* was the first novel to be published by a woman in Iran. The story, told from the prospective of the female protagonist, depicts a Shirazi landowning family that has become entangled in the politics of the 1940s. In the novel, Daneshvar's protagonist is Zari, a young woman who is roused by her husband's rebellion against the government and who begins to question the injustices of her society. In the end, Zari becomes a woman who dares to transcend her prescribed roles of wife and mother to become a symbol of the repressive nature of Iranian society.

The concerns that began in *Savushun* would continue in a collection of six stories that would appear under the title *Daneshvar's Playhouse.* The characters in the collection include the nanny in "Vakil Bazaar," the housewife in "The Accident," and the lonely wife in "To Whom Can I Say Hello?" These women are invariably trapped and have no control over their lives. The final piece in *Daneshvar's Playhouse* is a letter to Daneshvar's readers in which she discusses the difficulties of her life as a woman and as an outspoken academic under the theocratic rule of the Khomeini regime.

Simin Daneshvar was born in Shiraz, a town in south-central Iran, in April 1921, two months after Reza Khan, then a military commander, seized power. The Daneshvars were a middle-class family, and the young Simin was educated in a missionary school where she became fluent in English. This fluency would serve her well when her father, Dr. Mohammad Ali Daneshvar, a well-known physician, died in 1941. As the eldest child, Simin was forced to find a job to support her family. She was, for a short while, employed at Radio Tehran but was dissatisfied with the routine nature of radio production. She left Radio Tehran for a job as a journalist for the newspaper and from 1941 to 1945 she worked for the newspaper *Iran.* In 1942 she entered Tehran University, where, in 1949 she received her Ph.D. in Persian literature.

Daneshvar's early career as a journalist is quite evident in her writings as it gave her the objectivity to present the repressive nature of Iranian society while sidestepping ideology. In 1941, while she was working at *Iran,* Reza Shah Pahlavi, Iran's ruler, was forced to abdicate his throne by Russia and Britain, who proceeded to occupy the country. Shiraz, Daneshvar's birthplace, was occupied by the British while Russia controlled the oil fields on the Caspian Sea and in Iranian Azerbaijan. These events provide the background for *Savushun,* and her training as a journalist is evident in the position she takes. In 1950 Daneshvar met and married Jalal Al-e Ahmad, a writer and social critic whose essay "Gharbzadagi" was a bitter criticism of the influences of Western ideas on Iranian culture. In 1952 Daneshvar attended Stanford University as a Fulbright fellow, and when she returned to Iran, she joined the faculty of Tehran University. Along with her husband, she cofounded the Writer's Association of Tehran, which she continued to support after her husband's

death in 1969. The 1970s saw Daneshvar maintaining a low profile, and while she was promoted to associate professor of art history and made chair of the Department of Art History and Archaeology, she was never promoted to full professor because of interference from SAVAK, the secret police, who opposed her appointment because of her political writings. She retired from her post in Tehran University in 1979. In the 1980s, she continued writing, and that effort resulted in her third collection of short stories, which was followed in the 1990s by *Sutra and Other Stories.* In October 2003 she was awarded the Mehregan prize for lifetime achievement.

BIBLIOGRAPHY

Daneshvar, Simin. *Savushun: A Novel about Modern Iran.* Translated by M. R. Ghanoonparvar. Washington, D.C.: Mage Publishers, 1990.

———. *Sutra and Other Stories.* Translated by Hasan Javadi and Amin Neshati. Washington, D.C.: Mage Publishers, 1994.

"Introduction to Simin Daneshvar, the 81-Year-Old Away from Bustle." *Hayat-e Nou,* 16 May 2002, weekend supplement, p. 7.

Majd, Mohammad Gholi. *Great Britain and Reza Shah: The Plunder of Iran, 1921–1941.* Gainesville: University Press of Florida, 2001.

Nafisi, Azar. "The Quest for the 'Real' Woman in the Iranian Novel." *Social Research* 70, no. 3 (Fall 2003): 981–1000.

Stewart, Richard A. *Sunrise at Abadan: The British and Soviet Invasion of Iran, 1941.* Westport, Conn.: Greenwood Publishing Group, 1988.

Talatoof, Kamran. "Iranian Women's Literature: From Pre-Revolutionary Social Discourse to Post-Revolutionary Feminism." *International Journal of Middle East Studies* 29, no. 4 (November 1997): 531–558.

———. *The Politics of Writing in Iran: A History of Modern Persian Literature.* Syracuse, N.Y.: Syracuse University Press, 2000.

Nada Halloway

DAUGHTER OF FORTUNE (HIJA DE LA FORTUNA) ISABEL ALLENDE (1998)

Like all other novels by ISABEL ALLENDE (1942–   ), *Daughter of Fortune* was first written and published in Spanish. In some ways, this story represents a return to the motifs and themes of the author's earlier works, including her first novel, *The HOUSE OF THE SPIRITS* (1982). In *Daughter of Fortune,* Allende again creates an engaging female protagonist, Eliza Sommers, who struggles with both emotional attachments and social restrictions in a journey of self-discovery and self-realization.

Allende's *Daughter of Fortune* is positioned as the first part of a trilogy of novels that includes *Portrait in Sepia* and *The House of the Spirits* as the second and third books, respectively. The novels were not written in the sequence of their narrative action. Eliza Sommers, the central heroine in *Daughter of Fortune,* is the maternal grandmother of Aurora del Valle, the central figure of *Portrait in Sepia.* Published in 2000 and the middle book of the trilogy, *Portrait in Sepia* is the story of Aurora del Valle and her extraordinary, even epic, family struggles. Despite similarities in the characters of Eliza Sommers—the central protagonist of *Daughter of Fortune*—and Alba of *The House of the Spirits, Daughter of Fortune* is not a simple retelling of Allende's earlier story. The work stands on its own as the story of a young woman's difficult rite of passage into finding her own place in the world.

Daughter of Fortune also marks the development of Allende's individual style and movement away from the derivative qualities of her early work. In particular, the work does not contain as many overt examples of magic realism as *The House of the Spirits,* although elements of the book may still be categorized under that label. Magic realism is a mixture of realistic details and magical elements. Most notably, the characterization of Eliza Sommers, whose special talents include exceptional olfactory abilities and an excellent memory, steps only slightly into the magically real. Eliza's most "magical ability," her sense of smell, which inspires her fateful attraction to Joaquín Andieta, exhibits more of the sensual nature of Allende's writing than a tie to the magical realists of her heritage. Indeed, Allende directly links Eliza's sense of smell to her romantic adventures: She is drawn to the men she loves first by their enticing scents. For example, Eliza identifies Tao Chi'en, her second and truest love, by his faint, clean smell, like that of the sea.

Daughter of Fortune therefore partakes of a more immediately realistic style than Allende's early ventures into magic realism, but the novel maintains her interest and emphasis in social and feminist issues. The book does not explore social injustice as overtly as Allende's early novels, including *The House of Spirits* and *OF LOVE AND SHADOWS,* but it nevertheless deals with social status and class struggle. In *Daughter of Fortune,* Allende examines a multiethnic cast of characters living in the mid-1800s and based in several countries: The story moves from the Sommers family, originating in England and settling in Chile, to the impoverished plight of the Chilean Joaquín Andieta, to Tao's Chinese background, and to the wild liberties available to all comers in gold-crazed California.

Allende constructs a society driven and governed by class consciousness in Chile, where Eliza grows up and where the first part of the book takes place. Eliza, though an orphan and a foundling, is reared as a young lady; her adoptive mother, Rose Sommers, trains her with the hope of an advantageous marriage for the young girl. But the seemingly rigid class structure proves extremely impermeable and hypocritical. Jacob Todd, who eventually becomes a journalist in California, infiltrates the highest reaches of social gatherings as a false missionary until he is eventually revealed as a con artist. Feliciano Rodríguez de Santa Cruz, an upstart without a pedigree, succeeds in marrying Paulina del Valle, despite the intervention and anger of her long-pedigreed father. Even the cultured perfection of Rose Sommers and her brother John is revealed to be little more than a façade. John is really Eliza's father, though this fact is not revealed until Eliza has fled to California, and Eliza herself is never told. Rose, appearing as a proper woman, has her own scandalous love affair hidden in her past—and she writes pornographic books. Most significant, Eliza, despite Rose's best efforts, falls in love with Joaquín Andieta, a poor, illegitimate young man with political passion and no real opportunities to improve his social standing.

In contrast, Allende paints California as a land of possibilities, both real and imagined. The gold fever, the cause of the massive rush to California beginning in the middle of the 1800s, causes more loss and poverty than wealth, but in this new world there are, nonetheless, plentiful opportunities for financial success. Tao's healing knowledge is welcomed; Eliza, dressed as a boy, finds work in several unlikely places; and prostitution as well as legally acceptable trades offer immigrants opportunities for both financial gain and tragedy. California's gold rush draws prospectors from Chile as well as from the rest of the world, including Eliza's love, Joaquín. Though he is forced to steal from his employer to finance his voyage, and his leaving breaks the hearts of both his mother and his lover, Joaquín is resolute in his decision. California is his only chance for prosperity; if he remains in Chile, he will always be destitute. Pregnant and abandoned by Joaquín, Eliza drafts a drastic plan: She decides to follow her lover to California.

Tao Chi'en, who has been a victim of social injustice and poverty during his early childhood in China, proves instrumental to the dubious success of Eliza's plans. Not only does Tao smuggle Eliza on board a ship and save her life during her miscarriage, but he also protects and provides for her in California—at least initially. For much of her life, Eliza's actions and behavior have been scripted by social and familial standards. She has always felt both the literal and figurative threat of being cast out. At one point, Rose threatens to exile Eliza to an orphanage, and Eliza's unpardonable sin of being pregnant and unmarried has confirmed that early threat, forever casting Eliza out from the polite society of her adoptive family. In California, though Eliza depends upon Tao while she regains her strength and adjusts to the new world, she soon discovers that she must answer to no one except herself.

She finds that she must make adjustments to live in her new environment. Dressed as a boy, Eliza enters the dangerous, raucous, and lawless world of California, where the legal system equates with mob justice, and kindness originates in unlikely hearts, including that of the aptly named Babalú the Bad. Wearing men's clothes, Eliza also undergoes a metamorphosis. She travels as she pleases, though she still searches for her lover. As Eliza matures, she comes to know herself—and she loses her obsession with Joaquín, whom she never really knew. Instead, she gains a sense of individuality and an understanding of true friendship and love. In her friend Tao, she finds the steadfast affection of a lover; in turn, in Eliza, Tao finds strength and love.

As some critics have complained, the book ends with uncertainty. Tao and Eliza do not significantly explore their relationship; there are only hints through-out the book to suggest that they do, indeed, come to any mutual understanding of their love for each other. Significantly, too, Allende never reveals whether or not Eliza actually finds Joaquín Andieta in the decapitated head of Joaquín Murieta. Eliza herself does not state that the two are the same person, but she also decides, perhaps, that it does not matter.

In announcing "I am free" and holding tightly to Tao's hand, Eliza has abandoned her grasp on a restrictive, barren past and is taking hold of the possibilities inherent in herself and in her future. Eliza also aggressively reclaims her femininity, exploring the sight, feel, and smell of her naked body in lieu of an expected love scene with Tao. Eliza appreciates her body and her own identity, and she again adopts female dress—though without the imprisoning corset. Eliza has come to terms with herself as a woman, and she has seized both freedom and love, concurrent possibilities in the undefined world of California, but not in her socially restricted Chilean birthplace. In a disparate world characterized equally by crime and salvation, Allende's Eliza in *Daughter of Fortune* has integrated her femininity with her desire for liberty and love.

BIBLIOGRAPHY

Feal, Rosemary G., and Yvette E. Miller, eds. *Isabel Allende Today: An Anthology of Essays.* Pittsburgh, Pa.: Latin American Literary Review, 2002.

Novella, Cecilia. "Review of *Daughter of Fortune* by Isabel Allende." *Américas* 51, no. 5 (September 1999): 61, 63.

Winter S. Elliott

DEATH IN THE ANDES (*LITUMA EN LOS ANDES*) Mario Vargas Llosa (1993)

Written three years after the author's defeat in the 1990 presidential election in Peru, *Death in the Andes* won for Mario Vargas Llosa (1936–) the Planeta Prize, one of the most important literary awards in the Hispanic world. This novel marked a new start for Vargas Llosa, who had chosen to exile himself from Peru and acquire Spanish citizenship.

In contrast to Vargas Llosa's previous novels, the story is set in the Andes, a region that, though internationally renowned for scientific studies and tourist interests, had seldom been represented in his works. Featuring Lituma, Vargas Llosa's recurrent police-detective figure, this novel depicts the Andean world as an exemplar of Peru's social and cultural crisis. Critics suggest that this novel displays an ambitious narrative multiplicity, simultaneously juxtaposing and contrasting representations of Peruvian life. *Death in the Andes* also provides a way of observing the reality of Peru as a postmodern country that is beyond rational understanding.

The Andes, as depicted in this novel, is a world full of mysteries and conflicts in the eyes of the protagonist, Police Sergeant Lituma, who has been transferred from Peru's coastal region to a post in the mountainous area. His assignment is to protect a road construction project. The novel contains two parts and an epilogue. The first part is divided into five chapters. The story begins with three missing-person cases in the area of Lituma's jurisdiction. The missing people are Pedro Tinoco, a mute and retarded boy who used to be a servant for the police; Casimiro Huarcaya, an albino; and Demetrio Chanca, a highway construction foreman. The narrative in each chapter contains three sections, each following a different clue. The first section is about Lituma's investigation of the disappearance. The second section narrates incidents happening in the Andes, including guerrilla attacks and past encounters between this quasi-military force and the three missing people. The third is a love story between Tomás Carreño, Lituma's assistant, and Mercedes, a young prostitute from Lituma's hometown of Piura. Before coming to the Andes, Tomás was a fugitive who killed a drug dealer in order to save Mercedes. In this narrative structure, the first clue is based on the encounter between Lituma and the Andean world; the second is about the stories of the Andes; and the third is a story outside the Andes, tied to the police officer's past. The investigation of the crime is the link to the different stories.

During the investigation, Lituma frequents the bar owned by Don Dimnisio and Doña Adriana at the Naccos camp, as he suspects that the barkeepers may know some secret about the disappearances. There he hears different rumors about the three vanished people: killed perhaps by guerrillas or taken away by the *pishtacos* (vampires), the Andean monsters in which many local people believe. Lituma feels lonely and helpless in this strange land, as well as troubled by the lack of clues to the cases. Meanwhile, the next section focuses on the guerrillas' atrocities and reveals information about the social and political situations in the Andes. Under their stiff Marxist doctrines, the guerrillas maintain strong hostility to all government officials, property owners, and foreigners. Since the disappearances happened around the same time that the guerrillas attacked some other innocent people, Lituma suspects their guilt. Moreover, all three missing people have had previous encounters with the guerrillas. By the end of the first part of the novel, it seems that the guerrillas are at the center of the conflict in the Andes and a threat to everyone, including the two policemen. There also exists a major mystery that seems to connect the three missing people and the guerrillas.

However, in the second part of the novel, which consists of four chapters, the narrative focus changes from the guerrillas to Don Dionisio and Doña Adriana, the barkeepers. In this part, Lituma survives an avalanche and learns from a Danish engineer about the still-performed indigenous rite of sacrificing human beings to the Andean spirits or monsters. This discovery produces a link between the missing people and superstitions that abound in the local community. In parallel with Lituma's continuing investigation of the mystery, Doña Adriana talks about her legendary fights with the Andean vampires and subsequent marriage to Dionisio, a story that recalls the Greek myth of Ariadne rescued by Dionysus after she helped Theseus kill the minotaur. Her narration develops gradually from fantastic tales of human beings who once challenged the Andean monsters to more realistic observations of the depression in the region, which is connected to the cases of the missing people. Her stories help Lituma figure out the couple's role in the mystery.

The mystery is apparently solved at the end of the second part of the novel. The red herring initially leads the reader to suppose that these tragedies are caused by the superstitions of the indigenous people, who try to avoid the local economic recession by making human sacrifices to the Andean spirits. In the epilogue, however, while Tomás recalls his lost love, and the two policemen receive orders to abandon their post in Naccos, Lituma makes a final investigation into the mystery at the local bar. He finds that the guerrillas are in fact an indirect cause of the murders of the three victims. Thus, although different parts of the Andean community—the police, the road construction workers, the indigenous people, and the guerrillas—seem ideologically diverse or in contrast to one another, they prove to be interrelated and together form the world of mystery in Vargas Llosa's *Death in the Andes*.

BIBLIOGRAPHY

Kristal, Efraín. *Temptation of the Word: The Novels of Mario Vargas Llosa.* Nashville, Tenn.: Vanderbilt University Press, 1998.

Oviedo, José Miguel. *Mario Vargas Llosa: A Writer's Reality.* Barcelona: Seix Barral, 1985.

Vargas Llosa, Mario. *A Fish in the Water: A Memoir.* New York: Farrar, Straus, Giroux, 1994.

Haiqing Sun

DEATH IN VENICE (DER TOD IN VENEDIG) THOMAS MANN (1930)

The Nobel Prize–winning author THOMAS MANN (1875–1955) stands out as one of the most important figures of early 20th-century literature. Influenced by German philosophers Arthur Schopenhauer and Friedrich Nietzsche, Mann's fiction serves as a model of subtle philosophical examination of the ideas and characters in his stories. *Death in Venice,* like his first major novel *BUDDENBROOKS,* was inspired for the most part by actual events in Mann's life. He had lived on an island near Venice during a cholera outbreak in 1905, which initiated the setting for the story. Then, during a trip to Venice in 1911, he read an obituary for composer Gustav Mahler, leading to the creation of his fictional writer, Gustav von Aschenbach.

Death in Venice tells the story of an artist and the nature of art. The focal character, Aschenbach, is a man who possesses a latent sensuality but is able to keep his passions contained, refusing to grant them expression in either his life or his art. Aschenbach is a classic example of a Freudian "repressed" soul—a man existing in a state of imbalance that, it was believed, hindered and even extinguished the possibility of producing a work of truly inspired art. An aging German writer who serves as the paragon of solemn dignity and self-discipline, Aschenbach at first maintains his cerebral and duty-bound role, believing that true art emerges only through defiance of corrupting passions and physical weaknesses.

This defiance begins to weaken during a trip to Venice, a trip Aschenbach takes for the purpose of securing artistic inspiration from a change in scenery. The trip, however, serves as the first indulgence the restrained author has allowed himself and marks the beginning of his decline. Through the languid Venetian atmosphere and the peacefully rocking gondolas, Aschenbach is lured away from his rigid self-discipline. He later notices an extremely beautiful Polish boy named Tadzio. Initially, the aging writer convinces himself that his interest in the 14-year-old boy is only aesthetic, but as the novel progresses, Aschenbach falls deeply and obsessively in love with the boy, even though the two never have direct contact.

Tadzio's sensual hold on Aschenbach shatters the once firm resolve he employed to deny himself pleasure. Aschenbach spends his days secretly watching Tadzio as the boy plays on the beach. He even resorts to stalking as he follows Tadzio's family throughout the streets of Venice. Not even the cholera outbreak dampens his desire, his need to be near the boy. Aschenbach will become progressively more daring in his pursuit of Tadzio, more debased in his thoughts, and, true to Mann's literary use of irony, Aschenbach will die of cholera, a degraded slave to his passions, a man stripped of his dignity.

Mann portrays Aschenbach as a figure who undergoes a total displacement from one extreme of art to the other; readers experience his emergence out of the cerebral and into the physical, from pure form to pure emotion. Mann uses the novella to warn of the dangers posed by either extreme in a method he called "myth plus psychology." Each of these elements plays equally vital roles in tracing Aschenbach's decline. Tadzio is more than a flesh-and-blood boy posing as the object of Aschenbach's desires; he is a myth Mann compares to Greek sculpture, to Plato's Phaedrus, to Hyacinth, and to Narcissus. Aschenbach's journeys across the lagoon into Venice shows him in terms that mirror the legendary trip across the River Styx into the underworld. Strange red-haired figures frequently appear to Aschenbach, suggesting devils or demons. All of these references to the mythological serve the universalization of Mann's characters and their experiences within the story.

Psychological elements also figure prominently in *Death in Venice*. As the story initially unfolds, Aschenbach's libidinal drives are completely repressed, but as Freud would have noted, the writer's repression has only forced his drives to emerge by another means, in this case in daydreams holding the intensity of visions. Further into the story, Aschenbach has a daydream involving a tropical swamp, and later it is an orgiastic worship of a strange god epitomizing the Freudian longing for what is hoped to be the ultimate erotic abandon—death.

Mann's densely complex narrative represents the best of his ability to create layer upon layer of meaning and symbolism. Each reading evokes a new revelation or uncovers a new area of intellectual exploration. *Death in Venice* demonstrates the essence of the eternal struggle between the passions of nature and the restraints of rational man, but the disease to which Aschenbach succumbs acts as a metaphor for the question of passion as disease versus passion as natural and desirable. Mann takes the reader on a journey through the issue of doubt, challenging the reader to ask: Is it better to have loved obsessively and died, or to never have known this passion at all?

As a writer, Mann can be classified as oblique and economical. He writes with precision, wasting no words. Every detail he supplies to his reader should be explored as significant, as every detail serves Mann's strategy of hinting, implying, and suggesting, as opposed to directly revealing. What may seem to be only marginal particulars within Mann's prose—such as the black color of a gondola, a stonemason's yard for the selling of blank gravestones, or the stained, exposed teeth of a grimacing figure—are indeed all instrumental in establishing a foreboding atmosphere of imminent death. By weaving these threads throughout the story, by linking a variety of motifs working in concert, Mann makes the link between sensual art and death early on and then forges that link throughout the novel, leaving the reader not searching for a climax at the end of the story but, instead, closing the cover with a more deeply ingrained understanding of the multifaceted connection existing between sensual art and death.

BIBLIOGRAPHY

Brennan, Joseph Gerard. *Thomas Mann's World.* New York: Russell & Russell, 1962.

Bruford, Walter Horace. *The German Tradition of Self-Cultivation: Bildung from Humboldt to Thomas Mann.* New York: Cambridge University Press, 1975.

Burgin, Hans. *Thomas Mann, a Chronicle of His Life.* Mobile: University of Alabama Press, 1969.

Hatfield, Henry Caraway. *Thomas Mann: A Collection of Critical Essays.* Englewood Cliffs, N.J.: Prentice Hall, 1964.

Heilbut, Anthony. *Thomas Mann: Eros and Literature.* Riverside: University of California Press, 1997.

Heller, Erich. *The Ironic German, a Study of Thomas Mann.* London: Secker & Warburg, 1958.

———. *Thomas Mann, the Ironic German: A Study.* Mamaroneck, N.Y.: P.P. Appel, 1973.

Kahn, Robert L. *Studies in German Literature.* Houston: Rice University, 1964.

Masereel, Frans. *Mein Stundenbuch, 165 Holzschnitte Von Frans Masereel. Einleitung von Thomas Mann.* Munich: K. Wolff, 1926.

Mueller, William Randolph. *Celebration of Life: Studies in Modern Fiction.* New York: Sheed & Ward, 1972.

Reed, Terence. *Thomas Mann: The Uses of Tradition.* Oxford: Clarendon Press, 1974.

Robertson, Ritchie. *The Cambridge Companion to Thomas Mann.* Cambridge: Cambridge University Press, 2002.

Stock, Irvin. *Ironic Out of Love: The Novels of Thomas Mann.* Jefferson, N.C.: McFarland, 1994.

Christine Marie Hilger

DEATH OF ARTEMIO CRUZ, THE (*LA MUERTE DE ARTEMIO CRUZ*) CARLOS FUENTES (1962)

The third novel by internationally acclaimed Mexican writer CARLOS FUENTES (1928–), *The Death of Artemio Cruz* distills the history of postrevolutionary Mexico into one man's personal journey. Fuentes published this novel after he had established his reputation in communications and government, serving as press secretary for the United Nations information center in Mexico City, secretary for cultural affairs at the National University of Mexico, and head of the department of cultural relations at the ministry of foreign affairs. In addition to his novels WHERE THE AIR IS CLEAR (*La región más transparente,* 1958) and *The GOOD CONSCIENCE* (*Las buenas conciencias,* 1959), and short-story collection *The Masked Days* (*Los días emmascarados,*

1954), Fuentes had founded the literary journals *Revista Mexicana de Literatura* (1956) and *El Espectador* (1959). His travels to Cuba during 1959–61, immediately after Fidel Castro's revolution there, kept his interest focused on revolutionary idealism as he wrote *The Death of Artemio Cruz,* which established his reputation as a novelist of international standing.

The novel shows how the revolutionary ideals of an illegitimate son of a plantation owner and a mulatto servant are gradually eroded by disappointment and bitterness. His disillusionment transforms the brave, ethical revolutionary into a selfish and manipulative businessman who puts the interests of North American investors ahead of the welfare of the Mexican people. As he prepares for death and the last rites of the Catholic Church, he compulsively relives these pivotal experiences, presenting the reader with the power of judgment if not absolution.

Fuentes transforms the familiar deathbed scenario of a person's life review and summation by his creative use of tense and point of view as Cruz's mind wanders and refocuses between intervals of painful awareness. Three narrative forms, distinguished by the use of different tenses, signal the different modes of Cruz's consciousness. The first person and present tense convey his intense, immediate response to pain, disorientation, and proximity to death. This voice struggles in opposition to death itself and also to others, particularly his wife and daughter as they attempt to secure their inheritance. Cruz's unfulfilled potential is suggested by passages in the second person and future tense, which convey his dreams and desires at different periods of his life. This voice gives collective weight to Cruz's hopes and failures, bringing them in relation to those of the Mexican people and bringing the reader into a sympathetic relation with Cruz. The first- and second-person sections are written in stream-of-consciousness style. In contrast, the defining events of his life, when his ideals and potential are diverted, are portrayed in the historical form of third person, past tense. These sections represent Cruz as a man acting within the world's limitations, and the style is spare with simple sentence structures that contrast with the lyrical, elaborate style of the second-person meditations. At times throughout the novel, Cruz's aide is present with a tape recorder, and the limited, official record of Cruz's life is shown in relation to the fuller story given to the privileged reader.

Although the novel's presentation is not chronological, Cruz is grounded in and representative of his historical period, which is clearly identified with dates that are the focus of Cruz's remembrance. These crucial scenes involve abandonment or appropriation, and near the end Cruz lists these as regrets. He has repeatedly betrayed the ideals of love and revolutionary solidarity after his experience of both is warped by the execution of his first love, Regina, while he is fighting. Having lost his capacity for sacrifice, he makes subsequent decisions with his own survival and security as the primary objective. Using his acquaintance with an executed revolutionary soldier, he ingratiates himself with the soldier's family and acquires their land by marrying the soldier's sister. This deception poisons his marriage: His wife and daughter enjoy the privileges and benefits his materialism brings, but they do not love him, and Cruz moves on to extramarital affairs that multiply his failures and regrets. In a repetition of Mexico's colonial history, Cruz is, like all Mexicans, *hijo de la chingada* (child of a violated mother, Malinche, mistress and translator to Cortez). He is both product and perpetrator of abusive sexual relations by the powerful.

Cruz has used his revolutionary credentials to acquire land, influence, and control of the press, while increasing his own and his country's dependence on foreign investment. At his death, Cruz suffers from an intestinal obstruction, symbolic of the wealth that he has withheld for himself, blocking the flow of resources to the Mexican people to support the bloated, luxurious lifestyle of his own family. There is some benefit for others, however, in Cruz's survival and consolidation of power. The death of Cruz's son Lorenzo, who seems to have inherited the remnants of Cruz's revolutionary idealism, provides a contrasting image of cruelly wasted potential in an act of self-sacrifice. Cruz's wife blames him when Lorenzo is killed while fighting on the side of the Republicans in the Spanish civil war (1936–39), and Cruz's failing consciousness circles the painful last memories of riding with his virile, vibrant son, grieving for both the son he loved and his own younger, more ethical self. Unlike Lorenzo, Cruz has chosen to survive and be shaped by history, but his vitality has some virtue and value of its own.

As the end of the life story approaches, the reader is encouraged to empathize with Cruz's temptations and regrets, to mourn his wasted potential while condemning his sins of betrayal. His different narrative voices blend together at the end, fusing the suppressed idealistic dreams of all Mexicans, expressed by the use of the second person in the future tense, with suppressed details of their destruction by a representative, imperfect individual.

Carlos Fuentes has continued to build his reputation with well over a dozen more books translated into English and with prestigious academic appointments throughout the United States and worldwide. *The Death of Artemio Cruz,* written as he was coming into his full powers as a writer, remains one of the author's most widely read and respected novels.

BIBLIOGRAPHY

Faris, Wendy. *Carlos Fuentes.* New York: Frederick Ungar, 1983.

Schiller, Britt-Marie. "Memory and Time in *The Death of Artemio Cruz.*" *Latin American Literary Review* 15, no. 29 (January–June 1987): 93–103.

Tejerina-Canal, Santiago. "Point of View in *The Death of Artemio Cruz*: Singularity or Multiplicity?" *Review of Contemporary Fiction* 8 (1988): 199–210.

Tinnell, Roger D. "La Muerte de Artemio Cruz: A Virtuoso Study in Sensualism." *MLN* 93 (March 1978): 334–338.

Shiela Pardee

DEEP RIVER (DĪPU RIBĀ) ENDŌ SHŪSAKU (1993)

The Japanese writer ENDŌ SHŪSAKU (1923–96) was a Christian author who embraced a faith that combined both Eastern and Western spirituality. The novel *Deep River* centers on a visit to India by a group of Japanese tourists. The novel examines the internal journeys of four of the travelers—Isobe, Kiguchi, Numada, and Mitsuko—and explores their motivations for going to India, the fulfillment of their quests, and their discoveries along the way.

The novel begins with an account of the months just before and after the death of Isobe's wife. Isobe, confronted with the fact that his mate of 35 years has cancer, comes to realize his dependence on his wife, whom he had taken for granted up to that point. After her death, her final words haunt him: "I . . . I know for sure . . . I'll be reborn somewhere in this world. Look for me . . . find me . . . promise . . . promise!" In an attempt to fulfill her request, Isobe writes to a professor at the University of Virginia who is doing research on people who claim to have experienced previous lives. After learning of a young woman named Rajini Puniral, who lives in a village near Vārānasī and who professes to have been Japanese in a prior life, Isobe determines to go to India in search of the woman.

At an informational meeting prior to the trip, Isobe recognizes Mitsuko, a hospital volunteer with whom his wife had bonded in her last days. On the way home from the meeting, Mitsuko recalls the "hollowness in her heart" during her university days and remembers her attempts to draw Ōtsu, a classmate who practiced the Christian faith, away from God. Ōtsu had told her, "Even if I try to abandon God . . . God won't abandon me." After graduating from the university, Mitsuko had married in hope of becoming a typical housewife and ridding herself of the destructive element that "lurked within the depths of her heart." The marriage ended in divorce. Through the years she had carried on an intermittent correspondence with Ōtsu. His conversation and letters always spoke of a God who "made use even of my sins and turned me towards salvation." Perhaps, Mitsuko thinks that Ōtsu, who now lives in Vārānasī, is drawing her to India.

At the pretrip meeting, Numada, an author of stories with dogs and birds as the main characters, expresses a desire to visit a wild bird sanctuary during the trip. He had had a pet hornbill but had released it when he entered a hospital for treatment for tuberculosis. His wife, sensing his need for an animal companion, brought a myna bird to the hospital to keep him company. After recovering from a surgery during which his heart had stopped, Numada learned that the myna had died during the operation, and he reflects, *"I wonder if it died in place of me?"*

Kiguchi, another member of the tour group, fought in Burma during the war and now wishes to have a memorial service in India for his comrades who had died and for Tsukada, who had nursed Kiguchi when he had contracted malaria in the jungle. Years after the war, an American volunteer, Gaston, had comforted Tsukada as he died by assuring him of God's forgiveness for his having eaten meat from the body of a comrade. Kiguchi had felt that the peaceful look on Tsukada's face at his death "had been made possible because Gaston had soaked up all the anguish in Tsukada's heart."

Arriving in Vārānasī, Isobe sets about to fulfill the plea his wife had made on her deathbed. After meeting failure after failure, he cries out in his loneliness, "Darling! . . . Where have you gone?" Mitsuko answers his question with her comment: "At the very least, I'm sure your wife has come back to life inside your heart."

Numada and Kiguchi also fulfill their personal missions. Numada, after buying a myna and carrying it to a wildlife sanctuary where no hunting is allowed, opens the door of the cage, urges the bird out, and watches it enjoy its freedom. He feels "as though a heavy burden he had carried on his back for many years had been removed." On the banks of the Ganges, Kiguchi chants a sutra for Tsukada and his comrades who had died in the war. In so doing he carries out the wish he has had since the war.

Though Mitsuko remains unsure as to why she has come on the trip, she knows that she longs for something. After discovering that Ōtsu now devotes himself to carrying dying Hindus to the Ganges, she puts on a sari and approaches the river. A man beckons her to enter. She submerges her body and then acknowledges: ". . . there is a river of humanity. . . . I feel as though I've started to understand what I was yearning for through all the many mistakes of my past."

Deep River deals with the universal themes of love, loss, sacrifice, acceptance, and redemption. Isobe, Numada, Kiguchi, and Mitsuko take spiritual journeys which lead them to understand God as "a great life force" in man and in nature. They recognize sacrificial love in many forms and in so doing experience the God whom Ōtsu defined as "love itself."

BIBLIOGRAPHY

Endo, Shusaku. *Deep River.* Translated by Van C. Gessel. New York: New Directions, 1994.
Henry, Rick. "Review of *Deep River,* by Shusaku Endo." *Review of Contemporary Fiction* 16, no. 2 (1996): 182–183.
O'Connell, Patricia. "Review of *Deep River,* by Shusaku Endo." *Commonweal* 122, no. 10 (19 May 1995): 34–35.

Charlotte Pfeiffer

DEEP RIVERS (*LOS RÍOS PROFUNDOS*)

JOSÉ MARÍA ARGUEDAS (1958)   Generally regarded as the finest novel of JOSÉ MARÍA ARGUEDAS (1911–69), *Deep Rivers* marks a break with his earlier work, for in it the Peruvian author abandons conventional realism in favor of a lyrical manner more appropriate for communicating the Andean magical-religious worldview, as well as the love and tenderness he learned as a child raised among the Quechua people. Another significant evolution in the author's style, present in this novel, is his translating into the medium of Spanish the *sensibilité* of people expressing themselves in Quechua, the indigenous language. Arguedas wrote in correct Spanish but managed to communicate Andean thought.

The novel portrays Peru as immersed in a new paradigm, one of modernization and turmoil, and concentrates on the situation of a young boy pulled grievously in two different directions, the indigenous and the Western. Composing a representation of himself as a child, Arguedas mirrors his experiences through a recreation of a boy's narrative voice and worldview. The novel raises an important issue, that of intercultural and bicultural children who, unable to cope with difference, desperately long to *belong* and to be just like everyone else.

Ernesto, the adolescent protagonist and main narrator of *Deep Rivers,* is cut off from the beloved indigenous world of his childhood when he is sent to a church-run boarding school to receive the education that will supposedly equip and enable him to take his place in white society. Thus uprooted, he rejects the European world to which he belongs by birth and identifies affectively with the indigenous people among whom he had spent the happiest period of his childhood.

The Catholic Church–run school, whose value system is that of the landowning class it serves, stands as a microcosm of Andean society at large, and it is no wonder that Ernesto finds himself alienated in its oppressive atmosphere. Moreover, during the process of self-definition, the boy painfully feels a vast gulf between the world he longs for and the world in which he actually lives. In spite of this, he is able to recharge himself emotionally by listening to Quechua music in the town's native quarter and by making trips into the countryside to renew his bonds with nature and his human and sincere love for the Pachachaca River. These excursions become a magnificent vehicle for insights into Andean culture, for through them not only does the novel abound in observations on Quechuan music, language, folklore, and rituals, but it conveys how magical-religious thought functions by showing it at work at the level of Ernesto's subjective experiences.

Music is a constant theme in Arguedas's fiction, regarded as a privileged space in which matter is transformed into meaning and emotion. Music functions as an indispensable element of Arguedas's vision of the world. In the novel, Ernesto's attachment to music is so intense that the boy wonders if the song of the *calandra* larks can be composed of the same matter he is made of, and if it comes from the same widespread world of human beings he has been thrown into. At the same time, nature is understood as life itself. Indeed, Ernesto's relationship with music and his identification with the Pachachaca River provide some of the most beautiful passages in the book. Ernesto is an interstitial character living between two cultures and two languages, and as such he acts as a bridge between two worlds. Being aware of the fact that he is crossing borders, at times he senses that he lacks real roots and feels a deep sense of alienation.

As Ernesto confusedly adapts to his new circumstances, his perspective is ambivalent. He is partially absorbed into ruling society, for though he feels he is different, he has inherited many of the attitudes of his class. His teachers and classmates embrace him mostly as one of their own, although he is sometimes referred to as "the little stranger," "the fool," or "the little Indian who looks white." Furthermore, his experiences conspire to undermine his faith in indigenous values by calling into question their effectiveness in the world of the European culture. Not only does he see the Quechua people marginalized and humiliated at every turn, but even the magical forces of nature seem to lose their power when they come into conflict with Western culture.

In the latter part of the novel, however, a series of events occur that once again estrange Ernesto from the European world, forever consolidating his allegiance to the Quechua people. First, the *chicheras* (female vendors of maize beer) challenge the established dominant social order by breaking into the government salt warehouses and distributing the contents among the poor. Then, following an outbreak of plague, the *colonos* (hacienda tenant laborers) shake off their servility and become mobilized. Believing the plague to be supernatural and that it can be destroyed only by religious means, they march on the town to demand that a special mass be said for them and to force the authorities to comply with their wishes. In a triumphal climax, Ernesto and the Quechua are able to convert their suffering into cultural resistance. Indeed, in *Deep Rivers* the reader observes the emergence of a counter-hegemonic order represented by the *chicheras,* the *colonos,* Quechuan music and rituals, and the Pachachaca River. These elements, ignored and marginalized by those who hold the power (the priest who is the school director, the owner of the farm property where the Quechua people work, and the army that tries to repress the popular uprising), finally constitute a subversive paradigm, hegemonic in its own right.

The novel thus ends with a victory of the Andean population over the social order, a triumph that is paralleled on the internal plane by Ernesto's unreserved adherence to the Quechua ethos. His identification with the *chicheras* and the *colonos* against his own kind is much more than solidarity with the underprivileged, since his faith in the Quechuan values he has been raised to live by depends on the outcome of the conflict between the two ways of life. In more than one sense, his personal salvation hinges on the ability of the Quechua people to assert the validity of their culture by asserting themselves socially. With the victory of the *colonos,* Ernesto's rooting is vindicated.

Nevertheless, the ending is somewhat ambiguous. Even if Ernesto appears to have resolved his inner conflict by embracing Quechua culture with complete faith in its effectiveness, he clearly faces a future full of tensions, since he must live by its values in the "alien" world of European dominance. Thus, somehow *Deep Rivers* is a sort of rite of passage novel that stops at the point of change, when a new stage is about to begin in the character's evolution and growth.

The end may be regarded as the utopian vision of a dystopian reality. At the same time, however, Ernesto's deep faith in the Quechua culture reflects Arguedas's own confidence in the ability of that culture not only to survive, but, with increasing migration to the cities of the coast, to spread beyond its traditional geographical boundaries, to permeate and change the character of Peruvian society as a whole.

It is rather difficult to find another Latin American novel that has come near the intensity with which Arguedas portrayed the indigenous and bicultural people in *Deep Rivers,* depicting their dual surroundings, profound knowledge of good and evil, and tragic sense of life as beautiful and yet undermined by sorrow, in addition to the deep love they feel for one another, for nature, and for the whole universe. In Arguedas's view, indigenous Andean culture is not a static reality; on the contrary, it is pregnant with ideas of change and, hence, in a process of continuous redefinition with regard to its complex relationships to tradition and modernity.

Arguedas read and interpreted modernity from within Andean cultural reality. The author rejected the notion that the knowledge embodied in the Quechua oral culture—its music, rituals, and myths—is inferior to, or less valuable than, the knowledge associated with writing and reading in the Western tradition. His concept of literature is, for critics and readers alike, a fascinating and profoundly precious legacy.

BIBLIOGRAPHY

Amezcia, Francisco, ed. *Arguedas entre la antropología y la literatura.* Mexico City: Ediciones Taller Abierto, 2000.

Cornejo Polar, Antonio. *Escribir en el aire. Ensayo sobre la heterogeneidad socio-cultural en las literaturas andinas.* Lima: Horizonte, 1994.

Lienhard, Martin. *Cultura andina y forma novelesca. Zorros y danzantes en la última novela de Arguedas.* Lima: Horizonte/Tarea, 1990.

Ortega, Julio. *Texto, comunicación y cultura.* Los Ríos Profundos *de José María Arguedas.* Lima: Cedep, 1982.

Rama, Ángel. *Transculturación narrativa en América Latina.* Mexico City: Siglo Veintiuno, 1982.

Rowe, William. "Mito e ideología en la obra de José María Arguedas." *Hispania* 64 no. 3. (Sept. 1981) Lima: Instituto Nacional de Cultura: 486.

Sales Salvador, Dora. *Puentes sobre el mundo: Cultura, traducción y forma literaria en las narrativas de transculturación de José María Arguedas y Vikram Chandra.* New York, Bern, and Frankfurt: Peter Lang, 2004.

Dora Sales-Salvador

DEFENSE, THE (*ZASHCHITA LUZHINA*)

VLADIMIR NABOKOV (1930) VLADIMIR NABOKOV (1899–1977) wrote *The Defense,* his third novel, in Berlin in 1929 and published it serially under the penname Sirin in the Paris-based Russian journal *Sovremennye zapiski* (*Notes from the fatherland*). The novel was first published in Russian in 1930 and translated into English in 1964. Many contemporary critics, including the prominent Nabokov scholar Brian Boyd, regard *The Defense* as Nabokov's first masterpiece. Upon its appearance in book form in 1930, the Russian poet Vladislav Khodasevich first argued for the importance of *The Defense,* stating that art itself is the main subject of the novel.

Nabokov accomplishes his meditation on art in *The Defense* by brilliantly combining the emphasis on interiority of his first novel, *Mary* (1926), with the virtuosic structural precision of his second novel, KING, QUEEN, KNAVE (1928). In so doing, he manages to create his first memorable and well-rounded character, the chess player Luzhin, whose tragic story and isolated consciousness anticipate LOLITA's Humbert Humbert and *Pale Fire*'s Charles Kinbote.

As a chess player, Luzhin (whose name should be pronounced so that it rhymes with the English word *illusion*) creates beautiful patterns that attempt to deceive his opponents and, accordingly, is an image of the Nabokovian artist for whom art is a constellation of mysterious and meaningful symmetries. Luzhin's tragedy is that his consciousness, which is wholly formed by his genius for chess, does not fit into the world inhabited by the other characters in the novel. The reader feels sympathy for Luzhin due to the outcome of his displacement in the world—the suicide that results from the slow disintegration of his genius and inability to relate to other people.

Nabokov creates Luzhin as a sympathetic character by structuring the novel in three parts. In part one, which takes place between the years 1910 and 1912,

Nabokov presents Luzhin as a lonely 10-year-old boy straight out of a Dickens novel. Lacking parental love and suffering the cruelty of other children, Luzhin is an outsider and perceives the world as a continual threat. His mechanism for coping with his painful environment is to withdraw into himself. But when he discovers chess at the age of 11, he experiences relief and hope. With the reader now emotionally attached to Luzhin, Nabokov moves to the second part of the novel, which takes place in the summer of 1928 and covers Luzhin's preparation for the world chess championship. Luzhin now has an attractive and intelligent fiancée, Natalia, who understands and cares for him. But Luzhin suffers a mental breakdown during the tournament when he cannot balance the chess side of his mind with the love that he craves from Natalia.

Nabokov sets the third part of the novel during the winter of 1928–29, when Luzhin's doctor and Natalia convince him that chess is a danger to his mental health and encourage him to abandon the game. Luzhin valiantly tries to resist the intrusions of chess, but his natural predilection for the game causes him to confuse chess with reality and perceive irrational patterns and attacks in the world surrounding him. At the end of the novel, he commits suicide by jumping from the balcony of his apartment onto a courtyard whose flagstones look just like the squares of a chessboard. Luzhin's suicide is his final defense against the frightening and chaotic external world.

Nabokov suggests at the end of The Defense that Luzhin's tragedy derives from his ultimate inability to tell the difference between art and life. This inability, however, is not Luzhin's fault; rather, his harsh and cruel experiences as a child and as a rising chess star cause him to seek a refuge from reality in his art, with the eventual result being his confusion of art and life. His suicide—his final defense against the encroaching external world—demonstrates the self-destructive tendency of those who blur the boundary between art and life.

The Defense marks a significant advance in Nabokov's art because it introduces a subject that continued to fascinate him throughout his career: the relationship between artistic consciousness and the world. Most of Nabokov's following novels consider this relationship

in some way, with his greatest novels—Lolita (1955) and Pale Fire (1962)—finding their dark comedic brilliance in their presentation of the psychotic behavior of their artistically bent antiheroes. Luzhin, however, stands out among Nabokov's protagonists as a profoundly sympathetic figure whose tragedy evokes a truly pathetic response in readers.

A film version of The Defense, entitled The Luzhin Defense, appeared in 2000. Marleen Gorris directed the film, which was based on Peter Barry's screenplay and starred John Turturo as Luzhin and Emma Watson as Natalia.

BIBLIOGRAPHY
Alexandrov, Vladimir E. "The Defense." In The Garland Companion to Vladimir Nabokov, edited by Vladimir E. Alexandrov. New York: Garland, 1995. 75–88.
Boyd, Brian. Vladimir Nabokov: The Russian Years. Princeton, N.J.: Princeton University Press, 1993.
Fitzsimmons, Lorna. "Artistic Subjectivity in Nabokov's The Defense and Invitation to a Beheading." Journal of Comparative Literature and Aesthetics 24 (2001): 55–60.

Paul Gleason

DELEDDA, GRAZIA (1871–1936) Italian novelist, short story writer

Winner of the 1926 Nobel Prize in literature, Grazia Deledda was born in Nuoro, Italy, on September 27, 1871. She spent her childhood in a small isolated village, growing up in a family and in a country affected by the typical prejudices of the lower Sardinian middle class of that time. Her father was a prosperous landowner who served as a mayor of Nuoro for some years. Until the age of 10, Deledda attended the local elementary school; it was her only formal education. The rest of her cultural education was left to the recurrent but fortuitous lessons of a teacher for the royal household who lived in her uncle's house, and to her irregular and various readings. She was an avid reader of Russian novelists and of Giosuè Carducci, Gabriele D'Annunzio, and Giovanni Verga. However, her reading was unsystematic. Family concerns weighed heavily on her, since only a few members of her large family were not ill or involved in crime. As a consequence, she withdrew into herself, developing a fantastic and dreamy adolescence, full of romantic enthusiasms of love and glory.

Deledda had an early start to her career as a writer. Her first publications in local journals scandalized her provincial town because she wrote about her native customs using the community's own ethnic roots and history. At the age of eight she began to write poems, and her first short stories appeared in 1888–89 in magazines published in Rome and Milan. The dreams and disappointments of those years appear in her later novels, but they are more clearly seen in her youth correspondence, which is marked by endless love speeches, melancholy, and evidence of tears. Her adolescence was characterized by a fervid imagination and a literary romanticism.

In 1892 the death of Deledda's father instigated her gradual and progressive maturity, which was accompanied by a great literary production, bringing her renown in Sardinia and on the continent. In 1898 Deledda moved to Rome, where she lived until her death in 1936. She devoted herself entirely to literature, publishing a prodigious number of novels and short stories. In 1900 she married Palmiro Madesani, with whom she had two sons, Franz and Sardus. Her only travel abroad was in 1927, to Stockholm, when she attended the Nobel Prize ceremony.

Though Deledda lived in Rome with her husband, Sardinia was always the most important source of her inspiration. Her stories are usually set in Sardinia and describe the life and customs of simple people—small landowners, servants, farmers, and shepherds. Often her characters must find their own solutions to complex moral problems, a device that connects her work to the tradition of Fyodor Dostoyevsky. She kept in contact with her native region and made frequent visits there. Throughout her adult life, Deledda wrote novels at the average rate of one per year, producing around 40 altogether. She also translated Honoré de Balzac's *Eugénie Grandet* into Italian in 1930. Her first novel, *Flower of Sardegna* (*Fior di Sardegna,* 1892), was followed by *Honest Souls* (*Anime oneste,* 1895), which secured her fame. These early works reflected the influence of folklore on her writing and attracted the immediate attention of a number of critics. In *Tradizioni popolari di Nuoro in Sardegna* (1895) she examined the customs of the village where she was born.

The Old Man of the Mountain (*Il vecchio della montagna,* 1900) is the first of Deledda's many books dealing with simple characters and illustrating the destructive and tragic effects of overpowering sexual attractions. *After the Divorce* (*Dopo il divorzio,* 1902) is the moral story of a man, Constantino, who is condemned to a long prison term for murder, and his wife, Giovanna, who finally decides to divorce him. Constantino, however, is freed after a deathbed confession by the actual murderer.

Deledda's other major works include *Elias Portolu* (1903), which describes a shepherd who prepares to enter the priesthood because he falls in love with his brother's fiancée. His brother dies, and the protagonist must resolve the conflict between his love and the demands of society. *Ashes, A Sardinian Story* (*Cenere,* 1904) is the story of a young girl who sacrifices herself for her illegitimate child, killing herself in order not to harm her son's prospects in life. Apparently Deledda's own favorite piece of work was *Reeds in the Wind* (*Canne al vento,* 1913), where the author tells the story of an aristocratic family, the Pintors, who are sliding into deep poverty.

The Mother (*La madre,* 1920) is a tragedy set in an isolated Sardinian village. Paolo, a priest, has fallen in love, and his mother suffers more than she can bear. She has been working as a servant and has sacrificed herself so that her son would become a priest. Paolo conquers his passion, but the mother dies at the church during the service while her son looks on from the altar.

Deledda's later novels have a wider setting than the harshly beautiful Sardinia but continue to deal with moral and ethical themes, including *Church of Solitude* (*La chiesa della solitudine,* 1936), a work that deals with the subject of breast cancer. Deledda died in Rome on August 15, 1936. Her autobiographical novel *Cosima* was published posthumously in 1937.

BIBLIOGRAPHY

Bertone, Manuela, and Robert S. Dombroski. *Carlo Emilio Gadda: Contemporary Perspectives.* Toronto: University of Toronto Press, 1997.

Cavallini, Giorgio. *Lingua e dialetto in Gadda.* Messina-Firenze: D'Anna, 1977.

Dombroski, Robert S. *Creative Entanglements: Gadda and the Baroque.* Toronto: University of Toronto Press, 1999.

Gadda, Carlo Emilio. *Acquainted with Grief.* Translated by William Weaver. New York: George Braziller, 2005.

———. *Adalgisa.* Foreword Ian Thomson. Translated by William Weaver. New York: Modern Voices, 2007.

———. *That Awful Mess on the Via Merulana.* Introduction by Italo Calvino. New York: NYRB Classics, 2007.

Sbragia, Albert. *Carlo Emilio Gadda and the Modern Macaronic.* Gainesville: University Press of Florida, 1996.

Van der Linde, Gerhard. "The Body in the Labyrinth: Detection, Rationality and the Feminine in Gadda's *Pasticciaccio.*" *American Journal of Italian Studies* 21, no. 57 (1998): 26–40.

Raffaella Cavalieri

DEMIAN Hermann Hesse (1919)

The intense psychoanalytical novel *Demian* was published by the German Swiss novelist Hermann Hesse (1877–1962) in 1919. It was translated into English in 1923 under an English pseudonym (Emil Sinclair), at first in a series hosted by the cultural review *The Neue Rundschau* and immediately afterward as an autonomous book published by S. Fischer. It came out almost simultaneously with *Zarathustra's Return. A Word to the German Youth (Zarathustra's Widerkehr. Ein Wort an die Deutsche Jugend),* a rather short but flamboyant manifesto through which Hesse saluted the ending of World War I and expressed his ardent belief in the emergence of a new, spiritual era, rising like the phoenix from its own ashes.

Both works enjoyed great popular success, although the author of *Demian* remained unknown for a time both to the public and to literary specialists. Hermann Hesse later said that he had borrowed his pseudonym from the name of one of his deceased relatives, but also in order to express his intention of internationalizing the novel's ideology by taking it out of its strictly German, postwar context. Thomas Mann, who was highly enthusiastic about *Demian* (he even compared its author to James Joyce), contacted Samuel Fischer, the editor, in order to learn its author's identity. His inquiry marked the beginning of a strong friendship with Hesse, articulated in their vast correspondence; in Mann's family visit to Montagnola (southern Switzerland, where Hesse had settled with his second wife,

Ruth Wenger); and finally in Mann's strenuous lobbying efforts, which eventually led to his friend being awarded the Nobel Prize in literature in 1946.

In the novel the protagonist, Max Demian, whose name obviously recalls an ancient daimon, or demon, has the role of a guiding angel who helps the narrator, Emil Sinclair, to actualize the elementary, Faustian energies of his personality. The hero of the novel, depicted from his early boyhood up to his adulthood, is a typical doppelgänger figure, since he is torn apart, even from his earliest childhood, by the antithetical forces of light and darkness, which vie over his personality. Away from his family, who had provided him with a serene childhood, and removed from the presence of his tranquil sisters, Sinclair feels that his antisocial behavior is determined by some sort of metaphysical damnation. Max Demian, his more mature but peculiar classmate, helps him to act out the tormented energies of his soul, convincing him that he bears the "sign" of a demoniac elite whose roots can be traced back to Cain, the first prominent dark figure of the Bible.

The plot's motivation was determined by the complex existential and psychological turmoil that Hesse experienced at the dawn of World War I. In 1915 he published the novel *Knulp.* Its protagonist is a luminous social outcast and wanderer whose role as a paradoxical "anti-Christ" figure (in Nietzsche's terms) is to relieve people from the burden of their everyday life by helping them to act out their personality through play, joy, and artistry. In 1916, however, Hesse himself suffered a nervous breakdown, which was rooted, beyond his general psychic fragility, in three immediate causes: the war itself, experienced by Hesse as a German outcast, exiled to Switzerland; then the sudden death of the writer's father, Johannes Hesse (on March 8, 1916); and, finally, the prolonged recovery of his four-year-old son, Martin, from a severe bout of meningitis.

All this entailed Hesse's confinement to a mental sanatorium, Sommat bei Luzern, where he met Dr. J. B. Lang, who introduced him to the depths of Freudian and especially Jungian psychoanalysis. Hesse would later praise Lang for performing miracles by the new technique of analyzing the inner symbols of a tormented psyche. Hesse left the hospital within less than two months, apparently fully recovered. The cure had opened his interest in the relatively new discipline of psychoanalysis, which would produce deep imprints on his future literary work.

As a consequence, Hesse's character and style gradually changed and diversified. This was demonstrated in the Faustian, elementary darkness of the novel *Demian* (1919), articulated on the binary personality structure of the split man or double figure (doppelgänger), another theme derived from Nietzsche. The cataclysm of World War I and the relief that accompanied its conclusion drew Hesse into the frantic conviction that great historical anomalies can be avoided only if humanity generates a superior spiritual elite, comprising thinkers and artists who can represent a standard for the others and relegate malignity beyond the margins of a balanced, mutual social understanding. Hesse considered that each person should realize his individuation (opening up one's unconsciousness) by integrating the dark energies of his personality, rather than fighting against them, and by transforming the inner completion of his soul into a socially accepted moral norm. Light and darkness, considered as the intertwined parts of a split soul, would mark Hesse's spiritual formula well beyond the novels STEPPENWOLF and NARCISSUS AND GOLDMUND. They would become associated with another complementary dichotomy: the antithetical formative influence of the father and the mother, which was typical of the expressionist categories in Hesse's style at that time.

Demian tells of the disintegration of bourgeois identity, represented by the narrator, Emil Sinclair, and his accession to a new intellectual and spiritual elite, helped by his schoolmate, the strange and powerful Max Demian. Demian is the son of a somewhat mysterious aristocratic woman, Frau Eva. In the introductory part of the novel, the schoolboy Sinclair is depicted as the rebellious offspring of a humble bourgeois family. He is torn apart by the gap between the calm order provided by his parents and sisters and the call of the savage outside world, composed of villains, wrongdoers, and other attractive violent forces. Sinclair feels that he does not entirely belong to the strict milieu of his bourgeois order, as his propensity toward adventure, evil, and wandering exceed the serene wisdom of his ancestors. He also feels—rather hazily at the beginning, and more and more acutely as he progresses in life—that he bears a special existential "mark," identified by his schoolmate Max Demian as the "sign of Cain." Demian does not interpret Cain as a figure of damnation, as in the Bible, but as a hero whose metaphysical predestination—his "election"—entitles him to surpass his humble condition as a farmer, and to "go beyond," into the special order of the few who are allowed to act out of pure power, beyond restrictions and morality.

Demian teaches Sinclair that those who are marked by the sign should "go beyond" and become superior beings, rejoicing in the exuberant integrity of their existence, which is a combination of luminous and dark forces. "Going beyond," Demian explains, means living off-limits, beyond good and evil (as Nietzsche also argues), and experiencing liberty as a totalizing cosmic eruption, in which God and Devil come together.

Critics correctly argue that *Demian* is Hesse's first work in which the writer speaks about the energetic attraction of a universal, collective spiritual elite, while earlier writings as *Peter Camenzind* and *Knulp* had presented individualistic existential solutions. According to the classical psychoanalytical teachings, Max Demian also reveals to his disciple that the forces of transgression are not outside man but deeply rooted in the crevasses of his personality. Those few who are "elected" act out the inner forces of their spirit by merging evil and good into a complex integrity of power, not by turning the good half of their psyche against the bad one, as the great majority of the humanity does. It is the fervor of creating a "new religion," embraced by strong, solitary persons who march on their way toward human and cosmic completeness, that unites Demian and Sinclair. Although their social paths separate them for a while, they nevertheless share the belief that each person should find a spiritual twin who may help him to act out the repressed side of his personality.

The urge that each "selected" person should serve as a demonic catalyst for the others, helping them to act out the repressed cosmic light within their earthly bodies, is specifically Gnostic. Max Demian also suggests that those who enter the new "brotherhood" (or *Bund,* in German) should embrace a new religion, which goes beyond the split between good and evil promoted by the Bible. The word *Abraxas,* marking the god of the new religion, also sends us back to the ancient Gnostics. Another Gnostic theme is the ambivalence of the "two Eves." One of them is, of course, the biblical Eve, who brought into the world the bitter sorrows of the fall and temptation. The other is Frau Eva, Max Demian's mother, the spiritual double of the biblical character, who also recalls the Gnostic Sophia, the embodiment of cosmic and earthly wisdom. The author suggests that the adepts of the new, intellectual order should reunite under the spiritual guidance of a new Eve, against the larger resurrection background of the new mankind and civilization made possible by World War I. In this respect, the exclusive ideological message of the novel meets the topic of collective spiritual rejuvenation, as proclaimed by Hesse in *Zarathustra's Return.* Freud, Jung, Nietzsche, and even Max Scheler, with his powerful proclamation of the *Genius des Krieges* (*The Genius of War* (1915), highly prized by Hesse at the time of its printing) happily meet in the positive, energetic program of *Demian,* still praised by its readers as the spiritual manifesto of a new era.

BIBLIOGRAPHY

Bloom, Harold. *Hermann Hesse.* Philadelphia: Chelsea House, 2003.

Church, Margaret, et al., eds. *Five German Novelists (1960–1970).* West Lafayette, Ind.: Purdue University Press, 1971.

Farquharson, Robert H.: *An Outline of the Works of Hermann Hesse.* Toronto: Forum House, 1973.

Freedman, Ralph: *Hermann Hesse. Pilgrim in Crisis. A Biography.* New York: Pantheon/Fromm, 1997.

Mileck, Joseph. *Hermann Hesse and his Critics.* Chapel Hill: University of North Carolina Press, 1958.

———. *Hermann Hesse. Between the Perils of Politics and the Allure of the Orient.* New York: Peter Lang, 2003.

———. *Hermann Hesse: Biography and Bibliography.* Berkeley: University of California Press, 1977.

———. *Hermann Hesse: Life and Art.* Berkeley: University of California Press, 1981.

Otten, Anna, ed. *Hesse Companion.* Frankfurt: Suhrkamp Verlag, 1970.

Stelzig, Eugene L. *Hermann Hesse's Fiction of the Self.* Princeton, N.J.: Princeton University Press, 1988.

Tusken. Lewis W. *Understanding Hermann Hesse: The Man, His Myth, His Metaphor.* Columbia: University of South Carolina Press, 1998.

Zeller, Bernhard. *Hermann Hesse.* Reinbek: Rowohlt Taschenbuch Verlag, 2005.

Ziolkowski, Theodore. *The Novels of Hermann Hesse: A Study in Theme and Structure.* Princeton, N.J.: Princeton University Press, 1965.

Stefan Borbély

DERMOÛT, MARIA (1888–1962) *Dutch-Indonesian novelist, short story writer*

Maria Dermoût was born Maria Ingermann, the only daughter of an East Indies official who owned a Java sugar plantation. Her family, rooted in the Netherlands, had a tradition dating back four generations of working in the Dutch East Indies. Dermoût was born on Java on June 15, 1888. At the age of 11 she was sent to the Netherlands for her education, returning to Java at 18 years of age. She married Isaac Dermoût, a civil servant in the judiciary, in 1907. Two of their children and all but one grandchild were born in the Indies, extending her family's connection with that region.

Dermoût's literary work is dominated by memory and experience, distilled from a lifetime in the East. After spending more than 30 years in the Indies, traveling from island to island as she followed her husband's many postings, she returned to the Netherlands upon his retirement. It was at this time that she began to concentrate on her writing, making her professional debut in her 60s.

Dermoût's entire literary output runs to about 650 pages, a portfolio that she had been working on since her teens. She wrote two novels, which proved hugely successful at home and in translation. These were followed by a number of short stories, all of which were set in the Indies and share the same characteristics as her novels. A number of her stories were translated and published in *Vogue, Harper's Bazaar,* and *London Magazine.* These are stories of small things—a shell, a coin, a ring, and a garden—which stem from a love of all things and a belief that everything in the world has its own value. In Darmoût's world, objects have stories to tell, the dead return to teach the living, and the past and present are woven together.

Dermoût's first novel, *Only Yesterday* (*Nog pas Gisteren,* 1951), is a story-memoir, combining elements of the faraway world of the Dutch East Indies and the author's own childhood. The reader is introduced to this world by Riek, a young girl growing up on an isolated sugar plantation in Java. The novel explores the difficulties of loving, a prominent motif in the author's work. Lacking companions or siblings, she spends the majority of her time with the Indonesian servants and their children, learning about their culture and beliefs; the Dutch manners and customs of her parents and other adults are alien to her, proving that she must learn from and about two cultures as she grows older. Just as in Dermoût's other work, the exotic scenery provides a background to Riek's growing awareness of the emotional conflicts taking place within the household and her consequent loss of innocence. The novel ends with the end of her idyllic childhood, as she is old enough to return to the Netherlands for her education. It is then that she needs time in order to forget about all the memories of this early childhood that she has stored in her mind.

The Ten Thousand Things (1955) is set on the island of Ambon in the Moluccas, the original Spice Islands. In this novel Dermoût presents a series of interconnected worlds within a cycle of stories, heavily influenced by the work of the 17th-century naturalist Georg Rumphius. The tale encompasses the life story of Felicia van Kleyntjes (the lady of the Small Garden) and her attempts to change the island. In her idealism, the protagonist hopes to improve the island and reeducate its inhabitants, but Felicia's optimism comes well before she gains the wisdom not to interfere with the workings of an entire world.

Felicia is a Dutchwoman, but one whose family has lived in the Indies for many generations. The novel reveals that it takes even a woman of her exceptional background and experience many years to understand the true nature of life on the island, which is so different to European life and society. Ultimately, years after the sudden death of her son, she gains a greater understanding of life and death, realizing that they are not separate but linked, as are all events on the island. This creates a ripple effect where every detail has an effect on another part of this small universe and its inhabitants. Accordingly, not only the people but also objects and possessions are given their own story. This world is mysterious and often violent; the dead have as much influence as the living, which means that the past is as influential on the characters as the present.

In *The Ten Thousand Things,* Dermoût does not write from a colonialist perspective, but rather from a humanist one. Consequently, the dominant impressions are those of unity and beauty overcoming the ugliness in life, as the characters return to where they always should have been.

Dermoût continued to be fascinated by the art of description. The writer ignored established patterns in contemporary colonial literature, not writing about the rulers and the ruled but instead choosing to depict her own life between two cultures. Her work emphasizes the act of storytelling from myriad perspectives, thereby revealing the beauty of nature and the intricacies of character.

Experience and education gave Dermoût a background in Eastern and Western literatures and philosophies, both ancient and modern. She read widely in a number of languages, gaining a broad literary background, which in turn led her to incorporate eclectic elements in her work. She valued themes from diverse cultures and imported them into her work, whether images, stories, and inventions, all adding to the spun-out sentences that characterize her work. There is an inclusive aspect to her work that is as much linguistic as thematic and is also a reflection of Dermoût's personal beliefs in the value and function of language. Though language has multiple meanings, each meaning is dependent on one's perspective, so that the difficulty lies in understanding and accepting the views of both cultures.

BIBLIOGRAPHY

Dermoût, Maria. *The Ten Thousand Things.* Translated by Hans Koning. New York: NYRB, 2002.
———. *Yesterday.* New York: Translated by Hans Koning. Simon & Schuster, 1959.
Olsen, Tillie; and Deborah Silverton Rosenfelt, eds. *Tell Me a Riddle (Women Writers: Texts and Context)*. New Brunswick, N.J.: Rutgers University Press, 1995.

Lisa Migo

DESERT OF LOVE, THE (LE DÉSERT DE L'AMOUR) François Mauriac (1925)

One of François Mauriac's first novels, establishing his literary fame, *The Desert of Love* exhibits a recurring concern in his works, that of the tortures of the flesh and its world of loneliness and separation, as suggested by the title. This work by Mauriac (1885–1970) deals explicitly with themes of religion, salvation, and sin, as often seen in his works, but unlike many of his other novels, it also deals with themes of alienation, desperation, love, and desire, with a strange coincidental interweaving of time and people in the life of the individual. Mauriac, who won the 1952 Nobel Prize in literature, examines these themes boldly.

Similar to other Mauriac novels, such as THÉRÈSE, the novel begins at a moment of judgment or crisis and then moves back in time to trace what events led up to this plight. The story begins with Raymond Courrèges, an aging womanizer who, we are immediately told, has been secretly wishing to run into Maria Cross, years after their time together. Raymond's previous encounter with Maria had marked his transition into manhood, not in any sexual sense but certainly in the sense of losing innocence and choosing a path for one's life. Now 35, Raymond sits in a bar waiting for a younger friend, one of many to whom Raymond feels no sense of attachment or intimacy. Having devoted his life to "immediate satisfaction," he discards sentiment whenever it springs up between him and others, finding the greatest comfort in being able to dismiss any companion, whether mistress or friend, whenever he sees fit. He seems to have put his family through this same sort of emotional weeding, cringing in these first few paragraphs at the simple note from his father suggesting that they meet while he is in town.

Then, "she" comes into the bar. Maria does not take notice of Raymond, but he is abruptly transported: "She's forty-four, he thought; I was eighteen and she was twenty-seven." With that the reader goes back in time along with Raymond to his younger years, right before he first meets Maria. A bit of a bully, and certainly bearing no ambition, Raymond is a source of frustration to his father, Paul Courrèges, who finds his son a complete stranger; both are unable to communicate with their own flesh and blood. The author's background of Raymond details how utterly miserable he found himself within his own flesh, "ashamed of his body" at this most awkward stage of adolescence: "It never occurred to either his parents or his teachers that all his glorying in wildness and dirt was but the miserable bravado of the young which he assumed because he wanted to make them believe that he reveled in his own uncomeliness." The first person to look at him with desire or affection outside of condescension is Maria Cross, who gets caught looking at him while she shares the trolley ride back to their small town.

Paul Courrèges, a doctor, briefly mentions to Raymond in a conversation that the son of Maria Cross has died of meningitis, and that he is now tending to the mother. The small town in the Bordeaux region where the novel takes place sees Maria as a scandal, a kept woman belonging to Victor Larouselle, a rich, dissolute man who "leases" Maria her house and forces her to entertain his guests as a way of showing his power over the most beautiful pet in town. Rumors abound that orgies go on at Maria's, but we soon learn that she is actually quite frigid, in a sense kept "inert" by her son François's death. Maria seduces, but she never fully pleases, as we find out from Paul Courrèges, who has a terrible infatuation for her; he plunges himself into his medical practice and research so he can free himself from thoughts of her. We find out, however, that Maria admires the doctor for the fact that someone as honest and caring as he is could ever admire her. As Maria is but a parallel to Raymond's disgust with himself and his weakness, perhaps absorbing society's conceptions of herself as much as Raymond absorbs those same opinions of himself, Maria comes to be as much an extension for Paul Courrèges's desires as he is for hers. Much of the relationship in the doctor's mind, therefore, comes from his sanguine daydreams, as he imagines himself saying to her, "You can have no idea of the desert that lies between me and my wife, between me and my son and daughter."

Raymond, however, sees Maria as the way out of this desert, the chance to overcome the gulf between individuals that marks the world of the flesh. As Raymond and Maria take notice of each other, Raymond's awkwardness and frustration give way to a confidence and self-awareness. Raymond asks his father about her, finding Maria's reputation actually compelling, seeing her as audacious and rebellious, though in his passion there is his own desire to further revel in his own wretchedness by cavorting with the town's Jezebel. As they go from mere flirtation to secret rendezvous, Maria's role appears at first to be seductress, fulfilling the role that society has given her, becoming the debauched spoiler of innocence, but their first private meeting reveals a whole new tone for her in this relationship. Once Raymond arrives, she begins to talk about her recently deceased son, showing pictures and telling Raymond stories of how her son was when he was alive. Slowly, she becomes aware of the unconscious drive behind her actions, for she realizes that Raymond is but a surrogate for her lost son, a chance to again be beside that one oasis she once had in the desert. As she looks at Raymond, "the last traces of childhood in his face reminded her of her own lost boy."

Raymond, though, sees Maria as simply teasing and needing a shove to go that last step. In their second meeting, he seizes her, forcing her onto the sofa. Struggling, calling him a "nasty little creature," she finally frees herself and laughs at Raymond, mocking him by saying, "So you really think, my child, that you can take a woman by force?" Raymond feels humiliated, for in his mind he has been made into a fool, and he becomes "infuriated by defeat." The moment, however, turns into much more than just an awkward memory for him. To Raymond, it was the universe once again telling him that he was not worthy of love, again reminding him of his own inadequacy and loneliness. Raymond has at once been set on the path that will determine the rest of his life: "From now on, in all the amorous intrigues of his future, there would always be an element of unexpressed antagonism, a longing to wound, to extract a cry of pain from the female lying helpless at his mercy. He was to cause many tears to flow on many nameless faces, and always they would be *her* tears."

Paul Courrèges comes to quite another conclusion, however, as he comes to realize that he and Maria will never be anything more than participants in polite conversations. He is likewise disillusioned, but accepts a "predestined solitude" as his fate, understanding perhaps that his desire for Maria was projected and always would be, therefore never to be found outside of his own desert. Maria attempts to kill herself by jumping from a balcony, because she, like the doctor, realizes the futility of trying to change the situation in life that she has been given. When he arrives and examines the flesh that he once felt sure to be meant for him, he feels only pity and duty.

The story returns to the present, with Raymond still unnoticed by Maria in the bar. The man with the 44-year-old Maria is the even older, and now more pathetic, Victor Larouselle, who recognizes Raymond and invites him over to their table. Awkward silence passes between Raymond and Maria after Larouselle goes off to flirt with two women at the bar, until she finally blurts out, "My husband is really very indiscreet." Amazed that she is married, Raymond reaches for the opportunity to jab at her naïveté concerning Larouselle's rather infamous behavior. Their conversation reveals his anger and desire and her shame and contempt both of herself and of Raymond. Maria tries to recover her pride by bragging about Larouselle's son, who is on his way to being a success. She asks Raymond, after he mocks her stepson, "What do *you* do?" His reply, that he just "potters around," suddenly reveals to him "what a wretched mess he had made of his life." Catching himself in the mirror, he sees a pathetic man caught in the humiliation of a single, detestable moment, and he feels like one who "goes into battle with a broken sword."

Larouselle falls over from drinking too much, embarrassing Maria and pleasing Raymond. Raymond remembers that his father is in town for a conference and calls for him to meet them at Larouselle's hotel room. Once there, Paul Courrèges accidentally reveals Maria's "fall" from a balcony, which heartens Raymond even further. Maria makes a halfhearted attempt to ask Paul to write to her, which he dismisses rather abruptly but not coldly. Afterward, as father and son share a ride to their own rooms from Larouselle's hotel, Paul asks and Raymond reveals how he and Maria first met those years ago. Though he has ignored his father's advice to settle down, marry, and not squander things in life chasing ghosts, Raymond, true to his stubborn nature, forgoes the opportunity to change his life, despite having literally faced himself in the mirror.

At the book's conclusion, while his father and Maria seem to have taken stock of themselves after gaining insight into their own drives and passions, Raymond sees his frustration and disappointments as challenges, as more mockery from the impersonal desert of his life. The story ends with Raymond, recalling the words of a former mistress, telling himself that "it won't last, and until it's over, find some drug with which to stupefy yourself—float with the current." Ironically, he feels that despite his life amidst the flesh of one-night stands, he has become enthralled by a despair that makes him "condemned to a life of virginity."

BIBLIOGRAPHY

Flower, John E. *Intention and Achievement: An Essay on the Novels of François Mauriac.* Oxford: Clarendon Press, 1969.

Flower, John E., and Bernard C. Swift, eds. *François Mauriac: Visions and Reappraisals.* New York: St. Martin's Press, 1989.

O'Connell, David. *François Mauriac Revisited.* New York: Twayne Publishers, 1994.

Speaight, Robert. *François Mauriac: A Study of the Writer and the Man.* London: Chatto and Windus, 1976.

Wansink, Susan. *Female Victims and Oppressors in Novels by Theodor Fontane and François Mauriac.* New York: Peter Lang, 1998.

Matthew Guy

DEVIL ON THE CROSS (CAITAANI MUTHARABA-INI) NGUGI WA THIONG'O (1980)

Devil on the Cross was written during the year that the Kenyan writer NGUGI WA THIONG'O (1938–) spent in prison. During this same imprisonment, Ngugi put on a performance of the Gikuyu play *Ngaahika Ndeenada* (*I Will Marry When I Want*). He composed the novel on sheets of toilet paper and took great care to hide them in his cell. The novel stands as an indictment of the greed of capitalist neocolonial influences and the Kenyans who encourage these capitalistic influences to reign supreme over alternative movements toward modernization by native ideas.

The story centers on Wariinga, a young woman from Ilmorog who is trying to make her way through Kenyan society. This is a time when attractive young women become playthings for rich older men and where the values and aesthetics of the European bourgeoisie are very much in vogue. Her story is told by a Giccandi player, a "Prophet of Justice" who, though reluctant to tell the story, is compelled by a divine voice to share the "prophecy." This prophecy, he is told, "is not his alone." In telling Wariinga's tale, the Gicaandi player reveals the depth of the greed that plagues modern Kenyan life and the tragedies that beset one who tries to resist it.

Ngugi's use of a Giccandi player as the narrator is crucial to the complex interaction between form and content in *Devil on the Cross*. Giccandi is a genre of Gikuyu storytelling which, unlike much Gikuyu storytelling, consists of a duet of speakers rather than a single speaker who is backed up by a chorus. It is a competitive yet collaborative exchange of dialogue that ends up sounding much like an exchange of proverbial or riddle-like statements. As a genre, Kimani Njógu points out, Giccandi is "composed of hidden coded messages," a fact that led to its suppression by the colonial government. Much of the novel's dialogue occurs in duets and has this riddle-like quality, while the main event of the plot, the competition among the International Organization of Thieves and Robbers, is a corruption of the traditional precolonial Gikuyu poetry festivals.

The player begins by recounting the sadness of Wariinga's life, from her pregnancy by an older rich man who abandons her to her heartbreak when the kind, intelligent, and sensitive youth with whom she falls in love rejects her after she resists the advances of Boss Kihika and loses her job. In her distress, she decides to leave Nairobi and boards a matatu (minibus) bound for Ilmorog. There she encounters the rest of the novel's main characters, particularly Gatuiria, an educated man who later becomes Wariinga's fiancé.

The novel's action is divided between the matatu journey to Ilmorog and the competition to "select seven experts in modern theft and robbery," a competition held in Ilmorog by the International Organization of Thieves and Robbers. Over the course of the journey, the reader learns that all the passengers have reason to be at the competition, though only Mwireri, who is to be a competitor, has in his possession an authentic invitation. Everyone else has received a phoney invitation produced by a student protest group, which calls the gathering a "Devil's Feast" hosted by "Satan, The King of Hell." The message is clear: The greed of capitalism which subjugates the Kenyan people can be equated with the devil's work. Discussions of the devil emerge often in the novel. His power is feared and his existence debated by the characters who resist commercial greed, while those "thieves and robbers" never discuss or debate him, presumably because their interests are in league with his. However, he also emerges in Wariinga's narrative as an alternative resistance to the passive acceptance of Christian doctrine, which is Eurocentric and upholds and validates the oppressive values of Western capitalism.

As a child, Wariinga dreams of being a white man on a cross who is taken down and restored to life by black men in suits. Later in the novel she is tempted by a voice while she sleeps on a golf course. The voice is deemed to be that of the devil. He argues that Wariinga and her people need to reject the tenants of Christianity that emphasize passivity. He offers her a charmed life of beauty and respect if she will follow him. The chapter ends with Wariinga saying, "No! No! Get behind me, Satan"; however, readers are unsure whether she has totally rejected the devil's advice, particularly at the violent conclusion of the novel.

Indeed, when the action shifts forward two years to see Wariinga now living in Nairobi and employed as a skilled car mechanic, the cynical hopelessness on display at the competition is replaced by the possibility that Wariinga is making her way successfully through Kenyan society. She and Gatuiria are engaged, and the novel's concluding action sees Wariinga dressed beautifully in "the Gikuyu way" and prepared to meet Gatuiria's bourgeois parents. Tragedy strikes when the devil's urges to Wariinga to take an eye for an eye emerge. Wariinga meets her fiancé's father, and they are both surprised to realize that he is the man who had impregnated her and abandoned her years before. She shoots him and flees the house, knowing that "the hardest struggles of her life's journey lie ahead."

BIBLIOGRAPHY

Jussawalla, Feroza, and Reed Way Dasenbrock, eds. *Interviews with Writers of the Post-Colonial World.* Jackson and London: University of Mississippi Press, 1992.

Aine McGlynn

DIARY OF A MAD OLD MAN (*FŪTEN RŌJIN NIKKI*) TANIZAKI JUNICHIRO (1962)

The Japanese writer TANIZAKI JUNICHIRO (1886–1965) began his career as a writer of sensational, rather diabolical tales influenced in part by Western writers such as Edgar Allan Poe, Charles Baudelaire, and Oscar Wilde. Celebrated for his masterful plotting and psychological insight into perverse states of mind, Tanizaki was among the first 20th-century Japanese writers to receive international acclaim as a major literary figure. His last book before his death at the age of 75 is, as the title *Diary of a Mad Old Man* partially suggests, a first-person account of a man of similar age who suffers from a relatively benign form of erotomania rather than clinical insanity.

The ironic elements of this book are heightened by other biographical aspects, notably Tanizaki's own lifelong reputation as a sensualist. According to Gwenn Boardman Petersen in *The Moon in the Water: Understanding Tanizaki, Kawabata, and Mishima,* Tanizaki reputedly "act[ed] as a go-between for his own wife." Heightened irony also derives from his repudiation early in his career of the so-called "I" novel, a relatively plotless, naturalistic yet sentimental and poeticized, confessional narrative using material from the author's own life, which had been considered the ideal prose form by the earliest modernists of the Taisho era (the period between World War I and the mid-1920s). Although Tanizaki's diarist is not a professional writer, his bouts of libidinal reverie do lend themselves to being read as a parody of the I-novel decades after the genre had become moribund, or perhaps of Japanese aestheticism, generally. At the very least, the book both exemplifies and wryly comments on Tanizaki's lifelong preoccupation with the theme of the artist transfixed by sinister beauty.

Utsugi Tokusuke is an excitable, short-tempered old man with high blood pressure. As the reader might expect, Utsugi's high blood pressure, like the neuralgia in his left hand and his difficulty in keeping balance, has metaphoric implications. If he is testy, it is only in the modern sense of the term, since he is also impotent. But, as he observes in a mixed tone of lament and assertiveness, "even if you're impotent you have a kind of sex life." He goes on to declare, "Even so, I can enjoy sexual stimulation in all kinds of distorted, indirect ways." Although his diary begins by surveying his attraction to *onnagata*—handsome young men who play women's roles in Kabuki theater—it soon becomes clear that what sends his blood coursing is the female foot. Unfortunately, where it courses is to his own feet, which tend to swell up in the heat. As fetishistic objects, female feet provide Utsugi with meaningful indices of the profound cultural changes that have occurred in his lifetime; thus, at one point in his diary he launches into a sustained comparison of the tiny, dainty, but broad feet of women of the 1890s, who walked in a typically "mincing," "pigeon-like" manner, and the "elegantly long and slender" feet of more self-assured contemporary women.

While tending to propel him to the edge of comic absurdity (and occasionally beyond that brink), Utsugi's erotic sensibilities are played off against the prosaic aspects of everyday life. Eros provides a stay against disintegration and death, while disintegration and the possibility of death are themselves potent erotic stimuli. Utsugi is not content to measure out the short span of his remaining life in dosages of multivarious pharmaceuticals; but if too earthy and superficially "reckless" to play Prufrock, he is too "timid and cautious," by his own account, to truly rage against the dying of the light.

The intimate relationship between death and eros is played out in terms of physical symptoms that are in fact psychologically symptomatic: "When I crammed her toes into my mouth . . . my blood pressure reached its height . . . as if I might die of apoplexy that very instant. . . . I told myself that I *had* to calm down, that I mustn't let myself be excited, and yet I went on blindly sucking at her feet. I could not stop. No, the more I tried to stop, the more I suckled." The vague intimation of suicidal compulsion in this passage ("I don't care if it kills me") exemplifies the relief he often seems to derive from imagining his life finally ending, not just the pain but also the tedium: "Something is lacking unless my eyes get bloodshot and my blood pressure goes over 200."

Utsugi's preoccupation with his symptoms—the preoccupations of a narcissist as much as of an old, sick man—swells out of all proportion with his erotic obsession with his daughter-in-law, Satsuko, his most

dangerous symptom. Utsugi confides to himself about his attraction to cruel-looking women and, further, notes that "I might be all the more attracted to a woman knowing that she was a sneak thief." His fixation on feminine criminality waxes as he approaches closer to the inevitable end, until he feels genuine pleasure in the fantasy of being killed by such a woman, particularly since it offers the additional prospect of learning "how it feels to be brutally murdered." He asks himself, "Is it possible that physical suffering, the inability to enjoy the normal pleasures of sex, could distort a man's outlook this much?"

Utsugi never fully addresses the origin of his masochistic inclinations, other than to claim they had emerged only as he had grown old. Introspective speculation has its limits because, fortunately, Satsuko seems just his type—"a bit spiteful . . . a bit of a liar . . . cold." She is suitably coquettish, impudent, and malicious—to his exulting pleasure. Satsuko tantalizes Utsugi. On one occasion she proffers her leg for tongue caresses, extending it from behind a shower curtain in a gesture reminiscent of her days as a chorus girl. On another occasion she deposits a dollop of saliva into his mouth.

Satsuko further tantalizes Utsugi with her brutal sarcasm, as when she describes the effect of his tongue on her: "It made me feel queasy the rest of the day, as if I'd been licked by a garden slug." The two enter into what seems a mildly sadomasochistic compact, a "little erotic thriller" in which Utsugi uses his "almost unbearably rapturous" pain to play upon Satsuko's pity in order to extort a kiss. While howling in authentic pain, he quickly realizes that he can milk it for sympathy, and he begins to act the part of "a naughty, unruly child." However, the narrator is less than reliable, and the compact may not be all it seems. Although Satsuko benefits materially from the old man's lascivious beseeching, her motives may not be entirely self-serving or cruel. A nurse's report, which functions as a coda to the diary, reveals that his doctor had given the family a diagnosis entailing an implicit course of treatment: Utsugi "constantly needed to feel sexual desire" and that "in view of the fact that it helped to keep him alive you had to take [this] into account in your behavior toward him."

The old man displays his own sadistic tendencies in the reflexive manner common to many masochists. Out of petulance and a kind of vengeful malice, he flaunts the grotesqueness of his face once his false teeth are removed: "My nose flattened down over my lips. . . . I smacked my gums open and shut, and licked my yellow tongue around in my mouth." At the same time, he exults in the fact that the uglier he seems, the more beautiful Satsuko looks by contrast. An aesthete of sorts, he is able to imagine that were he to allow Satsuko to shave him he would be able to gaze up into her nostrils, where "[t]hat delicate transparent flesh would have a lovely coral gleam." His exquisite erotic hypersensitivity and narcissism encourage him on one occasion to suspect that Satsuko had sought to arouse him by arranging the food on her plate in an intentionally messy, uncouth manner that subtly contrasts with his wife's scrupulous cleaning of hers.

Utsugi's perverse, but by no means abnormal, psychology induces him to encourage Satsuko's adultery with another man because it stimulates his imagination; yet he is jealous of her dog for the time and attention she gives it. Somewhat doglike himself, he barters "petting" privileges for a 3-million-yen diamond ring, bought with money he had planned to spend Westernizing the family house inherited from his parents. Sick and in duress, he justifies his behavior with a Pascalian rationale: "When I think of Satsuko I feel like gambling on the slightest chance to *live* again. Anything else is meaningless."

His is a comically fleshy sort of wager, since he matter-of-factly acknowledges, "I have no religious beliefs, any sort of faith will do for me; my only conceivable divinity is Satsuko." Yet he hatches a "crazy, blasphemous scheme" to have Satsuko's face and figure carved on his tombstone as images of Bodhisattvas are often carved. Already lying under her image, psychologically, he fantasizes his ashes forever beneath Satsuko's feet. By logic of association, this fetishistic reverie propels his extravagance further inasmuch as he decides to integrate a Buddha's Footprint Stone carved on the model of Satsuko's foot. This conception is ambiguous—sensuously devotional, ridiculously pathetic, and outrageously nihilistic—insofar as the footprints of the Buddha (Buddhapada) is a highly revered symbol of the grounding of the transcendent and an imprimatur thought to evidence the Buddha's living presence, as well as an absence indicating the achievement of nirvana through nonattachment.

The obsessive Utsugi is nothing if not attached. This attachment is as much vindictive as erotic and aesthetic: "Then after I die . . . she'll find herself thinking: 'That crazy old man is lying under these beautiful feet of mine, at this very moment I'm trampling on the buried bones of the poor old fellow.' No doubt it will give her a certain pleasurable thrill, though I dare say the feeling of revulsion will be stronger. She will not easily—perhaps never—be able to efface that repulsive memory." Utsugi imagines his spirit coming alive under the sweet pain of "feeling the fine-grained velvety smoothness of the soles of her feet. . . . Between sobs I would scream: 'It hurts! It hurts! . . . Even though it hurts, I'm happy—I've never been more happy, I'm much, much happier than when I was alive! . . . Trample harder! Harder!'"

Although he is often ridiculous in his amorous cravings, it is hard to begrudge the old man his follies, even at his worst, when he stingily refuses to give a pittance to help his daughter and her children, while at the same time continuing to indulge Satsuko. Certainly the reader's rush to judgment is forestalled by the shifting ambiguity of his self-description: "I have Satsuko's taste for shocking people . . . yet in fact I am easily moved to tears. . . . I have enjoyed playing the villain. . . . [E]ven though I am sentimental and given to tears—as virtuous as that may sound—my true nature is perverse and cold-hearted in the extreme." But the reader's forbearance is also due to the way Tanizaki ironically undercuts his and his character's lyrical tendencies with more material concerns. This is perhaps best exemplified when the incessant chirping of a cricket induces the old man to dreamy reminiscences of childhood, until he abruptly realizes that he has been listening to the raspy sound of his own dry-mouthed breathing.

It is too much to claim, as Arthur G. Kimball does in *Crisis in Identity and the Contemporary Japanese Novel,* that Tanizaki's old man is a veritable Trickster figure in "his mischievous delight in stirring up family frictions, in his sexual urges, and most of all in his creative spirit which, one likes to think, transcends the inevitable." A more accurate assessment would identify him, as Kimball also does, with a type of folly described by Erasmus: "It is present whenever an amiable dotage of the mind at once frees the spirit from carking cares and anoints it with a complex delight."

BIBLIOGRAPHY

Boardman Petersen, Gwenn. *The Moon in the Water: Understanding Tanizaki, Kawabata, and Mishima.* Honolulu: University of Hawaii Press, 1992.

David Brottman

DICTIONARY OF MAQIAO, A (MA QIAO CIDIAN) HAN SHAOGONG (1996)

Written in the form of a dictionary, *A Dictionary of Maqiao,* by Chinese novelist HAN SHAOGONG (1953–), consists of 150 independent entries, each in length from a paragraph to a few pages, and not arranged alphabetically. The entries are regional, vernacular terms about local sites, people, customs, legends, and other phenomena in a place named Maqiao, a fictional village in the countryside of southern China in the 20th century. Each entry is essentially a narrative that consists of descriptions, stories, and comments about things related to Maqiao. There are no narrative bridges between entries; however, the same narrator provides all the information.

The narrator is an "intellectual youth," as the term is applied at that time to a young man who has relocated from a city to Maqiao and lives in the rural countryside for many years during the Chinese Cultural Revolution. Communist Party chairman Mao Zedong launched this wide-sweeping and radical change throughout China during the last decade he was in power (1966–76). In the novel, the narrator plays the role of an "ethnographic-lexicographer," one knowledgeable in language, word formations, and cultural backgrounds. This identity gives him the vantage point of representing local cultural ideas, values, and historical memories beyond a provincial perspective. The approach of lexicography does not limit the author's freedom of using more subject matters and writing styles than word definitions and explanations. Usually beginning with a semantic and functional interpretation of a word, it soon leads to an illustrative

narration, including stories, anecdotes, legends, historical events, as well as comments on things relevant in a wide sense. This way of representation was considered by many Chinese critics as innovative; however, in the eyes of some critics, the approach still bears the traces of traditional Chinese genres such as the anecdote fiction approach to fiction writing known as *biji xiaoshuo.*

The narrator's expressed intention is to write a biography for every individual thing in Maqiao, especially for those that seem unimportant and trivial but are meaningful by the narrator's standard. Some of them pose a challenge to the official discourses, while some help to grope into the depth of the texture of cultural traditions and historical memories. The "Maple Ghosts" entry is a good example. Not unlike any other trees in their physical features, these two "ghost-haunted" maples carry heavy historical, psychological, and cultural weight in Maqiao people's minds and memories. Once they were disastrously used by the Japanese invaders to navigate their bombing and killed villagers during World War II. Any challenging attempts, from felling the trees to portraying them, have failed. The narrator interprets the maple ghost in a perspective beyond the local "psychological reality": A tree has no will and freedom, but it can obtain significance in a complex network of meanings and cause-effect-relations in life, and thus the difference between one tree and another is as large as that between two such people as Adolf Hitler and Mahatma Gandhi. This consciousness can well account for the author's motivation and starting point of recording things in Maqiao and creating this dictionary-like novel.

In the undeveloped agricultural village of Maqiao, which is separated from the outside world, some backward sides can be found. The villagers seem to have a psychologically different time-space that has stranded Maqiao in an embarrassingly isolated, poor, and ridiculous state, and miserably out of step with the outside world. Nevertheless, with provincial cultural and geographical ideas, people here see Maqiao as the center of the world and view people from other places as marginal. The narrator is also surprised at the extreme male-centric character of Maqiao language and culture. Most words about femininity are dissolved into male discourses. Appellations such as *mom,* and *sister* are replaced by *little dad* and *little brother.*

The narrator does not hide his critical consciousness under the objective mask of an ethnographic lexicographer. His criticism is aimed at double targets: the cultural world of Maqiao and the outside ideological world. Sometimes these ideas are discussed as contrasting, opposite, or confrontational, and sometimes as similar, equivalent, or connective phenomena. In both senses, it is easy to discover a subversive and reflective function of Maqiao vocabulary to the dominant ideological discourses.

The local values that challenge the orthodox ideas are often connected to the special use of terms in Maqiao. In this dictionary, the Chinese character *xing* means "foolish" or "crazy," opposite to its usual meaning, "awake" and "vigilant." This brings a new understanding of the values embodied in the respected image of the ancient patriotic poet Qu Yuan (332–296 B.C.), who was exiled by his unwise king. Out of political loyalty to his country, he ended his own life in the Miluo River, a place where the ancestors of Maqiao people used to live. Long considered the father of Chinese poetry, Qu Yuan once described himself in his poetry as the only person who was *xing,*—that is, "awake" and "sagacious"—while other people were all "drunk" and "asleep," but the ambiguous double meaning of *xing* (foolish and awake) in the Maqiao terminology casts a new light on Qu Yuan's behavior and all the relevant values and ideology. The narrator supposes that Qu Yuan had already gone insane (*xing*) when he came to Miluo. From the linguistic relics of the historical memory, a different view rises, accompanied by a disengaged attitude toward power politics and a silent resistance to the official culture.

The Maqiao people exhibit their cultural ideas and consciousness in various dimensions. In their mind, science is the product of the "lazy-bone," since they describe any lazy phenomena as "scientific" in their everyday use of language. On the other hand, the "lazy" behaviors of some villagers, who refuse to participate in any organized labor and reject any benefit from the productive activities, are not only closer the spirit to the nature in of Taoism but also more "scientific," "reasonable," and "sagacious" in the sense of staying detached from the frenetic political movements before and during the Cultural Revolution.

In this dictionary-like work, a lot of comments are on language itself, based on the observation of the special qualities and uses of Maqiao terms. For example, the scarcity and low quality of food limit the meaning and functions of Maqiao words concerning taste. Maqiao people describe any palatable flavor as *sweet,* no matter how salty, spicy, or sour it is, and they use the word *candy* for anything that is delicious. The narrator immediately extends its meaning to a general level: Due to the ignorance brought by distance, we are always inclined to understand other people and their cultures in a similar simplified way. This phenomenon of Maqiao linguistic limitedness is even associated with the United States's undifferentiating view of the exiled Chinese as the "anticommunist heroes," regardless of the fact that a lot of them leave their country simply because they have failed in economic or cultural fraud. Some ideological and cultural stupidities of great powers are reflected in this tiny linguistic mirror.

Much attention is paid to another side of language in this dictionary. A considerable part of it describes how the creation, misuse, or abuse of words greatly influences people's lives and change their fates. The suggestive power of the unique term *street-sickness,* obviously an extension from words like *sea-sickness,* and *car-sickness,* always makes Maqiao people feel dizzy on urban streets, thus binding their lives in the agricultural zones generation after generation. There are many other relevant examples: An accidental mispronunciation of a word leads to a radio announcer being sentenced to years in prison; the miswriting in an invitation turns friendship into hatred and results in irreversible tragedy. In an ironic style, the narrator also tells stories about the similarity between the sheer meaningless words in everyday greetings in Maqiao and the politically clichéd language in China, in terms of their common characteristics and functions as the rubbish, or "shit," of language.

Influenced by magic realism and the local ghost cultures, *A Dictionary of Maqiao* provides stories with supernatural characteristics. A part of these create unique images and perspectives of viewing life. For example, the word *Wowei* refers to a legendary cabbage-formed thing that posthumously grows out of the mouth of a buried person. Its size is believed to be a conclusive measure of the degree of happiness, fortune, and physical satisfaction (basically nutrition) throughout his or her life. The naïve local people, while removing old waste tombs and scattered bones, search for Wowei among them and cannot help speculating how big, magnificent, and precious Chairman Mao's Wowei would be, because in their eyes, their greatest leader enjoys the most fortunate, satisfying, and fascinating life in the world. This experience gives the narrator a cynical, even nihilistic mood for days, casting his measuring gaze at every living person as walking Woweis, the sizes of which show their worldly status, happiness, and success. This exemplifies the use of magic realism in this novel in the way it represents the cultural psyche of the people of Maqiao and, further, the psychological reality and cultural imagination of the Chinese people during Mao's era.

BIBLIOGRAPHY

Han Shaogong. *A Dictionary of Maqiao*. Translated by Julia Kovell. New York: Columbia University Press, 2003.

Lee, Vivian. "Cultural Lexicology: *Maqiao Dictionary* by Han Shaogong." *Modern Chinese Literature and Culture* 14, no. 1. (Spring 2002). 145–177.

Leenhouts, Mark. "Is it a Dictionary or a Novel? On Playfulness in Han Shaogong's *Dictionary of Maqiao*." In *The Chinese at Play: Festivals, Games and Leisure,* edited by Bonnie McDougall and Anders Hansson. London: Kegan Paul, 2002. 168–185.

"Nanfan, Maqiao Cidian: Changkai yu Qiujin." (*A Dictionary of Maqiao*: Openness and Boundness.) *Dangdai Zuojia Pinglun* (*Contemporary Literary Review*) 5 (October 1996). 4–10.

Zhou Zhengbao. "Maqiao Cidian de Yiyi." (The Significance of *A Dictionary of Maqiao*) *Dangdai Zuojia Pinglun* (*Contemporary Literary Review*) 1 (February 1997) 4–10.

Tu Xianfeng

DICTIONARY OF THE KHAZARS (HAZARSKI REČNIK) MILORAD PAVIĆ (1984)

Dictionary of the Khazars is the first novel and first international success of the contemporary Serbian writer MILORAD PAVIĆ (1929–). A resident of Belgrade, Pavić gained an international reputation with his highly imaginative fiction. Pavić's novels break from traditional notions of the novel by means of an open-ended structure that allows for an unprecedented degree of reader participation. An enthusiastic admirer of magic realism, Pavić renders his stories through the characteristic entwining of the mythic and the historical. Demonstrating the infinite possibilities of instantiation in the postmodern narrative, Pavić's novels are classified as *hypertexts*. These works use gimmicks and generative devices to engage the reader in an interactive encounter. Heightened epistemological instability, formal innovation, and brilliant poetic language make Pavić's narratives a fascinating exercise in the limits of artistic representation.

Dictionary of the Khazars is a lexicon-format novel. The work's diverse reading paths converge in a story about the Khazars, the semifictional tribe whose bare appellation is the only historical trace of its nomadic existence in central and eastern Europe from the 7th to the 10th century. Creating a story out of these scant historical data, Pavić imagines a warlike tribe of hunters who inhabit other people's dreams in search of pieces of their primordial ancestry and identity. The parcels of dreams that the Khazars bring back from their oneiric voyages are molded into wholes—dictionaries. The tribe's sudden disappearance from the historical scene is presented as the consequence of an indecipherable dream's interpretation.

In the novel, the Great Khan of the Khazars has a dream that proves nearly impossible to interpret. To shed some light upon the vision, the khan summons representatives of the world's three great religions—a Christian, a Jew, and a Muslim. He asks for their respective elucidations of the dream, promising the conversion of his entire tribe to the religion whose explanation is most convincing. The scholars produce three dictionaries, or versions of the story. This trilogy in effect presents the novel itself: the Red Book (Christian), the Green Book (Islamic), and the Yellow Book (Hebrew). Each "dictionary account" is seasoned by the pseudo-scholarly apparatus and particularities of representation relevant to the respective culture. The three equally credible versions of the story indicate the complex and erratic nature of historical and ontological truth.

This summary barely touches on the surface plot of the *Dictionary of the Khazars,* for the novel always develops through a particularized path of reading, or "dream-hunting," which distinct for each reader. Thus, the very form of this hypertext indicates the extent of the indeterminacy and subjectivity that lie at the novel's core. The book is structured as an alphabetized series of dictionary entries about the people, events, and themes supposedly related to the Khazar polemic. The records include "subjects" as inventive as suicide by mirrors or romance between the living and the dead. The navigation through this fictionalized space may proceed along any conceivable path—cross sections, random choices of entries, from the end or the beginning of the printed text, via a certain book/dictionary (Christian, Islamic, or Jewish), and so forth. The nonlinear navigation generates the novel's outcome, which is always personalized and subjective.

The story merges fact and fiction, fantasy and reality in a manner reminiscent of the work of the Argentine short story writer Jorge Luis Borges. To render his "fictional reality" even more convoluted, Pavić has constructed his novel along gender lines, publishing female and male versions. The variation between the two is slight.

Written in a uniquely seductive language, *Dictionary of the Khazars* is a fine example of Pavić's distinctive blend of prose and poetry. His style is replete with unusual metaphors, unfamiliar imagery, rhythmic patterns, and poetic devices. In addition, the novel's language gains in its poetic power as its overall effect is subject to continuous jumping back and forth between the entries and their culturally differentiated modes of representation. The mastery of language combined with the unpredictability of sequence makes *Dictionary of the Khazars* an engaging text that not only invites but necessitates multiple readings.

The novel's elaborate structure hosts a myriad of myths, folklore and pseudo-folklore legends, incantations, and metaphysical meditations, all rendered in a subtly comic tone. The whole is a repository of quasi-facts and dreams.

The dictionary is an attempt to reconstruct a certain post-Khazar "dictionary of all Khazar's dictionaries" that appeared long after the tribe had vanished. The Khazar polemic was revitalized in the 17th century, Pavić explains in his fictionalized preface, and a special effort is made in the story to collect all dictionary entries in one book.

The text is based on a superimposition of historical gaps, with the narrative essentially disengaged from any historical, epistemological, or ontological reality or core. The sole anchorage of the novel is the reader's play of reading and cowriting. This ludic quality makes *Dictionary of the Khazars* an ebullient text, drawing readers into a world portrayed at the same time as joyous, mesmerizing, and uncanny.

Though written in 1984, Pavić's *Dictionary of the Khazars* has been praised as the first novel of the 21st century and the most powerful contemporary reconstruction of the novel's form. The success of Pavić's refiguration of the genre of the novel is substantiated by the writer's increasing popularity with readers, scholars, and critics.

BIBLIOGRAPHY

Coover, Robert. "He Thinks the Way We Dream" *New York Times Book Review* (20 November 1988).

Hayles, N. Katherine. "Corporeal Anxiety in *Dictionary of the Khazars*: What Books Talk About in the Late Age of Print When They Talk About Losing Their Bodies." *Modern Fiction Studies* 43, no. 3 (1997).

Milojkovic-Djuric, Jelena. "The Poetics of Epiphany: The Literary Oeuvre of Milorad Pavić." *Serbian Studies* 9, nos. 1–2 (1995).

Pavić, Milord. *The Inner Side of the Wind, or The Novel of Hero and Leander.* Translated by Christina Pribichevich-Zoric. New York: Alfred A. Knopf, 1993.

———. *Landscape Painted with Tea.* Translated by Christina Pribichevich-Zoric. New York: Alfred A. Knopf, 1990.

———. *Last Love in Constantinople: A Tarot Novel for Divination.* Translated by Christina Pribichevich-Zoric. Chester Springs, Pa.: Dufour Editions, 1998.

                            Sanja Bahun-Radunovic

DINESEN, ISAK (KAREN BLIXEN, KAREN CHRISTENTZE DINESEN, PIERRE ANDRÉZEL) (1885–1962) *Danish essayist, novelist, short story writer*

Isak Dinesen was the best-known pen name of the Danish author Karen Blixen. A writer primarily of short stories and essays, Dinesen achieved world fame late in her life when she was twice nominated for the Nobel Prize in literature (1954 and 1957). Written both in Danish and English (in many cases translated by Dinesen herself), her fiction had already been available in print outside Denmark since the 1930s, securing for the author an international reputation as one of the most accomplished and seductive storytellers of the 20th century. In an impressive border-crossing gesture, Dinesen's writings straddled not only two languages and authorial names but, equally, two distinct cultural and literary spaces. Yet her acclaimed reception in the United States in the late 1950s and in the 1980s, when her stories were rediscovered and widely read by feminist academics, was not paralleled by a similar immediate acceptance in her native Denmark. The Danish literary establishment was initially critical of her "fanciful" prose before allowing her to become one of the country's most revered literary institutions.

Part of the uneasiness Dinesen's fiction caused at first was the result of her opposition to the principles of social realism and abstract existentialism that were dominant in literary writing in Denmark before and after the end of World War II. Working against the moralizing rhetoric of her contemporary fiction, Dinesen wrote fantastic stories marked by duplicity, paradox, open-endedness, self-consciousness, and narrative complexity. Her fondness for the oral traditions of Europe and Africa enabled her to write stories that read like postmodernist fairy tales and challenged, through their indecisiveness, both the narrative predictability of realism and the inherited belief systems that Dinesen had experienced as stifling and restrictive. Nowhere is this more evident than in her engagement with women's position in society. Influenced substantially by the antiessentialist philosophy of Friedrich Nietzsche, Dinesen went on to rethink such highly loaded ideas as fate, good and evil, or tradition and progress in a manner that ultimately questioned patriarchal definitions of femininity and their immediate, lived effects on women's every day existence.

Her authorial positions are already well in place in *Seven Gothic Tales,* her first volume of stories, published in 1934. Set in a vanishing world of aristocratic valor, these are fantastic tales marked by a taste for the mysterious, the supernatural, and the unexplained. The book was repeatedly attacked as decadent by reviewers at the time of publication and by later critics, primarily for its snobbish class politics. Its perceived nostalgia for bygone ages was held to valorize the elitist values of a disappearing Danish aristocracy at the expense of more socially egalitarian scripts. Dinesen's defense of an aristocratic mode of living, though idiosyncratic in its conception, is hard to refute and can be partly traced in her life experiences.

Born in Rungsted in 1885 into an upper-middle-class family, Karen Christentze Dinesen lived her childhood torn between the two branches of her family: the Westenholzes, a maternal, bourgeois family that consisted of levelheaded, hard-working, affluent traders; and the Dinesens, the paternal side, aristocratic through its relationship with the country's nobility, frivolous and adventurous. Following her father's suicide in 1895, young Karen Dinesen transmuted her obsession with her idealist father into a love of aristocratic living, which she associated with freedom of movement, resistance to convention, and risk-taking. Strongly influenced by Nietzsche's thinking on the affirmative power of the "overman" (*der Übermensch*), Dinesen's class philosophy redefined nobility in a way that transcended conventional class divisions (since it included both upper-class and working-class "yes-sayers") to emphasize the transformative potential of saying "yes" to the dangers of the unknown and the firm rejection of the stability underwriting convention. This was a class politics especially tailored to empower Dinesen to question the stifling gender regulation that she was subjected to as a young woman in the prudish environment of her bourgeois family.

It is important, however, to see the oppositional force written into Dinesen's class politics as existing along with her insistence to maintain the privileges following from her titled position. It is well known that she never gave up the title of baroness, which she acquired through her marriage to Baron Bror von Blixen-Finecke, a distant cousin belonging to the Swedish aristocracy, in 1913. In the same year, she migrated with her husband to Kenya, where she ran a coffee farm for the next 19 years (1913–31). Her memoirs *OUT OF AFRICA* (1938) and *Shadows on the Grass* (1961), together with *Letters from Africa, 1914–1931* (published posthumously in 1981), record her life in colonial East Africa, dwelling more on her attachment to the land and its people and less on hard facts such as her divorce from Bror Blixen, the syphilis she contracted from her husband, and her love affair with the big-game hunter Denys Finch Hatton (romantically immortalized in Sydney Pollack's 1985 film).

In Dinesen's African writings, Africa is constructed as a space of freedom from social and gender convention. The author is shown to overcome difficulties, to educate, to cure, to judge, and to guide the people living on her farm in ways that highlight the unprecedented power she acquired as a woman but which at once obscure what made this empowering experience possible—namely, the privileges conferred on her by her race, family money, and aristocratic title.

In 1931, after the financial collapse of her farm that led to its liquidation, Dinesen returned to Denmark, where she launched a new career as a writer. She published widely in magazines at home and in the United States, lectured, read her work in live performances or on the radio, and became the mentor of a new generation of Danish writers who clustered around her. Despite the hardships of World War II, her difficult financial position, and deteriorating health, she published *Winter's Tales* in 1942, the most Danish of all her books as most of the stories are set in Denmark. She went on to write two of her most enduring stories in the 1950s: "Babette's Feast" (*Anecdotes of Destiny*, 1958) and "The Blank Page" (*Last Tales,* 1957). "Babette's Feast" is as much a story about Babette's culinary skills as it is a critique of the Protestant rejection of flesh and an exercise in duplicitous, ironic writing. "The Blank Page" reworks fairy-tale motifs to rethink women's socially prescribed fates and their power to change them. By all accounts, both stories are primarily about art and writing, their power to question the given and to create the new.

In an attempt to entertain herself during the bleak years of the war, Dinesen wrote her only novel, *The Angelic Avengers* (1944), which she considered too frivolous and light to acknowledge and so published it under the pen name of Pierre Andrézel. *Carnival: Entertainments and Posthumous Tales* (1977) and her novella *Ehrengard* (1963) were published posthumously, as were the essays included in *On Modern Marriage and Other Observations* (1987) and *Daguerre-otypes and Other Essays* (1979). Isak Dinesen lived in Rungstendlund for the remainder of her life; she died there in 1962.

BIBLIOGRAPHY

Hansen, Frantz Leander. *The Aristocratic Universe of Karen Blixen.* Translated by Gaye Kynoch. Brighton, Eng.: Sussex Academic Press, 2003.

Thurman, Judith. *The Life of a Storyteller.* New York: St. Martin's Press, 1982.

Woods, Gurli A. *Isak Dinesen and Narrativity: Reassessments for the 1990s.* Ottawa: Carleton University Press, 1994.

Effie Yiannopoulou

DING LING (JIANG BINGZHI) (1904–1986) *Chinese novelist*

Ding Ling, best known for her novel *The Sun Shines over the Sanggan River* (1998) and a collection of short stories, *Miss Sophie's Diary* (1927), is one of China's most famous female authors. Ding Ling's earlier work in the short story genre, initially praised for its exploration of female characters, was later criticized for its focus on bourgeois concerns. Her career alternately catapulted her to the top of the communist intellectual ladder and plummeted her to the depths in communist prisons and reform camps.

Ding Ling was born Jiang Bingzhi to a wealthy family in China's Hunan province. In her incomplete novel entitled *Mother,* she describes the suffering and courage of a woman who had to reinvent her life (including "letting out" her bound feet) after her husband died, leaving the family in debt. Ding Ling began her political activism at age 13, demonstrating for equal rights for women at the Hunan Provincial Assembly. After breaking off an arranged marriage, she wrote a denunciation of her uncle and the class to which he belonged. She traveled to Shanghai to live on her own and eventually continued on to Beijing, hoping to enroll at the university there. Moving frequently, she focused her education on Western writers and later came under the influence of Marxist literary theorist Qu Qiubai at Shanghai University.

Ding Ling participated in the May Fourth Movement of 1919, a cultural and intellectual turning point in China staged by students protesting the terms of the Treaty of Versailles, among other things, and working to overturn China's ancient imperial regime. The Western world became the touchstone of the May Fourth writers as they felt their way to a democracy. Western authors and educational theories were at the center of their writings. Ding Ling's early works as part of this movement focused on the concerns of the modern woman, including the shocking attention paid to female sexuality. They also borrow heavily from her readings of Western authors: The main character in several of her first short stories, for example, is based on Flaubert's Emma.

Ding Ling's early works focused on love and revolution and are seen as incipient Chinese feminism. In 1927 she published her story "Meng Ke," based on her failed attempt in the film industry. She went on to publish "The Diary of Miss Sophie" that same year. This story of a young woman and her sexual fantasies was to have long-ranging consequences for Ding Ling. In later years she was often identified with the narrator, and the story was used by her critics to attack her morals even though her later work de-emphasized the feminine and sexuality and instead emphasized Communist Party ideology.

In 1930 Ding Ling's husband, Hu Yepin, applied for membership in the Communist Party; two months later he was imprisoned and executed by the Kuomintang police, leaving Ding Ling with a two-month-old child. More committed than ever to the communist cause, she returned to Shanghai and was appointed editor of the League of Left-Wing Writers' periodical, *Beidou*. In it appeared her long serialized story "Flood," which depicts the 1931 floods that inspired the peasants to widespread rebellion. *Beidou* was shut down in 1932, and Ding Ling was imprisoned in 1933; rumors circulated about her presumed execution. In 1936 she escaped and arrived in the Shaanxi province, the headquarters of the Communist Party. There she was received by Mao Zedong as a hero, winning her important and influential posts.

In 1941 Ding Ling's critical article "Thoughts on March 8," about the gender inequalities in Yanan, prompted Mao's "Talks at the Yanan Forum on Art and Literature," a set of "rules" governing the purpose and use of literature under Communist rule. After this time, the Communist Party governed all aspects of art and literature, imposing narrow and severely constrained strictures on writers and punishing those who did not adhere to party guidelines. Ding Ling was among those punished in the frequent purges for her failings as an author for the Communist Party. Initially this took the form of brief periods of disfavor during which she had to publicly renounce her bourgeois ways and relinquish some of her positions.

In 1946 Ding Ling took part in a land reform movement in the southern Chahar province. While there, she conceived of the land reform novel entitled *The Sun Rises over the Sanggan River;* published in 1948, it received the Stalin prize in 1951. The novel depicts the events that unfold in the small village of Nuanshui as land reform officials arrive to redistribute land belonging to petty landlords and to indoctrinate the peasants in the official party ideology. In a 1979 interview, Ding Ling told a reporter that she was at work on a sequel to *Sanggan River, Zai Yanham de Rizili* (During the coldest days).

Ding Ling inexplicably fell out of favor with the Communist Party in 1958, amid accusations ranging from her arrogance as an author to her refusal to use literature for political purposes only. After a series of attacks, some of them brutally physical, she was expelled from the Communist Party and sent to do labor reform for 12 years. A series of imprisonments followed, lasting almost 20 years, until she was officially rehabilitated in 1979. She was finally released to rejoin her husband, whom she had married in 1942. Her works were no longer banned after her release; however, most of what she wrote for 20 years was lost forever.

Ding Ling's life, more than her writings, ensures her continued reputation. She wrote continuously, in many genres, for five decades, yet she is best known for her early fiction. Her career was spent trying to reconcile her personal views about literature and feminism with communist ideology, at times more successfully than others.

BIBLIOGRAPHY

Alber, Charles J. *Embracing the Lie: Ding Ling and the Politics of Literature in the People's Republic of China.* Westport, Conn.: Praeger Publishers, 2004.

Barlow, Tani E. "Feminism and Literary Technique in Ding Ling's Early Short Stories." In *Women Writers of 20-Century China,* edited by A. Palandri, 63–110. Eugene, Oreg.: Asian Studies Publications, University of Oregon, 1982.

Feuerwerker, Yi-tsi Mei. *Ding Ling's Fiction: Ideology and Narrative in Modern Chinese Literature*. Cambridge, Mass.: Harvard University Press, 1982.

———. "Ding Ling's 'When I Was in Sha Chuan (Cloud Village).'" *Signs, Journal of Women in Culture and Society* 2, no. 1 (1976): 255–279.

———. "In Quest of the Writer Ding Ling." *Feminist Studies* 10, no. 1 (Spring 1984): 65–83.

Patricia Kennedy Bostian

DISCIPLE, THE (LE DISCIPLE) PAUL BOURGET (1889)

The Disciple, one of PAUL BOURGET's (1852–1935) greatest literary achievements and his most famous novel, marked a change in the author's literary development. Prior to this work, his fiction consisted of highly dramatic tales set in high society; with *The Disciple,* Bourget began the transition into the moralistic tone that would mark his later oeuvre. The novel tells the tale of Adrien Sixte, a positivist philosopher living a rigidly ordered life in his Parisian apartment, with little or no variation in his daily routine. Those few people known to him include his housekeeper and the concierge of his apartment building. This regularity is upset one day when Sixte receives a letter requesting his appearance at an inquest: A young man, Robert Greslou, has been accused of murder.

Sixte remembers Greslou as a student, an exceptionally bright young man who had sought out his input as a teacher and mentor. Beyond two brief meetings at his residence, Sixte had no interaction with Greslou and is thus surprised to be called by the inquest. Before Sixte heads to the police station to assure the authorities that he can be of no use to the case, Greslou's mother arrives at his home, imploring him to help her son and offering him a monograph written by Robert.

The vast bulk of the novel is devoted to this tome, with Sixte's story serving merely as a frame for Greslou's memoirs, his autobiographical justification for the actions of his previous years. One of these actions is the incident that left a young woman dead; it is for her death that Greslou stands accused. His monograph details his obsessive adherence to philosophical treatises, Sixte's foremost among them. Greslou devoted his life to the sort of life he imagined Sixte would lead: hermitic, orderly, defined by thought over action and the mental life over the physical or sensual life. In this sense, Greslou's life functions as a test of Sixte's theories, his life's work.

After failing to gain acceptance at the university, Greslou takes a position as instructor to the children of aristocrat M. de Jussat. The elder son of the family, André, is a physical, strong sort, a direct opposite to the bookish, physically feeble Greslou. Second oldest is a daughter, Charlotte, simple and pretty, and the youngest boy is to become Greslou's pupil. The young tutor decides, as a matter of philosophical experimentation, to try and compel the daughter to love him. In the meantime, he develops feelings for her, though the overwrought self-analysis of his monograph makes it difficult to discern his true objectives or feelings from his "experimental" intentions.

Greslou eventually declares his love to Charlotte on a walk. Soon after her rejection of his love, she leaves for Paris and agrees to marry a friend of her brother's, a blow to Greslou. Upon her return, he again declares his love and suggests that he would commit suicide if she does not intervene. She does intervene, returning his love under the condition that he agree to a suicide pact, which he does. At the crucial moment, Greslou reneges, while she goes through with the plan. In his monograph, he argues that he bears no accountability for her death since she was responsible for the self-poisoning. Before her death, Charlotte had written to her older brother, and he remains the only person other than Greslou and Sixte aware of the truth: that she in fact killed herself. Charlotte's brother burns the letter but later relates to the court what he knows. Greslou is freed based on this evidence; the freedom is short-lived, as upon his release Charlotte's brother shoots Robert Greslou, killing him.

Faced with this confession and the needless deaths of two young people, Sixte realizes that it is an indictment of his views, his philosophy. The novel ends with Sixte, professed atheist, recalling lines from the only prayer he knows, the "Our Father," his transformation sealing the moral imperative of the story and offering critics ammunition for the characterization that *The Disciple* is more parable than novel.

BIBLIOGRAPHY

Austin, Lloyd James. *Paul Bourget, sa vie et son oeuvre jusqu'en 1889*. Paris: E. Droz, 1940.

Autin, Albert. *Le disciple de Paul Bourget*. Paris: Société française, 1930.

Mansuy, Michel. *Un moderne: Paul Bourget de l'enfance au discipline*. Paris: Les Belles Lettres, 1960.

Singer, Armand È. *Paul Bourget*. Boston: Twayne Publishers, 1976.

Rebecca N. Mitchell

DIVIDED HEAVEN (DER GETEILTE HIMMEL) Christa Wolf (1963)

Divided Heaven, the second novel by German author Christa Wolf (1929–) became an immediate best seller and a critical success upon publication: The initial 160,000 copies and 10 editions sold out within a few months. *Divided Heaven* chronicles Rita Seidel's reflections on her 'life when her boyfriend, Manfred Herrfurth, escapes from East to West Germany; after he leaves, Rita experiences a physical and mental breakdown. The novel's time span runs from 1959 to 1961 and ends with the erection of the Berlin Wall on August 13, 1961. The book's settings move from Rita's home village to Halle and West Berlin, and it includes autobiographical elements from Christa Wolf's life. *Divided Heaven* moves from the present (1961) to the past (1959) when Rita first meets Manfred, and then the book chronologically tells of the events that lead to her accident and hospital stay. In the course of the novel, she develops from a shy, uncertain woman to an independent, self-confident one.

The novel opens as Rita awakes from unconsciousness in a hospital and a doctor wonders what led to her mental breakdown. Rita them reflects on the events of the previous two years. As the story goes back two years, she meets Manfred Herrfurth, a chemist, at a dance in her village, and for her it is love at first sight. Rita decides to become a teacher and follow Manfred to Halle, where she moves in with his family. She must complete a practicum in a factory as part of her studies and volunteers to work at an all-male railroad car factory. During the novel, Rita moves between the worlds of workers at the factory and intellectuals as she studies and lives with the Herrfurths.

In fact, the novel's primary setting is the factory, where Rolf Meternagel, an older worker, becomes her mentor. At one time Meternagel had a prominent job,

but he was demoted after a series of dubious circumstances. The event that cost Meternagel his position turns out not to be his doing, and his reputation is later restored. Unfortunately, his health is now irreparably damaged. While Rita works at the factory, there is a crisis when not enough parts are delivered and production must be shut down. This crisis in the factory is reflective of the economic crisis then being experienced in the eastern part of Germany. Despite the human and economic problems, Rita becomes committed to socialism as she works in the factory.

In contrast, Manfred becomes frustrated in his work, and when an improved machine he has developed is rejected by company bureaucrats, he leaves for the West. Throughout the novel, mention is made of characters that have fled for the West. Although Rita follows him, she returns to the East and dedicates herself to socialism; she has confidence in the system, whereas Manfred does not. It is thus not only the two Germanys and the Berlin Wall that rip the couple apart, but also their different ideologies. The separation from Manfred precipitates a suicide attempt, which Wolf depicts as an accident. By doing this, the author assured that the East German government would accept the novel since it frowned on suicide.

The East German government followed the Soviet Union's model of socialist realism, which called for literature that reflected everyday human life. Novels or stories had to have positive heroes who set an example for everyone and coped well with life. *Divided Heaven* is an outgrowth of the Bitterfelder Weg, in which the East German government called for intellectuals and workers to work together to promote socialism. The Bitterfelder Weg was a cultural program created in 1959 by the Socialist Unity Party, which urged workers to write their own stories in writing circles. This, however, did not pan out, and instead writers worked on literature about workers and their problems. Christa Wolf's own life experiences make their way into *Divided Heaven* since Wolf worked in a railroad car factory herself, worked in a clerical office and had an extended stay at a hospital.

In *Divided Heaven,* Wolf examines the "German question" about the separation and distancing of Germany's two sections. The West was prosperous while the East went through economic difficulties, which led to skilled workers leaving the East for the West. This in turn led the East German government to build the Berlin Wall. While *Divided Heaven* does deal with the problems of the two Germanys growing apart, universal themes such as love, independence, finding one's purpose in life, and alienation abound in the work. While the novel speaks about divisions, Rita's accident is a result of the strain of the divisions and is depicted as an accident. At the time of Rita's accident, two railway cars are coming at her from two directions and she "falls" between two colliding cars. Rita's stay in hospital and subsequent therapy help her find her way to a new positive beginning in the East.

Divided Heaven was awarded the Heinrich Mann Prize and was made into a film for which Christa Wolf wrote the script.

BIBLIOGRAPHY

Baumer, Franz. *Christa Wolf*. Berlin: Colloquium, 1988.

Böthig, Peter. *Christa Wolf: Eine Biographie in Bildern und Texten*. Munich: Luchterhand, 2004.

Finney, Gail. *Christa Wolf*. New York: Twayne Publishers, 1999.

Resch, Margit. *Understanding Christia Wolf: Returning Home to a Foreign Land*. Columbia: University of South Carolina Press, 1977.

Karen Bell

DÖBLIN, ALFRED (1878–1957) *German essayist, novelist*

German novelist and essayist Alfred Döblin remains best known for his novel BERLIN ALEXANDERPLATZ (1929). He is considered one of the pioneers of the expressionist movement in German literature. In "The Crisis of the Novel," Walter Benjamin in his *Selected Writings* comments: "The flood of biographical and historical novels will cease to astonish him [Döblin]. Döblin, far from resigning himself to this crisis, hurries on ahead of it and makes its cause his own." Döblin's narrative response to what Benjamin considered the early 20th century's crisis of storytelling led him to develop a montage style that achieves a new intensity of expression and makes Döblin one of the most influential writers in German modernist literature.

Döblin was born in Stettin, Germany, on August 10, 1878. He was the son of a Jewish merchant, Max Döblin, who went to the United States and left behind his impoverished family. His mother was Sophie Freudenheim. Alfred Döblin was educated at the Gymnasium, Stettin. In 1898 the family moved to Berlin, where Döblin studied medicine at Berlin University, specializing in neurology and psychiatry. He completed his studies at Freiburg University, receiving a medical degree in 1905. During his student years, Döblin developed an interest in the philosophies of Immanuel Kant, Arthur Schopenhauer, and Friedrich Nietzsche. An early novel, *The Black Curtain* (*Der Schwarze Vorhang*), written between 1902 and 1903 and, like much of his early writing, is unpublished, was already beginning to reflect expressionist imagery and to show a clear indebtedness to Sigmund Freud's theories of sexuality. In 1911 Döblin began practicing medicine in a psychiatric practice in Berlin. During World War I he volunteered to serve on the front as a military physician.

In 1912 Döblin married medical student Erna Reiss, with whom he had four sons. Through his contributions to the expressionist magazine *Der Sturm* (*The Storm*), Döblin became known as a pioneer of the expressionist movement. Many of the pieces for *Der Sturm* were published in the collection *The Murder of a Buttercup* (*Die Ermordung einer Butterblume*, 1913). In 1915 Döblin gained fame with his novel *The Three Leaps of Wang-lun* (*Die drei Sprünge des Wang-lun*), which problematizes a political upheaval in 18th-century China; the book earned him the Fontane and Kleist Prizes. The novels *Wadzek's Battle with the Steam Turbine* (*Wadzeks Kampf mit der Dampfturbine,* 1918) and *Wallenstein* (1920) bolster Döblin's reputation as one of the leading figures in the expressionist movement.

Döblin used the pseudonym Linke Poot for a number of journalistic pieces and essays that expressed his critical opinion of the Weimar Republic. From 1921 to 1930 he was affiliated with the Social Democratic Party. He was a theater reviewer for *Prager Tageblatt* from 1921 to 1924, and a member of the cultural discussion circle Group 1925 together with Bertolt Brecht. In 1928 he became a member of the Prussian Academy of Arts. The novel *Berlin Alexanderplatz* appeared in 1929 and made Döblin a writer of international renown. In this work the author develops an original and, for the expressionist movement, a highly influential montage style: In a variety of narrative registers he incorporates printed matter (ads and market reports), public dialogue (political speech, weather reports), and bits of common and familiar songs. Through this montage technique, already common in film, *Berlin Alexanderplatz* grasps the modern metropolis's totality.

In February 1933, the day after the German parliament was set on fire, Döblin—a left-wing Jewish intellectual opposed to the National Socialism Party and despised as a representative of the so-called *asphaltliteratur* (asphalt literature)—left Berlin. He chose exile along with other famous writers such as Brecht, Heinrich Heine, THOMAS MANN, and Lion Feuchtwanger. He fled with his wife and four children to Switzerland and then to Paris, where he worked on antifascist propaganda for the Ministry of Information. His books were burned on May 10, 1933, in the Nazi book-burning campaign. In 1940, when the German military occupied Paris, he narrowly escaped the Nazis through the much-used route from southern France to Spain and Portugal to the United States. He lived in New York, Los Angeles, and Hollywood, where he worked as a scriptwriter for Metro Goldwyn Mayer (1940–41).

The difficulties of exile and emigration are movingly explored in the novel *Babylonian Wandering* (*Babylonische Wanderung,* 1938). In exile he also worked on the South American trilogy *The Journey to the Country without Death* (*Die Fahrt ins Land ohne Tod,* 1937), *The Blue Tiger* (*Der blaue Tiger,* 1938), and *The New Rainforest* (*Der neue Urwald,* 1948). These novels portray the clash between allegedly civilized Christian Europeans and the "savage" Inca empire and other native cultures. In 1941 Döblin converted to Roman Catholicism, a personal time on which he reflects in his essays "The Immortal Man" ("Der unsterbliche Mensch," 1946) and "Our Worry—The Man ("Unsere Sorge-der Mensch," 1948). By 1937 Döblin had started his multivolume novel *November 1918,* on which he worked throughout his years in exile, finally completing it in 1950. This work attempts a fictionalized but historically accurate account of Germany's failed 1918–19 revolution.

After World War II, Döblin returned to Germany and directed cultural affairs for the French military government. He also published the magazine *Das Gold-ene Tor* (*The Golden Gate*) from 1946 to 1951. In 1949 he was a cofounder and vice president of the literary section of the Academy of Science and Literature in Mainz. Disillusioned with the political development in postwar West Germany, Döblin moved to Paris—he had become a French citizen in 1936—where he lived from 1953 to 1956. After spending time in several spas in the Black Forest due to his poor health, he finally entered a sanatorium in Emmendingen, near Freiburg, where he died on June 28, 1957. His last novel, *Hamlet* (1956), represents an expression of his hope for a new Europe and reflects the author's Catholic faith. The work, written between 1945 and 1946, first appeared in East Germany in 1956 and in the Federal Republic of Germany in 1957. Today Döblin's huge oeuvre is part of the academic canon around the world. *Berlin Alexanderplatz,* his most famous work, was adapted cinematically in 1933 with Heinrich George in the leading role. Rainer Werner Fassbinder's 1980 version for television added to the novel's ongoing resonance.

BIBLIOGRAPHY

Barta, Peter I. *Bely, Joyce, and Döblin: Peripatetics in the City Novel.* Gainesville: University Press of Florida, 1996.

Bekes, Peter. *Alfred Döblin Berlin Alexanderplatz: Interpretation.* Munich: Oldenbourg, 1995.

Jelavich, Peter. *Berlin Alexanderplatz: Radio, Film, and the Death of Weimar Culture.* Berkeley: University of California Press, 2006.

Sander, Gabriele. *Alfred Döblin, Berlin Alexanderplatz.* Stuttgart: P. Reclam, 1998.

Schoonover, Henrietta S. *The Humorous and Grotesque Elements in Döblin's* Berlin Alexanderplatz. Berne and Las Vegas: Peter Lang, 1977.

Martin Blumenthal-Barby

DOCTOR FAUSTUS (DOKTOR FAUSTUS) THOMAS MANN (1947)

The creative portrayal of Germany's descent into evil comes to life in the pages of the acclaimed postwar novel by THOMAS MANN (1875–1955), *Doktor Faustus: Das Leben des Deutschen Tonsetzers Adrian Leverkühn, erzählt von einem Freunde,* translated as *Doctor Faustus: The Life of the German Composer, Adrian Leverkühn, as Told by a Friend.* This complex novel has been called many things by biographers, critics, and even Mann himself.

It has been deemed the most important work of Mann's career and the mark of his last treatise on German culture and its intellectual tradition. *Doktor Faustus* is a story that uniquely captures Germany's downfall following the adoption of national socialism, while allowing Mann as a writer to come full circle with his own personal development through the exploration of an artistically ambitious young man's upbringing in a traditional German environment. Readers are reminded of other Mann characters such as Hanno Buddenbrooks and Tonio Kröger, as the author wrestles again with themes from novels past; however, Mann approaches the character Doktor Faustus with a completely different intellectual framework.

Employing the greatest theme contributed by Germany to world literature, Mann constructs a retelling of the Middle Ages story of Faust. This "montage" technique allows Mann to present Adrian Leverkühn as a new Faust who receives the opportunity to secure his artistic desires by sealing a pact with the devil. However, Leverkühn is more than an embodiment of Goethe's Faust: He is also a representation of Nietzsche, whose stages in life Leverkühn mirrors; he is Luther and Beethoven and Schönberg and other musicians. In essence, the life of Leverkühn embodies the entirety of German cultural development.

Mann decides for the first time to change his narrative perspective and write the novel using a first-person narrator. Serenus Zeitblom, Ph.D., is a professor of literature and friend to main character Adrian Leverkühn. Representing the educated German, Zeitblom holds a clear intellectual perspective of the historical and political events that led Germany into the approaching catastrophes of National Socialism and another world war, but he raises no voice and takes no action against these developments; this is a point Mann makes against German intellectuals in his writings throughout the painful period of European fascism. Through Zeitblom, the reader encounters Adrian Leverkühn, a man who believes he was born too late, losing the possibility of creating true works of original art, a man driven to produce art (music) that has never existed before. Mann uses Leverkühn as the prototype of the German character unafraid of unleashing self-destructive forces to attain his goal, determined to go his own way without regard for the damage that may befall him or others from the choices he makes.

This choice of point of view, however, makes reading *Doktor Faustus* much more challenging. Zeitblom becomes to the reader an intimate, a confidant of sorts on whom the reader must rely in order to have Leverkühn's story fully revealed. Zeitblom is not a character with such charisma as to transfix the reader with pleasure. Instead, at times the reader finds Zeitblom to be the object of empathy, while at other times he draws only a mild or lukewarm reception and occasionally strikes the reader with a cold emptiness. His passionate histories of Ines and Clarissa Rodde build reader trust, while his too frequent references to his "Erschütterung" (shock or agitation) over Leverkühn's "humanly" behavior builds reader suspicion. Overshadowing all, the reader learns that Leverkühn is not the Leverkühn depicted by an omniscient narrator, but a different character, one that Mann seems to have generated, in part, to establish his structure of ambiguities.

Zeitblom, in fact, becomes a masterful vehicle of ambiguity for Mann through his consistent references to music that does not exist. Zeitblom conveys to the reader a music that expresses "unspokenness," a music that speaks without committing itself to any meaning. When Zeitblom tells the reader that a certain feature of the music is *unverkennbar* (unmistakable), the reader takes pause. Mann leaves the reader with the risky tool of choice and gives the freedom to choose whether to doubt or to believe. Leverkühn's music exists for the reader only in this form, but it is a form that stresses the unity between Zeitblom and Leverkühn, who make up Mann's two halves of one self, whose connectedness is underscored by the *du* (you) Leverkühn uses to address not only himself but also Zeitblom. To have used a real composer would have removed the hostile collusion Mann masterfully creates between narrator and subject. Instead, Mann is able, through Zeitblom, to sum up his own lifelong obsession with the description of music, to confront his own critical language with that of true musicians, and to allow the two languages (music and words) to criticize and complement each other.

In broad terms, Mann places considerable demands on his readers. *Doktor Faustus* becomes a tapestry of symbolic and literal meanings, of myth, realism, allegory, allusion, and ironic ambiguity. Mann utilizes parallels that are rarely direct equations. In addition, at times he consciously undermines the oppositions at the core of his complex thematic structure. This approach allows him to create a hero involved in trends from which he remains detached and transforms that tension into a fundamental paradox revealing a character that stands for the forces of fascism and yet is distinct from those forces. Through the character of Doktor Faustus—Zeitblom—Mann attempts to grasp the dialectics of subjectivity and objectivity, of compulsion and freedom, and the connections between politics and art, the bonds of collective experience, and individual psychological drive—all for the purpose of explaining an apocalypse. A skillfully orchestrated display of the dynamic command of language and of literary techniques comprising Mann's artistry makes *Doktor Faustus* one of the great 20th-century novels.

BIBLIOGRAPHY

Brennan, Joseph Gerard. *Thomas Mann's World.* New York: Russell & Russell, 1962.

Bruford, Walter Horace. *The German Tradition of Self-Cultivation: Bildung from Humboldt to Thomas Mann.* New York: Cambridge University Press, 1975.

Burgin, Hans. *Thomas Mann, a Chronicle of His Life.* Mobile: University of Alabama Press, 1969.

Hatfield, Henry Caraway. *Thomas Mann: A Collection of Critical Essays.* Englewood Cliffs, N.J.: Prentice-Hall, 1964.

Heilbut, Anthony. *Thomas Mann: Eros and Literature.* Riverside: University of California Press, 1997.

Heller, Erich. *The Ironic German, a Study of Thomas Mann.* London: Secker & Warburg, 1958.

———. *Thomas Mann, the Ironic German: A Study.* Mamaroneck, N.Y.: P.P. Appel, 1973.

Kahn, Robert L. *Studies in German Literature.* Houston: Rice University, 1964.

Masereel, Frans. *Mein Stundenbuch, 165 Holzschnitte Von Frans Masereel. Einleitung von Thomas Mann.* Munich: K. Wolff, 1926.

Mueller, William Randolph. *Celebration of Life: Studies in Modern Fiction.* New York: Sheed & Ward, 1972.

Reed, Terence. *Thomas Mann: The Uses of Tradition.* Oxford: Clarendon Press, 1974.

Robertson, Ritchie. *The Cambridge Companion to Thomas Mann.* Cambridge: Cambridge University Press, 2002.

Stock, Irvin. *Ironic Out of Love: The Novels of Thomas Mann.* Jefferson, N.C.: McFarland, 1994.

Christine Marie Hilger

DOCTOR'S WIFE, THE (HANAOKA SEISHŪ NO TSUMA) ARIYOSHI SAWAKO (1966)

The Doctor's Wife by ARIYOSHI SAWAKO (1931–86) gives a fictional account of the life of Hanaoka Seishū, who lived from 1760 to 1835 and performed the first known operation under anesthesia in 1805, 37 years before the use of ether in the United States and 42 years before the use of chloroform in England. The novel reveals the plight of women in a traditional Japanese household.

Since she was eight years old, Kae has admired the beautiful and clever Otsugi. She is thrilled when Otsugi visits her father to ask that Kae marry her son, Seishū, who is attending medical school at the time. After Kae's father rebuffs the request by saying that his daughter will be 24 when Seishū has completed medical school and thus will too old to marry, Otsugi arranges for the marriage to take place with the groom in absentia.

Kae adjusts to her life "with the family for which she had been longing." After her sisters-in-law, who treat her with kindness, do their jobs around the house, they spend the rest of the day weaving cloth at looms. When Kae learns that the cloth is sold for money which Otsugi saves and sends to Seishū in Kyoto, she joins Okatsu and Koriku at the weaving. Her love for her husband, whom she has never seen, grows, and she continues to revere her mother-in-law. When Seishū returns home, however, Kae begins to feel left out. She becomes jealous of Otsugi, and "the beautiful intimacy between the two—the bride and the mother-in-law who had sought her—terminated upon the arrival of the loved one they had to share."

Seishū begins experimenting with stray animals in an attempt to find a substance that will work as an anesthetic for surgery. He directs his energy and attention to his scientific research, and the household revolves around him and his medical pursuits. When he makes his discovery, he faces his next challenge: determining the proper dosage for a human being. Both mother and wife insist that he use them as subjects. Finally Seishū agrees to experiment on both. He administers an anesthetic on his mother but uses a weakened form and omits the poisonous part of the substance. Later, with Kae's urging, he uses a stronger dosage on his wife that includes the poison. Kae has headaches and trouble with her eyes after the first experiment and loses her eyesight completely after the second experiment. Seishū, absorbed in his medical interests, ignores the sacrifices of the women in his life who make his success possible—his two sisters as well as his mother and wife—and fails to recognize the rivalry and conflict between Otsugi and Kae as they compete for his affection.

Each of the two women, Otsugi and Kae, "risked her life to help the doctor achieve his dreams," announces Shimomura Ryoan, Seishū's younger brother, who is also a doctor. After their deaths, the two women and Seishū are buried in a row; Seishū's tombstone is larger than those of his mother and his wife. In the final sentence of the novel, Ariyoshi shows the fate of the two women—and her view of the prevailing condition of Japanese women: "If you stand directly in front of Seishū's tomb, the two behind him, those of Kae and Otsugi, are completely obscured."

BIBLIOGRAPHY
Ariyoshi, Sawako. *The Doctor's Wife.* Translated by Wakako Hironaka and Ann Siller Kostant. Tokyo: Kodansha International, 1981.

"Ariyoshi, Sawako." In *Contemporary Authors,* vol. 105. Detroit: Gale Research, 1982.

Schmieder, Rob. "Review of *The Doctor's Wife,* by Sawako Ariyoshi." *Library Journal* 104 (1979): 207.

Charlotte S. Pfeiffer

DOCTOR ZHIVAGO (DOKTOR ZHIVAGO)

Boris Pasternak (1957) The epic story by Russian poet and novelist Boris Pasternak (1890–1960), *Doctor Zhivago* was first published in Milan, Italy, in 1957, after the influential liberal journal *New World (Novy Mir)* had refused to publish the manuscript a year earlier. The editorial board of the Soviet journal justified the rejection by terming the novel a repudiation of the October Revolution of 1917 and describing the protagonist as a paradigm of bourgeois individualism. Equally, foreign critics praised the writer's courage in settling two world forces in opposition: the Western world's principle of individualism against that of Bolshevik collectivism. Nevertheless, Pasternak did not strike an allegiance with either; his belief rested in human personality as stemming from Christianity. Not surprisingly, *Doctor Zhivago* was considered irrelevant for the ideals promoted by Soviet propaganda and Bolshevik cultural standards. However, the novel enjoyed swift fame in the Western world, where readers saluted the honest depiction of the lone intellectual forced to confront a world that cannot be comprehended, and hence one to which a man cannot adapt.

Early critics compared *Doctor Zhivago* to Tolstoy's *War and Peace,* with which, admittedly, the novel has some points of intersection. Like Tolstoy's epic, Pasternak's narrative intermingles public events with family and love scenes, enthralling plot lines with meditations on human nature and history. Yet where Tolstoy succeeds in conveying a multidimensional fresco of human existence, Pasternak suggests a state of mind, communicating an inner experience that is more personal than even his rich poetical oeuvre. In fact, it can be asserted that *Doctor Zhivago* is a creative metafiction, at times where the main character becomes Pasternak's self-representation. Like Pasternak, Zhivago is a son of upper-class intelligentsia, denouncing both the evils of the prerevolutionary Russia and the methods and doctrines of the new Bolshevik regime, with which, after a period of brief enthusiasm, he becomes disenchanted. Exacting with his choice of words, Pasternak grants the name itself, Zhivago, with symbolic meaning. The name derives from the Russian word *zhiv* (alive), hinting at the novel's play on the themes of life, death, resurrection, and damnation that Pasternak engages in his narrative. The novel approaches these themes in the very opening chapter, "Five O'Clock Express": Yury's mother dies and is buried when he is only 10 years old, his father throws himself off the train, and his uncle defines the love of one's neighbor and the idea of free personality and sacrifice as basic attributes of modern man.

Doctor Zhivago spans four decades of modern Russian history, from the revolution of 1905 through World War I, the 1917 October Revolution, the ensuing civil war, the purges of the 1930s, the Nazi invasion of Russia, World War II, and the postwar aftermath. The novel spreads its plot far and wide over urban as well as rural Russia, from Moscow's high society to the faraway Siberian hamlet. The landscape, however, is hardly a realistic depiction of Russia, but more of a creative reflection of the outside world, a realm affectively personalized by Pasternak's poetic pen. The narrative brings together characters from various strata of the Russian society before and after the October Revolution. Yury Andreyevich Zhivago's destiny inexorably ties to that of Lara (Larisa Feodorovna), his great love and her husband, Pavel Pavlovich Antipov, who becomes the revolutionary leader Strelnikov. There are other characters, such as the lawyer Komarovsky, with whom Zhivago has a series of fateful, many times coincidental, encounters.

Zhivago, an upper-class doctor in prerevolutionary Moscow, sympathizes with the masses moving inexorably toward the October Revolution. His profession makes the protagonist a mediator between two worlds starting to clash, the Reds and the Whites. Yury briefly meets Lara when he tends to the wounds of his father's confidant and Lara's "protector," the dubious Komarovsky. Years later, married to Tonya and confronted with the spreading poverty of the revolutionary years, Zhivago, who at first was enthusiastic about the newly installed Bolshevik regime, becomes progressively disappointed and frustrated with the mentality of the "professional-revolutionary," the paradigm promoted by the Boshevik propaganda. Zhivago and his family leave Moscow for the Urals, where he tries to take a neutral position toward the multiple factions who are at war. He meets Lara again and tries to balance his life between his family and his lover until a Red partisan unit, in need of a physician, conscripts him. It is 18 months before Zhivago manages to escape the unit and go back to the Siberian town where he left his family, only to discover they have been dislodged by the civil war and forced to emigrate. Lara, however, is still there, with their daughter, waiting for his return, and at his homecoming they enjoy a brief but memorable time together. The love duet that Lara and Yury live amid a world of chaos and violence does not last long, yet it constitutes one of the most beautiful love intermezzos in Russian literature. Lara is soon saved by Comrade Komarovsky, and Yury returns to Moscow. There he witnesses the profound transformation of the capital's

intelligentsia, who are forced to compromise with the regime, to justify and propagate the ideology of self-enslavement. From here on, Zhivago's life and health quickly deteriorate; he suffers a fatal stroke in a crowded Moscow streetcar in 1929.

The epilogue to *Doctor Zhivago* is provided by Zhivago's friends, Gordon and Dudurov, who recall the events of 1930s and Yezhov's rule of terror. The last time frame of the novel is set a few years after the liberation of Russia from Nazis, and Zhivago's friends are looking over the 25 poems that embody Zhivago's literary heritage. Twenty years after his death, his slender volume of poetry lends sustenance and optimism to his readers and establishes his legacy. The other legacy that Yury Zhivago leaves behind is his daughter with Lara—Tanya, a laundry girl "redeemed" from the bourgeois heritage of her father, a child of the new Russia who emerges from the ashes of two world wars, a civil war, revolutionary upheavals, and several regimes of terror.

BIBLIOGRAPHY

Clowes, Edith W., ed. *Doctor Zhivago: A Critical Companion.* Evanston, Ill.: Northwestern University Press, 1995.

Livingstone, Angela. *Boris Pasternak: Doctor Zhivago.* Cambridge, Mass.: Cambridge University Press, 1989.

Pasternak, Boris Leonidovich. *Doctor Zhivago.* New York: Pantheon Books, 1997.

———. *The Poems of Doctor Zhivago.* Westport, Conn.: Greenwood Publishing, 1977.

Luminita M. Dragulescu

DOG YEARS (HUNDEJAHRE) GÜNTER GRASS (1963)

In *Dog Years,* the German novelist GÜNTER GRASS (1927–) gives his readers a panoramic view of German mentality before, during, and after World War II. The third book of the *Danzig Trilogy,* this work, following *The TIN DRUM* and *Cat and Mouse,* consists of three parts narrated by three different individuals. At the center of the novel is the story of the German shepherd dog that the party leadership of the city of Danzig presents to Hitler on the occasion of his 42nd birthday.

Through the reminiscing of Brauxel (who, the reader learns at the end of the work, is the persona of the novel's Eddi Amsel), the first narration introduces the land and people around the Vistula River during the years 1917–27. It presents the major participants: Eddi Amsel, the son of a Jewish merchant, who constructs scarecrows; and Walter Matern, the miller's son. Through Brauxel's reminiscing, the reader learns that Eddi's father was a well-to-do Jewish merchant who had fully integrated himself into the German community. He attended church, sang in the choir, and even fought and died for Germany in World War I. Given this integration, Brauxel debates with himself whether Alfred Amsel was a Jew and decides the case could be argued either way, "for all origins are what we choose to make of them."

At the age of five, Eddie starts building scarecrows that resemble people in the community. During his first school year, Eddi is often called names and beaten up by the anti-Semitic boys in the community, Walter Matern included. When Walter notices that Eddi has built a scarecrow figure that resembles him, he opts to defend Eddi against the other boys. A close friendship between the two boys develops.

The second portion of the novel, which covers the years 1927 to 1945, is conveyed through love letters that Harry Liebenau writes to his cousin Tulla Pokriefke. Tulla, a pale, pimply girl, is portrayed as conniving, cruel, and vicious. Through her, the reader is introduced to the German shepherd dog Harras, whose offspring, Prinz, becomes Hitler's birthday gift. In this portion of the novel, Grass shows the Jews increasingly persecuted as the Nazi Party gains prominence. One evening Eddi is badly beaten by a group of masked men. The perpetrator who exacts the harshest punishment grinds his teeth like Eddi's friend Walter. After this incident, Eddi leaves town, and Walter is promoted to platoon leader of a group of militia known as Storm Troopers (Strumabteilung, or SA men). War breaks out, and Walter joins the army. Walter and Harry, who is an air force auxiliary member, are transferred to the vicinity of Stutthof concentration camp. They notice a pervasive sickly-sweet odor that never fades. While they try to dismiss the cause of this acrid smell, Tulla forces them to acknowledge it as the burning of human flesh by confronting them with a human skull she has taken from a pile of bones dumped outside the camp. Harry's chronicle concludes with the collapse of the Third Reich and the final military operations, which are described as a hunt for Prinz, who has escaped from Hitler's bomb shelter and is now searching for a new master.

In the third and last section of the novel, spanning the years 1946–56, Prinz makes his way to a prisoner-of-war camp, where he finds Walter, who narrates this final portion. Upon his release, Walter wants to take revenge against all those who tormented him for being a communist sympathizer. He is not able to exact his vengeance on the men themselves, but upon contracting venereal disease, he makes every effort to infect as many of their wives and daughters as possible. In Berlin he meets Brauxel (Eddi), who takes him into the former potash mine. Here, deep in the bowels of the earth, Walter sees that Brauxel has created scarecrows that are now mechanical monstrosities. These monsters, created in the image of humankind, are able to express every emotion, thought, and act of man, including every aspiration and degradation. The tour of the mines ends with Walter watching a newly graduating class of robotic scarecrows offering an oath of allegiance to Brauxel & Co. When the two men prepare to leave, Brauxel ties Prinz to the entrance of the mine to guard it. Walter does not protest this act because he realizes that in Brauxel Prinz has now found his new master.

In his work Günter Gross, Keith Miles notes that in using three different narrators and perspectives, Grass attempts to convey the difficulty one mind has to "assimilate and describe the force, the horror and the complexity the material under review describes." By fragmenting the narration in this manner, Grass ensures that the reality, which the reader is invited to examine, is fractured and contradictory. Dog Years, however, does more than simply address the difficulty of dealing with the past. As scholar Alfred Hanel observes, the main thesis of this work is that Germany has not yet come to terms with its past and thus "has forced feelings of guilt underground."

BIBLIOGRAPHY

Cicora, Mary A. "Music, Myth, and Metaphysics: Wagner Reception in Günter Grass' Hundejahre." German Studies Review. 16, no.1: 49–60.

Goheen, Jutta. "Intertext-Stil-Kanon: Zur Geschichtlichkeit des Epischen in Günter Grass' Hundejahre." *Carleton Germanic Papers* 24: 155–166.

Miles, Keith. *Günter Grass*. New York: Barnes & Noble, 1975.

Reddick, John. *The "Danzig Trilogy" of Günter Grass: A Study of* The Tin Drum, Cat and Mouse, *and* Dog Years. London: Secker & Warburg. 1975.

Schuchalter, Jerry. "Otto Weininger and the Theme of German-Jewish Friendship in Günter Grass's Hundejahre." *Nordisk Judaistik: Scandinavian Jewish Studies*. 13, no. 2: 83–100.

Stephanie E. Libbon

DOÑA BÁRBARA RÓMULO GALLEGOS (1929)

Considered Venezuela's "national novel," *Doña Bárbara* vividly depicts the classic struggle between civilization and nature. Its author, RÓMULO GALLEGOS (1884–1969), was an important statesman, educator, and public figure during the first half of the 20th century, and his political service to his country rivals his literary contributions for their significance in Venezuela's early development. *Doña Bárbara* is Gallego's most widely read and translated work, and its title character one of the most memorable and polemic figures in Latin American literature.

The novel is set in Venezuela's llanos (plains), and its protagonists personify its archetypal clash: Doña Bárbara symbolizes—as her name suggests—the "barbaric," wild, untamed countryside; her nemesis, the citified Santos Luzardo, represents the forces of progress and civilization. The narrative unfolds as Santos returns to the plains to reclaim his family's ranch that has been appropriated by Doña Bárbara, who controls the latifundio (large landholding) like a feudal lord. The title character is described as a "strong woman," a "man eater," and a "sorceress," in contrast to Santos (whose name literally means "saints" in Spanish). The latter character clashes with Doña Bárbara, whose wild ways have broken down the boundaries between their properties and allowed her animals to run roughshod over neighboring lands. Luzardo engages in a legal battle with Bárbara and "civilizes" the ranch by branding cattle, erecting fences, and enforcing contracts to protect his holdings. At the same time, he seduces her daughter, Marisela, who had been living in the wild, unwashed and uneducated. He takes her to live in the ranch house, where he sets out to domesticate her through the teaching of language, manners, and city ways.

Doña Bárbara is one of Latin America's most important works of the region's postindependence period. As a creative force whose writing was inextricably tied to his politics, Gallegos advocated for "civilizing" the Venezuelans of the plains and bringing to them the urban sophistication of turn-of-the-century Europe. Like other writers and statesmen of the times, most notably the Argentine Domingo Faustino Sarmiento, Gallegos believed that his nation's successful future depended upon its ability to modernize and formally educate its population, and to "tame" the nature that surrounded him. His role model was the "mature" continent of Europe, which had much to teach the young nations of the Americas, and his message in the novel clearly points to that end. Thus, as Melvin S. Arrington, Jr., articulates, the novel manifests the basic dichotomy of civilization versus barbarism "in a series of dueling oppositions: urban versus rural, European (i.e., white) versus mestizo, rational thought versus superstition, progress versus tradition." Santos Luzardo—symbolizing civilization—wins the hand of Doña Bárbara's daughter in addition to recovering his property, and the "wild" woman of the plains is forced to admit defeat.

Although Gallegos grew up primarily in Caracas and spent little time in the countryside, his depiction of rural Venezuela is both poetic and realistic. He captures life on the plains vividly, painting accurate portraits of the novel's colorful characters. His description of the Altamira hacienda, or ranch, in its state of disrepair, lawlessness, and deterioration, reflects the work's portrayal of its untamed inhabitants. The original Spanish version captures the linguistic idiosyncrasies of the region, and the novel has been well translated to retain its unique vernacular.

Doña Bárbara was first published in Spain, during one of Gallegos's periods of exile there. Although the Spanish public received the work enthusiastically—it was named Book of the Month in September 1929—the author revised the novel substantially and released a second edition in 1930. This rewriting included the addition of 15 chapters and more than 20,000 words, converting it into the text's current form. The widely disseminated book was made into a popular film in

1943, with one of Mexico's best-known actresses, María Félix, playing the protagonist. *Doña Bárbara* has been translated into at least eight languages and forms part of the essential canon of Latin American literature.

BIBLIOGRAPHY

Alonso, Carlos J. *The Spanish American Regional Novel.* Cambridge: Cambridge University Press, 1990.

Bracho González, Adriana. *A la sombra del alma: Doña Bárbara en el quehacer venezolano.* Caracas: Monte Avila Editores Latinoamericana, 2000.

Gallegos, Rómulo. *Doña Bárbara.* Madrid: Cátedra, 1997.

Gordo, Francis and Lydia, eds. *Doña Bárbara: Analisis y estudio sobre la obra, el autor y su época.* San Juan: Ediciones Norte, 2005.

Rivas Rojas, Raquel. "Tales of Identity in the Shadow of the Mass Media: Populist Narrative in 1930s Venezuela." *Journal of Latin American Cultural Studies* 10, no. 2 (August 2001): 193–204.

Rodríguez-Alcalá, Hugo. *Nine Essays on Rómulo Gallegos.* Riverside: Latin American Studies Program, University of California, 1979.

Ruffinelli, Jorge. "Rómulo Gallegos." In *Latin American Writers,* edited by Carlos A. Solé, New York: Charles Scribner's Sons, 1989.

Shaw, Donald Leslie. *Gallegos: Doña Bárbara.* London: Grant and Cutler, 1972.

Jane Marcus-Delgado

DONOSO, JOSÉ (1924–1996) *Chilean novelist, short story writer*

José Donoso remains one of the most significant figures of the Latin American literary boom after World War II. Donoso's short stories and novels have a distinct tendency to depict dark human impulses bubbling beneath the surface of civility. His settings vary to parallel the social alienation, spiritual angst, and moral decay of his characters. Donoso's works reflect his effort to develop and refine a "pure" fictional discourse that conveys the essential underpinnings of human motivation—in terms of frustrated desires, impotence, impossible yearnings, and ultimately doomed protagonists. In his writing, Donoso never attempts to attach a fixed meaning to his characters and their experiences; rather, he constructs seemingly simple situations that belie their natural—and sometimes supernatural—impulses.

José Donoso was born in Santiago, Chile, on October 5, 1924. At an early age, he displayed the probing, precocious temperament that allowed him later to excel in academia. After graduating from the Grange English Preparatory School, he attended the University of Chile. During Donoso's third year of study in the liberal arts, he received a Doherty Foundation Scholarship to continue his studies at Princeton University. While at Princeton he wrote his first two short stories: "The Blue Woman" and "The Poisoned Pastry"; both were published in 1950 in the university's magazine. In 1951 Donoso earned his B.A. in English from Princeton University, and thereafter he became a lecturer, alternating between venues in the United States and abroad. He briefly returned to Santiago and taught English and literature at the Catholic University as well as journalism at the University of Chile.

In 1956 Donoso won both Santiago's Municipal Prize for his short stories and the Chile-Italia Prize for journalism. Further, he earned accolades in the subsequent year with the publication of his novel *Coronation* (*Coronación,* 1957). Later, with its English translation in 1962, *Coronation* won the William Faulkner Foundation Prize. Although he lived many years in Spain, Donoso intermittently returned to the United States to lecture at his alma mater and the famous writers' school at the University of Iowa.

After an 18-year absence from his native land, Donoso returned in the 1980s to find Chile firmly within the stranglehold of the dictator Augusto Pinochet and a ruthless totalitarian regime. A crisis of conscience led him to become an ardent spokesman for his countrymen and fellow artists who had been murdered, terrorized, and beaten into submission. He later left the rampant oppression in Chile and returned to Europe. After the collapse of the Pinochet regime, Donoso returned with his wife and children to Santiago, where he resumed his writing. He died of cancer on December 7, 1996, in Santiago.

Donoso's most popular novels include *Coronation* and *A House in the Country* (*Casa de campo,* 1984). *Coronation,* set in mid-20th century Santiago, depicts the decline of a wealthy, aristocratic family. Elisita Gray de Abalos, the elderly matriarch, exhibits symptoms that indicate the onset of Alzheimer's disease. Yet despite her dementia and frenetic behavior, she is able to viciously penetrate the deepest motivations, frustrations, and weaknesses of others with stunning clarity. Perhaps no other character is more deeply lacerated and emasculated than Andres, her middle-aged nephew and current caretaker.

A sullen, impotent bachelor, Andres psychologically grapples with his inability to experience true passion; however, years of affected dispassion and detachment have smothered his inner fire to live. He is, in a certain sense, a prisoner of a bygone era of aristocratic gentility and sensibilities. Andres craves an adventurous life of conquest, reward, and loss similar to Carlos Gros, his brother-in-law. When Andres hires Estela, a 17-year-old peasant girl, as Elisita's caretaker, he descends into a dark abyss of obsession. Estela represents the purest affirmation of life: youth, beauty, vulnerability, vitality, passion, and innocence. Naturally, she becomes the object of Andres's over-zealous conquest. Estela is his elixir of life, and he plots to have her without regard for her will—or the will of Mario, Estela's peasant fiancé, and the ire of the elder Elista. Andres ultimately destroys Estela's life and reputation.

In *A House in the Country,* Donoso explores themes of social and moral decay. *A House in the Country* is a political allegory based on the events surrounding Salvador Allende's coup and Augusto Pinochet's subsequent rise to power. Set in late 19th-century South America, the plot centers on the Ventura family's excursion to an opulent summer resort. The Venturas are a typical wealthy, noble family with an obsequious retinue of attendants; however, they are unable to remain detached from impending disaster and social upheaval. What follows is a grotesquely violent tale of exploitation, oppression, and murder.

BIBLIOGRAPHY

Craig, Herbert E. *Marcel Proust and Spanish America: From Critical Response to Narrative Dialogue.* Cranbury, N.J.: Bucknell University Press, 2002.

Magnarelli, Sharon. *Understanding José Donoso.* Columbia: University of South Carolina Press, 1993.

Nelson, Alice A. *Political Bodies: Gender, History, and the Struggle for Narrative Power in Recent Chilean Literature.* Cranbury, N.J.: Bucknell University Press, 2002.

Neshom Jackson

DON SEGUNDO SOMBRA RICARDO GÜIRALDES (1926)

Often hailed as Argentina's national epic and an elegy for a lost frontier past, *Don Segundo Sombra* is also regarded as the masterpiece of RICARDO GÜIRALDES (1886–1927). Completed and published just before his death, this novel brought Güiraldes the fame that he had so futilely sought throughout his literary career. It became an instant best seller primarily because it offers a romanticized account of gaucho life on the Argentine pampas as personified in its titular character, Don Segundo Sombra. In the process, it paints a rich portrait of the intimate details of gaucho life, such as their equipment, mannerisms, and speech—aspects that are even more apparent and richer in Spanish versions of the novel. In addition to such glorification, the novel offers somber commentaries on the racial and social strata within Argentine society, including prejudice and murderous violence, and even reveals the inherent ambiguity in the very term *gaucho.* Through Don Segundo's mentoring of the narrator, Güiraldes creates an analogy that casts the gaucho lifestyle as reformative for the decadence of contemporary, urban Argentine society. The narrator, a character in the novel, eventually discovers his own identity. Part documentary, part romance, the novel celebrates a lifestyle that resembles in many ways the iconic figure of the North American cowboy and his value system. The similarities are numerous and striking, even to the final scene showing Don Segundo riding into the sunset.

The novel is retold retrospectively by its narrator and chronicles his maturation under Don Segundo Sombra's tutelage. Don Segundo by sheer force of character rescues the youth as he teeters precariously on the edge of juvenile delinquency, becoming the boy's *padrino* (godfather) and thereby legitimating the boy's identity. The narrator, like almost everyone else in the story, is immediately and permanently impressed by the strength of Don Segundo's character. Güiraldes constantly stresses to his readers that it is Don Segundo's moral rather them physical stature that defines him as a paragon of virtue (though the author humanizes Don Segundo in many instances). So inspired by Don Segundo's character is the narrator that he flees his shady existence to follow the gaucho literally and figuratively across the Argentine pampas. While doing so, the narrator grows to physical and moral manhood while experiencing the rich freedom of the gaucho life.

Güiraldes represents this lifestyle as embodying almost exclusively positive values—everything from stoicism and loyalty to poetic sensibility and spirituality. He does so through a stylistic that mirrors these values. Two chapters perhaps best illustrate how Güiraldes accomplishes this goal. As noted above, chapter 2 introduces the laconic gaucho who shows exceptional mercy to his would-be murderer and exerts a magnetic influence over those he meets. Later in chapter 21, Güiraldes illustrates how central morality is to the gaucho lifestyle when he has Don Segundo narrate a story about Misery and Poverty. Don Segundo explains that the story, which recounts the foibles of a blacksmith named Misery, is a tool he is giving the narrator to help others in times of desperation. So intent is he on illustrating the power of narrative to rearticulate its audience that when one of their horses breaks loose, he dismisses the interruption. So influential is the story that the narrator christens his saddle blanket Poverty and his sheepskin pad Misery and promptly falls asleep on them—thereby demonstrating the power of narrative to redefine individuals and the necessity of accepting one's place with such privations as misery and poverty.

Despite the strength of such values, the novel ultimately must have the narrator (and, by extension, Güiraldes' contemporary Argentine audience) leave this idyllic world. At the novel's end, the narrator realizes how inextricable the gaucho is from this freedom: ". . . for Don Segundo trail and life were one and the same." In contrast, the boy's destiny lies within the confines of the city. However, Güiraldes argues that his urban audience, like the narrator, can and should continue to inhabit the moral high ground that they have vicariously explored in the novel. The audience can thereby revitalize the urban landscape with the vast freedom found on the pampas whereon the gauchos ride like the wind.

BIBLIOGRAPHY

Bordelois, Ivonne. *Un Triángulo crucial: Borges, Güiraldes y Lygones*. Buenos Aires: Eudeba, 1999.

Mata, Ramiro W. *Richardo Güiraldes, José Eustacio River, Rómulo Gallegos*. Montevideo [n.p.], 1961.

Previtali, Giovanni. *Ricardo Güiraldes and Don Segundo Sombra: Life and Works*. New York: Hispanic Institute in the United States, 1963.

Clay Smith

DURAS, MARGUERITE (MARGUARITE DONNADIEU) (1914–1996) *French novelist, playwright*

Much of renowned French author, playwright, screenwriter, and filmmaker Marguerite Duras's childhood in colonial Indochina provided her with endless avenues of exploration in her writing. Paradoxically, she would often use the parameters of storytelling in relaying her autobiography and, conversely, use elements of biography in her fiction, with her earlier work serving as source material for further work. Throughout her career, Duras boldly explored the boundaries of sex and gender. Many of her popular novels became plays and films, and Duras herself enjoyed a career as a filmmaker. Nonetheless, while her film work was respected by a small group of devotees, her popularity rests upon her literary and journalistic success.

Marguerite Duras was born Marguerite Donnadieu in Gia-Dinh, near Saigon, on April 4, 1914, to Henri and Marie Donnadieu. Biographical facts concerning Duras are often conflicting, due to her frequent effusiveness in response to inquiry or her deliberate realignment or alteration of her own chronology to suit her needs. What is commonly accepted is that the Donnadieus were French colonialists who had settled in Indochina (now Vietnam) as teachers. Soon after accepting a post in Phnom Penh in 1918, Marguerite's father returned to France in ill health and died shortly after, under somewhat shadowy circumstances. Madame Donnadieu returned with her family to France to settle her husband's estate, but she longed for her old life in the colonies. In 1924, upon her assignment to a teaching post in Sadek, and later Vinh-Long, the family returned to Indochina.

Duras's widowed mother was fiercely passionate about life in the colonies and detested the poverty that had affected her spirited clan of offspring during their time in France. Her unsuccessful attempts at farming and her construction of a wall to block the incoming tides on their land served as the central images in Duras's 1950 landmark novel *The SEA WALL* (*Un barrage contre le Pacifique*). Duras, whose later writings dealt more frequently than not with elements of autobiography, also used the mother figure as a prevalent trope in her work.

At the age of 15, Duras met an older Chinese man who took the girl as his lover. This real-life character—whose identity Duras refused to reveal—became the central focus of her 1984 novel *The* LOVER (*L'Amant*), a work which conflates memoir and fiction and explores the idea of examining desire from within oneself.

Following her liaison with "the Chinese lover," Duras returned to France with her family, where she studied law and political science in Paris, and, in 1939, married Robert Antelme. She adopted the surname Duras, taken from the region in France where her father had owned property, upon publication of her first book, *The Impudents* (*Les impudents*), in 1943. She became increasingly politically active during World War II and joined the French Resistance in 1943; she subsequently joined the Communist Party. In 1944 Antelme, a member of François Mitterand's Richelieu Resistance group in France, was arrested by the German Gestapo and deported to a concentration camp. These circumstances took their toll on Duras, leaving her unable to write for several years.

The year 1946 was bittersweet for Duras. Her husband returned from his imprisonment, and Duras helped nurse him back to health, but later that same year she divorced him. The following year she gave birth to a son, Jean, with her lover Dionys Mascolo. This painful period in her life later became the subject of her work *The War: A Memoir* (*Le douleur*, 1985). In 1950 she broke from the Communist Party amid controversy over her continued anger regarding the treatment of writers in the Soviet Union. She enjoyed tremendous success after the release of *The Sea Wall,* which narrowly missed being awarded the coveted Prix Goncourt, a prize she would eventually claim for *The Lover* in 1984.

In the mid to late 1950s, Duras continued to build both her list of publications and her activities, work done in protest against the war in Algeria, a country seeking its independence from France. Duras made the transition to film with her writing of the script for *Hiroshima mon amour* (1959). She was heavily involved in the production of the movie, which became a seminal piece in the French New Wave cinema. Throughout the 1960s she continued to write several books and movies, including *10:30 on a Summer Night* (*Dix heures et demie du soir en été,* 1960), *Another Long Absence* (*Une aussi longe absence,* 1961), *The Ravishing of Lol Stein* (*Le ravissement de Lol V. Stein,* 1964), and *The Vice Counsel* (*Le vice-consul,* 1965). She also found success in the theater, having adapted a 1955 collection of stories, *Whole Days in the Trees* (*Des journées entières dans les arbres*), in 1965 and, later, many of her novels into plays.

Though Duras continued to write in the 1970s, she turned her primary focus to filmmaking. In 1979 she embarked on a pivotal intimate relationship with a homosexual man, Yann Andrea, whose life inspired her 1992 work *Yann Andrea Steiner.* Alcoholism and smoking took a toll on her, and in 1988 she fell into a five-month-long coma; she later underwent a tracheotomy, which forced her to use a breathing apparatus for the remainder of her years. The 1991 film adaptation of *The Lover* was the source of much frustration for Duras: She cut ties with the director, then reasserted her claim on her life story by reworking the memoir-novel into what became the more fictitious and distant *The* NORTH CHINA LOVER (*L'Amant de la Chine du nord,* 1991). Duras died in Paris on March 3, 1996.

BIBLIOGRAPHY

Adler, Laure. *Marguerite Duras: A Life.* Translated by Anne-Marie Glasheen. Chicago: University of Chicago Press, 2000.

Best, Victoria. *Critical Subjectivities. Identity and Narrative in the Work of Colette and Marguerite.* Oxford and New York: Peter Lang, 2000.

Crowley, Martin. *Duras: Writing and the Ethical.* Oxford and New York: Clarendon, 2000.

Gunther, Renate. *Marguerite Duras.* Manchester, U.K., and New York: Manchester University Press, 2002.

Knapp, Bettina L., ed. *Critical Essays on Marguerite Duras.* New York: G. K. Hall, 1998.

Ramsay, Raylene L. *The French Autobiographies: Sarraute, Duras, Robbe-Grillet.* Gainesville: University Press of Florida, 1996.

Schuster, Marilyn R. *Marguerite Duras Revisited.* Boston: Twayne Publishers, 1993.

Winston, Jane Bradley. *Postcolonial Duras: Cultural Memory in Postwar France.* New York: Palgrave, 2001.

Lindsay R. Nemetz

E

EAGLE AND THE SERPENT, THE (EL ÁGUILA Y LA SERPIENTE) MARTÍN LUIS GUZMÁN (1928)

MARTÍN LUIS GUZMÁN's (1887–1977) best-known novel owes much to the genre of historical fiction, but it is often described as a seminal novel of the 1910 Mexican Revolution. *The Eagle and the Serpent,* first published in Spain in 1928 as *El águila y la serpiente,* depicts the revolution and its political aftermath in the next decade from the point of view of a journalist, a character-narrator who is never named but participates in the events and relates them from an autobiographical point of view. The book follows the wanderings and adventures of this journalist, a fellow traveler of the revolution.

The Eagle is bookended neatly by two flights from Mexico to the United States: The first has the main character, presumably Guzmán, fleeing from the forces of Victoriano Huerta (1854–1916), whose opportunistic reign was opposed by Guzmán and other advocates of the populist movement; the end chapter has the narrator fleeing to the United States again, having survived the fallout caused by the violent splitting of revolutionary factions led by Venustiano Carranza (1859–1920), Eulalio Gutiérrez (1881–1939), and Pancho Villa (1877–1923). Between these two flights, the narrator—a civilian journalist, propagandist, and fringe player who serves the revolution and its leaders in minor and major capacities—chronicles the historic and often extraordinary events that occur throughout Mexico during its major revolution of the 20th century. These events disappoint Guzmán because the idealism symbolized by the eagle at the beginning of the revolution gives way, toward its end, to a venality symbolized by the serpent.

The autobiographical narrative, a novel of more than 300 pages, dramatizes acts of sensational violence and recounts anecdotes of political intrigue. The narrator travels through Mexico, enduring arduous journeys and increasingly perilous hostilities, and out of his experiences he creates the novel, a hybrid between fiction and fact. Indeed, Guzmán's journalistic background is reflected in the fact that this novel was serialized in newspapers before its 1928 publication in book form. But *The Eagle* cannot be easily dismissed as a simple, prorevolutionary product of autobiographical journalism. To his journalistic perspective Guzmán adds historical distance and literary devices. Literary tropes and figures, such as varieties of humor, depictions of extreme violence, personification, and intertextuality serve to illuminate the major theme of the novel, the disillusionment and loss of faith in once-cherished ideals.

The Eagle contains many passages that sparkle with humor. One instance of comic farce comes during the screening of a vainglorious film about the revolution's triumphs. Guzmán and some cohorts watch from behind the screen, facing the audience. As the film is projected, the audience boos and hisses when unpopular generals are extravagantly lauded by the moving images. As the image of the general Venustiano Carranza, the most unpopular of all, enters Mexico City on horseback, two soldiers in the audience shoot at his screen image. The narrator and his companions behind the screen are lucky to escape the bullets meant for Carranza's cinematic projection. The narrator notes that if Carranza "had entered Mexico City on foot instead of on horseback, the bullets would have found their mark in us." Although self-effacing and good-humored, Guzmán underlines the fractiousness and easy violence of the revolutionary parties at that time.

A similar sort of humor is present as Guzmán writes about the meeting of revolutionaries at the Convention of Aguascalientes (1914), at which Carranza was replaced by Eulalio Gutiérrez as president of Mexico. One loquacious rebel, Antonio Díaz Soto, is—like many other participants—described with particular disdain. Guzmán notes ruefully that the long-winded Díaz Soto realized one day "that there was such a thing as socialism . . . [and] ruses devised by the classes in power to weld more tightly the chains of the proletariat." On one level, Guzmán here satirizes the inconsistent, improvised thinking of a minor revolutionary, but, more significant, he underlines the ideological vacuum in the Mexican revolutionary movement. The rebels have had no particular ideological drive, other than that of achieving some sort of self-determination for the Mexican people after years of autocracy by Porfirio Díaz (absolute ruler of Mexico for 35 years, served as president from 1876 to 1880 and from 1884 to 1911) and then Victoriano Huerta. The shallow Marxism of Díaz Soto merely draws attention to the revolutionaries' general lack of philosophical direction. On another occasion, Guzmán notes a rare sign of contentment on the face of perhaps the most fearsome revolutionary guerrilla, Pancho Villa. Villa's "expression was almost human," writes Guzmán. This impressionistic and highly subjective aside draws attention to the subjective, highly opinionated nature of Guzmán's narrative, but it also underlines the brutality of the revolutionaries: If Villa seems human at this point, he has appeared subhuman elsewhere.

Villa seems subhuman because of his ceaseless capacity for killing. Guzmán excoriates the propensity of revolutionary activists to pillage, rape, steal, and murder. Under what Guzmán refers to sarcastically as "revolutionary justice," many are executed for trivial crimes: Two looters are shot dead, five men are killed for counterfeiting money, a loyal revolutionary is shot for criticizing the boorish behavior of Villa followers in a restaurant, and a poor man is hanged simply to show that the rebels will kill anyone who fails to hand over exorbitant sums of money. Guzmán's distaste for casual violence is stressed through his depiction of cruelty inflicts on animals by trigger-happy revolutionaries. Soldiers shoot from a train at "peaceful animals grazing in the fields"; Guzmán's colleague shoots hapless rabbits for "target shooting"; and a harmless, "motionless" bird is shot by Rodolfo Fierro, a Villa lieutenant nicknamed El Carnicero (the Butcher). Fierro's killing of the bird prefaces the most excessive act of slaughter depicted in *The Eagle*. Fierro kills 300 soldiers from Huerta's defeated forces. He gives them a chance to escape, allowing them a chance to run for their freedom—but all except one are immediately cut down in the scramble. The 300 men have been held in a "barnyard." Before they "jumped like goats," they are rounded up "like cattle," treated like animals, and slaughtered as if they are useless beasts. The violence of the revolution has blurred the boundary between animal and human: Violence against both animals and humans is random, vicious, and omnipresent.

The revolution's dehumanizing of persons is contrasted with Guzmán's occasional use of personification—inanimate, nonliving objects are given human capacities of sense and thought. A clapped-out old train seems tired—"its resignation was apparent as it made ready for the return trip"; household objects in confiscated Mexico City properties become shabby as "though convinced of the futility of serving mankind"; and bullets have a malign, willful "personality" that causes them to maim and dismember. Through this literary trope of personification, Guzmán stresses the scale of the destruction wreaked against Mexico's infrastructure, as well as the violent capacities of its revolutionaries: Of course, bullets do not decide how they will injure their victim, the gunmen decide that. It is the human agents who willfully cause death and destruction, making objects look shabby and causing trains to become dilapidated.

Guzmán's deliberate allusions to other literary texts also underline the novel's major theme—that of disillusionment as sought-after change is lost to self-interested scrambling for power. A brief allusion to Shakespeare's *Macbeth*—when a prison guard cannot "screw his courage"—points to what Guzmán calls the "tragedy" of the Mexican Revolution, and to a general lack of valor and integrity. The reading of Plutarch by a high-minded colleague is also intertextual, as it contrasts the nobility espoused by Roman republicans and the civilized rhetoric of Cicero with the savage ignobility of Mexico's revolutionary leaders. Most significantly, though, Guzmán alludes to Cervantes's *Don Quixote*. Guzmán remembers the naïveté of the early phases of the revolution, when all involved were "building castles in the air around the person of Venustiano Carranza." It was thought that Carranza would bring the revolution through to a peaceful, democratic settlement. But Carranza disappoints. Like Don Quixote, Guzmán and his fellow intellectual and martial revolutionaries have been aiming too high, striving for impossible glories, for "castles in the air."

Guzmán's novel is steeped in Mexican culture, geography, and politics, but its theme of disillusionment and vanquished ideals has been received readily in other cultures. The novel has always been accessible to Hispanic readers, but *The Eagle* has been translated into Czech, Dutch, English, French, and German; the English translation by Harriet de Onís in 1930 is compelling and still available through reprints. These translations and the directness of Guzmán's theme of disappointment and frustration in the midst of a collapsed, idealistic project ensure that *The Eagle and the Serpent* will remain a seminal historical, political, and revolutionary novel.

BIBLIOGRAPHY

Langford, W. M. *The Mexican Novel Comes of Age.* South Bend, Ind.: University of Notre Dame Press, 1971.

Guzmán, Martín Luis. *The Eagle and the Serpent.* Translated by Harriet de Onis. Gloucester, Mass.: Peter Smith, 1969.

Morton, F. R. *Los Novelistas de la Revolución Mexicana.* Mexico City: Editorial Cultura, 1949.

Nicolás, Marta Portal. *Proceso Narrativo de la Revolución Mexicana.* Madrid: Cultura Hispánica, 1977.

Kevin De Ornellas

ECO, UMBERTO (1932–) *Italian essayist, novelist*

Umberto Eco is one of the most important writers in Europe, renowned not only for his best-selling novels but also for his cultural commentary and academic writing. Eco's fascination with language and the construction of meaning formed the basis for his work on semiotics and philosophy, but it also informs his fiction, which is notable for its linguistic punning and eclectic settings. His inventive use of language and humorous discussion of complex philosophical ideas demonstrate Eco's determination to present abstract discussions of meaning in an accessibly witty narrative.

Eco was born in Alessandria, northwestern Italy, in an area whose cultural life is informed by its French neighbors rather than the Italian south. Eco's family was resolutely nonpolitical, but when World War II broke out, he and his mother moved to a small village in the Piemonte mountains. Here the young Eco was afforded a viewpoint of the violence between the fascists and the partisan rebels, which he revisited through the character of Jacopo Belbo in his semiautobiographical second novel, *FOUCAULT'S PENDULUM*.

Because Eco's father, Guilio, wanted his son to be a lawyer, the young man duly entered the University of Turin. Eco soon gave up his law studies and, much against his father's wishes, began studying medieval philosophy and literature. He wrote his thesis on Thomas Aquinas, and after gaining his doctorate in 1954, he took up a job with the state-owned television network RAI as "Editor for Cultural Programs" in Milan. This change in direction was to mark the beginning of a period of reassessment, for the mid-to-late 1950s were a time of spiritual crisis for Eco. He had been a member of Catholic Action in his religious youth, but now his faith began to wane, eventually giving way to a humanist secularism. His work for RAI also gave him the chance to rethink his intellectual interests, which resulted in his fascination with modern culture and its representation in the media.

However, Eco had not entirely broken away from academia, and in 1956 he published a book based on his doctoral thesis, *Il problema estetico in San Tommaso.* This was also the year in which he began lecturing at the University of Turin. In 1959 he published his second book, *Sviluppo dell estetico medievale,* which established him as one of the central figures in medievalism. Eco lost his job at RAI, but he was quickly employed as the senior editor of the nonfiction department at the Milanese publishing house Casa Editrice Bompiani, in addition to writing a column for the avant-garde arts magazine *Il Verri;* these "Diario minimo" columns would later be collected into Eco's book *Misreadings*. It was during this time that he began formulating his ideas about semiotics and the "open" text, which culminated in the publication of *The Open Work* in 1962. This was followed by *Apocalyptic and Integrated Intellectuals* in 1964, a landmark study of popular culture and the effects of the media.

Although now a successful journalist, Eco began to concentrate increasingly on his academic work, taking up the position of lecturer at the University of Turin in 1961. This move was to be the first of several academic posts until he was appointed the first professor of semiotics at the University of Bologna in 1971, a post he still holds today. Meanwhile, Eco's academic writings had moved away from his initial interest in medievalism, and he spent the mid–1960s to mid–1970s working toward a theory of semiotics. His major publication from this time was *The Absent Structure* (1968), which was reworked into *A Theory of Semiotics* in 1976, but Eco's interests soon diversified again. While he continued with his work on semiotics, from the late 1970s onward he began to focus on theories of narrativity, leading to publication of *The Role of the Reader* in 1979, and issues of interpretation, which resulted in *The Limits of Interpretation* in 1990.

By the late 1970s, Eco had established himself as a highly respected academic, so his subsequent move into fiction came as something of a surprise. His first novel, *The Name of the Rose* (1980), gained international acclaim for its humorous blending of medieval theology and postmodern deconstruction of narrative; it represented the same union of medieval scholasticism and contemporary popular culture that had defined Eco's early research. The astonishing success of this book made Eco the center of global attention, a situation that increased with the release of Jean-Jacques Annaud's film of the novel in 1986. *The Name of the Rose* also exemplified the interconnected nature of

Eco's work: Each of his novels in some way revisits or revises an aspect of his theoretical writing.

This pattern continued with Eco's second novel, *Foucault's Pendulum* (1988), which also drew heavily on his interest in popular culture and medieval thought. However, whereas *The Name of the Rose* was an "open" text, a complex novel that could hold several layers of interpretation, *Foucault's Pendulum* had its roots in Eco's campaign against what he called "the syndrome of the secret," which he conducted throughout the 1980s. This syndrome was based on Eco's disdain for the idea of hidden meanings that consistently resist interpretation, which he thought literary philosophy had failed to address. In many ways this was an offshoot of his interest in the limits of interpretation, but for Eco there was a wider significance to this obsession with hidden meaning.

In *Foucault's Pendulum,* the protagonists' focus on and construction of The Plan, a medieval conspiracy concerning world domination, is based on exactly the kind of hidden meanings Eco reviled. The Plan is also a reference to the climate of paranoia and the fears of conspiracy that marked Italy's political history in the 1970s. Indeed, while *The Name of the Rose* was seen as being at least in part a comment on the political upheaval in Italy in the 1960s, this allusion was veiled by the historical setting of the 1320s. In contrast, *Foucault's Pendulum* is set in the near-present, with its action running from the 1960s to 1984, and the novel represents a working through of Eco's cultural theories about the nature of secrecy and the boundaries of interpretation, specifically the Italian obsession with political conspiracy.

In 1990 Eco gave the Tanner lectures at the University of Cambridge, focusing on his ideas about interpretation and secrecy. These lectures were subsequently published as *Interpretation and Overinterpretation* in 1992, and it is here that Eco's interest in hermetism comes into focus. Two particular elements of hermetic thought were to form the basis for Eco's third novel, *The Island of the Day Before* (1994): the idea of universal sympathy (the connection between all things) and the importance of similarity. The idea of universal sympathy recalls Eco's previous theories about the limits of interpretation, since a connection among all things results in an indefinite interpretation where a final, absolute meaning is impossible to attain. This drift in meaning is played out in *The Island of the Day Before* through the protagonist Roberto's confused grasp on reality, since everything he experiences on his adventures is somehow transformed for him into his lost love, Lilia. Roberto is also convinced of the existence of a conspiracy against him, which he believes is orchestrated by his imaginary half brother, Ferrante, a figure from Roberto's childhood who seems to have assumed solid form. In this novel Eco returns to a historical setting, framing Roberto's exploits against the politically uncertain world of 17th-century Europe, but the narrative itself is very similar to several 18th-century novels, such as Daniel Defoe's *Robinson Crusoe,* which further unsettles the reader. Indeed, Eco creates a collage out of these familiar narratives that allows him to rework his old ideas about interpretation and meaning into new forms, again illustrating the interconnected nature of his writing.

The linguistic instability of *The Island of the Day Before* is also carried over into Eco's fourth novel, Baudolino (2000), which again generates uncertainty about the reliability of meaning. The eponymous protagonist is, quite simply, a liar, and the reader is left to pick through his tales of exotic adventures and monstrous encounters in search of a recognizable truth. While the 12th-century setting of *Baudolino* returns Eco to his favored arena of medieval culture, this novel also revises Eco's theoretical writing, in this case his collection of philosophical essays, *Kant and the Platypus* (1997). This text, an attempt to rework and revise his earlier *A Theory of Semiotics* in light of his more recent reading in the field of cognitive sciences and the philosophy of perception, focused in part on the difficulties inherent in the perception and representation of reality. The platypus of the title was chosen because its discovery so confused 18th-century zoologists that in order to classify it they had to completely upend their systems of identification. In *Baudolino,* the protagonist is constantly encountering unknown monsters that need to be interpreted and understood as part of a wider system, but his inherent dishonesty leads us to question the validity of such an enterprise. Instead, Eco asks us to consider why we believe that we are

capable of ordering the world through such systems of classification, when really individuals have no way of verifying their perceptions or their understanding of reality.

Eco's novels reflect his academic interests, but their wide-ranging subjects also indicate the breadth of his writing and the prolific work rate that he has sustained for the last 40 years. Eco has also published extensively on medieval philosophy and aesthetics, most notably *Art and Beauty in the Middle Ages* (1986). He has also written children's books, translated the work of French writer Raymond Queneau, compiled a CD-ROM on the 17th century, and has continued his journalism as a cultural and social commentator and critic. The flexibility of his thought is seen in the variety of his novels, which, while commenting on and embodying his literary and cultural theories, never lose the wit and humor that make his fiction so entertaining.

BIBLIOGRAPHY

Bondanella, Peter. *Umberto Eco and the Open Text: Semiotics, Fiction, Popular Culture.* New York: Cambridge University Press, 1997.

Bouchard, Norma, and Veronica Pravadelli, eds. *Umberto Eco's Alternative.* New York: Peter Lang, 1998.

Caesar, Michael. *Umberto Eco: Philosophy, Semiotics and the Work of Fiction.* Cambridge: Polity Press, 1999.

Gane, Mike, and Nicholas Gane, eds. *Umberto Eco.* 3 vols. London: SAGE Publications, 2005.

Ross, Charlotte, and Rochelle Sibley, eds. *Illuminating Eco: On the Boundaries of Interpretation.* Warwick Studies in the Humanities Series. Aldershot, U.K.: Ashgate, 2004.

Rochelle Sibley

ELEVEN MINUTES (ONZE MINUTOS)

Paulo Coelho (2003)   Written by the brilliant Brazilian writer Paulo Coelho (1947–), *Eleven Minutes* was originally published in Portuguese. This novel differs from the rest of the writer's oeuvre as it deals with a subject which, Coelho states in the book's dedication, is "harsh, difficult, shocking." The novel explores the theme of the sanctity of sex by narrating the story of a young prostitute who eventually finds true love, realizing that sex for material gain is profane, and emotional love, if reciprocated by the partner, raises the sexual union to a holy act.

The title *Eleven Minutes* refers to the approximate duration for the act of coitus but connotes the infinite possibilities and meanings contained in this brief physical and emotional act. An invocation to the Virgin Mary, a dedication, a parable from the Bible, and an ancient hymn about the greatness of women serve as prologues to the main narrative. The novel's fairy-tale opening yokes the innocent with the profane: "Once upon a time there was a prostitute called Maria." The author immediately steps into the story to explain the difficulty in combining two contradictory mores, establishing the story's realistic nature. Authorial intrusions, however, do not recur in the narrative. The detailed portrayal of the protagonist Maria's quest for love helps to build her vibrant individualistic character. Excerpts from her diary appended at the end of every chapter, strikingly capturing Maria's perceptions and emotions at different junctures in her life.

Maria, a naïve, attractive Brazilian girl, becomes heartbroken during her teenage years through her realization that love is a terrible and disappointing emotion that brings only pain and suffering. During a holiday trip to Rio de Janeiro, Maria meets a Swiss tourist, Roger, who is looking for girls to hire as dancers for his club in Geneva. Maria is attracted by his promises of money and accompanies him to Switzerland. However, due to the restrictions he imposes on the dancers and the little money he pays them, Maria soon has a falling-out with the man she thought to be her benefactor. She prefers to think of herself as "an adventurer in search of treasure," like Santiago in Coelho's masterpiece *The ALCHEMIST* (1988), and, incidentally, has read a copy of that book.

In order to earn the money Maria requires for her return to Brazil, she starts working in another nightclub. She becomes fascinated by the ease with which a prostitute can earn money overnight, depending on the number of men she can charm and go to bed with. After a year of working as a prostitute, Maria meets in the nightclub a handsome young man called Ralf Hart, who is a renowned painter. Unlike the other men she has slept with, she realizes that Ralf looks at her not as a woman but as an individual with willpower and "inner light." Ralf is not focused on Maria as a mere sex object. Her distrust of emotional bonding with men

slowly wears off as she finds herself falling deeply in love with Ralf. Sex for the two young lovers becomes an exploration of the pleasures that the body promises when inspired by strong emotions. Maria starts hating her job as a prostitute. She feels that it is killing her soul, and she is also afraid that her discovery of true love and spiritual bonding with Ralf might be destroyed because of her carnal acts with other men.

Eleven Minutes also depicts other minor characters who are not given more narrative space than the work's functionality demands. Maria's experiences with Terence, an Englishman who teaches her about the relationship between pain, suffering, and pleasure, serve to titillate the reader. The librarian Heidi's discussions with Maria are limited to sex and orgasms. However, the novel does not read like a sex manual or a pornographic work due to the author's sensitive portrayal of Maria, which evokes the reader's empathy.

BIBLIOGRAPHY
Arias, Juan. *Paulo Coelho: The Confessions of a Pilgrim*. London: HarperCollins, 1999.
Coelho, Paulo. *Like the Flowing River: Thoughts and Reflections*. London: HarperCollins: 2006.

Preeti Bhatt

ELIADE, MIRCEA (1907–1986) *Romanian essayist, novelist, playwright*

A remarkably accomplished historian of religions and an orientalist whose abundant and influential scholarly work has long gained worldwide recognition, Mircea Eliade was also a prolific novelist. Although obliged to live in exile for 40 years, first in France and then in the United States, he never quite forsook his mother tongue: "Literature," he once said, "I can write only in Romanian, the language in which I dream." Without being merely fictional illustrations of his own philosophical concerns, Eliade's novels are nevertheless fundamentally connected with the scientific region of his oeuvre.

A fervent admirer of protean, Renaissance-like personalities, Eliade was not willing to suppress either of the two main branches of his spirit at the expense of the other, thus allowing the manifestation of both his artistic proclivity and of his penchant for systematic, technical research. He viewed literature and science as different yet complementary routes, at the end of which the intuition that the world constitutes an immense reservoir of signs waiting to be deciphered becomes certainty. Indeed, even in its most apparently banal forms, reality harbors the fantastic; the sacred and the profane may therefore be said to coexist, "camouflaged" in one another. Trying himself to personify the breadth and multiplicity of a polymath, Eliade also wrote a great number of essays on various topics, two plays, and a rich collection of personal literature. He was an impassioned journalist and a thoroughly enthralling academic figure.

Mircea Eliade was born in Bucharest on March 9, 1907. His father, Gheorghe, a captain in the Romanian army, had changed his last name from Ieremia to Eliade out of respect for the achievements of a 19th-century Romanian encyclopedic thinker and writer, Ion Eliade-Rădulescu. From an early age, Mircea Eliade was an avid reader despite what he described as his "galloping myopia." He began writing regularly when he was only 12 years old, and the great diversity of his interests—zoology, botany, chemistry, entomology—as well as the delight with which he let himself be immersed in the strange worlds of his fantasy prefigured the outstanding scope of his later pursuits.

In search of an elusive totality, young Eliade spent countless hours confined to the solitude of his attic, avidly reading book after book or outlining the course of his future more-or-less ambitious projects. He carefully cultivated the image of an odd, highly idiosyncratic individual, truly unique and as such chosen to fulfill an exceptional destiny. Fearing that his frequent outbursts of melancholia might weaken his determination, he devised and carried out a harsh, self-disciplining program that reached its zenith when he succeeded in reducing his hours of sleep to just four a night. By 1925, barely 18 years old, he had already published 100 articles and written several literary pieces, the autobiographical *Novel of a Nearsighted Adolescent* (*Romanul unui adolescent miop,* 1989) among them.

In 1925 Eliade enrolled at the University of Bucharest, Faculty of Letters and Philosophy, where he soon fell under the powerful spell of Nae Ionescu, his charismatic mentor. This gifted professor of philosophy, who would eventually become the chief ideologist of the Iron Guard, a fascist political party founded in 1927, both nurtured Eliade's extraordinary intellectual effervescence and instilled some of his most reactionary ideas: fiercely nationalistic, unapologetically anti-Western, and virulently anti-Semitic. A dark chapter in Eliade's life was about to begin. Much to the disappointment of his numerous critics, the older Eliade years later would neither reevaluate nor regret his youthful excesses, referring to them, rather vaguely, as "my imprudent acts and errors." In his *Autobiography,* for instance, not only did he choose to keep an awkward silence with regard to the lamentable excesses of his early years, he also continued to believe that the Legionary Movement, of which the Iron Guard was a part, had been, at least in its initial stages, a legitimate phenomenon of a purely spiritual and ethical essence, whose nonviolent ideals had subsequently been perverted by some thoughtless acts of a handful of terrorists. Based on a radically nationalistic, xenophobic, and anti-Semitic discourse, directed at those segments of the population increasingly frustrated by the purportedly anti-Romanian Jewish conspiracy, the Legionary Movement's infamous legacy culminated in a short-lived fascist dictatorship, which, between September 1940 and January 1941, elevated murder to the rank of state policy.

In November 1926 Eliade began writing for the daily newspaper *Cuvântul* on a regular basis, and one year later he published a series of articles entitled "Itinerariu Spiritual" (the spiritual itinerary). This influential manifesto demanded that young Romanian writers and thinkers—Emil Cioran, Mircea Vulcănescu, Constantin Noica, to name but a few—respond with a sort of intellectual heroism both to the window of opportunity that had briefly opened for their generation and to the conspicuous crisis of the West. The year 1927 saw Eliade's first visit to Italy, where he met Giovanni Papini, the icon of his adolescence, as well as other Italian intellectuals with whom he established long-lasting relationships. He returned there one year later in order to prepare his licentiate thesis on Italian Renaissance philosophy, which he successfully defended in October 1928. Having been granted a monthly scholarship by Maharajah Manindra Chandra Nandy of Kassimbazar, Eliade departed for India on November 22, 1928. He was to learn Sanskrit and gather material for his doctoral dissertation on yoga at the University of Calcutta, under the supervision of Surendranath Das-gupta, a renowned Indian professor of philosophy.

Concomitantly, Eliade concluded one novel, *Isabel and the Devil's Waters* (*Isabel și apele diavolului,* 1930), and began two others: *The Light that Fails* (*Lumina ce se stinge,* 1934) and *The Return from Paradise* (*Întoarcerea din rai,* 1934). His Indian adventure, which included six months of seclusion in a Himalayan hermitage as a result of a disagreement with Dasgupta, was cut short in December 1931 when he returned to Romania to complete his military service. Between 1931 and 1940, life treated Eliade rather well: He obtained his Ph.D. in philosophy (1933), published many literary and schol-arly books, engaged in public debates, and was unani-mously acknowledged as the incontestable leader of his generation. While the novels of those years—*Bengal Nights,* (*Maitreyi,* 1933, 1994), *The Hooligans* (*Huliganii,* 1935), *Mistress Christina* (*Domnișoara Christina,* 1936), *The Snake* (*Șarpele,* 1937), and *Marriage in Heaven* (*Nuntă în Cer,* 1939)—fail to stand out as major litera-ture, his studies already contained the theoretical arma-ture around which his key scientific opuses would later take shape: *Patterns in Comparative Religion* (*Traité d'histoire des religions,* 1949, 1958), *The Myth of the Eter-nal Return* (*Le mythe de l'éternel retour,* 1949, 1954), and *Shamanism: Archaic Techniques of Ecstasy* (*Le chamanisme et les techniques archaïques de l'extase,* 1951, 1964).

Fundamentally, Eliade's thought operates within two major categories: the sacred and the profane. Defined as a "structure of human consciousness," the former reveals itself in hierophanies, which thus act as portals to the sacred, cyclical time of myths and rituals. While archaic cultures retained a robust intimacy with these primordial, meaning-generating frameworks, human-kind's increasingly secular practices have thrown them into the empty and linear time of history. Therefore the imperative task of any historian of religions, which Eli-ade existentially assumed, consists in the attempt to provide a mediating bridge between modern Western and prehistoric Oriental civilizations, an operation that seeks to expose the deep-seated unity of all cultures and eventually inaugurate a "new humanism." Unfortu-nately, Eliade's uncompromising allegiance to a far-right ideology still casts a shadow today over what may otherwise be regarded as an extremely fruitful era.

After being imprisoned for several months in a camp during King Carol's anti-Legionary campaign (July–November 1938), Eliade was appointed a cultural atta-ché two years later, first to London and then to Lisbon. He returned only once to Romania, in summer 1942, and starting in 1945, he was forced to take refuge in exile until his death in 1986. Both in Paris and Chi-cago, he dedicated himself primarily to his scientific career without, however, totally abandoning literature. During this second wave of literary production, he wrote mostly short stories, of which "La Țigănci" ("With the Gypsy Girls," 1963, 1973) was to be recog-nized as a fine accomplishment. *The FORBIDDEN FOREST* (*Noaptea de sânziene,* 1955 in French, 1971 in Roma-nian, and 1978 in English), the great novel that was expected to bring Eliade international literary reputa-tion, ended up a failure. His 1968 fantastic novella *Pe Strada Mântuleasa* was translated into English as *The Old Man and the Bureaucrats* in 1979. A number of prestigious universities, Yale and the Sorbonne among them, have conferred honorary degrees on Eliade. He also received the Christian Culture Award Gold Medal for 1968 from the University of Windsor in Canada.

BIBLIOGRAPHY

Allen, Douglas. *Myth and Religion in Mircea Eliade.* New York: Garland Publishing, 1998.

———. *Structure and Creativity in Religion: Hermeneutics in Mircea Eliade's Phenomenology and New Directions.* Religion and Reason 14. The Hague: Mouton, 1978.

Carrasco, David, and Jane Marie Law, eds. *Waiting for the Dawn: Mircea Eliade in Perspective.* Niwot: University Press of Colorado, 1991.

Cave, David. *Mircea Eliade's Vision for a New Humanism.* New York: Oxford University Press, 1993.

Dudley, Guilford. *Religion on Trial: Mircea Eliade and his Critics.* Philadelphia: Temple University Press, 1977.

Eliade, Mircea. *The Autobiography of Mircea Eliade.* 2 vols. Translated by Mac Linscott Ricketts. Chicago: University of Chicago Press, 1981, 1988.

———. *Bengal Nights.* Translated by Catherine Spencer. Chicago: University of Chicago Press, 1994.

———. *Exile's Odyssey: 1937–1960.* Translated by Mac Lin-scott Ricetts. Chicago: University of Chicago Press, 1988.

———. *The Forbidden Forest.* Translated by M. L. Ricketts and M. P. Stevenson. South Bend, Ind.: University of Notre Dame Press, 1978.

———. *A History of Religious Ideas*. 3 vols. Translated by Willard R. Trask. Chicago: University of Chicago Press, 1978–85.

———. *Journey East, Journey West: 1907–1937*. Translated by Mac Linscott Ricketts. San Francisco: Harper and Row, 1981.

———. *The Myth of the Eternal Return, or Cosmos and History*. Translated by Willard R. Trask. Princeton, N.J.: Princeton University Press, 1971.

———. *The Sacred and the Profane: The Nature of Religion*. Translated by Willard R. Trask. New York: Harper and Row, 1961.

———. *La Țigănci și alte povestiri*. Bucharest: Editura Pentru Literatură, 1969.

———. *Yoga: Immortality and Freedom*. 2nd ed. Translated by Willard R. Trask. Princeton, N.J.: Princeton University Press, 1969.

Laignel-Lavastine, Alexandra. *Cioran, Eliade, Ionesco: L'oubli du fascisme*. Paris: Presses Universitaires de France, 2002.

Marino, Adrian. *L'Herméneutique de Mircea Eliade*. Translated by Jean Gouillard. Paris: Gallimard, 1980.

Simion, Eugen. *Mircea Eliade: A Spirit of Amplitude*. New York: East European Monographs, Columbia University Press, 2001.

Sorin Tomuța

ENCHI FUMIKO (1905–1986) *Japanese novelist, playwright, short story writer*

In her novels and short stories, Enchi Fumiko is known for her skillful portrayal of feminine sense and sensibility. One of the most prominent authors of the Showa period (1926–89), Enchi typically focused on the love and sexuality of women in a male-dominated society and, similar to the magic realists of Latin America, blended the real with the supernatural, fantastic, and bizarre. Enchi's literary fame also rests on her modern-Japanese translation of Murasaki Shikibu's *The Tale of Genji*, a masterful medieval novel that became a model for her own best-selling novel *MASKS*.

Enchi was born in Tokyo on October 2, 1905, the daughter of an eminent Japanese linguist, Ueda Kazutoshi (1867–1937). After attending Japan's University Girls High School from 1918 to 1922, she received tutorial education in English, French, and classical Chinese writing. Her education also consisted of reading Japanese literature and attending Kabuki, a popular form of Japanese theater.

At the age of 20, Enchi began her writing career as a playwright. Her one-act plays *A Birthplace* (*Furusato*) and *A Noisy Night in Late Spring* (*Banshu Soya*) came out in 1926 and 1928, respectively. In 1930 she married the journalist Enchi Yoshimatsu and, despite their unhappy relationship, stayed with him until his death in 1972; the couple had one daughter.

After the publication of a collection of her plays in 1935, Enchi turned her attention to writing fiction. Her earliest novels include *The Words Like the Wind* (*Kaze no Gotoki Kotoba*, 1939), *The Treasures of Heaven and Sea* (*Ten no Sachi, Umi no Sachi*, 1940), and *Spring and Autumn* (*Shunju*, 1943). She was afflicted with cancer for which she received a mastectomy in 1938 and a hysterectomy in 1949. Her personal misfortune was compounded in 1945 when an air raid by Allied forces destroyed her home and her possessions.

Enchi published some of her most important novels after the end of World War II; these included *The Waiting Years* (*Onna Zaka*, 1949–57), *Masks* (*Onna Men*, 1958), *A Tale of False Fortunes* (*Nama Miko Monogatari*, 1965), and *Growing Fog* (*Saimu*, 1976). *The Waiting Years* focuses on the lifelong suffering and endurance of a 19th-century matriarch, Tomo, who is constantly subjected to humiliation and mistreatment by her husband, an influential Japanese politician. At the beginning of the work, Tomo is in search of a mistress—a young and inexperienced girl—for her husband. In succeeding years, he brings more concubines home, further deepening her sorrow. However, accepting her role as a subservient wife in an upper-class family, she successfully manages the household and lives peacefully with and cares for the concubines.

Set in mid–20th century Japan, *Masks* concerns the anger, frustration, and vengeance of a middle-aged poetess named Mieko Togano. Apparently as sexual revenge, she manipulates her widowed daughter-in-law, Yasuko, into having simultaneous affairs with two men, Tsuneo Ibuki and Toyoki Mikame. Mieko then orchestrates the impregnation of her own daughter, Harume, by Ibuki—without his knowledge. *A Tale of False Fortunes* is an historical novel set in 10th-century Japan. An adaptation of the medieval romance *A Tale of Flowering Fortunes* (*Eiga Monogatari*), this work focuses on the lust for power in a Japanese aristocracy.

Public and critical reception of Enchi's work has remained favorable. Alongside such literary luminaries as TANIZAKI JUNICHIRO, KAWABATA YASIMARO, MISHIMA YUKIO, ABE KŌBŌ, ENDŌ SHUSAKU, and OE KENZABURO, Enchi is a major modern Japanese writer who has earned international fame. Her story "Starving Days" ("Himojii Tsukihi," 1952) won the Women Writers Prize, and *The Waiting Years* was awarded the Noma Prize for Literature, Japan's highest literary honor. Enchi's literary honors also included the Tanizaki Prize in 1969 and the Cultural Medal (Bunka Kunsho) in 1985. Enchi died on November 12, 1986, at the age of 81. Prior to her death, she became a member of the prestigious Art Academy in Japan. *The Waiting Years, Masks,* and *A Tale of False Fortunes* have been translated into English by Kodansha International, Knopf, and the University of Hawaii Press, respectively. *The Waiting Years* and *Masks* are also widely read and taught in the United States.

BIBLIOGRAPHY

Bargen, Doris G. "Twin Blossoms on a Single Branch: The Cycle of Retribution in *Onnamen.*" *Monumenta Nipponica* 46, no. 2 (Summer 1991): 147–171.

Cornyetz, Nina. *Dangerous Women, Deadly Words: Phallic Fantasy and Modernity in Three Japanese Writers.* Palo Alto, Calif.: Stanford University Press, 1999.

Enchi Fumiko. *Masks.* Translated by Juliet Winters Carpenter. New York: Knopf, 1983.

———. *A Tale of False Fortunes.* Translated by Roger K. Thomas. Honolulu: University of Hawaii Press. 2000.

———. *The Waiting Years.* Translated by John Bester. Tokyo and Palo Alto, Calif.: Kodansha, 1971.

Locascio, Lisa. "Legacy and Repetition: Heian Literature and Noh Theatre in Fumiko Enchi's *Masks.*" *Gallatin Undergraduate Journal* 1, no. 1 (Spring 2005).

John J. Han

END OF THE GAME, THE (FINAL DEL JUEGO) JULIO CORTÁZAR (1963)

In its English translation, published in 1963, *The End of the Game* offered international readers a representative sampling of JULIO CORTÁZAR's (1914–84) work as a master of short fiction. This book brings together stories from his first three collections of prose narratives: *Bestiary* (*Bestiario*), *The End of the Game,* and *The Secret Arms* (*Las armas secretas*). As such, *End of the Game* ranks as both an impressive introduction to and celebration of the Argentinean Cortázar's achievement as one of prose literature's true artists.

The book is divided into three sections that, interestingly, do not correspond to order of stories from the earlier collections. The first section contains some of the author's most famous fantastic works, beginning with the eerie "Axolotl," in which the narrator's fascination with the creatures of the title, a form of salamander he visits almost daily at an aquarium, becomes obsession and, then, an almost psychic connection. Finally the narrator loses himself, literally, in the creatures: His consciousness is transferred into one, leaving him swimming in the tank, watching as his human body, now home to the axolotl, walks away, condemning him to an existence moving "lucidly among unconscious creatures."

After the famous "House Taken Over" ("Casa tomada"), Cortázar's story of an otherworldly home invasion, the section moves to "The Distances" ("Lejana"), the story of a young woman suffering from a peculiar form of double consciousness: her own and, from a distance, that of a street woman who is routinely beaten and abused. At first the story seems to have similarities to "Axolotl" in that both deal with the subject of consciousness transferred. However, it becomes clear that, for Alina Reyes, the narrator of "The Distances," both are aspects of herself—one "real," the other projected—and thus the seemingly supernatural reveals, instead, the character's difficult psychology.

A standout of this first section, and of Cortázar's commitment to "lo fantástico," is his "Letter to a Young Lady in Paris" ("Carta a una señorita en París") in which the letter writer, addressing a woman named Andrea, laments his stay at her apartment; the damage it has undoubtedly caused; and his unfortunate tendency, at the root of his problems, to vomit live rabbits. "Letter to a Young Lady" is darkly comic: The narrator spends much time describing his strange habit—that is, his manner of pulling the bunnies from his throat and even his methods, humane or otherwise, of euthanizing them. However, as the rabbits continue to emerge from him at a rate beyond his control, it becomes clear that the occasion for the letter is more than a simple lamentation; it is, rather, a suicide note.

The story that begins the second section, "Continuity of Parks" ("Continuidad de los parques") is a brief but expert foray into the metafictional. The protagonist of the story, a businessman, settles into his favorite armchair to resume the reading of a suspense novel in which two lovers plan what will obviously be a murder. After a final embrace, the two separate, she toward the north and he, armed with a dagger, on a path that leads him to a stately house. He enters, walking through the hallways, checking each chamber door, until he reaches his victim, a businessman settled into his favorite armchair, reading a novel. A rich, almost Borgesian exercise in experimental prose, "Continuity of Parks" involves both the reader in the story and the one external to it in the noir novel-within-story to the point where one is compelled, at story's end, to peek up from the book and be reassured that its implications end on the page.

"The Night Face Up" ("La noche boca arriba") is the story of a motorcyclist who, having suffered a serious accident while rushing to keep an appointment, drifts in and out of consciousness in a hospital bed, suffering a series of feverish dreams in which he is an Aztec being hunted down for sacrifice. As these dreams become more terrifying and more sensory, the rider realizes that he has, in fact, fully awakened from the dream—the dream of the crash, the hospital, the future—and he closes his eyes to accept his fate on the stone of a sacrificial altar.

The second section also contains two of Cortázar's short-fiction masterpieces, "Bestiary" ("Bestiario") and "Blow-Up" ("Las babas del diablo"). In "Bestiary," the young Isabel has come to spend the summer with her aunt and uncle at the country estate they share with their son, Nino; his uncle, known as the Kid; and a foreboding and unwelcome guest: a tiger that roams the grounds and the house. As a result of rising familial tensions—stemming from the cruelty and crudity of the Kid, whose beating of Nino and licentious advances toward Isabel's Aunt Rema draw the child's fear and disdain—Isabel misleads the family as to the tiger's whereabouts. Thus, when the Kid, believing the tiger to be in his study, enters the library to find the creature waiting for him, his fate is sealed and his tyranny over.

"Blow-Up" is a complex narrative that takes as its subject the complexity of narrative. It is the story of a translator and photographer, Roberto Michel, who walks through Paris taking photographs on a particular Sunday in November and who may or may not be the sometimes-first-person, sometimes-third-person narrator. Indeed, the ambiguity of the story—meaning, the ambiguity inherent in telling any story, and, in particular, this one—is central to both its conflict and its theme. Michel and the narrator indulge in creating fictions by capturing, and thus reshaping, reality through various means, whether by film or language. The "plot" of the story—Michel's taking a photograph of a young boy speaking to an attractive blonde woman, a meeting for which he imagines an elaborate, and increasingly sinister, narrative—is inseparable from the narrator's difficulty in its telling. It is a matter not only of finding the right words, the right voice, and the right method for the story, but of dealing with its troubling implications or, perhaps, the troubled imagination behind it.

The final section begins with the title story, "End of the Game," in which three young sisters spend their summer afternoons playing the game of "Statue" by a stretch of tracks for the Argentine Central Railroad, drawing attention as the afternoon train goes by. The best at the game is Letitia, who excels at its requisite immobility due to a limiting physical handicap. Her performance earns her an admirer on the train, a young boy named Ariel who throws a note from his window complimenting her, which draws from Letitia an emotional and mysterious response.

The book ends with a former title story, the ghostly "Secret Weapons" from Cortázar's third collection, in which a young woman, Michéle, convinces her boyfriend, Pierre, to accompany her on a trip to her family's vacation home. Even before their departure, however, Pierre begins to experience a strange sense of déjà vu, remembering images of a home he has never seen and a horrifying past event: Michéle's rape, years earlier, by a Nazi soldier. Increasingly, Pierre begins to assume characteristics of the German—his mannerisms and his memories—becoming a kind of secret weapon for an attacker beyond the grave, thus propelling the story—and the collection—to a haunting conclusion.

BIBLIOGRAPHY

Bloom, Harold, ed. *Julio Cortázar.* Bloom's Major Short Story Writers. Philadelphia: Chelsea House Publishers, 2004.

Peavler, Terry J. *Julio Cortázar.* Twayne's World Author Series 816. Boston: Twayne Publishers, 1990.

Schmidt-Cruz, Cynthia. *Mothers, Lovers, and Others: The Short Stories of Julio Cortázar.* Albany, N.Y.: State University of New York Press, 2004.

Stavins, Ilan. *Julio Cortázar: A Study of the Short Fiction.* Twayne's Studies in Short Fiction 63. New York: Twayne Publishers, 1996.

Joseph Bates

ENDŌ SHŪSAKU (1923–1996) *Japanese essayist, novelist, short story writer*   Admired by such authors as MISHIMA YUKIO and Graham Greene, with whom he is often compared by critics, ENDŌ SHŪSAKU was one of Japan's preeminent 20th-century authors. Critics also find Endō's numerous works very accessible to non-Japanese readers and often categorize him as one of the Third Generation, an influential group of authors writing after World War II; however, his literary accomplishments and works distinguish him from his peers. For example, his many awards include every major Japanese literary prize and he has been included on the shortlist for the Nobel Prize in literature numerous times.

Endō's academic career informs his literary works. After World War II, he quickly returned to his studies, which the war had interrupted, and began publishing articles on Christianity in Japan. Following his graduation with a degree in French literature from Keio University in 1948, he continued his studies on one of the first state scholarships at the University of Lyon, where he was the first Japanese student to study. While at the university (1950–53), he focused on 20th-century French Catholic literature. However, his studies were cut short by the first bout of what would prove to be a lifelong illness requiring numerous extended hospitalizations. As many critics and Endō himself have argued, these events recur as metaphors (e.g., alienation, rejection, hospitalization, misperception) throughout his work.

After his return to Japan, Endō quickly turned his literary talents to fiction. These works were not his first published pieces (those were nonfiction essays on Christianity in Japan published while he was still at Keio University), but they were the ones that garnered him the most recognition as an author. In 1955 he published his first novellas, *White Man* (*Shiroi hito*) and *Yellow Man* (*Kiiroi hito*). Subsequently, he created several novels, short stories, plays, and editorial commentaries, not to mention numerous television interviews.

Throughout this range of genres, several themes recur in Endō's work. Many critics have argued that these themes reflect Endō's own struggles with his Christian faith and that his works provide a form of catharsis for what is often seen as his ambiguous beliefs. The basis for these claims comes in part from his life (he converted to Catholicism at age 11), his work, and his commentary (which often equates his Catholicism with a suit of clothes that he put on rather than a part of his being). Regardless of their source, Christian images and themes dominate most of his work.

Most notably and explicitly, Endō explores the concept of rejection and its consequences as manifested in Christ's life, a theme explicitly explored in novels such as SILENCE (*Chinmoku,* 1966) and *Wonderful Fool* (*Obaka-san*). Similarly, Endō reexamines the compatibility of Christianity with what he defines as a Japanese sensibility, often represented as a struggle of fundamental differences. While he frequently seems to represent these differences as irreconcilable, he also blends them into mutuality, as when he ends *Wonderful Fool* and *The Samurai* (*Samurai,* 1980) with their protagonists being transfigured into birds. Avoiding the simple dichotomies of East/West and Christian/non-Christian, Endō creates extremely complex and convoluted situations that offer no easy or final answer. Most often, his works end with the situation ambiguously resolved at best or his protagonists frozen in an absolute moral dilemma. This questioning reveals itself throughout his entire body of work, as demonstrated in *The Final Martyrs* (*Saigo no Junkyōsha,* 1994), which collects several of Endō's short stories from his decades of work into a single volume. As this collection also demonstrates, Endō reformulates this questioning by placing former characters in new situations, a strategy that he explains in his preface.

Although all of his works explore these dichotomies, most of Endō's works derive from historical events and autobiographical experiences. Many of his historically based works focus on Japan either during the 17th-century persecutions of missionaries or postwar rebuilding. As with most of his works, the ultimate formulation is tragic. For example, *Silence,* which is often cited as his masterpiece, chronicles the trials that Christian missionaries endured during this time. Through Father Ferreira's trial and eventual apostasy, Endō forces readers to question whether Christianity is compatible with Japanese sensibility, as he formulates it.

Endō returns to this same issue constantly throughout his other works as he does in *The Samurai,* where he personifies this theme in two figures from the same time period as *Silence*: Hasekura, a samurai who coverts to Christianity and the novel's protagonist, and Velasco, his missionary counterpart. "Caught up in the middle of this vortex," Hasekura searches desperately for meaning through his adopted Christian faith at home and across Europe as part of an ambassadorial mission. Like most of Endō's work, this novel ends with Hasekura's acceptance that he no longer belongs to either culture.

Shifting his focus to the devastation of postwar Japan, the author's *The Sea and the Poison* (*Umi to Dokuyaku,* 1958) charts Dr. Suguro's descent from a doctor dedicated to healing to the role of torturer, and thereby provides a searing commentary on the depths to which all humanity may plummet, especially in times of war. The novel's final commentary on the relativity and indeterminacy of human values coalesces in the "futility" that paralyzes Suguro in the final sentence of the novel. Set in a more contemporary period, *Volcano* (1959) returns to religious themes by placing the struggle between Christian and traditional Japanese beliefs literally at the foot of a volcano, Akadaké. Endō personifies this struggle through the competing perspectives of Durand, an unfrocked Catholic priest who sees the volcano as a potentially apocalyptic judgment against the villagers and Father Sato's religious retreat, and Suda, a retired volcanologist who is caught in an interpretive dilemma of determining the volcano's likelihood of eruption. As these works illustrate, this dialectic of indeterminacy and relativism informs much of Endō's oeuvre and illustrates why Endō Shūsaku

remains one of the most celebrated of Japan's authors in the 20th century.

BIBLIOGRAPHY

Endō Shūsaku. *The Final Martyrs: Stories.* Translated by Van C. Gessel. London: P. Owen, 1993.

———. *Five by Endo: Stories.* Translated by Van C. Gessel. New York: New Directions, 2000.

———. *Stained Glass Elegies: Stories.* Translated by Van C. Gessel. New York: Dodd, Mead, 1985.

Williams, Mark B. *Endō Shūsaku: A Literature of Reconciliation.* London and New York: Routledge, 1999.

Clay Smith

ESQUIVEL, LAURA (1951–) *Mexican essayist, novelist*

Laura Esquivel, a Mexican author of novels, screenplays, and essays, is best known for *LIKE WATER FOR CHOCOLATE: A Novel in Monthly Installments, with Recipes, Romances, and Home Remedies* (*Como agua para chocolate,* 1989). Continuing the magic realism tradition of GABRIEL GARCÍA MÁRQUEZ, Esquivel's highly read novel combines cooking and magic to tell a passionate and intriguing love story.

Much of Esquivel's writing is described as magic realism, a term first used in 1925 by Franz Roh when discussing a "quasi-surrealistic work of a group of German painters in the 1920s." Magic realism describes fiction that contains a mixture of realism and fantasy. Examples include Latin American writers Jorge Luis Borges and García Márquez. In an interview with Joan Smith, Esquivel explained her belief that "all objects have consciousness, that houses, for instance, guard the energies of the lives that have passed through them."

Esquivel was born the third of four children, and storytelling played an important part in her childhood in Mexico City. Her father, Julio Caesar Esquivel, worked as a telegraph operator and enjoyed making up and recording stories with his daughter on a reel-to-reel tape recorder. Esquivel lived in a Catholic household, but she describes her religious background as "eclectic," comprising her study of Eastern and other philosophies. In addition, the feminist movement of the 1960s and 1970s greatly shaped Esquivel's perspective on gender relations and artistic expression.

After finishing her education at Escuela Normal de Maestros (National Teacher's College), Esquivel worked as a kindergarten teacher and director of children's theater. When she could not find sufficient children's dramas to her liking, she began writing her own plays for adolescents. Between 1979 and 1980, she wrote children's shows for Mexican television.

Esquivel married Mexican director Alfonso Arau; during their 12-year marriage, they had one daughter, Sandra, and worked together professionally on several projects. He suggested that she write screenplays, and in 1985 Esquivel wrote the successful film *Chido One,* which her husband directed.

Following the success of her first movie, Esquivel began *Like Water for Chocolate* as a screenplay; however, producers told her that a period piece would be too expensive, so she reshaped the story into a novel, which was published in 1989 in Spanish and then translated into English in 1991. The unique tale of love and the kitchen quickly became an international best seller and gained critical acclaim for its innovative structure and style.

The book features 12 chapters, each beginning with a recipe that is stirred into the plot. The title of the novel refers to the process of boiling water for hot chocolate. As Claudia Loewenstein clarifies, "When someone is about to explode, we say that person is 'like water for chocolate.'" Thus, this romance tells the story of characters—Tita and Pedro—whose passion is so strong that they are about to explode. Even though they are in love, family tradition prevents their marriage—that is, because she is the youngest of three daughters, Tita must remain single and care for her mother, Mama Elena. Frustrated, Pedro decides to marry Rosaura, Tita's older sister, so that he may be near his true love. Esquivel conveys the tension of this triangle through magical elements, as seen in the wedding scene. Besides having to watch her sister marry her one true love, Tita must also bake their wedding cake. Her tears and sorrow become part of the cake as she prepares it, and when people consume it at the wedding they consume not just the cake but Tita's pain: "The moment they took their first bite of the cake, everyone was flooded with a great wave of longing."

Esquivel wrote the screenplay for the novel, and her husband directed the film, which achieved great success both financially and critically, receiving an Ariel Award nomination for best screenplay. The movie quickly became the top Spanish-language movie in the United States.

Although none of Esquivel's other writings have equaled the success of her first novel, she continues to create innovative fiction that possesses a cinematic quality. Esquivel wrote her next novel, *Law of Love* (1996), with the idea of it one day becoming a film. The story explores reincarnation and begins in the 16th century when the Spanish conquered Tenochtitlán (present-day Mexico City), where an Aztec princess was raped. The novel fast-forwards to the 23rd century to Azucena and Rodrigo, whose tale includes past lives, interplanetary travel, political intrigue, and romance. The layout of the book is noteworthy with its illustrations and a compact disk containing Puccini's opera songs. Similar to her use of recipes in *Like Water for Chocolate,* Esquivel guides the reader with instructions as to which tune to play between chapters.

In Esquivel's *Swift as Desire* (2001), Jubilo, a former telegraph operator (the profession of Esquivel's father), battles Parkinson's disease and has limited sight and communication abilities. His daughter, Lluvia, puts a telegraph in his room so he can communicate through Morse code. The novel then includes flashbacks of his life and shows how he helps people by editing their messages.

Esquivel's nonfiction includes *Between Two Fires: Intimate Writings on Life, Love, Food, and Flavor* (2001), a collection of essays about the spiritual power of food. The book blends recipes, musings on masculinity, personal anecdotes, politics, humor, and illustrations.

BIBLIOGRAPHY

Barbas-Rhoden. Laura. *Writing Women in Central America: Gender and the Fictionalization of History.* Athens: Ohio University Press, 2003.

Beer, Gabriella de. *Contemporary Mexican Women Writers.* Austin: University of Texas Press, 1996.

Colchie, Thomas. *A Whistler in the Nightworld: Short Fiction from the Latin Americas.* New York: Plume, 2002.

Esquivel, Laura. *Like Water for Chocolate.* Translated by Carol Christensen and Thomas Christensen. New York: Doubleday, 1992.

———. *Malinche.* Translated by Ernesto Mestre-Reed. New York: Atria Books, 2006.

———. *Swift as Desire*. New York: Crown Publishers, 2001.
Niebylski, Diana C. *Humoring Resistance: Laughter and the Excessive Body in Latin America Women's Fiction*. Albany: State University of New York Press, 2004.

Glenn Hutchinson

EVA LUNA ISABEL ALLENDE (1988)

The majority of the characters drawn by the writer ISABEL ALLENDE (1942–) possess some special talent or attribute. Eva Luna, the protagonist of the novel *Eva Luna,* is not an exception to that rule. In this novel, Allende experiments with a protagonist whose abilities mimic her own: Eva Luna, like her creator, the Chilean author Allende, is a storyteller. Fiction becomes both her reality and her livelihood.

In the character of Eva Luna, Allende adds another element to her usual mix of feminism and social commentary: She explores the nature of storytelling and, to some extent, the nature of reality. Both Eva Luna and her exceptional mother, Consuelo, possess the ability to recreate the world around them, shaping it so that people never really die and unpleasant events may be restructured. Consuelo, whose life has been both harsh and difficult, bequeaths to her daughter the ability to fill silences with words, and with words to create wondrous narratives and experience literally any event she can imagine. Consuelo, a servant woman, exemplifies both the oppression of the lower classes and the lack of freedom for women of her class and time, but she also values a particular type of liberty. With words, Consuelo does not merely escape reality but lives; "words are free," she instructs her daughter.

Eva Luna, the illegitimate daughter of Consuelo and an Indian gardener, whose snakebite Consuelo cures through an ingenious sexual remedy, does not benefit from the status or opportunities many of Allende's other female characters have enjoyed, including the upper-class heroines of her first two novels, Alba and her relatives in *The HOUSE OF THE SPIRITS* and Irene in *OF LOVE AND SHADOWS*. Instead, Eva Luna's life proceeds without the scripted education and wealth or professional jobs available to upper-class women. After her mother dies, the very young Eva enters the employment of a wealthy woman, whose petty abuse eventually inspires the child to snatch her wig from her head. Though she soon returns to her employer's house after a short break of freedom, Eva Luna eventually runs away for good—and begins to survive by telling stories.

Though Allende often includes colorful and marginal characters in her books, Eva Luna, because of her own plebian roots, finds herself surrounded by three very unusual people: her friend Huberto Naranjo, at first a street child and later a revolutionary; the inventive madam La Señora; and Melesio, the woman mistakenly equipped with a man's body. Eva practices her stories and gains worldly knowledge. After the police raid the red-light district, however, she finds sanctuary with another unusual character: Riad Halabí, called the Turk by his neighbors and whose benign presence in the novel perhaps reflects Allende's own early experiences in the Middle East.

Allende occasionally steps away from Eva Luna's story in order to relate the much shorter series of events that have brought Rolf Carlé, a native Austrian, to South America. The son of a brutal man whose favorite pastimes included sexually humiliating his wife and abusing his children, Rolf is scarred by more than his own virulent hatred of his father. Having witnessed firsthand the human bodies left behind at a German prison camp from World War II, and having helped to bury them, Rolf is fascinated with documentaries, the objective depiction of real events. As such, his interests contrast those of Eva Luna: fact versus fiction, with neither really able to tell the entire story.

With Riad, Eva experiences her first transcendent sexual encounter, and though she initiates a passionate relationship with Huberto Naranjo, Eva is fated to love Rolf. The two encounter each other against a backdrop typical of Allende's concerns and interests: guerrilla resistance against a tyrannical government. Notably, Allende recognizes a central flaw in the guerrilla movement that brings Rolf and Eva together: Though the ostensible goal of the "Revolution" is freedom, it would be an exclusive freedom, one in which Eva—being female—and many of her marginalized, socially unacceptable friends could not partake. Eva and Rolf meet at a party during which Eva tells one of her stories, a story that has the dual effect of convincing the director of national television to give her a contract and of attracting Rolf's interest.

Unlike both *The House of the Spirits* and *Of Love and Shadows,* the novel *Eva Luna* does not end with the immediate triumph of the existent government and a hopeful projection of change sometime in the future. Instead, the guerrilla movement to which Eva's former lover Huberto Naranjo now belongs succeeds in rescuing many of its members from a prison. Rolf captures the reality of the event on film, and Eva transforms it into the dubious fiction of her soap opera *Bolero.* Eva's soap opera mimics and reflects her own life: Its fictitious characters assume a reality of their own separate from the people who actually lived their lives. Eva spins the truth of her own experiences and the people around her into a complex web of illusion and fiction. Ultimately, Eva applies the same process to her own life.

Though the book is as full of sensuality as any other of Allende's books, Eva and her destined mate, Rolf, do not realize their love until the story's final pages. Nor do they exactly live happily ever after. Instead, Eva provides the reader with several projected future possibilities: Their love wears out, or perhaps Eva and Rolf luckily experience a love she does not have to continually invent. Eva ends the novel with an image of writing, an example of the type of recreation she has applied to both her life and her relationship with Rolf. She describes their honeymoon as exceptional, almost perfect, and she repairs the broken bits of her human characters; Rolf's nightmares disappear and she herself dances, envisioning stories with happy endings. While the "true" fate of Eva and Rolf remains ambiguous, Eva is nonetheless able to construct a happy ending for herself through the magical medium of storytelling.

BIBLIOGRAPHY

Diamond-Nigh, Lynne. "*Eva Luna*: Writing as History." *Studies in Twentieth Century Literature* 19, no. 1 (1995): 29–42.

Rojas, Sonia Riquelme, and Edna Aguirre Rehbein. *Critical Approaches to Isabel Allende's Novels.* New York: Peter Lang, 1991.

Winter S. Elliott

F

FALL, THE (LA CHUTE) ALBERT CAMUS (1956)

The Fall, the last novel penned by the Algerian-born French writer ALBERT CAMUS (1913–60) prior to his winning the 1957 Nobel Prize in literature, was written as a series of monologues delivered by a French expatriate and former lawyer currently living in the Netherlands. While *The Fall* lacks the action found in Camus's earlier novels *The STRANGER* (*L'étranger*) and *The PLAGUE* (*La peste*), it employs the same deceptively simple, journalistic prose and precise language found in those earlier works to explore similarly difficult existential questions about the nature of individual freedom, human relationships, power, and honest living.

The novel opens in a squalid bar called Mexico City, located somewhere in Amsterdam's wretched sailors' quarter. Jean-Baptiste Clamence, the novel's sole voice, has left Paris, the City of Light, behind and journeyed downward to Dante's hell. He approaches a fellow Frenchman under the pretext of assisting his countryman in communicating with the Dutch-speaking proprietor of the bar. Although his is the only voice actually "heard" during the course of the novel, Clamence occasionally responds to queries or comments presumably made by his listener. As a result of these periodic hints, Camus's reader learns that the unnamed Frenchman to whom Clamence speaks over the course of five days is a moderately educated Christian lawyer who has recently arrived from Paris and who expresses some curiosity about indulging in some of the more hedonistic pursuits available in Amsterdam's red-light

district. Initially taking the form of friendly barroom pleasantries, Clamence's monologue quickly assumes an air of seriousness and captures the listener's attention with ambiguously philosophical-sounding statements and phrases. The speaker's description of his occupation as "judge-penitent" causes the listener to ask for clarification.

Eventually it becomes clear to the reader that Clamence deliberately uses such ambiguous phrasing to elicit questions that will enable him to discuss himself without seeming too egocentric, a trait he seems particularly averse to despite his clear predilection for such self-centered discussion. Using vague language to describe his past, Clamence depicts his younger self as a perpetually smiling and popular man whose exceptional generosity, empathy, and kindness were matched only by his triumphs as a lawyer. An exceedingly happy young man, Clamence excelled in court, in sports, and with women and was, in his own estimation, one of the most widely respected Parisians of his time.

Although Clamence's earlier monologues seem to display an almost boundless self-satisfaction, a few cracks begin appearing in the speaker's otherwise saccharine recollections of courtroom munificence and extraordinary kindness to disabled people. Initially, Clamence offhandedly mentions that his hitherto unquestioned happiness suddenly hit a roadblock and that he has since changed into a very different sort of person. As these hints begin peppering Clamence's monologues with greater frequency, the listener seems to inquire about them enough to enable Clamence to promise to address them in future conversations. As a result, Clamence ensures that he will have a listener for several days.

As the two men continue to meet, either for drinks at Mexico City or for strolls around Amsterdam, he begins what is a highly calculated confession. At one point he recalls peals of laughter he heard one evening in Paris, the source of which he could not identify. The discomfort he felt at that moment coupled with two other seemingly unrelated occurrences prompted him to reevaluate his life. The first instance occurred when Clamence was driving and found himself stuck behind a stalled motorcycle when a red light had turned green. After blowing his horn politely, Clamence recalls, the motorcyclist responded with a vulgarity. When Clamence's second attempt to ask the man to remove his vehicle from the road in order to allow traffic to pass met with a similarly derisive remark, he exited his automobile with the intent of striking the cyclist. During the ensuing confrontation, someone punched Clamence for seeking to take advantage of the motorcyclist's unsteady, split-legged position. Stunned, Clamence returned to his car and drove off without retaliation. The second event Clamence recalls occurred during one of his customary late-night strolls through Paris. As he crossed a bridge that evening, he observed a young woman glaring into the Seine. Saying nothing, Clamence passed by the woman and continued walking home. As he walked away, he heard the unmistakable sound of a body hitting the water; he paused, then hastened home, doing nothing about the woman.

Whereas the former instance enabled Clamence to understand that he was not as universally well-regarded or dominant a figure as he had previously believed himself to be, the second instance taught him that his kindnesses were not genuine. In other words, Clamence had acted kindly in order to earn the esteem of others. Had his kindness been genuine, Clamence reasons, he would have done something to help the suicidal woman. These realizations disturbed him to such a degree that he sought solace in romance and alcohol. However, he soon learned that he lied to women in order to gain their affection and that the pursuit of false love was as isolating and unsatisfying as that of superficial charity.

Unable to enjoy his hedonistic pursuits and thoroughly dissatisfied with himself, Clamence fled Paris for Amsterdam in order to avoid the constant sourceless laughter he felt in his native city. Deciding that everyone on earth was guilty of something—including Christ, who, having survived the Slaughter of the Innocents, was guilty of letting others die for him—Clamence came to believe that such guilt enabled everyone to pass judgment on everyone else. A sinner himself, Clamence was thus vulnerable to judgment in the same way as a man guilty of a violent crime. Ultimately, it is this incessant judgment that plagues Clamence, and he creates the occupation of judge-penitent in order to elude the sentence levied upon him: laughter.

As an atheist, Clamence realizes that God cannot punish man; only man can pass judgment and punish man. However, since the man who judges is guilty of something, he will be subject to ridicule—that is, he will be judged a hypocrite if he judges someone else. From these realizations, Clamence devises his solution: He will confess his sins to others so that he will be clear to pass judgment on everyone else. By judging himself, Clamence prevents others from doing so, leaving him simultaneously unable to be judged and fit to pass judgment on others. Thus, Clamence regains the sense of power and superiority he had experienced when he believed himself to be the noblest, kindest man in Paris.

Widely considered an autobiographical novel, *The Fall* essentially implicates all of humanity. We all judge one another but seek to avoid judgment by any means necessary. Our disdain for Clamence, then, amounts to our disdain for our own hypocritical, selfish natures; his anti-solution to the problem of universal guilt and judgment is a challenge Camus poses to us all to find a real solution to suffering within the human condition. Only then will we be absolved of our human guilt.

BIBLIOGRAPHY
Brée, Germaine, ed. *Camus: A Collection of Critical Essays.* Englewood Cliffs, N.J.: Prentice Hall, 1962.
Lottman, Herbert R. *Camus: A Biography.* Garden City, N.Y.: Doubleday 1979.

Rhein, Phillip H. *Albert Camus*. New York: Twayne Publishing, 1969.

Todd, Oliver. *Albert Camus: A Life*. New York: Knopf, 1997.

Erik Grayson

FAMILY Ba Jin (1933)

This important work by Chinese author Ba Jin (a pen name for Li Feigan) tells an extremely intriguing and memorable story that is often taught in history courses. One snowy night, two young men hurry home. They wear the same uniform and study at the same academy; they are brothers. Jue Min is the elder one, with a pair of glasses on his round face, while Jue Hui, the younger sibling, is interested in the anarchic and democratic ideals influenced by the May Fourth Movement in 1919. The brothers have grown up in a wealthy family that belongs to a typical feudal clan controlled by their grandfather, Venerable Master Gao. The boys' elder brother is Jue Xin. Thus begins this quintessentially Chinese story, although the work was written in English by Ba Jin.

The three brothers display different characteristics and attitudes. Jue Min loves his cousin Qin and wishes they could study together after the academy rescinds its no-female rule, and then they could marry. Jue Hui likes a maidservant named Ming Feng, but he pays more attention to the rebellion against the autocracy than he does to the young woman. Jue Xin obeys the arrangement by Venerable Master Gao and marries Miss Li after graduating from a middle school, although he loves his cousin Mei very much and is eager to continue his studies. He knows that his two younger brothers are dissatisfied with his obedience, but he considers that he has no other choice. As the eldest son and the eldest grandson, has the filial duty to help his grandfather continue the family line, which has lasted for four generations. Fortunately, his marriage turns out to be happy. His wife, Rui Jue, is beautiful and mild, and their intense love produces their first boy, Hai Chen.

Jue Xin's lover, his cousin Mei, lives a miserable life. She marries and becomes a widow within one year, and returns home to live with her mother because she could not bear her mother-in-law's ill-treatment. The young people of the big family are sympathetic to her, especially Jue Xin.

Chinese New Year comes to the family, who live in Southwest China. Venerable Master Gao decides to celebrate the year's most important festival, despite the battles and fighting breaking out around the city. The family reunion banquet seems to go well, but the peaceful day ends when soldiers enter the city after the Festival of Lanterns. Some relatives of the family flee to the Kao compound, including Qin and Mei. At the garden of plum blossom, Jue Xin meets Mei. She tells her cousin that she would rather die than live with the sorrow of being alive. Jue Xin has no idea how to comfort her, but he weeps with her.

Ming Feng, another tragic woman in the family, is about 17 years old and has worked as a maidservant for more than eight years. She wishes to marry Jue Hui, but she is not a free woman: Venerable Master Gao plans to send her as a mistress to Milord Feng, an ugly man old enough to be her grandfather. The poor girl is unwilling and cries for help, but none dare to dispute the patriarch. Before being sent to Milord Feng, Ming Feng enters the room of Jue Hui at midnight. To her he represents her last hope of salvation, but he is too busy working on his academic articles to notice the lovely girl's depression. Finally, Ming Feng decides to commit suicide by diving into the pool in the backyard of the big house; a fresh life disappears soundlessly from the earth. Jue Min and others pity the girl, while Jue Hui now regrets his carelessness. However, none of the people could have changed Ming Feng's fate. Wan-er is sent to Feng's house instead, so that Venerable Master Gao can keep his promise to his friend. In his eyes, Ming Feng and Wan-er were only gifts; the only way they can avoid their unfair fate is to die.

Venerable Master Gao now directs his attention to Jue Min, deciding on a marriage between his grandson and the grandniece of Milord Feng. But this time his scheme fails. Jue Min refuses the marriage and goes into hiding with the help of Jue Hui. Venerable Master Gao grows angry and orders Jue Xin to find his younger brother. Furthermore, he intends to fulfill his arrangement by making Jue Hui the bridegroom. Jue Xin tries to persuade Jue Hui to agree, but his younger brother calls him a coward and says that it would lead to another tragedy. Presently the family hears the news of Mei's death, and Jue Xin is heart-stricken. He hurries to Mei's home to see his cousin for the last time and helps with the burial. The miserable experience awakes Jue Xin, prompting him to side with his brothers against their grandfather.

Venerable Master Gao grows weaker and weaker after his 66th birthday. He now wishes to see the whole clan reunited. He promised to release the engagement of Jue Min and encourages his grandson to study hard for the honor of the clan. Jue Min and Qin even receive his blessing to marry.

Jue Xin, although happy for his younger brother, is worried about his wife, who is soon due to give birth to their second baby. His uncles and aunts implore him to move his wife out of the city, as the coffin of Venerable Master Gao would be afflicted with the curse of the blood-glow. Jue Hui sees this as ridiculous and asks his elder brother to fight for his wife. But Jue Xin accepts the wrong decision again. Four days later, Rui Jue dies in childbirth without seeing her husband for the last time, as Jue Xin had been forbidden to enter the delivery room during the period of mourning for his grandfather.

Watching tragedy strike again and again, Jue Hui claims that he can no longer stay with his suffocating family. Supported by his elder brothers, he departs for Shanghai to begin his new life in the new world.

Family is the first volume of Ba Jin's trilogy named *Torrent.* Regarded as a semiautobiographical novel, it was finished when the author was in his 20s, a novel written by a young man and for the youth. Ba Jin demonstrates the common expression of intellectuals at a time when Chinese society was transforming from traditional Confucianism to enlightenment and individualism. He depicts the struggles and tragedies, love and hatred of the young generation. The novel is one of his representative works and has been studied for many years.

The most moving part of the novel reveals the deaths of three young women, Ming Feng, Mei, and Rui Jue. Neither the rich lady nor the servant girl has the right to choose her partner, but each is forced to accept her prearranged destiny, whatever it might be. They die miserably by an invisible killer—feudal rules. Ba Jin illustrates their tragedies with enormous sympathy and similarly enormous indignation. In this sense, some scholars point out that the novel projects feminist themes and criticism. Indeed, this is a primary reason that *Family* became so popular with China's young readers at the time of its publication in 1933 and throughout the 20th century.

In his treatment of the male characters, Ban Jin describes two men possessing very complicated feelings. One is Jue Xin, the eldest brother. On the one hand, he is a victim of conservatism, obliged to give up his idealism and act according to established traditions and rules. He loses his women one by one and does nothing rebellious but cries in the corner. On the other hand, Jue Xin is an accomplice, helping his grandfather to find out where Jue Min is in order to force an absurd marriage. He insists on nonresistance, even though he agrees with his younger brothers. Jue Hui has mercy on him but also is angered by his obedience, reflecting the author's own attitude toward this character.

Venerable Master Gao is another complex figure. He has a dream of a big family and does all he can to turn it into reality. Although he creates several tragedies, he makes his decisions according to ancestral rules and never considers that his decisions will hurt his children. On the contrary, he loves them. Withdrawing his order on his deathbed shows that he remained a kind grandfather at the end, even if he was an ironhanded patriarch.

As for Jue Hui, though he is a high-spirited youth rebelling against his family's restrictions, he still possesses ideas inherited from his feudal family. For example, though he likes the maidservant Ming Feng, he never expresses his love or his hidden dreams: If only Ming Feng were a lady like Qin, he would marry her in a heartbeat.

In essence, Ba Jin exhibits the reality of a troubled age though his novel *Family,* a mirror of Chinese society during the early part of the 20th century.

BIBLIOGRAPHY

Lang, Olga. *Pa Chin and His Writings: Chinese Youth between Two Revolutions.* Cambridge, Mass.: Harvard University Press, 1967.

Mao, Nathan K. *Pa Chin.* Boston: Twayne Publishers, 1978.

Ru Yi-ling. *The Family Novel: Toward a Generic Definition.* New York: Peter Lang, 1992.

Mei Han

FAMILY MOSKAT, THE (DIE FAMILIE MOSHKAT) ISAAC BASHEVIS SINGER (1950)

Published simultaneously in Yiddish and English, the novel *The Family Moskat* uses straightforward narrative as well as letters and diary entries to cover the decline of a well-to-do Jewish family, the Moskats, living in a *shtetl* (village) in Warsaw, Poland. ISAAC BASHEVIS SINGER's (1904–91) novel follows them from the end of the 19th century to the start of World War II. In a way, the family represents the decline of European Jewry, for many times their troubles are particularly Jewish troubles, and ultimately their fate is a Jewish fate. As with much of mankind's sufferings, however, the Moskat family's sufferings are caused most of all by the human heart, by the pangs of the soul, and are not the characteristics of ethnicity. The persecution of the Jews makes these universal sufferings pale by comparison, of course, but as Singer presents it within the staging of individual lives and not the general status of identity, such persecution becomes all the more tragic. *The Family Moskat* is not so much a novel about Jewish life as it is about human suffering amplified in the lives of Jewish individuals.

The novel begins with the third marriage of the Moskat patriarch, Meshulam Moskat, to a materialistic but endearing woman named Rosa from eastern Austria. She marries not so much for love as for security, for herself but especially for her daughter Adele, to secure an all-important dowry for marriage. Modernized as she is by European schools, Adele finds Warsaw is too "Asiatic," and like her Jewish identity, the city is foreign and unsettling. Meshulam does not tell his children about the marriage until after he returns from his trip; he does not even tell his right-hand man, the bailiff Koppel. But this air of mystery fits Meshulam perfectly. In the 50-odd years that he has been accumulating wealth and expanding his family, Meshulam has also been accumulating reputations, envy, adulation, and suspicions—a situation that parallels to Jews throughout European history.

Also coming into Warsaw is Asa Heshel Bannet, the prodigal son and grandson of rabbis in Tereshpol Minor, a small village world away from the urban chaos of Warsaw. Asa comes to Warsaw to find his intellectual fortune, and for the rest of the novel the young man squanders whatever worldly, familial, or spiritual fortune happens to come his way to pay for that quest. Intellectual yet undisciplined, he is just modern enough to stray from his Jewish tradition in search of answers to larger looming questions. For the most part, though, he is satisfied with merely formulating the questions, never bothering to take steps to find the answers, out of a lack of passion and a lack of confidence. He runs into Abram Shapiro, son-in-law to Meshulam Moskat, while showing a letter of recommendation to a Dr. Shmaryahu Jacobi in hopes of starting a long course of intense study. Jacobi is never seen again in the novel, as if Abram pulls Asa away from a life of purpose to a life of self-satisfaction, actively dodging all responsibility. Readers will recognize the story of Abraham from Genesis; Abram means "father" or "leader," but he is chosen by God, who tells him, "Your name will be Abraham, for I have made you a father of many nations." As his dissolute life unfolds before the reader, it is clear that Abram will never be an Abraham.

Abram finds Asa a room with Gina, a woman married to a religious fanatic named Akiba, who makes her life unbearable by indulging his mania for purification at every moment and shirking his duties as a husband. Abram brings Asa to the Moskat family's Chanukah celebration, intriguing two of the Moskat women, Rose's daughter Adele and Abram's niece Hadassah. Hadassah and Asa run off to Switzerland; the details of their time there are provided not by the regular narrator but through Hadassah's diary entries. Hadassah confesses that while she is troubled by the traditional Jewish religion, she cannot let go of her belief in God or in man, while Asa believes that man is morally "lower than the beasts." She believes that in Switzerland she and Asa will "recover our ideals together." Here it should be noted that *Hadassah* is the Hebrew name of Esther, who is celebrated for declaring her faith in the face of persecution, and the celebration of her selfless acts is the Purim holidays, which occur during Hadassah and Asa's misadventure. Hadassah returns to Warsaw in rags, barely alive, and escorted by police. This event adds to Meshulam's conviction that his family has been a disgrace to him, and he dies without writing out a will and dividing up their inheritance.

Adele leaves Warsaw for Switzerland, ostensibly to go back to school, but in her letter narrating her time with Asa in that country, she admits that school "wasn't really on my mind." The reader has enough familiarity with Asa by this time to know that she is lying to herself as well as to her mother when she talks of how affectionate Asa is, how in love he claims to be with her, and of the surety of their future. Hadassah, meanwhile, has been forced to marry Fishel Kutner, ensuring the disappointment of two more lives.

Years go by, and Hadassah, Adele, Asa, and many other members of the Moskat family are miserable. Despite the unfortunate outcome of their old elopement, Hadassah and Asa are still in love, and they soon begin an affair. Adele is well aware of this, as are the rest of the Moskat family. Abram's wife, Hama, finally leaves him despite her terror of living alone, while Abram periodically sleeps with his mistress, Ida Prager, who left her husband some time ago to be with Abram. Symbolically, these two adulterous relationships permeate the celebration of Yom Kippur, the Day of Atonement; in fact, Hadassah and Asa consummate their affair in Hadassah's bed on that holiest of days. Adele confronts Asa and tells him that he has talked himself into the affair, but he admits only to himself that he did not run to Hadassah as much as he ran away from the responsibilities of family and the burden of providing for others. Inevitably, he gets the chance to duck those responsibilities when Adele has David, her child by him, and Hadassah has their daughter, Dacha.

At the same time, the Moskats' former caretaker, Koppel, helps himself to much of the family's money, since they have never divided up Meshalum's inheritance. He also helps himself to one of Meshulam's daughters, Leah, who divorces her husband to run away with Koppel to America. Koppel divorces his wife, Bashele, leaving her and his children to scrape by until Bashele remarries. Koppel and Leah return at the end of the novel to reveal just how successful Koppel has become through bootlegging and other criminal activities in America. Their reappearance in the lives of the Moskat family shows how "modernized" and "Americanized" Leah's children have become. They return to a Poland weighed down with tension,

suspicion, and gloom as the Nazis prepare for their conquest.

The final chapters of the novel take place amid the Passover celebration, playing on the theme of exile and suffering, with members of the Moskat family making the matzo, "the bread of affliction which our forefathers ate in the land of Egypt." Hadassah, true to her name, wonders to herself if the new Haman (a notorious minister in the book of Esther) in Germany will "finish them off." The novel ends quite eerily, as the bombs are going off around Asa and Adele, and their attempt, along with others, to get to Israel by sea fails. As Asa tells another family member, "the ship wandered about on all the seas, and in the end they sent it back. That's what's happening to us Jews—pushed here and there, and then thrown out like garbage." Throughout the Jews hope for the Messiah to "come quickly while there are still a few pious Jews left," so when the final words of Gina's love interest, Hertz Yanovar, are given, among the rubble and bombs of Warsaw and upon news of Hadassah's death, it seems a cruel joke has been played: "The Messiah will come soon." Asked by Asa what he is talking about, he clarifies, "Death is the Messiah. That's the real truth."

The anguish of these family members form the basis of the novel, as relationships deteriorate or explode, as individuals are torn between love of tradition and the seduction of newer ideas, and as older members regret what has happened to the once strong bonds between families in particular and humankind in general. Outside forces thrust in now and again to turn the anguish into more emblematic suffering, as if to reinforce the real desolation of exile to Jews. As World War II breaks out, gentile neighbors turn on former Jewish friends, and Polish soldiers turn on fellow soldiers like Asa for being "Christ-killers," while as the Germans enter Warsaw, the Jews who welcome them in hopes of treatment better than they received under the Russians are kicked in the face by their glorious liberators. Masha Moskat, one of Leah's daughters, falls for a Pole named Yanek, an artist who finds himself drawn to Jews for various reasons. She converts to Christianity, is disowned by the Moskats, and is never accepted fully by her husband. In Yanek's mind his failures are wrapped up in the treachery of Jews, and as he chooses a military career and becomes successful, he starts to ape the anti-Semitism of others. Masha is led to make a halfhearted attempt at suicide.

The only real light of hope or transport from these sufferings comes, curiously, with the more faithful Jews—not that they suffer less, but that they are less wrenched by it. Hadassah's infidelity anguishes her husband Fishel, but he takes the situation to be divine choice, placing him where he is needed as he prays for her lost soul and even steps in to distribute Meshulam's inheritance and assure justice for the family. More tellingly, Jekuthiel the watchmaker and modern intellectual (as if Singer aligns the onslaught of modernity upon tradition with the indifferent progress of time) sarcastically greets a rabbi, who takes the greeting as a jibe at his thoroughly unmodern beliefs. In response, the rabbi takes up his Talmud and reads, wearing a "transported expression on his face," for "not in a long time had the rabbi found so much sweetness in poring over the ancient texts."

In the English version, the novel stops at Hertz Yanovar's declaration that death is the Messiah, with the fate of the Moskats left to the reader's imagination, stopping at the edge of annihilation. The Yiddish version, however, has one sole Moskat member escaping to Israel, thus leading one to assume that Singer wanted to portray to fellow Jews the undying hope that marks their identity after the Diaspora.

BIBLIOGRAPHY

Hadda, Janet. *Isaac Bashevis Singer: A Life.* New York: Oxford University Press, 1997.

Farrell, Grace. *Critical Essays on Isaac Bashevis Singer.* New York: G. K. Hall, 1996.

Singer, Isaac Bashevis. *Collected Stories.* New York: Penguin Putnam, 2004.

———. *Collected Stories: A Friend to Kafka to Passion.* New York: Penguin Putnam, 2004.

———. *More Stories from My Father's Court.* New York: Farrar, Straus, 2000.

Wolitz, Seth L. *The Hidden Isaac Bashevis Singer.* Austin: The University of Texas Press, 2001.

Matthew Guy

FAMILY OF PASCUAL DUARTE, THE (LA FAMILIA DE PASCUAL DUARTE)

CAMILO JOSÉ CELA (1942) The Spanish author CAMILO JOSÉ CELA (1916–2002) started his successful first novel in 1940 and finished it in 1942. After being rejected by several editors, the book was published in Burgos, Spain, in 1942, and it caused immediate opposing reactions. Most criticism of the novel, however, was based on its morality rather than its artistic value, as the public debated the bad example offered by Pascual Duarte's behavior. *The Family of Pascual Duarte* has often been associated with ALBERT CAMUS's *The STRANGER,* published the same year. Cela's novel includes meaningless violence and an apparent lack of morality, which can be easily linked to the works of existentialists like Camus. Cela's Pascual Duarte commits three murders, including matricide, and offers no hint of sincere remorse for killing his own mother. The Catholic Church condemned the text as depraved and morally harmful; nonetheless, the novel was an absolute success. A second edition was issued in 1943, but this time it was banned, and it could not be republished in Spain until 1946.

The first chapters work as the introduction—very much in the tradition of Spanish picaresque literature. These chapters look at Pascual Duarte's early years, not very happy ones as it transpires. In the novel, the writer presents a transcription of a long letter that Pascual Duarte himself has written from prison and from which the reader gets in contact with the details of his ominous crimes. Cela thus uses the well-known technique of the "found manuscript," very popular in Spanish literary tradition, from Cervantes to PÍO BAROJA. By this technique, the writer achieves the sense of distance from the actual text that is also a characteristic of the works by Cela.

The plot is simple and linear, although facts and real time do not fit on certain occasions. Pascual Duarte starts his story by describing his village and the customs of ordinary people in a realistic, but not too thorough, manner. It is notable that one of the houses prominent in the narration belongs to the person that will become Pascual's last victim. The five first chapters refer to his family and upbringing and are filled with details about himself, his parents, his brother Mario, and his sister Rosario. His brother will die very young, and Pascual's first sexual experience with his future wife, Lola, takes place not far from his brother's grave.

The narration is often interrupted by scenes that describe Pascual Duarte's life in prison and the thoughts and impressions he reveals while writing his life. After the first five chapters, the next six focus on his marriage to Lola and their honeymoon, which includes a dramatic ending: Pascual Duarte injures a man from his village in a bar row. The couple's first son is lost when Lola has a miscarriage, and the second dies when the baby is only 11 months old. Details of his misfortune and reflections from prison will follow up until chapter 14, in which Pascual Duarte tries to escape from his disgraceful fate by running away and trying to start a new life in a northern city of Spain. Happiness does not last long: In the following chapter he returns to his native village, where he witnesses the death of his wife and discovers that the lover of his sister has also been intimate with his Lola.

In chapter 16, Pascual Duarte stabs El Estirao, his sister's lover, to death. He suffers his first imprisonment as punishment for this crime, and he is released after three years. His sister tries to offer Pascual a new life and marriage. Esperanza—a name that means "hope" in Spanish—will become his second wife. But Pascual soon becomes conscious that his mother will make his new life impossible, as she had already done with his former marriage. Chapter 19 includes a meticulous description of her murder. The end of the novel incorporates another note from the transcriptionist and two "letters" that inform the reader about the end of the story, which concludes with Pascual Duarte's execution for his terrible crimes. These letters try to bring a sense of realism that makes the story even more thrilling.

Sometimes the words of Pascual Duarte seem to be simultaneously justifying and regretting his actions, which is perhaps the most important point for discussion when studying the novel. Violence is all around Pascual Duarte, but this antihero, instead of looking for an alternative to his situation, becomes even more violent toward those who surround him. The existential conflict between the man and his environs is eventually resolved by the victory of his sordid conditions, except that Pascual Duarte takes the situation further: From being a victim of the number of frustrations that he faces in life (the troublesome upbringing, the loss of a newborn son, his unhappy marriage, and so on), he becomes an insane, cold-blooded killer.

BIBLIOGRAPHY

Gibson, Ian. *Cela, el hombre que quiso ganar.* Madrid: Aguilar, 2003.

Perez, Janet. *Camilo Jose Cela Revisited: The Later Novels.* New York: Twayne Publishers, 2000.

Sánchez Salas, Gaspar. *Cela: El hombre a quien vi llorar.* Barcelona: Carena Editorial, 2002.

Tudela, Mariano. *Cela.* Madrid: ESESA, 1970.

Umbra, Francisco. *Cela: Un cadáver esquisito.* Barcelona: Planeta, 2002.

Rafael Ruiz

FAR FROM THE HIGHWAY (*LÅNGT FRÅN LANGSVÄGEN*) Vilhem Moberg (1929)

This is the first book in a two-novel set about life on the remote and isolated Ulvaskog farm in Småland, Sweden, at the end of the 19th century. The young farmer Adolf and his family are the fourth generation to cultivate the Ulvaskog farmland. Their struggles and destinies are put in perspective by detailed descriptions of the recurring aspects of farming and the repetitive elements of Christmas, weddings, and funerals. The second novel in the set is *Clenched Fist*. The two novels represent an early example of Swedish novelist Vilhelm Moberg's (1898–1973) literary primitivism and his use of the novel form as social criticism.

The old head of the Ulvaskog family, Bengt, catches pneumonia and dies during sowing. His son Adolf inherits the responsibility for the farm and his younger siblings and mother. Central to the story is Adolf's infatuation with Emma, the daughter of the lay assessor Otto, and the many disappointments that the two lovers must endure before they can finally marry. Their initial love results in a son born out of wedlock and sent off to live with foster parents. Otto, Emma's father, does not consider Adolf a worthy suitor and for years refuses to give his daughter in marriage to the young man. Meanwhile Adolf struggles to buy out his siblings, Hasse and Tilda, for their share of the farmstead. Hasse solves his money problem by marrying a rich woman. Signe is also preparing for marriage, but her fiancé drowns before the ceremony. She is heartbroken but gives birth to a daughter, Gärda, whom she raises on Ulvaskog. Adolf's youngest brother, Kalle, is cross-eyed and worries that as a consequence of his physical abnormality that he will never marry.

Death marks the changes of the seasons at Ulvaskog. Kalle succumbs to fever and dies. Soon after, Adolf's mother, Lotta, dies, but not before she has put up a long and stubborn fight against Emma, who is finally wedded to Adolf. Otto has been declared bankrupt and suddenly finds Adolf to be a most suitable son-in-law. But neither Adolf nor Emma can forget their first child, Per-Adolf, who is, according to Emma, still living with his foster parents. Adolf is also disappointed with his and Emma's first legitimate son, Emil, and worries that he cannot live up to the responsibility of managing a large farm. The real crisis occurs when Emma refuses to get Per-Adolf and bring him back to Ulvaskog. She finally reveals the truth about the fate of their first-born son. Because she could not part with him as her father had demanded, she drowned the baby in a ditch when he was just 17 days old, and she has been composing the letters from his imaginative foster parents ever since. Adolf's hatred and an all-consuming feeling of guilt lead Emma to take her own life. Her death is paired with a description of a group of parish members who wait in vain for the world to cease and the Savior to appear with the passing of the old century. The book ends with the beginning of the new century and the realization that there is no salvation from the daily toils and tragedies that humans must endure.

Moberg's pessimism is alleviated by his detailed descriptions of daily life on the farm. The beauty that is conveyed both in and through the many accounts of repetitive tasks such as sowing, plowing, and reaping suggests that there is meaning in life, but, as Adolf realizes after he learns about the death of Per-Adolf, the significance of any meaning lies beyond human understanding. The novel is an early example of the primitivism that would come to characterize much of Moberg's writing. Adolf has rejected the teachings of the church on the basis that he cannot ask forgiveness for sins that he does not regret, but his decision also corresponds with his increasing closeness and dedication to the land, which can be likened to a form of pantheism where nature and spirituality are closely linked. He realizes that he is but a link in a long chain of people who have lived and will continue to live off the farm's riches. Life and death surround the temporary home that is every person's lot.

BIBLIOGRAPHY

Holmes, Philip. *Vilhelm Moberg: En Introduktion Till Hans Författarskap.* Stockholm: Carlsson, 2001.
Platen, Magnus von. *Den Unge Vilhem Moberg: En Levnadsteckning.* Stockholm: Bonniers, 1978.

Malin Lidström Brock

FATELESSNESS (*SORSTALANSÁG*) Imre Kertész (1975)

Fatelessness is the first novel of Imre Kertész (1929–), a work that played a significant part in the author's receipt of the 2002 Nobel Prize in literature. A novel about a Hungarian-Jewish adolescent boy who is deported to Auschwitz and then imprisoned in Buchenwald, *Fatelessness* is written in a peculiar ironic-sarcastic tone that differentiates it from common Holocaust representations. The experience of the concentration camps has remained a central topic for Kertész in his subsequent works. Without questioning the singularity of the Holocaust, Kertész considers the postwar communist dictatorship in Hungary to be a "continuation" of the Nazi horrors. Having experienced several dictatorships, Kertész uses his oeuvre to find responses for the position of the individual within totalitarian systems and generally in the face of history.

Fatelessness consists of three main parts: the introduction to the world of György Köves, the 14-year-old protagonist, in the first chapters; his arrest and deportation to Auschwitz and his imprisonment in Buchenwald, comprising the major part of the book; and his return to postwar Hungary in the last chapter. The reader meets Köves, a Hungarian Jew, at the moment when his father is obliged to go to a forced labor camp. Although he does not reject religion explicitly, he is sceptical toward it as he speaks about everything around him with academic distance and reservation.

Köves accepts everything that happens to him and always seeks to understand the motives for even the most irrational and horrific events. His alienated character enables him to see through anti-Semitic ideology. In an emotional discussion with some girl neighbors, he explicates the significance of having to wear the yellow star, which upsets one of the girls. According to Köves, the yellow star needs to be worn so that Jews can be differentiated from the other people. Thus, there is no real internal or external difference between Jews and non-Jews, otherwise one would not need a sign to stigmatize them. This explanation, though, makes the girl even more despairing since it reveals the senselessness of her sufferings.

One of the novel's main motives is precisely to show this senselessness of mass murder, the breakdown of reason in and after Auschwitz. For this, Köves often uses reason to justify what happens to him, without ethical considerations. For instance, he describes the death of an elderly woman on the train trip as "understandable," since she was sick and suffered from lack of water for such a long time. Such justifications become more and more absurd and immoral to an extreme point, where Köves seems to "understand" the crematoria of Auschwitz. By this Kertész evokes and subverts the tradition of the Enlightenment and romanticism, both of which cherished the idea of the human individual who is able to know the world through reason, and by that progress to a better future. In contrast to Goethe's Wilhelm Meister, who through his adventures ends up being an experienced person, Köves is thrown into a world where the sequence of events leads to his own diminishment.

In the concentration camp, Köves is less and less able to preserve his will for life. Not only must he go through total physical deterioration, but he is also excluded from the community of the religious Jews, who all speak Yiddish and help one another. Soon he comes to a point where he is not able to keep up further, and he is transported to an infirmary nearby. After a minor recovery, he becomes the object of exclusion again. One of the other patients, for instance, is from Slovakia and does not like Hungarians. Thus, after having been excluded from the Hungarian society due to his Jewishness, he is now in the concentration camp stigmatized as Hungarian. Further, he is not considered as a real Jew by the orthodox inmates. These moments of the novel provide excellent examples of Kertész's subversive prose that touches on sensitive issues of national, religious, and ethnic identity.

After his liberation, Köves returns to Hungary, where the first man he meets denies the horror of Auschwitz and demands from Köves proof of the gas chambers' existence. Later, the conductor wants to fine him because he does not have a ticket. He cannot return to his home because someone else now lives there already, though he is eventually able to enter his neighbor's flat. Köves learns from the two elderly Jews who live there that his father never came back and that his mother remarried. In this discussion the motif of senselessness relates to the notion of fate. To accept his life as his fate would justify the Nazi mass murders and concentration camps. On the other hand, he cannot just forget his life story, as it needs to be rendered into a narrative. He comes to the conclusion that even though one needs to exist within circumstances contingent on fate, one needs also to make one's own destiny.

Fatelessness is a unique piece of literature that denounces the senselessness of discrimination and totalitarian systems, whereas it also expounds the problems of identity construction and linguistic representation. It is a novel that is able to talk about Auschwitz without a demand for moralization and discuss the possibility of human self and human agency in the face of history.

BIBLIOGRAPHY

Heller, Àgnes. *Auschwitz és Gulág.* Budapest: Múlt és Jövő, 2002.
Lányi, Dániel. "A Sorstalanság Kisérlete." (The attempt of fatelessness) *Holmi* 7, no. 5 (May 1995): 665–674.
Kaposi, Dávid. "'Narrativeless': Cultural Concepts and the [sic] *Fateless.*" *SPIEL: Siegener Periodicum zur Internationalen Empirischen Literaturwissenschaft* 21, no. 1 (2002): 89–105.
Radnóti, Sándor. "Auschwitz mint Szellemi Életforma." ("Auschwitz as a mental form of life") *Holmi* 3 (1991): 370–378.
Scheibner, Tamás, and Zoltán Gábor Szücs, eds. *Az Értelmezés Szükségessége.* (The necessity of interpretation) Budapest: L'Harmattan, 2002.

Eszter Susán

FEAST OF THE GOAT, THE (*LA FIESTA DEL CHIVO*) MARIO VARGAS LLOSA (2000) *The Feast of the Goat,* the seminal work by MARIO VARGAS LLOSA (1936–   ), describes the end of Rafael Leónidas

Trujillo's regime in the Dominican Republic. The novel begins in the present day with the return of Urania Cabral to Ciudad Trujillo (Santo Domingo) for the first time after a 35-year absence. Vargas Llosa develops her history as a woman who escaped her Dominican past, only to become haunted and fascinated by it in adulthood. A successful lawyer in Manhattan, Urania lives estranged from her family and country; however, she finds herself studying and reading about the Trujillo regime in her spare time. Upon her arrival in Santo Domingo, Urania appears fearful and agitated as she contemplates her return to her childhood house, yet she remains determined to confront her elderly and mute father, the deposed former president of Trujillo's senate.

As Urania speaks, first to her father and later to her aunt and cousins, Vargas Llosa uses her personal narrative as a vehicle for temporal shifts between present-day Santo Domingo and the oppression of Dominicans by the Trujillo regime during the early 1960s. Much of what Urania recalls from her life as a young girl involves the politics of the time, although often indirectly. Amid these fragmented memories, Vargas Llosa intermingles the experiences of Agustín Cabral, General Trujillo himself, and the assassins implicated in the 1961 anti-Trujilla revolt.

Vargas Llosa describes Trujillo's absolute control over the lives of his cabinet members and his demand for their constant loyalty. He routinely tests his officials' loyalty by marginalizing them with no explanation. One such test causes the permanent dismissal of Urania's father, who fails to reclaim his post despite his numerous pleas, attempts, and offers. In this section, Vargas Llosa additionally transitions to the metanarratives of Trujillo's assassins as they wait to shoot him along a dark ocean highway. The longest of these stories is that of José René "Pupo" Roman, the deposed secretary of the armed forces. His hope of killing Trujillo and precipitating a coup fails when Roman is unable to bring himself to take over the military. Instead of wresting the country from Trujillo's brothers and sons, Roman is captured and ruthlessly tortured by Trujillo's son Ramfis for many months before his merciful death.

As the immediate events surrounding Trujillo's death dissipate, Vargas Lloso provides a narrative salve for the harsh descriptions of the torture of the assassins and their accomplices through the story of President Joaquín Balaguer. Initially a figurehead, Balaguer alone convinces Trujillo's family and officials that the country must move toward democracy. In several deft decisions, he exiles Trujillo's brothers, sons, and wife and pacifies the United States as well as the Catholic Church.

Vargas Llosa now finally returns the readers to Urania, who discloses the true source of her anger toward her father. Throughout the story, Vargas Llosa makes references to Trujillo's failing prostate and his displeasure with a woman he invited to Mahogany House, his personal resort where he received women and young girls. Indeed, Urania reveals that her father sent her to Mahogany House as an offering to Trujillo in an attempt to curry his favor and return to his post as president of the senate. Her fear and Trujillo's impotency result in the general's fury, both at Urania and at his declining body. He expels her from Mahogany House, and she returns to school, where the Dominican nuns ensure her safe passage to their sister school in Michigan. Urania narrates the brutal story of her rape to her aunt, who provides her with little sympathy, and to her cousins, who are horrified. The novel concludes as Urania departs for the United States, unsure of any future for her involving her family or the Dominican Republic.

BIBLIOGRAPHY

Kristal, Efraín. *Temptation of the Word: The Novels of Mario Vargas Llosa.* Nashville, Tenn.: Vanderbilt University Press, 1998.

Oviedo, José Miguel. *Mario Vargas Llosa: A Writer's Reality.* Barcelona: Seix Barral, 1985.

Patterson, Richard E. "Resurrecting Raphael: The Fictional Incarnation of a Dominican Dictator." *Callaloo* 29, no. 1 (2006): 223–237.

Vargas Llosa, Mario. *A Fish in the Water: A Memoir.* New York: Farrar, Straus and Giroux, 1994.

Walford, Lynne. "Vargas Llosa's Leading Ladies." In *Leading Ladies: Mujeres en la Literatura Hispana y en Las Artes,* edited by Yvonne Fuentes and Margaret R. Parker, 70–80. Baton Rouge: Louisiana State University Press, 2006.

Emily Clark

FERNÁNDEZ, MACEDONIO (1874–1952)

Argentinean essayist, novelist, poet   The writer Macedonio Fernández was born on June 10, 1874, in

Buenos Aires, Argentina. He was the son of a wealthy rancher and landowner, also named Macedonio, and Rosa del Mazo. Known primarily by his first name, the younger Macedonio is widely considered to have propelled later developments in Argentine and Latin American literature, particularly among those writers considered to be part of the Latin American literary "boom." Macedonio's writing, encompassing prose and poetry, fiction and nonfiction, is extremely fragmented, complex, and experimental. Given the difficulty and outlandishness of his writing, his thought and conversation are considered by many to have been the primary medium of his influence; however, several literary critics have recently contested that idea through in-depth studies of his oeuvre, much of which was published decades after his death. In any case, his immense influence is indisputable and clearly evident in the fiction of Argentinean writers Jorge Luis Borges and JULIO CORTÁZAR.

Macedonio attended the University of Buenos Aires, where he received the degree of doctor of jurisprudence in 1897. He read widely in psychology, philosophy, and metaphysics—especially the works of Arthur Schopenhauer—and wrote humorous, costumbrista (literary interpretation of everyday life), and philosophical articles for the periodicals El Tiempo and El Progreso. While still a student, Macedonio began to hold philosophical conversations with his classmate Jorge Borges, father of the writer Jorge Luis Borges. In 1905 Macedonio began a correspondence with the American philosopher William James, a man he admired greatly; their epistolary exchange ended only upon the latter's death in 1911.

In 1901 Macedonio met Elena de Obieta, who became his wife and the mother of his four children. Elena died in 1920 after abdominal surgery, and her death had an immense effect on Macedonio and his later writing. He ceased practicing law, sent his children to live with relatives, and began to live his life in a combination of vagrancy and seclusion, moving from one boardinghouse to another, with few material possessions.

When Jorge Borges and his family—including Jorge Luis—returned from Switzerland in 1921, Macedonio began a friendship with the younger Borges. Borges and other writers from his generation eventually adopted Macedonio as a beloved literary father figure, the Socrates of Buenos Aires. As a poet, Macedonio came to be considered a "precursor" of the ultraist movement endorsed and later rejected by Borges. Along with Borges, Macedonio contributed to the launch of the literary magazine Proa, founded in 1922. In the July 1923 issue, Borges published a review of a nonexistent work by Macedonio called El Recienvenido (The newly arrived), thus giving birth to Macedonio's literary persona, Recienvenido. Macedonio began publishing his essays in Proa in earnest in 1924.

Perhaps the oddest aspect of Macedonio's biography was his bizarre 1927 campaign for the presidency of Argentina, an undertaking barely distinguishable from his literary projects and carried out through random acts of propaganda, such as scattering pieces of paper marked "Macedonio" throughout Buenos Aires. In 1928 Macedonio published No toda es vigilia la de los ojos abiertos (Not everything is visible), a collection of his thoughts on philosophy and metaphysics. This was followed in 1929 by Papeles de Recienvenido (Notes on the return), a collection of miscellany, which appeared in later, expanded editions in 1944 and 1966. During this time, Macedonio also began work on his best-known novel, Museo de la Novela de la Eterna (Museum of the eternal novel), which made its first appearance in 1938 as "Novela de Eterna" y la Niña del dolor (Daughter of pain), la "Dulce-persona" de amor que no fue sabido (Sweet-person of unknown love). In 1941 Una Novela que comienza (A novel begins) and Continuación de la Nada (Continuation of nothingness) were published, and a book of his poetry, called simply Poemas, appeared in 1953.

Macedonio's writing combines humor and philosophy into elaborate, fragmentary, and idiosyncratic mind games that upend literary conventions, particularly those of the realist novel. His fictional work culminated in the pair Adriana Buenos Aires: última novela mala (the last bad novel) and Museo de la Novela de la Eterna: primera novela buena (the first good novel), both of which appeared many years after his death (1971 and 1967, respectively), and were edited by his son, Adolfo de Obieta. While Adriana Buenos Aires takes many novelistic commonplaces to their not so logical conclusions, reducing them to absurdity, Museo *de la Novela de la Eterna* explodes narrative conventions, calling into question the expectations most readers bring to the novel. *Museo* contains 59 prologues that attempt to spell out, albeit cryptically, the author's goal of enlightening the reader and drawing him or her into the process of the novel's creation, so that by the end the reader is active (*lector salteado*) rather than passive (*lector seguido*). As part of this project, Macedonio even envisioned creating a "living novel" of scenes acted out on the streets of Buenos Aires.

After the publication of *No toda es vigilia la de los ojos abiertos,* Macedonio apparently ceased to take an active role in publishing his work; this was left to his friends, and later to his son and editor, Adolfo de Obieta. After 1943, Macedonio lived with Adolfo until his death in Buenos Aires on February 10, 1952. Although his work remains largely untranslated and little known outside of Latin America, recent scholarly attention may soon bring the author greater international recognition.

BIBLIOGRAPHY

Garth, Todd S. *The Self of the City: Macedonio Fernandez, the Avant-Garde and Modernity in Buenos Aires.* Cranbury, N.J.: Associated United Presses, 2005.

Genette, Girard. *Paratexts: Thresholds of Interpretation.* Cambridge; New York: University of Cambridge Press, 1997.

Peavler, Terry J. and Peter Standish. *Structures of Power: Essays on Twentieth-Century Spanish-American Fiction.* Albany: State University of New York Press, 1996.

Heather Dubnick

FIRST CIRCLE, THE (*V PERVOM KRUGE*)

ALEKSANDR SOLZHENITSYN (1968)   Regarded as the author's most elaborate novel, with a vision, scope, and breadth befitting its topic, *The First Circle* addresses the recurrent theme of ALEKSANDR SOLZHENITSYN's oeuvre, namely the "internal freedom" which even the most totalitarian of political and cultural systems is unable to deny the individual. The title of this text by the Nobel Prize–winning Solzhenitsyn (1918–) is drawn from Dante's epic poem *The Divine Comedy,* the first circle of the Inferno, or hell. Solzhenitsyn's hell in his fictional universe is represented by a Soviet forced-labor camp system.

The First Circle of the title is a higher echelon, an upper stratum that constitutes an institute oriented around scientific and technological research based on the periphery of Moscow. The employees of this institute are scientists and mechanical engineers who are promoted from lower circles of the labor camp system and then assigned to urgent, sensitive, and high-priority security assignments.

The majority of Solzhenitsyn's narrative is structured around a project designed to create a scientific process that will allow a detailed analysis of telephone calls where the contents of the conversations have been monitored and the identities of the speakers are unknown. This creates a position where the "advantaged" members of the Soviet society are forced to use their cerebral superiority to trap their comrades. Solzhenitsyn compounds this scenario by revealing that a common motivation for working above and beyond the required levels is not just the prospect of imminent demotion, but a misguided intellectual curiosity and long-lasting loyalty to their party.

The central plot of the novel, which is narrated over three anxious and frantic days, is a suspense-laden technological problem. On December 24, 1949, an ambitious young Soviet diplomat, Innokentii Volodin, calls a childhood friend and colleague from a public telephone booth to warn him against revealing a medical innovation known only to him and his French cohorts. The conversation is monitored, recorded, and intercepted. After two days, a philologist and linguistic expert who works in the field of acoustics announces that a serious development in "voice identification" has taken place. Hours later, Innokentii Volodin is placed in the notorious Moscow Lubianka jail, his status as a political doyen downgraded to that of another number within the all encompassing political system.

One potential hero figure to emerge from *The First Circle* is Gleb Nerzhin, the central protagonist, who possesses a number of biographical links with Solzhenitsyn as well as sharing a name with a character from another of Solzhenitsyn's works, *The Feast of Victors.* Nerzhin, born in 1918, has been brought up and steeled against the extreme rigors of Stalinist Russia. Following his imprisonment, Nerzhin is sent to the institute to work alongside the third narrator of *The First Circle,* an intellectually minded linguist named Lev Rubin. Although Nerzhin has knowledge of the client who will benefit from his developing a more efficient voice-monitoring system, he is immediately wary of and unhappy about his complicity with the regime. The vision that Solzhenitsyn conveys is bleak and chilling, with his characters informed by an overtly paranoid political sensibility. Everyone, from the head of the secret police to the security forces in the research institute, operates under the constant expectation and fear that their times of comparative freedom are about to be withdrawn and their privileges swiftly commuted to sanctions.

Critics have often pointed out one particular sequence within the narrative, Solzhenitsyn's portrayal of Joseph Stalin. Stalin was the premier of the Soviet Union from the 1920s to his death in 1953. His iron rule was punctuated by state terror, mass deportations, and political repression. Solzhenitsyn portrays the Soviet leader as a paranoid, cunning, vindictive, vituperative, and isolated tyrant. The writer was also criticized for authorial self-indulgence, outright political jockeying, and assimilating unnecessary fictions that intrude upon factual, well-documented testimony. The portrayal of the Russian dictator Stalin is not only scathing but also lacks the depth ascribed to other characters, as well as lapsing into outright sarcasm in some parts of the novel.

Moreover, there is a claustrophobic quality to *The First Circle* that embellishes the dominant theme: incarceration. Although Solzhenitsyn represents Russia as a giant prison, he also ironically suggests that it is only when one is imprisoned within the system that one can achieve a degree of true freedom. Even though the principal protagonists have lost their relationships with their wives, their material possessions, their influence, and their power, their positions within the Institute still afford them a dignity and basic humanity that also seems to threaten the tyranny of Stalin.

BIBLIOGRAPHY

Dunlop, John B., ed. *Solzhenitsyn in Exile.* Palo Alto, Calif.: Hoover Institution, 1985.

Ericson, Edward E. *Solzhenitsyn and the Modern World.* Washington, D.C.: Regnery Gateway, 1993.

Krasnov, Valdislav. *Solzhenitsyn and Dostoevsky: A Study in the Polyphonic Novel.* Athens: University of Georgia Press, 1980.

Rothberg, Abraham. *Alexandr Solzhenitsyn: The Major Novels.* Ithaca, N.Y.: Cornell University Press, 1971.

Thomas, D. M. *Alexander Solzhenitsyn: A Century in his Life.* New York: St. Martin's Press, 1998.

Martyn Colebrook

FLOUNDER, THE (DER BUTT) GÜNTER GRASS (1977)

The Flounder is a 4,000-year-long history of the sexes, based loosely on the Grimms' fairy tale "The Fisherman and His Wife." The narrator of this novel by Germany's highly revered writer GÜNTER GRASS (1927–) is a present-day man, Edek, who, along with his female companion, Ilsebill, has seen nine or more reincarnations since the Stone Age period. To entertain his present-day partner, who is pregnant, the narrator tells her the stories of their previous incarnations, introducing one story for each month of her pregnancy. By portraying the various epochs in which this couple lived, Grass explores the sexual roles of men and women down through the ages. In particular, he looks at the denouement of primeval matriarchy as patriarchy came to the fore and the subsequent emergence of feminism as a counteraction to and emancipation from the aggressive male-dominated world.

Having been caught (or allowed itself to be caught) by the prehistoric fisherman Edek, the Flounder bargains for its life by promising to mentor the man and show him how to overthrow the matriarchal society in which he lives. One of the results of man gaining the upper hand is that woman is now transfigured from a three-breasted being into a two-breasted one, in order to accommodate man's desires. More important than man's opportunity, under patriarchy, to reconstruct woman is his chance to reconstruct history, as men now take over the business of writing. With this newly won opportunity to become the scribes of history, men portray their own gender in a more flattering light as they simultaneously erase all positive contributions made by women. Grass undermines this male propaganda, however, by depicting the female as the nurturer and promoter of humankind. The male, by contrast, he portrays as possessing a bloodthirsty, destructive nature that inclines him ever toward war, be it in the form of Neolithic rocks and spears or in the modern deployment of intercontinental missiles.

In the 20th century, the Flounder allows himself to be caught by three fisherwomen who turn out to be members of a highly organized group of feminists. With the Flounder now their captive, they put him into a tank and proceed to put him and Edek, as his cohort, on trial for the overthrow of the matriarch. Grass uses this trial as a means to go back over history, recounting mythology, fairy tales, and actual historical events, as he chronicles not only the development of patriarchy but man's uses and abuses of women as well. As Edek recapitulates to the female tribunal all that he has done over the centuries, the Flounder has reconfirmed what he has known for a long time—that men are stupid, incapable of learning anything, especially when it comes to women. For this reason, the Flounder now offers to ally himself with the women. In his new role as their mentor, he warns these women that while their time has come, they must beware lest they make the same mistakes as the men.

BIBLIOGRAPHY

Durrani, Osman. *Fiction of Germany: Images of the German Nation in the Modern Novel*. Edinburgh: Edinburgh University Press. 1994.

Pickar, Gertrud Bauer, ed. *Adventures of a Flounder: Critical Essays on Günter Grass' Der Butt*. Munich: Wilhelm Fink. 1982.

Preece, Julian. *The Life and Work of Günter Grass: Literature, History, Politics*. New York: Palgrave Macmillan, 2001.

Stephanie E. Libbon

FORBIDDEN COLORS (KINJIKI) MISHIMA YUKIO (1953)

The third novel by Japanese writer MISHIMA YUKIO (1925–1970) returns to themes earlier explored in his semiautobiographical first novel, CONFESSIONS OF A MASK. The title, a euphemism for homosexuality roughly equivalent to "forbidden love," frankly announces the novel's subject matter and setting: the inner workings of Tokyo's post–World War II gay subculture. When first published, *Forbidden Colors* was considered shocking and controversial, not only for its portrayal of gay bars and homosexual relationships but also for its depiction of postwar economic and social corruption.

The novel's plot revolves around the cruel and perverted mentorship the aging writer Shunsuke offers to the bland, but powerfully attractive male Yuichi. Viciously misogynistic, Shunsuke sees the much younger Yuichi as the perfect weapon with which to revenge himself upon womankind. Not only is Yuichi physically irresistible, but as Shunsuke shrewdly notes, as a gay man he is incapable of heterosexual romance. He forms a deal with Yuichi, offering to make him sole heir of his considerable estate in return for Yuichi's help. He then proceeds to tutor the younger man in the arts of emotional betrayal, encouraging him to make a loveless marriage while continuing affairs with both women and men of diverse ages and social backgrounds.

At Shunsuke's urging, Yuichi makes a socially approved marriage to a conventionally naïve young woman. His marriage to Yasuko becomes a kind of laboratory where both Yuichi and Shunsuke experiment with all shades of female suffering: He provokes her jealousy with careless evidence of affairs, he refuses to share her simple domestic pleasures, and he heartlessly rejects her real love and affection on every front. Shunsuke manages affairs for Yuichi with two of his former lovers, the beautiful and sophisticated Kyoko and the older bourgeois socialite, Mrs. Kaburagi. Behind the scenes, he scripts Yuichi's advances and arranges endless accidental meetings between the rivals, actions designed for maximum female unhappiness and humiliation.

Yuichi's exploration of Tokyo's gay underground is also warmly encouraged by Shunsuke. Yuichi pursues liaisons throughout every venue in Tokyo's homosexual demimonde: public restrooms and parks, bars and tea shops catering to gay clientele, and elaborate and decadent house parties frequented by men from every sector of postwar Japanese society. Because of his beauty, Yuichi rapidly becomes a tea shop star at the popular Ginza rendezvous, Rudon's, where both men and boys compete for his attention—including, eventually, Mrs. Kaburagi's husband.

Between lessons in social manners, Shunsuke lectures the youth on classic Western literature and traditional Japanese poetry. Yuichi becomes a sounding board for Shunsuke's aesthetic theories, as well as an example of the cruelty of perfect beauty at the heart of Shunsuke's philosophy.

A number of ironic twists threaten the perfect resolution of Shunsuke's plans. Shunsuke himself becomes jealous of Yuichi's attention to others, notably the cultured businessman Kawada. Further, Yuichi grows fond of Yasuko, their bond symbolized by Yuichi's choice to stay by her side and share her pain during the delivery of their child. Even Shunsuke's grudge against the Kaburagis goes awry. Instead of being devastated by discovering their mutual involvement with Yuichi, the couple becomes closer, united by this shared interest. And the shallow and self-centered Mrs. Kaburagi performs a nearly motherly gesture of self-sacrifice in helping Yuichi mend his relationship with his own mother.

In a final irony at the novel's close, Yuichi visits Shunsuke to declare his independence. Unwilling to continue as a pawn, Yuichi has come to return all the money Shunsuke has so far lent him and to break with his influence completely. But before he can make his intentions known, Shunsuke surreptitiously drinks poison, leaving Yuichi forever in his financial and spiritual debt.

Mishima's novel would seem to have some parallels with other narratives of fatal beauty and revenge. The contrast between the beautiful young man and the ugly older writer who aesthetically idealizes him is reminiscent of THOMAS MANN's DEATH IN VENICE. Shunsuke and Yuichi's relationship also alludes to the vengeful mentoring Miss Havisham provides for Estella in Charles Dickens's Great Expectations. In terms of Mishima's own oeuvre, the relationship exemplifies the opposition between the irrational realm of physical beauty and the rational power of intelligence and spiritual maturity, a dialectic never finally synthesized.

The novel contains themes developed in Mishima's later work such as the incompatibility of perfection and mortal existence and the opposition between morality and aesthetics. It also offers an early example of the careful attention to the ironic nuances of personal and social relationships Mishima later perfected in such short stories as "The Pearl," "Three Million Yean," and "Thermos Bottles." As in all his writing, Mishima makes his social critique through an emphasis on psychology: the shallow and hypocritical inner world of his characters mirrors the larger corruptions of modern Japan. The novel also contains Mishima's most extensive examination of gay life and culture. His frank and vivid portrayal of postwar gay Tokyo, groundbreaking at the time of its publication, still gives the work an almost sociological interest.

BIBLIOGRAPHY
Mishima Yukio. After the Banquet. Translated by Donald Keene. New York: Alfred A. Knopf, 1963.
———. Death in Midsummer and Other Stories. (Manatsu No Shi) Translated by Edward G. Seidensticker. New York: New Directions, 1966.
———. The Decay of the Angel Translated by Edward G. Seidensticker. New York: Alfred A. Knopf, 1974.
Napier, Susan J. Escape from the Wasteland: Romanticism and Realism in the Fiction of Mishima Yukio. Cambridge, Mass.: Harvard University Press, 1991.
Nathan, John. Mishima: A Biography. Boston: Little Brown, 1974.
Scott-Stokes, Henry. The Life and Death of Yukio Mishima. New York: Noonday Press, 1995.
Starrs, Roy. Deadly Dialectics: Sex, Violence and Nihilism in the World of Yukio Mishima. Sandgate, Folkestone, U.K.: Japan Library, 1994.
Wolfe, Peter. Yukio Mishima. New York: Continuum, 1989.
Mina Estevez

FORBIDDEN FOREST, THE (FORÊT INTERDITE) Mircea Eliade (1955)

MIRCEA ELIADE (1907–86) considered his epic novel The Forbidden Forest to be his best work. Written between the years 1949 and 1954, the novel was originally published in French as Forêt interdite the following year. It finally appeared in Eliade's native Romania as Noaptea de Sânziene in 1971 and in English as The Forbidden Forest in 1978.

Well known for numerous studies on comparative religion, including The Myth of the Eternal Return (1949) and Patterns in Comparative Religion (1958), Eliade received little attention for his fiction. Yet both his nonfiction and his fiction demonstrate Eliade's vast knowledge of religious and mythological history and symbolism. The Forbidden Forest demonstrates major themes evident in Eliade's scholarly work, including the ordeal by labyrinth, initiation rites, and the conflict between sacred time and historical time.

Divided into two parts and set in major European cities (including Bucharest and London) from 1936 to 1948, Eliade's novel is Proustian in scale (almost 600 pages) and consists of a tapestry of intertwining characters and story lines. The central character, Stefan, is a handsome, thoughtful man who works for the Romanian Ministry. His daily life is tedious and routine, quite the opposite of his personal life. Stefan maintains a flat where he pursues his interest in painting and spends much of his time eavesdropping on the conversations of his neighbors, including those of Spiridon Vadastra, an awkward lawyer with a glass eye. Stefan is married to Ioana, a young woman whom he meets after she mistakes him for her current lover, Ciru Partenie, a well-known Romanian writer. Stefan is also having an affair with Illeana, a young woman whom he initially meets on the Night of St. John, or Midsummer's Eve. The significance of this day is central to the theme of the novel, as not only is it the day on which his relationship with Illeana begins and ends, but it is traditionally known as a night to celebrate fertility and new life.

Stefan is on a spiritual quest, trapped in a metaphorical labyrinth from which he is desperately trying to escape. Not only is Stefan torn between his love for both Ioana and Illeana, he longs to rediscover a time that transcends history, a time that is not susceptible to the terror and destructive nature of history that is so evident during World War II. It is through the wide range of people and events in Stefan's life that Eliade gives the reader a sense of Stefan's ordeal by labyrinth.

The first part of the novel deals with Stefan's developing friendships and conflicting romantic feelings. Biris, a consumptive philosopher and teacher, serves as Stefan's confidante and is able to shed light on Stefan's preoccupation with history. Biris realizes that Stefan is horrified by historical events and that the young man longs for "the paradise of his childhood." Yet Biris knows that man cannot escape history, for when he eventually dies at the hands of communist intelligence agents in the second half of the novel, unlike Stefan, he understands that both men and civilizations are mortal. Stefan also befriends Antime, a scholar of the works of Partenie, Stefan's doppelgänger. It is Antime who introduces Stefan to an Iron Guardist, a member of the ultra-nationalist, anti-Semitic and fascist Legion of the Archangel Michael movement and political party that existed in Romania from 1927 into the early years of World War II. After providing refuge to the guard, Stefan is placed in a prison camp and loses his job at the

ministry. Eventually, however, he is released and reinstated at the ministry.

Stefan's relationships with women are also a source of conflict. Despite the birth of their son, Stefan is unsure of his love for Ioana. His relationship with Illeana is also unstable. Unable to gain a commitment from Stefan, Illeana becomes engaged to an officer. However, her fiancé is killed in a tragic car accident, resulting in Illeana deciding to leave both Stefan and Bucharest indefinitely.

Stefan's quest to find Illeana is the focus of the novel's second half. After his wife and son are killed in the bombing of Bucharest in spring 1944, Stefan realizes that he truly loves Illeana and sets out to find her. After much searching, he finally finds her on the Night of St. John, 1948, in the forest where they had first met 12 years earlier. As they leave the forest together, they are killed in a car accident. Despite realizing his true feelings and finding his true love, Stefan is still a victim of history and the terrifying events it brings to mankind.

Many critics have written that Eliade's *The Forbidden Forest* serves as a fictional representation of his scholarly work on religion and mythology. Ultimately, Eliade's novel not only tells the tale of the initiation rites man must endure in order to gain an understanding of his self, but it also conveys the anxiety that permeated society during and after World War II. Long underrated, Eliade's fiction, like his popular religious studies, should be considered essential to those who wish to gain an understanding of the human condition and the history and myth that has shaped it.

BIBLIOGRAPHY

Allen, Douglas. *Myth and Religion in Mircea Eliade.* New York: Garland Publishing, 1998.

———. *Structure and Creativity in Religion: Hermeneutics in Mircea Eliade's Phenomenology and New Directions.* Religion and Reason 14. The Hague: Mouton, 1978.

Carrasco, David, and Jane Marie Law, eds. *Waiting for the Dawn: Mircea Eliade in Perspective.* Niwot: University Press of Colorado, 1991.

Cave, David. *Mircea Eliade's Vision for a New Humanism.* New York: Oxford University Press, 1993.

Dudley, Guilford. *Religion on Trial: Mircea Eliade and his Critics.* Philadelphia: Temple University Press, 1977.

Eliade, Mircea. *The Autobiography of Mircea Eliade.* 2 vols. Translated by Mac Linscott Ricketts. Chicago: University of Chicago Press, 1981, 1988.

———. *Bengal Nights*. Translated by Catherine Spencer. Chicago: University of Chicago Press, 1994.

———. *Exile's Odyssey: 1937–1960*. Translated by Mac Linscott Ricetts. Chicago: University of Chicago Press, 1988.

———. *The Forbidden Forest*. Translated by M. L. Ricketts and M. P. Stevenson. South Bend, Ind.: University of Notre Dame Press, 1978.

———. *The Myth of the Eternal Return, or Cosmos and History*. Translated by Willard R. Trask. Princeton, N.J.: Princeton University Press, 1971.

———. *The Sacred and the Profane: The Nature of Religion*. Translated by Willard R. Trask. New York: Harper and Row, 1961.

Laignel-Lavastine, Alexandra. *Cioran, Eliade, Ionesco: L'oubli du fascisme*. Paris: Presses Universitaires de France, 2002.

Marino, Adrian. *L'Herméneutique de Mircea Eliade*. Translated by Jean Gouillard. Paris: Gallimard, 1980.

Simion, Eugen. *Mircea Eliade: A Spirit of Amplitude*. New York: East European Monographs, Columbia University Press, 2001.

Gehrett Ellis

FORGOTTEN, THE (*L'OUBLIE*) Elie Wiesel (1989)

"For the dead *and* the living, we must bear witness," Elie Wiesel stated in his work *And the Sea Is Never Full: Memoirs, 1969–*, a motto now adopted by the United States Holocaust Memorial Museum in Washington, D.C. But how can the Shoah survivor who suffers from Alzheimer's disease "bear witness"? Wiesel explores this problem in *The Forgotten*, the novel he has described as his most depressing because its kindly, scholarly protagonist, Elhanan Rosenbaum, is victimized yet again, this time not by the Nazis but by a disease that goes unnamed in Wiesel's novel. Wiesel writes in his memoirs that he kept this manuscript in a drawer for several months until he figured out how he could communicate some kind of hope by its conclusion. *The Forgotten*, first published in French as *L'Oublie* in Paris by Editions du Seuil, was translated into English in 1992.

The hope revealed by Wiesel in what could be perceived as a totally tragic novel stems from the deep love between Elhanan and his son Malkiel. Devoted to each other self-sacrificially and constantly, they gradually learn how to "transfuse" memory from the survivor to his descendant. As a scholar and psychotherapist, Elhanan understands both the importance of telling stories from his rich life and the horrible inevitable mental deterioration that Alzheimer's disease causes, ultimately reducing its victim to jumbled phrases, potential loss of identity, silence, and death. Elhanan's prayer to the God of Abraham, Isaac, and Jacob opens this modernistic novel: "Do not abandon me, God of my fathers, for I have never repudiated You." Elhanan spends many hours during the early stages of his disease narrating his memories to Malkiel and Tamar, Malkiel's fiancée, plus writing personal journal entries and tape recording autobiographical anecdotes. His biggest assignment for his son is to send him to Feherfalu, Romania, his hometown, in order to visit the place where Elhanan grew up happily with his family and returned brokenhearted upon discovering that all of them had been murdered by the Nazis.

There is also a mystery to be solved in this town, complicated by Elhanan's inability to recall the events and persons involved in this intrigue. Its gravity is so great that he believes God is punishing him via his disease for his failure to act appropriately. By the close of the novel Malkiel does indeed solve the mystery so that he can lift Elhanan's guilt by reassuring him with the truth.

Wiesel's novel is challenging because of its fragmented style and Elhanan's increasingly confused speech as his disease progresses and his rationality decreases. Yet Wiesel displays his consummate literary artistry by joining his story's serious content with this most appropriate approach. Displaying an uncanny ability to understand the mental disintegration of a victim of Alzheimer's while remaining totally in control of his novel's fragmented content, Wiesel provides a realistic glimpse of the horrors of this malady and of how a devoted family member can best love and preserve the Shoah survivor's important memories.

Further, Malkiel's self-sacrificial love for his father helps him to grow from a nomadic, somewhat irresponsible journalist into a mature man ready to take on marriage, children, and his father's dark but beautiful memories:

> Despite the pain and sorrow, we'll [Malkiel and Tamar] put our trust in what exalts us—my father's relentless sufferings—and in what

thwarts us, too—the ambiguities of life, most of all Jewish life in the diaspora. We'll forge new links from which new sparks will rise. Spoken words will become signs, words unspoken will serve as warnings. And we'll invent the rest. And my father's memory will sing and weep in mine. And yours will blossom in our children's.

BIBLIOGRAPHY

Kolbert, Jack. *The World of Elie Wiesel: An Overview of his Career and Major Themes.* Selinsgrove, Pa.: Susquehanna University Press, 2001.

Roth, John K. *A Consuming Fire: Encounters with Elie Wiesel and the Holocaust.* Atlanta: John Knox Press, 1979.

Wiesel, Elie. *And the Sea Is Never Full: Memoirs, 1969–.* Translated by Marion Wiesel. New York: Alfred A. Knopf, 1999.

———. *Memoirs: All Rivers Run to the Sea.* New York: Alfred A. Knopf, 1995.

Carole J. Lambert

FORTRESS BESIEGED Qian Zhongshu (1947)

Considered by most critics to be either the most important or one of the two most important works of modern Chinese literature, *Fortress Besieged,* by Qian Zhongshu (1910–98), depicts the complicated and often conflicted lives of a set of Chinese intellectuals on the eve of the Second Sino-Japanese War (1937–45). However, this summary in no way reflects the novel's complex layers, which unfold in surprising and satisfying ways to form a unique masterpiece of the modernist condition.

Fortress Besieged distinguishes itself from other contemporary Chinese works in a number of ways. For example, where Ding Ling's The Sun Shines over the Sanggan River (1948) concentrates on the land reform movement among farming communities, this novel focuses on the pseudo-intellectual community in China at the end of the 1930s. However, Qian's representations of that community create a novel of seemingly infinite complexity, comparable to works by Western authors such as James Joyce. Throughout the novel, Qian embeds multiple references to and quotes from a wide range of cultural, historical, and political events from the East and West: everything from classic works of Chinese literature like *The Analects* and *The Great Learning* (*Ta Hsüeh*) and satires such as Li Ju-chen's *Ching-hua Yüan* and Wu Ching-tzu's *Ju-lin Wai-shih* and the conflict between traditional and contemporary social practices to references to Shakespeare's *A Midsummer Night's Dream* and Sheridan's *The School for Scandal* and popsicles.

Qian also explicitly embeds numerous quotes from many different languages in the book: Readers frequently find excerpts from Chinese poetry as well as French and Latin phrases sprinkled throughout the novel, often on the same page as when Qian juxtaposes his descriptions of Kao Sung-nien with a commentary on Mandarin phraseology and a Latin epithet, or when he reveals the conflation between Pao's mispronunciation of "Su Tung-p'o" and the French term *tombeau.* Qian's frequent and extensive allusions and quotations create an extremely cosmopolitan world through which his characters must struggle. Perhaps the most important quotation is the novel's epigraph, the French proverb from which Qian derives the novel's title: "Marriage is like a fortress besieged: those who are outside want to get in, and those who are inside want to get out."

This reference to marriage as a conflicted, relative state informs the novel's main themes of multiple readings and the tragic consequences of misunderstanding. Through such means, Qian reveals how many of his characters may gain knowledge but lack understanding. Moreover, he reveals how the constant demands by societal norms create a tenuous position for everyone, especially for Qian's protagonist, Fang Hung-chien. By focusing on the travails that Hung-chien, his wife, Sun Jou-chia, and their friends undergo as they fruitlessly pursue happiness and meaning, Qian ultimately crafts a tragedy in which actual and metaphorical marriages assume, as the novel's title suggests, competing and irreconcilable meanings. Through this tragic series of events, Hung-chien comes to represent the competing tensions that define his time. Moreover, Hung-chien demonstrates a constant lack of insight into events that propel him into a hopeless situation at the novel's end. For example, he does not perceive until it is too late how others manipulate their relationships with him for their own gratification, whether those relationships are romantic (with Pao and T'ang) or political (with Kao and Han Hsüeh-yü). Qian dramatizes the tragic consequences of misinterpretation at the minute level when he has Hung-chien confusing T'ang with Su on the phone. These events are equally accidental (like his misinterpreting Aunt Li's conversation with Jou-chia) and intentional (Kao's deceptive offers for teaching positions). These and other incidents compound Hung-chien's situation to the point of paralysis. Qian's formulation of these individuals presents a bleak portrait of modern life.

BIBLIOGRAPHY

Huters, Theodore. *Qian Zhongshu*. Boston: Twayne Publishers, 1982.

Zhang Wenjiang zhu. *Guan zhui bain du jie*. Shanghai: Shanghai gu ji chu ban she, 2000.

Clay Smith

FOUCAULT'S PENDULUM (IL PENDOLO DI FOUCAULT) UMBERTO ECO (1988)

Foucault's Pendulum is the second novel by the highly prolific Italian writer UMBERTO ECO (1932–), and continues the pattern of linguistic games and narrative proliferation established in *The NAME OF THE ROSE*. This time the focus is more contemporary, with the unfortunate narrator-protagonist Casaubon and his colleagues Belbo and Diotellevi becoming immersed in an international conspiracy that involves the Knights Templar, the Holy Grail, and the Milanese publishing community.

In a story that spans the political turmoil of Italy in the 1970s, Casaubon's friendship with Belbo leads to his involvement with the Garamond/Manutius publishing house and his exposure to the Diabolicals—self-financing occult writers—as well as Agliè, a man who may or may not be the immortal Count Saint-Germain. Casaubon's interest in the Templars is initially focused on his doctoral thesis, but his curiosity is piqued by the appearance and almost immediate disappearance of Colonel Ardenti, who claims to have decoded the mystery of the Templars' fate. As the years pass, Casaubon is continually drawn to the esoteric, and while these links to the Templars seem innocuous at first, he soon becomes enmeshed in the world of hermetic knowledge and is unable to extricate himself. He, Belbo, and Diotallevi combine computer technology with the numerology of the cabala to create the Plan, a system that uses a computer program to generate random connections between seemingly unconnected facts. Very soon they are rewriting world history in order to explain the coded message from Provins that was passed on to them by Colonel Ardenti, and which supposedly alludes to the secret of the Templars. The trio see this as a game, but it soon becomes apparent that their far-fetched explanations are drawing unwelcome attention from the very secret society whose existence they have been debating.

Unlike *The Name of the Rose*, *Foucault's Pendulum* casually whisks the reader across continents as well as through the finer points of the cabala and occult beliefs. This reinforces the all-pervasive nature of the conspiracy that Casaubon and his friends uncover, but it also encourages the reader to make his or her own connections between apparently disparate events and ideologies. The novel is structured around the 10 *sefirot,* creative forces that intervene between God and our creative world of the cabala and has 120 chapters, a number of great numerological significance, which plays on the idea that there might be some hidden meaning in the text. Eco may well have cultivated this response in his readership to illustrate the human desire for order and to comment on the climate of postmodern paranoia, a reality in which to think of something is to create it.

This is an extension of the ideas found in *The Name of the Rose,* but while the earlier novel celebrates the free exchange of thought, *Foucault's Pendulum* warns against a society that is completely "open" to interpretation. Casaubon and Belbo's idle musing about the order of history endanger their lives, while Diotallevi is prepared to attribute the breakdown of his health to their work on the Plan. While none of their theories can be proved, they cannot be disproved either, but rather than accept uncertainty, the trio are intent on finding an answer.

It is this arrogance that is condemned in the novel: Eco's characters cannot live their lives in the physical present; they must constantly seek to know the secrets of history. Oedipus and other Greek figures certainly come to mind. The most telling episode occurs when Lia, Casaubon's girlfriend, creates an alternative and innocent interpretation of the message of Provins.

Casaubon admits that the list may be about laundry rather than a plan for world domination, but he is unable to control his obsessive hypothesizing, and so the Plan destroys them all.

Foucault's Pendulum is a clear reflection of Eco's work on semiotics and the meaning of signs. The novel is a mischievous realization of unconstrained open interpretation, which results in a chaotic and unworkable reality. Although technically a thriller, *Foucault's Pendulum* combines literary puns, social observation, and popular culture to comment on the nature of human curiosity and the ultimately transformative effect of narration on reality.

BIBLIOGRAPHY

Cannon, JoAnn. "The Imaginary Universe of Umberto Eco: A Reading of *Foucault's Pendulum*." In *Umberto Eco,* edited by Mike Gane and Nicholas Gane, vol. 3, 55–68. London: SAGE Publications, 2005.

Hutcheon, Linda. "Eco's Echoes: Ironizing the (Post)modern." In *Umberto Eco,* edited by Mike Gane and Nicholas Gane, vol. 3, 25–41. London: SAGE Publications, 2005.

Rochelle Sibley

FRIED, HÉDI (EDWIGE SZMUK) (1924–   )

Swedish novelist   Born in Sighet, Transylvania, later a resident of Sweden, Hédi Fried was of Romanian origin. She is best known for her novel *The Road to Auschwitz: Fragments from a Life* (1990). In its content, an archetypal Holocaust survivor testimony of witness, *The Road to Auschwitz* also provides the reader with a new way of reading literature after the Holocaust. Fried, who was born as Edwige Szmuk in 1924, begins her story in a very different way from Sighet's more famous native writer, ELIE WIESEL. The latter mostly narrates his life from within the German concentration camps of World War II. Fried, however, weaves her story of incarceration into her life narrative. Her testimony neither begins with Auschwitz and the Nazis nor ends with them, which metaphorically disallows the Nazis any power over her narrative or her life. And perhaps because of this, Fried's writing lacks Wiesel's bitterness and angry tone.

The Road to Auschwitz is a testimony of Fried's life before World War II in Romania, through her incarceration in a Hungarian ghetto to her short stay in Auschwitz before being moved to Bergen-Belsen and her eventual settlement in Sweden after liberation. It is only 40 years after the war, living far away from the tragic events in Germany, that she realizes she is a witness. However, the real power in her narrative does not so much lie in witnessing itself, but in its ability to reinforce the ways in which so much literature in the West is the literature of destruction, which forces us to reconfigure our sense of Western literary history, particularly after the Holocaust has taught us the dual nature of its survivors. As Fried's contemporary, TADEUSZ BOROWSKI confirms, survivors did not survive on morality, virtue, or the literature of Western humanism. Survivors served a dual role as both victim and executioner. To those who survived the concentration camps, a survivor is one who made sure someone *else* went to the gas chamber.

In this respect, Fried's narrative is like that of many others. Like Borowski and PRIMO LEVI, she narrates her own coming to terms with the truth in which a fellow prisoner destroys the illusion and pulls back the veil over the lie of *Arbeit Macht Frei,* or work brings freedom. She has the scene common to all testimonies where one hardened inmate explains the truth to those newly arrived who still harbor the hope that they will see their parents again. The difference between Fried and other survivors is striking. The later survivors seem to use their literary pasts to help make sense of living in their incomprehensible present time (one remembers the touching account of Levi teaching a fellow prisoner Italian by reciting passages of Dante to him). Fried, on the other hand, writes as a way of rebelling against her Nazi persecutors.

Because Fried uses rather than creates literature while in places such as Bergen Belsen, she poses a challenge to both the enlightened system of reason that the Nazis perverted to enslave her and the past literature of this enslavement. Levi uses Dante as both self-therapy and as a way of preserving the literary, cultured, and civilized past he remembers prior to Auschwitz. For him, Dante is a bridge of communication between human beings in a new world where communication, understanding, and reason are now impossible. Fried, on the other hand, does not use poetry to sustain the world of the past;

rather, she uses it to fight the new world of antihumanism in the camp. While Fried remembers as much of her native Hungarian poets as Levi remembers his Italians, she and her block mates in the camps often risk death to preserve them on organized scraps of paper, scraps most prisoners see as only toilet paper.

This drive to preserve harkens back to her deportation from her home in Sighet when she had to leave her books behind. Leaving her home for the last time, she made a vow to never allow herself to be attached to physical things again. But the rebellious, even proletarian François Villon she had to leave on her shelf has not left her. Every desire she has to write, as expressed in her account, is an act of resistance along the lines of Villon, who, we remember, was banished from Paris in 1463 after killing a priest in self-defense over a loaf of bread. His *Testament* is a moral defense of his troubled life on the streets of Paris. Like Villon, Fried's use of literature is to rebel, not reinforce.

What is also unique in Fried is that she is not alone in her acts of literary rebellion. Some of the most moving passages of her narrative are when she recounts how many of the girls in her block participated in "study groups," as she calls them. She recounts how every girl is charged with writing down every poem she could remember, so that each night, they can recite them to the group. While they often recite their Hungarian, Romanian, and French favorites, those who evoke the most emotional responses are poets such as Villon, Charles Baudelaire, and Jozsef Attila—often labeled today as either literary terrorists or certified paranoid schizophrenics: poets burdened with not too little a connection to reality, but too much of it.

Similarly, over time, Fried notes hidden talents emerging from these hardened girls of the compound, as they venture poems of their own. Others draw or even act. But these literary acts of Fried and her block mates are not reifying acts by any means, even though they are imitative. They are what we would call today, acts of terrorism—last-ditch, irrational attempts to thwart the mechanisms of power that systematically disenfranchise, demoralize, and destroy its opponents. The literary culture in Bergen-Belsen, for example, is in the tradition not of Homer but of Villon—not nation building, but nation sabotaging.

For Fried, then, the act of inscription comes to supersede the memory of literature or even its content, which suggests a new way of theorizing literature not so much *after* the Holocaust, but always already as a product of it. From the vantage point of Auschwitz today, "looking back at the end of the world," as French theorist Jean Baudrillard has said, we have been able to see our Western history for what it is: not the story of enlightened progress emerging from the savagery and toil of barbarism, but as a revelation of the double bind of humanism that reveals the barbaric and the irrational emerging from within the civilized and rational. While it may have taken a Holocaust survivor—one who is both victim and perpetrator—to state that history is a series of the happenings at Auschwitz, the whole of the humanistic tradition since the rationalism of Descartes is now visible from its endpoint, for according to Hédi Fried, Auschwitz was the final stage of 500 years of humanism, not its negation.

BIBLIOGRAPHY

Bauer, Yehuda. *Rethinking the Holocaust.* New Haven, Conn.: Yale University Press, 2002.

Fried, Hédi. *Fragments of a Life: The Road to Auschwitz.* Translated by Michael Carl Meyer. London: Robert Hale, 1990.

Schabas, William A. *Genocide in International Law: The Crime of Crimes.* Cambridge: Cambridge University Press, 2004.

Brent M. Blackwell

FRISCH, MAX (1911–1991) *Swiss essayist, novelist, playwright*

German-speaking Switzerland during the 20th century produced numerous writers who became famous far beyond its borders. Among those writers was Max Frisch, a prolific novelist, playwright, essayist, and diarist, one of the most representative writers of European literature after World War II. His texts have been translated into many languages, and his plays remain in the repertoire of theaters today. Critical studies on Frisch's impressive oeuvre abound, with scholarly debate ongoing. He kept a finger on the pulse of his time; nevertheless, his texts are inscribed with the timeless substance of human experience. Some of the major topics in Frisch's work include individual identity, guilt and innocence, and technological omnipotence versus fate. Often compared to ROBERT MUSIL, James Joyce, or MARCEL PROUST, Frisch is considered a writer who explicitly depicted the moral dilemmas of 20th-century modernist life.

Max Rudolf Frisch was born on May 15, 1911, in Zurich. While a youth in school, he started to write. At age 16, he sent his first attempt at playwriting, a drama entitled *Steel* (*Stahl*), to a director who encouraged the young man to continue writing. After graduating from high school, Frisch enrolled at Zurich University in 1930 as a student of literature, art history, and philosophy.

Frisch soon had to abandon his studies and started working as a journalist for the *Neue Zürcher Zeitung* (*NZZ*), one of the major newspapers in Switzerland. He also published two novels, but was disappointed by their poor critical reception. After burning all of his manuscripts, Frisch began to study architecture at the Federal Institute of Technology in Zurich. Upon graduating in 1941, he joined an architectural firm, however, his career in architecture, although successful, proved unfulfilling.

Encouraged to write for the stage again, Frisch completed his first successful play, *Santa Cruz,* in 1944. Already in this early text, he introduced the basic components of what was later called his "dramaturgy of permutation," alluding to a recurring motif in his work in the form of the characters' attempts to rewrite their lives. Frisch then turned to more political issues: the horrors of war, racism, fascism, and their devastating effect on humanity. This was largely inspired by the German playwright Bertolt Brecht, whose concept of the epic theater influenced Frisch's playwriting.

After spending a year in the United States on a Rockefeller grant in 1951, Frisch devoted his time fully to writing. His lifelong habit of traveling made him a true cosmopolitan and provided further creative impulse. On the international stage, *The Firebugs* (*Herr Biedermann und die Brandstifter,* 1953), first written as a radio play, as well as *Andorra* (1961) became Frisch's most successful political parables. Both plays share a multilayered composition open to different interpretations: *Firebugs* deals with the rise of fascism and the self-destructive complacency of the bourgeoisie unable to recognize imminent doom; *Andorra* illustrates the deadly effect of the bigoted image a society imposes upon a presumable Other, one who is marginalized, ostracized, and ultimately killed.

Encouraged by his stage success, Frisch returned to the novel. His three major texts—*I'M NOT STILLER* (*Stiller,* 1954), *HOMO FABER* (1957), and *A WILDERNESS OF MIRRORS* (*Mein Name sei Gantenbein,* 1964)—can be read as a trilogy connected by the recurring motif of their protagonists' struggles with the immutability of their respective biographies. Unwilling to accept their personal identities, Stiller and the hypothetical protagonist Gantenbein in *A Wilderness of Mirrors* attempt possible alternatives to their lives. *Homo Faber* treats the subject of humanity's blind faith in technological progress.

Frisch's late oeuvre is more private in character. For example, *Montauk* (1975) appears to be an autobiographical story about an aging author. However, close reading reveals a complex reflection on human consciousness, one in which the individual remains painfully aware of past experiences while trying to grasp the present. Frisch's final narrative, *Bluebeard* (*Blaubart,* 1982), mixes interior monologue, flashbacks, and fantasy to analyze the complexity of an innocent man's guilt feelings.

Stiller, published in 1954 and translated into English as *I'm Not Stiller* in 1958, raised Max Frisch into the class of international writers. In this novel, the author combines fact and fiction to extend the possibilities of narrative: He uses numerous perspectives, each serving to highlight the limitations of the others. *I'm Not Stiller* follows the tribulations of a man who changes his identity only to be eventually unmasked, showing the dilemma of contemporary humanity caught up unwillingly in prescribed roles and patterns. The protagonist is a prisoner in Switzerland, a country "so clean one can hardly breathe for hygiene." The Swiss officers who arrest him are convinced he is a certain Anatol Stiller who disappeared some years earlier, leaving behind a wife, mistress, and moderately successful career as a sculptor. Stiller is further suspected to be involved in a spy case. However, he does not want to identify with his past and therefore denies being the man in question, insisting that he is Jim White (white like a blank page). To prove his claim in prison, he produces seven notebooks, telling his version of the truth.

At closer inspection the reader recognizes these tales of Stiller's American past as parables that illustrate the protagonist's emotional background, detailing his desires and fears. The reader is left with the task of reconstructing Stiller's story by means of limited and necessarily subjective information. What sets the protagonist's dream of a free life in the United States under a new identity in motion is his failure as an artist and lover. However, he cannot escape his past. Stiller is finally exonerated and released. His final attempt to find happiness with Julika, his wife, is doomed to failure because of their separate needs. Stiller still seeks security in erotic relations instead of spiritual or family inclusion. Only after Julika's death is Stiller able to accept and live with his deficiencies.

The story probes many existential questions, including self-expectation and guilt in human relations. For Frisch, loving means not making a "graven image" of the Other, an image that leads to indifference, prejudice, or hatred among humans. Furthermore, *I'm Not Stiller* challenges a specifically Swiss self-perception for being stagnant and backward-looking, and for refusing to reexamine values in the light of changing circumstances.

A new narrative technique of Frisch's emerges in the postwar German novels of the 1960s. Instead of presenting the fictional world as a reality, this new kind of novel offers the reader several possibilities, each of which could be replaced by any number of variations in the narrative. Instead of describing past actions, the narrator engages in a game with future possibilities. Critics recognize the importance of Frisch's *Mein Name sei Gantenbein* (1964) in establishing this trend. Published the following year as *A Wilderness of Mirrors* (1965), the novel *Gantenbein* is narrated in the subjunctive: A stranger walks out of a bar and is later found dead. Based on this initial occurrence, an anonymous narrator creates a story—or, rather, several stories. "A man has been through an experience, now he is looking for the story of his experience." And with this purpose, the narrator explores multiple feasible events that may occur to this character.

The narrator proposes, for example: "Let's say my name is Gantenbein," and goes on, "Let's pretend I am blind." What does it entail to fake blindness in the realm of everyday life? Is there any room for jealousy when blindness prevents one from seeing reality? In order to investigate these questions further, the narrator creates fictional roles for himself, imagining the characters of Enderlin, Svoboda, and Lila, with whom he identifies to differing extents. He invents situations in which these characters might act. In an attempt to reconstruct the past, he imagines being the deceiver and the one deceived simultaneously. Having once projected these imaginary roles and scenes, the narrator retracts or cancels them, either by reminding the reader that the scene is no more than hypothetical or provisional, or by rejecting the scene as unsatisfactory. The narrator's intention is not simply to express the experiences of his past life by means of his fantasy, but also to "try on" stories like clothes—that is, to explore alternatives to his past behavior. His inventions are equally an attempt at self-escape and self-discovery.

Frisch's final years brought him a multitude of honors such as honorary doctorates and prizes from universities and governments in the United States and Europe. The award of the prestigious Peace Prize bestowed by the German book publishing industry in 1976 honored Frisch for "defending the rights of the independently thinking, the minorities, and the powerless ones." In 1990 the author was diagnosed with cancer; he died in Zurich on April 4, 1991.

BIBLIOGRAPHY

Koepke, Wulf. *Understanding Max Frisch*. Columbia: University of South Carolina Press, 1991.

Probst, Gerhard F., and Jay F. Bodine, eds. *Perspectives on Max Frisch*. Lexington: University Press of Kentucky, 1982.

Sharp, Francis Michael. "Max Frisch: A Writer in a Technological Age." *World Literature Today* 60, no. 4 (1986): 557–561.

White, Alfred D. *Max Frisch, the Reluctant Modernist*. Lewiston, N.Y.: Edwin Mellen Press, 1995.

Andrea Heiglmaier

FUENTES, CARLOS (1928–) *Mexican essayist, novelist, playwright*

An internationally acclaimed Mexican writer, Carlos Fuentes ranks as a major contemporary Latin American writer. He has lived and studied in Latin America, Europe, and the United States, and his works have been translated into numerous languages. In the 1950s Fuentes belonged to a group of intellectuals who referred to themselves as the generation of Medio Siglo. These young intellectuals came from the elite intelligentsia of Mexican society, a group trained in both traditional history and contemporary politics. As writers they became equally knowledgeable regarding the literature and work of Miguel de Cervantes, Fernando de Rojas, and René Descartes and politically conversant with the writings of Niccolò Machiavelli, Desiderius Erasmus, David Hume, Jean-Jacques Rousseau, and Karl Marx. Fuentes and the others of the generation of Medio Siglo were particularly influenced by the socialist ideology of the extreme political left of the 1950s, and they were destined to become Mexico's leaders in the fields of both politics and literature, their main goal being to modernize Mexico.

The only son of Mexican diplomat Rafael Fuentes Boettiger and his wife, Berta Macías Rivas, Carlos Fuentes was born in Panama City on November 11, 1928. At a time when the majority of Mexicans were conservative Catholics, his father was a progressive liberal atheist. When American president Woodrow Wilson ordered the April 1914 landing of U.S. Marines in Veracruz, Mexico, in a show of force opposing Victoriaro Huerta, the self-declared military dictator, Rafael Fuentes Boettiger participated in the Mexican defense of his native city, Veracruz. Although Carlos Fuentes had not yet been born, this historic military failure and the Mexican Revolution (1910–20) would deeply affect his life and his writing. As a result, Fuentes's literature would reflect the search of Mexican identity and cultural heritage, and years later he would personally reject the colonialist term *Latin America* in favor of his own term *Indo-Afro-Ibero-America,* which he coined in the 1990s.

Because of his father's diplomatic career, Fuentes spent his childhood years in a variety of cities in Latin America and the United States, and he became a fully bilingual and bicultural child, attending school year-round from 1934 to 1940, in English at the Henry Cook Public School in Washington, D.C., during the academic year, and in Spanish in summer school in Mexico City. In 1941 his father transferred to South America, then to Chile, and later Argentina. In Chile

Fuentes attended the exclusive private Cambridge School and the Grange School, a private British school, where he published stories in a literary magazine and where his teacher encouraged him to become a professional writer. During a brief stay in Argentina, his parents became displeased with the conservative school curriculum, and they allowed Carlos a break from attending school, a hiatus during which he discovered the modern narratives of short story writer Jorge Luis Borges. In Borges's stories he found a new style of literature, one that avoided mimetic realism and epic individualism and pointed to an alternative tradition, that of "verbal exuberance and intellectual ingenuity," as Fuentes explained in his 1999 lecture on Borges.

In the 1940s the Fuentes family left Argentina and moved to Mexico, where they witnessed the transformation of the small town which had been Mexico City into a modern industrial center. Fuentes attended the Colegio México from 1944 to 1946 and the Colegio Francés Morelos from 1947 to 1950; these were his most intellectually formative years. After graduation in 1950, Fuentes enrolled at the University of Geneva in Switzerland and spent a year studying international law. On the flight to Switzerland, Fuentes stopped in Paris and had the unexpected good fortune of meeting the young Octavio Paz (1914–98), already a compelling voice in Mexican letters and later a Nobel laureate (1990). Paz would become a lifelong friend, collaborator, and important influence in Fuentes's search for an authentic Mexican cultural identity. After graduating from law school at the National University of Mexico in 1948 and a year studying economics at the Institut des Hautes Études Internationales in Geneva, Carlos Fuentes followed his father's path and began a career in politics and international diplomacy. In 1950 he became a member of the Mexican delegation to the International Labor Organization, and he later headed the Department for Cultural Relations at the Mexican Ministry of Foreign Affairs.

Fuentes began to publish articles on literature, the arts, and politics in the 1950s. He edited the journal of the Universidad de México and was a founding member of the progressive literary journal *Revista Mexicana de Literatura,* which published the work of other Latin American authors such as Borges and JULIO CORTÁZAR.

The success of *Revista Mexicana de Literatura* gave the generation of Medio Siglo prominence.

In 1954 Fuentes published his first collection of fiction, *The Masked Days* (*Los días enmascarados*), which consists of six stories written in a style that combines the fantastic with what became known as magical realism. The stories reveal Fuentes's genuine concern with the past and the present of Mexico City, a concern evident in later modernist works such as WHERE THE AIR IS CLEAR (*La región más transparente,* 1958), The DEATH OF ARTEMIO CRUZ (*La muerte de Artemio Cruz,* 1962), The HYDRA HEAD (*La cabeza de la hydra,* 1979), the postmodern The OLD GRINGO (*El gringo viejo,* 1985), and The CAMPAIGN (*La campaña,* 1991).

Fuentes's first novel, *Where the Air Is Clear,* has as its subject a fusion of Mexico City's past and present. The novel's ironic title speaks of smog and the environmental price of modernization and industry. Told through the eyes of several characters, the novel criticizes the failure of the Mexican Revolution to resolve serious social issues such as poverty, racism, and class bias in Mexico's largest city.

In 1959 Fuentes married famous Mexican actress Rita Macedo, and published his second novel, *The GOOD CONSCIENCE* (*Las buenas conciencias*). *The Good Conscience* narrates the saga of the powerful Cebollos family, a tale that symbolizes and represents the old aristocracy of historic Guanajuato, Mexico. The novel focuses on the moral struggle of the young protagonist, Jaime Cebollo, as he faces the difficult decision of whether to follow his principles and become a man of good conscience or silently compromise his integrity and accept his place as heir to a prosperous but hypocritical system.

In the 1950s and 1960s, Fuentes became an intellectual radical, a Marxist, and member of the Communist Party. He began to write *The Death of Artemio Cruz* during his visit to Cuba in 1958. Fuentes become a great defender and supporter of the Cuban Revolution, and shortly after Castro's victory, he traveled to Cuba to show his support. *The Death of Artemio Cruz* represents another socialist criticism of the Mexican Revolution. The plot is somewhat reminiscent of William Faulkner's *As I Lay Dying,* utilizing the narrative voice of the main character recalling his own life at his time of death. Fuentes dedicated this novel to Marxist scholar C. Wright Mills.

Fuentes's daughter Cecilia was born in 1962, and the Fuentes family lived in Paris until he and Rita Macedo divorced. Fuentes then returned to Mexico. In 1972 he married Sylvia Lemus, a television journalist. The couple moved to Paris, where their son Carlos Rafael and their daughter Natascha were born. Both children tragically died young: Carlos Rafael Fuentes Lemus died at the age of 25 from complications associated with hemophilia, and Natascha Fuentes Lemus died at the age of 29.

In 1962, while in Paris, Fuentes began the horror novella *Aura,* about a young historian, Felipe Montero, who starts to work in the strange, old house of Señora Consuelo, an elderly widow. His job requires him to edit the memoirs of her deceased husband, General Llorente. Felipe falls passionately in love with Aura, the young, beautiful, green-eyed niece of his employer. Eventually, however, he discovers Aura's true frightening identity. This novella received critical acclaim as a literary masterpiece of magical realism.

During the 1970s, Fuentes accepted the position of ambassador to France during the administration of Mexican president Luis Echeverría, but he later resigned in protest over the appointment of former Mexican president Díaz Ordaz as ambassador to Spain. As a result of this resignation, Fuentes was exiled from Mexico for several years. In the late 1970s he wrote the spy thriller *The Hydra Head,* a novel of international political intrigue involving Arabs and Israelis trying to obtain control of Mexico's oil reserves.

In the 1980s Fuentes accepted several teaching positions in the United States, including Princeton, Dartmouth, and Harvard. He served as the Lewin Visiting Professor at Washington University in St. Louis, spent a semester at Cornell University, and also taught at Merton House in St. John's College of Cambridge University. Fuentes received honorary degrees from Harvard, Cambridge, and Dartmouth and was awarded Mexico's highest literary award, the National Prize in Literature, in 1984. In 1988 Spanish king Juan Carlos presented Fuentes with the Cervantes Prize, Spain's highest award for a Spanish-language author.

Fuentes returned to the Mexican Revolution as the setting for *The Old Gringo,* the first American best seller written by a Mexican author. The story explores possibilities concerning the mysterious fate of real-life American writer Ambrose Bierce. According to a widespread rumor, Bierce reportedly disappeared in Mexico after joining the ranks of Pancho Villa's rebellion in 1914. Fuentes's novel focuses on the complex relationships of an American woman (Harriet Winslow), a Mexican general (Tomás Arroyo), and Bierce, and the relationship of Mexican identity and American culture. The character Ambrose Bierce is old and dying, and he finds sudden death preferable to a lengthy and painful demise. The novel was transformed into a movie in 1988, with Gregory Peck and Jane Fonda in starring roles.

In the 1990s Carlos Fuentes broke with Octavio Paz in a much-publicized dispute over a series of divergent political, literary, and intellectual views. Paz had deeply influenced Fuentes in his early years, but in later years Mexico's two literary giants were at odds and broke off all communication, although their public dialogue continued in the press until the death of Octavio Paz in 1998.

In 1991 Fuentes published *The Campaign,* a novel about the history of the Americas' struggle for independence from Spain. The following year, French president François Mitterand presented Fuentes with the Legion of Honor, France's highest distinction. The author has received countless prizes, nurtured hundreds of writers, and promulgated a wealth of ideas. In September 2006 he published another collection of stories, *Todas las familias felices (All the Happy Families).* Carlos Fuentes remains Mexico's most erudite and internationally acclaimed man of letters and its most ardent proponent of Mexican culture and identity.

BIBLIOGRAPHY

Boland, Roy, ed. *Specular Narrative: Critical Perspectives on Carlos Fuentes, Juan Goytisolo, Mario Vargas Llosa.* Auckland, New Zealand: VOX/AHS, 1997.

De Guzman, Daniel. *Carlos Fuentes.* Boston: Twayne Publishers, 1972.

Faris, Wendy B. *Carlos Fuentes.* New York: Ungar, 1983.

Shirey, Lynn. *Latin American Writers. Global Profiles.* New York: Facts On File, 1997.

Stavans, Ilan, ed. *Latin American Essays.* New York: Oxford University Press, 1997.

Williams, Raymond L. *The Writings of Carlos Fuentes.* Austin: University of Texas Press, 1996.

Rhonda Saldivar

G

GADDA, CARLO EMILIO (1893–1973) *Italian novelist*

Carlo Emilio Gadda was one of the most radical experimental writers of the 20th century and a foremost representative of the transition of Italian society and culture into modernity. He was close to the literary and cultural environment of the intellectuals of Lombardia (northern Italy) but remained a solitary figure in the panorama of Italian letters. His innovative narrative, often called baroque, comprised a radical shattering of language and aesthetic forms. Many of his writings underwent constant reworking and never reached a final format. Only late in his prolific career was he recognized as a literary model by important writers and critics, such as Pier Paolo Pasolini and the neo-avant-garde poets known as Gruppo 63.

Gadda was born in Milan into an upper-middle-class family. His father, Francesco Ippolito, worked in the textile industry and his mother, Adele Lehr, who was of Hungarian descent, taught history and geography in high school. After his father died in 1909, Gadda and his two siblings, Clara and Enrico, were able to pursue their studies only through their mother's hard work and sacrifices. He describes the difficulties of these teenage years in his most autobiographical novel, *Acquainted with Grief* (*La cognizione del dolore,* 1963). A promising student both in literature and in mathematical sciences, Gadda escaped the harshness of everyday life by immersing himself in a variety of readings, ranging from adventure novels to the long poems of Dante and Ludovico Ariosto.

When Italy entered World War I in 1915, Gadda was immediately drafted. He joined the war with enthusiasm, hoping to overcome the anguish and troubles tormenting him as well as the social environment, which he criticized sharply; this idealism brought him close to the futurist movement with its motto "war is the only hygiene of the world." Yet he did not subscribe to the nationalist ideology of nation building and territorial conquest. The war also made him reflect on the senselessness of human actions and the chaos and irrationality that govern the reality of life, while his capture by the Austrian army led to feelings of despair and humiliation. Out of this time came the diary *Giornale di guerra e di prigionia* (1955), a diary recording Gadda's World War I experiences, including combat and years as a war prisoner in Austria. The work has not been translated into English. At the end of the war, the news of the death of his brother Enrico engendered the sense of deep grief and torment that underlie Gadda's entire literary production.

In 1920 Gadda earned a degree in electronic engineering. With the exception of a short period when he taught mathematics, he worked as an engineer for most of his life and traveled extensively in Italy, Europe, and South America, always dividing his time between his profession and writing. Although he began writing more regularly, he was unable to complete or publish his works. At this same time he came into contact with some writers from the literary circles of Milan. Gadda's intellectual development and cultural affiliation belong definitely within the context of Lombardy, Italy's most industrial region, which, under Austrian rule prior to the country's unification, still maintained strong ties to the continental European culture. Out of this period came *About Manzoni* (*Apologia manzoniana,* 1924) and *Milan Meditation* (*Meditazione Milanese,* 1928). He collaborated with the Florentine review *Solaria,* which was opposed to the official cultural politics of the fascist regime—nationalism and cultural provincialism. The synergy generated by the review led to cultural impulses to join the great modernist, European tradition of FRANZ KAFKA, ROBERT MUSIL, MARCEL PROUST, and James Joyce.

In *La Madonna dei filosofi* (1931) and *Il Castello di Udine* (1934), his abandonment of classic language and style and his interest in experimentation became apparent. The death of his mother in 1936 prompted the writing of *Acquainted with Grief,* one of his central works. The novel, with strong autobiographical elements, centers on a mother-son relationship and childhood traumas. It is a psychological analysis of the condition of grief, positioned against the claustrophobia of middle-class life.

In 1940 Gadda moved—like Alessandro Manzoni a century earlier—to Florence, where he hoped to surrender himself to the linguistic environment of the "cradle" of Italian language. Here he met such renowned writers as the novelist ELIO VITTORINI and the poet Eugenio Montale, and he started working on the drafts of *The Adalgisa* (*L'Adalgisa,* 1944) and *Milan Designs* (*Disegni Milanesi,* 1944), which incorporates Milan's dialect and portrays the social reality of everyday middle-class life. At the end of World War II, he started working on the mystery novel *That Awful Mess on Via Merulana* (*Quer pasticciaccio brutto de via Merulana,* 1957), which had been previously published partially in the review *Letteratura* in 1946–47. His economic difficulties were temporarily relieved by the work he obtained with the national broadcaster RAI, until the publication of *Quer pasticciaccio* in 1957 brought him a long-awaited fame.

That Awful Mess on via Merulana, a parody of the mystery novel, is linguistically the most experimental of his works. The protagonist is a police investigator from Rome, Francesco Ingravallo, known as Don Ciccio, who resembles Gadda in his obsessions, passion

for reading, and distaste for the superficiality and passivity of the average individual in the early years of the fascist regime. The sociohistorical context is a country paralyzed by the seamless and false quietude induced by the fascist culture, where women are made responsible for the breeding of the nation, the press is censored, news of homicides and social scandals are erased from public knowledge, and the regime is increasingly favored by the sanitized, industrial middle class.

The novel revolves around a crime—the murder of a woman—in an apartment house in Via Merulana, where businessmen, professionals, and shopkeepers live. The investigation unfolds relentlessly, uncovering the complexity of social relations, but it does not lead to a conclusion. Refusing to produce a novel for entertainment, Gadda subverts the mystery genre through the novel's lack of closure. The reader is not gratified by the investigative efforts or by the aesthetic finality of the crime and the novel. The solution does not exist because it is always located elsewhere, as no solution to the enigma of life is possible.

Eros and Priapo: From Fury to Ash (*Eros e Priapo,* 1967) is an analysis of fascism and the culture of the 1920s in a format that borders on the essay-novel. Gadda was interested in unraveling the dynamics of collective behavior and the psychological traces of collective action. In *Eros e Priapo* he identifies in fascism the power that leads to individual narcissism and condemns it.

Gadda's philosophical interests informed his vision of reality and his literary production. He was particularly influenced by the German philosopher Gottfried Wilhelm Leibniz and the French thinker Henri Bergson in envisaging a structure of reality that is constituted by the infinite possibilities among its parts and spaces. But the most important contribution to writing came through his attention to and experimentation with language, which also became the object of theoretical reflections. Gadda's "laboratory" of language merges the solemnity of the Italian literary tradition with Latinisms, archaisms, and scientific and legal jargon, while the regional dialects, which he forced himself to learn during his travels, serve as strong contrasts to the literariness of the language. The frequent use of onomatopoeia, the transformations of adjectives into nouns and vice versa, and the richness of figures of speech are meant to liberate the semantic, intrinsic potential of words. This linguistic hybridity often parodies high literature and makes use of pastiche, humor, and the grotesque.

BIBLIOGRAPHY

Bertone, Manuela, and Robert S. Dombroski. *Carlo Emilio Gadda: Contemporary Perspectives.* Toronto: University of Toronto Press, 1997.

Cavallini, Giorgio. *Lingua e dialetto in Gadda.* Messina-Firenze: D'Anna, 1977.

Dombroski, Robert S. *Creative Entanglements: Gadda and the Baroque.* Toronto: Universisty of Toronto Press, 1999.

Maraini, Dacia. "Intervista a Gadda." In *E tu chi eri?* Milan: Bompiani, 1973.

Sbragia, Albert. *Carlo Emilio Gadda and the Modern Macaronic.* Gainesville: University Press of Florida, 1996.

Van der Linde, Gerhard. "The Body in the Labyrinth: Detection, Rationality and the Feminine in Gadda's *Pasticciaccio.*" *American Journal of Italian Studies* 21, no. 57 (1998): 26–40.

Alessandra Capperdoni

GALLEGOS, RÓMULO (1884–1969) *Venezuelan essayist, novelist*

Rómulo Gallegos was a leading Latin American novelist, essayist, and statesman who vividly depicted Venezuelan rural life of the first half of the 20th century. His greatest and most celebrated work is considered by many to be his country's national novel—DOÑA BÁRBARA (1929). Gallegos's work reflects the relative youth of his nation, describing its tumultuous processes of modernization, racial conflict, and economic development. In addition to *Doña Bárbara,* Gallegos is well known for his novels dealing with rural and socioeconomic themes, namely the two episodic works *Cantaclaro* (1934) and *Canaima* (1935).

Gallegos is remarkable among Latin American writers for his dual role as an artistic voice for his nation as well as one of its most important public figures. Throughout his most productive years as an author, he pursued a career in politics and was an outspoken opponent of Venezuela's military dictatorships. One of his earliest political activities took place in 1930 when he was appointed to the country's senate by the ruling strongman, Juan Vicente Gómez. Shortly after taking office, in 1931 Gallegos went into exile in Spain to protest the leader's illegal and unconstitutional regime. He remained there for four years, returning to his native land when Gómez died in 1935.

After returning from exile, Gallegos became increasingly involved in political life. He served as Venezuela's secretary of education, as a member of the National Congress, and as president of the Caracas city council. In addition, Gallegos was one of the founders and leaders of the Acción Democrática party, which dominated the Venezuelan political arena for much of the 20th century. In 1948 his political involvement culminated in his election to the presidency, which he won with 80 percent of the vote. After only four months in office, Gallegos was overthrown in a military coup, forcing him into exile for the following decade.

Throughout the 1950s, Gallegos traveled extensively through the Americas and Europe. After the departure of his nation's last dictator, Marcos Pérez Jiménez, who ruled the country from 1948 to 1958, Gallegos returned once again to Caracas. He continued an active career as Venezuela's elder statesman, serving as a senator for life in Congress and also as president of the Organization of American States. From 1958 until his death a decade later, Gallegos received tributes and numerous awards, including the Venezuelan National Literature Prize; the Order of San Martín, Liberator of Argentina; the Alberdi-Sarmiento Prize in Buenos Aires; the Order of the Sun of Peru; the Order of Andrés Bello; and the Cross of the Venezuelan Air Force. He was also a candidate for the Nobel Prize in literature and was named "Illustrious Son of Caracas." In addition, he was awarded honorary doctorates from several universities, and many schools were named after him, including a prestigious award in literature created by the government in 1964.

Although Gallegos developed an extraordinary career as a writer and political leader, the years of his childhood and early formation were fairly unremarkable. The eldest son of Rómulo Gallegos Osío and Rita Freire de Guruceaga, he was born in Caracas on August 2, 1884, and given the name Rómulo Angel del Monte Carmelo Gallegos Freire. While spending his childhood in the nation's capital city, he was greatly impressed by the natural beauty and lifestyle of the surrounding countryside, and much of his later work reflects a preoccupation with improving the quality of life for his rural compatriots.

Gallegos began his postsecondary studies in law at the Universidad de Caracas after completing high school, but he was forced to leave school for economic reasons. In 1912 he married Teotiste Arocha and became director of the Colegio Federal de Barcelona de Venezuela, followed by a position as deputy director (1912–18) and then director (1922–30) of the Colegio Federal de Caracas (renamed Liceo Andrés Bello). Between 1918 and 1922, he served as deputy director of the Escuela Normal de Caracas.

Gallegos's writing career flourished from an early age, beginning with essays on social and political themes in the Caracas magazine *La Alborada,* which he cofounded. His essays were soon complemented by his fictional works, including a volume of short stories, *Los aventureros* (The adventurers, 1913), and followed by a dramatic work, *El milagro del año* (The miracle of the year, 1915). He then became director of a successful weekly publication, *Actualidades,* in 1919, and by the 1920s Gallegos had begun his career as an educator. It was during that decade that he produced *Reinaldo solar* (first published 1920 as *El último solar* [The last solar]) and *La trepadora* (The grapevine, 1925). The two works directly following *Doña Bárbara, Cantaclaro* (1934) and *Canaima* (1935) are often considered a part of a trilogy that includes the initial novel. These three works were succeeded by *Poor Black Man* (*Pobre negro,* 1937), *The Stranger/The Foreigner* (*El forestero,* 1942), *On the Same Earth* (*Sobre la misma tierra,* 1943), and *The Reed in the Wind* (*La brizna de paja en el viento,* 1952). The latter, written during Gallegos's exile in Havana, is based on political events that took place in Cuba after the fall of the dictator Gerardo Machado. His final work, *La tierra bajo los pies* (Earth under the feet), describes the social changes in Mexico that resulted from the country's post-revolutionary land reform. It was published in 1971, two years after Gallegos's death.

Many of the underlying themes in Gallegos's work can be traced to 19th-century Spanish American writings on socioeconomic relationships, situated in the context of historical works on the struggle of civiliza-

tion versus barbarism. The most noteworthy and influential of these was the Argentinean Domingo Faustino Sarmiento's *Civilización i barbarie* (1845), which pitted the barbarism of "backward," less-developed regions of the continent to the "civilization" of Europe and Latin America's urban centers. Like Sarmiento, who was also a political figure and a distinguished author, Gallegos was committed to reforming his nation's social, educational, and political institutions through his scholarly production as well as his life in public service. Gallegos felt that this goal could be accomplished by eliminating "backward cultural patterns in which the majority of the people were poor, ill-fed victims of regimes based on force," according to Jorge Ruffinelli's "Rómulo Gallegos" in *Latin American Writers.* Many of the characters in Gallegos's novels symbolically represent the struggle of civilization versus barbarism, including the protagonist of *Doña Bárbara,* whose very name reflects the untamed forces of nature she embodies. As Melvin J. Arrington describes in the *Encyclopedia of Latin American Literature,* she represents Venezuela's untamed llanos, or backlands, personifying not only its lawless brutality but also the other dichotomies that echo throughout Gallegos's work: "urban versus rural, European (i.e., white) versus mestizo, rational thought versus superstition, progress versus tradition."

Doña Bárbara became a best seller soon after its publication, and it was translated into English in 1931. Its popularity proved fortunate for the author, opening doors for him during his first period of self-imposed exile in 1930. While in Europe, the author wrote his two subsequent works, *Cantaclaro* and *Canaíma.* The former continues the writer's portrayal of life on the Venezuelan plains in a more nuanced and psychologically complex manner than its predecessor, *Doña Bárbara,* while the latter situates these "civilizing" struggles in the jungle of the country's Orinoco river valley.

Gallegos's contribution to Spanish American literature is significant both for its aesthetic value as well as for the role it plays as historical testimony to the social conditions of its time. Documenting the evolution of Venezuela's identity as a nation, his writing illuminates the most important struggles that were taking place—politically, economically, and culturally. As both a statesman and an author, Rómulo Gallegos played a critical role in his country's development and is one of its best-known and most respected national treasures.

BIBLIOGRAPHY

Alonso, Carlos J. *The Spanish American Regional Novel.* Cambridge: Cambridge University Press, 1990.

Rivas Rojas, Raquel. "Tales of Identity in the Shadow of the Mass Media: Populist Narrative in 1930s Venezuela." *Journal of Latin American Cultural Studies* 10, no. 2 (August 2001): 193–204.

Rodríguez-Alcalá, Hugo. *Nine Essays on Rómulo Gallegos.* Riverside: Latin American Studies Program, University of California, 1979.

Ruffinelli, Jorge. "Rómulo Gallegos." In *Latin American Writers,* edited by Carlos A. Solé. New York: Charles Scribner's Sons, 1989.

Vazquez Amaral, Jose. *The Contemporary Latin American Narrative.* New York: Las Americas Publishing, 1970.

Jane Marcus-Delgado

GAO XINGJIAN (KAO TSING-JEN) (1940–) *Chinese essayist, novelist, playwright, short story writer* An acclaimed novelist, playwright, critic, and artist, Gao Xingjian (also known as Kao Tsing-jen) became the first Chinese writer to receive the Nobel Prize in literature, winning the award in 2000. He is known for such important novels as SOUL MOUNTAIN (*Lingshan*, 1989) and ONE MAN'S BIBLE (*Yigeren de Shengjing*, 2000).

Born on January 4, 1940, in the province of Jiangxi during the crisis period of the Japanese invasion of China, Gao developed his talents in music, art, and literature through the encouragement of his mother, an actress and enthusiastic reader of Western literature. Educated in the government schools of the People's Republic of China, Gao took a degree in French in 1962 at Peking University. During the period of persecutory reforms of the Chinese Cultural Revolution (1966–76), instigated by Chairman Mao Zedong, Gao's mother was sent to live in the countryside, where she later accidentally drowned. During the same period, Gao was sent to a reeducation camp for five years. Assigned to labor in the fields, he secretly wrote novels, plays, and articles, but his fear of punishment for his literary interests forced him to burn a suitcase filled with his writing.

In 1975 Gao was allowed to return to Beijing to help the government with the French translation of one of its publications. He became a member of the liaison committee of Chinese Writers Association, and in 1979 he became resident playwright at the People's Art Theater in Beijing. Between 1980 and 1987 he produced numerous short stories, essays, and plays and was permitted to travel abroad to France and Italy. A new period of political ferment in his life began with the publication in 1981 of a critical work, *A Preliminary Discussion of the Art of Modern Fiction* (*Xiandai Xiaoshuo Jiqiao Chutan*), which ended with a denunciation by the government and with the author placed under surveillance.

The next year, Gao pioneered experimental theater in China with his play *Alarm Signal* (*Juedui Xinhao*) at the Theater of Popular Art in Beijing in 1982. This endeavor resulted from Gao's newfound inspiration from such European modernist playwrights as Germany's Bertolt Brecht, France's Anton Artaud, and Ireland and France's Samuel Beckett. As a result, Gao came under increasing political attack, and rumors circulated that he would be sent to a prison farm. Adding to the crisis in Gao's life was a mistaken diagnosis of lung cancer. Responding to what appeared to be a death sentence medically and a penal colony politically, Gao took a five-month journey through the forest and mountains of southwest China, following the Yangtze River from its source to the sea. The notes he took on this journey formed the basis for his major novel *Soul Mountain*. Because Gao never expected to be able to publish this novel, it was written without any self-censorship or inhibition with regard to either content or style. The countryside not only liberated him from the watchful eyes of the authorities, but the landscape inspired him to create a dreamlike, meditative series of interrelated fragments that touched on a variety of subjects. These images include nature as a great power but also a fragile target of human greed; folk cultures suppressed by modernity; the searing intimacy between men and women; the mysterious nature of the self; the recovery of childhood; and, most important, Buddhist spirituality, symbolized by the elusive Soul Mountain. Begun in 1982, *Soul Mountain* was completed seven years later in France, but it was never published in China. After finishing *Soul Mountain,* Gao wrote a short essay in which he stated that literature did not serve politics or the social consensus but was purely a matter of free artistic expression.

While working on *Soul Mountain,* Gao returned to the theater in 1983, with the production of his controversial avant-garde play *Bus Stop* (*Chezhan*). Inspired by Beckett's absurdist drama *Waiting for Godot* and written in French, the play was condemned as "spiritual pollution" by the authorities. Gao's play *Wild Man* (*Yeren,* 1985) was also perceived as provocative; and with the production in 1986 of his play *The Other Shore* (*Bi'an*), the author found it impossible for his plays to be performed in China. As a result, Gao voluntarily left his country in 1987 and established himself as a political refugee in Paris, where two years later he completed *Soul Mountain.* In 1992 he was named a chevalier de l'Ordre des Arts et des Lettres by the French government, and in 1998 he acquired French citizenship. After the Tiananmen Square massacre in China in 1989, Gao published *Fugitives* (*Taowang*), which takes place against the background of this tragic event in which Chinese protesters were gunned down by government troops. Upon the book's publication, he was declared persona non grata by the Chinese government; and his works were officially banned.

In addition to his literary output, which includes plays, short stories, novels, and nonfiction, Gao is a noted painter, with 30 international exhibitions. Gao's black-and-white ink paintings blend Eastern and Western artistic traditions, continuing his literary style. Gao also provides cover illustrations for his own books.

In 2000 Gao's autobiographical novel *One Man's Bible* was published. Written in the same meditative, dreamlike style as that which characterizes *Soul Mountain, One Man's Bible* concentrates on Mao's Cultural Revolution, exploring the damage done to the individual under a repressive regime in which an extreme of social conformity and ideological control led to the utter disempowerment of the individual and the complete loss of spontaneity, freedom, and even a sense of common decency. As in *Soul Mountain,* the recovery of the lost self is also a major theme; here a love affair with a German-Jewish woman, Margarethe, initiates an emotional awakening on the part of the narrator, allowing him to drop his protective mask and confront the suppressed memories that will give him back his identity.

In 2004 Gao moved from Paris to Marseilles and began work on *Snow in August* (*Bayue Xu*) for the Bei-jing Opera in Taiwan. This work once again demonstrates Gao's capacity for artistic innovation and his ability to create new forms out of a fusion of Eastern and Western artistic perspectives. In 2004 Gao also gathered together his early short stories into a collection, *Buying a Fishing Rod for My Grandfather* (*Gei Wo Laoye Mai Yugan*), and collected his artwork in a volume titled *Return to Painting* (*Per un'altra estetica*), which features more than 100 of his paintings that span his career.

Upon receiving the Nobel Prize in literature in 2000, Gao was once again condemned by the Chinese government, whose furious political response to the award threatened a rupture with Sweden, home to the academy that administers the prize. While opposed to all forms of oppression, Gao himself remains determinedly aloof from the political arena, insisting that literature serves neither the state nor the market, but is a medium through which one individual comes to know himself and to express himself with complete freedom.

BIBLIOGRAPHY

Draguet, Michel. *Gao Xingjian: Le gout de l'encre.* Paris: Hazen, 2002.

Engdahl, Horace, ed. "Gao Xingjian." In *Literature, 1996–2000* (Nobel Lectures: Including Presentation Speeches and Laureates' Biographies), 133–153. Singapore: World Scientific, 2003.

Kwok-Kan Tam, ed. *Soul of Chaos: Critical Perspectives on Gao Xingjian.* Hong Kong: Chinese University Press, 2001.

Quah Sy Ren. *Gao Xingjian and Transcultural Chinese Theatre.* Honolulu: University of Hawaii Press, 2004.

Zhao Yiheng. *Towards a Modern Zen Theatre: Gao Xingjian and Chinese Theatre.* London: University of London, 2000.

Margaret Boe Birns

GARCÍA MÁRQUEZ, GABRIEL (1928–)

Colombian essayist, novelist   Foremost Latin American writer and 1982 Nobel laureate, Gabriel García Márquez is the author of many works, particularly the extraordinary ONE HUNDRED YEARS OF SOLITUDE (*Cien años de soledad,* 1967), an epic novel that is a landmark in Latin American fiction and universally acclaimed as a masterpiece of the 20th century.

Gabriel José García Márquez was born on March 6, 1928, in Aracataca, a town in northern Colombia overlooking the Caribbean, in the same year of the Banana Stuke Massacre (October, 1928) when 32,000 native workers went on trike against the American United Fruit Company. He was raised by his maternal grandparents and nurtured by the stories, memories, and legends of the coastal region. His grandfather, Colonel Nicolás Ricardo Márquez Mejía, was a veteran of the War of a Thousand Days (1899–1902), an outspoken critic of the banana massacres that resulted from the 1928 strike, and an excellent storyteller. His grandmother, Tranquilina Iguarán Cotes, told tales filled with superstitions, omens, and ghosts in a deadpan style rendering them as irrefutable truth. After the death of his grandfather, eight-year-old "Gabito" (little Gabriel) was sent to live with his parents. They in turn sent him to a boarding school in Barranquilla, a port city on the Magdalena River. From 1940, he studied on scholarship at the Jesuit Liceo National in Zipaquirá, north of Bogotá, and after graduation in 1946, he enrolled in the Universidad Nacional in Bogotá to study law and, eventually, journalism. On a visit to his parents, he met Mercedes Barcha Pardo, the 13-year-old pharmacist's daughter who would become his wife 14 years later.

García Márquez first considered writing stories at 19 years of age, when he read FRANZ KAFKA's *The META-MORPHOSIS,* in which Gregor Samsa realizes upon waking that he has turned into an insect. The Kafkian novella relates this fantastic occurrence as a natural—though problematic and absurd—event and continues the narration in a relentlessly realistic tone. The mode of this narrative reminded García Márquez of the stories of his youth and of the narrative voice of his grandmother, who would recount extraordinary and fantastic things in a completely natural voice. His first story, "The Third Resignation," appeared in 1946 in *El Espectador,* the liberal Bogotá newspaper, which published 10 more of his stories in the next several years.

The 1948 assassination of the liberal popular candidate Jorge Eliécer Gaitán (1903–48) closed the university in Bogotá (and led to a decade of violent political unrest in Colombia known as *la violencia*), and García Márquez moved north to Cartagena, where he continued studying law and began writing a daily newspaper column. By 1950 had abandoned his law studies and moved to Barranquilla to devote himself to writing. He wrote for newspapers and frequented a literary group that discussed important writers: Ernest Hemingway, James Joyce, Virginia Woolf, and, most especially, William Faulkner, whom García Márquez considered his teacher and "master." In Faulkner's creation of a place, the mythical Yoknapatawpha County set in the state of Mississippi, García Márquez found a model for writing fiction that is both regional and historic while treating universal topics and classical themes.

In Barranquilla, García Márquez wrote newspaper columns for *El Heraldo,* and completed his first longer work, *Leaf Storm* (*La hojarasca,* 1955), inspired by his visit to Aracataca to sell his grandparents' house. The novella is set in a place that he called Macondo (meaning "banana" in the Bantu language), modeled after a banana plantation near Aracataca, and it describes a period in the history of the region between the civil wars that ended about 1903 and 1928, the year of his birth. Dissatisfied with the work, however, he threw the manuscript in a drawer, and *Leaf Storm* did not appear in print until three years later in 1955 when, while he was traveling in eastern Europe, some friends submitted it to a publisher.

In 1954 García Márquez became a staff writer for *El Espectador* in Bogotá, and in 1955 he was sent to Italy, nominally to cover what was thought to be the imminent death of Pope Pius XII. As a foreign correspondent in Europe, García Márquez reported from the Continent until the Pinilla government (Gustavo Rojas Pinilla claimed the presidency in a coup in 1953 and ruled Colombia until 1957) shut down the newspaper *El Espectador* and left him adrift and abroad without a job. He traveled through Geneva, Rome, Poland, and Hungary, and finally settled in Paris, where he lived meagerly in the Latin Quarter and wrote fiction, like Hemingway, whom he once saw on the street but did not approach. He wrote multiple drafts of *No One Writes to the Colonel* (*El coronel no tiene quien le escriba,* 1961) and then *Este pueblo de mierda* (literally, this town of shit), which would eventually become *IN EVIL HOUR* (*La mala hora,* 1962). In Europe he also investigated socialist and communist governments and considered whether these were solutions to the corrupting power and persistent violence that plagued his native Colombia and elsewhere in Latin America.

In 1957 García Márquez married Mercedes Barcha and was back writing in Latin America, in Venezuela, first for *Elite,* a Caracas newsweekly edited by his friend Plinio Apuleyo Mendoza, and then for *Momento.* As a journalist, García Márquez covered the Cuban revolution, developed a friendship with Fidel Castro, and represented the Cuban news agency, *Prensa Latina,* in New York City in 1959. After a year in the United States, he grew disillusioned by the fractious infighting of the Cuban movement, packed his family, and headed south, riding deliberately through Faulkner territory. He established residence in Mexico City, where he eked out a living writing subtitles and screenplays. During this time, two sons were born, and several of his fictional works finally appeared in print. These included *No One Writes to the Colonel,* the novella of hunger, painful survival, and bitter political frustration, set in a place referred to only as "the town" but richly extending the description of the fictional Macondo. *In Evil Hour* won a fiction prize, but publishers in Spain edited out the raw Latin American flavor and the Colombian colloquialisms, so García Márquez retracted it. He also completed the stories for *Big Mama's Funeral (Los funerales de la Mamá Grande,* 1962), a work rooted in extravagant but very real events before which the narrator assumes a type of guileless astonishment in the face of political corruption and social distress. In this book García Márquez employs exaggeration and hyperbole to inject symbolically significant but impossible details into an otherwise realistic narrative. This intrusion of the marvelous does not so much express inner states of the characters as it creates a fantastic other dimension that parodies both the inflated rhetoric and the monstrous events of historical reality.

The stories for a larger work set in the coastal Colombia of his youth had been germinating for some time, but the writing did not come until he had an epiphany. He was driving between Mexico City and Acapulco in January 1965 when he was struck by a revelation about the novel's format. Fortified with paper and cigarettes, he shut himself away from extraneous activity and wrote. He emerged 18 months later, intoxicated with nicotine, thousands of dollars in debt, but with a manuscript of 1,300 pages, which he promptly sent off to a publisher in Buenos Aires.

One Hundred Years of Solitude appeared in June 1967 and within a week sold out its first run of 8,000 copies; each subsequent week a new printing sold out. Success and fame followed immediately. The novel won the Chianchiano Prize in Italy, the Best Foreign Book in France, the Rómulo Gallegos Prize, and the Neustadt Prize. The famed Mexican writer CARLOS FUENTES hailed García Márquez as a master, and the already famous Peruvian MARIO VARGAS LLOSA wrote a book about his life and work.

One Hundred Years of Solitude is an epic tale, both comic and tragic, of a family named Buendía in a place called Macondo in the banana region of the coastal Caribbean of Colombia. A nostalgic chronicle of a century in the life of a town and a family, the work dramatizes the universal story of creation, discovery, nomenclature, and loss—of memory and of paradise. The narrative seamlessly combines actual and miraculous events and disregards conventional time and reader expectations. The plot is structured with patterns and repetitions both unique and archetypal. The story is historical and mythical, individual and collective, actual and literary.

Harold Bloom has called this work a miracle, less a novel than a scripture, "the Bible of Macondo." Like the Hebrew Bible, it recounts a time so ancient that things still do not have a name and stories so primitive that they anticipate recurrent patterns. Many consider this the most important book written in Spanish after Cervantes's *Don Quixote de la Mancha.* Like that book, *One Hundred Years of Solitude* is self-reflexive: It creates and peoples a new world and simultaneously records and reflects the creation in a book. Also like *Don Quixote,* which some consider the genesis of the modern novel, García Márquez's work signaled a new form in fiction which would define a generation of writers— the modern Latin American novel. In *One Hundred Years of Solitude,* García Márquez brings the modernist sensibilities of the new novel—the formal precision and the plays on memory and time—to a continent that Cuban writer ALEJO CARPENTIER had already described in the 1930s and 1940s as simultaneously virginal and corrupt and imbued with *lo real maravilloso*—the marvelous at every step.

One Hundred Years of Solitude marked the emergence, and perhaps the pinnacle, of a literary boom in Latin America, an era characterized by realistic fiction that played with expectations of readers, particularly in relation to time and the structure of plots. The format of these works is both experimental and politically and socially motivated. *One Hundred Years of Solitude* includes a flight into the marvelous, into the dimension of hyperbole and myth, that is more than surreal: It is at once imaginative, magical, and politically responsible. This novel affected people's ideas about the contemporary novel, challenged their sense of reality, and changed their perception of Latin America.

In his Nobel lecture entitled "The Solitude of Latin America," delivered on December 8, 1982, in Stockholm, García Márquez explained that the wonders of Latin America, real or imaginary, stretch the imagination and strain the comprehension. The story of Latin America has been no less inventive and fantastic than its history, which is filled with corrupting power and horrific violence that seems to make no progress or brook any borders. In this reality, the poets, singers, prophets, and fighters have needed very little imagination or invention to make that reality credible. García Márquez hoped that the creativity and originality ascribed to the artists of this American continent be allowed to pervade and to find solutions for that area's social problems. He invoked the 1949 Nobel lecture of William Faulkner on faith in the endurance of man to say that, 30 years later, there is the possibility of a colossal disaster and that man may not endure unless the teller of tales are able to create an alternate reality where love and happiness are possible and where multitudes are not condemned to 100 years of solitude.

García Márquez has continued to promote and produce writing that is imaginative and yet socially committed to solving the problems of Latin America. He examines the topic and themes of arrogance and power in his fictional treatment of leaders and despots, life fabricated and life usurped by fiction in *The Autumn of the Patriarch* (*El otoño de patriarca,* 1977) and later *The General in His Labyrinth* (*El general en su laberinto,* 1989). Power and politics, love and freedom, both real

and symbolic, are treated in a group of stories collected as *Innocent Eréndira and Other Stories* (*La increíble y triste historia de la cándida Eréndira y de su abuela desalmada,* 1997).

Love in the Time of Cholera (*El amor en los tiempos del cólera,* 1985) is a masterful compendium of the multiple varieties and manifestations of love, a treatise on the inexorable passage of time, and a labyrinthine study of memory and experience. The story takes place between 1880 and 1930 in an unnamed Caribbean seaport city, a composite of Cartagena and Barranquilla, within García Márquez's well-known fictional universe. Love, both adolescent and mature, in the face of death and as a means of valuing life is a key theme in his more recent works, *Of Love and Other Demons* (*Del amor y otros demonios,* 1994) and *Memories of My Melancholy Whores* (*Memoria de mis putas tristes,* 2004).

The autobiography of this excellent writer is recounted in a touching self-portrait that begins with *Living to Tell the Tale* (*Vivir para contarla,* 2002), a memoir of the early years from Aracataca to his first venture into the larger world.

BIBLIOGRAPHY

Bell-Villada, Gene. *García Márquez: The Man and his Work.* Chapel Hill: University of North Carolina Press, 1990.

Bloom, Harold, ed. *Gabriel García Márquez.* New York: Chelsea House, 1989.

Bowers, Maggie Ann. *Magic(al) Realism.* New York: Routledge Taylor & Frances Group, 2004.

Dolan, Sean. *Gabriel García Márquez.* New York: Chelsea House, 1994.

Janes, Regina. *Gabriel García Márquez: Revolutions in Wonderland.* Columbia: University of Missouri Press, 1981.

Rodriguez Monegal, Emir. *El Boom de la Novela Latinoamericana.* Caracas: Editorial Tiempo Nuevo, 1972.

Vargas Llosa, Mario. *García Márquez: historia de un deicidio.* Barcelona: Barral Editores, 1971.

Williams, Raymond L. *Gabriel García Márquez.* New York: Twayne Publishers, 1984.

Arbolina Llamas Jennings

GARDEN WHERE THE BRASS BAND PLAYED, THE (DE KOPEREN TUIN) SIMON VESTDIJK (1950)

SIMON VESTDIJK (1898–1971) wrote *The Garden Where the Brass Band Played* in the form of a memoir, narrated in the first person by Nol Rieske, the younger son in a bourgeois household, who is looking back on his youth. The story is set in the late 1920s or early 1930s in the provincial town of W. (seemingly based on Leeuwarden, the Dutch town where Vestdijk attended university). This psychological novel with clearly autobiographical overtones is a complex coming-of-age story about the emotional development of the main character, Nol Rieske, and his unattainable, tragic love for Trix Cuperus. Tracing an arc through the life of a young man, from childhood to adulthood, this bildungsroman offers extraordinary insight into adolescent psychology and reflects upon missed opportunities and the irretrievable loss of the past.

The key scene of *The Garden* occurs when Nol is eight years old. His mother takes him to the city park, where he is enchanted by the music of the brass band and its conductor, Cuperus. Upon hearing the maestro conduct a Sousa march, Nol discovers the compelling power of music. Spontaneously, he dances with Trix, Cuperus's 12-year-old daughter, with whom he immediately falls in love. The memory of this occasion takes hold of the protagonist and serves as a leitmotif throughout the novel.

Music, extensively commented upon and wonderfully evoked by Vestdijk, plays a major role in the novel. Cuperus comes to the Rieske residence to give piano lessons to Nol, who feels great affection and admiration for his erratic teacher and mentor. Cuperus's reputation as a drunk, however, causes the town to disapprove of his behavior, and he gradually becomes an outcast, even more so after the disastrous amateur performance of the opera *Carmen,* which he directs. This production—a lengthy intermezzo in the main section of the book—dissolves into chaos when the throaty baritone, drunk with rum to attempt to restore his voice, tries to kill the tenor onstage. Cuperus subdues him, but the audience's unruly reaction to this disruption, along with accusations of public drunkenness directed against Cuperus, suspends the opera production.

Nol grows up, goes to the university to study medicine, and almost loses track of Trix, who becomes a waitress at the town's garden restaurant. When he returns to W. to visit the dying alcoholic Cuperus, Nol's love for the young woman is rekindled. After her father's death, however, she refuses to allow Nol to write or to visit her because she considers herself unworthy of his affection. Although Nol belongs to the upper social stratum of the town, his love for the worldly and simple yet fiercely proud Trix seems to undermine class distinctions in a society where the bohemian and bourgeois stand irreconcilably opposed.

For three years Nol hears little about the young woman, but thoughts of her nevertheless continue to haunt him. Before his mother's death, Nol meets Trix again and proposes marriage. However, tragedy enters their relationship. After revealing to Nol that, following the opera performance of *Carmen,* she was seduced by Vellinga, the editor of the local newspaper, and later on by a number of Nol's friends, Trix commits suicide because she had become public property. Nol had failed to grasp his love's psychological exhaustion and despair, and he continued to cling to the image of Trix as inscrutable, indomitable, and superhuman. His self-centered impulse to idealize Trix in nearly metaphysical terms rather than to accept her in the real world blinds him from seeing her self-destructive tendencies.

The implacable opposition of moral pettiness and a more open attitude toward dissent and difference clearly surfaces in *The Garden Where the Brass Band Played.* The novel offers a razor-sharp analysis and harsh critique of small-town parochialism and brilliantly evokes its weariness and apathy.

The mood in the novel is one of nostalgic reflection, seizing time past in quasi-cinematic images. In the elegiac final chapter, the garden turns into an almost mythic setting. After Nol's recovery from the emotional tribulations, he returns to the park where he finds himself surrounded by dark trees, bearing leaves that have the brassy colors of autumn. In trying to come to terms with the deaths of his mother and Trix, the protagonist is reminded of his own inevitable death. *The Garden Where the Brass Band Played* is simultaneously a subtle metaphorical interpretation of the platonic love theme and a lament for its demise.

Among 20th-century Dutch novels, Vestdijk's books best present and shape the universe of adolescence with superb descriptions of emotional insecurity, the discovery of mentors, and the experience of first love.

Particularly, *The Garden Where the Brass Band Played* is a masterful study of melancholic romanticism. It represents the apex of the author's novelistic achievement. The work received great acclaim among critics and readers, gaining Vestdijk a reputation as one of the most accomplished novelists of his generation in the Netherlands.

BIBLIOGRAPHY

Kralt, P. *Paradoxaal is het gehele leven. Het oeuvre van Vestdijk.* Amsterdam: Amsterdam University Press, 1999.

Meijer, R. P. *Literature of the Low Countries. A Short History of Dutch Literature in the Netherlands and Belgium.* The Hague and Boston: Martinus Nijhoff, 1978. 342–349.

Vestdijk, S. *The Garden Where the Brass Band Played.* Leyden: Sythoff/London: Heinemann, 1965.

———. *Rumeiland.* Translated by John Calder. Rotterdam/Gravenhage: Nijgh en Van Ditmar, 1963.

———. *Terug tot Ina Damman.* Amsterdam: Nijgh en Van Ditmar, 1934.

———. *De toekomst der religie.* Arnhem: Van Loghum Slaterus, 1947.

Arvi Sepp

GENERAL IN HIS LABYRINTH, THE (EL GENERAL EN SU LABERINTO) GABRIEL GARCÍA MÁRQUEZ (1989)

More than 20 years after first gaining international acclaim with ONE HUNDRED YEARS OF SOLITUDE, GABRIEL GARCÍA MÁRQUEZ (1928–   ) fulfilled a lifelong ambition in *The General in His Labyrinth,* an historical novel about the last months in the life of General Simón José Antonio Bolívar, the great liberator and leader of Latin American independence. Bolívar is an almost mythical figure for the Latin American peoples and has been the subject of numerous biographies, but it takes the mastery of García Márquez to narrate the general's life as a journey through a labyrinthine river voyage, with a plot that dwells on the realistic and tragically human without diminishing the majesty of the life.

Simon Bolívar, or The Liberator—so named because he liberated the northern part of South America from Spanish domination—had a dream of a Grand Colombia, a vast arc of allied nation-states that his populist revolution wrested from the Spanish, starting with the takeover of Venezuela in 1821. After 20 years of wars, which failed to hold together his Grand Colombia, also undermined by Mexican federalists, Bolívar was, at 47 years of age, fragile and debilitated physically, a condition at odds with the extreme ardor and passion that characterized his life and campaign in Latin America. It is at this point in his life that the novel *The General in His Labyrinth* begins.

The General and His Labyrinth traces Bolívar's final river journey along the Magdalena River, starting from Bogotá, Colombia, in May 1830, until his death on an estate near Santa Marta in December 1830. On this last voyage, Bolívar revisits the triumphs, passions, and treacheries of his life. His great personal charm and prodigious success in love, war, and politics are evoked and recalled through dreams, flashbacks, and memories, interspersed with his battle against debilitating illness. During this melancholy and tumultuous journey, Bolívar is disoriented, caustic, distressed by an assassination attempt, and saddened by the loss of the presidency of the Republic of Colombia.

The novel is organized into eight unnumbered chapters, which almost correspond to the ports along the river and the thematic threads in the narrative. A major theme is the juxtaposition of the deteriorating physical condition of Bolívar the man and the glorious exploits of Bolívar the legendary hero. In flashbacks that develop chronologically, there appear his major military and political exploits, his great friends, and his significant enemies. His amorous adventures, real and apocryphal, are interspersed and exaggerated with a Rabelaisian relish that recalls the García Márquez of *One Hundred Years of Solitude.* The novel's frame and each chapter are marked by the presence of the seven aides who accompany Bolívar on the voyage—in particular, José Palacios, who identifies with the great man and serves as witness to his floating demise.

At each port there is a stream of visitors who add interest, conflict, and incidental satire. Bolívar confronts a multitude of tribulations including ghastly weather conditions, enemies—Francisco de Paula Santander, in particular—his illness, and his paralyzing desire to return to his former glory. He wanders from port to town to house with his entourage, but he is not always treated with love and admiration.

During the seventh month of his journey down the Magdalena River, the general continues to visit his past life. Through stream of consciousness, the general relives battles, lost loves, and the political campaigns that brought him the greatest recognition. However, because of Bolívar's illness, his memories become diluted, distorted, and ambiguous. His declining health becomes the focus of his last days, and yet his illness humanizes him. On a journey that is fraught with nightmares, delusions, and fantasy, what becomes clearly evident is the vitality, heroism, and heart of Simón Bolívar.

The General in His Labyrinth is an excellent historical novel that can qualify as a biography; however, it is also a literary labyrinth—a maze to be explored, discovered, and created as one does a life. García Márquez takes the time to present an intricate and detailed study of Bolívar the hero and of the complexity and chaotic world of Latin America during the time of The Liberator. This novel is not a departure for Gabriel García Márquez: It is to some extent a fulfillment of the dream of Colombian greatness in the hero Simón Bolívar and his love for Latin America.

BIBLIOGRAPHY

Bloom, Harold, ed. *Gabriel García Márquez.* New York: Chelsea House, 1989.

Kelly, Brian. "The Legacy of a Liberator Named Bolívar." *U.S. News & World Report,* 07 May 2006, pp. 10–11.

Menton, Seymour. *Latin America's New Historical Novel.* Austin: University of Texas Press, 1993.

Iris M. Lancaster

GENET, JEAN (1910–1986) *French essayist, novelist, screenwriter, playwright*

A French modernist writer with a proclivity for both high poetic diction and underworld slang, Jean Genet was also a cinephile who made abundant use of motion picture techniques in his narratives. His works attack established bourgeois values and focus on social outcasts, with criminal actions and homosexuality as recurrent themes. His novels depict the world of gloomy prisons, daring thieves, cold-blooded criminals, male prostitutes, and cruel pimps. The impact that Genet's fiction has had on French readers and intellectual circles ranges from admiration to disgust. While, for instance, Jean Cocteau and JEAN-PAUL SARTRE praised his literary genius, ANDRÉ BRETON, Louis Aragon, and ALBERT CAMUS showed contempt for the author and aversion to Genet's writings. Outside of France, particularly in the United States, Genet's influence was felt by Allen Ginsberg, Jack Kerouac, and Paul Bowles.

Jean Genet was born on December 19, 1910, in Paris, and died from throat cancer in a small hotel in the same city on April 15, 1986. His father was unknown, his mother was Camille Gabrielle Genet, and seven months after his birth he was abandoned to a foundling home, the Hospice for Welfare Children in Paris. In early July 1911 he became a ward of the state, and by the end of the month he was placed with a foster parents, Eugenie and Charles Regnier, artisans living in the village of Alligny-en-Morvan. The couple was offered a small monthly salary to take care of Genet until he was 13. They gave him a Catholic education and had him baptized at the village church.

From the age of six, Genet attended the village public school that was within walking distance of his foster parents' house. He fared extremely well, and at the age of 13 he passed his primary school examination with honors, achieving the highest grades in his district and earning him a *certificat d'études*. This, however, marked the end of Genet's formal education; thereafter, he guided his own instruction, reading books that he stole from bookstalls and bookshops.

The same period coincided with Genet's change of status from foster child to domestic servant, helping his foster parents with farm duties, though he hated manual tasks. Thanks to his high educational achievement, he was sent to a prestigious school near Paris, L'École d'Alembert, to become a typographer; days later, he ran away from the school. From 1923 on, his life was a series of moves, escapes, episodes of stealing, and stays in jail. In September 1926, after he had spent 42 days in prison, the court condemned him to the Mettray agricultural penitentiary colony, where he was incarcerated for over two years. The Mettray reformatory, a harsh, brutal environment, was later to haunt Genet's life and fiction. It is the key setting for both *The MIRACLE OF THE ROSE* (*Miracle de la rose,* 1946) and the film script *The Language of the Wall.*

To escape Mettray prison's bleak conditions, Genet joined the French army in March 1929, serving for two years. He was assigned to a regiment of army engineers and sent to Montpellier, then to Avignon, before volunteering in January 1930 to serve in a sapper's battalion. His 11-month service in Syria made him familiar with the Arab world, to which he was closely tied throughout his life.

After Syria, in June 1931, Genet joined the colonial troops in Morocco, where he was assigned to an artillery regiment. In April 1934 he signed up for another three years to serve in the Algerian artillery, but he deserted the garrison in June 1936. To avoid imprisonment, he began a year-long journey in Europe, wandering through Spain, Italy, Albania, Yugoslavia, Austria, Poland, Czechoslovakia, Germany, Belgium, and France. This European odyssey, including prison sentences in some countries, is randomly related in The THIEF'S JOURNAL (Journal du voleur, 1948). On his return to France, Genet went back to stealing, and on September 16, 1937, he was arrested in a department store for stealing handkerchiefs and was sentenced to one month in prison.

The period stretching from 1937 to 1942 may be summed up as one of sustained delinquency, with theft and imprisonment as a recurring pattern. The same period was also one of poetic creativity, for it was in Fresnes Prison that Genet wrote his first novel, OUR LADY OF THE FLOWERS (Notre-Dame-des-Fleurs, 1944) which he had to rewrite later from memory after his manuscript had been confiscated by the prison guards. The rewritten manuscript was later smuggled out of prison and fell into the hands of Jean Cocteau, who admired Genet's story "The Man Condemned to Death." This work was written in Fresnes prison in 1942 and printed at the author's own expense. After initial hesitation, Cocteau urged his secretary and publisher, Paul Morihien, to publish Our Lady of the Flowers anonymously. The first copies of Our Lady of the Flowers circulated clandestinely owing to the novel's celebration of crime and criminals, and also because of its overt homosexual content (Genet himself was homosexual).

This phase corresponding to Genet's birth as a writer was also a time during which his personal circumstances took a serious turn. After stealing a rare edition of Paul Verlaine's Fêtes galantes on May 29, 1943, he was sentenced to La Santé prison. While incarcerated there, he wrote The Miracle of the Rose. He was later transferred from La Santé to the Camp des Tourelles, a militia-controlled prison and a deportation center for the Nazi concentration camps. Thanks to the help of his admirers and Cocteau's friends, he was released from the Camp des Tourelles on March 15, 1944. Following a petition signed by Jean-Paul Sartre and Jean Cocteau and other French eminent intellectuals, France's president, Vincent Auriol, granted Genet clemency on August 12, 1949, thus sparing him further incarceration.

Genet's literary career saw its most prolific phase from 1944 to the late 1950s. After Our Lady of the Flowers and Miracle of the Rose, he published three other novels: Funeral Rites (Pompes funèbres, 1947), dedicated to the memory of a young communist resister, Jean Decarnin, who died on the barricades while fighting for the liberation of Paris; Querelle (1947), a work adapted later by German director Rainer Werner Fassbinder and presented at the 1982 Venice film festival; and The Thief's Journal, an autobiographical work relating the author's thefts and sexual adventures. Genet also wrote poems, plays, essays, and film scripts and directed the film A Song of Love (1950). His plays include The Maids (1947), Deathwatch (1947), The Balcony (1956), The Blacks (1958), and The Screens (1961). Bitterly critical of French colonialism in Algeria, The Screens stirred a huge controversy and violent demonstrations in Paris, where it was performed in 1965, three years after Algeria's independence.

For his written work, Genet won the Le Prix des Pleiades (1947) and the Grand Prix des Arts et des Lettres (1983). He also befriended most of the French major literary figures of his time, including Sartre, SIMONE DE BEAUVOIR, Michel Foucault, and Jacques Derrida. Both Sartre and Derrida devoted books to Genet: Saint Genet: Actor and Martyr and Glas, respectively.

A dexterous stylist and versatile writer, Genet was a voracious, insatiable reader who pored indiscriminately over popular literature and the French classics. As a boy, he relished adventure books, especially the works of Emile Gaboriau, a leading writer of crime novels in France, and those of Paul Ferval, whose exotic settings and intrepid criminals fascinated Genet. An enthusiastic reader with an unquenchable thirst for knowledge and culture, Genet also absorbed the works of Pierre de Ronsard, François-René de Chateaubriand, Jean Racine, Charles Baudelaire, Paul Verlaine, Arthur Rimbaud, Stéphane Mallarmé, Fyodor Dostoyevsky, and MARCEL PROUST. He regarded these authors as masters of style and creators of a "noble" literature. His admiration for these authors, and for Proust in particular, is notable.

Throughout his life, Genet tried to separate the *sacred* sphere of poetic creation from the *profane* world of politics, expressing a marked hatred for all governments. He stuck to his apolitical stance until May 1968, when he was gradually drawn into the French political scene. During students' protests at that time, he upheld the protesters, publishing a political article, "Les Maîtresses de Lénine" (May 30, 1968), that paid homage to Daniel Cohn-Bendit, one of the key leaders of the demonstrations. Genet's political engagement later gained momentum. In the 1970s, for instance, he met MARGUERITE DURAS and Gilles Deleuze and joined forces with them to protest against the living conditions of African immigrants in France.

If, before the 1970s, Genet had conceived of literature as a purely aesthetic exercise, devoid of ideological and political import, he ultimately acknowledged the close links between literature and politics. In October 1970 he declared in *Le Monde*: "Literature, as I practiced it formerly, was gratuitous. Today it is in the service of a cause. It is against America"; one may add against Israel, too, given Genet's support of the Palestinian cause.

From the 1970s, Genet wrote little fiction but grew more engaged politically, supporting the Palestinian struggle against the Israeli occupation and the Black Panthers' fight for equal rights. *Prisoner of Love,* published posthumously in May 1986, is a hymn to these two causes that offered the rootless Genet an anchor, a precarious home among the oppressed black American and Palestinian communities of which he became an adopted member. After his death in April 1986, he was buried in the Spanish cemetery of Larache, Morocco.

BIBLIOGRAPHY

Barber, Stephen. *Jean Genet.* London: Reaktion Books, 2004.
Chevaly, Maurice. *Genet.* Marseille: Temps Parallel, 1989.
Coe, Richard N. *The Vision of Jean Genet.* London: Owen, 1968.
Dattas, Lydie. *La chaste vie de Jean Genet.* Paris: Gallimard, 2006.
Driver, Tom F. *Jean Genet.* New York: Columbia University Press 1966.
Gaitet, Pascale. *Queens and Revolutionaries: New Readings of Jean Genet.* Newark: University of Delaware Press, 2003.
Reed, Jeremy. *Jean Genet: Born to Lose.* London: Creation, 2005.
Ringer, Loren. *Saint Genet Decanonized.* Amsterdam, New York: Rodopi, 2001.
White, Edmund. *Genet: A Biography.* New York: Alfred A. Knopf, 1993.
Winkler, Josef. *Flowers for Jean Genet.* Translated by Michael Roloff. Riverside, Calif.: Ariadne Press, 1997.

Amar Acheraiou

GIBRAN, KAHLIL (1883–1931) *Arabic novelist, poet*

Kahlil Gibran is widely considered to be one of the most influential literary figures of the Arab world in the 20th century, along with the Egyptian novelist NAGUIB MAHFOUZ and the Syrian poet Adonis. Although he lived for only a short time and wrote his later work in English, Gibran became a model for those who aspired for a fundamental transformation in the content and form of the inherited literary tradition in the Arabic language. His writing style and aesthetic formation resulted from a peculiar mixture of Eastern Christianity, Islamic Sufism, Nietzschean romanticism, and modernism. Moreover, he was one of the early émigré writers in American literature whose work has appealed to a broad range of readership beyond the Arab immigrant community in the United States.

Kahlil Gibran was born as Gibran Kahlil Gibran in Bsharri, a Maronite Christian village in northern Lebanon, then an Arab province in the Ottoman Empire. Gibran's father was a tax collector, and his mother was the daughter of a Maronite clergyman. When Gibran's father was imprisoned under the charge of tax evasion, his mother decided to emigrate to the United States. In 1895 the family settled in Boston's South End, which at the time had the second largest Syrian immigrant community after New York.

In the midst of the cultural, financial, and linguistic difficulties that any first-generation immigrant family had to endure, Kahlil Gibran furthered his interests in art and literature. Impressed by his sketches and drawings, Gibran's art teacher introduced him to Fred Holland Day, a wealthy and ardent follower of the European avant-garde movement. Under Day's tutelage, Gibran entered the Bostonian art circles and began to read much of literature's Western canon, including William Shakespeare, Leo Tolstoy, John Keats, William Blake, Maurice Maeterlinck, and Walt Whitman. Day was also influential in convincing young Gibran to complete his education back in Lebanon.

In 1898 Gibran arrived in Beirut to study at the Maronite college Madrasat-al-Hikmah. Despite his disappointment with the school's strict discipline and dogmatism, Gibran got on well with his Arabic teacher, Father Youssef Haddad. Under his teacher's guidance, Gibran read the Arab classics, translations from the French and contemporary Syrian novelists and poets. In his final year at the college, Gibran became the "college poet" and editor of a student magazine called *The Beacon* (*Al-Manarah*). More important, his experiences in Lebanon would later shape the themes of his early works in Arabic. Subsequent to his graduation from college in 1902, Gibran returned to Boston deeply disturbed by the negative aspects of religious or sectarian dogmatism, patriarchal traditions, imperial oppression, and feudal customs he witnessed in his native land.

Within a year of his return, Gibran lost three members of his family: his sister, mother, and half brother. It was only through his immersion in creative work and support from the circle of Fred Holland Day that Gibran could recover from this tragedy. In 1904 he held his debut art exhibition and published his first journalistic essay in the Arabic newspaper *Al-Mouhajir* (The Emigrant). This first piece, "A Vision," is an allegorical take on the question of human freedom and sets the tone for Gibran's later newspaper articles, which he would publish in a collection entitled *A Tear and A Smile* (*Dam'ah wa-Ibtisamah*) in 1914.

Between 1905 and 1919, Gibran had a productive period in terms of literary output in Arabic. In addition to a pamphlet on music (*Nubdah fi Fan al-Musiqa*) and a long poem titled *The Procession* (*Al-Mawakib*) that appeared in 1905 and 1919, respectively, he published three works of narrative prose: *Nymphs of the Valley* (*Ara'is al-Muruj*) in 1906, *Spirits Rebellious* (*Al-Arwah al-Mutamarridah*) in 1908, and *The Broken Wings* (*Al-*

Ajnihah al-Mutakassirah) in 1912. Each of these narratives is set in Lebanon and focuses on pressing social issues such as the oppression of women under patriarchal norms, religious corruption and hypocrisy, the exploitation of the poor, and the abusive and tyrannical power of the feudal lords. Despite an orientation toward social criticism, Gibran's narratives do not reproduce the conventions of generic realism. They are highly allegorical and aphorismatic, filled with interior monologues and constant shifts in the narrative voice. In that sense, the form of these narratives reflects the modernist's tendency to view the external world subjectively as opposed to the classical realist's objective, panoramic vision.

The reception of Gibran's work among the Arabic-speaking readership was varied. Within progressive circles it was considered a commendable and timely challenge against both the literary conventions and the social taboos of a deep-seated oriental tradition. Conservatives, however, were offended by Gibran's negative portrayal of the clergy and feudal lords, along with abusive father and husband figures.

After a sojourn in Paris from 1908 to 1910, Gibran moved to New York with the encouragement of his patroness, Mary Haskell, and his friend, Ameen Rihani. Gibran was more comfortable in New York's vibrant and cosmopolitan cultural atmosphere than in his enclosed circle in Boston. He rapidly gained status among expatriate Arab intellectuals and began to contribute to émigré magazines such as *The Arts* (*Al-Funun*) and *The Traveler* (*As-Sa'ih*). He later became a founding member of The Pen Club (Al-Rabitah al-Qalamiyyah), arguably the first avant-garde movement in Arabic literature. In addition, along with several art exhibitions, Gibran launched a series of drawings called The Temple of Art, which included portraits of well-known figures such as the Irish poet W. B. Yeats, the Swiss psychiatrist Carl G. Jung, and the leader of the Bahai faith, Abdu'l-Baha.

Of more importance, following his settlement in New York, Gibran began to pursue writing in English. In order to appeal to a wider American audience, he composed his later narratives in the form of universal parables. Rather than concentrating on themes specifically derived from his native land, he developed a visionary discourse of the human condition in modern times. At the center of Gibran's later work was a humanized Jesus figure, a wordsmith forging the eternal truth of mankind. The titles of his books reflect this tendency clearly: *The Madman* (1918), *The Forerunner* (1920), *The* PROPHET (1923), and *Jesus, the Son of Man* (1928).

Of these works that envision the unity of God, nature, and mankind, *The Prophet* was received with enormous enthusiasm. The book has powerful philosophical and mystical undertones and is composed of the words of wisdom of a prophet, Almustafa ("The Chosen"), on his return to his native land from exile. A great lament on the spiritual crisis of modern times, *The Prophet* has continued to be one of the most remarkable best sellers in the English language. By 1957 it had sold its millionth copy and by 1970 it reached 4 million copies in sales. It has also been translated into all major world languages.

Kahlil Gibran, along with FRANZ KAFKA and SADEQ HEDAYAT, is a major 20th-century representative of what French critics Gilles Deleuze and Felix Guattari call "minor literature"—namely, literature that articulates a marginalized position from a collective and universal perspective.

BIBLIOGRAPHY

Bushrui, Suheil B. *Kahil Gibran of Lebanon: A Re-evaluation of the Life and Works.* Gerrards Cross, U.K.: C. Smythe, 1987.

Gibran, Jean. *Kahil Gibran: His Life and World.* Boston: New York Graphic Society, 1974.

Waterfield, Robin. *Prophet: The Life and Times of Kahil Gibran.* London: Allen Lane, Penguin Press, 1998.

Firat Oruc

GIDE, ANDRÉ (1869–1951) *French essayist, novelist, playwright*

Prose writer, dramatist, translator, literary critic, letter writer, essayist, autobiographer, diarist, poet, and renowned novelist, André Gide was a leading literary figure of the first half of the 20th century. At the center of Gide's oeuvre lie the recording of self-contradiction and the ruthless interrogation of culture and institutions, especially the moral aspects of thought systems. While many of Gide's early works did not receive the immediate critical and public recep-

tion they deserved, as the author perfected his craft, his body of work became recognized for its importance. As a result, he was made an honorary fellow of the Royal Society of London (1924), received an honorary doctorate from the University of Oxford (1947), and was awarded the 1947 Nobel Prize in literature for "his comprehensive and artistically significant writings, in which human problems and conditions have been presented with a fearless love of truth and keen psychological insight."

Gide was born on November 22, 1869, in Paris. His early life had a profound influence on his writing. His father, a professor of law at the Sorbonne, died when Gide was 11 years old, leaving the young boy's upbringing to his mother, a harsh, puritanical stoic who instilled self-discipline in her only son. Despite his repressive home life, Gide was sexually aware at an early age, as recorded in his *Journal,* notations covering the years 1889–1949, and his autobiography, *If It Die* (*Si le grain ne meurt,* 1920–21). Both lengthy and confessional in nature, these works not only serve as invaluable tools for interpreting his literary works but also combine to form a magnum opus. They reveal much about Gide's psychological struggles and his creative process, as well as the literary culture of the first half of the 20th century.

In addition to these self-disclosing works, Gide published *Corydon,* a Socratic dialogue justifying homosexuality and lambasting the suppression of it by existing social norms. While the work was commercially published under his own name in 1924, it had been previously published anonymously as *C.R.D.N.* in 1911. In the work, he describes his own sexual escapades and also promotes the sort of sexual relationship so often attributed to the ancient Greeks, one in which adolescent boys developed intellectually and sexually under the guidance of an elder male lover.

In 1895, two years after a sexually and emotionally liberating trip to North Africa, Gide married his cousin, Madeleine Rondeaux, with whom he had been in love for many years. They never consummated the marriage, however, and shared a platonic life. Madeleine was a stabilizing figure, yet her presence did not keep Gide from his many homosexual encounters, including a long-term affair with Marc Allegrét, and his fathering of a daughter, Catherine, with his friend Maria Van Rysselberghe.

In 1908 Gide and other French writers founded the prestigious *La Nouvelle Revue Française,* which serialized many of Gide's works. During the 1930s he became a strong voice on the political left, but after a trip to the Soviet Union in 1936, he became disillusioned with strident political ideologies. During World War II, Gide fled Nazi-controlled France and lived as an exile in Algeria. Upon returning to Paris after the war, the author enjoyed considerable fame as an honored man of letters.

Gide's early works—*Urien's Voyage* (*Le voyage d'Urien,* 1893) and *The Lover's Attempt* (*La tentative amoureuse,* 1893)—bear a marked symbolist influence. He attended weekly symbolist gatherings in the living room of Stephen Mallarmé to discuss the centrality, purpose, and destiny of poetry. For the young Gide, symbolist aesthetics provided a bridge between the sensual and spiritual worlds, a way that bodily pleasure and metaphysical conceits could be wedded through language. After his 1893 journey to North Africa, however, he found the Paris salons stifling and ridiculed them in *Marshlands* (*Paludes,* 1894), a comical satire and animal parable in which the characters, choosing not to use their sight, live in the darkness.

Gide expressed his North African awakening in *The Fruits of the Earth* (*Les nourritures terrestres,* 1897), a prose poem addressed to "Nathaniel," in which the narrator acknowledges the need to follow his impulses when sensuality stands against logic, reason, and knowledge. These oppositional positions continued to fascinate him throughout his writing career.

Gide's mature works, often referred to as his "great creative period," include *The* IMMORALIST (*L'Immoraliste,* 1902), LAFCADIO'S ADVENTURES (*Les caves du Vatican,* 1914), and his masterwork *The* COUNTERFEITERS (*Les faux-monnayeurs,* 1925). Although today these three works are classified within the novel genre, Gide designated each work a distinct form, calling *The Immoralist* a *récit* (account or narrative), *Lafcadio's Adventures* a *sotie* (a term he borrowed from the medieval theater performance of fools, meaning a playful, ironic "variation"), and only *The Counterfeiters* a *roman* (novel).

Gide's *récits,* such as *The Immoralist,* are told by first-person narrators, although the artistry in these works lies in the novel's ability to undercut the authority of the narrative voice, resulting in open-endedness and ambiguity. *The Immoralist* stands as an example of Gide's skillful use of psychological realism. It is a tale in which the reader encounters a disjunction between the interior narrator, the protagonist Michel, and the exterior narrator, a friend of Michel's who writes a letter to his brother. By using this technique, Gide creates distance between the two narrators, calling the story's reality into question, and, as in all his works, breaks from the traditions of verisimilitude and naturalism.

While the *soties* are primarily a comic form, they employ stock characters that often stand for abstract ideas, puppets that bear the brunt of Gide's scathing social satire. *Lafcadio's Adventures* is often remembered for its "gratuitous act," a deed done without motivation and purpose, in which the protagonist, Lafcadio, pushes a man from a train for no reason. In this act, like the Russian author Fyodor Dostoyevsky in *Crime and Punishment,* Gide explores moral boundaries. Significantly, Gide presented a series of lectures on Dostoyevsky in 1921 and 1922, focusing on the psychological acumen of the writer and the complexity of his characters, who, like Gide and the characters he created, are filled with paradoxes.

The Counterfeiters is the work for which Gide remains best known. The novel's play with perspective and technical innovations make it a modernist work of art that has been compared to James Joyce's *Ulysses,* Virginia Woolf's *Mrs. Dalloway,* and Marcel PROUST's *IN SEARCH OF LOST TIME.* Here Gide uses a technique he called *composition en abyme,* a form of self-reflexivity in which one of the protagonists, Edouard, writes on the same subject that Gide's narrative explores. Gide often employs characters who express themselves through writing or journals. While this makes for a complex narrative technique, it also foregrounds the journeys and self-reflection that form the core of Gide's works. *The Immoralist, Lafcadio's Adventures,* and *The Counterfeiters* demonstrate the author's range of style, his social concern, and his formal experimentation with artistic technique. The Frenchman Gide was quite fluent in English and supervised most of the English translations of his works, many of which were done by his friend Dorothy Bussy.

After traveling to French Equatorial Africa in 1925, Gide published *Travels in the Congo* (*Voyage au Congo,* 1927), which sharply criticized French colonial policies. In the last phase of his life, he was known for his humanism and political activism, championing the rights of the dispossessed and exploring communism, which he finally rejected after a trip to Russia in 1936.

Gide wrote to understand the self while processing his lived reality. His aesthetic is one of the personal and subjective at a time when many were questioning the worth of concepts such as nationalism and socialism. Gide had a bizarre, absurd sense of humor, one that can be attributed to the way he juxtaposes thought systems, ideals, and ways of seeing the world, for which he was highly noted. His works reveal a restless quest to integrate aspects of the personality and a deeply held belief in art as a means of synthesizing intrapersonal, interpersonal, and sociopolitical concerns, many of which may seem at odds with one another. Despite his self-descriptions and his characterization of his early narrative fictions as *récits* and *soties,* Gide is acknowledged as one of the most significant novelists of the first half of the 20th century. His works continue to draw a diverse audience, including those who appreciate his psychological realism, his formal, modernist experimentation, his classical style, his literary criticism, his moral vision, and his championing of the homosexual cause. Gide died on February 19, 1951.

BIBLIOGRAPHY

Bettinson, Christopher D. *Gide: A Study.* Totowa, N.J.: Rowman & Littlefield, 1977.

Brachfeld, Georges Israel. *André Gide and the Communist Temptation.* Geneva: Librairie E. Droz, 1959.

Brennan, Joseph Gerard. *Three Philosophical Novelists: James Joyce, André Gide, Thomas Mann.* New York: Macmillan, 1964.

Cordle, Thomas. *André Gide.* New York: Twayne Publishers, 1969.

Delay, Jean. *The Youth of André Gide.* Translated by June Guicharnaud. Chicago: University of Chicago Press, 1963.

Fowlie, Wallace. *André Gide: His Life and Art.* New York: Macmillan, 1965.

Freedman, Ralph. *The Lyrical Novel: Studies in Hermann Hesse, André Gide, and Virginia Woolf.* Princeton, N.J.: Princeton University Press, 1963.

Hytier, Jean. *André Gide.* Translated by Richard Howard. Garden City, N.Y.: Doubleday, 1962.

Littlejohn, David, ed. *Gide: A Collection of Critical Essays.* Englewood Cliffs, N.J.: Prentice Hall, 1970.

O'Neill, Kevin. *André Gide and the Roman d'aventure: The History of a Literary Idea in France.* Sydney: Sydney University Press for Australian Humanities Research Council, 1969.

Rossi, Vinio. *André Gide: The Evolution of an Aesthetic.* New Brunswick, N.J.: Rutgers University Press, 1967.

Sheridan, Alan. *André Gide: A Life in the Present.* Cambridge, Mass.: Harvard University Press; Oxford: Oxford University Press, 1999.

Walker, David H., ed. *André Gide.* London & New York: Longman, 1996.

Watson-Williams, Helen. *André Gide and the Greek Myth: A Critical Study.* Oxford: Clarendon Press, 1967.

Blake G. Hobby

GIFT, THE (DAR) VLADIMIR NABOKOV (1952)

The Gift is the final and most important Russian novel (English translation, 1963) by VLADIMIR NABOKOV (1899–1977). The semiautobiographical story of a young Russian émigré writer living in Berlin in the 1920s, *The Gift* was first serialized in the Paris journal *Sovremennye zapiski* (*Notes from the Fatherland*) between 1937 and 1938. Nabokov conceived the novel in 1932 but let it germinate during the early to mid-1930s as he wrote and published the novels *Laughter in the Dark* (1933) and *Despair* (1936). He wrote chapter 4 out of sequence and stopped production altogether to write and publish his surreal political novel *Invitation to a Beheading* in 1938. The editor of *Sovremennye zapiski* refused to publish the novel's fourth chapter because of its irreverent and unconventional parody of the life of the 19th-century Russian novelist and political writer Nikolai Gavrilovich Chernyshevsky, whom Nabokov saw as a bad writer and dangerous precursor to bolshevism. *The Gift* finally appeared in its entirety in book form in 1952.

Because it tells the story of a young man's development as a writer, *The Gift* immediately recalls the work of two writers whom Nabokov greatly admired: James Joyce and MARCEL PROUST. Like *A Portrait of the Artist as a Young Man, Ulysses,* and IN SEARCH OF LOST TIME, the novel shows the development of artistic consciousness. However, Nabokov's Fyodor Godunov-Cherndyntsev differs from Joyce's Stephen Dedalus and Proust's narrator in the number of texts he produces in the course of the novel. The novel includes many samples of Fyodor's writing, from the poems that he writes as a child to his controversial biography of Chernyshevsky. Nabokov also incorporates supposed reviews of Fyodor's work.

The structure of *The Gift* is strikingly similar to that of the "Oxen of the Sun" episode of *Ulysses,* in which Joyce writes passages that illustrate the development of English prose from Anglo-Saxon to modern times. Nabokov uses Joyce's method throughout *The Gift* to trace the development of Russian literary history and Fyodor's own progression as a writer. The first chapter, which contains Fyodor's childhood poems, imagines the first, innocent stages of Russian literature. The second chapter then narrates the grand adventures of Fyodor's naturalist father in a romantic style that recalls Aleksandr Sergeyevich Pushkin. In its satiric style and antic comedy, the third chapter imitates the work of Nikolay Gogol, another of Nabokov's heroes. Chapter 4 presents Fyodor's biography of Chernyshevsky and defends Nabokov's idea that Russian literature declined when it became politicized and didactic in the late 19th century. The fifth and final chapter is written in a new style, one that, as the work of the mature Nabokov, may be seen as signifying the rebirth of Russian literature. *The Gift* concludes with a Proustian intimation that Fyodor will go on to write the very novel the reader just read.

The Gift is also notable for its semiautobiographical elements, specifically Nabokov's touching portrayal of Fyodor's loving relationship with his father and wife. As chapter 2 relates, Fyodor's father disappeared on an exploratory trip to Tibet. This disappearance is a romanticized version of the fate of Nabokov's own father, an important liberal Russian politician who was assassinated by a right-wing radical in 1922. Like Nabokov, Fyodor has learned his passion for butterflies from his father, as well as the detailed precision with which he views the world. Fyodor's notion that, in his writing, he can accompany his father on his final voyage and his acknowledgment of the possibility that his father may one day return suggest a particularly Nabokovian intimation of immortality. In addition, *The Gift* indicates its author's love and appreciation for his wife, Véra. At the end of the novel, Fyodor overcomes the passage of time and his own loneliness through his love for Zina, feeling that with her support and encouragement, he can create brilliant works of literature such as *The Gift*. Nabokov, too, recognized Véra's love for him as the ultimate gift that made all his books possible.

Despite its Proustian and Joycean complexities and reputation as one of the finest Russian novels of the 20th century, *The Gift* has received scant critical attention. Brian Boyd's commentary in his two-volume biography of Nabokov is the only lengthy English-language study of the novel. Moreover, *The Gift* has not found a significant readership in America, with most readers preferring Nabokov's "American Trilogy"— LOLITA (1955), *Pnin* (1957), and *Pale Fire* (1962)—to this, his greatest Russian masterpiece.

BIBLIOGRAPHY

Blackwell, Stephen H. *Zina's Paradox: The Figured Reader in Nabokov's "Gift."* New York: Peter Lang, 2000.

Boyd, Brian. *Vladimir Nabokov: The Russian Years.* Princeton, N.J.: Princeton University Press, 1993.

Dolinin, Alexander. *"The Gift."* In *The Garland Companion to Vladimir Nabokov,* edited by Vladimir E. Alexandrov, 135–169. New York: Garland, 1995.

Livak, Leonid. "The Novel as Target Practice: Vladimir Nabokov's *The Gift* and the 'New Malady of the Century.'" *Studies in the Novel* 34 (2002): 198–220.

Píchová, Hana. *The Art of Memory and Exile: Vladimir Nabokov and Milan Kundera.* Carbondale: Southern Illinois University Press, 2002.

Weir, Justin. *The Author as Hero: Self and Tradition in Bulgakov, Pasternak, and Nabokov.* Evanston, Ill.: Northwestern University Press, 2002.

Paul Gleason

GIGI COLETTE (1944)

The prolific author COLETTE (1873–1954) was born in Saint-Sauveur-en-Puisaye, Burgundy, France. Author of over 50 novels and numerous short stories and articles for periodicals of her era, she wrote from her early 20s through her mid-70s. *Gigi* was published late in the author's career, when Colette was 72 years of age. This popular 20th-century French writer was known for blurring the lines of fiction and autobiography and being the first modern woman to live in accordance with her sensual and artistic desires.

Gigi is a collection of four short vignettes published in 1944, the title story making it the most famous of Colette's works. It became a Broadway play and an Oscar-winning film. *Gigi* was written in 1942 when Colette was aging and bedridden with painful arthritis, and just after her third husband had been arrested by the Nazis and sent to a concentration camp. Many of Colette's novels focus on the loss of love and the resultant solitude, but *Gigi* may be considered the exception, for it ends with marriage and love as the path toward human freedom.

Gigi is set in the world of the demimonde in 1900. It is the love story of the uninhibited 16-year-old Gigi, who is from a family most concerned with money and success rather than love. Coltish, filled with life, and determined—much like the central character Claudine in Colette's earlier CLAUDINE novels—Gigi is Colette's last creation of youthful energy and innocence. As in other of Colette's novels, many of the characters prefer living in an idealized past rather than the present. In the novel, Gigi is raised by her aunts (two aging courtesans) to be a courtesan—a mistress for wealthy, debonair aristocrats. One such man, Gaston, falls for her and attempts to make her his mistress, but Gigi refuses, to the incredulity of her aunts. Gigi wants love, telling Gaston she does not want to lose him. To this, Gaston proposes marriage. The novel's dialogue is witty and humorous, carrying the love story to the matrimonial end.

BIBLIOGRAPHY

Conte-Stirling, Graciela. *Colette, ou la force indestructible de la femme.* Paris: Harmattan, 2002.

Moers, Ellen. "Willa Cather and Colette: Mothers of Us All." *World* 2 (27 March 1973): 51–53.

Laura Madeline Wiseman

GINZBURG, NATALIA (NATALIA LEVI) (1916–1991) *Italian essayist, novelist, playwright*

Natalia Ginzburg was one of the foremost women writers of Italian postwar culture. Her writing straddled literary genres—novels, plays, poetry, and essays—always returning to the exploration of the family microcosm, the notion of memory, and the articulation of female identity and voice.

Born Natalia Levi in Palermo, Sicily, on July 14, 1916, Ginzburg grew up and was educated in the cultural environment of Turin. Her Jewish father, Giuseppe Levi, and Catholic mother, Lidia Tanzi, were not religious, and her upbringing was marked by the cultural openness of her secular family. Her father was a professor of comparative anatomy at the University of Palermo and later a renowned professor of biology and histology at the University of Turin. Her mother came from a militant socialist family.

Ginzburg's childhood years coincided with the coming to power of the fascist regime and its political and cultural triumph, a development that met little opposition during the buildup to World War II. Early on she became aware of the political upheaval as her antifascist family assisted Filippo Turati, one of the founders of the Socialist Party, in his escape to France. Her family's political affiliations as well as their nonreligious background made her often feel as belonging to a "special" minority, at times engendering a sense of marginalization. Introverted and sensitive, she became a solitary teenager, and her introspective nature and critical alertness to the outside reality became woven into the autobiographical tension and intimate narrative of her mature writing.

During this time Ginzburg began writing poetry and short stories. The publication of her second tale, "I Bambini" (1933), in the revue *Solaria* brought her in contact with the publisher Giulio Einaudi and the writers and intellectuals he fostered: Filippo Turati, the Rosselli brothers, CARLO LEVI, CESARE PAVESE, and Leone Ginzburg.

In 1938 Natalia Levi married Leone Ginzburg, an Italian author and patriot of Jewish-Russian descent. The two became actively involved with the publishing house Einaudi, founded in 1933, which had become a center of inspiration and "conspiracy" for antifascist intellectuals. Much earlier, in 1934 Leone had been arrested. Released two years later, he became a professor of Russian literature at the University of Turin. He was soon forced to abandon his teaching position and was exiled to Abruzzo, a region southeast of Rome, where Natalia soon joined him. The village where they spent the first years of World War II was to turn up repeatedly in Natalia's novels and marked a period in her life of both serenity and melancholy.

Although the young couple endured financial hardships, they found friendship and support among the local people, whose simplicity and kindness struck a chord with Natalia. However, this brief period of happiness, and its deeply felt intimacy with her family and the Abruzzo region, was short-lived. Her central work, *Family Sayings* (*Lessico famigliare,* 1963), captures her life at Abruzzo it at its best. Out of this period came a tale, "Mio marito" (1941), and the novella *The Road to the City* (*La strada che va in città,* 1942). *The Road to the City* was written under the pseudonym of Alessandra Tornimparte to elude existing restrictive racial laws. Natalia Ginzburg also worked on a translation of MARCEL PROUST's SWANN'S WAY (*La strada di Swann,* 1946), for the publishing house Einaudi. Her choice to translate Proust's novel from the French marked her increasing interest in the subject of memory and loss, which became a nodal point in her narrative work over her lifetime.

With the fall of the fascist government in 1943, Leone and Natalia were able to leave for Rome. Two weeks later, the city's occupation by German troops left the population and the country in chaos, and Leone was arrested again by the German Gestapo for antifascist activities. Natalia tried in vain to free him, but he was tortured to death in jail in 1944.

After the end of World War II, Ginzburg returned to Turin, where she worked for Einaudi and rejoined the cultural scene and the publishing house's intense literary activity. Her relationship with writers and intellectuals such as Pavese, Felice Balbo, Emilio Einaudi, and ELSA MORANTE nourished these first postwar years. Ginzburg also maintained her contacts with the Communist Party, though she abandoned her former activism. In 1948 she wrote the strongly autobiographical tale *La madre,* in which the widow protagonist, left alone with two children, is torn by feelings of aimlessness that will lead to her suicide.

Natalia Ginsburg continued her commitment to literary and socialist endeavors throughout her entire career. In 1950 she married Gabriele Baldini, a musicologist and professor of English literature. From 1959 to 1962 she headed the Italian Institute of Culture in London. In 1983 Ginzburg was elected to the Italian parliament as a member of an independent left-wing party.

Although her literary production straddled several genres, Ginzburg returned almost obsessively to core themes: the exploration of everyday and ordinary family life, with its quotidian language and conversations, lies and fictions, dominating characters, banality, and exceptional events, as well as its grappling with profound cultural transformations. Among her writings, the novels *A Light for Fools* (*Tutti i nostri ieri,* 1952), *Dead Yesterdays* (1956), *All Our Yesterdays* (1985), *Family Sayings* (*Lessico famigliare,* 1963), and *The Things We Used to Say* (1999) are overtly autobiographical. Yet, her introductory comments to *Family Sayings* challenge the traditional understanding of the genre of autobiography.

Family Sayings is Ginzburg's highest achievement. Both satirical and nostalgic, the novel is centered on the microcosm of the Levi family, their ordinary conversations and everyday occurrences. In many ways it deconstructs the fascist ideal of the family as foundation of the nation and source of collective identity. The parents loom large in this picture but do not fit the ideal patriarchal family. The father, though domineering and irascible, undercuts his authority through his own absurd behaviors that ridicule the ruling function of the paterfamilias. The mother is dedicated to her family, but she often fails as a caretaker and nurturer. Her interests lie in wandering about the city and enjoying exotic, foreign things. Ginzburg's insistence on the small details of life and on the everyday family vocabulary provides a counterpoint to the official dogma and language of fascism that privileges nationalism over the individual and family. Memory is therefore not a strictly nostalgia but, instead, a remembering of the alternative histories of the particular and everyday reality.

The exploration of family life is woven into epistolary form in the novels *The City and the House* (*La città e la casa,* 1984), *Dear Michael* (*Caro Michele,* 1973), and *No Way* (1976), and into the narrative/historical reconstruction of *The Manzoni Family* (*La famiglia Manzoni,* 1983). Here the writing attempts to articulate the voice of the Manzoni family while absorbing the literary figure of Alessandro Manzoni—father of Italian nationalist literature—into the larger workings of family life. *Dear Michael* was adapted for the screen by the Italian film director Mario Monicelli in 1976. Ginzburg's other novels include *The Dry Heart* (*E stato così,* 1947) and *Voices in the Evening* (*Le voci della sera,* 1961).

Natalia Ginzburg died on October 7, 1991.

BIBLIOGRAPHY

Adalgisa, Giorgio. "Natalia Ginzburg's 'La madre': Exposing Patriarchy's Erasure of the Mother." *The Modern Language Review* 88, no. 4 (October 1993): 864–880.

Bullock, Alan. *Natalia Ginzburg: Human Relationships in a Changing World.* New York: Berg/St. Martin's, 1991.

Jeannet, Angela M., and Giuliana Sanguinetti Katz, eds. *Natalia Ginzburg: A Voice of the Twentieth Century.* Toronto: Toronto University Press, 2000.

Picarazzi, Teresa L. *Maternal Desire: Natalia Ginzburg's Mothers, Daughters and Sisters.* Madison, N.J.: Fairleigh Dickinson University Press, 2002.

Woolf, Judith. "Silent Witness: Memory and Omission in Natalia Ginzburg's *Family Sayings.*" *Cambridge Quarterly* 25, no. 3 (1996): 243–262.

Wright, Simona. "La guerra al femminile, tra eperienza e comunicazione letteraria: *L'Agnese va a morire, Lessico famigliare, Prima e dopo.*" *Forum Italicum* 32, no. 1 (Spring 1998): 63–85.

Alessandra Capperdoni

GIRONELLA, JOSÉ MARÍA (1917–2003)

Spanish novelist, short story writer, essayist   The Spanish author José María Gironella is best known for an epic novel that dramatizes the forces and conflicts of the Spanish civil war (1936–39), the key event for Spain and a defining epoch for many Westerners in the 20th century. *The Cypresses Believe in God* (*Los cipreses creen en Dios,* 1953) describes Spain as it endured this historic conflict and, through the dissension within a family, chronicles the harrowing divisions that resulted in a bloody civil war and wounded an entire generation. The book came out in the middle of the Francisco Franco years (1892–1975) and evaded political censorship, perhaps because it portrayed the nationalist cause with particular sensitivity. It was read avidly, criticized ferociously, and discussed everywhere. The novel won the National Prize for Literature in Spain and, more important, afforded the Spanish readers a serious, detached, and arguably objective view of their still-recent and very painful history.

Gironella was born in Darnius, Gerona, in the province of Catalonia. He attended school in a Roman Catholic seminary and worked at various jobs until he entered the army in 1937 at the age of 20, when he and his *quinta* (his draft-age mates) were required to serve in the military. Although Gironella lived in Catalonia, a leftist-leaning province with separatist aspirations, he joined the Nationalist forces, the coalition of political right-wing parties under Franco.

A Republican government in which Socialists were in the majority had drafted a constitution enacting political reforms and anticlerical measures between 1931 and 1933. A backlash of strikes and uprisings eventually put a conservative government in power (November 1933–February 1936). Socialists and anarchists rebelled, and Catalonia was placed under martial law because of lawlessness. Eventually the liberal Republican government was restored (February 1936–39), but the civil war began when General Franco and other army officers attempted a coup on July 18, 1936. This rebellion from the right began a brutal, fratricidal three-year struggle which was played out in every town and city of Spain. General Franco, aided by fascist Italy and the German Nazi Condor Legion, would unite the "Nationalist" forces and defeat the parties of the liberal Republican left, known as the Popular Front. The sides on the left were called "Reds" and were aided by the International Brigades (republican military units) and socialist volunteers, Soviet Red Army regulars, and anarchist militias. The Spanish civil war, with its direct military aid from abroad and the destruction of a town by aircraft bombardment at Guernica, has been seen by many as the de facto beginning of World War II in Europe. The Republican government lasted until February 1939, when the republic formally fell, and Franco marched into Madrid on April 1, 1939. Francisco Franco declared Spain a monarchy and himself regent, and he ruled Spain as a dictator until his death in 1975.

After the war ended in 1939, José María Gironella tried a variety of trades and eventually found work as a newspaper reporter and foreign correspondent. In 1945 he published a volume of poetry. In 1946 his first novel, *Where the Soil Was Shallow* (*Un hombre*), set in Ireland, won the Nadal Prize, and he married Magdalena Castañer. In Paris between 1949 and 1952, he wrote what would become the first part of a trilogy about the Spanish civil war. *The Cypresses Believe in God* chronicles the period immediately preceding the war, from the period of the first republic in 1931 to the army rebellion in 1936. The second volume, entitled *One Million Dead* (*Un millón de muertos,* 1961) is a sequel and covers the actual conflict, the entire period of the war, which lasted from July 18, 1936, to April 1, 1939. The third installment, *Peace after War* (*Ha estallado la paz,* 1966), deals with the aftermath of the war.

In the trilogy, the Alvear family is the psychological nucleus of a large cast of characters, both fictional and historic, whose members or components are changed permanently by the war. The city of Gerona is the geographic center, but as the episodes of the conflict broaden, the narrative extends to the four corners of Spain. The story gives both an immediate and a panoramic view of the struggle. It dramatizes the myriad fragmentary ideologies, the conflicts, the revolts, and the alignment of sides, one called "Nationalist," comprising royalists, monarchists, Catholic, and the other called "Red," consisting of, among others, Republicans, socialists, communists, and anarchists. The perspective achieves an objectivity based on a combination of Gironella's own lived experience, though he calls memory a distorted image; the testimony of other people, which he found exaggerated and sometimes fanatical; research into the contemporaneous documentation in newspapers and photographs; and, perhaps most important, historic and geographic distance because he wrote much of the novel abroad.

Gironella's trilogy narrates major actual and ideological conflicts of the 20th century in classical 19th-century narrative style. This is primarily a family saga of the Alvear family, including Matias, a telegraph operator in Gerona; his wife, a devout Catholic woman; and their three children, especially their son Ignacio, who represents idealistic youth searching for a way amid the tumult and chaos around him. The family forms the nucleus of fictional characters, which include priests, monarchists, communists, socialists, Trotskyites, the Republican left, the Catalan League, anarchists, Masons, militiamen, professional soldiers, international volunteers, regional representatives, and guerrilla freedom fighters. The story of the conflict is told from a multiplicity of angles with an apparent attempt at impartiality. The characters, whether fictional or historical, are caught in gripping human conflict, their choices and ideologies mirroring the complicated turmoil of historical reality.

Gironella's epic novel combines the fictional with the historic. The cast of real personages include government leaders; officers of the Spanish Nationalist Army, the Spanish Red Army, Nationalist air force, and Red air force; officers of the International Brigade; political leaders of the international brigades; guerrilla commanders; Spanish and Russian communists; Trotskyites; members of the Iberian Anarchist Federation; German and Italian fascists; and correspondents for Spanish papers and for the foreign press, including Russian, American (Ernest Hemingway), and English. In fact, the success of the books lies in the hunger for information about the facts and the issues that led to the failed republic and the long years under Franco rule.

Cypresses was one of the most-read books in Spain after and about the Spanish civil war. Gironella's apparent impartiality was tinged with his Francoist background, and he is particularly eloquent on the Nationalist side. However, his meticulous research and journalistic background give a credible voice and a lesson in history—if not to accept, at least to dispute.

Gironella attempts, particularly in *One Million Dead,* to make a methodical reply to several works written outside of Spain that have been very influential in Europe and America. Among these are MAN'S HOPE by ANDRÉ MALRAUX, *For Whom the Bell Tolls* by Ernest Hemingway, *A Spanish Testament* by Arthur Koestler, and *Diary of My Times* by GEORGES BERNANOS. Gironella has said that these books contain mostly folklore, that they are full of personal saga and individual dogma, but are devoid of a clear appraisal of what actually occurred in Spain. The staging area was Spain, but the participants—and the repercussions—involved Germans, Italians, Frenchmen, Englishmen, Americans, and Belgians. In the preface to the second volume, *One Million Dead,* Gironella explains the title; he says that three years of fratricidal war in Spain left 1 million dead, not in actual cadavers, which added up to approximately 500,000, but in spirits destroyed. To the half-million who were killed he adds those who became killers, "the murdered among the dead—all those who died at the hands of men who, in the grip of hatred, killed their own capacity for pity, their own souls."

In addition to the highly acclaimed and much discussed Spanish civil war trilogy, Gironella wrote *Condemned to Live* (*Condenados a vivir,* 1971), a story of two families of Barcelona during 1939–67, which won the Premio Planeta, the Spanish national prize for literature. *The Men Cry Alone* (*Los hombres lloran solos,* 1986), is a fourth volume devoted to the causes and effects of the Spanish civil war. A prolific writer, Gironella also wrote short stories; memoirs; travelogues based on trips to China and Japan; and essays on politics, philosophy, and religion. José María Gironella continued to write about Spain and to comment on the compelling issues of the 20th century until his death in 2003.

BIBLIOGRAPHY
Schwartz, Ronald. *José Maria Gironella.* New York: Twayne Publishers, 1972.
Suarez-Torres, J. David. *Perspectiva humorística en la trilogía de Gironella.* New Cork: Eliseo Torres, 1975.
Thomas, Gareth. *The Novel of the Spanish Civil War (1936–1975).* Cambridge: Cambridge University Press, 1990.

Arbolina Llamas Jennings

GLASS BEAD GAME, THE (DAS GLASPERLENSPIEL) HERMANN HESSE (1943)

The last novel by the Swiss German author HERMANN HESSE (1877–1962), *The Glass Bead Game* is a serene bildungsroman conceived in the form of a "eutopia" (positive, happy utopia) set in the year 2200, somewhere in the German-speaking areas of Europe. The English translation by Richard and Clara Winston appeared in 1969. The author's portrait of an ideal geography envisions a cloistered, spiritual province, Castalia, flourishing unharmed and protected from the vicissitudes of everyday history and politics within the borders of a wider state or nation. Its inhabitants belong to a highly respected male elite, governed by the strict laws of willingly obeyed intellectual hierarchies that reflect the main disciplines of the humanities. Everybody, however, acknowledges the serene organizational superiority of music and mathematics as the sole pathways to a comprehensive celestial harmony.

Each specialized discipline of the humanities inside Castalia is ruled by a master (*magister*), who is elected by the community itself as a sign of collective respect and in recognition of his spiritual excellence. In addition to these particular disciplines, the elite of the province also gather in the community of the glass bead game players, which needs a special, interdisciplinary initiation. To play the glass bead game supposes the gift of linking apparently unrelated disciplines (for instance, medieval music and gardening, or Bach and mathematics) into a higher, sublimely spiritual synthesis. The German philosopher Leibniz (1646–1716), who besides his famous *Monadology* also wrote esoteric texts, imagined knowledge as the skill of detecting abstract and subtle correspondences between the different sciences and the divine plenitude of the cosmos, based on the art of a generalized calculus, or mathematics, which he called *characteristica universalis*. Accordingly, the glass bead game is practiced by its participants as a universal science (*mathesis universalis*), governed by the pure and abstract equations of mathematics and music. The cast of the glass bead game players form the generally admired extreme spiritual elite of Castalia. They also serve worldly values, since the general plan of the annual festival elaborated by the master of the glass bead game—Magister Ludi—is advertised on the radio and in the press, in order to rally the players from outside the province in a feast of ethereal spiritual communion.

Hesse's novel presents the career of an outstanding glass bead game player, Josef Knecht (his name means "servant" in German), from his early classes in a grammar school up to the peak of the provincial hierarchy, as Magister Ludi. Meditating on his cloistered, ethereal existence within an enclave that willingly ignores the perils of everyday struggle and history, Knecht finally decides to quit his appointment and become a teacher to a worldly, decadent aristocratic Italian family. Unfit for the outside world, however, he dies almost immediately, while swimming in an alpine lake. Hesse seems to take great lengths to point out that Knecht's sudden death, provoked by the rising sun, must be interpreted as a ritual of sacrifice, performed by nature itself against an outstanding member of a community whose spiritual formation has always had as its prerequisite an inorganic and abstract aestheticism.

Indeed, the members of Castalia—all men, no women—exclude love, instincts, psychology, suffering, and even death from their cycles of existence. Within the province, nature itself is a cultural object, similar to history, politics, war, diplomatic intrigue, entertainment, or sport. Accordingly, Castalia is presented by the author as an extremely sophisticated and impeccable artificial society, which, though a financial burden, is sustained by a state that remains unnamed throughout the text. Josef Knecht's unexpected resignation is determined by his deep awareness that no society or person can live outside history forever. In a letter addressed to the president of the Order, the abdicating Magister Ludi claims that history will necessarily engulf Castalia in an unpredictable future, destroying the very sense of protected permanence and eternity that form the most cherished identity marks of this enclave.

Two main, intermingled thematic blocks structure the narrative. The former relies on Knecht's intellectual evolution, from his boyhood up to the high ranks of Castalia. The latter consists in the analysis of an enclaved cultural system experiencing a decadent crisis. Both meet in Knecht's outstanding destiny as a very gifted member of the order of the glass bead game players and in his decision to quit his artificial, cloistered life in order to encounter the true rhythms of nature. As such, a main topic of the novel is the relation between eternity and time. Castalia and its members live outside time: The vicissitudes of the surrounding politics and history come sifted to its inhabitants through the sieve of a pure and crystal-clear inner tradition. To a certain point, Knecht's career is marked by the same certainty provided by eternity. However, several of his personal experiences—such as his vivid addresses on the existence of the order delivered before a visitor of Castalia, the *hospitant* Plinio Designori, or his long visit to a Benedictine monastery, where he meets an influential Catholic figure, the historian Pater Jakobus—teach him that in the evolution of humanity, time cannot be obliterated since it contains two basic elements of civilization: decadent erosion and death. In view of that,

the novel's plot is built on the scheme of archaic sacrificial rituals, whereby ferocious Time devours everything, including Eternity.

In the 19th century, Germany's educational system was built on a general school hierarchy, available to everyone, and on a few elite schools, which could only be accessed by strict intellectual selection and invitation. One of them was Pforta, a school that specialized in the humanities and was attended by Friedrich Hölderlin, Friedrich Nietzsche, and other highly qualified "geniuses." Its rules went against any family contacting the gymnasium directly; that was possible only after the student had gone through a very tough selection trial. The nomination procedure usually seized the attention of the entire country, as there were towns (even regions) whose schooling system had been unable to provide, for long and "shameful" years, any suitable candidate to qualify for the elite schools. Hermann Hesse described the system in an early, rather bitter novel, *Beneath the Wheel* (*Unterm Rad,* 1906), whose protagonist, the young Hans Giebenrath, had managed to enter the elite school but failed to meet its inhuman, extremely strict requirements, suffering a nervous breakdown.

In *The Glass Bead Game,* a rather gifted, parentless schoolboy, the young Josef Knecht, is selected for the elite schooling system of Castalia by the venerable master of music (Magister Musicae), who pays a short visit to the student's small town in order to verify his outstanding local references. Gently protected by his master, but recommended by his excellent personal qualities and intellect, Knecht rises in the province's spiritual hierarchy and is selected for the inner cloister of the glass bead game players. They finally make him their Magister Ludi, following the venerable Thomas von der Trave, whose name is actually an innocent pun, secretly referring to THOMAS MANN, Hermann Hesse's great friend. (Trave is the river that flows through Lübeck, Thomas Mann's native town in northern Germany.)

Becoming an outstanding glass bead game player, whose intellectual qualities go far beyond his colleagues' psychological uncertainties, symbolized by Fritz Tegularius, Knecht's very gifted but unruly friend, the future Magister Ludi is selected by the order as an "ambassador" for two special missions, which enable him to reach the highest rank in the hierarchy. At first he is encouraged to take up a debate with a clever visitor (*hospitant*) of Castalia, the young Plinio Designori, offspring of an old patrician Italian family, who challenges the province's eternity and artificial rules by contrasting them to the relative, changing dialectics of the outside world's politics and history. Later on, after leaving Castalia, Designori becomes a highly influential politician and member of Parliament, still favorable to Castalia, even though the financial burden represented by the province proves to be more and more difficult to sustain by this nurturing political body. Plinio Designori plays a conclusive role in Knecht's death as well: The dissident Magister Ludi is employed as the tutor of Designori's unruly son Tito, who indirectly kills Knecht by beating him in an uneven alpine swimming competition. Before entering the cold lake, Tito Designori performs an orgiastic dance honoring the rising sun. Knecht dies because of the sun, which represents, in Hesse's symbolical intention, nature's everlasting ferocious energy.

On his second ambassadorial mission, Knecht is an envoy to the powerful Benedictine monastery of Mariafels, whose abbot, Gervasius, has asked the order of Castalia to send over a member who might initiate the monks into the mysteries of the glass bead game. Castalia is happy to fulfill the request, hoping to get support from the Benedictines at the Vatican. Knecht manages to complete this secret task during his prolonged visit, persuading the famous historian Pater Jakobus to further plead the cause of the province. The intellectual debate between these two gifted men occupies a considerable part of the narrative episode dedicated to Mariafels, and it effects a complete change in Josef Knecht's intellectual thinking. While getting valuable information on the glass bead game, Pater Jakobus teaches Knecht historiography and determines him to envisage the evolution of cultural systems as part of a wider dialectic of time, death, and history.

Knecht's personal crisis concerning Castalia springs from his debate with the Benedictine monk, who makes him understand that culture is an organic, vivid flow of inspiration, maturity, and decadence, deeply rooted in the evolution of society and history. As a consequence, it cannot be contained in a spiritual province that cultivates artificial values, as Castalia does, by privileging the art of endless analyses and combinations of the past to the detriment of spontaneity and fresh creation. Such a collective existence, the learned monk suggests, is a glamorous but decadent mystification, built on extremely fragile pillars, which might easily collapse because of a sudden historical or political move.

The analysis of Castalia as a dying cultural system will obsess Magister Ludi Josef Knecht's mind while in office and will finally determine him to resign in order to try his powers in the outside world. In Hesse's mind, Castalia is a "pedagogical province," of the kind defined by Goethe in his *Wilhelm Meister*. On the other hand, it is a postmodern form of purely spiritual collective existence, as Hesse places his order in a period consecutive to modernism, which is defined in the book as "the Age of the Feuilleton,"—that is, the period of a sketchy and hyper-personalized, exacerbated form of culture, entirely dominated by the urge of novelty, which does not allow ideas to solidify and structure into eternal and universal strata.

The modernist period—the historians of Castalia used to say—had deepened collective unrest by privileging wars, politics, sport, and entertainment. In contrast, the future province would be built on abstract, purely spiritual—that is, universal—humanistic values, concentrated in a superior but necessarily cloistered cultural body. In order to train its members, Castalia must carefully eliminate from their souls such organic turbulences as love, family life, psychology, and fear, committing them to a highly sophisticated science of interdisciplinary cultural associations based on numerology and music. No member of Castalia can generate fresh creation: Originality is the art of detecting magical interrelations between apparently unrelated topics, like European music and Chinese philosophy or medieval architecture and scholastics.

One should not forget that Hesse published his work in the midst of the violent rage of World War II, presenting Castalian life as a serene spiritual alternative to collective hate, bloodshed, and sufferance. But apart from being a mild political manifesto, the novel relies on the German philosopher Oswald Spengler's famous

Decline of the West (Das Untergang des Abendlandes, 1918–23) in order to define its main categories. In his seminal work, Spengler claims that the history of antiquity stipulated the existence of two kinds of societies, defined by their representation of time. The so-called happy, eudaemonistic, a-historical societies (like ancient Greece, for instance) understood time as a succession of present moments of energetic plenitude, which actually obliterated the sense of evolution and history. On the contrary, profoundly historical civilizations, like those of the Egyptians and the Jews, kept strict records of their traditions, developing a sharp sense of caducity and progress. Spengler also demonstrates that the collective sense of time has always been associated with the representation of death. For the Greeks, who incinerated corpses, the underworld was but a counterpart to the existing world; the Egyptians, on the other hand, developed a sober culture of death based on the idea of continuity, while the Jews brought into the Mediterranean culture the logic of the future coming of a Messiah and the image of the apocalypse.

In Spengler's terms, Castalia is conceived by its author as an a-historical, artificial society, built on the logic of the spiritual "province." In The Decline of the West, Spengler also stipulates an antithesis between two cultural destinies, defined respectively as the culture of the city and the culture of the province. Both represent a way of spiritual survival within the organic process of turning organic "culture" into a hyper-organized "civilization," which represents the decadent end of each culture. Spengler asserts that the culture of the city is based on the social logic of the impulsive and faceless mob, which fixes the destiny of cultural evolution by turning it into distraction and intelligence. In contrast, the culture of the province keeps tradition alive, preserving its organic vividness through wisdom and originality. Spengler imagines that in a hyper-socialized, incessantly massifying Europe, the spiritually cloistered enclave can be a solution for culture, given the natural tendency of the "cultural province" to produce a highly qualified and dedicated elite.

Hesse was familiar with Spengler's idea. His other great novels—DEMIAN, Journey to the East, STEPPENWOLF, and NARCISSUS AND GOLDMUND—are built on the logic of the spiritual elite. Hesse also believed that the Oriental way of serene, absolute life could save European culture from disintegration. Josef Knecht is himself attracted by the call of the East, as a chapter of his development centers on his voluntary obeisance to a Chinese monk, who lives outside civilization in a tiny oasis of bamboo trees he planted. Knecht eventually introduces the Chinese I-Ching book (The Oracle of Predictions) into his spiritual meditation and proposes it later as the main combinatory topic of a surprisingly original annual glass bead game.

The very meaning of the glass bead games remains a mystery, although millions have tried to solve its logic. Initially the game was played with tokens, but thereafter pure spiritual formulas prevail. The game is an exquisite and almost magical art of combination, which is specific to the decadent phase of various cultures, seized by an aesthetic fatigue which they experience as a lack of genuine creativity. In order to explain the cultural logic of combinatory decadence, Hesse evokes ancient Alexandria and the fall of Greek spirituality within magic and mysticism. Another analogy is the dawn of the Renaissance, driven into the flamboyant effervescence of the baroque or the exquisite skill of inventing magical, unpredictable resemblances between humans, things, and symbols. It might also be said that the functioning principles of the Internet lend new and unexpected meanings to the classical glass bead game imagined by Hesse. Therefore, by simply searching the Web, one could find many sophisticated surfers belonging to a worldwide community of glass bead game players. As Hesse died in 1962, he could not, of course, foresee postmodernism and the World Wide Web, but his novel projects a future fascination for what is considered by many to be the serene, purely spiritual solution to our everyday wars, sorrows, and disasters.

BIBLIOGRAPHY

Bloom, Harold. Hermann Hesse. Philadelphia: Chelsea House, 2003.

Church, Margaret, et al., eds. Five German Novelists (1960–1970). West Lafayette, Ind.: Purdue University Press, 1971.

Farquharson, Robert H.: An Outline of the Works of Hermann Hesse. Toronto: Forum House, 1973.

Freedman, Ralph: Hermann Hesse. Pilgrim in Crisis. A Biography. New York: Pantheon/Fromm, 1997.

Mileck, Joseph. *Hermann Hesse and his Critics.* Chapel Hill: University of North Carolina Press, 1958.

———. *Hermann Hesse. Between the Perils of Politics and the Allure of the Orient.* New York: Peter Lang, 2003.

———. *Hermann Hesse: Biography and Bibliography.* Berkeley: University of California Press, 1977.

———. *Hermann Hesse: Life and Art.* Berkeley: University of California Press, 1981.

Otten, Anna, ed. *Hesse Companion.* Frankfurt: Suhrkamp Verlag, 1970.

Stelzig, Eugene L. *Hermann Hesse's Fiction of the Self.* Princeton, N.J.: Princeton University Press, 1988.

Tusken. Lewis W. *Understanding Hermann Hesse: The Man, His Myth, His Metaphor.* Columbia: University of South Carolina Press, 1998.

Zeller, Bernhard. *Hermann Hesse.* Reinbek, Germany: Rowohlt Taschenbuch Verlag, 2005.

Ziolkowski, Theodore. *The Novels of Hermann Hesse: A Study in Theme and Structure.* Princeton, N.J.: Princeton University Press, 1965.

Stefan Borbély

GOD'S BITS OF WOOD (*LES BOUTS DE BOIS DE DIEU*) Ousmane Sembène (1960)

God's Bits of Wood is the third and most famous novel of award-winning author and filmmaker OUSMANE SEMBÈNE (1923–), who was born in Ziguinchor, Senegal, then a French colony. *God's Bits of Wood,* a panoramic novel of social realism, chronicles a 1940s railroad strike on the Dakar-Niger line. Though several heroic figures, most notably Ibrahima Bakayoko, distinguish themselves at the head of the strike, the true heroes of the novel are the common people of Africa who rise against the colonial oppressors to demand their rights.

Returning to Senegal in 1947 from service in the French army, Sembène found the capital, Dakar, in a state of political and social upheaval. That year he took part in the famous railroad workers' strike on the Dakar-Niger line, which brought transportation to a halt across French West Africa. Though he left for France before the successful conclusion of the strike on March 19, 1948, Sembène was deeply affected by the experience and later drew on the events he had witnessed to create *God's Bits of Wood.*

God's Bits of Wood does not take its shape from the actions of an individual character, but rather attempts to chronicle the effects of the strike on a wide swath of West African colonial society. For this panoramic view, the book is frequently compared to Émile Zola's 1885 social realist novel *Germinal. God's Bits of Wood* has a cast of more than 40 characters from all ranks of life, including Bambara and Peul ethnic groups as well as French colonial officials. Its action alternates between Bamako (today the capital of Mali), Thiès, and Dakar.

The novel begins with the child Ad'jibid'ji, daughter to Ibrahima Bakayoko, sneaking into a railway worker's union meeting in Bamako; in concert with similar meetings up and down the Dakar-Niger line, the workers vote to strike for the same higher wages and family stipends enjoyed by white workers. The first month's enthusiasm for the strike begins to wane, however, as the families of workers start to go hungry. The railroad retaliates against the workers by cutting off water to their homes and by attacking the workers with private police and strikebreakers. The strike becomes a struggle for survival for both the men who oppose the railroad directly and the women who fight to keep their families from starvation. Though the community rises to the challenge, it also begins to disintegrate under the pressures of poverty.

Violence between the strikers and the railroad continues to escalate, resulting in the senseless shooting of two children by the panicked railroad official Isnard. In one of the novel's most extended and moving scenes, the women of Thiès march on Dakar in protest, drawing such attention to their cause that the railroad is forced to open negotiations. The strike's main spokesman, Bakayoko, returns to face the railroad officials in Dakar and, through a dramatic, nationally publicized speech, succeeds in expanding the strike into a general strike across West Africa, forcing the railroad to capitulate.

Heavily influenced by Marxist ideology, Sembène creates a novel in which the proletariat itself is the hero. Though individuals continue to distinguish themselves in the struggle, the victory is won through broad-based community action, particularly the mutual support between the wives of strikers in finding food and water for their families. Similarly, though the march of the Thiès women is in large part organized by the heroic Penda, a returned prostitute who is murdered by police on entering Dakar, the accomplishment is communal rather than individual.

Even the novel's ostensible hero, Ibrahima Bakayoko, acts more as an embodiment of this communal force than as an individual. The strikers often speak of Bakayoko as their leader, but until his appearance in the final third of the novel, the reader has little sense of his personality. Even after arriving, he remains mysterious and highly idealized, leading some critics to attack Sembène's portrayal as overly romantic; however, others have argued for Bakayoko as one of the great revolutionary figures of modern fiction.

A major concern throughout *God's Bits of Wood* is the racism of the colonial government and railroad officials, and the corresponding self-assertion of the black strikers. Though the workers strike to improve their economic situation, they also strike for racial equality, demanding equal benefits with the railroad's white employees. The railroad, headed by the bitterly racist M. Dejean, refuses their demands in part because to grant stipends to the worker's families would mean acknowledgment of their polygamous marriages, implicitly accepting the differences of their culture. M. Dejean holds the black strikers in such contempt that it takes months to even arrange a meeting. Meanwhile, scenes of "the Vatican"—the opulent, protected neighborhood of the colonial officials—alternate pointedly with descriptions of the slums that house the workers. This conflict can also be seen in the characters of N'Deye Touti and Beaugosse, Africans whose European education has left them with conflicted loyalties throughout the strike.

Though Sembène was a staunch warrior for black rights, he never embraced the negritude movement of Léopold Sédar Senghor and Aimé Césaire, believing that an all-black ideology would needlessly isolate Africa from the world. Accordingly, the struggle in *God's Bits of Wood* does not fall neatly along racial boundaries. One colonial official, ironically named Leblanc ("the white"), secretly supports the strikers with part of his salary. The movement receives solidarity contributions not only from other African countries (such as Dahomey, now Benin), but also from left-wing groups in France. Blind Maïmouna's song seems to close the book with hope for further interracial reconciliation; though she recalls the terrible violence, she ends by singing, "Happy is the man who does battle without hatred."

The changing role of women serves as another recurring theme. Just as the strike creates a "new breed" of self-confident, assertive African man, so does it create a new breed of empowered African woman, prepared to fight for her family and her political rights alike. Though the nominal leaders of the strike are male, women such as Ramatoulaye, Mame Sofi, and Penda perform equally brave deeds, supporting their families and defying the French authorities. In one notable scene, the women of Dakar even repulse a police cavalry charge, though their torches tragically destroy their own homes in the process.

As in many of Sembène's works, religion appears in *God's Bits of Wood* only as a repressive force. The police first set on the women of Dakar because Ramatoulaye has killed a ram belonging to El Hadji Mabigé, her imam brother, to feed her starving children and the other striking families. El Hadji is finally prevailed on to withdraw his complaint, but he remains loyal to the French colonial government and refuses to aid his sister. Throughout the strike, El Hadji, like other Islamic and Christian religious leaders across French West Africa, preaches that to rebel against French rule is to rebel against God.

Though some have criticized *God's Bits of Wood* for its episodic structure and touches of melodrama, it remains one of the most celebrated novels produced in 20th-century Africa, a moving recounting of the power of ordinary people.

BIBLIOGRAPHY

Aire, Victor O. "Ousmane Sembene's *Les Bouts de bois de Dieu*: A Lesson in Consciousness." *Modern Language Studies* 8, no. 2 (1978): 72–79.

Bestman, Martin T. *Sembène Ousmane et l'esthetique du roman negro-africain*. Sherbrooke, Quebec: Éditions Naaman, 1981.

Cooper, Frederick. "'Our Strike': Equality, Anticolonial Politics and the 1947–48 Railway Strike in French West Africa." *The Journal of African History* 37, no. 1 (1996): 81–118.

Gadjigo, Samba, ed. *Ousmane Sembène: Dialogues with Critics and Writers*. Amherst: University of Massachusetts Press, 1993.

Jones, James A. "Fact and Fiction in *God's Bits of Wood*." *Research in African Literatures* 31, no. 2 (2000): 117–131.

Murphy, David. *Sembène: Imagining Alternatives in Film and Fiction*. Oxford and Trenton, N.J.: Africa World Press, 2000.

Petty Sheila, ed. *A Call to Action: The Films of Ousmane Sembène*. Trowbridge, U.K.: Flicks Books, 1996.

Tsabedze, Clara. *African Independence from Francophone and Anglophone Voices*. New York: Peter Lang, 1994.

· David Yost

GOLSHIRI, HUSHANG (1938–2000) *Iranian novelist, short story writer*

The writer, critic, and editor Hushang Golshiri was born in Esfahan, Iran, into a working-class family. He was raised in Abadan, in the southern part of Iran, where his father worked for an oil company. From 1954 to 1974 he lived in Esfahan, where he obtained his high school diploma and then worked at many odd jobs, including in a factory, a bazaar, a confectionery shop, and a dye shop. He was also a teacher in a small village and started to write short stories in his spare time.

In 1959 Golshiri entered a B.A. program in Persian literature at Esfahan University; his studies were interrupted by six months of imprisonment because of his political activities. He received his degree in 1962. At one time he attended Sa'eb Literary Society, which was devoted to the study of classical literature. However, after his release from prison, he started a new society with a group of his friends for the purpose of reading and discussing modern poetry and short stories. These meetings led to the establishment in 1965 of *Jong-e Esfahan*, a literary magazine devoted to modern literature in which Golshiri printed some of his own stories and poems. It was an important journal attracting and influencing many talented young people until it was closed down in 1981.

Golshiri's first collection of short stories, *As Always* (*Mesl-e hamisheh*), was published in 1968. This was quickly followed by the novel *Prince Ehtejab* (*Shazdeh Ehtejab*), a 1969 work that brought him fame and has been translated into several languages. A story of the Qajar dynasty's decadence, the novel has also been made into a film. A later autobiographical novel, *Christine and the Kid* (*Christine va Kid*, 1971), the story of a love affair with a British woman, was less successful.

Golshiri started teaching in high schools, but after being imprisoned again for six months in 1973, he was forced to quit teaching and was also denied his social rights for five years. He then traveled to Tehran and, with a few friends, established weekly meetings that resulted in the publication of a collection of short stories called *My Little Prayer Room* (*Namazkhaneh-ye Kuchek-e Man*) in 1975. The first part of a novel called *Ra'I's Lost Lamb: Burial of the Living* (*Barreh-ye Gomshodeh-ye Ra'i: Tadfin-e Zendegan*) appeared in 1977.

In 1968 Golshiri joined a large number of Iranian writers who signed a petition objecting to the government-organized International Congress of Writers and Poets. This led to the establishment of the independent Iranian Writers Association, and Golshiri remained one of its elected directors and its most committed and influential member to the day he died.

In 1975 Golshiri was invited to teach theater students at the Faculty of Fine Arts, University of Tehran, but he was banned from this post for political reasons in 1982. In 1978 he was invited to attend the International Writing Program at Iowa University, Iowa City, in the United States. In the 1980s he published a number of his writings: the novella *The Fifth Innocent or The Tale of Hanging Dead of the Rider Who Will Come* (*Massoum-e Panjom ya Hadis Mordeh bar Dar Kardan an Savar keh Khahad Amad*, 1980); *The Antique Chamber* (*Jobbeh'khaneh*, 1983); a novella for children, *The Story of the Fisherman and the Demon* (*Hadis-e Mahigir va Div*, 1984); and *Five Treasures* (*Panj Ganj*, 1989 in Stockholm). *Book of Jinns* (*Jen Nameh*, 1990) was also published in Sweden.

Golshiri traveled to the Netherlands in 1989 and Germany in 1990. He was granted a nine-month writer's retreat at Heinrich Böll House by the H. B. Foundation in 1997. He was also awarded by Hellman-Hammett Prize by Human Rights Watch in 1997 and the Erich-Maria Remarque Peace Prize in 1999 for his literary and social efforts to fight oppression and promote human rights.

Golshiri was instrumental in promoting a generation of young fiction writers in 1990 through his creative workshop, where he presented analyses of modern fiction techniques and supervised readings of Persian classical works. He implemented new techniques of narrative in his fiction. Language and narrator were important elements for the author in order to portray a society in crisis.

Hushang Golshiri died in 2000 after a long illness. His estate presents an annual award to young fiction writers.

BIBLIOGRAPHY

Ghanoonparvar, M. R. *In a Persian Mirror: Images of the West and Westerners in Iranian Fiction.* Austin: University of Texas Press, 1993.

Golshiri, Hushang. *Black Parrot, Green Crow.* Translated by Heshmat Moayyad. Washington, D.C.: Mage Publishers, 2003.

Talattof, Kamran. *The Politics of Writing in Iran, A History of Modern Persian Literature.* Syracuse, N.Y.: Syracuse University Press, 2000.

Farideh Pourgiv

GOMBROWICZ, WITOLD (1904–1969)

Polish novelist, short story writer   One of the most prominent Polish writers of the 20th century, Witold Gombrowicz established his reputation with his novel *Ferdydurke* (1937). His distinctive style mingles the grotesque, satire, and parody together with numerous formal and linguistic experiments. Frequently associated with existentialism, his work escapes any rigid labeling in terms of philosophical movements. An author of novels, short stories, dramatic texts (pre-absurdist in character), and renowned journals, Gombrowicz tends to straddle the line between the fictional world and autobiographical material. Regarded as a nonconformist, he spent most of his adult life outside Poland. His international reputation was established in the 1960s when translations of his works were published in Paris.

Gombrowicz was born on August 4, 1904, in Maloszyce near Opatow, about 200 kilometers from Warsaw, the son of a well-to-do Polish family of landowners. His father, Jan Onufry Gombrowicz, was a wealthy lawyer and industrialist, while his mother, Antonina Marcela, was a daughter of Ignacy Kotkowski, a landowner. Before he moved to Warsaw, Witold Gombrowicz spent his early childhood on his family's provincial estate in Maloszyce. After he moved to Warsaw, he attended an aristocratic Catholic school and then, between 1922 and 1927, studied law at Warsaw University. After a short period spent in Paris, where he attempted to study philosophy and economics at the Institut des Hautes Etudes Internationales, Gombrowicz began his work as a lawyer in Warsaw's municipal district in 1928.

Dissatisfied with his professional career, Gombrowicz began writing and, in 1933, published a collection of short stories entitled *Memoir of a Time of Immaturity* (*Pamietnik z czasu dojrzewania*), in which he plays on the conventions of "low literature." Even though the collection was completely misunderstood and attacked by conservative critics for its extravagance and antipatriotic nature, the author decided to give up law and to pursue a literary career.

In 1937 Gombrowicz published his masterpiece, *Ferdydurke.* The novel immediately provoked a vivid critical discussion. Admired for its sardonic humor by a large part of the more liberal—avant-garde—intellectual elite, *Ferdydurke* was harshly condemned by the nationalistic part of the Polish establishment. Its grotesque protagonist, Jozio, is an adult whose immaturity is tested to the extreme by rigid conventions and worn-out clichés that diminish his role in society to that of an adolescent. A parody of numerous educational, cultural, and national stereotypes, *Ferdydurke* is also an uncompromising search for both artistic and intellectual honesty that ennobles notions associated with immaturity, adolescence, and inferiority. The novel has a distinctive style packed with neologisms. The author's artistic originality is based on parody and intertextual associations. The American writer Susan Sontag reportedly called *Ferdydurke* "one of the most important overlooked books of the 20th century."

In 1938 Gombrowicz published his first stage play, *Yvonne, the Princess of Burgundy* (*Iwona Ksiezniczka Burgundii*), a grotesque drama whose main concern is the oppressive influence of form, habits, and traditional ceremonies on the development of an individual. In the late 1930s, however, the play was anything but a literary success.

In August 1939 Gombrowicz was commissioned to write a series of articles on Argentina, and he set sail for Buenos Aires. Several days later, however, World War II broke out, prompting the author to stay in Argentina, where he resided until 1963. Due to the communist regime in the postwar Poland, he never returned to his home country. Settling down in Buenos Aires, he earned his living by teaching French and working for the Banco Polaco between 1947 and 1955. In the Argentine capital, he met his future wife, Rita.

Despite financial problems and his uncertain artistic status (his works were blacklisted in Poland), Gombrowicz continued writing in Polish. Fortunately, Kutura—a Polish publishing house that was established in Paris—published Gombrowicz's works, enabling him to reach his Polish-speaking audience. Before that, however, in Buenos Aires, he published a Spanish translation of *The Marriage,* his second stage play, in 1947. Grotesque in character, the play was praised for its satiric portrayal of aristocratic and Christian values. Its Polish original, *Slub,* was published in Paris six years later together with his semiautobiographical novel *Trans-Atlantic (Trans-Atlantyk).* Based on Gombrowicz's experience of his first years in Argentina, *Trans-Atlantic* once again criticizes—in a hilarious, if provocative, way—patriotic stereotypes and additionally takes up the theme of homosexuality, which in itself challenges Catholic system of values.

Beginning in 1953 and extending until Gombrowicz's death, *Kultura,* a Paris-based Polish émigré magazine, published installments of the author's *Diaries* (*Dzienniki*), in which he deals not only with various matters of everyday life but also presents a serious critical dispute with Marxist ideology, existentialism, and the Catholic religion, in addition to discussing his understanding of the fragile borderline between the fictional and the autobiographical.

In 1960 Gombrowicz published *Pornography* (*Pornografia*), his third novel. The book was regarded as provocative because it makes extensive use of erotic associations and presents the world deprived of any absolute transcendental power. Once again, its reception aroused controversy, which contributed to establishing the author's literary status. In 1963, thanks to a Ford Foundation grant, Gombrowicz managed to return to Europe, and after spending a year in Berlin, he moved to Paris and then settled down in Vence, in the south of France. In 1965 he published his fourth novel, *Cosmos* (*Kosmos*), and in 1966 his last play, *Operetta* (*Operetka*).

Gombrowicz seriously suffered from asthma and became practically speechless in the late 1960s. He died in Vence on July 24, 1969. At the end of his life, he was an internationally recognized writer, having won the prestigious International Prize for Literature in 1967 for *Cosmos* and having been considered as a candidate for the Nobel Prize in literature in 1968. In the late 1970s and 1980s, after the publication of his oeuvre in Poland, he became a cultural icon there. The year 2004 was officially announced by the Polish parliament as the year of the author's centenary celebration.

BIBLIOGRAPHY

Berressem, Hanjo. *Lines of Desire: Reading Gombrowicz's Fiction with Lacan.* Evanston, Ill.: Northwestern University Press, 1998.

Cataluccio, Francesco, and Jerzy Illg, eds. *Gombrowicz Filozof.* Krakow: Znak, 1991.

Glowinski, Michal. *Gombrowicz i Nadliteratura.* Krakow: Wydawnictwo Literackie, 2002.

Jarzebski, Jerzy. *Gombrowicz.* Wrocław: Wydawnictwo Dolnośląskie, 2004.

Majchrowski, Zbigniew. *Gombrowicz i cien Wieszcza: Oraz inne eseje o Dramacie i Teatrze.* Gda sk: Wydawnictwo Uniwersytetu Gda skiego, 1995.

Ponowska-Ziarek, Ewa, ed. *Gombrowicz's Grimaces: Modernism, Gender, Nationality.* Albany: State University of New York Press, 1998.

Tomasz Wiśniewski

GOOD CONSCIENCE, THE (*LAS BUENAS CONCIENCIAS*) CARLOS FUENTES (1961)

A follow-up to the first novel by legendary Mexican writer CARLOS FUENTES (1928–), *WHERE THE AIR IS CLEAR* (1958), *The Good Conscience* is a taut character study of a young man: Jamie Ceballos, who hails from the provinces of Mexico, struggles desperately to make sense of his fledgling identity, which is mired in a setting filled with spiritually prohibiting elements. The novel was dedicated to the Spanish filmmaker Luis Buñuel (1900–83), who has been hailed as the father of modern surrealist filmmaking. Fuentes and Buñuel were in constant contact with each other, relaying their thoughts about literature, art, and philosophy. Fuentes has been particularly attracted to Buñuel's penchant for pairing opposites in emotion and action. For example, a character can be gifted with insight, but that person may be unable to view his or her world in realistic terms; or there can be beauty where there is also tremendous ugliness. In the case of *The Good Conscience,* the pairing of oppositions is perhaps most striking in the novel's setting, as well as in the characters that inhabit a kind of setting that is backward, trite, and repressive.

Readers will recognize Jaime Ceballos as a character from the final chapters of Fuentes's debut novel, *Where the Air Is Clear,* the unsophisticated suitor of Betina Régules, the fashionable young woman whose peers are of Mexico City's social elite. Despite being much shorter than the novel preceding it (148 pages versus 373 pages), *The Good Conscience* is a definitive account of a protagonist tempered by rebellious, curious, individuated, and religious ideals. Jaime must choose between being at peace with the prestige and comfort his family's wealth has afforded him, the fiery idealism of his youth, and the sober morality his religious education has instilled in him. This struggle is set against life in the city of Guanajuato. It is important to note that Guanajuato's provincial setting is unkind to those unwilling to play along with its habitually narrow-minded way of life.

Throughout the novel, Jamie Ceballos attempts to come to terms with the kinds of societal, political, and familial surroundings that he finds repressive, while simultaneously trying to rediscover his own roots, sense of purpose, and direction. If Fuentes's first novel, *Where the Air Is Clear,* is about an entire country's search for its own collective identity, then *The Good Conscience* is about the search for individual identity.

Fuentes's creative canvas in *Where the Air Is Clear* is vast and panoramic, encompassing a multitude of characters, settings, and story lines. In *The Good Conscience,* however, the story of a young boy's coming of age has a much narrower focus; this lends an air of familiarity and intimacy that readers do not experience while reading Fuentes's first novel. In addition, *The Good Conscience* is also written in a more realistic tone; absent are the heavy mythical overtones and nonlinear time frames. *The Good Conscience* has a classic omniscient narrator, but the narrator does not seamlessly and magically jump from one temporality into another and then back again, as is the case in *Where the Air Is Clear.*

Not unlike Fuentes's first novel, *The Good Conscience* is politically charged. Nineteenth-century political machinations are central to the novel, so much so that political undertakings are nearly as fully developed as any character in the novel. These political maneuvers drive the Ceballo family from one scheme to the next, as, for example, they seek important political allies in order to secure their traditional way of life.

Jaime is caught in the middle of these two planes of existence. On the one hand, he can choose a life of leisure, the sort of lifestyle his parents lead; on the other hand, he can choose to resist the norm and instead embrace a fulfilling life that is free of modern-day excesses. Although Jaime has choices, he is inhibited, repressed from choosing the lifestyle he wants to lead. When Jaime matures into an adult, his elders fear that he will not choose to fall into the Guanajuato way of life: hypocritical, banal, and socially and spiritually stifling. Readers come to understand early on that Jaime is not content to follow the status quo; rather, his nature is to question, to test, and to experiment, not to merely blindly accept that which is hailed as truth or perceived as reality. Reality is relative, and Jaime realizes this, which makes him a dangerous ingredient in the mix of daily life in provincial Guanajuato.

The reader is witness to Jaime's tribulations as he grows up in such a difficult setting, one that problematically affects his spiritual and individualistic growth, otherwise, despite his unwillingness to follow Guanajuato's way of life. In the end, Jaime succumbs: His idealistic and individual spark dies out, giving way to conformity. Readers will sympathize with Jaime's struggles to remain steadfast to his own unique ideals, to keep the company of those whose spirits are untainted by excess and conformity, despite eventually being subsumed by what he has long been trying to stave off. In the end, the "good conscience" in the title of the novel belongs to Jaime, a conscience that remains in spite of his failure to resist the status quo.

The "good conscience" is represented by Jaime's recognition of his failure, of his own shortcomings, of his own inability to maintain his idealistic fervor in the face of such immediate repression. It is in this way that Jaime Ceballo is partially redeemed in the reader's estimation, despite his failure to amend a corrupted establishment.

Although Jaime does not remain as fiercely independent and individualistic as he is at the beginning of the novel, letting go of his "childhood illusions" in favor of becoming a man, readers are nonetheless left with lingering feelings that, somehow, this sensitive, insightful character will not be consumed by the provincial setting for long.

BIBLIOGRAPHY

Bertie Acker. *El Cuento mexicano contemporáneo: Rulfo, Arreola y Fuentes: Temas y cosmovisión.* Madrid: Playor, 1984.
Durán, Gloria. *The Archetypes of Carlos Fuentes: From Witch to Androgyne.* Hamden, Conn.: Archon, 1980.
Faris, Wendy B. *Carlos Fuentes.* New York: Ungar, 1983.

Rosemary Briseño

GOOD SOLDIER SCHWEIK, THE (OSUDY DOBRÉHO VOYÁKAŠVEJKA ZA SVĚTOVÉ VÁLKY) Jaroslav Hašek (1921–1923)

The most famous novel by the Czech writer Jaroslav Hašek (1883–1923), *The Good Soldier Schweik and His Fortunes in the World War* was published in sections from 1921 until the author's death in 1923. The book is actually a third of Hašek's stories about Josef Schweik, a character who has been the subject of much debate. Although frequently seen as a patriotic but blundering soldier, Schweik is seen by many critics as simply a shrewd malingerer. A series of five stories was published in *Caricatures* in 1911 and *The Good Soldier Schweik in Russian Captivity* was written in 1917. However, it is the author's post–World War I novel *The Good Soldier Schweik and His Fortunes in the World War* that gained Hašek a place in literary history.

The book is usually accompanied by Josef Lada's illustrations, which help the reader to see Schweik as an amiable and simpleminded hero. However, such an analysis ignores Schweik's clever attempts to avoid active duty and his keen insight into the army's operations. Schweik always has a story or lie at the ready; artifice and subterfuge are used to escape trouble and outwit his military superiors, as seen in his shrewd manipulation of the guards in chapter 10 of the novel. Although Schweik is quick to identify himself as feebleminded, the majority of his actions go against this claim. This can perhaps be traced back to Hašek's statement to a friend: "In this world, you can only be free if you're an idiot." Although Schweik is obviously bright and cunning, he seems to hide behind a veneer of idiocy to excuse his hidden disapproval of the war effort.

The novel is subversive in many ways, reflecting Hašek's own rejection of authority. The story begins by downplaying the assassination of Archduke Franz Ferdinand on June 28, 1914, in Sarajevo, Bosnia, igniting World War I. The author's treatment of the assassination sets the stage for a narrative that presents an unflattering portrayal of the Austro-Hungarian Empire. Although Schweik claims to regret the act that spawned such military devastation, his statements and actions indicate otherwise, particularly when he visits a local bar and engages in a humorous discussion of the murder of Archduke Ferdinand.

The episode at the bar sets up the story by leading to Schweik's first arrest. Bretschneider's interrogation of Schweik and Palivec, with his underhanded tactics, reflects what many saw as an increasingly authoritarian government. The arrest of the innocent on framed-up charges was a reality of the war years, although they are better known in Soviet Russia and through such dystopian texts as George Orwell's futuristic novel *1984*. Schweik is frequently suspected of subversion against his country, leading to his frequent confrontations with the police and his superior officers.

It is not surprising that Hašek would make light of World War I in this novel. As a Czech, he had more sympathy for the Slavic opponents in Russia and Serbia than the German elites in Bohemia. If Schweik is meant to represent Hašek, it follows that the soldier's actions, though seemingly well-intentioned, often result in sabotaging his own regiment. Hašek's description of the Austro-Hungarian officers contributes to the negative portrayal of the war efforts of the Central Powers (Germany, Austria-Hungary, their allies in World War I).

Many of Schweik's unfortunate experiences are borrowed from Hašek's own life, including the author's trouble with the police, employment, wartime insubordination, and capture by Russian soldiers. However, Hašek's personality is also reflected by the portrayal of Marek, a newly enlisted volunteer. Due to his contempt for authority, Marek spends the war in military prison for insubordination and minor offenses in his attempt to avoid combat.

Hašek's novel can be read as a surrealist text through its conflation of life and art. Trivial anecdotes are given great prominence by Schweik, who has two or more such stories or explanations for every occasion and situation. Although Hašek was not part of the surrealist movement, he frustrates readers' expectations by not describing a single battle in his war novel. This, combined with his emphasis on everyday people, makes his work similar to such surrealist texts as ANDRÉ BRETON's *NADJA*.

Hašek's novel was released one volume at a time; however, he died before he could complete Schweik's story. Several authors have attempted to finish the novel, but none have matched Hašek's writing abilities. The best-known ending comes from Karel Vanâk, but he takes several liberties with Schweik's personality, leading most critics to reject his efforts. The novel is almost always published in its incomplete form.

Due to public anger over Hašek's connection with Russian Bolshevism and doubt as to his true concern for Czech nationalism, the novel was initially poorly received in 1923. Society was insufficient distanced from World War I to properly appreciate a humorous novel about the recent horror. Within a decade, however, some critics were praising *The Good Soldier Schweik* as one of the 20th century's greatest works. It has since been translated into dozens of languages and is one of the best-known novels inspired by World War I.

BIBLIOGRAPHY

Frynta, Emanuel. *Hasek: The Creator of Schweik*. Translated by Jean Layton and George Theiner. Prague: Artia, 1965.

Parrott, Cecil. *The Bad Bohemian: The Life of Jaroslav Hasek, Creator of "The Good Soldier Svejk."* London: Bodley Head, 1978.

———. *Jaroslav Hasek: A Study of "Svejk" and the Short Stories*. Cambridge: Cambridge University Press, 1982.

Pytlik, Radko, and Miroslav Laiske. *Bibliografie Jaroslava Haska (Soupis Jeho Dila a Literatury o Nem)*. Prague: Statni Pedagogicke, 1960.

Kevin Hogg

GORKY, MAXIM (ALEKSEI MAXIMOVICH PESHKOV) (1868–1936) *Russian novelist, playwright*

Remembered today primarily as a Russian dramatist, much of Maxim Gorky's reputation rests on his 1902 play *The Lower Depths* (*Ha Ahe*), a tragic picture of Russian lower classes at the turn of the 20th century, and on his 1906 novel *Mother* (*Mat*), subsequently adapted for the screen in Vsevolod Pudovkin's 1926 film of the Russian revolution of 1905. Politically outspoken, Gorky on occasion found himself on the wrong side of the government. He was at the forefront of the Russian realist movement, co-opted by the Soviet government as the father of Soviet literature and popular internationally as much for his lifestyle and outspoken nature as for his literary output.

Born Aleksei Maximovich Peshkov in Nizhnii Novgorod on March 28, 1868, he would adopt the pseudonym Gorky (Russian for "bitter") over two decades later, in 1892. His father died of cholera in 1871, and he and his mother soon moved in with her parents. Gorky's grandfather was a brutal man, and much of the young boy's early life was marked with violence and hostility. In *My Childhood* (*Detstvo*, 1913) Gorky describes the turbulence of his childhood. His mother died in 1878, and at the age of 11 he was put out of his home by his grandfather, believing the young boy was old enough to fend for himself. For several years after leaving his grandparents' home, Gorky worked at almost any available job, from fishery worker to religious icon maker, all the while reading great works of Russian and international literature. Gorky was virtually self-educated, his goal of university studies thwarted by bis paltry financial means. In 1887 his grandmother, whom he loved dearly, died. Soon after her death, Gorky attempted to end his own life by shooting himself in the heart; the unsuccessful attempt likely made his life more difficult by leaving him with decreased lung function.

Gorky married Ekaterina Pavlovna Volzhina in 1896. In 1898 he published *Stories and Sketches* (*Ocherki i rasskazy*), which sold well and brought him literary recognition. In 1900 he followed his first novel with *Foma Gordeev*, the story of an unhappy young man who is unable to carry on with his father's family business. Throughout his works, Gorky heaped much criticism on his characters' inability to take any sort of action. He also developed a popular character type that would become the center of many of his novels: the wanderer. An outsider as a youngster, Gorky was skilled in drawing characters who were outside society and did not necessarily fit with their surroundings.

Around the same time that he began publishing, Gorky also began to develop a reputation as a man with a strong political voice. Arrested and imprisoned for distributing seditious materials, he was released and returned to his hometown, where he was put under close watch. He was arrested again in 1901, and this time he was sent to central Russia to live in exile. Shortly thereafter, while recovering from tuberculosis in Crimea, he met Anton Chekhov and subsequently Leo Tolstoy, developing a lasting friendship with the former and a tolerable acquaintance with the latter. His relationship with Chekhov, coupled with an introduction to the Moscow Art Theatre, gave him the encouragement to try his hand at drama, beginning with *The Lower Depths,* which opened to international acclaim in Moscow in 1902. It offered a complex and tragic depiction of lower-class life in a dilapidated flop-house, characterized by helpless and hopeless characters who have little control over their own lives.

Gorky became involved with the Social Democrats, Vladimir Lenin's party, in 1903. During the revolution of 1905, he allied himself with both the workers and the intellectuals, organizing a workers' march and then asking unsuccessfully that the tsarist government not interfere with it. Helping the main organizer escape from Russia, and frequently writing inflammatory articles for newspapers, Gorky found himself once again in jail. Freed due in large part to his international renown, he could not resist political involvement and had to leave Russia, going to Finland, then to Germany, and finally to the island of Capri, where he would stay until 1913 when amnesty was granted to political exiles.

After Gorky was freed in 1905, an ensuing trip to America to raise funds for the cause of the Russian workers, an elaborately planned tour, was derailed when the Russian embassy exposed moral weaknesses in his personal life: He was traveling with his mistress, Maria Fedorovna Andreeva, not his wife. In spite of the disastrous reception, Gorky used his free time completing his novel *Mother,* among many others. Divorce was difficult in Russia, and consequently he and Ekat-erina stayed married as a result, with little animosity felt between the author and his legal wife. In 1906, however, while staying on Staten Island with a rich socialist, he learned that his five-year-old daughter had died in Russia.

Living out his exile in Capri, Gorky continued his prolific literary career, and his insistent political activism. Frequently combining the two interests, Gorky's literary output expressed his political concerns. He received many other Russian activists at his home and his school on Capri. During this time, and henceforth, Gorky devoted much of his attention to "God-building"— roughly, a concept that suggests that man can accomplish greatness as part of a collective effort, and that gods are the energy that comes from a human collective.

Gorky was finally allowed to return to his homeland during a 1913 general amnesty in celebration of the 300th anniversary of the Romanov dynasty. Not long after this, he was again involved in political controversy. With Russia's role in World War I, followed by the Russian Revolution of 1917, Gorky's political impulses were not to be controlled, and he voiced his displeasure with the Bolsheviks, Lenin, and the war, consequently becoming the object of criticism himself. Gorky also developed the Commission for the Protection of Monuments and the Institute of World Literature, in untiring efforts to keep artists and intellectuals safe in a tumultuous time. He had a turbulent friendship with Lenin, who ultimately recommended that Gorky leave Russia in 1921 as the author again found himself on the wrong side of the Politburo. He moved to Sorrento, Italy, in 1924, and continued to add volumes to his continuously growing autobiographical series (*Childhood,* 1913; *My Apprenticeship,* 1916; *My Universities,* 1924). He also began his four-volume saga *The Life of Klim Samgin,* which was written over a 12-year period, 1924–36.

After Lenin's death, Joseph Stalin wanted Gorky to return to the Soviet Union, and in 1928 the Soviet leader renamed the writer's hometown in honor of the author. (This and many other landmarks named in honor of the author reverted to their original names after the fall of the Soviet Union in 1991.) Gorky moved back in 1931, settling in Moscow with his wife. Treated well by the government, he no longer had the freedom of an activist, and, beholden to the Stalinist government, he produced political propaganda—but the price was his own moral conviction. In 1934 he was named head of the newly created Union of Soviet Writers, and that same year his son Maxim died, presumably from pneumonia. Suspicions were that the young Maxim, a reputed communist, was instead killed as a Stalinist move to silence resistance. Gorky decided it was time for him to leave the Soviet Union, but he was denied permission to travel outside of the country, probably because of his international celebrity and the potential danger it posed to the Stalinist regime. He died on June 18, 1936, and was given an honorable burial between Lenin's wife and sister in the Kremlin. Two years later several doctors and political officials suggested that the deaths of both father and son were not natural, but rather were carried out at the hands of the Stalinist machine.

Gorky wrote *The Life of Klim Samgin* between 1924 and 1936. The final novel of his career, it moves from the Russian provinces to the cities and finally to an international arena. A pointed critique on Russian intellectuals between the 1870s and 1917, the year of the revolution, the book comprises four volumes and features a distinctly unlikable protagonist. As the representative of the intelligentsia, Samgin posits himself as a progressive proponent of the political left, but his actions betray a disconnect between his self-perceived politics and the reality of his actions—an unwillingness to truly identify with the revolutionaries. He claims political allegiances, but in reality his politics are nonexistent. True only to his own fiscal success and comfort, he cannot make a move toward political commitment and is accidentally killed in the 1917 Russian Revolution. Samgin represents what Gorky found fault with in the Russian intelligentsia—self-importance, apolitical views, and a clear double standard between thought and action.

The novel is not an artistic masterpiece, suffering at once from a wholly unsympathetic main character and also from its extreme length. The reader is allowed to see events of Russian history played out through Samgin's point of view of, weaving real-life events and characters into the fabric of the story—including characters who discuss Gorky's writings. Gorky exploits an interesting narrative method in displaying history through the eyes of a fictional character, but because of Samgin's distinct unpleasantness and the occasional uneven balance of fiction and history, the novel is generally considered flawed. Nevertheless, it paints an interesting and fairly accurate picture of Russian life in the decades around the turn of the last century.

Gorky wrote *Mother,* one of his most well-known novels, in 1907, and it was first published in English and later translated into Russian. Although it was not recognized as one of his most artistically strong novels, it was seen all the same as a preeminent example of the socialist novel, or of socialist realism. It has fared better than many of Gorky's novels over the decades, due in large part to the Vsevolod Pudovkin film from 1926. The novel, which found its inspiration in the revolution of 1905, centers on a faction of the Russian Social Democratic Party who were working to encourage rebellion among the workers and peasants prior to the 1905 Revolution. Gorky creates a distinct dichotomy between the members of the party and the workers and peasants—the workers reflecting a pure attachment to social betterment and the workers and peasants reflecting an inert group unaware of the potential for change and unmoving in any attempt to better their lot. Young Pavel Vlasov fanatically and single-mindedly leads the revolutionaries from the Social Democratic Party, and he is ultimately arrested, tried, and sent to live in exile—steadfastly believing in and asserting his conviction that the revolutionary activities will prevail and bring a change to the current tsarist regime under Nicholas II.

After Pavel's sentencing, his mother, Pelageia Nilovna Vlasova, takes on the mantle of her son's revolutionary activities, disseminating copies of his rousing courtroom speech. This action on the part of the eponymous mother shows that her son was able to affect social change even in his mother, one of the most resistant members of his community to social change. Pelageia is an Orthodox Christian who had felt that man need not try to change his predestined fate, but she has grown disillusioned with institutional religion and—through a friendship with Rybin, a peasant—begins to see God in everyday life. She believes that she must do God's work in order to truly live her faith. While organized religion has perpetuated the social inequity rampant under the tsarist regime, living a life based on the teachings of Christianity ideally leads to a society in which political power does not have to bring repression and violence with it. Pelageia is also arrested while distributing revolutionary treatises. In spite of the novel's bleak outcome, Gorky conveys a sense of optimism and a belief in the possibility of social change.

BIBLIOGRAPHY

Barratt, Andrew. *The Early Fiction of Maksim Gorky*. Nottingham, U.K.: Astra Press, 1993.

Clowes, Edith W. *Maksim Gorky: A Reference Guide*. Boston: G. K. Hall, 1987.

Ovcharenko, A. I. *Maxim Gorky and the Literary Quest of the Twentieth Century*. Translated by Joy Jennings. Moscow: Raduga Publishers, 1985.

Terry, Garth M. *Maxim Gorky in English: A Bibliography*. Nottingham, U.K.: Astra Press, 1986.

Troyat, Henri. *Gorky*. Translated by Lowell Bair. New York: Crown, 1989.

Angela Courtney

GOYTISOLO, JUAN (1931–) *Spanish essayist, novelist*

A Spanish expatriate novelist and critic, Juan Goytisolo embodies the tradition of the contemporary intellectual rebel in exile. He is considered Spain's greatest writer living at the beginning of the 21st century, yet he has lived abroad since the 1950s, most recently in Marrakesh. His more than 30 works of fiction, autobiography, essays, and journalism have been called subversive acts of aggression toward both history and language. His vantage point is the estrangement and marginality of the willfully dispossessed, and his mode of narration is experimental, highly allusive, postmodern, poststructural, and postcolonial. Juan Goytisolo backed the struggle for Algerian liberation from the French with ALBERT CAMUS, supported the 1959 Cuban revolution and reported on Fidel Castro with GUILLERMO CABRERA INFANTE, explored the psychology of homosexuality with JEAN GENET, and collaborated with noted writers such as the Peruvian MARIO VARGAS LLOSA and the Mexican CARLOS FUENTES. He even appeared as himself in Jean-Luc Godard's *Notre Musique* (2004), a film billed as an indictment of modern times. In 2004 Goytisolo received Mexico's prestigious JUAN RULFO prize for lifetime literary achievement, an award presented by the Colombian GABRIEL GARCÍA MÁRQUEZ.

Juan Goytisolo was born Juan Goytisolo Gay in Barcelona, Spain, on January 5, 1931, to a Catalan mother, Julia Gay, and a businessman father whose heritage was Basque. During the Spanish civil war (1936–39), the family lived in a mountain village in Catalonia. When Juan Goytisolo was eight years old, a German air raid killed his mother while the family was on a visit to Barcelona. The Republican side briefly imprisoned his conservative father, a Francisco Franco loyalist. Goytisolo considers himself a child of the Spanish civil war, a bitter casualty of the schism that went deeper and extended far beyond the three years of fighting, well into the three decades of repression and stagnation that marked the Franco regime in Spain (1939–75). A bitter critic of all things related to Francoist Spain, Goytisolo's writing takes off from his own life. His obsession with Spain transcends its history (the Moorish and Jewish roots of Spain before the Spanish Inquisition), its politics (the repressive calm of the Franco years), and its popular culture (the "Sunny Spain" of vacation brochures). His essays, reportage, and novels are frequently self-referential, with recurring characters and incidents, and his prose uses parody and pastiche to blur the boundaries between the genres.

Goytisolo attended universities in Barcelona and Madrid, and began his writing career while still living in Spain. However, from 1957 he lived in self-imposed exile outside of Spain, first in Paris and later in Marrakesh. In Paris he took a job with the editorial firm of Gallimard, where he influenced and was influenced by the publications, politics, and philosophy of a wide range of contemporary writers, particularly the proponents of the "new" novel in Latin America.

In Paris, Goytisolo also began a relationship with Monique Lange (1926–96), whom he married in 1978 and to whom he remained married until her death in 1996. Though he is an avowed homosexual, Goytisolo considers Lange the love of his life; Lange, herself a journalist, novelist, and screenwriter, wrote in her novel *Les poisons-chats* of the heroine's difficult love for a homosexual man. Goytisolo credits Jean Genet with helping him overcome sexual taboos in order to explore the transgressive nature of sexuality and of fiction and to align himself with the marginalized and the dispossessed.

Goytisolo's early publications in Spain were short stories and novels in a neorealist style, a type of reportage using authentic settings and simple plots that revealed contemporary social problems. *The Young Assassins* (*Juegos de manos,* 1954) deals with a group of students who plot to murder a politician and kill the one they have chosen as assassin; *Children of Chaos* (*Duelo en el Paraíso,* 1955) recounts the violence visited upon a small town in Spain after the civil war, when children gain control. *Fiestas* (1958), *Island of Women* (*La isla,* 1961; UK title, *Sands of Torremolinos*), and *The Party's Over* (*Fin de fiesta,* 1962) are realistic narratives imbued with trenchant social criticism. Critic Helen Cantarella, writing in the *New York Times Book Review* in 1962, says that "what distinguishes Goytisolo from other writers in the ever-widening international confraternity of young protesters is the clinical objectivity of his vision and the vigorous control he displays over his powerful, driving style. His works—short, violent and frightening—are like pages torn out of the book of experience."

With the publication of MARKS OF IDENTITY (*Señas de identidad,* 1966), Goytisolo renounced the realism of his early novels and developed a discourse of both the experimental and the avant-garde. He regards *Marks of Identity* as his first adult work, and with it he disavowed his previous eight books. *Marks of Identity* was followed by *Count Julian* (*Reivindicación del conde don Julián,* 1970), which some critics consider his masterwork, and *Juan the Landless* (*Juan sin tierra,* 1975). These fictional but essentially autobiographical novels shocked Spanish Roman Catholic society with their sexual openness and savage criticism. In them the same narrator renounces his homeland and wanders as a nomad through history, celebrating 700 years of Moorish and Arabic influence and excoriating Spain for its historical hypocrisy, cruelty, and fixation with racial "purity." He condemns the denial of diversity in Spain and explores and embraces a marginalized identity while experimenting with transforming the Spanish language, which he sees as a tool of political power. These books were banned in Spain and would be throughout Franco's life, but they were published in Mexico and Argen-

tina, and they established the author's international reputation. The trilogy is perhaps Goytisolo's greatest literary achievement.

During the 1960s and 1970s, Juan Goytisolo traveled widely throughout North and South America, serving as a visiting professor at the University of California at San Diego (1969), Boston University (1970), McGill (1972), and New York University (1973–74). Just after the English publication of the sensational *Marks of Identity* and its sequel *Count Julian,* Goytisolo impressed students at New York University as articulate, erudite, politically engaged, witty, and easily conversant with the diverse authors and works that were part of the New York community at the time.

Goytisolo's books are on the cutting edge of avant-garde narrative fiction: Linguistically experimental, densely allusive, self-referential, and multilayered, they employ interior monologues, sudden shifts in perspective, parody, and pastiche. Among his later novels are *Makbara* (*Makbara,* 1980); *Landscapes after the Battle* (*Paisajes después de la batalla,* 1982); *The Virtues of the Solitary Bird* (*Las virtudes del pájaro solitano,* 1988); *Quarantine* (*La cuarentena,* 1991), set during the first Gulf War; *The Marx Family Saga* (*La saga de los Marx,* 1993); *State of Siege* (*El sitio de los sitios,* 1995), written to mimic the siege of a city; *The Garden of Secrets* (*Las semanas del jardín,* 1997); *A Cock-Eyed Comedy* (*Carajicomedia,* 2000), lampooning the Opus Dei movement specifically and the Spanish Catholic Church generally; and *The Blind Rider* (*Telón de boca,* 2002).

Goytisolo is a regular contributor to the Madrid newspaper *El País* and has published collections of essays, memoirs, and reportage. His 1960 *Campos de Níjar,* a report on poverty in Andalusia, shocked European readers. A collection of essays on the Muslim world, *Landscape of War,* warns repeatedly against the mobilization of radical Islam. Astute in appraising the liberalizing movements of the 20th century in Algeria, Indochina, and Cuba, Goytisolo sees that these events eventually turned into entrenched repressive regimes, such as that of Fidel Castro, who turned that "ex-paradise of a Caribbean island . . . into a silent and lugubrious floating concentration camp."

In a *New York Times Magazine* feature article on April 16, 2006, Fernanda Eberstadt emphasizes Goytisolo's savage revolt against the family, class, religion, and nation into which he was born; his passion for a Muslim tradition that is tolerant and syncretic and predates the fundamentalist revival; his predilection for the marginalized and dispossessed; and his plea for ethnic, religious, and sexual pluralism. In both his life and novelistic work, Juan Goytisolo has turned bitter alienation into optimistic authenticity.

BIBLIOGRAPHY

Boland, Roy, ed. *Specular Narrative: Critical Perspectives on Carlos Fuentes, Juan Goytisolo, Mario Vargas Llosa.* Auckland, New Zealand: VOX/AHS, 1997.

Doblado, Gloria. *España en tres novelas de Juan Goytisolo.* Madrid: Playor, 1988.

Epps, Bradley S. *Significant Violence: Oppression and Resistance in the Narrative of Juan Goytisolo, 1970–1990.* Oxford: Clarendon Press; New York: Oxford University Press, 1996.

Gonzalez, Bernardo Antonio. *Parábolas de identidad: Realidad interior y estrategia narrativa en tres novelistas de postguerra.* Potomac, Md.: Scripta humanística, 1985.

Lazaro Serrano, Jesús. *La novelística de Juan Goytisolo.* Madrid: Editorial Alhambra, 1984.

Pérez, Genaro J. *Formalist Elements in the Novels of Juan Goytisolo.* Madrid: Ediciones José Porrua Turanzas, S. A., 1979.

Pope, Randolph D. *Understanding Juan Goytisolo.* Columbia: University of South Carolina Press, 1995.

Ribeiro de Menezes, Alison. *Juan Goytisolo: The Author as Dissident.* Rochester, N.Y.: Tamesis, 2005.

Six, Abigail Lee. *Juan Goytisolo: The Case for Chaos.* New Haven, Conn.: Yale University Press, 1990.

Ugarte, Michael. *Trilogy of Treason: An Intertextual Study of Juan Goytisolo.* Columbia: University of Missouri Press, 1982.

Arbolina Llamas Jennings

GRACE, PATRICIA (1937–   ) *Maori novelist, short story writer*   Patricia Grace was born in Wellington, New Zealand. She is of Maori descent, specifically of Ngati Raukawa, Ngati Toa, and Te Ati Awa ancestry; her marriage also affiliates her with the Ngati Porou heritage. Grace's Maori heritage is integral to her style and the content she explores as an author. She writes primarily adult fiction and short stories, although her writing of children's books has brought her acclaim. She also experiments with poetry and translation.

Grace's writing is characterized by its evocative imagery and lyricism, both traits of the oral Maori tradition. Her juxtaposition of Maori language and words within English language skillfully presents a text of diverse cultural interest. Through this aesthetic tension and balance, the writer at once embraces her readers of non-Maori descent while distancing them from the experiences specific to Maori culture and experience.

Grace studied to be a teacher and has taught in primary and secondary schools, in addition to being a writing fellow at Victoria University of Wellington (1985). She began writing while teaching and helping to raise seven children. Her first fiction publication, *Waiariki and Other Stories* (1975), is the first collection of short stories ever published by a woman of Maori descent. Each of the 10 stories presents the distinct voice of a different Maori character. *Waiariki* won the PEN/Hubert Church Award for Best First Book of Fiction. Publication of Grace's first novel came three years later. *Mutuwhenua: The Moon Sleeps* (1978) is about the interracial relationship between a Maori woman and a Pakeha (non-Maori) man.

In 1980 Grace published another collection of short stories, *The Dream Sleepers and Other Stories.* This collection features memorable child characters. Grace used her ear for children's voices and experience to begin writing picture book texts. Many of these stories are published in English, Maori, and Samoan. Her 1981 story *The Kuia and the Spider* (*Te Kuia me te Pungawerewere*), won New Zealand's Children's Picture Book of the Year Award. *Watercress Tuna and the Children of Champion Street* (*Te Tuna Watakirihi me Nga Tamariki o te Tiriti o Toa,* 1985) and *The Trolley* (1993) are other picture book titles.

Grace's 1986 work *Potiki* combines her skill with the short story, the novel, and children's writing. Using multiple perspectives, the work tells the story of an extended family's battle against encroaching development, experienced from different family member's perspectives and told in their different voices. The title won the New Zealand Book Award for Fiction and has been widely translated.

In 2001 Grace published *Dogside Story,* another powerful book about an extended Maori family. Its protagonist is a disabled young man coming to terms with secrets hidden by himself and his community. The novel won the Kiriyama Pacific Rim Book Prize, was nominated for the Booker Prize, and short-listed for the 2002 Montana New Zealand Book Awards.

In 2001 Grace collaborated on *The Silent Migration: Ngati Poneke Young Maori Club 1937–1948,* a collection of first-person oral stories about Maori urban migration. She also collaborated on the book *Earth, Sea, Sky: Images and Maori Proverbs from the Natural World of Aotearoa New Zealand* (2004). The book pairs scenic photographs of New Zealand with translations of traditional Maori poems and proverbs.

Patricia Grace's work is unique because, as a Maori female author, she gives voice in her writing to a drastically underrepresented and marginalized demographic in world literature, simultaneously describing the history of a people for outside readers while embracing her Maori readership. However, this extratextual information—writing that lies outside traditional and popularized texts—is not the only reason Grace's works are revered. Her language is lyrical without being melodramatic, dreamlike while rooted in realism, and harmonic with notes of dissidence. Patricia Grace's diverse talents across diverse genres reinforce her importance within the field of world literature.

BIBLIOGRAPHY
Fitzgibbon, Tom, and Barbara Spiers. "Patricia Grace." In *Beneath Southern Skies: New Zealand Children's Book Authors and Illustrators.* Auckland: Ashton Scholastic, 1993.

Knudsen, Eva Rask. *The Circle and the Spiral: A Study of Australian Aboriginal and New Zealand Maori Literature.* Amsterdam: Rodopi, 2004.

Markmann, Sigrid. "On Women's Writing in Aotearoa/New Zealand: Patricia Grace, Keri Hulme, Cathie Dunsford." In *English Postcoloniality: Literatures from Around the World,* edited by Radhika Mohanram and Gita Rajan. Westport, Conn.: Greenwood, 1996.

Mvuyekure, Pierre-Damian. "Patricia Grace." In *A Reader's Companion to the Short Story in English,* edited by Erin Fallon, et al. Westport, Conn.: Greenwood, 2001.

O'Brien, Greg. "Patricia Grace." In *Moments of Invention: Portraits of 21 New Zealand Writers.* Auckland: Heinemann Reed, 1988.

Panny, Judith Dell. *Turning the Eye: Patricia Grace and the Short Story.* Auckland: Dunmore Press, 1997.

Roberts, Heather. *Where Did She Come From? New Zealand Women Novelists 1862–1987.* Wellington: Allen & Unwin, 1989.

Elissa Gershowitz

GRAIN OF WHEAT, A NGUGI WA THIONG'O (1967)

Following the shocked response in Britain to the author's two first novels, *WEEP NOT, CHILD* (1964) and *The RIVER BETWEEN* (1965), and in response to what he considered distorting revisions, NGUGI WA THIONG'O (then writing as James Ngugi) abandoned his master's thesis on Caribbean literature at the University of Leeds, England, and returned to his homeland, Kenya. With only his baccalaureate from Makerere University in Kampala, Uganda, Ngugi became the first African lecturer for the English Department at the University of Nairobi. He then worked to change the name (and focus) of his department from English to Literature, eventually accomplishing this goal the year following the publication of his third novel, *A Grain of Wheat,* in 1967. Ngugi would write only one more novel in English, *Petals of Blood* (1977), before abandoning this language to write in his mother tongue of Gikuyu, in his own pursuit of decolonized literary expression and dissemination.

A Grain of Wheat is a spiraling, multivoiced account of the years of Kenya's state of emergency (1952–60) during its struggle for independence from Britain (which was achieved on December 12, 1963). Villagers caught up in rebuilding their lives and pursuing late and ill-defined justice in the bitter aftermath of their entangled pursuit of Uhuru (liberation or freedom) reflect on their poisonous memories of jealousy, meanspiritedness, betrayal, and disillusionment. Regarding the legacy of the fictional martyr Waiyaki, the opening of the book gives the biblical explanation of sacrifice: "That which thou sowest is not quickened, except it die" (1 Corinthians 15:36). This quote has led to various optimistic efforts to read the book's multilayered betrayals, guilts, and secrets in a positive light.

The heroic hermit Mugo is burdened by the festering secret that his envy of the idealistic rebel Kihika led him to fatally betray this true hero of the liberation movement to effect his own escape. Kihika's sister Mumbi has betrayed her imprisoned husband, Gikonyo, with the opportunistic new regional chief, Gikonyo's former friend, Karanja. But this is not sycophantic Karanja's only foray into betraying the man who most trusts him, for he has an affair with the English commander Thompson's emotionally starved wife as well. But is Karanja, the officially recognized Kenyan traitor to the cause of liberation, the only antipatriot? The reader eventually learns that Gikonyo, the imprisoned freedom fighter, also nurses memories of betraying Kenya in order to reclaim his life.

As the intricately intertwined disillusionments of *A Grain of Wheat* spiral to their point of closure, the villagers pass judgment on their former hero, Mugo. Ironically, the aging, maddened mother of Mugo's victim, Wambui, hears her son's voice for the first time since his death in the voice of the man who brought about his death, and Mugo in turn sees the face of the aunt who tortured his childhood in the ravaged face of the woman whom he has driven insane with grief. In short, not only the struggle for liberation but even its follow-up pursuit of tardy and imperfect restitutions is distorted by each individual's immersion in his own suffering rather than recognizing the impact of his or her interaction with others. Only Gikonyo and Mumbi's discovery that they will have a child of their own, following the child she bore for Karanja, seems to present an opportunity for reading optimism into *A Grain of Wheat*'s bleak questions about the ultimate fitness for national reconstruction in a country left morally annihilated after generations of psychosocial colonialist assault.

The novel's ending tends to elicit critical optimism that sacrificial suffering will, in the long run, purify, nourish, and eventually strengthen what has been depleted by colonialism or destroyed in the war for independence. This analysis of the book's title certainly reflects Ngugi's traditional Gikuyu interweaving of myth into the literal stories of people searching out truths in the enmeshment of lies that their lives have become. Notably, wheat is a European grain not indigenous to East Africa. Therefore the necessity of bloody sacrifice to grow a grain of wheat in Kenya emphasizes Ngugi's inescapably bitter point that all the bloodletting may purify but can never reconstruct the original indigenous societies and the moral and spiritual tradi-tions they upheld, destroyed by colonization. In short, perhaps Ngugi's choice of title invites the reading that the sacrifices that melded the ancient independent nations of tribes such as the Kikuyu, Luo, and Swahili into the modern creation of Kenya can at best only produce a European import that ensures the body's survival.

BIBLIOGRAPHY

Jussawalla, Feroza, and Reed Way Dasenbrock, eds. *Interviews with Writers of the Post-Colonial World.* Jackson and London: University of Mississippi Press, 1992.

Makoni, Sinfree. *Black Linguistics: Language, Society and Politics in Africa and the Americas.* London and New York: Routledge, 2003.

Ngugi wa Thiong. *Matigari.* Translated by Waugui wa Goro. Oxford: Heinemann, 1989.

———. *Moving the Centre: The Struggle for Cultural Freedom.* London: J. Currey, 1993.

———. *Writers in Politics: A Re-engagement with the Issues of Literature and Society.* Oxford: Heinemann, 1997.

Sander, Reinhard, and Bernth Lindfors. *Ngugi wa Thiong Speaks: Interviews with the Kenyan Writer.* Trenton, N.J.: Africa World Press, 2006.

Alexis Brooks de Vita

GRASS, GÜNTER (1927–   ) *German novelist, poet*   "A rat hangs crucified on a wooden cross while two other rodents look on. A flounder whispers in the ear of a fisherman. A woman sews a button to her cheek. A dwarf bangs on a tin drum." These images, as Jan Biles notes in the article "Germany's Günter Grass," are part of the legacy being built by Günter Grass, one of Germany's most provocative contemporary artist-authors.

Günter Grass was born on October 16, 1927, in Danzig, Germany (now Gdansk, Poland), of German-Kashubian parents. His father came from a family of working-class Protestant Germans; his mother was a Catholic Kashubian, a Slav minority distinct from the Poles also living in the Danzig area. Little biographical information about Grass's early life is available beyond the fact that he grew up under circumstances similar to his protagonist, Oskar Matzerath, in *The Tin Drum*. During his formative years, Grass spent much time drawing and writing. His artistic interests were influenced by a drawing teacher who showed the youth catalogues depicting works by the Spanish cubist painter Pablo Picasso, the German expressionist sculptor Ernst Barlach, and other artists. Unable to fully appreciate this art at his early age, he nevertheless was fascinated by these visual arts and avidly followed their latest trends. Although he knew even less about literature than about pictorial art, he began writing poetry at a very young age. At 13 years old he attempted to write a novel about the medieval Kashubians, an ancient ethnic group of Slavonic Balts from northern Poland.

Along with these more solitary interests, Grass, like most boys of his age, was first a member of the Jungvolk, a version of the Hitler Youth for children between 10 and 14 years of age; when he turned 14, he became a member of the Hitler Youth. In 1944, at the age of 16, Grass became an air force auxiliary member, serving in an anti-aircraft battery. Drafted into the German army a year later, he was assigned to an antitank unit on the front line of World War II. Wounded at Cottbus in 1945, he was hospitalized at Marienbad in Czechoslovakia, and then held at an American prisoner of war camp until his release in 1946. At the end of the war, Grass and others were forced to visit the Dachau concentration camp in Germany. This event became a turning point for Grass. He would now dedicate his life to describing the German experience, first under the Nazis, then during Germany's postwar period of reconstruction, and finally as his country struggled with reunification.

Grass wandered around West Germany in search of his family and employment after his release as a prisoner of war in 1946. Ending up in Cologne, he worked first as a black marketeer and then in a potash mine. In December 1946, with the help of the Red Cross, he found his family living as refugees on a farm near Cologne. For a few weeks he stayed with them, working as a farmhand, but he then made his way to Düsseldorf, where he worked as an apprentice stonecutter. During this time he also studied sculpture under Sepp Mages and drawing under Otto Pankok at the Academy of Art. In the spring and summer of 1952 he traveled through France and Italy. In 1953 he moved to West Berlin, where he found a job as a graphic designer and studied at the State Academy of Fine Arts under Karl Hartung. In 1954 he married a Swiss ballet student, Anna Schwarz, whom he had met two years earlier during his travels; this marriage would end in divorce in 1978.

Grass's first recognition as a writer came at a poetry contest put on by Stuttgart Radio in 1955, when his poem "Lilies Out of Sleep" ("Lilien aus dem Schlaf") won first prize. The following year he published his first volume of poems and drawings. This collection, *Advantages of Wind-Fowl* (*Die Vorzüge der Windhühner,* 1956), distributed by Luchterhand Publishers, contains the allegorical imagery and diverse style that would become his trademark in the coming years. In 1956 Grass and his wife moved to Paris, where they lived until 1960. During this period, he continued to work as a sculptor, graphic artist, and writer. He also began working on his first novel, *The Tin Drum.* In 1958 he was invited to read portions of this work at the Berlin meeting of Gruppe 47, a loose conglomerate of socially critical writers of which he subsequently became a member. He won international acclaim in 1959 with the publication of *The Tin Drum,* which was quickly translated into most major languages. The film version of the novel in 1979, directed by Volker Schlöndorff, won the best award at the Cannes Film Festival and an Oscar for best foreign film.

In 1960 Grass, his wife, and their two-year-old twin sons returned to Berlin. That same year he published another volume of poetry. A year later his novella *Cat and Mouse* (*Katz und Maus*) was published, and DOG YEARS (*Hundejahre*) appeared in 1963. These three works, collectively known as *The Danzig Trilogy,* portray the rise of Adolf Hitler, the atrocities and horrors of World War II, and the guilt that has lingered with the German people in the postwar years.

The 1960s saw a shift in Grass's focus as his works began to reflect a period of intense political activism. Having sided against the communists and the conservatives in the late 1940s, and against West German chancellor Konrad Adenauer in the 1950s, Grass now became a supporter of the Social Democrat Party. In addition to editing speeches for Willy Brandt, who served as the West German chancellor from 1969 to 1974, Grass also wrote political tracts and contributed nearly a hundred election speeches in which he advocated a Germany free from fanaticism and totalitarianism. Grass's campaign work brought the realization that political progress moves at a snail's pace. Grass reflects this insight in his work *From the Diary of a Snail* (*Aus dem Tagebuch einer Schnecke,* 1972), in which he summarizes his election experiences and personal views as a campaigner in 1969 for the Social Democrats and Brandt. Two other of Grass's works that reflect the political influence of this period are *The Plebeians Rehearse the Uprising* (*Die Plebejer proben den Aufstand,* 1966) and LOCAL ANAESTHETIC (*Örtlich betäubt,* 1969).

Taking a critical stance on Bertolt Brecht's behavior during the Berlin street riots of June 17, 1953, in *The Plebeians Rehearse the Uprising,* Grass portrays Brecht as more concerned with his own theatrical productions than with the reactionary efforts of the workers who are rebelling against the state's latest edicts. This anti-Brechtian position evoked a strong backlash from those who felt Grass was attempting to disparage the Brecht legacy. *Local Anaesthetic,* which attempts to come to terms with the student movements and other protests during the Vietnam War, received just as poor a reception in Germany as did the former work. The book was, however, highly successful in the United States, where it landed Grass a *Time* cover story in the April 13, 1970, issue.

In the 1970s and 1980s, Grass expanded his subjects from German history and contemporary politics into issues such as feminism, ecology, and developing-world poverty. In *The FLOUNDER* (*Der Butt,* 1977) one sees Grass's commitment to both the women's movement and the peace movement as he explores the battle of the sexes and the development of civilization from the Stone Age to the present. In *The Rat* (*Die Rättin,* 1986) once again Grass's commitment to peace and the environment can be seen as he presents an apocalyptic world where mutant rats take over a radioactive Earth after mankind has deployed a neutron bomb amd destroyed itself.

Grass's concern with humankind's impact on the environment also extends to a concern with how the West affects the rest of the world. In 1975 he took his first trip to India. Eleven years later, in 1986, he returned there to live for several months in a suburb of Calcutta with his second wife, Ute Grunert, whom he married in 1979. His 1987 diary-form novel, *Show Your Tongue* (*Zungen Zeigen*), depicts his impressions of India during these months, but simultaneously also addresses the role played by the West in contributing to the poverty and misery of the Indian people.

The 1990s saw Grass's growing disillusionment with the Social Democrat Party as well as his increased desire to side with the underdog. During the drive for unification of East and West Germany that followed the fall of the Berlin Wall in 1989, Grass argued against Germany's hasty reunification. His novel TOO FAR AFIELD (*Ein weites Feld,* 1995), set in East Berlin during the collapse of communism, reflects Grass's opposition to Germany's reunification. Seen as showing too much sympathy for the former German Democratic Republic, while simultaneously overly critical of the Federal Republic of Germany for its "annexation" of East Germany, this work prompted vehement debate and criticism in the mainstream German media.

Despite the negative public reaction and a political stance that put him at odds with most of the intellectual and political elite of Germany, Grass's position did not change. In 1990 he joined others who were demanding reconciliation with Eastern Europe. In 1992 he left the Social Democrat Party in protest against the tighter constraints it had applied to political asylum laws at a time when there were increasing attacks against asylum seekers. In addition to criticizing Germany's domestic politics, Grass also took umbrage with its international policies. In 1995 he became a cosigner of the Heilbronner Manifest, which called for members of the artistic and scientific communities to reject mandatory military service as a show of protest against the Pershing II missiles the United States was then deploying in Germany. Currently, Grass's political focus is on the war in Iraq. He has signed and written several antiwar appeals.

Controversy surrounded Grass's interview with the German newspaper *Frankfurter Allgemeine* on August 11, 2006, in which, while discussing his forthcoming autobiography *Peeling Onions,* he revealed that he had been a member of Hitler's Waffen SS. Nevertheless, Grass has been admired around the world for many years for the body of his works. For his writings, cultural critiques, and political activism, he has received honorary doctorates from Kenyon College, Ohio, and from such universities as Harvard, Poznań, and Gdańsk.

For his literary achievements he has been the recipient of more than 20 awards, both domestic and international. For the body of his work, he was awarded the highest honor in 1999 when he received the Nobel Prize in literature. In its announcement of the award, the Swedish Academy cited his first novel, *The Tin Drum,* and praised the author's exploration of war as it affected his hometown of Danzig. "Here he comes to grips with the enormous task of reviewing contemporary history by recalling the disavowed and the forgotten: the victims, losers and lies that people wanted to forget because they had once believed in them," noted the citation. "It is not too audacious to assume that *The Tin Drum* will become one of the enduring literary works of the 20th century."

With his extraordinary first novel, *The Tin Drum,* Günter Grass, distinguished German novelist, playwright, sculptor, and poet, became, according to Katharena Eiermann in "Günter Grass and the Theatre of the Absurd," "the literary spokesman for the German generation that grew up in the Nazi era and survived the war." Considered one of the most significant and controversial authors to emerge in Germany after World War II, Günter Grass has described himself as a belated apostle of enlightenment in an era that has grown tired of reason. In his acceptance speech for the Nobel Prize in 1999, Grass said that storytellers, by giving audiences "mouth-to-ear artificial respiration, spinning old stories in new ways" help to keep humanity alive. In Grass's attempts to do just this, he has been described by Eiermann as a moral watchdog and the "conscience of his generation."

BIBLIOGRAPHY

Mayer-Iswandy, Claudia. *Günter Grass.* Munich: Deutscher Taschenbuch Verlag, 2002.

Øhrgaard, Per. *Günter Grass: Ein deutscher Schriftsteller wird besichtigt.* Vienna: Paul Zsolnay, 2005.

O'Neill, Patrick. *Günter Grass Revisited.* New York: Twayne Publishers, 1999.

Preece, Julian. *The Life and Work of Günter Grass: Literature, History, Politics.* New York: Palgrave Macmillan, 2004.

Stolz, Dieter. *Günter Grass, der Schriftsteller: Eine Einführung.* Göttingen: Steidl, 2005.

Zimmermann, Harro. *Günter Grass unter den Deutschen: Chronik eines Verhältnisses.* Göttingen: Steidl, 2006.

Stephanie E. Libbon

GREEN HOUSE, THE (*LA CASA VERDE*)

Mario Vargas Llosa (1966)   Mario Vargas Llosa's *The Green House* won the Crítica Prize in Spain (1966), and the Rómulo Gallegos Prize in Venezuela (1967), the latter being most important literary prize in Hispanic America. The novel was inspired by a trip that Vargas Llosa (1936–   ) made to the Amazon area in 1958, during which he observed the major differences between advanced regions and the indigenous territory of his country, as well as the exploitations of the Indian people by various external and colonial economic and political forces.

The Green House presents a panorama of ordinary people's lives and legends in northern Peru during a time span of 40 years following the 1920s. The setting stretches from the coastal desert area to the forest region, with a background of ideological and moral conflicts rooted in Peru's historic and political realities. The major plots in the novel include the history of a brothel called the Green House in Piura, a small town turned modern city in the coastal desert, and the stories of the small town Santa María de Nieva in the forest region, where the economy is undeveloped and the indigenous people are threatened by forces of nature and foreign adventurers and colonists.

The novel contains four parts and an epilogue. Each part contains three to four chapters, and each chapter consists of five episodes from the lives of the five major characters: Don Anselmo, founder of the Green House, whose role is later taken by his daughter Chunga; Bonifacia, also known as Selvatica, a prostitute in the Green House; Fushía, a Japanese fugitive from Brazil who is hiding in the forest region; Jum, an Indian tribe leader in the forest area; and Lituma, a native Piuran. The burning and rebuilding of the brothel Green House in Piura provide the main narrative in terms of time, and the story of Lituma and his wife, Bonifacia, who are married and then move from the forest area to the coastal city of Piura, is the major link in terms of setting, as their relocation connects the stories in the two different regions. The five plots in each chapter develop in a criss-cross way due to the author's narrative technique of "stream of dialogue," as seen in *The Time of the Hero* and *Conversation in the Cathedral*. In this technique a character's words in one story are often used as a lead in another story. Such a technique smoothly carries the multiclued narrative and successfully illustrates life in the two regions through the fates of the five main characters.

In early 20th century, Don Anselmo, a musician and founder of the first brothel in Piura, seduces a blind girl, Antonia, who becomes pregnant and later dies at the birth of their daughter Chunga. Her death ignites the fury of the local people, who, led by Padre García, burn the brothel. Since then Don Anselmo lives humbly in a notorious district of Piura, where he witnesses the development of the area from a small town to a modern city. He also observes his daughter Chunga build a second Green House. By the time Don Anselmo dies, other people, including Padre García, have begun viewing his life more open-mindedly. The stories of other main characters from Piura also take place in the second brothel, founded by his daughter Chunga.

Bonifacia is an orphan who grows up in a convent in Santa María de Nieva, a small town in the forest region. One of her friends in the convent is Lalita, who later becomes mistress of the Japanese-born smuggler Fushía. Bonifacia falls in love and marries Lituma, a police officer. Later she moves with her husband to Piura, where Lituma and his childhood friends become involved in a fatal conflict with a local rich man. Lituma is imprisoned in Lima due to his rival's death. He subsequently returns to Piura after serving his prison term, only to find that his wife has been enticed by his friend Josefino to become a prostitute in Chunga's Green House. She has also changed her name to Selvatica, or "girl from the forest."

The stories of Fushía and Jum take place in Bonifacia's home region. Fushía is a smuggler and a fugitive from Brazil. He seizes control of a remote island in the region, organizes a gang to rob the local Indians of their resources, and thus accumulates a large amount of money. Fushía later falls ill with leprosy and is sent to San Pablo for isolation and treatment. His lover Lalita has run away from him and married Nieves, a sailor on the rivers. In his last days, Fushía relates his adventurous life to his former partner Aquilino.

Jum is an Indian tribe leader who has tried to resist the outside world's exploitation of his people. After fruitless efforts to get fair prices for the Indians' agri-cultural products in the surrounding towns, he decides to organize a company owned by the local Indians. However, he is captured and tortured by the police because of his involvement, and the Indians' commercial organization eventually fails.

At the end of the novel, the death of Don Anselmo reunites all the characters in Piura. Lituma and Bonifacia reconcile, and Padre García agrees to perform a Christian burial for Don Anselmo, who they discover is, like Bonifacia, from the forest region.

BIBLIOGRAPHY
Kristal, Efraín. *Temptation of the Word: The Novels of Mario Vargas Llosa.* Nashville, Tenn.: Vanderbilt University Press, 1998.
Oviedo, José Miguel. *Mario Vargas Llosa: A Writer's Reality.* Barcelona: Seix Barral, 1985.
Vargas Llosa, Mario. *A Fish in the Water: A Memoir.* New York: Farrar, Straus and Giroux, 1994.

Haiqing Sun

GROUP PORTRAIT WITH LADY (GRUP-PENBILD MIT DAME) Heinrich Böll (1971)

The German author Heinrich Böll's (1917–85) *Group Portrait with Lady* is widely considered one of his most important novels because it was likely the deciding work in his selection for the 1972 Nobel Prize in literature. Though the text reaches back in history to address the war—and is therefore often regarded as the summation and completion of his long engagement with World War II—it also lodges a trenchant critique of postwar Germany, deepening Böll's concerns with continuities from the Nazi time in the German psyche and society.

With the novel's fictional biographical account of Leni Pfeiffer between the 1920s and 1970–71, Böll is able to reconsider and recast German history in those crucial 50 years. Leni is another of Böll's nonconformists whose lonely distance from society highlights the inhumane character of institutions, including family, state, and church. For the first time, however, Böll foregrounds a woman protagonist in this nonconformist role. Leni extends the series of renegade protagonists that Böll developed in *The Clown* and ABSENT WITHOUT LEAVE, but the hopes of such social rebels are now placed in a woman, anticipating *The Lost Honor of*

Katharina Blum (1974), in which Böll would concentrate more specifically on contemporary society. In *Group Portrait with Lady,* the 54-year-old Böll continued to develop his literary interests and style to create a watershed work that both completes his fiction until that point and sends him in surprising new directions.

The novel, set at the beginning of the 1970s, is narrated by an unnamed researcher who is piecing together information about the adamantly silent, elusive, and even mystical Leni—that is, Helene Maria Pfeiffer (née Gruyter). Because Leni resists talking to this researcher, he relies on reports, meeting minutes, memories, and interviews with people (friends and those who are not friends), which are presented in the novel in a quasi-documentary style. In a series of chapters narrated from varying perspectives, the novel offers important elements of her life in retrospect, as document, memory, and trauma. Leni's father was a successful builder during the Nazi years, a time during which Leni was sent to a convent school and came under the intellectual and moral guidance of a Jewish nun, Rahel Ginzburg. This relationship points her in a nonconformist direction, but her life otherwise fits other female biographies under the Nazis. With her father's encouragement, she joined the Nazi girls' group, married a soldier who was killed on the eastern front soon thereafter, and was left a young widow when Germany was filled with women in black. The darker side of the Nazi years becomes increasingly clear along with this seemingly banal biography: Leni's brother and cousin are shot for desertion, her father is sentenced to life in prison for alleged fraud in Denmark, and Rahel dies in hiding, concealed but also neglected in an attic by her fellow nuns.

Leni's life takes a radically different turn when, working during the war, she makes a small gesture of charity by offering a cup of coffee to a slave laborer, a Russian prisoner of war named Boris. This strictly forbidden but fundamentally humanizing moment changes both of their lives: They fall in love, meet during air raids in a "graveyard-paradise," and eventually conceive a child, Lev, who will follow in his mother's nonconformist footsteps by rejecting postwar society. At the end of the war, Boris, carrying German identification papers, is arrested by forces from the United States and handed over to the French; he dies soon thereafter in a coal mine.

Since the end of the war, Leni has remained a "statue," working as a gardener while refusing to join the capitalistically competitive and materialist postwar society. She prefers instead to rent out cheap rooms in her house to people whom society has mostly rejected or forgotten. Relatives of hers, excited by the real-estate opportunity, are trying to remove her from the Gruyter family house, but a Help Leni Committee has formed, and local garbage men, with whom her son works, helps obstruct the eviction.

By the end of the novel, the narrator who has offered this varied and variegated material has joined the Help Leni Committee, and it is clear that he has fallen in love with his subject. In this relationship and in these materials, Böll is both building on and parodying the documentary style that had been popular in 1960s literature. In *Group Portrait with Lady,* Böll emphasizes how all documents are selective, subjective, and fictional and how the researcher has his or her own agenda, interests, and affective attachments. The narration is episodic and fragmentary, pointing to a complex relationship between reality and fiction, particularly concerning a figure of whom readers never receive a direct picture.

Certainly an important aspect of this elusive and quasi-mystical portrait is its religious overtones: One critic has called Leni a "subversive Madonna," and the indications are there in her middle name, her social importance, and in the form of a holy family with Boris. Typical for Böll, however, his Madonna leads an emphatically sexually free life and otherwise resists the dictates of the institutionalized church, which was, after all, at least partially responsible for the death of her Jewish mentor. Even as he hints at the importance of a refigured Christian humanism, Böll undercuts its realization in institutions, preferring instead a character who leads her own life and a reader who cultivates his or her own image of this renegade and the history that surrounds her.

BIBLIOGRAPHY

Böll, Victor, and Jochen Schubert. *Heinrich Böll.* Munich: Deutscher Taschenbuch Verlag, 2002.

Butler, Michael, ed. *The Narrative Fiction of Heinrich Böll: Social Conscience and Literary Achievement.* Cambridge and New York: Cambridge University Press, 1994.

Conrad, Robert C. *Understanding Heinrich Böll.* Columbia, S.C.: Camden House 1992.

Crampton, Patricia, trans. *Heinrich Böll, on his Death: Selected Obituaries and the Last Interview.* Bonn: Inter Nationes, 1985.

Prodanuik, Ihor. *The Imagery in Heinrich Böll's Novels.* Bonn: Bouvier, 1979.

Reed, Donna K. *The Novels of the Nazi Past.* New York: Peter Lang, 1985.

Zachau, Reinhard K. *Heinrich Böll: Forty Years of Criticism.* Columbia, S.C.: Camden House, 1994.

Jaimey Fisher

GÜIRALDES, RICARDO (1886–1927) *Argentinean novelist*

Best known as the author of DON SEGUNDO SOMBRA, a romanticized portrait of the gaucho and his way of life, Ricardo Güiraldes is one of Argentina's most celebrated authors. However famous he may be today, he enjoyed virtually no recognition as an author during his brief lifetime; only just before his death in 1927 did he receive recognition when *Don Segundo Sombra* became an instant best seller, an ironic end to a tragic literary life.

Born into a family of wealth and power, Güiraldes led a frustrated personal life that was defined by Hodgkin's disease and his lack of literary fame. From an early age, he had to negotiate the disparate worlds of the urban and the rural—first between his family's home located in the heart of Buenos Aires and the family's ranch, La Portena, where he frequently visited. At this ranch, Güiraldes first met the gauchos, and here he fell in love with their culture, a lifestyle that he would celebrate in his final and most famous novel, *Don Segundo Sombra*. Although his heart was on the pampas, physically he was most often in the city, a place that exercised a seductive lure for him.

Güiraldes's early education prepared him for the sorts of urban and social situations that he most often found himself in. Encouraged to write at an early age by his tutor, Güiraldes soon began an intense period of reading during which he also mastered foreign languages, such as German. Despite his literate facility, Güiraldes was a problem student who was not inter-ested in school. Graduating without distinction, he soon embarked on a series of jobs, all of which proved frustrating to the restless young man. In contrast to these failures, or perhaps because of them, Güiraldes was a success in the Buenos Aires social circles. In 1910, to remove him from these influences, his family sent him to Paris for a two-year stay, but as he had done in Buenos Aires, Güiraldes pursued a life of extravagance and self-indulgence. Leaving Paris, Güiraldes embarked on a grand tour of several countries, including India, China, Japan, Egypt, and Russia. He and his father disagreed over his apparent vagrancy and lack of direction. While on his tour, Güiraldes realized that the gaucho was the preeminent figure of integrity in a world otherwise corrupted.

After returning to Argentina in 1912, Güiraldes married Adelina del Carril, whose influence empowered him to create what became his literary masterpiece. She actively encouraged and enabled his writing, thereby keeping him from frittering away his life in pursuit of social status. Back in Argentina, he quickly became part of the modernist movements in literature, arts, and ideas that were being debated at this time by other Argentineans, including his friend Jorge Luis Borges.

Despite this nurturing atmosphere, Güiraldes struggled to realize his dreams as a writer. He paid to have his first literary work published, *Tales of Death and Blood* (*Cuentos de muerte y de sangre,* 1915). Notably, Don Segundo Sombra first appears as a character in one of this book's short stories, although Güiraldes would not start the actual writing of *Don Segundo Sombra* until 1920. That same year he also published the autobiographical *Raucho* (1917), again with no literary or financial success; nonetheless, Güiraldes continued writing. Struggling with this lack of success, he began to question his life's ambition. In this mood, he and Adelina returned to Paris, where he soon fell under the stimulating influence of the French Left Bank, inspiration to so many other authors, including Ernest Hemingway, F. Scott Fitzgerald, and Gertrude Stein.

Rededicated to his writing, Güiraldes returned to Argentina, where he continued working on *Don Segundo Sombra* and also published *Rosaura* (1922) and *Xaimaca* (1923); these works, however, also failed to gain the author recognition. This failure continued until *Don Segundo Sombra* appeared, winning him the National Prize for Literature. Finally, Güiraldes had the literary success that had eluded him for so long. Cruelly, though, this fame was also fleeting: Güiraldes died within a year of the novel's publication, but not before he had achieved the recognition of his literary talent.

BIBLIOGRAPHY

Bordelois, Ivonne. *Un Triángulo crucial: Borges, Güiraldes y Lygones*. Buenos Aires: Eudeba, 1999.

Mata, Ramiro W. *Ricardo Güiraldes, José Eustasio Rivera, Rómulo Gallegos*. Montevideo [n.p.], 1961.

Previtali, Giovanni. *Ricardo Güiraldes and Don Segundo Sombra: Life and Works*. New York: Hispanic Institute in the United States, 1963.

Clay Smith

GULAG ARCHIPELAGO, THE (ARKHIPELAG GULAG) Aleksandr Solzhenitsyn (1973–1975)

The Gulag Archipelago is a compelling, encyclopedic, erudite, and scathing history and memoir of life in the Soviet Union's prison camp system. In many respects it marks the most ambitious literary effort by the 1970 Nobel Prize–winning author Aleksandr Solzhenitsyn (1918–). The original editor for *The Gulag Archipelago* was to be Dmiti Petrovich Vitkovsky, but as a consequence of spending half of his life in the Solovetsky Island camp, Vitkovsky suffered paralysis and was left without the ability to speak. Solzhenitsyn's dedication in the work is telling: "I dedicate this to all those who did not live to tell it. And may they please forgive me for not having seen it all nor having remembered it all, for not having divined all of it."

In terms of its critical history, *The Gulag Archipelago* was first published in Paris as *Arkhipelag Gulag* in three volumes (1973–75). The word *gulag* is an acronym for the Soviet government administration systems that oversaw and maintained the exhaustive sequences of forced-labor camps. Solzhenitsyn's use of the word *archipelago* in the title acts as a metaphor for the camps, which were scattered through the Soviet Union in a manner that Solzhenitsyn himself compared to being like a series of islands that moved from the Bering Strait through to the Bosporus Sea.

In terms of its structure and content, *The Gulag Archipelago* is an attempt to assimilate information gathered from Solzhenitsyn's fellow prison inmates, Solzhenitsyn himself, historical documentation, and letters that he successfully committed to record during his eight-year period of imprisonment. At once a novel and a vital piece of personal testimony, *The Gulag Archipelago* represents the author's attempt to create a record of the Soviet regime's totalitarian and highly paranoid use of terror, intimidation, and fear-inspiring techniques against its own population, and it illuminates the apparatus of Soviet repression.

A portrayal of Stalinist and historical violations, *The Gulag Archipelago* was a shocking indictment of the Soviet Union for those readers living outside of its borders. Joseph Stalin was the Soviet leader from the 1920s to his death in 1953. His iron rule was one of state terror, mass deportations, and political repression. Characterized by descriptions of the horrors within the Soviet regime, *The Gulag Archipelago* provided further momentum for critics of the Soviet system and caused those who had sympathy with its motives to feel their position was less viable than previously. The first two volumes describe sequences of arrests, convictions, transportation, and imprisonment meted out to the gulag's victims. Solzhenitsyn moves skillfully between a detached historical portrayal and the harsh personal accounts from the lives of those within the prison system. The third volume documents attempted escapes and subversions that proved to be momentary provocations against an all-encompassing governmental machine.

Following publication of the first volume in Paris in 1973, official Soviet journalism virulently attacked Solzhenitsyn in print, and he was arrested and exiled from the country in February 1974. An earlier volume of the novel is believed to have been confiscated by the KGB. Solzhenitsyn donated the proceeds from the book's sale to the Russian Social Fund for Persecuted Persons and Their Families.

BIBLIOGRAPHY

Dunlop, John B., ed. *Solzhenitsyn in Exile*. Palo Alto, Calif.: Hoover Institution, 1985.

Ericson, Edward E. *Solzhenitsyn and the Modern World*. Washington, D.C.: Regnery Gateway, 1993.

Krasnov, Valdislav. *Solzhenitsyn and Dostoevsky: A Study in the Polyphonic Novel.* Athens: University of Georgia Press, 1980.

Rothberg, Abraham. *Alexandr Solzhenitsyn: The Major Novels.* Ithaca N.Y.: Cornell University Press, 1971.

Thomas, D. M. *Alexander Solzhenitsyn: A Century in his Life.* New York: St. Martin's Press, 1998.

Martyn Colebrook

GUZMÁN, MARTÍN LUIS (1887–1976)

Mexican essayist, novelist Martín Luis Guzmán is regarded as one of the 20th century's most distinguished chroniclers of political revolution and upheaval. Through his journalism and fiction, he conveyed the chaos and frustrations that came hand in hand with the Mexican revolution of 1910 and subsequent rebellions. An insider and writer who worked on behalf of many Mexican leaders, Guzmán offers a unique perspective of political revolution in his prose because of his insight into the vicissitudes of revolt and social upheaval. Guzmán's writings are unique in the intensity with which they contrast idealistic hopes with thwarted ambitions and the dark descent into despotism.

Guzmán was born in Chihuahua, Mexico, on October 6, 1887, the son of a colonel in Mexico's federal army. He honored his father's wish that he should never lose his civilian status and take up a military career. Although Guzmán worked for many revolutionary leaders, he never called himself a guerrilla or a soldier. He spent his childhood in Mexico City and Veracruz. At the age of 13, the precocious young man started the journal *Juventud* (*Youth*), and at the age of 15 he won a placement at the National Preparatory School. He received a degree in jurisprudence in 1913 from the National University of Mexico.

Even at an early age, Guzmán was active in Mexican politics. He was a part of the editorial staff of *El Imparcial;* served as chancellor of the Mexican consulate in Phoenix, Arizona; and joined many groups opposed to the dictatorial presidency of Porfirio Diaz. Guzmán was delighted in 1911 when the progressive Francisco Madero won the presidency in Mexico after a popular uprising, but he was dismayed when Victoriano Huerta had Madero assassinated.

During the years 1913–15, when Mexico was ravaged by fighting between various self-appointed provisional governments, Guzmán supported revolutionary leaders, including Venustiano Carranza, Álvaro Obregón, and Francisco "Pancho" Villa, who opposed the seated rulers. He worked in various capacities, including administration, communications, and propaganda. Eventually he became disillusioned with each of these rebel partisans because of what he perceived as their pursuit of self-interest rather than the egalitarian goals of the revolutionary movement.

Having fallen out of favor with all of the squabbling forces, Guzmán fled Mexico in 1915, spending periods in America, France, and Spain. His first book, *The Dispute of Mexico* (*La querella de México*), was published in Spain in 1915. The work is a pessimistic essay about the alleged unwillingness of many Mexicans to accept fundamental change and modernization. In the United States, he taught at the University of Minnesota; wrote most of another book, *On the Banks of the Hudson* (*A orillas del Hudson*), which combines nonfictional prose with poetry; and wrote for the U.S.-based Spanish-language publications *El Gráfico* and *Revista Universal.*

The few years Guzmán spent back in Mexico after 1920 were turbulent. He founded the newspaper *El Mundo* and supported the uprising of Adolfo de la Huerta against the presidency of Álvaro Obregón. Obregón's forces seized the paper because its staff supported de la Huerta, forcing Guzmán into a decade-long exile. Guzmán then became a naturalized Spanish citizen, writing for publications such as *El Debate, Ahora, El Sol, La Voz,* and *Luz.*

In Spain, Guzmán published his two most important works: the novels *The EAGLE AND THE SERPENT* (*El águila y la serpiente,* 1926) and *The Shadow of the Tyrant* (*La sombra del caudillo,* 1929). The former is a direct, reportage-style, first-person narration of Guzmán's inside view of the disillusioning breakdown of revolutionary ideals; the second book takes a more generic approach, presenting a roman à clef about the venality of Mexican politics in the 1920s. The "tyrant" of the title of the second novel is based on a conflation of two real-life figures in Mexican politics detested by Guzmán: President Obregón and President Plutarco Elías Calles. The novel's chief source material is the failed rising of de la Huerta against Obregón's government in 1923 and the Calles government's ruthless suppression of the uprising in 1928 by Arnulfo Goméz and Francisco Serrano, two generals who were executed.

Although very different from *The Eagle and the Serpent, The Shadow of the Tyrant* retains its predecessor's stress on the perceived disparity between the revolutionary party's laudable early collectivity and its degeneration into vicious, self-seeking individualism. The novel was filmed by the Mexican director Julio Bracho in 1960, but it was quickly banned because the revolutionary party that benefited from the violence shown in Guzmán's novel and film was still in power. It was 1990 before the film received a Mexican premiere.

In 1936, at the invitation of President Lázaro Cárdenas, Guzmán returned to Mexico, remaining in his homeland for the rest of his life. He worked as a correspondent for *El Universal* and founded the important newsweekly *Tiempo*. Guzmán also continued to write book-length prose. Other than the two novels on political revolutions of the late 1920s, his only work still widely read is his massive but incomplete account of the life of Pancho Villa. He had initiated a project to write a semifictional, 10-volume account of the revolutionary Villa's life, *Memoirs of Pancho Villa* (*Las memorias de Pancho Villa*), and between 1938 and 1964 he published five volumes; the other five were never written. A scholarly translation by Virginia H. Taylor has made this sprawling work accessible to English-speaking readers. *Memoirs* was written by Guzmán in the first-person narration of Pancho himself, as the author went to extraordinary lengths both to frame the action with historical accuracy and to faithfully represent Villa's rough-and-ready manner and speech. The first volume begins with an account of Villa's break from conventional society, when he shoots a landowner for raping his sister. From this point, Guzmán's Villa is an emancipatory fighter for justice, for his family, and for a broader Mexican society. Guzmán's novels always explicitly follow his political prejudices: He believed that Villa was prone to excessive violence, but that the rebel was motivated by genuine revolutionary aspirations of political and social inclusion.

Guzmán wrote many other book-length works in the 1950s and early 1960s, including biographies, memoirs, historical studies, political speeches, and polemics about postrevolutionary Mexico. He became, like aging revolutionaries in many nations, a revered elder of the state. Elected to the Mexican Academy in 1954, he was awarded both the National Prize for Literature and the Manuel Ávila Camacho Prize in 1958. He also served as a senator in Mexico, beginning in 1969. He died in Mexico City on December 22, 1976.

Guzmán's place in the canon of 20th-century novelists is guaranteed because of the universality of the ideas found in *The Eagle and the Serpent* and *The Shadow of the Tyrant,* two great novels of the 1920s. Many revolutionary movements have begun with idealistic dreams, only to degenerate into ferocious violence, selfish interests, and disillusionment. Guzmán's two major novels capture this agonizing decline of idealism into dismay with poignancy and unpretentious directness.

BIBLIOGRAPHY

Delpar, Helen. "Mexican Culture, 1920–1945." In *The Oxford History of Mexico,* edited by Michael C. Meyer and William H. Beezley, 543–572. New York: Oxford University Press, 2000.

Franco, Rafael Olea. "Martín Luis Guzmán." In *Encyclopedia of Contemporary Latin American and Caribbean Culture,* 3 vols., edited by Daniel Balderston et al., vol. 2, 703–704. London: Routledge, 2000.

Gómez, Ermilo Abreu. *Martín Luis Guzmán.* Mexico City: Empresas Editoriales, 1968.

Perea, Héctor. "Martín Luis Guzmán Franco." In *Encyclopedia of Mexico: History, Society and Culture,* 2 vols., edited by Michael S. Werner, vol. 1, 622–623. Chicago: Fitzroy Dearborn Publishers, 1997.

Rutherford, John. *Mexican Society During the Revolution: A Literary Approach.* Oxford: Clarendon Press, 1971.

Kevin De Ornellas

H

HAMSUN, KNUT (KNUT PEDERSEN) (1859–1952) *Norwegian essayist, novelist, short story writer, playwright*

Over the course of a literary career spanning more than seven decades, the Norwegian Knut Hamsun addressed many of the psychological, philosophical, and political concerns of Western society during the spread of the Industrial Revolution, through both world wars, and into the paranoid political milieu marking the onset of the cold war. Abandoning the neoromanticism that characterized his earliest writing and popular among his Norwegian contemporaries, Hamsun's midlife fiction charts the psychological and philosophical terrain frequently associated with Fyodor Dostoyevsky and Friedrich Nietzsche.

Haunted by the existential malaise permeating much of his prewar fiction, Hamsun eventually promoted agrarian primitivism—a return to working the land—as the only redemptive possibility for humankind. Recognizing the considerable philosophical importance of these primitivist works, the Swedish Academy awarded Hamsun the 1920 Nobel Prize in literature. Hamsun's legacy, however, remains the existentially concerned fiction he produced during the last years of the 19th century. With writers as varied as FRANZ KAFKA, Charles Bukowski, and Paul Auster acknowledging Hansun's influence, he is considered by many as, after only the playwright Henrik Ibsen, Norway's most important literary figure.

Knut Pedersen, who eventually assumed the surname Hamsun, was born on August 4, 1859, in the town of Lom in Gudbrandsdal, Norway. The fourth of six children, Hamsun spent his earliest years in a small two-room cottage in Garmotreet with his parents, Peder and Tora (*née* Olsen) Pedersen, three older brothers, and two younger sisters. In the summer of 1863, the Pedersens left Garmotreet for Hamarøy, a town located some 100 miles north of the Arctic Circle, where Hamsun's uncle, Hans Olsen, had established a tailor's shop, a post office, and a library. With his earnings, Olsen invested in Hamsund, a farm located a few miles west of Hamarøy, and invited the Pedersens to work the land there.

As a child, Hamsun enjoyed working as a shepherd for his family, but as he grew older the boy developed a vocational restlessness that was to plague him for much of his adult life. Between 1873 and 1880, Hamsun worked as a store clerk in Lom and Hamarøy, as a nomadic peddler in northern Norway, as a cobbler's apprentice and a dock hand in the town of Bodø, as a grade school teacher and a bailiff's assistant in Vesterålen, and as a highway construction worker north of Oslo. During this time of transition and change, Hamsun managed to publish numerous essays, articles, poems, and short stories, as well as three novels, *The Enigmatic Man* (*Den Gaadefulde,* 1877), *Bjørger* (1878), and *Frida* (1879).

In 1882, convinced that the United States would offer prosperity on a scale unavailable to him in Norway, Hamsun joined his oldest brother, Peter, in the town of Elroy, Wisconsin. Although he carried letters of introduction from such prominent Norwegians as the 1903 Nobel laureate in literature, Bjørnstjerne Bjørnson (1832–1910), Hamsun had difficulty establishing contact with Scandinavian literary figures in the United States. Despite bouts of depression and loneliness exacerbated by his poor English skills, however, he managed to find work as a secretary to the Norwegian émigré writer Kristofer Janson, and he also gave several public lectures on literature. In 1884, suffering from a severe case of bronchitis misdiagnosed as tuberculosis, Hamsun returned to Norway to die in his homeland.

During a brief period of convalescence spent in the fjord town of Aurdal, Hamsun began publishing stories influenced by Ibsen and Émile Zola, essays on American culture, and articles on Mark Twain in Norwegian newspapers. Additionally, having already altered his name from Pedersen to Pederson and having published novels as Knut Pedersen Hamsund, the young writer finally settled on the name Knut Hamsun in 1886. Hoping to earn enough money to settle in Norway and live as a writer, the newly christened Hamsun returned to the United States that summer to work in Chicago as a common laborer and railroad conductor.

After a brief stint as a farmhand in North Dakota, Hamsun moved to Minneapolis to give a series of lectures on Scandinavian literature, impressionism, and criticism. Finally established as a member of the Scandinavian expatriate intelligentsia, he published articles, written in both English and Dano-Norwegian for various Scandinavian newspapers, on topics ranging from August Strindberg to life in Minneapolis. Despite his scholarly successes, however, Hamsun grew disillusioned with life in America and returned to Scandinavia permanently in 1888.

Despite having spent his time in the pioneer regions of the midwestern part of the United States among a predominantly poor, ill-educated Scandinavian population, Hamsun felt his experiences were broad enough to write *The Cultural Life of Modern America* (*Fra Det Moderne Amerikas Aandsliv,* 1889), a book criticizing American civilization. The work accuses American democracy of reducing all standards of excellence and denounces American patriotism for causing isolationism and stunting cultural growth. Meeting with great popular success, *The Cultural Life of Modern America* and the early published excerpts of *Hunger* (*Sult*) earned Hamsun a place among the Scandinavian literary elite by the end of the 1880s.

With the publication of his most famous novel, *Hunger,* in 1890, Knut Hamsun joined the ranks of the world's most acclaimed authors, forging a thematic and stylistic link between the great 19th-century Russian authors and the existentially concerned modernist writers of the early 20th century. In *Hunger,* Hamsun chronicles the exploits of a young writer struggling to survive in Oslo (then called Christiania) by writing idealistic articles for local newspapers. An anxious, neurotic loner in the same vein as Fyodor Dostoyevsky's Raskolnikov in *Crime and Punishment,* and something of a precursor to Samuel Beckett's pathetic writer Molloy, Hamsun's nameless narrator exists on the periphery of urban Norwegian culture, belonging to neither the literati he wishes to join nor the uneducated, impoverished mass of homeless tramps and criminals he seems to resemble most. Strangely, the narrator's hunger is more the result of a self-imposed regimen of fasting than true necessity, since he steadfastly refuses to abandon freelance writing for steadier employment.

As his situation becomes increasingly dire, the narrator's thoughts turn frenetic, and his behavior alternates between a nihilistic disregard for the consequences of one's actions and a tragicomic attempt to preserve dignity in the face of public pity and scorn. In the end, the narrator, having failed at writing, romance, and self-preservation, finds work as a deckhand on a Russian ship headed toward England. In a sardonic parody of the fresh-faced young man heading abroad to find his fortune, Hamsun leaves his reader with an image of a mentally unstable man, weakened by weeks of malnourishment, unable to keep even the most meager meals in his stomach and dressed in rags, sailing off into the vast emptiness of the ocean.

During the following three decades, Hamsun published nearly two dozen novels, plays, collections of verse, and collections of short stories. Although most of his books are set in northern Norway or the American Midwest, Hamsun's work deals less with physical geography than psychological and emotional geography. A literary descendant of Dostoyevsky and Nietzsche,

Hamsun plumbs the depths of human despair, isolation, perception, and madness in a style presaging the modernist school of literature. With his liberal use of fragmentation, flashbacks, and stream-of-consciousness techniques, Hamsun represents an important bridge linking the great 19th-century novelists to the literary modernism of writers such as Kafka and James Joyce.

As his literary reputation spread internationally, Hamsun's vociferous support of conservative polemics began tarnishing his image at home in predominantly liberal Norway, and a series of pro-German articles published during World War I brought a degree of international vilification to the writer. Nevertheless, in 1920, prompted by his 1917 novel, *The Growth of the Soil* (*Markens Grøde*) Knut Hamsun received the Nobel Prize in literature at the age of 60. On his 75th birthday, he received the Goethe prize, and at the age of 80 he was further honored when a collection of his articles met with great popular and critical success.

Among the world's most highly regarded novelists at the outset of World War II, the octogenarian Hamsun nearly destroyed his reputation by vociferously defending his Anglophobic views and praising Adolph Hitler's Third Reich in a string of more than a dozen articles published after the German invasion of Norway on April 9, 1940. Insisting that Germany was not at war with Norway but merely defending the Nordic nation's neutrality, Hamsun criticized Norway's King Haakon and the parliament for establishing a government-in-exile in England. Subsequent articles praised Vidkun Quisling and his Norwegian Nazi party, attacked young Norwegians for developing a resistance movement, and lauded various German military victories.

Despite accusations to the contrary, Hamsun never joined the Norwegian Nazi Party, the Nasjonal Samling, but he did meet with Joseph Terboven, the *reichskommissar* for Norway in 1941. Two years later, he traveled to Germany to visit Joseph Goebbels and Hitler. Despite the führer's complete dismissal of Hamsun, the writer penned a passionate obituary for Hitler in *Aftenposten* on May 7, 1945.

Three weeks after Hamsun published his eulogy for Hitler, the Norwegian government interned the writer and his second wife, Marie, at their home in Nørholm.

Just under a month later, on June 14, Hamsun was transferred to Grimstad Hospital before being sent to the Landvik Nursing Home, just outside of the town. After a series of interrogations, Hamsun was sent to a psychiatric hospital in Oslo. He openly professed his support for Germany and seemed capable of lucid thought. After an interrogation of his wife suggested that the author might be emotionally unstable, Hamsun refused to speak with Marie for more than four years. On February 11, 1946, after four months in the psychiatric institution, Hamsun returned to the nursing home in Landvik. Though his psychiatric examiners did not consider the writer insane, they considered him to be "a person with permanently impaired mental faculties."

Due to his mental impairment and deafness, Hamsun was not forced to undergo a criminal trial for treason, but he was subjected to a trial to determine whether the aged writer should pay reparations to the Norwegian government for his Nazi sympathies. On December 16, 1947, after passing a guilty verdict, a Norwegian court sentenced Hamsun to a fine amounting to 85 percent of the writer's estimated estate. Returning in poverty to Landvik Nursing Home after the trial, the 90-year-old Hamsun published his memoirs, *On Overgrown Paths* (*På Gjengrodde Stier*) in 1949. Shortly afterward, he mended his broken marriage to Marie. Knut Hamsun died on February 19, 1952, at age 92.

BIBLIOGRAPHY

Ferguson, Robert. *Enigma: The Life of Knut Hamsun.* London: Hutchinson, 1987.

Hamsun, Knut. *Selected Letters.* Edited by Harald Naess and James McFarlane. Norwich, U.K.: Norvik Press, 1990.

Næss, Harald. *Knut Hamsun.* Boston: Twayne Publishers, 1984.

Erik Grayson

HAN SHAOGONG (1953–) *Chinese novelist*

Han Shaogong is an important figure in 20th-century literature as the leader of the "root-searching movement" (*xungen pai*), a group of contemporary Chinese writers who were formerly displaced youths of the so-called Lost Generation—those who were "sent down" to the countryside for reeducation during the Great

Proletarian Cultural Revolution. Celebrating the new-found freedoms of a post-Mao era, root-seekers explored literature free of political propaganda and instead extolled their historical background; the psychology, sociology, and aesthetics of past and present Chinese culture; and regional language, dialect, themes, and "color." In his essay "Literature of the Wounded," Han Shaogong describes the concept of "root seeking" as "releasing the energies of modern ideas, recasting and broadening the self among our people, and uniting global consciousness of one's roots."

Han Shaogong was born on January 1, 1953, in Changsha, capital of central China's Hunan Province. Like many youths during the Cultural Revolution, Han was a self-described "enthusiastic Red Guard." He was assigned to write slogans and paint signs espousing the teachings of Chairman Mao Zedong and to spout publicly words of wisdom from the *Little Red Book, The Quotations of Chairman Mao.* The Red Guards comprised hundreds of thousands of youths in military-green "army uniforms" who performed a ritualized dance (*zhongziwu,* the dance of devotion) with the *Little Red Book* in their right hand each morning as they sang "The East Is Red."

At a period in Chinese history when intellectuals were scorned and titles were deemed "bourgeois" and antithetical to the principles of collectivism, Han became part of a cadre of millions of high school and university students (*zhiqing*) sent to the countryside to become "reeducated" and labor for life alongside peasants in an attempt by the Chinese government to squash "elitism" and renew the spirit of the Chinese Revolution. In 1970, after graduating from junior secondary school at the age of 16, Han was relocated to small villages in northern Hunan to till the fields and plant rice and tea as an "Educated Youth."

Han later translated his experiences as a "relocated" youth of the Lost Generation in Ma Qiao, a small village in Hunan Province, into the novel *Ma Qiao Cidan,* or *A DICTIONARY OF MAQIAO* (1996). This novel, loosely written in the form of a dictionary, is reminiscent of Samuel Johnson's famous dictionary, in that the entries, while providing insight into usage and definition of certain terms, are interspersed with the author's personal beliefs, observations, and predilections. In *A Dictionary of Maqiao,* Han gives the trappings of a formal reference work, beginning with a list of entries; his translator, Julia Lovell, even provides the reader with a pronunciation guide. However, all other similarities of dictionary conventions are abandoned. For one, the entries are not written in alphabetical order, nor are they consistent in length; while some may provide synonyms or antonyms, there is no consistent organization. Furthermore, while some entries may provide insight in usage and meaning, many are simple anecdotes, some amusing, some bizarre, and others somber and thought-provoking. Under the guise of providing definitions for terms, Han provides insight into the constrictions, atrocities, illogical ideology, propaganda and indoctrination, and harshness of existence during the Mao regime.

Han's criticism of Maoist policies, relocation, and restrictive thought control infuses several definitions. In "Tincture of Iodine," he mocks Chairman Mao's "reeducation," stating, "I was born in the city and reckoned myself really quite advanced until I went down into the countryside." He further derides Mao's assertion that rural is better and the simple are actually those better educated. The label used is "Little Brother," where Han begins by saying that "Little Brother" is really a sister, meaning women have no name or role in society and thus are unworthy of consideration. This lack of standing, he further contends, is the reason that Chinese women were degraded by having their breasts and feet bound, why they walked in "little steps, eyes downward." He segues this entry and the "namelessness" of women into an analogy of the disdain of purveyors of the Cultural Revolution for intellectuals and the danger they represented: "Thus in the Cultural Revolution, names like 'professor,' 'engineer,' 'Ph.D.,' 'artist' were expunged . . . because any form of title can provide the breeding ground for a body of thought or entire belief system." Finally, in his definition of "Streetsickness," Han shows that rural life is "superior." A Maqaio man, Benyi, loses the opportunity for gainful employment and advancement in government because of his "streetsickness." The entry supposedly shows the Chinese people's "enmity" of class and status in society.

In his definition of "Scientific," Han explains the Maoist doctrine that "science" or industrialization causes the masses to become lazy and shows that the Maqaio villagers eschew modern conveniences such as airplanes, trains, automobiles, and even technological advances in agriculture and animal husbandry. However, restrictions placed to ensure simplicity have a negative effect, demonstrated by the "Model Operas," an indication of the dearth of fine works of art, as the eight operas written during the Cultural Revolution were the only ones deemed "politically correct" enough to be performed. In "Striking Red," the author describes the absurdity of attempts to control language through the "arts propaganda teams," which performed works "sent down from above to the sound of clappers." He further mocks such Maoist terms as "checking on production," relating an incident in which the character falls into a manure pit, and euphemistically uses the phrase "checking on production" to mean "covering up difficulties," and the words "having respect" as a more genteel way of stating that one is "being fined."

Further condemnations of Mao's practices are seen in "Maple Demon," where huge, shady, beautiful ancient trees that are a part of the history and culture of the Maqaio people are sawed down, to the dismay of the people, to make seats for cultural teaching session; and in "Public Family," where land reform policies are enforced and where land ownership, family tradition, and the loss of legacy are lamented as field workers labor on the lands that their families used to own and for which they still hold attachment and fondness.

Han also speaks to the atrocities suffered by Chinese people at the hands of their own rulers and through those forces that sought to conquer them. In "Scientific" he speaks of the "red terror" of the Cultural Revolution, when many Chinese citizens perished. In "Striking Red," Han comments on the Maqaio men's prior practice of marrying pregnant women to ensure that they are fertile, only to kill or have the women abandon their firstborn offspring. Han states that the practice was discontinued once the Communist Party came into power, but that when songs such as "Farewell to the Riverbanks" were sung, "the song evoked for its female listeners the misery of earlier days." In "Dear Life" he relates the incident of a young boy who is killed by an unspent artillery shell left by the Japanese, and in "Eating" he speaks of the hunger suffered

by the peasants, who, when asked if they had eaten while visiting others, were expected to say they had done so that the person visited would not feel obligated to feed them. Finally, in "Bandit Ma" Han relates the incident of the capture of bandits (actually local freedom fighters) who were required to dig their own graves and then were machine-gunned to fall into them. This incident is reminiscent of the great purge when millions of Chinese citizens, opponents to Mao Zedong's regime as well as many intellectuals, were either imprisoned or executed.

Han also shows admiration for those who stood on principle and resisted the propaganda and constrictions of the Cultural Revolution. In "Qoqo Man" he relates the tale of Wanyu, the best singer in the province, who refused to participate in a local opera extolling simple labor and sacrifice, in which he was to sing with a "carrying pole and buckets of manure." In "House of Immortals" (also titled "Lazy Bones") Han characterizes the Taoist Ma Ming as a filthy man who subsists on bugs and raw rice, yet who is content to scrape lazily and proudly along because he refuses to work in the fields; he thus feels content in his poverty and accepts none of the fruits of others' labor.

Han is evenhanded, however, in his criticism of the disdainful attitude outsiders take to Chinese culture. In his definition of the term *Sweet*, he shows the Maqaios' confusion of the term, stating its use for everything that is good, yet showing a lack of sophistication of subtle nuances of language. This example he further elucidates to show Westerners' lack of understanding of Chinese culture and politics, noting that they are unable to differentiate between Oriental peoples of various races and cultures and deriding their belief that anything anticommunist is "sweet," even if the object of that admiration is a charlatan and a thief. In "Old Man," he also chastises those "Educated Youth" like himself who felt superior to the locals among whom they were sent to serve and who suffered from a lack of understanding of and appreciation of local culture and language. When a young woman is resentful of being called "Old Man," Han uses this example to show the lack of understanding of language and culture on the part of outsiders and the importance of respect for the elderly, stating "age should be more prized than youth."

Han spent six years in the countryside, returning to Changsha in 1976 to attend Hunan Normal University, where he studied Chinese, and Wuhan University, where he studied English. He won the National Excellent Short Story Prize in 1980 and 1981 while still an undergraduate at Hunan Normal University. Han also studied ancient Chinese culture, especially the pre-Confucian culture of Chu (present-day Hunan and Hubei provinces), Manchu, and Wu-Yue, as well as Islam.

In 1985 Han wrote the essay "Wenxue de Gen" ("The Root of Literature") and a novella, *Pa Pa Pa*. His major works include *Ba ba ba* (1993), *Moon Orchid* (1985), *Womanwomanwoman* (1985), *Deserted City* (1989); a collection of short fiction, *Homecoming and Other Stories* (1995); and the novels *Intimations* and *Leaving the World to Enter the World*, in addition to *Dictionary of Maqiao*. He has also published a Chinese translation of MILAN KUNDERA's *The UNBEARABLE LIGHTNESS OF BEING* and Fernando Pessoa's *The Book of Disquiet*.

A Dictionary of Maqiao has been named one of the top 100 works of 20th-century Chinese fiction by *Yazhou Zhoukan* (*Asian Weekly*) and awarded the China Times Prize for best novel in Taiwan. Han Shaogong has also been named the winner of the Shanghai Literary Prize and was honored with the Chevalier de L'ordre des Arts et des Lettres from the French Ministry of Culture and Communication for his contribution to Sino-French cultural relations. He is only the second Chinese writer to have won this award.

Han has lived in South China's Hainan province since 1988, serving in various capacities, including chairman of Hainan Provincial Federation of Literature and Art and editor of *Hainan Jishi Wenxue* (*Hainan Documentary Literature*) and the literary magazine *The Edge of the Sky* (*Tianya*). He has also served as editor of *Hainan Review* and *Frontiers* and as vice chairman of the Hainan Writers' Association.

BIBLIOGRAPHY

Duke, Michael S. *Worlds of Modern Chinese Fiction*. Armonk, N.Y.: Sharpe, 1991.

Han Shaogong. *A Dictionary of MaQiao*. Translated by Julia Lovell. New York: Colombia University Press, 2003.

———. "After the 'Literature of the Wounded': Local Cultures, Roots, Maturity, and Fatigue." In *Modern Chinese Writers' Self-Portrayals,* edited by Helmut Martin and Jeffrey Kinkley. Armonk, N.Y.: M. E. Sharpe, 1992.

———. *Homecoming and Other Stories.* Translated by Martha Cheung. Hong Kong: Chinese University of Hong Kong, 1992.

Xia Yun (Helen Hsia). "Zhimian beilun de Han Shaogong." ("The Frank and Unconventional Han Shaogong.") Translated by David Wakefield. *Meizhou Huaqiao riboa* (*China Daily News,* New York) February 27, 1987.

Donna Kilgore

HAN YONGUN (MANHAE) (1879–1944)

Korean novelist, poet, essayist Han Yongun—also called Manhae, meaning a myriad of seas—was one of the most beloved writers in modern Korea. He is defined as a resistance poet who established a unique world of poetry embracing religious spirituality and Korean sensibility. His writing of novels was limited. Through his diverse writings, he explored the complex truths of existence for spiritual and romantic fulfillment. Generally, his poems are characteristic of deep meditation and mystical, philosophical, and passionate love. Also, as a Buddhist philosopher, revolutionary activist, cultural critic, Han Yongun contributed to the radical reformation of Korean Buddhism, social and political revolution, the anticolonial movement, and national enlightenment. He is well known as one of 33 national leaders for "the 1919 Declaration of Korean Independence" against Japanese colonial occupation. From the 1970s, international scholarly interest in Han Yongun has steadily increased, and his writings have been translated into English and other languages.

Han was born the second child of an impoverished *yangban* (upper-class noble) family in Hongsung, South Chungcheong Province, on August 29, 1879. At age nine he mastered the liberal arts including Chinese literature and Confucianism. Young Han Yongun was inspired by his father's stories about historical heroes who saved the country in great crises. From 1896 to 1897, he joined the guerrilla army of a civil resistance against Japanese imperialism and pro-Japan bureaucrats, called the Eulmi Uibyung, which was caused by Queen Min's (Min Bi) assassination by the Japanese troops. The resistance movement failed, forcing Han into hiding and then to wander around the world. In 1905 he entered the Buddhist priesthood at the Baekdam Temple in Seorak Mountain, where he studied Western philosophers such as Rousseau, Kant, Bacon, and Descartes. Han absorbed Western modern knowledge with his adventurous spirit and combined it with Buddhism.

Han Yongun was active in the progressive reformist movement of Korean Buddhism to bring spiritual practice to modern society and to nationalize Korean Buddhism. In his controversial *Treatise on the Reformation of Korean Buddhism* (*Chosun Bulgyo Yusinron,* 1910), he argued against a traditional requirement of Buddhist monks to adhere to celibacy.

In March 1919 Korea declared its independence, and this event became one of the most memorable moments in Han Yongun's life as well as in Korean history. Japan reacted to the unarmed nationwide movement, called the March First Independence Movement, by killing or injuring more than 20,000 Koreans and jailing an additional 40,000. As a representative of the Buddhist society, Han was arrested and sentenced to three years in prison, but he was released in the fall of 1919.

Upon issuing the monthly periodical *Mindfulness* (*Yusim*) in 1918, Han devoted himself to writing, and he published various essays about spiritualism, Buddhism, Korean independence, and women's liberation; titles included "Agony and Pleasure," "Praise and Censure," and "The Self-Awakening of Women." In May 1926 Han's poetry collection *Your Silence* (*Nim ui Chimmuk*) was released. His poetic language is distinctively paradoxical and contradictory in tragic and erotic ways and evokes splendid images of Korea during the nation's hardest time—that is, the loss of sovereignty. In the title poem, "Your Silence," he succinctly declares, "*Nim* is gone. Ay, my *nim* is gone." The concept of the Korean word *nim,* translated as "love" or "beloved," is central to his poems. In his own preface, "To Readers," Han opens up dialectical possibilities of the manifold meanings of the word *nim* by defining it as not only a lover but everything missed and yearned for. For example, all creatures are the *nim* of Buddha, and philosophy is *nim* for Kant.

While many contemporary critics conservatively interpreted Han Yongun's *nim* as Buddha, homeland, or the Korean nation from a religious or nationalist perspective, modern critics object to such strict readings but pay attention to a unique union of earthly love and religious spirituality in Han's writings. Nevertheless, through his writings inspired by Gandhian civil disobedience and based on the Buddhist concept of perpetual couplets such as birth and death, separation and unification, and presence and absence, he envisioned a hopeful future for Koreans suffering under Japanese colonial rule.

From 1935 to 1936, Han serialized two novels, *Dark Wind* (*Heukpung*) and *Repentance* (*Whohoe*), in the *Choson* newspaper. These unfinished works followed his spiritual ideas. But as the newspaper was discontinued, the novels remained unfinished.

Han Yongun suffered paralysis and died on June 29, 1944. To honor his literary achievement and inherit his spirit for freedom and peace, in 1973 the Manhae prize for literature, in honor of Han Yongun, was founded by the Changbi publishers an award representing critical writers and intellectuals in Korea. In 2004, for the first time since the division of the Korean peninsula, North Korean novelist Sukjung Hong won the Manhae prize, and 1986 Nobel laureate WOLE SOYINKA was named the 2005 winner of the prize. This prestigious award demonstrates that Han Yongun holds an important place in the Korean literary world and appeals to the international aspirations of the Korean literary achievement.

BIBLIOGRAPHY

Evon, Gregory N. "Eroticism and Buddhism in Han Yongun's *Your Silence.*" *Korean Studies* 24 (2000): 25–52.

Huh Woosung. "Manhae's Understanding of Buddhism." *Korea Journal* 40, no. 2 (2000): 65–101.

———. "Gandhi and Manhae: Defending Orthodoxy, Rejecting Heterodoxy and Eastern Ways, Western Instruments." *Korea Journal* 41, no. 3 (2001): 100–124.

Lee, Peter H., ed. *A History of Korean Literature.* Cambridge: Cambridge University Press, 2003.

McCann, David R., ed. "Han Yong' Un." In *The Columbia Anthology of Modern Korean Poetry,* edited by David R. McCann, 27–36. New York: Columbia University Press, 2004.

Yom Moo-Ung. "A Study of Manhae Han Yong-un." *Korea Journal* 39, no. 4 (1999): 90–117.

Heejung Cha

HARP AND THE SHADOW, THE (EL ARPA Y LA SOMBRA) Alejo Carpentier (1979)

The Harp and the Shadow (1979) is the fifth novel by Cuban writer Alejo Carpentier (1904–80). Carpentier, a master of the modern Latin American novel, is credited with coining the term *magic realism*. As implied by its title, the novel explores the darkness that often resides beneath a glorious and beautiful facade. Carpentier identifies this duality in the figure of Christopher Columbus, who reveals his sinister side in a deathbed monologue. Through integrating historical, mythic, and fictional material, Carpentier's narrative moves from a valorous and altruistic depiction of Columbus ("the Harp") to an egotistical and duplicitous one ("the Shadow"). Written during a time when cancer was spreading throughout Carpentier's body, *The Harp and the Shadow* is a poignant examination of the distortions to which worldly works are subject after the death of their creator.

The novel takes as its starting point the prospect of Christopher Columbus's saintly canonization. In the opening chapter, Pius XI reflects upon his long-standing conviction that "the perfect way to join together the Christian faithful of the old and new worlds . . . was to find a saint whose fame was unlimited, incontrovertible, a saint of planetary wingspan, a saint so enormous, even larger than the Colossus of Rhodes." The pope is also compelled by the political advantages that signing such a decree would bring to his papacy. But while Columbus's achievements seem to symbolize Catholicism's global reach and resonance, the explorer's less laudable acts (allegedly including adultery, enslavement, and fraud) would seem to contraindicate sainthood. These qualities begin to emerge in the second chapter of the novel, where a dying Columbus recalls his voyages to the Americas. He confesses to profound greed, referring to a section in his diaries where the word *gold* appears more than 200 times, while God is mentioned only 14 times. Columbus speaks at length about his sexual conquests, his unbridled lust for glory, and the "deceptions and intrigues [he] practiced for years and years, trying to gain the favor of the princes of the earth, hiding the real truth behind feigned truths, citing authority for my claims with allusions expertly selected from the Writings."

Columbus admits that when his professed treasures failed to materialize in the New World, he "requested license for the slave trade." At the end of the novel, the ghost of Columbus witnesses the investigation into his canonization, at which the Catholic ministers find him to be unworthy of sainthood. With the canonization rejected, Columbus's ghost is left to wander the earth aimlessly, repeatedly lamenting, "They screwed me."

Historical accuracy in *The Harp and the Shadow* is subordinated to the demands of characterization and the development of the novel's larger themes—namely, the deceptiveness of veneers and the addictive nature of fame. In his reconstruction of Columbus's undertakings, Carpentier often swerves from the historical record. The explorer's affair with Queen Isabella, for example, is unsubstantiated in the historical literature; the queen's apparent sexual motivation for funding Columbus's voyages is particularly suspect. Although in itself a probable embellishment, the erotic element introduced by Carpentier may be read as a metaphor for Columbus's general drive to conquer territory at whatever cost—financial, ethical, or otherwise. "I penetrated them all," boasts Columbus after cataloguing his lovers, but the statement could equally be applied to the lands and cultures he invaded. Furthermore, Carpentier's distortion of the truth emulates Columbus's own fabrications; the explorer admits: "I speak of gold mines where I know of none. I speak of pearls, many pearls, merely because I see some mussels that 'signal their presence.'" When arguing for enslavement, Columbus insists that the Indians are docile and obedient, but when required to explain his severe disciplinary methods, Columbus describes the slaves as ferocious cannibals. Indeed, Columbus claims different things depending upon his objectives—and Carpentier, in his historiography, exercises similar liberties.

Carpentier's blend of fact and fiction reflects a (quintessentially postmodern) suspicion of historical "truths." This suspicion is implied in *The Harp and the Shadow* when Pius XI unwisely attributes infallibility to one biographer's account of Columbus; he thinks, "Count Roselly of Lorgues could not have been mistaken. He was a scrupulous, dedicated historian, completely trustworthy; and he had maintained that the great mariner had lived his entire life with an invisible halo over his head." But as literary critic Hayden White has argued, "To historicize is to mythologize. History is never history of, it is always history for. It is not only history for in the sense of being written with some ideological aim in view, but also history for in the sense of being written for a specific social group or public." By drawing from sources that are generally excluded from officially sanctioned representations of the past—such as folklore, fable, autobiography and psychological speculation—Carpentier casts historical scholarship as but one of many lenses through which the past can be studied.

In *The Conquest of America,* Tvzetan Torodov asserts, "We are all direct descendants of Columbus." Although the explorer's cultural and geographical legacies are profound, the figure of Columbus also exemplifies the ambitious drives to which all people are, to varying degrees, susceptible. It is this aspect—Columbus as monomaniacal "wielder of illusions"—that renders the man particularly evocative as a literary subject. In *The Harp and the Shadow,* Carpentier describes Columbus "pursuing a country never found that fades away like a castle of enchantments . . . [following] vapors, seeing things that never become intelligible, comparable, explicable, in the language of the Odyssey or in the language of Genesis." Though on an epic scale, Columbus's struggles and self-deceptions are universal ones, encoded again in the "mystical vision" that the young Pius XI contemplates while crossing the Chilean plains; he recalls "an allegory in which a man is placed in a corridor without beginning or end and spends years trying, through science and learning, to push back the enclosing walls that limit his vision; gradually he succeeds, gradually he makes them recede, but no matter how far he pushes them, he can never manage to destroy them."

BIBLIOGRAPHY

Gonzalez Echevarria, Roberto. *Alejo Carpentier: The Pilgrim at Home.* Ithaca, N.Y.: Cornell University Press, 1977.

Harvey, Sally. *Carpentier's Proustian Fiction: The Influence of Marcel Proust on Alejo Carpentier.* London: Tamesis, 1994.

Pancrazio, James J. *The Logic of Fetishism: Alejo Carpentier and the Cuban Tradition.* Lewisburg, Pa.: Bucknell University Press, 2004.

Shaw, Donald Leslie. *Alejo Carpentier.* Boston: Twayne Publishers, 1985.

Tulsay, Bobs M. *Alejo Carpentier: A Comprehensive Study.* Vaencia and Chapel Hill, N.C.: Albatros Hispanófila, 1982.

Kiki Benzon

HAŠEK, JAROSLAV (1883–1923) *Czech essayist, novelist, short story writer* Jaroslav Hašek, born in Prague, a city in the Bohemian region of Austria-Hungary, was an influential and noted Czech novelist, humorist, and journalist. Hašek and FRANZ KAFKA were considered the most noted literary figures in Prague during their lifetimes. The Czech-born author is perhaps best known for his satiric masterpiece *The GOOD SOLDIER SCHWEIK.*

Growing up with an alcoholic father, the young Jaroslav lived in relative poverty, which was made worse by the early death of his father Josef, a failed high school teacher, when the boy was 13 years of age. Although he showed academic potential, the young Hašek dropped out of school and took a job with a pharmacist. He attended the Prague Commercial Academy and graduated at the age of 19. He held a number of short-lived jobs over the next several years and later set out on an extended tour of central Europe. Many of his adventures were published as short humorous stories. He would go on to publish more than 1,500 articles and short works. Because of the turbulent political situation, many of these writings were published under one of his more than 100 pseudonyms.

From 1904 to 1907, Hašek worked for several anarchist papers, including *Olmadina* (The younger generation). His involvement with the movement ended after his arrest at a demonstration. For the next few years, he supported himself with such odd jobs as buying and selling dogs. He was briefly married to Jarmila Majerová, but he left his wife shortly after the birth of their son Richard.

Hašek's writing reveals an opposition to the elite position of writers. He wrote in Czech rather than the German language favored by the upper class. His writing was marked by realistic dialogue, long stories, and rambling sentences. The author sought to render a more realistic portrayal of life by focusing on everyday people in everyday locations.

In his life and writing, Hašek opposed the monarchy, the Catholic Church, the military, and almost all other organized structures. As an editor for *Svet Zvírat* (The world of animals), he showed much evidence of the antiestablishment views that characterized his career. He made false additions to articles and published articles about such imaginary animals as werewolves. These mischievous antics continued throughout his journalistic career. In his biography of Hašek, Václav Menger tells of a dispute involving Hašek lasting for 14 issues of a magazine. The debate became so heated that the editors feared lawsuits. In the end, it was discovered that Hašek had been writing both sides of the argument.

His tricks were not limited to his writing. In 1911 Hašek became politically active by founding a party to parody Austria-Hungary's other political groups. With the Party of Moderate Progress Within the Limits of the Law, Hašek gained a few dozen write-in votes for a seat in parliament. This movement later became a cabaret act of the same name, highlighting Hašek's policy of combining life and art in the surrealist fashion.

In February 1911 an event occurred that has been frequently debated. Late at night, a man discovered Hašek allegedly trying to climb over the guardrail of a bridge. Believing this to be a suicide attempt, he held the author back and alerted the authorities. Hašek was placed in an asylum for observation. He later claimed to simply be looking at the river, but critics have disagreed over whether this was a suicide attempt, a publicity stunt, or simply another of his hoaxes.

Much of Hašek's life is reflected in his writings, most notably in his unfinished masterpiece, *The Good Soldier Schweik*. Like Schweik (alternately translated as Svejk), Hašek served in the 91st regiment at České Budějovice and Galicia. After only 11 days, however, he was taken prisoner by Russian soldiers. As a prisoner of war in Russia, he became a supporter of the Bolsheviks following the October Revolution. He supported the newly formed Czech Legion in Russia, working as a recruiting agent in the fight against Austria-Hungary. Following the war, he returned to what had become Czechoslovakia to work with the Social Democrats.

Hašek was not welcomed back by many of his former friends, who were upset by his involvement with the Bolsheviks. He spent his few remaining years with his second wife, Aleksandra Lvova, whom he married without having divorced Jarmila. He died of heart failure on January 3, 1923, and his funeral was attended by his few remaining friends and his son Richard.

BIBLIOGRAPHY

Frynta, Emanuel. *Hasek: The Creator of Schweik.* Translated by Jean Layton and George Theiner. Prague: Artia, 1965.

Parrot, Cecil. *The Bad Bohemian: The Life of Jaroslav Hasek, Creator of* The Good Soldier Svejk. New York: Bodley Head, 1978.

———. *Jaroslav Hasek: A Study of "Svejk" and the Short Stories.* Cambridge: Cambridge University Press, 1982.

Kevin Hogg

HATCHET, THE (BALTAGUL) MIHAIL SADOVEANU (1930)

Romanian novelist MIHAIL SADOVEANU's *The Hatchet* is the most widely translated Romanian novel, except perhaps for MIRCEA ELIADE's works, though the latter's audience was tremendously increased by the author spending most of his life in the Western world and by his outstanding career as a historian of religion. Sadoveanu (1880–1961), however, never left Romania but for short periods of time. *The Hatchet*'s international fame started as early as 1936 in France and Germany, continuing with the Czech version two years later, followed by the Finnish translation in 1944 and by the Italian edition in 1945. The Communist regime, which came to power in Romania after World War II, strongly promoted the writer and his books, especially those works that contributed to the reenactment of an heroic and idealized national past. Thus, *The Hatchet* was published in translation even in such far-reaching places as Shanghai (1957), Tehran (1958), and Damascus (1964), which ensured the author a widespread world audience.

The plot, inspired by the everyday life of rural Moldavia (the eastern region of current Romania, where Sadoveanu was born and lived), is quite simple and reworks old folklore legends and ballads. However, the covert cultural code of the novel goes further back in time and space, reiterating an archaic Egyptian fertility rite. Sadoveanu was already a high-ranking Freemason (grade 33) when he wrote this novel; accordingly, *The*

Hatchet's literary composition combines two complementary levels of cultural codes and symbols. The manifest, so-called exoteric cultural code evokes the world of some well-known Romanian myths and legends, especially that of the ballad *Miorita* (*The Little Sheep*), which tells the hypothetical story of a crime committed among the shepherds. One of the herdsmen is informed by a prescient sheep that he is going to be murdered by his two companions, and the ballad goes on with the imaginative cosmic projection of the shepherd's death, constructed by himself. The would-be victim does nothing to prevent the murder; on the contrary, he makes all the imaginative arrangements for the time he will be killed and projects into cosmic myths and rituals all the symbols of his funeral, asking the sheep to carry out the details of his burial.

The ballad *Miorita* is the central legend of Romanian ontology: Hundreds of writers, philosophers, and artists have tried to capture its inner wisdom concerning the nature of human being and existence. It has been interpreted as the textual description of an archaic rite of passage and as the ultimate luminous stage in an ontological tragedy in which a man is facing the call of death and giving vent to his happiness at leaving his transitional earthly incarnation in order to regain the pure wholeness of the cosmos. Another famous interpretation turns the ballad into the main key to understanding the psychological drama of the Romanian people: Its persistence throughout centuries is attributed to an archaic capacity to avoid the traps of history by pessimistically "leaping out of time" into imagination or myth whenever the people face a challenge or catastrophe.

Mihail Sadoveanu's personal artistic ideology, based on luminous reenactments of the heroic past (especially that of the Moldavian Renaissance of the 15th century), made him the best candidate for the fictional rewriting of *Miorita*. At its overt level, the plot of *The Hatchet* is indeed in analogical synchronicity with that of the ballad: Vitoria Lipan, a simple wife of a proud and distinguished shepherd, is disturbed by the long and unexpected absence of her husband and suspects that he has been murdered. Long journeys are not uncommon among the shepherds, so it seems there is no need to worry, but Vitoria "reads" the secret signs of nature and of her soul and concludes that her husband lies dead and unburied somewhere along his pasture trails. Determined to find her husband, she sets out together with her son on a long journey and finally comes across his body, his bones scattered all over the place. The most intense psychological fragment of the text reenacts the tragedy of the mourning *mater dolorosa* who carefully gathers the bones and prepares them for the burial; she then identifies the murderer who knocked down her husband with a hatchet in order to rob him of his sheep.

Like many other novels written by Sadoveanu, *The Hatchet* is also an initiation rite whose plot revolves around the story of a master and his disciple. Through her painful descent into death, the mother teaches her son to "read" the archaic "signs" of eternity, encrypted in myths, rituals, and symbols, and to distrust the empiric evidence of everyday life. The subtle counterpoint of the two levels of justice presented in the novel serves the same aim of contrasting eternity with fleeting time.

Vitoria Lipan "feels" that her husband is dead, and she is almost certain about it, but the human authorities that represent earthly justice are reluctant to accept her allegations, since it not uncommon among the shepherds to stay away from home for unpredictable periods of time. The suspecting wife chooses the cosmic justice of immemorial customs and rituals. Although she does not know exactly where her husband pastures his herds, she sets out on the trails of her ancestors, the only paths leading to the truth. Strolling from village to village, on archaic pathways whose knowledge she has inherited from her ancestors, Vitoria Lipan disregards the authorities and completes the detective work by herself. She is guided only by the secret "signs," symbols, and rituals of an organic wisdom shared exclusively by the peasantry.

The deepest, must esoteric level of the work combines two complementary sets of symbols: one is taken from the *mater dolorosa* complex of Christianity, while the other, even more basic, comes from the classic Egyptian Isis-Osiris fertility myth. The secret "key" lies both in *The Hatchet*'s overall narrative structure and in the aforementioned mourning scene, as the Romanian essay writer Alexandru Paleologu shows in a brilliant study of Sadoveanu's multilevel narrative, published in 1978.

Another clue is the protagonist's name: *Vitoria* is, of course, the Moldavian rural equivalent for "Victoria"; while *Lipan* designates a fish, the grayling, which lives in the same waters as the trout. Leaving all the biological details aside, the complete name suggests the "victor over the waters," which leads both to the central fishing symbols of Christianity and to the tragic destiny of the mourning Egyptian goddess Isis, who sets out to search for the body of her husband and brother Osiris. She finds the body in the Nile delta and resurrects it by carefully gathering the bones together. These symbols are intertwined with a plot evidently taken from *Miorita* and with a profusion of words and gestures inspired by the archaic Moldavian countryside. By mixing analogical cultural elements taken from mythical complexes, which do not usually communicate, Sadoveanu suggests the existence of a universal, unique, synthesizing wisdom, whose access is reserved only for the initiates.

BIBLIOGRAPHY
Sadoveanu, Mihail. *The Hatchet.* Translated by Eugenia Farca. New York: Columbia University Press, 1991.

Stefan Borbély

HEDAYAT, SADEQ (SADEGH HEDAYAT)
(1903–1951) *Iranian novelist, short story writer*
Sadeq Hedayat is one of the most famous Iranian writers of the 20th century. He was born in Tehran in 1903 into an old aristocratic family widely known for their literary and political affiliations. His great-grandfather was Reza Qoli Khan, famous as a poet and historian in the 19th century. Hedayat's life spans the first half of 20th-century Iran—the upheavals of initiating a constitution for the country, the change of one dynasty into another, and the effects of the two world wars in every aspect of Iranian life.

Sadeq Hedayat is best known for his short but intense novel *The BLIND OWL* (*Buf-e Kur,* 1931), which has been translated into many languages. He also wrote one play, two historical dramas, and many short stories, and translated the works of many European writers into Persian. Hedayat was instrumental in the revival of Persian folklore studies. He published *Owsaneh* (folk

tales and popular proverbs) and *Nayrangestan* (Persian folklore) in 1933.

Sadeq Hedayat attended Elmiyeh School in Tehran when he was six years old; later he was sent to Dar al-Fonun, the first Iranian polytechnic school established in the 19th century in Iran. The graduates of this school were usually sent to Europe on a grant to study modern arts and sciences so that on their return they would introduce these subjects in Iran. At the age of 15 Hedayat suffered from a severe eye problem and had to postpone his education. In 1919 he was sent to École St-Louis, a French missionary school in Tehran, where he was not an outstanding student but read Persian and French literature avidly. In 1921, when he was 18 years old, he published his edition of Omar Khayyam's quatrains; this book shows the scope of his knowledge of classical Persian poetry as well as Arabic and European literature.

Hedayat was sent to Europe to study in 1925. However, he could not conform to academic study or, later on, to a safe and routine job. As a result, he left Ghent, his first place of education, and moved first to Paris, then to Reims, to Besancon, and back to Paris, changing his field of study several times before finally giving up education altogether. Despondent, he attempted suicide by jumping into the River Marne but was saved by a young man. He returned to Tehran in 1930.

Hedayat was very much interested in pre-Islamic Persian literature and had a strong dislike for Islamic and Arabic influences in Persian culture and civilization. His dislike is displayed in his satirical portrayal of many of the characters in his short stories and novellas such as *Alaviyeh Khanom* (1933), *Haji Aqa* (1945), and *The Pearl Cannon* (*Tup-e Murvari,* 1947). He translated many stories from European writers such as Arthur Schnitzler, Alexandre Lange Kielland, Anton Chekhov, Gaston Cherau, FRANZ KAFKA, and JEAN-PAUL SARTRE, stories that were published in Persian magazines. He also wrote short stories in French, including "Sampingue" and "Lunatique."

Hedayat was a vegetarian from his youth and even wrote a book entitled *The Benefits of Vegetarianism* in Berlin in 1927. All through his life he harbored a wry sense of humor toward everything and everyone, which is displayed in most of his works.

In 1936, at the invitation of a friend, Hedayat went to India and studied Pahlavi, an ancient Persian language. He translated into Persian several Pahlavi texts such as *Karnameh Ardeshir-e Babakan* (the Record of Ardeshir-e Babakan), and *Gojasteh Abalish* (Abalish the damned). It was in Bombay that he wrote the final draft of *The Blind Owl* (*Buf-e Kur*). Fifty copies of this novel were printed and sent to his friends in Europe. While in India he also wrote several short stories.

Hedayat came back to Iran in 1937, and after working for a construction company and Bank Melli, he joined the State Office of Music and became the editor of *Music Magazine,* to which he contributed several articles. However, the conditions in Iran were becoming more and more repressive, and Hedayat became so frustrated by the turn of the political events that he left for Paris again in 1950 with the hope finding a job and writing. But with no job and no money and not being able to write as he wanted, he committed suicide in April 1951. He was buried in Père Lachaise Cemetery in Paris.

Undoubtedly Hedayat has had a great and lasting impact on fiction in Iran. His realism and social criticism in his multifaceted writings does not spare any specific group, and the edge of his satire is focused on the middle and lower middle classes. He was one of the few writers of his time who broke away from the traditional uses of prose and poetry and used a realistic approach in his fiction.

Though Hedayat was not recognized in his lifetime, his posthumous success was monumental. Numerous books and hundreds of articles have been written about Hedayat and his works. Mostafa Farzaneh's *Acquaintance with Sadeq Hedayat* (*Ashna'i ba Sadeq Hedayat,* Paris, 1988) in two volumes contains useful information and a personal point of view. Homa Katouzian's *Sadeq Hedayat: The Life and Legend of an Iranian Writer* is a very valuable text, as it provides the social and literary background of the first half of the 20th century. In 2003 Sadeq Hedayat Centenary Conference took place at Oxford University. There is an annual literary award given in his honor in Iran.

BIBLIOGRAPHY

Ghanoonparvar, M. R. *In a Persian Mirror: Images of the West and Westerners in Iranian Fiction.* Austin: University of Texas Press, 1993.

Katouzian, Homa. *Sadeq Hedaya: The Life and Legend of an Iranian Writer.* London: I. B. Tauris, 2002.

Talattof, Kamran. *The Politics of Writing in Iran, A History of Modern Persian Literature.* Syracuse, N.Y.: Syracuse University Press, 2000.

Farideh Pourgiv

HESSE, HERMANN (1877–1962) *German novelist, poet*

The 1946 Nobel Prize laureate, German-Swiss prose writer, poet, and painter Hermann Hesse represented the European postromantic, decadent modernism of the first half of the 20th century. Hesse developed a warm friendship with THOMAS MANN, whose literary themes he partially shared, especially those concerning the relation between the sound, solid order of the bourgeoisie as opposed to the solitary, bohemian, exuberant sensuality of the artist. Hesse was also attracted by the Oriental way of life and by Buddhist mysticism, which he came to know both through the personal remembrances of his family, some of its members having served as missionaries in India, and from a personal journey to Sri Lanka and Indonesia, undertaken in 1911 together with his friend, painter Hans Sturzenegger from Schaffhausen. (Details about the writer's life and work can be found in Gunther H. Gottschalk's excellent *Hermann Hesse Project,* run since 1996 at the University of California, Santa Barbara: www.gss.ucsb.edu/projects/Hesse.)

Hermann Hesse turned his traveling experience into a diary, published in 1913 as *From India* (*Aus Indien*) and into a famous novel, *SIDDHARTHA,* published in 1923 (the English translation did not appear until 1951). Oriental motifs are ubiquitous in his work, as he considered that Oriental plenitude and serenity can constitute an antidote to gloomy, modernist, European self-isolation and alienation. Being rebellious and rather neurotic, his characteristic inconsistency drew him into several deep psychotic crises, such as repeated conflicts with his parents, an escape from school (depicted in a short story, "Beneath the Wheel" ["Unterm Rad," 1906]), an early suicide attempt in 1892, as well as several internships in mental institutions, where he also learned Jungian psychoanalysis.

In order to compensate for his personal sensitive fragility, Hesse tried to protect himself by continuously building up an Oriental simplicity around him, in the midst of a raging, violently political Europe. He left Germany for Switzerland in 1912 (following the example of his obsessive model, the philosopher Friedrich Nietzsche); gave up German citizenship in 1923; took up gardening and painting; settled in tiny villages like Gaienhofen (together with his first wife, photographer Maria Bernoulli, a neurotic herself); and finally moved to Montagnola, in southern Switzerland, where he tried to integrate into the organic mildness of everyday peasant life, until his death in 1962. Although he firmly shared the belief that artists should live a marginal and Bohemian life, outside political and social constraints, his little essay "Oh Friends, Not These Tones! ("O Freunde, nicht diese Töne!"), published in the November 3, 1914, issue of the *Neue Zurcher Zeitung,* was widely read as a warning against public hatred and German nationalism on the threshold of World War I. During the war, Hesse helped refugees and committed himself to humanitarian work; later on, when the Nazis came to power in Germany, he—as "first voluntary émigré"—also helped Thomas Mann and other refugees to find their way to freedom.

Hesse was obsessed by his former countryman Nietzsche, whose incandescent style he took up in an ardent manifesto saluting the end of the World War I and the coming of a "new era," *Zarathustra's Return. A Word to the German Youth* (*Zarathustra's Widerkehr. Ein Wort an die Deutsche Jugend,* 1919–1920), the first edition of which was published anonymously. Hesse turned Nietzsche's perception of the complementary ambivalence of the "Apollonian" form and "Dionysian" energy into the dual typology of the antithetical protagonists of his novels *DEMIAN* (1919; English translation 1923), *Klingsor's Last Summer* (*Klingsors letzter Sommer,* 1920), *NARCISSUS AND GOLDMUND* (*Narziss und Goldmund,* 1930, also known as *Death and the Lover*). These works also exhibit the novelist's vivid interest in Carl Jung's analytical psychology. As the author pointed out in a later recollection, the plot in *Demian* was meant to approximate the classical individuation process. Goldmund's sunny career outside the monastery in *Narcissus and Goldmund* also resembles the individuation frame by adding to the basic psychological complex the distinct traits of a maternal mythology,

whose profound explanation can also be detected in Hesse's early childhood trauma.

Hesse came across Jungian psychoanalysis in May 1916, when he was treated for a nervous breakdown in a private sanatorium near Lucerne. There he met a young physician, J. B. Lang, who made a great impression on him by treating his illness with unorthodox, Jungian methods, based on the hermeneutic of profound cultural symbols and archetypes. Dr. Lang was also the man who urged Hesse to "act out" his fears and complexes by taking up painting. The writer remained faithful to this "therapy" by completing more than 3,500 oil paintings and drawings, some of them now housed in the Hermann Hesse Museum in Montagnola.

A sample of this prestigious collection was brought to the United States in 1999 by the Oglethorpe University Museum. The style of Hesse's paintings shows colorful, mild (not radical) expressionist traces, which also reflect the style of Klingsor, the painter from the novella *Klingsor's Last Summer.* The color palette of these paintings also evinces sensual chaos and mental exuberance, bordering on a sense of death and extinction. Painting a wild, Dionysian self-portrait on the brink of his death, Klingsor deliberately turns the dreamy surface of his forms and colors into a destructive, elementary, "artistic" energy, inspired by demonic forces surging from the underworld. Drawing on Nietzsche's philosophical text *The Birth of Tragedy* (1871–72), itself inspired by Arthur Schopenhauer's *The World as Will and Representation* (1816), the topic of artistic creation is conceived as a decadent, self-destructive process—a theme that provides the in-depth structure of Thomas Mann's major novels. Hesse's flamboyant protagonist is, in Nietzsche's specific terms, a Dionysian, exuberant "mid-day man," and a sun worshipper who drives his art beyond form, into torment and extinction.

Hesse's characters are primarily reclusive figures who enjoy shadowy places, in spite of their precious bohemian solitude, which drives them out of towns and houses and into the open spaces of the forest and the plain. As a consequence, the sun is mostly associated in his writings with destructive exuberance. For example, after leaving the spiritual enclave of Castalia, Josef Knecht, the master of *The GLASS BEAD GAME, (Das*

Glasperlenspiel, 1943; English translation 1957), is subdued by the power of the rising sun.

Hermann Hesse's typical hero is the antibourgeois, bohemian, anarchist artist and wanderer, illustrated in the early novel *Peter Camenzind* (1904), in *Knulp* (1915), and particularly in STEPPENWOLF (*Der Steppenwolf,* 1927; English translation 1929). *Steppenwolf* constituted one of the main "bibles" of the young counterculture movement of the 1960s in the United States and Western Europe. A famous Californian rock group, Sparrow, changed its name to Steppenwolf; their song *Born to Be Wild,* released in 1968, is featured in the cult film *Easy Rider* (1969). Harry Haller, the novel's social outcast protagonist, attracted the young rebels of the 1960s precisely because of his split, half-male, half-female personality, which he transcends by means of love and magic. Numerous hippies of the sixties considered themselves "steppenwolves" in their urge for transgressing social order and discipline. They also loved Harry Haller because of his refusal to take up adult values and his desire to remain a paradoxically immature child of the universe. Many characters depicted in Hesse's great novels bear childish traces, recalling Nietzsche's famous Zarathustra and his teachings. The utopian province of Castalia, which hosts the elite fraternity of the glass bead game players, is also depicted as a "childish" spiritual enclave, surrounded by the "mature" forces of politics and history.

The artist as a melancholic, bohemian social outcast obsessed Hesse from the beginning of his literary career. Furthermore, this image brought into his stories the structural opposition between the sterile fixity of the social settler, such as the family man, the bourgeois or the philistine, and the exuberant, spiritual richness of the wanderer. Hesse also shared with Nietzsche and Mann the attraction toward the "artistic," brilliant, Italian, or Mediterranean South as a counterpart to the foggy, gloomy German North. In this antithesis, which explains many characteristics of his protagonists, the German North plays the role of the structuring, restrictive form, while the Mediterranean South engages the destructive, Dionysian energies of the underworld, similar to what happens in Mann's DEATH IN VENICE.

This structural opposition is used by Hesse for the first time in his early novel *Knulp,* whose protagonist is an elderly social outlaw. Knulp wanders back to his place of birth in order to find a tranquil passage to death and reintegration into the simple rhythms of nature. Old Knulp has always been a bohemian wanderer who, despite his shabby attire and outworn shoes, seems endowed with an outstanding rhetorical style and human distinction. In his youth, Knulp left behind his northern place of birth in order to travel south in search of ecstatic artistry. He has never had a job or a house of his own, but has always managed to please everybody because he is capable of relieving people from their sorrows, pains, and unpleasant thoughts.

According to an ancient, classical definition, used among others by the Greek Athenaios in his *Deipnosophistai* (third century A.D.), Knulp could be seen as a charming parasite, a social magician. Everywhere he stops, he is able to act as the perfect mirror of the others. Happily socializing with Knulp, who appears to know every person he meets in his Bohemian wanderings, people feel their life turning into a feast. Accordingly, men, women, and children (animals as well) experience enthusiasm when he shows up and treat him well, urging him to stay as long as he desires. Knulp is Nietzsche's perfect "mid-day man," a social charmer without shadows, which means both social sincerity and the absence of sufferance and dark interiority. Hesse said about *Knulp* and the earlier *Peter Camenzind* that they both embody the antidecadent figure of the "natural man" espoused by Jean-Jacques Rousseau. Due to his playful serenity, Knulp also appears—in Nietzsche's terms—as an "anti-Christ" figure, rather similar to Dionysus, the eternal *xénos* (alien) and wanderer. The last chapters of the novel openly depict Knulp as God's favorite son on his way up to heaven, where he hopes that Good Old Father will save him from heavy burdens, as a reward for making people's lives on Earth easier.

The romantic antithesis between natural, organic existence and social alienation already marked Hesse's first success story, *Peter Camenzind* (1904), a bildungsroman whose protagonist is the offspring of an isolated, archaic community (Nimikon), which lives in timeless harmony with nature somewhere at an extremely high altitude in the Alps. Peter grows up with the creed that there can be no essential difference between persons, flowers, and trees, since all of these share the spiritual plenitude of the universe. While growing up, Peter's archaic wisdom turns into a humanitarian ideology based on altruism and simplicity. He develops a vivid cult for Saint Francis of Assisi, praises Buddha's nirvana and Leo Tolstoy's ascetic retirement from life, and sings exuberant hymns to a generic divinity called Dionysus-Hermes-Eros, which he finds in wine and in his love for an aged, enigmatic painter, Erminia Aglietti.

Traveling down to "civilization" (in his particular case, Florence and Italy, the hotbed of the European bourgeoisie), Peter experiences—similar to what occurs in RAINER MARIA RILKE's *The NOTEBOOKS OF MALTE LAURIDS BRIGGE*—the complexity of modern life. He eventually becomes contaminated by it as he becomes a skilled journalist and gets to know Paris, a city he perceives as the quintessence of human inconsistency. Nevertheless, these tribulations cannot alienate Peter's natural and harmonious character inherited from his mountaineer ancestors. Despite his bitter experiences, he remains related to the destructive effect of civilization, a positive person who is unharmed by chaotic challenges and negativities. Hesse depicts him as a new Zarathustra, one who fulfils his call by retreating into his high-altitude native village, where he manages an inn he used to patronize when his father was alive. It is there that he regains the simple certainties of the cosmic natural energies connecting him to eternity.

Following Hesse's 1916 nervous breakdown, which entailed his confinement to a mental sanatorium after his father's sudden death, the writer's style and his character presentation gradually changed and diversified. The most relevant new topic was the Faustian, elementary darkness of the novel *Demian* (1919), articulated on the binary personality structure of the split man or double figure (doppelgänger)—another theme derived from Nietzsche. The cataclysm of World War I and the relief that accompanied its conclusion drew Hesse into the frantic conviction that great historical anomalies can only be avoided if humanity generates a superior spiritual elite, comprising thinkers and artists who can represent a standard for the others and relegate malignity beyond the margins of a balanced, mutual social understanding. Hesse considered that each person should realize his individuation, not by fighting against but by integrating the dark energies of his personality and transforming the inner completion of his soul into a socially accepted moral norm. Light and darkness, considered as the intertwined molds of a split soul, will mark Hesse's spiritual formula well beyond the novels *Steppenwolf* and *Narcissus and Goldmund*. They would become associated with another complementary dichotomy: the antithetical formative influence of the father and the mother, which was typical of the expressionist categories adopted by Hesse's style at that time.

Embroiled in this conflictual relationship, which also underlies Thomas Mann's works (*BUDDENBROOKS, Tristan, Tonio Kröger, DEATH IN VENICE,* and so on), the figure of the father embodies the structuring force that makes things stay within the form. Motherhood, on the other hand, is associated with the sensual, dispersive, exuberant drive of artistry. German expressionism shares Schopenhauer's and Nietzsche's belief in the existence of a dark, elementary energy that comes to the surface in order to guide the artist toward extinction and the underworld. According to this formula, each artist belongs primarily to a dark, formative "Urmutter" (primeval God-Mother), whose energies flow into each creation, whatever its style or form of expression. As such, each artist is, metaphysically speaking, a "double" figure (doppelgänger), since his or her personality combines the structuring, paternal consistency of the form and the opposite, maternal call of the primal underworld.

This dichotomy brings into Hesse's work a cherished theme, that of "going beyond" one's limits and personality, of "surpassing" the inner separation of the soul through integration. In *Narcissus and Goldmund,* young Goldmund is brought to a monastery by his oppressive father in order to give the young man instruction and to remove the sensual, artistic remembrance of an "indecent" mother from his memory. Put into the care of Narcissus, a fatherly figure and one of the young masters of the monastery, Goldmund ends up in a rebellion against the masters. He leaves the monastery (a similar gesture to Hesse's own departure from the theological seminary in Maulbronn), becomes an artist and a lover, and thus actualizes the repressed, maternal energies of his being. It is therefore not surprising to learn that in each new girl he meets, in each new clay figure he molds, and even in the figure of the Virgin Mary, what he discovers is the immersed image of a mother archetype, calling him from beneath, toward exuberance and extinction.

The revolt against the father figure (which can be also Gautama Buddha and his classical teaching) represents a main topic of *Siddhartha* (English translation 1951). Hermann Hesse's Indian story is based on the paradoxical spiritual evolution of a young Buddhist Brahmin. Siddhartha is, to a certain extent, an anti-Buddha, because Hesse's protagonist reverses the classical story of the historical Gautama Buddha who lived in the sixth century B.C. According to the standard Indian legend, the founding master of Buddhism got the name Siddhartha at birth (Gautama was his family name) and became Buddha Shakyamuni ("the sage of the Shakya clan") through a spiritual rebirth after several years of asceticism and contemplation. He reached perfection through severe fasting and contemplation and managed to attain complete spiritual insight, which yielded to him a sense of the self's pure concentration and the possibility of transcendence toward the heavenly beauty of Nirvana.

Hesse's unorthodox plot starts with the revolt of the young Siddhartha against his condition as a Brahmin. He feels that the doctrine of sacrifice, which he learns as a very promising future Brahmin, cannot help self-exploration, since it leaves aside the very idea of asceticism, which is inner peace and self-understanding. In order to explore his soul, Siddhartha leaves his father's house and joins the tribe of the wandering ascetics called *samanas,* who live in the forest and engage in relentless reclusion and concentration. Followed by his friend Govinda, and meeting eventually the great Gautama Buddha, who teaches in a nearby region, Siddhartha achieves a highly spiritual detachment. But he also experiences the paradoxical revelation that by yielding to extreme asceticism and mortification, he risks ending up in self-alienation, given the gap that may widen between himself and the surrounding world.

To compensate for his estrangement, Siddhartha decides to leave the *samanas* behind and to make a step toward the sensual beauties of everyday life. By doing this he rediscovers many empirical details he has ignored so far: the vivid colors of nature, people's faces and their smell, the unpredictable metamorphoses of material beings, and, of course, love. Lured by a beautiful girl, he feels sensual rejuvenation in spite of his long years of mortification. Reaching a town, he meets an attractive courtesan, Kamala, who initiates him into the art of sexuality. In order to please her with precious gifts, he becomes a successful merchant under the guidance of an older tradesman, Kamaswami, but he practices trade with detachment and joy, more as an art than as a way of living. In spite of his success as a merchant, he finally decides to leave Kamala and Kamaswami, seeking to join his old friend Vasudeva on the banks of a huge river and become a humble ferryman.

The characters and situations of the novel are structured according to well-defined old Buddhist realities and symbols. Kamala, the courtesan, symbolizes the earthly world as illusion, and Samsara represents the endless flow of births and reincarnations. According to the old Hindu teaching, due to the cumulative effect of one's actions in his former lives (called *karma*), the soul is condemned to be reborn again and again, remaining captive in the endless chain of reincarnations. The Buddhist teaching also says that through penance, asceticism, and contemplation, a perfect soul can escape the cycle of reincarnations, reaching the pure realm of Nirvana. By leaving the *samanas*, Siddhartha voluntarily decides to continue his life within Samsara: Kamala and his captivity in the world of illusions are represented by a bird living in a cage, released by the courtesan when Siddhartha abandons his career as a merchant and goes down to the great river.

On the other hand, Govinda, Siddhartha's disciple, stays close to Nirvana, refusing to join his master when the latter decides to leave the ascetic life of the *samanas*. Siddhartha reveals to him that his decision to take up the earthly world is based on an unorthodox interpretation of the classical Buddhist doctrine—that is, on a solitary revolt against the very meaning of the master's teaching. He explains to Govinda that in order to achieve perfection, Buddha separates Nirvana and Samsara, although the universe as we see it does not show any sign of separation. On the contrary, it is a vivid integrity, an organic whole, in which Nirvana and Samsara do not oppose each other but coexist in mutual completion.

The river is the main symbol of completeness in the novel. Siddhartha and Vasudeva venerate it as a cosmic teacher who binds the two sides of the universe together and links Earth to eternity. The great river marks the center of the imaginary geography in Hesse's novel. Siddhartha crosses it several times: At first, when he is still a wandering ascetic or *samana,* he learns from the river that everything passes away in an endless flow that links life to death in the cosmic cycle of reincarnations. Later on, when he comes back to the river as a ferryman, he experiences the revelation that the river contains, simultaneously, since time immemorial, all the nurturing energies and "images" of the world.

The novel *Demian* (English translation 1923) was published in 1919 under an English pseudonym (Emil Sinclair). It came out almost simultaneously with *Zarathustra's Return. A Word to the German Youth* (*Zarathustra's Widerkehr. Ein Wort an die Deutsche Jugend*), a rather short but flamboyant manifesto through which Hesse greeted the end of World War I and expressed his ardent belief in the emergence of a new, spiritual era, rising like the phoenix from its own ashes. Both writings enjoyed great popular success, although their author remained for a while unknown both to the public and to the specialists. Thomas Mann, who was very enthusiastic about *Demian* (he even compared its author to James Joyce), contacted Samuel Fischer, the editor, in order to find out the author's identity. Mann's inquiry marked the beginning of a strong friendship with Hesse, articulated in their vast correspondence, in Mann's family visit to Montagnola (southern Switzerland, where Hesse had settled with his second wife, Ruth Wenger), and finally in his strenuous lobbying efforts, which eventually led to his friend being awarded the 1946 Nobel Prize in literature.

Demian, whose name obviously recalls an ancient daimon, or demon, features a guiding dark angel who helps the protagonist, Emil Sinclair, to actualize the elementary, Faustian energies of his personality. The hero of the novel is a typical doppelgänger figure, since he is torn apart, even from his earliest childhood, by the antithetical forces of light and darkness, which battle over his personality. Away from his family, who had provided him with a serene childhood, and removed from the presence of his tranquil sisters, Sinclair feels that his antisocial behavior is determined by some sort of metaphysical damnation. Max Demian, his more mature but peculiar classmate, helps him to act out the tormented energies of his soul, convincing him that he bears the "sign" of a demoniac elite whose roots can be traced back to Cain, the first prominent dark figure of the Bible.

Max Demian teaches Sinclair that each person should "go beyond" and become a superior being, rejoicing in the exuberant integrity of his existence, which is a combination of luminous and dark forces. "Going beyond," Demian explains, means living off-limits, beyond good and evil (as Nietzsche also claims), and experiencing liberty as a totalizing cosmic eruption in which God and Devil come together. It is the fervor of creating a "new religion," embraced by strong, solitary persons who march on their way toward human and cosmic completeness, that unites Demian and Sinclair. Although their social paths separate them for a while, they nevertheless share the belief that each person should find a spiritual "twin" who may help that person to act out the repressed side of his or her personality.

The solitary wanderer, presented as the dark side of the character Knulp, also features in the deep structure of *Steppenwolf.* Its protagonist, Harry Haller lives in a tragic and distant self-isolation, but, like Detlef Spinell, Thomas Mann's grotesque writer from *Tristan,* he is attracted to respectable and thoroughly organized bourgeois milieus. These he praises as the epitome of solidly outlined and well-structured forms. Harry Haller is also a doppelgänger figure: In a tragic contrast, his soul unites the passion for order and the "call of the wolf," which drives him to live as a social outcast, apart from human understanding and compassion. Hesse has a penchant for associating this renegade figure with the generic society of the "underclass artists," which includes illusionists, circus workers, wandering magicians, and acrobats. What Hesse also shares with Thomas Mann is the desire to show that art itself has two levels of self-expression: a sublime one, belonging to the genius, and a sarcastic, grotesque one, which is associated with the jester figure. Harry Haller's love for a girl named Hermine, who also bears the androgynous marks of Hermes Psychopompos (the Greek god of the gateway to the underworld), drives him into a "magic theater," where both halves of his fractured soul will finally come together.

Hermann Hesse's elitist belief in the existence of a "pure order" of poets and thinkers guided him throughout his whole life, playing a decisive role in his option for the Swiss citizenship in 1923. His perception of Switzerland was twofold. On the one hand, it represented the politically independent, "perfect" country of the Alps, which hosted J. J. Bachofen, Jacob Burckhardt, and Nietzsche, all of them illustrious professors at the University of Basel. On the other hand, this was the luminous realm of pacifist, culture-centered, pure, nonpolitical German spirituality, which Hesse himself tried to express in his articles and manifestos against Hitler and Nazi Germany. His vibrant belief that artists should gather in a superior fraternity, guided by sublime values and mutual generosity, went into the novels *Journey to the East* (*Die Morgenlandfahrt,* 1932; English translation 1956) and *The Glass Bead Game,* a luminous, spiritual utopia set in the year 2200.

The belief that people should act out the mission that lies within them guided Hesse throughout his life. This programmatic feature was inherited from the writer's family, comprising on both sides serene religious missionaries. Born in 1847 in Estonia, his pietistic father, Johannes Hesse, served in India as a Christian missionary. There he met Hesse's mother, Marie Gundert (born in 1842), who also belonged to a missionary family. Returning to Germany in 1873, they settled down in the small town of Calw, by the Black Forest, in the land of Württemberg, and began running a missionary publishing house, under the guidance of Hesse's grandfather, Hermann Gundert. As a consequence, Hesse would always believe that each person should become a pacifist humanitarian and that culture, built by a superior elite of thinkers and artists with pure humanitarian drives, can heal all the wounds of a tormented, materialistic civilization.

Journey to the East (*Die Morgenlandfahrt,* 1932) evokes the atmosphere of the medieval crusades, although the novel is firmly anchored in the realities of the 20th century. The protagonist, called H.H. (most of Hesse's heroes are hidden autobiographical projections), joins a bohemian spiritual movement, which unites the cultural elites of the period. Their members, gathered in exuberant flocks, travel all across Europe, heading purportedly for the Far East. The sole goal of their spiritual crusade is the cultural fulfillment of each of them. The wandering community is run by a strict hierarchy, which benevolently surveys its members' devotion and self-realization. There is no place for politics on the journey: The participants act and think outside time and history, being guided exclusively by the inner rules of their community.

A similar timeless place is Castalia, the islandlike republic that is home to the glass bead game players in *The Glass Bead Game.* This novel was published in 1943, at the height of World War II, as a personal pacifist manifesto and protest. The young Josef Knecht, future Magister Ludi (master of the game), is featured as a pupil with brilliant personal qualities. These enable him to be selected for a special school inside Castalia, a spiritual order controlled by a strict but very kind hierarchy of high officials and masters in the 12 branches of the humanities. The most distinguished elite of the hierarchy consists of the highly qualified glass bead game players, an exquisite way of combining all arts and their symbols into a dynamic synthesis based on the associative rules of mathematics and music. The game requires a special, Pythagorean initiation, which accustoms its players to the art of spiritual correspondences. Success consists—as happened earlier with the gnostics and the alchemists—in the complete neutralization of the players' emotions.

The novel is a utopia; its action is set in the year 2200, which also marks, in Hesse's belief, the end of the "belligerent" and "sketchy" period of our heroic modernity. The new era, whose spiritual quintessence resides in the geographical enclave of Castalia, is deprived of genius and intellectual creativity, but has an extremely sophisticated capacity of recycling old symbols and formulas into a very elaborate network of cultural analogies. All the inhabitants of Castalia are outstanding masters of their fields, having been extremely carefully selected and controlled during the decades of their formation. They live outside of time and history, in a state of neutral, nonpsychological serenity. Castalia nonetheless represents a heavy financial burden for the altruistic state (whose name is not disclosed in the novel) that supports it. When history in the outside realm accelerates its rhythms, entering a new era of political turmoil and belligerence, the very existence of the spiritual enclave is blown apart.

The novel tells the story of Josef Knecht, who completes his hierarchical ascension by becoming a respected Magister Ludi—Master of the Glass Bead Game. On his way to the top, he is sent by the officials of Castalia to carry out various outdoor missions. One such journey takes him to an important Benedictine monastery where he meets Pater Jakobus, one of the spiritual leaders of the Catholic Church. Hesse presents the old monk as a replica of Jacob Burckhardt, professor and an older colleague of Nietzsche's at the University of Basel. This is another playful gesture of reverence to Hesse's own personal circumstances as a voluntary émigré in the political enclave of Switzerland, surrounded by the rage of World War II. Under Pater Jakobus's guidance, Knecht immerses himself in the art of history and realizes that even Castalia is prone to destruction and relativity, given its reluctance to acknowledge conflicts (except spiritual ones) and its crystal-clear fragility.

Having served for many years as a brilliant Magister Ludi, Knecht experiences a crisis caused by his belief that, though he is a distinguished Castalian, he nonetheless contributes to the mystification that allows the province to survive while being incapable of controlling its own destiny. In order to solve the dilemma, Knecht decides to leave Castaglia and continue his life as a private teacher in the worldly house of a friend and former debate adversary, the politician Plinio Designori. Unfit for his new condition, he dies almost immediately while swimming in a cold, alpine lake, cherished by the heat of a rising sun.

BIBLIOGRAPHY
Bloom, Harold. *Hermann Hesse*. Philadelphia: Chelsea House, 2003.
Mileck, Joseph. *Hermann Hesse and his Critics*. Chapel Hill: University of North Carolina Press, 1958.
———. *Hermann Hesse: Biography and Bibliography*. Berkeley: University of California Press, 1977.
———. *Hermann Hesse: Life and Art*. Berkeley: Universisty of California Press, 1978.
Otten, Anna, ed. *Hesse Companion*. Frankfurt: Suhrkamp Verlag, 1970.
Stelzig, Eugene L. *Hermann Hesse's Fiction of the Self*. Princeton, N.J.: Princeton University Press, 1988.
Tusken. Lewis W. *Understanding Hermann Hesse: The Man, His Myth, His Metaphor*. Columbia: University of South Carolina Press, 1998.
Zeller, Bernhard. *Hermann Hesse*. Reinbek, Germany: Rowohlt Taschenbuch Verlag, 2005.
Ziolkowski, Theodore. *The Novels of Hermann Hesse: A Study in Theme and Structure*. Princeton, N.J.: Princeton University Press, 1965.

Stefan Borbély

HIVE, THE (*LA COLMENA*) Camilo José Cela (1951)

The Hive was the second great success in the career of one of the most influential Spanish writers of the 20th century, Camilo José Cela (1916–2002). Written in the bitter aftermath of the Spanish civil war (1936–39), the novel remains a superb depiction of the social and economic distress the country was experiencing.

Cela wrote *The Hive* between 1945 and 1950. His first novel, *The Family of Pascual Duarte* (*La familia de Pascual Duarte*), was denied a second publication edition in Spain due to strict censorship policies. With *The Hive*, censorship became a greater threat, as a first edition of the novel was immediately banned. It was eventually published in 1951 in Buenos Aires, Argentina, but remained unpublished in Spain until 1966.

The Hive was conceived as the first part of a trilogy that would never be completed. In *The Hive*, Cela experimented with a radically new approach to novelistic structure. The book is made up of a series of fragmented slices of reality, verbal vignettes that record three days in the difficult lives of the characters. The novel is divided into six chapters and an epilogue; these parts constitute brief, spontaneous dialogues taken from everyday situations. Though we know very little about the speakers—just what we can get from what they say, the way they talk, and what other people say about them—their interactions are always meaningful and vivid. Cela provides the reader with flashes from real life, a sampler of the good and evil inside each human being.

The stories included in *The Hive* are fragmentary; none appears to reach a conclusion, and the book seems to lack a clear linear plot. But the parts of the novel taken as a whole depict the beehive of activity that was life in Madrid during the early years of the dictatorship of Francisco Franco (1939–75). This social function of the novel has led many critics to affirm that the real protagonist of the novel is the city of Madrid, portrayed through the hopes and fears of its inhabitants. Cela used a mixture of the objective and omniscient narrator's voice, as well as irony, as the main vehicle of his subjective intent.

At first glance, the reproduction of the characters' conversations can be interpreted as an apparently objective and realistic approach to Cela's subject matter, but masterful selection and editing of the seemingly random dialogues produce revealing portraits. The Hive is a superb assortment of variations in levels of speech and diction, depending on the status of the speaker and the relationship with the person addressed. With this novel, Cela reveals a gifted ear for dialogue, as the conversations are both appropriate to the speaker and imbued with passages of lyrical poetry. Cela's technique reveals the personal and societal alienation and anonymity of the individual within a throbbing, often corrupt, modern city. This novelistic approach has often been associated with John Dos Passos's *Manhattan Transfer* (1925). In *The Hive,* Cela portrays an urban landscape through the words of a collective character, and every dialogue acts as a sort of dramatic counterpoint to the previous one.

Although the formal structure of *The Hive* differs fundamentally from the traditional and linear approach of *The Family of Pascual Duarte,* many of the author's ideas contained in his first novel are also present in *The Hive.* Cela was interested in the depiction of the hardships endured during the post–civil war period in Spain, revealing them primarily through dialogue. *The Hive* is a powerful piece of documentary realism portraying the poverty, moral degradation, and hypocrisy of the society of the time. All social layers are present, from the well-to-do man looking for forbidden pleasures to the beggar desperately searching for a place to spend the night.

Although the form of this narrative is experimental, the substance of *The Hive* is not a departure from the ideas of Cela's long association with existentialism. *The Hive* proceeds from immediate situations to the suggestion of higher ideals. The characters pose questions as they try to grasp the meaning of human life and the universal problems of mankind. The voice of the narrator is not as hard and detached as in *The Family of Pascual Duarte.* Human weakness articulated by the characters implies the possibility of concern and understanding. Behind the perceptible distance that separates the narrator's voice and the characters, there is a hidden philanthropic tenderness in the latter's definition.

The Hive is considered the greatest social-realistic novel of the Spanish postwar period. Cela's realism, however, is a genre in which there are no descriptions. The author is not at all interested in the presence of objects or urban landscapes. He is concerned only with people's feelings, their hunger and poverty, and the number of ways in which their misery comes to the surface. The novel focuses exclusively on characters: There are more than 300 in the novel, and the reader is informed through the many dialogues what these individuals love and hate, because *The Hive* is, above all, a comprehensive catalogue of universal human attitudes and feelings.

BIBLIOGRAPHY

Gibson, Ian. *Cela, el hombre que quiso ganar.* Madrid: Aguilar, 2003.

Perez, Janet. *Camilo José Cela Revisited: The Later Novels.* New York: Twayne Publishers, 2000.

Sánchez Salas, Gaspar. *Cela: el hombre a quien vi llorar.* Barcelona: Carena Editorial, 2002.

Tudela, Mariano. *Cela.* Madrid: ESESA, 1970.

Umbra, Francisco. *Cela: Un cadáver esquisito.* Barcelona: Planeta, 2002.

Rafael Ruiz

HOLY SINNER, THE (DER ERWÄHLTE)

THOMAS MANN (1951) The novel immediately following the publication of the epic work *DOCTOR FAUSTUS* by THOMAS MANN (1875–1955), *The Holy Sinner* led Mann and his readers through an entirely different literary experience. Published four years before the author's death, *The Holy Sinner* seemed a needed respite for Mann after his magnum opus, a form of a satyr play following the great tragedy. Where *Doctor Faustus* gives the reader a dense but intimate treatise of Mann's central thematic concerns, *Der Erwählte* offers readers a lighter, almost playful experience.

Based on Hartman von Aue's manuscript of 1187 titled *Gregorius, The Holy Sinner* is transformed by Mann from the medieval work into far more than a simple parody of a saint's legend. *Der Erwählte* displays Mann's use of his highly developed powers of symbol-making while concealing questions of extreme serious-ness within lively storytelling that alternately delights and shocks the reader. *The Holy Sinner* recounts the incestuous events leading to the crowning of a fictional Pope Gregory IV. Born of noble but incestuous par-ents, Grigorss experiences a Moses-type journey as a babe put out to sea. Taken in by fishermen and raised by an abbot, Grigorss leaves his home after discovering his true history. His aimless wandering, however, comes to an end when he comes across a distressed nation plagued by war that is ruled by a pious and beautiful queen. After saving the nation, Grigorss weds the queen and impregnates her. Mann then reveals to the reader that this royal couple are not only husband and wife but also mother and son as well as aunt and nephew. Representing the epitome of all sin, the devout Grigorss journeys to a rock out at sea, where he is shackled for 17 years before pilgrims sent by God arrive to crown him pope.

Echoing the Dostoyevskian theme *Beati quorum tecta sunt peccata* (Blessed are they who are covered with sins, Psalm 31), Mann explores the depths of the Judeo-Christian concept of original sin. Through Grig-orss, the reader must challenge the notion that a soul cannot attain the highest levels of sanctity without passing through the deepest levels of sinfulness. With-out sinfulness, the saint cannot acquire knowledge of human nature; without sinfulness, the power of pen-ance and the overwhelming mightiness of grace is never tested. Mann takes the character of the kind-hearted abbot who has taken the infant—born in great sin—into his care and symbolically demonstrates the continual effort of God to make our sin his own agony, sin, and cross, thus becoming the God of sinners who allows his grace to spring up from the abyss of sin, pro-viding hope to all.

Reared in a fisherman's hut and later a monastery, the child Grigorss displays the physique and disposi-tion of his noble origins, and despite a delicate consti-tution, he fares better than the robust fishermen's sons in competitions because of his intensely disciplined nature. His nobility has a flaw, however—the flaw of alienation, which Mann has used to pester his heroes since his novel *Tonio Kröger* (1903). For Grigorss the alienation begins with a long-held, unconsciously sensed feeling of not belonging that is also shared by the fishermen's children, who see the scholarly Grig-orss as somehow mysteriously superior. Their reaction is to shun the boy, causing him further feelings of alienation.

The situation reaches an apex following an altera-tion between Grigorss and his brother Flann. Clearly the underdog to Flann's brute strength, Grigorss man-ages a decisive blow that breaks his brother's nose. Their mother, disturbed over the injury to her true son Flann, reveals to Grigorss that no blood relationship exists between them; he is a foundling, one whose ori-gins will hinder his belonging in the spiritual realm. The flaw of alienation is now complete in Grigorss: He belongs neither to the people of his community nor to the people of his own family.

Mann uses this flaw as a backdrop to reveal the full scope of the boy's sinful origins. Armed with the truth, Grigorss sets out on a self-imposed quest, a crusade to atone for the sins of his parents. Outfitted as a knight, he chooses the fish for his crest as a symbol of St. Peter. He begins his journey across a channel of water, across the same waters he drifted along as a baby. His arrival brings him the answer to his wishes—to deliver a lady of innocence from the most dire peril. The woman hints at knowing him, at recognizing the material she used to cast her infant son onto the turbulent waters of the channel. Even though she finds an exact match to the brocade of his garments, she allows the truth to elude her conscious mind and takes her son to be her husband. Extending the oedipal parallels of the Greek myth, Grigorss fathers two daughters—his sisters.

Once an inquisitive maid brings the truth to the foreground, Grigorss inflicts a penance upon himself: He ventures back to the lands of the fishermen dressed in beggar's robes and carrying neither bowl nor bread. Allowed to sleep in a shed, he takes their insults and jeering as a salve to his deep wounds, but it is not enough. Cast in a leg iron, he goes to an uninhabited island where his only nourishment is a few drops of "earth milk" oozing from a rock. His physical being is reduced under the strain, but his spiritual being renews. Grigorss becomes Gregorious, the new pope, a man brought back to human life through events explained only by his elevation into saintliness.

The Holy Sinner as parable demonstrates the transformation of extreme sin by extreme penance into salvation. Mann seizes the opportunity to develop a situation (bordering on caricature and burlesque) to its extreme while providing a story that at a deeper level masterfully illuminates the spirit of Christian doctrine. Mann uses incest to represent the summit of human presumption and self-idolatry equated to Adam's original rejection of God and his divine providence. Mann reminds his readers that no one can claim pure innocence. More important, Mann reminds us that no sin exists that cannot be redeemed by grace.

BIBLIOGRAPHY

Brennan, Joseph Gerard. *Thomas Mann's World.* New York: Russell & Russell 1962.

Bruford, Walter Horace. *The German Tradition of Self-Cultivation: Bildung from Humboldt to Thomas Mann.* New York: Cambridge University Press, 1975.

Bürgin, Hans. *Thomas Mann, a Chronicle of His Life.* Mobile: University of Alabama Press, 1969.

Hatfield, Henry Caraway. *Thomas Mann: A Collection of Critical Essays.* Englewood Cliffs, N.J.: Prentice-Hall, 1964.

Heilbut, Anthony. *Thomas Mann: Eros and Literature.* Riverside: University of California Press, 1997.

Heller, Erich. *The Ironic German, a Study of Thomas Mann.* London: Secker & Warburg, 1958.

———. *Thomas Mann, the Ironic German: A Study.* Mamaroneck, N.Y.: P. P. Appel, 1973.

Kahn, Robert L. *Studies in German Literature.* Houston: Rice University, 1964.

Masereel, Frans. *Mein Stundenbuch, 165 Holzschnitte Von Frans Masereel. Einleitung von Thomas Mann.* Munich: K. Wolff, 1926.

Mueller, William Randolph. *Celebration of Life: Studies in Modern Fiction.* New York: Sheed & Ward, 1972.

Reed, Terence. *Thomas Mann: The Uses of Tradition.* Oxford: Clarendon Press, 1974.

Robertson, Ritchie. *The Cambridge Companion to Thomas Mann.* Cambridge: Cambridge University Press, 2002.

Stock, Irvin. *Ironic Out of Love: The Novels of Thomas Mann.* Jefferson, N.C.: McFarland, 1994.

Christine Marie Hilger

HOMO FABER: A REPORT (*HOMO FABER. EIN BERICHT*) MAX FRISCH (1957)

The life of 50-year-old engineer Walter Faber is suddenly disrupted by a series of odd but intertwining coincidences in the splendid novel *Homo Faber* by the Swiss author MAX FRISCH (1957–   ). The novel opens with the protagonist on a flight from New York to Caracas in April 1957. Faber discovers that next to him sits the brother of his former friend Joachim Henkes. He quickly learns that Joachim was married for a time to Hanna Landsberg, a woman Faber himself was in love with 20 years earlier and who called him "Homo Faber" ("Man the Maker")—a very revealing nickname for an engineer whose only belief is in the machine. Faber sadly recalls that at the time Hanna was pregnant with his child, but because of his reluctant acceptance of her pregnancy, she broke off their relationship, planning instead to abort the baby.

Back in New York, Faber decides to book an ocean crossing on a ship instead of a flight to Paris, where he has planned to attend a conference. This decision will change his life, for during the voyage he falls in love with Sabeth, a 20-year-old woman who is traveling home after spending one year at Yale University on a scholarship. Once in Paris, he decides to take a break to accompany the young woman through France and Italy. He then plans to travel with Sabeth back to her mother's home in Athens. During this sightseeing trip they quickly become a couple. Faber is startled by the discovery that Sabeth is actually the daughter of Hanna, the woman with whom he was in love 20 years before. He takes refuge in thinking that Joachim is Sabeth's father. However, tragedy follows Faber and Sabeth. Near Athens she is bitten by a snake and suddenly collapses to the ground. Faber rushes her to the hospital, where he meets Hanna and finally understands that Sabeth is his own daughter. In the meantime, the young Sabeth dies from an undiagnosed fracture at the base of her skull.

After these tragic events, Faber flies to Caracas, where he fails to attend an important business meeting because of a severe stomachache. Lying in bed at the hotel, he tries to understand the events of the last three months by writing what he calls a report. He spends more than two weeks writing, the product of which constitutes the first part—titled "First Stop"—of Frisch's novel. He then flies to Cuba, where he spends "four days doing nothing but look." Significantly, he stops using his camera to film the world and starts experiencing the world in a more direct way. He resolves to make meaningful changes in his life. Determined now to marry Hanna, he returns to Athens. Once in the Greek capital, he consults a doctor about his stomach trouble and learns that he has cancer. He must remain in the hospital to undergo an operation. There he writes the second part of his report—"Second Stop"—which ends abruptly when the doctors take him to the operating room: "*8:45 A.M. They're coming.*"

Frisch's novel has often been considered a modern variation of the Oedipus myth. In addition to Faber's incest, the numerous allusions to antiquity, and the omnipresent question of fate and coincidence, there is an explicit reference to the famous Greek myth at the end of the novel, when Faber realizes his blindness and considers destroying his eyes, as Oedipus does at the end of the myth. Faber laments: "Why not take these two forks, hold them upright in my hands and let my head fall, so as to get rid of my eyes?" These parallels with the Oedipus myth have fascinated many literary critics.

Yet *Homo Faber* is much more than that. The novel deals with many universal themes, including man-woman relationships (as in all novels by Max Frisch), ageing, and death. (Faber behaves as though age did not exist. In the end he has to recognize that one cannot go against time: "We cannot do away with age . . . by marrying our children.") One of the novel's central concerns is also the technological society, as experienced by Frisch during several visits to the United States in the 1950s. The protagonist of the novel is a "technologist," a "maker"; he evolves in a world of machines, trying to avoid human feelings. But after his sightseeing trip through Europe, the love affair with his daughter, and her tragic death, he starts to change. He is obliged to recognize his emotional weakness and discover a new way of living. In the second part of his report, he condemns the "American way of life," a very harsh criticism leveled not only at America but also at himself.

By choosing to give the novel the form of a first-person report, Frisch confronts his readers directly with Faber's perspective, allowing them to witness how the protagonist gradually becomes aware of his mistakes and consequently starts to change his life. Max Frisch's *Homo Faber* was adapted for a film entitled *Voyager* in 1991.

BIBLIOGRAPHY

Knapp, Mona. "Temus fugit irreparabile: The Use of Existential versus Chronological Time in Frisch's Homo faber." *World Literature Today.* 60, no. 4 (1986): 570–574.

Meurer, Reinhard. *Max Frisch, Homo faber: Interpretation.* 3rd ed. Munich: Oldenbourg, 1997.

Müller-Salget, Klaus. *Max Frisch, Homo faber.* 5th ed. Stuttgart: Reclam, 1994.

Schmitz, Walter, ed. *Max Frisch, Homo faber. Materialien, Kommentar.* 3rd ed. Munich: Hanser, 1984.

———, ed. *Frisch's "Homo faber."* 6th ed. Frankfurt: Suhrkamp, 1995.

Sharp, Francis Michael. "Max Frisch: A Writer in a Technological Age." *World Literature Today* 60. no. 4 (1986): 557–561.

Céline Letawe

HOPSCOTCH (RAYUELA) Julio Cortázar (1963)

Hopscotch is not only Julio Cortázar's most celebrated literary achievement, it stands alongside Gabriel García Márquez's *One Hundred Years of Solitude* as one of the most important and influential novels of the Latin American literary boom of the 1960s. Referring to it as a single novel, however, is misleading, as Cortázar (1914–84) himself explains via an audacious "Table of Instructions" that precedes the opening chapter: "In its own way, this book consists of many books, but two books above all. The first can be read in a normal fashion and it ends with Chapter 56. The second should be read by beginning with Chapter 73."

Hopscotch is thus two novels—and perhaps many more—in one, the first to be read straight through, in the traditional, linear fashion and the second emerging by reading the chapters out of sequence, according to the author's instruction. Though this type of structural, and thus narrative, conceit is perhaps more readily digested by 21st-century readers, having been familiarized with the postmodern literary experiments of the 1960s and beyond, to the public that initially received *Hopscotch* it was an outrageous risk that earned both the book and its author immediate international fame and infamy.

In the first reading, the book is divided into two main sections, "From the Other Side" and "From This Side," with a third, "From Diverse Sides," that the author claims the reader "may ignore . . . with a clean conscience." The protagonist of *Hopscotch* is the bohemian Horacio Oliveira, a writer and Argentinean expatriate living in Paris, heartsick over the dissolution of his relationship with his estranged lover, the beautiful La Maga. As the novel opens, Oliveira is shown for the lost soul he has become: drifting through the streets of Paris, searching in vain for a sight of La Maga, tortured by his memory of her. He spends much of his time with his circle of friends, known as the Snake Club—intellectuals, failed artists, and discontents like himself, with strong appetites for jazz, art, metaphysics, and self-indulgence—though his engagement with them offers him little clarity or peace. Haunted by time and memory, and by his own failings, Oliveira is unable to reconcile the pieces of his past and present into a unified whole.

In the second section, "From This Side," Oliveira has returned to Buenos Aires, by way of deportation, and has taken up residence with a former girlfriend, Gekrepten, though he is no closer to resolving his grief over the loss of La Maga. Indeed, his obsessions begin to have dire psychological and real-life consequences: He falls in with an old friend, Traveler, and his wife, Talita, in whom he comes to see first remembrances and, then, the reincarnation of his lost love. In the resulting and escalating tension—which sees the three working together at a local circus and, later, living under the same roof, that of an insane asylum purchased by the Travelers' employer—Oliveira's fixation takes him, literally, to the edge of suicide: perched on a windowsill, contemplating jumping, while Traveler and Talita look on from the street below, standing on the chalk outline of a hopscotch board. Thus ends the first reading of the text.

However, although the method of reading this first novel is indeed linear, the narrative itself is far from straightforward, alternating between first-person and third-person chapters—the first person, Oliveira's, in the present tense, the third person in the past. Consequently Cortázar develops character through a process both of aggregation and juxtaposition, the chapters not always directly prefiguring or responding to one another and shifting in time, space, and voice. This technique is significant in developing the dominant themes of the book: Oliveira is a man fragmented, a modern figuration of the mythological Janus, the two-faced Roman god of gateways, of beginnings and endings. Oliveira likewise has a face in the uncertain future and a face in the disorienting past, and as a result he finds no unifying sense of the present or the self. In this regard, the first reading of the book perhaps prepares the reader, both structurally and thematically, for the supposed disjunction of the second.

Interestingly, though, the second reading, despite its seemingly disparate structure, proves in fact a far richer, more personal and introspective text than the first. The Oliveira of the second reading, before the discordant Janus, has become a Hamlet figure whose contemplations of being and not being seem more philosophical than psychological. This change is due, in part, to an important situational difference: As the second reading opens, Oliveira is recuperating—from his strained mental state, or perhaps from a failed suicide attempt, or from both—under the care of Gekrepten, Traveler, and Talita. This Oliveira, in contrast to the first, reflects on not only suffering but on the ability of art and, in particular, of language to heal. In other words, the Oliveira of the second reading is revealed as a man searching for, and perhaps even hopeful for, the possibility of recovery.

The metaphysical focus of the second reading is furthered by the recurrent referencing of another character: the enigmatic Morelli, a writer and intellectual whose philosophies, particularly of narrative, seem to resemble both those of Oliveira, if he is the author of these pages, and of Cortázar himself. The Morelli passages—many of them, apparently, taken directly from his works—link fundamental questions of time, memory, and consciousness—questions that plague Oliveira in the first reading and which he intellectually and aggressively pursues in the second—with theories of narrative. Indeed, Morelli argues for a new kind of literary art, a "narrative that will act as a coagulant of experiences," which will create, in turn, a new kind of man by creating a new kind of reader, making him "an accomplice, a traveling companion." Thus the metaphysical becomes the metafictional, and the kind of novel argued for becomes the one in the reader's hands.

But Cortázar is an artist who prefers provocation to pronouncement, and Oliveira's search in the second reading remains ultimately, and fittingly, unresolved: The concluding two chapters of the reading refer back to each other ad infinitum, effectively leaving the reader inside the labyrinth. In the final analysis, *Hopscotch,* in true Cortázar fashion, offers no definitive or delineating solutions or conclusions, only possibility.

BIBLIOGRAPHY

Alonso, Carlos J. *Julio Cortázar: New Readings.* New York: Cambridge University Press, 1998.

Peavler, Terry J. *Julio Cortázar.* Twayne's World Author Series 816. Boston: Twayne Publishers, 1990.

Standish, Peter. *Understanding Julio Cortázar.* Columbia: University of South Carolina Press, 2001.

Yovanovich, Gordana. *Julio Cortázar's Character Mosaic: Reading the Longer Fiction.* Toronto: University of Toronto Press, 1991.

Joseph Bates

HOSSAIN, ROKEYA SAKHAWAT (BEGUM RAKEYA) (1880–1932) *Indian essayist, novelist* Rokeya Sakhawat Hossain, also known as Begum Rokeya, was a pioneering Bengali Indian feminist, social activist, and writer who crusaded for the cause of education for girls and condemned the repressive social customs forced upon women in the name of religion. Her radical articles and works of fiction depicting and questioning the subjugation of women in a patriarchal world, when originally published, shook the whole of Bengal, and these writings remain relevant in the orthodox communities of South Asia. They have contributed to a great extent in enlightening readers about the rights of women as individuals and as independent human beings.

Hossain was born in the village of Pariaband in the district of Rangpur, a part of Bengal in British colonial India, which is now the northern part of Bangladesh. Her father was an influential Muslim landowner who adhered strictly to orthodox religious and cultural traditions. Rokeya experienced gender discrimination early in her life when she was made to wear a veil from the age of five and was not allowed to go outdoors or be seen in public. While her brothers attended Xavier's College in Calcutta, Rokeya and her sisters were denied formal education. The young girls were taught only Urdu and Arabic at home to prevent their being polluted by radical ideas from the outside world. However, Rokeya's eldest brother, Ibrahim Saber, favored the education of women due to his awareness of the Western world lifestyle. Ibrahim covertly taught the young Rokeya English and Bengali, a benevolent act that influenced her whole life.

In 1896 she married Khan Bahadur Syed Sakhawat Hossain, a widower in his late 30s and the father of a daughter. He was the deputy magistrate in the Bengal civil service, a broad-minded intellectual who had studied in London. They settled in Bhagalpur, Bihar, where Syed Hossain encouraged his wife to further her learning to read and write in English. Both Rokeya and her husband believed that education was the panacea for the suffering and victimization of women, and Syed Hossain set aside 10,000 rupees to start a school for Muslim girls. He also motivated Rokeya to write, and between 1903 and 1904 her articles on the oppression of women were published for the first time in journals in Calcutta. None of their children lived, and in 1909 Syed Hossain died in Calcutta from diabetes. In 1909 Rokeya Hossain established the Sakhawat Memorial Girls' School in Bhagalpur in her husband's memory. The school became the focus of strong opposition from prominent Muslim leaders who were against Muslim women's education.

In 1910 Hossain closed down the school, abandoned her home, and left Baghalpur due to a dispute with her stepdaughter's husband over family property. She settled in Calcutta, where she reopened the Sakhawat Memorial Girls School in 1911. The number of students increased from eight to 84 by 1915. In 1917 the school was inspected by Lady Chelmsford, wife of the governor general and viceroy of India. This brought the school into the public eye, and later well-known figures such as the Agha Khan, Sir Abdur Rahim Moulana Mohammad Ali, and others assisted in its development. By 1930 the school had been upgraded into a high school, which still flourishes in Calcutta with financial aid from the government.

In 1916 Hossain founded the Anjuman-e-Khawatine-e-Islam, Bangla (Bengali Muslim Women's Association) to change public opinion about the rights of women, their education, and their independence. She actively participated in debates and conferences and spoke strongly in favor of emancipation. She argued for moderating the Muslim traditional use of purdah (concealment of women), an oppressive custom that isolated females from society. In 1926 she presided at the Bengal Women's Education Conference in Calcutta.

All through her life, Hossain wrote passionately about the plight of Muslim women and for the need for the reform of obsolete traditions. Writing mostly in Bengali as a way to reach the masses, she used humor, irony, and satire to criticize injustice. In 1905 Hossain wrote SULTANA'S DREAM (*Sultana'r Shopno*), which was initially published in the *Indian Ladies Magazine* in Madras and later published in book form in 1908. *Sultana's Dream* envisions an early feminist utopia called Ladyland, in which women rule with love and compassion and men observe the custom of wearing veils. The tale uses metaphor to subvert traditional notions about women as the weaker sex and pleads for equal rights based on gender. Hossain's novella *Padmarag* (1924) portrays several women of different religious and cultural backgrounds oppressed by their family and community coming together and working successfully in an organized manner for the advancement of uneducated girls and women. In 1928–30 Hossain drew attention to the discrimination and exploitation experienced by Bengali Muslim women by publishing in the monthly *Mohammadi* a series of columns titled "The Secluded Ones" ("Abarodhbasini"), which denounced the system of women forced to wear veils.

On her last public appearance, Rokeya Hossain presided at a session of the Indian Women's Conference held in Aligarh in 1932. Soon after the meeting, she died of a heart attack. She was buried in Sodpur, near Calcutta. The memorial service was attended by many Hindu and Muslim social workers and educators, both men and women, in Albert Hall in Calcutta. Condolences were sent by the governor of Bengal. The monthly journal *Mohammadi* published a special memorial issue to honour Rokeya Sakhawat Hossain.

December 9 is celebrated annually in Bangladesh as Rokeya Day.

BIBLIOGRAPHY

Chaudhuri, Maitrayee, ed. *Feminism in India.* New Delhi: Kali for Women, 2004.

Pereira, Lindsay, and Eunice de Souza. *Women's Voices: Selections from Nineteenth and Early-Twentieth Century Indian Writing in English.* New Delhi: Oxford India Paperbacks, 2002.

Ray, Bharti. *Early Feminists of Colonial India: Sarala Devi Choudhurani and Rokeya Sakhawat Hossain.* New Delhi: Oxford University Press, 2002.

Preeti Bhatt

HOUSE OF THE SLEEPING BEAUTIES (*NEMURERU BIJO*) KAWABATA YASUNARI (1961)

In *House of the Sleeping Beauties,* by the Japanese Nobel Prize–winning author KAWABATA YASUNARI (1899–1972), the protagonist, 67-year-old Eguchi, visits an inn where old men pay to spend a chaste night with beautiful young women who have been drugged. During his time there, he muses on the lives of the women, reflects on his past, and confronts the loneliness of old age and death.

Having heard of the inn from his friend Kiga, Eguchi makes his first visit. A woman in her 40s (Eguchi wonders if she is "the proprietress or a maid") welcomes him and explains the rules of the house: the staff, guests, and women are to respect the anonymity of both the guests and the women, and the guests are not to have sexual relations with the women. The innkeeper shows Eguchi to a suite of rooms in the upstairs of the house, where tea, a sleeping woman, and sleeping medicine for himself await him. She gives him the key to the room where the drugged girl lies, and she assures him that the woman will not awaken until after he has left in the morning. As Eguchi examines the young woman, he ponders her circumstances. The sight of her and the smells emanating from her elicit memories of women he has enjoyed in the past as well as thoughts about family members.

Each time Eguchi returns to the inn he is assigned a different woman—or two women in the case of his last visit. Always, though, he experiences the same sensations: "melancholy comfort" and "youthful warmth."

Eguchi prides himself on the fact that he has "not ceased to be a man" and imagines that the other men who visit the house are no longer able to "use women as women." He contemplates "the longing of the sad old men for the unfinished dream, the regret for days lost without ever being had" and comforts himself with the thought that he does not yet have their "ugly senility." Eguchi is aware, however, that "the ugliness of old age pressed down upon him" and that "the impotence of the other old men was probably not very far off" for him. After learning of the death of one of the guests during a visit to the house, he asks himself, "Would this not be a most desirable place to die?" and "To die in his sleep between, for instance, the two young girls tonight—might that not be the ultimate wish of a man in his last years?"

The process of drugging the young women is, Eguchi realizes, a dehumanizing one. He understands that the contentment that he and the other old men experience during their visits to the house is "a happiness not of this world." On one occasion he looks at a beautiful woman and acknowledges that "she had been stripped of all defenses" and questions, "Was she a toy, a sacrifice?" On another visit he recognizes that the only distinction between the sleeping girl and "a corpse was that she breathed and had warm blood."

Eguchi confronts the degree of callousness during his last visit to the house. He awakes from a sleep and finds that one of the two women provided for him that evening has died; after he calls for the innkeeper, she tells him, "Go on back to sleep. There is the other girl."

In *House of the Sleeping Beauties,* Kawabata Yasunari, winner of the 1968 Nobel Prize in literature, deals with themes that run throughout his works: the beauty of women, a yearning for the past, a search for an illusory happiness, and death. He allows the reader to enter the interior world of the protagonist and experience with Eguchi the misery and longings that come with old age. Kawabata writes in a compact, lyrical style. His use of details adds realism; at the same time, the writer creates an impressionistic effect by leaving much unsaid and having the reader see, feel, and evaluate from Eguchi's limited point of view.

BIBLIOGRAPHY

Kawabata Yasunari. *House of the Sleeping Beauties and Other Stories.* Translated by Edward Seidensticker. Tokyo: Kodansha International, 2004.

"Kawabata Yasunari." In *Contemporary Authors.* Vol. 91. Detroit: Gale Research, 1980.

"Kawabata Yasunari." In *World Authors, 1950–1970.* New York: H. W. Wilson, 1975.

Mishima Yukio. "Introduction." In *House of the Sleeping Beauties and Other Stories,* by Yasunari Kawabata, 7–10. Tokyo: Kodansha International, 2004.

Charlotte S. Pfeiffer

HOUSE OF THE SPIRITS, THE (*LA CASA DE LOS ESPÍRITUS*) ISABEL ALLENDE (1982)

The first novel by the Chilean writer ISABEL ALLENDE (1942–   ), *The House of the Spirits* remains the author's best-known and most popular work, despite the subsequent success of her following novels, memoirs, and children's books. Although the book received tremendous critical acclaim and acknowledgment soon after its publication in Spain as *La casa de los espíritus* in 1982, the road to publication was difficult. Unable to secure a positive response from a Latin American publisher, Allende turned to Plaza y Janés in Spain, and the book was soon translated into French, German, and, in 1985, English. As the first significant novel of its kind authored by a woman, *The House of the Spirits* has since had a tremendous impact on Latin American literature.

The House of the Spirits revolves around memories more than spirits. Even so, the book contains sufficient supernatural elements—including the character Clara's fascination with spirits—to tie it strongly to the genre of magic realism. The novel portrays a generational story, a saga, examining not just the history of one family but also the contrasts between a younger and an older generation against a backdrop of political and social turmoil in modern Latin America.

Allende began the book as a retrospective look at her own family. She has famously stated that *The House of the Spirits* began as a letter to her grandfather, and the book does encapsulate elements of her own family. Allende's writing quickly turned from an epistolary form to imaginative fiction. Indeed, though many of the characters are based on members of Allende's family, they do not represent the reality of those people.

Esteban Trueba, for example, bears little resemblance to Allende's memories of her grandfather. The resemblance between Allende's relatives and her fictional characters persists, however. At her mother's urging, for example, Allende altered the name of Alba's father, for the author had unconsciously given the character one of her own father's surnames.

The book's central character, Alba, eventually reveals that she, too, writes in order to preserve her family's— and her country's—past. Although Alba narrates most of the story, her grandfather, Esteban Trueba, forms the core of the novel. It is he who is first infatuated with Rosa, whose untimely death delays his union with her family. Later, Esteban returns and marries Rosa's clairvoyant sister Clara, who, after years of silence, foretells their marriage with characteristic aplomb. Esteban occasionally speaks for himself in the novel, relating his own point of view and his sometimes twisted rationale for events and actions. *The House of the Spirits* thus combines several points of view: the first person adopted sporadically by Esteban throughout the novel and by Alba in the book's explanatory epilogue, and the more general third person through which the narrative typically proceeds.

Alba and Esteban, linked by both familial bonds and by shared narrative roles, establish a set of opposites at the heart of the novel. Esteban is the product of both his generation and his class, the landed aristocracy; Alba, in contrast, entangles herself with progressive social upheavals and radical beliefs—many in direct opposition to her grandfather's views. Yet these two individuals are united by love. Esteban has a dubious, sometimes violent relationship with the other women in his family, including his wife, Clara, who punishes physical abuse with punitive silence, and his daughter Blanca, who persists in a long-term, passionate relationship with a peasant, Pedro Tercero García, in the face of her father's violent disapproval and anger. But the old man truly loves, respects, and perhaps understands his granddaughter.

Their platonic, familial love, however, is not the only passion portrayed in the novel; sexual, romantic love also abounds. The book proceeds through its several generations of women with reflective names, from Nívea to her daughters Rosa and Clara to Clara's daughter Blanca and finally to Alba, with an examination of the rewards and difficulties of passion.

The women love their respective men in a practical manner. Although they enjoy the sexual pleasure that their relationships bring, Allende's women do not give their spirits or their minds with the abandon that their lovers would wish. Esteban loses Rosa to death and shares with her only a kiss; likewise, he never manages to possess Clara completely. Their relationship is passionate but violent, and Clara withdraws into a spiritual world characterized by séances. Similarly, though Blanca's relationship with Pedro Tercero persists for decades, she imbues and controls it with a sense of caution and restraint. Only Alba seems to love Miguel without reserve, choosing at the end of the novel to remain in a country dominated by a military dictatorship in the hope of eventually gaining a life together with her lover.

The emphasis on the lives and loves of several generations of women, an important element of Allende's writing, blends particularly well with the novel's magical and supernatural elements. The novel also determinedly portrays the sudden upheaval and personal damage caused by the victory of a military dictatorship. Using an unnamed country in the novel, but easily recognizable as Allende's homeland of Chile, *The House of the Spirits* examines the social changes and governmental actions leading to the development of the country's dictatorship. From the feminist changes advocated by Nívea to the communist government preceding the military takeover and vehemently despised by Esteban, the novel presents a segment of the history of the author's country. The book's primary vehicle for that historical progression is Esteban Trueba, who unifies the various generations of women presented. He marries Nívea's daughter Clara, having first loved and lost her other daughter; he provides his daughter Blanca with somewhat dubious parenting; and he protects and loves his granddaughter, Alba.

More important, Esteban's development—for he does not remain a static, misogynist, imperious aristocrat for the entirety of his life—mimics the country's conservative attitude toward its own social change and sequential governments. At first glance, Esteban appears to be a typical landed aristocrat: He rules his peasants with unflinching and sometimes brutal control and arrogance, to the point of raping the powerless women inhabiting his lands. This general abuse of the lower classes and more specific abuse of women are the result of generations of social strife and a cyclical pattern of hatred and violence. Esteban also fathers an illegitimate son, ironically named after him, and detests his daughter's alliance with Pedro Tercero García, her lover and a singer of radical songs.

Indeed, at every turn Esteban advocates the continuation of the traditional social strata that have given him his power and authority. Marxism, or communism, the movement overthrown by the military dictatorship, threatens his unquestioned power and his continued oppression of the lower classes. But despite his initial support of the dictatorship, Esteban does not thrive under its rule. He is unable to protect Alba from "disappearing" into its prisons and unable to save her from the torture, rape, and abuse inflicted by Esteban García, the product of her grandfather's rape of a young peasant girl. Although Esteban does eventually secure Alba's release by calling in a favor owed to him by a prostitute, all of his power and authority are ultimately proven worthless. Like everyone else, he and his loved ones are subject to the unreasoning tyranny of the dictatorship.

Alba, however, breaks the cycle of hatred and revenge perpetuated by Esteban García. Though she contemplates the pleasures of "getting even" with her torturers, she finally concludes that any revenge would result in yet another generation of violent abuse, torture, and rape. Instead, Alba chooses to remember, rather than to repeat, the past. Having returned to her grandfather's house, the eponymous house of the title, Alba explores the notebooks of her grandmother Clara and turns to her own writing. Recording the past, exploring the experiences of other women in her family and the ubiquitous connection between those women and their country, allows Alba to come to terms with both her immediate past—torture and abuse at the government's hands—and her uncertain future. At the end of the novel, Alba finds herself pregnant with a child that could be Miguel's but is just as likely to be the product of the rapes she endured as a prisoner. However, in recognizing her child as her daughter, who becomes another link in the novel's progression of strong and mystical women, Alba acknowledges life and love, and not hatred, in her determined documentation of the past and her anticipation of the future.

BIBLIOGRAPHY

Correas Zapata, Celia. *Isabel Allende: Life and Spirits.* Translated by Margaret Sayers Peden. Houston: Arte Público Press, 2002.

Frick, Susan R. "Memory and Retelling: The Role of Women in *La Casa de los espíritus.*" *Journal of Iberian and Latin American Studies* 7, no. 1 (2001): 27–41.

Gough, Elizabeth. "Vision and Division: Voyeurism in the Works of Isabel Allende." *Journal of Modern Literature* 27, no. 4 (2004): 93–120.

Hart, Patricia. *Narrative Magic in the Fiction of Isabel Allende.* Rutherford, N.J.: Associated University Presses, 1989.

Meyer, Doris. "'Parenting the Text': Female Creativity and Dialogic Relationships in Isabel Allende's *La Casa de los espíritus.*" *Hispania* 73, no. 2 (1990): 360–365.

Winter S. Elliott

HRABAL, BOHUMIL (1914–1997) *Czech novelist, poet, short story writer*   Bohumil Hrabal was one of the most important and original Czech writers of the 20th century. He was born in Brno-Židenice, Moravia, but grew up in the small, provincial town of Nymburk, east of Prague, where he lived in a local brewery with his parents and beloved uncle Pepin. Hrabal studied law at Prague's Charles University, obtaining a degree in 1946. During World War II Hrabal worked as a train dispatcher in a small railway station at Kostomlaty, memories of which he used later in his best-known work *Closely Watched Trains* (1965). After the war he did not pursue a legal career but, instead, all kinds of odd jobs, working as a clerk, an insurance agent, a traveling salesman, a steelworker, and a wastepaper baler. These firsthand experiences became a major source of inspiration for his humorous, lively works, in which real-life events and people are on rearranged and displaced in time. Full of deep existential joy and a sense of the comically absurd in life, Hrabal's prose elevates ordinary experiences into poetic acts.

In the early 1950s Hrabal moved into Prague's working-class district of Libeň, where he spent the next 20 years as a manual laborer and a regular visitor to the local pubs and taverns. Hrabal's apartment at Libeń became a center of fruitful cooperation of various intellectual and artistic circles, bringing together writers and other artists, including graphics designer Vladimír Boudník, poet and philosopher Egon Bondy, and members of the famous Art Group 42. Hrabal and other artists like Kamil Lhotak and Jiří Kolář from the "42" group distanced themselves from the vision of socialist realist culture enforced by the Stalinist regime in Czechoslovakia.

Hrabal started writing poetry in the 1930s and 1940s, strongly influenced by the avant-garde (especially the French surrealists and dadaists), and printed his verses only occasionally in local newspapers. Later, these first literary steps evolved into longer prose pieces: short stories, novellas, and novels. An admirer of James Joyce and Jaroslav Hašek and of stream-of-consciousness writing and surrealist "automatic writing" techniques, Hrabal created his own original narrative style: the so-called *pábení*, or palavering. Using the principles of collage and montage, the writer combined an abundance of stories, anecdotes, eavesdropped conversations, gossips, and jokes into the practically unlimited flow of narration, as if he were recording it directly in his favorite pub, U zlatého tygra (At the Golden Tiger) in Prague. On the level of language, *pábení* resembles natural spoken speech encompassing a number of nonliterary elements, local idiom, slang, colloquialisms, archaic expressions, and other unique word constructions. Hrabal's *pábení* creates a sense of "total realism" and provides an access to what the writer called "The Flood of Sparkling Experience"—authentic life stories of common, working-class people.

Hrabal's first collection of stories *Lark on a String* (*Skřivánci na niti*) was to be published in 1959; however, because of communist censorship, the work appeared four years later as *Pearl on the Bottom* (*Perlička na dne,* 1963) and marked his official literary debut as a prose writer. It was quickly followed by two other collections of stories: *The Palaverers* (*Pábitelé,* 1964) and *An Advertisement for the House I Don't Want to Live in Anymore* (*Inzerát na dům, ve kterém už nechci bydlet,* 1964). Two works appeared shortly thereafter: *Dancing Lessons for the Advanced in Age* (*Taneční hodiny pro starčí a pokrocile,* 1964), a story written in a single unfinished sentence about the amorous adventures of an elderly man; and *Closely Watched Trains* (*Ostře sledované vlaky,* 1965), a subversive novel portraying a little Czech train station during World War II. The international success of this last work was ensured by the Czech new wave filmmaker, Jiří Menzel, whose screen adaptation of Hrabal's prose won the Academy Award for best foreign film (1967).

After the uprising in Prague in spring 1968 had been crushed by tanks of the Warsaw Pact, Hrabal was silenced again. The so-called normalization of the 1970s brought back censorship and periods when the writer was totally banned. As a result, he was rarely able to engage his readers in a dialogue over contemporary issues. Nevertheless, some of his most important books were published in the *samizdat* (underground copies), in émigré editions, or in official, bowdlerized versions. This was the fate of *I Served the King of England* (*Obsluhoval jsem Anglického krale*), a picaresque "from rags to riches" story of an apprentice waiter, written in the early 1970s and circulating in the *samizdat* from 1975. Hrabal's finest work, *Too Loud a Solitude* (*Příliš hlucna samota*), appeared the following year. The author created a portrait of a "subtle idiot," a man who, working as a trash compactor, educates himself from the books he salvages from destruction. Full of allusions and philosophical undertones, the novel's free-flowing narration impresses the reader with passages of stunning associations and invites numerous readings of the novel.

Despite problems with censorship, Hrabal remained a prolific writer. Between 1976 and 1979 he published a trilogy of memoirs: *Cutting it Short* (*Postřižingy*), *Lovely Wistfulness* (*Krasosmutnění*), and *Harlequin's Millions* (*Harlekýnovy milióny*), as well as *The Little Town Where Time Stood Still* (*Městečko ve kterem se zastavil čas,* 1978)—a tribute to his vigorous uncle Pepin. In the 1980s Hrabal's friends abroad published his three-volume autobiography narrated by his wife, Eliska: *The Weddings in the House* (*Svatby v domě*), *Vita nuova*, and *Vacant Lots* (*Proluky*). Between 1989 and 1991 Hrabal wrote *Total Fears: Letters to Dubienka* (*Totální starchy*), a mixture of personal history and poetic prose in a form of letters to an American student of Czech, April Gifford.

Hrabal's prose has been translated into 27 languages, and 3 million copies of his books were published in Czechoslovakia during his lifetime. After the Velvet Revolution in 1989, his previously banned works appeared; however, as the writer grew older and ill, he became increasingly desperate and obsessed with his own "loud solitude." During his final years Hrabal devoted himself to his beloved cats and visits to favorite Prague pubs. He died on February 3, 1997, after falling from a window at the Bulovka hospital in Prague.

BIBLIOGRAPHY

Hrabal, Bohumil. *Closely Watched Trains.* Translated by Edith Partgeter. Evanston, Ill.: Northwestern University Press, 1995.

———. *Dancing Lessons for the Advanced in Age.* Translated by Michael H. Heim. New York: Harcourt Brace, 1995.

———. *I Served the King of England.* London: Chatto & Windus, 1989.

———. *Krasosmutneni.* Prague: Praha-Litomysi, 2000.

Ewelina Krok

HUSSEIN, ABDULLAH (1931–) *Pakistani novelist* Born in Rawalpindi in 1931 and raised in Gujarat, a small town near Lahore, Abdullah Hussein began his remarkable literary career in an unusual way: as a bored chemical engineer at a cement factory in the Punjab. Prior to his career as an engineer, Hussein had enjoyed reading. As he reveals in an interview with Rehan Ansari in 2000, he had read extensively works from local and colonial libraries: works by Urdu authors (Manto, Krishan Chandar, Bedi, Ismat, Hyder, and Umrao Jaan Ada), European authors (Tolstoy, Dostoyevsky, Chekhov, and Maupassant) as well as American authors (Hemingway, Fitzgerald, Faulkner, Steinbeck, Kerouac, and Mailer). While this reading kindled a desire in him to write, it was boredom with his job after college that fanned these coals into a blaze: "The boredom was killing me so I thought I might write something," Hussein jokingly explained.

With this new desire burning inside him, he started to face new challenges. Since he lacked the experiences that would center his novel, he began interviewing people about their experiences before and during the partition of India and Pakistan in 1947. Many of these people thought his goal of writing a novel was ridicu-

lous. Further, Hussein was a completely unknown author: He had neither written nor published anything before. Despite such obstacles, he persisted in his writing because he knew that he had to tell the story he had conceived. Consequently, he produced *The Weary Generations* (*Udās Naslēň,* 1963) an epic novel that redefined Urdu prose.

Chronicling the period before the India partition in 1947, *The Weary Generations* provides vital insight into the forces that led to the division. Hussein's adept portrayal of this epic struggle, as embodied in the lives of the novel's protagonists, Naim and Azra, won him Pakistan's highest literary prize, the Adamjee Award. The novel became an instant best seller and remains in print today after more than 40 editions and several translations into other languages. By translating the novel into English in 1999, Hussein has expanded access to his portrait of the historical, religious, and political forces that created Pakistan and that reverberate today throughout the Indian subcontinent and the world.

Now retired and residing in England, Hussein has continued his literary creation and success with several works, including *Night and Other Stories* (1984), *Stories of Exile and Alienation* (1998), and *Downfall by Degrees* (2004). Hussein's latest novel, *Emigré Journeys* (2001), is also his first novel written in English. As *The Weary Generations* had done, this novel provides readers with moving and compelling insights into the intercultural issues defining the world. By so doing, Hussein continues the literary legacy that he started a half century ago and that distinguishes him as one of the preeminent Pakistani writers of all time.

BIBLIOGRAPHY

Ahmad, Aijaz. *In Theory: Nations, Classes, Literature.* London; New York: Verso, 1992.

Hooker, Virginia M. *Writing a New Society. Social Change through the Novel in Malay.* Honolulu: University of Hawaii Press, 2000.

Hussein, Abdullah. *The Weary Generations.* London Peter Owen, 1999.

Clay Smith

HWANG SEOKYEONG (1943–) *Korean novelist* Leading his life as a migrant laborer, social

activist, Vietnam War veteran, and political exile, in addition to his career as a prolific novelist, Hwang Seokyeong has undauntedly confronted the history of modern Korea through the lens of his probing realism with deep compassion for its socially underrepresented and marginalized people. Critically acclaimed at home and gaining worldwide attention, his novels have been translated in several languages. Hwang not only pinpoints crucial moments in modern Korean history in his novels, he also persistently delves into the roots of social contradictions of Korean society, examining the imposition of Western cultures since the late 19th century, 35 years of Japanese colonial rule, the partitioning of the Korean peninsula, and the political struggle in present-day Korea as a continuation of the larger dynamics of the cold war.

Hwang's early novels vividly depict the uprooted and isolated lives of the impoverished and working-class masses in the 1970s, when South Korea was engrossed in industrialization and modernization. *Strange Land* (1971) and *The Road to Sampo* (1973) deal with the increasing distinction of classes amid this rapid economic development. Hwang's works came at a time when the subject of those victimized by being excluded from the country's economic growth was taboo for writers under the state's dictatorial leadership during that era. Through his portrayal of migrant laborers drifting from one place to another in *Strange Land* and *The Road to Sampo,* and his depiction of the poverty-stricken lives of people on the outskirts of a city in *A Dream of Good Fortune* (1973), Hwang reveals the other side of the period's economic growth and development, which he described as "a wretched condition of uprootedness sweeping over the whole country." Alongside his critique of the nationalist rhetoric of industrial development, Hwang delicately weaves his belief in the perennial strength of the lower, working-class people into his gritty portrayal of the people's suffering and tribulation.

Despite his consistent interest in the everyday life and problems of the masses, Hwang hardly remains within the confines of realism and social engagement. He continues to adopt different narrative techniques and place his novels in a variety of spatiotemporal settings to gain a more comprehensive and critical perspective on the present day. In his multivolume saga *Jang Gilsan,* originally published in serial form in a newspaper between 1974 and 1984, Hwang makes a subtle charge against the politically oppressive situation of Korean society in the form of a historical novel. Displaying Hwang's mastery of rich vernacular expressivity and ingenious reinvention of folklore tradition, *Jang Gilsan* captures both the actual conditions of the oppressed and their indomitable spirit of resistance against the ruling class through the life of the Robin Hood–like title character in the late 17th century.

The Shadow of Arms (1987) reflects Hwang's Vietnam War experience as a Korean marine. At the heart of this first Korean novel about the Vietnam War are Hwang's scathing comments on the intervention of Western powers in Vietnam and his remorse for his country's complicity in that "dirty war." Drawing a parallel between the history of Korea and that of Vietnam, *The Shadow of Arms* prefigures Hwang's broadening range of vision and global outlook on the world in his recent novels.

The most formative event in Hwang's career as a writer came in 1989 with his visit to North Korea. This "unauthorized" travel resulted in his exile to Germany, his arrest, and his five-year imprisonment. Released in 1998, he published *An Old Garden* (2000) and *Guests* (2001). As a revised version of the "Sampo" in *The Road to Sampo,* which is less a geographical location than a place fraught with ideological investments of the 1970s, a "garden" is sought out in *An Old Garden* to bridge the gap between the haunting past and an uncertain future. This comes after Hwang witnessed the fall of the Berlin Wall in 1989 and the dissolution of the Soviet Union. *An Old Garden* treats the turbulent political events in South Korea in the 1980s through the prism of the years before a new millennium.

The beginning of the 1980s in Korea was marked by the Kwangju Democratization Movement (May 1980). A military group seized power through a coup d'état and crushed the people's demand for democratic rule by ruthlessly killing hundreds of civilians in Kwangju. The main character of *An Old Garden* is a student activist who dedicates himself to the democratization of his country in that era. When he is released after 18 years of imprisonment, what awaits him are enervated "fighters" of the 1980s now disillusioned with their own utopian dreams and a still-vague outlook for the future. The anguish of disillusionment predominant in the novel is symbolized by the death of his lover, who had supported his political activism with selfless devotion. Only a diary she left and their 18-year-old daughter bear the evidence of her existence. Ending the novel with the main character waiting to see the daughter he has never seen before, Hwang poses a question of what should be done now and how to come to terms with both the achievements and the limitations of the generation of those who strived to realize their utopian visions.

Guests revolves around the massacre in Sincheon, Hwanghea Province, in North Korea during the Korean War. Based upon Hwang's research and interviews during his stay in present-day North Korea, *Guests* discloses through mosaiclike multiple points of view that innocent people were killed by Christians rather than by the U.S. Army, as the North Korean authorities propagated. Using the word *guests* to define the enforced modernity on his country by such outside influences and philosophies as Marxism and Christianity, Hwang seeks to resolve the enmity in the Korean peninsula—the last site still teeming with the contradictions of cold war politics. *Guests* ends with the visit to North Korea of Reverend Ryu, who had settled in the United States after the war. Describing Reverend Ryu performing a shamanistic ritual for the dead in the final page, Hwang intimates that he will continue to grapple with social and historical issues in and about the Korean peninsula by playing the role of shaman through his literary creation.

BIBLIOGRAPHY

Kim, Hunggyu. *Understanding Korean Literature*. Translated by Robert J. Fouser. Armonk, N.Y.: M. E. Sharpe, 1997.
Kim, Yoon-shik. *Understanding Modern Korean Literature*. Translated by Jang Gyung-ryul. Seoul, Korea: Jipmoon-dang, 1998.

Seongho Yoon

HYDRA HEAD, THE (*LA CABEZA DE LA HIDRA*) CARLOS FUENTES (1978)

As a major literary figure and significant contributor to not only literature of the developing world but to world literature in general, CARLOS FUENTES (1928–   ) is a vital literary tour de force, providing the world outside of Latin America with important insight into Mexico's political and social milieu. A forerunner of the earliest stages of the Latin American literary boom—the sudden prominence of Latin American writers and their works in the 1960s—Fuentes explicates Mexico's political, societal, and cultural makeup by focusing on the development and definition of Mexican national identity. *The Hydra Head* is a political spy thriller about the tensions between the Middle East and Mexico's newly discovered oil reserves, involving the ineptness of a well-meaning but less-than-capable man of mystery and intrigue, Félix Maldonado.

Some critics have argued that *The Hydra Head* is probably better as a film than as a novel. The protagonist is perhaps too much of a failure to carry out his prescribed role, one that calls for stealth, intelligence, and streetwise common sense. Some critics also argue that *The Hydra Head* cannot be regarded as serious fiction because it is a spy novel, a genre typically regarded as noncanonical and, therefore, unlikely material for serious study.

Although *The Hydra Head* has many factors distinguishing it as a espionage thriller, Fuentes does not remain completely faithful to the genre. In a classic spy novel, most crimes committed usually end up resolved, questions do not remain unanswered, and story lines are neatly culminated into compact resolutions. In *The Hydra Head,* however, several incidents, most notably Sara Klein's murder, are never solved.

The novel is dedicated to four Hollywood actors: Conrad Veidt, Sydney Greenstreet, Peter Lorre, and Claude Rains. Each actor is memorialized by the roles they played in the American iconic film *Casablanca* (1942). It is interesting to note that *Casablanca* can be interpreted as a political allegory; some of the main characters in the film are tested by the political climate of World War II. In general, major characters in *Casablanca* evolve and change for the better. However, Fuentes, staying true to form, juggles with opposing forces of existence. In the case of *The Hydra Head,* the extremes range between good and evil, between anonymity and a strong sense of self, between corruption and honesty. And as with the majority of his books, Fuentes is concerned with power structures.

Fuentes's ruminations regarding the political, national, moral, and cultural circumscribe most of the action in the novel. A major source of this kind of multifaceted dialogue concerns Mexico's newly discovered oil reserves. Suddenly, Mexico becomes a brand-new force to be reckoned with in the theater of world economics. At the same time, the country also risks losing its sense of autonomy if it allows itself to become involved in the dangerous global game of oil deals. In *The Hydra Head,* power struggles between the Israeli and Arab nations regarding control over Mexico's oil reserves are important. In other novels, Fuentes makes definite demarcations between opposites or extremes, but in *The Hydra Head* he somewhat skews what could be defined as definitive hero and villain archetypes. For example, Félix Maldonado is bumbling, unsophisticated, hotheaded, and unassuming; however, he is passionate. Genuinely concerned with ideals of nationalism, he thinks it would be beneficial to his country if control over oil reserves remains in Mexico.

Although Félix's nationalism is clearly evident, his individual identity is not. Because he is unable to control opposing and influential forces, his own individuality becomes skewed; in fact, his identity is completely eradicated, and a new one is given to him. The plastic surgery on Félix's face is perhaps the most obvious symbol of an existential disregard for individual identity. In this way Fuentes alludes to Shakespeare's *Timon of Athens,* where heroic ideals are neither revered nor fully realized.

The mythical monster in the title of the novel, the hydra, is the nine-headed monster from Greek mythology. It symbolizes the inability of each character to control both his emotions and the incidents revolving around the characters; this is significant because oil has the power to make a country self-destruct. Since moderation and foresight are necessary in order to maintain control of oil, the question of whether or not Mexico is equipped to handle such an important undertaking is also symbolized by the Greek monster.

Because oil symbolizes wealth, power, prestige, and control, these factors attract negative human factors, such as greed, corruption, and shortsightedness. Mexico's position in the world theater of power plays teeters on the precipice of massive success and a legacy of corruption. However, oil is also regarded as only one part to a whole—only one part of the hydra, the monster representing power and wealth. Should the hydra lose one of its nine heads, it is immediately replaced. This cycle of destruction and construction is perpetuated by the sometimes dangerous passion driving whoever and whatever controls this significant global resource.

The Hydra Head is much more than a genre-driven spy thriller: It engages such topics as metaphysics, existential realities, and the issue of a Third World country with the capacity and the means to provide great economic promise to future generations. However, contemporary world geopolitics and the corruption it invariably brings represent Fuentes's belief that there must always be balance in the world. As a result, Fuentes's own preoccupation with Mexican national identity is regarded as somewhat of a cliché: The issue of identity is not seen individually in the characters; rather, each one represents a singular part to a collective identity.

The Hydra Head, therefore, is a novel examining a developing world country suddenly thrust into the theater of developed world politics as it tries to ensure its own wealth, control, and power. The characters, however, soon discover that this is a risky endeavor with little to no guarantee of the country's social, cultural, or political survival.

BIBLIOGRAPHY

Aguilar, Georgina Garcia-Gutierrez, ed. *Carlos Fuentes desde la crítica.* Buenos Aires: Altea, Taurus, Alfaguara, 2001.

Brody, Robert, and Charles Rossman, eds. *Carlos Fuentes: A Critical View.* Austin: University of Texas Press, 1982.

Gonzáles Alfonso. *Carlos Fuentes: Life, Work, and Criticism.* Boston: York, 1987.

Rosemary Briseño

I

I, THE SUPREME (YO, EL SUPREMO)

Augusto Roa Bastos (1974) *I, the Supreme* is based on the life of Paraguayan dictator José Gaspar Rodríguez de Francia (1766–1840). Francia came to power in 1811, and in 1814 he designated himself "perpetual dictator." He ruled Paraguay with a stern hand and violent oppression, assassinating the leader of the opposing party. Although he promoted the Paraguayan Catholic Church, Francia forbade marriage within any group in order to advance the mixture of blood among different races. During his regime, Paraguayan industry and agriculture did well on a national basis, but Francia's isolationist policy against foreign trade damaged imports and exports and cut off Paraguay from other countries. Francia maintained power in Paraguay until his death in 1840.

Using the prototype of the real-life Francia, Augusto Roa Bastos (1917–2005) created one of the greatest fictional characters and works in Latin American narratives. In showing how a dictator tries to bend his country to his own will, the text covers different aspects of Paraguayan life: politics, economy, society, religion, diplomacy, culture, historical events, and daily life. The stories in this novel are derived from various sources, including Francia's own diary; records of his speeches and conversations with his secretary; observations of his life from an omnipresent narrator; and notes and quotations from a "compiler," who uses library resources such as books, journals and government and personal documents to explain the personal life of the dictator and his ambitions to "save" Paraguay. The novel also has an "appendix" in which Paraguayan historians in a national conference discuss how to recollect the remains of the "supreme dictator."

The structure of *I, the Supreme* is loose compared to traditional Western narratives. The author uses multiple times and spaces to illustrate the dictator's life. For example, Francia exists in two time frames; in one, he reigns over his country during his lifetime, while in the other he continues to observe the fate of his nation in the hundred years following his death. In this second, post-death time, he criticizes the treaty Argentina, Brazil, and Uruguay signed against Paraguay in 1865; the Chaco war with Bolivia from 1932 to 1935; and the growing influence of the United States in South America in the 20th century. The "compiler" of Francia's documents lives in a historical time following his tracing of information from the dictator's contemporaries. The narration of Francia's dying experience uses a normal time as in human life.

The author uses realistic time in narrating historical events. Francia's monologue is supported by a plethora of stream of consciousness, comments that introduce the reader to various aspects of and events in Paraguayan history, especially after his death, when his soul is freed from time restraints. The compiler inhabits an independent space from which he can launch criticism toward the dictator. There erupts a confrontation between the dictator's discourse and the documents collected by the compiler, and this directs the narrative toward multiple genres such as bibliography, history, and fiction. There is also a discussion about dictatorship as a recurrent phenomenon in Latin America from the 19th to the 20th century. Francia desired a dictatorship and absolute power. All the events in the narrative are related to the activities of Francia and are connected by his stream of consciousness. The nine political reports written by the dictator also serve as a major thread in the narrative, in which the dictator provides detailed analysis of Paraguay's social political situations, and the danger of invasions from Argentina and Brazil, which want to absorb Paraguay into their own territory. These reports also include the dictator's belief in saving his country from foreign invasion by policies of isolation, by constructing fortresses along the borders, and by war.

This novel provides a thorough and profound analysis of the dictator's personality. Francia is a complicated character. He has worked as a professor and has avidly followed the French Revolution (as a result of which he adds Francia to his last name. He is also a cold-blooded politician—not a hero like Simón Bolivar or Antonio José de Sucre, but rather a legendary figure with twisted characteristics. He is a person representing Paraguay's collective will, a paradox of morality and viciousness, a giant and a dwarf to his enemies.

Like other dictators in Latin American history, Francia lives in profound loneliness, isolated from the rest of the world, and only hears his own voice. In the novel, he reads Rousseau and Voltaire and particularly admires Napoleon. As a ruler, he has carried out his mission of defending his country's freedom and independence, although at great cost in terms of of life and property. He is also merciless against his political enemies and lacks a sense of justice. Since the early stage of his rule, most of the noble families, religious leaders, and high-ranking military officers have stood against him; meanwhile, he has gained strong support from the lower classes. He tries to realize the grand ideas of the French Enlightenment in his country, but unfortunately foreign threats and territory crises never allow him a chance to complete these reforms.

The novel's narrative is marked by techniques of magical realism. Francia's monologues after his death strengthen the image of a dictator who is lost in his own absolute power and tends to identify himself as the nation. The narrative also contains many magical scenes—for instance, when the dictator and his general make their horses fly through the clouds, and when the rebels (who have been murdered by the dictator) show up in a march, displaying wounds that are as shiny as the medals on their chests.

Roa Bastos reported that he studied piles of documents before writing *I, the Supreme.* He considered this novel a collective book rather than an individual story, as he worked with multiple historical and biographical clues, rewrote the stories, and reordered the times. The whole book is like a huge game of varying times and perspectives. The author's narrative techniques strengthen his power of expression and criticism, transforming Francia from a historical and legendary figure into a fictitious one.

BIBLIOGRAPHY

Celballos, René. *Der transversalhistorische Roman in Lateninamerika: Am Beispiel von Augusto Roa Bastos, Gabriel Garcia Marquez und Abel Posse.* Frankfurt: Vervuert, 2005.

Foster, David W. *Augusto Roa Bastos.* Boston: Twayne Publishers, 1978.

Tovar, Paco. *Augusto Roa Bastos.* Lleida: Pagès Editors, 1993.

Haiqing Sun

I, TITUBA, BLACK WITCH OF SALEM (MOI, TITUBA, SORCIÈRE . . . NOIRE DE SALEM) MARYSE CONDÉ (1986)

With her controversial 1986 novel *I, Tituba, Black Witch of Salem,* one of the most respected of Guadeloupe's several powerful writers, MARYSE CONDÉ (1934–   ) has produced one of the African diaspora's literary classics. *I, Tituba* explores the interwoven psychosocial, racial, and historical effects of the Atlantic slave trade and the sacrificial personal cost of rebellion against it. Winner of the 1986 Grand Prix Litteraire de la Femme, the novel has been translated into English through a grant from the U.S. National Endowment for the Humanities.

In this work, Condé's earlier efforts to envision a precolonial African past enrich her return to what she knows of the Caribbean and what she imagines about the African diaspora and colonization. As suggested in the first edition's afterword by Ann Armstrong Scarborough, in *I, Tituba,* anglophone pan-Africanism finds itself queried by Condé's negritude through an inspired vision of North American slavery's comparative relationship to the maroon movement of the Caribbean.

In the Condé/Scarborough interview included in the book's afterword, the author describes how, while in residence as a Fulbright scholar at Occidental College in Los Angeles and doing research in a UCLA library, she stumbled upon the story of the Salem, Massachusetts, witch trials. Like many descendants of the Atlantic slave trade who discover that they are unaware of links between ports in the enslavement triangle, Condé realized that she had never heard of the enslaved Barbadian woman persecuted at the start of the Salem trials. After gathering what little historical information exists about Tituba, Condé went on to ask a feminist Jewish professor about Puritan New England and to visit Salem. There, Condé was struck by the home of Nathaniel Hawthorne, whose *The Scarlet Letter* Condé professes to like and reread often. This outsider view of the early North American colonies inspired Condé's masterpiece about what she perceives as the present tenacity of historical American narrow-mindedness, hypocrisy, and racism.

Condé's Tituba is a Barbadian woman of mixed race; most members of the enslaved Pan-African community were of mixed race by the end of the 17th century. Tituba recounts the emotional and physical torments suffered by her grandmother and mother before her birth and her own rather idyllic childhood, growing up in the islands as a free person. However, love leads her into marriage with an enslaved man, the historically named John Indian, and she fatefully sets sail with him to the Puritan colonies of North America.

As Condé wrote the book, she dreamed of Tituba, conversed with her, and felt that Tituba checked her manuscript. The author seems to have approached Tituba as the embodiment of historical erasure that Condé believes plagues all peoples of the African continent and its forced dispersion. (Historical erasure is the discovery that one's cultural or racial community has been so misrepresented or underrepresented by a dominating culture's values and perception of events as to be effectively erased from history.) In her foreword to the English translation, African American social revolutionary Angela Y. Davis shares the author's perception of rehistoricizing the African diaspora community through the revoicing of Tituba. However, despite her acknowledgment of the novel's sobering overall themes, Condé insists that the reader keep in mind her heavy-handed employment of parody throughout the book, such as in the intrusive village-chorus advice offered by the spirits of Tituba's deceased mother and grandmother, and in the 20th-century feminist enlightenment Tituba receives when she finds herself wrongfully imprisoned with the equally persecuted Hester Prynne of *The Scarlet Letter*.

In the complexity of the book's rendering of the "power/need" dynamics among women and men, the enslaved and their enslavers, Europeans, Africans, Caribs, and their mixed-race descendants, Condé's no-holds-barred exploration of colonial racism, gender bigotry, and disenfranchisement of the poor, and of an enslaved woman who survived all three, remains a definitive literary study of the personal impact of a colonial-era atrocity.

BIBLIOGRAPHY
Alexander, Simone A. James. *Mother Imagery in the Novels of Afro-Caribbean Women*. Columbia: University of Missouri Press, 2001.
Barbour, Sarah, and Gerise Herndon, eds. *Emerging Perspectives in Maryse Condé*. Trenton, N.J.: Africa World Press, 2006.
Condé, Maryse. *Tales from the Heart: True Tales from my Childhood*. Translated by Richard Philcox. New York: Soho Press, 2001.
Ouédraogo, Jean. *Maryse Condé et Ahmadou Kourouma*. New York: Peter Lang, 2004.
Pfaff, Francoise. *Conversations with Maryse Condé*. Lincoln: University of Nebraska Press, 1996.

Alexis Brooks de Vita

I AM A CAT (*WAGAHAI WA NEKO DE ARU*) NATSUME SŌSEKI (1905)

A satire on human foibles from the standpoint of a cat, *I Am a Cat* is one of the most original novels of the *Wagahai wa Neko de aru*, one of the best loved works by the Japanese writer SŌSEKI NATSUME (1867–1916). The work chronicles the adventures of an alley cat as he recounts with disarming candor the details of his life story. Saved from starvation by de facto adoption into a middle-class family, the cat proceeds to comment in a learned and quizzical manner on his dealings with humans. Through him we meet various eccentric and engaging personalities. Mr. Sneaze, the head of the household, is a high school English teacher and also an exaggerated caricature of the author. He is lazy, stubborn, dilettantish (dabbling in poetry, drawing, and music), and greedy. He buys expensive foreign books, but his main use for them is narcotic, for once he starts reading he will invariably fall asleep.

We also meet the spirited Mrs. Sneaze, who fights a running battle with her husband over his masculine and pigheaded ways. From there the circle widens to include the friends who gather at the Sneaze household to while away the time with food and conversation. These include the scientist Coldmoon, a former student of Sneaze; the layabout Waverhouse, an aesthete who loves to make up tall tales to poke fun at pretentious people; and the poet Beauchamp.

The novel has no formal, fully developed plot or structure. The primary plot sequence concerns the possibility of marriage between Coldmoon and Opula Goldfield, the daughter of a prosperous businessman who lives nearby. At the close of the novel, Opula's hand is won by the careerist Sampei; Coldmoon, coming to his senses, marries a girl from his hometown. Nevertheless, the essence of the book lies not in the development of story but in the humor and aptness of the cat's mordant observations of social conditions and human relationships. The satire is sometimes biting and acerbic, as for instance when Sneaze and Waverhouse make fun of the new acquisitive, money-grubbing ways symbolized by the Goldfields. At other times wit is preferred, as when the cat muses on the irrationality of human actions compared to the superiority of cats, although this is quickly countermanded by his own misadventures when he bites into a piece of sticky rice cake and struggles to free himself from its demon clutches. We also get to see slices of Meiji life (the 45-year reign of the Meiji emperor from 1868 to 1912, during which time Japan modernized as a country). These images are presented with affectionate good humor: An episode in which a robber steals into the Sneaze house, finds nothing of value, and runs away with a box of yams is a skilled demonstration in the use of bathos. Another squabble between Sneaze and high school students underscores the generation gap: The students like to throw balls into his garden to goad him into anger—predictably he does not disappoint them.

In place of plot, the author offers a profusion of witty conversations between the protagonists at the Sneaze household; in fact, much of the novel's interest comes from these conversations. With Waverhouse leading the way, the talk moves from reminiscence about student days to the details of ancient Greek athletic contests. Other topics include the origins and functions of noses, the possibility of new artistic genres (something called a "haiku-play" is facetiously discussed at one point), 14 different ways to use a pair of scissors, the dynamics of death by hanging, the direction of human civilization, and the correct way to eat buckwheat noodles.

While the satirical elements reflect the influence of Jonathan Swift, the digressive, irreverent, and occasionally self-referential asides in these conversations reflect the influence of Laurence Sterne's visionary novel *The Life and Opinions of Tristram Shandy, Gentleman* (1759). As the preeminent scholar of English literature of his time, Sōseki knew both authors well. He belonged to that generation that was the first to receive the new Western-style education and also the last to have a traditional Japanese one. Thus, the novel is peppered with a heady mixture of references to Oliver Goldsmith, William Thackeray, Thomas Carlyle, Socrates, Aristotle, Friedrich Nietzsche, as well as a number of Chinese and Japanese poets, Confucian sages, and Zen Buddhist philosophers.

The episodic structure adumbrated above also reflects the book's publishing history. What was to later become the first chapter of *I Am a Cat* appeared in a literary journal in January 1905 as a story. However strange the idea, a talking cat proved so popular that Sōseki went on to write 10 more chapters, eventually producing an enormous work running more than 600 pages in its English translation. Over a century later, the novel still never fails to appeal or to engage; all in all, it is an impressive testimony to Sōseki's immense learning and comic talent.

BIBLIOGRAPHY

Gessel, Van C. *Three Modern Novelists: Soseki, Tanizaki, Kawabata.* Tokyo and New York: Kodansha, 1993.

S seki Natsume. *My Individualism and the Philosophical Foundations of Literature.* Translated by Sammy I. Tsunematsu. Boston: Tuttle, 2004.

———. *Rediscovering Natsume Soseki.* Translated by Sammy I. Tsunematsu. Folkestone, U.K.: Global Oriental, 2000.

Yiu, Angela. *Chaos and Order in the Works of Natsume Soseki.* Honolulu: University of Hawaii Press, 1998.

Wai-chew Sim

IBUSE MASUJI (1898–1993) *Japanese novelist, short story writer*

Ibuse Masuji is one of Japan's most nationally acclaimed writers of the 20th century. In a career that spanned almost 60 years, he produced 30 books and short story anthologies, only a handful of which have been translated into English. Despite this lack of appreciation outside his native Japan, his most famous text, BLACK RAIN (*Kuroi ame*), is one of the best-known literary treatments of the atomic bombing of Hiroshima. However, this popularity is due more to its theme than any appreciation of Ibuse's style, which, although varied, often focused on rural characters and natural imagery.

The reason for Ibuse's fascination with the natural world is perhaps due to his birth and upbringing in the village of Kamo, near Hiroshima. Born on February 15, 1898, to a family of independent landowners, Ibuse left Kamo in 1917, traveling to Tokyo to attend Waseda University and eventually the Japanese School of Art. Although he never graduated, his studies of French literature and his interest in the influential Russian writers of the 19th century, such as Tolstoy and Chekhov, were important to his later development as a novelist. His thematic focus rested on the so-called unchanging people, the farmers and landowners who continue to exist regardless of the individual circumstances or the prevailing social regime.

Ibuse began writing in 1923 (the year of the great Tokyo earthquake), publishing *Confinement* (*Yu hei*), which was later revised as *The Salamander* (*Sanshuo,* 1926), a story about a salamander whose head grows so big that the animal cannot leave its home. *Confinement* failed to impress critics until Ibuse's cause was taken up by an influential literary critic, Hideo Kobayashi. The delicacy of expression with which Ibuse treats this theme is echoed in another of his famous stories, "Carp," about a man who receives a white carp from his friend. During the 1930s, Ibuse continued writing in this pastoral manner in his short stories, although his most famous work of this period is *Jon Manjiro, the Castaway* (*Jon Manjiro hyoryuki,* 1937), a fact-based historical novel about a castaway visiting the United States during the 1800s. *Jon Manjiro* in many ways opened Japan to the Western influence and can be credited in part with the acting as a catalyst for the modernization of Japan.

This focus on "international" matters contrasts with Ibuse's other major work of the 1930s, *Waves: A War Diary* (*Sazanami gunki,* 1930–38), a coming-of-age story about the defeat of the Heike clan by the Genji in the 12th century. Nonetheless, *Jon Manjiro* and *Waves* are linked through their stories of individuals being caught up by larger forces. This link is clearly due to the fact that the 1930s and 1940s were a tumultuous time in Japan, with the annexing of Manchuria in 1932, the "China Incident" (when Japan attacked China) in 1937, and the onset of World War II (which ultimately led to the Japanese attack on Pearl Harbor). Ibuse could not ignore such events, and in 1941 he went to Singapore to act as a war correspondent/propagandist. However, he was never comfortable with either his role or military life, and he continued writing during the war. When he returned to Japan in 1942, he published *City of Flowers* (*Hana no machi,* 1942), an account of his experiences in occupied Singapore, and "A Young Girl's Wartime Diary" ("Aru shojo no senji nikki," 1943), both of which have yet to be translated.

In the postwar era, Ibuse continued to use his wartime experiences as a basis for stories. Of those books translated into English, the satirical *Lieutenant Lookeast and Other Stories* (*Yohai taicho,* 1950) and *No Consultations Today* (*Honjitsu kyushin,* 1952) are both based on his experiences of military life. *Lieutenant Lookeast* is about a fiercely patriotic lieutenant who forces cadets always to bow to the east (toward the emperor), and *No Consultations Today* is concerned with the foibles of an army doctor. The very publication of these works indicates the extent to which Japanese society had altered as a result of the war; it is almost unthinkable that Ibuse's humor (a trait for which his writings are renowned) could be directed toward such previously unapproachable targets as the military without the upheavals brought about by the war.

There is a large gap in Ibuse's works unavailable to anglophone audiences from this period until the publication of *Black Rain* (1965–66). His most famous work known across the world, *Black Rain,* won Ibuse both the Noma Prize and the Order of Cultural Merit upon its publication, the high point of an already prestigious career. Dealing with the atomic bomb dropped on Hiroshima, *Black Rain* in many ways unites the disparate themes seen throughout Ibuse's oeuvre. This "documentary novel," mixing both factual accounts and fictional structure, deals with how a small family survives after the devastation of the bombing, as well as Ibuse's distrust of the military mindset and the effect of radiation on the natural landscape. Unusually for such difficult material, Ibuse's trademark humor is also present; one such example is when Shigematsu, the protagonist, sternly describes a woman's behavior as "improper" because she hitches her skirt "unnecessarily high"—this is only six days after the destruction of Hiroshima. The inclusion of such anecdotes (demonstrating how some Japanese traditions survive even an atomic explosion) clearly demonstrates Ibuse's skill as a writer, adding a very human element to an otherwise disturbing text.

After the success of *Black Rain,* Ibuse's later works suffered by comparison but are by no means poor works of literature. Ibuse went on to publish an autobiography, optimistically entitled *The First Half of My Life* (*Hanseiki,* literally "half-century," 1970) as well as two other works, *Under Arms* (*Choyochu no koto,* 1977–80) and *An Ogikubo Almanac* (*Ogikubo fudoki,* 1981), all of which have yet to be translated into English. In the end, Ibuse outlived his contemporaries, such as KAWABATA YASUNARI (1899–1972) and Eiji Yoshikawa (1882–1962), as well many of his literary successors such as MISHIMA YUKIO (1925–70) and ABE KŌBŌ (1924–93). Ibuse Masuji died in Tokyo on July 10, 1993.

BIBLIOGRAPHY

Cohn, Joel R. *Studies in the Comic Spirit in Modern Japanese Fiction.* Cambridge, Mass.: Harvard University Press, 1998.

Liman, Anthony V. *A Critical Study of the Literary Style of Ibuse Masuji.* Lewiston, N.Y.: E. Mellen Press, 1992.

Treat, John Whittier. *Poets of Water, Pillars of Fire: The Literature of Ibuse Masuji.* Seattle: University of Washington Press, 1988.

William George Slocombe

IF NOT NOW, WHEN? (*SE NON ORA, QUANDO?*) PRIMO LEVI (1982)

This novel by the famed Italian author PRIMO LEVI (1919–87) can be read on multiple levels. First, it is an exciting story, with the heroes (and heroines), a roving resistance band of Jews, trying whenever possible to wreak havoc in the lives of the villains, the Nazis and their collaborators. The band interrupts German radio communications, deflects supply drops, blows up bridges, and derails trains. When the Nazis cannot fight these marauders directly, they shoot local villagers whom they believe to be assisting the roving band with food and information.

A deeper level of interpretation reveals the horrors and complexities of war: Who can be trusted to be included in the band? How can love relationships between some of the men and the few women combatants be developed and nurtured amidst death, destruction, distrust, and depression? Where will members of the resistance go after the war when their families and original homes have been destroyed? Finally, how can this almost anarchic group risk giving up its weapons after the war, those weapons which have preserved its existence on the run from 1943 to 1945?

Perhaps the deepest level of interpretation focuses on Primo Levi's humanitarian, compassionate inclusiveness, which filters through this text. Although using a third-person omniscient narrator, the novel focuses on Mendel, son of Nachman, the thoughtful, level-headed "watchmender" from a Russian village whose loving wife, Rivke, was murdered by the Nazis: "My name's Mendel, and Mendel is short for Menachem, which means 'consoler,' but I've never consoled anybody," he tells the taciturn Leonid, who later will die on a suicide mission to liberate inmates from a small German *Lager* (camp) in Poland.

Yet Mendel's honest, caring reflections do indeed console at least the reader throughout the bloody chaos of resistance combat. As an artilleryman separated from the Red Army, Mendel "must go underground and continue to fight. And at the same time he has grown tired of fighting: tired, empty, bereft of wife, village, friends. He no longer felt in his heart the vigor of the young man and soldier, but only weariness, emptiness, and a yearning for a white, serene nothingness, like a winter snowfall."

Mendel overcomes his feelings of apathy toward war to become Dov's "lieutenant," although ranks in this band have no official military meaning. Yet he does not value killing: "Only by killing a German can I manage to persuade the other Germans that I'm a man. And yet we have a law that says: 'Thou shalt not kill.'" This he explains to Piotr, a clever combatant and Orthodox Christian who likes this band of Jews and even decides to accompany them to Palestine after the war. Levi's humanistic inclusiveness is shown in the band's esteem for Piotr and their acceptance of his desire to remain with them despite his not being a Jew.

Levi's compassion for all good men is further demonstrated when he introduces a 23-year-old Polish medical student turned partisan: Edek. Ancient prejudices between Poles and Jews are overcome when, together, the band of Jews and the band of Poles battle the Germans. Mendel reflects, "Edek is a gentle man who has learned to fight; he has chosen as I did and he's my brother, even if he's a Pole and is educated, and I am a village Russian and a Jewish watchmender."

The greatest test of fraternity occurs when Gedaleh, the charismatic, shrewd, violin-playing leader, befriends Ludwig, a German railway worker and flutist. Levi, the chemist, describes Gedaleh as a chemical compound: "In him, Mendel recognized, well fused as in a precious alloy, heterogeneous metals: the logic and the bold imagination of Talmudists, the sensitivity of musicians and children, the comic power of strolling players, the vitality absorbed from the Russian earth." Gedaleh and Ludwig enjoy playing their instruments together as the war is winding down in 1945, and Ludwig ends up securing an entire railroad freight car in which the band journeys west, making their way to Italy. When Pavel complains that Ludwig is "still a German," Gedaleh replies: "Well so what? He didn't go to war; he's always worked on the railroad, he plays the flute, and in 'thirty-three he didn't vote for Hitler." Levi provides no response from Pavel, who must, like

the reader, ponder the roots of prejudice in everyone, the power of indoctrination, and the need to judge people individually, not stereotypically.

Levi's powerful, multilayered novel is summed up well by the band's theme song, which reiterates the title: "Do you recognize us? / We're the sheep of the ghetto, / Shorn for a thousand years, resigned to outrage. / We are the tailors, the scribes and the cantors, / Withered in the shadow of the cross. . . ."

BIBLIOGRAPHY
Angier, Carole. *The Double Bond: Primo Levi—A Biography.* New York: Farrar, Straus and Giroux, 2002.
Anissimov, Miriam. *Primo Levi: Tragedy of an Optimist.* Translated by Steve Cox. London: Aurum Press, 1998.
Levi, Primo. *The Drowned and the Saved.* Translated by Raymond Rosenthal. New York: Vintage, 1989.
———. *Survival in Auschwitz: The Nazi Assault on Humanity.* Translated by Stuart Woolf. New York: Collier, 1993.
———. *The Voice of Memory: Interviews 1961–1987.* Translated by Robert Gordon. New York: New Press, 2002.

Carole J. Lambert

IF ON A WINTER'S NIGHT A TRAVELER (SE UNA NOTTE D'INVERNO UN VIAGGIATORE) ITALO CALVINO (1979)

If on a Winter's Night a Traveler is a novel by ITALO CALVINO (1923–85) from late in his writing career. Calvino was an Italian fiction writer well known for stories and novels that range in character from fables to neorealist tales. *If on a Winter's Night a Traveler* incorporates these disparate elements into a single text. The book meditates on the art of storytelling and features a character simply named the Reader as its protagonist.

Written largely in the second person, the story begins with the Reader starting to read a novel that proves defective in its printing. Irritated by the mistake in the book's manufacturing, the Reader decides to return it to the bookseller. While at the bookstore, the Reader meets the same book's "Other Reader," whose name he learns is Ludmilla. The two become fast friends as they find they share a great love of reading. They pick up what they believe to be good copies of the volume they had been reading. The two agree to read the novel at the same time and to share with each other their impressions of the book. Once the Reader delves into the text, however, he quickly realizes that he is now reading an entirely different novel from the one he had begun before.

If on a Winter's Night a Traveler continues in this way, as the Reader finds over and over again that the book he begins reading breaks off at precisely the moment it becomes interesting, and out of frustration to know what happens next in the book, the Reader is driven to find the rest of the text, each time only to start a new book. Through this process, the Reader goes through 10 novels in total. These novels vary greatly in subject matter and in tone. One concerns a young man named Nacho Zamora, who seeks his mother in a South American setting; another centers on a young university student who lives with his mentor, Mr. Okeda, but cannot resist his desire for Mr. Okeda's wife and daughter; and yet another tells of a man living incognito in France who is desperately trying to dispose of the body of the rival, named Jojo, he has killed. Each book contains different characters and a different plot, but each breaks off as its suspense increases.

Mimicking the different situations and locations of the books he reads, the Reader's search for novels to read leads him on a number of adventures. With Ludmilla, the Other Reader, he encounters Professor Uzzi-Tuzii, who is an expert on the literature of the lost Cimmerian culture of Europe, and meets Mr. Cavedagna, an absentminded editor at a publishing house. (Calvino himself was an editor at the Italian firm Giulio Einaudi, which published his books). The Reader eventually finds himself arrested for bringing a banned book into the country of Ataguitania. Through his knowledge of books, the Reader finally frees himself, but not without first trying to locate all the missing books in a special library. Here, again, however, his search proves futile, and he learns that the titles of the novels he has been looking for can all be strung together into a single sentence that yet another reader in the series of readers notes represents the opening of yet another novel.

Just as the books all fold into one another, so too do the authors of these books overlap in puzzling ways. The Reader searches for information on the authors until finally learning that the person of his affection,

Ludmilla, has carried on a relationship with one particularly intriguing writer named Ermes Marana. The Reader's pursuit of information about Marana proves as empty as his quest for the novels, however. The novel closes with the Reader, despite the jealousy that he feels concerning Ludmilla's affair with Marana, deciding that he must marry Ludmilla.

The style of *If on a Winter's Night a Traveler* is often called metafiction, a writing approach that concentrates on its own status as artifice. Instead of a work that seeks to pull the reader into a fictional world, metafiction reminds the reader that he or she is always reading a contrived text. Metafiction was a popular style in Calvino's work of the 1960s and 1970s as well as in the work of his contemporaries such as the Americans Donald Barthleme and John Barth. In Calvino's hands, metafiction is taken to a new level in *If on a Winter's Night a Traveler,* as it is the very act of reading—and all it entails—that proves to be the subject of the story.

BIBLIOGRAPHY

Bloom, Harold, ed. *Italo Calvino. Bloom's Modern Critical Views.* New York: Chelsea House, 2000.

Bondanella, Peter, and Andrea Ciccarelli, eds. *The Cambridge Companion to the Italian Novel.* New York: Cambridge University Press, 2003.

Weiss, Beno. *Understanding Italo Calvino.* Columbia: University of South Carolina Press, 1993.

Joe Moffett

IMMORALIST, THE (L'IMMORALISTE)

ANDRÉ GIDE (1902) Despite ANDRÉ GIDE's claims otherwise, his novel *The Immoralist* is clearly autobiographical. Gide (1869–1951), one of the most significant novelists of the first half of the 20th century and winner of the 1947 Nobel Prize in literature, went to great lengths to differentiate events in the main character's life from events in his own. Yet the resemblance is apparent and uncanny. For example, Michel, the protagonist in *The Immoralist,* wrestles with his own sexual identity, as did Gide, both seeing in their homosexual desires an ideal existence that contrasted with their lived realities. Additionally, the name Gide chose for Michel's wife, Marceline, closely resembles Gide's wife's name, Madeleine. These parallels are significant.

When the novel, which Gide referred to as a *récit* (account or narrative), was published, many critics recognized the close resemblance between Michel and Gide. Notably, Gide himself insisted that *The Immoralist, Strait Is the Gate* (1909), and LAFCADIO'S ADVENTURES (1914) together formed a set, each exploring a similar theme of morality.

Doubly removed from the time that the events take place in the novel, a friend of Michel's relays the story via a letter to his brother. Thus, the novel's narrator is unreliable, an authorial presence that, in its distance from the actual happenings, causes the reader to doubt the story's authenticity. Rather than provide a moral guide or authoritative narrative voice, Gide presents questions to which the narrative does not provide answers. In doing so, the author creates a text contingent upon the reader to complete its formation.

The Immoralist is a psychological novel, one dealing with repressed desires and the deep rift that exists between the central character's interior world and the moral demands of the exterior world. The story focuses on Michel, who gathers his friends so he may share his story. Michel tells of his harsh, Protestant mother and disciplined, academic father (more Gide correspondences), both of whom contribute to his puritanical disposition. Yet despite these foundational early childhood experiences, Michel seeks to explain a change that has taken place, a self-transformation that he finds troubling but that affords a resolution to his distress: the conflicted existence of a homosexual man who, after having led a hypocritical existence, wishes to leave the moral confines of his life and enter an "immoral" world where he can follow his passions, his instincts, and his ardent will. Michel's inner struggle is mirrored in his physical maladies, and his cross-continental travels provide him with sensual experience necessary for his psychological awakening.

Even though Michel does not love her, he marries his 20-year-old cousin Marceline (he is 24) after his father dies. The marriage fulfills his father's deathbed wish, but Michel remains divided in his ability to make a complete commitment, and the marriage is not consummated for several years. After marrying in Paris, Michel and Marceline travel to North Africa, where Michel at once confronts new sensations, sensual feelings he has not known before. Unfortunately, he is also stricken with tuberculosis at the same time, an outward, visible sign of his inner, invisible conflict. While recovering, he is inspired by a young, attractive Arab boy; Michel then vows to live. After Michel convalesces, he and Marceline travel to Italy, where he sunbathes in the nude and shaves off his beard, signs of his recovery and transformation. His metamorphosis removes layers of constraints. Michel describes what is left: the original being, a manuscript hidden underneath all the layers of fiction. Before leaving, Michel and Marceline consummate their marriage for the first and only time.

The second part of the novel begins in Normandy, where the two live on their farm, La Moliniére. There Michel prepares for his Paris teaching duties and spends considerable time with the 17-year-old son of the farm's caretaker, another one of the many homoerotic relationships that sustain him. When Michel returns to Paris, however, he resents the "false" life he leads. He works these feelings into lectures on Roman civilization. After one of these lectures, he stays up all night with his friend Ménalque, who embodies what Michel wants to be: a free, independent spirit who can travel on his own and experience the sensual world. Ménalque rebels against the forces and institutions that have formed him: Christianity, middle-class society, Parisian culture. He is a Nietzschean man, one who personifies the "immoralist" ideal Michel develops. Upon returning to his Paris apartment, Michel finds that Marceline has contracted tuberculosis. He takes her to the farm to recover, but he soon becomes restless and insists that they sell the farm.

The third and final part of the novel opens with Marceline struggling to recover from her illness. The two set out for an air cure in the Swiss mountains, although Michel soon insists that they follow the route of his own convalescence, a journey that takes them through Italy and back to Africa. As Michel again regains his passion for life, Marceline's health worsens, and she dies. Left alone, Michel struggles to find the will to live and pleads for his friends to come and listen to his story.

The Immoralist ends ambiguously. Michel remains at a terminal point, a watershed where he must decide whether to follow his own path or the path defined by society. This moral struggle not only encompasses the dominant concerns of the novel but also becomes the central concern for the rest of Gide's works. Michel is weak at the novel's close, a seemingly failed Nietzschean superman who faces an existential dilemma.

By ending the narrative with an open-ended question, Gide created a modernist work of art posing many of the same questions about human existence that JEAN-PAUL SARTRE and ALBERT CAMUS raised in the middle of the 20th century. In this way, *The Immoralist* is not only representative of its age but also foreshadows philosophic thought to come.

BIBLIOGRAPHY

Apter, Emily. *André Gide and the Codes of Homotextuality.* Saratoga, Calif.: Anma Libri, 1987.

Bettinson, Christopher D. *Gide: A Study.* Totowa, N.J.: Rowman & Littlefield, 1977.

Cordle, Thomas. *André Gide.* New York: Twayne Publishers, 1969.

Pollard, Patrick. *André Gide, Homosexual Moralist.* New Haven, Conn.: Yale University Press, 1991.

Walker, David H., ed. *André Gide.* London and New York: Longman, 1996.

Blake G. Hobby

I'M NOT STILLER (STILLER) MAX FRISCH (1954)

With *I'm Not Stiller,* the author's third novel, the Swiss playwright and novelist MAX FRISCH (1911–91) established himself as a major contributor to postwar German literature. The English title is also the first sentence of the novel, whose central themes are generally held to be the existentialist quest for the modern self and, in close connection with that, the intricate dynamics of male-female relationships.

This focus of the novel on individuals and their private lives was perceived as unusual in the highly politicized literary field of the 1950s and '60s, especially when applied by a writer whose dramatic work stood firmly in the tradition of the German playwright Bertolt Brecht. Despite the novel's inbuilt satire of Swiss state officialdom and, for its time, shockingly matter-of-fact explorations of adultery, most early critics would either accuse *I'm Not Stiller* of being comparatively apolitical (and hence bourgeois) or—as MARIO

VARGAS LLOSA does as late as 1988—justify their high esteem of the novel by overemphasizing its political implications. Among modern academics, by contrast, critical discussions of the text primarily center on its philosophical background, narrative techniques, and multilayered imagery.

Whereas the style of *I'm Not Stiller* seems almost colloquial and deceptively straightforward, its structure is highly complex. Questioning personal identity not only with regard to the protagonist but also on the levels of narrator and author, Frisch communicates his story through several different and sometimes contradictory perspectives. Their organization and the general blueprint of the novel could be summarized as follows: Carrying an American passport under the name Jim White, the protagonist/first-person narrator travels back to Zurich. At the border, he is recognized as the Swiss sculptor Anatol Stiller, who has been missing for the last six years and is suspected of espionage and other illegal activities. During his imprisonment—he is released after 10 weeks—White/Stiller attempts to put his case in writing and thereby convince the court of his "true" American identity. He fills seven notebooks, which are, for the most part, what we read. Books one, three, and five contain his persistent claims to being Jim White (which he upholds even when faced by wife and friends); various diary entries about his current prison life; and his reflections and fantasies of, or related to, his years in America, where he seems to have been vainly searching for his personal version of the American Dream—that is, an authentic existence diametrically opposed to the stifling mediocrity of contemporary Switzerland.

Books two, four, and six are different. The mysterious narrator remains the same, as is clear from his occasional interjections. Yet here he produces seemingly objective third-person accounts of the missing Stiller. By means of focalization, he successively adopts the viewpoints of Stiller's beautiful, fragile, and sexually unresponsive wife, Julika (book two); his well-intentioned but habit-governed prosecutor, Rolf (book four); and his sensible, thoroughly emancipated ex-lover, Sybille (book six). Finally, in book seven, the narrator caves in and hesitantly acknowledges his identity with Stiller. All this is then followed by a 50-page epilogue written by the prosecutor, Rolf, who also happens to be Sibylle's husband but has nevertheless become a friend of the accused, and now presents himself as the editor of Stiller's prison notebooks. "The Prosecutor's Epilogue" describes Stiller's renewed but doomed attempt at married life with Julika, which ends bleakly with her illness and death after two and a half years.

This skeletal summary at least hints at the numerous ambiguities in connection with narrative authority that Frisch plays with and at times quite explicitly highlights in the text. From whom do we learn about the various figures and how far can we trust their views of themselves and one another? The epilogue, for example, has been read as anything from a negligible and artistically misguided add-on to a thinly veiled authorial statement. What is less evident is the extreme and yet lucid subtlety with which Frisch, as in all his major novels, traces the difficulties, especially among lovers, of one understanding the other.

There are also Stiller's exuberantly vivid descriptions and adventure fantasies—for instance, when he talks about the Chihuahua desert or his subterranean cave experience in Texas. Crammed with allusions ranging from popular media culture to ancient myth, from Calvinism to westerns to Hades to matriarchy, these narrative excursions allegorically prefigure and reflect the more soberly realistic events of the novel. Perhaps, with its alternating creation of absorbing illusions and alienations of the reader, *I'm Not Stiller* might be considered Brechtian after all.

BIBLIOGRAPHY

Koepke, Wulf. *Understanding Max Frisch.* Columbia: University of South Carolina Press, 1991.

Probst, Gerhard F., and Jay F. Bodine, eds. *Perspectives on Max Frisch.* Lexington: University Press of Kentucky, 1982.

Sharp, Francis Michael. "Max Frisch: A Writer in a Technological Age." *World Literature Today* 60, no. 4 (1986): 557–561.

White, Alfred D. *Max Frisch, the Reluctant Modernist.* Lewiston, N.Y.: E. Mellen Press, 1995.

Rudolph Glitz

INDIFFERENT ONES, THE (GLI INDIFFERENTI) ALBERTO MORAVIA (1929)

The Italian author ALBERTO MORAVIA (1907–90) began writing his masterpiece *The Indifferent Ones* in 1925, when he was 17 years old. Publication came in 1929, when he was 21. *The Indifferent Ones* is the story of a Roman bourgeois family during the fascist regime in Italy. Moravia explicitly stated that he meant not to write a moral or satirical novel: His desire was to infuse the Italian novel with drama. A case in point is that Moravia read out loud what he wrote, and the original draft contained almost no punctuation, which he added afterward.

Moravia's novel recalls the great 19th-century French realist writers, Greek tragedy, and the influence of the Russian Fyodor Dostoyevsky. The action takes place over a couple of days (adhering closely to Aristotle's unity of time in which the action takes place in a concentrated period, usually one day). Mariagrazia, a widow, is the mother of Carla and Michele. She is sentimental, hypocritical, and ignorant of others. Her lover, Leo, seduces Carla, whom he has known since she was a child; the idea of incest is mentioned on several occasions. Carla thinks that this affair will enable her to begin a new life. Leo acts not merely from lust but also because he wishes to lay hands on the family's villa, which he graciously offers to buy for a tiny portion of its real value. Michele is the only one of the family to realize this. He tries to act, but is unable: He suffers from apathy. His attempts to react fail: Once he manages to pitifully insult Leo; another time, he throws an ashtray at Leo but misses and hits his mother instead. Finally he buys a revolver and goes to Leo's house to kill him, but he forgets to load his gun, cutting a pathetic figure.

Michele is the story's moral conscience, yet he is unable to love anyone; he cannot even successfully make love to his mother's best friend, Lisa (a former lover of Leo's before Mariagrazia stole him away). Michele is disgusted by duplicity and inauthenticity of feelings, sentiments, thoughts, and actions. At the end, Leo proposes to marry Carla, and Michele makes a last-ditch effort to persuade his sister not to go through with it. This is to no avail: Carla tells Michele she will marry Leo, and the last scene of the book reveals Carla and Mariagrazia dressed up in masks to go to a ball, invited by another family who assumes Carla will become their son's fiancée.

The Indifferent Ones was enormously shocking and influential upon its release. Though the editor demanded that Moravia contribute the necessary money for its publication, the book went through many reprints. This is all the more surprising because Moravia, gravely ill, was shuttled between various hospitals and sanitariums during the second half of his childhood. Indeed, he began writing the novel while convalescing in bed. He had had little experience of the social world, but the scenes and dialogue in this book strike one as genuine.

The style of the book is sober and direct, in contrast with the prevailing trends in Italian literature, which were oriented toward *prosa d'arte* (poetic prose). Italian contemporary critics' attacks on the book tended to focus on its language, though they really meant to criticize its content. It is certainly one of the most cynical Italian novels of the first half of the 20th century. Nonetheless, this cynicism is not at odds with what is loosely called the book's existentialism. Many readers and critics have persisted in calling *The Indifferent Ones* the first existential novel, though the birth of existentialism was years away. More rigorously, it would be correct to say that the theme of not knowing what to do (morally and philosophically) is repeated throughout the novel. This, however, is different from the sense of the abyss underlying one's very step, as in JEAN-PAUL SARTRE's *NAUSEA* (*La nausée,* 1938). Moravia's novel is fundamentally not a tragic novel—it is a tragedy manqué. There are no bullets—the gun is empty—nor is the antihero, as Michele can be called, part of a comedy of manners. The cold analysis of the characters' motives precludes this.

Moravia was to write many more novels, stories, and travel writings, but he was never again to give such a detailed glimpse of the rottenness of hypocrisy, societal conformity, and acute indecision as he did in *The Indifferent Ones.*

BIBLIOGRAPHY

Moravia, Alberto, and Alain Elkann. *Life of Moravia.* Translated by William Weaver. South Royalton, Vt.: Steerforth Italia, 2000.

Peterson, Thomas. *Alberto Moravia.* New York: Twayne Publishers, 1996.

Jacob Blakesley

IN EVIL HOUR (LA MALA HORA) GABRIEL GARCÍA MÁRQUEZ (1962)   This novel—published after *Leafstorm* (*La hojarasca,* 1955) and *No One Writes to the Colonel* (*El coronel notiene quien le escriba,* 1957)—was begun earlier in 1956, completed as *This Shitty Town* by 1959, and, in a shortened form (purged of "Faulknerisms") and under its current title *In Evil Hour* (*La mala hora,* 1962), won the Esso Literary Prize and was subsequently published in Spain in 1962. About a year later, GABRIEL GARCÍA MÁRQUEZ (1928–) noticed that the Spanish edition had been heavily edited, "purified" of the colloquialisms and linguistic barbarities peculiar to the language of Latin America in general and the Colombian town of the setting, so he repudiated it and had a second, restored edition published in Mexico in 1966.

In Evil Hour is an early novel by García Márquez, but it contains subjects—the horror of *la violencia,* the violent years, in Colombia—and techniques—elaborate construction and discontinuous episodes—characteristic of all of his work. The book is political yet broadly human; panoramic yet particular; highly symbolic yet rooted in realistic detail; organized in continuous, present-time narrative, yet also containing both the past and the future. The narrative emerges with energy and power, but it is essentially a story told by indirection. The tale of horror and repression is narrated without a protagonist by focusing on the reaction, futile or complicit, of an entire town. *In Evil Hour* contains some of the strange, extreme realism and the verbal dexterity of *ONE HUNDRED YEARS OF SOLITUDE* (*Cien años de soledad,* 1967), but it has none of that novel's serendipitous magic.

In Evil Hour begins and ends with similar incidents: Father Angel is obsessed with mice in the church and sets his servant, Trinidad, to finding ingenious ways to trap them. In an early scene, she looks into the box containing the trap and finds her first corpses, "a small massacre . . . with repugnance and pleasure." The last scene in the novel shows a new, younger servant, Mina, presenting the cynical Father Angel with an empty box. He refers, as in the first scene, to music he has heard playing in the night, but Mina says that the music was made "[of] lead . . . There was shooting until just a little while ago." The seemingly trivial opening conversation and the obviously not trivial closing conversation frame the town mayor's obsession with, and inability to get rid of, both a searing toothache and a series of writings, lampoons pasted like handbills on walls and doorways. The lampoons, running like a leitmotif through the narrative, contain humorous political commentary as well as oblique references to the secrets of individual residents. All the lampoons attack hypocrisy or power misused. The narrative does not reveal the exact contents of the missives but shows the consternation of the targets and the rage of the mayor as he realizes the political nature of the lampoons and becomes more and more determined to find the perpetrators.

Other more sinister events and powers beset the town, as well: the seemingly unmotivated murder of the town musician, a flood that destroys the homes of many residents, the putrefaction of a dead cow stuck in the river that runs through the town. Gradually, the reader learns by indirection that the mayor was installed by a "new government," but that this government, although promising change, is just as repressive as the old one. The mayor's gendarmes present him with a young man seen putting up a lampoon. The mayor orders torture in an attempt to find out the names of other participants, and the young man is killed, having revealed nothing. Earlier political violence also emerges, as in a secretary who says to the new judge, as he sits in his chair, "When they killed Judge Vitela, the springs broke, but they've been fixed." The secretary adds, "And all because when he was drunk he said he was here to guarantee the sanctity of the ballot."

García Márquez colors this depiction of political repression with absurdity. When the mayor has a new decree read in the town square, there is, ironically, silence "too great for the voice of the crier." The narrator comments: "The decree had been read with the same authoritarian ritual as always; a new order reigned in the world and she [the widow Monteil] could find no one who had understood it." The widow adds that "ever since the world has been the world, no decree has ever brought any good." Only at the end of the novel does the reader learn, obliquely, that underneath the absurdity lies a long-standing, national plot against the regime: The dentist, who pulled the mayor's rotten

tooth, hides weapons underneath his floor, and those few who have not been shot have taken to the countryside to join rebels.

The pieces of García Márquez's narrative thus come together in powerful protest of the political evil besetting his native Colombia. Underlying his political commentary, however, is a much more general, moral one, most powerfully expressed through an indictment of the church and of human complacency and desire for power in general. At the end of the novel, when Mina tells the priest about the shooting, he says, "I didn't notice anything." Although *In Evil Hour* is political, few areas of human experience portrayed in the novel remain apolitical. Yet the novel also upholds the power of life to survive. The undercurrent of bodily functions—characters are often shown eating, shaving, bathing, making love—shows that life goes on in spite of politicians and priests and flawed human nature. *In Evil Hour* reveals García Márquez not as complex in technique as he later became but certainly as broadly human in his themes.

BIBLIOGRAPHY

Bell, Michael. *Gabriel García Márquez: Solitude and Solidarity.* New York: St. Martin's Press, 1993.

Janes, Regina. *Gabriel García Márquez: Revolutions in Wonderland.* Columbia: University of Missouri Press, 1981.

Minta, Stephen. *Gabriel García Márquez: Writer of Colombia.* London: Jonathan Cape, 1987.

Zamora, Lois Parkinson. *Writing the Apocalypse: Historical Vision in Contemporary U.S. and Latin American Fiction.* Cambridge: Cambridge University Press, 1989.

Rita Saylors

INFANTE'S INFERNO (LA HABANA PARA UN INFANTE DIFUNTO) GUILLERMO CABRERA INFANTE (1984)

Described by the author as "hell with women and sex and songs," GUILLERMO CABRERA INFANTE's book *Infante's Inferno* (1984) is a brilliantly written chronological catalog of a young man's coming-of-age experiences, both triumphant and disastrous, in prerevolutionary Havana, Cuba. Embellished by the writer's trademark puns and other forms of wordplay, this book presents an unnamed narrator who shares intimate details of such milestones as his first peek at a naked woman, his first kiss, his first taste of alcohol, and his first sexual conquests and defeats, many of which significantly take place in various darkened movie theaters throughout Havana. Because the narrative becomes, at times, explicitly erotic—as when the young man details his masturbatory techniques—the book was first published in Spain in 1979 under the title *La Habana para un infante difunto,* a parody of French composer and pianist Maurice Ravel's famous *Pavane pour une infante défunte* (*Pavane for a Dead Princess*).

Cabrera Infante (1929–2005) has commented in many interviews that his discovery of this title influenced the writing of the entire book. He explains that "*infante défunte* rhymes very well in French; it is both homophonic and cacophonic at the same time. That is to say, the words sound the same and yet they are shocking together. The word *pavane* was brought in because it is an archaic musical form, while *infante* was used because of the fascination foreigners have with that term, which in Spanish designates the sons of the king who will not ascend to the throne. When the title came to me, I became convinced it was perfect, so I set out to rewrite the entire book."

Written entirely in the first person, the book is often marketed as the memoir of Cuban-born writer Guillermo Cabrera Infante, but in a 1980 interview with Marie-Lise Gazarian Gautier, the author adamantly denies that *Infante's Inferno,* which took over two years to write, is autobiographical. The self-proclaimed writer of fragments admits that there are snippets of his own life within the text, but in a later interview with Gazarian Gautier in 1984, he insisted that "*Infante's Inferno* is a book full of memories of Havana. Those memories are manipulated to such an extent that even those people who participated in them are unaware of it. There is a constant manipulation of my own nostalgia, and I use it as a wellspring for my literature." Thus, with this book, as with the majority of Cabrera Infante's writing, attempts at strict genre classification become problematic.

Regardless of the label—whether the work is autobiography or novel or something in between—Guillermo Cabrera Infante offers here a revealing glimpse into male adolescence that is authentic enough to resonate with readers even as it sheds a curious light on the sights and sounds of Havana. *Infante's Inferno* seeks not to tell the whole truth about its author, but rather "the truth in part and in art."

BIBLIOGRAPHY

Alvarez-Borland, Isabel. "The Pícaro's Journey in the Structure of *La Habana para un Infante Difunto.*" *Hispanofila* 90, no. 3 (1987): 71–79.

Feal, Rosemary G. *Novel Lives: The Fictional Autobiographies of Guillermo Cabrera Infante and Mario Vargas Llosa.* Chapel Hill: University of North Carolina Press, 1988.

Hall, Kenneth E. "Cabrera Infante as Biographer." *Biography: An Interdisciplinary Quarterly* 19, no. 4 (1996): 394–403.

Dana Nichols

INFINITE PLAN, THE (EL PLAN INFINITO) ISABEL ALLENDE (1991)

The Infinite Plan: A Novel, first published in Spanish as *El plan infinito* in 1991, denotes a significant turning point in the career of ISABEL ALLENDE (1942–). Allende's fifth book is distinctly different from her earlier work in two ways. Unlike Allende's prior books, which have a Latin American setting, *The Infinite Plan* takes place mostly in the United States, with occasional forays into other countries. Also significant is the book's main character, Gregory Reeves, son of a traveling evangelist and member of a diverse, sometimes bizarre, cast. Previously, Allende focused on female characters and female issues, and imbued her novels with an intense exploration of love in many forms. With *The Infinite Plan,* however, Allende investigates the lifelong journey of a male character, probing his problematic and lengthy maturation.

The Infinite Plan, as critics have observed, lacks Allende's usual intense focus on social issues, particularly the politics of her homeland, Chile. But *The Infinite Plan* nevertheless evolves from an origin similar to that of even Allende's first novel, *The HOUSE OF THE SPIRITS* (1982). In writing this book, Allende transformed elements of her own family—names, people, events—into a grand-scale fictional narrative. *The Infinite Plan* also suggests Allende's tendency to write of the real people and real stories around her into her books. Allende combines both third- and first-person points of view in order to present Gregory Reeves's story from childhood to adulthood. As the story progresses, it becomes evident that Gregory is *telling* his own story to a definitive audience, a person he addresses directly as "you" in the book's final paragraph. With Gregory Reeves, Allende blurs the line between fiction and nonfiction; the character and his story are based on the real life of her husband, William Gordon, and the audience Gregory speaks to throughout the book is Isabel Allende herself.

The story begins in the 1940s. Gregory is introduced as a little boy, son of an unlikely pair of parents: Charles Reeves, ambitious, larger-than-life, and possibly unfaithful to his wife; and Nora Reeves, who finds her husband's "Infinite Plan" admirable. Olga, part witch and part siren, is thoroughly indispensable to the family. Gregory's sister Judy carries a dark secret of sexual abuse. The family meets a young black man, King Benedict, who reappears much later in the novel, lending the work a subtly cyclical structure. As a lawyer, Gregory finds some redemption and validation by winning a legal case for Benedict.

The family eventually finds itself stranded in a Hispanic section of Los Angeles, rescued and assisted in no small part by the Morales family, followers of Reeves's "Infinite Plan." Allende does not contrast the Reeves family with the Morales family; both groups have serious issues. For example, Carmen Morales, Gregory's friend, nearly dies from an abortion and never becomes the perfect, married "good girl" her father had wanted. Instead, her free spirit leads her across the world, allows her to adopt her dead brother's half-Vietnamese child, and eventually gives her wealth and security. In Carmen, Allende constructs one of her familiar free and passionate female characters, but she does not allow the focus of her story to drift from Gregory to Carmen. Unlike Carmen, Gregory's future is not promising or pleasant.

In Gregory, Allende finds an opportunity to depict and criticize some of the most notable excesses of the United States, from the libertine 1960s through the materialistic 1980s. Gregory is not, by any means, a successful husband, father, or even lawyer. Though gifted and idealistic, Gregory lacks the practical ability to fulfill his wishes. He loses touch with his children, and at the end of the book he has lost his oldest child to the streets and is forced to confront the clinging, unstable nature of his youngest. He marries for a romantic vision of love, but disappointingly learns that he has mistaken physical beauty and sex for true affection.

But Allende is not entirely unsympathetic to her character's plight. Though he does not receive the same tolerant, indulgent treatment Allende generally affords her female characters, she does not entirely blame Gregory for his mistakes, finding his social setting—the tumultuous sixties, Vietnam, the greed of the eighties—also culpable in creating the darker, and weaker, aspects of his character. Nor does Allende leave Gregory ultimately without salvation. Instead, through the help of the psychiatrist Ming O'Brien, Gregory comes to understand himself, to know the motivations for his actions. Although Gregory nearly loses his law practice, his friends rally to his side, offering him money and support. Ultimately, the character continues the fight on his own terms and begins to regain control over both his legal practice and his own life. Gregory has at least begun to comprehend the "Infinite Plan" of the book's title—not the sham religion of his father, but the progression of actions and events that have made him the flawed but reparable human being that he is.

BIBLIOGRAPHY

Hunt, Daniel P. "Women Writing Men: Leslie Marmon Silko's *Ceremony* and Isabel Allende's *El plan infinito.*" *Selecta: Journal of the Pacific Northwest Council on Foreign Languages* 14 (1993): 16–19.

Perricone, Catherine R. "*El plan infinito*: Isabel Allende's New World." *SECOLAS Annals: Journal of the Southeastern Council on Latin American Studies* 25 (1994): 55–61.

Winter S. Elliott

IN SEARCH OF LOST TIME (À LA RECHERCHE DU TEMPS PERDU; REMEMBRANCE OF THINGS PAST) MARCEL PROUST (1913–1927)

The reclusive French writer MARCEL PROUST, now considered by many scholars as the greatest novelist of the 20th century, labored for more than 14 years and died while still adding to what would eventually be a seven-volume masterpiece. The novel is so singular, so complete, and so monumental that it has become the brilliant exemplar of modernism and the distillation of 20th-century aesthetics. Proust's admirers included great thinkers and writers such as José Ortega y Gassett, Samuel Beckett, Virginia Woolf, Graham Greene, ANDRÉ GIDE, JEAN GENET, Gérard Genette, Roland Barthes, Ralph Ellison, and many more. His work effaced the realism of the 19th-century novel and set a standard for narrative fiction. *In Search of Lost Time* is a brilliant treatment of the universal human condition, of the quest of the individual for the meaning of life, of the birth of the artist, and of the transcendence of art.

In the original French, *À la recherche du temps perdu* is a verbal tour de force, an exquisite rendering of the narrator's perception and apprehension of a shifting universe and of the incalculable losses to time. From the very first line, the novel draws the reader into the conscious and unconscious realm of a speaker who is author-narrator-protagonist and who exists alternately and simultaneously in all the times and places of his life.

Since 1922, *À la recherche du temps perdu* has been read in English as *Remembrance of Things Past,* in the translation by C. K. Scott Moncrieff, which immediately became the basis for other translations. Moncrieff took the title from Shakespeare's Sonnet 30 ("When to the sessions of sweet silent thought/ I summon up remembrance of things past,/ I sigh the lack of many a thing I sought,/And with old woes new wail my dear time's waste"). The Moncrieff translation is poetic but much wordier than the original French. Moncrieff had a tendency to give several synonyms for many words and to gratuitously embellish, and his focus on rumination and memory in the title does not allow for the multiple possibilities of wordplay inherent in the original French. In 1993 the Modern Library edition (the translation of C. K. Moncrieff, Terence Kilmartin, and D. J. Enright) recast the work more literally as *In Search of Lost Time,* a title now universally preferred.

In Search of Lost Time consists of seven volumes, although the various editions and translations have split the work in different ways. Proust did not readily find a publisher for his work (André Gide rejected it for publication by the Nouvelle Revue Française, which later became Gallimard). The first volume, SWANN'S WAY (*Du côté de chez Swann,* 1913), was published by

Grasset in 1913, at the expense of the author, as the first of a two-part work. *The Guermantes Way,* originally the title of the second part, was scheduled to appear the following year; however, World War I (1914–18) intervened. Grasset closed its doors, and Proust continued to expand and enrich the text. In 1919 Gallimard published the entire, much longer novel, beginning with *Swann's Way* and continuing with *Within a Budding Grove* (or *In the Shadows of the Young Girls in Flower; À l'ombre des jeunes filles en fleurs,* 1919), which was awarded the Prix Goncourt. *The Guermantes Way* (*Le côté de Guermantes*) and *Sodom and Gomorrah* (*Sodome et Gomorrhe*) appeared in 1922. The remaining volumes came out posthumously under the direction of Marcel Proust's brother, Robert Proust. *The Prisoner* (*La prisonnière*) appeared in 1923; *The Fugitive* (*La fugitive,* 1925) was first published as *Albertine disparue* to differentiate it from another book with a similar title; and, finally, *Time Regained* (*Le temps retrouvé*) closed the cycle in 1927, at a total 4,300 pages.

The French text now considered the most authoritative is *À la recherche du temps perdu,* edited by Jean-Yves Tadié (Gallimard, 1987). The finest and most ambitious English translation of the entire masterpiece is the Penguin UK Modern Classics edition, which came out between 1996 and 2001, based on the Tadié 1987 Gallimard edition. Under the general editorship of Christopher Prendergast, each of the seven volumes of Proust's novel has been translated into English by a different scholar. The first volume, *Swann's Way,* is by Lydia Davis; *In the Shadows of the Young Girls in Flower* is by John Grieve; *The Guermantes Way* is by Mark Treharne; *Sodom and Gomorrah* is by John Sturrock; *The Prisoner* is by Carol Clark; *The Fugitive* is by Peter Collier; and *Finding Time Again* is by Ian Patterson, a translation that John Updike calls sublime. The first four parts have been published in New York by Viking (2003–04). The remaining three volumes are not scheduled until 2019, due to revised American copyright laws.

In Search of Lost Time in any version is a literary masterpiece that has dissolved the boundaries of genre, incorporating the elements of musical and artistic composition. The novel combines reflective essay, autobiography, and panoramic human comedy. Originally conceived as two books, each in two parts and orchestrated, some say, in homage to the four-opera *Ring* cycle of Richard Wagner (1813–33), the novel achieves Wagnerian fullness and amplitude in its fully developed score. Critics see the template for *In Search of Lost Time* in Parsifal's quest of the Holy Grail, with its symbolic swan, attendant flower maidens, and the Gurnemanz, leader of the Grail Knights. *In Search of Lost Time,* like *Parsifal,* is the epic story of a young man who, through trial and suffering, is destined to restore harmony to his world and direct the mind to a higher divinity.

In Search of Lost Time has become the seminal work of modernism and the novel that best exemplifies the narrative style of the early 20th century. Proust destroys 19th-century novelistic conventions of chronology and causality while incorporating Freudian psychology and the subjective apprehension of time and sensation into the narrative. The novel dramatizes the vast panorama of Belle Époque society, with recurring characters in the style of Honoré de Balzac's *Human Comedy,* in sharply drawn vignettes and set-pieces as memorable and comic as those of Charles Dickens but with the modulations of perception and shading of a Henry James. This work is a wonderfully nuanced application of impressionism to novelistic narrative; it sheds the vestiges of photographic realism by shredding light and color into component wavelengths, the multiple superimposed impressions of the narrator. It is a bildungsroman, a novel of growth and development, but from the inside out; it advances from a narrative stance in the present of the adult narrator and moves backward in time in a series of images and recurring motifs. Gerard Genette says that the narrative is polymodal (both internally and externally focused) and polyvocal (both in the voice of the internal narrator Marcel and the heightened voice of the external narrator Proust) and, therefore, stretches the literary genre and enlarges the possibilities of fiction.

The chronology of *In Search of Lost Time* corresponds essentially to the life of the narrator, who is remarkably like the author, even in first name, except that the main portion of *Swann's Way,* "Swann in Love," takes place before the births of the narrator and his first love, Gilberte, in the 1890s. The last episode of *Time Regained,*

the afternoon at the Guermantes, takes place in 1925, after the death of the author, as does perhaps the very beginning, the "Overture," which introduces the very book we are reading, but from the vantage point of the future, after *Time Regained.*

The work begins with that famous reflexive line: "For a long time, I went to bed early" (*Longtemps, je me suis couché de bonne heure*). This is followed by recollections of awakenings appearing as free associations but subtly intertwining a series of leitmotifs that end in the resurrection of the village of Combray through involuntary memory, the episode of the madeleine cakes dipped in a cup of tea. "Combray 2" goes back to the childhood family walks through the country gardens, differentiating the two main paths, the path by their neighbor Swann and the path by the Guermantes, the haughty aristocrats. The next section flashes back to a time before the birth of the narrator, to Swann's infatuation with Odette, to their affair, to Odette's poses, to Swann's jealousy, to the ironies and cruelties inherent in every aspect of love. Swann is rich and Jewish and has artistic ambitions, but he squanders his talents on the pursuit of society and the love of a woman he does not even like. The last part of the first book is devoted to dreams of place names and to the meeting in the Champs-Élysées, the main thoroughfare in the middle of Paris, of Gilberte, the little girl with red hair who is the narrator's first love. The last is an image of Mme Swann in the Bois (park) one late autumn morning, the memory which becomes a regret for the lost moments and places as fleeting as the years.

Within a Budding Grove includes "Madame Swann at Home," in which the narrator as a boy makes friends with Gilberte Swann and begins to experience stirrings of longing, jealousy, and desire. The Swann's household opens to him, and he has glimpses of Odette, Swann, the artists, the concerts, and the exhibits then current, while getting varying and often opposing critiques of both personalities and performances. The narrator's parents wish he would do something useful with his life, but he continues a dilettante in pursuit of society and pleasure. From Gilberte, he first hears of Albertine. The narrator has snatches of revelation: In love, happiness is abnormal; love secretes a permanent pain. In "Place-Names: The Place," the narrator leaves for the seaside town of Balbec with his grandmother. There among the visits, the names, the seascapes, the churches, the dinners, he meets the little band of beautiful young girls, today's young buds, and has a glimpse of future ugliness. He makes friends with Charlus, his alter ego, and begins his fixation with Albertine.

The Guermantes Way, named for the alternate walk in the village of Combray, was once planned to be the counterpart to the volume of *Swann's Way* and a middle section before *Time Recaptured.* In the finished work, *The Guermantes Way* forms a two-part treatment that begins with a move of the narrator's family to a new apartment in Paris. It encompasses a variety of social episodes that underscore the narrator's fascination with nobility and are punctuated by the grandmother's illness and death. *The Guermantes Way* has an accretion of themes, among them death and loss, notations on theatricality, role playing, social aspirations, snobbery, and sexual ambivalence. The narrator is essentially recording the world of dispersion and dissimulation and the distractions of social life to his creative energies.

Sodom and Gomorrah, sometimes translated as "Cities of the Plain," begins with a forty-page essay on homosexuality, "the race of inverts," in Proust's words, both beautiful and repellent. It concludes at a reception at the palace of the prince de Guermantes, the pinnacle of aspirations for the caste-conscious narrator, though he is now aware that every level of society is swarming with illicit lusts. Sodom is to be understood as synonymous with the affinity of men for other men, and Gomorrah with lesbianism. The narrator is haunted by his suspicion of Albertine's preferring girls, and the entire book is redolent with the illusive nature of love and the spectacle of man turned into slave through obsessive passion.

The Captive and *The Fugitive* (sometimes called *The Sweet Cheat Gone*) narrate, in almost 1,000 pages, the relationship between Marcel and Albertine, an epic love story totally devoid of idealism, glamour, romance, or enjoyment—except as suffering. The sleeping Albertine evokes lyrical descriptions but awakes only exquisite pain. Love for Proust is an exercise in futility because it is never requited, and although the loved one can be captured, the captive can never be held.

The universe is ever changing and the personality ever fleeting. The narrator says that we love only what we do not wholly possess; he is physically ill, discouraged with life, and disillusioned with society.

Time Regained begins years later in a world dramatically altered, a world that the old literary forms can no longer reflect accurately. This is underscored when the narrator, a guest at a lavish estate, reads a pastiche of pages purportedly from the *Goncourt Journals,* which describe an earlier time in a "realistic" style, a description which differs markedly from the experience of the narrator. Marcel, dejected and ill, withdraws from society to a sanitarium and returns to Paris in 1916 only to capture in potent satire the continuing search for pleasure, luxury, and dissipation in the midst of the bitter and bloody war.

Yet amid the pessimistic details of daily life during this time of wrenching upheavals, in the tasting of tea and madeleine, the narrator experiences a great joy, a glimmer of the past, long lost. He experiences through involuntary memory a repeated pattern of revelations, of illuminations through the medium of sensory perception that can unite the present to the past. He becomes aware that in these favored moments, he is liberated at least temporarily from the passage of time, and he reflects that he must capture these sacred moments into a literary creation. The narrator has to work against time, as his illness is progressing, but he is elated that now he has a literary vocation. He is finally able to detach himself from society and to produce in the ensuing time and short space available to him a voluminous novel, the most lyrical and compassionate treatment on the human condition.

In Search of Lost Time is not easily read, especially in the sequential order advised by critics and informed readers. It is long (seven volumes) and longwinded (4,300 pages). The prose is a labyrinth, the sentences transcontinental, the plot seemingly motionless, and the author one of the great megalomaniacs of literature. Yet Roger Shattuck, a most incisive reader of Proust's work, says that neither the novel form nor human nature remains unchanged after Proust has passed. The endless reflections and contradictions found *In Search of Lost Time* contain the multitudinous self, the fragmentary nature of perception, the conflicting aspects of reality, and the fluctuations and partial realization of the personality.

Reading Proust has afforded wisdom, pleasure, and satire, as well as self-discovery. The now-classic Monty Python comedy troupe paid homage to Proust's novel in a sketch first broadcast on November 16, 1972, called The All-England Summarize Proust Competition. The winner was the contestant who could best summarize *À la recherche du temps perdu* in 15 seconds: "once in a swimsuit and once in evening dress." Many others have attempted to summarize the novel in as few words as possible. Here are some worthy examples: Gérard Genette in *Figures III: "Marcel devient écrivain"* ("Marcel becomes a writer"). Vincent Descombes in *Proust: philosophie du roman: "Marcel devient un grand écrivain"* ("Marcel becomes a great writer"). Gérard Genette, again in *Palimpsestes: "Marcel finit par devenir écrivain"* ("Marcel ends up becoming a great writer"). A Web site *temps perdu.com* lists many other reductive summaries and invites submissions.

In 1977 Alain de Botton created another distillation of Proust's novel and an affectionate view of the brilliant and often bizarre author in a best seller, *How Proust Can Change Your Life*. He reveals Proust's ideas on, among other things, how to revive a relationship, how to select a good doctor, and how to turn suffering to advantage. Alain de Botton says that Proust's book is a search for causes behind dissipation and sloth. Far from being a memoir tracing the passage of a more lyrical age, it is a practical, universally applicable story about how to stop wasting time and start appreciating life. The object of reading Proust is to come away with a heightened sense of perception that can be employed wherever you are and in whatever time you live. Though many of us have traditionally been concerned with the pursuit of happiness, far greater wisdom lies in pursuing ways to be properly and productively unhappy.

Readers find *In Search of Lost Time* a dramatization, or perhaps a novelization, of many, if not most, of the ideas and the aesthetic approaches that define the 20th century. Among these—this list is not exhaustive—are the scientific studies of light, matter, memory, and sensation; the feelings of alienation, disillusionment, and ennui; the fragmentation of consciousness; Henri Bergson's *élan vital,* the life force, that stresses duration and the fluidity of time; Freudian psychoanalysis, Gestalt psychology, and Jungian collective unconscious; Einstein's theory of relativity; and Heisenberg's uncertainty principle, more accurately called, as it pertains to pinpointing reality in time and space, the theory of indeterminacy.

Proust's novel also serves as an exemplar of the techniques and the modes of modern art. It explains Belle Époque decadence, synesthesia (the interplay of the senses), symbolism, impressionism, cubism, montage, telescoping, stream of consciousness, epiphany, objective correlative, even magic realism. In *The Proust Project* (FSG/Turtle Point Press, 2004), André Aciman, a distinguished critic, asks literary figures from our time to select a passage of three or four pages in length from *In Search of Lost Time* and to respond to it. The comments of prominent literary figures tell us something about Proust, and a lot about our own era. Aciman remarks in his preface that *In Search of Lost Time* is a novel about intimacy, but its long and densely populated story is filled with brutality, with malice and envy, with lacerating desire, with jealousy and betrayal, with all sorts of little cruelties.

Proust saw the underside of humanity and the nothingness of society and depicted it with incisive intelligence and understanding, but he was not a nihilist. A passage in the last volume of the novel may serve as manifesto: "Real life, life at last laid bare and illuminated—the only life in consequence which can be said to be really lived—is literature, and life thus defined is in a sense all the time immanent in ordinary men no less than the artist." Edmund White has remarked that Proust was no ordinary man: Proust happened to live at one of the high points of culture and civilization; he had unusual natural gifts of eloquence, analysis of psychology, and assimilation of information; and he was willing to sacrifice his life for his art.

BIBLIOGRAPHY
Barthes, Roland, and Gérard Genette, Tzvetan Todorov. *Recherche de Proust.* Paris: Seuil, 1980.
Beckett, Samuel. *Proust.* New York: Grove Press, 1931.
Booth, Wauce C. *The Rhetoric of Fiction.* Chicago: University of Chicago Press; London: Penguin, 1983.

Bouillaguet, Annick, and Brian G. Rogers. *Dictionnaire Marcel Proust.* Paris: Honoré Champion, 2004.

Brée, Germaine. *The World of Marcel Proust.* Boston: Houghton Mifflin, 1966.

Genette, Gérard. *Palimpsestes: la littérature au second degré.* Paris: Seuil, 1982.

Hindus, Milton. *A Reader's Guide to Proust.* New York: Farrar, Strauss, 1962.

Kogten, Igor van. *Proustian Love.* Asterdam/Lisse: Swets & Zeitlinger B.V., 1992.

Landy, Joshua. *Philosophy as Fiction: Self, Deception, and Knowledge in Proust.* New York: Oxford University Press, 2004.

Proust, Marcel. The Prisoner *and* The Fugitive. Translated by Carol Clark and Peter Collier. London: Penguin Books, 2003.

Rogers, B. G. *Proust's Narrative Techniques.* Genève: Librarie Droz, 1985.

Scholes, Robert. *Structuralism in Literature.* New Haven, Conn.: Yale University Press, 1974.

Shattuck, Roger. *Proust's Binoculars: A Study of Memory, Time and Recognition in* À la recherche du temps perdu. New York: Random House, 1963.

———. *Proust's Way: A Field Guide in Search of Lost Time.* New York: W.W. Norton, 2000.

Tadié, Jean-Yves. *Marcel Proust/Biographie.* Paris: Gallimard, 1996.

———. *Marcel Proust.* Translated by Evan Cameron. New York: Viking, 2000.

Terdiman, Richard. *Present Past: Modernity and the Memory Crisis.* Ithaca, N.Y.: Cornell University Press, 1993.

Trouffaut, Louis. *Introduction á Marcel Proust.* Munich, Germany: Max Hueber Verlag, 1967.

White, Edmund. *Marcel Proust.* New York: Viking, 1999.

Wilson, Edmund. *Axel's Castle: A Study in the Imaginative Literature of 1870–1930.* New York: Scribner, 1931, 1948.

Arbolina Llamas Jennings

INTERPRETERS, THE WOLE SOYINKA (1965)

The Interpreters is the first of two novels written by the prominent Nigerian intellectual WOLE SOYINKA (1934–). He is best known for his prolific career as a playwright, already well established at the time of the publication of *The Interpreters,* as well as for his poetry and literary criticism. Educated in Nigeria and the United Kingdom, Soyinka has worked as a dramatist, lecturer, and professor at numerous universities in both countries as well as in Ghana and the United States. In 1986 he became the first African writer to be awarded the Nobel Prize in literature.

The Interpreters is a complex work that has often been overlooked in favor of Soyinka's other literary forms, derided for what some regard as its lack of organization, and hailed as the first modernist African novel of exquisite intricacy and innovation. The novel portrays a group of friends, recently graduated from the university, as they try to find their way through a complicated and often contradictory Nigerian society toward an authentic sense of self. Each is faced with difficult choices through which he or she must work out a relationship to society, in all its diverse and troubled forms.

A thoughtful and often heavily satirical novel, *The Interpreters* does not have a traditional, linear plot, but moves around in time, often incorporating flashbacks, in a way that is minimally signaled and sometimes difficult to follow. Yet this technique has the effect of isolating experience from fixed chronology, perhaps challenging our reliance on predictable sequences of cause and effect and reflecting the sometimes confusing inundation of messages and experiences the characters themselves are subjected to as they struggle to make sense of their world.

The novel is likewise unusual in that it does not have a clearly identifiable single protagonist, but shifts around from character to character in its focus. Egbo is the grandson of the king of Osa, a rich creek-town, and now that he is grown he is heavily pressured to return and take the throne. He is torn between undertaking this responsibility and keeping his comfortable job at the Foreign Office; although he decides on the latter, he is never fully comfortable with his choice. He must later face another troubling choice: whether to leave his girlfriend, Simi, for the undergraduate whom he hardly knows but has made pregnant and who holds a certain elusive fascination for him. In many ways Egbo seems caught between past and future, and no easy solutions offer themselves to him.

Sagoe has created a bizarre philosophy, which he terms *voidancy,* centered on death and excrement. Moreover, although as a journalist he executes incisive criticism of society, he nonetheless seems to exhibit a certain escapism as his response to life's stresses. His eventual development toward engagement with the world, manifested directly through maturity in his relationship to his girlfriend Dehinwa, ultimately brings some measure of resolution to his character.

Sekoni, on the other hand, possesses an idealism and creative force so strong as to be nearly impossible to negotiate within his immediate contexts, and in fact he dies midway through the novel. He is deeply spiritual and full of vision, which unfortunately is only frustrated by engagement with the petty and often mundane world around him. He leaves a legacy, however, through the compelling sculpture he creates: "The Wrestler."

The principled Bandele, although quiet, is a powerful character in that he often helps the others to be reconciled to their own lives, while at other times drawing attention to their internal conflicts and contradictions. Meanwhile, Kola, devoted to art, provides a rich locus of symbolism for the novel through his painting of a Yoruba pantheon, in which each character is depicted in the form of a divinity.

Throughout *The Interpreters,* Soyinka deploys a trenchant critique of Nigerian society along with a sophisticated contemplation of the predicament of the individual struggling to find a tenable position within it. The author often focuses his satire on the superficiality of society, the unexamined contradictions inherent in the lives and conduct of many, and the pervasiveness of corruption. He does engage the tension between traditional and modern values and practices, but for him it is clear that neither offers wholly satisfying treatments of life's quandaries. Instead of championing one over the other in a simplistic manner, Soyinka pushes for a critical examination of both as crucial to honest engagement in a complex world.

BIBLIOGRAPHY

Hederman, Mark P. *The Haunted Inkwell: Art and Our Future.* Blackrock, Co. Dublin: Columba Press, 2001.

Jeyifo, Biodun. *Wole Soyinka: Politics, Poetics and Postcolonialism.* Cambridge, and New York: Columbia University Press, 2004.

Jones, Eldred D. *Wole Soyinka.* New York: Twayne Publishers, 1973.

Moore, Gerald. *Wole Soyinka.* New York: Africana Publications, 1971.

Okome, Onookome, ed. *Ogun's Children: The Literature and Politics of Wole Soyinka since the Nobel.* Trenton, N.J.: Africa World Press, 2003.

Omotoso, Kole. *Achebe or Soyinka: A Study in Contrasts.* London: Hans Zell, 1996.

Soyinka, Wole. *The Man Died: Prison Notes.* New York: Harper & Row, 1972.

Megan K. Ahern

IN THE FLESH (LEIBHAFTIG) Christa Wolf **(2002)** This novel by the German author Christa Wolf (1929–   ) details a writer's illness and recovery from a burst appendix and its resulting infections during the last weeks of the German Democratic Republic (GDR). John S. Barrett translated the work into English in 2005. The novel's protagonist is Wolf's alter ego, while the character Hannes Urban is based on the historical figure Hans Koch, an important leader of the GDR who committed suicide in 1986. While Wolf had criticized the GDR, she did not want East and West Germany to unify, and her stance caused her a great deal of controversy. In a November 4, 1989, speech she urged fellow East Germans to remain and work toward a true socialism. Like Cassandra, the mythical character and a previous novel's protagonist, Wolf's calls were not heeded, East Germans fled the country for the West, and the GDR collapsed.

Wolf has often used illness in her works, but *In the Flesh* represents a departure since the main character is in the present time, with the illness and recuperation taking place at an East German hospital. Previously in Wolf's books, the illness was set in the past and the protagonist recovered, as in *DIVIDED HEAVEN* (1963) or succumbed to illness as in *The Quest for Christa T.* (1969). *In the Flesh* is told in the first and third person by the unnamed narrator in a stream-of-consciousness manner. When her body fails or she is being examined by doctors and nurses, the perspective changes to the third person, and the character is viewed as an object. The novel is a detailed look at a hospital stay, which begins with the ride in an ambulance to the facility. The novel then recounts the seemingly countless examinations and operations and ultimately the protagonist's slow recovery, during which she must relearn such basics as eating and walking. The narration not only slips back and forth from first to third person but also from clarity to unconsciousness and from the present to the past. Due to the fever caused by the infection in her body, painkillers, and anesthesia, the patient drifts in and out of consciousness. Kora Bachmann, her anesthesiologist, aids in this process and, like her mythical namesake, takes the narrator on journeys into the underworld or, in this case, the subconscious. Here the character remembers and then extensively reflects on Hannes Urban, who embodies the GDR as a dignitary of the state. The narrator, who initially considered Urban as a friend and believed in the government's socialist vision, distances herself from Urban and the state. During her hospital stay, Urban goes missing and is later found dead. He has killed himself, and his suicide makes the protagonist want to live and experience the future.

In the Flesh takes place in the mind of a writer and therefore contains many literary quotes and allusions. The protagonist is both admired by the state as well as put under surveillance, something the author Christa Wolf herself experienced. The novel reflects the decline of the East German state a few months before the fall of the Berlin Wall, which is illustrated in the difficulty the doctors have in obtaining the medicine that is vital to the protagonist's recovery. The pharmaceutical must be ordered and shipped from West Berlin, since it is not available in the East. Though the patient begins to recover from her illness, the country does not—it dies.

BIBLIOGRAPHY

Baumer, Franz. *Christa Wolf.* Berlin: Colloquium, 1988.
Böthig, Peter. *Christa Wolf: Eine Biographie in Bildern und Texten.* Munich: Luchterhand, 2004.
Finney, Gail. *Christa Wolf.* New York: Twayne Publishers, 1999.
Resch, Margit. *Understanding Christa Wolf: Returning Home to a Foreign Land.* Columbia: University of South Carolina Press, 1977.

Karen Bell

IN THE LABYRINTH (DANS LE LABY-RINTHE) ALAIN ROBBE-GRILLET (1959) *In the Labyrinth* constitutes a prime example of the New Novel, a term given by critics to works created in France mostly in the 1950s by writers such as CLAUDE SIMON, NATHALIE SARRAUTE, MARGUERITE DURAS, Jean Ricardou, and ALAIN ROBBE-GRILLET, who became the most visible exemplar and spokesperson for the movement.

As in most works classified with the New Novel, *In the Labyrinth* by Robbe-Grillet (1922–) defies traditional reader expectations as to narrative coherence, character, and plot. The novel is full of stops and starts, incomplete scenes and actions, and indeterminacy in matters such as who the characters are, why they are doing what they are doing, whether a scene takes place in day or night, rain or snow, and so forth. Robbe-Grillet in his later career has collaborated with surrealist and abstract expressionist painters (such as René Magritte and Robert Rauschenberg), and it may be useful to view this novel through the lens of nonrealistic artwork. *In the Labyrinth* evokes for some readers the feeling of M. C. Escher prints, with their elaborate and dreamlike patterns, passageways, connections, and disconnectedness. Robbe-Grillet is also a prominent filmmaker, and one can see in this novel an attention to visual detail from a writer with a photographic sensibility.

As its title implies, *In the Labyrinth* evokes movement through passages, some of which are dead ends, others of which wind back upon themselves or connect in unexpected, nonlinear ways. These labyrinthine movements are both linguistic—the author's use of recursive language that comes back upon itself, then branches off in new directions—and plot-related. The central motif of the book involves a mysterious soldier traveling through unfamiliar city streets in a quest to locate someone he has never met, so as to deliver a package whose contents—along with the nature and purpose of the soldier's quest—are only revealed to the reader at the book's denouement.

In the Labyrinth begins and ends with first-person observations of the speaker's setting; these are the novel's only first-person referents. The book may thus be seen as the speaker or author setting out for himself the challenge of taking ordinary objects in the room—a box, a painting, a dagger, some slippers—and weaving from those bare materials a sort of narrative involving the enigmatic soldier, only to return to the initial setting briefly at the book's close. This experimental quality of the narrative—as though the speaker were spontaneously taking on the challenge of creating a story from the objects in his studio—also brings a pervasive narrative indeterminacy. A passage that describes in great specificity an object or scene is often immediately undercut by an alternative view.

The narrative is full of qualifying words such as *but, or, instead, may, might,* and *could be.* For example, the novel's second sentence declares that it is raining outside; then it elaborates on a detached someone walking in that rain; the next sentence declares that outside the sun is shining and then expands on that new premise. The next paragraph notes that nothing from outside penetrates the chamber—including dust—but the next sentence and many subsequent pages of the novel are devoted to describing dust and the patterns made by objects in the dust.

Robbe-Grillet has been accused of a mathematical attention to detail, which some critics have seen as inhuman and cold. Many pages of *In the Labyrinth* are indeed devoted to long, seemingly mundane descriptions of walls, streets, footprints in the snow, patterns on wrought iron lampposts, and so forth. These descriptions are not only given but repeated numerous times, accruing variation and elaboration as the novel progresses. In a famous article ("Literature Objective"), influential critic Roland Barthes noted that Robbe-Grillet's detailed descriptions of objects were not, as in the traditional realistic novel, background for the more important elements of character and plot, but were in themselves primary. Barthes applauded what he termed the "objectivity" of Robbe-Grillet's writing as authentic rather than lacking in human empathy and warmth.

Since the novel is so lacking in traditional elements such as exposition, characterization, and coherent plot, a reader may naturally be tempted to wonder what symbolic or allegorical significance one can find—for example, what does the soldier's quest symbolize? In the headnote to *In the Labyrinth,* Robbe-Grillet counsels against such attempts, telling readers: ". . . the reality in question is a strictly material one; that is, it is subject to no allegorical interpretation. The reader is therefore requested to see in it only the objects, actions, words, and events which are described, without attempting to give them either more or less meaning than in his own life, or his own death."

BIBLIOGRAPHY

Hellerstein, Marjorie H. *Inventing the Real World.* Selinsgrove, Pa.: Susquehanna University Press and London: Associated University Presses, 1998.

Ramsay, Raylene L. *Robbe-Grillet and Modernity: Science, Sexuality and Subversion.* Gainesville: University Press of Florida, 1992.

Smith, Roch C. *Understanding Robbe-Grillet.* Columbia: University of South Carolina Press, 2000.

Stoltzfus, Ben. *Alain Robbe-Grillet: The Body of the Text.* London & Toronto: Associated University Presses, 1985.

Douglas J. King

INTIMACY (*INTIMITÉ*) JEAN-PAUL SARTRE (1938)

The novel *NAUSEA* (*Le nausée,* 1938) and the collection of short stories and novellas *The Wall* (*Le mur,* 1939), which includes *Intimacy,* brought the French author JEAN-PAUL SARTRE (1905–80) immediate recognition and success as a writer and philosopher. Previously, he had been relatively unnoticed, even with the publication of his early, largely psychological studies. *Le nausée* and *Le mur* both express Sartre's early existential themes of alienation and commitment to individual freedom and authenticity. *Intimacy,* a work included in *The Wall,* particularly elaborates on the contradictions between the bourgeoisie and existentialism as well as on Sartre's well-known concepts of bad faith, or self-deception, and how hell is other people, as portrayed in his remarkable play *No Exit* (*Huis-clos,* 1947). *Intimacy* is told through the perspectives of multiple characters, a technique that Sartre would use in many of his fictional works, such as the trilogy *The Roads to Freedom* (*Les chemins de la liberté*), comprising *The Age of Reason* (*L'âge de raison,* 1945), *The Reprieve* (*Le sursis,* 1947), and *Troubled Sleep* (also known in translation as *Iron in the Soul; La mort dans l'âme,* 1949). The novella deconstructs Lulu's decision, negatively influenced by her friend Rirette, about whether or not to leave her impotent husband, Henri, with whom she is unhappy, for her lover, Pierre.

For Sartre, the bourgeoisie came to stand for all that existentialism was not; it was impossible to be an existentialist and a bourgeois in his mind, which Lulu's actions and decision-making process reflect in *Intimacy.* When Lulu meets Rirette at the Dome café to tell her that she has left Henri, Rirette painfully observes how Lulu is more concerned with the waiter's delay in taking her order for a café-crème. While Lulu is sitting at the café with her friend, her valise beside her and her coat on after she has left her husband, she still believes that she deserves better attention and service. She does not care if she runs into her husband after she and Rirette leave the Dome as long as she buys her lingerie at a particular store and location before going to the hotel. During her brief stay at the Hotel du Théâtre, she is more concerned about the shoddy conditions of her room and the untrustworthy Algerian who works at the front desk and, she believes, wants to break into her room.

Although Rirette encourages Lulu to make decisions for herself rather than as Henri's wife, Rirette's life is controlled by capitalism and her urge to be recognized as part of the middle class. While Rirette acts concerned about Lulu's attitude toward their waiter, she believes that the waiters are inferior to the people that they serve, including herself and Lulu. Rirette notes with pleasure how the waiter at the Dome makes conversation with her and hurries to their table when she calls him over for service, not understanding that perhaps his behavior is motivated by the slim monetary allotment that she will give him when she leaves the table. Rirette objectifies their male waiter into a source of sensual pleasure for herself because she is lonely and has no one with whom she shares her life. Although she appears to yearn for the company of a man, Rirette is more proud that she is the best saleswoman at her office and therefore makes more money than the other ladies, and she is glad that she is competing with them for the same commissions.

Bad faith, or what Sartre considers self-deception, clearly drives the thoughts and behaviors of all of the characters in *Intimacy*. They shift responsibility for their decisions and actions from themselves to outside influences. Lulu believes that Henri's impotency is the cause of their marriage's problems, rather than her successive sexual affairs. She does not take responsibility for her behavior as his wife and her decision not to communicate with him, and Henri does not acknowledge his behavior toward her, until the night that she comes over to their house from her hotel to talk about her leaving him. Nor does Lulu take responsibility for not telling her lover, Pierre, that their sexual relationship leaves her unfulfilled, choosing instead to write in her letter to him that she wants to continue meeting with him frequently anyway and that her body is his even though she has returned to her husband. Rirette, even though she claims to be Lulu's good friend, abstains from telling her that Pierre is attracted to her and acts in an inappropriately sexual manner toward her. Pierre, positioning himself as Lulu's savior from her difficult marriage, is evidently using Lulu purely for convenient sexual gratification, as Lulu notices that he does not tell her he loves her after she has told him that she has left Henri. Pierre is relieved when Lulu returns to Henri and thus will not be accompanying him to Nice because he has not told her that she will be unable to stay in his mother's flat. However, he chooses to share this piece of information with Rirette, knowing that she is trustworthy and will not tell Lulu because she is such a good friend.

While hell emerges as the togetherness of other people in Sartre's play *No Exit,* published in 1947, Lulu's relationship with her husband, friend, and lover exemplify Sartre's beliefs. Lulu's quandary about whether to stay with her husband, although he is unable to satisfy her sexually, is complicated by the fact that she can only satisfy herself because of her own medical condition; therefore she does not enjoy the sexual relationships she finds outside of her marriage. When, after coming into contact with Henri on the street, Lulu is overpowered by Rirette and pushed into a taxi, she announces that she hates Rirette, Pierre, and Henri. She wonders what each one has against her and why they would want to torture her. Lulu covers her honest admission to Rirette with the excuse that she has been overcome by nerves upon seeing her husband. Her decision to return to her distraught marriage with Henri and continue her unsatisfying affair with Pierre and false friendship with Rirette reaffirms Sartre's belief that members of the bourgeoisie are incapable of acknowledging their individual freedom and the anguish and responsibility that comes with that freedom.

BIBLIOGRAPHY
Bloom, Harold. *Jean-Paul Sartre*. Philadelphia: Chelsea House, 2001.

Farrar, Roxanne C. *Sartrean Dialectics.* Amsterdam: Rodopi, 2000.

McBride, William L., ed. *Existentialist Literature and Aesthetics.* New York: Garland, 1997.

Poisson, Catherine. *Sartre and Beauvoir.* Amsterdam and New York: Rodopi, 2002.

Sartre, Jean-Paul. *What Is Literature?* Translated by Bernard Frechtman. New York: Harper & Row, 1965.

Wardman, Harold W. *Jean-Paul Sartre: The Evolution of his Thought and Art.* Lewiston, N.Y.: Edwin Mellen, 1992.

Tara J. Johnson

INVENTION OF MOREL, THE (LA INVENCIÓN DE MOREL) ADOLFO BIOY CASARES (1940)

Inspired by his fascination with the movie star Louise Brooks, ADOLFO BIOY CASARES's novel *The Invention of Morel* is on one level a stoic evocation of the pains and frustrations of romantic love and on another level a profound metaphysical mystery story. Along with his friend and mentor Jorge Luis Borges, Bioy Casares (1914–99) believed that the mission of the 20th-century writer was to react against the effusiveness of 19th-century realist and psychological novels and their representations of human experience. Against the notion held in the previous century that the production of a voluminous novel with a condensed or nonexistent story was the height of skill, Bioy Casares sought to redeem the overlooked centrality of plot, inspired by the adventure, mystery, and science fiction of writers such as Robert Louis Stevenson, G. K. Chesterton, and Edgar Allan Poe. With *The Invention of Morel,* he achieved his most successful synthesis of metaphysical speculation and taut and suspenseful plotting.

The narrative, written by an unnamed narrator and presented by an editor who makes occasional interjections to clarify or contradict details of the narrative, takes the form of a record of time spent on an island. The beginning of the novel details the narrator's arrival at the supposedly deserted island, despite having received warnings that it is the focal point of a mysterious and deadly disease. His decision to make the journey is not rationalized, but it has a distinctly fatalistic resonance: "But my life was so unbearable that I decided to go there anyway . . . . I have the uncomfortable sensation that this paper is changing into a will." Before

arriving, he is told that around 1924 a group came to the island and built a museum, a chapel, and a swimming pool, abandoning the island as soon as the work was completed. One night, another group of people unaccountably appears on the island and occupies the built-up part of it to "dance, stroll up and down, and swim in the pool, as if this were a summer resort."

The narrator satisfies himself by observing the visitors from the marshy lowlands of the island and exploring the buildings under the cover of night. On one excursion, he discovers a strange-looking generator and a series of what look like bomb shelters in the museum's basement. Soon after, he encounters a young woman who regularly comes to sit on some rocks to watch the sun set. The narrator quickly becomes fascinated by her and eventually summons the courage to address her. When he does so, she gives no response and behaves as though she has not seen him. As his love for her deepens, he conceives of several ways to attract her attention: He cultivates a garden and spells out messages for his with flowers, yet she continues not to notice these. Further events on the island puzzle the narrator: Some of the other guests fail to notice him despite his proximity; a bearded man named Morel appears and speaks to Faustine, the woman on the rocks, the narrator, consumed with jealousy, eavesdrops on the pair only to find that their conversations and actions are strangely repetitive. One day, two moons and two suns appear in the sky.

Several explanations are considered by the narrator to account for the unusual occurrences on the island: that he has caught the island's fabled disease; that he is invisible; that the visitors are either extraterrestrial or insane; or that the island is a kind of purgatory for the dead. None of these are satisfactory, though, so the narrator takes advantage of his apparent invisibility to watch the other inhabitants of the island more closely. He attends a gathering of the group hosted by Morel, who explains his titular invention: Morel confesses to the visitors that he has been filming them since they came to the island, and, coupled with the aid of recorders and projectors, his invention will ensure that the week they have spent there will be recreated and replayed for the rest of eternity on the island. His audience is incredulous and then grows angry at the suggestion that for those who have been "taken" by Morel's invention, fatal consequences await. The narrator soon comes to realize that the figures he shares the island with are projections of the people recorded by Morel's invention for one particular week in the past, after he had purchased the island and had its few buildings erected. When he recognizes that Faustine's image may correspond to a dead woman, or to one he might never meet, his life on the island becomes intolerable. He investigates the machines in the museum basement and learns how to operate them so that he can turn on the recorders and insert himself alongside Faustine into the eternal projection: "I hope that, generally, we give the impression of being inseparable, of understanding each other so well that we have no need of speaking." This accomplished, the narrator discovers that the island's illness is a result of having been recorded by Morel's invention; the narrative closes as he is dying, pleading to be allowed to enter the heaven of Faustine's consciousness.

One of the most noticeable features of the novel is its terse style, which maintains a constant mood of suspense throughout. The reader has no authority upon which to rely but the narrator's, and because his motives are ambiguous and undefined, one finds oneself doubting the veracity of his statements. Might it be possible that the island and its inhabitants do not exist, and the invention is the narrative itself? Like many South American writers of the period, Bioy Casares delighted in exploiting the indeterminate status of the writer in his fiction. Who, he asks, is controlling what happens in the novel; is it Morel, the narrator, or the author?

Aside from drawing inspiration from the intricate plotting of those writers mentioned above, the novel has a very specific reference point in H. G. Wells's *The Island of Doctor Moreau*. Both novels take the form of a found manuscript of questionable legitimacy and feature an island dominated by a strange personality engaged in hubristic activity. While the novel contains many elements of Wellsian science fiction, its eventual investigations and implications are of a more metaphysical than scientific nature. Doctor Moreau's grotesque creations appear early in Wells's narrative to create a sense of shock, and the novel can be read as a direct engagement with contemporary issues in Victorian science, such as vivisection. Bioy Casares adopts Wells's framework but only allows Morel's decidedly banal creations to reveal their dreadful nature at the novel's climax, thus prompting his metaphysical enquiry about the nature of time, materiality, and immortality.

As with the best science fiction writing, *The Invention of Morel* proved to be intuitive and prophetic in its anticipation of the moral and philosophical debates surrounding everything from monitoring and surveillance to reality television. Inspired in part by the early years of film, the novel played its part in the stylistic development of the genre. *L'année dernière à Marienbad* (*Last Year at Marienbad,* 1961), scripted by ALAIN ROBBE-GRILLET and directed by Alain Resnais, was heavily influenced by *The Invention of Morel* and was the first cinematic depiction of two people who coexist spatially in two separate temporal dimensions. The notions underlying this innovative idea preoccupied Bioy Casares throughout his writing: the comic and tragic lengths to which lovers will resort, the inability to master one's ultimate destiny, and the essential solitude of life.

BIBLIOGRAPHY

Bioy Casares, Adolfo. *The Invention of Morel.* Translated by Ruth L. C. Simms. New York: New York Review Books, 2003.

———. *Memorias.* Barcelona: Tusquets Editores, 1994.

Camurati, Mireya: *Bioy Casares y el alegre trabajo de la inteligencia.* Buenos Aires: Ediciones Corregidor, 1990.

Curia, Beatriz. *La Concepción del cuento en Adolfo Bioy Casares.* Mendoza: Universidad Nacional de Cuyo, Facultad de Filosofía y Letras, Instituto de Literaturas Modernas, 1986.

Levine, Suzanne Jill: *Guía de Adolfo Bioy Casares.* Madrid: Fundamentos, 1982.

Martino, Daniel. *ABC de Adolfo Bioy Casares.* Madrid: Ediciones de la Universidad, 1991.

Snook, Margaret L. *In Search of Self: Gender and Identity in Bioy Casares's Fantastic Fiction.* New York: Peter Lang, 1998.

Suárez Coalla, Francisca. *Lo fantástico en la obra de Adolfo Bioy Casares.* Toluca: Universidad Autónoma del Estado de México, 1994.

Toro, Alfonso de, and Susanna Regazzoni, eds. *Coloquio Internacional en Homenaje a Adolfo Bioy Casares: Homenaje a Adolfo Bioy Casares: una retrospectiva de su obra (litera-*

tura, ensayo, filosofía, teoría de la cultura, crítica literaria). Frankfurt, Vervuert, and Madrid: Iberoamericana, 2002.

Justin Tonra

ISLAND OF THE DAY BEFORE, THE (*L'ISOLA DEL GIORNO PRIMA*) (1995)

UMBERTO ECO   The third novel by Italian author UMBERTO ECO (1932–   ), *The Island of the Day Before* is another extended meditation on the subjective nature of reality that demonstrates the deceptive nature of all signs and metaphors. Eco presents his historical romance as the collected letters of Roberto de La Griva, a shipwrecked 17th-century nobleman who becomes stranded on an abandoned ship, the *Daphne,* anchored off a mysterious Pacific island. With no way of locating himself or finding a way home, Roberto abandons himself to philosophical contemplation, roaming the crewless ship and composing letters to his beloved Lilia, a woman he has admired from afar.

The novel intercuts Roberto's writings with recollections of his earlier life when, as a teenager, he survived the siege of Casale in the Thirty Years' War. It is during his time in Casale that a fantasy figure from his childhood, his older and illegitimate half brother Ferrante, starts to intrude into Roberto's reality. A young captain who bears a striking resemblance to Roberto is involved in a treacherous plot to end the siege, and Roberto only just avoids being punished for this interloper's actions. Even after the war, when he travels to Paris and meets Lilia in the salon of a society hostess, the spectre of his half brother haunts Roberto. When he is arrested on unspecified charges of treason, Roberto suspects Ferrante's involvement, seeing any adversity in his own life as an attempt by Ferrante to assume Roberto's place as the heir to the de La Griva estate. However, after his arrest, Roberto is offered a chance of freedom by the sinister Cardinal Mazarin, who sends him to spy on the English attempt to locate the "fixed point" of longitude that allows for the measuring of nautical time. This results in Roberto's being shipwrecked and finding the *Daphne,* a ghost ship full of clocks and tropical plants whose absent crew were also engaged in searching for the elusive "fixed point." Although Roberto's loneliness is temporarily alleviated by a German Jesuit, Father Caspar Wanderdrossel, the presence of the priest intensifies Roberto's religious and philosophical confusion until he is no longer able to distinguish reality from fiction.

Like Eco's previous novels, *The Island of the Day Before* is told retrospectively but in this case by an increasingly intrusive and anonymous narrator who constantly mocks and parodies Roberto's words, turning the story into an extended metatextual joke. Roberto's authority is further undermined by his own attempts at writing, since all narrative is shown to be subjective and open to revision. This is a familiar topic in Eco's fiction, but the multiple strands of this novel generate further questions about the nature of individual identity and the idea that every person is the author of their own reality.

The metatextual component of the story is further emphasized by its resemblance to several popular early novels, such as *Robinson Crusoe, The Man in the Iron Mask,* and *Gulliver's Travels.* Eco combines elements of these familiar narratives with the dramatic political intrigue and religious upheaval of the 17th century to create an encyclopedic collage or "essay novel" that constantly reworks his favorite themes into infinite variations. This process is mirrored by Roberto's own writing, in which everything he sees on board the *Daphne* is transformed into his lost would-be love, Lilia. Even his retelling of his adventures in Casale and Paris concentrates on courtly love and romance, making Lilia the central concern of Roberto's entire life.

The single-mindedness of his narrative is a source of endless amusement for the narrator, but it also raises issues about the importance of narratorial credibility. Although Roberto is confused or even delusional, his account of his experiences is still entertaining, suggesting that the point of Roberto's far-fetched romance is to emphasize the enjoyment that can be found in literature regardless of its relationship to reality. This attitude is reinforced by the style of the novel, which is packed with Eco's usual linguistic puns and intellectual puzzles.

The Island of the Day Before is one of Eco's more challenging novels, but the complexity of Roberto's narrative is undercut by the innate humour with which Eco approaches this discussion of linguistic communication. The novel reveals time, space, and even reality to be humanmade concepts that refuse to manifest themselves consistently and continually defy comprehension, but for Roberto the most important consideration is his love for Lilia. So for all his metaphysical questioning and abstract philosophy, human emotions and desires are what motivate Roberto's narration and serve as signposts by which he can navigate his way through the web of texts, signs, and images that make up Eco's view of culture.

BIBLIOGRAPHY

Bouchard, Norma. "Umberto Eco's *L'isola del giorno prima*: Postmodern Theory and Fictional Praxis." In *Umberto Eco,* 3 vols., edited by Mike Gane and Nicholas Gane, vol. 3: 103–117. London: SAGE Publications, 2005.

Rice, Thomas J. "Mapping Complexity in the Fiction of Umberto Eco." In *Umberto Eco,* 3 vols., edited by Mike Gane and Nicholas Gane, vol 1: 369–389. London: SAGE Publications, 2005.

Vlasselaers, Jose. "*The Island of the Day Before*: A Quest for the Semiotic Construction of a Self." In *Umberto Eco,* 3 vols., edited by Mike Gane and Nicholas Gane, vol. 3: 137–146. London: SAGE Publications, 2005.

Rochelle Sibley

J

JANSSON, TOVE (1914–2001) *Finnish-Swed-ish novelist, children's book author, short story writer* Finnish-Swedish novelist and artist Tove Jansson was best known for her stories about the Moomins, a family of enchanting trolls. These creatures are white, round, and furry, with large snouts that make them look like hippopotamuses. Jansson's creatures are loved throughout the world. Of her novels aimed at an adult readership, *The Summer Book* is considered a modern classic. She was also famous for her children's book illustrations and several commissioned murals, which can still be still seen in many public buildings in Finland.

Tove Jansson was born in Helsinki, Finland, as the oldest child of the sculptor Victor Jansson and the graphic artist Sigge Hammarsten. The family belonged to Finland's Swedish-speaking minority, and Jansson's childhood was characterized by great tolerance for the eccentric and a deep love of nature. Despite the bohemian lifestyle of her parents, her upbringing was also infused with a certain drawing room formality and fin-de-siècle elegance, which originated in her father's aristocratic Finno-Swedish background.

In Jansson's autobiographical *The Sculptor's Daughter* (1968), written from her perspective as a young girl, her father is depicted as a formidable patriarch. He is thought to have provided Jansson with the inspiration for Moominpappa, the benevolent but absentminded father in the Moomin family. The Janssons spent many summers on the Porvoo islands just outside Helsinki, and Tove Jansson continued to visit the islands as an adult. The Finnish archipelago became the setting for many of her children's books and novels.

At the age of 15, Jansson contributed cartoons and comic illustrations to the Finnish liberal magazine *Garm*. Her political signature was a little troll that she later developed into the Moomintroll. She moved to Stockholm in 1930 and later to Paris to study art. By the time her first independent art exhibition opened in Helsinki in 1943, she had already published a picture book for children. Two years later she wrote her first children's book, but it was the third book, *Finn Family Moomintroll* (1950), that was her breakthrough as a writer. Jansson wrote a total of eight books about the Moomin valley. She continued to paint, and wrote and illustrated several picture books for children. She also illustrated other people's work, among them translations of Tolkien's *The Hobbit* and Carroll's *Alice in Wonderland* and *The Hunting of the Snark*.

Between 1953 and 1959, Jansson drew a comic strip based on the Moomin family for the *Evening News* in London. Later, her brother Lars took over the creation of the strip. At its most popular, it appeared in 120 papers in 40 countries, and reached an estimated daily readership of 20 million. Today, the rights to the Moomin figures are licensed and the Moomins appear in comic books and Japanese animated movies, as toys, and as decorations on china.

In the 1970s, Tove Jansson began writing novels and short stories for adults. She was then living with the woman who became her life partner, the graphic artist and professor Tuulikki Pietila. The relationship is described in fictitious form in the novel *Fair Play* (1989), a book about two women artists who struggle to combine love with artistic independence. Jansson was appointed an honorary doctor at Abo Akademi University in Finland and was given the title honorary professor in 1995. She died in 2001.

The novels and picture books about the Moomintrolls owe much of their charm to Jansson's use of the harsh but beautiful Scandinavian landscape and her understated, sparse use of language, which emphasizes the comic and mildly anarchic aspects of the Moomins' many adventures. The Moomins are white, smooth trolls with small ears and large noses who reappear in their valley every spring after a long hibernation during the cold Finnish winter. Their approach to life and other creatures is spontaneous and tolerant, especially to their many uninvited summer guests. In *Finn Family Moomintroll* (1950), the young Moomintrolls find a magician's hat, which magically transforms everything that ends up inside it. The short chapters deal primarily with the chaos that is caused by the hat. They also include short portraits of Moominmamma, whose maternal presence provides the safe core around which the adventures take place, and the eccentric Moominpappa, who spends most of his time in his study, writing or thinking about his memoirs.

Aimed primarily at children, the books can also be read as explorations into the psychology of family structure and more general philosophical inquiries into the meaning of life. Jansson's first children's book, *The Little Trolls and the Great Flood* (1945), was an allegory of the Russo-Finnish Winter War of 1939–40. In *Moominpappa at Sea* (1965), Moominpappa decides that the family will spend their summer vacation in a lighthouse, set on a small, isolated island in the Finnish archipelago. As they are cut off from the rest of the world, conflicts soon occur, and each family member is forced to question his or her attitude to life and to the others. Moominpappa, especially, must face up to his patriarchal grip over the rest of the family. The books about the Moomin family have been translated into 34 languages and are sometimes compared to the stories by J. R. R. Tolkien and C. S. Lewis. They also bear some resemblance to Lewis Carroll's *Alice in Wonderland* and Anton Chekhov's family plays.

The Moomin stories are sometimes interpreted as investigations into what Jansson saw as a fundamental tension between a desire for love and safety and the often solitary and insecure life of the artist. *Who Will Comfort Toffle? A Tale Of Moomin Valley* (1960) is one her best-loved picture books and has been interpreted by some critics as a search for love between two women. Another theme that returns in books for adults is the world viewed from a child's perspective. *The Summer Book* (1972) is considered Jansson's masterpiece among her adult novels. The friendship between a young girl and her paternal grandmother is at the center of the story, which takes place on an island in the Finnish Gulf. The girl's mother has died, and her father's grief has reduced him to a melancholy shadow in the background of her stay on the island. The young girl is left with her solitary and eccentric grandmother for company. The girl and the old woman are forced to adjust to each other's fears and yearnings through long talks and silences spent in each other's company. As in many of Jansson's books, each chapter may be read a separate story, describing life as a series of moments rather than a developing narrative.

In 1992 the Amos Anderson Art Museum in Helsinki organized a retrospective exhibition of Jansson's art. She also received numerous awards for her literature, among them the Pro Finlandia medal and the H. C. Andersen Award for children's literature. In 1994 she was awarded the Swedish Academy's Gold Medal.

BIBLIOGRAPHY

Jansson, Tove. *Sculptor's Daughter.* Translated by Kingsley Hart. London: Ernest Benn, 1969.

Jones, Walton Glyn. *Tove Jansson.* Boston: Twayne Publishers, 1984.

Westin, Boel. *Familjen I Dalen: Tove Janssons Muminvärld.* Stockholm: Bonniers, 1988.

Malin Lidström Brock

JEALOUSY (LA JALOUSIE) ALAIN ROBBE-GRILLET (1957)

Born in Brest, France, into a family with a strong background in the sciences, ALAIN ROBBE-GRILLET (1922–) was an agricultural engineer by training but became one of the leading exponents of what was known as the *nouveau roman,* or "new novel." The term was coined in the late 1950s to describe the work of a group of French writers who rejected the conventional features of the novel, dispensing with traditional methods of plotting and characterization in favor of concentrating on an objective representation of the world's details (the physical things in the novel's story). Robbe-Grillet has been a leading figure in the movement and has written theoretical pieces on its behalf, in addition to fiction; *Jealousy* is seen as a particularly representative distillation of the movement's main concerns, with its methodical, geometric, and repetitive descriptions of objects replacing the psychological portrayal of its characters.

The action of *Jealousy* takes place in and around a house on a colonial banana plantation, and is narrated by a voice that may be that of a jealous husband. What creates this doubt is the fact that the first-person pronoun does not appear in the novel, attributing to the narrator an altogether vague and mysterious presence. Because no "I" is present, the reader cannot be quite sure whether the accumulation of details is taking place within the mind of an obsessive narrator or whether it is an objective description of external reality. Though this indeterminacy is a feature of one of the central preoccupations of the *nouveau roman,* the absolute incompatibility of subjective and objective experience, there are many details in the novel that encourage the identification of the narrator as the jealous husband, suspicious that his wife (who is referred to throughout as A . . .) is having an affair: There is an extra place setting at the dinner table, an extra chair on the veranda. Nothing is made explicit, however, and this identification depends to a large extent on the reader's expectations and assumptions. When A . . .'s cheerful greeting is described as that "of someone who prefers not to show what she is thinking about—if anything—and always flashes the same smile, on principle; the same smile, which can be interpreted as derision just as well as affection, or the total absence of feeling whatever," the objective style of the narrative voice remains, though it is tempting to attribute a certain tone of resentment therein to the husband.

The jealousy implicit in the repetitive detail of the narrative is directed toward two of the other protago-

nists: the narrator's wife, A . . . , and a local plantation owner, Franck. Much of the novel's significant detail is revealed through observation and remembrance of fragmentary encounters between these two characters, though there is equal space devoted to minutely detailed descriptions of objects, the house, and the banana plantation. Franck comes to visit for dinner and drinks, and he squashes a centipede against the dining-room wall; he and A . . . sit on the veranda and discuss a novel they are reading and engine trouble that Franck is having with his car; they plan a day trip to the nearest town; the trip goes ahead, but an apparent fault with the car means that they stay overnight in a hotel in the town: These are the details that are presented in the narrative a number of times from a number of different viewpoints as they are seen and remembered by the narrator. As the accumulation of details continues, additional pieces of information are yielded, such as a letter that apparently passes between A . . . and Franck, yet there is nothing conclusive to convince the narrator or the reader that adultery has taken place.

At one point the narrative refers to a song that is sung a number of times by a laborer on the plantation: "Yet these repetitions, these tiny variations, halts, regressions, can give rise to modifications—though barely perceptible—eventually moving quite far from the point of departure." Though the catalogue of details continues to grow, A . . .'s husband is ultimately left undecided about whether his wife is having an affair, and this is an appropriate reflection of the central question posed by the curious style of the novel: Can anything be learned from a repeated examination of material detail, or is reality simply a series of meaningless phenomena with no underlying significance? For Robbe-Grillet, the rigorously materialist writer, to postulate any kind of emotional relationship between human beings and the material world is fraudulent and illusory. He condemns the use of what John Ruskin called the "pathetic fallacy," where in natural phenomena are described in art as though they can feel emotion in the manner that humans do, to reflect the artist's mood.

Robbe-Grillet's writing owes a debt to earlier French existentialist novelists ALBERT CAMUS and JEAN-PAUL SARTRE, though he once criticized them for compromising their vision by yielding to the sentimentality of the traditional novel. To avoid this, Robbe-Grillet eradicates the use of metaphor in *Jealousy,* considering its use to be the beginnings of capitulation and the pathetic fallacy. Human consciousness and the material world are irreducibly distinct, and to learn anything from the latter is to foist the workings of the former upon it. For example, jealousy is just one way in which the mind seeks to impose order on the chaotic meaninglessness of objective reality. In the novel, the narrator's jealousy is a result of his struggle to impress meaning upon the series of exchanges that he witnesses between his wife and Franck. The repetition of these scenes in the narrative might then be seen as the jealous husband's concern growing into an obsession, as he repeats the details in his mind, trying to elicit meaning from them; the repetition intensifies up to the sixth chapter, when A . . . and Franck have gone to town, and the narrator supposes the adultery is taking place.

Symbols play an important role in the novel and draw further attention to Robbe-Grillet's assertion that an unmediated relationship with reality is impossible. One of the windows of the house is made from a pane of flawed glass, and looking through it, the narrator can make objects outside appear and disappear according to the angle at which he is looking. This is essentially what is happening throughout the novel: Different viewpoints create different versions of the same scene, none of which is its truly faithful or accurate reproduction. The narrator thus struggles to glean meaning from a disinterested reality.

The French title of the novel, *La jalousie,* offers another clue that is lost in its English translation: It can mean both jealousy and Venetian blind. On a number of occasions, the narrator views a scene through one of the house's window blinds, and the subsequent implication is that both jealousy and a Venetian blind can obscure an objective view of reality. By the end of the novel, neither the reader nor the narrator can be sure that anything has actually happened since the novel's beginning. *Jealousy* creates something of a void, one in which the very conventions and traditions of the novel are brought into question in a most remarkable and arresting way.

BIBLIOGRAPHY

Hellerstein, Marjorie H. *Inventing the Real World.* Selinsgrove, Pa.: Susquehanna University Press, and London: Associated University Presses, 1998.

Ramsay, Raylene L. *Robbe-Grillet and Modernity: Science, Sexuality and Subversion.* Gainesville: University Press of Florida, 1992.

Smith, Roch C. *Understanding Robbe-Grillet.* Columbia: University of South Carolina Press, 2000.

Stoltzfus, Ben. *Alain Robbe-Grillet: The Body of the Text.* London and Toronto: Associated University Presses, 1985.

Justin Tonra

JELINEK, ELFRIEDE (1946–) *Austrian essayist, novelist, playwright, poet*

Winner of the 2004 Nobel Prize in literature, Elfriede Jelinek has written a large, varied body of work consisting of poetry, plays, novels, essays, radio plays, screenplays for television and film, and libretti. While she has enjoyed some positive critical and audience reception in German-speaking countries, she has also engendered a great deal of controversy, particularly in her native country of Austria. Jelinek, a member of the Austrian Communist Party from 1974 until 1991, uses Marxist and feminist approaches to write complex, experimental examinations of power structures, male/female sexual relationships, popular culture, and Austrian history.

Jelinek was born on October 20, 1946, in Mürzzuschlag, Styria, Austria, but her family moved to Vienna when she was very young. Her father was of Czech-Jewish origin and trained as a chemist. Since he worked on a sensitive government project during World War II, he was not pursued by the authorities for his Jewish heritage. Jelinek's mother was from a well-to-do Viennese family and was the dominant partner in the marriage. As a young child, Jelinek began music lessons and studied piano and organ at the Vienna Conservatory of Music. She also completed six semesters in theater at the University of Vienna. Jelinek began her writing career after a year-long convalescence following a nervous breakdown. In 1975 she married Gottfried Hüngsberg, a German. Since her husband lives and works in Munich in the information technology industry, Jelinek divides her time between her home in Vienna and Munich.

Elfriede Jelinek's first publication was a collection of poetry in 1967 entitled *Lisa's Shadow* (*Lisas Schatten*). She followed that with the first of 10 novels, *We Are Decoys Baby* (*Wir sind lockvögel baby*) in 1970, in which she uses montage and parody to satirize and take on consumerist society and popular culture. Her next major novel was *Women as Lovers* (*Die Liebhaberinnen,* 1975), which details the attempts of two women, one from the working class and another from the middle class, to establish their independence in a patriarchal society. In 1983 Jelinek published her best-known and least experimental novel, *The Piano Teacher* (*Die Klavierspielerin*). This novel has autobiographical elements since its protagonist is a musician with a weak and absent father and overbearing mother. As mentioned previously, Jelinek had studied music for a long time, and she has openly stated that her mother dominated her and her father's lives. The novel's protagonist, Erica Kohut, seeks to gain independence from her mother and establish a sexual life for herself by attending peep shows and spying on couples. During the course of the novel, she enters into a relationship with one of her students, but it ultimately ends badly for Kohut. Another novel, *Lust* (1992), examines the life of a middle-class woman trapped in a marriage in which she is a mere commodity for her capitalist husband. Jelinek's 1995 novel *Children of the Dead* (*Die Kinder der Toten*) examines Austria's fascist past, and her latest novel is *Greed* (*Gier,* 2000).

Elfriede Jelinek has written 15 plays and is often more widely perceived as a playwright than a novelist. Her first play, produced in 1979, was *What Happened after Nora Left her Husband; or, Pillars of Society* (*Was geschah, nachdem Nora ihren Mann verlassen hatte; oder, Stützen der Gesellschaften*). This rewriting of two Henrik Ibsen plays—*Hedda Gabler* and *Pillar of Society*—questions whether the Ibsen character Nora really would have found emancipation, given that male and female roles are determined early in childhood. *Clara S.: Musical Tragedy* (*Clara S.: Musikalische Tragödie*), focusing on Clara Schumann, the composer Robert Schumann's wife as the pivotal character, was produced in 1982. In 1992 Jelinek portrayed women as vampires engaged in a battle of the sexes that they, and ultimately any woman, cannot win in *Disease; or, Modern Women* (*Krankheit; oder, Moderne Frauen*). Her criticism of sports and hero worship of sports figures in the 1998 play *A Sportpiece* (*Ein Sportstück*) is her biggest theater success to date.

Since Elfriede Jelinek casts a critical eye on her homeland and its recent history, mass culture, class, and gender, she is a controversial figure in the literary and cultural scene. Jelinek views language as a weapon and uses it to explore some uncomfortable themes that have unsettled a wide audience. Many male critics dislike her crass portrayals of sexual relations, and many feminists disapprove of her portrait of female sexuality and masochistic behavior. Elfriede Jelinek is considered to be a *Nestbeschmutzerin* (someone who fouls the nest) because of her examination of Austria's role during the Nazi era. Indeed, her pieces were not performed until the 1990s, especially in Austria, due to some of their themes. Her play *Burgtheater* (the actual Burgtheater is the national home of Austrian theater) has never been performed at its namesake since she implied that the actors of the Burgtheater were involved with the National Socialists during the Third Reich.

Despite the controversy that surrounds her oeuvre and her person, Elfriede Jelinek's talent has garnered her many awards. She won the Austrian Youth Culture award in 1969 and the Austrian State Scholarship for Literature in 1972, was honored for Education and Art by the Austrian Minister in 1983, and received an honorary Award for Literature of Vienna in 1989. In 1979 Jelinek won an award for best screenplay in West Germany and the Büchner prize of 1998. In 2004 she received the Franz Kafka Prize from the Czech Republic. It was also in 2004 that Jelinek was awarded the Nobel Prize in literature, the first Austrian to earn this honor.

BIBLIOGRAPHY

Fiddler, Allyson: *Rewriting Reality: An Introduction to Elfriede Jelinek.* Oxford and Providence: Berg, 1994.

Gurtler, Christa. *Gegen den schönen Schein: Texte zu Elfriede Jelinek.* Frankfurt: Verlag Neue Kritik, 1990.

Hoffmann, Yasmin. *Elfriede Jelinek: une biographie.* Paris: Chambon, 2005.

Mayer, Verena. *Elfriede Jelinek: ein Porträt.* Reinbek bei Hamburg: Rowohlt, 2006.

Karen Bell

JELLOUN, TAHAR BEN (1944–   ) *Morrocan essayist, novelist, playwright, poet* Tahar Ben Jelloun is a prolific Moroccan novelist, essayist, poet, playwright, and pamphleteer. He published his first

collection of poems, *Hommes sous linceul de silence,* in 1971, and his first novel, *Harrouda,* appeared in 1973. Since then he has published more than 20 books, which have been translated into many languages. Ben Jelloun is one of the best-known North African writers and the first Arab author to be awarded Le Prix Goncourt, France's most prestigious literary prize, for his book *The SACRED NIGHT* (1987).

Born in 1944 in Fez, Morocco, Jelloun now lives in Paris with his wife and children. He comes from a modest social background: His father was a shopkeeper, his mother a housewife. At 18 Jelloun moved to Tangier, where he attended a French high school, the Lycée Reynault. In 1963 he went to the University Mohammed V in Rabat and studied philosophy. After graduation, he taught philosophy at high schools in Tétouan and Casablanca.

The year 1965 was important in Ben Jelloun's life: He took part in a student revolt against the Moroccan police and King Hassan II's repressive regime. In 1966 he was arrested along with many other students and sent to a military camp for 18 months. It was in the barracks there that he wrote his first poem—in secret, since camp prisoners were not allowed to read or write. This very oppression, he declared, urged him to write and denounce state oppression. His later novel, *The Last Friend* (*Le dernier ami,* 2004), relating the appalling conditions of Moroccan political prisoners, contains some autobiographical elements reminiscent of the many months he spent in the military camp.

After his release, Jelloun went back to teaching until 1971, when the Moroccan government decided to Arabize the teaching of philosophy. Jelloun consequently left Morocco for France, where he pursued studies in social psychiatry. He completed a doctoral dissertation in Paris in 1975 on "The Sexual Misery of North African Workers in France," published in 1977 as *The Highest of Solitudes* (*La plus haute des solitudes*). Before becoming a full-time writer, Ben Jelloun practiced psychiatry as a consultant in a French hospital. His experience as a psychotherapist enabled him to discover aspects of humanity that he was not initially aware of, his previous knowledge being "merely theoretical." He confessed that "from the moment I was party to the truth about people who suffered for serious psycho-

logical reasons, I started to discover more about human life." His second novel, *Solitaire* (*La réclusion solitaire,* 1976), draws widely on this psychoanalytic work, fictionalizing his patients' disorders and sufferings.

Ben Jelloun defines himself as a man of words rather than of action. Just as he uses speech to help his patients to overcome their traumas, he writes fiction to comment on Moroccan society and try to change its archaic structures. Inspired by the French ideals of secularism, equality, and social justice, Jelloun militates for a free, egalitarian, and secular society in which religion does not interfere in politics and where women and men have equal rights. His novels focus on Morocco, which he criticizes for its "feudal" institutions based on tyranny, sexual and religious hypocrisy, and women's oppression.

A fervent social critic, Jelloun is an *intellectuel engagé* (engaged intellectual), involved in world politics and in issues relating to Morocco, North Africa, and the Middle East. Owing to his knowledge of the Arab world and engagement in Maghrebian and Middle Eastern causes, he is constantly solicited by European media on questions pertaining to the Muslim world. His views and critical contributions often appear in *Le Monde, Le Monde Diplomatique, Le Nouvel Observateur, El País,* and *La Repubblica.*

An honored novelist and a respected intellectual, Jelloun is a humanist and a man of dialogue, urging understanding and fraternity between people. He condemned racism in his essays "French Hospitality" ("Hospitalité française," 1984) and "Racism Explained to my Daughter" ("Le racisme expliqué à ma fille," 1998), and in "Islam Explained to Children" ("L'Islam expliqué aux enfants," 2002), written in the wake of September 11, 2001, terrorist attacks, he warned against cultural conflicts and religious hatred, in the process attempting to highlight Islam's ideals and contributions to human civilization.

While Ben Jelloun is acclaimed in Europe, he is disparaged by many at home, accused of giving French and European audiences stereotypical ideas of Moroccan society. He is especially criticized for writing in French, the language of the former colonizer, a critique to which he responded saying that he writes in French for two major reasons: first, to be read by as wide a circle of readers as possible; second, to preserve the distance between himself and his native country. According to the author, French is more suitable for addressing contemporary issues than Arabic, the language of the Koran. Referring to the erotic scenes in *The Last Friend,* Jelloun writes: "I am not sure I would have been able to write all that in Arabic."

BIBLIOGRAPHY

Amar, Ruth. *Tahar Ben Jelloun: Les stratégies narratives.* Lewiston, N.Y.: E. Mellen Press, 2005.

Aresu, Bernard. *Tahar Ben Jelloun.* New Orleans: Tulane University, 1998.

Bousta, Rachida Saigh. *Lecture des récits de Tahar Ben Jelloun: écriture, mémoire et imaginaire.* Casablanca: Afrique Orient, 1992.

Elbaz, Robert. *Tahar Ben Jelloun ou l'inassouvissement du désir narratif.* Paris: L'Harmattan, 1996.

Gaudin, Francoise. *La Fascination des images: les romans de Tahar Ben Jelloun.* Paris: Harmattan, 1998.

Kohn-Pireaux, Laurence. *Etude sur Tahar Ben Jelloun: L'Enfant de sable, La Nuit sacrée.* Paris: Ellipses, 2000.

Orlando, Valerie. *Nomadic Voices of Exile: Feminine Identity in Francophone Literature of the Maghreb.* Athens: Ohio University Press, 1999.

Amar Acheraiou

JENSEN, JOHANNES V. (1873–1950) *Danish novelist, journalist, travel writer, nonfiction writer, essayist, poet*

The 1944 winner of the Nobel Prize in literature, Johannes Vilhelm Jensen, was born in the small Danish town of Farø. His father was a district veterinarian with very broad scientific, historical, and anthropological interests. Under his influence, the young Jensen developed a fascination for Darwinism and studies of nature that is reflected in his writing career, making him, according to critics, the most outstanding portrayer of animals in Danish literature. Jensen's mother, a strong and temperamental woman, was opposed to traditional Christianity but was also strongly attached to the peasant culture, an attitude she passed on to her son.

Jensen's parents decided that their son deserved the best education available in Denmark, which meant the University of Copenhagen, with Viborg Cathedral School as the intermediate stage. Although Jensen had always been an avid reader, his years in Viborg opened to him the richness of world literature. The German classics influenced him most, with the 19th-century poet Heinrich Heine his favorite writer, but he was also familiar with the French naturalists, especially Émile Zola. Of his fellow Danish writers, Jensen was mostly influenced by JOHANNES JØRGENSEN.

In 1893 Jensen was accepted by the University of Copenhagen to study medicine. The university disappointed him, and he sought refuge in writing. Under the pseudonym Ivar Lykke, Jensen wrote 10 serial thrillers that helped to support him during his studies. Apparently he was not proud of these pulp works since later he never considered these novels part of his life's work.

While working at the hospital in 1895–96, Jensen wrote his novel *Danes* (*Danskere*) and used the proceeds from its success to travel to New York in September 1896. Returning home, he published his second novel, *Einar Elkœr* (1897). After this he gave up his medical studies and became a fiction writer for the newspaper *Politiken.* In 1898 Jensen went to Spain and Germany as a correspondent, and in 1900 he attended the World's Fair in Paris. Jensen developed a taste for travel and a longing for foreign places, and in 1902 he left for Singapore, from where he went to Malaysia, Shanghai, Japan, and then, crossing the Pacific, to San Francisco, Chicago, New York, returning to Denmark in 1903. Jensen's travels spurred him into a period of intense productivity. In 1904 he published the novel *Madame D'Ora,* a collection of stories, *New Himmerland Stories* (*Nye Himmerlandshistorier*); and the travelogue *The Woods.* The novel *The Wheel* (*Hjulet*) and a collection of poems appeared in 1905.

Also in 1905, Jensen married Else Marie Ulrik and renewed his collaboration with the publication *Politiken,* both unions lasting for the rest of his life. In October 1906 Jensen and his wife traveled to New York, and after this trip he started translating American novelist Frank Norris's novel *The Octopus.* The translation was published in Denmark in the same year. Jensen also wrote a preface to Jack London's *The Call of the Wild,* introducing another American writer to the Danish people, and published a series of newspaper articles on the United States.

The year 1906 was decisive for Jensen: He embarked on writing about the problems concerning the theory of evolution. In 1908 there appeared the first volume of Jensen's great epic in six volumes, *The Long Journey* (*Den Lange Reise*), in which he portrays the rise of man from the primitive times to the discovery of America by Columbus. One of the leitmotifs of the novel becomes the longing of the northerner for the lost land and eternal happiness. The epic was published from 1908 to 1922 and demonstrates Jensen's poetic skills and his talent as an amateur anthropologist.

In 1912 Jensen started on his second great journey, traveling to Berlin, Colombo, Singapore, Peking, Manchuria, and returning home through Siberia. In 1914 he traveled to the United States for the fourth time, resulting in another period of intense productivity. During the years of World War I, Jensen focused on writing *The Long Journey*.

Another voyage Jensen undertook started in 1925. This time he went to Berlin, Egypt, and Palestine, regularly sending travel letters to the newspaper *Social-Demokraten*. He reflected on the journey in two books, *The Light of the World* (*Verdens Lys*) and *The Transformation of the Animals* (*Dyrenes Forvandling*, 1927), presenting a development of evolutionary theories. After his next journey (Madeira, the Canary Islands, Berlin, and Rome) in 1928, Jensen continued writing *The Stages of the Mind* (*Aandens Stadier*, 1928), incorporating his travel observations and thoughts on evolution.

By this time Jensen was widely recognized as a prominent author, and in 1929 he received an honorary doctorate from the University of Lund in Sweden. In the 1930s he remained prolific, publishing translations; essays on evolution, ethics, and art; and newspaper articles on contemporaneous topics, including American politics and collections of poetry. Jensen also tried theater projects but was unsuccessful in that arena. Before World War II, Jensen visited the United States again, but the outbreak of the war prevented his planned travel to France. When the Germans occupied Denmark on April 9, 1940, Jensen burned his diaries and letters that chronicled the past 30 years, so this part of his writing is lost to posterity.

Strongly opposed to World War II, Jensen, preferred to stay uninvolved. During the war years he wrote mostly articles on art criticism and anthropology as well as a history of civilization, *Our Origin* (*Vor Oprindelse*, 1941). In 1944 Jensen received the Nobel Prize in literature "for the remarkable force and richness of his poetic imagination, combined with a wide-ranging intellectualism and bold, innovative sense of style." The Nobel committee especially recognized Jensen's monumental *The Long Journey*.

In the last years of Jensen's life, his productivity decreased, and his writings mostly concentrated on the studies of evolution and popularization of the theory of evolution. The purpose of Jensen's last trip to France in 1948 was to study the regions from which knowledge of prehistoric man originated. In 1949 he published the book *Africa* (*Afrika*), a work again reflecting his interest in natural science.

Jensen died on November 25, 1950, leaving a rich heritage of poems, essays, novels, and myths, works that would influence generations of Danish writers and readers.

BIBLIOGRAPHY
Gerhart Hauptmann, Verner von Heidenstam and Johannes V. Jensen. New York: A. Gregory, 1971.
Rossel, Sven H., ed. *A History of Danish Literature.* Lincoln: University of Nebraska Press, 1992.

Maria Mikolchak

JØRGENSEN, JOHANNES (1866–1956)
Danish novelist, poet, hagiographer, essayist The writer Jens Johannes Jørgensen is known in Denmark mainly as a poet, particularly for two collections of verse, *Digte 1894–98,* (1898); and *Udvaglte Digte 1884–1944* (1944). However, he is best known in other countries for his novelistic hagiographies, especially ST. FRANCIS OF ASSISI (1907) and *St. Catherine of Siena* (1915). The strong Catholic content of Jørgensen's prose, which the average educated Danish reader would find unacceptable, placed the writer outside the traditional scope of Danish literature. At the same time, Jørgensen's Catholicism earned him recognition outside Denmark, especially among Catholic writers.

Born in the small provincial town of Svendborg in 1866, Jørgensen was 15 when he moved to Copenhagen to continue his education. Feeling like a poor outsider in the country's rich capital contributed to turning the young boy into a left-wing radical, one who denounced Christianity and societal conventions. After several years of revolt, however, the traditional moralist and Christian within Jørgensen eventually won this tug of war between convention and conscience. He worked as a journalist writing on foreign affairs and literature and gradually turned away from his earlier nihilism.

In 1887 Jørgensen published his first volume of poems, *Verse* (*Vers*). Four years later he married Amalie Ewald and settled down. Around this time he met Mogens Ballin, a Catholic Jew with a strong personality, under whose influence Jørgensen began his conversion to Catholicism. Previously insecure and vacillating in religious acceptance, unable to take a stand or make a final decision whether to join the church, Jørgensen started taking Catholic instruction in 1895 and was received into the church in February 1896. He took this step during a time when the climate of Danish public opinion ran against Christianity in general and Catholicism in particular. The writer's decision required strength of character and persistence.

Jørgensen now commenced a period of hard work and prolific literary production. His early Catholic works, *Roman Mosaic* (*Romersk Mosaik,* 1901) and *Pictures of Roman Saints* (*Romerske Helgenbilleder,* 1902), however, were viewed as too impersonal and uncritical to be a success. *The Book of Pilgrim* (*Pilgrimsbogen,* 1903) that followed earned Jørgensen acclaim in Denmark and abroad despite the fact that he was a Catholic writer. Readers in Germany and France viewed Jørgensen as a writer of philosophical importance.

In 1894, with Mogens Ballin, Jørgensen traveled to Italy and visited Assisi for the first time. That was the beginning of what would become his predominant literary preoccupation for the rest of his life: hagiographies of the saints, in particular St. Francis, who was allegedly born in Assisi and lived there until his death in 1226. In 1907 Jørgensen published his biography, *St. Francis of Assisi* (*Den Hellige Frans af Assisi*), which brought him world fame and earned him honorary citizenship, first in Assisi and later in his native town of Svendborg. The Franciscan spirituality influenced Jørgensen to such extent that he settled down in Assisi in

1915. In the same year he published another of his famous hagiographies, *St. Catherine of Siena* (*Den Hellige Katerina af Siena*).

Jørgensen's Catholicism, along with financial difficulties, caused family problems. When his wife became openly anti-Catholic, Jørgensen left her and their seven children in 1913, later obtaining a divorce in 1915. In 1914 he met a young Frenchwoman, Andrée Carof, who became his strongest influence. Andrée Carof followed Jørgensen to Assisi, Italy, where he lived until her death in 1933. Their relationship, however, was considered a father-daughter relationship and a spiritual union rather than a romantic involvement.

As a devout Catholic, Andrée Carof provided Jørgensen with the firm guidance for which he had always been searching to fight his insecurities and religious doubts. Carof's sudden death in 1933 left Jørgensen lost and adrift, having lost his companion of almost 20 years and the guiding hand he had desperately needed. Living in Italy, he felt completely alone, but in his home country he also felt neglected and unappreciated, even by the Danish Catholics. He therefore decided to stay in Italy to devote his time to writing a book, *Charles de Foucauld* (1934), a work filled with Andrée Carof's presence without mentioning her by name.

In 1937 in Assisi Jørgensen met a young Austrian woman, Helena Klein, whom he fell in love with and married. This happy event spurred his creativity, leading him to produce a book of essays, *The Assisi-Salzburg Axis* (*Omkring Axen Assisi-Salzburg,* 1938), showing a distinct German cultural influence. His major effort from this period was the two-volume work *St. Bridget of Sweden* (*Den Hellige Birgitta af Vadstena,* 1941–43), to which he dedicated many years of writing. During the war years of 1943–45, Jørgensen worked on his book in Sweden, and although he returned to Assisi after the war, he remained fond of Sweden.

It was not until 1953 that Jørgensen returned to Denmark and settled in his childhood home in Svendborg. The house was now arranged for him as a residence of honor, which doubtless contributed to Jørgensen's uplifted spirits; he was now more settled than at any time in the past. He died in his old home on May 29, 1956, six months short of his 90th birthday, and was buried at the local cemetery.

Jørgensen's life was outwardly uneventful, but inwardly it shows constant spiritual turmoil. In his youth he experienced a major change from being a provincial religious boy to that of an ardent atheist and nihilist; later, from a revolutionary he turned into an uncompromising Catholic suffering constant religious doubts and mental anguish. For a long time he remained unappreciated in Denmark, and his work was seen as in opposition to largely socialist and atheist Danish literature. At one time Jørgensen contemplated writing in German so that he could reach a wider audience and his reputation would not solely depend on the translations of his work. He decided, however, to remain a Danish writer since, despite all the years abroad, he never lost his love of Denmark and the Danish language.

Jørgensen's poetry remains very Danish in quality, and this body of work eventually earned him acclaim in his home country, where he is admired for his sublime sense of the language and great poetic artistry. His prose, however, might have fared better in Denmark had he chosen Danish saints for his hagiographies. On the other hand, the hagiographies earned Jørgensen a worldwide reputation, alongside with such Danish authors as Hans Christian Andersen and Søren Kierkegaard in the 19th century and Jens Peter Jacobsen and JOHANNES V. JENSEN in the 20th century. Jørgensen's book on St. Francis is said to have been translated into more languages than any other Danish work, with the exception of Andersen's *Fairy Tales*. In the United States the book was published in a paperback edition. Jørgensen's other famous hagiography, that of St. Catherine, triggered modern research into that saint and is considered to be an outstanding book among the many works written about her. In 1944 an attempt was made in Sweden by the author and literary critic Harald Schiller to formally propose Johannes Jørgensen for the Nobel Prize, and, although that year the prize went to another Danish writer, Johannes V. Jensen, the attempt itself is indicative of Jørgensen's international reputation and significance in world literature.

BIBLIOGRAPHY
Jones, W. Glyn. *Johannes Jørgensen*. New York: Twayne Publishers, 1969.

Maria Mikolchak

JOSEPH AND HIS BROTHERS (*JOSEPH UND SEINE BRÜDER*) THOMAS MANN (1933–1943)   The series of four biblical novels by renowned German author THOMAS MANN (1875–1955) chronicles the ancient history of the Jews and evolves as a refutation of prolific racist mythmaking during the Nazi era. Mann wrote the tetralogy over a 16-year period, collectively titled *Joseph and His Brothers: The Tales of Jacob* (*Die Geschichten Jaakobs*), *Young Joseph* (*Der junge Joseph*), *Joseph in Egypt* (*Joseph in Aegypten*), and *Joseph the Provider* (*Joseph der Ernaehrer*). The novels focus on the biblical story of Joseph, great-grandson of the Jewish patriarch Abraham and a young man of amazing talents, self-confidence, and divine trust in God's providence. Joseph must and does survive his own egotism, the resentment and envy of his brothers who sell him into slavery, as well as false imprisonment in order to become the savior of his Egyptian tormentors during a time of deadly famine.

Mann takes this biblical narrative and transforms it into a blend of mythology and psychology, adding subtle motivations not apparent in the biblical account and creating a variation on Friedrich Nietzsche's *Overman* (*Ubermensch*). Joseph starts out as a boy raised in Israel. Cherished by his father, the young Joseph does not possess the maturity or the discernment to realize the damage his father's favoritism has created between himself and his brothers. This wedge culminates in Joseph's forced journey into the complexities of Egyptian civilization and his initiation into the new horizon of modernity. Mann uses this new horizon as a vehicle by which Joseph frees himself from the unhappy circumstances of his boyhood. Joseph grows, matures, and transforms into a leader who does not turn his back on his own culture but instead leads his people into a future removed from the legends of the past. Joseph avoids the trap of tyrannical patriarchy and evolves into a concerned and wise statesman, a model through whom new myth can be formulated.

Mann chose to present a theme that is set in the distant past and not in the familiar mode of novelistic inquiry where the writer approaches the story from the present time and looks backward. Mann chose to get behind the epoch of the story and look forward. This innovative approach begins with a prologue, a masterpiece in itself, which engages the latest scientific discoveries concerning the beginnings of human existence on earth. Scouring the depths of our origins long before histories were written, Mann takes his readers up through the eras of orally transmitted legend, demonstrating his belief that every legend contains a relevant fact, an event of decisive importance to humanity. From this initial exploration of the bottomless depths of human origins, the story begins, but Mann does not provide the reader with a simple narrative retelling of the Joseph story. Instead, he provides a modern concern, and it is this double theme that holds his narrative together—the age-old questions addressing why the members of this one family, Joseph's family, were chosen by God to hear his voice, to enter into his covenant, and to experience his blessing. Mann offers a glimpse into this complicated theological and psychological arena by revealing the family as having a deep, unappeasable, and at times troubling concern or caring for things spiritual and for God. With a holy obsession, the members of Joseph's family—past, present, and future—are willing to risk life and limb for the right and godly way of life; they will turn away from the enticements and temptations of the temporal world, and they will hold contempt for those who put their trust in monuments of stone (the pyramids).

A second question deals with whether or not the actions, episodes, and events in the lives of humanity are predestined or predetermined by a single, divine plan. Joseph's family believes, accepts, and surrenders to the notion of a divine plan, but Mann presents this facet with a bit of a twist: He allows the characters to share in the connection and motivation of the episodes, and he thus builds the theme. The main characters—Jacob, Joseph, Judah, Potiphar, and the young Pharaoh—exist as historical personages from a specific moment in time, but Mann also allows moments in which the lives of the historical figures blend with those of their forefathers. In addition, the characters are at times given moments of consciousness allowing them to see themselves, and even one another, as part of the mystical divine plan, the preordained "whole." This approach, however, lessens the novel's dramatic quality, if only somewhat, by eliminating the character's exposure to the consequences of a final, critical, or irrevocable decision. Other factors, however, minimize or eliminate the dramatic finality within a story, such as the various literary tools (leitmotif, anticipation, irony) and analytical devices (Jungian topology and Freudian analysis) available that are also designed to lessen the finality of experience, thus demonstrating experience to be repeatable. While Mann may imperil the definitive motivation of the "whole," he produces a spiritual effort that receives its validation not from something it aims at or strives for, such as a goal, but from within itself and its own intensity. The main characters, chosen by God, therefore appear to the reader as parts of a fully determined divine plan.

Joseph and His Brothers offers a four-part series of novels chronicling the biblical story of Joseph and marks what many biographers and critics claim is the furthest point from the "German question" that Mann could venture. Nonetheless, parallels exist. Joseph's brothers, like the German people, act as a collective whole in the dastardly deed that sold young Joseph into slavery. Not one of his brothers intervened on Joseph's behalf, leaving Mann to take his readers to the precipice of a difficult question reeking of Mann's classic sense of irony: If one's own brother will not face up to an evil action, should we be so shocked by the appalling reaction of a population bewildered by the actions of the fascist regime who also did not protest?

BIBLIOGRAPHY

Brennan, Joseph Gerard. *Thomas Mann's World.* New York: Russell & Russell, 1962.

Bruford, Walter Horace. *The German Tradition of Self-Cultivation: Bildung from Humboldt to Thomas Mann.* New York: Cambridge University Press, 1975.

Bürgin, Hans. *Thomas Mann, a Chronicle of His Life.* Mobile: University of Alabama Press, 1969.

Hatfield, Henry Caraway. *Thomas Mann: A Collection of Critical Essays.* Englewood Cliffs, N.J.: Prentice-Hall, 1964.

Heilbut, Anthony. *Thomas Mann: Eros and Literature.* Riverside: University of California Press, 1997.

Heller, Erich. *The Ironic German, a Study of Thomas Mann.* London: Secker & Warburg, 1958.

———. *Thomas Mann, the Ironic German: A Study.* Mamaroneck, N.Y.: P.P. Appel, 1973.

Kahn, Robert L. *Studies in German Literature.* Houston: Rice University, 1964.

Masereel, Frans. *Mein Stundenbuch, 165 Holzschnitte Von Frans Maserel. Einleitung von Thomas Mann.* Munich: K. Wolff, 1926.

Mueller, William Randolph. *Celebration of Life: Studies in Modern Fiction.* New York: Sheed & Ward, 1972.

Reed, Terence. *Thomas Mann: The Uses of Tradition.* Oxford: Clarendon Press, 1974.

Robertson, Ritchie. *The Cambridge Companion to Thomas Mann.* Cambridge: Cambridge University Press, 2002.

Stock, Irvin. *Ironic Out of Love: The Novels of Thomas Mann.* Jefferson, N.C.: McFarland, 1994.

Christine Marie Hilger

JOURNEY TO THE END OF THE NIGHT (*VOYAGE AU BOUT DE LA NUIT*) LOUIS-FERDINAND CÉLINE (1932)

The 1932 publication of the cynical and darkly comic *Journey to the End of the Night* by LOUIS-FERDINAND CÉLINE (1894–1961) sent immediate shock waves into a French literary world still reeling from the social and artistic disruptions of World War I. Its audacious literary use of spoken French—a colloquial Parisian slang, itself vulgar, funny, street-smart, and corporeal—together with its running first-person commentaries on the imbecilities of war, colonialism, industrialism, and what Henry Miller would call the "air-conditioned nightmare" of 20th-century life, were embraced in the anti–status quo intellectual atmosphere of 1930s Paris. The novel has since remained a brilliant and insightful, if bitter and often misanthropic, commentary on the modern condition. Its influence has extended beyond the postwar French existentialists to the United States, where it can be felt in writers as diverse as Henry Miller, Kurt Vonnegut, Jack Kerouac, and William Burroughs.

Episodic in structure, picaresque in form, *Journey to the End of the Night* is told in the first person and covers the experiences of the narrator, Bardamu, from his early 20s until his mid-30s, tracing his adventures across three continents and chronicling his "aimless pilgrimage" toward self-knowledge. It opens as the young medical student, caught up in the martial spirit that engulfed Europe in the weeks preceding the outbreak of war in 1914, enlists in the army. Suddenly, he informs us, "The music stopped. Then I said to myself, as I saw how things were going, 'It's not such fun, after all. I doubt it's worth it.' And I was going to go back.

But it was too late! They'd shut the gate behind us, quietly; the civilians had. We were caught, like rats in a trap." Bardamu's journey begins.

The horrors of war scenes, drawn from Céline's own experiences on the front, are justly famous. Bardamu's early naïve idealism quickly gives way to cynicism; the war is civilization's death wish. "You can see," he says of the dead, "that they died for nothing. For nothing at all, the idiots. I swear that's true; you can see that it is. Only life itself is important." For Bardamu, the carnage exposes the language of glory, country, and patriotism as a deadly lie. "The poetry of heroism," he argues, "appeals irresistibly to those who don't go to war, and even more to those whom the war is making enormously wealthy. It's always so." Bardamu himself becomes its victim. Wounded and subject to hallucinations and panic attacks, he survives the war in and out of hospitals, always walking a dangerously fine line between being permanently institutionalized, ordered back to the front, or executed as a coward.

Finally, invalided out of the regular French army, Bardamu next finds himself a minor official in a remote French African trading post, a lone European wracked with fevers and no real duties or purpose. He soon discovers the horrors and insanities of the colonial system are equal to those he endured at the front. "The wielder of the lash," he finds, "gets very tired of his job in the end, but the white man's heart is brimful of the hope of power and wealth that doesn't cost anything." Yet if the native peoples must be whipped to force compliance in the absurd farce, "the whites carry on on their own; they've been well schooled by the state." Nevertheless, in this unlikely place, Bardamu encounters the selfless officer, Alcide, who reenlists in hell to provide an education for his crippled niece, giving her "the gift of years of torment, the annihilation of his poor life in this torrid monotony, without making conditions and without bargaining, uncalculating."

After escaping the European wars and African jungles, America beckons to Bardamu as the 20th-century's Promised Land. It is a false promise, a desire-driven trance induced by that "two hour whore," the movies. A different reality confronts Bardamu, first in New York and later in Detroit, where he works on the Ford assembly line. Urban America is "an insipid carnival of vertiginous buildings," a "cancer of promiscuous and pestilential advertising," and its factories and workplaces merely dehumanizing machines, better designed to employ well-trained chimpanzees than thinking, feeling humans. Always on the move, always in a hurry, America fascinates Bardamu. "What is it that frightens all these bloody people so?" he wonders. "It's probably somewhere at the farther end of the night. That's why they don't go into the depths of the night themselves."

The last sections of the novel find that Bardamu has finished his studies and is practicing medicine as best he can in the poor, working-class suburbs of Paris. Twenty years older, and more resigned than indignant, he is no longer running from either life or himself. Yet, in the face of the medical establishment's complete indifference, he cannot prevent the innocent young Bebert from dying of typhoid or save a young woman from slowly bleeding to death of an abortion when the family, to avoid a scandal, refuses to send her to a hospital. There is "no exit" from life but death, an exit which, as Germaine Bree notes in *The French Novel from Gide to Camus,* is held in check by Bardamu's "unreasoning animal instinct for physical survival."

Throughout the novel, Bardamu's adventures parallel and often intersect with those of his alter ego or double, the shadowy and mysterious Robinson, whose experiences more than once prefigure Bardamu's own. When the two first meet on the battlefield, Robinson has already made his plans to drop out of the war. When Bardamu reaches his remote African post, he discovers he is replacing Robinson, who had just absconded with the company funds. In Detroit he again encounters Robinson. Even in the Paris suburbs, he cannot escape Robinson, whose active nihilism mirrors Bardamu's passivity. Now a petty criminal, Robinson has agreed to murder an old woman for a thousand francs. When the plot falls through and he is injured in the failed attempt, Bardamu oversees his recovery. The novel ends with Robinson's death. The murder accomplished, Robinson is shot by a jilted girlfriend, leaving Bardamu both free and alone. "Try as I might to lose my way, so as not to find myself face to face with my own life, I kept coming up against it everywhere. My aimless pilgrimage was over. Let others carry on the game! The world had closed in. We had come to the end."

BIBLIOGRAPHY
Ostrovsky, Erica. *Céline and His Vision.* New York: New York University Press, 1967.
Thomas, Merlin. *Louis Ferdinand Céline.* New York: New Directions, 1980.
Vitoux, Frederic. *Céline: A Biography.* New York: Paragon House, 1992.

Michael Zeitler

JÜNGER, ERNST (1895–1998) *German essayist, novelist* The German-born Ernst Jünger is mainly known as an author of diaries. Spanning eight decades, these diaries reflect, together with his novels and essays, most major political, social, and ecological developments of the 20th century. They often establish a cosmological or mythical context that helps to subvert positivistic discourse. An extraordinary historical knowledge informs and legitimizes Jünger's evaluation of modernity. His dual strategy of being both at the heart of events and a detached observer has been called "stereoscopic." His work is the focus of fierce, often ideologically biased debate.

At the age of 16, Jünger fled from his bourgeois home and boarding school in the northwest German province of Lower Saxony and enlisted in the French Foreign Legion. He was shipped to Morocco but deserted into the Sahara. After only a few weeks, his father arranged for his return to Germany.

The reason for this African journey was the young man's disillusionment, which also caused its result. Jünger's next attempt to escape was volunteering for the German army at the beginning of World War I, during which he experienced the atrocities in the trenches of the western front. His eagerness to become an audacious leader and courageous individual dwindled amid the horrors of fighting and waiting. Jünger was wounded several times, and in 1918 he was awarded Germany's highest military decoration, Pour le Mérite. His account of the war, *In Stahlgewittern* (*Storm of Steel,* 1920, later editions significantly revised), based on his diaries, instantly became a best seller. In the Weimar Republic, Jünger tried his fortunes as a political journalist in Berlin, writing furiously against democracy and liberalism. His aggressive nationalism culminated in *Der Arbeiter* (*The Worker,*

1932), a controversial expansive essay on the state of modern society. It has been labeled fascist in its tendency to affirm man's role merely part of some great machinery. Problematic in its advocacy (which Jünger himself later revoked), the essay is brilliant in its observations of functionality and efficiency as key values of modernity.

Jünger declined the offer of a seat in the German national parliament, the Reichstag, and he never joined the National Socialist Party or the purged Academy of Arts. He turned his back on political activism, and on National Socialism in particular. In 1933 his house was searched by the Gestapo. In 1939 Jünger was called up again as a soldier in World War II. He spent most of the war in occupied Paris serving in the staff of General von Stülpnagel, the German army commander for France. Jünger established contacts with a large number of French intellectuals and with the German resistance. In 1944, after the attempt to assassinate Hitler had failed, he was dismissed from the Wehrmacht because of the inspiration his essay Der Friede (Peace) had provided for the conspirators.

Having published two prose works of fiction, Sturm (Storm, 1923), and Afrikanische Spiele (African Diversions, 1936), Jünger's first novel appeared in 1939. On the Marble Cliffs (Auf den Marmorklippen) is an account of the terror exercised by a brutal and licentious regime. Two brothers living in a reclusive library become the center of an opposition that is eventually crushed. The novel's outlook on history is pessimistic and fatalistic. It has been read as an allegory of the Third Reich and thus as a courageous act of resistance. Other critics, however, condemned the work for its stylized and too-sensuous language. Jünger initially endorsed an interpretation focusing entirely on National Socialist Germany, but he later stated that his depiction could characterize other modern states as well. Ironically, Hitler, on whom the protagonist is modeled, personally saved Jünger from being sent to a concentration camp after the novel was published. On the Marble Cliffs is now seen as the main example of "inner emigration" literature. This term was coined to characterize the writing and life of authors who stayed in Germany or in countries occupied by Germany during the Third Reich (1933–45) but did not actively participate in institutions or activities of the National Socialist Party. Inner emigration writing is politically indeterminate and explicitly open to interpretation (in writing or in life).

One of Jünger's first publications in postwar Germany, the essay Der Waldgang (The Retreat into the Forest, 1951), can be read as a document of a second inner emigration: from modernity. The walk into the woods is a walk away from society, called "the Ship." Jünger's oppressive system stands alike for National Socialist Germany, the Allied regime after the war, and the Federal Republic of Germany. The archetypal opposition between wood and ship is not dependent on the character of changing political systems but represents the fundamental dichotomy of individual and society. For Jünger, as for many other modern writers, every system is oppressive. It will eventually use its rules as weapons against its own citizens. Other essays, including his early theory of global governance, Der Weltstaat (The Global State, 1960), continue this reasoning.

Jünger's interest in LSD (which resulted in expansive essays on how perception is affected by hallucinogenic drugs), his being made honorary chief of a Liberian tribe (on one of his countless, adventurous intercontinental journeys), and his conversion to Catholicism shortly after his 100th birthday can all be seen as part of a questioning or oppositional attitude toward Western modernity.

Jünger was also a passionate entomologist. His essay Subtile Jagden reflects this interest, which is grounded in a feeling of connectedness to the earth and its ecosystem. In 1950 Jünger moved to a Swabian (southwestern Germany) village, where he continued to write without being involved in politics or academia. Nonetheless, he received the highest honors of the Federal Republic of Germany (the Bundesverdienstkreuz three times) and was visited by its presidents Heuss, Carstensen, and Herzog, several times by Chancellor Kohl, and by dignitaries from other countries, though he remained indifferent to their overtures and never engaged with the discourse of politicized writers. Jüngers's 100th birthday, however, was celebrated almost like a state event. Writing virtually until his last days (documented in the diaries Siebzig Verweht, 1980–97), he died in 1998.

Two postwar utopian novels by Jünger present societies in crisis. *Heliopolis* (1949) is set in a city after a devastating war. Two factions fight for power. The protagonist, Lucius de Geer, finds refuge from an almighty state and technology in love and meditation. The novel has been criticized for its imagery and stereotypical depiction of gender roles, but it has also been praised for its visionary insight into technological developments. The proximity of power and mystery and the role of fear in politics remained leitmotifs in Jünger's writing. They are also present in *Eumeswil* (1977), another city novel. Eumeswil, after the collapse of global governance, is ruled by an autocrat who placates his citizens by granting them access to technologies that make their life more comfortable. Public morale is at a low. Only an existence completely detached from society, in a dreamlike fantasy world, can restore individual independence.

The Crotch (*Die Zwille,* 1973) is a novel of adolescence in which a boy, Clamor Ebling, along with his older friend Teo, attacks the house of a headmaster who, as it turns out, has abused one of his pupils. Modernization and a call for action provide the historical context, while sexual awakening and escapism provide the individual reaction.

First drafts for *Eine gefährliche Begegnung* (*A Dangerous Encounter,* 1985) date back to 1949. A first version was published in volume 18 (*Die Zwille* [*The Crotch*]) of Jünger's *Collected Works* (1983). The novel is set in Paris around 1900; Jünger conducted thorough research into the period. His only crime novel is rich in psychological detail and presents illegal acts as a hopeless attempt to counter the power of a modern state and administration. A dreamer, a dandy, and an adventurer encounter a detective who will not be fooled by half-hearted attempts at opposition.

Jünger's narrative works often include essayistic or aphoristic passages, diary entries, or dream protocols. They treat subjects that are also present in his works of other genres. Jünger's contribution to modern and postmodern literature is his often explicit invitation to interpretation, the mosaiclike structure of his work, and his assertion of the power of the individual who is not to be defined by the state but is subject only to forces transcending human activity.

BIBLIOGRAPHY

Figal, Günter, and Heimo Schwilk, eds. *Magie der Heiterkeit: Ernst Jünger zum Hundertsten.* Stuttgart: Klett-Cotta, 1995.

Koslowski, Peter. *Der Mythos der Moderne: Die dichterische Philosophie Ernst Jüngers.* Munich: Fink, 1991.

Meyer, Martin. *Ernst Jünger.* Munich: Hanser, 1990.

Nevin, Thomas. *Ernst Jünger and Germany: Into the Abyss, 1914–1945.* London: Constable, 1997.

Noack, Paul. *Ernst Jünger: Eine Biographie.* Berlin: Fest, 1998.

Strack, Friedrich, ed. *Titan Technik: Ernst und Friedrich Georg Jünger über das technische Zeitalter.* Würzburg: Königshausen & Neumann, 2000.

Christophe Fricker

K

KAFKA, FRANZ (1883–1924) *Austrian novelist, short story writer* "A picture of my existence," Franz Kafka wrote about himself, "would show a useless wooden stake covered in snow . . . stuck loosely at a slant in the ground in a ploughed field on the edge of a vast open plain on a dark winter night." The sense of alienation, loneliness, and futility evoked by this image runs throughout Kafka's short stories and novels such as *The TRIAL* (1914) and *The CASTLE* (1922), which are considered to be among the most important in modern literature. Kafka's work often portrays a scorned individual struggling against an unintelligible and dehumanizing totalitarian or bureaucratic regime. Kafka's fatalistic subject matter, combined with the detached quality of his prose, has become a literary mode in modernism unto itself, aptly termed *Kafkaesque.*

Kafka was born in Prague (now in the Czech Republic, but then part of Austria) on July 2, 1883. His parents, Hermann and Löwy, belonged to the German-speaking Jewish community of Prague. Kafka had two brothers, both of whom died in infancy, and three sisters, all of whom died in Nazi concentration camps. The domestic environment in which the young Kafka grew up was tense, conditioned by the family's Jewish marginality in society and Hermann's profound temper. Kafka's turbulent relationship with his browbeating father is repeatedly played out in the author's work: "My writing was all about you," states Kafka in "Letter to My Father"—"all I did there, after all, was to bemoan what I could not bemoan upon your breast. It was an intentionally long-drawn-out leave-taking from you."

Kafka excelled as a student at prestigious German schools in Prague, and in 1906 he was awarded a doctorate in law from Ferdinand-Karls University. Around this time, he began to take writing seriously and became involved in a circle of writers and intellectuals, which included Franz Werfel, Oskar Baum, and Max Brod. Still living with his parents, Kafka secured a relatively lucrative position in the Workers' Accident Insurance institution and was professionally successful; his office work—writing reports on industrial accidents and health hazards—influenced the formal, legalistic language of his creative prose. Kafka considered his fiction to be the most important part of his life, as evinced in a 1913 diary entry: "When it became clear in my organism that writing was the most productive direction for my being to take, everything rushed in that direction and left empty all those abilities which were directed toward the joys of sex, eating, drinking, philosophical reflection and above all music." Thus, Kafka diligently wrote late into the evenings, after he had finished the day at the insurance office. In 1917, however, the onset of tuberculosis forced him to take frequent sick leaves, and after several years in and out of sanatoriums, the illness became so severe that Kafka retired altogether in 1922.

Much of Kafka's early writing is lost; what does remain was largely unfinished by the author. Famously, Kafka asked his close friend Max Brod to destroy his work once he had died. Brod, however, defied this request and, after Kafka's death, set about editing the work for publication. In organizing and refining the manuscripts, which were in complete disarray, Brod is considered to be largely responsible for Kafka's posthumous fame. Rather than diminishing the narrative and philosophical power of Kafka's literary legacy, the rough and unfinished quality of his existing work intensifies its remarkable sense of the open-endedness and uncertainty that define existentialism.

In 1912 Kafka wrote some of his most compelling stories, including "The Judgment" ("Das Urteil"), his novella The METAMORPHOSIS (Das Verwandlung), and much of his novel AMERIKA. This was also the year when Kafka met Felice Bauer, to whom he was engaged (and disengaged) twice over the next five years; he warned her that marriage to him would mean "a monastic life side by side with a man who is fretful, melancholy, untalkative, dissatisfied and sickly." Their erratic relationship, which was conducted largely through letters, expresses Kafka's general ambivalence to matrimony. His desire to marry was at once fueled by the wish to escape his father's influence and, somewhat paradoxically, impeded by a deep-seeded emotional attachment to his parents. Kafka's approach to sexual matters was similarly conflicted; he referred to intercourse as "the punishment for being together" but had encounters with prostitutes; in 1910 he wrote in his diary, "I passed by the brothel as though past the house of a beloved." Traveling to Vienna and Venice in 1913, Kafka began a brief relationship with Grete Bloch, who, unbeknownst to Kafka, had a son by him; the child, however, died at a young age. In 1914 Kafka began work on The Trial, his most famous novel and, though unfinished, the only long work for which he wrote an ending.

The next few years found Kafka moving among apartments in an effort to get away from his parents' noisy home and to avoid his father's incessant criticism. He finally broke off his engagement to Felice Bauer. In hopes of alleviating the symptoms of his tuberculosis, he moved from Prague to his sister Ottla's farm. During this time, Kafka dreamed aimlessly of becoming a potato farmer or moving to Palestine. In 1919 he wrote "Letter to His Father," which catalogues his every impression of their fraught relationship and, indirectly, illuminates issues of power that permeate his fictional work. Kafka gave the "Letter" to his mother to pass on, but it never reached its addressee.

He soon fell in love with Milena Jesenská, a 24-year-old writer who had translated some of Kafka's stories into Czech, but Milena, who was married, ultimately refused to leave her husband to live with him. In 1922 Kafka wrote The Castle, which portrays the destructive power of indifference, and "A Hunger Artist" ("Ein Hungerkunstler"), a brilliant exposition of the artistic drive.

Retirement from the insurance company brought a period of relative good health, and in 1923 Kafka moved to Berlin to live with Dora Dymant, a 20-year-old woman from an Orthodox Jewish family who worked in the kitchen of a holiday camp. This was perhaps the period of greatest liberation for Kafka, cohabiting with a woman he loved, far from the pressures of Prague. The couple dreamed of moving to Tel Aviv, but this aspiration was thwarted by the dire reality of Kafka's tuberculosis. He was left with no option but to return to Prague for treatment—a move that deprived him of both the love and freedom he had finally attained. He died of his ailment in 1924.

Kafka's work is centrally concerned with power dynamics in which the individual is trapped in a web of institutions and bureaucracy. Several of his writings depict the gradual degradation of someone ensnared in the "due process" of a judicial or otherwise bureaucratic system. In "The Great Wall of China" ("Beim Bau der Chinesischen Mauer," 1917), Kafka explains his thesis about the individual's urge to freedman, yet failure to attain it: "Human nature, essentially changeable, as unstable as the dust, can endure no restraint. . . . [I]t soon begins to tear madly at its bonds, until it rends everything asunder, the wall, the bonds, and its very self." Invariably, the ensnared individual in Kafka's stories is revealed to be utterly impotent against those who implement their inscrutable laws, codes, and penalties.

Power, for Kafka, is an end unto itself, and its expression in terms of the human factor in his work usually occurs at the middle and lower hierarchical levels—the "source" or ultimate legislator remaining conspicuously absent and inaccessible. The author's focus rests on individuals from the lower and middle class who are lost and alienated from a traditional world. These and other themes classify Kafka's work, particularly *The Trial,* as modern literature. In *The Trial,* Kafka positions an arbitrarily accused man, Joseph K., before a board of menacing judiciaries, who deem him a criminal without ever specifying the nature of his crime; even the status of the trial itself is determined by the enigmatic logic of those in authority, as one magistrate informs Joseph K., "You may object that it is not a trial at all; you are quite right, for it is only a trial if I recognize it as such."

Kafka's short story "In the Penal Colony" ("In der Strafkolonie," 1914) features a condemned person who is put to death by means of a machine that inscribes upon its victims the "reason" for their execution. Power dynamics are also played out, as an Oedipal reference, in "The Judgment," where a father's predetermination that his son will kill himself results, indeed, in the son's suicide. The stories are riddled with stairs, labyrinths, and other claustrophobic spaces, which function as physical indicators of the hierarchical structures in which Kafka's pawnlike heroes are made to exist. "So if you find nothing in the corridors open the doors," says a character in "The Advocates," "if you find nothing behind these doors there are more floors, and if you find nothing up there, don't worry, just leap up another flight of stairs."

Although Kafka's renderings of individual subjugation to forms of authority are often set in explicitly institutional or legal contexts, his stories are heavily allegorical and offer commentary on domestic, social, and even existential forms of confinement. The procedural aspect of *The Trial,* for example, evokes the process of life in general as a series of struggles culminating in death; "trial" commences at the moment of birth, and as the priest in the story explains, "the judgment does not arrive at once, [but rather] the trial transforms itself gradually into the judgment."

In *The Castle,* Olga describes her family's lamentable life as an ongoing penalty: "We did not fear something to come," she says, "[because] we had suffered already under the present [conditions], we were in the midst of the punishment." For the protagonist in *Amerika,* Karl Rossman, life is a sequence of assaults and dismissals, so that his final decision to join the Nature Theatre of Oklahoma may be seen as the ultimate ceding to marginality, an opting for exile and oblivion over a slave-like participation in the prevailing social and economic systems. Instead of progressing toward an objective—even if what is sought is an understanding of the very system that contains them (its rationale, its alleged purpose)—Kafka's heroes become increasingly aware of the insurmountable distance separating them from knowledge and freedom. The quest *toward,* then, reveals itself, finally, nightmarishly, to be a quest *away from.*

In all of his work, as indeed in most of Kafka's mature writing, the lucid, concise prose style forms a striking contrast to the world it represents—the labyrinthine complexities, the anxiety-laden absurdities, and the powerfully oppressive symbols of torment that are at the center of Kafka's ideology and artistic vision. Somewhat like a Rorschach test, Kafka's fiction is open to variable interpretation, at once eliciting and resisting attempts at conclusive explanation. Practically every major school of literary criticism—from deconstruction to psychoanalysis, from gender theory to historical materialism—has generated its own body of analysis of Kafka's work. Kafka's particular wisdom, according to MILAN KUNDERA, is "wisdom of uncertainty."

In a letter to his sister Ottla, Kafka wrote, "I write differently from what I speak, I speak differently from what I think, I think differently from the way I ought to think, and so it all proceeds into deepest darkness." Despite the pessimistic tenor and sinister autobiographical content of his fiction, Kafka himself is said to have possessed a compassionate and often uplifting personality. Brod recalled an incident when, accidentally awakening Brod's napping father, Kafka said, "Please look on me as in a dream."

In person, Kafka had a dry wit and was capable of making light of his misfortunes with a kind of self-mocking exasperation. Remarking on his job writing industrial accident reports for an insurance company, Kafka quipped, "I have a headache from all these girls in porcelain factories incessantly throwing themselves down the stairs with mountains of dishware." Although Kafka denounced hierarchical religious structures and answers, accounts of his character frequently point to an almost inhuman perspicacity and search for truth:

Friedrich Thieberger, the son of a Prague rabbi, described Kafka as "a sort of saint," and Emil Utitz, who had known Kafka since his high school years, remembered him as "quiet, delicate and almost saintly." Gustav Janouch, a friend during Kafka's last four years of life, held that the writer was a "visionary" and "prophet" of a "private religion," while Brod characterized Kafka "a saint possessed by truth." In a letter to Brod, Kafka's onetime girlfriend Milena Jasenská described his "absolute, unchangeable urge to perfection, to purity and to truth . . . till his last drop of blood." Indeed, nothing defined Kafka more than his valuation of writing, which, he maintained, "should both retain its natural, heavy rise and fall and at the same time and with equal clarity be recognized as nothing, a dream, a hovering."

Franz Kafka died on June 3, 1924, at the age of 40, leaving behind an inimitable literary legacy.

BIBLIOGRAPHY

Bridgwater, Patrick. *Kafka's Novels: An Interpretation.* Amsterdam: Rodopi, 2003.

Brod, Max. *Franz Kafka, a Biography.* New York: Schocken Books, 1960.

Cooper, Gabriele von Natzmer. *Kafka and Language: In the Stream of Thoughts and Life.* Riverside, Calif.: Ariadne Press, 1991.

Kafka, Franz. *Kafka—The Complete Stories.* Edited by Nahum N. Glatzer. New York: Schocken Books, 1976.

Karl, Frederick Robert. *Franz Kafka: Representative Man.* New York: Ticknor & Fields, 1991.

Mailloux, Peter Alden. *A Hesitation before Birth: The Life of Fanz Kafka.* Newark: University of Delaware Press, 1989.

Pawel Ernst. *The Nightmare of Reason: The Life of Franz Kafka.* New York: Farrar, Straus, 1983.

Kiki Benson

KANAFĀNĪ, GHASSĀN (1936–1972) *Palestinian essayist, novelist, short story writer, playwright* Ghassān Kanafānī is among the most innovative and influential Palestinian authors of the 20th century. His diverse writings include novels, short stories, plays, children stories, literary criticism, and political essays, all of which engage the Palestinian realities of his day. He was also a journalist and spokesman for the National Front for the Liberation of Palestine (NFLP), whose weekly publication he edited.

Kanafānī was born in Acre on April 9, 1936, during the time of the Palestine mandate. Before the first Arab-Israeli war (1948), he studied in French missionary schools. Once the war broke out, Kanafānī and his family fled as refugees to Lebanon and then to Damascus, where he later graduated from a UNRWA (United Nations Relief and Works Agency) school in 1952. He studied Arabic literature for three years at the University of Damascus but was expelled in 1955 because of his activities with the Movement of Arab Nationalists (MAN). Kanafānī met the MAN leader, George Habbash, in 1953. This encounter launched his lifelong engagement in fighting for the Palestinian cause.

In 1955, after leaving the University of Damascus, Kanafānī moved to Kuwait, where he taught art and physical education at a UNRWA school for Palestinians. He also continued his political activities and joined the editorial board of the MAN newspaper *al-Ray'* (*The Opinion*), which was located in Kuwait. During this time, he began composing short stories, his first attempts at fiction writing.

In 1960 Kanafānī returned to Beirut and joined the editorial board of the MAN newspaper *al-Hurriya* (*Freedom*). He became the editor in chief of the socialist newspaper *al-Muharrir* (*The Liberator*) in 1962. In the following year, Kanafānī published his first and most-popular novel, MEN IN THE SUN (*Rijal fi al-Shams*). Other fiction published during the 1960s include the short story collection *The Land of the Sad Oranges* (*Ard al-Burtuqal al-Hazin*, 1963), the modernist novel *What's Left for You* (*Maa Tabaqqaa Lakum*, 1966), the detective novel *The Other Thing: Who Killed Layla al-Hayk?* (*al-Shay' al-Akhar: Man Qatal Layla al-Hayk*, 1966), the resistance novel *Umm Sa'ad* (1969), and *Returning to Haifa* (*A'id ila Hayfa*, 1969). In addition to these works, all of which met with critical acclaim, Kanafānī published two important literary studies that examined the effects of the Israeli occupation on Palestinian literature. Through these two studies, Kanafānī established and popularized the concept of resistance literature.

Kanafānī joined the editorial board of the newspaper *al-Anwar* (*Illuminations*) in 1967. By 1969 he had become the official spokesman of the recently founded Popular Front for the Liberation of Palestine (PFLP), a radical Marxist-Leninist offshoot of the now inactive

MAN. He then became the editor in chief of the PFLP's weekly newspaper *al-Hadaf* (*The Goal*).

On July 9, 1972, at 36 years old, Ghassān Kanafānī—together with his young niece Lamees—was killed in a car-bomb explosion in Beirut. His death came approximately a month after the PFLP claimed responsibility for a terrorist attack at the Lod Airport in Tel Aviv that claimed 24 victims. Kanafānī was survived by his wife, Anni, and two children. The author's work remains popular and influential.

BIBLIOGRAPHY

Akaichi, Mourida. *Un Théâtre de voyage: dix romans de Mohammed Dibet de Gass an Kanaf.* Paris: Harmattan, 2005.

Harlow, Barbara. *After Lives: Legacies of Revolutionary Writing.* London; New York: Verso, 1996.

Jonathan Smolin

KAWABATA YASUNARI (1899–1972) *Japanese novelist*

Kawabata Yasunari, one of Japan's most outstanding authors, has received recognition both in his home country and abroad. In 1968 he received the Nobel Prize in literature for his terse, lyrical writing, which focuses on the themes of love and loss.

Born in Osaka on June 11, 1899, Kawabata was orphaned at the age of three. His grandmother died when he was seven, and the death of his sister followed when he was nine. Reared by his maternal grandfather, Kawabata attended Japanese public schools. When he was a boy, he planned to become a painter, but he decided to become a writer when his talent became obvious during his high school years. He began his studies at Tokyo Imperial University in 1920, graduating in 1924.

In the 1920s Kawabata associated with the neosensationists, a group of young writers who shunned the social realism popular at the time and used lyricism and impressionism in their writing. Kawabata was one of the founders of the journal *Bungei Jidai,* which published contemporary literature. In the late 1960s he campaigned for politically conservative candidates and publicly condemned the Cultural Revolution in China. Toward the end of his life, Kawabata experienced ill health, and on April 16, 1972, he committed suicide.

Kawabata's works, which have a melancholy tone, deal with human sexuality and examine the feminine mind. Many of the protagonists are lonely men who seek fulfillment through beautiful women. Kawabata's writing relies heavily on suggestion and impression and often leaves the reader with unanswered questions.

The Izu Dancer (*Izu no odoriko,* 1927), Kawabata's first published work, has a student as the protagonist. He becomes infatuated with a 14-year-old dancer but recognizes the girl's innocence. At the end of the novel the two young people part.

In SNOW COUNTRY (*Yukiguni,* 1948), the work which secured Kawabata's place as a leading writer, Shimamura, a wealthy man, periodically escapes the world of Tokyo by visiting a hot springs area. There he enjoys a liaison with Komako, a geisha. Although she loves him with abandon, Shimamura remains emotionally detached. Both are aware that the relationship is temporary.

THOUSAND CRANES (*Sembazuru,* 1949–52), which has numerous references to the tea ceremony, centers on the relationship of a young man, Kikuji, with two of his father's mistresses. He has a brief sexual encounter with one of the women, who commits suicide soon after. The other woman attempts to match Kikuji with a young lady whom he finds attractive, but Kikuji fails to pursue the relationship because of his disdain for his father's former mistress.

The Sound of the Mountain (*Yama no oto,* 1949–54), *The Master of Go* (*Meijin,* 1951), HOUSE OF THE SLEEPING BEAUTIES (*Nemureru bijo,* 1961), and *The Old Capital* (*Koto,* 1962) focus on regret and the past. In *The Sound of the Mountain,* set in Kamakura during the Allied occupation after World War II, the protagonist, an aging man, deals with the family problems of his married children and reflects on his past life. In *The Master of Go,* Kawabata suggests the passing of the old world by having a young challenger defeat an elderly champion at the game of Go. The protagonist of *House of the Sleeping Beauties* seeks to deny the aging process through visits to a home where men are paired with young women who have been drugged to sleep. In *The Old Capital,* twin sisters separated since birth meet in Kyoto. The novel reveals the beauty of the old city—which the Nobel Prize presentation called the "leading character"—and mourns the disappearance of the old traditions associated with it.

Throughout his life Kawabata also wrote palm-sized stories. Usually two or three pages in length, they have open endings. Their lyrical quality causes some people to consider them more poetry than prose.

Kawabata's canon of works validates his selection to receive the Nobel Prize in literature. His economical and lyrical literary style, detailed imagery, vivid brooding characters, and piercing meditative studies on love and loss have well earned Kawabata his reputation as one of Japan's greatest writers.

BIBLIOGRAPHY

"Kawabata, Yasunari." In *Contemporary Authors*. Vol. 91. Detroit: Gale Research, 1980.

"Kawabata, Yasunari." In *World Authors, 1950–1970,* edited by John Wakeman. New York: H. W. Wilson, 1975.

Ueda, Makoto. "Kawabata Yasunari." In *The Mother of Dreams and Other Short Stories,* edited by Ueta, 20. Tokyo: Kodansha International, 1989.

Charlotte S. Pfeiffer

KEMAL, YAŞAR (1922–) *Turkish essayist, novelist, poet*

Yaşar Kemal is one of the most well-known Turkish novelists read in and outside of his home country of Turkey. He is an exceptional author in successfully harmonizing the social realism of such classical novelists as Honoré de Balzac and MAXIM GORKY with the epic style of such 20th-century modernists as William Faulkner and James Joyce. At a deeper level, Yaşar Kemal affiliates his work with the art of Homer and Miguel de Cervantes in the sense of creating narratives of human plights, utopias of emancipation from oppression, and secular representations of a heroic sensibility toward life. Nonetheless, it is the native raw material (tales, legends, proverbs, epics, and idioms of Anatolia) that constantly feeds Kemal's rich dialogue with his Western colleagues. In brief, Kemal's literary career could be described as an extraordinary project of novelization of the Anatolian lifeworld in the face of its extinction in the second half of the 20th century.

Yaşar Kemal was born as Sadık Kemal Göğçeli in a South Anatolian village named Hemite. During World War I his family moved to the southern plains from the Kurdish province in eastern Turkey. Despite his well-to-do background, Kemal experienced a troubled childhood. At the age of five, he witnessed his father's murder and the shock of this tragedy left Kemal with a speech impediment that would last until his 12th year. At approximately the same period, Kemal lost his right eye due to an accident.

The absence of a primary school forced Kemal to leave his village at an early age. Because of financial hardships, however, he had to work as a laborer in a cotton gin factory while attending school. When it became clear that he could not handle both, he had to put an end to his formal education. Before he established his career as a journalist in 1951 at *Cumhuriyet* (*The Republic*), an Istanbul-based national newspaper, Kemal took various jobs, including work as a clerk, substitute teacher, field boss, tractor driver, and public letter writer (a person who writes letters for others). In these odd jobs he was self-taught.

Kemal had a keen interest in Anatolian folklore and oral tradition. His early acquaintance with Turkish folk elegies prompted him to write poetry in that traditional style. His early poems were published in 1939 in a local newspaper. In the subsequent years he published poetry in literary journals of the south Anatolian region and became linked with the intellectual circles in bigger cities such as Adana and Istanbul. During the same period, he traveled extensively among the villages of the region in order to compile undiscovered folkloric material. In 1943 he published the accumulated material under the title *Ballads* (*Ağıtlar*). Kemal's early ethnographic work left an impact on his later careers in journalism and creative writing.

As a journalist, Kemal reported on the deprived conditions of Anatolian peasantry. These writings proved to be unique in style and highly influential in bringing the peasants' poverty to the attention of the urban readership. Kemal's reporting won the annual Journalists' Association Prize, and his works were later published in book form. He continued to work as a journalist until 1963, ending his career as the director of National News Service at *Cumhuriyet*.

Upon his arrival in Istanbul, Kemal's literary interests shifted from poetry to prose. His first stories, "Memet and Memet" ("Memet ile Memet"), "The Dirty Story" ("Pis Hikaye"), and "The Shopkeeper" ("Dükkancı"), appeared in 1952 in a collection named *Yellow Heat* (*Sarı Sıcak*). These stories were vignettes from the toil of the peasants of the Chukurova plain.

With the 1995 publication of his first novel, MEMED, MY HAWK (*İnce Memed*), Kemal gained outstanding popularity as a creative writer. *Memed, My Hawk* became an instant best seller and was quickly translated into other languages. In this novel, Kemal created an epic hero out of Turkey's centuries-long history of feudalism. Ince Memed is a noble outlaw who exposes the exploitations of feudal landlords and the complicity of the state authorities in the oppression of the peasantry. At the end of the novel, Ince Memed flees to the mountains and assumes a spectral quality that haunts the unjust society. In another novel published in 1955, *The Drumming Out* (*Teneke*), Kemal narrates the efforts of a young and progressive mayor to weaken the power of the rice plantation owners. In his work the author invoked the politically committed urban intellectual in the figure of Ince Memed.

Following the publication of these two novels, Kemal began to work on a trilogy that offered a more sophisticated picture of the south Anatolian peasantry than *Memed, My Hawk* accomplished. In 1960 the first volume of the trilogy *The Wind from the Plain* (*Orta Direk*) appeared. In this novel, Kemal focuses on the issue of migration to the plains of Chukurova with the false expectation of receiving better wages there. *Iron Earth, Copper Sky* (*Yer Demir Gök Bakır*, 1963), the second volume in the trilogy, diverges significantly from the conventions of realism as the peasants create a myth as a form of salvation from their miseries. In the final volume, *The Undying Grass* (*Ölmez Otu*, 1968), the myth is destroyed and the reader is brought back to the everyday life of the peasants in the search for social transformation.

In the early 1970s Yaşar Kemal published two novels: *Murder in the Ironsmiths' Market* (*Demirciler Çarşisi Cinayeti*, 1974) and *Yusuf, Little Yusuf* (*Yusufçuk, Yusuf*, 1975). In these novels the focus is on the vanishing power of the feudal landlords under industrialization and urbanization. With the gradual deruralization of Anatolia, the feudal norms became obsolete and outmoded. Both novels portray the corrupted but hopeless attempts of the Chukurova landlords to retain their privileges and status against new capitalist urban interests.

Kemal did not give up his interest in Anatolian folklore during his career as a novelist. In 1967 he published *Anatolian Tales* (*Üç Anadolu Efsanesi*), in 1970 *The Legend of Mount Ararat* (*Ağrıdağı Efsanesi*), and in 1971 *The Legend of Thousand Bulls* (*Binboğalar Efsanesi*).

The author's later novels mark certain stylistic and thematic differences from his earlier novels, which had centered on the social fabric and landscape of the south Anatolian plains. In such works as *Seagull* (*Al Gözüm Seyreyle Salih*, 1976), *The Birds Have Also Gone* (*Kuşlar da Gitti*, 1978) and *The Sea-Crossed Fisherman* (*Deniz Küstü*, 1978), the setting shifts from peasant communities to fishing towns, from land to sea. Moreover, Kemal's later works tend to be more allegorical and in close parallel with the narrative strategies of magical realism. The controlling theme of the later novels is not human oppression but psychological and ecological alienation.

Yaşar Kemal retained his political commitments throughout his literary career. His devotion to the rights of the underprivileged led him to embrace socialism as an emancipatory ideology. He was first sentenced to prison at the age of 17. In 1950 he was tried on charges of disseminating communistic ideology but was acquitted a few months later. In 1962 Kemal joined the Turkish Labor Party and took up an active role as a member of the party's central committee. He established a Marxist weekly called *Ant* in 1967 and was sentenced to 18 months in prison when he published *The Guide to Marxism* in *Ant*. Under national and international pressure, the sentence was suspended. In 1995 he was sentenced again, to 20 months in prison (this too was later suspended), for an article he wrote for the German weekly *Der Spiegel*, criticizing the Turkish government's policies toward the Kurdish population in the country.

Kemal has remained an important author in contemporary world literature. Most of his novels have been translated into major European languages. His *Memed, My Hawk* has been translated into as many as 40 languages. He has received numerous awards in his own country as well as France, Germany, the United States, Spain, and Italy. In the words of the German

Nobel laureate GÜNTER GRASS, Yaşar Kemal is one of the few authors who has chosen to "take up residence" in the patches of earth now condemned to marginal existence.

BIBLIOGRAPHY

Bissinger, Manfred, and Daniela Hermes, eds. *Zeit, sich einzumischen: Die Kontroverseum Günter Grass und die Laudatio auf Yaşar Kemal in de Paulskirche.* Göttingen, Germany: Steidl, 1998.

Kemal, Yaşar. *Memed, My Hawk.* Translated by Edouard Roditi. New York: Pantheon Books, 1961.

———. *The Sea-Crossed Fisherman.* Translated by Thilda Kemal. New York: Braziller, 1985.

———. *Seagull.* Translated by Thilda Kemal. New York: Pantheon Books, 1981.

———. *The Undying Grass.* Translated by Thilda Kemal. London: Collins & Harvill Press, 1977.

Firat Oruc

KERTÉSZ, IMRE (1929–   ) *Hungarian essayist, novelist*

A Holocaust survivor, Hungarian writer Imre Kertész received the 2002 Nobel Prize in literature. Though Kertész's most famous novel, FATELESSNESS (*Sorstalanság*), was published in 1975, his work has been accorded international literary acclaim only in recent years, particularly since the 1989 demise of socialist governments in Eastern Europe. His unconventional approach to writing about the Holocaust troubled many critics in the past. In *Fatelessness,* the 14-year-old narrator György Köves admires the efficacy and shrewdness of the Nazi regime and does not resist imprisonment and torture: He accepts the degrading horrors as they unfold. Kertész's dry, objective writing style portrays the horror and injustice of concentration camps as mundane, everyday events.

Such an approach to writing about the Holocaust led publishers initially to regard *Fatelessness* as indifferent and possibly anti-Semitic. Kertész's style clearly differs from the efforts of other writers who have written about Holocaust experiences, such as PRIMO LEVI, Paul Celan, or Jean Améry. Yet Kertész has perhaps paid as much attention to the systemic causes of the Holocaust as to the experience of it, as his novels tend to focus on totalitarian structures and methods that make such events possible. As declared in his Nobel Prize acceptance speech, which he dedicated to all Holocaust victims, Kertész refuses to excuse the Holocaust as "an inexplicable historical error" that "cannot be rationalized," as many are tempted to do. Rather than writing off the Holocaust as an isolated, unfathomable tragedy, Kertész provocatively regards it as the inevitable result of modern European civilization, with its totalitarian governments and Christian-based education system.

Kertész was born on November 9, 1929, in Budapest to middle-class parents, a clerk and a lumber trader. His parents divorced in his infancy, and he was sent to boarding school as a child. Along with some 7,000 other Hungarian Jews in 1944, Kertész was deported from Budapest and sent first to Auschwitz and then to Buchenwald, from which he was freed in 1945. He returned to Budapest and wrote for *Spark* (*Szikra*), a journal published by the Ministry of Heavy Industry. Though Kertész graduated from high school in 1948, he actively self-educated himself by reading such authors as FRANZ KAFKA, Immanuel Kant, and Friedrich Hegel. Kertész worked as a journalist for *Illumination* (*Világosság*), a Social Democrat publication, though he was fired from his position in 1951 after the newspaper assumed a communist stance. After a stint working in a factory, Kertész was drafted into the Hungarian military, serving from 1953 to 1955. Thereafter, he married and began translating German literature into Hungarian, an endeavor that would support him financially for many years. These translations included works of Freud, Nietzsche, Roth, Schnitzler, Wittgenstein, and Hofmannsthal.

Kertész began writing *Fatelessness* in 1960 and did not complete the novel until the early 1970s. Since the publication of *Fatelessness,* for which he is best known, Kertész has become a prolific novelist and essayist. All of his work concerns the Holocaust on some level. "When I am thinking about a new novel," Kertész has said, "I always think of Auschwitz." *Fatelessness* is commonly regarded as the first novel in a tetralogy, also comprising *Failure* (*A kudarc,* 1988), *Kaddish for a Child Not Born* (*Kaddis a meg nem született gyermekért,* 1990), and *Liquidation* (*Felszámolás,* 2002). Extending the story of György Köves from the nonautobiographical *Fatelessness, Failure* is an autobiographical narrative, as the life of György Köves becomes that of Kertész himself. Like *Fatelessness, Failure* offers a damning indictment of totalitarian regimes, if in a distant, objective style. *Kaddish for a Child Not Born* is the story of a marital conflict between a husband and wife, each of whom has been affected by the Holocaust. The wife desires a child, but the husband (named B., the novel's narrator) refuses, desiring to beget not a child but only a written account of his experiences at Auschwitz. Kertész's most recent work, *Liquidation,* concerns B.'s decision to commit suicide and request that his ex-wife destroy his written account of his Holocaust experiences.

Other works include *The Path Finder* (*A nyomkeresó,* 1977); *The English Flag* (*Az angol labogó,* 1991); and *Galley Diary* (*Gályanapló,* 1992); a host of essays and lectures, which appear in *The Holocaust as Culture* (*A holocaust mint kultúra,* 1993); *Moments of Silence While the Execution Squad Reloads* (*A gondolatnyi csend, amíg kivèzöoztag újratölt,* 1998); and *The Exiled Language* (*A száműzött nyelv,* 2001). In addition to winning the 2002 Nobel Prize in literature, Kertész has been awarded the Brandenburger Literaturpreis (1995), the Leipziger Buchpreis zur Europäischen Verständigung (1997), the Herder-Preis (2000), the WELT-Literaturpreis (2000), and the Ehrenpreis der Robert-Bosch-Stiftung (2001).

Since 1989, Kertész has spent most of his time in Berlin because he finds his political and literary work unfit for Hungarian culture. Kertész believes that Hungary, unlike post–1989 Germany, has not yet confronted the legacy of the Holocaust past. The refusal to openly recognize the Holocaust has led to what Kertész calls a stultifying "culture of hinting" in Hungary, which continues to tolerate Nazis and anti-Semitism. Though he believes that in recent years the situation has improved somewhat in Hungary, Kertész still considers himself an exile in Berlin. He maintains no formal ties to any Hungarian organizations.

Eschewing postmodernism and relativism, Kertész believes in literature with a purpose. In an interview for the German newspaper *Die Zeit,* he stated that he would reread ALBERT CAMUS's Nobel Prize acceptance speech before penning his own, as if to remind himself of the very philosophies he deems detrimental to society. "We need to take positions again," Kertész argues, as "[t]here is a need for a literature that takes itself seriously."

BIBLIOGRAPHY
Vasvári, Louise O., and Steven Tötösy de Zepetnek. *Imre Keretész and Holocaust Literature.* West Lafayette, Ind.: Purdue University Press, 2005.

Jessica Gravely

KING, QUEEN, KNAVE (*KAROL' DAMA VALET*) VLADIMIR NABOKOV (1928)

Originally published in Russian in 1928 under the penname Sirin, *King, Queen, Knave* is the second novel by famed author VLADIMIR NABOKOV (1899–1977). The work was translated into English in 1968 after its publication in Germany. Unlike his first novel, *Mary* (1926), which is autobiographical in theme and features mainly Russian characters, Nabokov's *King, Queen, Knave* tells the story of a German love triangle. The author's virtuosic use of the stock plot of a love triangle results in a highly comic narrative that departs significantly from his first novel, whose meditations on memory, loss, and the passage of time recall the work of the great French modernist MARCEL PROUST. As an early divergence from modernism, and as an inspired parody of genre fiction, *King, Queen, Knave* forecasts the great English-language novels of Nabokov's maturity: *LOLITA* (1955), *Pale Fire* (1962), and *Ada* (1969). Nabokov wrote in Russian until 1940.

King, Queen, Knave begins in a compartment of a train traveling to Berlin and then quickly establishes the love-triangle plot. Franz, a hopelessly nearsighted and bland young man, is on his way to the German capital, where he hopes to gain employment in his uncle's clothing store. Also occupying Franz's compartment are Dreyer and his wife, Martha, who Nabokov later reveals to be Franz's uncle and aunt. Seen through Franz's poor eyes, Martha, appears extremely sensual and more passionate than her husband, a self-satisfied and successful businessman. Nabokov knowingly employs the clichéd language of romance novels in this scene and throughout the novel to parody the love-triangle genre, as well as to reveal the limited intelligence of his characters. This parodic use of clichéd language recalls the techniques of Gustave Flaubert, whose *Madame Bovary* Nabokov considered to be the best French novel of the 19th century.

Nabokov's characterization of Martha also evokes the heroine of Flaubert's great novel. Like Emma Bovary, Martha wants to have an affair to relieve her ennui—and she singles out her husband's nephew. But what begins as a simple distraction from her boring life with her husband ends up as a raging passion. Because this passion is for an inept, clumsy, ordinary, and distinctly unromantic young man, Nabokov is able to turn the traditional love-triangle story on its head to great comic effect. The early scenes of Franz and Martha's clandestine affair, as well as those of Franz's encounters with his uncle, are hilarious parodies of common scenes in triangular relationships in fiction.

The plot, however, eventually takes on a darker comedic tone when Martha decides that Franz should murder his uncle. She thinks that with Dreyer dead, she and Franz can inherit his money and live together forever. The lovers consider many schemes for the murder, but they finally decide that they want to fake Dreyer's accidental death by drowning during their summer vacation at a Baltic resort. On a rainy day during the vacation, they manage to entice Dreyer to take a ride in a dinghy, but just as they prepare themselves to push him overboard, he reveals that he has recently made a business deal that will pay him $100,000 in a few days. With the knowledge that she and Franz will inherit more money upon Dreyer's death, Martha decides to wait a few days before attempting the murder again. But Martha's decision results in the undoing of the murder plot—and the loss of her own life. The rain causes her to catch pneumonia, and she dies two days later.

Throughout the novel, all three of the main characters are unable to break out of their roles in the triangular relationship because of flaws in their ability to perceive the world. Nabokov as narrator has the deck stacked against the characters, as the title suggests. The self-satisfied Dreyer—the novel's "king"—remains blissfully unaware of his wife's affair with Franz and the murder plot throughout the novel. Even after his wife dies as a result of the attempt on his life, Dreyer considers Franz amusing and his wife cold and passionless. The misperceptions of the king parallel those of Martha, the novel's "queen." Indeed, Martha never perceives Franz's antagonism to the murder plot because she succeeds in breaking his autonomous will. And Franz, the novel's "knave," does not perceive that he can resist Martha's plot; thus, he never displays the craftiness and intelligence of the true knave.

Taken as a whole, *King, Queen, Knave* succeeds in parodying the mechanics of the love-triangle plot, with Nabokov acting as the grand master of the narrative game. His comic interest in deconstructing a particular narrative genre, however, leads to the novel's main flaw—namely, that the characters never really come alive. Despite this, *King, Queen, Knave* exemplifies the gifts that Nabokov more successfully displays in his later novels.

BIBLIOGRAPHY

Boyd, Brian. *Vladimir Nabokov: The Russian Years.* Princeton, N.J.: Princeton University Press, 1993.

Connolly, Julian W. *"King, Queen, Knave."* In *The Garland Companion to Vladimir Nabokov,* edited by Vladimir E. Alexandrov, 203–214. New York: Garland, 1995.

Merkel, Stephanie L. "Vladimir Nabokov's *King, Queen, Knave* and the Commedia dell'Arte." *Nabokov Studies* 1 (1994): 83–102.

Paul Gleason

KINGDOM OF THIS WORLD, THE (EL REINO DE ESTE MUNDO) ALEJO CARPENTIER (1949)

The Kingdom of This World, the second novel by Cuban author ALEJO CARPENTIER (1904–80), deals with the events surrounding the Haitian Revolution (1791–1804). The novel is divided into four sections, each of which chronicles an important stage in the country's independence movement. In the first section, Mackandal, a one-armed insurgent slave, uses ancient magic in an attempt to poison the French; though they bring about tremendous carnage, Mackandal's machinations ultimately fail, and he is put to death. The second part of the novel describes a rebel outbreak led by Jamaican-born Dutty Boukman; although Boukman is executed, by 1803 the insurgents are sufficiently galvanized to overthrow the colonialists. The third section concerns the postrevolution reign of Henri Christophe, a former slave and self-designated king who lords over his minions with even greater cruelty than his French predecessors. The final chapter of the novel is set during the mulatto Boyer's rule, which constitutes yet another phase of tyranny in Haitian history.

Although there is no traditional plot as such, the novel is unified by Ti Noel, who appears in each of the four sections and is depicted by turns as a slave, a squatting farmer, a disillusioned voodoo practitioner, and an advocate for humanity. Noel's subjective interpretation of events functions to augment the novel's historical material, which, sourced from a handful of records and documents, is necessarily limited in scope. When, for example, Noel is forced to partake in the construction of Christophe's sumptuous palace, Sans Souci, he notes that this postrevolution regime is simply another version of the one implemented by the French colonialists: "Walking, walking, up and down, down and up, the Negro began to think that the chamber-music orchestras of Sans Souci, the splendor of the uniforms, and the statues of naked white women soaking up the sun on their scrolled pedestals among the sculptured boxwood hedging the flower beds were all the product of a slavery as abominable as that he had known on the plantation of M. Leonormand de Mezy." Noel is mortified to see that the legacy of slavery has gone full circle—that his fellow black men are oppressed by an autocrat who is himself black.

Imbued with notions of human corruptibility and the insidious lure of dominance, Noel's observations allow Carpentier not only to supplement and "humanize" the historical record but also to move beyond the novel's particular context to produce a more general critique of power. Noel's final transformation—he decides that voodoo is best applied toward the betterment of humankind—is likewise a moment of prescriptive commentary. Dwelling within the turbulence of the Haitian revolution and emerging enlightened, Noel comes to represent the possibility of conscience for a human species that is too often vicious, self-serving, and ignorant.

The Kingdom of This World, as with several of Carpentier's other novels, both adheres to and deviates from the historical literature. In several key respects, Carpentier's rendering of actual figures and events is accurate: The Haitian movement for independence unfolded much as the novel suggests; Mackandal, Boukman, Christophe, the French general Leclerc, and Paulina Bonaparte are characters drawn from history, and the ruins of Sans Souci are still visible in Haiti. These verisimilar elements work to advance Carpentier's condemnation of surrealism, which, in the prologue to *The Kingdom of This World,* he deems fantastic to the point of being socially irrelevant. Furthermore, Carpentier's efforts to "return to the real" produce a rich and rare account of revolutionary Haiti.

Although the Haitian Revolution was, in fact, the only successful slave revolution in the history of the Americas, it is largely absent from historical literature. In *Tropics of Discourse,* Hayden White states that "Our explanations of historical structures and processes are determined more by what we leave out of our representations than by what we put in"—and indeed the relative dearth of information about Carpentier's topic speaks to the greater political forces of colonialism triumphing over the Occidental. Even during the Haitian Revolution, the reality of black slaves overthrowing the white French alarmed other colonial regimes, who were fearful of similar uprisings in their own states. As a consequence, alternate reasons (such as epidemic or white vs. white conflict) were commonly used to explain French deaths in Haiti during the revolutionary period. But as Michel-Rolph Troullot writes in *Silencing the Past: Power and the Production of History,* "The silencing of the Haitian Revolution is only a chapter within a narrative of global domination." Thus, in addition to restoring a pivotal event to Latin America's historical record, Carpentier's novel works to expand cultural awareness of politically motivated historical omissions.

As well as making audible previously "silenced" historical episodes, Carpentier redefines what constitutes historical material per se by stressing the cultural significance of magic. In the prologue to *The Kingdom of This World,* the author muses, "For what is the history of Latin America but a chronicle of magical realism?" Magical realism, Fredric Jameson submits, "is not a realism to be transfigured by the supplement of a magical perspective, but a reality which is already in and of itself magical or fantastic." Latin American culture, according to Carpentier, cannot be realistically represented without invoking supernatural and marvelous phenomena because these things form part of that culture's conception of the real.

Carpentier is often credited with coining the term *magic realism*. In his essay "On the Marvelous Real in America," Carpentier explains: "The marvelous begins to be unmistakably marvelous when it arises from an unexpected alteration of reality (the miracle), from a privileged revelation of reality an unaccustomed insight that is singularly favored by the unexpected richness of reality or an amplification of the scale and categories of reality perceived with particular intensity by virtue of an exaltation of the spirit that leads it to a kind of extreme state. To begin with, the phenomenon of the marvelous presupposes faith." The real consequences of this "faith" are evinced in *The Kingdom of This World* when Mackandal is executed: Witnesses believe that he has escaped death by transforming into an insect; Noel, who is later believed to have similar powers, decides to employ magic toward improving the lives of his fellow people and not merely in service of his own needs and desires. The emancipation of slaves and the construction of a durable and civilized Haitian culture are thus aided by a magical worldview—a worldview that Carpentier scrupulously depicts in his fiction.

BIBLIOGRAPHY

Gonzalez Echevarria, Roberto. *Alejo Carpentier: The Pilgrim at Home*. Ithaca, N.Y.: Cornell University Press, 1977.

Harvey, Sally. *Carpentier's Proustian Fiction: The Influence of Marcel Proust on Alejo Carpentier*. London: Tamesis, 1994.

Pancrazio, James J. *The Logic of Fetishism: Alejo Carpentier and the Cuban Tradition*. Lewisburg, Pa.: Bucknell University Press, 2004.

Shaw, Donald Leslie. *Alejo Carpentier*. Boston: Twayne, 1985.

Tulsay, Bobs M. *Alejo Carpentier: A Comprehensive Study*. Vaencia; Chapel Hill, N.C.: Albatros Hispanófila, 1982.

Kiki Benzon

KIŠ, DANILO (1935–1989) *Yugoslav essayist, novelist, short story writer*

Danilo Kiš is one of the most significant Yugoslav writers of the second half of the 20th century. A translator, essayist, and fiction writer, he gained international recognition with his semiautobiographical examination of the dehumanizing forces of totalitarian regimes. The distinctive feature of his novels is an interlacing of metaphysical reflections and pseudodocumentary records in a voice that is both poetic and ironic. This subtly humorous tone presents the writer's formal victory over his own subject, the trials and misery of the individual in political history.

Kiš was born in Subotica, Yugoslavia in 1935. A Jewish Hungarian on his father's side, a Montenegrin on his mother's side, and fluent in French and Hungarian, Kiš wrote in the language he deemed his own heritage: Serbo-Croatian. Three years after his birth, his family moved to Novi Sad, where, fast on the heels of the news about the anti-Semitic laws and regulations recently passed in Hungary, the future writer was hurriedly baptized in the Orthodox Christian Church. Kiš would later attribute his survival to this event. With the occupation of Yugoslavia by German forces, widespread persecution of Jews swept through the country. In 1942 the family moved to Hungary, with the intention of hiding in a remote village. Two years later Kiš's father was found and deported to a concentration camp from which he never returned. This unfortunate legacy predisposed the writer's interest in the topic of camps, from Germany's Auschwitz to Russia's gulag, forced-labor and prison camps that killed millions of people.

After World War II, the Red Cross repatriated Kiš's mother and her two children to Cetinje, Yugoslavia. There Kiš completed his elementary and high school education and relearned the Serbo-Croatian language. When he was 16 years old, his mother died. Two years later Kiš published his first piece of writing, a poem focusing on this intimate loss. In 1954 the young man moved to Belgrade, where he entered the university. He received his undergraduate and master's degrees in comparative literature at the University of Belgrade.

Kiš's first novels, *The Mansard* and *Psalm 44,* were both published in 1962. *The Mansard* is a poetic and satiric account of a provincial writer's life in a big city, while *Psalm 44* relates a true story about a Jewish couple who revisit a concentration camp in which their child was born years earlier. Later the writer would critique his first novelistic attempts as being too lyrical and devoid of ironic distance.

While living in Strasbourg between 1962 and 1964, Kiš wrote *Garden, Ashes* (1965). The novel is structured around attempts by Andreas Scham (Kiš's alter ego) to reconstruct the identity of his father, who had disappeared during the Holocaust. In *Garden, Ashes* Kiš finds a balance between lyricism and irony. This precarious equilibrium is achieved by the introduction of postmodern narrative contrivances such as lexicon entries, lists, and pseudodocuments. *Garden, Ashes* lives up to its title: Mourning is presented as a life-giving activity by means of which the hero comes to terms with his childhood, his family, and, most important, his father.

This novel also initiates a Kiš trilogy consisting of *Garden, Ashes;* the collection of short stories *Early Sorrows: For Children and Sensitive Readers* (1970); and the novel *Hourglass* (1972). These works dissect a family history, revealing political forces and a nurturing but tyrant father. The nature of this exploration is as much general as intimate. Kiš's own lost father emerges as the prime subject, as the writer attempts to reconstruct his father's personality from accounts, pictures, medical records, and disjointed memories. Coming last in the series of writings, *Hourglass* relates the final months in one man's life before he is ordered to a concentration camp. The novel unfolds in a poetic series of authorial meditations and digressions, which unexpectedly build a suspenseful narrative. Structured as a metafictional commentary on the detective novel, *Hourglass* refutes the very teleology implied by the genre. There is no final conclusion to this narrative—the letter that closes the novel only opens a wider semantic space of uncertainty.

During another period of living in France (1973–76), Kiš wrote his masterpiece *A TOMB FOR BORIS DAVIDOVICH* (1976). Having earlier examined the terror of the Holocaust, Kiš now felt obliged to speak out about another horrifying totalitarian system—the Soviet regime. This short novel takes the form of seven stories, based on real and pseudo-real documents. Here Kiš's attention focuses on the Soviet trials and camps in which even loyal communists such as Boris Davidovich disappeared. These stories are interlinked by a common theme, yet their final coalescence in a novelistic structure relies completely upon the controversial source of the stories—the Moscow Trials (1936–38). This was a series of trials against individuals accused of plotting against Joseph Stalin and other Soviet leaders during the Great Purge in Russia. The verdicts were widely considered to be predetermined. The use of authentic and pseudo-authentic documents incited critics to charge Kisš with plagiarism upon the novel's publication. The writer soon found himself in the center of a heated literary and political controversy.

To answer these harsh charges, Kiš published the polemical *The Anatomy Lesson* (1978), in which he expounds on the creative precepts that govern his writing. Soon afterward he left Yugoslavia and settled down permanently in France. The two most important writings of Kiš's French years are the selection of essays *Homo Poeticus: Essays and Interviews* (1983) and his masterpiece collection of short stories *The Encyclopedia of the Dead* (1983). Kiš died in Paris in 1989.

Structuring his novels around a sensitive examination of the human condition in a totalitarian society, Kiš avoids the danger of pathetic rendition by high stylization, quizzical juxtaposition, and challenging experimentation. In his novels, the quotidian and universal interlace and modify each other in a pseudohistorical record. Sympathetic to magic realism, Kiš developed his own idiom out of journalist style, historical-record narration, personal testimony, and dynamic lyricism. The singular achievement of Kiš's fiction is a narrative voice that is emphatically distant and painfully intimate simultaneously. This ambivalent voice has the effect of rendering the tragic historical subject of his novels terrifyingly proximate. Kiš's literary reputation has been disseminated worldwide by supporters such as Susan Sontag, Joseph Brodsky, and Paul Auster. His work has been translated into more than 30 languages.

BIBLIOGRAPHY

Bernbaum, M. D., and R. Trager-Verchovsky, eds. *History, Another Text: Essays on the Fiction of Kazimierz Brandys, Danilo Kiš, György and Christa Wolf.* Ann Arbor: University of Michigan Press, 1988.

Kiš, Danilo. *Homo Poeticus: Essays and Interviews.* New York: Farrar, Straus and Giroux, 1995.

Prstojevic, Alexandre. *Le roman face à l'historie: essai sur Claude Simon and Danilo Kiš.* Paris: Harmattan, 2005.

Schulte, Jörg. *Eine Poetik der Offenbarung: Isaak Babel, Bruno Schulz, Danlio Kiš.* Wiesbaden: Harrassowitz, 2004.

Sanja Bahun-Radunovic

KISS OF THE SPIDER WOMAN (EL BESO DE LA MUJER ARAÑA) MANUEL PUIG (1976)

The novel *Kiss of the Spider Woman* by Argentina's MANUEL PUIG (1932–90) has become the author's most popular work due in large part to its successful screen adaptation in 1985.

Kiss of the Spider Woman depicts the evolving relationship between two prison inmates: Valentin, a Marxist revolutionary, and Molina, a homosexual window display artist. Valentin's crime is political subversion and Molina's the seduction of a minor. Much of the novel takes place as a conversation between these two inmates. As a means of passing time while incarcerated, Molina relates to Valentin the plots of his favorite films—mostly 1930s and 1940s melodramas. While Valentin is initially critical of Molina's romantic and "escapist" stories, he gradually comes to enjoy and find solace in Molina's narratives. The title *Kiss of the Spider Woman* refers to Molina's favorite movie star Aurora, whose roles include an evil spider woman who symbolizes death to Molina.

In discussing the films, the men inevitably reveal themselves to each other, and their intimacy deepens. Valentin explains how his political ideas have rendered all other aspects of his life insignificant; he laments, in particular, having destroyed a relationship with a woman from a bourgeois background in favor of political activism. For his part, Molina is plagued by concerns for his mother and predicts that, in his absence, she is likely to become mortally ill. Their discussion progresses from the verbal to the sexual. Although Molina's treatment of Valentin appears sincere (he shares his food and nurses Valentin when he is ill), his motives become suspect when the reader learns that Molina is a mole being used by the prison authorities. He hopes that his subterfuge will earn him an early release. Ultimately, however, Molina's sympathy compels him to assist Valentin in the Marxist cause, and he agrees to deliver information to Valentin's cohorts upon his release from prison.

Kiss of the Spider Woman portrays a collision of opposing values: human emotion and political activism. At the outset of the novel, the gulf between the two men is vast; Valentin considers interpersonal relationships to be insignificant in comparison to revolutionary activism, while Molina concerns himself almost exclusively with romance and sentiment. By placing these contrasting personalities in close quarters, Puig explores the limitations of their particular standpoints and intimates both means and motivation for compromise. Valentin and Molina, through long conversations in their cells, come to see each other's point of view somewhat clearer. Puig is suggesting that when profound human relations are formed, the line between seemingly incompatible values becomes blurred. This blurring can be personally enriching, but—as demonstrated by the novel's tragic conclusion—this enrichment comes with its own set of limitations and potential dangers. Molina is ultimately killed during his dealings with the revolutionaries.

Commonly situated within the "new" narrative movement of the 1960s and 1970s, Puig's fiction is characterized by structural and material experimentation. Exploring the narrative possibilities of nontraditional literary forms, Puig incorporates letters, police and hospital reports, advertisements, song lyrics, and shopping lists into his fiction. He is one of the few novelists to employ paratextual devices; *Kiss of the Spider Woman,* for example, includes extensive footnotes, which provide a history of psychological and cultural interpretations of homosexuality. The novel furthermore favors dialogue over exposition as a means of advancing the plot and conveying character psychology. Perhaps the most stylistically inventive aspect of *Kiss of the Spider Woman* is its lengthy film synopses, which account for over half of the novel's textual body.

Although Puig's work has been criticized for drawing heavily upon "frivolous" melodrama, Molina's film accounts function as much more than sentimental and sensational diversion. The combination of intensive dialogue and cinematic description transforms the prison environment into something of an extended psychoanalytic session. Molina's description of a zombie-horror film, for example, prompts Valentin to voice his deeply guarded feelings about the love he has lost. Molina is recounting a moment in the film when a newlywed woman realizes that the zombie she has seen is her husband's first wife, and Valentin suddenly interrupts the storyteller: "I'm very depressed . . . I'm just aching for Marta, my whole body aches for her."

Although Valentin's current partner is a fellow political rebel, he misses his former love, Marta—and Molina's narrative about a zombified (neither alive nor dead) former wife prompts Valentin to finally articulate his regret at her loss. Emotion erupts from the hitherto unsentimental Valentin, who goes on to dictate a letter for Marta: "Inside, I'm all raw, and only someone like you could understand. . . . The torturer I have inside of me tells me that everything is finished, and that this agony is my last experience on earth." Thus, what may seem to be a solely experimental exercise in narrative style—Puig integrates cinematic, literary, and epistolary forms—is finally a strategy of psychological elucidation. Indeed, Puig's fiction is concerned above all with analysis—of self, other, and society. Writing, in Puig's estimation, "is an analytic activity, not a synthetic one."

BIBLIOGRAPHY

Bacarisse, Pamela. *Impossible Choices: The Implications of the Cultural References in the Novels of Manuel Puig.* Calgary, Alberta: University of Calgary Press, 1993.

Craig, Linda. *Juan Carlos Onetti, Manuel Puig and Luisa Valenzuela: Marginality and Gender.* Rochester, N.Y.: Tamesis, 2005.

Giordano, Alberto. *Manuel Puig: La conversación infinita.* Buenos Aires: Beatriz Viterbo, Editora, 2001.

Kerr, Lucille. *Suspended Fictions: Reading Novels of Manuel Puig.* Urbana: University of Illinois, 1987.

Marti-Pena, Guadalupe. *Manuel Puig ante la critica: Bibliografia analitica y comentada.* Madrid: Iberomericana, 1997.

Tittler, Jonathan. *Manuel Puig.* New York: Twayne Publishers, 1993.

Kiki Benzon

KITCHEN (KITCHIN) YOSHIMOTO BANANA (1988)

Kitchen, the debut novel by YOSHIMOTO BANANA (1964–), was a phenomenal success, catapulting the young author into instant celebrity status in her native Japan. The novel quickly won three literary prizes: *Kaien* magazine's New Writer's Prize, the *Umitsubame* first novel prize, and the *Izumi Kyoka* literary prize, which established her presence as a serious new voice of late 20th-century Japan. The book became extremely popular among young readers, first in Japan, then globally as it was released in more than 20 foreign translations. *Kitchen* has also been filmed twice, once by Japanese television and also in a more widely released version directed by Hong Kong filmmaker Yim Ho.

The novel comprises two seemingly unrelated stories: the longer "Kitchen" and the much shorter "Moonlight Shadow." The protagonist of "Kitchen" is Mikage Sakurai, a young girl who finds herself alone and disoriented after the death of her grandmother. With no other relatives to turn to and unsure about her future, Mikage continues to live in her grandmother's house, cleaning and delaying the advent of her relocation. Her solitude is unexpectedly broken by the arrival of Yuichi Tanabe, a college classmate who had befriended her grandmother. Concerned, Yuichi offers to take Mikage in until she can pull herself together and find a new place to live. Together with Yuichi's transsexual father-turned-mother Eriko, Mikage finds an odd but emotionally generous surrogate family.

Eventually Mikage overcomes her grief while living with and happily cooking for Yuichi and Eriko. Her days in the kitchen provide not only therapy but also a future as she takes a job working for a famous television chef after leaving them. Though they grow apart, Mikage and Yuichi are reunited after the tragic murder of his mother/father. The tables turned, Mikage sustains Yuichi through his grief, aided by the culinary skills she had first honed in his home.

"Moonlight Shadow" also takes up the theme of sudden bereavement and grief though with a slightly more supernatural flavor than the first story "Kitchen." The protagonist Satsuki has lost her teenage sweetheart Hitoshi in the same automobile accident that killed his sister Yumiko, the girlfriend of Hiiragi. Satuski and Hiiragi find comfort in each other's presence despite developing very different rituals to assuage their sorrow: Satsuki takes up early morning jogging, while Hiiragi finds solace in wearing the dead Yumiko's schoolgirl uniform.

Satsuki meets a woman while resting during her usual morning jog over the bridge where she and Hitoshi used to meet. The rather strange Urara tells Satsuki about a mystical experience, the Weaver Festival Phenomenon, which happens only once every hundred years near a large river. The event may allow the living a parting glance of the dead and thus emotional closure, something Urara senses that Satsuki needs.

When the day arrives, Satsuki is granted a final vision of Hitoshi and makes her peace with his death. Though not at the river, Hiiragi too is seemingly visited by Yumiko, after which he can no longer find her school uniform in his closet.

Upon reflection, the two initially unrelated stories in *Kitchen* mirror each other thematically and also in term of plot details: Both deal with the emotional devastations of love and loss and both contain instances of a character's cross-dressing. Both stories revel in sensually rendered descriptions, particularly the smells of food like Mikage's *katsudon* and Satsuki's *Pu-Arh* tea. Loss sits at the dead center of *Kitchen,* and while the novel is written in the hyper-deadpan style of modern Japanese pop culture, this is a quintessentially traditional Japanese theme: the impermanence that is the defining condition of human life.

BIBLIOGRAPHY

Yoshimoto Banana. *Goodbye, Tsugumi, a Novel.* Translated by Michael Emmerich. New York: Grove Press, 2002.
———. *Lizard.* Translated by Ann Sherif. New York: Washington Square Press, 1996.
———. *Kitchen.* Translated by Megan Backus. New York: Washington Square Press, 1993.
———. *N.P. A Novel.* Translated by Ann Sherif. New York: Grove Press, 1994.

Mina Estevez

KNOT OF VIPERS, A (LE NOEUD DE VIPÈRES) FRANÇOIS MAURIAC (1932)

Considered by many to be the best novel by France's FRANÇOIS MAURIAC (1885–1970), *A Knot of Vipers* contains those recurring central themes of alienation, error, and delusion, or simply "sin," seen in most of his stories. The work also reveals Mauriac at the height of his technical powers, with the novel's curious structure of invective turned confession turned memoir. The story begins as a letter written by the narrator, Louis, to his wife, Isa, and their children. Louis envisions the letter being placed among his documents and securities in his safe, to be discovered when the family members dash for their inheritance once he is in the ground. The letter drips with hatred, spite, anger, resentment, accusation, and disappointment, all seasoned with enough rationalization and justification to make it that much more bitter for his family to hear. Beginning this way, the work soon changes to a confession, a diary of sorts, that Louis uses to explore his past to see why his present life repulses him so. Isa dies before he gets to finish this hateful apology, and in the end his exposition becomes part of Louis' ultimate redemption.

Part one of the novel has Louis admitting that the letter is an act of vengeance that he has been brooding upon for decades. He tells his family that he could, if he wanted, deny them what they have been so anxiously awaiting, this fortune of his for which he has been sacrificing all of his life. These sacrifices, he admits, have "poisoned" his mind, "nourishing and fattening" the "vipers" in his heart. "I am by nature," he coldly confesses, "Nature's wet blanket," though he moves on to describe a life that somehow suggests that his nature was in fact corrupted and turned over to what it is now.

The narrator, Louis, was an only child, with his father having died early in his life and his mother showing affection but no understanding. Louis envies those who have childhood memories that they cherish; all he has are memories of sacrifice and alienation. Education for him came at a high price, and he received no sense of guidance or enlightenment despite his hard work and success. Socially awkward and detached, he becomes a bit of a skirt chaser, seeking only to humiliate and dominate whenever he can. He was a brute, he says, and he has paid and continues to pay for his behavior, but at this point he regrets nothing. All that will soon change, however. Louis points out that he had cherished a hatred for religion, even taking to eating his "Good Friday cutlet" in front of his pious wife and family, as if to show that he will not yield nor will he be owned. An indifference to religion would have been more expected, but to throw such energy at blasphemy as Louis does reveals the deeper struggles and confusions at the heart of his dedication to anger.

Along with the focus on striking out at God is Louis's lifelong cruelty to his wife. In the discussions of his wife and their early marriage, hatred gives way to regret, revision ("I shouldn't say that, that's not fair to you"), and short glimpses into his pain and disappointment. Louis did love his wife in those first years, he writes, ironically for her "spiritual elements." However,

Louis also reveals that what he loved about Isa was her love for him, how much her personality reflected his own worth. In his long invective he tells Ira that what fascinated him was that she found him "no longer repellent." In a moment of misunderstanding, Isa soon after the wedding confesses to her husband that she had been involved with a man named Rodolphe. The reader realizes, as Louis does not, that Isa here is opening herself up, making sure that no mystery will come between them. Louis, however, thinks that Rodolphe now haunts their marriage, and that Isa is still secretly in love with the man.

After these miscommunications, Louis writes and begins what he calls the "era of the Great Silence," ignoring Isa for the rest of their marriage. She, of course, turns to her children for affection, which causes further resentment from Louis. He enters a life of secret debauchery, indifferent to his children in their "grub stage," as he calls it. The children for the rest of their lives take on the brunt of their father's hatred and cold indifference. Louis becomes a great lawyer in Paris, revealing that his skills in the courtroom prompt others to offer him opportunities at being a writer for journals and newspapers, and others to suggest that he run for political offices. Dismissing them, Louis says that he stuck it out to keep getting the "big money."

A few people in particular show Louis brief moments of love, possible connections to others, but they are taken away too soon for him to be truly redeemed. First there is his daughter, Maria, whom he loved, he says, because she never was afraid of him and did not "irritate" him. An affair with a schoolteacher, perhaps the mother of the illegitimate son in the second part of the novel, was to Louis the one time that he knew "real love," but he also admits that the woman intrigued him because she so easily became his "property." Isa's sister, Marinette, catches the interest of Louis not out of lust but for the simple fact that she is not suspected of any plots or jealousies. Her son, Luc, becomes Louis's emotional surrogate, most likely to spite his own family, but Luc goes off to war and never returns.

These disappointments and misreadings of others stand beside Louis's revelation of the mess that he has made of his life. He tells Isa here that he is tormented by having "nothing out of life," nothing to look forward to "but death," and no sense of any world beyond this one, no hint of a solution, no response to his provocations to a silent God (this "nothingness" that he rages at will become important for his ultimate redemption). He confesses that he has chosen wrongly, that he never learned how to live. "I know my heart," he writes, "it is a knot of vipers."

Part two of the novel shows that this letter, now turned notebook, has been brought along unwittingly by Louis as he leaves to go to Paris in search of his illegitimate son, Robert, little realizing it is an attempt to find someone that he can love and with whom he can finally communicate. Completely broken off from his family, he admits that he is projecting onto Robert the qualities that he cherished from Luc and Phili, family members for whom he apparently has a certain affection. Louis initiates his search after overhearing them asking Isa to have their father committed. In retaliation, Louis looks to give Robert the entire fortune, robbing the family of yet one more thing.

Louis relates one scene in which Isa, prompted by her children, asks Louis about some stock shares that she had brought into the marriage. He assures Isa that they are safe, and she breaks down, asking why he hates his children. He screams back at her, "It is you who hate me, or rather, it's my children. *You* merely ignore me." Isa confesses to her husband that the entire time they were married, she never let the children come to sleep with her due to her hope that one day Louis may have possibly come to her bed to be with his wife. The true effect of their disappointed relationship on both Isa and Louis is realized, but far too late to prevent lasting damage.

Isa dies, and Louis laments that "she had died without knowing me, without knowing that there was more in me than the monster, the tormentor, that she thought me to be." At the funeral, Louis and his children hurl their anger and rage at one another, they at him for his cruelty, he at them for lying about not knowing where he was to tell him about Isa's death. Louis catches them in the lie because he had seen family members meeting with Robert to discuss what their father was plotting. His son, Hubert, exasperated at the intrigues, says that he only fought for his children, for their honor, but now they are all faced with "nothing."

The word *nothing* suddenly strikes at the knot of vipers that Louis has been cultivating all these years, echoing the "nothingness" in his life and the "nothingness" that is Isa's death. Immediately, Louis feels his hatred die, his "desire for reprisals" dissipate, and his fortune simply no longer of interest to him. He hands everything over to them, unburdening himself of his fortune and, symbolically, his torments. The reader is apt to suspect that Louis had unconsciously kept his children away from the very thing that caused his life to become so odious. "Fancy waking up at sixty-eight," says Louis, adding, "I must never stop telling myself that it is too late." At one point he remembers what he had always loved about Isa—her piety—recalling her nightly prayers, "I thank Thee that Thou hast given me a heart to know and love Thee."

Louis's final act is one of compassion and understanding, as Phili has left his wife, Louis's granddaughter Janine. Recognizing both the family's mistreatment of Phili and the affection that Janine still clings to, Louis comforts his granddaughter, asking her finally if she really thinks Phili is worth all of her "pain and torment." The question never gets answered, as Louis dies, ironically, while writing in his notebook.

The novel ends with two letters, the first from Hubert to his wife, Genevieve, addressing the discovery of the notebook and the curious confessions of his inscrutable father. He tells his wife of the blasphemy and hatred therein, admitting that his father now seems noble and more human. Still, he suspects Louis of actually turning a defeat into a moral victory. The second letter is from Janine to her uncle Hubert, defending her grandfather, saying that he was the most religious man she has ever known. She says that the rest of the family acts piously but never lets principle interfere with their lives, and she praises Louis for living his according to principles he felt to be true to his heart. She asks at the end of this assessment of Louis's life if it can be said that for him, "where his treasure was, there his heart was *not*?"

BIBLIOGRAPHY

Flower, John E. *Intention and Achievement: An Essay on the Novels of François Mauriac.* Oxford: Clarendon Press, 1969.

Flower, John E., and Bernard C. Swift, eds. *François Mauriac: Visions and Reappraisals.* New York: St. Martin's Press, 1989.

O'Connell, David. *François Mauriac Revisited.* New York: Twayne, 1994.

Speaight, Robert. *François Mauriac: A Study of the Writer and the Man.* London: Chatto and Windus, 1976.

Wansink, Susan. *Female Victims and Oppressors in Novels by Theodor Fontane and François Mauriac.* New York: Peter Lang, 1998.

Matthew Guy

KO UN (1933–) *Korean essayist, novelist, poet*

Ko Un is one of the leading figures in 20th-century Korean literature. As a poet, novelist, essayist, literary critic, and political activist, Ko has published more than 120 books. His prolific writing often explores or recalls the tumultuous events of Korea's modern history, ranging from Japanese colonization to the Korean War to authoritarian dictatorships and military coup d'états, to democratization and labor movements, and to the first summit of the South and North Korean leaders in Pyongyang after the division of the Korean Peninsula. Although Ko's writing is deeply entrenched with nationalism and Buddhism, his politically controversial and aesthetically innovative works have been internationally admired and translated into many other languages. Ko has been short-listed for the Nobel Prize in literature twice, in 2002 and 2004.

Ko was born on August 1, 1933, as the first child of a peasant family in Gunsan, North Cholla Province, southwestern Korea. This region was under Japanese occupation from 1910 to 1945. He was a precocious child who mastered the Chinese classics at age eight. Inspired by the leper-poet Han Ha-Un, Ko began to write poems at the age of 12. His parents enthusiastically supported his education, and his grandfather taught him the Korean language and history, which were strictly prohibited and systematically erased during Japanese colonialization of Korea. Once Ko audaciously told his Japanese headmaster in the third grade that he wanted to be emperor of Japan, for which he was almost expelled from the school. This childhood episode shows his early awakening of historical and political consciousness.

During the Korean War (1950–53), Ko was forced to work as a gravedigger. Feeling surrounded by countless innocent deaths and unimaginable madness, he experienced an existential crisis, which resulted in a failed suicide attempt and, consequently, permanent damage in one ear. Ko then decided to become a Buddhist monk. Under the Buddhist name Il Cho, he lived a monastic life for 10 years by practicing Son, a meditation similar to the Japanese Zen; publishing the first Korean Buddhist newspaper, *Pulgyo Shinmun;* and traveling around his home country. These experiences are continuously and productively implicit in his writing. Ko's first collection of youthful poems, *Other World Sensibility* (*Pian Kamsang*), and first novel, *Cherry Tree in Another World* (*Pian Aeng*), were released in 1960 and 1961, respectively.

Even though he served as venerable head monk of several major temples, Ko became dissatisfied with religious formalism and thus wrote "Resignation Manifesto" in 1962. Upon returning to a secular life, he taught Korean language and art at a charity school on Cheju Island for three years. Yet he also suffered from severe insomnia and alcoholism and became excessively involved in nihilism. In 1970 Ko attempted suicide again, this time by taking poison and falling into a 30-hour coma.

When, however, the young garment worker Chon Tae-Il burnt himself in the 1990s to draw public attention to terribly poor labor conditions, Ko awoke to his need to engage in political struggle and labor movements as a social and political activist. This was also a turning point in his poetic world, which transformed from nihilistic sensibility with self-doubt and despair to revolutionary awareness with historical and critical insight to social injustice and oppressive reality.

In 1973 Ko was deeply involved in political demonstration and protest against President Park Chung-Hee's Yusin reforms (constitutional amendments), which included suppression of civil rights and support of his presidency for life. In 1974 Ko became the official spokesman for the National Association for the Recovery of Democracy. Consequently, he was blacklisted as a leading dissident writer and speaker, and his writing was censored during military dictatorial regimes. During the years 1973–82, Ko endured such political ordeals as imprisonments, detentions, and house arrests. In particular, in 1980, along with Kim Dae-Jung, the 2000 Nobel Peace Prize winner, Ko was arrested on charges of treason after Park Chung-Hee's assassination. The death of South Korea's president was followed by General Chun Do-Hwan's military coup d'état and the Kwangju uprising against it. Ko's prison term for life was suspended after two and a half years. During his imprisonment, he conceived a project he titled *Ten Thousand Lives* (*Maninbo*), in which he planned to depict people he had met in his life and historical figures he admired. The 20 volumes of *Maninbo* were published between 1986 and 2003, and another five volumes are expected.

In 1983 Ko married Lee Sang-Wha, a professor of English literature, and moved to the countryside of Ansong, Kyonggi Province, two hours away from Seoul. His marriage and the birth of his only daughter generated a new sense of stability and happiness for the author. As a result, Ko wrote prolifically and completed seven volumes of epic poems including *Paekdu Mountain* (*Paekdu-san*, 1987–94), *Homeland Stars* (*Chokuk ui Byol,* 1984), *Your Eyes* (*Nei Nundongja,* 1988), *Song of Tomorrow* (*Neil ui Norae,* 1992), and other works. He also published biographies; numerous essays; and several novels, including *The Desert I Made* (*Naega Mahndeun Samak,* 1992), *Their Field* (*Gudeul ui Bulpahn,* 1992), and *Chongsun Arirang* (1995). The English edition of *The Sound of My Waves* (*Na ui Pado Sori*) first appeared in 1992, followed by poetry collections *Beyond Self* (1997), *Travelersmaps* (2004), and *Ten Thousand Lives* (2005).

Ko's novels are acclaimed for the author's insightful descriptions of religious life and asceticism in relation to a secular world. He skillfully interweaves mythical elements and historical facts. Moreover, even though it is generally considered that a cardinal point of Son Buddhism, which is meditation for deliverance, is incompatible with the nature of language, he successfully incorporates the world of Son with a literary form of novel called "Son Novel." For example, in 1991 Ko published the lengthy Buddhist-inspired novel *The Garland Sutra,* or *Little Pilgrim* (*Hwaomkyung*). *Hwaomkyung* is the scripture of Mahayanist Buddhism, *Hwaom* refers to "Buddha land" full of harmony and peace. The novel is based on the young boy Sun-jae's pilgrimage to seek truth, in the course of which he is taught ascetic practices and the secret succession of religious tradition by 53 masters. The boy comes to attain the ultimate stage of deliverance (*Vimutti*)—full enlightenment self-mastery—and complete mental health. By presenting a typical paradigm of a scriptural narrative, Ko makes Son a literary genre.

Likewise, in the saga novel *Son: Two Volumes* (1995), Ko fictionalizes the history of Son masters in China and Korea. The novel begins with the Indian monk Dharma, the founder of Son, on the way to China and ends with Son's division into the southern Son and northern Son. The long, colorful journeys of Son masters to acquire spiritual wisdoms and the supreme security from bondage (nirvana) are intertwined with worldly affairs and politics of empires. Critics note that through his Son novels, imbued with his experience of Buddhist existentialism, Ko expertly adapts the world of meditation to the world of language.

Ko's 1999 novel *Mt. Sumi* (*Sumi-san*) is also structured with spiritual elements of Son Buddhism in the 18th century Choson dynasty, when anti-Buddhist policies were severely reinforced. Mt. Sumi which Ko models on the Himalayas, is imaginary. He poetically depicts various characters who accidentally come to a deserted island named Muyok, meaning "no earthly desire." The story is initiated with Indam's dream in which an old monk guides him to find a tragic poet's collection of works and a mysterious book whose title means "the load to Sumi." It displays various characters and their wandering lives tied with anguish and contentions of their previous incarnations (karma). What is interesting in this novel is that Ko reinterprets the orthodox doctrine of Buddhism, which teaches that transmigration of souls (samsara) is a bridle of life, and the ultimate goal of Buddhists is to be delivered from worldly existence. Instead, he affirmatively redefines samsara as deliverance itself within the energy of the universal order and "life and death" not as agony but as the process of self-training.

Ko has received many prestigious literary awards in Korea, including the Korean Literature Prize in 1974 and 1987, Manhae Literary Prize in 1989, and Danjae Prize in 2004. In June 2000, a truly memorable time in his life as well as in post–Korean War history, Ko accompanied President Kim Dae-Jung on his historic visit to Pyongyang. In front of the leaders and people of the two Koreas, he read his poem "At the Taedong River" ("Taedong-gang eso") expressing his lifetime longing for a peaceful reunification of the two Koreas. The following year he became the first annual Snyder-Soderquist lecturer at the University of California at Davis in a new lecture series of internationally distinguished writers and cultural figures.

While passionately committed to writing and continually publishing—such as a collection of poems, *South and North* (*Nam gwa Buk,* 2000), and a book of essays, *The Road has Traces of Those Who Went Before* (2002)—Ko is also committed to sharing Korea's artistic and cultural accomplishments with the world by giving lectures and poetry readings around the globe. A critic once described Ko as a myth that appeared in the history of literature and mental world of Koreans.

BIBLIOGRAPHY

Brother Anthony of Taize. "From Korean History to Korean Poetry: Ko Un and Ku Sang." *World Literature Today* 71, no. 3 (1997): 533–540.

Hass, Robert. "Poet of Wonders." *New York Review of Books,* 3 November 2005, pp. 59–62.

Kim Young-moo. "The Sound of My Waves." *Korea Journal* 33, no. 3 (1993): 100–107.

Paik Nak-chung. "Zen Poetry and Realism: Reflections on Ko Un's Verse." *Positions* 8, no. 2 (2000): 559–578.

Sunoo, Harold Hakwon. *Life and Poems of Three Koreans: Kim Chi-ha, Ko Un, Yang Song-oo.* Philadelphia: Xlibris, 2005.

Teague, Anthony. "Ten Poems of Ko Un." *Korea Journal* 33, no. 3 (1993): 109–114.

Heejung Cha

KOKORO NATSUME SŌSEKI (1914) *Kokoro* by NATSUME SŌSEKI (1867–1916) is one of the great classics of Japanese literature. A translation of the title produces a wide range of meanings: "heart," "soul," "spirit," "feelings," and "the heart of things." *Kokoro* is divided into three parts: "Sensei and I," "My Parents and I," and "Sensei and his Testament." The first part describes the initial meeting and growing friendship between the young narrator and the sensei, an honorific term meaning master or teacher. The second part traces the relationship between the narrator and his family. The last part is a lengthy letter written to the narrator by the sensei in which he describes his past, his involvement in the suicide of a friend years earlier, and his present decision, partly for atonement, to kill himself.

A meditation on love, friendship, and the mysteries of the human heart, *Kokoro* brings together with great simplicity and drama many of the recurrent themes of Sōseki's fiction, including human isolation, the perils of modernization, and the paradox of individuality. These themes are skillfully adumbrated in an early exchange when the sensei, speaking to the narrator, states that "loneliness is the price we have to pay for being born in this modern age, so full of freedom, independence, and our own egotistical selves."

A large part of the novel's appeal lies in Sōseki's adroit use of mystery as the author depicts the growing friendship between the two men. Although their acquaintance happens by accident, the narrator nonetheless feels a mysterious attraction to the elderly sensei. The more the narrator knows about the sensei and his beautiful wife, the more attached he grows to them, yet he is unable to get the sensei to reveal the reasons for the misanthropic attitudes that make him shun all social intercourse. The mentor appears to despise himself and to reject all intimacy; he tells the youth that loving always involves guilt, and yet he also states that "in loving, there is something sacred."

The second part of the novel deftly sets the scene for the concluding section. It describes the narrator's return home upon graduation, his estrangement from his older brother, and the course of his father's illness as he lies dying from a kidney disease. With his father on the verge of death, however, the narrator receives a long letter from the sensei in Tokyo. As he leafs absentmindedly through the letter, he catches the following sentence: "By the time this letter reaches you, I shall probably have left this world." In desperation, the young narrator deserts his dying father and rushes to Tokyo to find his old friend.

The letter is both dignified and affecting. In it the sensei describes how he was cheated of a large portion of his patrimony by a rapacious uncle. He further describes his determination to finish his education and never to return to the provinces. The letter explains how in Tokyo he came to live with a respectable widow, Okusan, and her pretty daughter, Ojosan. The sensei, falling in love with Ojosan, found that his close friend and fellow student named K was also in love with the daughter. Finally, the sensei reveals how he had capitalized on K's simple honesty and betrayed him by stealthily importuning the young girl's mother for Ojosan's hand.

K subsequently killed himself, and the sensei married Ojosan upon graduation. Although devoted to his wife, the sensei never reveals to her his complicity in K's death. Furthermore, he can never wholeheartedly accept her love for him, and over the years this impasse causes his wife great distress. To assuage his gnawing sense of guilt, he tries many ways to hide his sense of responsibility and complicity in his friend's death, including alcohol for a time. He makes monthly visits to K's grave and has tended dutifully to his mother-in-law, Okusan, as she lies critically ill before dying. Eventually he decides to take his own life.

In a number of ways, *Kokoro* delineates the cultural and social dislocations of the Meiji era (1868–1912), when Japan in one generation hauled itself out of feudalism and plunged precipitously into the 20th century. The death of the narrator's biological father underscores the sensei's surrogate or spiritual-father status, but, as he himself puts it, he and the narrator belong to different eras—nothing will bridge the gap. The ancient Japanese regime emphasized honor, loyalty, and collective human relationships, but the new social atmosphere favors robust self-assertion. The sensei's death highlights the scale of the task facing the narrator. In a period of accelerated change, he—and by implication, the country—have been cut adrift without cultural or ethical moorings. With great sensitivity and economy, the novel broaches these issues. And more important, Sōseki's work sheds a perspicacious light on such critical social concerns.

BIBLIOGRAPHY

Gessel, Van C. *Three Modern Novelists: Soseki, Tanizaki, Kawabata.* Tokyo and New York: Kodansha, 1993.

Natsume Sōseki. *My Individualism and the Philosophical Foundations of Literature.* Translated by Sammy I. Tsunematsu. Boston: Tuttle, 2004.

———. *Rediscovering Natsume Soseki.* Translated by Sammy I. Tsunematsu. Folkestone, U.K.: Global Oriental, 2000.

Yiu, Angela. *Chaos and Order in the Works of Natsume Soseki.* Honolulu: University of Hawaii Press, 1998.

Wai-chew Sim

KRLEŽA, MIROSLAV (1893–1981) *Yugoslav essayist, novelist, short story writer, playwright, poet*

Miroslav Krleža was a prolific novelist, poet, playwright, essayist, and major cultural figure in former Yugoslavia. He is considered the most important Croatian writer of the 20th century. Whereas Krleža's reputation in his native country rests primarily on his work as a playwright, he wrote prolifically and, according to some critics, more successfully in other genres. His oeuvre includes more than 10 collections of poetry, several collections of short stories, 20 books of essays, almost 50 plays, and several books of polemics and memoirs. Krleža's opus also includes four novels, all of them exemplary of the writer's existentialist concerns and his distinctive synthesis of expressionist and neorealist techniques.

Krleža was born in 1893 in Zagreb, Croatia (then port of the Austro-Hungarian Empire), where he completed his primary and secondary education. In 1908 he entered a preparatory military school in Peczuj, continuing his education at the military academy in Budapest. Krleža spent World War I on the battlefields from Galicia to the Carpathians. The onset of the war, however, marked the beginning of Krleža's literary career. In 1914 he published his first poems and plays, written in the vein of Nietzschean-influenced romanticism. The war experience disillusioned the young writer, and his later embrace of expressionism was reflective of this stance.

The expressionist attentiveness to the occluded, sinister aspects of human nature and the technique of baroque colors and exaggerated imagery permeated Krleža's writing even when he turned away from overt experimentation in the genre. Expressionist antiwar lyrics, plays, and prose (published cumulatively in 1918) reflected Krleža's leftist political orientation at the time. In 1918 the writer enthusiastically joined the Yugoslav Communist Party. In a constant confrontation with everything that, for him, embodied the threat of totalitarian and homogenizing forces in society, Krleža was one of the party's most boisterous and unruly members; he was officially expelled from the party in 1939.

Krleža's most innovative literary writings as well as his most important polemic work belong to the interwar period. Marked by the writer's move from expressionist experimentation to neorealist hypernarration, the decade from the late 1920s to the late 1930s was extremely prolific. Krleža wrote a great number of plays, among which the dramatic trilogy *The Glembajs* (*Gaspoda Glembajevi,* 1928), *In Agony* (*U agoniji,* 1928), and *Leda* (1932) are considered the peaks of Yugoslav dramaturgy. Krleža also published numerous collections of poetry, the foremost among which is *The Ballads of Petrica Kerempuh* (*Balade Petrice Kerempuha,* 1936), written in the Croatian *kajkavski* dialect. The collection of short stories *The Croatian God Mars* (*Hrvatski bog Mars,* 1922) is undoubtedly most representative of Krleža's short fiction. Three out of Krleža's four novels were also written in this period.

Krleža's first novel, *The RETURN OF PHILIP LATINOVICZ* (1932), relates a story about a modernist painter who returns from Paris to his small hometown in rural Slavonia. Philip's attempts to confront his complex psychological cluster of childhood memories lead everyone affected by his self-purging to doom. Krleža's psychological acuity is matched here by his pronounced social concerns. Realist as much as symbolist, this novel also offers a unique conjunction of the naturalist style and expressive imagery.

Krleža's short novel *On the Edge of Reason* (1938) is a tale about a lawyer who commits a social blunder by speaking too honestly about a prominent industrialist. While the hero sinks through the depths of political and social disfavor, the reader recognizes the main targets of Krleža's critique: hypocrisy, the volatile nature of societal labeling, the deafening fixedness of political strata, and the individual's own instability.

Krleža's third novel, the tripartite satire *The Banquet in Blitva* (1939–62) recounts the political happenings in an imaginary country named Blitva. The novel, written in the expressionist style, is an allegory of the political and artistic reality in the Balkans after the collapse of the Austro-Hungarian Empire.

During this period, Krleža also devoted his energy to the founding of literary journals (*Fire, Literary*

Republic, Today, Stamp) and to various literary and political polemics (published as *My Settling of Accounts* [1932] and *Dialectic Anti-Barbarus* [1939]). After World War II, however, he became the foremost cultural figure in Yugoslavia: He served as vice president of the Yugoslav Academy of Science and Arts and president of the Yugoslav Writers Union, and was the lifelong head of the Yugoslav Lexicographical Institute. Krleža's close friendship with the Yugoslav leader Josip Broz Tito shielded him politically from the confrontations that the writer's cynical nature occasionally created. Krleža's most ambitious literary project in this period was the six-volume novel *The Banners* (1967). This realist memoir-narrative offers a broad picture of European history in the decade between 1912 and 1922. After this capacious novel, Krleža wrote comparatively little, but his major works were continuously republished. Until his death in 1981, Krleža remained one of the most influential intellectual figures in former Yugoslavia.

In many respects Krleža was a typical central European novelist of the time. The style and themes of his novels are comparable to those of ROBERT MUSIL or Karl Kraus. Contextualized within the outskirts of the disintegrating Austro-Hungarian Empire, Krleža's literary oeuvre was thematically structured around psychosocial barriers for those in the margins, forces of modernization in a provincial setting, social role of the artist, ideological snares of the state, and distrust of totalitarian systems. Yet social alertness coupled with baroque imagery and an intensive attention paid to the dark sides of the human psyche position Krleža's writings in the heritage of expressionism. Expressive verbiage and vigorous imagery were uncommonly fused with Krleža's own bent for satire in two of his four novels. There, Krleža is an exponent of another important central-eastern European narrative tradition: the sardonic representation of bureaucracy and petty-bourgeois mentality (exemplified by FRANZ KAFKA and JAROSLAV HAŠEK). Finally, Miroslav Krleža's work is uniquely marked by the writer's profound humanism, persistent intellectual questioning, and mistrust of all politico-social systems.

BIBLIOGRAPHY

Bogert, Ralph. *The Writer as Naysayer: Miroslav Krleza and the Aesthetic of Interwar Central Europe.* Columbus, Ohio: Slavica Publishers, 1991.

"Miroslav Krleza." *Contemporary Literary Criticism* 114 (1999).

Sanja Bahun-Radunovic

KUNDERA, MILAN (1929–) *Czech essayist, novelist, playwright, poet, short story writer*

Milan Kundera is one of the most important contemporary Czech writers, renowned internationally as a novelist, essayist, poet, playwright, and literary critic. His career often reflects the tumultuous events of post–World War II Czechoslovakia. Although Kundera explicitly rejects political readings of his works, his experiences with the artistic constraints imposed by Nazism, revolutionary socialism, Stalinism, and Soviet military intervention have influenced his philosophical views and literary aesthetics. On a formal level, he is known for an ironic tone, experimental techniques, and the intrusion of the author-figure in his novels.

The author's novels frequently probe the incongruities between the private and public realms, sex and love, memory and forgetting, history and the life of the individual, body and soul, lightness and weight, and lyricism and skepticism. In his novels, Kundera exposes individual frailties by interrogating and demystifying human behavior.

Kundera was born in Brno, the capital of Moravia, on April 1, 1929, to Milada (Janosikova) Kundera and the musicologist and pianist Ludvík Kundera. In his youth he studied piano with his father, a student of the composer Leoš Janáček and rector of the Brno Janáček Academy of Music, as well as musical composition and theory with Paul Haas and Vaclav Kapral. After graduating from the gymnasium (secondary school) in 1948, he continued his studies in musicology at Charles University and then transferred to the film faculty of the Prague Academy of Art, where he pursued film writing and directing. Graduating in 1952, he was appointed lecturer in world literature at the Prague Film Academy, where he taught until 1969.

In the first years after World War II ended in 1945, communism was perceived by Czech intellectuals and avant-garde artists as radical, dynamic, and forward-thinking. Yet by as soon as 1948, advocates found that their aesthetic freedoms were severely restricted under the Soviet regime. Artists were obliged to follow strict aesthetic guidelines, demonstrating realism, optimism, and romantic idealism.

Kundera joined the Czechoslovakia Communist Party in 1947, at age 18, only to be expelled in 1950 after the Stalinist purges for antiparty activities. He was readmitted in 1956, after the party's 20th congress, and expelled again in 1970. At the time of his readmission, Kundera became a member of the editorial board of the literary magazines *Literarni Noviny* and *Literarni Listy*. By 1970, however, the Soviet-supported regime banned Kundera from publication, removed his books from shelves, and dismissed him from his positions at the Academy of Music and Dramatic Arts.

In 1975 Kundera accepted an invitation to teach as a professor of comparative literature at the University of Rennes in France, where he remained until 1979. Kundera's Czech citizenship was revoked in 1979 after the publication of *The BOOK OF LAUGHTER AND FORGETTING* (*Kniha Smichu a Zapomněni*, 1978). He was naturalized as a French citizen in 1981.

Kundera began his literary career as a poet, publishing his first poem in 1949, followed by three volumes of poetry: *Man, A Broad Garden* (*Člověk, zahrada širá*, 1953), *Last May* (*Poslední Máj*, 1955), and *Monologues* (*Monology*, 1957). Although his first collection of poems espoused a communist outlook, the verse was regarded as a radical departure from "socialist realism," the only artistic style officially accepted following the communist takeover in 1948. His second book, *Last May*, is a tribute to Julius Fučík, a leader of the anti-Nazi resistance in Czechoslovakia in World War II. A writer and journalist, Fučík had been imprisoned, tortured, and executed. *Last May* complies with the regime's official aesthetics and has been regarded as an example of communist political propaganda.

In *Monologues*, Kundera turned to love poetry, using erotic encounters as a means of examining tensions between rational intellect and emotion.

After its publication, however, he renounced poetry. He found that lyricism, which relies on emotion as the purveyor of truth, was too easily manipulated and inevitably led to reification.

Kundera became increasingly involved in drama, literary theory, and fiction. In 1960 he published *The Art*

of the Novel (*Umění románu*), a critical study of the Czech avant-garde novelist Vladislava Vančury and a defense of the novel as a modern genre. In 1962 he launched his career as a playwright with the production of *The Keepers of Keys* (*Majitelé klíčů*) by the Prague National Theatre. Set in the period of Nazi occupation of Czechoslovakia, *The Keeper of Keys* concerns the political and ethical decisions of a young student. The play was well received and was produced in several European countries, the United States, and Great Britain.

By the 1960s, Kundera had become a major literary figure in Czechoslovakia. He entered his most productive stage as a writer with the publication of three consecutive books of short stories, known collectively as *Laughable Loves* (*Směšné lásky*, 1963, 1965, 1968) and his first novel, *The Joke* (*Žert*, 1967). The appearance of *The Joke* in a French translation the following year earned Kundera international recognition, as did its adaptation to the screen in 1969.

Kundera's best-known novels include *The Joke, The Farewell Party* (*Valčík na rozloučenou*, 1971), *The Book of Laughter and Forgetting*, and *The UNBEARABLE LIGHTNESS OF BEING* (*Nesnesitelná lehkost byti*, 1982). *The Joke* introduces several recurring themes found in his novels, including the arbitrary nature of life, human powerlessness, the loss of personal and historical memories, and the exploitation of love. Kundera experiments with narrative form in *The Joke* by employing multiple narrators, disrupting linear time, presenting conflicting accounts of overlapping stories, and introducing various discourses. The novel illustrates how a meaningless act or "joke" can result in tragedy, and how such dramas are ultimately trivialized by virtue of their arbitrary origins.

The author's darkest novel, *The Farewell Party*, examines moral guilt and despair in the face of failure. Set in a spa for middle-aged women with infertility problems, the novel follows several frustrated individuals who devise strategies to redirect their lives, only to become further mired in their insurmountable predicaments.

The Book of Laughter and Forgetting (1978) considers the implications of collective forgetfulness, evoking the events of the Prague Spring in the early 1960s in which strict restraints were finally lifted to allow Western ideas, culture, and art to thrive in Czechoslovakia. Kundera also alludes to the Soviet invasion of Czechoslovakia in 1968. Divided into seven interrelated sections, the novel traces the attempts of several characters, living in a police state in the 20th century, to recover or destroy powerful memories. The novel's ending portrays a group of naked men and women on a beach. Isolated, they trade ideas about the fate of Western civilization and individual freedom. The characters recall the past to reexperience the innocence of youth and idealism, a past that is juxtaposed with the present. A central theme in the novel is the distinction between self-satisfied and skeptical laughter, and between public and private longings. This novel brought Kundera his first international success.

In *The Unbearable Lightness of Being*, Kundera examines the tenuous boundary between polarized, binary qualities such as weight and lightness, body and soul, eroticism and love. Through an investigation of the characters' sexual relationships, the author elucidates their various metaphysical dilemmas. He emphasizes the relativity of language systems, demonstrating that objects can signify multiple meanings consecutively or even simultaneously. Finally, he refines his definition of *kitsch,* an aesthetic that prohibits all forms of dissent and conceals the existence of death.

Kundera successfully exposes the relative nature of symbolic and ideological systems of knowledge and illustrates the ubiquity of self-delusion and misapprehension. He attends to tensions between dichotomous states of being to discover what occurs when conflicting conceptions of "reality" collide. Kundera's more recent novels include *Immortality* (first published in French as *L'Identité* in 1990, later in Czech as *Nesmrtelnost* in 1993), *Slowness* (1995), *Identity* (1997), and *Ignorance* (*Totoznost,* 1996). He has received numerous awards and honors, including the 1973 Prix Médicis for the best foreign novel published in France, *Life is Elsewhere* (*Zivot je jinde,* 1970); and the 1994 Jaroslav-Seifert Prize for his novel *Immortality*.

Milan Kundera remains one of Europe's most outstanding contemporary novelists.

BIBLIOGRAPHY

Aji, Aron, ed. *Milan Kundera and the Art of Fiction: Critical Essays.* New York: Garland, 1992.

Pifer, Ellen. "*The Book of Laughter and Forgetting*: Kundera's Narration Against Narration." *Journal of Narrative Technique* 22, no. 2 (1992): 84–96.

Straus, Nina Pelikan. "Erasing History and Deconstructing the Text: Milan Kundera's *The Book of Laughter and Forgetting*." *Critique* 28, no. 2 (1987): 69–85.

Weeks, Mark. "Milan Kundera: A Modern History of Humor amid the Comedy of History." *Journal of Modern Literature* 28, no. 3 (2005): 130–148.

Shayna D. Skarf

L

LAFCADIO'S ADVENTURES (LES CAVES DU VATICAN, THE VATICAN CELLARS, THE CATACOMBS OF THE VATICAN, THE VATICAN SWINDLE) ANDRÉ GIDE (1914)

The prodigious French Nobel laureate ANDRÉ GIDE (1869–1951) originally published *Lafcadio's Adventures* in *La Nouvelle Revue Française* in four installments, from January through April 1914; it appeared as a book later the same year. In 1933 Gide adapted it for the stage, and it was eventually performed at the Comédie-Française in 1950. In English, the book has appeared under three titles: *The Catacombs of the Vatican, The Vatican Cellars,* and *Lafcadio's Adventures,* with the last being the preferred. The story was the product of many years of work, with the first reference to it in Gide's *Journal* dating from 1905. When it appeared, it was suggested that Gide had plagiarized an earlier, historical work by Jean de Pauly, *The False Pope,* published in 1895. Both works deal with a hoax—which actually occurred in the early 1890s—involving the collection of a ransom to rescue the pope kidnapped (allegedly) by Masonic elements within the Catholic Church. Although such a plot does form a backdrop to the action of Gide's story, he writes in his *Journal* in 1909 that "the story of Lafcadio" illustrates the claim "that there is no *essential* difference between the honest man and the knave."

Gide insistently referred to *Lafcadio's Adventures* as a *sotie,* a sort of parody popular in France during the Renaissance, a popular theme of which was to depict the world as governed by fools. According to Emile Picot's study *Sotie en France* (1878), the *sotie* was often staged as the first piece in a comedic trilogy: The *sotie* led into a farce and was concluded with a morality play. Gide's *sotie* manages to preserve the ridiculous, madcap character of its predecessors but introduces an axis for the action through persistent concern for the possibility and consequences of a crime without motive—a concern that effectively combines parody, farce, and morality play into a single work stitched together by the work of chance. Composed of five books, temporally sequential but involving a number of characters whose actions interweave in a dizzying variety of combinations, *Lafcadio's Adventures* relentlessly explores the consequences of fortuitous decisions, deliberately eschewing any sort of psychological realism.

The first three books of the novel set out the characters and their conditions before their respective motions combine, in the final two books, to yield the action of the story proper. The first book focuses on a highly ranked Masonic scientist, Anthime Armand-Dubois, and his wife Veronica, who have recently moved to Rome in order to seek a cure for Anthime's rheumatism. Just before the arrival of Veronica's sister and her family, Anthime discovers that Veronica has been interfering in his experiments out of concern for his animal subjects. When Veronica's sister Marguerite arrives with her husband, the prominent author Julius de Barraglioul, Anthime vents his spleen by sparring with the devotion of their young daughter Julie, who piously rebuffs him. Over dinner, Anthime learns that Veronica has secretly been praying for him at a shrine to the Virgin and, further enraged, leaps from the table and vandalizes the statue. That night Anthime has a dream in which the Virgin appears and reproaches him. Awakening alone later that night, Veronica finds her husband in his laboratory, cured of his rheumatism and praying. Given his prominence in the lodge, Anthime is encouraged to make a public announcement of his conversion, and he is reassured by the church that he will receive support when he is deserted by the Masons. Anthime makes his announcement, but the support never arrives, and he and Veronica are forced to move to Milan for financial reasons.

The second book opens with Julius and his family returning to Paris from their trip to Italy. Arriving home, Julius finds a letter from his ailing father, a count, asking him to look up a young man named Lafcadio Wlouki. The letter closes with what Julius takes to be some disdainful comments concerning Julius's most recent novel, which was based on his father's life and upon which rest his chances for being elected to the Académie Française. Julius dutifully seeks out Lafcadio, finding him in a seedy lodging house where, after being admitted to Lafcadio's room in the latter's absence by Lafcadio's mistress, Carola, he is surprised by Lafcadio as he is searching through the room. After an awkward conversation, Julius arranges for Lafcadio to visit him the next day under the pretext of needing a secretary and then departs hastily, leaving Lafcadio to destroy the scant personal articles that Julius has found. Piecing together a number of coincidences, Lafcadio surmises that he is an illegitimate child of Julius's father and sets out to visit the count immediately. On the way, Lafcadio rescues two small children from a burning house and meets an attractive young woman who rewards him with her handbag. The count confirms Lafcadio's suspicions and assures him of a generous but discreet inheritance. Visiting Julius the next day, Lafcadio discovers that the young woman from the scene of the fire the previous day is Julius's daughter Genevieve. In the subsequent conversation with Julius, again remarkable for its awkwardness, Lafcadio relates his life story, Gide taking care to emphasize the contrast between the "paradoxical" (Julius's term) nature

of Lafcadio's aleatory existence and the "hash of bare bones" (Lafcadio's term) that constitutes the logical coherence of Julius's novels. Their meeting ends abruptly when news arrives that the count has died, and Lafcadio leaves to prepare for his departure from Paris—buying Carola an ostentatious pair of cufflinks as a parting gift.

The third book again opens with Julius's younger sister, Valentine, returning to her country home from the count's funeral in Paris. Waiting for her there is a priest who confides in her a story about the kidnapping of the pope and asks for money in order to ransom the pontiff. The exceptional nature of this story leads Gide to interpose himself into the narrative and provide an aside on the nature and relation of fiction and history. Writing that some "have considered that fiction is history which *might* have taken place, and history fiction that *has* taken place," Gide cautions that the present story is not intended for readers who would disavow the extraordinary out of hand. The priest is actually Protos, a boyhood friend of Lafcadio, and when he leaves, Valentine immediately contacts her friend, Arnica Fleurissoire, in order to relate the story to her. Arnica, in turn, is the youngest sister of Veronica and Marguerite. She tells her husband Amédée, who, unable to contribute any money to the ransom, quixotically resolves to go in person to Rome. Drawing the final threads into place, the book ends with Julius visiting with Anthime on his way back to Rome for a meeting and vowing to intercede on Anthime's behalf with the pope himself.

The fourth book is entirely devoted to Amédée's bumbling crusade. After a series of misadventures, Amédée finally arrives in Rome, his skin a comically repulsive mass of insect bites, and he is immediately swept up by a young French boy who installs him in a seedy lodging house where Amédée discovers to his horror that he is to share his room with a woman: Lafcadio's former mistress Carola. The boy, Baptistin, and Carola prove to be confederates of Protos and "the Millipede," the group perpetrating the swindle involving the kidnapping of the pope. Surmising Amédée's purpose in visiting Rome, Protos, along with a false cardinal in Naples, enlists Amédée's aid in cashing a check by disguising himself as a priest and convincing Amédée that he represents those who are "truly" working to free the pope. The devout and idealistic Amédée readily assents to aid Protos and returns to Rome, where be goes to meet with Julius to ask his advice on the situation. Julius has just come from his audience with the pope and is agitated by its apparent fruitlessness, leading Julius to question his principles, both personal and artistic. Struck by the uncharacteristic impiousness of his brother, Amédée wonders for a moment if he is not speaking to a "false Julius." At lunch, Julius reveals the source of his disquiet: It certainly still seems to him that self-interest is not the sole source of all human actions, but it now seems that self-sacrifice cannot be the sole source either, that there must be a third possibility, neither good nor evil: gratuitousness or disinterested actions. Their conversation is cut short by a note from an anxious Protos, and Julius takes Amédée to cash the check and loans him his ticket for the trip to Naples.

The final book opens with Lafcadio, having taken possession of his inheritance, on his way by train through Italy from whence he plans to sail to Java. As his thoughts wander, Lafcadio is joined in his compartment by Amédée. Lafcadio immediately forms a desire "to impinge upon that fellow's [Amédée's] fate." He satisfies this desire when, in accordance with a spurious circumstance that he sets for himself, he commits a gratuitous act, "a crime without a motive," and throws Amédée from the train. At the next station, Lafcadio's bag is mysteriously stolen as he throws a die to determine whether he should retrieve his hat, which Amédée had pulled off as he fell. Remaining on the train, Lafcadio discovers the Millipede's money, as well as Julius's ticket, in Amédée's coat and decides to return to Rome to ascertain the effects of his action upon Julius. On the way to visit his brother, Lafcadio learns from the newspaper that Amédée was wearing the cufflinks Lafcadio had given to Carola in Paris.

The conversation between Julius and Lafcadio is the climax of the novel. When Lafcadio presents himself, Julius immediately begins speaking of the recent transformation of his principles occasioned by his audience with the pope. He is beginning to compose a new novel, one no longer governed by the overly structured logic and ethics of conventional literature; it will consist of an account of the character of a young criminal, which, of itself, engenders an utterly gratuitous crime. As the two men together develop a more particular

account of such a character, Gide switches to the format of a play and indicates the speaker by a marginal notation as they proceed, "each in turn overtaking and overtaken by the other." Their exchange concludes with Julius reading to Lafcadio the latest account of Amédée's murder, which reveals to Lafcadio that someone had tampered with the body after the murder, but which Julius uses to argue that the motive for the crime was robbery, making it deliberate rather than gratuitous. When Lafcadio corrects Julius's error, the latter, far from recognizing the model for his own villain, abruptly concludes that Amédée's "outrageous" story about the kidnapping of the pope must in fact be true and the reason he was murdered. Julius immediately departs for the police, while Lafcadio sets Julius's train ticket on the table and then leaves to retrieve Amédée's body for the funeral.

On his return trip to Rome, Lafcadio encounters Protos, now disguised as a lawyer, who reveals himself as the one who helped to cover up Lafcadio's murder of Amédée by removing evidence from the body. Protos attempts to induce Lafcadio to continue along the path opened by the murder and to blackmail Julius, but Lafcadio, horrified, refuses. In Rome, after the funeral, Julius attempts to reassure Anthime as to his misfortune by relating the story of the kidnapped pope, but Anthime instead renounces his conversion and reveals that his rheumatism has returned. Meanwhile, having been denounced by Carola, Protos strangles her just before the police arrest him, discovering in the process the evidence that he had taken from Amédée's body. That night, Lafcadio, having heard of Protos's arrest, confesses his crime to Julius, who advises him to confess to the church but to allow Protos to be blamed for Amédée's murder since Lafcadio's inheritance allows him the possibility of a "new life." Unconvinced, Lafcadio retires but is woken by Genevieve, who declares the love that she has harbored since seeing Lafcadio rescue the children from the fire. She too counsels Lafcadio to confess only to the church and Gide ends the novel— "here begins a new book"—with Lafcadio waking at dawn, Genevieve beside him, his decision unmade.

Lafcadio's Adventures is narrated in the third person, sometimes with a distant perspective and other times revealing the characters' interior space. Repeatedly a first-person, authorial "I" voice intrudes, reflecting on the story, and how to tell it, and on the relationship between fiction and reality. Although Lafcadio desires his spontaneous act to be viewed as a meaningless, amoral adventure, Gide ends the narrative with disquieting ambiguity, leaving the reader to wonder whether Lafcadio will escape his crime unpunished or face his moral duty through the courts.

As the original French title *"Caves"* implies, the characters, save for Lafcadio and Protos, are hollow shells, each blindly following a belief system without foundations. Ultimately, even Lafcadio and Protos can be viewed as being torn by institutional forces and playing socially governed roles. Protos takes on the guise of various institutional representatives (cleric, lawyer, confidence man), and Lafcadio is torn between the injustice of his act on the one hand and his own desire for autonomy on the other. Despite its ambiguous ending, *Lafcadio's Adventures* does not present the Gidean ideal—a person capable of dealing with contradiction and paradox. Although Lafcadio tries to break free of social and moral claims, aspiring to become a Nietzschean superman—one who stands aloof from the masses—he still struggles with the conventions provided by his lineage and class. Protos, ever shifting from one system to another, exploits the external, superficial elements of all systems, including the swindler system he chooses to follow. Here Gide foregrounds the contradictions that will become the central conflict of his masterwork, *The COUNTERFEITERS* (1925).

Gide himself insisted that he conceived *Lafcadio's Adventures, The Immoralist* (*L'Immoraliste,* 1902), and *Strait Is the Gate* (*La Porte Etroite,* 1909) as a set, each exploring a similar theme of problematic moral attitudes. As in *The Immoralist,* homoerotic descriptions accompany many of the male characters, especially Lafcadio, to whom both men and women are attracted. *Lafcadio's Adventures* drew stern criticism from the Catholic right, both for its depiction of Lafcadio's motiveless crime and for a pederast passage involving the young Lafcadio and one of his mother's many lovers, all of whom seem more attracted to the son than to the mother. *Lafcadio's Adventures'* anti-institutional views, its anti-deterministic philosophy, and its disdain of the church endeared the work to the iconographers of the dadaists and the surrealists.

Like many of Gide's other works, *Lafcadio's Adventures* is often compared with the existential novels and philosophy of ALBERT CAMUS and JEAN-PAUL SARTRE. Like Camus' Mersault in *The STRANGER* and Fyodor Dostoyevsky's Raskolnikov in *Crime and Punishment,* Lafcadio is often seen as an existential hero, a man who is troubled over his own existence and purpose in the world. One of Gide's first mature works, *Lafcadio's Adventures* remains an early 20th-century literary milestone for its break with novelistic conventions, ironic tone, and iconoclastic outlook.

BIBLIOGRAPHY

Bettinson, Christopher D. *Gide: A Study.* Totowa, N.J.: Rowman & Littlefield, 1977.

Brachfeld, Georges Israel. *André Gide and the Communist Temptation.* Geneva: Librairie E. Droz, 1959.

Brennan, Joseph Gerard. *Three Philosophical Novelists: James Joyce, André Gide, Thomas Mann.* New York: Macmillan, 1964.

Cordle, Thomas. *André Gide.* New York: Twayne, 1969.

Delay, Jean. *The Youth of André Gide.* Translated by June Guicharnaud. Chicago: University of Chicago Press, 1963.

Fowlie, Wallace. *André Gide: His Life and Art.* New York: Macmillan, 1965.

Freedman, Ralph. *The Lyrical Novel: Studies in Hermann Hesse, André Gide, and Virginia Woolf.* Princeton, N.J.: Princeton University Press, 1963.

Hytier, Jean. *André Gide.* Translated by Richard Howard. Garden City, N.Y.: Doubleday, 1962.

Littlejohn, David, ed. *Gide: A Collection of Critical Essays.* Englewood Cliffs, N.J.: Prentice-Hall, 1970.

O'Neill, Kevin. *André Gide and the Roman d'aventure: The History of a Literary Idea in France.* Sydney: Sydney University Press for Australian Humanities Research Council, 1969.

Rossi, Vinio. *André Gide: The Evolution of an Aesthetic.* New Brunswick, N.J.: Rutgers University Press, 1967.

Sheridan, Alan. *André Gide: A Life in the Present.* Cambridge, Mass.: Harvard University Press; Oxford: Oxford University Press, 1999.

Walker, David H., ed. *André Gide.* London & New York: Longman, 1996.

Richard Ford and Blake Hobby

LAGERLÖF, SELMA (1858–1940) *Swedish novelist* The Swedish novelist Selma Ottiliana Lovisa Lagerlöf was the first woman writer to win the Nobel

Prize in literature. Her award in 1909 reflected her sensitive, thoughtful, and expansive exploration of the Nordic legends and history of her country in her fiction. Writing during a period dominated largely by realism in Europe and the United States, Lagerlöf chose instead to explore imaginative romanticism—that is, neoromanticism, a genre identified by its refreshing freedom and imaginative fervor as well as its reaction to naturalism and the scientific view. Her contemporary rival in this genre was the Swedish poet and prose writer Carl Gustaf Verner von Heidenstam (1859–1940), to whom the Nobel Prize in literature was awarded in 1916. Both authors died in 1940. Although Lagerlöf wrote many novels, she is best remembered for *The Story of Gosta Berling* (*Gösta Berlings Saga*) and her fascinating fairy tale *The Wonderful Adventures of Nils* (*Nis Holgerssons underbara resa genom Sverige*, 1906–07).

Selma Lagerlöf was born in Mårbacka, in the province of Värmland in southern Sweden. She grew up in a household run by a retired army officer and a caring mother. She enjoyed what today is described as home schooling. In addition to a broad academic education, her childhood was filled with a rich exposure to fairy tales, legends, and superstitions that she heard from her family and townspeople. These elaborate tales, involving animals, nature, human transformations, great epic struggles, and human passion, took root in her fertile mind, later to blossom as the basis of her fiction. In her Nobel Prize address, she would acknowledge her debt to this rich and colorful past: "It is not too much to ask that you should help, Father, for it was all your fault right from the beginning. Do you remember how you used to play the piano and sing Bellman's songs to us children and how, at least twice every winter, you would let us read Tegnér and Runeberg and Andersen? It was then that I first fell into debt. Father, how shall I ever repay them for teaching me to love fairy tales and sagas of heroes, the land we live in and all of our human life, in all its wretchedness and glory?"

Lagerlöf studied to become a teacher, graduating from the Royal Women's Superior Training Academy in Stockholm in 1882. She taught at a girl's secondary school at Landskrona from 1885 to 1895. During those years she began writing her first novel, *The Story of Gösta Berling*. The development of the book involved many stages over a period of years. The initial chapters received a prize and a publishing contract by the Swedish weekly publication *Idun*. When the complete book was published in 1891, it received a poor response from readers. The novel might have fallen into oblivion had not its Danish translation brought it positive reviews.

The Story of Gösta Berling, which is charged with romantic pathos, became a part of the Swedish romantic revival of the 1890s. A period piece, it is set in Värmland, the author's home region of Sweden, and chronicles the adventures of 12 free-spirited and reckless cavaliers, hardy marauders who are led by the inimitable and charming young Gösta Berling. The Countess Elisabeth is inescapably attracted to Gösta, whom she eventually marries after her husband divorces her. The novel was transformed into a film directed by Mauritz Stiller in 1924, starring Greta Garbo.

Lagerlöf's most popular children's book is *The Wonderful Adventures of Nils*, a work inspired by the famous British author Rudyard Kipling's exotic animal tales about such memorable characters as Mowgli, Baloo, and Bagheera in *The Jungle Book* (1894). The impetus behind Lagerlöf writing *The Wonderful Adventures of Nils* was that she was granted a commission by a school board to write a text for young readers as an aid to learn about Swedish geography. In the fantasy story, Nils Holgersson, a 14-year-old boy, appears at first as lazy and self-centered. Of course, he must change his attitude about himself and the world around him. As punishment for his idleness and mischievous actions, he goes though a metamorphosis and becomes diminutive in size, like an elf. The central action of the novel has Nils take flight on the back of an adult male goose from his father's farm. The gander joins a flock flying north, to Lapland. High above the Swedish landscape, the boy is carried along on the wind currents. He crosses the great expanse of the country, bonding with the geese and the world of nature and experiencing a rite of passage. A moral transformation occurs, and he suddenly discards his selfish, self-centered nature. From his high perspective, Nils records the geography of Sweden. Nature is the great teacher and healer, as other romantic authors such as William Wordsworth and Percy Bysshe Shelley noted in the opening decades of the 19th century.

Lagerlöf finished *The Miracles of Antichrist* (*Antikrists Mirakler*) in 1897 and a later novel, *Jerusalem,* in 1902. In 1914, five years after she received the Nobel Prize in literature, she was appointed to the prestigious Swedish Academy. During World War I, the author wrote several important works, including *The Emperor of Portugalia* (*Kejsaren Av Portugallien,* 1914) and the pacifist, antiwar novel *The Outcast* (*Bannlyst,* 1918). *The Emperor of Portugalia* was made into the 1925 film *The Tower of Lies,* starring Lon Chaney and directed by Victor Sjöström.

In the 1920s Lagerlöf became active in advancing women's rights. She wrote the Värmland trilogy *The Lovenskold Ring* (*Löwensköldska Ringen,* 1925), *Charlotte Löwensköld* (1925), and *Anna Svärd* (1928), as well as a biography of the Finnish author Zachris Topelius. She finished her autobiography in the 1930s.

World War II proved to be another moral test for Lagerlöf, as it did for artists around the globe, and she worked against the Nazi persecution of many people, including fellow artists. She turned her pen toward writing petitions that were instrumental in gaining a Swedish visa for the German-born dramatist and poet Nelly Sachs, an action that is purported to have saved the poet, later a Nobel Prize winner herself, from the German death camps. Sachs lived the rest of her life in Sweden after escaping from Germany in 1940.

As a final testament to Lagerlöf's personal sacrifice for the peace effort, she donated her gold Nobel Prize medal to help raise funds for Finland's struggle against Soviet aggression during the bitter Winter War (also known as the Soviet-Finnish War or the Russo-Finnish War), which began on November 30, 1939, just three months after the start of World War II. When she died of a stroke at her home on March 16, 1940, Lagerlöf was still working on raising funds and hope for the Finnish people.

BIBLIOGRAPHY

Berendsohn, Walter Arthur. *Selma Lagerlöf: Her Life and Work.* Port Washington, N.Y.: Kennikat Press, 1968.

Edstrom, Vivi Bloom. *Selma Lagerlöf.* Boston: Twayne Publishers, 1982.

Lagerlöf, Selma. *The Diary of Selma Lagerlöf.* Translated by Velma Swanston Howard. Millwood, N.Y.: Kraus Reprint, 1975.

Larsen, Hanna Astrup. *Selma Lagerlöf.* Millwood, N.Y.: Kraus Reprint, 1975.

St. Andrews, Bonnie. *Forbidden Fruit: On the Relationship between Women and Knowledge in Doris Lessing, Selma Lagerlöf, Kate Chopin, Margaret Atwood.* Troy, N.Y.: Whitston Publishing, 1986.

Michael D. Sollars

LAMPEDUSA, GIUSEPPE TOMASI DI (1896–1957) *Italian novelist, short story writer*

Giuseppe Tomasi di Lampedusa was not a professional writer and was discovered by the critical establishment only after his death. He is renowned mainly for his historical novel *The* LEOPARD (*Il gattopardo,* 1958), published posthumously and made into a film by director Luchino Visconti in 1963.

Lampedusa was born in Palermo, Sicily, into an aristocratic family on December 23, 1896. He lived a happy childhood in the protected cultural milieu and social advantages enjoyed by his noble family, dividing his time between the city of Palermo and their summer residence in Santa Margherita Belice. The memories of this time of happiness would be incorporated into the narration of *The Leopard.* He was accorded the privileges of an education consistent with his noble class, marked by the early 19th-century values of the world prior to Italy's unification (1861), yet he distanced himself from the young elitist nobility who were often also provincial. Long sojourns abroad were also part of his upbringing. He spoke fluent English, German, and French; he could read Spanish and started learning Russian. He had a passion for European literature, including works by William Shakespeare, Jonathan Swift, Charles Dickens, Montaigne, Racine, Pascal, Saint-Simon, MARCEL PROUST, Goethe, and Fyodor Dostoyevsky. The one exception was Italian literature, which he criticized for its high tone and lack of concreteness and for having decayed since the great Renaissance tradition of Torquato Tasso. Yet he did read many Italian authors—his preference seemed to be for the diaries of Garibaldi's fighters and for historians, including Gramsci—and was always well informed on any new trends in Italian and European writing.

During World War I Lampedusa was captured and, following his escape, walked through Europe to return to Palermo. Despite the fact that he served in the war, his liberal ideas meant he was never a "patriot," nor did he sympathize with the fascist government. In London, during one of his extensive journeys, he met the Latvian baroness Alessandra Wolff-Stomersee, of Italian descent, whom he married. They developed a close companionship and deep understanding, and she became his confidante and probably the only believer in his literary gifts.

By the early 1930s the family's financial resources were depleted when the inheritance left by Lampedusa's grandfather was divided among his many relatives. Through careful husbandry of his resources, he was nevertheless able to maintain a standard of living suitable to his status. During World War II, with the bombing of Sicily, the Lampedusa Palace was almost completely destroyed. It had belonged to his grandfather and was the basis for Lampedusa's reconstruction of the prince's residence in *The Leopard*. He was able to save only part of the family's library and was deeply saddened by the loss.

Lampedusa led a quiet and almost reclusive existence, with few friends and little social life. In 1954 he was invited to take part in a literary event where well-established authors and poets would introduce the work of emerging and unknown writers. This was his first foray into the literary world, and he met the poet Eugenio Montale and the novelist Giorgio Bassani, who would later facilitate the publication of his novel. After 1954, Lampedusa started to entertain literary friendships and socialize with like-minded individuals, often from the younger generation. He befriended and subsequently adopted one of these young people, Gioacchino Lanza, who became the model for Tancredi in *The Leopard*. Lanza and Francesco Orlando, also from the same group, became Lampedusa's most enthusiastic supporters and biographers after his death.

At this time, Lampedusa also began to work seriously on his novel which, according to his wife and adopted son, he had toyed with writing for more than 20 years. *The Leopard* was originally intended to be 24 hours in the life of an aristocratic Sicilian prince. Yet Lampedusa soon realized that the structure would not support an entire novel and instead decided to portray the life of the prince and his family spanning 25 years; the time period would mark the developments of the Italian risorgimento (reorganization), from the Independence Wars and Giuseppe Garibaldi's fighting for the establishment of a new regime under the king of a unified Italian peninsula.

In his detailed account of the lives of the characters—with the old patriarch dominating the scene but representing the end of an era—Lampedusa celebrated both Sicily and the aristocracy of his upbringing. He did not spare any criticism or pointed barbs, making his characters appear ruthless at times. Yet the novel also shows a nostalgia for a world soon to be gone forever. Thus, its interest lies both in its historical approach and in its portrayal of the mores of a social class at the end of its supremacy after centuries of domination. The story is told in the naturalist mode that the author always admired in great French novelists, but it does not lack an underlying psychological study of individual characters.

Upon publication, *The Leopard* was highly acclaimed by critics across Europe. Unfortunately Lampedusa was not able to enjoy this recognition. Initially the manuscript was refused several times until the writer Giorgio Bassani was able to read it and persuade Feltrinelli to publish it in 1958, a year after the author's death.

Although the novel was Lampedusa's most important writing, it did not remain his only work. In 1955 he transcribed the Stendhal lectures he had presented informally to a group of friends and also began writing his short stories. Both were published posthumously; *Lezioni su Stendhal* appeared in 1959 in the revue *Paragone,* and *Racconti* came out in 1961. In *Racconti* are found many of *The Leopard*'s motifs. The social milieu is still the aristocracy in Sicily toward the end of its power, but the ascendant and greedy bourgeoisie is given more attention. He wrote the short stories in the French naturalism mode, but they were not successful and reveal the author's difficulty in going beyond autobiographical subjects. The first of these stories, *The Morning of a Sharecropper* (*Il Mattino di un mezzadro*), was originally planned as a follow-up to *The Leopard* with the title *The Blind Kittens* (*I gattini ciechi*). The other stories are *Joy and Law* (*La gioia e la legge*), *Siren* (*Lighea*), and *The Places of My Childhood* (*I luoghi della mia prima infanzia*).

Lampedusa became ill with cancer, a condition he did not disclose to his family. When his health declined drastically, he was taken for emergency surgery to a hospital in Rome, where he died on July 23, 1957.

BIBLIOGRAPHY

Carrera, Alessandro, and Lanza Tomasi, eds. "Giuseppe Tomasi di Lampedusa: Italian and American Perspectives Forty Years after the Publication of 'The Leopard'." *Anello Che Non Tiene: Journal of Modern Italian Literature* 13–14, nos. 1–2 (Spring 2001–Fall 2002): 185.

Gilmour, David. *The Last Leopard: A Life of Giuseppe Tomasi di Lampedusa.* New York: Pantheon 1988.

Salvestroni, Simonetta. *Tomasi di Lampedusa.* Florence: La Nuova Italia, 1973.

Sciascia, Leonardo. *Pirandello e la Sicilia.* Milano: Adelphi, 1996.

Tosi, Giuseppe Maria. "Letteratura e solitudine: Gli anni '50 e il 'caso Lampedusa'." *Forum Italicum* 30, no. 1 (Spring 1996): 65–79.

Alessandra Capperdoni

LAND **PARK KYONG-NI (1969–1994)** *Land* tells an epic saga of the Choi family's ups and downs during the turbulent period of modern Korean history from 1897 to 1945. The setting ranges from Pyongsa-ri, Hadong, a typical farming village in the southern region of South Korea, to Seoul, China, Russia, and Japan. The work features about 14 main characters and numerous minor characters, covering virtually every historical event up to the emancipation of Korea from the Japanese in 1945. It took 25 years for PARK KYONG-NI (1926–) to finish this 16-volume, five-part monumental epic narrative of the vicissitudes of three generations of the Choi family.

The first part depicts the disintegration of the traditional relations among four castes from 1897, in the years following Donghak Farmers Rebellion (1894–95), to 1905, when the Eulsa Treaty was signed, making Korea a protectorate of Japan. The main narrative involves the complicated fate of the main characters, beginning with Choi Chi-soo, son of the renowned Yangban family. Unknown to Chi-soo, he has a stepbrother, Hwan, who participates in the Donghak Rebellion, is chased by officials, and steals his way into Chi-soo's house, hiding there as a servant under the name of Goo-chon. However, he falls in love with his stepbrother's wife, Pyoldang Ahssi, and finally elopes with her to Mt. Chiri. The lovers are tracked down by Chi-soo, who shoots Pyoldang Ahssi and then becomes a Buddhist monk named Woo-kwan at Yeongoksah. However, Chi-soo is himself eventually killed by Kim Pyong-san, who was manipulated by the concubine Guinyuh.

Chi-soo's mother, Mrs. Yun, is a widow and matriarch of the Choi family. She has been harboring a tragic secret: She had once been raped at a temple and given birth to an illegitimate son, Hwan. Because of her shame and guilty conscience, she treats everyone around her coldly, including her own son and servants. Doubtful about her son Chi-soo's sudden death, however, she keeps tracing clues and finally inflicts a severe punishment on Pyong-san and Guinyuh.

Yet as the nation's destiny declines, she watches helplessly as her family's fortune dwindles due to severe famine. At last she is inflicted with cholera, like many people in the village, and experiences an untimely death, leaving only a little granddaughter to hold the family name. Young Seo-hee, who is intelligent and austere like her grandmother, tries to rebuild the Choi family with a loyal servant, Kil-sang. Her plan, however, is continually thwarted by vicious and greedy Cho Jun-koo, a distant family relative who comes with a wife and a hunchbacked son, Byong-soo, to manage the Choi household. With the Russia-Japan War and the Eulsa Treaty, circumstances favor Jun-koo, who claims the Chois' family land as his own. Having failed to kill the Chos, Seo-hee and Kil-sang leave Pyongsa-ri with a little money Seo-hee had secretly inherited from her grandmother and head for Yong-jeong (also called Kando), in the Manchu area of China.

The second part of the novel describes how the young Seo-hee is reborn as the strong-willed matriarch of the Choi family. Barely escaping from Japan's oppressive reign, Seo-hee starts a business of trading beans and lands and makes a great fortune in Yong-jeong. She is helped by an old man named Kong and Kil-sang, who has been a faithful servant since her childhood days. In spite of loving Sang-hyon, son of her father's friend from the same social class, the independent Seo-hee decides not to become an obedient housewife to Sang-hyon but instead marries her servant Kil-sang. She later gives birth to two sons, Hwan-kuk and Yun-kuk. Assured of her financial situation, she starts her longtime plan of avenging her family's disgrace. Via Mr. Kong, she manipulates Jun-koo into investing big money in a gold mine, which leads him to fall into serious financial trouble. Triumphant, Seo-hee buys Jun-koo out of trouble and finally regains the land her family had once owned.

Kil-sang, meanwhile, has long been disturbed by Seo-hee's insatiable obsession to avenge her family and restore the Chois' land. He has also anguished over the insurmountable class difference between him and his wife. Kil-sang comes to learn the secret of Seo-hee's grandmother and meets with Hwan. Sharing the vision of Korea's liberation from Japan, he leaves Seo-hee behind so that he can join Hwan in the resistance movement. Seo-hee then decides to go back to her beloved hometown alone with two sons and a nanny.

The third part of the novel depicts the Japanese's brutal treatment of Koreans and the ensuing resistance activities deployed by domestic and international organizations. Seo-hee, who previously did not care about others but had concentrated on rebuilding her family's prestige, now takes charge of resistance activities and helps keep the independent spirit going in her village. In the fourth part, hearing about the positive progress in international politics, Seo-hee hopes for the country's independence. Her son Hwan-kuk, who has cherished great respect and warm love toward his father Kil-sang, takes care of him when he is arrested and sentenced to two years in prison, where he finally dies. In the final part, Japan announces its defeat in the World War II, and Seo-hee and her two sons express their deep gratitude toward all the ordinary heroes who sacrificed their lives to achieve their beloved country's liberation.

Land is a great and much-beloved historical epic that represents how Korean people survived the dark period of the Japanese occupation. Despite being a period novel with local color, it has universally appealing classic themes such as romance overcoming class difference, a daughter's revenge for her family's honor, an uncle's greed so great that he makes an alliance even with the enemy Japanese to rob his niece's wealth, and the hope and belief of people fighting for independence in the dark period of oppression. It also has numerous colorful characters, and among them is the indomitable and memorable heroine Seo-hee. Having lost everything—her parents, social status, and wealth at a young age—she struggles to restore the family's name and wealth during the chaotic period of the occupation. She ultimately becomes a legendary char-

acter who manifests two distinctive spiritual characteristics of Korean women: determination and patience. This landmark epic narrative was dramatized into a TV miniseries twice and received tremendous accolades. Tojimunhakgwan (The *Land* Writing Center) for resident writers has been built in Wonju, memorializing the birthplace of *Land*.

BIBLIOGRAPHY
Cheong Hyeon-kee. *Han and Life: Criticism of Toji*. Seoul: Sol, 1994.
Choi You-chan et al. *The Cultural Topography of Toji*. Seoul: Somyeong, 2004.
Kim Chi-su. *Park Kyong-ni and Yee Cheong-jun*. Seoul: Minumsa, 1982.
Yee Deok-hwa. *Park Kyong-ni and Choi Myeong-hee: Two Women Novelists*. Seoul: Taehaksa, 2000.
Yee Sang-jin. *Glossary of Toji Characters*. Seoul: Nanam, 2002.

Jihee Han

LAO SHE (SHU QINGCHUN) (1899–1966)

Chinese novelist, playwright Lao She is a pseudonym of Shu Qingchun. He grew up in a Manchu family and was a native of Beijing. After graduating from high school in 1917, he became principal of a preliminary school and then a teacher in a middle school. In 1924 he traveled to England, where he taught Chinese at London University for six years. In 1930 he returned to China and became a professor at Jinnan and Qingdao universities. During World War II, Lao She was in charge of the All China Art Cycle Anti-Japanese Aggression Association and wrote numerous plays and novels encouraging Chinese resistance against the Japanese. After the war, in 1946, he went to the United States, staying for three years. In 1949 he returned to China, where he served as vice president of the China Authors Association and continued his writing until the end of his life. One of the most famous writers in China, Lao She was given the title of "The People's Artist" in 1951, and his works have become well known in many countries around the world.

Lao She's first novel, *The Philosophy of Lao Zhang* (*Lao Zhang de Zhexue*), was written in 1928 when he was in England. *Camel Xiangzi* (*Luotuo Xiangzi*) remains one of the author's most popular and highly regarded novels. The work is based on Lao's firsthand knowledge of rickshaw boys and demonstrates his unique narrative style. Other major novels include *Two Mas* (*Er Ma,* 1984), *Cat City* (*Mao Cheng Ji,* 1932), *The Divorce* (*Li Hun,* 1933), and *Four Generations under One Roof* (*Si Shi Tong Tang,* 1946). *Tea House* (*Cha Guan*) was published in 1957 and became Lao She's representative play. The author's last work is an unfinished autobiographical novel, *Beneath the Red Banner,* which was published posthumously in 1980.

BIBLIOGRAPHY

Vohra, Ranbir. *Lao She and the Chinese Revolution.* Cambridge, Mass.: East Asian Research Center, Harvard University, 1974.

Wang, David Der-Wei. *Fictional Realism in Twentieth-Century China: Mao Dun, Lao She, Shen Congwen.* New York: Columbia University Press, 1992.

Mei Han

LAXNESS, HALLDÓR (1902–1998) *Icelandic novelist, short story writer, playwright, poet, essayist*

Considered the most important Icelandic author since the writers of the sagas, Halldór Laxness is credited with fusing Icelandic history and the epic tradition into a series of powerful novels that renewed Icelandic literature and helped to shape Icelandic national consciousness in the 20th century. He is also a significant figure in world literature and was awarded the 1955 Nobel Prize in literature. Laxness's protagonists are often humble rural Icelanders, made memorable by the author's compassionate portrayals of their strength and resiliency when confronted with trying circumstances and a harsh natural environment. In prose marked by empathy, wry humor, understatement, and a timelessness that evokes the saga style, Laxness's characters often respond with the hearts and souls of poets.

A consistent theme in Laxness's works is how best to respond to the outside ideologies and forces that have buffeted Icelandic society in the modern era, particularly during the rapid modernization and urbanization of the post–World War II years. Also explored in various works is the question of remaining in one's native place versus leaving for broader experiences or a larger stage.

Laxness himself was a restless citizen of the world, living abroad in Europe and North America for a number of years when young and traveling widely throughout his life. His philosophical interests were also extensive, including serious commitments to, in turn, Catholicism and socialism and a continuing interest in Taoism. While best known for his novels, his prolific writings include short stories, poetry, plays, memoirs, and essays.

Laxness was born in Reykjavík on April 23, 1902. When he was three years old, his family moved to a farm in Mosfellsveit outside Reykjavík. The extended family included Laxness's maternal grandmother, from whom he first heard Icelandic folk tales and songs. Traces of this folklore are evident in the timeless and sometimes fantastical qualities of the writer's style, linked by some with magical realism. By his late teens, Laxness had decided on a career as a writer, and he left school, traveling to Denmark in 1919. He spent most of the next decade abroad, working first as a journalist in Copenhagen and then traveling throughout Europe, immersing himself in the varied literary, philosophical, and religious ideas of these regions.

Laxness's first mature novel, *The Great Weaver from Kasmír* (*Vefarinn mikli frá Kasmír,* 1927), records this period, chronicling the spiritual searching of young Steinn Ellidi, who, like Laxness, rejects his traditional upbringing. Steinn explores a multitude of modern belief systems and ultimately turns to Catholicism, retreating from the world to a monastery. His psychological struggles continue, however, as they did for Laxness, who by the end of the 1920s had left Catholicism. In the later part of that decade, Laxness lived in the United States for three years, hoping initially to write for the emerging movie industry. His observations there of unbridled capitalism radicalized his political beliefs, making him a supporter of socialism and later a public defender of communism, which sometimes embroiled him in controversy.

Laxness's politics can be seen in his great novels of Icelandic rural folk in the 1930s, which made his international reputation. *Salka Valka* (2 volumes, 1931–32), his first work translated into English, describes the harshness of life in a remote fishing village near the Arctic Circle. Salka Valka and her mother are both abused by the fisherman Steinþór, while the village is under the economic control of a local merchant. Salka Valka, strong-willed, passionate, and resilient, resists the forces that seem destined to limit her life. She gains a measure of financial independence and becomes passionately involved with Arnaldur, a childhood friend who has returned to the hamlet as a labor organizer. Arnaldur is unable to make the union a reality, however, and while Salka Valka is clearly the stronger person, it is she who stays while Arnaldur leaves for California.

Independent People (*Sjálfstœtt fólk: hetjusaga,* 2 volumes, 1934–35) is often considered Laxness's masterpiece and was a best seller in several languages. Bjartur is a crusty and persevering peasant who succeeds finally in purchasing his own farmland from the local bailiff, for whom he has worked as a farmhand for 18 years. Moving there as a newly married man, Bjartur faces numerous obstacles to maintain his hard-won independence, including the curse that the land reputedly carries. Bjartur's most serious problems turn out to be more earthbound, however, out of which Laxness shapes his ironic epic. Bjartur's wife, pregnant by the son of the bailiff, dies after giving birth and leaves him with a daughter. The protagonist remarries, and in the following years the household ekes out a meager living, with Bjartur suffering great privations from all to maintain the land and his precious sheep.

World War I brings Bjartur increased prosperity when demand for his farm products rises, but he is increasingly alone as his second wife dies and his children are driven away by his indefatigable devotion to the farm. When the postwar downturn comes, Bjartur is bankrupted and his property sold at auction, reverting to the bailiff. Bjartur, however, clings to his ideal and makes plans to work a new, more remote piece of land. At the novel's end he is reconciled with his tubercular daughter, but she dies as they travel to his new farm. Bjartur ultimately serves as a poignant symbol of the yeoman farmer who faces constant challenges from forces beyond his control.

Laxness's protagonist in *World Light* (*Heimsljós,* 4 volumes, 1937–40) is based partially on the Icelandic folk poet Magnús Hjaltason. Ólafur Kárason's life is one of suffering and ineffectualness. Abandoned by his mother and reduced to a foster child, sickly and considered somewhat eccentric, Ólafur prefers to write poetry about the world rather than live in it. His sensitivity to beauty and sense of mission to convey it to others is authentic, however, and Laxness makes clear he feels he is noble and even Christ-like.

Iceland's Bell (*Íslandsklukkan,* 3 volumes, 1943–46) is set in the late 17th and early 18th centuries, the period of Iceland's worst colonial exploitation by Denmark. The lives of an impoverished farmer, a manuscript collector, and the daughter of the local magistrate are interwoven with a story that confronts the nature of justice and the significance of the sagas to Icelandic national identity. Laxness's novel, written during the years Iceland gained its independence from Denmark and his most popular work in Iceland, made its own contribution to the nation's identity.

Satirizing contemporary culture and politics, *The Atom Station* (*Atómstöðin,* 1948) follows Ugla, a young woman from northern Iceland, as she travels to Reykjavík to study the organ. Put off by the capital's false sophistication and other troubling postwar cultural changes, she comes to sympathize with communism as a means to a more authentic life. As background and subplot to the novel are the political machinations surrounding the newly independent Icelandic government's agreement with the United States to continue its military base at Keflavík in 1946. The pact, of which Laxness was one of Iceland's most influential opponents, was perceived by some as a betrayal of the nation.

The Happy Warriors (*Gerpla,* 1952), based on saga themes and using their stylistic conventions, pays homage to saga literature while working for pacifist ends by satirizing the convention of hero worship and heroic ideals found in the saga.

Laxness's later novels proclaim the worth and sufficiency of traditional Icelandic mores in the face of religious ideologies and other external influences. In *The Fish Can Sing* (*Brekkukotsannáll,* 1957), the customs, folk knowledge, and gentle morality instilled in a traditional Icelandic childhood are lyrically invoked by the narrator Álfgrímur's episodic retelling of his early years in a fishing village outside Reykjavík, which much resembles Laxness's own experiences. *Paradise Reclaimed* (*Paradísarheimt,* 1960), based on the writings of an Icelandic Mormon convert of the late 1800s, shows how a sudden and solo immigration to Utah in the United States by Steinn Steinsson, a formerly devoted family man, leads to unforeseen consequences that break his family apart even as its remaining members rejoin him in America. Returning to Iceland, he is last seen contemplating rebuilding the ruins of his old farmstead.

In *Under the Glacier* (*Kristnihald undir Jökli*, 1968) the bishop of Iceland sends an emissary to investigate what seems to be a disturbing lack of formal observance by the pastor of a rural parish, but the spiritual life of the pastor and locals, reported on in a series of facetious pseudo-objective reports, is found to be rich.

Much of Laxness's writing in his later years was in the form of memoirs, and he published little during his last 10 years, as Alzheimer's disease took an increasing toll on his faculties. Laxness died at Mosfell on February 8, 1998, where he had lived since 1945 in a mountainside home with his second wife.

BIBLIOGRAPHY

Hallberg, Peter. *Halldór Laxness.* New York: Twayne Publishers, 1971.

Hallmundsson, Hallberg. "Halldór Laxness and the Sagas of Modern Iceland." *Georgia Review* 49 (1995): 34–45.

Kress, Helga. "Halldór Laxness." In *Dictionary of Literary Biography,* vol. 293, *Icelandic Writers,* edited by Patrick J. Stevens, 125–149. Detroit: Gale Research, 2004.

Leithauser, Brad. "A Small Country's Great Book." *New York Review of Books,* 11 May 1995, pp. 41–45.

Magnússon, Sigurdur A. "The World of Halldór Laxness." *World Literature Today* 66 (1992): 457–463.

Sue Barker

LAYE, CAMARA (LAYA, CARAMA) (1928–1980) *African novelist*

The African-born writer Camara Laye (sometimes referred to as Laya Camara, the latter being his family name) was born in Karoussa, French Guinea. His father was a goldsmith, a member of the Malinke tribe. Laye was reared as a Muslim; some of his family were familiar with Sufi traditions. After Koranic school, he attended French schools in Karoussa and Conakry and then technical schools in France, earning a diploma in engineering in 1956. He married his childhood friend Marie Lorifo in 1953; they had four children.

Laye worked at various jobs, including that of auto mechanic, in and around Paris, then at the ministry of youth. In 1956 he returned to Africa, living in Dahomey (now Benin), Ghana, and then Conakry, Guinea, where he worked as an engineer for the colonial regime there. Laye then served as diplomat for the new, independent government of Guinea in several African countries. Under President Sekou Toure, he served as director of the National Institute of Research and Documentation but became increasingly uncomfortable with some of Toure's policies. Laye therefore left Guinea in 1966 for the Ivory Coast and then Senegal, where he worked as a research fellow and teacher in Dakar while continuing to oppose Toure. When his wife returned to Guinea to visit her mother in 1970, she was imprisoned there for seven years. During that period Laye married a second wife, Mamtoulaye Kante, perhaps partly to obtain help in caring for his children while their mother was imprisoned; his first wife subsequently divorced him. Sources vary regarding his total number of children. In 1975 he became ill from a kidney infection and returned to Paris for treatment, paid for by an international fundraising campaign. He died in Dakar in 1980.

Laye's first book, *L'Enfant Noir,* was published by Plon in France in 1953, then translated as *The Dark Child* by Noonday Press in the United States in 1954 and as *The African Child* by Collins in England in 1959. Based on the author's own early experience, the book describes an idyllic childhood in the context of a traditional Malinke culture still largely untouched by Western influence, even though railroad tracks ran right next to the family compound of mud huts in a city. The young boy called Fatoman watches his father ply his trade as the preeminent goldsmith of the region, in the company of a small black snake that he is told is his father's "guiding spirit." Both his parents have magical powers (the father says his powers are derived from the snake), for which they are widely respected; both exhibit exceptional integrity based on traditional values.

Although a city boy and a schoolboy, Fatoman regularly visits his mother's village and participates in rural agricultural life, with its rich rituals. He also participates in traditional rites of passage, culminating in his circumcision. Throughout the book Laye emphasizes the dignity and cultural richness of his people's traditional lifestyle. Conversely, he says very little about his gradual introduction through schooling into Western culture, except the bullying and exploitation of younger students by older ones (eventually curtailed by parental intervention) and the severe discipline (also exploitive in some respects) imposed by his teachers. The book concludes with his progressive movement away from family and African culture as his schooling takes him first to the capital city of Conakry on the coast and then to France.

Laye's second and most renowned book is *Le Regard du Roi,* published in 1956 by Plom in Paris, by Collins in 1965 in Britain, and in 1971 as *The RADIANCE OF THE KING* by Collier (Macmillan). Whereas the protagonist of *The Dark Child* moves progressively further from his African roots, Laye's second book focuses on the increasingly confusing and disorienting journey of a white European, ironically named Clarence, into the magical and dreamlike world of African culture. Expelled by the local European enclave in an African town for unpaid gambling debts, Clarence desperately seeks employment from a visiting African king, who turns out to be an adolescent boy so laden with gold ornaments that he can barely stand, much less walk. This boy king nevertheless exerts a mysterious attractive power over Clarence, even though a huge, adoring crowd separates them. Despite the proffered assistance of a mysteriously authoritative beggar and two rascally twin boys, Clarence fails to win an audience with the king. Later that evening, he is charged with stealing his own coat in a surreal encounter with the local justice system that seems a mixture of FRANZ KAFKA and magical realism. Then he, the beggar, and the two boys set out on a southward journey through an enchanted forest toward the boys' home village, where they will await the arrival of the king. From his first encounter with the black, sweaty masses awaiting the king's arrival, Clarence becomes increasingly absorbed into the fluid, shifting African world, in which Western values are often inverted or turned inside out. He finds himself regressing into a primal state in which his main concerns are his overpowering daytime sleepiness, the blurring together of dream and reality, and his rampant nocturnal sexuality, whether real or imaginary.

While awaiting the king's arrival in the southern village, Clarence gradually becomes aware that he has been exploited as a breeding stud to impregnate the many wives of the impotent local chief's harem. After more dream visions involving sirens/manatees and a clairvoyant hag who apparently copulates with her serpentine familiars (and perhaps with Clarence himself), he becomes so disgusted with himself that when the king he now adores actually arrives, he refuses to join

the welcoming crowd. Yet the king's magnetic gaze draws Clarence out of his hut, stark naked, to rest against the god-king's faintly beating heart, at which point Clarence is apotheosized, and the novel ends.

The Radiance of the King seems to blend European modernism with an African version of what has come to be known as magical realism. It inverts Western racial and cultural stereotypes regarding Europeans and Africans as Clarence's rationalism dissolves in the enchanting fluidity of the African world, and he becomes, in his own estimation, more primitive and degraded than the Africans he initially disdained. Yet in Laye's comic novel, Clarence's journey into the heart of his own hitherto unexplored darkness culminates in his salvation, in contrast with the apparent damnation of Kurtz that so fascinates Joseph Conrad's character Marlowe in *Heart of Darkness.*

The novel has been considered Laye's masterpiece, yet a controversy has recently arisen concerning whether Laye himself actually wrote it. In her earlier book, *The Writings of Camara Laye* (Heineman, 1980), Adele King did not question the authorship of either of his first two books. However, in a later book, *Rereading Camara Laye* (University of Nebraska Press, 2004), she argues elaborately that, by his own admission, Laye did not write *The Radiance of the King* and that he had help writing *The Dark Child.* Moreover, she claims that the French government supported the publication of these books, which are not critical of French colonial rule in Guinea, as part of a campaign to resist pressure to grant independence to French colonies in Africa. Thus King has raised critical but as yet unresolved issues about the authorship of the two books for which Laye is most renowned and the political context in which they were produced.

Laye's third book, the novel *Dramous,* was published by Plon in Paris in 1966, then translated by James Kirkup as *A Dream of Africa* (Collins, 1968; Collier, 1971). The novel extends the story of Fatoman, the protagonist of *The Dark Child,* after his return from Paris to Africa. The now more sophisticated African is critical of European materialism and individualism, but he is even more critical of the murderous political violence perpetrated by his fellow countrymen shortly before political independence, which Fatoman fears will culminate in an

African dictatorship worse than colonial domination. While imprisoned by the book's stand-in for Sekou Toure, Fatoman dreams of Guinea's return to peace, brought about by a black lion.

Laye's most recent book, *Le Maître de la parole: Kuoma Lafolo Kuoma* (The *Guardian of the World: Kuoma Lafolo Kuoma,* 1980), is a historical epic.

BIBLIOGRAPHY

Laye, Camara. *The Dark Child.* Translated by James Kirkup. New York: Noonday Press, 1954.

———. *The Radiance of the King.* Translated by James Kirkup. New York: Collins Books, 1971.

Palmer, Eustace. *An Introduction to the African Novel: A Critical Study of Twelve Books by Chinua Achebe, James Ngugi, Camara Laye, Elechi Amadi, Ayi Kwei Armach, Mongo Beti, and Gabriel Okara.* New York: Africana Publications, 1972.

Thorpe Butler

LEAVETAKING (ABSCHIED VON DEN ELTERN) PETER WEISS (1961)

The two novels PETER WEISS (1916–82) wrote relatively early in his career, *Leavetaking* and VANISHING POINT (*Fluchtpunkt,* 1962) are ambitious and unsettling works of prose fiction, styled, in terms of genre, in a Proustian manner of fictionalized autobiography, though charged with a more forceful sense of political urgency. Written in the aftermath of World War II and the Holocaust brutalities, these works reflect an effort on the part of the author to analyze and understand, if only in retrospect, the cultural logic that made the catastrophes of the Second World War possible. They are rooted in the assumption that any serious investigation of an age must begin at home—in unabashed self-scrutiny.

The first work, *Leavetaking,* opens, characteristically, with the narrator's memory of his parents' death. What begins as belated sorrow for family estrangement and disintegration serves as a prelude to a more rigorous examination of "the yawning emptiness" that has been a mark of the narrator's childhood and youth. Cruelty is a central subject. From instances of "ritual beatings" that took place in the traditional bourgeois household of his childhood, through the more fearful experiencing of classroom spanking or ritual persecution and stoning by the gang leader Friederle and his cronies, cruelty, the narrator suggests, and the consequent fear

of punishment and persecution, have been the major facts of this lingering feeling of emptiness. As the narrator's early exposure to the morbidly sadistic world of German fairy tales also suggests, the cultural sanctioning of cruelty not only drives the traumatized subject to a state of early alienation, but it also overcasts his early years with a premonition of a fate that, due to his exile, he was to escape later in life.

With a compulsion that to a great degree explains the germination of Weiss's writing here and in his later pieces, the narrator of *Leavetaking* repeatedly looks back on those scenes from his early life. In the aftermath of the historical disaster of World War II, these scenes loom large with the horror of their premonitory potential. Here the narrator spares no one. This includes neither society, which has made the existence of degraded conditions possible, nor his youthful self, who—prior to his exclusion from the system of which, due to his Jewish origins, he learns he can no longer be a part—had internalized many of its laws.

The childhood experience of persecution by the bully Friederle and his menacing group, the narrator realizes, may have been shattering in itself, but it does not put him on a par with real historical victims of the cruelty of the war years. Weiss studied in Prague with Peter Kien, for instance, a young writer and painter who later died at Auschwitz in 1944. Quite ironically, in fact, the narrator reveals how the trauma of victimization had often been followed by a fantasy of power, or worse, by his literal projections of cruelty upon others. Remembering one such episode in which the brutalities acted out upon a small boy had turned him into a Friederle-like thug, the narrator remarks, "I was filled with brief happiness to be able to be one of the strong ones, although I knew that my place was among the weaklings."

It is this astonishing sincerity with which Weiss is prepared to examine his own place in the processes of "merciless development" at the time that distinguishes his writing from any easy attempts, popular in postwar German literature, at "coming to terms with the past." What only saves the young Weiss from being thoroughly overcome, with many others, by Hitler's screaming speeches summoning to self-sacrifice and death, is the shock of his father's Jewishness. This knowledge is closely tied in his memory with the experience of another loss, the death of his sister Margit. The two events, both fostering the already present sense of dislocation and alienation, stand as overtures to two major departures in the narrator's life: the "leavetaking" of his family and the self-conscious embracing of the challenges of an émigré existence. For Weiss, neither comes easily.

The years of later exile in Prague are full of guilt and foreboding, not the least of which are induced by the narrator's struggle and rebellion against his parents, from whose control he cannot seem to liberate himself totally. It is only after realizing that his defeat "was not the defeat of the emigrant in face of the difficulties of living in exile, but the defeat of someone who does not dare to free himself from his independence" that the narrator decides to make power of his non-belonging and sever his ties with the past. Stirred by the ominous force of a dream about a huntsman who could also be the dreamer—that is, the narrator—and under the threat of a forthcoming war, eventually Weiss's narrator in *Leavetaking* takes leave of his parents by embarking on a train that would lead him to a new life of his own.

BIBLIOGRAPHY

Berwald, Olaf. *An Introduction to the Work of Peter Weiss.* Rochester, N.Y.: Camden House, 2003.

Cohen, Robert. *Understanding Peter Weiss.* Columbia: University of South Carolina Press, 1993.

Hernand, Jost, and Marc Silberman, eds. *Rethinking Peter Weiss.* New York: Peter Lang, 2000.

Mina Zdravkovic

LEM, STANISŁAW (1921–2006) *Polish novelist, short story writer*

Since his debut as a novelist in the late 1940s, Stanisław Lem has become the most acclaimed and widely read science fiction writer from eastern Europe. In his numerous short stories and novels, he has exposed and explored the boundaries of human consciousness and knowledge through a satirical mixture of fantasy and realism. A Marxist, the Polish-born Lem likewise has critiqued the social and political reality of his country during the cold war. His literary criticism defines science fiction exclusively as a genre that rigorously questions existing assumptions and extrapolates beyond genre clichés.

Lem was born in Lwów, Poland (now L'viv, Ukraine), in 1921 to the family of a prosperous physician. In 1940 he commenced medical studies at Lwow University. However, the German occupation of the city in 1942 forced him to postpone his education. During World War II, he found employment as an assistant mechanic and welder for a German firm, and he also worked for the resistance. When the Soviets reclaimed the city in 1944, Lem resumed his studies. Soon after, in 1946, Lem and his family moved to Krakow, Poland, as a result of repatriation laws. There he finished his medical program at Jagiellonian University but did not take his final exams in order to avoid a position as a military physician. From 1947 to 1950, Lem worked as a junior assistant at the hospital Konwersatorium Naukoznawcze and began to write fiction. In 1953 he married Barbara Lesniak, a radiologist. Their son was born 15 years later, in 1968.

Lem's prose frequently interrogates the optimistic role of the scientist and of science in society; his artistic expression has been interpreted as a critique of scientific socialism. Although his scientists are experts in their fields, their knowledge and analytical expertise often fails them. Instilled with the 20th century's confidence in the power of reason and the scientific method, Lem's protagonists confront phenomena that remain ambiguous and inexplicable. His stories approach this subject matter with either a playfully satirical style or a dry, ironic, and highly philosophical treatment. In the latter, space exploration is rarely a romantic adventure at the speed of light, but rather a gritty, introspective contemplation of the real.

In *SOLARIS* (1961), the best known of Lem's novels, the author explores the limitations of the human imagination and assumptions surrounding the search for alien life. The novel tells the story of scientist Kris Kelvin's visit to Solaris, a planet believed to be inhabited by a giant sentient ocean. Kelvin is an expert in Solaristics, a fictional scientific field that, despite a multitude of theories and publications on the subject, has failed to adequately explain the true nature of the planet's ocean. Yet the ambiguity of this result also touches upon subsequent themes of the novel.

Lem's long and successful literary career commenced with the appearance of his serialized novel *A Man from Mars (Czlowiek z Marsa,* 1946). He began the series *Hospital of the Transfiguration (Szpital Przemienienia)* in 1948, in which a young doctor named Stefan Trzyniecki finds work in a Polish insane asylum to escape the realities of the German occupation of the country. He discovers that life inside the hospital is not at all different from life outside. While this book began to establish Lem's ironic literary style, *The Astronauts* (*Astronauci,* 1951) is a space opera that portrays the horrors of an accidental nuclear holocaust on Venus. The success of this story established science fiction as a valid literary genre in many countries of the Eastern Bloc (communist central and eastern European countries then in the Warsaw Pact). Kurt Maetzig directed the joint Polish/East German film production of the story, *The Silent Star* (*Der Schweigende Stern,* 1959).

The most prolific period of Lem's life was the 1950s and 1960s, when he gained an international reputation. In 1957 he published the groundbreaking *Star Diaries* (*Dzienniki Gwiazdowe*), which inaugurated the exploits of Ijon Tichy. Not only is this comical space adventure highly amusing, it also contains complex philosophical and scientific questions as to the nature of time and causality. Two years later, both *Eden* and *The Investigation* (*Sledztwo*) further established Lem's intensely satirical style, in which he employed science fiction editor Darko Suvin's concept of the "new" in science fiction to displace contemporary issues into a distant, alternate reality. *Memoirs Found in a Bathtub* (*Pamietnik znaleziony w wannie,* 1961) is a dystopian parody set in the year 3149. A man is sent on a mission so secret that no one has the proper security clearance to explain it to him. In the same year, *Return from the Stars* (*Powrot z gwiazd,* 1961) and *Solaris* (1961) appeared. *The Invincible* (*Niezwyciezony,* 1964) examines the limitations of human reliance on technology. *The Cyberiad* (*Cyberiada,* 1967) is a humorous, fantastic, and, at times, surreal tale of scientific competition told in "seven sallies." *Tales of Pirx the Pilot* (*Opowiesci o pilocie Pirxie,* 1968) is a diverse collection of stories. The fictitious Professor Peter E. Hogarth remembers his part in attempts to decipher a mysterious alien transmission in *His Master's Voice* (*Glos Pana,* 1968).

Further publications include additional adventures of Ijon Tichy in *The Futurological Congress* (*Kongres futurologiczny,* 1971), and *A Perfect Vacuum* (*Doskonala Próznia,* 1971), which consists of reviews of non-existent academic and creative books. *Imaginary Magnitude* (*Wielkosc urojona,* 1972) expands on Lem's fictional

library and contains a number of introductions from books of the author's own invention. With *The Chain of Chance* (*Katar,* 1976), Lem returned to genre writing. The book is a mathematically based, spy and science fiction novel in which an ex-astronaut aids Interpol in solving a series of mysterious murders.

In the 1970s, Lem was honored for his achievements both at home and abroad, but not without controversy. In 1970, 1973, and 1976, he received recognition from the Polish government for his accomplishments, including the State Prize for Literature. In 1973 he became an honorary member of the international Science Fiction and Fantasy Writers of America (SFWA). Yet, due to a bitter polemical attack on American pulp science fiction writers, he was expelled from the organization in 1976. Referring to it as "kitsch," or inferior art, Lem considered that other authors sacrificed the genre's unique qualities to placate and feed a mass audience and for financial gain.

The year 1981 saw the beginning of a period of martial law in Poland as a result of efforts by the worker's union Solidarity to bring about political reform. Consequently, in 1982 Lem took a one-year academic position in West Berlin. From 1983 to 1988 he lived in Vienna, where he published *Fiasco* (*Fiasko,* 1987) and *Peace on Earth* (*Pokoj na Ziemi,* 1987), both books with cold war themes. Lem returned to Poland as cracks in the Iron Curtain began to widen in 1988. He was awarded Poland's highest national honor, the Order of the White Eagle, and received numerous literary awards, including the Austrian Kafka Prize for Literature in 1991. He also received honorary degrees from several universities.

Lem wrote a number of book reviews, essays, and commentaries on science fiction. *Microworlds* (1986) is a collection in English of selections from his critical book *Fantasy and Futurology* (*Fantastyka i Futurologia*) and related material. His autobiography of life during the interwar period is entitled *Highcastle: A Remembrance* (*Wysoki Zamek,* 1975). *A Stanisław Lem Reader* (1997) includes several interviews with Lem, essays on his work, as well as a bibliography of his writings in English.

In 2000 Lem published *A Blink of an Eye* (*Okamgnienie*), a series of essays on the technological potential of the 21st century. He became an honorary citizen of

Kraków, Poland, where he died on March 27, 2006, at the age of 84.

BIBLIOGRAPHY

Lem, Stanisław. *Highcastle*. Translated by Michael Kandel. New York: Harcourt, Brace, 1995.

Swirski, Peter. *Between Literature and Science: Poe, Lem, and Explorations in Aesthetics, Cognitive Science, and Literary Knowledge*. Montreal and Ithaca: McGill-Queen's University Press, 2000.

Ziegfeld, Richard E. *Stanisław Lem*. New York: F. Ungar, 1985.

Sonja Fritzsche

LEOPARD, THE (*IL GATTOPARDO*) GIUSEPPE TOMASI DI LAMPEDUSA (1958)

A historical novel by GIUSEPPE TOMASI DI LAMPEDUSA (1896–1957), *The Leopard* was one of the most successful literary works of 20th-century European literature. The plot is straightforward: In 1860 Giuseppe Garibaldi and his forces have landed in Marsala (Sicily) to free the island. For centuries Sicily and southern Italy had been under the rule of the Spanish line of the Borboni (Bourbons), supported by the local aristocracy of landowners. With Garibaldi's landing, the Sicilian aristocrats fear this moment, which will mark the end of their class privileges and replacement by the increasingly powerful *mezzadri*—sharecroppers, renters, and administrators who took advantage of the aristocracy for personal gain and now constitute the new middle class of professionals. At the same time, the aristocrats are mired in their mores and inability to take action.

The aristocrat protagonist of the novel is Don Fabrizio Corbera, prince of Salina, whose family herald is the leopard. Although he is not different from the others, he is a sharp observer of the events that are precipitating his own demise as well as dramatically changing the destiny of southern Italy. He can see clearly that the "liberation" of the island by the king of Savoy's forces led by Garibaldi is, in fact, an "occupation" of the south on the part of a northern prince-state. Unable to counteract the course of history yet understanding his nephew Tancredi's words "to keep everything unchanged, we need to change everything," Don Fabrizio realizes that to hold any power, the family and aristocrats must side with Garibaldi's forces but make sure that a new kingdom is established under the rule of the king of Savoy and not, as Garibaldi hoped, be made a republic. Don Fabrizio lets Tancredi join Garibaldi and also marry the beautiful but unrefined Angelica, the daughter of a rich peasant, dashing the hopes of one of his daughters, Concetta, who is in love with Tancredi. The prince observes the course of the events in a detached way: New masters will replace the old ones, but the world will always be divided between masters and servants, exploiters and exploited.

Don Fabrizio's disillusionment with the political state of the Italian peninsula is complete. A representative of Savoy's government, Chevalley, arrives to offer him, as a prominent figure on the island and an aristocrat, a seat in the new senate in Rome. Don Fabrizio refuses since he is too tied to the old order to belong, and contribute effectively, to the new. Instead, Angelica's father, Don Calogero Sedara, will become senator, Tancredi will become ambassador, and the new powers are reconstituted. Don Fabrizio keeps his role of meditative and detached observer until his death in a small hotel in Palermo while he was traveling, marking the end of the family line.

The strength of the novel is in the minute descriptions of the landscape of Sicily, the palace and estate of the prince, the everyday habits of the family, and the social and cultural changes in the turmoil of an era that is central to the definition of the new course of Italy. Some central scenes are particularly successful, such as the ball given in honor of Tancredi's engagement to Angelica (with the depiction of sumptuous rococo furniture, lavish but already decadent clothing, and the social interaction of the guests) and the encounter between Chevalley and Don Fabrizio (with Chevalley's humorous slip of the tongue referring to the "conquest" of Sicily).

But the success of the novel lies especially in the abundance of detailed moments and actions perfectly and intricately bound together in a social tapestry of costumes, types, and manners: Don Fabrizio's secret encounters with a woman from the lower class; the piety and bigotry of his wife; his insipid daughters, with their rosaries and relics; Tancredi's brashness; Angelica's provocative beauty; Don Calogero's unlimited ambitions; and the tensions (carefully controlled and manipulated) between aristocrat landowners and the ascendant bourgeoisie, as well as between the pragmatic and industrial northerners and the somnolent and traditional southerners. In many ways the novel lends itself to a great social portrait of an era, and its atmosphere was perfectly captured by Luchino Visconti's film. But above all, the novel remains an endeavoring homage, as well as critique, to the advantages and ills of Sicily, in which the author had deep roots; its hostile but fascinating landscape, light, and perfumes conveyed through a sensual prose; and the splendor of a past forever gone.

The posthumous publication of *The Leopard* resulted in immediate success despite the author's many difficulties in finding a publisher while he was alive. Lampedusa was not a professional writer nor was he associated with any literary group, and he was therefore unfamiliar with the details of publishing. Furthermore, the historical genre of the novel, at a time when new trends were slowly emerging, did not attract the interest of any publishers. The last refusal came from Elio Vittorini, who, although a respected writer and literary critic, openly favored works with strong and positive messages in his publications and failed to recognize the work's value. Nevertheless, *The Leopard* was immediately appreciated by the writer Giorgio Bassani, who facilitated its publication by Feltrinelli after Lampedusa's death. The novel's poignant prose and intriguing characterization have ensured the lasting interest of readers and made possible not only its entry into the world literary canon but also its continuing critical attention.

BIBLIOGRAPHY

Cupolo, Marco. "Tomasi di Lampedusa's *Il Gattopardo* and Postwar Italian Political Culture." Translated by Norma Bouchard. In *Risorgimento in Modern Italian Culture: Revisiting the Nineteenth-Century Past in History, Narrative, and Cinema,* edited by Norma Bouchard, 57–72. Madison, N.J.: Fairleigh Dickinson University Press, 2005.

Hampson, Ernest. "Visconti's *Il Gattopardo*: Aspects of a Literary Adaptation." *Spunti e Ricerche: Rivista d'Italianistica* 15 (2000): 69–78.

Lucente, Gregory L. "Lampedusa's *Il gattopardo*: Figure and Temporality in an Historical Novel." *MLN* 93, no. 1 (January 1978): 82–108.

Sartarelli, Stephen. "The Classic on the Margin." *Anello Che Non Tiene: Journal of Modern Italian Literature* 13–14, nos. 1–2 (Spring 2001–Fall 2002): 63–70.

Tosi, Giuseppe. "Le Cosmogonie aristocratiche: *Il Gattopardo* di Tomasi di Lampedusa." *Italica* 74, no. 1 (Spring 1997): 67–80.

———. "Letteratura e solitudine: Gli anni '50 e il 'caso Lampedusa'." *Forum Italicum* 30, no. 1 (Spring 1996): 65–79.

Alessandra Capperdoni

LEROUX, GASTON (1868–1927) *French essayist, novelist*

Today the French author Gaston Leroux is remembered best for writing *The PHANTOM OF THE OPERA* (*Le Fantôme de l'opéra* 1910), a novel that has long since been overshadowed by its various reincarnations on film and on the stage, including a 1925 film starring Lon Chaney and, most recently, a popular musical by Andrew Lloyd Webber that was also put on film (2004). Leroux was, however, an important figure in the development of the detective novel, and his influence can still be seen in the genre today. Although few of his novels are available in print, and he is now just one of the many long-past-popular authors who have largely lost their literary prominence, his legacy nonetheless lives on through the mystery and horror writers that followed him.

Born in Paris on May 6, 1868, Gaston Louis Alfred Leroux was the only child of successful store owners, Julien and Marie-Alphonsine Leroux. He began his education at the College of Eu, a grammar school in Normandy, where he began to develop a love for reading and writing. After completing his secondary education at Caen, he moved to Paris and studied law while still dabbling in fiction, but upon beginning his law practice, he quickly became disillusioned and abandoned his legal career. In 1889, the same year in which Leroux became certified to practice law, his father died. The young man inherited a million francs from his father's estate and proceeded to spend most of it quickly and unwisely, living out his desires for fine food and drink as well as exercising his propensity for gambling. He was a popular man for his personality as well as for his money, and his wealth dissipated within six months. The short period of his wealth brought with it the keen awareness that his carefree decadence must come to an end, but he was not willing to return to his decidedly unrewarding career in law.

In his early 20s, Leroux embarked upon his first true career, that of a journalist, working first for *L'Écho de Paris* as a court reporter. Not one to be satisfied with retelling what had already happened, Leroux became a proactive participant in a case he was covering, masquerading as an investigator for the prison system, complete with falsified documents, and gaining admission to the suspected prisoner. With the resulting interview, he exposed the truth and vindicated the accused man. This type of eager reporter would figure in Leroux's novels in later years. After this groundbreaking journalistic success, Leroux went to work for the daily paper *Le Matin,* reporting on international and political stories from such exotic locations as Morocco, where he covered the tense Moroccan crisis of 1905, and Russia, where he covered the Russian Revolution of 1905. He also reported on the long-running Dreyfus affair and delighted in Dreyfus's eventual acquittal—a political scandal in which newspapers played a large role by exposing corruption. During the Boer War, Leroux was forcibly removed from colonial secretary Joseph Chamberlain's office, which he had entered unauthorized, and instead of the interview he had hoped for, he wrote a story on his escapades in the thwarted attempt. While an international reporter, Leroux frequently used costumes and assumed identities in order to get the story he wanted.

Although he loved his career as a reporter and believed wholeheartedly in his responsibilities to his reading public, Leroux nevertheless realized that the time had come for him to step back from the exciting but dangerous life he had been living. He changed careers again in the early 20th century, shifting from journalism to fiction. As was typical at the time, his novels were first serialized in French newspapers or magazines. Once complete, they would be bound and sold in France as well as translated and exported. His first novel was *The Seeking of the Morning Treasures* (*Le Chercheur de trésors,* 1903), which was serialized in *Le Matin* in 1903. However, it was in 1907 with *The MYSTERY OF THE YELLOW ROOM* (*Le Mystère de la chambre jaune,* 1907) that Leroux achieved true critical success and a stage adaptation. In this novel, Leroux depicts what is still considered to be the quintessential example of the sealed room mystery, in the vein of Edgar Allan Poe's *Murders in the Rue Morgue:* An attack takes place in an apparently inescapable room from which the attacker then mysteriously escapes. The following year Leroux reprised his popular characters in *The Perfume of the Lady in Black* (*Le Parfum de la dame en noir,* 1908), and he would continue to exploit the memorable protagonist Rouletabille's popularity for several more novels. He was now in the fortunate position to be able to rely on his creative writing as his sole source of income, which finally afforded him the ability to leave his tiring journalistic career.

Leroux had been writing novels on the side while working for the newspapers. In 1903, shortly after his divorce from his first wife, Marie Lefranc, Leroux published *The Seeking of the Morning Treasures* in *Le Matin.* Inspired by the life of Louis Cartouche, an infamous thief from the 1700s, Leroux's serialized novel became popular reading. *Le Matin* fueled the fire by hiding small caches of money around the Paris environs, which readers had to find based on clues in the novel.

Leroux met Jeanne Cayatte in 1902, and they soon began living together, remaining unmarried until 1917. Scandalously, she accompanied him to Russia in 1905 while obviously pregnant, flaunting conventional norms. In 1908, long before their marriage, the couple began living in Nice, where Leroux enjoyed easy access to his old vice of gambling and its social trappings. Financially, they were comfortable, although Leroux readily threw money away to the casinos, deriving great joy from gambling. He could recoup his losses, should he incur them, by relying on his popularity as a novelist and writing another book, always with a contract and an advance.

By 1911, Leroux had written five more novels when he published *The Phantom of the Opera,* the stimulus apparently resulting from a tour he made through the Paris Opéra that had included its labyrinthine cellar levels. As a novel, it did not fare as well in the popular opinion of the day. At this time, however, the nascent film industry began adapting his novels for the screen, beginning in 1913 with a novel entitled *Balaoo* and then again in 1919 with the still-popular *Mystery of the Yellow Room.* In 1925 Universal Pictures, hoping to repeat the success of *The Hunchback of Notre Dame,* selected *The Phantom of the Opera* and cast Lon Chaney as the star. Though it was not the first film version of

Leroux's novel, it was the most enduring of all the many adaptations made subsequently.

On April 16, 1927, two years after the success of the film *The Phantom of the Opera,* Leroux died at the age of 59, in Nice, where he is buried.

BIBLIOGRAPHY

Hogle, Jerrold E. *The Underground of the Phantom of the Opera.* New York: Palgrave, 2002.

Husson-Casta, Isabelle. *Le Travail de l'"obscure clarté" dans le Fantôme de l'opéra de Gaston Leroux.* Paris: Lettres Modernes, 1997.

Wolf, Leonard. *The Essential Phantom of the Opera.* New York, Plume, 1996.

Angela Courtney

LEVI, CARLO (1902–1975) *Italian essayist, novelist* Carlo Levi, born in Turin, Italy, at the beginning of the 20th century, was a writer, painter, journalist, and senator. He grew up in an environment of Italian Jewish intellectuals and received his degree in medicine at the University of Turin in 1924. He did not, however, practice medicine except later for a period in Lucania, where he was held as a political prisoner. In 1922, even before receiving his medical degree, he began writing for *La Rivoluzione liberale* (a liberal-socialist newspaper edited by Piero Gobetti). The next year he submitted a painting to the quadriennale of modern art in Turin; it was accepted and highly praised.

From this time on, Levi painted in earnest. In 1929 he was one of the founders of the group called the "six painters of Turin." By the next year he was firmly entrenched in the antifascist movement in Italy, as head of the local branch of Carlo Rosselli's Giustizia e Libertà. Several years later, in 1935, after having been arrested by the fascist authorities, Levi was sent to southern Italy, to Lucania (now called Basilicata), for political confinement. After repeated requests were made of him, Levi decided to practice medicine again, and he continued painting and writing. He was freed in 1936 after a general amnesty following a victory of the Italian forces in Ethiopia. In 1939, because of severe racial laws, he left Italy for Paris. He returned to Italy in 1942 and was an active partisan during World War II. He was subsequently arrested and freed in 1943.

Levi then went into hiding, during which time he wrote CHRIST STOPPED AT EBOLI (*Cristo si è fermato a Eboli*), drawing on his notes, poems, drawings, and paintings. This book, first published in 1947, has been translated into more than 20 languages. The memoir-novel won an important literary prize and launched Levi's fame in Italy. It is a stupendous and humane account of his time in Lucania, in the town of Aliano (which he renamed Gagliano). Part anthropological survey, part sociological study, part political theorizing, and part poetic narrative, the work describes inimitably the culture of Gagliano and the timelessness in which the populace lives. In Levi's narrative, Christ stops at Eboli, never going further south, where the majority of the citizens do not believe in Christianity but are pagans. The people exist in a world inside another world (Italy).

In 1944–46, Levi was editor of two different journals, one antifascist, and the other left-wing. In 1946 he published an earlier work he had written, entitled *Fear of Liberty* (*Paura della libertà*), containing his thoughts on the relationship between politics, culture, and the sacred. In 1948 he published *Watch* (*L'orologio*). This is a historical novel set between Rome and Naples immediately after the Second World War. Levi formulates his distinction between the *contadini*—the minority of people, belonging to every social group and profession, who contribute to the construction of a democratic nation—and the *luigini,* named after the corrupt fascist podesta (magistrate) in *Christ Stopped at Eboli,* the majority of people who are parasitic, living off the work of others. The revolution Levi held so much hope for, as he realized, was betrayed.

In 1954 Levi, who considered himself first and foremost a painter, not a writer, had an entire room of his paintings shown at the prestigious Venice Biennale. The next year he wrote *Words are Stones* (*Le Parole sono pietre*), winner of the Viareggio Prize. This nonfiction book consists of descriptions of three trips Levi made to Sicily and focuses on the lower classes and the battle of the peasants for land and rights. Levi speaks of a courageous union leader killed by the Mafia, turning him into a hero. In 1956, after a trip to Russia, he wrote *The Future Has an Ancient Heart* (*Il Futuro ha un cuore antico*). Here Levi recounts his trip and the generally positive impression he received of the mixture of economic classes. In 1959 he wrote *The Linden Trees* (*Doppia notte dei tigli*), in which he criticizes the governments of both West and East Berlin.

In 1963 Levi was elected an independent senator on the Communist ticket. He was reelected once and then lost his seat. Most important, however, he chose to represent Lucania (Aliano), keeping a promise he had made to the peasants there in 1935. In 1964 he wrote *Tutto il miele è finito,* a lyrical account of the poor in Sardinia and their contrast between the archaic and the modern, a theme that fascinated him. In the last years of his life, almost completely blind and gravely ill, he managed to write down some memories of his childhood, and even draw and paint. He died in January 1975 and was buried at the location of his choice: Aliano.

BIBLIOGRAPHY

Brand, Peter, and Lino Pertile, eds. *Cambridge History of Italian Literature.* Rev. ed. Cambridge: Cambridge University Press, 2000.

Levi, Carlo. *The Linden Trees.* Translated by Joseph M. Bernstein. New York: Knopf, 1962.

———. *Words Are Stones: Impressions of Sicily.* Translated by Antony Shugaar. Hesperus, 2005.

Ward, David. *Antifascisms: Cultural Politics in Italy, 1943–1946: Benedetto Croce and the Liberals, Carlo Levi and the "Actionists."* Madison, N.J.: Fairleigh Dickinson University Press, 1996.

Jacob Blakesley

LEVI, PRIMO (1919–1987) *Italian novelist, short story writer*

Primo Levi was born in Turin, Italy, in 1919, into a middle-class Jewish family. He lived there all of his life except for 1944–45, when he was captured, sent to Auschwitz, and later freed. He is known primarily as the writer of books that have deeply and irrevocably marked the human conscience: *If This Is a Man* (*Se questo è un uomo*), and *The Drowned and the Saved* (*I Sommersi e i salvati*).

In 1941 Levi graduated from the University of Turin with a degree in chemistry. He began working as a chemist shortly thereafter, until in late 1943 he joined the resistance against the fascists. Soon betrayed and captured, he declared himself a Jew (rather than a partisan) and was sent to Auschwitz. He remained in Auschwitz for 11 months, and after the camp was freed, he began a circuitous trip home.

Levi quickly wrote *If This Is a Man,* which was published in 1947 by a small Italian press and then in 1956 by Einaudi, at which point Levi's rise to fame began. As the author noted, *If This Is a Man* was not specifically written to formulate accusations (though it does accuse): It was written in the spirit of a "concise investigation of some aspects of the human character." There is no other book quite like it, given its high moral seriousness, its complete lack of presumptuousness, and its earnest attempt to comprehend the human soul in terrestrial hell. Indeed, Levi based part of the book on the structure of Dante's *Inferno;* in fact, one of the most moving passages depicts Levi speaking to his friend Jean about Ulysses in the *Inferno.* The character Levi has to translate Dante into French, reciting from an imperfect memory. Yet no language barrier resists the verses of Dante: "Consider your origins: / You were not made to live like brutes / But to follow virtue and knowledge." After this brief interlude, Levi and Jean are once more drowned, like Ulysses: "Finally the sea was closed above us."

During the following years (and until the end of his life) Levi gave hundreds of presentations at schools and other locations about his experience in the concentration camp, trying to explain to others and himself how such horror could have occurred in an apparently civilized world. As he insisted, his survival was not due to his goodness, but to chance—and to his knowledge (however rudimentary) of German, which many Italians fatally did not have.

In 1963 Levi wrote *The Truce* (*La tregua*), an account of his long journey home from Auschwitz. After this, he said he would write no more about the concentration camps. His prose is significantly humorous, a departure from all his previous writing. For this book he won the Campiello Prize for Literature.

Levi's next two books, *Storie naturali* (*Natural Stories,* 1967) and *Vizio di forma* (1971), are collections of science-fiction stories, begun in 1946. The first collection was published under a pseudonym (Damiano Malabaila) and won the Bagutta Prize for Literature. Levi thought of them as "dressed-up moral tales." In 1975 he published *The Periodic Table* (*Il Sistema periodico*), an intriguing and fascinating sort of autobiography told in 21 chapters, each dedicated to a single chemical element. His love of science shines through, as does his devotion to reason and analysis.

Levi's next work, the novel *The Monkey's Wrench* (*La Chiave a stella,* 1978), tells the story of a Turinese mechanic named Faussone. Written in a mixture of Italian and Piedmontese dialect, the book incorporates Levi's specific positive vision of work. For Levi, work is important precisely because it gives an end and meaning to one's life: It provides structure and gives responsibility. This is clearly distinguished from the useless work one was forced to do in Auschwitz and elsewhere. *The Monkey's Wrench* won the prestigious Premio Strega.

In 1981 Levi composed an anthology of favorite texts, entitled *The Search for Roots* (*La Ricerca delle radici*), ranging from his favorite chemistry textbook to *Moby-Dick*. In 1982 he published IF NOT NOW, WHEN? (*Se non ora, quando?*). A story of Jewish partisans set in World War II, this novel won two literary prizes. In 1984 Levi published a book of poems, *At an Uncertain Hour* (*Ad un'ora incerta*); some of its verses are regularly anthologized.

Levi's next book—*Other People's Trades* (*L'Altrui mestiere*, 1985)—is a collection of articles about various topics, showing what ITALO CALVINO called his "encyclopedic curiosity." Indeed, Levi was a wide reader in many disciplines. The book opens with a passage from the Book of Job, which, according to Levi, includes all the questions to which humanity has not and will not find an answer. Above all, the perpetual demand of justice will never find an adequate response.

In 1986 Levi published his final book: *The Drowned and the Saved*. He returned to the subject of Auschwitz in a series of profound reflections on the notion of guilt (the "gray zone"), shame, and useless violence at Auschwitz. The book concludes with letters from Germans and Levi's measured response to them. The epigraph to the book is from Coleridge (and thus ties together with Levi's *At an Uncertain Hour*): "Since then, at an uncertain hour, / That agony returns: / And till my ghastly tale is told / This heart within me burns." Levi additionally quotes Jean Amery, the Austrian philosopher: "Who is tortured will always remain tortured." This was true for Levi as well: Ill and depressed, he committed suicide in 1987.

BIBLIOGRAPHY

Angier, Carole. *The Double Bond: Primo Levi—A Biography.* New York: Farrar, Straus and Giroux, 2002.

Anissimov, Miriam. *Primo Levi: Tragedy of an Optimist.* Translated by Steve Cox. London: Aurum Press, 1998.

Levi, Primo. *The Drowned and the Saved.* Translated by Raymond Rosenthal. New York: Vintage, 1989.

———. *Survival in Auschwitz: The Nazi Assault on Humanity.* Translated by Stuart Woolf. New York: Collier, 1993.

———. *The Voice of Memory: Interviews 1961–1987.* Translated by Robert Gordon. New York: New Press, 2002.

Jacob D. Blakesley

LIKE WATER FOR CHOCOLATE (*COMO AGUA PARA CHOCOLATE*) LAURA ESQUIVEL (1989)

Mexican writer LAURA ESQUIVEL (1950–   ) wrote *Like Water for Chocolate: A Novel in Monthly Installments with Recipes, Romances, and Home Remedies* as an extraordinary tale of the unique relationship between the magic of love and the sensuality of food. Actual cooking recipes abound in the novel as epigraphs to introduce chapters. Her unique admixture of physical passion and flavorful sustenance is cast in the hyperbolic style of magic realism. *Like Water for Chocolate*'s colorful union of realism and fantasy make the novel a tour de force as Esquivel's extremely sensual language reaches a highly descriptive plane. Brewing and boiling like an incredible spicy bouillabaisse, it carries the reader through an enchantingly entertaining journey that is compelling and innovative.

Esquivel first wrote *Like Water for Chocolate* as a screenplay; however, when she was unable to get it produced, she reshaped the story into a novel, which was published in 1989 in Spanish and then translated into English two years later. The novel quickly became an international best seller and gained critical acclaim the world over for its innovative structure and style.

Much of Esquivel's writing is identified as partaking of the genre of *magic realism,* a term first used in 1925 by Franz Roh when describing a "quasi-surrealistic work of a group of German painters in the 1920s." Magic realism came into its own in literature in the latter part of the 20th century. In *Like Water for Chocolate,* scenes of magic realism include Esquivel's description of the house in which the protagonist Tita lives. This house, always bursting with the preparation of wonderful tasty delights, belies the constant undercurrent of passions and descriptive catastrophic occurrences in the lives of the author's characters. Esquivel has maintained that "all objects have consciousness." Other Latin American writers engaged in magic realism include short story writer Jorge Luis Borjes and novelist GABRIEL GARCÍA MÁRQUEZ.

Beginning in the late 19th century and continuing through the Mexican revolution that began in 1910, the story of *Like Water for Chocolate* takes place on a ranch in Coahuila, located on the border between the United States and Mexico. The story is told in the first person by a young woman whose great aunt is Tita, a main character in the work. The title of the novel refers to the process of boiling water for hot chocolate, and "when someone is about to explode, we say that person is 'like water for chocolate,'" explains scholar Claudia Loewenstein in her interview with Esquivel published in *Southwest Review*. Fittingly, Esquivel's romance tells the story of two characters, Tita and Pedro, whose passion is so strong that they are about to explode.

Even though they are in love, these two young star-crossed lovers cannot marry. According to her mother, Mama Elena, because she is the youngest of three daughters, Tita must remain single and care for her widowed mother. In despair, Pedro chooses to marry Rosaura, Tita's older sister, so that he can at least live near his true love. Esquivel shows the tension of this triangle through magical elements, as evident in the wedding scene. Besides having to watch her sister marry her one true love, Tita must also bake their wedding cake. Her tears and sorrow become part of the cake as she cooks it, and when people eat it at the wedding, they consume not just the cake but Tita's pain.

The 12 chapters of the novel correspond to 12 months in a year, and each chapter begins with a recipe that relates to the plot. Some critics have pointed out that many readers enjoy the novel as a romance, while other readers may find the work more of a parody of what Maria Elena de Valdes explains as "the Mexican version of women's fiction published in monthly installments together with recipes, home remedies, dressmaking patterns, short poems, moral exhortations, ideas on home decoration, and the calendar of church observances." Also, exaggeration in the book suggests a playful twist on traditional romance: Tita's sister Rosaura suffers a smelly death due to excess flatulence. Pedro, the hero, has a stroke during an intense sexual climax, and Tita decides to kill herself by swallowing a box of matches, with bursting flames devouring both Tita and Pedro. The scholar Dianna C. Niebylski cautions the reader from attaching a sentimental or romantic view to the novel: "What is so romantic about an ending where practically everything in the novel is burned to a crisp?" However, Esquivel resists calling the novel a parody.

Parody or not, Esquivel's novel challenges patriarchy and celebrates the domestic sphere of the kitchen. Mama Elena, a strong leader of the family, shows little compassion toward Tita's situation. One reason to explain her harshness is that she loves someone outside tradition, suffers a broken heart, and spends the rest of her life obeying and enforcing tradition. Esquivel comments that she sees "the mother as being equal to the masculine world and masculine repression, not feminine. Mama Elena is the one who wants to impose norms and a certain social organization," according to Loewenstein. And like her mother, Rosaura does not challenge convention and follows family and cultural tradition. Other women in the novel make different choices. Gertrudis shows one version of feminism when she leaves home and joins the revolution and becomes a general. Esperanza, part of the next generation, goes to the university. Tita pursues her romance with Pedro to its fiery end.

BIBLIOGRAPHY

Barbas-Rhoden, Laura. *Writing Women in Central America: Gender and the Fictionalization of History*. Athens: Ohio University Press, 2003.
Beer, Gabriella de. *Contemporary Mexican Women Writers*. Austin: University of Texas Press, 1996.
Colchie, Thomas. *A Whistler in the Nightworld: Short Fiction from the Latin Americas*. New York: Plume, 2002.
Esquivel, Laura. *Like Water for Chocolate*. Translated by Carol Christensen and Thomas Christensen. New York: Doubleday, 1992.
———. *Malinche*. Translated by Ernesto Mestre-Reed. New York: Atria Books, 2006.
———. *Swift as Desire*. New York: Crown Publishers, 2001.
Niebylski, Diana C. *Humoring Resistance: Laughter and the Excessive Body in Latin America Women's Fiction*. Albany: State University of New York Press, 2004.

Glenn Hutchinson
Linda Loya

LISPECTOR, CLARICE (1920–1977) *Brazilian essayist, novelist, short story writer* The extraordinary talent of the Brazilian writer Clarice Lispector remains an indelible part of that country's lit-

erary legacy. Her contribution to the Portuguese language in the way of fiction and nonfiction has been described by Portuguese writer Fernando Pessoa to be "as significant as that of author Guimarães Rosa." The critic and writer Benedito Nunes has remarked, "The development of certain important themes in the fiction of Clarice Lispector belongs in the context of the philosophy of existence, composed of doctrines which, although differing in their conclusions, have the same starting point: the Kierkegaardian intuition of the pre-reflexive, individual and dramatic character of human existence. It deals with issues such as angst, nothing, failure, language, communication between consciousness, some of which traditional philosophy had ignored or relegated to a second plane."

Clarice Lispector was born on December 10, 1920, in Tchechelnik, a remote village in Ukraine, to Pedro and Marietta Lispector. Her early years were marked with many turbulent upheavals and changes. In early 1921 the family of five (including two other daughters) moved from Ukraine to Maceió, capital of the state of Alagoas, Brazil. Brazilian Portuguese consequently became Lispector's native language. In 1928, when the young Clarice was eight years old, her mother died. Several years later her father moved the family to Rio de Janeiro, where he died in 1940.

Following her father's death, Lispector started work as a journalist for the Brazilian News Agency (Agência Nacional) and the newspaper *The Night* (*A noite*). This was the period of the Estado Novo, or New State, under the presidency of Getúlio Vargas. In 1943 Lispector graduated from college and married Maury Gurgel Valente. Her husband soon joined the Brazilian Diplomatic Corps and entered a career in diplomacy that forced Clarice to leave Brazil for extended periods.

Lispector published her first novel, *Close to the Wild Heart* (*Perto do coração selvagem*) in 1944. This brilliant work, filled with passionate ideas and descriptions of the challenges of modernism's perplexity, reveals the carefully wrought style that would reemerge throughout Lispector's writing. The work was awarded the Graça Aranha Prize by the Brazilian Academy of Letters. Later in 1944, Lispector and her husband moved to Europe.

The postwar years proved productive for Lispector's writing. Her work *The Lamp* (*O lustre*) was published in 1946, and *The Besieged Town* (*A cidade sitiada*) was completed in 1949. After traveling and living in Italy, England, and other European destinations, Lispector moved to Washington, D.C., with her family in the early 1950s. Her second son, Paulo, was born in the United States. Despite absences from her South American homeland, she remained a constant figure of national interest and importance there. Abroad, her reputation was gaining interest, and the famous Italian artist De Chirico painted her portrait.

The decades of the 1950s and 1960s proved very successful for the author. The first French edition of *Close to the Wild Heart* was published by Editions Plon in 1954, with a cover designed by the famous avant-garde artist Henri Matisse. In 1956 Lispector completed *The Apple in the Dark* (*A maçã no escuro*), a modern novel that probes such metaphysical questions as existence, language as it constructs reality, and the plague of uncertainty. Her work, unlike that of Samuel Beckett and other late modernists, offers affirmation that answers are possible.

The year 1960 saw the publication of Lispector's short story collection *Family Ties* (*Laços de família*). In 1961 her novel *A Maçã no Escuro* (*The Apple in the Dark*) was published, and her second collection of short stories, *The Foreign Legion* (*A Legião Estrangeira*), was published to great acclaim in 1964.

Lispector remained active as a writer during the 1970s. In 1977, months before her death, she received the Fundação Cultural do Distrito Federal prize (Federal District Cultural Foundation) for her life's work. Clarice Lispector died of cancer in Rio de Janeiro on December 9, 1977. Following her death, many of the books that now comprise her complete oeuvre were published posthumously. Three works that were brought out in the year following her death include *A Breath of Life* (*Um sopro de vida*), *Pulsations* (*Pulsações*), and *Not to Be Forgotten* (*Para não esquecer*), the latter a compilation of short stories. Other compilations of her short stories followed in the 1980s, as interest in the author and her writings continued. Maria Consuelo Campos, writer and scholar, once remarked about Lispector's literary achievement in the modernist movement: "There is a Brazilian literature B.C. (before Clarice) and another A.C. (after Clarice)." Hélène Cixious in *The Hour of Clarice Lispector* remarks: "Clarice represents an inimitable turning point in Brazilian literature. What she does, in an original and inaugural manner, is to create moments of illumination and revelation. Using a word so dear to Joyce and to Clarice, she creates an epiphany."

BIBLIOGRAPHY

Alonso, Claudia Pazos, and Claire Williams, eds. *Closer to the Wild Heart: Essays on Clarice Lispector.* Oxford: Legenda, European Humanities Research Centre, 2002.

Brasil, Assis. *Clarice Lispector.* Rio de Janeiro: Organização, 1969.

Cixous, Hélène. *Reading with Clarice Lispector.* Minneapolis: University of Minnesota Press, 1990.

Fitz, Earl E. *Clarice Lispector.* Boston: Twayne Publishers, 1985.

Peixoto, Marta. *Passionate Fictions: Gender, Narrative, and Violence in Clarice Lispector.* Minneapolis: University of Minnesota Press, 1994.

Santos, Cristina. *Bending the Rules in the Quest for an Authentic Female Identity: Clarice Lispector and Carmen Boullosa.* New York: P. Lang, 2004.

Michael D. Sollars

LITTLE BALL LAUNCHED BY A DWARF, A (NANGAENGYEEGA SSOAOLLIN JAGEUN GONG) CHO SE-HEE (1979)

A Little Ball Launched by a Dwarf (Nangaengyeega ssoaollin jageun gong), by Korean author CHO SE-HEE (1942–   ) is a collection of 12 sequential stories, including such diverse titles as "Knifeblade," "Moebius Strip," "A Little Ball Launched by a Dwarf," "Spaceship," "On the Footbridge," "The Cost of Living," "Mr. Klein's Bottle," "God Is Guilty Too," and "Spinyfish Headed for My Net." This collection of interrelated stories challenges and redefines the limits of the novel. The work was translated into English in 2002. With great use of irony, these stories manifest Cho's sharp criticism of the modern democratic and capitalistic society, an economic system in which the have-nots are structurally destined to be ruled, exploited, and defeated.

The title story follows the frustration and anger of a dwarf's family in the 1970s. The father, named Kim Bool-yee, is a 46-inch, 70-pound dwarf who has been trying to make a living doing all sorts of manual labor and currently works as a plumber. The mother works at a printing factory, and two sons, Young-su and Young-ho, who were once honor students, have quit their school and now work at the factory to ease their parents' financial burden. The daughter, Young-hee, is very pretty and devoted to her parents and brothers. This poor but loving family of five have managed to live in a humble shanty in a slum area of Seoul named Haengbok (Happiness)-dong and Nahkwon (Paradise)-ku. These overstated names poignantly suggest not only the hellish struggle that the family members have to wage in order to survive but also the tragic ending they will suffer in return for their efforts to be happy. The story is narrated by the three siblings, Young-su, Young-ho, and Young-hee, and each brings social charges against inhumane, capital-oriented rich land developers and speculators, incorporating intellectual, humanist, and feminist point of views.

In the first part, Young-su presents the government's inhumane, cruel treatment, which drives out the poor and powerless from their homes with a disguised policy of improving the slum area with a new housing project. One day his family receives a demolition notice from the government, though they are also given a ballot for a new apartment house that will be built in the same slum area. Most of shanty residents in Haengbok-dong, however, decide to sell their rights to rich land speculators and move to a less-expensive area called Seongnam because they cannot afford the new apartment expenses. Young-su's family also decide to sell their right, but his father Kim Bool-yee and sister Young-hee have a hard time digesting the shock that they have to leave their home and start their lives all over in a strange place. In particular, Kim Bool-yee, who has long been depressed by the guilt of not supporting his family due to his weak health, finally becomes deranged and disappears: He has been talking of becoming a circus hand like his friend, and when he hears the family's decision to move, he decides to search for a circus company to make his fortune. Young-hee, who wants her family to live in the new apartment house instead, goes to the rich land speculator who bought her family's ballot, without telling her family. Unable to find his father and sister, Young-su and the rest of the family finally move to Seongnam and start their illegal residence there.

In the second part, Young-ho tells the tragic story of his family after the move. His father, Kim Bool-yee, falls off the roof of a brick-making factory; the accident happens while he is trying to shoot a small iron ball on a paper plane toward the moon. Young-ho's mother, after her husband's death, tries to make a living but becomes depressed by the prospect that they will never get out of the cycle of poverty and suffering. Young-ho's older brother, working at a printing house, joins the labor union but is accused of being a communist and beaten harshly by the managers. His girlfriend, Myong-hee, who became a caddy at a golf course, is raped and commits suicide. Young-ho, watching his unfortunate mother and brother, decides to stick to his underpaid job at a small electricity shop and becomes the family's most substantial supporter.

In the third part, Young-hee, who had gone to the rich land speculator and became his secretary and lover, finally retrieves her family's ballot for the new apartment house. She then runs away from the man she has hated and returns to her shanty house with a fully paid contract for the new apartment. However, despite her self-sacrificing efforts for her family, she learns from a neighbor that her father has died and the rest of her family has moved elsewhere. Shocked and frustrated, she faints and falls into a deep sleep. In her dream, she meets her brother and cries: "Kill the villains who call my dad a dwarf!" There the sequence of stories forming a novel ends.

This heart-wrenching story of the poor family of a dwarf has resonated in Korean society since its publication. Kim Bool-yee starts to lose his mind after he hears from a neighbor that if someone works hard, abides the law, prays faithfully, and still finds an unfortunate life, he should leave this dead, indifferent world and move to the moon. Taking these words literally, he begins to dream of life on the moon, and whenever something goes wrong, he goes outside and shoots a small iron ball high into the air. Even though he sees all of his balls fall back to the earth, he keeps shooting and dreaming. One day he climbs up on the chimney of the factory where he had once worked in order to stand closer to the moon. There he makes a last but his most passionate try to launch his dream up to the moon, but this time, like all of his past iron balls, he falls down to the earth—and dies.

Perhaps the dwarf's wish to live in a place where he is not discriminated against gets justly rewarded. However, the fact that his small, ordinary dream is presented as something impossible to realize on the planet Earth, and possible only on the distant moon, poignantly suggests the deteriorating living conditions of the poor, powerless people in 1970s Korean society. The author Cho wanted to give a warning sign to his society: The story of the dwarf Kim Bool-yee remains a sad portrait of those countless poor urban laborers whose dream of educating their children and living a happy life with their family members continues to be dwarfed if not totally eclipsed by the rich and powerful.

BIBLIOGRAPHY

Choi Gap-jin. "A Study of Hwang Suhk-young and Cho Se-hee." *Woorimalgeul* 24 (Winter 2002): 149–164.

Kim Woo-chang. "History and Human Reason: Twenty-five Years Since Cho Se-hee's *A Little Ball Launched by a Dwarf*." *Dongnam Uhmunnonjip* 7 (1997): 51–76.

"On Cho Se-hee." *Jakgasehgye* (special edition) 7 (1990).

Shin Myung-jik. *The Dream of Impossible Subversion.* Seoul: Shiinsa, 2002.

Yee Kyong-ho. "Interview with Cho Se-hee." *Jakgasehgye* 54 (Autumn 2002): 18–35.

Jihee Han

LITTLE PRINCE, THE (LE PETIT PRINCE)

ANTOINE DE SAINT-EXUPÉRY (1943)   This last novel by the popular French writer ANTOINE DE SAINT-EXUPÉRY (1900–44) is ostensibly a children's book, set in the author's familiar and cherished landscape of the Sahara of northern Africa. Although the central character is a pilot, this tale has little to do with actual flight; the storytelling of *The Little Prince* is far removed from the quasi-biographical and autobiographical musings of the author's earlier works that often deal with an airplane pilot's exploits. These earlier works include *NIGHT FLIGHT* (*Vol de nuit,* 1931) and *SOUTHERN MAIL* (*Courrier sud,* 1929). The pilot as narrator in *The Little Prince* does appear as he is forced to land in the desert, but this is where the biographical familiarity ends, for it is here that the protagonist encounters the eponymously small prince who tells wise and enchanting stories of other worlds that he has visited. The simple beauty of this charming parable has delighted adults and children alike over the many decades since it was written in the late years of World War II. In addition, Saint-Exupéry's own illustrations of *The Little Prince* have appeared on a plethora of merchandise, perpetuating the success of the novel and its author.

The book was dedicated to Leon Werth, Saint-Exupéry's closest friend, and more particularly to Werth when he was a child. The dedication states that Werth—unlike many adults—does in fact remember when he was a child. This assertion sets the tone for the tale proper, which ponders the loss of innocence in the world and rejoices in the simple joy and vast imagination that children possess. The narrator begins his story with a picture of a boa constrictor digesting an elephant, drawn when he was six years old; he relates to his readers the frustration he felt when the adults who viewed it thought it looked like a hat and therefore discouraged him drawing any further pictures. Disillusioned from his dream, the narrator becomes a pilot and remains distrustful of grown-ups; when he does meet any adults who appear clear-sighted, the pilot shows them his childhood drawing as a means of testing their true understanding, but unfortunately they always see a hat, and their lack of imagination and interest allows them to see no further.

The pilot is so truly disappointed by the other adults he meets that he chooses the solitary existence familiar to many of Saint-Exupéry's characters. He lives his life alone until he crashes his plane in the Sahara desert and meets a very serious and very small person. The little prince teaches the narrator to appreciate the beauty in life and the joy that is to be found in the mutual appreciation that one obtains from love and friendship. The little prince relates his adventures around numerous planets and his curious encounters with several adult characters, grown-ups who all occupy themselves with so-called matters of consequence, restricted by the ridiculous rules and regulations they impose upon themselves. Saint-Exupéry exposes the peculiarity of everyday adult activities through the man who drinks to forget that he is ashamed of drinking and the businessman who counts the stars so obsessively that he is barely aware of what it is he is counting. Once again, Saint-Exupéry urges his readers to find freedom from modern life and materialism and stresses the importance of a responsibility to something beyond ourselves, a duty to others, the value of living for the good of someone else, be that through friendship, love, or work; after all, "what is essential is invisible to the eye."

The narrator urges his readers not to read this book thoughtlessly, as he has experienced so much grief recording his memories; this perhaps is a little insight into the spirit in which Saint-Exupéry writes and wishes to be read. Certainly the personal nature of all his stories resonates clearly, and there is an intimacy in *The Little Prince* that inspires a feeling of conspiracy between the author and those to whom he relates the memories of his dear friend. The pilot laments his own growing up and his diminishing ability to see beyond the immediate, unlike his little prince, who can see the elephant inside the boa constrictor and the sheep inside the box.

BIBLIOGRAPHY

Des Vallières, Nathalie. *Saint Exupéry: Art, Writing and Musing.* Translated by Anthony Zielonka. New York: Rizzoli, 2004.

Higgins, James E. *The Little Prince: A Reverie of Substance.* New York: Twayne Publishers, 1996.

Saint Exupéry, Antoine de. *Wartime Writings, 1939–1944.* San Diego: HCJ, 1986.

Schiff, Stacy. *Saint Exupéry, A Biography.* New York: Knopf, 1994.

Webster, Paul. *Antoine de Saint Exupéry: The Life and Death of the Little Prince.* London: Macmillan, 1993.

Eadaoin Agnew

LOCAL ANAESTHETIC (ÖRTLICH BETÄUBT) GÜNTER GRASS (1969)

Eberhard Starusch has a number of problems: His teeth hurt, his dentist constantly quotes Seneca, and one of his students is trying to devise a dramatic protest against the Vietnam War. In this 1969 allegorical novel by the renowned German novelist GÜNTER GRASS (1927–), a middle-aged teacher in Berlin needs extensive dental work—a perennial motif in Grass's novels, signifying the "postwar moral decay of the German nation." *Local Anaesthetic,* told through the reminiscing and imagination of a teacher of German and history, is for the most part an inner monologue that is punctuated only occasionally by questions and commentary from the dentist. When his dentist places him in front of a television to distract him, Starusch projects his past and present onto the screen, resulting in a combination of reality, repressed memories, and fantasy that provide a mirror image of German history. At the same time that the television is functioning as a projection for Starusch's musings, it is also reporting current events. In this manner Grass intermingles Germany's Nazi past and the ensuing period under West German chancellor Konrad Adenauer, as well as the student movements of the 1960s and in particular the student revolts of 1968.

The current events become increasingly more pertinent for Starusch once his favorite student, Philipp Scherbaum, decides to protest the American napalming of the Vietnamese by burning his dog, Max, on the Kurfurstendamm, a popular shopping boulevard. By setting Max on fire, Scherbaum expects to shock Berliners out of their materialistic complacency. While he realizes that the awareness of human rights abuses taking place in Vietnam will not cause this realization to occur, sacrificing his dog will break through the people's complacency because, as Scherbaum notes, "Berliners love dogs more than anything else." Starusch knows from his own anarchistic days, however, that this reaction will get his student nowhere. Even the dentist notes that this event will simply offer a vicarious thrill equivalent to that of a Roman circus. In a discussion between Starusch and his dentist, the two agree that if one wants "to eliminate human failings . . . [one must] eliminate man."

In this work, the leftist students dismiss the older generation and anyone else who does not share their point of view. Ironically, they exhibit the same type of idealism, self-righteousness, and narrow-mindedness they criticize in their elders. Scherbaum seems to recognize this contradiction on some level as he notes that the protest culture, by using popular media such as posters and pop music, has no true impact but "only lulls people to sleep." Given this potential for a sedating effect, this protest culture runs the risk, as literary critic Cloe Paver notes, "of gratifying unconscious emotional needs instead of awakening critical faculties, and thus of becoming a substitute for action, rather than inspiring action." The fascinating and exciting allure of this movement as well as its potential to initiate a loss of restraint reminds Starusch of the heightened emotions that infected those caught up in the thrill of the Nazi rallies. It is particularly through the teacher Irmgard Seifert that Grass portrays the initial seductive quality of the Nazi assemblies, the ability to forget or repress this earlier fervor after the war, and finally the confronting of one's past and its accompanying shame that must be resolved.

Grass employs a course of dental treatment as a metaphor for political activism and protest. Activism, like a local anaesthetic, only works for a short amount of time. Unless the root problem is addressed and eliminated, the pain will always return. The healing is thus a process of self-discovery that Germany must undergo, and in so doing a *Vergangenheitsbewältigung*—a coming to terms with its past—must be endured in order to move into the future free of pain.

BIBLIOGRAPHY

Friedrichsmeyer, Erhard. "The Dogmatism of Pain: *Local Anaesthetic*." *Dimension* 36–49.

Paver, Cloe E. M. "Lois Lane, Donald Duck and Joan Baez: Popular Culture and Protest Culture in Günter Grass's *örtlich betäubt*." *German Life & Letters* 50, no. 1: 53–64.

Taberner, Stuart. "Feigning the Anaesthetisation of Literary Inventiveness: Günter Grass's *örtlich betäubt* and the Public Responsibility of the Politically Engaged Author." *Forum for Modern Languages* 34, no. 1: 69–81.

Stephanie E. Libbon

LOLITA Vladimir Nabokov (1955) The Russian-born novelist Vladimir Nabokov (1899–1977) wrote *Lolita,* his 12th published novel, between 1948 and 1953. *Lolita* is a reworking of an earlier version of the story *The Enchanter* (*Volshebnik*), written in 1939 in Paris. Writing the text on index cards, Nabokov worked on the novel in the time available to him when he was not teaching literature at Cornell and Harvard universities. He composed much of the novel in his and his wife Véra's aging Oldsmobile as they traveled the United States on summertime butterfly-gathering expeditions.

When the novel, which recounts a consummated love affair between a middle-aged college professor and a barely pubescent girl, was finished in 1953, it was rejected by American publishers because of its controversial subject matter. After Olympia Press published the novel in France in 1955, important critics such as Graham Greene hailed it as a masterpiece. When G. P. Putnam's Sons finally brought out *Lolita* in the United States in 1958, the novel became a best seller and allowed its author to retire from teaching to concentrate on writing. Today many critics recognize *Lolita* as one of the best novels of the 20th century and a foundational text of postmodernist metafiction.

Like Nabokov's earlier novels KING, QUEEN, KNAVE and *Laughter in the Dark, Lolita* tells the story of a love triangle. As the novel opens, Professor Humbert Humbert, a teacher and scholar of French literature, becomes a tenant in the home of a widow, Charlotte Haze, and her 12-year-old, barely pubescent, "nymphet" daughter, Lolita. Having been obsessed with nymphets from an early age, Humbert quickly develops a passion for Lolita, eventually marrying her mother so that he can be close to her. After Charlotte finds about his obsession for her daughter and dies in a freak automobile accident, Humbert becomes Lolita's guardian and attempts to control her through gifts, extended vacations throughout the United States, and parental decisions. For example, Humbert tries to prevent Lolita from dating boys her own age by enrolling her in an all-girls school. On their second vacation, Lolita escapes Humbert's control and runs away with Claire Quilty, who writes and directs *The Enchanted Hunters,* a school play in which Lolita appears. Humbert searches for Lolita for two years, finds her pregnant and poor, and murders Quilty for depriving him of the love of his life. Humbert is arrested for his crime, and the text of *Lolita* is his memoir of the events leading up to the murder.

Because Nabokov constructs *Lolita* as a memoir, he is able to use metafictional strategies to explore the relationship between art and truth. The fictional psychologist John Ray, Jr.'s "Foreword" precedes the memoir, highlighting Humbert's madness and acknowledging that many of the names in the text are pseudonyms, including "Humbert Humbert." Knowing at the outset that the text is the fictional construct of a madman, the reader recognizes the way in which human consciousness distorts events. Despite the reader's constant awareness that Humbert presents events in ways that make him look innocent, he or she is seduced by the text's wit and beauty, so that Humbert becomes a sympathetic character. In effecting this literary seduction, Nabokov places the reader in Lolita's position as an individual susceptible to Humbert's linguistic charms.

Nabokov also uses the theme of susceptibility to language to explore the relationship between art and power. Like Paduk, the insane dictator in Nabokov's anti-authoritarian novel *Bend Sinister* (1947), Humbert uses language as a means of attaining power. When he and Lolita begin living together after her mother Charlotte's death, Humbert makes many rules that deprive her of her freedom, the most important of which is his decision to send her to the school for girls. In aesthetically admiring Humbert's facility with language and not ethically evaluating his relationship with Lolita, the reader risks absolving the character of moral responsibility. One of Nabokov's great triumphs in the novel is the way in which he uses the tension between Humbert's aesthetic prowess and moral depravity to invoke an ethical response in the reader and make him or her evaluate the relationship between art and ethics.

Another of Nabokov's triumphs in *Lolita* is his extended meditation on the dangers of nostalgia. At the novel's outset, Humbert writes of his boyhood affair with a nymphet named, Annabel. When Humbert meets and seduces Lolita as a middle-aged man many years later, he attempts to relive an experience of childhood happiness. The violence and pedophilia that characterize the novel's action demonstrate Nabokov's contention that nostalgia can lead to unhappiness and destruction.

Lolita has twice been made into a major motion picture. Stanley Kubrick's version appeared in 1962, starring James Mason as Humbert, Sue Lyon as Lolita, and Peter Sellers as Quilty. In 1997 Adrian Lyne's *Lolita* came out, featuring Jeremy Irons as Humbert, Dominique Swain as Lolita, and Frank Langella as Quilty.

BIBLIOGRAPHY

Boyd, Brian. *Vladimir Nabokov: The American Years.* Princeton, N.J.: Princeton University Press, 1993.

Clegg, Christine, ed. *Vladimir Nabokov's Lolita: A Reader's Guide to Essential Criticism.* New York: Palgrave Macmillan, 2002.

Nabokov, Vladimir: *The Annotated* Lolita. Edited by Alfred Appel, Jr. New York: Vintage, 1991.

Nafisi, Azar. *Reading* Lolita *in Tehran: A Memoir in Books.* New York: Random House, 2003.

O'Rourke, James. *Sex, Lies, and Autobiography: The Ethics of Confession.* Charlottesville: University of Virginia Press, 2006.

Pifer, Ellen, ed. *Vladimir Nabokov's* Lolita: *A Casebook.* New York: Oxford University Press, 2002.

Paul Gleason

LOVE IN THE TIME OF CHOLERA (EL AMOR EN LOS TIEMPOS DEL CÓLERA)

GABRIEL GARCÍA MÁRQUEZ (1985)   *Love in the Time of Cholera* appeared eight years after the extraordinary ONE HUNDRED YEARS OF SOLITUDE and three years after the author GABRIEL GARCÍA MÁRQUEZ (1928–   ) received the 1982 Nobel Prize in literature. Less magical but no less inventive than the earlier blockbuster work, *Love in the Time of Cholera* is, nevertheless, a major work by a mature artist at the peak of his narrative powers; it is a resplendent narrative that in its own way illuminates the scope of fiction and the form of the modern novel.

Love in the Time of Cholera is, first of all, an old-fashioned love story about love lost and love regained. It is also an anatomy of love and a compendium of the multiple varieties and manifestations of love: young love, old love, lustful love, platonic love, conjugal love, redemptive love; love as affliction, love as therapy, and love as a hedge against mortality. It is, in addition, a treatise on the inexorable passage of time, a labyrinthine study of memory and experience and a meditation on age and death. The story takes place between 1880 and 1930 in an unnamed Caribbean seaport city, a composite of Cartagena and Barranquilla, within the well-known fictional universe of García Márquez. The location is both exotic and familiar, a new-world postcolonial outpost subject to the flow of the river Magdalena and the intermittent bouts of pestilence and war. The era is the end of the 19th century and the beginning of the 20th, a time that is violent, full of discoveries, inventions, and concerted attempts to apply science and technology to a primeval world resistant to progress.

The plot is structured in blocks, beginning at the end with a death and then flashing back 50 years to the beginning of love in a previous century. The book follows the parallel lives of Florentino Ariza, Fermina Daza, and Juvenal Urbino through the disparate stages of love—infatuation, lust, and love, young and mature, carnal, conjugal, and transcendent. As an adolescent, Florentino Ariza falls in love with Fermina Daza, who, in spite of flowers and poetry, rejects him and marries Dr. Juvenal Urbino. Florentino, the consummate romantic, is undaunted; he pledges constancy and heartfelt loyalty, if not corporeal fidelity. During a long career of liaisons, seductions, and work for the River Company, Florentino persists in his unquenchable hope for life

with Fermina. Juvenal Urbino, an eminent doctor, civic leader, and staunch Catholic, dedicates his life to eradicating cholera by introducing modern science to putrid swamp areas. He and Fermina Daza are almost inseparable through a 50-year marriage, devoid of great matrimonial catastrophes but full of trivial everyday miseries.

The first chapter follows the course of Dr. Urbino's last day of life. The illustrious physician, still active at 80 years old, attends to the death of a friend and contemplates his own mortality, celebrates the anniversary of a colleague, and finally climbs a ladder trying to coach his loquacious parrot out of a mango tree, unsuccessfully, and dies. Arriving at the house to pay his respects to the deceased, Florentino Ariza expresses his vow of eternal fidelity and everlasting love to Fermina, but the elderly widow, in an act of rage, rejects him again.

Fermina Daza, much aged but still almond-eyed and naturally haughty, realizes that she has chosen one man over the other as much out of fear and whim as reason or attraction. She has achieved security, relative harmony, and conjugal happiness as wife of one man, and in old age she is astonished that she has remained the love object of the other. In spite of age, societal mores, infirmity, and incredulity, Florentino Ariza and Fermina Daza have a last chapter in a riverboat together, alone under the cholera flag. The events in *Love in the Time of Cholera* are typical and ordinary, but they are narrated with such exuberantly rich detail that they become curiously and ironically recognizable and archetypal.

Setting and plot notwithstanding, this novel is rich with language—the prodigious use of language, the fluidity and evocative power of language. The chronology—1880s–1930s—and the geography—a town in the Caribbean Colombia of Latin America—are both specific, yet the treatment of topic and theme is both timely and timeless. Just as Gustave Flaubert a century earlier created the magnificently realistic novel *Madame Bovary* out of the discards and detritus of romantic illusion, marital mismatch, and adultery, García Márquez creates a postmodern though realistic novel about the most clichéd subject of all—love. He does this by the judicious choice of the right word—the *mot juste*—and by parodying the various literary forms used to dramatize and illuminate the vicissitudes and the manifestations of love. The episodes of the complex lives of Florentino Ariza, Fermina Daza, and Juvenal Urbino, together and apart, are narrated with generous humor, skepticism, and mercy, in a panoply of love genres. These include romance (love letters, assignations, flowers, tokens, refusals, suffering); erotica (the 622 affaires as well as countless fleeting adventures of just one character); comedy of manners ("the daily incomprehension, the instantaneous hatred, the reciprocal nastiness, and the fabulous flashes of glory in the conjugal conspiracy"); soap opera; and even the improvisational, and often ridiculous, commedia dell'arte.

The *cólera* of the Spanish title is cholera, a disease that sweeps through in terrible intermittent epidemics caused by contaminated drinking water or untreated sewage. It is a fact of life in the time of the story and always portent of death. *Cólera,* in Spanish, is also defined as choler, anger, ire, and violence. In the novel, the symptoms of cholera are said to be identical to those of love. The defense against cholera is hygiene, science, and work; the reaction to an outbreak, at least at the time of the story, is isolation and quarantine. In *Love in the Time of Cholera,* cholera as affliction and illness is emblematic of a time when outbreaks were devastating because there was no effective treatment. Cholera also applies to the places in Latin America that suffer regularly the carnage of civil wars and the cruelty of oppression. Cholera is allied to love in that both afflictions can be virulent and resistant to effective treatment or cure; cholera, like primordial passion, is as difficult to control as the flow of the river or the rage of blood.

The novel carries us through half a century in words stately and colonial, through the advances and progress in long pastoral phrases, and through the river voyages in terms rhythmic and flowing. The novel is a journey which gives the reader a shining vision of a hopeful world, although as Florentino comes to learn, "nobody teaches life anything."

BIBLIOGRAPHY

Bloom, Harold, ed. *Gabriel García Márquez.* New York: Chelsea House, 1989.

Janes, Regina. *Gabriel García Márquez: Revolutions in Wonderland.* Columbia: University of Missouri Press, 1981.

Kakutani, Michiko. "'Garcia Marquez Novel Covers Love and Time': A Review of Gabriel García Márquez's *Love in the Time of Cholera.*" New York Times, 6 April 1988, p. C21.

McGuirk, Bernard, and Richard Cardwell, eds. *Gabriel García Marquez: New Readings.* Cambridge: Cambridge University Press, 1987.

Pynchon, Thomas. "'The Heart's Eternal Vow': A Review of Gabriel García Márquez's *Love in the Time of Cholera.*" New York Times, 10 April 1988, pp. 442–445.

Arbolina Llamas Jennings

LOVER, THE (*L'AMANT*) MARGUERITE DURAS (1986)

The novelistic memoir *The Lover* by MARGUERITE DURAS (1914–96) is a modernist story of sexual coming of age in French colonial Vietnam. It is also a portrait of the young author. It is the most accessible and by far the most popular of Duras's works, not the least because its interracial eroticism and exotic locale lent itself to film (director Jean-Jacques Annaud's movie version appeared in 1992). Yet it retains traces of the postmodern fiction and screenplays that have been the basis of Duras's critical reputation. (Her screenplay for Alain Resnais's *Hiroshima, Mon Amour* might be usefully contrasted with *The Lover,* since it is an avant-garde evocation of much the same kind of sexual relationship.)

In adherence to the modernist paradigm, Duras's young girl finds herself in conflict with the petty pretensions and narrow ambitions of her lower-middle-class family. Typical of such portraits, she is precociously mature and self-assertively willful in her hunger for experience, yet she is also hypersensitive, moody, and prone to brooding on self-destruction as a means of releasing herself from the tensions of desires that cannot be satisfied. Unlike Duras's enigmatic postmodern fictions, in which disembodied voices are overheard referring in fragmentary speeches to possibly sinister actions in an obscure past, *The Lover* provides the semblance of psychological interiority, which serves to provide partial motivation for the transgressive activities that reflect, and further affect, the girl's alienation from family and community. Like many modernist narratives, it describes a flirtation with abjection and madness in the course of tracking a self-awareness so intense that it produces a yearning for the oblivion of death. But because events are evoked in a sporadic manner—ostensibly as they return to memory—the relationships they might illuminate remain deliberately murky. That said, the narrator does not allow the reader to forget that memoirs are subject to more reconstructive shaping than other forms of fiction. For this reason, many of the implications of the book emerge out of the dialectic of disjunction and continuity as the mature narrator remembers the girl who lived the experiences.

The narrator refers to the younger self she is evoking in her memoir as "the child who crossed the river." This is literal inasmuch as the girl's liaison with her Chinese lover necessitates crossing a geographical boundary marking racial and cultural difference. But by speaking of *the* girl and *the* river, Duras bestows a mythical, if not allegorical, status on each. The girl becomes an archetype in the archetypal act of crossing or transgressing a boundary that is itself an age-old symbol of time.

At the level of the plot, the crossing constitutes the initiation of sexual life, which, because it requires a crossing of the color line, also constitutes an embrace of the expansive world of otherness that forever cuts the girl off from the circumscribed world of conventional behavior and frames of reference. But the act of crossing the river must also be read as the very act that led the mature woman to be able to write the memoir. That is, the act of crossing the river expresses in symbolic terms the idea of a crucial existential act of self-definition, whose full import could not be known at the time. The girl returns across the river when she abandons her lover; but in a sense the narrator is the one who crosses the same river twice by going back to retrieve the feelings, thoughts, and actions of her younger self. Only the retrospective gaze of the mature author can fully appreciate the transgressive traversal of demarcations as a metaphor for the necessary artistic, and prideful, defamiliarization of an all-too-familiar shame of family impoverishment.

Duras leans toward the manner of her postmodern fictions when she suggests that the attempt to trace the erotic impulse necessarily produces gaps and uncertainties in the narrative because the ambiguities of the impulse are ultimately inexpressible. Yet she also seems to suggest that the erotic desires of her 15-year-old girl originated less as a response to isolation than as an expression of deep antagonism toward her hapless mother that also involves shame, resentment, and desire for revenge. The girl's ambivalence and some-time antagonism toward her mother is linked to the latter's personality, which tacitly demands that the girl grow up. Her mother is said to be childish and even mad, possessing no awareness of what her manifest displays of "despair" produce in her children. Her mother's inability to cope with the demands of supporting her family is documented in the grotesque description of 600 chicks that her inept brooding had rendered deformed and incapable of receiving nourishment—a description that has metaphoric applicability to the emotionally maladjusted girl and her brothers.

The girl resents the mother for her persistent desire to "escape" from wherever she is, which the girl identifies as a manifestation of the desire to be released from the burden of her female child. She also resents her mother's bourgeois pretensions and ambitions because they, too, seem to reflect obsessive fantasies of escape. This resentment is exacerbated by the shame of abjection. The girl is ashamed of her family's déclassé condition, for which she holds her mother largely responsible. This shame is exacerbated by the mother and daughter's shared recognition that in Indochina Europeans are not supposed to be poor: "We were ashamed, we sold our furniture but . . . we had a houseboy and we ate."

But shame's self-loathing produces shamelessness, which is how pride displays its abjection. However much contempt the girl has for her mother's obsessions about escape, she also recognizes that she is motivated by much the same fantasy. The mature woman who narrates her younger self acknowledges that she too is someone who has always sought to leave. It was that impulse that had motivated the girl's taking a wealthy Chinese lover—that and "a sort of obligation." The ambiguity of the mother and the ambivalence of her daughter can be seen in the indirect way that the narrator tacitly links the girl's amorous activities with prostitution and identifies the mother as a kind of pimp in denial: "The child knows what she's doing is what the mother would have chosen for her to do, if she'd dared." That is, the family needs the money that the lover provides.

Duras's work is often analyzed in terms of its seeming affinity with the ideas of Jacques Lacan, whose revision of classic Freudian theory has been a major influence on the postmodern feminist analysis of feminine reflexivity. Duras seems to be aware of the psychodynamic foundations said to determine the daughter's animosity toward the mother, particularly the special difficulties girls are said to have in negotiating their traumatic recognition that they lack a phallus, the signifier of autonomous selfhood. According to psychoanalytic theory, the daughter might well resent the mother inasmuch as she shares that lack. Furthermore, a son is said to afford the mother a more satisfying fetish substitute for the missing phallus than does a daughter. With regard to *The Lover,* the need to symbolically disavow her own castration—social, cultural, and psychological—might explain the mother's greater love for her two sons, which is resentfully alleged by both the girl and the grown woman who narrates the story. What is more certain is that the acquisition of the phallus through sexual activity figures as one of the unconscious elements in the girl's relationship with her lover.

A key scene in *The Lover* suggests Duras's ambivalence toward the feminist critique of the way that the feminine desire for autonomous phallic selfhood, as a free agent capable of willing her life, becomes reconfigured as the attempt to become an object of masculine desire. Posing before a mirror wearing a man's fedora, the girl imagines with satisfaction how she will look to others: "Suddenly I see myself as another, as another would be seen, outside myself, available to all, available to all eyes in circulation." Duras repeatedly indicates that throughout the affair the girl has little sexual desire for the man, until just as she leaves him. Her pleasure and satisfaction is in being an object of desire—and not just the object of *his* desire, since she claims to like the fact that she is just one of his lovers, "indistinguishable" from the others. It is important to note that the mature woman who tells her story continues to define herself as an object of the desiring masculine gaze. She acknowledges that her reminiscences have been stimulated by a male's admiring gaze, together with his comment that she now looks more attractive than she had looked back then.

This anecdote may be intended to function strategically as a means of further consolidating Duras's erotically charged persona so that she seems the very embodiment of a feminine desire too strong to be abated by aging. But the anecdote does more than serve to discursively induce a commodifiable fantasy of the predominance of erotic desire in the organization of Duras's life and writing. The narrator invites, indeed demands, the reader "look" at her as she crosses the river as one might access an image in a photo album. And there are passages when she seems to endorse her younger self's insistence that to be looked at (that is, to be in the object position) is preferable to looking (that is, occupying the position of the subject—the position of being the willing free agent who chooses): "No one you look at is worth it. Looking is always demeaning."

Duras makes it clear that the desire to be the object of the masculine erotic gaze does not entail subordination. The girl achieves subjectivity by choosing to be a cool, indifferent object of desire; and in so doing she dominates her lover from the seemingly passive position. Duras often describes the girl as fatalistic: "She doesn't feel anything in particular, no hate, no repugnance either, so probably it's already desire. . . . It's as if this must be . . . what had to happen especially to her." Detachment gives the girl the power of inexplicable enigma, the power that "perverseness" bestows. It also helps to establish the shadowy atmosphere of reverie that consolidates in the liminal space of the lover's tryst. This space is an emotional or psychological space where the girl can act out, through sex, her alternating moods and contradictory impulses—such as her abiding, self-defining sense of sadness ("I could almost call it by my own name") and the intimation of destined disaster that her mother has given her.

The girl's detached passivity also serves to transform the lover into a means of achieving oblivion, a reflection of a suicidal desire that is also a form of aggression toward herself and toward her family: "Everyday we try to kill one another, to kill." Duras makes little attempt to give the lover an objective existence, rendering him an insubstantial and vulnerable apparition, which for that very reason allows him to represent a set of interrelated preoccupations central to the girl's inner life. He represents masculinity, adulthood, the social status of wealth and a more sophisticated cultural heritage; at the same time, he also represents racial Otherness, the lack of social status of the colonized, and a lack of autonomy, since he remains dominated by his father both financially and by the code of filial obligation that contrasts strikingly with the Western girl's blithe transgression and conflicted relationship with her mother. These categorical designations are not stable. For example, being Asian, the lover is necessarily conceived as feminine by Europeans like her older brother, insofar as the feminine gender is a culturally defined position of shameful abjection that even she has internalized: "In my brother's presence he becomes an unmentionable outrage, a cause of shame who ought to be kept out of sight." Both she and her lover are hyperaware of the disparity between how he *should* be seen and judged in terms of the wealth-standard and how he *is* seen and judged in terms of the racial standard.

Ironically, the lover's racialized self-consciousness is largely what constructs his erotic desire for the girl, while at the same time it serves to weaken him as a person and as a lover. Racial and economic differences both fuel his erotic obsession with the white girl and allow her to have more power in the relationship than she would otherwise have, given her age: "His heroism is me; his cravenness is his father's money." In her precociously intuitive way, the girl seems to recognize that being white makes her a fetish object that allows her lover to see himself as more alive than he actually is, while rendering him powerless in his dependency.

As with so many figures of Duras's more experimental works, the girl commands power over the lover's gaze precisely to the degree that she remains strangely blank. This quality of blank detachment and seeming self-sufficiency is dimly understood by the Chinese lover to reflect the desirable but ultimately unpossessable essence of whiteness itself. His desire is fetishistic inasmuch as she is an object whose unacknowledged function is to tacitly deny the possibility of his own castration. The girl has retained the phallus: She is uncastrated in a way that the lover is not once he leaves the social world of his own race and enters the white world.

A girl begins to know her self in the eyes of the lover: This is the book's romance and the source of its mass popularity. The book has academic respectability because the self that she discovers is one whose perversity appalls her, even as she cannot resist claiming it as her own. In Duras's postmodern fiction, the speakers are not necessarily reliable, and versions of events are meaningful only in their status as versions inasmuch as all humans construct narratives around nebulous incidents. In the manner of these metafictions, *The Lover* sometimes refers obliquely to acts of transgression while deliberately leaving the nature and consequences of these acts obscure. The narrator, for example, refers to a harsh, event but never makes clear what that event was. Neither does she identify her older brother's terrible crimes, to which she darkly refers in a piecemeal way that creates a sense of mystery, but also risks frustrating the reader.

BIBLIOGRAPHY

Mazzola, Robert L. "Coming to Terms: Images and Masquerade in Marguerite Duras's *L'Amant*." In *Marguerite Duras Lives On,* edited by Janine Ricouart, 137–149. Lanham, N.Y. and Oxford: University Press of America, 1998.

Schuster, Marilyn R. *Marguerite Duras Revisited.* New York: Twayne Publishers, 1993.

Selous, Trista. *The Other Woman: Feminism and Femininity in the Work of Marguerite Duras.* New Haven and London: Yale University Press, 1988.

Varsomopoulou, Evy. "Eros, Thanatos, I: The Sublimity of Writing the Family Romance in Marguerite Duras' *L'Amant*." In *The Poetics of the Kunsterlinroman and the Aesthetics of the Sublime.* Burlington, Vt.: Ashgatge, 2002.

Vickroy, Laurie. "Filling the Void: Transference, Love, Being and Writing in Duras's *L'Amant*." In *Marguerite Duras Lives On,* edited by Janine Ricouart, 123–136. Lanham, N.Y. and Oxford: University Press of America, 1998.

David Brottman